1 MONTH OF
FREE
READING

at

www.ForgottenBooks.com

By purchasing this book you are eligible for one month membership to ForgottenBooks.com, giving you unlimited access to our entire collection of over 1,000,000 titles via our web site and mobile apps.

To claim your free month visit:
www.forgottenbooks.com/free932844

ISBN 978-0-260-18113-8
PIBN 10932844

This book is a reproduction of an important historical work. Forgotten Books uses
state-of-the-art technology to digitally reconstruct the work, preserving the original format
whilst repairing imperfections present in the aged copy. In rare cases, an imperfection in
the original, such as a blemish or missing page, may be replicated in our edition. We do,
however, repair the vast majority of imperfections successfully; any imperfections that
remain are intentionally left to preserve the state of such historical works.

CALIFORNIA
UNREPORTED CASES

BEING THOSE

DECISIONS DETERMINED IN THE SUPREME COURT AND
THE DISTRICT COURTS OF APPEAL OF THE
STATE OF CALIFORNIA

BUT NOT

.OFFICIALLY REPORTED

WITH

ANNOTATIONS
SHOWING THEIR PRESENT VALUE AS AUTHORITY

REPORTED AND EDITED BY

PETER V. ROSS
Of the San Francisco Bar
'Author of "Inheritance Taxation," "Probate Law and Practice," etc.

VOLUME 7

SAN FRANCISCO
BENDER–MOSS COMPANY
1913

San Francisco
The Filmer Brothers Electrotype Company
Typographers and Stereotypers

CASES DETERMINED

IN THE

SUPREME COURT OF CALIFORNIA

BUT NOT

OFFICIALLY REPORTED.

RIEBLI v. HUSLER.

S. F. No. 2842; September 4, 1902.

69 Pac. 1061.

Community Property.—The Presumption That Cattle Bought by the husband during the marriage were community property is not overcome by the wife's mere testimony that they were bought with her money, and that she had a certain amount of money in banks and loaned when she was married, three years before the purchase; they having been placed on a ranch occupied by them under a lease to the husband alone, and treated as his property by his afterward giving her, when he was insolvent, a bill of sale thereof.[1]

Sale—Change of Possession.—A Recorded Bill of Sale from Husband to wife of cattle, possession of which remained as before on a ranch occupied by husband and wife, but leased to him alone, is within Civil Code, section 3440, providing that a transfer of personalty, made by one having the possession or control thereof, and not accompanied by delivery and followed by change of possession, is void against the seller's creditors.

APPEAL from Superior Court, Sonoma County; Albert G. Burnett, Judge.

Action by Christina A. Riebli against E. A. Husler. Judgment for defendant. Plaintiff appeals. Affirmed.

J. P. Rodgers for appellant; Lippitt & Lippitt for respondent.

---

[1] Cited in the note in Cof. Pro Dec. 65, on what is community property.

COOPER, C.—This action was brought to recover four-teen head of cows, or the value thereof, which are alleged to be the separate property of plaintiff. The defendant at the time of taking the property was a constable of Petaluma township, and justified under a writ of execution in favor of one Keegan against A. B. Riebli, the husband of plaintiff. The case was tried before the court, findings filed, and judgment entered for the defendant. Plaintiff prosecutes this appeal from the judgment, and from the order denying her motion for a new trial.

The court found that, at the time of the taking, the property was not the property of plaintiff, but was the property of her husband, against whom the writ of execution issued. The sole point contended for by plaintiff is that there is not sufficient evidence to sustain this finding. We have carefully examined the evidence, and find it sufficient. The cows were bought by plaintiff's husband in October, 1899. They were not owned by plaintiff before her marriage, nor were they afterward acquired by her by gift, bequest, devise or descent. At the time they were purchased they were not conveyed to her by an instrument in writing. The cattle, therefore, having been purchased during marriage, the presumption is that they were community property. The burden was upon plaintiff to overcome this presumption by evidence clear and convincing. In the absence of such evidence the presumption as to the community character of the property must prevail: Civ. Code, secs. 162, 164; In re Boody's Estate, 113 Cal. 686, 45 Pac. 858; Fennell v. Drinkhouse, 131 Cal. 451, 82 Am. St. Rep. 361, 63 Pac. 734.

While there is some evidence tending to show that the cows were purchased with the separate money of the plaintiff, it is not clear, nor, in our opinion, sufficient to overcome the presumption as to the community character of the property. The only evidence on the point is that of plaintiff. She did not produce the evidence of her husband, nor of the party from whom the cattle were purchased. She testified that the cattle were bought by her husband out of her money; that at the time of her marriage—more than three years before—she had between $900 and $1,000 in the Sonoma County Bank, and some money in the German Loan Society, and some loaned out in Washington. She did not say that she had this money or any money in any bank at the time the cattle were purchased. She did not show that she drew any money from any bank about the time of the purchase, nor that she gave her husband or anyone a check on any bank or on any party in payment of the cattle. The cattle were bought and placed on the ranch, which was occupied by plaintiff and her husband, under a lease to the husband alone, and turned on the range with the other cattle. They were not branded or marked by plaintiff in any way so as to identify them from the cattle owned by her husband. No one testified to any claim made by her to the cattle at or about the time of the purchase. Afterward, in June, 1900, the plaintiff and her husband went to an attorney for advice, and thereupon the husband executed and delivered to the plaintiff a bill of sale for "twenty-six head of cows, one bull, seven calves, seven head of horses and harness, wagons, and farming implements, now on the ranch of Charles Lynch, in Vallejo township; also all chickens, pigs, and hay on said ranch." The bill of sale included the cows in controversy. It was recorded, and plaintiff said concerning its execution: "Q. How came he [Riebli] to make that bill of sale? A. Well, he lose all his property where he had all his money he had—he lose on the Lynch place— and, of course, I want to be sure of my property; and that's why we had the bill of sale drawed up, so I could do as I pleased, because it was bought out of my own property, and was my own property, that I worked thirteen long years for." It is evident that this bill of sale was an afterthought. Plaintiff had taken no bill of sale of the property at the time it was purchased, but when her husband had lost his money she took the precaution to take a bill of sale from him of that which she says she already owned, and to have the bill of sale recorded. It is evident that at the time the bill of sale was made the plaintiff and her husband regarded the property as community property, or the separate property of the husband, and we will so regard it. It has been held that the contemporaneous and practical construction of a contract by the parties to it is strong evidence as to its meaning if its terms are equivocal: Keith v. Engineering Co. (Cal.), 68 Pac. 598. We think it equally clear that the plaintiff and defendant, by the bill of sale, treated the property as subject to the control and dominion of the husband, and not as the property of the wife. We will assume that they each knew its character, and that the husband would not have conveyed, nor the wife have demanded a conveyance of, property the title of which was already in the wife. We fully recognize the right of the wife to her own separate property, and her right to invest and reinvest it as she pleases. But we know that the wife is often a willing tool in aiding her husband to escape his just debts. In such case the better rule is to require the character of the property to be proven by clear and convincing evidence. It is not clear to us that property bought by the husband, and mingled with his own, and afterward conveyed by him to his wife, was all the time her separate property. The bill of sale conveyed the property to the wife as between husband and wife. But there was no immediate delivery nor change of possession. It remained upon the ranch in the possession of the husband as before. The ranch was leased by the husband, and no claim is made as to any change of possession. There had been no change of possession when Keegan became a creditor, and the bill of sale was therefore void as to him: Civ. Code, sec. 3440.

It follows that the judgment and order should be affirmed.

We concur: Haynes, C.; Smith, C.

PER CURIAM.—For the reasons given in the foregoing opinion the judgment and order are affirmed.

HART v. HOYT et al.

Sac. No. 978; September 12, 1902.

70 Pac. 19.

Water Rights—Trespass—Prescription.—It is Immaterial That the Quantity of water owned by defendant and conducted through the ditch to her land is left indefinite by the evidence, in an action for trespass, where defendant justified under a prescriptive right to the use of a ditch across plaintiff's land as a conduit of water to her lands, and a right of entry for repairing it.

APPEAL from Superior Court, Siskiyou County; **J. S. Beard, Judge.**

Action by E. C. Hart against Elizabeth Hoyt and others. Judgment for defendants. Plaintiff appeals. Affirmed.

Gillis & Tapscott for appellant; Warren & Taylor for respor·'ents.

SMITH, C.—This is a suit for trespass on plaintiff's land. The defendant Mrs. Hoyt justifies under an alleged prescriptive right to the use of a ditch across plaintiff's place as a conduit of water to her lands, and a right of entry for repairing the same. The other defendants justify as her servants. The case was tried by a jury, whose verdict was for defendants, and judgment was accordingly entered in their favor. The plaintiff appeals from the judgment and from an order denying his motion for a new trial. The main question involved is as to the sufficiency of the evidence of Mrs. Hoyt's alleged right of entry to justify the verdict. The plaintiff's lands lie to the eastward of those of Mrs. Hoyt, and the ditch in question runs westerly through the lands of the plaintiff, and at the present time to and upon her lands. Formerly, according to the testimony of plaintiff's witnesses, the ditch did not quite reach the land of Mrs. Hoyt; but there is evidence tending to show the contrary. There is also evidence tending to show that Mrs. Hoyt is the owner of water from the Shasta river, flowing in a ditch to the eastward of plaintiff's lands, known as the Miller, Casedy and Hoyt ditch, which for many years she has been conducting to her lands through the ditch in question. Nor is it material to the issues in this case that the quantity of water thus owned by her, and conducted through the ditch to her land, is left indefinite by the evidence. We think, therefore, that the jury was justified in finding that she had acquired a prescriptive right to the use of the ditch.

As to entries on plaintiff's lands, made by her, in the exercise of her right, for the purpose of repairing the ditch, the evidence on her part is somewhat meager, and is stoutly contradicted by the plaintiff and his witnesses. But assuming, for the purposes of the decision, that the right to the use of the ditch would not imply the right of entry to repair it, she testifies unequivocally that she and her husband, who was her predecessor in title, have been using the ditch since 1864 or 1865, and have habitually sent men onto plaintiff's land to clean it out whenever necessary; and her testimony is strongly confirmed by her habitual use of the ditch, which, it appears from the evidence, required frequent repairing. We cannot say, therefore, that the verdict of the jury was not justified by the evidence.

Objection is made by the appellant to several rulings of the court with regard to evidence, but none of these seem to be of sufficient importance to require consideration.

We advise that the judgment and order appealed from be affirmed.

We concur: Gray, C.; Chipman, C.

PER CURIAM.—For the reasons given in the foregoing opinion the judgment and order appealed from are affirmed.

UNION PAVING AND CONTRACT COMPANY v. MOWRY.

S. F. No. 2069; September 17, 1902.

70 Pac. 81.

Ostensible Agency.—Evidence in an Action for Labor Done in Street Paving that defendant told plaintiff, who was negotiating with her to do street paving for her, that all street work was arranged by A, and the fact that A executed another contract with plaintiff, as defendant's agent, for such kind of work, which she recognized, justifies a finding that A, in making and modifying such a contract, had ostensible agency, defined by Civil Code, section 2300, to be when the principal causes a third person to believe another to be his agent.

APPEAL from Superior Court, City and County of San Francisco; John Hunt, Judge.

Action by the Union Paving and Contract Company against Ellen M. Mowry. Judgment for plaintiff. Defendant appeals. Affirmed.

R. Percy Wright for appellant; D. H. Whittemore for respondent.

HARRISON, J.—The plaintiff brought this action to recover for the labor done in paving with bituminous rock a

portion of a public street under a contract between the
defendant and one Reed, and by him assigned to the plaintiff. The execution of the contract, as well as its performance by the plaintiff, was denied by the defendant. The
cause was tried by a jury and a verdict rendered in favor
of the plaintiff. From the judgment entered thereon, and
from an order denying a new trial, the defendant has appealed.

1. The contract on the part of the defendant was signed,
"Ellen M. Mowry, by Chas. Alpers." There was no evidence
that Alpers had express authority from her to sign the contract, but evidence was presented to the jury which the
plaintiff claimed created an ostensible agency, and showed
that he had implied authority to sign the contract. It was
shown that Alpers had been residing in the same house with
the defendant and her mother for many years, during which
time he had been accustomed to take part in making contracts in her behalf for street work; that several contracts
for doing street work in front of or adjacent to the property
of the defendant had been made in her behalf; and that,
with two exceptions, all of these contracts had been made
by Alpers, and signed by him in the same manner as was
the present one. Mr. Reed, the plaintiff's assignor, testified
that several of these contracts had been made with him, and
that all of the business that he had transacted in regard
thereto for the property of the defendant had been with Mr.
Alpers; that he had had several conversations with her about
street work, and that she then referred him to her mother
or to Mr. Alpers, saying that these matters were all fixed
or arranged by Mr. Alpers; that for one of these contracts
the defendant had given him her notes; and that the same
were afterward paid by Alpers. It was also shown that, at
the same time that the contract in question was made, another contract on her behalf for street work upon an adjacent block was made with Mr. Reed, and signed by Alpers
in the same manner as the one in suit; that at that time
Reed made a "side agreement" with her respecting the time
for doing the work and the payment therefor, and delivered
the same to Alpers; that, the work named in the other contract not having been completed, the defendant some months
afterward recognized the validity of this contract by send-

ing a written notice to Reed that he complete the same according to its terms, in which she referred to the contract as "our contract," and as having been "made and entered into between you and myself." The defendant was a witness in her own behalf, and did not contradict the testimony of Reed, or state that she had not given to Alpers authority to make the contract. Mr. Alpers was a witness in behalf of the defendant, and testified that he negotiated with Mr. Reed with reference to this contract, and signed the same for the defendant, and he did not testify that he did so without her authority. Under this evidence the jury was authorized to find an ostensible agency in Alpers, within the terms of section 2300 of the Civil Code, and that he had an implied authority from her to make the contract.

2. The contract provided that the gutters should be paved with basalt blocks, but that, in the event of the city not allowing such gutters, the city specifications should be adopted. In the ordinance prescribing the manner of performing street work, which was offered in evidence, no mention is made of stone gutters where the roadway or street is to be paved with bituminous rock. After the contract had been entered into, a resolution was passed by the board of supervisors directing Mr. Reed to omit the construction of the basalt block gutters thereon. This resolution was afterward repealed before the work was commenced. Evidence was offered on behalf of the plaintiff to the effect that thereafter an agreement was entered into between Mr. Reed and Mr. Alpers for the modification of the contract by omitting therefrom the basalt gutters, and deducting $25 from the agreed price for the work. Testimony was offered on behalf of the defendant in contradiction of this evidence; but, upon this conflict of evidence, we are not at liberty to disregard the verdict of the jury, and it must be assumed in this court that such agreement was made. The work was thereupon completed to the satisfaction of the superintendent of streets, and the street was afterward accepted by the board of supervisors. The authority of Alpers to make such agreement was the same as his authority to make the original contract. The statement of the defendant to Reed that all street work was arranged by Alpers included such modification, and justified him in acting thereon. It must be held, therefore, that per-

formance of this part of the contract was waived by the parties.

The judgment and order are affirmed.

We concur: Van Dyke, J.; Garoutte, J.

————————

MILLER et al. v. KERN COUNTY LAND COMPANY.

S. F. No. 2014; September 17, 1902.

70 Pac. 183.

Quieting Title—Venue.—The Answer, as Well as the Complaint, may be looked to, to determine whether the action is one to quiet title—that is, to determine the right to an easement—within constitution, article 6, section 5, requiring actions to quiet title to real estate to be brought in the county in which the land is situated.

APPEAL from Superior Court, City and County of San Francisco; Edw. A. Belcher, Judge.

Action by Miller & Lux against the Kern County Land Company. From an order, refusing change of venue, defendant appeals. Remanded, with direction to dismiss.

Charles W. Willard, Page, McCutchen & Eells and Page, McCutchen, Harding & Knight for appellant; Houghton & Houghton, E. B. & Geo. H. Mastick and W. B. Treadwell for respondent.

TEMPLE, J.—This is an appeal from an order refusing to grant a change of venue on the ground of the convenience of witnesses. Both parties are corporations which have their principal places of business in San Francisco, where the suit was brought. The action was to recover damages for injury to real property situate in Kern county. A former motion for a change of venue was made, based on section 392 of the Code of Civil Procedure, which provides that actions for injuries to real property must be tried in the county where the land is situated. An order denying a change of venue was affirmed here, on the ground that section 16, article 12, of the constitution denied a defendant corporation that right in such actions: 134 Cal. 586, 66 Pac. 856. The complaint shows that plaintiff had constructed and was maintaining a canal over land belonging to the defendant, which defendant, as is alleged, wrongfully obstructed, to the damage of plaintiff in the sum of $25,000. Instead of directly averring that it owns an easement over the land of defendant, plaintiff states in its complaint a great many facts and circumstances from which it is supposed the right to such an easement must necessarily follow. The answer admits the obstruction charged of the canal or ditch, but denies the easement and the facts alleged upon which plaintiff's claim is founded, as also the damages. This leaves the principal issue whether plaintiff has such easement. The affidavits upon which the change of venue is asked, and also those offered by plaintiff in opposition to the motion, show very clearly that in the opinion of both parties the only real question to be tried is whether plaintiff has such easement. The case is brought within the decisions in Fritts v. Camp, 94 Cal. 393, 29 Pac. 867, and Pacific Yacht Club v. Sausalito Bay Water Co., 98 Cal. 487, 33 Pac. 322, except that in those cases the complaint showed expressly that the action was brought to quiet title to real estate, to wit, to determine the right to an easement, while that such will be the effect of a judgment in this case appears only after answer. Upon this point respondent's counsel contends that on the question of jurisdiction the court can only look at the complaint. The constitution only prohibits the bringing of suits to quiet title in counties other than where the land is situated. If the complaint does not show that the action is of that character, it was properly commenced, and the defendant cannot, by the nature of his defense, cause it to be decided that the action was wrongly brought. This is a very narrow construction of the constitutional provision, and under which the rule could be systematically evaded. An action for a trespass is a very common and easy method of trying title to real estate, and could often be substituted for an action to quiet title, at the option of a plaintiff. The provision is jurisdictional, as was held in the case of Urton v. Woolsey, 87 Cal. 28, 25 Pac. 154. Whenever this point is made to appear, therefore, it is shown that the court has no jurisdiction of the action, and must dismiss it. This must be so whenever it clearly appears that the purpose of bringing the action was, in whole or in part, to determine a disputed right to real estate. Some of the inconveniences which may result from such a rule are quite obvious, but the people have seen fit, in the very clause of the constitution which defines the jurisdiction of the superior court, to impose this limitation, and the courts cannot disregard it, or allow it to be evaded. It might have been provided that such action should be sent to the proper county for trial, but a different mode was adopted.

Counsel contend that this matter was disposed of on the former appeal, which has been mentioned. But the question was not, and could not have been, raised on that appeal.

The cause is remanded, with directions to the superior court to dismiss the action.

We concur: Henshaw, J.; McFarland, J.

BUCKMAN v. HATCH et al.*

S. F. No. 2548; September 22, 1902.

70 Pac. 221.

Street Improvements.—In Pleading the Determination of a **Board of Supervisors** as to certain public improvements, it is not necessary to state the facts conferring jurisdiction, but the determination may be pleaded as duly given or made.

Street Improvements.—In an Action to Foreclose a Street Assessment, where no objection is taken to the complaint by demurrer, and the proceedings on the trial do not appear in the record, the court on appeal must presume that evidence was given to uphold every allegation of the complaint, whether defectively stated or not, and, to this end, that the original resolution of intention describing the work was put in evidence, and that the resolution contained a full description of the work as required by statute, including a specific description of the materials of which cesspools and culverts were to be constructed.

Street Improvements—Time for Work.—Under Vrooman Act, section 6 (Stats. 1885, p. 151), requiring that the superintendent of streets "shall fix the time for the commencement, ... and for the completion of the work under all contracts entered into by him," it is not necessary that the time be fixed in the contract itself, but only that the superintendent shall in writing, authenticated with his official signature, fix the time.

---

*For subsequent opinion in bank, see 139 Cal. 53, 72 Pac. 445.

APPEAL from Superior Court, City and County of San Francisco; Frank J. Murasky, Judge.

Action by A. E. Buckman against Mary Hatch and others. Judgment for plaintiff, and William Nicol, one of the defendants, appeals. Affirmed.

John H. Henderson for appellant; E. G. Knapp and Wm. H. Chapman for respondent.

GRAY, C.—This is an action to foreclose a street assessment. There was no demurrer to the complaint, but defendants answered, and on a trial plaintiff obtained judgment. Defendant Nicol appeals from the judgment, and the record on said appeal consists of the judgment-roll without a bill of exceptions.

Two points are made by appellant, both directed to the sufficiency of the complaint.

1. It is claimed that it appears from the face of the complaint that the resolution of intention describing the work was insufficient to confer jurisdiction on the board of supervisors, in that it did not show of what materials the cesspools and culverts mentioned therein were to be constructed. The complaint does not contain a copy of the resolution of intention, but the same is set out in the complaint according to its legal effect. We quote from the complaint as follows: "That under and in pursuance of said act approved March 18, 1885, and the acts amendatory thereof and supplementary thereof, the following proceedings were duly had and taken, to wit: That on the eighth day of July, 1895, the board of supervisors of said city and county, at a regular meeting thereof, duly made and passed a resolution, to wit, resolution of intention No. 12,603, describing the work, wherein and whereby said board resolved that it was their intention to order the following work in said city and county to be done and improvement to be made," etc. And further: "Said board of supervisors, deeming that the public interest and convenience required the above-described work to be done, duly gave, and made, and at a regular meeting of said board passed, its order and resolution designated as 'No. 12,893,' providing for and ordering said work to be done, and thereby duly gave and made its determination to order

the said work done, which said order and resolution No.
12,893, after it was so duly given, made, and passed, was
signed by the said clerk of said board of supervisors, ...
and by its order and resolution of award No. 13,113, duly
given and made and passed therefor, ... did duly award
the contract for said work and improvement to F. Leffler.''
And again: "And all and singular the proceedings aforesaid
and determinations of said boards and officers hereinbefore
referred to, and of each of them, including those of said
contractor and of his agents and assigns, were each and all
duly given and made, and each and all acts aforesaid were
duly performed, within the time and in the manner required
by law." We think such allegations are sufficient to show
that the board had jurisdiction to award the contract, and
to sustain the judgment—at least in the absence of any demurrer to the complaint, and with no question appearing to
have been made upon the trial as to the sufficiency thereof.
If the reference to the resolution as "describing the work,"
and the allegations to the effect that said resolution was
"duly given and made," "duly had and taken," "and in the
manner required by law," and that the resolution awarding
the contract was "duly given, made, and passed," are all
true, it must be that the first resolution fully described the
materials of which the cesspools and culverts were to be constructed, for, if it did not contain such a description, the several resolutions were not "duly given, made and passed";
and the action of the board was not "duly had and taken" in
the premises. "In pleading a judgment or other determination of a court, officer or board, it is not necessary to state
the facts conferring jurisdiction, but such judgment or determination may be stated to have been duly given or made,"
etc.: Code Civ. Proc., sec. 456; Improvement Co. v. Fulton,
4 Cal. Unrep. 151, 33 Pac. 1117; Williams v. Bergin, 127
Cal. 578, 60 Pac. 164.

Aside from the statute and decisions above cited, and the
principle therein laid down, we think that every reasonable
presumption may be resorted to to uphold the judgment. No
objection having been taken to the complaint by demurrer,
and the proceedings upon the trial not appearing in the record, it is not unreasonable to presume that at the trial evidence was given to uphold every allegation of the complaint,
whether such allegation was defectively stated in the plead-

ing or not, and to this end we may presume that, without
objection thereto, the original resolution of intention describing the work was put in evidence, and that said resolution
contained a full description of the work as required by the
statute, including a specific description of the materials of
which the cesspools and culverts were to be constructed. We
may admit, then, for the purpose of this decision, that the
complaint was defective in its statement as to the description of the work contained in the resolution of intention;
yet this defect in the pleading was not of such a nature that
it could not be cured or waived by the reception of evidence,
without objection, as to the matters imperfectly pleaded; and
we will, therefore, assume that it was so cured or waived
upon the trial of the case. It is too late for a defendant,
after verdict, to object to defective allegations in the complaint, which, if pointed out by special demurrer before the
trial, or by objections to the evidence at the trial, might have
been obviated by amendment: Larkin v. Mullen, 128 Cal.
449, 60 Pac. 1091.

2. It is also contended that the complaint does not show
that the contract fixed the time for the commencement or
completion of the work. It does appear from the complaint
that the superintendent of streets in his official capacity as
such, fixed the time for the commencement of said work at
fifteen days from and after the date of said contract, and
for the completion thereof at ninety days from the date of
said contract. This allegation shows a compliance with section 6 of the Vrooman act, under which these proceedings
were had: Stats. 1885, p. 151. It was not necessary that
this time be fixed in the contract, for the act does not require
that it shall be so fixed: Fletcher v. Prather, 102 Cal. 413,
36 Pac. 658; Buckman v. Ferguson, 108 Cal. 33, 40 Pac. 1057.
It is only necessary that within fifteen days after the execution of the contract the superintendent shall, in writing,
authenticated with his official signature, fix the time: Buckman v. Ferguson, supra. In the absence of a demurrer, the
allegation of the complaint as to the fixing of the time is
clearly sufficient to sustain the judgment.

We advise that the judgment be affirmed.

We concur: Chipman, C.; Haynes, C.

PER CURIAM.—For the reasons given in the foregoing opinion the judgment is affirmed.

TEMPLE, J.—I concur in the judgment.

HARTLEY v. VERMILLION et al.*

Sac. No. 951; October 4, 1902.

70 Pac. 273.

Highways—Dedication.—Use by the Public Generally of a Road for fifteen years, to the knowledge and with the acquiescence of the owner of the land on which it is located, does not show a dedication.[1]

Highway—Prescription.—A Permissive Use of a Road, without anything to show the owner an adverse claim, will not give a right by prescription.[2]

APPEAL from Superior Court, Solano County; A. J. Buckles, Judge.

Action by Eliza M. E. Hartley against Frank M. Vermillion and another. Judgment for plaintiff and defendants appeal. Reversed.

Raleigh Barcar and O. R. Coghlan for appellants; Wheaton & Kalloch and Geo. A. Lamont for respondent.

GAROUTTE, J.—This action was brought to restrain the defendants from obstructing a road which plaintiff alleged was a public highway. The court found as a fact that the

*For subsequent opinion in bank, see 141 Cal. 339, 74 Pac. 987.

[1] Cited and approved in Garvin Co. v. Lindsay Bridge Co. (Okl.), 124 Pac. 326, where it is held that a company's permitting the public to use its bridge does not amount to a dedication.

Cited with approval, and applied to the question of water rights, in Village of Hailey v. Riley, 14 Idaho, 494, 17 L. R. A., N. S., 86, 95 Pac. 691.

Cited in the note in 129 Am. St. Rep. 582, on dedication to a public street.

[2] Cited and followed in Board of Commrs. of Sheridan County v. Patrick, 18 Wyo. 139, 104 Pac. 533, which involved the question of the rights of highway as acquired by prescription.

road was a public highway, and granted the relief asked. The appeal is taken from the order denying a motion for a new trial.

Some point is made that the road is a statutory private road, but. in view of the fact that it was never opened and laid out in accordance with the provisions of the statute relating to the laying out of private roads, there is nothing in that point; and the single question presented relates to the sufficiency of the evidence to sustain the findings of fact. The evidence in all substantials is uncontradicted, and, weighing that evidence in the balance furnished by the law, the court is convinced that it fails to support the finding of fact to the effect that the road was a public highway. The evidence of plaintiff is all to the effect that the people generally had used the road in dispute for fifteen years or more, to the knowledge and with the acquiescence of the defendants, the original owners of the land upon which the road is located; and this is all. Cooper v. Monterey Co., 104 Cal. 438, 38 Pac. 106, 107, was just that kind of a case, and there the court said: "The finding that the strip of land in question was traveled and used by the public ever since 1872, with the knowledge of plaintiff, and without objection on his part, is only the finding of probative facts tending to prove a dedication; but the fact of dedication—which, by the way, is neither alleged nor found—does not necessarily follow from these probative facts, since they are not necessarily inconsistent with a total absence of intention to dedicate, and may indicate merely a license. The finding that the strip of land 'is a public highway,' whether deemed an ultimate fact or a conclusion of law, is not justified." In the same case the court also said: "The evidence on the part of the defendant was sufficient to justify the finding as to the user by the public with the knowledge of plaintiff, and without objection from him, but nothing more in favor of defendant. As this finding is obviously insufficient to support the judgment, I think the order and judgment appealed from should be reversed." While the court finds a statement in Hope v. Barnett, 78 Cal. 14, 20 Pac. 245, which might be construed as supporting the doctrine that mere user of a highway with knowledge of the owner, and with his consent, or without objection upon his part for a certain period of time, creates a dedication, yet such cannot be said to be the law in this state. Dedication is a pure question of fact. The intention of the owner to dedicate is a vital element in every case, and that intention also is a pure question of fact. A mere permissive user, by the owner, of land for a highway, never can amount to a dedication. That is a user by license, and nothing more, and of itself never would ripen into a dedication, no matter how long continued. An expression is found in Schwerdtle v. Placer Co., 108 Cal. 596, 41 Pac. 448, to the effect that a conclusive presumption of dedication to the public arises from long-continued adverse user. Technically speaking, this statement does not contain a sound expression of the law. Long-continued adverse user by the public may create an easement in that public by prescription, but it cannot amount to dedication. It is not plain that the user of a highway by the public could be adverse if the owner consented to the user; and dedication always involves the assent of the owner of the land. If he objects to the use, if the use is against his assent, that fact disproves any intention upon his part to dedicate. It is said in City of Los Angeles v. Kysor, 125 Cal. 465, 58 Pac. 91: "In all those cases where it is claimed that a dedication is created in pais it may be said that there is no amount of evidence which will justify a court in instructing a jury that dedication is conclusively shown. The owner's intention is the all-important element in creating a dedication, and that intention is a question of fact. It never can be a matter of law. Hence, when the particular intention in doing an act is the all-important element involved in the trial of a question of fact, it is peculiarly the province of the jury or the trial court to say what that intention is." A dedication of land for a highway is an appropriation of it by the owner for that purpose. It is perfectly evident that the appropriation of the land by the public is not a dedication, and, to justify a finding of fact by a trial court that the owner has dedicated his land to public use as a highway, the evidence must be plain and convincing that such was his intention. It is said in San Francisco v. Grote, 120 Cal. 62, 65 Am. St. Rep. 155, 52 Pac. 128, 41 L. R. A. 335: "It is not a trivial thing to take another's land without compensation, and for this reason the courts will not lightly declare a dedication to public use. It is elementary law that an inten-

2

tion to dedicate upon the part of the owner must be plainly
manifest.'' And while long-continued user without objection, and with the knowledge and consent of the owner, is
some evidence of a right in the public, still there must be
joined to that user an intention upon the part of the owner
to dedicate, or no dedication will be consummated; for the
long-continued user by the public without objection by the
owner is entirely consistent with a license to the public to
use the land, and therefore evidence of long-continued user
alone will not support a finding of fact that a dedication was
created. Neither will a finding of fact of mere long-
continued user support a conclusion of law that a public
highway was created. As previously stated, in order to constitute a dedication of a highway by evidence in pais, there
must be convincing evidence that the owner intended to
appropriate the land to the public use. The present case
shows mere user by the public for a long number of years.
This evidence does not amount to a dedication; but, beyond
this, the evidence of the defendants shows clearly that they
never intended to dedicate these lands for a public highway.
For many years the road was obstructed by gates, and during
all of those years they exercised acts of ownership over it entirely inconsistent with an intention upon their part to dedicate it to the public. They spent large sums of money
annually in improving it, and the county, whose business
it was to care for and improve and protect its public highways, during all of these years never claimed any rights in
this road, and is not now a party to this litigation. The
court concludes that the evidence is too weak to support a
finding of fact to the effect that the land in dispute was a
public highway, created by the dedication of its owners.

Some claim is made that the public have obtained rights
to the road by prescription. There is nothing in this claim.
Time of user is not a material element in creating a dedication of a highway; but, for the public to acquire an easement
in land by prescription for a highway, it is a most material
element. Yet continued user by the public for the statutory
period of limitations is not sufficient to vest rights. As in all
other cases of title acquired by prescription, the user must
be adverse. A permissive user will never ripen into a right
by prescription. In this case there was no adverse user and
no claim of right that this court can discover from the evi-

dence. Certainly, defendants never thought the public was claiming a right in this land adverse to them. They saw nothing to put them upon inquiry as to that kind of a claim. The claim of right, as in all other cases of adverse possession, must be open and notorious, and here there was nothing of that kind.

For the foregoing reasons the order denying a new trial is reversed and the cause remanded.

We concur: Harrison, J.; Van Dyke, J.

—————

BRYAN v. BRYAN.

Sac. No. 1016; October 11, 1902.

70 Pac. 304.

Divorce—Time for Appeal.—Under Code of Civil Procedure, section 939, allowing an appeal from a final judgment within six months from entry, where judgment was entered January 15, 1901, and notice of appeal served October 17, 1901, the appeal cannot be considered.

Divorce—Questions Reviewable.—The Question Whether a Judgment is the legal conclusion from the facts found cannot be considered on appeal from an order denying a new trial, but only on an appeal from the judgment.

Divorce—Cruelty.—In Divorce Plaintiff Testified That Defendant often, in the presence of others, accused her of being intimate with other men; that he had a venereal disease, and accused her of giving it to him; that he many times threatened to take the minor child away from plaintiff, and on one occasion took the child away for about two weeks and would not tell plaintiff where it was; that he called her a prostitute, and left her often without means of support; that she had to support herself; and that the conduct of defendant caused her mental suffering and bodily injury. Held, that such testimony sustained a finding of extreme cruelty.

Divorce—Appeal.—Where the Testimony is Conflicting, findings of fact thereon cannot be disturbed on appeal.

Divorce—Motion for New Trial—Statement.—The Statute Provides that when the notice of the motion for a new trial designates, as the ground of the motion, the insufficiency of the evidence to justify the decision, the statement shall specify the particular insufficiency. In divorce defendant, in his answer and cross-complaint alleged acts of adultery with five men, and with others unknown to defendant, and the court found against defendant as to each charge. Defendant assigned that the evidence did not sustain the findings that plaintiff was entitled to a divorce, for defendant had pleaded and proved recrimination under Civil Code, section 122, and that a divorce should have been denied plaintiff for that reason. Held, that the assignment was insufficient to raise any question as to the sufficiency of the evidence.

Divorce.—In Divorce the Court Found That the Allegations of the complaint and cross-complaint as to the date of marriage were true, but that the allegations of the supplemental cross-complaint were untrue. The supplemental cross-complaint set up a charge of adultery, and "realleged every allegation in the cross-complaint." Defendant contended the findings were inconsistent. Held, that the contention was of no merit, there being no issue as to the date of marriage, nor necessity for a finding thereon.

Divorce.—On Appeal from an Order Denying a New Trial in divorce the supreme court has no power to modify the provision of the decree providing for the support of a minor child until its majority.

APPEAL from Superior Court, Yolo County; E. E. Gaddis, Judge.

Action by Frances Bryan against S. A. Bryan. From a judgment for plaintiff and from an order denying a new trial defendant appeals. Affirmed.

R. Clark for appellant; Arthur C. Huston and Harry L. Huston for respondent.

COOPER, J.—Action for divorce and custody of minor child. Findings were filed, and judgment thereupon entered in favor of plaintiff, awarding her the custody of the child. Defendant appeals from the judgment and order denying his motion for a new trial.

The judgment was entered January 15, 1901, and the notice of appeal was served and filed October 17, 1901. The appeal from the judgment was, therefore, not taken within six months after its entry, and cannot be considered: Code Civ. Proc., sec. 939. Nor can we consider the question as to whether or not the judgment is the legal conclusion from the facts found, for the reason that such question can only be raised by appeal from the judgment. We are therefore confined to questions properly involved in the appeal from the order denying a new trial.

The complaint alleges facts showing extreme cruelty on the part of defendant toward plaintiff, and the court below found the allegations to be true. It is claimed that the finding as to extreme cruelty is not supported by the evidence, but we think the evidence of plaintiff is sufficient to sustain the finding. She testified that defendant often, in the presence of other parties, accused her of being intimate with other men; that he had a venereal disease, and accused her of giving it to him; that he many times threatened to take the minor child away from plaintiff, and on one occasion took the child away for a period of about two weeks, and would not tell plaintiff where it was; that he called her a prostitute, and left her often without means of support; that she had to follow dressmaking in order to support herself; that the acts and conduct of defendant caused her great mental suffering and bodily injury. The court below, by the finding, gave credence to the many acts narrated by the plaintiff, and under the rule we cannot disturb the finding.

The defendant, in his answer and cross-complaint, alleged five different acts of adultery committed by plaintiff with different men, and that at divers other times and places plaintiff "committed adultery with divers and sundry other men unknown to defendant." Defendant prayed for a decree of divorce against plaintiff upon these affirmative allegations. The court found against defendant as to every such allegation, and the findings are in no way attacked. There is no specification as to the insufficiency of the evidence to sustain either of said findings, or any portion of either. The only attempted assignment as to the insufficiency of the evidence to support the findings of the affirmative matters set forth by defendant is the following: "The evidence does not sustain the findings that plaintiff is entitled to a divorce, for the defendant pleaded and proved a case of divorce against plaintiff, which pleadings and proof amounted to a showing of recrimination under section 122 of the Civil Code of this state, and a divorce should have been denied plaintiff for that reason." It will be readily seen that the above is merely a statement to the effect that evidence does not sustain the conclusion of law that plaintiff is entitled to a divorce. It is true the reason is attempted to

be given in the statement that "defendant pleaded and
proved a case of divorce against plaintiff." The defendant's grounds of divorce, as pleaded by him, consisted of
several distinct acts of adultery, and the court found each
allegation to be untrue. If the separate findings, or either
of them, was not supported by the evidence, it was incumbent
upon defendant to specify such finding, and the respects
wherein the evidence was insufficient. Not having done so,
we cannot examine the pleadings and proof in order to see
whether the defendant proved "recrimination" under section 122 of the Civil Code. We must be governed by the
findings. They can be attacked in the manner clearly
pointed out in the code, and not otherwise. It has been the
tendency of this court of late to look with great liberality
upon specifications of insufficiency of evidence, but it has
never been held that it was sufficient to say "the evidence
does not sustain the findings." If we were to adopt such
rule, it would set at naught the express provision of the
code: "When the notice of the motion designates, as the
ground of the motion, the insufficiency of the evidence to
justify the verdict or other decision the statement shall specify the particulars in which such evidence is alleged to be
insufficient."

The claim is made that the findings are contradictory in
this: that the allegation of the complaint and cross-complaint
to the effect "that plaintiff and defendant intermarried on
the twenty-third day of November, 1894, and ever since have
been, and now are, husband and wife," is found to be true,
and elsewhere the court finds all the allegations of the second
supplemental cross-complaint to be untrue. If we could consider the question on this appeal from the order denying a
new trial, we think the finding would have to be held sufficient. The criticism is exceedingly hypercritical. The second supplemental cross-complaint "realleges each and every
allegation in his original cross-complaint and first supplemental cross-complaint." In this way, and in this way
only, is the former allegation of marriage realleged. The
supplemental cross-complaint of itself contains only the single allegation as to adultery by plaintiff with one Brumfield
on July 2, 1900. This the court found to be untrue. There
was no issue made by the pleadings as to the marriage, and
no necessity of any finding upon the question. The plaintiff

alleged it, and defendant did not deny it, but reiterated and alleged it in his cross-complaint and answer.

It is finally claimed that the court had no power to provide in the decree for the support of the minor child—a girl— until it should reach the age of twenty-one years. We cannot modify the judgment on this appeal from the order denying a new trial. If it goes beyond the power of the court in the respects pointed out, it can at any time be modified: Crater v. Crater, 135 Cal. 633, 67 Pac. 1049.

We advise that the appeal from the judgment be dismissed and the order denying a new trial affirmed.

We concur: Gray, C.; Smith, C.

PER CURIAM.—For the reasons given in the foregoing opinion the appeal from the judgment is dismissed and the order denying a new trial affirmed.

SWIFT et al. v. OCCIDENTAL MINING AND PETRO-
LEUM COMPANY et al.*

L. A. No. 1037; October 18, 1902.

70 Pac. 470.

Appeal.—The Sufficiency of the Complaint, and whether findings of the court sustain the judgment, cannot be considered on appeal from an order denying a motion for a new trial.

Appeal.—A Specification of Error, in a Notice of Motion for a new trial, that the decision is against law for any reason appearing on the judgment-roll, can only be considered on appeal from the judgment.[1]

---

*For subsequent opinion in bank, see 141 Cal. 161, 74 Pac. 700.

[1] Cited with approval in Kaiser v. Dalto, 140 Cal. 169, 73 Pac. 829, where the court says: "It must now be regarded as the settled rule that, where all the issues of fact raised by the pleadings are found upon by the court and the findings are correct, an erroneous judgment drawn from those facts cannot be corrected by means of a motion for a new trial."

Cited and approved in Swett v. Gray, 141 Cal. 70, 74 Pac. 441, where it is said that the question of the sufficiency of the complaint is not to be considered on motion for a new trial, where there is no appeal from the judgment.

Appeal—Assignment of Error.—Under Code of Civil Procedure, sections 657, 659, requiring assignments of error to point out the particulars in which the ruling objected to is erroneous, an assignment "that the evidence is insufficient to justify the court in finding," followed by the language of the finding, but containing no specification of any particular wherein the finding is unsupported, is insufficient.[2]

Custom and Usage.—Where, in an Action Against a Mining Company, the court made a finding of fact, which was not reviewable, that plaintiff acquiesced in and consented to the use of certain oil for fuel, error, if any, in the introduction of evidence of a custom in the community to permit lessees of land for prospecting purposes to burn oil found to run their engines and pumps, was harmless.

APPEAL from Superior Court, Santa Barbara County; B. T. Williams, Judge.

Action by C. E. Swift and others against the Occidental Mining and Petroleum Company and another. Judgment for defendants, and from an order denying a new trial plaintiffs appeal. Affirmed.

B. F. Thomas for appellants; Eugene W. Squier and John J. Squier for respondents.

CHIPMAN, C.—The complaint alleges the ordinary action in ejectment to recover possession of eighty acres of land leased by plaintiffs to the assignors of defendant Occidental Mining and Petroleum Company for mining purposes. Defendant High was an employee of defendant company, and has no interest in the subject matter of the action. In the opinion the word "defendant" will have reference to the company. Defendant filed an answer and also a cross-complaint, both of which were amended by leave of court. The amended cross-complaint of defendant alleges the execution of a lease of the land by plaintiffs, setting forth the document in haec verba; the assignment to defendant; performance by defendant and its predecessors; offer to execute a renewal, and tender by defendants to plaintiffs. In a second count allegations much the same as in second defense in the answer are set forth, praying that the renewal pro-

---

[2] Cited and followed in Robson v. Colson, 9 Idaho, 220; 72 Pac. 952, the court there construing a statute of Idaho similar to sections 657 and 659 of the California Code of Civil Procedure.

vided for in the lease be decreed to be specifically performed; or, in other words, that plaintiffs be required to execute a new lease. Plaintiffs, answering the cross-complaint, denied the allegations as to performance, and alleged discontinuance of the work for periods specified; alleged also the wrongful cutting of timber, and the burning of oil for fuel; failure to pay royalties as required by the lease. The pleadings are verified. The court made findings substantially in accordance with the allegations in the amended answer and amended cross-complaint, and entered its decree enforcing specific performance of the covenant for a renewal of the lease as prayed for in the cross-complaint. Plaintiffs moved for a new trial upon a statement of the case, which being denied, they appeal from the order. There is no appeal from the judgment. There was no demurrer to the cross-complaint or answer.

It is urged by appellants that the findings are insufficient to suport the judgment, and that the cross-complaint does not state a cause of action, and that the conclusions of law are unsupported by the findings. The insufficiency of the complaint cannot be considered on an appeal from an order denying a motion for a new trial, nor on such motion can the question whether the findings sustain the judgment be considered: Martin v. Matfield, 49 Cal. 42; Brison v. Brison, 90 Cal. 323, 27 Pac. 186; Bode v. Lee, 102 Cal. 583, 36 Pac. 936; Rauer v. Fay, 128 Cal. 523, 61 Pac. 90; and numerous other cases. Where the conclusions of law are claimed to be erroneous, and not consistent with or not supported by the findings, the moving party may proceed under sections 663, 663½ of the Code of Civil Procedure (Shafer v. Lacy, 121 Cal. 574, 54 Pac. 72); and where this course is not pursued, there must be an appeal from the judgment, or the sufficiency of the findings to support the judgment cannot be considered (Patch v. Miller, 125 Cal. 240, 57 Pac. 986). In a specification in the notice of motion that "the decision is against law" for any reason appearing on the judgment-roll, such as a failure to find upon a material issue, or that wrong conclusions of law have been drawn from the findings, such specification can only be considered upon an appeal from the judgment: Thompson v. City of Los Angeles, 125 Cal. 270, 57 Pac. 1015. This court is limited in its review

of the action of the lower court, on appeal from the order
denying a new trial, to the grounds upon which the new
trial was asked: Wheeler v. Bolton, 92 Cal. 159, 28 Pac. 558.
Appellants cite Simmons v. Hamilton, 56 Cal. 493, and claim
that it was there held that the conclusions of law found by
the court and the sufficiency of the pleadings could be considered on motion for a new trial. This case has been
referred to on the point but once, so far as I can find (In re
Doyle's Estate, 73 Cal. 564, 15 Pac. 125), and it was there
said that: "A party cannot demand a new trial upon the
ground that the court erroneously applied the law to the
facts, or drew wrong conclusions of law from the facts found.
The remedy in such case is by appeal. . . . . Nothing to the
contrary was decided by a majority of this court in Simmons
v. Hamilton, 56 Cal. 493." If there is anything in the Simmons case contrary to the rules above stated, it must be
deemed to have been long since overruled. We must, therefore, confine our inquiry to alleged errors of law properly
specified in the statement, and determine whether the evidence is insufficient to justify the findings in so far as it
is so specified.

Turning to the specifications of the insufficiency of the
evidence to sustain the findings, it will be seen that all but
two of the twenty findings of fact are challenged, and in no
single instance is there the slightest attempt to specify
wherein the evidence is insufficient, except as to an incon-
sequential part of finding 12. The form of specification
is "that the evidence is insufficient to justify the court in finding," and then sets out the language of the finding, but no
specification of any particular wherein the finding is unsupported. The court has many times stated the requirements
of Code of Civil Procedure, sections 657, 659. In De Molera
v. Martin, 120 Cal. 544, 52 Pac. 825, this was done with much
care, and the earlier cases on the point were cited. In Kyle
v. Craig, 125 Cal. 107, 57 Pac. 791, the assignment was substantially the same as here, and it was said: "Unless the
particulars in which the evidence is said to be insufficient
to justify any particular finding or part thereof are pointed
out in the assignment of error, we cannot notice the assignments here." In the case of Taylor v. Bell, 128 Cal. 306, 60
Pac. 853, the assignment was in much the same form as here,

and, after stating the finding, continued as follows: "But, on the contrary, the court should have found," etc., stating what, in the opinion of appellant, should have been found. The court said: "These specifications fail to comply with the requirements of section 659 of the Code of Civil Procedure that the statement shall specify the 'particulars' in which the evidence is alleged to be insufficient." It was said by Mr. Justice Temple in the still more recent case of Type Founders' Co. v. Packer, 130 Cal. 459, 62 Pac. 744: "Whenever there is a reasonably successful effort to state 'the particulars,' and they are such as may have been sufficient to inform the opposing counsel and the court of the grounds, and the court has entertained and passed upon the motion, in my opinion this court ought not to refuse to consider the case on appeal; and especially where, as in this case, the transcript shows that all the evidence has been brought up." But in the case before us there is not even a "reasonably successful effort to state the 'particulars,'" for there is no effort at all. What is said is no more than if counsel had said "the evidence is insufficient to justify any one or all of the findings," and had let it go at that.

There are numerous assignments of error in the admission and exclusion of evidence. We have examined these alleged errors with some care, and do not find any ruling that was necessarily prejudicial. Defendants were permitted to prove that it was a custom in the vicinity of the property to permit lessees of land prospecting for oil to burn oil extracted in producing power to run their engines and pumps. Defendants pleaded no such custom, and nothing in the written lease authorized them to use the oil for this purpose, and the lease required defendants to pay to plaintiffs monthly, on demand, "one-tenth of their gross earnings derived from the sale of the products or substances aforesaid" (referring to mineral substances). The court found, among other facts, that plaintiffs "acquiesced in and consented to the use of said oil for fuel." As the evidence in support of this finding cannot be considered, the admission of the evidence could not have affected the plaintiffs' appeal. If plaintiffs consent to the use by defendants of oil for fuel, it is immaterial whether there was or was not such a custom, and, if the evidence should have been excluded, no harm was done in admitting it.

The order should be affirmed.

We concur: Gray, C.; Cooper, C.

PER CURIAM.—For the reasons given in the foregoing opinion the order is affirmed.

BELL v. STAACKE et al.*

L. A. No. 1155; October 18, 1902.

70 Pac. 472.

Appeal—Specification of Error.—Code of Civil Procedure, section 648, provides that when the exception is to the verdict or decision, upon the ground of the insufficiency of the evidence to justify it, the objection must specify the "particulars" in which such evidence is alleged to be insufficient. Held, that specifications in a bill of exceptions that the evidence "is insufficient to justify the finding" are defective.

APPEAL from Superior Court, Santa Barbara County; W. S. Day, Judge.

Action by John S. Bell against George Staacke and others. There was judgment for plaintiff, and from an order denying a new trial defendants appeal. Affirmed.

T. Z. Blakeman and Canfield & Starbuck for appellants; Jas. L. Crittenden and Richards & Carrier for respondent.

VAN DYKE, J.—The appellants' appeal from the judgment in this case has been dismissed: 137 Cal. 307, 70 Pac. 171. The matter now before the court for consideration is their appeal from the order denying their motion for a new trial.

In the notice of motion for a new trial, appellants assign, among other grounds, errors of law occurring at the trial, excepted to by such parties, and insufficiency of the evidence

---

*For subsequent opinion in bank, see 141 Cal. 186, 74 Pac. 774.

to justify the decision. The bill of exceptions, however, contains no specification on the ground of errors of law. The so-called specification of insufficiency of the evidence is in the following form: "The evidence is insufficient to justify the finding," followed by a statement of what the finding contains; and this is repeated in the same language in reference to each of the twenty-two different findings. The code requires: "When the exception is to the verdict or decision, upon the ground of the insufficiency of the evidence to justify it, the objection must specify the 'particulars' in which such evidence is alleged to be insufficient": Code Civ. Proc., sec. 648. The specification in this case clearly does not comply either with the code or repeated decisions of this court. From the specification it is impossible to ascertain in what particular the evidence fails to support any finding referred to. It is presumed that the findings are supported by the evidence, and it is only proper to require the party who challenges their correctness to point out specifically wherein the evidence fails to support the same. In Kyle v. Craig, 125 Cal. 116, 57 Pac. 795, fifteen errors were assigned, in which it was claimed the evidence was insufficient to justify the findings. This court says: "The only specification wherein the evidence is alleged to be insufficient is, 'The evidence is insufficient to justify,' etc. Unless the particulars in which the evidence is said to be insufficient to justify the particular finding, or part thereof, are pointed out in the assignment of error, we cannot notice the assignments here." In Taylor v. Bell, 128 Cal. 306, 60 Pac. 853, the specifications are like this: "The court should have done" so and so; "The evidence shows," etc.; and, as stated by the court there, "This is a form of specification which has been repeatedly held to be insufficient": See, also, Dawson v. Schloss, 93 Cal. 194, 29 Pac. 31; De Molera v. Martin, 120 Cal. 544, 52 Pac. 825. The evidence contained in the bill of exceptions in this case comprises pages from 154 to 760 of the transcript, embracing 1,820 folios, and, aside from the imperative requirement of the code referred to, it would be quite unreasonable to ask the appellate court to grope through this mass of evidence for the purpose of ascertaining whether any particular finding was supported by the evidence.

In the brief of appellant Staacke's counsel, the attention of the court is not directed to any of the alleged erroneous errors of law occurring at the trial, and counsel for the other appellants calls attention to but three alleged errors of law. These three consist of the following rulings: (1) Sustaining plaintiff's objections to the following question asked Staacke on his direct examination: "Did he [James Wheeler] make any remark to you at the time about the purpose of that deed?" (2) Sustaining the objections to the following question asked Staacke: "Did you have any conversation then with Thomas Bell?" (3) Sustaining objections to the introduction of the letter of George Staacke to Louis Jones dated September 21, 1892. The question asked called for a conversation with James Wheeler, Thomas Bell's attorney, about the purpose of the deed of March 7, 1889; and the conversation referred to occurred two months after such deed was executed and recorded, and after plaintiff had taken possession of the ranch. It is not shown that the plaintiff was present at the time of the supposed conversation, or that James Wheeler was his attorney or agent, or was authorized to speak or act for him. So in reference to the question, "Did you have any conversation then with Thomas Bell?" that conversation occurred after the deed from Thomas Bell was executed and recorded; and it is not shown that John S. Bell was present or within hearing at the time of such supposed conversation, and no foundation was laid for the introduction of the alleged conversation between Bell and Staacke. The objections were properly sustained to the introduction of the letter of George Staacke to Louis Jones. It was a private letter written after the death of Thomas Bell, and it was not shown that it had ever been seen by John S. Bell, or that he ever knew anything about its existence. Under the circumstances, the rulings of the court complained of were not erroneous.

The order appealed from is affirmed.

We concur: Garoutte, J.; Harrison, J.

HOBSON v. SILVA et al.

S. F. No. 2575; October 31, 1902.

70 Pac. 619.

Lease—Construction—Surrender.—A Contract of Lease and an Amendment thereof provided for the payment of rental as follows: A rental of $30 per month; $4,000 to a bank (the amount being secured by mortgage on the premises), together with $26.65 per month as interest thereon; also $900, which is "now a lien on the premises," as follows: $200 in one year, $200 in two and one-half years, and $350 "at the expiration of the lease," or whenever the lessee purchases the premises, under an option. The lease was to run for twenty years, unless sooner terminated. Thereafter the lessee surrendered possession, a part of the monthly rental and interest, and also the first installment of the $900, having accrued. Held, that the lessee could not object to a construction of the lease which merely made her liable for the sums mentioned, and released her from liability for the $4,000 and the two installments of the $900 which had not matured, etc.

Lease—Gas and Water Bills.—A Lessee Who Makes a Lease, knowing that other tenants are in possession, who are to attorn to her, cannot recover from the landlord for gas and water bills overdue when she takes possession, where it does not appear that they are not the personal bills of the other tenants.

Lease.—A Lease Provided That the Lessee's Liability should not commence until a certain suit is "finally adjudicated and determined in favor of G." It was admitted that the suit was adjudicated in favor of G. by a judgment rendered on September 3d, as alleged in the complaint. After said date an amended lease was made, making no mention of the lawsuit. Defendant from the very first paid rent, regardless of the provision. Held, that, even if the allegation of the complaint was not as broad as the language used in the lease, it might be assumed that the provision was regarded as fully complied with.

APPEAL from Superior Court, Alameda County; John Ellsworth, Judge.

Action by H. F. Hobson against Louisa Silva and husband. Judgment for plaintiff and defendants appeal. Affirmed.

Edward A. Holman for appellants; Oscar G. Heaton and F. W. Sawyer for respondent.

CHIPMAN, C.—This action is brought to recover certain money claimed to be due under a contract of lease and an amendment thereof. The contracts stipulate for the payment of sundry sums, which were to be treated as rental. The lease was to run for twenty years, unless sooner terminated, and defendants had the right to purchase the leased premises on certain conditions. Among the payments agreed to be paid by defendants was a rental of $30 per month; also $4,000 to the Oakland Savings Bank, secured by mortgage on the premises, together with $26.65 per month as interest thereon; also the sum of $900, which is "now a lien on said premises," as follows: $200 in one year, $200 in two and one-half years and $350 "at the expiration of the lease, or whenever she [Louisa] purchases said premises." The original document was made on April 13, 1897, but defendants did not go into personal possession until December 15, 1897, on which day the amendment to the lease was executed. The lessees did not exercise the option to purchase, but surrendered possession on January 11, 1899. At this time they had paid interest to the bank from the date of the lease, up to October 19, 1898, but no more. They paid no part of the $4,000 and no part of the $900, and there was then due the monthly rental for seven months next preceding January 11, 1899. The court found of these amounts, as due plaintiff, seven months' rental, $210; the first installment of the $900 payment, $200; and interest due the bank, for which plaintiff was liable to it, being two months and some nineteen or twenty days, $70.29; or, in all, $480.29. The court did not allow any part of the principal sum of $4,000, nor any of the installments of the $900 payment not yet due. It is not easy to understand the meaning of the original contract. It reads like the handiwork of a not very skillful layman. The amendment is almost complete in itself, and is prepared with some sort of comprehension of what the parties were aiming at; and, read in connection with the original contract, it is possible to arrive at the intention of the parties with reasonable certainty. So far as we can discover, the court gave the agreements a construction as fair to defendants as they could ask.

1. Appellants' principal contention is that under the terms of the agreements they were discharged from all liability on surrender of possession, as well for liabilities accrued as to accrue. They surrendered the possession voluntarily at a time when they were in default. They commenced paying

interest to the bank the day after the execution of the
original lease, to wit, April 14, 1897.   They paid rental also,
although not in possession, until in December; and this was
because they were collecting rents from tenants in occupation
during that time.   Appellants ask that all these items be
eliminated from the account, and that their liability shall
begin from the date they themselves took possession.   This
we do not think should be allowed.   We can find nothing in
the contracts warranting the claim that the surrender of
possession released the lessees from obligations already incurred.   The court seems to have acquitted them of the
liabilities yet to accrue, but not yet discharged, and this was
as favorable to appellants as they could reasonably claim.

2. Defendants offered to prove by Frank Silva, one of defendants, that when they took possession there were overdue
gas and water bills, and that plaintiff refused to pay the
same; this in support of a counterclaim pleaded in the answer.   The testimony was excluded on objection as irrelevant and immaterial.   Defendants claim that this was error.
It appeared from Silva's testimony that he knew there were
tenants in possession when the lease was made, who, by an
agreement between plaintiff and defendants, were to attorn
to defendants.   It was not shown that these bills were
chargeable to plaintiff, nor when they accrued.   So far as
anything to the contrary appears, they were or might have
been the bills of the tenants from whom defendants were collecting rents, and for which plaintiff was in no way liable,
and which he might well have refused to pay.   Defendants
took the lease with such possession as could then be given,
and they apparently accepted the situation, and went into
full possession later on without objection, in the meantime
having paid rent to plaintiff, and interest to the bank, as
though satisfied.   The court did not err in excluding the
testimony.

3. It is urged that the demurrer to the complaint should
have been sustained.   So far as we can discover from defendants' brief, the reason for this claim is based in part on
the assumption that, by the terms of the lease set out in the
complaint, the defendants were released from all past
liability on surrender of the premises.   We have already
seen that this is a mistaken view of the agreements.

3

4. It is also claimed that by the terms of the lease there was no liability of defendants until a certain lawsuit, entitled "Gooby v. Graf," "is finally adjudicated and determined in favor of John Gooby." It was admitted that said lawsuit was "adjudicated and determined in favor of John Gooby by a judgment in said superior court duly given and made" on September 3, 1897, as alleged in the complaint. Even if it be conceded that the allegation is not as comprehensive as the language used in the lease, it is not true that defendants were to incur no liability whatever unless this lawsuit was "finally" adjudicated. The amended lease makes no mention of this lawsuit, and as it was entered into after the lawsuit was in fact determined, and as defendants had from the beginning paid, regardless of this provision, it is altogether probable that the provision was regarded as fully complied with. At any rate, we do not think the general demurrer to the entire complaint should be sustained, if it be conceded that, as to some of the payments to be made, they were not payable until after this event had happened.

We discover no error in the record, and therefore advise that the judgment and order be affirmed.

We concur: Gray, C.; Haynes, C.

PER CURIAM.—For the reasons given in the foregoing opinion the judgment and order are affirmed.

BACOME v. BLACK.

S. F. No. 2399; October 29, 1902.

70 Pac. 620.

Money Lent.—In an Action to Recover Money Loaned, a Finding that the money was loaned defendant and another jointly, and that defendant promised to repay the same, is not inconsistent, so as to be insufficient to support a judgment for plaintiff.

Money Lent—Evidence.—In an Action for Money Loaned, it was contended by defendant that the credit was given and the money loaned another. Plaintiff showed the loan was brought about by the other, but that defendant got the money to assist him in purchasing a newspaper route. Held, not prejudicial error to admit testimony that on the following day plaintiff loaned defendant a sum to make up the amount necessary to purchase the route.

APPEAL from Superior Court, City and County of San Francisco; J. C. B. Hebbard, Judge.

Action by Sarah Bacome against Thomas Black. From a judgment for plaintiff, and from an order denying a new trial defendant appeals. Affirmed.

Arnold W. Liechti for appellant; Rodgers, Paterson & Slack (J. E. Barry of counsel) for respondent.

CHIPMAN, C.—Action to recover $1,000 alleged to have been loaned by plaintiff to defendant, at the latter's instance, upon agreement to pay the same within six months. It is alleged that plaintiff has frequently demanded and as often defendant has refused payment. The complaint is verified, and the answer denies its allegations specifically and denies any indebtedness. Plaintiff had judgment, and defendant appeals from the judgment and order denying his motion for a new trial. The court found the following facts: (1) "That on August 28, 1897, ... plaintiff did, at the special instance and request of defendant and Jeanie Black, loan and deliver to defendant and Jeanie Black jointly the sum of $1,000"; (2) "defendant promised to repay the same to plaintiff, with interest, within six months from date"; (3) "that plaintiff has demanded of defendant at various times the payment of said amount since the same became due, but that defendant has failed and refused to pay the same, or any part thereof, or the interest thereon."

1. It is claimed that the findings do not support the judgment, for the reason that the court found (finding 1) that the loan, which is the basis of the suit, was made to two persons (defendant and another) jointly at their request, but fails to find a breach of contract (nonpayment of the debt) on the part of both parties, the debtors (finding 3). The action is against one of the parties to whom the loan of $1,000 was made, and as to the one sued (defendant) the court found that he alone and not both, "promised to repay the same to plaintiff, with interest" (finding 2). The breach was the failure to pay the money when due, as promised. There is no allegation in the complaint that Jeanie Black agreed to pay anything, and there is no finding that she so agreed. The promise of defendant to pay the amount is not inconsistent with the fact found that plaintiff furnished the money to both jointly.

2. It is claimed that the evidence does not support the findings. It appears from the testimony that defendant desired to purchase an "Examiner" route in San Francisco, but had not the money necessary to do so. His sister Jeanie undertook to borrow $1,000 for defendant for this purpose from plaintiff, who was then an unmarried servant girl, named Sarah O'Connor. Plaintiff testified that she went with Jeanie to the Hibernia Bank and drew out the money. "Mr. Black [defendant] was waiting outside of the bank for us to come out." When the two came out Black said: "Sarah, I am much obliged to you for your kindness. It is doing me a great favor." It appeared from the testimony of other witnesses that Black got the money and used it to purchase the route. Plaintiff testified "that the money was loaned to Miss Black to give to her brother to purchase the 'Examiner' route." There is evidence tending to show that Black acknowledged the indebtedness and promised to settle it. There is some evidence tending to show that plaintiff gave the credit to Jeanie, and looked to her, and not to her brother, the defendant. At the same time it is clear that the money was obtained for and was used by defendant. Jeanie had no use for the money, and acted only as an intermediary or agent for her brother. The evidence is perhaps sufficient to show that Jeanie was also liable, but not necessarily to the exclusion of defendant's liability. The defendant offered no evidence, but rested wholly on plaintiff's failure of proof. Considering all the facts as testified to by plaintiff's witnesses, we think there was sufficient evidence to justify the findings of the court.

3. Maggie Larsen, a witness, testified that on the day following the day on which defendant got the money from plaintiff she loaned him $450 to make up the amount necessary to complete the purchase of the route. An objection to the testimony as immaterial and irrelevant was overruled, and defendant claims that the ruling was error. We can not see that the evidence was material. Neither can we say that it was prejudicial error to admit it.

The judgment and order should be affirmed.

We concur: Haynes, C.; Cooper, C.

PER CURIAM.—For the reasons given in the foregoing opinion the judgment and order are affirmed.

MORRISON v. McAVOY et al.

S. F. No. 2520; October 30, 1902.

70 Pac. 626.

Sidewalks—Openings—Liability of Tenant.—A city ordinance provided that no person should obstruct any sidewalk so as to interfere with its convenient use, and that every one should keep around every flight of stairs descending from the sidewalk to the basement a fence or railing at least two feet high. Held, that where the owner of a building had made an opening in the sidewalk, with stairs running to the cellar, the opening being provided with iron doors that constituted part of the sidewalk when closed, a use by the tenant of the opening and doors so as to violate the ordinance rendered only the tenant liable, and not the landlord.

Sidewalks.—An Opening in a Sidewalk With Stairs leading to the cellar, the doors forming part of the sidewalk when closed, and the sides of the doors affording a protection when open, was not a violation of the ordinance.

APPEAL from Superior Court, Alameda County; F. B. Ogden, Judge.

Action by Georgie Morrison against J. C. McAvoy and others. From a judgment for defendants, plaintiff appeals. Affirmed.

Fred W. Fry and Edward A. Holman for appellant; Fitzgerald & Abbott and Johnson & Shaw for respondents.

CHIPMAN, C.—A demurrer was sustained to plaintiff's third amended complaint and, plaintiff declining to further amend, judgment passed for defendants, from which plaintiff appeals. The demurrer was by two of the defendants, but seems to have been treated by counsel and the court as filed in behalf of all the defendants, and we will so treat it.

The complaint alleges that defendant Eletta Brown was the owner and the other defendants were tenants of the premises, situated in the city of Oakland, where the alleged injury occurred; that an ordinance of said city provided that "no person shall . . . . so occupy or obstruct any sidewalks as to interfere with the convenient use of the same by all passengers"; also that "every person shall keep around

every . . . . flight of stairs descending from the sidewalk
to the basement owned or occupied by him, a fence or railing at least three feet high." It is alleged that in 1892
said Brown leased the premises to one M. Beaudry, now
deceased, and defendant G. Peladeau, for a term of six
years; that at the time said Brown so leased said lot she
"maintained without any license, ... underneath the sidewalk which is in front of said premises, ... an unauthorized
and unprotected excavation, and also an unauthorized and unprotected opening thereto, with doors to said opening about
sixteen inches in height when opened, and which are fitted
to and usually cover said opening and form part of said
sidewalk, ... and which opening . . . . has an unauthorized flight of stairs . . . . leading into said cellar underneath said premises, and which said doors, ... when
opened, and which said excavation and opening thereto and
said flight of stairs, each and all constituted an impediment
. . . . in, under, upon, and over said sidewalk," contrary to
said ordinance; that "said cellar, doors, and opening and
flight of stairs were used for ordinary business purposes";
that said "Brown never furnished any other means of access
to said cellar, and never provided any guard, ... or protection whatsoever against accidents, or any fence or railing . . . . about said" opening, and said "opening, doors,
and flight of stairs each and all constituted and caused at
all times herein mentioned an unauthorized trap, obstruction, and nuisance upon, in, and under said sidewalk," that
when the said Brown so leased said premises she well knew
the condition of the said opening, etc., as above described,
and she received rent for said premises at all said times in
their then condition; that defendant Hugh B. McAvoy was appointed administrator of the estate of said Beaudry, deceased, in 1895; that said defendants, Hugh McAvoy, as
administrator, and said Peladeau, wrongfully sublet a
portion of the first floor of said premises and the said cellar
with its said approaches, for the month of October, 1897, to
their codefendant, J. C. McAvoy; that when said administrator and said Peladeau so rented said premises for the
month of October, 1897, they knew the said condition of
said cellar, door and stairway, and knew that they constituted a nuisance, but did not furnish any fence, railing or
guard, or protection around said opening and stairs, or any

other means of access to said cellar, and they received rental for the use thereof. It is then alleged that defendant J. C. McAvoy "maintained and used said unauthorized and unprotected flight of stairs, excavation, and opening with said doors, in the same condition in which they were so originally leased to him"; that on October 27, 1897, each and all said defendants "permitted the said doors to be opened and raised from the position in which they were kept while forming a part of said sidewalk, and carelessly and negligently suffered .... said doors to remain opened and raised, and said flight of stairs .... to remain uncovered without any guard, fence, railing, barricade, or protection whatever," and plaintiff, during the daytime of said day, while "carefully traveling along said .... sidewalk, ... and while wholly unaware of said obstruction, ... with said doors raised in said sidewalk, ... was, without fault or negligence on her part, ... precipitated into .... said .... opening .... and down said flight of stairs and into said cellar," and was thereby injured.

The demurrer is on several grounds: (1) That Hugh McAvoy is improperly joined as a defendant, although it appears from the complaint that he individually was not a tenant, and the only interest he had was as administrator of Beaudry, deceased. (2) Misjoinder also as to J. C. McAvoy, although he was the surviving partner of Beaudry & McAvoy, and as such surviving partner was engaged in winding up the partnership business, and the accident happened after Beaudry's death. (3) That the complaint does not state facts sufficient to constitute a cause of action against any one or all of the defendants. (4) The complaint is uncertain in several particulars, and especially it does not appear how the doors could be open and the opening unguarded, and the doors constitute an obstruction over the sidewalk, or interfere with its safe use, or how the doors were in disregard of plaintiff's safety. It does not appear whether the doors or the opening constituted the impediment; nor does it appear whether plaintiff was injured by reason of the doors or the opening, "or whether she stumbled over the doors into the opening, or simply stepped into the opening without touching the doors." It does not appear how plaintiff, in the daytime, while carefully traveling over the sidewalk, was unaware of said doors, or opening, or stairs, or whether she did not see them, or was unfamiliar with the premises.

As to defendants Brown, Hugh McAvoy and Peladeau, the complaint fails to show any liability. The iron doors appear not to have been an obstruction when closed, and no defect in the manner of their construction is alleged, and it is averred that they constituted part of the pavement when closed. Such doors, as means of ingress and egress to and from the basement of buildings in towns and cities, are not unusual, and do not constitute a nuisance per se, and are not forbidden by the ordinance pleaded. It is the failure to properly use the doors that introduces the element of danger, and for this improper use the tenant in possession alone is liable. If the complaint shows that the tenant, J. C. McAvoy, failed to protect the opening when the doors were open, he alone must answer the consequences. The principles governing such cases were fully discussed in Rider v. Clark, 132 Cal. 382, 64 Pac. 564.

The first part of the ordinance above quoted was not infringed by the construction of the doors, for they formed part of the sidewalk, and were safe when closed, so far as is alleged. The second portion of the ordinance refers to open stairways as they are sometimes constructed next to the buildings or next to the curb, and where the protection around the stairs is by a railing; in which case the protection or railing must be three feet high, and is permanent, and is the only protection required. The iron door openings in the present case are entirely different, and the usual protection to pedestrians are the sides of the door, as was the case of Rider v. Clark. The complaint seems to proceed upon the theory that the opening, with the doors, the stairs, and the cellar, were all unauthorized, and in violation of the ordinance, and together constituted a nuisance. There is nothing to show that the use of the basement by these means was unauthorized, except the ordinance, and this does not go so far. Indeed, it impliedly permits access to the basement of buildings from the sidewalk by means of stairs. When the accident occurred, the doors were open, and, as near as we can understand the complaint, the pleader left us ground to assume that he intended to allege that the doors were standing upright, and offered an impediment sixteen inches high to protect and warn persons passing along the sidewalk. The complaint does not show how long these doors were, or how much space they occupied. If there had been a distinct allegation—which there is not—that the sides of the door were not high enough to offer reasonable protection to footmen in the daytime, or had alleged clearly that the doors were opened out and laid flat on the pavement, offering no protection, there would have been a different case presented. The complaint, as we have said, seems to rest on the assumption that the only right defendants had was to make an opening for a stairway and provide a fence or railing around such opening three feet high. The ordinance justifies no such position.

Plaintiff might have presented the distinct issue, on which she would have the right to be heard, that the iron doors, when open and standing upright, was a negligent and dangerous use made of the opening to the basement, irrespective of the ordinance. She evaded this issue, and relied on the prohibitions of the ordinance, which, as we have seen, does not cover her case.

The judgment should be affirmed.

We concur: Gray, C.; Haynes, C.

PER CURIAM.—For the reasons given in the foregoing opinion the judgment is affirmed.

METZ et al. v. BELL.

L. A. No. 1154; November 5, 1902.

70 Pac. 618.

Nonsuit.—Where, in an Action on a Promise Made in a Letter written by defendant's intestate, the court struck out the testimony of the intestate's wife that the letter was the writing of her husband, and there was no other evidence in the record showing that he wrote it, the refusal to grant a nonsuit was erroneous.

Appeal.—Where the Record Purports to Contain All the Evidence taken at the trial of an action, the court on appeal will not presume that resort was had to evidence not disclosed by the record.

APPEAL from Superior Court, Los Angeles County; D. K. Trask, Judge.

Action by George E. Metz and another against Susan W. Bell, as administratrix of the estate of Nathaniel Bell, deceased. From a judgment for plaintiffs, defendant appeals. Reversed.

Henry C. Dillon and George A. Corbin for appellant; Oscar Lawler and Carroll Allen for respondents.

PER CURIAM.—This is an action upon a promise in writing alleged to have been contained in a letter written by Nathaniel Bell, now deceased, on October 18, 1896, and addressed to one of the plaintiffs, by which said Bell agreed to pay plaintiffs $5,000 in the event of a sale by Bell of certain mining property of his situate in Grant county, New Mexico, to any of the parties to whom plaintiffs had endeavored to sell the same, said sum to be paid upon payment in full of the purchase price obtained at such sale.

The plaintiffs' case depended almost entirely for evidence to support it upon the letter above referred to, and without said letter in evidence the case would be entirely without support. Against the objection and exception of defendant a foundation was laid for the introduction of this letter through the testimony of the defendant Mrs. Bell, she testifying that the letter was the writing of Mr. Bell. After the letter had been placed in evidence the court expressed some doubt as to the correctness of its ruling in permitting the witness to testify to her husband's handwriting, and seemed to think that it should have been excluded under the provision of subdivision 1, section 1881 of the Code of Civil Procedure, forbidding the examination of a husband or wife as a witness for or against each other without the other's consent, etc. On the suggestion of this difficulty in the mind of the court, the attorney for plaintiffs said: "Before the case is finished we will call an expert to testify as to handwriting." Subsequently a motion for nonsuit was made by defendant at the conclusion of plaintiffs' evidence, and on another suggestion of doubt in the mind of the court as to the competency of Mrs. Bell's evidence the motion to strike it out was renewed and granted in following language by the court: "Then the motion will be granted, and her testimony stricken out, as I consider all of her testimony immaterial in any event. She was called to prove nothing but the handwriting,

and they have proven that by the testimony of Mr. Metz.''
The motion for a nonsuit was immediately thereafter denied
by the court. At no time was any evidence of experts introduced to prove that the letter of October 18th was written
by Bell, nor was Metz at any time asked anything concerning
the handwriting of that particular letter. He did testify
that the letters attached to this deposition, or that would be
attached thereto, were in the handwriting of Bell, and were
received by him from Bell; but we have searched the record
in vain for anything to show that the letter of October 18th
was attached to the deposition. The letter itself was duly
objected to when offered in evidence, and the only foundation for its introduction being stricken out, the letter necessarily also went out of the case. There is nothing to show
that the other letters of Bell were used in any way to establish the handwriting of the letter of October 18th, and, inasmuch as the record purports to contain all the evidence
taken at the trial, we cannot presume that resort was had to
any evidence not disclosed by the record.

There is nothing in the argument that the circumstances
of the case established the fact that the letter was written
by Bell. As plaintiffs' case depended entirely upon this letter, the motion for a nonsuit should have been granted. And,
as a new trial must be had for this reason, it will be unnecessary to discuss the other errors complained of. The failure
to introduce the testimony of experts to prove the handwriting of the letter of October 18th doubtless resulted from the
mistake of court and counsel in supposing that the handwriting of that letter had been established by the testimony of
Metz in his deposition. This mistake will doubtless be remedied upon a new trial in such a way as to leave it unnecessary to determine whether Metz would be a competent witness
to prove the handwriting of the deceased, Bell.

The judgment and order are reversed.

HILDRETH v. MONTECITO CREEK WATER COMPANY.*

L. A. No. 1256; November 6, 1902.

70 Pac. 672.

Water Company.—A Complaint Seeking to Compel a Water Company to Supply plaintiff's premises with water, which alleged, in terms, that the water controlled by the defendant had been appropriated to public use, was not so deficient in that regard as to be subject to a general demurrer, though the facts might have been more specifically stated.

Water Company—Right of Consumer to Demand Water.—The waters of a certain creek had been diverted by a ditch and distributed among the neighboring inhabitants, including plaintiff's grantor, for more than five years prior to the formation of a company for the principal purpose of supplying water to the stockholders and others entitled thereto, whether as riparian owners or as appropriators. This company, with the acquiescence of all parties, diverted the water into pipes, and for twenty-five years delivered it to those entitled thereto. Held, that by a prescription of thirty years, confirmed by an implied contract, plaintiff was entitled to demand that the company continue to supply him his share of the water on payment of reasonable rates.

Water Company—Action to Compel Supply.—Constitution, Article 14, section 1, declares the use of water "appropriated for sale, rental, or distribution" to be a public use. A complaint alleged that the waters of a certain creek had been appropriated by a company to public use. It was proved that the company controlling the water of the creek was formed for the principal purpose of distributing it to those entitled thereto by a prior appropriation to public use or as riparian owners. Held, that there was no variance.

Water Company—Public Use.—Where Several of Those Entitled to the waters of a certain creek, as a public use, formed a corporation for the purpose of distributing the water, and all but one of those entitled thereto subsequently became stockholders, the use was not thereby rendered any the less a public one.

Water Rights.—Where the Rights of a Community to the water of a certain creek were appurtenant to the lands of the individuals composing the community, each individual land owner had an appropriative right to his share of the water.

Water Rights.—Where One had an Appropriative Right as a land owner to his share of the water of a certain creek, and the

*For subsequent opinion in bank, see 139 Cal. 22, 72 Pac. 395.

water was afterward taken by a corporation for the purpose of distributing it to those entitled thereto, the land owner could not be restricted, by way of estoppel or contract, in the appropriative right to his share, by by-laws of the corporation of which he had no notice.

Water Rights—Adverse User.—Where One had an Appropriative right as a land owner to his share of the water of a certain creek, and the water was afterward taken by a company for the purpose of distributing it to those entitled thereto, and the land owner for eight years was not supplied by the company, after which he regularly received his share from it, he did not lose his right by an adverse user of the company during the intervening period.

APPEAL from Superior Court, Santa Barbara County; W. S. Day, Judge.

Action by Edward Hildreth against the Montecito Creek Water Company. From a judgment in favor of plaintiff, defendant appeals. Affirmed.

G. H. Gould for appellant; Canfield & Starbuck for respondent.

SMITH, C.—This is an appeal from a judgment adjudging plaintiff entitled to have his premises in the Montecito, in the county of Santa Barbara, known as the "Lorenzana Place," supplied with water from the pipes and waterworks of defendant corporation, as the same were being supplied at the time of the commencement of the suit, at the rate of one dollar per month, or such other reasonable rate as may hereafter be lawfully fixed for such water supply, and that defendant, its officers, etc., provided the rates be paid, be perpetually enjoined from shutting off from said premises the water supply aforesaid. The grounds urged for reversal, in addition to some alleged errors of law that will not require consideration, are that the complaint does not state a cause of action, that the judgment is not supported by the findings, and that certain of the findings are not justified by the evidence.

The objection to the complaint is, in effect, that it is not sufficiently alleged that the waters controlled and managed by the defendant have been appropriated or dedicated to public use. But it is so, in terms, alleged; and, though the facts might have been more specifically stated, the complaint, in the absence of special demurrer, is, we think, sufficient.

The objections to the findings are that there is a fatal variance between the case as found and as alleged, and that the findings are otherwise insufficient to support the judgment. The case, as affected by these objections, is as follows: For more than five years prior to the year 1877, the waters of Hot Springs creek, to the extent of its entire summer flow, had, by means of a ditch, been diverted from their natural channel and distributed generally among the inhabitants of the Montecito, in the neighborhood of the creek, including plaintiff's predecessors in title, and by them appropriated and adversely used on their respective lands, and as appurtenant thereto; and the said inhabitants had thereby become entitled, as appropriators, to the use of said waters. But in June of that year certain of the inhabitants, riparian owners on Montecito creek and its tributaries, of which Hot Springs creek was one, posted above the head of the ditch used by the inhabitants, and caused to be recorded, a notice of appropriation of the waters of the creek, for the purpose, as expressed in said notice, "of furnishing themselves and other riparian proprietors upon said [Montecito] creek and its tributaries with water for household and domestic purposes, watering stock, bathing, irrigating grounds, lands, and premises, propelling machinery," etc., "and for the purpose of selling and supplying for like purposes water to other inhabitants," etc.; and in August, 1877, a corporation was organized by these parties, named the Montecito Water Company, having, as expressed in its articles, the same objects, but, as found by the court, its principal object being to supply with water themselves and others entitled, as riparian proprietors or as appropriators, to the use of the waters of said creek. By this corporation the waters of the creek were diverted, by means of a pipe connecting with the creek above the head of the old ditch, and distributed among the inhabitants of the Montecito "who were riparian owners of said creek, and to other persons in said Montecito whose lands were in the neighborhood of said creek, though not riparian thereto." Of the persons thus supplied, most were stockholders of the company, who were supplied with water as such; but others who were not stockholders were also supplied, and charged monthly rates for the use of the company's works and for the water supplied them. Among the latter were Lorenzana and wife, the occupants of the place now owned by the plaintiff; and they and the plaintiff have respectively ever since been supplied with water by the Montecito Water Company and its successor, the defendant, at the monthly rate of one dollar. After the formation of the former company most of the persons entitled to water, and finally all other than the Lorenzanas and the plaintiff, became stockholders of the corporation.

Upon this state of facts, leaving out of view the question of variance, it is clear the plaintiff was entitled to recover. His predecessors in title, the Lorenzanas, it is expressly found, were in the year 1877 entitled to the use of the water of the Hot Spring creek in common with other owners of land in the Montecito. Nor were any of the subsequent transactions of the parties of a character to affect their rights or those of the plaintiff. The appropriation and use of the water by the predecessor of defendant were not adverse. On the contrary, it is found that the principal object of the original incorporation was the distribution of the waters of the creek among those entitled to it; and the conduct of the defendant in carrying out this object, and the acquiescence of the other parties, must be taken as constituting a contract between them and the defendant, imposing upon the latter the obligation to distribute the water according to the rights of the parties, and upon the former the obligation of paying a reasonable proportion of the expenses incurred in carrying out this object. It may be said, therefore, that the plaintiff's right to the water he has been using is supported by an uninterrupted prescription of over thirty years, confirmed by contract, and that, so long as the defendant continues to divert the water of the creek, it will remain subject to the obligation of delivering to the plaintiff his share upon the payment of reasonable rates.

As to the supposed variance, we do not see there is any. For not only has the water in question been appropriated for sale, rental and distribution, within the language and intent of the provisions of section 1, article 14, of the constitution (Price v. Irrigating Co., 56 Cal. 433; McCrary v. Beaudry, 67 Cal. 120, 7 Pac. 264; Merrill v. Irrigation Co., 112 Cal. 426, 44 Pac. 720; Crow v. Irrigation Co., 130 Cal. 309, 62 Pac. 562, 1058), but the original appropriation of the water to the use of the inhabitants of the Montecito was itself an appropriation to public use, and the waters thus appropriated came, impressed with this use, into the hands of the predecessor of the defendant, which thus became charged, and its successor after it, with the administration of the use (Bouv. Law Dict., "Public Use"; Pocantico Waterworks Co., v. Bird, 130 N. Y. 249, 259, 29 N. E. 246, and authorities cited; Witcher v. Holland Waterworks Co., 66 Hun, 619, 20 N. Y. Supp. 560; Lewis, Em. Dom., c. 7). Nor is the use to which the water was originally appropriated any the less a public use because of the fact that all of the beneficiaries, other than plaintiff, have become stockholders of the company. Upon the facts found, the original corporation is to be regarded, so far as the water in question is concerned, as a mere agency of the parties entitled to the use of the water, whether stockholders or others, for the purposes of distribution: Shorb v. Beaudry, 56 Cal. 446. It acquired no rights to the water by its notice of appropriation, except to the surplus after the satisfaction of the public use. Nor does it appear to have since acquired any further rights, either by purchase or by prescription.

It is, however, objected that the evidence is insufficient to justify the finding as to the rights of the predecessors of the plaintiff and other inhabitants of the Montecito to the use of the waters in question; the specific objection being "that no use is shown that is definite enough to constitute an appropriative right in any individual." But it is well settled that an easement may be acquired by an unincorporated community, as well as by individuals—the only difference being that in the former case it is said to be acquired by custom; in the latter, by prescription: Washb. Easem. 7, 137, 146; Godd. Easem. 18; Co. Litt. 113a et seq. But where the rights thus acquired by the community are appurtenant to the several lands of the individuals composing it, there is acquired also by each owner an individual right; the relations of the parties being analogous to those of partners, or the members of unincorporated associations, or other joint owners. There may be, therefore, at the same time a public easement in the community, and a private easement in each of its individual members (Jones, Easem., sec. 82); and the individuals entitled to the use may, where their rights are attacked. avail themselves of either or both.

It is further objected that the plaintiff and his predecessors received the water allowed them under certain conditions prescribed by the by-laws of the company, and thus became restricted, either by way of contract or estoppel, to the use of the water at the option of defendant. We do not quite understand the argument, but, whatever might otherwise be its force, it is sufficiently met by the fact that there is nothing to show that they knew of or accepted any conditions affecting their rights.

Finally it is claimed that it appears from the evidence that from 1877 to 1885 Lorenzana was not supplied from the pipes of the company, but got such water as leaked from its flume only. But how this is, we need not inquire. The question is not whether Lorenzana acquired a right by user, but whether he lost his right by adverse user of the defendant or its predecessor, and we find nothing in the evidence to justify the latter conclusion. So, also, it is not denied that he has received water from the defendant ever since 1885.

We advise that the judgment appealed from be affirmed.

We concur: Gray, C.; Chipman, C.

PER CURIAM.—For the reasons given in the foregoing opinion the judgment appealed from is affirmed.

MURPHY v. CROWLEY et al.[*]

S. F. No. 2481; December 8, 1902.

70 Pac. 1024.

Limitation of Action—Recovery of Property Obtained by Fraud. A complaint states a cause of action, not for recovery of real estate, but for relief on the ground of fraud, which, by Code of Civil Procedure, section 338, subdivision 4, is barred in three years, it being by a daughter of C., deceased, against his second wife, and alleging that C. being addicted to drink, so as to partially disqualify him from business and render him the prey of designing persons, defendant resolved to get possession of his property, and for this purpose married him, and shortly thereafter, in pursuance of this purpose,

------

[*]For subsequent opinion in bank, see 140 Cal. 141, 73 Pac. 820.

4

while from drinking he was not able to intelligently transact business, she, by influence of her superior will, got him to deed property
to her, and title to property which he bought was taken in her name
at her instance and dictation, he being compelled thereto and overpowered by her will; and the prayer being that it be adjudged that
the conveyance was obtained by fraud and undue influence, and that
it be set aside, and that the title to the second lot was taken in her
name through fraud and undue influence, and that she holds it in
trust.

APPEAL from Superior Court, City and County of San
Francisco; Jas. M. Troutt, Judge

Action by Ellen E. Murphy against Margaret E. Crowley
and another. Judgment for defendants and plaintiff appeals.
Affirmed.

A. E. Nathanson and T. M. Osmont for appellant; Sullivan
& Sullivan and Theo. J. Roche for respondents.

VAN DYKE, J.—The court below sustained a demurrer
to the amended complaint, and, plaintiff failing to amend
again within the time allowed for such purpose, judgment was
entered for the defendants. The appeal is taken from the
judgment upon the judgment-roll. The amended complaint
states substantially the following facts: That the plaintiff is
of the age of twenty-three years, and the wife of John P.
Murphy; that at the age of one and a half years, to wit, in
1877, plaintiff was an orphan of the name of Ellen E. Barry,
and was then received into the family of Daniel F. Crowley
and his wife, Elizabeth Crowley, and was by them reared,
nutured, and educated the same as though she had been their
child, and until the death of Elizabeth Crowley, June 24,
1890; that she thereafter continued to reside with Daniel F.
Crowley as his daughter, and that in January, 1890, a few
days after the death of Elizabeth, his wife, the plaintiff was
adopted by said Daniel F. Crowley by an order and decree
of the superior court of the city and county of San Francisco;
that, about three months after the death of his said wife,
Crowley became addicted to the use of alcoholic liquors to
such an extent as to partially disqualify him for business,
and render him the prey of artful and designing persons;
and, upon information and belief, the plaintiff alleges that
defendant Margaret E. Crowley "looked with covetous eyes

upon the lands and possessions, hereinafter described, of said Daniel F. Crowley, and with languishing eyes upon Daniel himself, and resolved to possess herself of Daniel first, and to annex his estate later, and in pursuance of this ingenious scheme she beguiled Daniel into a marriage with her, and accordingly, on the second day of June, 1890, the said Daniel F. Crowley married the said Margaret, who thereupon moved into his home and took possession; that said Daniel F. Crowley was at the time of said marriage the owner and possessed of a certain lot of land firstly hereinafter described, the same being the lot upon which he and plaintiff were then residing; that after their said marriage the said Daniel and his wife, Margaret, occupied and resided continuously on said lot . . . . until the death of said Daniel, as hereinafter stated; that the defendant Margaret E. Crowley was and is a woman of strong will and imperious and domineering disposition; that for more than a month after his marriage with said defendant said Daniel F. Crowley indulged his drinking habit to such an extent that he was not able to intelligently transact business, as plaintiff is informed and believes; that immediately after their said marriage the defendant, Margaret, as plaintiff is informed and believes, in execution of said previously formed design on her part, sought to obtain a conveyance to her from said Daniel F. Crowley of said property; that to that end she urged said Crowley to make a deed to her of said premises, using all the strength and influence of her superior will power to accomplish her purpose; that accordingly, on the tenth day of June, 1890, about the eighth day after the said marriage, said Daniel F. Crowley signed a deed purporting to convey said premises to said defendant Margaret; that the same was made without consideration and at a time when, as plaintiff is informed and believes, the said grantor's will power and judgment were greatly weakened by his long-continued habit of inebriety; that said deed was the result of impaired intellect and will power on the part of said Crowley, and of the dominating mind and influence of the defendant Margaret E. Crowley; and that, in the debilitated condition of said Crowley's faculties, he was unable to resist said defendant's importunities, or to wrestle successfully with her aggressive spirit and arbitrary disposition.'' It is further alleged that said Crowley continued to indulge in alcoholic liquors, and on the fifth day of July,

1890, at the instance of said defendant, as plaintiff is informed and believes, he was committed to the Home of the Inebriates in San Francisco, for treatment of persons laboring under diseases of alcoholism. It is further alleged that, immediately after defendant became the wife of said Daniel F. Crowley, she began a course of persecution of plaintiff, and insisted that plaintiff should leave the roof of her adopted father, and seek employment to earn her own living, and finally, in the month of July, 1890, the plaintiff was driven from her home and compelled to seek shelter among strangers, to earn her own support by the labor of her hands, without any assistance from defendant or plaintiff's adopted father, and from said date she never received any help or assistance of any kind from her said adopted father or from defendant, "and, with her forced exile from her home, plaintiff's education entirely ceased, as she had no means of her own, and her wages were consumed in her daily support." It is further alleged that down to the death of said Daniel F. Crowley, which occurred on July 11, 1898, the defendant exercised a controlling influence over his mind and actions. It is further alleged that in August, 1895, said Daniel F. Crowley purchased the lot of land in the complaint secondly described; that the title to the said property was taken in the name of the defendant Margaret E. Crowley "at her instance and at her dictation, as plaintiff is informed and believes, said Daniel being compelled thereto and overpowered by the dominant will and aggressive energy of said defendant"; and, upon information and belief, it is alleged that the consideration paid for said lot was the separate estate of Daniel F. Crowley, and not community property. It is averred that the plaintiff has not been able to ascertain whether said Daniel F. Crowley died testate or intestate, and alleges that his only heirs at the time of his death were his said widow, the defendant Margaret E. Crowley, and the plaintiff, and that no administration had been taken out on his estate. It is also averred that on the third day of November, 1898, the defendant Margaret E. Crowley conveyed the said parcel of real estate first in the complaint described to the defendant Richard O'Connell, who now claims the same adversely to the plaintiff. She avers, upon information and belief, that the conveyance was made without consideration, and for the purpose of complicating the title, obstructing and defeating plaintiff's recovery of said property, and that said O'Connell took the said conveyance with notice of the fact above alleged. The demurrer was based upon several grounds— among others, that the cause of action was barred by the provision of section 338, subdivision 4, of the Code of Civil Procedure, and was sustained upon this latter ground. This provision requires that an action for relief on the ground of fraud or mistake shall be commenced within three years, provided that the cause of action shall be deemed to have accrued only after the discovery of the facts constituting the fraud by the aggrieved party.

The appellant, however, contends that this is an action for the recovery of real property, and falls within section 318 of the Code of Civil Procedure, which extends the limitation to five years, instead of the section under which the court sustained the demurrer. This contention of the appellant cannot be sustained. There is nothing in the averments of the complaint of the nature of an action for the recovery of real property. On the contrary, all the allegations show very clearly that the gravamen of the action is fraud and undue influence. The prayer of the complaint is that "it be adjudged and decreed that said conveyance by said Daniel F. Crowley to the defendant Margaret E. Crowley, made on the tenth day of June, 1890, of the lot first hereinabove described, was obtained by fraud and undue influence on the part of said defendant, and that the same be set aside and annulled; that said lot constitutes part of the estate of said Daniel F. Crowley, deceased, and that plaintiff is the owner of an undivided one-half thereof; that the title to said lot secondly hereinabove described was taken in the name of said defendant through her fraud and undue influence; that she held the title thereto in trust for said decedent, and now holds the same in trust for this plaintiff, as to an undivided one-half thereof; that said decedent was mentally incapacitated to make said first-named conveyance, or to consent to the making of said conveyance to the said defendant secondly above mentioned; that the deed of said first parcel of land from defendant Margaret to her codefendant, Richard O'Connell, be annulled; that plaintiff's title to an undivided moiety of said parcels of land, and of each of them, be quieted, and that she be let into possession thereof as a tenant in common with defendant Margaret E. Crowley; and that the defendants be required to account to plaintiff for one-half of the rents and profits of said real estate received by them, or either of them, since the death of said Daniel F. Crowley." Daniel F. Crowley was competent to execute the deeds, and they had the effect to convey his title to the property therein described. "A conveyance or other contract of a person of unsound mind, but not entirely without understanding, made before his incapacity has been judicially determined, is subject to rescission, as provided in the chapter on rescission in this code": Civ. Code, sec. 39. It had not been declared, judicially or otherwise, that he was incapacitated; and the conveyances, therefore, stood on the same ground as the conveyance of any other person, but subject to rescission as in other cases. In Castro v. Geil, 110 Cal. 296, 52 Am. St. Rep. 84, 42 Pac. 804, after citing the code provisions as above, it is said that "this language applies with equal force and propriety to the case before us." It is therefore conclusively settled that the deed in question vested the title in appellant, and that it could not be devested otherwise than by a judicial action, or the voluntary conveyance of the grantee, and, if by judicial action, that the complaint must allege facts which show upon the face of it that the action is not barred by the statute of limitations: See, also, People v. Blankenship, 52 Cal. 619; People v. Noyo Lumber Co., 99 Cal. 456, 34 Pac. 96. In Castro v. Geil it was held that the action was barred by the provision of the code in reference to actions for relief on the ground of fraud, already referred to. In this case there is no pretense that the plaintiff had not discovered the facts constituting the fraud until within three years before the commencement of the action. On the contrary, all the averments of the complaint show that the alleged fraud and undue influence were known to her at the time they were said to have been perpetrated. In Goodnow v. Parker, 112 Cal. 437, 44 Pac. 738, relied upon by the appellant, it was held that that was not an action for relief upon the ground of fraud or mistake, but an action for the recovery of real property, "and that the correction of the mistake in the deed is merely incidental to that action." This action, however, as already stated, is based upon the fraud and undue influence alleged in the complaint, and has none of the features of an action for the recovery of real property. Until the deeds in question are set aside, the plaintiff has no standing in court, as she has neither title nor right of possession, and therefore could not maintain an action for the recovery of real property, even if this were such.

We think the demurrer was properly sustained on the ground assigned by the court below, and this renders it unnecessary to consider or to pass upon the question whether the complaint was insufficient on the other grounds assigned in the demurrer.

The judgment is affirmed.

We concur: Garoutte, J.; Harrison, J.

WILLIAMS v. BAGNELLE.*

Sac. No. 1005; December 20, 1902.

70 Pac. 1058.

Mandamus—Adequate Remedy.—The Writ of Mandate will not Issue where there is a plain, speedy and adequate remedy in the ordinary course of law.

Mandamus—Teacher's Salary.—Political Code, title 3, article 12, section 1699, provides that any teacher whose salary is withheld may appeal to the superintendent of public instruction, who shall require the superintendent of schools to investigate the matter, and that the judgment of the superintendent of instruction shall be final, and that on receiving it the superintendent of schools, if it is in favor of the teacher, shall, if the trustees refuse to issue an order for such salary, issue his requisition in favor of such teacher. The salary of a teacher was withheld by the superintendent of schools, and she applied for a peremptory writ of mandate directing him to draw a requisition in favor of petitioner. Held, that the writ would not issue, plaintiff not having pursued the remedy under the statute, which applied to a case where the salary was withheld by such superintendent, as well as where withheld by the trustees.

Mandamus—Teacher's Salary.—Code of Civil Procedure, section 1085, provides that the writ of mandate may be issued to compel the performance of an official act required to be done by law. Political Code, section 1543, requires the county superintendent of schools to draw requisitions on the county auditor against the school fund of the district, and provides that no such requisition shall be drawn unless the order states the monthly salary of teacher, and names the

---

*For subsequent opinion in bank, see 138 Cal. 699, 72 Pac. 408.

months for which it is due. An order drawn by trustees in favor of a teacher was "on account of balance on yearly contract for $1,000 from ——— to ——— during the present school year. . . . . Monthly salary . . . . $———." Held, that the writ of mandate would not issue to compel the superintendent to issue a requisition for the teacher's salary, as the superintendent was not authorized to draw a requisition; the monthly salary not being mentioned in the order, nor the month for which it was due.

APPEAL from Superior Court, Madera County; M. L. Short, Judge.

Proceedings by W. L. Williams against Estelle Bagnelle, as school superintendent of Madera county, to compel defendant to draw a requisition on the county auditor in favor of plaintiff. From a judgment awarding the writ defendant appeals. Reversed.

R. R. Fowler and W. H. Larew for appellant; Francis A. Fee for respondent.

COOPER, C.—Appeal from the judgment awarding a peremptory writ of mandate against defendant, as school superintendent of Madera county, directing her to draw a requisition in favor of plaintiff upon the county auditor of said county for $111.20 in payment of balance claimed to be due plaintiff for salary as teacher in said district. The plaintiff claims that the above-named sum is due him for one month's salary as teacher in the public schools of Madera school district, under a contract with the school trustees of said district, for nine months' teaching therein. The defendant contends and claims that only eight months of school were authorized or taught in the said district, and that the plaintiff drew the full amount of his salary for said eight months.

The extraordinary writ prayed for in this case will not issue where there is a plain, speedy and adequate remedy in the ordinary course of law: Code Civ. Proc., sec. 1086; Kimball v. Union Water Co., 44 Cal. 173, 13 Am. Rep. 157; Wood v. Strother, 76 Cal. 545, 9 Am. St. Rep. 249, 18 Pac. 766. The Political Code, under the head of "Education" (title 3, article 12, section 1699), provides: "Any teacher whose salary is withheld may appeal to the superintendent of public instruction, who shall thereupon require the superintendent of schools to investigate the matter and present the facts thereof

to him. The judgment of the superintendent of public instruction shall be final; and upon receiving it, the superintendent of schools, if the judgment is in favor of the teacher,
shall, in case the trustees refuse to issue an order for said
withheld salary, issue his requisition in favor of said teacher.''
The salary of the plaintiff in this case was withheld, and he
cannot come into court and ask for a writ of mandate without having made any attempt to pursue the plain and speedy
remedy pointed out in the above section. The language is
plain, and the judgment of the superintendent of public instruction is made final. The legislature intended to confer
upon the state officer whose position and duties require him
to familiarize himself with the common schools and the school
laws of the state the power to examine the facts and pass
judgment upon the question as to salary. The section does
not, as contended by respondent, apply only to cases where
the salary is withheld by the trustees of the district. It applies to ''any teacher whose salary is withheld.'' If it is
withheld by the superintendent of schools, as in this case, the
teacher may appeal to the superintendent of public instruction. If the decision is in favor of the teacher, it is the duty
of the superintendent of schools to issue his requisition.
Again, the writ will only issue to compel the performance of
an act which the law specially enjoins as a duty resulting
from an office, trust or station: Code Civ. Proc., sec. 1085;
Crandall v. Amador Co., 20 Cal. 73. The duties of the
county superintendent are provided for in Political Code, section 1543. In certain cases it is made his duty to draw requisitions upon the county auditor against the school fund of the
district. In regard to requisitions for teachers' salaries it is
provided: ''Nor shall any requisition for teachers' salaries
be drawn unless the order shall state the monthly salary of
teacher, and name the months for which such salary is due.''
The order in this case drawn by the trustees of the district
in favor of plaintiff specified that it was ''on account of balance on yearly contract for $1,000 from —— to —— during
the present school year, in the Madera school district.
Monthly salary of teacher, $——.'' It will be readily seen
that the monthly salary of the teacher is not mentioned, nor
is the month for which the salary is due. The defendant cannot be compelled to draw her requisition unless the order for
such requisition complies substantially with the law. In

fact, it is the duty of defendant to see that all moneys of the district are paid out only for legal claims, and in compliance with the rules and safeguards provided by statute.

We advise that the judgment be reversed and the proceeding dismissed.

We concur: Haynes, C.; Gray, C.

PER CURIAM.—For the reasons given in the foregoing opinion the judgment is reversed and the proceeding dismissed.

January 19, 1903.

Application for order granting a hearing in bank.   Granted.

PER CURIAM.—Order for hearing in bank granted.

McFARLAND, J.—I concur in the order granting a hearing in bank, because I am not prepared at present to sanction that part of the opinion which holds that the judgment of the state superintendent is final. I think, however, that clearly the appellant should have first appealed to the superintendent, and in other respects I think the opinion of the department correct.

HARLOE v. BERWICK et al.

L. A. No. 1164; December 16, 1902.

70 Pac. 1060.

Appeal.—Where the Order Granting a New Trial Does not Disclose the ground on which it is made, but it appears from the record that it might well have been made on the ground of the insufficiency of the evidence to sustain the verdict, the court on appeal may presume that it was made on that ground.

Appeal.—An Order Granting a New Trial for Insufficiency of Evidence to sustain the verdict is not reviewable on appeal if there is any appreciable conflict in the evidence.

APPEAL from Superior Court, San Luis Obispo County; E. P. Unangst, Judge.

Action by Flora Harloe against J. C. Berwick and wife and W. Schnocker. Judgment for defendants, and from an order granting a new trial they appeal. Affirmed.

William Graves and Louis Laing for appellants; Robert Bouldin and Frank Walden for respondent.

CHIPMAN, C.—Claim and delivery. The answer is a general denial of plaintiff's complaint, and a further answer that the personal property in question belonged to defendants Mrs. Berwick and W. Schnocker when taken into possession by plaintiff after seizure by the sheriff; also claiming damages in the sum of $300 for the alleged unlawful taking and detention by plaintiff. The cause was tried before a jury, and defendants had a verdict for the return of the property or its value, fixed at the sum of $350, and for damages in the sum of $200, and the court entered judgment accordingly. In due time, plaintiff moved for a new trial, which was ordered by the court. The appeal is by defendants from this order.

The controversy is over certain barley grown on plaintiff's ranch while under lease to J. C. Berwick and F. C. Cherry. This lease had expired and was surrendered to plaintiff on November 24, 1899, and, by arrangement with plaintiff, Berwick & Cherry were allowed to remain a few days to close up their business. Defendants Mrs. Berwick and W. Schnocker were creditors of Berwick & Cherry, Mrs. Berwick being the wife of J. C. Berwick. The barley in question was sacked and stored in a building called a barn or granary, situated on the ranch. Plaintiff desired to purchase this grain to seed the land formerly rented by Berwick & Cherry. She employed one Fiske to make the purchase for her, and he went with plaintiff to the premises for that purpose on November 25th, the day following the surrender of the lease; and there is evidence tending to show that Fiske purchased the barley that day, and placed George Harloe, plaintiff's son, in charge of it, with instructions to weigh the grain and report the amount to Fiske, who would then pay for it; that the sale was with the full knowledge and consent of Berwick and Cherry, both of whom were present; that the purchase price was subsequently paid by Fiske to a receiver, who had been put in possession of Berwick & Cherry's property, and they drew this money out of the hands of the receiver by orders on him to pay creditors; that Berwick assisted Harloe in counting the sacks and arriving at the weight of the grain. The sale was on Saturday. Harloe closed all the doors but one to the barn or granary, and left that door open, at the request of Berwick, to allow a hired man (Phoenix) to go in to sleep there as he had previously been doing. On Monday morning Harloe, with Berwick's assistance, counted the sacks, and ascertained the weight in the course of the day, and Harloe sent a report to Fiske. Monday night defendants, Mrs. Berwick and Schnocker, aided by the hired man Phoenix, hauled all this grain to an adjoining ranch and stored it, working all night to accomplish the removal. These defendants claim under an alleged sale made to them of the barley in question by Berwick in payment of claims they had against the firm of Berwick & Cherry. It is claimed that these sales were made on the 25th of November, the same day of the sale to Fiske. and that Mrs. Berwick and Schnocker did not know of the sale to Fiske. The good faith of the purchase by Fiske is not attacked by any evidence, the only claim being that there was not sufficient delivery. Cherry, one of the partners, testified fully as to the sale to Fiske for plaintiff, and that he knew nothing of the alleged sale to defendants, and never consented to any sale to them. There is some evidence, at least circumstantial if not direct, tending to show that defendants did know of the sale to Fiske when they purchased. Without going further into the matter, it is sufficient to say that the evidence is conflicting upon the question as to which of the several purchasers acquired the better right to the barley. Appellants concede that the verdict for $200 damages was error, and they claim that they were willing to waive this item of damage, and so offered to the trial court. There is nothing in the record to show any such offer. The order does not disclose the ground on which it was made. Among the grounds urged for a new trial was insufficiency of the evidence to justify the verdict. The court might well have reached the conclusion that such was the fact here. Where the court grants a new trial on this ground, as we may presume it did in the present case (Condee v. Gyger, 126 Cal. 546, 59 Pac. 26), its order is not open to review if there is any appreciable conflict in the evidence: Newman v. Overland Pac. Ry. Co., 132 Cal. 74, 64 Pac. 110.

The order should be affirmed.

We concur: Gray, C.; Haynes, C.

PER CURIAM.—For the reasons given in the foregoing opinion the order is affirmed.

CAHILL v. BAIRD.*

S. F. No. 2498; December 16, 1902.

70 Pac. 1061.

New Trial—Statement.—Under Code of Civil Procedure, section 659, subdivision 3, providing that on motions for new trial for insufficiency of the evidence the.notice shall specify the particulars in which the evidence is alleged to be insufficient, where a statement which does not contain all the evidence is stipulated to be correct, and is certified by the judge to have been settled and allowed, it will be inferred that only so much of the evidence has been inserted as is necessary to explain the grounds specified in the notice.

Attorney—Right to Compensation.—Under Code of Civil Procedure, section 1855, subdivision 5, providing that "there can be no evidence of the contents of writings other than the writing itself, except . . . . when the original consists of numerous documents, ... and the evidence sought from them is only the general result of the whole," it would not be necessary, in order to prove the character and value of the services rendered by an attorney in an action, to produce the record.

Attorney—Entire Contract of Employment.—The General Employment of an attorney to defend a case is an entire contract, and, if he withdraws without cause, or is discharged for justifiable reasons, before the contract is completed, he cannot maintain an action for the value of his services.

APPEAL from Superior Court, City and County of San Francisco; George H. Bahrs, Judge.

Action by William Cahill against Veronica C. Baird. From an order denying defendant's motion for a new trial after a verdict for plaintiff she appeals. Reversed.

John S. Partridge for appellant; Wm. J. Herrin for respondent.

SMITH, C.—This is an appeal by the defendant from an order denying her motion for a new trial. The suit was brought to recover the sum of $1,500 alleged to be due to the plaintiff's assignor, of which amount the principal item was a charge of $1,000 for services in a suit brought against the defendant here by her daughter, Mrs. Baldwin, to recover

*For subsequent opinion in bank, see 138 Cal. 691, 72 Pac. 342.

stock transferred by her to her mother. The jury found for
the plaintiff in the sum of $925, for which judgment was en-
tered. The grounds urged for reversal are: Misconduct of
the jury, the specific form of the objection being that the
assent of the jurors, or of one or more of them, was induced
"by a resort to the determination of chance"; remarks made
by the judge in the course of the trial claimed by the appellant to have evinced a prejudgment of the case, and to have
prejudiced the jury; the exclusion of certain testimony; and
error in instructing and failing to instruct the jury.

1. To the first point the preliminary objection is made that
the affidavits relied on are not incorporated in a bill of exceptions, as required by rule 29 (64 Pac. xii) of this court.
But, under the view we take of the case, it will be unnecessary
to consider this point. Objection is also made to the statement on the ground that it is stipulated that "it does not
contain all the evidence." But in view of the stipulation of
the attorneys that "the statement is correct," and of the certificate of the judge that it is "settled and allowed," this is
to be commended, rather than complained of, since it is to
be inferred that only so much of the evidence has been inserted as was necessary to explain the grounds specified in
the notice: Code Civ. Proc., sec. 659, subd. 3; Adams v. Lam-
bard, 80 Cal. 436, 437, 22 Pac. 180.

2. As to the first of the three remaining points of error assigned, we find nothing objectionable in what was said by the
judge. All except one of the instances of supposed injurious
remarks are merely rulings of the court on the admission and
exclusion of evidence, couched in appropriate and unobjec-
tionable terms. The remaining instance was a question to
the attorneys as to a point of law suggested by the evidence
offered, and was not only altogether appropriate, but could
have suggested nothing to the jury that was not favorable to
appellant.

3. With regard to the third point, we do not understand—
as stated in appellant's brief—that the court refused "to
allow defendant to introduce any testimony as to former
charges made by Mr. Hurd," plaintiff's assignor, etc. The
actual ruling was to exclude the judgment-roll in the former
case of Baird v. Baird (in which defendant as trustee was a
party), and, as this does not appear in the statement, we cannot determine whether it was admissible, or, if admissible,

whether the error would have been prejudicial. Possibly the appellant's attorney understood the ruling to be as stated in his brief, but, if he desired to prove the character and value of the services rendered by the plaintiff's assignor in the former case, it was unnecessary to produce the record: Code Civ. Proc., sec. 1855, subd. 5. The question whether evidence on the point was admissible is not presented by the record, and is therefore not passed on.

4. The court charged the jury, in effect, that, while the employer may terminate the contract of employment where the one employed uses improper, insulting or profane language, especially where the employer is a lady of refinement, etc., in such case the attorney would be entitled to recover the reasonable value of his services up to that time, "unless there has been a contract by which he has bound himself to do some work which in its nature would be indivisible—where it would necessarily be an entire and complete contract; but there is no evidence of such contract in this case," etc. And the court refused to give the following instructions asked by the defendant: "You are instructed that, when a client employs an attorney for a specific action, that is an entire contract; and if you find that the attorney broke the contract himself, or acted in such a manner as to make the relation of attorney and client no longer possible, you must find that the attorney is not entitled to any compensation." The latter instruction should have been given, and the instruction given, in so far as it conflicts with it, and especially the instruction to the jury that "there is no evidence of such a contract in this case," and the part of the instruction following, which was, in effect, to find for the plaintiff as to services rendered by his assignor in the case of Baldwin v. Baird, were erroneous. We have no doubt that the general employment of an attorney to defend a case is an entire contract, or that, if the contract is terminated by his withdrawal from the case without cause, or he is discharged for justifiable reasons, he cannot maintain an action for the value of his services: Holmes v. Evans, 129 N. Y. 140, 29 N. E. 233; Walsh v. Shumway, 65 Ill. 471; McArthur v. Fry, 10 Kan. 233; Moyers v. Graham, 15 Lea (Tenn.), 57. In the Illinois case cited the effect of the decision is somewhat impaired by the observation of the court, after stating that the contract in question was an entirety, that "of course it differs from a case where an attor-

ney has been retained without a specific contract.'' But in every case where an attorney is employed to represent a party in a suit generally, there is, we understand, a specific contract to do so, as there is in all cases of executory contracts to perform services: Moyers v. Graham, 15 Lea (Tenn.), 60.

We advise that the order appealed from be reversed and the cause remanded for a new trial.

We concur: Haynes, C.; Gray, C.

PER CURIAM.—For the reasons given in the foregoing opinion the order appealed from is reversed and the cause remanded for a new trial.

PEOPLE ex rel. SANDERS v. JONES et al.

S. F. No. 2336; December 16, 1902.

70 Pac. 1063.

Appeal—Time—Review of Evidence.—Under Code of Civil Procedure, section 939, providing that "an exception to the decision on the ground that it is not supported by the evidence cannot be reviewed on appeal from the judgment unless the appeal is taken within sixty days after the rendition of the judgment," on an appeal taken in May from a judgment entered the preceding August the bill of exceptions cannot be examined for the purpose of reviewing the sufficiency of evidence.[1]

APPEAL from Superior Court, City and County of San Francisco; J. M. Seawell, Judge.

Action by the people of the state of California, on the relation of Cornelius T. Sanders, against M. P. Jones and others. From a judgment for defendants, plaintiff appeals. Affirmed.

Tirey L. Ford, attorney general, Fisher Ames and Rodgers, Paterson & Slack for appellant; Lloyd & Wood for respondents.

---

[1] Cited and followed in Gilbert v. Kelly, 138 Cal. 690, 72 Pac. 344, where it is given as authority for saying that section 939 of the Code of Civil Procedure has been adhered to by the supreme court of the state.

COOPER, C.—This is an appeal from a judgment on the judgment-roll and a bill of exceptions. The only point relied upon by appellant is that the evidence is insufficient to support the findings of fact. Respondents contend that the bill of exceptions cannot be examined for the purpose of reviewing the evidence, and we see no escape from the contention. The judgment was rendered August 23, 1897, and the notice of appeal filed and served May 10, 1898. It is provided in the Code of Civil Procedure (section 939) that "an exception to the decision or verdict, on the ground that it is not supported by the evidence, cannot be reviewed on appeal from the judgment unless the appeal is taken within sixty days after the rendition of the judgment." It has been univer- sally held here that the evidence could not be reviewed in such case where the appeal is not taken within sixty days after the judgment is rendered: Handley v. Figg, 58 Cal. 579; Forni v. Yoell, 99 Cal. 172, 33 Pac. 887; Wise v. Ballou, 129 Cal. 45, 61 Pac. 574.

It follows that the judgment must be affirmed.

We concur: Chipman, C.; Haynes, C.

PER CURIAM.—For the reasons given in the foregoing opinion the judgment is affirmed.

DENMAN v. WEBSTER.*

S. F. No. 3057; December 16, 1902.

70 Pac. 1063.

City Attorney—Duty to Defend Board of Education.—Under the charter of San Francisco, authorizing the election of a city attorney, and in article 5, chapter 2, section 1, requiring him to prosecute and defend for the city and county all actions at law or in equity, and to give advice to all officers, boards and commissions, and in article 7, chapter 3, section 1, subdivision 3, authorizing the board of education to require the services of the city attorney in all actions, suits and proceedings by or against it, it is the duty of the city attorney, when so required, to appear for and defend such board in all suits brought against it.

---

*For subsequent opinion in bank, see 139 Cal. 452, 73 Pac. 139.

City Attorney—Refusal to Defend Board of Education.—Under the charter of San Francisco, article 16, section 18, providing that any elected officer may be suspended by the mayor for cause, and that he "shall appoint some person to discharge the duties of the office during the period of such suspension," on the refusal of the city attorney to defend the board of education in a suit brought against it the board is not authorized to employ another attorney, but should notify the mayor of such refusal.

Board of Education—Power to Employ Counsel.—Political Code, section 1617, subdivision 7, authorizing boards of education and trustees of school districts to employ teachers, "janitors, and other employees of the schools," and subdivision 20, relating to the powers of trustees only, do not authorize a board of education to employ counsel to defend an action brought against it.

City Attorney—Duty to Defend Board of Education.—The charter of San Francisco, in requiring the city attorney to prosecute and defend suits by or against the board of education, does not impose any "school function" on him, but his "function" remains that of an attorney.

Board of Education—Power to Employ Counsel.—Under the charter of San Francisco, requiring the city attorney to defend the board of education in suits brought against it, and authorizing the mayor to suspend such attorney if he refuses to act, and appoint someone to act in his place, such board has no implied power to employ private counsel either in place of or to assist the city attorney to defend the board in a suit.

APPEAL from Superior Court, City and County of San Francisco; J. M. Seawell, Judge.

Petition for mandamus by William Denman against Reginald H. Webster, as superintendent of schools of the city and county of San Francisco. From a judgment for defendant the petitioner appeals. Affirmed.

William Denman for appellant; Carlton W. Greene for respondent.

HAYNES, C.—Appellant applied to the superior court of said city and county for a writ of mandate requiring the defendant, as such superintendent of schools, to draw his requisition upon the auditor of said city and county for the sum of $500, to be paid to appellant upon the order of the board of education. The defendant demurred to the petition, the demurrer was sustained, the writ denied, and the petitioner appeals.

The circumstances under which appellant's said services were rendered, as alleged in his petition, were that in October, 1900, the respondent, as superintendent of schools in said city and county, sued out an alternative writ of mandate to compel the board of education "to admit to its deliberations one W. D. Kingsbury"; that the said board of education made its order upon the city attorney requiring his services in its defense in said proceeding so brought against it; that "the city attorney, denying his jurisdiction to render said services," refused to render the same, and that the board of education thereafter employed appellant to defend it in said proceeding, and that he did defend said board and continued to do so until March 25, 1901, when judgment was rendered therein in favor of said board; that the board approved his demand for the said sum of $500, but respondent refused to make a requisition upon the auditor to issue a warrant therefor, and still refuses to do so. We think the demurrer was properly sustained. The charter provides for the election of a city attorney, and authorizes him to appoint four assistants. Article 5, chapter 2, section 2 (Treadwell's Charter, p. 132), provides: "He must prosecute and defend for the city and county all actions at law or in equity, and all special proceedings for or against the city and county. . . . . He shall give legal advice, in writing, to all officers, boards and commissions named in this charter, when requested to do so by them, or either of them, in writing, upon questions arising in their separate departments involving the rights or liabilities of the city and county." And among the powers of the board of education the following is specified: "To require the services of the city attorney in all actions, suits and proceedings by or against the board of education": Charter, art. 7, c. 3, sec. 1, subd. 8 (Treadwell's Charter, p. 266). The provision last above quoted, while declaring one of the powers of the board of education, also specifies a duty of the city attorney as effectively as if it had been embodied in the section first above quoted. The obvious purpose of the charter in providing for the election of a city attorney and prescribing his duties and compensation was to take from the various city officers and boards the power to employ other counsel and burden the city and county or school district with the payment of fees, to be fixed by the officer or board employing them, thus nullifying the charter provision, which impliedly limits the compensation for legal services rendered in all actions, suits and proceedings by or on behalf of the board of education to the salary of the city attorney and his subordinates. At the least, there is no power, express or implied, given by the charter to the board of education to employ counsel and fix his compensation. Appellant inquires, however, whether the board is compelled to appear in person, the city attorney having declined to defend the action. To this it may be replied that the city attorney is not only the law officer of the city and county as a municipal corporation, but is the law officer of the board of education in all actions, suits and proceedings by or against it; and section 18 of article 16 of the charter (Treadwell, p. 376), provides: "Any elected officer, except supervisor, may be suspended by the mayor and removed by the supervisors for cause; and any appointed officer may be removed by the mayor for cause. The mayor shall· appoint some person to discharge the duties of the office during the period of such suspension." The city and county having assumed the responsibility of representing the board by its law officer in all suits and proceedings by and against it, the proper city authority should have been informed of the refusal of the city attorney to represent the board, inasmuch as the charter had provided for the emergency by an appointment of a city attorney during suspension.

Appellant also contends that subdivisions 7 and 20 of section 1617 of the Political Code authorized the board of education to employ counsel to defend said action. The first of these subdivisions authorizes boards of education and trustees of school districts to employ teachers, "janitors and other employees of the schools," and to fix and order paid their conpensation. The words "other employees" refer to persons employed in or about the several schools and school buildings in like character or capacity to those named. No such position or employment as "attorney of the schools" has ever before been suggested. Subdivision 20 refers to boards of trustees, and not to boards of education.

As to appellant's contention that the city attorney is a municipal, and not a school, officer, and that the charter can impose no school function upon him, it is sufficient to say that his office and his duties are created and defined by the charter, and that in prosecuting and defending actions by or against the board of education he exercises no "school func-

tion." His "function" is that of an attorney, no matter
whom he represents, or what may be the character of the action. If appellant were employed to prosecute an action of
ejectment to recover farming land, it could hardly be said he
was exercising the functions of a farmer; or, if the property
were a mine, that he exercised the function of a miner.

We have seen that no power has been expressly conferred
upon the board of education to employ counsel, and we think
it equally clear that it has no implied power to do so. This
conclusion results from the fact that provision has been expressly made for counsel to represent it, and in case of the
refusal of the city attorney to discharge that duty the charter provides for the appointment of another by the mayor
during his suspension, so that there cannot be a vacancy in
the office of such duration as to imperil the rights of the
board. Appellant contends, however, that, even if the city
attorney could have been compelled to defend the action, the
board would have had the power to employ private counsel,
and cites Hornblower v. Duden, 35 Cal. 670. In that case
the board of supervisors of El Dorado county employed
counsel other than the district attorney in certain important
litigation, and this employment was sustained under the general power given to the board of supervisors "to do and perform such other acts and things as may be strictly necessary
to the full discharge of the powers and jurisdiction conferred
on the board," and the action of the board was sustained.
But no such general powers have been conferred upon the
board of education. "Boards of supervisors are creatures of
the statute, and the authority for any act on their part must
be sought in the statute": Modoc Co. v. Spencer, 103 Cal.
498, 37 Pac. 483. In that case it was held that the board of
supervisors had no power to employ counsel on behalf of the
county to prosecute or assist in the prosecution of criminal
cases prosecuted in the name of the state, and any allowance
for such services created no legal claim against the county.
In Merriam v. Barnum, 116 Cal. 619, 48 Pac. 727, it was held
that the power of the board of supervisors to employ special
counsel to assist the district attorney in the prosecution or defense of suits to which the county is a party did not authorize the appointment of special counsel to advise the board,
and mandamus would not lie to compel the auditor to draw
a warrant therefor. Mr. Justice Henshaw concluded his

opinion in that case as follows: "However valuable the services of the appellant may have been to the county in this instance, to permit compensation for them would be to override the law, and to destroy one of the strongest safeguards cast about the expenditure of county funds." This language is equally applicable to the present case. The other cases cited by appellant mostly relate to the action of boards of supervisors under general and implied powers. None of them conflict with the conclusions we have reached upon the facts of this case, or the law applicable thereto. Dillon on Municipal Corporations, section 89, lays down the rule that "any fair, reasonable doubt concerning the existence of the power is resolved by the courts against the corporation, and the power is denied." In view of our conclusions upon the main question, it is not necessary to consider the special demurrers interposed to the complaint.

The judgment should be affirmed.

We concur: Gray, C.; Cooper, C.

PER CURIAM.—For the reasons given in the foregoing opinion the judgment is affirmed.

In re WICKERSHAM'S ESTATE.*

S. F. Nos. 2873, 2874; December 19, 1902.

70 Pac. 1079.

Community Property—Will.—A Husband has No Power to Provide in his will for a sale of community property except to pay debts.

Community Property.—An Executor's Return of Sale of Community property under a power in the husband's will is defective where it fails to show that the property was sold for the payment of debts, though it appears that it was sold under the power in the will.

Community Property—Power of Sale in Will—A Wife's Interest in community property is adversely affected by a sale thereof under a power in her husband's will.

Community Property—Sale Under Power in Will—Appeal.—Under Code of Civil Procedure, sections 153, 940, 956, providing that the notice of appeal shall state the judgment, order, or specific part

---

*For subsequent opinion, see 138 Cal. 355, 70 Pac. 1076.

thereof, appealed from, and that the court on appeal from a judgment may review the verdict or decision and any intermediate order or decision which involves the merits or affects the judgment, the court, on appeal from an order of sale of community property under a power in the husband's will, can review error in including the wife's interest in the order, though it was correct as to the interest of the husband.

Community Property—Sale Under Power in Will.—On Appeal from an order of sale of community property under a power in the husband's will on the ground that the wife's interest in the property was erroneously included, the executors of the husband could not represent the wife's estate, their interest being adverse.

Community Property—Sale Under Power in Will—Appeal.—Under Code of Civil Procedure, section 1452, providing that heirs or devisees may themselves, or jointly with the executor, maintain an action for the possession of real estate or to quiet title to the same, the heirs of a deceased person are entitled to all actions and defenses necessary to the protection of their property, except those depending on the right of possession; and hence the heirs of a deceased wife are entitled to prosecute an appeal from an order obtained by the executors of the husband for the sale of community property under a power in the husband's will.

APPEAL from Superior Court, Sonoma County; Albert G. Burnett, Judge.

Judicial settlement of the estate of I. G. Wickersham, deceased. From orders confirming sales of certain realty by the executors, Mrs. Cora Wickersham, as executrix of Frank Wickersham, and guardian of I. G. Wickersham, an infant, appeals. Reversed.

Francis J. Heney and Cowan & Juilliard for appellant; Lippitt & Lippitt and Campbell, Metson & Campbell for respondents.

PER CURIAM.—These are appeals from orders of the court confirming sales of real estate made by the executors under a power of sale in the will of deceased. They involve the same questions, and are submitted on the same briefs. In what we have to say, the former appeal is directly referred to, but the decision will apply to both. The appellants are the same as the appellants in the case of the same title, S. F. No. 3037, and as the respondents in case S. F. No. 3157, just decided (138 Cal. 355, 70 Pac. 1076); and as in those cases the principal question involved is as to their right to be heard in opposition to the sale. On this question the court held the negative. But the case presented by the appellant's written opposition to the sale is substantially the same as presented in the former cases, and on the authority of the decision there, and under the provisions of section 1553 of the Code of Civil Procedure, this ruling of the court must be held to be erroneous.

It is objected, however, by the respondents' counsel, that the appellant's opposition does not show that the order was in fact erroneous, which is apparently the case. But assuming the objection to be material, it is answered by the fact that the executors' return of sale is itself materially defective in failing to show that the sale was made for the payment of debts, for which alone they were authorized to sell: Sharp v. Loupe, 120 Cal. 89, 52 Pac. 134, 586. The petition does, indeed, allege that the sale was made under the powers of the will, and ordinarily this would be sufficient (Code Civ. Proc., secs. 1561, 1562); but where the property sold is community property, this is not so, for it is a cardinal rule of practice that the decision of the court is, or at least ought to be, merely the application of the law to the facts presented to it, and that, in the absence of facts justifying it, the decision is at least erroneous. But the testator had no power to authorize the sale of his wife's interest, except for payment of debts (Sharp v. Loupe, supra); and hence, as it appears from the appellant's allegations that the property sold was community property, the return is insufficient to show the executors' power to sell, which, to justify the action of the court, should have been made to appear.

Other points made by respondents seem hardly to require consideration. Thus it is objected that, assuming the correctness of appellant's contention, the sale could not affect the wife's interest in the community property. But the contrary is expressly held in the case of Sharp v. Loupe, cited above. The case of King v. Lagrange, 50 Cal. 328, holding the contrary, involved the construction of the law as it stood in 1853, of which it may have been a correct exposition. Otherwise its authority must give way to that of the later decision. Still less can the objection be entertained that, the appeal being from the whole order of sale, and the sale being valid as to the husband's interest, the order cannot be reversed because the wife's interest was erroneously included. Anything that may be reviewed on appeal from a part of a judgment may be reviewed also on an appeal from the whole judgment, though the converse is not true: Code Civ. Proc., secs. 153, 940, 956. Again, still less can the point, waived and yet argued in one of the briefs, be maintained that the executors alone could represent the estate of Lydia Wickersham in the present proceeding. As to themselves, occupying as they did a position hostile to that estate, they, at least, could not represent it: Townsend v. Tallant, 33 Cal. 52, 91 Am. Dec. 617; Norton v. Walsh, 94 Cal. 564, 29 Pac. 1109. On the other hand, the heirs of a deceased person succeed at once to their respective interests, from which it follows, as in the case of other owners, they are entitled to all actions and defenses necessary to the protection of their property, except those depending on the right of possession; which, as essential to the performance of their functions, are exclusively vested in the executor: Code Civ. Proc., sec. 1452; Bates v. Howard, 105 Cal. 183, 38 Pac. 715.

For the reasons given, the orders appealed from in the two cases must be reversed, and it is so ordered.

- - - -

REESE v. BELL et al.

S. F. No. 2321; December 18, 1902.

71 Pac. 87.

Bills and Notes—Alteration by Inserting Interest.—In an Action on a note a defense was that the note had been altered by the insertion therein of writing calling for interest. The plaintiff in a verified complaint had alleged indorsement and transfer of the note by the payee to another for value before maturity, and a like indorsement by him to plaintiff. He testified that he had not received payment. Held, that such testimony tended to establish a prima facie case for plaintiff. On cross-examination of such witness defendant had a right to show by him facts which would dispute his testimony that the payee assigned the note to him before maturity to show why he had not received payment, and to dispute that the note had not been in his possession as testified by him.[1]

---

[1] Cited in Luin v. Chicago Grill Co., 138 Iowa, 270, 115 N. W. 1025, as authority for holding, in an action for compensation for services, that the plaintiff might be cross-examined so as to bring out facts of

Bills and Notes—Evidence.—Where, in a Suit on a Note, a Witness Testified that he had been attorney for the maker after the note was given and at the time certain indorsements were made by the payee, but that he was not the attorney for the payee, his testimony was not rendered incompetent because the payee subsequently testified that such witness was his attorney, the evidence being conflicting, and the court accepting that of the attorney.

Bills and Notes—Doctrine of Relation.—Where the Payee of a Note made a mere equitable assignment thereof, and after maturity indorsed the same, the doctrine of relation would not apply to cut off the right of the makers to set up any defense good against the payee.

Bills and Notes—Indorsement After Maturity.—Civil Code, section 3123, provides that an indorsee in due course is one who in the ordinary course of business and for value before its apparent maturity, and without knowledge of the dishonor, acquires a negotiable instrument duly indorsed to him or indorsed generally. Held, that, where a note was not duly indorsed to plaintiff before its apparent maturity, in an action thereon by him the maker might set up any equitable defense.[2]

APPEAL from Superior Court, City and County of San Francisco; Frank H. Dunne, Judge.

Action by E. L. Reese against Teresa Bell and another. From a judgment for defendants, plaintiff appeals. Affirmed.

Black & Leaming for appellant; T. Z. Blakeman for respondents.

CHIPMAN, C.—The action is on a promissory note executed by defendants, payable to the order of one George R. Eaton, bearing date November 1, 1895, due one year from date, for $5,000, and purporting to bear interest from date until paid at the rate of three per cent per month. It is alleged in the complaint that on August 6, 1896, Eaton, the payee, indorsed, sold and assigned said note to R. C. Hopkins for value, and that thereafter said Hopkins, ''and prior

---

contrary significance to statements of his made on direct examination, even though the facts themselves were not touched upon in the direct examination.

[2] Cited in Bank of Houston v. Day, 145 Mo. App. 425, 122 S. W. 760, where the court says that the element of good faith with respect to the holding of commercial paper is essential to holding in due course.

to the commencement of the action (date not stated), indorsed, sold, assigned and transferred to this plaintiff, for value, said promissory note," and that plaintiff is now the owner and holder thereof, alleges nonpayment, and demands judgment for the amount of the note and interest. The answer denies the execution of the note as set out in the complaint; denies the alleged indorsements and assignments and denies ownership in plaintiff; denies that no part of the principal or interest has been paid. For further answer alleges the execution of a note reading in all respects as the note sued upon, except that when said note was delivered to Eaton the clause relating to interest did not contain the words "from date" after the word "coin," and did not contain the word "three" just preceding the words "per cent," but was blank as to any date from which interest was payable and as to any rate of interest. It is also averred that the consideration for the note was that for one year from its date the said Eaton would "devote the whole of his time and service for said Teresa Bell 'in looking up the affairs of the Thomas Bell estate,'" and the answer sets forth the agreement of the same date, signed by Teresa Bell, one of the makers of said note, and by Eaton, and is witnessed by defendant M. E. Pleasant, and is an agreement to pay the note of even date for $5,000, for Eaton's said services. It is averred that, when delivered, said note mentioned in the agreement and in the complaint did not bear any interest, but since the delivery thereof it has been by some person or persons altered, without defendants' knowledge or consent, by inserting the omitted words as above stated; that said Eaton failed to keep his said agreement except for a portion of the time of the months of November and December, 1895; that thereafter Eaton and defendant Teresa Bell mutually agreed that Eaton would receive $1,500 in full payment for all his services performed under said agreement, and should surrender said note; and in accordance with said agreement of settlement said Teresa, on December 31, 1896, executed and delivered to Eaton an order on the executors of the last will of Thomas Bell, deceased, for said sum, and that Eaton accepted the same in full payment of said note, and he "then and there promised to said Teresa Bell to return said promissory note to her, but he has ever since failed to do so." The court found (1) the

execution of the note as alleged and under the agreement
set forth in the answer; (2) that Eaton did not indorse or
assign the note as is alleged in the complaint, nor did Hopkins indorse it to plaintiff, and plaintiff did not become the
holder of the note until after its maturity; (3) that the
blanks as to date and rate of interest were filled in after
the note was delivered, as alleged in the answer; (4) that
Eaton did not keep his agreement set forth in the answer,
and, as there alleged, that on December 31, 1896, defendant
Bell paid him in full for any services rendered by him.
Judgment accordingly passed for defendants, from which
and from the order denying his motion for a new trial plaintiff appeals.

Appellant concedes that the testimony is in conflict as to
the partial failure of the consideration, settlement of the note
as alleged in the answer, and the alteration as alleged. It
is contended, however, that there is no evidence whatever to
support finding 2. This finding is that Eaton did not, on
August 6, 1895, or at any time prior to the maturity of the
note, assign it to Hopkins for value at all, nor did Hopkins
assign it to plaintiff before the commencement of the action
for value at all, nor did Eaton indorse the note to anyone
prior to its maturity, and plaintiff did not become the holder
until after maturity. This finding in some respects depends
upon testimony which appellant claims was improperly admitted in evidence, and this point will first be disposed of.

Plaintiff testified in his own behalf. He was shown the
note, and testified that he brought the suit at the request of
Mr. Schooler (plaintiff's attorney); that he had not received
any payment on the note, and so far as he knew it had not
been paid; that the note had not been in his possession;
that it was assigned to him by Mr. Eaton; and added, "I
think it was before the maturity of the note." On cross-
examination he testified that the note was assigned to him
for collection by Eaton in Mr. Schooler's office in San Francisco. "The note was not delivered to me. I did not see it
at that time. Mr. Eaton assigned it to me for collection
just for the use of my name to sue on. I don't know how
long that was before the beginning of the suit. It was possibly a few days or a week." (The complaint was filed July
24, 1897, nearly nine months after the note had matured.)
He was asked to "state what was said by Mr. Eaton, Mr.

Schooler, or yourself on that occasion at Mr. Schooler's office, when you say the note was assigned to you for collection.'' Plaintiff objected to the question as not proper cross-examination. The objection was overruled and plaintiff excepted. The answer was that ''they merely asked to have the note assigned to me to sue for collection, and Mr. Eaton retained the note; that is as much as I can remember. It was to use my name for suing on the note a third party.'' This was followed by the question: ''The first time that you saw this note . . . . was there any rate of interest on it? Mr. Schooler: I object to the question; it is not proper cross-examination. Nothing asked at all but as to whether that was the note, and the witness said it was. Now, the answer of the defendants in this case is in their first count,—that this note has been altered by inserting the word 'three' and inserting the word 'from date.' The Court: It seems to me he should be allowed to answer whether he saw it or not; answer the question. Mr. Schooler: We take an exception.'' The witness answered that he saw the note in November, 1895, in Eaton's possession, ''and there was no rate of interest in it. . . . . The next time I saw the note was, I believe, some time in December, 1895. It bore interest at that time. The note was then in Mr. Eaton's possession, in San Francisco. Mr. Eaton wanted to borrow $500 from me on the note. . . . . I told him I did not like to loan him $500 on the note. I said at that time I noticed there was three per cent a month interest on the note, and said, 'Is that lawful?' and said, 'Did they agree to sign that three per cent interest?' He said, 'No, I put that on myself'; and I said, 'I did not think that that was lawful'; and he said, 'I could put on ten per cent and it would be lawful.' '' The examination then proceeded without objection, and witness was asked: ''When did you next see that note? A. I had that note in my possession then for about eight months, having loaned him $500 on it, from December, 1895. Mr. Eaton then took the note up and paid me the $500 and interest. I cannot give the exact date when he took the note up. I never saw the note after that until I saw it just here. I do not remember any transaction concerning the note after Mr. Eaton took it up until it was assigned to me for collection.'' He was then asked if he paid any money for the transfer of the note to him, which was objected to as immaterial, in-

competent and not cross-examination, and the objection
overruled and exception. He answered: "Yes, sir; money
passed, and passed right back to me again. They asked to
have this note assigned to me, and wanted it in the hands
of a third party, and wanted a money consideration to pass,
which there was." He was asked to state where and how
the money was passed. "Mr. Schooler: I object as immaterial, irrelevant, and incompetent." Objection overruled
and exception. "A. The amount was twenty-three hundred
dollars, if I remember rightly, and it was cashed in the
Nevada Bank, and it was handed to Mr. Hopkins, and Mr.
Hopkins handed it back to me after we got outside the
bank." Witness was then asked what was said and done at
that time by Eaton, Hopkins and witness. Objected to as
not cross-examination, and objection overruled. "A. Well,
we just went to the bank. It was at the request of Mr.
Schooler and Mr. Eaton that this note should be assigned to
me. . . . . I think this money consideration was the same
day Mr. Eaton assigned the note to me for collection. We
went to the bank, and I gave a check to Mr. Hopkins for
$2,300, and the money was carried out, and it was handed
back to me by Mr. Hopkins. Mr. Eaton was there. Mr.
Eaton knew that Mr. Hopkins handed it back to me. I do
not know that the note was produced on that occasion; I did
not see it. . . . . I have no interest in the note other than
that heretofore stated."

Witness was the plaintiff in the case. In a verified complaint he had alleged the indorsement and transfer of the
note by the payee, Eaton, to Hopkins before maturity, for
value, and the indorsement to him for value before the commencement of the action. He testified in chief that the note
was assigned to him by Eaton before its maturity; that he
had not received payment, and so far as he knew it had not
been paid; that the note had not been in his possession. This
testimony tended to establish a prima facie case for plaintiff, and went to the material issues presented by the
complaint. We think it was proper for defendants, on cross-
examination, to go to the bottom of this witness' connection
with the note, and draw from him all he knew about it,
even though the facts within his knowledge might tend to
prove the allegations set up in defense. Defendants had the
right to show facts by this witness which would dispute his

testimony that Eaton assigned the note to him before maturity; to show why he had not received payment, and why the note had not been paid; and to dispute that the note for which he was asking judgment had not been in his possession; and to show that it had been in his possession, and the facts relating to that possession. By his testimony plaintiff challenged the fullest inquiry, by cross-examination, into his connection with the note.

Fisher Ames testified that he had been attorney for Mrs. Bell, and was her attorney at the time the matters occurred concerning which he testified, but that he was not Eaton's attorney. His testimony was not objected to at the trial, but because Eaton testified that Ames was his attorney it is now urged that the evidence was incompetent. This contention cannot be maintained, if for no other reason than that the evidence is in conflict as to the fact of the alleged relation of attorney and client, and the lower court accepted the testimony of Mr. Ames. He testified to some important facts bearing upon finding 2. He testified that he was not Mr. Eaton's attorney; that he saw the note in question about the middle of November, 1895; ''at that time it bore no interest. . . . . I next saw the note in July, 1897, and at that time it bore three per cent interest per month. . . . . . It was not indorsed. Q. Not indorsed by either of the names that are upon it now? A. Neither of the names were upon it at that time.'' On cross-examination he testified that Eaton showed him the note in witness' office about the middle of July, 1897, at which time he testified it bore no indorsement. This was long after the maturity of the note, shortly before the suit was brought, and it was then in Eaton's possession. It is not necessary to pursue the evidence at length. The remaining findings are not now attacked, and there is enough, in the testimony of plaintiff and Ames, without resort to the testimony of defendants (which is quite explicit in support of the findings), to justify finding 2. Section 3123 of the Civil Code provides: ''An indorsee in due course is one who, in the ordinary course of business, and for value, before its apparent maturity or presumptive dishonor, and without knowledge of its actual dishonor, acquires a negotiable instrument duly indorsed to him, or indorsed generally, or payable to bearer.'' The evidence in the case was sufficient to support the finding that the note was not indorsed to Hopkins for value before maturity, or, indeed, to anyone prior to maturity, although plaintiff held it for a while as security for the loan before maturity. Conceding that it was not necessary to show that plaintiff took the note before maturity, if his assignor, Hopkins, took it by indorsement before maturity, without notice of any infirmity in it (Eames v. Crosier, 101 Cal. 260, 35 Pac. 873), it appears that Hopkins did not so take the note. According to plaintiff's testimony Eaton assigned the note to plaintiff just before the suit was brought, and when Mr. Ames saw the note, a few days earlier, it bore no indorsement.

There is evidence to support the finding that the consideration for the note was services to be performed by Eaton, the payee, and also that he failed to perform all the services agreed to be performed by him. There is sufficient evidence also to support the finding that the note was altered in the particulars claimed in the answer, without the knowledge or consent of the makers, at some time after it was delivered to Eaton, and that this alteration was made before the alleged transfer to Hopkins. There is also evidence sufficient to support the finding that on December 31, 1896, Eaton received $1,500 in payment of his said services, which constituted the consideration for the note. On these points the evidence was either in conflict or sustained the findings without conflict, and, as we understand appellant, he concedes that under the rule the facts cannot be inquired into here. It is claimed, however, that the note was transferred to Hopkins before maturity for value and without notice of any infirmity. The claim that there was at most but a partial failure of consideration by reason of Eaton's not performing service for the full term agreed upon is found adversely to appellant on sufficient evidence which tended to show that Eaton and Mrs. Bell had an agreement by which he was to surrender the note in consideration of the payment of $1,500 to him by Mrs. Bell. But it is said that this agreement was entered into after the transfer of the note to Hopkins. There is evidence that the note was not indorsed by the payee or the indorsee until just before the complaint was filed, and that it did not pass from Eaton to anyone by indorsement before maturity. Conceding that he transferred the note to Hopkins in August, 1896, it was at most but an equitable assignment, and did not shut out the defense set up by defendants unless the indorsement in July, 1897, related back to the date of the transfer, as claimed by appellant, and operated as an indorsement at that date. But we do not think that the doctrine of relation can apply to cut off the right of the makers of the note to set up their . defense. The doctrine of relation is but a fiction of the law adopted by the courts solely for the purposes of justice: Shay v. McNamara, 54 Cal. 169; Hawkins v. Harlan, 68 Cal. 236, 9 Pac. 108.

When the note was executed it bore no interest, and the contemporaneous agreement shows that it was not intended to bear interest, at least until the year's services were performed, which constituted its consideration (Civ. Code, sec. 1917); and respondent urges that by section 1700 of the same code the intentional alteration of the note was in a material particular, and extinguished "all the executory obligations of the contract" in favor of the payee against the makers who did not consent to the alteration. We are cited to Walsh v. Hunt, 120 Cal. 46, 39 L. R. A. 697, 52 Pac. 115, where it was said that "any unauthorized change in a material respect destroys the integrity of the instrument as the contract which the maker has executed; it ceases to be his contract, and is avoided, even in the hands of an innocent holder for value"; and the principle applies as well to commercial paper—citing cases. If the alteration was material this fiction of the law, now invoked, could not be used to override the salutary rule enunciated in Walsh v. Hunt, supra. But if it be true, as is claimed by appellant, that the alteration was not material, and would not affect the validity of the note in the hands of an innocent holder (citing Fisher v. Dennis, 6 Cal. 577, 65 Am. Dec. 534; Visher v. Webster, 8 Cal. 112; and First Nat. Bank v. Wolff, 79 Cal. 69, 21 Pac. 551, 748), the fact remains that the note was not "duly indorsed" to Hopkins or plaintiff "before its apparent maturity," and neither Hopkins nor plaintiff was "an indorsee in due course" (Civ. Code, sec. 3123), and defendants could plead their equitable defense.

The judgment and order should be affirmed.

We concur: Gray, C.; Haynes, C.

PER CURIAM.—For the reasons given in the foregoing opinion the order appealed from is affirmed.

6

CALLAHAN v. JAMES.*

Sac. No. 964; December 18, 1902.

71 Pac. 104.

Public Lands — Townsite — Construction of Statutes.— Revised Statutes of the United States, section 2322 (U. S. Comp. Stats. 1901, p. 1425), confers on the locator of a mining claim a possessory title. Section 2324 (U. S. Comp. Stats. 1901, p. 1426) requires such locator to do a certain amount of work annually. Section 2386 (U. S. Comp. Stats. 1901, p. 1457) subjects townsite titles to whatever possessory right in the locator is recognized by local authority, as does also Statutes of 1867–68, page 696, section 10, so long as the locator shall comply with the laws. Section 2392 (U. S. Comp. Stats. 1901, p. 1459) provides that no town lot title shall be acquired "to any mine of gold, silver, cinnabar or copper, or to any valid mining claim or possession held under existing laws." Section 2387 (U. S. Comp. Stats. 1901, p. 1457) authorizes townsite lands to be conveyed to occupants, and the balance to be sold, or otherwise disposed of. Held that, construing section 2392 (U. S. Comp. Stats. 1901, p. 1459), in the light of previous legislation which it embodies (Acts March 2, 1867, 14 Stats. 541 (U. S. Comp. Stats. 1901, p. 1460), and June 8, 1868 (15 Stats. 67), showing that the intent was merely to confer on mining titles acquired from the United States the same superior quality given by section 2386, enacted March 2, 1865 (U. S. Comp. Stats. 1901, p. 1457), to those recognized by local authority, and construing it also in view of section 2387 (U. S. Comp. Stats. 1901, p. 1457), showing an intent that the entire townsite be disposed of, and also in view of its own wording, the clause, "or to any valid mining claim or possession held under existing laws," must be taken to refer to the possessory title conferred by section 2322 (U. S. Comp. Stats. 1901, p. 1425), and not to any mine subject to a valid claim or possession; and hence locators, whose claim had been patented as a townsite, and who afterward failed to do the work required by section 2324 (U. S. Comp. Stats. 1901, p. 1426), thereby lost, under section 2386 (U. S. Comp. Stats., p. 1457), and Statutes of 1867–68, page 696, section 10, their paramount title.

Public Lands—Townsite—Mining Claim.—Even if the clause, "or to any valid mining claim or possession," be construed as applying to any mine subject to such claim or possession, the effect would be the same, since, construing it in connection with the previous clause, "to any mine of gold, silver," etc., "any valid claim or possession" must be a valuable mine, and not a mere worthless claim, as, for aught that appeared, the one in suit was.

*For subsequent opinion in bank, see 141 Cal. 291, 74 Pac. 853.

Quieting Title.—A Defendant in a Suit to Quiet Title Sufficiently Connects his title with that of his predecessor, on which he relies, by showing that the predecessor's estate was assigned to his widow, who, with two of the children, conveyed to defendant, though the third child was a minor, and the order assigning the property to the widow might have been in excess of the court's jurisdiction in view of her remarriage, as the title of the two adult heirs vested in defendant which was sufficient for purposes of defense.

Public Land—Townsite—Delivery of Deed.—In a Suit to Quiet Title it was found that the trustee of a townsite platted on public lands of the United States executed deeds to persons whose names appeared on the official map as being entitled thereto, who had not previously obtained conveyances, and, among others, to defendant's predecessor; and that the trustee left "all of said deeds so executed" with one T. Held, that this was sufficient to show delivery, since, if not to be regarded as express finding thereof, delivery was to be inferred therefrom.

Public Land—Townsite—Payment of Purchase Money.—In a Suit to Quiet title, the omission of a finding that defendant's predecessor paid the purchase money for a town lot to the trustee of a townsite is immaterial, it appearing from the evidence that the money was paid by another for him.

Public Land—Townsite—Quieting Title.—Statutes of 1867–68, page 696, section 24, relating to conveyances of townsite lots platted on public lands, provides that every certificate or deed granted to any person pursuant to the act shall be taken as conclusive evidence that all preliminary proceedings have been correctly performed. Held, that the payment of the purchase money would be presumed from the fact of conveyance, and hence the omission of a finding thereof in a suit to quiet title was immaterial.

Public Land—Townsite—Quieting Title.—Civil Code, section 870, provides that, when a trust in relation to real property is expressed in the instrument creating the estate, a deed in contravention of the trust is void. Statutes of 1867–68, page 696, section 15, relating to the conveyance of the lots of a townsite platted on public lands, provides for the sale of unoccupied or vacant land to possessors of adjoining lands or other citizens of the town, and, if any lands remain unsold at the end of six months after filing the plat, they are to be sold at auction. A federal statute provides that any act of the townsite trustees not in conformity to the regulations prescribed by the legislative authority of the state shall be void. Held, that the trustee's deed was sufficient to convey the legal title, though made to one who is not an occupant of the land.

Public Land—Townsite—Quieting Title.—Statutes of 1867–68, page 696, section 15, authorizes conveyances of the lots of a townsite platted on public land, being unoccupied, to possessors of adjoining land, or other citizens of the town. Held, that it could not be in-

ferred from findings in a suit to quiet title that defendant's predecessor was never "in possession of any part or portion" of the lot
in controversy, that he was not an occupant, or otherwise qualified
to receive a conveyance.

APPEAL from Superior Court, Tuolumne County; G. W.
Nicol, Judge.

Action by John F. Callahan against John P. James. Judgment for plaintiff and defendant appeals. Reversed.

F. W. Street for appellant; J. B. Curtin for respondent.

PER CURIAM.—This is a suit to quiet the plaintiff's title
to land described in the complaint, situate in the town of
Groveland, and known as the "Rhode Island Mining Claim."
The plaintiff had judgment, from which, and from an order
denying his motion for a new trial, the defendant appeals.

The plaintiff deraigns title to the land in question under
a mining location, originally made in the year 1854 by one
Reid, and renewed by Reid and one Austin January 1, 1876.
The defendant, under the patent of the townsite of Groveland, issued under the federal laws (Rev. Stats., sec. 2387
et seq. [6 Fed. Stats. Ann. 344; U. S. Comp. Stats. 1901,
p. 1457]), and a deed of the patentee to Lawrence Murray,
of date September 5, 1879, purporting to convey to him lot
8, block 6, as designated on the official map of the townsite,
of which lot the land in question is part. The date of the
patent is February 10, 1886; that of the original entry of
the townsite, October 3, 1877. It is found by the court that
the land in question was duly located January 1, 1876, by
plaintiff's predecessors, whose title became vested in him
March 26, 1896, and that "plaintiff ever since has been the
owner and in the possession of said Rhode Island mining
claim [specifically described in the findings], and has been
working and developing the same as a mining claim." And
as conclusion of law it is found that at the date of the townsite entry, October 3, 1877, the land lying within the Rhode
Island mining claim was withdrawn from sale or disposition
by the government of the United States, and hence was
reserved from the operation of the patent to the trustee of
the townsite. It is urged by the appellant's counsel that
this conclusion of the court was erroneous, and that on the
facts found the judgment should have been for defendant.

By respondent's counsel the contrary is asserted; and it is further contended, on the facts found, that defendant has not acquired the trustee's title, and hence that plaintiff was entitled to recover on his naked possession.

In this statement of the questions involved we use the expression "naked possession" advisedly, because it does not appear from the findings that the "possessory title" given to plaintiff's predecessors, the locators of the mine, by section 2322 of the Revised Statutes (5 Fed. Stats. Ann. 13; U. S. Comp. Stats. 1901, p. 1425) has been kept alive by the performance of the annual amount of work required by section 2324 (5 Fed. Stats. Ann. 19; U. S. Comp. Stats. 1901, p. 1426). Accordingly, it is not contended by the respondent counsel—so far as appears from this brief—that the case comes within the operation of the provisions of section 2386 of the Revised Statutes (6 Fed. Stats. Ann. 343; U. S. Comp Stats. 1901, p. 1457), by the terms of which titles under the township act are made "subject" to the possessory rights of locators. Nor can such contention be successfully made. The possessory title of plaintiff's predecessors was, indeed, valid at the time of the entry of the townsite (which was within the year following the year of the location, and therefore within the time allowed the locators to do the work required), and, had it been kept alive to the time of the commencement of the suit, would have been sufficient to sustain plaintiff's action. For by the express provisions of the law (Rev. Stats. 2386 [6 Fed. Stats. Ann. 343; U. S. Comp. Stats. 1901, p. 1457]) all titles under the townsite act are made subject to the possessory rights of miners; and to the same effect in section 10 of the state law: Stats. 1867–68, p. 696. But by the terms of the statute the right is granted to locators for "so long" only as the law shall be complied with; and upon default of compliance the term of the possessory right or lease given by the statute terminates, and the provisions of the statute no longer apply. The judgment can be affirmed, therefore, if at all, only upon one of two grounds urged in the respondent's brief; that is to say, upon the ground that the land in question was reserved from the operation of the patent by the provisions of section 2392 of the Revised Statutes (6 Fed. Stats. Ann. 351; U. S. Comp. Stats. 1901, p. 1459), or, failing this, upon the ground that (defendant having failed to connect himself with the patent title) plaintiff's action can be successfully maintained on his possession.

1. The former contention turns upon the construction of section 2392 of the Revised Statutes (6 Fed. Stats. Ann. 351; U. S. Comp. Stats. 1901, p. 1459), the provisions of which are that "no title shall be acquired, under the foregoing provisions of this chapter, to any mine of gold, silver, cinnabar, or copper, or to any valid mining claim or possession held under existing laws." It is not, however, nor can it be, contended, that the case comes within the exception provided for in the first of the two clauses of the section; for under the unvarying decisions of the courts, federal and state, the term "mine" is defined as including only mines valuable for their minerals, or, as expressed in the statute, "valuable mineral deposits" (Rev. Stats., sec. 2319 [5 Fed. Stats. Ann. 4; U. S. Comp. Stats. 1901, p. 1424]; Davis v. Weibbold, 139 U. S. 517–519, 523, 35 L. Ed. 238, 11 Sup. Ct. Rep. 628; Richards v. Dower, 81 Cal. 50, 22 Pac. 304; Dower v. Richards, 151 U. S. 662, 663, 38 L. Ed. 305, 14 Sup. Ct. Rep. 452, and cases therein cited; Smith v. Hill, 89 Cal. 125, 26 Pac. 644; Barden v. Railroad Co., 154 U. S. 288, 38 L. Ed. 992, 14 Sup. Ct. Rep. 1030; Standard Quicksilver Co. v. Habishaw, 132 Cal. 123, 64 Pac. 113; 1 Lindley on Mines, secs. 86, 94), and there is nothing in the case to show that the mine in question is of that character. The contention of the respondent, therefore, more specifically stated, is that the case comes within the exception made by the latter clause of the section, and it is therefore the construction of this clause only that is involved here. This, it is obvious, is susceptible of two constructions. It may refer either to the mine claimed or possessed, or to the claim or possession of the mine. Under the former construction, supplying omitted words, it would read "or to any mine subject to a valid mining claim or possession," etc. Under the latter it would refer to the "possessory right" given to mining locators by the provisions of section 2322 of the Revised Statutes (5 Fed. Stats. Ann. 13; U. S. Comp. Stats. 1901, p. 1425); and, thus construed, its effect would be substantially the same as that of the provisions of section 2386 of the statute (6 Fed. Stats. Ann. 343; U. S. Comp. Stats. 1901, p. 1457) and of section 10 of the state act; that is, it would except such rights from the operation of the patent so long as they should continue

to exist, and, if ultimately patented, forever. The latter construction seems to be most in consonance with the language of the act, and also with its intention as shown by the obvious purposes and the circumstances of its enactment. The chapter of the Revised Statutes relating to townsites (chapter 8, title 32 [6 Fed. Stats. Ann. 341; U. S. Comp. Stats. 1901, p. 1454]) is simply a revision of former statutes, including among others the act of March 3, 1865 (from which section 2386 is taken), and the acts of March 2, 1867 (14 Stats. 541 [6 Fed. Stats. Ann. 353; U. S. Comp. Stats. 1901, p. 1460]), and of June 8, 1868 (15 Stats. 67). In the act of 1867 the only proviso was: "That no title shall be acquired, under the provisions of this act, to any mine of gold, silver, cinnabar or copper." Under the act of 1868 the proviso was: "That no title under [the former act] shall be acquired to any valid mining claim or possession held under the existing laws of Congress": Richards v. Dower, 81 Cal. 50, 22 Pac. 304. In the Revised Statutes both provisos are run together in section 2392, now under consideration. Comparing the several acts enumerated, it appears that prior to the act of 1867 the only saving clause was that referring to mining possessions in the act of 1865, now embodied in section 2386 of the Revised Statutes; the original enactment being prior to the enactment of any mining laws by the government of the United States, and hence apparently not referring to those laws. The purpose of the act of 1868, if we have rightly construed it, would, therefore, be to correct this defect, and to make the former reservation unmistakably applicable to possessions of lands recognized or provided for by the federal laws thereafter enacted; and the general effect of the acts and of the provisions in the Revised Statutes would be simply to preserve both reservations—that is to say, the reservation made in the act of 1865, and that made in the act of 1867. So as to the effect of the legislation, taken together, it can be readily understood that it was intended to except from grants of townsites all valuable mines—as, indeed, was required by section 2318 of the Revised Statutes (5 Fed. Stats. Ann. 4; U. S. Comp. Stats. 1901, p. 1423); and also that it was intended, pending the development of mineral deposits, and the ascertainment of their character, to protect miners in the enjoyment of the possessory rights given to them by section 2322 of the act (5 Fed. Stats. Ann. 13; U. S. Comp. Stats. 1901, p. 1425), as was required by the provisions of section 2319 (5 Fed. Stats. Ann. 4; U. S. Comp. Stats. 1901, p. 1424). But it is impossible to conceive of any reason why exception should be made of lands occupied by miners, demonstrated by subsequent development to be of no value for mining purposes, or, in other words, not to be mines in the statutory sense. The case would, therefore, seem to come within the principle embodied in the maxim, "Cessante ratione legis, cessat et ipsa lex." So, also, it is the obvious intention of the act to dispose of the whole title of the townsite land, either to the mining claimant or to the trustee of the town; that is to say, to the former, in case the land claimed is presently known to be a valuable mine, or subsequently, on final application, proves to be such; to the latter, should the contrary be the case. For by the express provisions of the act (section 2387 [6 Fed. Stats. Ann. 344; U. S. Comp. Stats. 1901, p. 1457]) the lands granted to the trustee are to be disposed of, not only by conveyance to occupants, but—as to lands not thus disposed of—by sale or otherwise, as directed by the state. But upon the construction contended for in the innumerable cases in which mining locations are in fact not of lands of the kind contemplated by the mining laws, and, as the result of development, are subsequently demonstrated not to be such, the lands located would remain undisposed of, contrary to the general intent of the statute, which would be to extend indefinitely the unauthorized possession of the claimant for purposes other than mining, though in continued and designed default in performing the acts required by the law as essential to his title. Thus in the present case, though the mine should prove to be not a mine in the sense of the statute, and though all statutory requirements should be designedly omitted, the lapsed location would, in effect (upon the construction of the law contended for), be made the equivalent of a fee simple title, which was clearly not contemplated by the law. For it is at least clear that it was not the intent of the act to give to miners any other rights than those conferred upon them by the mining laws—that is to say, the land itself—in the event only it should prove to be a mine of the kind described in the decisions cited above, and in the meanwhile the possession of it for purposes of mining upon the terms defined in the law. Nor would the result be different should we construe the proviso as referring not to the possessory right of the miner, but to the mine itself. For in such case, under the familiar rule embodied in the maxim, ''Noscitur a sociis,'' and the decisions cited above, the terms used in the latter clause must be interpreted in the same general sense as those in the former; that is to say, as referring to actual or valuable mines only: Cases supra. Thus construed, the agreement and disagreement between the cases provided for in the two clauses would be simply thus: In either case the mine must be a valuable mine; but in the former, it must be known to be such at the time of the townsite entry, while in the latter it may not be known until a later period, as the result of subsequent development. We therefore conclude that the case as presented by the findings does not come within the exception prescribed by section 2392 of the act (6 Fed. Stats. Ann. 351; U. S. Comp. Stats. 1901, p. 1459). On the other hand, it is equally clear that it does come within the provisions of the other saving clause, section 2386 (6 Fed. Stats. Ann. 343; U. S. Comp. Stats. 1901, p. 1457); for the entry of the townsite October 3, 1887, was within the period of two years after the location of the mine, January 1, 1876, during which the work required by the law could be performed; and hence, under the express provisions of the section quoted, all titles acquired under the patent were taken subject to ''the possession and the necessary use of the land'' by the locators. Though, as we have seen, the findings fail to show that at the time of the commencement of the action the ''possessory title'' acquired by the locators under section 2322 (5 Fed. Stats. Ann. 13; U. S. Comp. Stats. 1901, p. 1425) of the statute had been kept alive by performance of the work required annually by section 2324 (5 Fed. Stats. Ann. 19; U. S. Comp. Stats. 1901, p. 1426). If, however, on a new trial, it should be shown that work has been performed as required by the law, and other conditions complied with, the plaintiff will then come within the reservations of section 2386 of the statute (6 Fed. Stats. Ann. 343; U. S. Comp. Stats. 1901, p. 1457), and of the corresponding section (being No. 10) of the state law (Stats. 1867–68, p. 696); and he would then be able to maintain his action. But what would be the effect of a resumption and continuance of work on his claim—if, as seems to be suggested by evidence, he was in default at the date of the filing of the complaint—cannot be determined in this suit.

2. The remaining objections made to the deed are: That the deed from the trustee of the townsite to the defendant's predecessor, Murray, was void for want of delivery, or, if delivered, because in contravention of the terms of the trust; and that the title of Murray has not vested in the defendant. The last objection may be briefly disposed of. The defendant deraigns title under a deed from Mrs. Joanna Wilson, formerly Murray, to whom, by an order of the superior court of date March 5, 1900, the whole of the estate—being under the value of $1,500—was assigned, as the widow of the deceased, Murray, for the use and support of the family of said deceased, two of the three children of Murray joining in the deed, and the other being a minor. The point of the respondent's objection is that "the order setting aside the property to Joanna Wilson was in excess of the jurisdiction of the probate court," she having, by her remarriage, ceased to be the widow of the deceased. If such be the case (and we do not deem it necessary to pass on the point), it would follow simply that the order would be void, and the titles of the heirs would remain unaffected. Nor can we conceive of any process of reasoning to lead us to the conclusion that the effect of the void order could be to vest the title of the whole estate in the minor heir. It would have been, no doubt, in the power of the court, upon the assumption made, to assign the estate to the minor; but until such assignment her rights remain the same as those of the other heirs. The interests of the grantors in the deed as heirs therefore passed to the defendant which is sufficient to meet the objection. Nor are the objections that the deed of the trustee was not delivered to Murray, and that the purchase money was not paid by him, more tenable. It is expressly found that the trustee, on September 5, 1879, being about to go abroad, "did make and execute [deeds] to the persons whose names appeared upon [the] official map of the townsite, ... as being entitled thereto, and who had not previously obtained conveyances," and among others to Murray, "whose name appeared upon said map on lot 8,

block 6, of said townsite"; and that at the same time the grantor did "leave all of said deeds so executed" with one Tannahill. From this, if not to be regarded as an express finding of delivery (Hill v. Den, 54 Cal. 20), delivery is to be inferred (McDougall v. McDougall, 135 Cal. 319, 67 Pac. 778). Nor is the finding material that Murray never paid to the trustee the purchase money. It is sufficient that it was paid by another for him, as appears from the evidence to have been the case; and, though it is not so found, the fact, if essential to the validity of the conveyance (which we do not hold), will, under the provisions of section 24 of the act, be presumed.

The remaining objection is that the trustee had no power to convey to anyone other than to occupants of the land conveyed, and that it is found that Murray did not come within this description. But neither the fact relied on nor the conclusion drawn from it can be admitted. As to the latter, it is a universal principle, except where affected by express statutory provisions, that a deed of conveyance conveys all the interest of the grantor; and this applies equally to a legal title held in trust as to any other. For in the view of a court of law, or of a court exercising legal, as distinguished from equitable, functions, the equitable title is nonexistent, and the legal is, in fact the only title. Nor, with regard to the present case, is there any law making it an exception to the rule. It is, indeed, provided by section 870 of the Civil Code that, "when a trust in relation to real property is expressed in the instrument creating the estate," a deed in contravention of the trust is void. But here the trust expressed in the federal statute, and presumably in the patent, is not expressed otherwise than by reference to regulations thereafter to be enacted by the legislature of the state. The cases cited by the respondent do not affect this proposition. In Biddick v. Kobler, 110 Cal. 191, 42 Pac. 578, all that was held was that in a suit to recover possession by a grantee of the trustee, who was never the occupant, or entitled to the occupancy of the land conveyed, against one who was such occupant, and so entitled at the date of the entry, the equity of the latter could be relied on as a complete defense; all of which follows from familiar principles of equity, and also from the express provisions of section 10 of the state law, providing that the deeds of the trustees shall not "be deemed to conclude the rights of third persons." But we find nothing in the decision to lead us to suppose that the court intended to hold that the deed in question was ineffectual as a conveyance of the legal title, and though, in some of the cases from other jurisdictions cited by the court, it is held, under the statutory provisions governing them, that such a deed would be void, yet it is said by this court that these "authorities . . . . go much further in the same direction than we are called upon to go here." In one of the cases cited by the court, and perhaps others (Treadway v. Wilder, 8 Nev. 91, 9 Nev. 71), it may be noted the conclusion of the court was based upon the provisions of the federal law there involved, which expressly declared that all deeds made in contravention of the trust should be void. But in the act involved here there is no such provision. It is, indeed, provided that the acts of the trustee in contravention of the regulations to be imposed by state legislation shall be void. But by the state act provision is made for conveyances not only to occupants of lots (as provided in section 10), but also (as provided in section 15) for the sale of "any unoccupied or vacant lands" "to possessors of adjoining lands, or other citizens of said town, at a price not less than one dollar per acre," etc.; and, if any lands remain unsold at the end of six months after the filing of the town plat, they are to be sold at auction: Amador Co. v. Gilbert, 133 Cal. 51, 65 Pac. 130. As to the facts of the case, there is nothing in the findings of the court to indicate that the conveyance was not in accord with some one of the powers of the trustee as above specified. It is not found that Murray was not an occupant of lot 8, block 6, at the date of the entry of the townsites; but merely that he was never "in possession of any part or portion of lot 8, block 6, ... within the boundaries of said Rhode Island mine." Nor was it found that he was not of the class described in section 15 of the act as "possessors of adjoining lands," as in fact appears from the evidence was the case; or that he was not a citizen of the town. The findings therefore fail to show that the deed was in contravention of the trust.

We are of the opinion, therefore, that the land in question was conveyed by the patent, and that the title is vested in the defendant, and, consequently, that the judgment can-

not, on the facts found, be sustained; and for these reasons
the judgment and order appealed from are reversed and
the cause is remanded for a new trial.

McMULLIN v. McMULLIN.*

S. F. No. 2533; December 30, 1902.

71 Pac. 108.

Divorce—Desertion—Voluntary Separation.—In an action for
divorce for desertion, evidence held insufficient to support a finding
that the separation between plaintiff and defendant was voluntary,
and with defendant's consent.

Divorce—Desertion—Curing by Offer to Return.—Where a husband deserted his wife against her consent, he could not, eighteen
years thereafter, cure such desertion by an offer to return, so as to
entitle him to a divorce for desertion on the wife's refusal of his offer.

APPEAL from Superior Court, City and County of San
Francisco; George H. Bahrs, Judge.

Action by Thurlow McMullin against Virginia McMullin.
From a judgment in favor of plaintiff, defendant appeals.
Reversed.

Denson & Schlesinger for appellant; Chas. S. Wheeler
and Bishop & Wheeler for respondent.

VAN DYKE, J.—This is an action for divorce, in which
plaintiff had judgment. Defendant moved for a new trial
on a bill of exceptions, which was denied. The appeal is
from the judgment and order denying the motion for a new
trial. The suit is prosecuted by the plaintiff on the ground
of desertion. The parties intermarried on the 15th of
February, 1871. A son was born March 17, 1872, and this
suit was commenced April 9, 1898, in which it is charged
the defendant deserted the plaintiff on April 10, 1896. The
court finds: "That in the year 1877 plaintiff voluntarily
separated himself from the defendant, and thereafter, until
on or about the tenth day of April, 1897, continued to live

---

*For subsequent opinion in bank, see 140 Cal. 112, 73·Pac. 808.

separate and apart from the defendant; but that the said separation was not against the wish or will of said defendant, but was wholly acquiesced in and consented to by the said defendant. That plaintiff did not, in the year 1877, willfully desert or abandon the defendant, nor was plaintiff's separation from the said defendant with the intent then and there to desert the defendant, nor has the plaintiff ever since or at any time continued to or kept up or continued the said or any separation or abandonment, but that, on the contrary, the separation of plaintiff from defendant in the year 1877 was, and thereafter until the tenth day of April, 1895, continued to be, with the full acquiescence and consent of defendant.''

1. The contention on the part of the appellant that this finding is unsupported by the evidence we think is well taken. In reference to the desertion, or, as called by the court, "separation," in 1877, the defendant testifies as follows: "In the morning when we were down to breakfast, and sat there, and he started to go, he went back first into the kitchen, and discharged the cook, in my presence, and I told the cook not to pay any attention; that he must remain. He told the nurse to pack his trunk; that he would send for it that day; and then he left, and during the day he sent for the trunk by an expressman, and when I saw that he was there I interrogated him to find out where he was going to take the trunk, and the expressman did not tell. That was the last time that he ever was in the house. The trunk was ready to go. The nurse had packed it. It was not closed, and just before it was closed I put in a little shoe—one of the pair of shoes; a little kid shoe, the first my baby had ever worn—and laid it on the tray of the trunk after the things were all packed. That was one of my baby's shoes. And I had a pair of cuff buttons that I had given him Christmas before we were married and rather too handsome for him to wear daily, and liable to be broken, and he asked me to put them aside, and take care of them for him. I put those on top of the tray of the trunk, and I wrote a few words on a piece of paper, and put them on top of the cuff buttons. I have not seen the piece of paper since. I remember about what the words were. I said: 'I married you for love. I have lived with you for love, and I would have clung to you forever for love.

You have broken my heart. You have wrecked my life. May those who have done this thing meet with just punishment. God help us all, and keep you from harm. Your wife.' I directed it, 'My husband.' I laid it on top of the buttons, that he must see it. It was impossible for it to get lost. I know he must have seen it. I put it in the tray of the trunk beside the little shoe. The trunk was locked by the nurse, and the expressman took it away. I have never at any time had any agreement or correspondence or talk with Mr. McMullin, or anyone in his behalf since then, to live separate." Plaintiff's attorney here admitted that Mrs. McMullin was a woman of education and refinement. The defendant further testified:."I lived with my father up to the time of his death, about fifteen years ago, and since then with my mother; and they have supported me and my child, barring the time that I was working for my living. I worked in the mint for over eight years, and devoted my salary to the support of my boy and myself." In reference to this the plaintiff testified as follows: "Q. By his Counsel: Did you say to your wife, on the 14th of November, 1877: 'I am going to desert you. My relatives are unwilling I should live with you. I wish you would pack my trunk?' " to which he answered: "I do not remember anything about the relative part. I remember asking to have—I do remember asking her to pack my trunk. Q. Did you, on the morning of November 15, 1877, before leaving the house, discharge, or attempt to discharge, the Chinese servant? A. I do not remember anything about the occasion of discharging either the servant or nurse. I have no recollection of any such occurrence. I don't remember of speaking to the servant about it. I sent for my trunk by an expressman, and got it. I have no recollection of seeing that little shoe in the trunk, and am sure I would remember it if I had seen it, and think I would have it now." On cross-examination the witness said: "I don't remember that shoe. I think, if I had received it, I would have it yet; but I can't recall it. I remember the pair of cameo cuff buttons. She gave them to me for a birthday or Christmas present before marriage. I guess they came in the trunk, but I can't remember about that. At any rate, I think they are somewhere among my effects now, but I have not seen them for years. She put them in the trunk, and I took them out.

I don't remember whether they were in a case when they came in the trunk. . . . . I don't remember about any note being put in the mirror or otherwise. I don't remember whether I sent any communication to her in any manner. After one, two, or three days I went back for the purpose of getting my things, or having them packed to leave. There might have been a request made for these things to be packed while I was away, but I don't know. When I went back for my things, she begged me to stay." He admits receiving the cuff buttons. "She put them in the trunk, and I took them out." He does not deny receiving the note and the baby's shoe which the wife says she sent with the cuff buttons, but merely says, "I don't remember." Here we have the direct and positive testimony of the wife that her husband left against her consent—in other words, deserted her—and that she did not acquiesce in his doing so; and the plaintiff, in his testimony, does not deny this; and there is no evidence whatever of a voluntary separation in 1877, as found by the court, or that the defendant consented or acquiesced in the desertion of the plaintiff.

2. The court also found: "That on the tenth day of April, 1895, while the plaintiff and defendant were living separate and apart by mutual acquiescence, the plaintiff offered in good faith to return and live with the defendant, and sought a reconciliation and restoration; that the defendant then and there refused it, and ever since has refused to accept said offer." We have already shown that the finding of the court that there was a separation by mutual acquiescence is not supported by the evidence. At the time of the pretended offer for reconciliation on the part of the plaintiff, an action for maintenance against him, instituted by the defendant herein, was pending. Judge Paterson, it seems, was the attorney of the defendant here, Mrs. McMullin, in her suit for maintenance. In his testimony herein he says: "During the pendency of that case I had a good many talks with Mr. Wheeler and Mrs. McMullin. . . . . I know that McMullin was exceedingly anxious to have the matter disposed of, and that there should be a divorce. Mr. Wheeler told me that Mr. McMullin would be willing to give her a liberal half of all the property he had, and would acquaint us fully what those properties, where they were, and what they were worth. Mrs. McMullin, basing her objection

on religious grounds, declined to listen to any proposition which would result in a divorce. She claimed to have religious scruples against such a thing as divorce, and said she never could have a happy day if she were a divorced woman. Necessarily, and taking these views, and being very positive about them, the matter of divorce was dropped, so far as she was concerned, in the negotiations.'' Then he refers to other negotiations, and on cross-examination he says: ''I intended to say that Mr. McMullin's desire, communicated to me, that there should be a divorce from his wife, to which she would not assent. Subsequently, I stated that I learned from either Mr. McMullin or Mr. McMullin or Mr. Wheeler—I don't know which or where—that, unless that were done, Mr. McMullin would lay the foundation of a divorce himself by an offer of a home.'' Under these circumstances the so-called offer for reconciliation was made by the plaintiff. It is quite a formal document, in which he refers to the negotiations testified to by Judge Paterson, and concludes by saying: ''I therefore ask that you return and fulfill the marriage contract, and I offer to do and will do likewise. I will wait for you to-night at the parlors of the Occidental Hotel from 7 P. M. until 7:30 P. M.'' From the tone of the document and from all the surrounding circumstances detailed in the evidence, this offer was not made with the expectation of it being accepted, or for the purpose of reconciliation. When on the stand giving his testimony in reference to sending this communication, he was asked on cross-examination: ''When you sent this letter to Mrs. McMullin, did you expect that she would accede to it? A. I didn't know. Q. I asked you if you expected? A. I think I answered I didn't know. Q. Of course you didn't know whether she would accept or not. Did you expect she would? A. I did not know at that time. Q. You didn't know whether you expected it? A. I didn't know whether she would accept it or not. Q. Then I understand from you, you did not know whether she would accept that or not? Did you expect she would accept it? A. How could I tell that?'' The court then interposes: ''Did you have any expectation about it one way or another? A. Yes, naturally so, Judge; I would rather expect she would accept it. Q. By Defendant's Counsel: What reason did you have for expecting, after these

7

eighteen years of separation, under all these conditions, that she would accede to this letter, and go and live with you again?'' The court sustained an objection to this question, and thereby saved the witness from being compelled to answer it. Cross-examination is one of the most valuable means of eliciting truth, and, when properly conducted, should be upheld by the court, and not suppressed. This was the crucial point—whether the offer was made in good faith—and the defendant's counsel had a right on cross-examination to test the conscience of the plaintiff upon the question of his motive or good faith in making the offer. The wife, as it appears, had conscientious scruples against a divorce, and would not listen to any separation in that direction. She is rather to be admired for that than to be punished. Divorces for slight or trivial causes, or by collusion and connivance, are becoming so common as to be a scandal. The marriage relation is the foundation of all society, and, on the contrary, divorces, unless for special reasons, are demoralizing, and are not favored in the law. The code declares: ''If one party deserts the other, and before the expiration of the statutory period required to make desertion a cause of divorce, returns, and offers in good faith to fulfill the marriage contract, and solicits condonation, the desertion is cured'': Civ. Code, sec. 102. The statutory period referred to is one year, so that the plaintiff in this case could not avail himself of this provision of law, inasmuch as he had not sought condonation for nearly eighteen years. The code also declares: ''Consent to a separation is a revocable act, and, if one of the parties afterward, in good faith, seeks a reconciliation and restoration, but the other refuses it, such refusal is desertion'': Civ. Code, sec. 101. It is upon this section of the code that the plaintiff relies, but, as already shown, the separation was not by consent.

The judgment and order are reversed and cause remanded.

We concur: Harrison, J.; Garoutte, J.

LEONARD v. LEONARD et al.

S. F. No. 2525; December 26, 1902.

70 Pac. 1071.

Bills and Notes.—Where One of the Makers of a Note Who Had Paid it sued the other, on the ground that the note was for defendant's benefit and that it was agreed he would reimburse plaintiff if he paid it, and no objection was made to plaintiff's evidence because the note itself was not introduced in evidence or its absence accounted for, the absence of such evidence was no ground for a nonsuit.

Bills and Notes—Limitation of Actions.—Where Plaintiff and Defendant gave a note for the benefit of defendant, the money being to pay an obligation of defendant's and defendant agreed to pay the note or repay plaintiff if he paid it, the transaction was not a loan by plaintiff, and his cause of action against defendant for the purpose of the statute of limitations did not arise until payment by him of the note.

Bills and Notes—Joint and Several Obligation.—Civil Code, section 1659, relative to interpretation of contracts, provides that, where all the parties who unite in a promise receive some benefit from the consideration, whether past or present, their promise is presumed to be joint and several. Section 1431 provides that an obligation imposed on several persons is presumed to be joint, and not several, except in the cases mentioned in the title on the "Interpretation of Contracts." Held, that, where a note was given by two persons to obtain money for the benefit of one of them, the obligation was joint as well as several.

APPEAL from Superior Court, Santa Cruz County: Lucas F. Smith, Judge.

Action by James Leonard against T. W. Leonard and another. There was judgment for plaintiff, and the above-named defendant appeals from an order denying him a new trial. Affirmed.

John H. Leonard and Charles B. Younger, Jr., for appellant; Chas. M. Cassin for respondent.

PER CURIAM.—The plaintiff recovered, in the lower court, a verdict and judgment for the sum of $439.40 and costs. The appeal is from an order denying the defendant's motion for new trial. The case as alleged in the complaint is as follows: The action originates in a note of the plaintiff and T. W. Leonard to the City Bank of Santa Cruz, of date April 30, 1894, for the sum of $600, and another note of the same to the same, of date March 16, 1897, for the sum of $200—the balance then due on the former note. The plaintiff paid on the original note, March 16, 1897 (the date of the latter note), the sum of $207.70; and afterward, March 13, 1899, the second note in full. The complaint, in addition to the above facts, alleges that the first note was given "at the request of and for the sole benefit of said defendants, and upon their promise to him that they, the said defendants, would pay the same, ... and would pay to plaintiff any sums of money that plaintiff might pay thereon," etc. The verdict and judgment are for the amounts thus paid, with interest.

It is urged by the appellant's counsel, as ground of reversal, that a nonsuit should have been granted for the several reasons assigned, viz.: (1) That the execution of the original note of April 30, 1894, was not proven; (2) that the transaction as described in the testimony of the plaintiff was simply a loan by him to the defendants, and the cause of action, therefore, barred by the statute; and (3) that the joint liability of the defendants was not proven. But these objections, we think, are untenable. The execution of the original note was in fact proved; but the point of the objection is that the note itself was not introduced in evidence nor its absence accounted for. But as no objection to the evidence was made on that score, this was unnecessary. As to the second and third points, the evidence establishes that the money was borrowed, with the knowledge and consent of the defendants, for the purpose of paying their note to a third party; and there is evidence tending to show that they agreed to pay the note, or to repay him, if he paid it; from which it is clear that the cause of action on the latter promise to repay arose upon the payment, and is not barred by the statute; and also that the obligation thus created was joint, as well as several: Civ. Code, secs. 1431, 1659.

It is further urged by the appellant that it appeared from the uncontradicted testimony of T. W. Leonard that the plaintiff was indebted to him in the sum of $245, which, it is claimed, should have been allowed on his counterclaim. But, from the previous evidence of the witness, this claim seems to refer to payments made by him on the real property of himself and his codefendant, and was therefore not due from plaintiff otherwise than on the assumption that he was the real owner of half the property, which is negative by the verdict.

Other points are made by the appellant, but it will be sufficient to say we do not regard them as tenable.

For the reasons given, the order appealed from must be affirmed, and it is so ordered.

————

In re PINA'S ESTATE.

S. F. No. 3108; December 30, 1902.

71 Pac. 171.

Appeal — Costs, Review of Questions Relative to. — Where a Transcript on appeal did not set out the orders from which the appeals were taken, and in the notice of appeal the appeals were stated to be "from the order and judgment of the court striking out petitioner's bill of cost and disallowing the same," etc., but the bill of exceptions did not contain any bill of costs, or make reference to any, or to any action of the court thereon, questions relative to the court's action concerning costs could not be reviewed.

Administrator. — Where an Application for Letters of administration was supported by a petition stating that petitioner was a brother of deceased, and as such entitled to administer on his estate, and requesting that applicant be appointed in his stead, but the petition was not verified—merely having attached thereto a certificate in the form of an acknowledgment for a conveyance of real estate—and no evidence was offered that petitioner was a brother of deceased, or in any way related to him, the petition was properly excluded. There being no other evidence in support of the application, it was properly refused.

APPEAL from Superior Court, Sonoma County; S. K. Dougherty, Judge.

Judicial settlement of the estate of Antonio Pina, deceased, in which one Carrillo applied for letters of administration. From orders disallowing applicant's bill of costs, and dismissing the application for letters of administration, applicant appeals. Affirmed.

George Pearce for appellant; Thomas Rutledge, E. M. Norton, A. B. Ware and Clarence F. Lea for respondent.

HARRISON, J.—The orders from which the appeals herein are taken are not set forth in the transcript, but in the notice of appeal the appeals are stated to be "from the order and judgment of said court, made on the thirtieth day of September, 1901, striking out petitioner's bill of costs, and disallowing the same; also the judgment and order of said superior court denying and dismissing petitioner's application for letters of administration with the will annexed, made on the fifteenth day of October, 1901." The bill of exceptions does not contain any bill of costs, or make reference to any, or to any action of the court thereon, and this part of the appeal must therefore be disregarded.

It appears from the bill of exceptions that an application for letters of administration with the will annexed upon the estate of the deceased was before the superior court, and in support thereof certain evidence was introduced on behalf of the applicant as to his competency for the position. Certain other evidence was offered, but was not admitted by the court, and the rulings in excluding this evidence are relied upon as error.

The appellant offered in support of his application a petition by Luis Pina setting forth that he was a brother of the deceased, and as such entitled to administer upon his estate, and requesting that the appellant be appointed in his stead. This petition was not verified, but had attached thereto a certificate of acknowledgment in the form of an acknowledgment for the conveyance of real estate, and, upon the objection of the contestants, was excluded by the court. No evidence was offered on the part of the applicant that Luis Pina was a brother of the deceased, or in any way related to him, and the court very properly excluded the petition. This was the only evidence offered by the applicant in support of his right to have letters of administration issued to him.

Certain exceptions were taken to other rulings of the court, but none of these rulings are of such a character as would justify a reversal of the orders.

The orders are affirmed.

We concur: McFarland, J.; Van Dyke, J.

SNOW v. MASTICK et al.

S. F. No. 2588; December 31, 1902.

71 Pac. 165.

Sale—What Constitutes.—Defendant S., Son of Plaintiff, engaged with defendants M. and N. in working a mine, plaintiff agreeing to back his son for his share, and to send him either money or provisions to put in for his share, and, pursuant thereto, sent him provisions. Held, that there was no sale to the others, so as to make them liable therefor.

APPEAL from Superior Court, City and County of San Francisco; J. C. B. Hebbard, Judge.

Action by Louis T. Snow against Reuben Mastick and others. There was a judgment of nonsuit and plaintiff appeals. Affirmed.

I. F. Capman for appellant; Mastick, Van Fleet & Mastick for respondents.

PER CURIAM.—This action was brought to recover of defendants the sum of $353.74 for groceries and provisions alleged to have been sold and delivered by plaintiff to defendants at their instance and request. The defendant Snow is the son of the plaintiff. He was not served with summons, and did not appear in the case. At the close of plaintiff's evidence the defendants Mastick and Nahl moved for a nonsuit, which was granted, and judgment accordingly entered. This appeal is from the judgment, and the sole question is as to the ruling on the motion for a nonsuit.

After carefully examining the evidence, we think the court did not err in granting the nonsuit. The theory of plaintiff was that the merchandise was furnished to defendants at the request of each and all of them. The testimony offered was that of plaintiff and his son, one of the defendants here. The plaintiff is, and was at the time named in the complaint, engaged in the grocery business in the city and county of San Francisco. In October, 1897, the defendant Snow was engaged in the business of mining, with the other defendants, in a mine called the "Bull Dog," in Siskiyou county. The defendant Snow testified that he entered into the mining venture with the other defendants, and that his father, the plaintiff, agreed to pay his share; that, "after we had decided to take this property and try to work it, he agreed to back me in the proposition; . . . . that, in case we did not succeed in making a go of the property up there, my father was to assume the loss of my third." The plaintiff testified: "I expected to back my son to the extent of his interest in the concern." On October 1, 1897, before the goods in question were shipped, plaintiff wrote to his son, the defendant Snow, and in the letter said: "I have not seen Mr. Mastick yet. Your scheme is all satisfactory. You put your money in as fast as the others do. I can send you food and pay freight to Gazelle for your part. Your share would be about $17 per month, and I suppose you would use that much in grub. At any rate, you can call on me for your share as fast as each contributes, and have either cash or groceries." The following questions were asked of plaintiff, and the answers given as herein stated: "Q. And Mr. Mastick came to you, you say, and asked you to back your son up there, did he not? A. I expected to back my son to the extent of his interest in the concern. Q. And in conformity with that agreement you sent these goods to your son? A. Yes, sir. Q. You understood, did you not, that these goods were sent as payment of your son's interest in that concern? A. To such extent as he was interested in the property." Taking the evidence all together, it is clear that the intention to hold the defendants Mastick and Nahl was an afterthought of plaintiff.

The judgment is affirmed.

SAMBUCK v. SOUTHERN PACIFIC COMPANY.

S. F. No. 2554; January 3, 1903.

71 Pac. 174.

Damages for Personal Injuries — Examination of Plaintiff's Person.—Where, in an action for injuries, plaintiff's physician testified that on examination there were no objective signs of injury on his body, and no bruises, and that his injuries were subjective, rather than objective, and defendant's physician had thoroughly examined plaintiff, and fully detailed his condition, as a witness, defendant was not prejudiced by the court's refusal to compel plaintiff to submit to an examination of his person at the trial.

Carrier of Passengers—Presumption of Negligence.—In an action for injuries to a passenger from a railroad collision, it is presumed in the first instance that the collision was the result of the carrier's negligence, to rebut which defendant must affirmatively show that the collision was the result of inevitable casualty, or of some cause which human care and foresight could not prevent.

Carrier of Passengers—Liability for Slight Negligence.—In an action for injuries to a passenger, the carrier is liable for the slightest negligence.

APPEAL from Superior Court, Santa Cruz County; Lucas F. Smith, Judge.

Action by Nicholas Sambuck against the Southern Pacific Company. From a judgment in favor of plaintiff, defendant appeals. Affirmed.

Charles B. Younger and Foshay Walker for appellant; John H. Leonard for respondent.

PER CURIAM.—The plaintiff brought this action for damages for personal injuries of a permanent nature received in a collision and train wreck while traveling as a passenger on defendant's railroad train. On a trial with a jury, plaintiff had a verdict and judgment for $6,000. The defendant appeals from said judgment and from an order denying it a new trial.

1. The principal contention of appellant is based on an alleged error of the court in refusing to compel the plaintiff to submit his body to an examination, on motion of appellant. Conceding that the plaintiff refused to permit an inspection of his person at the trial, and for the purposes of the argument that the court erred in refusing to order him to submit, yet we think it is plain, from the record before us, that defendant was not injured thereby. The most that such an inspection could disclose in aid of defendant would have been to establish the fact that there was no external evidence of any injury; but this fact was subsequently fully established, and without conflict, by one of plaintiff's own witnesses. W. R. Congdon, the doctor who was still treating plaintiff at the time of the trial, testified that he examined him about the 5th or 6th of December, 1899, which was more than eleven weeks

after he was hurt and about three months before the trial, and that he had him stripped, "his clothes all taken off of him," and that "there were no objective signs on his body, no bruises." This was uncontradicted, and, coming from the plaintiff's witness, the plaintiff was bound by it; and an inspection of plaintiff's body could have added nothing to it more favorable to the defendant. The plaintiff, in his testimony, did not claim, nor was there any evidence to show, that at the time of the trial there were any marks, scars or other evidences of injury to be discovered by an inspection or examination of any particular part of plaintiff's person; but, on the contrary, the testimony of the physicians in the case shows that evidence of plaintiff's injury was, as they term it, "subjective," rather than "objective." In addition to this, it also appears that the defendant's physician had examined plaintiff thoroughly at least twice, and had reported the result thereof to the defendant, and detailed it fully as a witness upon the trial of the case. He said that on his examination at the time of the injury he found some scratches and a slight puff of the skin in the lumbar region, between the ribs and the hip bone, about two inches to the right of the spine. He examined him a day or two later, and these scratches and this puff were entirely gone, and he was in a normal condition, so far as the doctor could see. Without intimating what the rule would be in a case where a motion is squarely made for an order compelling the plaintiff to submit to an examination, and where it appears that such an examination might result in some evidence beneficial to the moving party, we must hold that it appears affirmatively here that the appellant could not have suffered any injury from the action of the court in refusing to order any further examination or inspection of plaintiff's body.

2. There is some substantial evidence tending to show that plaintiff's injuries were not slight, but severe, and of a permanent nature, and this evidence prevents us from saying that as a matter of law the verdict for $6,000 is excessive.

3. The rule that an injury to a passenger in a railroad collision is presumed in the first instance to be the result of the carrier's negligence is well established in this state. It is equally well established that, to rebut the presumption of negligence arising from a collision, the defendant must affirmatively show, where a passenger is plaintiff, that the collision

was the result of inevitable casualty, or of some cause which human care and foresight could not prevent, and that the law holds the carrier responsible in such cases for the slightest negligence. The instructions complained of by appellant involve the foregoing principles, and two of them are copied from the case of Mitchell v. Southern Pac. R. R. Co., 87 Cal. 62, 11 L. R. A. 130, 25 Pac. 245, in which the court says: "We have carefully examined the instructions of the court to the jury and find no error in any of them." The other instruction complained of is copied from the language of the opinion in Bush v. Barnett, 96 Cal., at page 204, 31 Pac. 2. This latter case has since been cited in an opinion of the court in bank in McCurrie v. Southern Pac. Co., 122 Cal. 558, 55 Pac. 324, and in the very recent case of Bosqui v. Sutro R. R. Co., 131 Cal. 390, 63 Pac. 682; and it must now be regarded as the settled rule in this state that (in the language of the instruction), "the presumption that the injury was caused by the negligence of the carrier, which is raised upon the proof by the plaintiff that he was injured while being carried as a passenger, is itself a fact which the jury must consider in determining its verdict, and which, in the absence of any other evidence in reference to the negligence, necessitates a verdict in favor of the plaintiff."

The judgment and order appealed from are affirmed.

LACRABERE v. WISE et al.[*]

S. F. No. 2590; January 3, 1903.

71 Pac. 175.

Unlawful Detainer.—**Evidence in an Action for Unlawful detainer** examined, and held to sustain a finding that defendants had agreed to pay $50 a month rent for the leased premises.

Parol Evidence.—**A Receipt may Always be Explained by parol.**

Lease.—**A Notice to Quit, Requiring the Tenants to pay their** rent, amounting to $100, "being the amount now owing from me to you," or deliver possession, was good, and entitled the landlord to maintain unlawful detainer, notwithstanding the mistake in the phrase "me to you."[1]

---

[*] For subsequent opinion in bank, see 141 Cal. 554, 75 Pac. 185.

[1] Cited in the note in 120 Am. St. Rep. 53, on unlawful detainer.

APPEAL from Superior Court, Santa Cruz County; Lucas F. Smith, Judge.

Unlawful detainer by John Lacrabere against John H. Wise and others. Judgment for plaintiff, and from an order denying a new trial defendants appeal. Affirmed.

Frank J. Murphy (Fred H. Hood of counsel) for appellants; George P. Burke for respondent.

VAN DYKE, J.—The appeal is from the order denying defendants' motion for a new trial. The action is for unlawful detainer, the complaint being in the usual form.

1. Appellants contend that the evidence does not show that the defendants ever agreed to pay any rent to the plaintiff. The court finds that on or about April 1, 1898, the plaintiff, by an agreement and lease, at Watsonville, in the county of Santa Cruz, leased, demised and let to the said John H. Wise and H. E. Wise, associated and transacting business under the firm name of Christy & Wise, certain premises situated in said county of Santa Cruz, for the term of one year, or as long as there was sufficient pulp on said premises adjoining the said demised premises to feed 2,600 head of sheep upon the said demised premises at the monthly rent of $50, payable monthly on the first day of each and every month, the first month's rent to be paid on the first day of May, 1898. The testimony of the plaintiff was positive to the making of the lease according to the foregoing finding, but it is contended by appellants that this evidence was entirely neutralized by the receipt which the plaintiff gave the defendants for the first month's rent. That receipt reads:

"$50.00.   San Francisco, April 15, 1898.

"Received from J. B. Joyaux fifty dollars as one month from date in advance for hauling with my windlass the pulp needed by Christy & Wise sheep on the land of W. Silverer.
                    "JOHN LACRABERE."

The plaintiff testifies that on the fifteenth day of April, 1898, "John Esponda gave me $50 as one month's rent for the premises. When I received the $50 I signed a receipt" (being the receipt in question); and in this connection it was "admitted that at all times mentioned in the complaint J. B. Joyaux was acting as the agent of Christy & Wise, and

acted as such agent when renting lot No. 1, and that the sum
of $50, paid as aforesaid, was the money of Christy & Wise."
The receipt shows upon its face that the word "rent" should
have been inserted between "month" and "from" in order
to make sense. It states that the pulp is needed by Christy
& Wise sheep on the land of W. Silvarer. It appears from
the testimony that the plaintiff was the lessee of Silvarer,
and sublet to the defendants the premises in question. A
receipt is not like a written contract, but may always be explained by parol testimony. It appears from the testimony
that the pulp referred to could not be used excepting upon
the premises described in the complaint, and which it is
claimed were leased to said defendants. Taking the testimony of the plaintiff with the admission, the court was justified in its finding that defendants, Christy & Wise, through
their agent, leased the lot No. 1, as claimed, for the rent and
upon the terms stated.

2. It is claimed that the evidence does not show that the
three days' notice was served upon the defendants. The
finding is that on the thirtieth day of July, 1898, at the city
of Watsonville, county of Santa Cruz, three days' notice in
writing was duly given to and served by plaintiff upon said
defendant John H. Wise, and on August 11, 1898, at the city
and county of San Francisco, a like three days' notice was
given to and served by plaintiff upon said defendant Harry
E. Wise, demanding the rent due, stating the amount, or the
delivery of possession of the premises to the plaintiff. The
notice addressed to the defendants contained in the bill of
exceptions reads: "You are hereby required to pay the rent
of the premises hereinafter described and which you now
hold possession of, amounting to the sum of $100, being the
amount now due and owing from me to you, said Christy &
Wise, for two months' rent from the first day of May, 1898,
to the first day of July, 1898, or deliver up the same to my
agents [giving their names and place in the city of Watson-
ville], or I shall institute legal proceedings against you to
recover possession of said premises with treble rents."
(Here follows description of premises as contained in the
complaint.) In the notice as copied in the transcript there
is an evident mistake in this respect: "me to you" should
be transposed as "you to me" in order to make sense, and
the mistake is so patent as not to mislead anyone. The no-

tice in question was served upon the defendant John H.
Wise at Watsonville, county of Santa Cruz, on July 30, 1898,
and upon defendant Henry F. Wise at the city and county of
San Francisco on August 11, 1898. The defendants having
failed to pay the rent or deliver up the premises demanded,
the action was commenced upon August 25, 1898. A tenant
of real property is guilty of unlawful detainer where he continues in possession after default in the payment of rent
pursuant to the lease or agreement under which the property
is held and three days' notice in writing, requiring its payment, stating the amount which is due, or possession of the
property, shall have been served upon him: Code Civ. Proc.,
sec. 1161, subd. 2. The next subdivision of the same section
provides that within three days after the service of notice the
tenant may perform the conditions or covenants in the lease,
or pay the stipulated rent, as the case may be, and thereby
save the lease from forfeiture. As said in Ivory v. Brown
(opinion filed November 17, 1902), 137 Cal. 603, 70 Pac. 657:
"The defendants neither paid rent, nor heeded the notice, but
remained in possession. The action was commenced May 11,
1900. It is thus apparent that defendants had ample and
statutory notice." In this case the defendants failed and
refused to pay the rent or to surrender the possession of the
premises within the time specified, or at all, and more than
three days after the service of the notice elapsed before the
suit was brought. The defendants are supposed to have
known the law, and they could not have misunderstood the
purport of the notice.

Order affirmed.

We concur: Harrison, J.; Garoutte, J.

BEN LOMOND WINE CO. v. SLADKY.*

S. F. No. 2468; January 3, 1903.

71 Pac. 178.

Appeal—Order Granting New Trial.—Where one of the grounds
of the motion for a new trial is insufficiency of evidence to justify
the verdict, and the order granting the new trial is general in its
terms, it must be affirmed.

---

*For subsequent opinion in bank, see 141 Cal. 619, 75 Pac. 332.

Appeal.—Where the Order Granting a New Trial was general in its terms, the supreme court, on appeal therefrom, was not limited to a consideration of the reasons given therefor by the lower court in an opinion filed by it at the time.

APPEAL from Superior Court, Santa Cruz County; Lucas F. Smith, Judge.

Action by the Ben Lomond Wine Company against Charles Sladky. Judgment for defendant, and from an order granting a new trial defendant appeals. Affirmed.

Lester H. Jacobs and Frohman & Jacobs for appellant; Kierce, Sullivan & Gillogley for respondent; Geo. R. Eaton and Black & Leaming for defendant.

PER CURIAM.—This action was tried before a jury, and a verdict rendered in favor of the defendant. A motion for a new trial was granted, from which the present appeal has been taken.

One of the grounds for the motion was the insufficiency of the evidence to justify the verdict, and the order granting a new trial, being general in its terms, must, under the well-established rule, be affirmed.

The contention of the appellant that because the court, at the time it made the order, filed an opinion setting forth certain reasons for its action, the consideration of the appeal is limited to those reasons, is untenable: Newman v. Overland Pac. Ry. Co., 132 Cal. 73, 64 Pac. 110. As said in that case: "The order which is entered in the minutes is the only record of the court's action, and is to be measured by its terms, and not by the reasons which the court may give for it." Objection is also made to the form in which the specifications of insufficiency of evidence are set forth in the statement, but, as was said in Bledsoe v. Decrow, 132 Cal. 312, 64 Pac. 397: "The specifications as to the insufficiency of the evidence to justify the findings resulted in getting all the evidence in the record, and seems to have informed defendant's attorneys as to the respects wherein the evidence was alleged to be insufficient." It is recited in the statement herein at the close, "The foregoing comprises all the testimony given in this action": See, also, Churchill v. Flournoy, 127 Cal. 355, 59 Pac. 791; Standard Quicksilver Co. v. Habishaw, 132 Cal. 115, 64 Pac. 113.

The order is affirmed.

SILVEIRA v. REESE.

L. A. No. 1273; February 4, 1903.

71 Pac. 515.

Partnership.—The Loaning of Money by a Partner to the Firm does not change the original contract of partnership.

Appeal.—That a Specification as to the Insufficiency of Evidence may avail, it must be directed to a material finding of fact, and it must be clearly shown that there is no substantial testimony to sustain the finding. If there is, the credibility of witnesses, and the weight to be given their testimony, will not be considered.

Partnership.—Refusal to Appoint a Receiver in an Action for Dissolution of a partnership and an accounting is in the sound discretion of the trial court.

APPEAL from Superior Court, Los Angeles County; Lucien Shaw, Judge.

Action by John Silveira against A. D. Reese. From the judgment plaintiff appeals. Affirmed.

Hester & Ladd for appellant; E. E. Powers for respondent.

COOPER, C.—The plaintiff and defendant were partners in the manufacturing of bricks. This action was brought to obtain a dissolution of the partnership, and a settlement of the partnership accounts. The case was tried before the court, findings filed, the accounts settled, and the judgment ordered and entered dissolving the partnership as prayed. The plaintiff made a motion for a new trial, which was denied, and this appeal is from the judgment and order denying the motion for a new trial.

The appellant contends that the evidence is insufficient to sustain the findings in many respects, but we do not deem it necessary here to follow counsel through all the various specifications of insufficiency. We have carefully examined the evidence, and find it sufficient as to all material findings.

The first specification argued is that the evidence does not sustain the finding "that defendant did not agree after the original contract of partnership to advance money to carry on the business." The defendant testified: "I never promised and agreed to put in $1,000 after the original $500 put

into the business by me was exhausted. . . . . I did not agree
to furnish the said firm with all the money necessary to carry
on the business.'' The evidence shows that the partnership
continued under the original contract. The various conversations between the parties as to the necessity for more money
to carry on the business, and the fact that defendant loaned
the partnership money to carry on the business, did not
change the original contract of partnership.

It is specified that the evidence does not sustain the finding
"That appellant and respondent had a settlement of their
partnership accounts at the time the first kiln was burned."
By looking at the record, we do not discover any such finding.
The finding is: "At the time that the said kiln of 110,000
bricks was burned, the said plaintiff and defendant had a
settlement as to money advanced by the said defendant for
the said partnership, and it was then ascertained and agreed
that the defendant had advanced for and on behalf of the
plaintiff the sum of $234.87.'' The defendant testified: "I
had loaned or advanced to him [the plaintiff] the sum of
$234.87, and on that day I went to see him, and wrote out a
promissory note for the amount, bearing interest at the rate
of eight per cent per annum, and read and explained it to
the plaintiff and his wife, who was present, and he signed it
in my presence, and the note has not been paid.'' And in regard to the same transaction the plaintiff testified: "Defendant came to my house, and we had a settlement of all our accounts up to that time. It then appeared that defendant had
advanced a considerable amount of money more than I had.
He then had me to sign a paper which he said represented
the interest I was to pay him on his advances.'' It is claimed
that the evidence is insufficient to justify the finding that defendant laid out and expended $230.56 for wood used in mak-
ing bricks, and that only part of the wood was used in making
bricks. The defendant did testify that he bought thirty
cords of wood, and that he used ten cords in burning the kiln,
and sold the remaining twenty cords. It does not appear
how much per cord the wood cost, nor how much the twenty
cords were sold for. Neither does it appear that the partnership was charged with the twenty cords. The defendant
testified that he paid "$230.56 for wood partly used in burn-
ing the same; that all the said sums of money were paid,

8

laid out and expended in putting the said kiln in condition
to be burned, and in burning the same, and in putting the
bricks in condition to be put on the market for sale, and the
said expenditures were all necessary for that purpose; that I
have never been paid or received anything for and on account of the money paid out by me, or on said promissory
note, save and except the sum as follows: $140.20 for bricks
sold, and hay, horses, or barley sold, and the proceeds retained by me." The court found and charged the defendant
with this $140.20. We think that the finding, while some-
what indefinite as to the item for wood, is supported by this
evidence. While defendant testified that the wood for which
he paid $230.56 was partly used in burning the kiln, at the
same time he says that said sum was used and expended in
putting the kiln in condition to be burned, and in burning
the same. He further says positively that the $140.20 is all
that he has received for sales of property.

The above is sufficient to show the character and want of
merit as to the specifications. Specifications as to the insufficiency of evidence must be directed to material findings of fact.
It must also be clearly shown that there is no substantial testimony to sustain the finding objected to. We do not attempt
to pass upon the credibility of witnesses, or the weight to be
given to their evidence in case of substantial conflict. The
question as to insufficiency of evidence to sustain findings is
urged in so many cases, and takes up so much of the time of
this court, that the attention of the bar should be called to
the necessity of care in urging such questions. This suggestion, if adhered to, would save this court much time and
labor, and enable it to give its attention to other business.

It is finally claimed that the court failed to find upon the
issue as to whether or not the 210,000 kiln of bricks was injured by the unskillful firing of the same by defendant. If
it be conceded that, where two persons engage in the business
of manufacturing bricks as partners, one could recover damages against the other for negligence or want of skill in
the manufacture thereof by the other, we are of the opinion
that the court found upon the issue. The allegation of the
complaint shows that the negligence relied upon was the firing of the kiln with oil instead of wood, and that "plaintiff
then refused to consent to the use thereof in firing said kiln."
The court found that "it is not true that the plaintiff re-

fused to consent to the use of oil in the firing and burning of said kilns,'' and in regard to the use of oil in firing the said kilns the court found that it is not true "that the market value of said brick was greatly damaged or depreciated thereby, or that the said firm lost $165 thereby, or any other sum.''

It was not error, under the circumstances, for the court to refuse to appoint a receiver. That rested in the sound discretion of the court below, and we see no abuse of such discretion.

We advise that the judgment and order be affirmed.

We concur: Haynes, C.; Gray, C.

PER CURIAM.—For the reasons given in the foregoing opinion the judgment and order are affirmed.

SCHMIDT v. BITZER et al.

S. F. No. 3160; February 11, 1903.

71 Pac. 563.

Injunction — Refusal to Dissolve.—Where an Injunction is granted on a verified complaint, the court, in its discretion, may refuse a dissolution, provided the complaint states facts sufficient to authorize the granting of the injunction in the first instance.

Injunction—Breach of Trade Agreement.—A Complaint Alleged that plaintiffs and defendants were each engaged in the butcher business, and had agreed not to handle trading stamps, vegetables, or to give premiums as "inducements tending to draw trade" from one to the other, but that, to the irreparable injury of plaintiffs," defendants did handle and give trading stamps, vegetables, etc., and an injunction was prayed. Held, that in the absence of averments that defendants were giving the stamps to draw trade, or giving them to persons trading with the parties, or that defendants were insolvent, or the damages not ascertainable, the complaint was insufficient.

APPEAL from Superior Court, City and County of San Francisco; J. C. B. Hebbard, Judge.

Suit by H. F. H. Schmidt against Albert Bitzer and another. From an order refusing to dissolve an injunction, defendant Bitzer appeals. Reversed.

A. S. Newburg (H. G. W. Dinkelspiel of counsel) for appellant; Salomon, McClellan & McClellan for respondent.

COOPER, C.—This appeal is from an order refusing to dissolve an injunction. As the injunction was granted upon a verified complaint, it may be conceded that the court, in its discretion, could have refused to dissolve the injunction, provided the complaint states facts sufficient to show that the restraining order should have been granted in the first instance. The complaint sets forth a written contract, by the terms of which the plaintiff and defendants, after reciting that they were engaged in the butcher's business in the city of San Francisco, mutually agreed "not to handle trading stamps, vegetables, or to give premiums as inducements tending to draw trade from one of us to the other, with the exception of calendars or New Year's cards, which may be distributed by either." The complaint then alleges that about the sixteenth day of January, 1902, the defendants, in violation of said agreement, "did handle and give trading stamps, vegetables and other premiums," and that they are continuing and will continue to do so, to the great detriment and irreparable injury of plaintiff's business; that pecuniary compensation will not afford adequate relief, that a restraining order is necessary to prevent a multiplicity of judicial proceedings, and that plaintiff has not a sufficient or adequate remedy at law.

The complaint does not state facts sufficient to justify the order granting the injunction. If it be conceded, for the purposes of this case, that the contract is valid, it is not alleged that the trading stamps, vegetables or other premiums were given by defendants as an inducement to draw trade from plaintiff. The agreement was not that defendants would not handle trading stamps, vegetables or premiums, but that they would not do so "as inducements to draw trade" from plaintiff. The complaint must be most strongly construed against plaintiff, and it is necessary that it should clearly and unequivocally show that defendants are violating the agreement. It not only does not appear that defendants handled or gave trading stamps, vegetables and other premiums for the purpose of drawing trade from plaintiff, but it does not appear that such trading stamps, vegetables or premiums were given to any person trading with, or intending to trade with, either plaintiff or defendants. The trading stamps, vegetables and premiums might have been given to the inhabitants of the Russian empire or of Greenland, and yet the complaint be true. The complaint is also destitute of any allegation showing that the plaintiff will suffer irreparable damage by reason of the alleged acts. No statement .is made that defendants are insolvent or in any way unable to respond in damages, nor that the amount of damages cannot be readily ascertained. The words "in violation of the said agreement," and "to the irreparable injury of plaintiff," may be regarded as mere phrases, in the absence of facts. They probably made the complaint sound more emphatic to the pleader, but the facts must be stated so as to show that the damages will be irreparable.

It follows that the order must be reversed as to appellant.

We concur: Haynes, C.; Gray, C.

PER CURIAM.—For the reasons given in the foregoing opinion the order is reversed as to appellant.

PARRISH v. ROSEBUD MINING AND MILLING COMPANY et al.*

S. F. No. 2631; February 21, 1903.

71 Pac. 694.

Fire Insurance—Insertion of False Answers by Agent.—Where an insurance company's agent inserted false answers in an application for a fire policy after full information as to the facts had been given him by insured's manager, such answers constituted no defense to an action on the policy though the answers were declared to constitute warranties.

Fire Insurance—Insertion of False Answers by Agent.—The falsity of such answers constituted a valid defense to a policy issued by another company, not represented by such agent, on the same property, based on such application.

Fire Insurance—Payment During Litigation—Bond for Repayment.—Where, pending a controversy as to the liability of several insurance companies for a loss, the L. Co. paid insured ninety-five per cent of the face of its policy, and took from insured a bond for repay-

---

*For subsequent opinion in bank, see 140 Cal. 635, 74 Pac. 312.

ment in case a judgment should be rendered adverse to insured in any of the actions contemplated against the other insurance companies, such bond was a guaranty, and not a contract of suretyship, and no recovery could be had thereon if the principal obligation was void for any cause other than the personal disability of the principal obligor.[1]

Fire Insurance—Payment During Litigation—Bond for Repayment.—Pending a controversy as to the liability of insurers for a olss, one of them paid ninety-five per cent of its liability, and took a bond from insured, obligating it to repay such amount in the event that in any of the actions contemplated by insured against any of the other companies named, which had concurrent insurance on the property, a final judgment should be rendered in favor of the "defendant herein." Held, that the word "herein" could not be stricken out, and the word "therein" substituted, since the term "defendant herein" was not improperly applied to the obligee as being defendant in one of the cases enumerated, or as expressing an intention that the "adverse judgment" should be on grounds favorable to such obligee.

Contract.—In Construing a Contract the Intention of the parties is to be determined not from the facts as they actually were, but as the parties supposed them to be.

Fire Insurance—Payment During Litigation—Bond for Repayment.—Pending a controversy between insured and several insurance companies concerning the latter's liability for a loss, the L. Co. compromised the claim against it, and took a bond from insured, by which the latter agreed that, in the event that in any of the actions contemplated against the other insurers named, a final judgment should be rendered in favor of the "defendant herein," then insured should repay to the L. Co. the amount so paid. Held, that the intention of the parties was to make such repayment contingent on a judgment adverse to insured on the merits in a case involving the same questions as were involved in the controversy with the obligee, and hence a judgment against insured in one of such actions on a defense not available to the obligee did not justify a recovery on the bond.

Fire Insurance—Payment During Litigation—Bond for Repayment.—Where insured gave a bond obligating it to repay the proceeds of a policy in the event an adverse judgment should be rendered in suits against other insurers, a recovery could not be had in an action on the bond against an obligor other than insured in an action to which insured was not a party.

APPEAL from Superior Court, City and County of San Francisco; Edward A. Belcher, Judge.

---

[1] Cited in the note in 105 Am. St. Rep. 508, on contracts of guaranty.

Action by Edwin Parrish against the Rosebud Mining and Milling Company and others. From a judgment in favor of defendant W. S. McCormick plaintiff appeals. Affirmed.

Chickering, Thomas & Gregory for appellant; Lloyd & Wood for respondents.

SMITH, C.—This is an appeal from a judgment for the defendant W. S. McCormick (doing business as McCormick & Co.), and from an order denying the plaintiff's motion for a new trial. The other defendants were not served, and did not appear. The plaintiff is the assignee of the Lion Insurance Company, of London, for collection, and brings the suit upon a bond in the sum of $7,125 executed to the company by this and another defendant. The condition of the bond is: "That if· the Rosebud Mining and Milling Company of Colorado, or its assigns, shall in all things stand to and abide by and well and truly keep and perform the covenants and conditions and agreements as set forth in the instrument attached hereto, then the above obligations shall be void; otherwise to remain in full force and virtue." The instrument attached relates to a policy of insurance in the sum of $7,500, issued by the London company to the defendant Rosebud Mining and Milling Company, upon which there has been a loss by fire. It is recited in the instrument: That the Rosebud company is about to institute suits against the London company, the Western Assurance Company of Toronto and other companies enumerated (twelve in all); that "the same questions. both of law and of fact, are or will be involved in all of said actions concerning the liability of said insurance companies"; and that the London company "is desirous of adjusting the said loss without the necessity of litigation, in consideration of the covenants and agreements hereinafter contained on the part of the said" Rosebud company. Then follows: "First," an acknowledgment of the receipt of $7,125 from the London company, "and in consideration of the said payment" a release of the London company from liability on the policy; and, "second," the promise following, that is to say·: "The said Rosebud Mining and Milling Company does hereby agree that in the event that in any of said actions by said Rosebud Mining and Milling Company against any of the aforesaid insurance companies to recover upon the said policies a final judgment be rendered herein, that the said Rosebud Mining and Milling Company will immediately repay upon demand to the said Lion Fire Insurance Company of London the said sum of seven thousand one hundred and twenty-five ($7,125) dollars,'' being ninety-five per cent of the face of the policy. It is also agreed that upon a settlement with any of the companies the London company "shall receive as favorable terms of settlement for such loss as shall any other company interested therein now or hereafter ob-tain." But, as the other companies have been settled with on the same terms as the London company (except as to agreement to repay), this part of the agreement may be left out of view. Afterward, in a suit brought by the Rosebud company against the Western Assurance Company of Toronto, judgment was rendered in favor of the latter. But from the facts alleged by the defendant and found by the court to be true it appears that this judgment was based on facts constituting a defense of which the London company could not have availed itself, and that the latter in fact had no meritorious defense to an action on the policy.

The allegations of the answer and the findings of the court in this regard are extremely circumstantial, and therefore too voluminous to be given in detail. Suffice it to say, an application for insurance in the sum of $50,000 was made by the Rosebud company to one Packard, the agent of the London company, by whom the policy in question was issued, with policies of other companies of which he was agent; and by his procurement; and on the same application, the policy of the Toronto company, of which he was not agent, was also issued. In this application, which, by the terms of the latter policy, was made a warranty of the truth of the facts stated, there were two false answers to questions on material points. But these were inserted by Packard himself, after full information as to the facts from the manager of the company, who was assured by him that they were correct, and that he would be responsible for them. Of these facts Toronto company had no notice, but issued its policy exclusively upon the faith of the written application; and in the case against it the decision in its favor was put by the court exclusively on the falsity of the two answers alluded to, and "upon no other." Hence it is apparent—if the facts are as found—that this, which was a sufficient defense in the case of the Toronto company, could not have been maintained by the London company in a suit on the policy: Wheaton v. North British etc. Ins. Co., 76 Cal. 420, 9 Am. St. Rep. 216, 18 Pac. 758; Farnum v. Phoenix Ins. Co., 83 Cal. 257, 17 Am. St. Rep. 233, 23 Pac. 869; La Marche v. New York Life Ins. Co., 126 Cal. 502, 58 Pac. 1053; Wood on Fire Insurance, sec. 152; Ostrander on Fire Insurance, pp. 131, 384, 385. Hence, it is claimed by the respondent a suit could not be maintained against the former company on its promise to repay the money paid on the policy; nor, such being the case, can the present suit be maintained.

Assuming the former proposition to be correct, the latter must be admitted. The obligation sued upon is a guaranty, as distinguished from the contract of a surety, or an original obligation of the promisor: Civ. Code, secs. 2787, 2794, subd. 2, and sec. 1605, and note to Ann. Civ. Code 1872 and 1901, and Civ. Code N. Y., sec. 1534. It follows, ex vi termini, that, to give it validity, there must be a principal obligation; and that, if the supposed principal obligation be void from any cause other than that of personal disability of the principal obligor, the guaranty is also of no validity: Civ. Code, secs. 2809, 2810; Glassell v. Coleman, 94 Cal. 266, 29 Pac. 508; Kilbride v. Moss, 113 Cal. 434, 54 Am. St. Rep. 361, 45 Pac. 812. The question involved is, therefore, the same as though the suit were on the principal obligation, instead of being on the guaranty. In other words, the question is whether, under the terms of the contract, the plaintiff would be entitled, on the facts found, to recover in a suit against the Rosebud company. If so, he is entitled to recover against the defendant here; otherwise not. The findings of the court, we think, are fully sustained by the evidence, and the plaintiff's case must, therefore, turn upon the sufficiency of the facts found to support the affirmative of this question. On this point the theory of the plaintiff's case is that the rendition of the judgment against the Rosebud company in the case against the Toronto company was one of the contingencies upon which, as provided in the agreement, the promise of the former was to take effect. But in support of this theory it is necessary to assume, and it is in fact tacitly assumed by the appellant, that the agreement is to be read as though, in lieu of "herein" (the word occurring in the instrument as set forth both in the complaint and the findings), the word "therein" was inserted; for, under the contract as it stands, the contingency described is not merely the rendition of a judgment against the plaintiff, but the rendition of such a judgment "in favor of the defendant herein," which apparently refers to the London company, and, at least, cannot be made to apply to the defendant in the judgment. But no reasons are given by the counsel why such an assumption is either necessary or admissible; nor do we know of any principle or authority to justify it. It is, indeed, true that, where the main intent of a contract is clear, inconsistent words will be rejected (Civ. Code, sec. 1653), or subordinated to it (section 1650); and that, when it can be "seen on the face of the instrument" that the wrong word has been inadvertently used, and that another was intended, the latter may be substituted (Wilson v. Wilson, 5 H. L. Cas. 53, [10 Eng. Reprint, 811]). But to justify such an amendment it must appear upon the face of the contract that the words used by the parties are unsusceptible of a reasonable construction (Civ. Code, secs. 1638, 1641, 1643, 1652), or inconsistent with "the main intention of the parties"; or that the substituted word is in fact the word, or the equivalent of the word, intended. But here none of these conditions occur. That the word intended was other than the word used is nothing more than a bare surmise or guess; nor would the proposed amendment be consistent with the general or main intention of the parties; and, finally, the agreement as it stands admits of a rational construction, consistent with that intention, for the term "the defendant herein" is not improperly applied to the London company as being defendant in one of the cases enumerated, and, if the intention was to designate as the condition of the promise a judgment in any of the cases specified favorable, or upon grounds favorable, to the London company, this is not inaptly expressed by the terms used; i. e., "a final judgment . . . . rendered in favor of the defendant herein." Nor is there any grammatical impropriety in the use of the term "defendant," as relating to the cause of action or claim existing in favor of one of the parties against the other, on which, it is recited, a suit was contemplated.

These considerations of themselves dispose of the proposed alteration of the agreement—as to which it is sufficient that there is nothing on the face of the instrument to justify it.

But the substituted term is also open to the objection that it would be inconsistent with the general or main intention of the parties as manifested by the agreement itself, and the circumstances attending it. The effect of the agreement, briefly stated, was that the money was to be repaid upon a judgment adverse to the promisor and of the character specified in any of the suits enumerated as "involving the same questions both of law and fact," from which it must necessarily be inferred that the main intention of the parties was to make the stipulated repayment contingent upon a judgment adverse to the promisor in a case involving the same questions, which is, in effect, to say, on the merits; for the intention of the parties is to be ascertained, not from the facts as they actually were, but from the facts as the parties supposed them to be, and hence it must be supposed that the ultimate end or purpose of the agreement was to leave the question between the parties to be determined on the merits, and that the enumeration of the cases supposed to be of the character described was merely subsidiary. The actual intent or understanding of the parties was, therefore, in no wise different from what it would have been had the instrument, without enumerating cases, provided for the return of the money in the event of a judgment for the defendant in any case of the character described. This conclusion is also confirmed by the circumstances of the case, which render any other incredible; for, not to mention other circumstances, the amount paid on the claim (ninety-five per cent of its face value) indicates that the parties were practically satisfied of its validity, and this is unmistakably shown by the written opinion of the attorneys of the London company, based upon a thorough discussion of the facts of the case, and of the several questions of law and fact involved, and by their advice to the company "to adjust the loss on reasonable terms." Nor is there anything in the agreement to indicate any substantial doubt as to the validity of the claim. The recital that the London company "is desirous of adjusting the . . . . loss without the necessity of litigation," indicates nothing more than a desire to avoid the impending litigation against itself by leaving the question to be determined in another and similar case; and as the London company, in the event it should turn out it was mistaken as to its liability, might otherwise be precluded from recovering the money paid in consideration of the release. it was but a reasonable precaution to exact from the Rosebud company a promise to repay the money in such event.

It is clear, therefore, that the terms proposed for substitution would be inconsistent with the general or main intention of the parties; and hence, were the substitution made, it would still be a question whether, under the familiar rules governing the interpretation of contracts, it would not be necessary to disregard the word substituted as inconsistent with that intention. We do not propose to pass definitely on this question, but as the principles and authorities bearing upon it bear also upon the question we have been discussing, and the questions themselves are closely related, it will not be out of place briefly to refer to them as confirmatory of the conclusion we have reached. "An agreement," it is said, "ought to receive that construction which will best effectuate the intention of the parties, to be collected from the whole of the agreement"; and, to effect this, greater regard is to be had to the clear intention of the parties than to any particular words which they have used in the expression of their intent. "These two rules," it is added (referring to the rule above stated and the rule that words "are to be understood in their plan and literal meaning") "would seem sometimes to be in conflict, but they came substantially to this: 'Men will be taken to have meant precisely what they have said, unless, from the whole tenor of the instrument, a definite meaning can be collected, which gives a broader interpretation to specific words than their literal meaning would bear' ": Anson on Contracts, 252, 253. The same rules are given no less definitely in the Civil Code: "A contract must be so interpreted as to give effect to the mutual intention of the parties": Sec. 1636. "The language of a contract is to govern its interpretation, if the language is clear and explicit, and does not involve an absurdity": Sec. 1638. "The intention of the parties is to be ascertained from the writing alone, if possible; subject, however, to the other provisions of the title": Sec. 1639. "A contract must receive such an interpretation as will make it .... reasonable, ... if it can be done without violating the intention of the parties": Sec. 1643. "A contract may be explained by reference to the circumstances under which it was made and the matter to which it relates": Sec. 1647. "However broad may be the terms of a contract, it extends only to those things concerning which it appears that the parties intended to contract'': Sec. 1648. Hence, ''particular clauses of a contract are subordinate to its general intent'' (section 1650); and ''words in a contract which are wholly inconsistent with its nature, or with the main intention of the parties, are to be rejected'' (section 1653): See, also, Pollock on Contracts, 434–437; Anson on Contracts, 159. Under these rules it might be held—were the agreement as it is assumed to be—that the name of the Toronto company, mistakenly inserted in the list of cases enumerated, should be rejected, or disregarded as inconsistent with the main intention of the parties, and hence, a fortiori, the proposed amendment of the language used by the parties must be held to be inadmissible.

It is proper to add that the present suit cannot be regarded as ultimately determining the question of liability of the defendant. Whether or not the Rosebud company has a good defense to the plaintiff's action can be determined finally only by a judgment to which it is a party—the cases of all the other companies having been settled. The plaintiff may, therefore, upon proof of the invalidity of the claim of that company on the policy, yet recover judgment against it either in this suit or in another. In such case he would then be entitled to recover on the guaranty, though until then he cannot do so.

I advise that the judgment and order appealed from be affirmed.

PER CURIAM.—For the reasons given in the foregoing opinion the judgment and order appealed from are affirmed.

WITHERS v. MOORE.[*]

S. F. No. 2541; February 26, 1903.

71 Pac. 697.

Sale—Coal to be Imported—Construction of Contract.—A San Francisco merchant cabled to a coal dealer in New South Wales an offer to purchase two cargoes of coal, which read: "Offer subject to immediate reply twenty-four shillings cost freight and insurance exchange duty paid two cargoes," etc. The coal dealer replied, "Ulti-

---

[*]For subsequent opinion in bank, see 140 Pac. 591, 74 Pac. 159.

matim twenty-four shillings and three pence." The merchant cabled, accepting this offer, and later wrote the coal dealer, "We beg to confirm having purchased from you [stating kind of coal and price] 'cost,' 'freight,' 'insurance,' 'exchange,' 'duty paid,'" etc. Held, that the contract would be construed to mean that the coal should be delivered at its destination with all enumerated charges, including customs duties, paid by the seller, whatever they might happen to be at the time of delivery, the purchaser having no advantage of an intermediate reduction in customs duties.

Sale—Coal to be Imported—Customs Duties.—The Purchaser's First Cablegram contained the words, "Our usual form of charter-party," and in writing to the seller, confirming the contract, the purchaser said, "The vessels to be chartered under our usual form of charter-party as per copy previously sent you, and to contain all the clauses contained therein." He also stated that he forwarded by that mail a few originals and copies of the charter-party. The charter-party taken by the seller provided that, "being so loaded shall therewith proceed to San Francisco Harbor and deliver the said full and complete cargo in the usual and customary manner"; and again, "All port charges, pilotages, wharfage dues, and charges at port of discharge," etc., "to be paid by the ship as customary." Held, that if the purchaser had contemplated an advantage to him from a reduction of custom duties, as a feature of his form of charter-party, it should have been specifically mentioned, failing which he could not rely on the charter-party as conferring on him that advantage, in obedience to a claimed custom of the port.

Custom and Usage.—Where the Court Hold That a Contract has not Been Made with reference to a custom, evidence as to the existence of the custom is properly struck out as immaterial.

Custom and Usage.—Code of Civil Procedure, Section 1870, Subdivision 12, provides that evidence of usage may be given to explain the true character of an act, contract or instrument, where such true character is not otherwise plain, but usage is never admissible except as in an instrument of interpretation. A San Francisco merchant cabled to a coal dealer in New South Wales, "Offer subject to immediate reply twenty-four shillings cost freight and insurance exchange duty paid two cargoes." The coal dealer replied, "Ultimatim twenty-four shillings and three pence." The merchant responded by letter confirming his cabled acceptance, and saying, "We beg to confirm having purchased from you [stating kind of coal and price] 'cost,' 'freight,' 'insurance,' 'exchange,' 'duty paid,'" etc. Held, that the contract of sale thus evidenced was free from ambiguity, so that extrinsic evidence of a custom of the port of San Francisco giving to the purchaser of imported goods the advantage of a reduction of customs duties was inadmissible.

Payment.—A San Francisco Merchant Purchased Coal from a Dealer in New South Wales. The dealer drew a draft on the merchant for an amount less than the agreed price under the existing customs duties. Afterward the customs duties on the purchase were reduced, and later the cargo arrived. Held, that payment of the draft was on account and not in full satisfaction.

Charter-party.—A San Francisco Merchant Purchased Coal from a Dealer in New South Wales, stipulating that his form of charter-party should be used by the dealer. In violation of this stipulation, the charter-party actually employed omitted a clause providing that, if the vessel should be free from wharfage during discharge, the freight was to be reduced 4½d. per ton. Held, that this breach of contract would not justify the purchaser in rejecting the cargo, it being his duty to perform his part of the contract, and seek compensation in damages.

APPEAL from Superior Court, City and County of San Francisco; Edward A. Belcher, Judge.

Action by Henry J. Withers against John J. Moore. From a judgment for plaintiff and from an order denying a motion for a new trial defendant appeals. Affirmed.

Gordon & Young for appellant; Richard C. Harrison for respondent.

CHIPMAN, C.—Action on contract for the purchase of coal to arrive at San Francisco from Newcastle, New South Wales. Plaintiff had judgment, from which, and from the order denying his motion for a new trial, defendant appeals.

It is alleged in the complaint that defendant agreed in writing with plaintiff about October 12, 1893, to purchase from plaintiff two cargoes of coal at 24s. 3d. per ton, delivered alongside wharf at Oakland or San Francisco, the first to be shipped from Newcastle, New South Wales, between March 1 and May 31, 1894, and the second August 1, 1894, and October 31, 1894, "in vessels to be chartered under the usual form of charter-party of the defendant"; that on September 15, 1894, a cargo was delivered to and accepted by defendant as and for the first of said two cargoes, on account of the purchase price of which defendant paid a part, leaving still due and unpaid $1,657.75; that about October 31, 1894, plaintiff shipped a cargo by vessel named "Poltalloch" for the second of said cargoes; that said ship had theretofore been chartered by plaintiff for said voyage, under a charter-party of said form, and that plaintiff fully complied with said contract of October 12, 1893; that said ship arrived at San Francisco about January 23, 1895, prior to which defendant notified

plaintiff that he would not accept said cargo when the same
should arrive; that plaintiff tendered said cargo to defendant,
and offered to deliver the same to him, but defendant refused
to accept it, whereupon plaintiff sold the same for the best
obtainable price, realizing therefor the sum of $4,428.49 less
than defendant had agreed to pay therefor. In two other
counts the cause of action is set forth in somewhat different
form. Defendant admits the contract, but claims in his answer that the charter-party was "subject to the custom and
usage in the city and county of San Francisco among coal
dealers and coal merchants, and sellers and buyers and shippers of coal, which custom and usage is, and was at all the
times mentioned in the complaint, and for many years prior
thereto, 'that any alteration in present rate of import duty
to be for or against the purchaser,'" meaning thereby that,
if the rate of duty should be less at time of importation than
at the date of contract, the purchaser should receive the benefit, but, if greater, then the purchaser should be liable to pay
such excess of duty in addition to the price of coal. It is also
alleged that the charter-party made by plaintiff was in some
material particulars different from the form usual with defendant; that the payment made on the first cargo was in full
satisfaction thereof. It was alleged in one of the counts of
the complaint that disputes had arisen prior to September 28,
1894, touching the meaning of the contract of October 12,
1893, which had been settled by plaintiff and defendant agreeing that defendant should have deducted from the price of
said coal the sum of £43 2s. 9d., from the price of the first
cargo. This is denied in the answer which alleges that the
agreement was that the sum of 4½d. per ton should be deducted for wharfage by reason of the fact that said coal would
be free from wharfage, and also thirty-five cents per ton import duty, being the difference between the duty at the date
of the contract and the date of delivery. The court found
the contract as alleged in the complaint; that it was not made
subject to any custom or usage; that the usual form of
charter-party of defendant provided for a reduction of 4½d.
from the freight to be charged in the charter-party, should
the vessel be free from wharfage; that plaintiff and defendant agreed after the contract was made that, if the vessel
paid no wharfage, the price of the coal should be reduced
4½d. per ton; that the first cargo was received by defendant

under the contract as and for the first cargo; that the second cargo was shipped and arrived and was tendered to defendant as alleged in the complaint, and refused by defendant, and the cargo sold, as alleged; that neither of said cargoes paid wharfage at this port. The court also found the facts as to the value of said cargoes, the amount paid on account of the first, the amount still due thereon, the amount for which the second cargo sold, and the amount still due thereon, as alleged, and, as conclusion of law, found that there was due plaintiff from defendant the sum of $4,126.43. As near as we can ascertain from the record, the court arrived at this balance by deducting from the contract price of each cargo 4½d. per ton for free wharfage, and by allowing plaintiff the reduction in the rate of duty which went into effect July 1, 1894, and by allowing plaintiff, also, the difference between the contract price on the second cargo, less 4½d. per ton, and what it brought in the open market when sold to the best advantage.

1. The point most seriously urged by appellant, and apparently the only one on which the court found against him, is, that the contract was subject to the custom alleged in the answer.

Plaintiff resided in London, England, and the contract was entered into by cable messages with defendant, who resided in San Francisco. Plaintiff testified: "I have never had any other dealings in coal with any other firm or person in San Francisco, other than as set out above"; i. e., with defendant and one other shipment. "The contract in suit . . . . was made quite independent of the custom or usage in the port of San Francisco." He testified that he knew of no custom such as is alleged when he made the contract, and did not learn of it until some months afterward, when defendant claimed the benefit of it. Appellant relies on the following clauses of the charter-party: ". . . . and being so loaded shall therewith proceed to San Francisco Harbor . . . . and deliver the said full and complete cargo in the usual and customary manner," etc.; again, "all port charges, pilotages, wharfage dues, and charges at the port of discharge and half cost of weighing at port of discharge to be paid by the ship as customary." Respondent contends that the contract on which the suit was brought was a contract of sale and pur-

9

chase, entirely distinct from the charter-party, which latter
was between the charterer (the plaintiff and seller in this
case) and the ship owner, in which defendant was not known,
and by which he is not bound, and the provisions of the charter do not concern defendant. The terms of the sale were
settled by cable, afterward confirmed by mail. Defendant's
cable offer was made October 10, 1893, for two cargoes of
coal, and read as follows: "Offer subject to immediate reply
twenty-four shillings cost freight and insurance exchange
duty paid two cargoes 2,500 tons to 3,500 tons March, April,
May loading August, September, October loading. Our
usual form of charter-party. Advise you to accept offer. No
prospect of doing better." Some further correspondence by
cable ensued, and on October 12, 1893, plaintiff cabled: "Ultimatum twenty-four shillings and three pence. Others appear to be able to do better. Telegraph confirmation." On
the same day defendant cabled: "Offer accepted. We have
guaranteed equal to Elinshire." On October 14, 1893, defendant wrote plaintiff in further confirmation, and inclosing copies of the cable messages which had passed between the
parties, stating, among other things: "We beg to confirm
having purchased from you [stating kind of coal and price]
'cost,' 'freight,' 'insurance,' 'exchange,' 'duty paid,' alongside wharf in this city or Oakland. . . . . The vessel to be
chartered under our usual form of charter-party (as per copy
previously sent you) and to contain all the clauses contained
therein," except as stated in the letter. It was also stated
that defendant was forwarding by that "mail a few originals
and copies of our charter-party." On April 18, 1894, plaintiff chartered a ship named "Highfields" to carry the first of
the two cargoes referred to in defendant's letter of October
14th. This charter-party did not conform in all respects to
the form furnished by defendant, but complaint is now urged
only as to the clauses above quoted relating to custom, and a
clause reading: "Should vessel be free from wharfage during
discharge, the above freight to be reduced by 4½d. per ton."
As to this latter clause the court found in favor of appellant
but the finding is that the allowance for free wharfage was
because of a subsequent contract. However, as appellant got
the benefit of the clause, he is not injured by the finding, if
it be conceded to be based on a subsequent, rather than the
original, contract.

By the terms of the contract the seller agreed to pay the duty, whatever it might be. He did not agree to make a rebate on the price of the coal, should the duty be less when the coal was delivered than when the contract was first made; nor did the purchaser agree to pay more by reason of an increase in the rate of duty. It would be as reasonable to say that the price to be paid for the coal was to vary; i. e., was to be less or more as the cost, freight, insurance or exchange might vary. The plain meaning of the contract was that the coal should be delivered at Oakland wharf with all the enumerated charges paid by the seller, whatever they might happen to be, at the time of delivery. The seller took the chance of any advance in the duty, and the buyer took the chance of the seller being the gainer by any reduction in the duty. It is clear to our minds that the language of the contract will bear no other consideration.

The charter-party made no mention of the provision in the contract of purchase and sale as to the payment of duty by the seller, and it would not naturally or necessarily be included, for it was no part of the charges which the ship owner would ordinarily be concerned with. If this item had been in contemplation of defendant as a necessary part of his form of charter-party, it should have been included, and not left to such vague and uncertain expressions as "port charges" or delivery to be "in the usual and customary manner," which suggests nothing contrary to the terms of the contract. Not being included, we can look only to the contract to determine what the agreement was as to payment of duty, and there the provision is plain, as we have already said, that plaintiff was to pay the duty, whatever it might be. The only debatable question is whether the court erred in its finding that this contract was not subject to the custom alleged by defendant, and also erred in finally striking out all evidence as to custom. The evidence on both sides was taken subject to a motion to strike out. There is a conflict on the question whether such a custom in fact prevailed generally among coal dealers in San Francisco. But the court reached the conclusion that the contract was not made with reference or subject to any custom, and, if it was not so made, certainly the evidence relating to custom or usage was immaterial.

Aside, however, from other considerations which fully sustain the trial court in excluding the evidence where the intention of the parties is clearly expressed, parol evidence is inadmissible to prove a different intention. In Burns v. Sennett, 99 Cal. 363, 33 Pac. 916, cited by appellant, the court said: "A usage, of course, cannot be given in evidence to relieve a party from his express stipulation, or to vary a contract certain in its terms, but it has a legitimate office in aiding to interpret the intention of parties to a contract, the real character of which is to be ascertained, not from express stipulations, but from general implications and presumptions." And so the provision of the Code of Civil Procedure cited by appellant (section 1870, subdivision 12) provides that evidence of usage may be given "to explain the true character of an act, contract, or instrument, where such true character is not otherwise plain; but usage is never admissible except as an instrument of interpretation."

The cases cited by counsel are in harmony with the rule of our code—for example, Nordaas v. Hubbard (D. C.), 48 Fed. 921, holding that "evidence of usage is . . . . admissible to explain a contract, where otherwise the intention of the parties cannot be ascertained"; and Robinson v. United States, 13 Wall. 363, 20 L. Ed. 653, where such evidence is received to explain the intention of the parties to a contract, "the meaning of which could not be ascertained without the aid of extrinsic evidence." The contract here is quite plain and free from ambiguity or uncertainty. Not only is extrinsic evidence unnecessary to explain the meaning of the contract, but to admit proof of the custom would change the obligation of defendant to pay 24s. 3d. per ton for coal to an obligation to pay thirty-five cents less per ton.

As to the evidence, it appears that a controversy arose early in the business about the alleged variance in the Highfields charter-party, and this was finally settled by plaintiff conceding the point as to the free wharfage. The reduced duty on coal did not go into effect until July 1, 1894. Much correspondence was carried on concerning both charters before and after July 1, 1894; but defendant made no claim that any custom prevailed in San Francisco, such as is pleaded, until in his letter of September 26, 1894, which was a month after the second charter-party was made, and some time after the "Poltalloch," (the second chartered ship) had been loaded. This was a letter in reply to plaintiff's letter to defendant of September 5th, in which he wrote: "In regard to the Highfields cargo I presume you only paid the reduced duty and that you will shortly remit difference as desired in my former letters.''

2. It was alleged in the answer of defendant, and it is now urged, that the payments made by defendant to plaintiff on account of the first cargo were in full satisfaction and payment therefor. We find nothing in the evidence to support this claim. Plaintiff on June 1, 1894, drew a draft on defendant for a certain sum, but there is no evidence to show that this was intended by plaintiff to be for the full balance he then claimed to be due him from defendant. At that time the duty had not been reduced, and the cargo had not yet arrived. The payment was on account, and not in full satisfaction.

3. A breach relied on in the contract relating to the second or ''Poltalloch'' shipment, as justifying the rejection of the cargo, is the omission of the free wharfage clause from the charter-party. Assuming that it was a condition of the contract that defendant's form of charter-party was to be used, this omission was a breach which could be, and was in fact, by the judgment of the court, fully compensated by allowing defendant credit for the amount of wharfage charges which plaintiff was relieved from paying, and defendant cannot complain. His duty was to perform his part of the contract, and seek compensation in damages. The court gave him his compensation, and he can ask no more. The principle will be found stated in Fountain v. Semi-tropic L. & W. Co., 99 Cal. 677, 34 Pac. 497.

The judgment and order should be affirmed.

We concur: Gray, C.; Haynes, C.

PER CURIAM.—For the reasons given in the foregoing opinion the judgment and order are affirmed.

PRYAL v. PRYAL.

S. F. No. 2427; March 5, 1903.

71 Pac. 802.

Homestead — Deed from Husband to Wife—Death of Wife.— Code of Civil Procedure, section 1474, provides that if the homestead selected by the husband and wife be selected from community property, it vests absolutely in the survivor on the death of either spouse. A homestead selected from community property was deeded to the wife by a deed signed by the husband alone, and the wife alone deeded it to a third party. Held, that the deed from the husband did not destroy the homestead, nor the husband's right of survivorship, and on the death of the wife the husband, and not the wife's grantee, was entitled to the property.

Community Property—Conveyance by Wife—Action by Husband's Heirs.— Act of March, 1897, amending Civil Code, section 164, so as to make a conveyance to a married woman by instrument in writing presumptive evidence that title is thereby vested in her, provides that in cases where married women have conveyed real property which they acquired prior to May 19, 1889, "the husbands or their heirs or assigns, of such married women," shall be barred from maintaining any action to show that the real property was community property, unless begun within one year from the date of the taking effect of the act. Code of Civil Procedure, section 434, declares that if no objection be taken to the complaint, either by demurrer or answer, defendant must be deemed to have waived the same, except, etc. Held, that where the wife's grantees failed to object that an action by the husband's heirs to recover alleged community property conveyed by her to them was not brought within the time prescribed by the act of 1897, they could not raise that objection on appeal.

APPEAL from Superior Court, Alameda County; F. B. Ogden, Judge.

Action by Andrew D. Pryal against William A. Pryal. From a judgment for plaintiff, defendant appeals. Affirmed.

Fitzgerald & Abbott for appellant; Nye & Kinsell for respondent.

COOPER, C.—Action to quiet title to two separate pieces of real estate situate in Alameda county. Plaintiff had judgment and defendant appeals from the judgment on the judgment-roll.

1. In November, 1867, plaintiff resided with his wife, Mary
A. Pryal, upon the first piece of property described in the
complaint, and on said day he made in due form a declaration of homestead thereon, which was duly recorded. At the
time of making the declaration the property was community
property, and it will be hereafter called the homestead. In
the year 1879 the plaintiff, by deed of gift, signed by himself
alone, conveyed the homestead to his wife. In August, 1896,
the wife, by deed of grant, bargain and sale, purported to
convey the homestead to defendant, the son of plaintiff and
his deceased wife. Plaintiff, with his wife and family, resided upon the homestead from the date of the making thereof
until the death of the wife, in September, 1896. In whom
is the title to the homestead?

It is provided in Code of Civil Procedure, section 1474:
''If the homestead selected by the husband and wife, or either
of them, during their coverture, and recorded while both were
living, was selected from the community property . . . . it
vests, on the death of the husband or wife, absolutely in the
survivor.'' The homestead was selected from the community
property, and hence vested, on the death of the wife, in the
surviving husband. It is claimed by appellant that the deed
made by the husband to the wife in 1879 had the effect of
destroying the community character of the property, and
making it thereafter the separate property of the wife. If
we concede such to have been the effect of the deed, it does
not follow that it destroyed the homestead, nor the right of
survivorship therein given under the statute. The homestead
cannot be conveyed, nor encumbered in any way, so as to destroy its homestead character, unless the instrument by which
it is sought to convey or encumber it is executed and acknowledged by both husband and wife. The purpose of the law
is to place it beyond the power of either spouse, acting alone,
to destroy the homestead character impressed upon the real
estate or to encumber it in any way. The deed of gift to
the wife, therefore, did not in any way destroy the homestead, nor the rights of the husband and wife, or either of
them, thereto as a homestead.

It is said that the deed to the wife did not affect the homestead, but made it thereafter a homestead upon the separate
property of the wife, to be treated as if selected on her separate property, without her consent, for the reason that the

deed to the wife carried the husband's title subject to the
homestead. The case of Burkett v. Burkett, 78 Cal. 310, 12
Am. St. Rep. 58, 3 L. R. A. 781, 20 Pac. 715, is relied upon,
and it is claimed that that case holds to the effect that after
the deed to the wife the homestead must thereafter be treated
as selected from the separate property without the consent of
the wife. That case does not go to the extent claimed here.
It was held there that the conveyance by the husband to the
wife passed the title to the wife subject to the homestead.
The court was discussing a question as to the disposition of
property on divorce proceedings, under subdivision 4, section
146 of the Civil Code, which provides: "If a homestead has
been selected from the separate property of either it shall be
assigned to the former owner of such property, subject to the
power of the court to assign it for a limited period to the
innocent party." The object of the section is to give to the
owner of separate property his or her property, freed from
the homestead, subject to the right of the court to set it aside
for a limited period to the innocent party. The section sets
forth a rule as to the separate property of husband or wife,
and evidently refers to the character of the property at the
time of granting the divorce. There the homestead had been
selected. It had been selected from the property that was,
at the time of granting the divorce, the separate property of
the wife. The court was dealing with such separate property which had been impressed with the character of a homestead. The disposition of the homestead is not, under the
section, made to depend in any degree upon the question as
to who made the homestead declaration, but it is intended to
give the separate property to the owner of such separate
property, even though it has been impressed with the character of a homestead. That was the ruling of the court, as
we understand the decision, for therein it is said: "At the
time the divorce proceeding was instituted and the decree rendered therein, the property was a homestead upon the separate property of the wife, by virtue of the declaration of
the husband, and his subsequent conveyance to her. . . . . .
The husband having conveyed the property to the wife, by a
valid deed, prior to the commencement of the divorce suit,
she must be regarded as the 'former owner' under this section, and entitled to the property, subject only to the power
of the court to set the same apart to the husband, for a lim-

ited time, if he appeared to be the innocent party.'' What is there said is not in the least inconsistent with our conclusion here. The court was not dealing with a homestead selected from community property after the death of one of the spouses. The views we have expressed are not only consistent with Burkett v. Burkett, supra, but supported by the later case, In re Lamb's Estate, 95 Cal. 406, 30 Pac. 568. It is there said: ''When the statute speaks of the selection of a homestead from the 'separate property of the person selecting or joining in the selection of the same,' it has reference to the status of the property at the time when the selection is made.'' We therefore conclude that the title in the homestead vested in the plaintiff on the death of the wife.

2. The second tract of land will be called the ''Oakland Property.'' This was purchased by Mary A. Pryal in September, 1887, with community funds, and therefore became community property. In August, 1896, the said Mary A. Pryal executed and delivered to defendant a deed of grant to the Oakland property. The husband alone has the power to dispose of community property: Civ. Code, sec. 172; Parry v. Kelley, 52 Cal. 334. Therefore, the deed, made to defendant by his mother in her lifetime, did not convey the title.

In March, 1897, section 164 of the Civil Code was amended so as to make a conveyance to a married woman, by an instrument in writing, presumptive evidence that the title is thereby vested in her. This section as amended contains the provision: ''And in cases where married women have conveyed, or shall hereafter convey, real property which they acquired prior to May 19, 1889, the husbands or their heirs or assigns, of such married women, shall be barred from commencing or maintaining any action to show that said real property was community property, or to recover said real property, as follows: As to conveyances heretofore made from and after one year from the date of the taking effect of this act.'' This action is, in effect, for the purpose of showing that the Oakland property was community property within the meaning of the section as amended. It was commenced in August, 1898, more than one year from the date of the taking effect of the act. The action, therefore, would appear to have been barred by the above statute, if the statute had been pleaded.

The section clearly lays down a limitation as to the time of commencing or maintaining such actions. It is referred to

and treated as a statute of limitations by this court in Peiser
v. Griffin, 125 Cal. 14, 57 Pac. 690. But in this case the defendant did not raise the question as to the statute of limitations, either by demurrer or answer. There is no finding as
to the question, and evidently no such issue was made in the
court below. Defendant will not be allowed to raise the question here for the first time: Code Civ. Proc., sec. 434; Brown
v. Martin, 25 Cal. 91; People v. Broadway Wharf Co., 31
Cal. 34; Manning v. Dallas, 73 Cal. 420, 15 Pac. 34; Reagan
v. Justice's Court, 75 Cal. 255, 17 Pac. 195. The Oakland
property was therefore correctly held to be the property of
plaintiff.

It follows that the judgment should be affirmed.

We concur: Haynes, C.; Smith, C.

PER CURIAM.—For the reasons given in the foregoing
opinion the judgment is affirmed.

HOGAN et al. v. GLOBE MUTUAL BUILDING AND
LOAN ASSOCIATION et al.*

S. F. No. 2516; March 6, 1903.

71 Pac. 706.

Bills—Acceptance—Time of Payment.—Plaintiff furnished lumber for a building, and took an order to secure the purchase price,
indorsed by defendant corporation: "Accepted, payable as follows
$375 upon completion of the house. . . . ." Held, the acceptance was
not conditional on the completion of the building, but merely fixed a
time of payment, and liability on the acceptance matured on the destruction of the building by fire and the determination of the owner
not to rebuild.

APPEAL from Superior Court, City and County of San
Francisco; J. M. Seawell, Judge.

Action by Hugh Hogan and T. P. Hogan, partners under
the firm name of Humboldt Lumber Company, against the
Globe Mutual Building and Loan Association and Frederick

*For subsequent opinion in bank, see 140 Cal. 610, 74 Pac. 153.

Esty. From a judgment of dismissal plaintiffs appeal. Reversed.

F. A. Berlin for appellants; Joseph Hutchinson and F. W. Sawyer for respondents.

GRAY, C.—In this action the demurrer of the above-named corporation defendant to plaintiffs' amended complaint was sustained, and judgment of dismissal was thereupon entered in favor of said corporation. Plaintiffs appeal from said judgment, and the only question presented relates to the sufficiency of the complaint. The respondent contends simply that the complaint does not state a cause of action, and therefore the demurrer to it was properly sustained, and the action rightly dismissed.

The complaint is based upon an order for $386, drawn on the respondent corporation by defendant Esty in favor of appellants, and accepted by the corporation with an indorsement on its face, signed by the corporation, in the following language: "Accepted, payable as follows: $375 upon completion of house, $11 thirty-five days after, provided no liens are filed." The order in question is dated and addressed to "Globe Mutual Loan Assn.," and runs as follows: "Please pay to Humboldt Lumber Co., or order, three hundred and eighty-six dollars, for material furnished on your building, w. s. Grant st. and Bancroft, Berkeley, and charge same to my account."

It is shown by the complaint that the defendant Esty was a contractor constructing the building referred to in the order for the owner of premises upon which it was located; that the building and loan association had in its hands, at the time of said acceptance by it, moneys and securities belonging to the owner of the building, more than sufficient to pay said order; that soon after the order was drawn, and when the house was nearly completed, it burned down, without any fault on the part of plaintiffs or the contractor, and thereby it became impossible to complete it. It also appears from the complaint that the house, when destroyed, was insured against fire for its full value, in the name of the owner, and for the benefit of the building and loan association, mortgagees of said property, and that the contractor offered to rebuild the house at the original contract price, but the owner thereof refused to allow him to do so, and that the owner thereof does not, nor do the defendants, or either of them, intend to rebuild said building. It further appears from the complaint that the material furnished by plaintiffs and mentioned in the order was actually used in the construction of the building, and that the order was given to secure the purchase price thereof, $386, and that after the fire the corporation refused to pay the order when told by plaintiffs that it would be looked to for its payment.

The precise question to be determined here is this: Was the completion of the house a condition precedent to respondents' liability on its acceptance? The intention of the party executing the acceptance should govern in answering this question, and this intention is to be determined by the language used in the acceptance, and this language should be construed by the light of the circumstances under which the language was used, having a due regard for the relation of the parties; and the courts will not import a condition into a contract, unless compelled to do so by the language employed. Looking, then, first, to the language, we find the first word used in the acceptance is "accepted"; the words which immediately follow relate to the time when the order is to be paid. The event of the completion of the house was evidently fixed upon merely as the time of payment. It is not reasonable to suppose that the parties intended that the payment should be contingent upon the house not being destroyed by fire, because they expressed nothing of that kind, and in all probability the thought of fire did not occur to them. We are further impelled to the conclusion that the acceptance was meant to be absolute and unconditional from the fact that the lumber company had parted with all title and right to the material furnished, and there was nothing left for the company to do to earn the money mentioned in the acceptance; and, further, the respondent was under the mortgage and insurance policy secured in the very property which the acceptance was to pay for against any possible loss by reason of paying the acceptance when it should fall due. The material sold was a part of the house upon which respondent held a mortgage, and respondent may be said to have succeeded to the title to these materials to the extent that his mortgage gave him an interest therein. The house is treated as the property of respondent, and is referred to as "your building" in the order addressed to and accepted by respondent. The respondent seems, then, to have accepted an order covering a debt for which it may have well regarded it necessary to its own interest to see that it was paid, even in the absence of the order. This debt, in its origin, was not encumbered with any condition, and we do not believe that respondent intended to add any condition to it when he became responsible in writing for its payment, but his purpose was merely to fix a convenient time for its discharge. The only condition that appears from the language of the acceptance attaches to the $11 payable thirty-five days after the completion of the house, ''provided no liens are filed.'' This sounds like it was intended as a condition precedent to the payment of the $11, and we do not intend that the former part of this opinion shall apply to the $11 item; but as it is shown that, the house being destroyed, no liens can ever be filed against it, it is impossible that the condition referred to can ever happen, and it may, therefore, be disregarded.

From the foregoing facts we conclude that the times and dates mentioned in the acceptance were intended merely to prescribe the time of payment by reference not to days or years, but to events that in all probability would happen. It having become impossible that these events should ever occur, it is but reasonable that the money should be due and payable whenever the fact of the impossibility of their occurrence has become certain. In other words, the money was due on the acceptance immediately on the destruction of the house by fire and the determination of the owner not to rebuild; provided, of course, the owner did not unreasonably delay the making of a decision on that question, in which case it would be due upon the lapse of a reasonable time after the fire within which to make such decision: Ubsdell & Pierson v. Cunningham, 22 Mo. 124. The parties having neglected to provide for the contingency of a fire, the law in this case, as in many other cases, supplies the omission by implying such a promise as is necessary to do justice between the parties. The foregoing propositions find support in the following cases: De Wolfe v. French, 51 Me. 420; Crooker v. Holmes, 65 Me. 195, 20 Am. Rep. 687; Nunez v. Dantel, 19 Wall. 560, 22 L. Ed. 161.

The case of Clark v. Collier, 100 Cal. 256, 34 Pac. 677, contains nothing out of harmony with the foregoing. In that case the suit was by the contractor to recover the final installments under his contract, and his right of recovery was admittedly conditioned upon the completion of his contract, and it was held that he had not completed the work that he agreed to do; in other words, he had not earned the money he sought to recover. In the case at bar the money has been earned; the plaintiff has done everything required to be entitled to recover. The amended complaint shows that the acceptance was due when the suit was brought, and the demurrer to it should have been overruled.

We advise that the judgment be reversed.

We concur: Haynes, C.; Smith, C.

PER CURIAM.—For the reasons given in the foregoing pinion the judgment is reversed.

VINSON et al. v. LOS ANGELES PACIFIC RAILROAD COMPANY.*

L. A. No. 1360; March 13, 1903.

72 Pac. 840.

Appeal—Statement.—Code of Civil Procedure, Section 950, provides: "On an appeal from a final judgment, the appellant must furnish the court with a copy of the notice of appeal, of the judgment-roll, and of any bill of exceptions or statement in the case on which the appellant relies. Any statement used on motion for a new trial, or settled after decision of such motion, when the motion is made upon the minutes of the court, as provided in section 661, or any bill of exceptions settled, as provided in sections 649 or 650, or used on motion for a new trial, may be used on appeal from a final judgment equally as upon appeal from the order granting or refusing the new trial." Held, not to give a party intending to appeal from a judgment an independent right to have settled a statement of the case for use on such appeal, but to limit him to the use of such statements only as have been regularly and legally settled in the course of some proceeding on motion for a new trial.

Appeal — Extension of Time for Filing Transcript.—Supreme court rule 2 provides: "The appellant in a civil action shall, within forty days after the appeal is perfected and the bill of exceptions

---

*For subsequent opinion in bank, see 141 Cal. 151, 74 Pac. 757.

and the statement (if there be any) are settled, serve and file the printed transcript of the record." Code of Civil Procedure, section 661, provides: "The judgment-roll and a statement to be subsequently prepared, with a copy of the order, shall constitute the record on appeal from the order granting or refusing a new trial. Such subsequent statement shall be proposed by the party appealing . . . . within ten days after the entry of the order . . . . but the statement shall only contain the grounds argued before the court for a new trial, and so much of the evidence or other matter as may be necessary to explain them." Held, that the pendency of proceedings to settle a statement on motion for a new trial after the time for appeal from the order denying a new trial had expired, no appeal having been taken from the order, did not operate to extend the time for the filing of the transcript on the appeal from the judgment, nor authorize the filing of such transcript more than forty days after the time of perfecting the appeal.

APPEAL from Superior Court, Los Angeles County.

Action by Jennie Vinson and another against the Los Angeles Pacific Railroad Company. From a judgment for plaintiffs, defendant appeals. Dismissed.

John D. Pope and Bicknell, Gibson & Trask for appellant; Waters & Wylie for respondents.

SHAW, J.—This is a motion by the plaintiffs to dismiss the defendant's appeal from the judgment of the court below. The ground of the motion is that the transcript was not filed within forty days after the appeal was perfected. Rule 2 of this court (64 Pac. vii) provides that "the appellant in a civil action shall, within forty days after the appeal is perfected and the bill of exceptions and the statement (if there be any) are settled, serve and file the printed transcript of the record." The judgment was rendered in the court below on May 15, 1902, and the appeal was perfected on November 17, 1902. It is conceded that, if the time for filing the transcript began to run on November 17th, the appeal must be dismissed for failure to file the same within time. But the appellant claims that the time had been extended by the pendency of proceedings to settle a statement on motion for a new trial, and this presents the sole question in the case. The notice of the motion to dismiss was served and filed on January 10, 1903. It is claimed that a statement on motion for a new trial was settled on

December 16, 1902, and that within forty days after that date, but after the filing of the notice of motion to dismiss, the transcript on appeal was filed. If the statement so settled was settled under authority of law, and can be used on the appeal, the motion must be denied.

The motion for new trial was made on the minutes of the court, and was denied in the court below on July 21, 1902. No appeal was ever taken from the order. The respondent contends that after the lapse of sixty days from the entry of the order, without the taking of an appeal, the right to have a statement settled upon the motion ceased, that the subsequent settlement of the so-called statement was a mere idle and useless ceremony, and that the statement so settled is without force or effect. The appellant relies on section 950 of the Code of Civil Procedure, which is as follows: "On an appeal from a final judgment, the appellant must furnish the court with a copy of the notice of appeal, of the judgment-roll, and of any bill of exceptions or statement in the case, upon which the appellant relies. Any statement used on motion for a new trial, or settled after decision of such motion, when the motion is made upon the minutes of the court, as provided in section 661, or any bill of exceptions settled, as provided in sections 649 or 650, or used on motion for a new trial, may be used on appeal from a final judgment equally as upon appeal from the order grant· ing or refusing the new trial." The contention of the appellant is that the effect of this section is to give the party who intends to appeal from a judgment an independent right to have settled a statement of the case for use upon such appeal, and that, by virtue of its provisions, he is not limited to the use of such statements only as have been regularly and legally settled in the course of some proceeding upon motion for a new trial. This contention cannot be sustained. The section is found in the chapter relating to appeals, and has no specific provisions relating to the settlement of statements. The phrase, "any statement used on motion for a new trial, or settled after decision of such motion when the motion is made upon the minutes of the court, as provided in section 661," limits the right to use statements on motion for new trial made on the minutes of the court to such as have been properly settled under section 661. The obvious purpose of the section was to provide that any statement or bill of exceptions regularly settled in any proceeding in which such statement or bill of exceptions might be lawfully settled could be used on an appeal from a judgment, although it was not originally intended for that purpose. And this is the construction which has been given it. Thus in Foley v. Foley, 120 Cal. 33, 65 Am. St. Rep. 147, 52 Pac. 122, it was held that bills of exceptions settled for the purpose of reviewing an order refusing to set aside a default, although originally made for that purpose alone, could nevertheless be used upon an appeal from the judgment. In that case the bill of exceptions had been regularly and lawfully settled. But the section goes no further than this, and cannot be given any greater effect.

We must therefore look to the provisions of section 661 to ascertain whether the statement in question can be used. That section, so far as applicable with respect to motions for new trial upon the minutes of the court, is as follows: "The judgment-roll and a statement to be subsequently prepared, with a copy of the order, shall constitute the record on appeal. Such subsequent statement shall be proposed by the party appealing, or intending to appeal, within ten days after the entry of the order . . . . but the statement shall only contain the grounds argued before the court for a new trial, and so much of the evidence or other matter as may be necessary to explain them." It is quite obvious from this language that the purpose for which such subsequent statement is to be prepared and settled is to present to the appellate court such matter as may be necessary to enable it, upon appeal, to review the order disposing of the motion for a new trial. The appeal referred to is manifestly not an appeal from the judgment, but an appeal from the order upon the motion. There is nothing in the section which calls for a broader meaning than this. Therefore, it would follow that, after the time for an appeal has expired, no appeal having been taken, the right to have such subsequent statement ceases to exist, and any further proceeding toward the settlement of such a statement is wholly unauthorized. Any statement settled under such circumstances would be void as a statement, and would be stricken from the files upon motion. The decisions of this court tend to support this conclusion. In Flagg v. Puterbaugh, 98 Cal. 134, 32

Pac. 863, the court, speaking of the settlement of a bill of exceptions upon an order, after the time for the appeal from the order had expired, none having been taken, says: "It would be a vain thing to settle a bill of exceptions if there is no appeal, and the court would not order it." For that reason alone the court in that case refused to issue a mandamus compelling a judge of the court below to settle the bill. In Estate of Franklin, 133 Cal. 584, 65 Pac. 1081, this court held that, as there was no law providing for motions for a new trial of an order settling an executor's account, there was no authority for the settlement of any statement of the case upon such a motion, and therefore the transcript on appeal must be filed within forty days after the perfecting of the appeal, and that the time was not extended by the pendency of proceedings to settle such a statement. In Buckley v. Althorf, 86 Cal. 643, 25 Pac. 134, it is held that a statement which was not served until six days after the time allowed by law was one "which the court was not called upon to settle, and which could not be used upon the appeal," and that therefore the time for the filing of the transcript was not extended by the continuance of proceedings to settle such a statement. It follows that the pendency of proceedings to settle the statement in controversy after the time for appeal from the order denying a motion for a new trial had expired, no appeal having been taken from the order, did not operate to extend the time for the filing of the transcript, nor authorize the filing of such transcript more than forty days after the time of perfecting the appeal.

It is therefore ordered that the appeal be dismissed.

We concur: Angellotti, J.; Van Dyke, J.

In re DELMAS.

Cr. No. 1015; April 9, 1903.

72 Pac. 402.

Attorneys—Disbarment.—Since the **Superior Court has Concurrent Jurisdiction** with the supreme court to disbar attorneys, an original application for disbarment will not be entertained by the supreme court unless the proceeding is instituted or supported by a bar association, or the misconduct is alleged to have direct connection with matters pending in the supreme court.[1]

Attorneys—Disbarment.—An Application for the Disbarment of an attorney on the ground that he had deprived prosecutor of certain money by fraud will not be entertained by the supreme court until prosecutor had established his cause of action against the attorney in the ordinary tribunals of the county in which the cause of action accrued by either criminal or civil process.

Application by H. W. Hutton for the disbarment of D. M. Delmas. Dismissed.

H. W. Hutton in pro. per.; D. M. Delmas pro se.

BEATTY, C. J.—An accusation in writing, entitled as above, has been filed here by H. W. Hutton, upon which he prays that a citation may issue to Mr. Delmas, requiring him to answer certain charges therein contained. Without waiting for the issuance of a citation, Mr. Delmas has voluntarily appeared, filed a denial of the charges, and has requested an immediate hearing thereon. The court, however, must decline to proceed in the matter. For a long time, and in a number of cases, we have refused to entertain proceedings to disbar attorneys for alleged professional misconduct, unless the proceeding was instituted or supported by a bar association, or the misconduct was alleged to have direct connection with matters pending in this court. This course is sufficiently justified by the fact that the superior courts—which have a concurrent jurisdiction in proceedings to disbar attorneys—have time to spare for the necessary investigation, while the time of this court is more than exhausted in the effort to dispose of matters which cannot be litigated elsewhere. It is also a weighty consideration that the convenience of witnesses requires that the issues of fact involved in any proceeding should be tried in local tribunals, rather than in a court which sits in only one place in a state, and it is no reason for departing from this practice that in a particular instance the state court happens to be located in the county to which the proceeding properly belongs; or, to put the proposition in its concrete form, the fact that

[1] Cited in Matter of Danford, 157 Cal. 429, 108 Pac. 324, where it is distinguished from a case in which, although the prosecution was also at suit of a private individual, it was brought before a lower court, the supreme court not being asked to take original jurisdiction.

the supreme court of this state sits in San Francisco is no reason why it should take cognizance of a proceeding which, if the controversy had originated in another county, would have gone naturally and properly, and upon considerations of convenience, to the superior court of that county. For these reasons it is the invariable practice of this court in the case of applications for writs of certiorari, mandamus, prohibition, procedendo, or any prerogative writ, where there is a concurrent jurisdiction in the superior court, to require the petitioner to allege and satisfactorily establish the facts which render it proper and necessary that the writ should issue originally from this court: Rule 26. Proceedings to disbar attorneys, although not within the express terms of this rule, are clearly within its reason, and, as above stated, they have been disposed of accordingly.

Another reason why this accusation should not be entertained in this court, or in any court, as the matter now stands, is found in principle decided in the Tilden case, 3 Cal. Unrep. 383, 25 Pac. 687, and the Stephens case, 102 Cal. 264, 36 Pac. 586. In the latter case, speaking of the charges against Stephens, we said: "So far as these allegations tend to show that the accused attorney has been guilty of a criminal offense, the charge here falls within the rule announced in the case of Tilden, 3 Cal. Unrep. 383, 25 Pac. 687, in which we distinctly announced that we would not investigate such charges until after regular proceedings in the courts having jurisdiction of the offense. The present case presents even stronger objections to the proceedings which we are asked to institute. If the facts alleged are true, the accuser has an undoubted right to recover in a civil action, by the verdict of a jury, the money of which he claims to have been defrauded. But without making any attempt to establish his right, or the guilt of the accused, in the ordinary tribunals, by either criminal or civil process, he asks this court to lay aside the important and pressing business with which every moment of its time is fully occupied, in order to investigate, in the first instance, a charge which may be tried and determined in the courts of the country. We should feel entirely justified in refusing to accede to such a demand even if the pressure of more imperative engagements did not render it necessary. When an accusation of this kind is preferred, not by a bar association, or any responsible public officer charged with the conservation of the public interests, but merely by a party complaining of a private injury, we must decline to investigate it until such party has shown his good faith by first resorting to regular proceedings in the ordinary tribunals.'' The above language is strictly applicable to the present charges, which, whether criminal in their nature or merely importing a civil liability, are properly triable in the usual method, and in the ordinary tribunals.

The proceeding is dismissed.

We concur: Van Dyke, J.; Shaw, J.; Angellotti, J.; Henshaw, J.; Lorigan, J.

PEOPLE v. GEHRIG.

Cr. No. 974; May 13, 1903.

72 Pac. 717.

Criminal Law—Appeal— Failure to Appear.—Under Penal Code, section 1253, providing that a judgment may be affirmed if the appellant fail to appear, but can be reversed only after argument, though the respondent fail to appear, a judgment of conviction could only be affirmed where defendant filed no brief, made no appearance, and submitted the case on the record without argument.

APPEAL from Superior Court, Sierra County; Stanley A. Smith, Judge.

Frank Gehrig was convicted of manslaughter, and he appeals. Affirmed.

F. D. Soward and L. W. Fulkerth for appellant; U. S. Webb for the people.

GRAY, C.—In this case the defendant was convicted of manslaughter, and sentenced to ten years' confinement in the state prison. He appealed from the judgment and from an order denying a new trial. He has filed no brief and made no appearance upon the appeal. The appeal is ''submitted on the record'' without argument. Section 1253 of the Penal Code reads as follows: ''The judgment may be affirmed if the appellant fail to appear, but can be reversed only after argument, though the respondent fail to appear.'' Under this provision of the law but one disposition can be made of the case in its present condition; it can be affirmed. We therefore advise that the judgment and order appealed from be affirmed.

We concur: Haynes, C.; Chipman, C.

PER CURIAM.—For the reasons given in the foregoing opinion the judgment and order appealed from are affirmed.

PEOPLE v. ELPHIS.

Cr. No. 962; May 19, 1903.

72 Pac. 838.

Forgery.—Where an Information for Uttering a forged check failed to charge that such uttering was with intent to defraud any person, or that defendant at the time knew that the check was false and forged, it was insufficient to sustain a conviction.

Forgery—Appeal—Reversal for Insufficiency of Indictment.—Under Penal Code, section 1262, providing that, if a judgment against a defendant is reversed without ordering a new trial, the appellate court must, if he is in custody, direct him to be discharged therefrom, on the reversal of a conviction for uttering a forged check, for insufficiency in the indictment, the defendant, who was in custody, was entitled to be discharged.

APPEAL from Superior Court Contra Costa County; Wm. S. Wells, Judge.

B. F. Elphis was convicted of forgery and he appeals. Reversed.

John O'B. Wyatt for appellant; U. S. Webb, attorney general, and E. B. Powers, deputy attorney general, for the people.

SHAW, J.—This is an appeal by the defendant from a judgment of conviction on a plea of guilty. The charge is that the defendant, at the time and place alleged, did ''feloniously, willfully and unlawfully, falsely utter and pass to one Louis Grunauer a certain false, forged and counterfeit check as a true and genuine check of one F. C. Wright on the First National Bank of Fresno .... for the payment of thirty-eight dollars which aforesaid check then and therein the words and figures, to wit: 'Fresno, Nov. 15, 1901. No. 24. The First National Bank pay to the order of J. H. Wilder, thirty-eight $38.00 dollars. [Signed] T. C. White. Endorsed, J. II. Wilder.' Contrary,'' etc.

It is admitted that the information is fatally defective because it neither charges the intent to defraud any person, nor that the defendant at the time knew that the check was false and forged: People v. Mitchell, 92 Cal. 590, 28 Pac. 597, 788; People v. Turner, 113 Cal. 278, 45 Pac. 331; People v. Smith, 103 Cal. 563, 37 Pac. 516. It appears from the record that the defendant is in custody. Section 1262 of the Penal Code provides that, ''if a judgment against a defendant is reversed without ordering a new trial, the appellate court must, if he is in custody, direct him to be discharged therefrom.'' The defendant appears to be entitled to a discharge, and the section quoted, on the face of it, does not give this court discretion to do otherwise than discharge him. It is possible that the errors which require a reversal are not substantial, with respect to the actual guilt of the defendant, but might be cured by another information. The defendant pleaded ''Guilty.'' If prosecuted again, it should be upon a new information after another preliminary examination.

The judgment of conviction is reversed, without prejudice to another prosecution if the district attorney thinks it advisable, and it is ordered that the defendant be discharged from custody upon the present charge.

·We concur: Angellotti, J.; Van Dyke, J.

WILLEY v. CROCKER-WOOLWORTH NATIONAL BANK OF SAN FRANCISCO.*

S. F. No. 2741; May 22, 1903.

72 Pac. 832.

Partnership.—A Bank Receiving Deposits from A. B. P. & Co. is put on inquiry as to whether the depositor is not a partnership, rather than the individual A. B. P.

Partnership.—A Bank Receiving Deposits from, and Doing Business with, a partnership consisting of an individual and a corporation, is estopped to deny the validity of the partnership, when sued by it for a deposit.

Partnership—Death of Partner.—Code of Civil Procedure, section 1585, gives a surviving partner the right to continue in possession of the partnership, and to settle its business and account with the executor or administrator, and to pay over such balances to him as may be payable to him in the right of the decedent. Held, that, as the right of a corporate surviving partner to close up the partnership business after the death of its individual partner was not affected by the question of the legality of a partnership between a corporation and an individual, the estoppel of a bank receiving deposits from and doing business with such partnership to deny its legality was not terminated by the individual partner's death.

APPEAL from Superior Court, City and County of San Francisco; Frank J. Murasky, Judge.

Action by Charles G. Willey against the Crocker-Woolworth National Bank of San Francisco. Judgment for plaintiff and defendant appeals. Affirmed.

Henry E. Monroe and Monroe & Cornwall (Loyd & Wood of counsel) for appellant; Crandall & Bull (H. M. Barstow of counsel) for respondent.

PER CURIAM.—This is an appeal from a judgment on a bill of exceptions. The facts are substantially as follows: A. B. Perry & Co., a copartnership composed of Alvan B. Perry and W. P. Fuller & Co., a corporation, did their banking business with defendant, a banking corporation, and had a deposit account with defendant. On February 14, 1899, the said copartnership had on deposit with defendant

---

*For subsequent opinion in bank, see 141 Cal. 508, 75 Pac. 106.

the sum of $1,720.64, being the amount in controversy herein. On February 16, 1899, the said Alvan B. Perry died, leaving the said W. P. Fuller & Co. as the sole surviving partner. After the death of Perry, the said W. P. Fuller & Co. presented a check, properly drawn, to the defendant, and demanded the payment of said sum, but payment was refused, and has at all times since been refused. The plaintiff is now the holder of the demand by assignment from W. P. Fuller & Co., as the surviving member of the partnership. Defendant attempts to justify its refusal to pay upon the following facts: The said A. B. Perry & Co. had their account and did their banking business with the Tallant Banking Company from August 4, 1897, up to November 28, 1898, but the said Alvan B. Perry had no personal account with the said banking company. On August 4, 1897, the said Alvan B. Perry, individually, borrowed from the Tallant Banking Company the sum of $1,600, giving his personal note therefor, payable ninety days after that date, which transaction was entered in their books and carried forward in separate account of Alvan B. Perry under and as bills receivable. On November 12, 1898, said Tallant Banking Company transferred to defendant certain of its assets, including the said note, and thereupon defendant assumed certain liabilities of the Tallant Banking Company, including the liability for the deposit to the credit of A. B. Perry & Co. The said deposit account was thereafter kept by defendant with the said A. B. Perry & Co., but said Alvan B. Perry had no individual account with defendant at any time. After the transfer by said Tallant Banking Company to defendant, it sent notices of interest due on said note to Alvan B. Perry, and the interest on said note was paid by said Perry from time to time. After the transfer of the said account to defendants, it gave to said A. B. Perry & Co. a passbook inscribed "A. B. Perry & Co.," and the account was so kept on defendant's books, and it dealt with said copartnership as such—received its deposits and honored its checks—without prosecuting any inquiry as to who were the members constituting such copartnership. On February 16, 1899, the day of Alvan B. Perry's death, and without any authority or request from Alvan B. Perry or from A. B. Perry & Co., defendant charged up to the account of A. B. Perry & Co. the sum of $1,604.96, being the amount due upon the said note. Defendant claims that it had the right to pay the said note from the amount due on the said account of A. B. Perry & Co., for the reason that it did not know that anyone other than Alvan B. Perry was a member of or interested in said firm, and for the further reason that the corporation of W. P. Fuller & Co. could not legally enter into a copartnership with an individual, and that for this reason there was no copartnership.

If the money on deposit in the name of A. B. Perry & Co. belonged to a copartnership doing business under the name and style of A. B. Perry & Co., it is clear that defendant had no right to appropriate the deposit for the purpose of paying the individual indebtedness of A. B. Perry. It had made the loan to Perry individually, and had taken his unsecured note for the amount. It knew that it had two different names on its books, and that one, at least apparently, was that of a firm or association of individuals. The words "A. B. Perry & Co." were sufficient, upon their face, to put defendant upon inquiry. And that defendant knew it was dealing with a different person from Alvan B. Perry further appears from the fact that in November, 1898, it loaned the sum of $3,000 to and took the note of A. B. Perry & Co. for the amount. This note was paid by A. B. Perry & Co., and not by Alvan B. Perry. Defendant had no agreement whereby it had any lien or claim on the funds of A. B. Perry & Co. It received the deposit under that name. It cannot, of its own volition, repudiate the obligation by showing that the name was that of something having no legal existence. It is not necessary to decide the question as to whether or not a corporation can legally enter into a copartnership. It will be sufficient to decide that question when it is properly raised by someone who is interested and who has the right to raise it. There is no doubt, in case this suit had been brought by the copartnership during the lifetime of Perry, the defendant would have been estopped from denying that it was a copartnership. Defendant, having voluntarily treated it as such for the purpose of receiving its deposits and business, will be compelled to treat it as such for the purpose of repaying such deposits. Defendant's attorneys, in their closing brief, very frankly and fairly admitted this proposition, and say: "If Perry were alive, and had joined with W. P. Fuller & Co. as plaintiff, or had joined in an assignment of this claim, we frankly and fully admit that the question as to the power of this corporation to enter into a copartnership would not be before the court." And such was the ruling of this court in Yancy v. Morton, 94 Cal. 561, 29 Pac. 1111, where it was held that the owner of a building was estopped from setting up the illegality of the formation of a partnership by two corporations which furnished materials for the building, in an action to foreclose a lien therefor by an assignee of the partnership.

The defendant was therefore estopped during the lifetime of Perry from making any such defense as it is attempting to make here. It was so estopped at the time it made the transfer of the partnership account to the payment of the note of Alvan B. Perry. Then the question arises as to whether or not such estoppel continued after the death of Perry, and as to his surviving partner. The heirs and administrators of Perry succeed to his rights, and therefore are in privity with him: Bigelow on Estoppel, 5th ed., pp. 148, 347. In such case the estoppel applies to the privies in estate: Bigelow on Estoppel, 5th ed., pp. 142, 143. The corporation of W. P. Fuller & Co. was in fact a copartner, whether it was so in a legal sense or not. It had acted as such. Perry, in his lifetime, by express agreement, had made it such. He was estopped by his agreement from denying that it was such. Defendant had, by its conduct, treated it as such. Therefore, when Perry died the corporation was a surviving partner in fact. Whether it was so legally or otherwise, it certainly was so as a matter of fact. As such surviving partner, Code of Civil Procedure, section 1585, gave it the right "to continue in possession of the partnership, and to settle its business . . . and account with the executor or administrator, and pay over such balances as may from time to time be payable to him in right of the decedent." The estoppel continued after the death of Perry as to his heirs and legal representatives, as to the condition of affairs that had been brought about by the surviving partner, and to any balance that might be due deceased from the assets of the copartnership. On the other hand, the assets were liable, for the partnership debts. They were also liable for any balance due the surviving partner. The money left in the bank may have been the money of the surviving partner. Its acts were not ultra vires as to the deceased partner, nor as to defendant. None of its stockholders appear to have objected to its business transactions with deceased. In Block v. Fitzburg R. R., 139 Mass. 310, 1 N. E. 348, where two railroad corporations formed a company called the Despatch Company, and made a contract, as such company, to carry plaintiff's goods from Boston to Chicago, it was held that they were liable to plaintiff for damage to his goods. In the opinion it is said: "They are, so far as plaintiff is concerned, partners, and liable jointly and severally for any loss or damage to his goods between Boston and Chicago." In French v. Donohue, 29 Minn. 111, 12 N. W. 354, where an association or corporation and a third person had assumed to enter into partnership, and jointly transacted business together, it was held that they might recover, by reason of their joint interest, upon obligations made to them in their partnership names. The court said: "The defendant has obligated himself to whomsoever the name represents, and he will not now be permitted to repudiate such obligations or to deny the legal competency of said partnership, in so far as it may be necessary to enforce the same." A corporation may enforce an accounting in a partnership of which it is a member: Standard Oil Co. v. Scofield, 16 Abb. N. C. 372. It cannot avoid a liability for the debt of a firm, in which firm it is a member, on the ground that it had no power to become a partner: Cameron v. First Nat. Bank of Decatur (Tex. Civ. App. 1896), 34 S. W. 178. Where a corporation does in fact enter into a copartnership, it must account to the other partner, even though it had no legal right to enter into the copartnership: Boyd v. American Carbon Black Co. et al., 182 Pa. 206, 37 Atl. 937. It is therein said: "While public policy demands that the court should declare such contracts by corporations unlawful, and that they will make no decree which prolongs their life, in fact, for a single day, every principle of equity demands that the corporation receiving a benefit from such contract shall account for what it has received from him who has fully performed. The contract is not malum in se, but malum prohibitum. It was illegal, but not iniquitous. If the corporation has had the benefit of $15,000 paid by Boyd for the construction of the second plant, has received the proceeds of the manufactured product, and has used and continues to use his gas, it ought to and must account. It is wholly immaterial whether the partnership be declared dissolved because it is illegal to carry it on, or it be declared at an end, in fact, because of want of power on part of the corporation to enter into it. In either case the plaintiff is entitled to his property in possession of defendants, and whatever money they may have received, more than their share.'' The reasoning of the above case, which holds that a corporation is liable to an accounting as a partner, would make it liable to an accounting as a surviving partner. To be such, it must necessarily have the right to collect the assets. In this case the partnership was dissolved by the death of Perry. No decree of court could more effectually have dissolved it. Its affairs must be settled. Its creditors, if any, must be paid. The surviving corporate partner must settle with legal representatives of the deceased. To do so, it must be allowed to maintain this action.

The judgment is affirmed.

Ex parte LAPIQUE.

Cr. No. 1040; June 9, 1903.

72 Pac. 995.

Habeas Corpus.—A Petition for Habeas Corpus on the ground that the petitioner has been committed without reasonable cause, which does not set forth the evidence taken at the preliminary examination, is insufficient.

McFARLAND, J.—The petition herein for a writ of habeas corpus is on the alleged ground that the petitioner is held under a commitment issued without reasonable or probable cause; but the petition does not set forth the evidence taken at the preliminary examination, and is therefore insufficient: Ex parte Walpole, 84 Cal. 584, 24 Pac. 308. The petition is denied.

PORCO v. STATE BOARD OF BARBER EXAMINERS.

S. F. No. 3259; June 24, 1903.

73 Pac. 168.

License—Mandamus to Issue.—Where an Action was Brought against the State Board of Barber Examiners to compel the issuance of a license to plaintiff, and during the pendency of the suit the act creating such board was repealed, and no successor in interest or obligation was provided for, the action abated.

APPEAL from Superior Court, Napa County; E. D. Ham, Judge.

Mandamus by John Porco against the State Board of Barber Examiners. From a judgment in favor of plaintiff, defendant appeals. Dismissed.

Tirey L. Ford, attorney general, George A. Sturtevant, deputy attorney general, and R. C. Van Fleet for appellant; George E. Caldwell for respondent.

SMITH, C.—This is an appeal from a judgment in a suit for mandamus, requiring the defendant to issue to plaintiff a barber's license, as required by act of February 20, 1901, "To regulate the practice of barbering," etc.: Stats. 1901, p. 15, c. 25. But the act in question has been repealed by an act of the legislature approved March 16, 1903 (Stats. 1903, p. 166, c. 151), which took effect on its passage; and the defendant has thus ceased to exist, leaving no successor in interest or in obligation. It follows that the action, which "is deemed to be pending . . . . until its final determination on appeal" (Code Civ. Proc., sec. 1049), was thereby abated (Code Civ. Proc., sec. 385; Bouvier's Law Dictionary, "Abatement," p. 6; Green v. Watkins, 6 Wheat. (19 U. S.) 261, 5 L. Ed. 256), and, with it, the judgment and this appeal. The appeal should therefore be dismissed, without costs (Estate of Baby, 87 Cal. 200, 22 Am. St. Rep. 239, 25 Pac. 405; Estate of Shaver, 131 Cal. 221, 63 Pac. 340; Bienenfeld v. Fresno Milling Co., 82 Cal. 426, 22 Pac. 1113), and we so advise.

We concur: Gray, C.; Haynes, C.

PER CURIAM.—For the reasons given in the foregoing opinion the appeal herein is dismissed.

In re SANFORD'S ESTATE.

S. F. No. 2797; July 17, 1903.

73 Pac. 466.

Appeal—Remittitur—Motion to Recall.—May 3d an appeal was dismissed. May 25th a remittitur was issued. June 9th the remittitur was filed in the lower court. August 11th notice of motion to recall remittitur was served. Affidavit of moving counsel stated that he left the city May 2d, and was absent nearly two months, and on his return one of the members of the firm associated with him in the case, and who had taken part in the appeal, was, and till the filing of the motion continued to be, absent from the city, and that he was unable to consult with him. Held, that excuse for not making the motion within the time fixed by law was not shown, so that the motion would be denied.

On motion to recall remittitur.   Denied.

LORIGAN, J.—An appeal was taken to this court in the above estate from an order denying a motion for a new trial of the application for final distribution of the estate of said decedent. On the 3d of May, 1902, said appeal was by this court dismissed, and the remittitur therein issued on May 25, 1902, and filed in the superior court June 9, 1902. On August 11, 1902, counsel for appellant served notice that on September 8th thereafter he would move to recall said remittitur on various grounds specified therein. It will be observed from the recited dates that this application was made long after the expiration of the thirty days within which the court had control over its decision, and long after the decision became final. The moving counsel for appellant attempts to obviate the effect of this delay by a recital of facts in his affidavit accompanying the motion which he insists excuse it. He states therein that he left the city and county of San Francisco on May 2, 1902, and was absent from the city for nearly two months thereafter; that upon his return one of the members of the firm of attorneys associated with him in the case, and who had taken part in the appeal, was, and thereafter up to the time of the filing of said motion still continued, absent from the city and county of San Francisco; and that he was unable to consult with him as to what steps should be taken in this matter. Placing the most liberal construction upon this statement in the affidavit, it falls far short of showing any of that measure of diligence which the law requires to excuse him from the stringent application of the rule governing the recall of remittiturs. As above stated, the remittitur was issued on the 25th of May, 1902, and it is apparent from the affidavit that the affiant must have returned to the city and county of San Francisco at least as early as July 2, 1902, and as notice of the present motion was not served until the 11th of August, 1902, it is evident that there was a month intervening between the time of his return and the service of this motion, within which he did nothing, and for which inaction he nowhere in his affidavit accounts. His affidavit is equally silent as to where any member of the firm associated with him on the appeal was in the interval between the issuance of the remittitur and the notice of this present motion. It is nowhere stated that they were not in San Francisco during the two months that he was absent therefrom. It only states that upon his return he found that the particular member of the firm with whom he wished to consult was absent. Nor does it appear when the latter departed from the city. Non constat but that he was in the city during the entire time while the affiant was away, knew of the issuance of the remittitur, and deemed it inadvisable to petition for a rehearing, or to make such motion as is now made here. It is presumed that each attorney is fully advised as to all proceedings had in cases in which he is interested, and that presumption will be indulged in until the contrary is shown. The showing here in no manner overcomes that presumption, and not only does not show sufficient excuse for the nonpresentation of this motion earlier, but, to the contrary, shows an unnecessary delay of over a month, as far as the attorney making the affidavit is concerned, and fails to show that his associates were not advised of the issuance of the remittitur, or that they had not ample time and opportunity to present this motion within the time allowed by law.

There appearing no sufficient excuse, or in fact any excuse, why this motion was not made within the time fixed by law, the motion to recall the remittitur is denied.

We concur: Beatty, C. J.; McFarland, J.; Shaw, J.; Van Dyke, J.; Henshaw, J.

O'NEIL v. McLENNAN.

Sac. No. 1085; August 4, 1903.

73 Pac. 576.

Appeal—Record.—In the Absence of a Bill of Exceptions and statement in the record, the contentions that the court never duly appointed a receiver and did not acquire jurisdiction to order a sale cannot be considered.

Appeal—Judgment-roll.—Orders, Stipulations and an Oath and account of a receiver in the transcript, not being authenticated, cannot be considered on appeal, being no part of the judgment-roll.

Appeal—Record.—Complaint cannot be Made on Appeal that the court made no disposition of a demurrer, the record not showing it was presented to the court.

APPEAL from Superior Court, Madera County; W. M. Conley, Judge.

Action by Timothy O'Neil against Alexander McLennan. From the judgment defendant appeals. Affirmed.

H. M. Owens and W. M. Gibson (T. C. West of counsel) for appellant; Robert L. Hargrave for respondent.

COOPER, C.—This action was brought to dissolve the partnership existing between the plaintiff and the defendant, to have a receiver appointed, the partnership property sold, and the debts paid. On the eighteenth day of November, 1901, after trial, the court found the allegations of the complaint to be true, made its decree dissolving the partnership, and settling the accounts of the copartners and the account of the receiver. This appeal is from the judgment. It is not claimed that the judgment is not the legal conclusion from the facts found, nor is it claimed that the findings are not supported by the evidence. The sole errors relied upon are, that the court never duly appointed the receiver in the action, that it did not acquire jurisdiction to order the sale of a certain leasehold interest, and that no disposition was ever made of defendant's demurrer to the complaint. As to the first two propositions, there is no bill of exceptions and no statement in the record, and therefore we cannot say as to the correctness of the contentions of de-

11

fendants. We must presume in favor of the regularity of the proceedings of the lower court. If there was a receiver, we must presume that he was regularly appointed, took the proper oath, and gave the proper bond. If a leasehold interest was sold, we must presume that the proper proceedings were taken for the order of sale. The burden is upon the party who claims error to show it affirmatively. In the transcript there is printed what purports to be certain orders, stipulations, oath of receiver, and receiver's account, but they are in no way authenticated, and we cannot consider them. They are no part of the judgment-roll (Code Civ. Proc., sec. 670), and hence cannot be considered (Esert v. Glock, 137 Cal. 533, 70 Pac. 479). There is printed in the transcript a demurrer of defendant, "filed June 15, 1900," but there is nothing to show that it was ever served upon plaintiff or called to the attention of the court. We must presume that it was abandoned by defendant. A copy of an order made on demurrer is a part of the judgment-roll. Here there is no copy of such order. We are told in defendant's brief that no disposition was made of the demurrer by the court. If this be true, it must be shown by defendant that he presented it, or in some way called the court's attention to it. A party will not be allowed to file a demurrer, and print it in the transcript, and claim here that it was error for the court not to pass upon it, unless he shows that he presented it.

The judgment should be affirmed.

We concur: Gray, C.; Haynes, C.

PER CURIAM.—For the reasons given in the foregoing opinion the judgment is affirmed.

GOLDSCHMIDT v. MAIER et al.

L. A. No. 1050; September 14, 1903.

73 Pac. 984.

Trustee—Action Against Cotrustee.—A Trustee cannot Maintain an action to recover possession of the trust property from his cotrustee, nor can he maintain an action for conversion on the sale of the trust property by the cotrustee when the trustees are authorized to sell the property.

Trover and Conversion.—A Leasehold Estate is not the Subject of an action for conversion.

Trust.—A Debtor Agreed to Transfer His Property to His Two Creditors, who agreed to take possession and sell the same, and turn over to the debtor any balance after the payment of the debts and expenses. The property was transferred to one of the creditors, who accepted the same as trustee for himself and the other creditor, and sold the property for a sum insufficient to reimburse himself for expenses and to pay any part of the claim of the other creditor. Held, that the other creditor, as beneficiary under the trust, could not maintain an action in trover for damages, his remedy being in equity for an accounting.

Trust.—Where, in Trover by a Beneficiary Against the Trustee under a trust authorizing a sale for the benefit of creditors, the court properly decided that trover could not be maintained, the admission of testimony of witnesses as to their failure to conduct the assigning debtor's business at a profit was not prejudicial error.

Trust.—A Finding That a Creditor had Made a Written Demand on another creditor, who had accepted the possession of the debtor's property as trustee for the creditors, to share pro rata in the distribution of the proceeds of any sale, and to be consulted as to the management of the property, and that the trustee did not comply with the demand, sufficiently covers an allegation in the former creditor's complaint that the trustee "refused to recognize the rights" of the former creditor, "and took exclusive possession of the property."

APPEAL from Superior Court, Los Angeles County; W. F. Fitzgerald, Judge.

Action by Max Goldschmidt against Joseph Maier and another. From a judgment for defendants, plaintiff appeals. Affirmed.

McKinley & Graff for appellant; Louis Gottschalk and A. W. Hutton for respondents.

PER CURIAM.—The plaintiff appeals from the judgment and from an order denying a new trial. In May, 1897, McInnis Bros. were the owners of a liquor saloon conducted in a leased building in Los Angeles, and, as found by the court, were then indebted to the copartners of Goldschmidt Bros. in the sum of $1,115.36, and to said corporation in the sum of $1,500; that said McInnis Bros., for the purpose of paying said indebtedness, proposed to said Goldschmidt Bros. and the defendants that they would transfer to them

all their interest in said property and business; said creditors, Goldschmidt Bros. and the defendants, should take
possession, and either sell the same or do the best they could
therewith, in order to pay said debt; that, if any balance
remained after paying said debts and the expense of carrying on the business to the time of sale, it should be paid
to McInnis Bros., but, if less was realized, the proceeds
should be divided pro rata between Goldschmidt Bros. and
said corporation in proportion to the amount of said indebtedness; that both of said parties consented thereto, but said
proposal was not then carried out, but McInnis Bros. remained in possession about ten days, carrying on said business on their own account, and then delivered possession to
said corporation defendant, which accepted the same as trustee for Goldschmidt Bros. and itself to sell said property, and apply the proceeds to the payment of the said
respective claims, and neither the plaintiff nor Goldschmidt
Bros., whose claims were assigned to plaintiff, obtained or
had possession of said property at any time. Defendant
Maier was the lessee of the building in which said saloon business was conducted, McInnis Bros. paying the lessor the rent.
No sale of the property and business was made until April
1, 1899, when it was sold for $1,775, which was insufficient
to reimburse said corporation for the expenses of carrying
on the business and to pay any part of plaintiff's claim.
On May 11, 1897, plaintiff's assignors gave notice to the
corporation that it held said property as trustee for the
purposes hereinbefore stated, and demanded that they be
consulted as to the management of the property; that the
corporation refused to do so, and that neither plaintiff nor
his assignors produced any purchaser or claimed an accounting, or made any application to have said corporation declared a trustee, or to be recognized as cotrustees; that the
value of said property and business, exclusive of the lease,
did not, with the goodwill, exceed $500; and as to plain-
tiff's allegation that defendants took exclusive possession,
and converted said property to their own use, the court
found that neither of the defendants converted any part of
the property; and as a conclusion of law the court found
that plaintiff could not maintain this action for the alleged
conversion, and is not entitled to judgment against the defendants, or either of them, but that said conclusion is

without prejudice to the right of plaintiff to maintain an action for an accounting, and that this action be dismissed, and entered judgment accordingly. Plaintiff moved for a new trial upon a statement of the case, and his motion was denied, and on appeal specifies several errors of law in ruling upon evidence, a failure to find upon certain issues, and also that the evidence is insufficient to justify certain findings.

We do not think it necessary to consider in detail the sufficiency of the evidence to justify the findings specified by appellant. As to each of them there was a material conflict in the evidence. Nor is it contended that the findings are not sufficient to support the judgment, though it is argued that a different judgment might and should have been rendered upon the same facts. It is said that the plaintiff had two remedies for the wrongful acts of the defendants—that they could have brought an action for an accounting, or an action for damages for the wrongful acts of the defendants; that, as defendants refused to manage the property according to the terms of the trust, plaintiff had the right to treat the acts of the defendant as a tort, and recover damages therefor. But appellant further says: "The Goldschmidts occupied a double relation to defendants; that both they and defendants were trustees and beneficiaries for themselves and each other." The possession of one trustee, however, is the possession of all, and each is entitled to the possession to the same extent, and the character of the possession of each is like that of copartners, joint tenants, or tenants in common: See Balch v. Jones, 61 Cal. 234. Prior to the sale made by defendants, neither the plaintiff nor his assignors could have maintained an action in claim and delivery to recover possession of the trust property, or any part of it, from their cotrustee; and, as the trustees were authorized to sell the property, a sale by defendants was not a conversion. Appellant's contention that the evidence was sufficient to maintain an action in trover cannot be sustained. If any additional reasons for our conclusion were required, it may be added that the property delivered by McInnis Bros. in trust included the business of said firm conducted in a building occupied under a lease which included certain personal property of the lessor, and a leasehold of real estate is not the subject of an action

of trover.   As beneficiaries under a trust authorizing a sale,
the Goldschmidt Bros. could not maintain an action in
trover for damages.   It is true a trustee may not use the
influence or power which his position gives him to obtain
any advantage over his beneficiary, and section 2234 of the
Civil Code provides, "Every violation of the preceding provisions of this article is a fraud against the beneficiary of
the trust," and fraud in the administration of a trust is
peculiarly cognizable in equity.

The question whether defendants were authorized to sell
the property on credit might be material in an action for
an accounting, but here there is no allegation that a sale
was made.   The allegation is that defendants took exclusive
possession, and converted the property and business to their
own use; that the value thereof was $3,000, and plaintiff's
damages $1,400.   None of the several cases cited by appel-
lant have any application to this case.   As to what constitutes conversion, in its general application, there is no controversy.   The case of People v. Van Ness, 79 Cal. 88, 12
Am. St. Rep. 134, 21 Pac. 554, was the case of a state officer
who retained certain moneys received by him as such officer
under a claim of right; but the state was not a cestui que
trust or beneficiary under a trust, but a principal, and the
officer its agent.   Another was that of a factor who had disregarded the instructions of his principal.   Others were
bailees for hire.   In all, the plaintiffs had the legal title.
Counsel quote largely from Chetwood v. California National
Bank, 113 Cal. 414, 45 Pac. 704.   In that case Chetwood, the
plaintiff, was a stockholder in the bank, and brought the
action—the corporation refusing to sue—to recover a large
sum for the use and benefit of the corporation.   The complaint was in form and was entitled a bill in equity for an
accounting and settlement of a trust, but contained "nothing more than a charge ex delicto against certain directors
for a breach and nonperformance of their duties" by the
three directors who constituted the executive committee, who,
not regarding their duties, "and contriving together to injure and deceive the said corporation, neglected and omitted,
etc.," and prayed that the defendants Thomas, Thompson
and Wilson be held to an accounting of their said trust,
that they restore the sum of $400,000, etc.   The court made
an "order of judgment" for the plaintiff, but the court was

unable to determine the amount, and ordered a reference to take proof thereof, etc. Pending further proceedings under the "order of judgment," the plaintiff settled with two of the three directors for the sum of $27,500, which was paid, and caused a formal judgment of dismissal to be entered as to those two defendants, and prosecuted the action against the third director, and a judgment against him for the remainder of the amount found by the referee ($139,419) was rendered, from which the appeal was taken. The complaint charged the three defendants constituting the executive committee with a conspiracy to injure and deceive the corporation, and, having settled with two of the conspirators and received from them $27,500, and dismissed the action as to them, the court held that the plaintiff could not prosecute the action against the remaining conspirator, and said: "For these wrongful acts defendants are liable in tort, and the fact that there might be another cause of action ex contractu is a matter entirely apart." In the case at bar a trust is alleged, as well as a tort for the conversion of the property, and the trial court found against the plaintiff as to the conversion, and we think the evidence, though conflicting, is sufficient to support the finding. And the court further found that McInnis Bros. delivered possession of said saloon to said corporation, which accepted the same as trustee for the benefit of itself and plaintiff's assignors, to manage and sell the same, and apply the proceeds to the payment of the claim of the said corporation and of the plaintiff. This finding clearly shows that the proceeding should have been in equity for an accounting, and that a sale under the trust was not a conversion.

It is further said by appellant that the court erred in permitting various witnesses to testify as to their failure to conduct the business of the saloon at a profit; but, in view of our conclusion that the judgment of the court should be affirmed upon grounds already stated, the exclusion of the evidence would not have benefited the plaintiff, nor did its reception injure him.

Lastly, it is contended by appellant that the court failed to find upon the following allegation of paragraph 7 of his complaint: "That defendants refused to recognize the rights of Goldschmidt Bros. in the business and property and the management thereof, and took exclusive possession of the

property and business." This allegation is fully covered by
the sixth finding, which recites the substance of the written
demand of Goldschmidt Bros. of May 11, 1897, to the effect
that they were entitled to share pro rata with the corporation in the distribution of the proceeds of any sale, and to
be consulted before any sale be made, and offered to pay
their share of the expenses, "and also demanded to be consulted in all matters relating to the management of said
property, and that said brewery did not comply with the
terms of said notice, and refused to do so." We think this
finding quite sufficient to cover said allegation.

The judgment and order appealed from are affirmed.

WEIS v. CAIN et al.

L. A. No. 1027; September 17, 1903.

73 Pac. 980.

Summons—Publication.—Where an Affidavit for the Service
of summons by publication stated that the summons had been placed
in the hands of the sheriff of the county for service, that the sheriff
had returned the same with his return indorsed thereon to the effect
that he could not find the defendant within the county, and that
affiant did not know the residence of defendant, etc., it was sufficient
to justify the court in ordering service by publication.[1]

---

[1] Cited and followed in Roberts v. Jacob, 154 Cal. 308, 97 Pac.
672, where the affidavit showed that the plaintiff had made inquiries
in all conceivable ways to inform himself of the defendants' whereabouts.

Cited in People v. Wrinn, 143 Cal. 13, 76 Pac. 647, together with
Rue v. Quinn, 137 Cal. 651, 66 Pac. 216, 70 Pac. 732, as sustaining the
jurisdiction of a court in ordering publication of summons upon the
sheriff's return of non est without first scrutinizing the diligence
exercised in seeking the address of the defendant in the summons
named.

Cited in the note in 37 L. R. A., N. S., 209, on character of
inquiry as to whereabouts of party necessary to sustain constructive
service of process.

Cited and followed, along with numerous other California cases,
in Cargile v. Silsbee, 148 Cal. 260, 82 Pac. 1045, a suit to set aside
a judgment annulling a certificate for the purchase of state school

APPEAL from Superior Court, San Diego County; J. W. Ballard, Judge.

Action by H. F. Weis against Ben P. Cain and others. From an order setting aside a judgment in favor of plaintiff, he appeals. Reversed.

Stearns & Sweet for appellant; Mills & Hizar for respondent.

GRAY, C.—Action to quiet title. Plaintiff had judgment, and nearly five years later the defendant and respondent, Mrs. Goss moved to set aside the judgment on the ground that there was no proper service of summons. The service was by publication, and the particular points made on the motion were that the affidavit for publication was insufficient, and that the summons had once been placed in the hands of the sheriff, and by him returned to the clerk of the court, and no other summons was issued. The motion was granted, and the plaintiff appeals from the order.

The points urged on this appeal by appellant and respondent respectively were all considered and reconsidered by this court in the very recent case of Rue v. Quinn, 137 Cal. 651, 66 Pac. 216, 70 Pac. 732, and there determined favorably to the contentions of this appellant. The only difference between the two cases is that in the Rue case the affidavit for publication contained a statement not to be found in the corresponding affidavit in the case before us, which statement reads as follows: "I have also made inquiry of all other persons from whom I could expect to obtain information as to the residence or whereabouts of each of the said defendants." In all other respects the affidavits in the two cases are entirely similar, and the difference of this added statement in

lands, on the ground that the judgment had been obtained by fraud on a fraudulent affidavit for publication of summons.

Cited and followed, along with many decisions to similar effect, in Shepard v. Mace, 148 Cal. 272, 82 Pac. 1046, the court merely referring to these without further comment, as though the point needed none.

Cited and followed, together with other cases, notably Rue v. Quinn, 137 Cal. 651, 66 Pac. 216, 70 Pac. 732, in Emory v. Kipp, 154 Cal. 85, 129 Am. St. Rep. 147, 19 L. R. A., N. S., 983, 97 Pac. 18, the plaintiff's interest having been acquired from the plaintiff in Rue v. Quinn, and concluded by the decision in that case.

the one is not important. Without that statement it can still be reasonably said of the affidavit in this case, as was said in that case: "The facts set forth therein afford some evidence of diligence on the part of the plaintiff to find the defendant, and also that, notwithstanding such diligence, she could not be found within the state; and although the facts are based upon information of others, it cannot be said that the affidavit is of no legal effect to authorize the court to be satisfied therefrom, or that it did not have a tendency to establish both the fact of diligence and of a failure to find the defendant."

On the authority of Rue v. Quinn, supra, we advise that the order appealed from be reversed.

I concur: Chipman, C.

For the reasons given in the foregoing opinion the order appealed from is reversed: Shaw, J.; Angellotti, J.; Van Dyke, J.

POLK v. BOARD OF EDUCATION OF CITY OF SANTA BARBARA.

L. A. No. 1168; October 9, 1903.

74 Pac. 47.

Schools—Employment of Teacher—Proof of Contract.—A contract of a school board employing plaintiff as a teacher for the ensuing year at a salary of $1,100 is proved by minutes of the board showing she was elected teacher for the ensuing year, a letter from one of the members to her informing her of her election, a letter from her to him accepting the employment, and proof that for several years previously she had been employed by the board at a salary of $1,100, and that, in pursuance of the employment for the year in question, she entered on her duties and taught for the first four months, receiving the due proportion of the salary at that rate.

APPEAL from Superior Court, Santa Barbara County; W. S. Day, Judge.

Action by Mary Polk against the board of education of the city of Santa Barbara. Judgment for plaintiff. Defendant appeals. Affirmed.

Henley C. Booth for appellant; Richards & Carrier for respondent.

SHAW, J.—This action is, in all respects but one, similar to the action of Hancock v. Board of Education, 140 Cal. 554, 74 Pac. 44, this day decided, and what is said in that case applies equally to this case. This also is an appeal by the defendant from a judgment in favor of the plaintiff, the evidence being before the court by virtue of a bill of exceptions. The only particular in which the claim of the appellant in this case differs from the other is in relation to the contract under which the plaintiff claims. The contention is that the contract alleged is not proved. The allegation is that the contract entered into by the Santa Barbara high school district was a contract whereby the board employed the plaintiff as teacher in the high school for the school year beginning in September, 1899, at the annual salary of $1,100. In proof of this allegation, the plaintiff introduced in evidence the minutes of the board of August 8, 1899, showing that the plaintiff was elected teacher of English for the ensuing year, a letter from one of the members to the plaintiff informing her of her election, and a letter from the plaintiff to the same member in substance accepting the employment. In addition to this, there was proof that the plaintiff had been employed for several years previously by the same board at an annual salary of $1,100, and that in pursuance of the employment for this year she entered upon her duties, and taught for the first four months of the year in question, receiving the due proportion of the salary at the same rate. The liability of the defendant in this action necessarily depends on the liability of the board or organization to which it succeeded. If there was a contract by which that body was bound to continue the employment of the plaintiff during the school year, it necessarily follows that the board of education which succeeded to its obligations is also bound to the same extent. We think the evidence was sufficient to justify the findings of the court in that respect, and that the judgment is correct.

For the reasons here given, as well as those in the case of Hancock v. Board of Education, the judgment is affirmed.

We concur: Angellotti, J.; Van Dyke, J.

In re DONNOLLY.

Cr. No. 1029; October 10, 1903.

74 Pac. 139.

Mandamus—Dismissal—Costs.—Where, After Submission of an application to compel a judge to settle a bill of exceptions, he signs it, the application will be dismissed, without costs.

Application for mandate by Charles Donnolly against William P. Lawlor, judge of the superior court of the city and county of San Francisco, to compel him to settle a bill of exceptions. Dismissed

H. W. Hutton for appellant; Thos. M. O'Connor for respondent.

SHAW, J.—This is an application for a writ of mandate to compel the judge of the court below to settle a bill of exceptions to be used on appeal by the petitioner, as defendant in the case of People of the State of California v. Charles Donnolly. Since the submission of the application for a mandate the transcript on appeal in the case of People v. Donnolly has been filed, showing that the bill of exceptions in question has been settled by the judge, and it is made a part of the record on appeal. In view of this fact, there is nothing remaining before the court for decision. It is therefore ordered that the petition be dismissed, without costs.

We concur: Van Dyke, J.; Angellotti, J.; McFarland; J.

In re MOSS.

Sac. No. 1120; November 4, 1903.

74 Pac. 546.

Guardian—Appeal.—Where a Guardian Ad Litem, After Taking an appeal, failed to file a bill of exceptions or statement on appeal, and did not request the clerk of the trial court to certify any transcript of the record on appeal, and none was filed, the appeal will be dismissed.

Guardian.—Where an Appeal in a Proceeding to Appoint a guardian for an incompetent, tried by his guardian ad litem, was taken by the incompetent himself, it was subject to dismissal on his application, on notice to his attorneys.

APPEAL from Superior Court, San Joaquin County; Joseph H. Budd, Judge.

Proceedings for the appointment of a guardian for the person and estate of William S. Moss, an alleged incompetent. From an order appointing a guardian of his person and estate, the alleged incompetent and his guardian ad litem appeal. Dismissed.

Nicol & Orr for appellants; Budd & Thompson for respondents.

PER CURIAM.—Two appeals were taken in this matter from an order appointing a guardian of the person and estate of said Moss, one by Moss himself, the other by his guardian ad litem. The notice of appeal by the guardian ad litem was served and filed November 13, 1897, and an undertaking on appeal was filed the same day. No bill of exceptions or statement on appeal has been settled or filed by said guardian, nor has he requested the clerk of the lower court to certify any transcript of the record on appeal, and none is on file here. Respondents move to dismiss that appeal for failure to file a transcript on appeal within the time prescribed. The motion to dismiss the appeal taken by Moss himself is based upon his written request, after notice to his attorneys thereof, that his appeal be dismissed. No appearance was made by the attorneys for appellants at the hearing of these motions, though due notice was given them thereof, and as it appears that said appeals should both be dismissed—one for failure to file a transcript, the other on appellants' application—it is so ordered: Lorigan, J.; McFarland, J.; Angellotti, J.; Van Dyke, J.; Henshaw, J.

In re BILL'S ESTATE.

BILLS et al. v. FULLER.

L. A. No. 1478; November 24, 1903.

74 Pac. 704.

New Trial.—On Appeal from an Order Granting a new trial, the supreme court has no jurisdiction to reverse the judgment.

APPEAL from Superior Court, Los Angeles County.

Proceedings by Joseph B. Fuller for the probate of the will of Anna May Bills, deceased. From an order granting a new trial, Robert John Bills and another appeal. Reversed, and previous order reversing judgment vacated and remittitur recalled.

Isidore B. Dockweiler for appellants; Bower & Hutchinson for respondent.

PER CURIAM.—This is an appeal from an order granting a new trial. In pursuance of an agreement of compromise, by which the controversy between the parties to the appeal has been settled, the respondent has stipulated that the order appealed from may be reversed. By inadvertence, the court, upon the presentation of the stipulation, made and entered an order reversing the judgment. This order was, of course, nugatory, not only because it was inadvertently made, but because, in the absence of an appeal from the judgment, we had no jurisdiction to reverse it. Nevertheless a remittitur thereon has been issued and sent to the superior court. It is therefore ordered that said remittitur be recalled, and the order reversing the judgment vacated. It is further ordered, in pursuance of the stipulation heretofore filed, that the order granting a new trial be, and the same is hereby, reversed. Remittitur forthwith.

McCAUGHEY v. McDUFFIE et al.

L. A. No. 1358; December 2, 1903.

74 Pac. 751.

Mortgage—Deed Absolute.—Where Plaintiff's Land was Conveyed to M. as security for a loan, to be conveyed by the latter to W., or his order, on repayment of the amount—the agreement being for plaintiff's benefit—evidence held not to support a finding that the reconveyance was conditioned on plaintiff's paying W. a certain additional sum.

Mortgage—Deed Absolute—Strict Foreclosure.—Where a conveyance of land, absolute in form, is intended as a mortgage to secure a loan, a decree of strict foreclosure, vesting title in the grantee upon nonpayment within a specified time, and without a foreclosure sale, will not be made.

APPEAL from Superior Court, Santa Barbara County; W. S. Day, Judge.

Action by Ann Elizabeth McCaughey against M. B. McDuffie and another. Judgment for defendants and plaintiff appeals. Reversed.

Wm. G. Griffith for appellant; C. A. Storke for respondents.

CHIPMAN, C.—Plaintiff sets forth two causes of action: First. That during all the times mentioned in her complaint she was the owner and in possession of certain real estate situate in Santa Barbara county; that on November 9, 1900, defendant McDuffie loaned her $2,000, which she promised to repay, with interest at ten per cent per annum, on or before November 6, 1901, to secure which one Susan McCaughey, who had or claimed some interest in the land, conveyed the same to McDuffie by grant deed, which was, however, executed as, and intended to be, a mortgage, defeasible upon the condition of the payment of said indebtedness and interest; that, to carry out the intention of the parties, defendant McDuffie executed to defendant Wylie, an uncle of plaintiff, a contract in writing agreeing to convey said land to Wylie, or his order, upon the payment to said McDuffie of said sum and interest on or before November 6, 1901; that said contract was executed for, and intended to be for the benefit of, plaintiff, in respect of which Wylie acted as agent or trustee of plaintiff, and that the intent of said contract was that upon the payment of said sum to McDuffie the said land was to be reconveyed to plaintiff, all of which facts were well known to McDuffie; that on November 6, 1901, plaintiff tendered to McDuffie $2,200 in gold coin, and demanded a reconveyance of said land to plaintiff, and is still ready and willing and able to pay said defendant said sum, but said defendant refused to accept said money or to reconvey said land; that at the time plaintiff demanded of Wylie that he assign said contract to plaintiff, but he refused to do so; that said Susan McCaughey on November 5, 1901, conveyed said land to plaintiff by grant deed, which was duly recorded on November 7, 1901. As a second cause of action, that on November 9, 1900, defendant McDuffie was in possession of said land, claiming title thereto, and on said day executed a contract in writing by which he agreed to convey said land to defendant Wylie, or his order, upon the payment of $2,200. Allegations follow similar to those in the first cause of action as to the meaning of said contract and the intention of the parties thereto; tender of said sum by plaintiff, and demand upon defendants. The prayer is: (1) That said deed be declared to be a mortgage; that said contract be adjudged to be for the benefit of plaintiff and that said Wylie be required to assign said contract to plaintiff. (2) That plaintiff be allowed to redeem said land on payment of said sum to McDuffie. (3) That McDuffie be required to reconvey said land to plaintiff on such payment being made. (4) For the specific performance of said contract according to its intent and meaning, and for general relief.

Defendant McDuffie denies the allegations of the first cause of action. Answering the second cause of action, denies the alleged agency of Wylie, and avers that the only contract entered into with Wylie was the written contract, Exhibit A, set out in the answer, and referred to in the complaint, and denies that it was for the benefit of plaintiff; admits the tender alleged, and demand made for reconveyance, and refusal, but alleges willingness to convey in accordance with the contract, Exhibit A. This contract is signed by McDuffie alone, and purports to be between McDuffie and Wylie, and recites that on the payment to McDuffie of the sum of $2,000 on or before November 6, 1901, he agrees "to sell to Joseph Wylie, or order," the land in question, and recites as follows: "For this agreement and in consideration thereof, the said Joseph Wylie has paid to me the sum of $200, but said $200 is to be considered as no part of the purchase price of said lands but is simply the consideration for the option hereby given to him by me to purchase said lands. If said Joseph Wylie shall not pay to me on or before the 6th day of November, 1901, said sum of two thousand dollars, then this agreement to be void and of no effect, and I am not to be obliged to sell to him said land . . . . and time is especially agreed to be of the essence of this contract." Defendant McDuffie also filed a cross-complaint, asking to have his title quieted to the land as against all claims of plaintiff. Defendant Wylie, answering, denies plaintiff's ownership and possession of the land; denies that McDuffie loaned her any money; denies that the deed to McDuffie was intended to be a mortgage; admits the execution of the contract by McDuffie, but denies that it was for the benefit of plaintiff, or that defendant Wylie acted as plaintiff's agent or trustee, or that said land was to be reconveyed to plaintiff instead of Wylie; alleges payment by him of $200 to McDuffie for said agreement, and that said agreement was his own individual property; denies that plaintiff made the demand on him alleged in the complaint, or that he refused to assign the contract to plaintiff; alleges that he has expended the sum of $300 of his own money on and about said contract; as an affirmative defense, alleges that he purchased from McDuffie the right to buy said lands for the sum of $200, and, in addition, paid to said Susan McCaughey $100 for said right to buy the lands.

The court found that McDuffie was the owner of the land and in possession and entitled to possession at the commencement of the suit, subject, however, to said contract, Exhibit A; that plaintiff was not the owner, nor entitled to possession, and had no rights in said land, "except those provided for in said agreement and the trust relations existing between her and defendant Wylie"; "that defendant McDuffie did not loan to plaintiff any sum of money, nor did plaintiff borrow of said defendant any money." Other facts explanatory of the transaction as found by the court cannot well be abbreviated, and are as follows: "That prior to the ninth day of

12

November, 1900, plaintiff and one Susan McCaughey had
been the owners of the lands and premises described in the
amended complaint herein, but their interests had been on
said ninth day of November, 1900, foreclosed and sold, and
one Mary Pierce held the sheriff's deed of all the rights of
said plaintiff and said Susan McCaughey thereto; that on
said day the defendants herein, acting upon the request of
said Susan McCaughey, who, having obtained the consent of
Mary Pierce to convey the lands in consideration of the
amount which she had invested therein, undertook to put it
within the power of said Susan McCaughey or the plaintiff,
to whom she afterward conveyed her interest in said land, to
repurchase said land, and the said defendants and the plaintiff and Susan McCaughey then and there agreed that the
defendant M. B. McDuffie should buy the land for the sum of
$2,000, and that Susan McCaughey and the defendant Joseph
Wylie should pay to said Mary Pierce the excess over $2,000
necessary to procure the conveyance of her interest in said
lands; that, in consideration of the premises, and the further
consideration of $200 then and there secured by the defendant
Wylie, the defendant McDuffie agreed to convey to the said
Wylie or to his order on the payment to him of the sum of
$2,000 at any time prior to November 6, 1901, the said prem-
ises; that all the parties understood the transaction was made
and entered into for the benefit of the plaintiff and Susan
McCaughey, provided they should pay the said consideration
of $2,000, and the additional amounts advanced and expenses
incurred in the transaction; that said defendant McDuffie
purchased said lands for the sum of $2,000, taking absolute
deeds therefor from the said McCaugheys and Mary Pierce,
and, in consideration of $200 secured by said Wylie, agreed
to convey said premises to him or to his order on or before
November 6, 1901, upon the payment to him of the sum of
$2,000, all of which was with the consent of the plaintiff and
said Susan McCaughey; that, in addition to the payment of
the said $200 for the option of purchase, the defendant Wylie
furnished $50 of the excess paid to Mary Pierce as aforesaid,
and incurred a liability in said transaction of $25 for at-
torney's fees, $20 to Ramon Malo, a real estate agent, and
$15, expense of abstract.'' The court finds the tender to
McDuffie as alleged in the complaint, but that plaintiff did
not tender to Wylie his alleged additional expenses, and that

for this reason Wylie refused to consent to the execution of the deed by McDuffie, and for like reason the latter refused to make the deed; also that Wylie has not offered to pay the $2,000, the purchase price of said land. As conclusions of law, the court found that the plaintiff tendered McDuffie $2,000, and Wylie $310, within thirty days from March 25, 1902 (the findings are dated April 21, 1902), the date of the announcement of the decision from the bench, and thereupon she will be entitled to a deed to said land, failing in which the title be quieted in McDuffie "as against all claims of the parties hereto." Judgment passed for McDuffie November 1, 1902, quieting his title to the land "against the said plaintiff," but not against Wylie. The appeal is by plaintiff from the judgment, and from the order denying her motion for a new trial.

We do not deem it necessary to present the evidence in detail, nor does the view we take of the case require that the alleged errors of law committed in the course of the trial be passed upon. The court found, and the evidence was, that the McDuffie contract, Exhibit A, was made for the benefit of the plaintiff, and hence whatever right Wylie had under it plaintiff also had. So far as concerned McDuffie, he was tendered all he was entitled to by the terms of the agreement; and whether he held the absolute title to the land as purchaser, or only as security for the money used to redeem from Pierce, it was his duty to reconvey the land to plaintiff when tendered his money and interest, unless he was excused from doing so by the failure of plaintiff to pay Wylie what he (Wylie) claimed to have paid out in the transaction. It appears that to redeem from Pierce required $2,264.65. McDuffie furnished $2,000 of this amount. Mrs. McCaughey and plaintiff got together enough money to pay the balance ($264.65), of which Wylie testified that he furnished $50 of his own money. He also gave a chattel mortgage on two horses to secure the accruing interest on the contract with McDuffie; and the evidence is undisputed that he paid no money to McDuffie, although the contract recites the payment of $200. This $200 interest was tendered by plaintiff to McDuffie, so that, as between McDuffie and Wylie, nothing stood in the way of a deed from the former on payment of $2,000 tendered. Wylie testified that his deal with McDuffie was wholly on his own account, and that plaintiff had nothing to do with it, and had no interest in it or in the option contract. The evidence was clearly to the contrary, and the court found that the contract was made for plaintiff's benefit. Wylie testified: "There is no other agreement than that shown by the deed and that agreement. I don't think Mrs. McCaughey ever saw the original of that agreement before she made the deed in evidence here, dated November 9, 1900." McDuffie testified: "I did not know of any agreement between Mrs. McCaughey and Mr. Wylie in regard to a reconveyance, or in regard to any interest Mrs. McCaughey or Miss McCaughey might have in this transaction." Attorney Storke testified that he drew the rough draft of the contract, and showed it to McDuffie, who made some pencil changes in it; that the same day he also showed it to Mrs. McCaughey and Wylie. But whether this was before or after McDuffie had seen it and made some changes in it does not appear. Mr. Storke testified that it was before deeds had passed to McDuffie. He further testified: "I read her that agreement, and told her that those were the circumstances under which she could act, and she said, 'All right'; and Mr. Wylie came in, I think, at the same time. I wanted her to distinctly understand that the agreement was with Wylie," but that she could make any arrangement she chose with Wylie. It was after this that Wylie advanced $50 to make the amount to be paid to Pierce.

The agreement between McDuffie and Wylie is dated December 15, 1900, more than a month after the deeds were made to McDuffie by Pierce and the McCaugheys. There is evidence showing that, in addition to paying the $264.65 over and above the $2,000 paid to Pierce, plaintiff, through Mrs. McCaughey, was compelled to consent that McDuffie should also have the rentals of the land for the ensuing year; that Wylie was the tenant, and was in possession of the land as such, but the McCaugheys occupied the residence situated thereon. When the tender was made to McDuffie and Wylie to assign the contract to plaintiff, or authorize McDuffie to reconvey the land, Wylie made no demand for any advances, except the $50 claimed by him to have been advanced to Mrs. McCaughey to pay Pierce. The undisputed testimony on this point is by Attorney Griffith, as follows: "I asked Wylie if he had the contract—if he was ready to assign the contract to Ann McCaughey—and he said he was when the money was paid him that she owed him, pointing to Mrs. McCaughey.

He said it was $50. Mrs. McCaughey denied that she owed him $50. We could arrive at no agreement, so I turned to Mr. McDuffie, who was present, and said, 'You refuse, then, to make the deed, do you?' and he says, 'Yes, except on Mr. Wylie's order.' Mr. Wylie said he would not assign the contract to Ann McCaughey unless Mrs. McCaughey paid him the $50. We walked out then.'' He could have referred to no other money than the $50 loaned to Mrs. McCaughey before the deeds were made to McDuffie, and before the contract was signed.

There was some controversy between Wylie and Mrs. Mc-Caughey arising out of the collection by Wylie of the proceeds of the land for the year 1900, and she testified that all but $29 of this $50 had been paid, which fact is not contradicted. She testified (and we think the evidence bears her out) that what she owed Wylie was a matter apart from the agreement relating to the reconveyance of the land, and that Wylie had no right to refuse to assign the contract to plaintiff, and McDuffie had no right to refuse the amount due him.

The finding that Wylie, in addition to furnishing $50 to pay Pierce, ''incurred a liability in the transaction of $25 for attorney's fees, $20 to Ramon Malo, a real estate agent, and $15 expense of abstract,'' has no support in the evidence. The attorney's fee referred to was incurred to Mr. Storke by Mrs. McCaughey, and he presented his bill to her, and it has not been paid. Wylie testified that he ''engaged Mr. Storke for an attorney to go and see about getting the place back. I went into his office, and told him that I would pay him for his work.'' Mr. Storke, however, must have understood that Wylie was acting for Mrs. McCaughey, and that he was to look to her for the services rendered by him, as he presented his bill to her. He said nothing about this item in his testimony, and Wylie made no claim that anything was due him when the tender was made but the $50 referred to above. As to the $20 item to Ramon Malo, and $15 for an abstract, there is no evidence that Wylie incurred any such liability. Whatever services Malo rendered were at the instance of Mrs. Mc-Caughey, and there is no evidence to show who made the abstract, or who became liable for it. Witness Durfee was employed by Mrs. McCaughey to raise the money to pay McDuffie. He met plaintiff and Mrs. McCaughey to find out what money was necessary. He testified: ''At that time Mr. Wylie told me that there was $2,200 to be paid to Mr. Mc-

Duffie; there was $25 to be paid to Mr. Storke; there was $15 to be paid for an abstraction; there was $20 for Mr. Malo; then there was a compensation for getting the money. I made it $2,300, or that would leave $40, which would be for my commission and to pay Mr. Perkins. There was nothing said by the defendant Wylie at that time about any money owing him by Mrs. McCaughey. . . . . Mr. Wylie stated that the items given were all there was; that, 'If there is any little business between me and the McCaugheys, that is our business. That has nothing to do with this.' On the 6th of November, 1901 (the expiration of the option), Mr Wylie met me on the street, and told me that there was about $50 that he wanted out of it. That was the first I knew that he wanted anything." There is nothing in the evidence to warrant the finding that Wylie had incurred any liability for these items, or that he had a lien on the property, through the McDuffie option, to secure payment. As the money was being raised for plaintiff's benefit, and to redeem this land, the inference is that the liability, if any, was hers.

When Wylie made the contract with McDuffie, it was for the benefit of plaintiff, and the option was given to Wylie, and not directly to plaintiff, as the evidence showed, because he wanted some security for the $200 he had agreed to see McDuffie paid as interest on his $2,000 for the year the option was given to run. There was nothing said about other claims of Wylie, and the evidence clearly shows that neither plaintiff nor Mrs. McCaughey ever understood that they were to do more than pay McDuffie $2,200 in order to get a reconveyance from him, and certainly McDuffie never understood it otherwise. The evidence shows that the $50 advanced to Mrs. McCaughey when she paid Pierce was a loan to her, and nowhere does it appear that she was given to understand when the agreement was made for plaintiff's benefit that it was conditioned on her repayment of this $50. There was evidence that the property was of the value of $4,000 in November, 1900, but this fact is probably immaterial.

The findings of the court on the matters commented upon above are challenged, and, we think, are unsupported by the evidence.

It is advised that the judgment and order be reversed.

We concur; Smith, C.; Haynes, C.

For the reasons given in the foregoing opinion, the judgment and orders are reversed. We add that if, upon another trial, the evidence discloses the same facts as before, the court should find that there was a loan by McDuffie to plaintiff as alleged, and that the transaction was intended as a mortgage of the land to secure the same, and the decree should so declare. The law would not, upon such a finding, warrant a decree of strict foreclosure, vesting title in McDuffie upon nonpayment within a specified time, and without a foreclosure sale: Shaw, J.; Angellotti, J.; Van Dyke, J.

PEOPLE v. CHRONES.

Cr. No. 1043; January 13, 1904.

75 Pac. 180.

False Pretenses—Failure of Proof.—Penal Code, Section 1110, provides that if a false pretense was expressed in language, unaccompanied by a false token or writing, or by some note or memorandum thereof in writing subscribed by the defendant, there can be no conviction, unless the pretense is proved by the testimony of two witnesses. The information charged that defendant falsely represented that he owned the goods and fixtures in his place of business, and that he was not indebted to any person, and by means thereof obtained the goods in question. Held, that as but one witness testified to the pretense, and there was no token or writing given or shown, there could be no conviction.

APPEAL from Superior Court, City and County of San Francisco; F. H. Dunne, Judge.

Lewis Chrones was convicted of the crime of obtaining goods under false pretenses, and appeals. Reversed.

Denson & Schlesinger for appellant; U. S. Webb, attorney general, J. C. Daly, deputy attorney general, and Lewis F. Byington, district attorney, for the people.

SHAW, J.—The defendant was convicted in the court below of the crime of obtaining goods by false pretenses. He appeals from the judgment and from the order denying his motion for a new trial.

The principal error assigned is that the pretense by means whereof it is alleged the goods were obtained was not established by sufficient evidence. The information charges that the defendant falsely represented that he owned the goods and fixtures in his place of business, and that he was not indebted to any person, and by means thereof obtained the goods in question. Section 1110 of the Penal Code provides that if a false pretense was expressed in language, unaccompanied by a false token or writing, or by some note or memorandum thereof in writing subscribed by, or in the handwriting of, the defendant, there can be no conviction, unless the pretense is proved by the testimony of two witnesses, or of one witness and corroborating circumstances. The only witness who testified to the pretense in this case was W. J. O'Brien, the agent of the owners of the goods. There was no token or writing given or shown. We have carefully read the testimony presented in the bill of exceptions, and fail to find therein any evidence of circumstances constituting any substantial corroboration of testimony of O'Brien with relation to the pretense.

It is not necessary to discuss the other errors assigned. Upon another trial the district attorney will doubtless make clearer the point that the goods in question were sold by the agent, O'Brien, duly authorized to do so, and that the owners of the goods had no part in the transaction, except to deliver the same in pursuance of the sale made by O'Brien, and in reliance upon his report.

The judgment and order are reversed and the cause remanded for a new trial.

We concur: Angellotti, J.; Van Dyke, J.

PEOPLE v. KENNEDY.

Cr. No. 1051; February 15, 1904.

75 Pac. 845.

Homicide—Insufficiency of Evidence—New Trial.—The court properly granted a new trial in a prosecution for murder where the only direct testimony against defendant was that of an accomplice, and the corroborating testimony was insufficient to connect him with the commission of the offense so as to justify a conviction, even assuming that the accomplice's testimony, if true, was sufficient for that purpose.

APPEAL from Superior Court, City and County of San Francisco; Carroll Cook, Judge.

William B. Kennedy was convicted of murder, and from an order granting a new trial the people appeal. Affirmed.

U. S. Webb, attorney general, E. B. Power, Lewis F. Byington, district attorney, and I. Harris, assistant district attorney, for the people; William H. Schooler and A. S. Newburgh for respondent.

SHAW, J.—The defendant was charged with the crime of murder, and upon the trial a verdict was returned finding him guilty of murder of the first degree. Thereupon, on his motion, the court granted a new trial, on the ground, among others, that the only direct testimony against the defendant was that of an accomplice, and that there was no sufficient corroborating testimony to connect him with the commission of the offense. From this order the plaintiff appeals.

Upon an examination of the testimony we are of the opinion that the action of the court was correct. There is scarcely any corroborating evidence tending to connect the defendant with the commission of the crime, and certainly not enough to justify a conviction, even if it be assumed that the testimony of the accomplice, if true, was sufficient for that purpose. From a reading of that testimony we are in grave doubt whether the court should not have granted the motion upon the ground that there was no evidence sufficient to convict.

The order appealed from is affirmed.

We concur: Angellotti, J.; McFarland, J.; Lorigan, J.; Henshaw, J.; Van Dyke, J.

MABB et al. v. STEWART et al.

L. A. No. 1260; June 7, 1904.

77 Pac. 402.

Remittitur—Filing—Presumption.—Under Statutes of 1895, page 269, chapter 207, and Code of Civil Procedure, section 1963, subdivisions 15 and 17, providing that it will be presumed that official duty has been performed, and that a judicial record, when not conclusive, still correctly determines or sets forth the rights of the parties, it will be presumed that failure to file the remittitur for four months after it was sent down was because the fee for filing had not been paid or tendered, or for some other sufficient reason.

Costs—Time for Filing Memorandum.—A memorandum of costs filed three days after the filing of the remittitur is filed in due time.

APPEAL from Superior Court, San Bernardino County; Benjamin F. Bledsoe, Judge.

Action by J. W. Mabb and others against Lyman Stewart and others. On appeal there was a decision for defendants, and, from an order allowing them to file a memorandum of their costs on appeal, plaintiffs appeal. Affirmed.

Cramer B. Morris and J. L. Murphey for appellants; Otis & Gregg (Howard Surr of counsel) for respondents.

SMITH, C.—The parties here are the same as in the case of the same title heretofore decided by this court (133 Cal. 556, 65 Pac. 1085), and the appeal is from an order of the lower court, of date January 6, 1902, allowing the defendants to file a memorandum of their costs on appeal.

The case is: The decision of this court, which was for the defendants, was rendered August 7, 1901. The remittitur was issued September 7, 1901, and received by the clerk of the lower court September 9th of the same year, but was not filed by the clerk until January 3, 1902. The reason of the clerk's delay in filing does not appear, but, in support of the correctness of the record and of the regularity of the officer's proceeding, it will be presumed it was because the fee for filing had not been paid or tendered, or that there was some other sufficient cause (Stats. 1895, p. 269, c. 207; Code Civ. Proc., secs. 1963, subds. 15, 17); for otherwise it would have been the duty of the court, on proper motion, to have ordered the filing to be corrected so as to show the right date. The order appealed from (after some further proceedings that need not be particularized) was made January 6, 1902, and the memorandum of costs therein referred to was presumably filed on the same day—that is to say, three days after the filing of the remittitur. The memorandum was therefore filed in due time. It might have been filed without any order of the court, but it was within the power of the court to make the order, and, in view of the misunderstanding of the parties as to the defendants' rights, such action was not inappropriate.

Under this view of the case, the facts shown in the bill of exceptions, other than those above stated, and the various points made by the appellants' counsel, become immaterial, and need not be stated or considered.

We advise that the order appealed from be affirmed.

We concur: Gray, C.; Chipman, C.

For the reasons given in the foregoing opinion the order appealed from is affirmed: Van Dyke, J; Angellotti, J.; Shaw, J.

In re SCOTT'S ESTATE.

S. F. No. 3894; June 6, 1904.

77 Pac. 446.

Executors—Settlement of Account—Appeal.—It is only necessary for an executor to serve notice of appeal from an order settling his account on the persons who appeared and contested the account.

APPEAL from Superior Court, City and County of San Francisco; J. V. Coffey, Judge.

Proceedings for the settlement of the account of the executors of the estate of Angelia R. Scott, deceased. From the order entered after hearing objections of legatees under will of deceased, the executors appeal. On motion to dismiss appeal. Motion denied.

A. E. Bolton (Philip G. Galpin of counsel) for appellants; Houghton & Houghton, L. Seidenberg and R. P. Clement for respondents.

SHAW, J.—Motion to dismiss the appeal. Upon the hearing of the account of the executors of the estate of Angelia R. Scott, deceased, certain legatees under the will appeared and filed objections to the account, and, upon the contest ensuing thereon, items for which the executors had claimed credit, amounting to over $7,000, were rejected, and an order was made settling the account accordingly. From this order the executors appealed. Notice of appeal was served on all the legatees who had appeared at the hearing, and attempt was made also to serve the same upon all the parties interested in the estate, including a number of other legatees who did not appear at the hearing, or otherwise make themselves parties to the proceeding. As to some of these parties, the notice was defective, and, for the failure to properly serve these parties, the respondents who filed the objections move to dismiss the appeal upon the ground that it is necessary to serve the notice of appeal upon all the parties interested in the estate, whether they made themselves parties to this proceeding or not. The question involved in this case is substantially the same as that involved in the Estate of McDougald (this day decided by the court in bank), 143 Cal. 476, 77 Pac. 443. Upon the authority of that case, it must be held that the only parties upon whom it is necessary to serve notice of appeal in proceedings of this sort are those who make themselves parties in the court below by appearing at the time of the settlement and contesting the account.

The motion is denied.

We concur: Angellotti, J.; Van Dyke, J.

PEOPLE v. CHIN YUEN et al.

Cr. No. 1126; July 26, 1904.

77 Pac. 954.

Robbery—Perpetrators — Accomplices — Instructions.—Though Penal Code, section 31, makes accomplices principals, they are not "perpetrators," so that, on a prosecution for robbery of two of the five persons present when the crime was committed, a requested instruction that the jury must be satisfied of the identity of defendants as the perpetrators is properly refused, as misleading, in ignoring the fact that they may have been accomplices.

APPEAL from Superior Court, City and County of San Francisco; Carroll Cook, Judge.

Chin Yuen and Yee Hung were convicted of robbery, and appeal. Affirmed.

A. S. Newburgh for appellants; U. S. Webb, attorney general, C. N. Post, assistant attorney general, and Lewis F. Byington, district attorney, for the people.

SMITH, C.—The defendants were convicted of the crime of robbery, and appeal from the judgment, and from an order of the court denying their motion for new trial.

The crime was committed upon the person and in the room of Lai Sin, a Chinese woman. The defendants were two of five Chinamen present when the crime was committed. The only point made by the appellants' counsel is that the court erred in refusing to give the following instruction: "I instruct that in order to justify a conviction of these defendants, or either of them, you must be satisfied beyond a reasonable doubt of the existence of every fact necessary to constitute the crime of robbery, and *of identity of the defendants, or either of them, as the perpetrators or perpetrator.* The evidence in a criminal case must satisfy the jury to a moral certainty and beyond a reasonable doubt—that is, must entirely satisfy the jury of the guilt of the defendants—before they can convict. If the jury are not entirely satisfied, they should acquit." This instruction was refused by the court on the ground, in effect, that, in the passage italicized, it ignored the fact that the defendants may have been guilty as accomplices, and was misleading. Otherwise the instruction was covered by the charge of the court. The argument of appellants' counsel is that by the statute "all persons concerned in the commission of a crime . . . . whether they directly commit the act constituting the offense, or aid and abet in its commission," etc. ". . . . are principals": Pen. Code, sec. 31. And hence, it is argued, "as a logical conclusion, an accomplice is likewise a perpetrator." But this is contrary to the plain meaning of the term—not to the crime, but to the act constituting it, which is to be understood as referring to the act constituting the principal crime. Nor has the meaning of the term been in any way affected by the statutory provision. There was no error in the ruling of the court.

We advise that the judgment and order appealed from be affirmed.

We concur: Harrison, C.; Gray, C.

VAN DYKE, J.—For the reasons given in the foregoing opinion the judgment and order appealed from are affirmed.

ANGELLOTTI, J.—I concur in the judgment. In my opinion, the requested instruction discussed in the opinion was substantially covered by the charge of the court.

SHAW, J.—I concur with Angellotti, J., and I also consider the instruction liable to mislead the jury, though not technically incorrect.

WARREN y. McGOWAN.

S. F. No. 4035; July 28, 1904.

77 Pac. 909.

Appeal—Delay.—An Appeal will be Dismissed; it having been perfected and the bill of exceptions settled and filed in the clerk's office for eight months, said clerk not having been requested to certify to the correctness of any transcript on appeal, no such transcript having been filed in the supreme court, and no extension of time to file it having been granted.

APPEAL from Superior Court, City and County of San Francisco; Thomas F. Graham, Judge.

Action by F. M. Warren against James P. McGowan. From an order setting aside a judgment for plaintiff he appeals. Dismissed.

Rigby & Rigby and Wal. J. Tuska for appellant; Eugene D. Sullivan and Thomas P. Boyd for respondent.

PER CURIAM.—This is a motion to dismiss an appeal taken from an order made by the superior court vacating and setting aside a judgment that had been rendered in favor of plaintiff. From the affidavits and the certificate of the clerk it appears that the appeal was perfected on the third day of December, 1903, and that the bill of exceptions to be used on said appeal was settled by the judge who made the order on the eleventh day of December, 1903, and on the same day filed in the office of said clerk. It further appears from the certificate of the clerk that said clerk has never been requested to certify to the correctness of any transcript on appeal, and no such transcript has been filed in this court. It further appears that no extension of time to file such transcript has been granted.

It is ordered that the appeal be dismissed.

PEOPLE v. McFADDEN.*

L. A. No. 1452; August 17, 1904.

77 Pac. 999.

Summons—Order for Publication.—It cannot, on Appeal, be said that the court erred in construing its order for publication of summons in the "San Diego Union" as referring to the "San Diego Union and Daily Bee," in which it was published.

Summons—Time for Publication.—The Requirement in an order for publication of summons that it be published for two months must yield to Political Code, section 3549, making four weeks' publication sufficient; so that it is enough that it was published four weeks.

APPEAL from Superior Court, San Diego County; E. S. Torrance, Judge.

Action by the people against Sarah J. McFadden. From the judgment defendant appeals. Affirmed.

F. D. Brandon and Edwin A. Wells for appellant; U. S. Webb, attorney general, Geo. A. Sturtevant, deputy attorney general, and Cassius Carter, district attorney, for the people.

PER CURIAM.—In this case, which is otherwise similar to the case of People v. Norris, L. A. No. 1336 (just decided), 144 Cal. 422, 77 Pac. 998, the order of the court directed publication ''in the San Diego Union,'' and the

---

*Rehearing denied September 16, 1904.

actual publication was in the "San Diego Union and Daily Bee," and the order of publication ordered that publication be made for two months, and publication was made for five weeks only. We cannot say that the court was not justified in construing its order as referring to the paper in which it was published, and the requirement of the order as to time of publication must yield to the provisions of section 3549 of the Political Code, under which four weeks' publication is sufficient.

On the authority of the decision cited, and for the reasons here given, the judgment is affirmed.

PEOPLE v. MILLER.

Cr. No. 1166; September 28, 1904.

78 Pac. 227.

Rape.—An Indictment Alleging That Defendant on a certain day had intercourse with H., a female under sixteen years of age, "and not the wife of defendant," unequivocally alleges that the female was not the wife of defendant at the time of the commission of the offense.[1]

Evidence.—Evidence as to the Number of Boxes witness could pack in a given time is not admissible to show how many defendant could pack.

APPEAL from Superior Court, San Bernardino County; Frank F. Oster, Judge.

Clarence T. Miller was convicted of rape, and appeals. Affirmed.

Henry M. Willis for appellant; U. S. Webb, attorney general, and C. N. Post, assistant attorney general, for the people.

SMITH, C.—The defendant was convicted of the crime of rape, and sentenced to a term of seven years' imprisonment in the state prison at Folsom. He appeals from the judgment

[1] Cited in People v. Miles, 9 Cal. App. 316, 101 Pac. 527, a similar prosecution, the court saying that the cited case was the only previous instance of the question being before the supreme court, and that there it was held that the information did allege that the female was not the wife, etc.

and from an order denying his motion for a new trial. The grounds for reversal alleged are: (1) The insufficiency of the indictment in failing to allege that the prosecutrix was not the wife of the defendant at the time of the commission of the offense; (2) error of the court in allowing a question to the prosecutrix, and the insufficiency of her answer to establish an essential element of the crime; (3) the exclusion of certain testimony; and (4) that the verdict is contrary to the evidence.

The objection to the indictment is obviously untenable. The actual allegation is that the defendant on the day named "did willfully, etc., ... commit an act of sexual intercourse with one Eva Hilberg, a female person under the age of sixteen years, and not the wife of said Clarence T. Miller"; and this, whether we have regard to the mere grammatical construction or to the manifest intent of the allegation, unequivocally alleges that the act was committed on a female under the age of sixteen years, and not the wife of the defendant at the time of the act. Nor is the allegation susceptible of a different meaning.

As to the second of the grounds urged, the question asked we regard as proper, and the answer of the witness as susceptible of but one inference, which is adverse to the appellant on the point complained of.

The third ground is also without merit. The evidence excluded related to the number of boxes of oranges the witness Hilberg could pack in a given time, which could furnish no grounds for any inference as to how many the defendant could pack, which was the purpose for which it was offered: Code Civ. Proc., sec. 1832.

As to the appellant's fourth point, the evidence against the defendant is, indeed, not so strong as to exclude doubt. But it cannot be said there was no evidence to sustain the verdict, nor can we say there was such abuse of discretion in the lower court in refusing a new trial as to justify the interference of this court: Const., art. 6, sec. 4.

We advise that the judgment and order appealed from be affirmed.

We concur: Gray, C.; Cooper, C.

For the reasons given in the foregoing opinion, the judgment and order appealed from are affirmed: Shaw, J.; Van Dyke, J.; Angellotti, J.

13

MAZOR v. SPRINGER et al.

S. F. No. 3054; October 8, 1904.

78 Pac. 474.

New Trial—Newly Discovered Evidence—Time of Discovery.—
In an action against two defendants for work and labor, one defendant admitted that the work was performed at his request, and plaintiff and another witness testified that the other defendant also
requested the performance of the work. On motion for a new trial
on the ground of newly discovered evidence it was claimed that the
defendant last mentioned was not at the place where this request was
claimed to have been made on the date at which it was claimed to
have been made; but no witnesses other than those present at the
trial were mentioned as able to testify to this effect. No excuse for
not calling these witnesses was produced, except the statement in the
affidavit of the defendant who requested the services that the fact
of the other defendant's absence at the time of the alleged interview
had not occurred to defendants until after the trial. Held, that as
the new evidence would not affect the liability of affiant, and as he
was not qualified to speak for the other defendant, a new trial was
properly refused.

APPEAL from Superior Court, Santa Clara County; M.
H. Hyland, Judge.

Action by Stanislaus Mazor against Mary Springer and
another. From a judgment for plaintiff, and from an order
denying a motion for a new trial, defendants appeal.
Affirmed.

J. H. Campbell for appellants; B. A. Herrington for respondent.

SHAW, J.—This is an action to recover wages for labor
performed. Defendants appeal from the judgment and
from an order denying their motion for a new trial.

There was sufficient evidence to prove the allegation that
the plaintiff performed the work in question at the request
of the defendant Mary Springer. The plaintiff testifies positively to that effect, and he was corroborated by the witness
Gilman. The answer does not deny the request so far as
the defendant Sage is concerned. The plaintiff also testified, in effect, that the agreement was that he was to receive
$15 for the first month and $25 per month thereafter, and

that he worked the entire time for which he claims, except seventeen days. This was sufficient to support the verdict. We cannot say, from the evidence, that the jury did not deduct the wages for the time he was absent, nor can we disturb the verdict, where the evidence is conflicting, although the preponderance may now seem to be for the defendants.

The court did not err in denying the motion for a new trial on the ground of surprise at the testimony of Gilman concerning the contract made in his presence between the plaintiff and the defendant Springer, and of the discovery of new evidence relating thereto. The new evidence was to the effect that on the afternoon on which Gilman said the conversation took place at the house of Mary Springer she was "many miles distant" from the house. It is not alleged that there was any witness, other than those present at the trial, by whom her absence at that time could have been proven; nor is her whereabouts at that time stated. The only excuse for not calling the witnesses present at the trial to testify to her absence was that contained in the affidavit of the defendant Sage, that the "fact of the absence of Mary Springer from the said Springer farm did not occur to their (defendant's) minds until several days after the trial was concluded." Her absence, if proven, would not affect the liability of Sage, who admits making the request. He was not qualified to speak concerning the mind and memory of Mrs. Springer, and she made no affidavit. Under these circumstances the court did not abuse its discretion in refusing a new trial upon these grounds.

The judgment and the order denying the defendants' motion for a new trial are affirmed.

We concur: Angellotti, J.; Van Dyke, J.

ALEXANDER v. WILSON, Sheriff, et al.

Sac. No. 1069; December 28, 1904.

79 Pac. 274.

Attachment—Preserving Property.—A Sheriff is Entitled to an Allowance of his necessary expenses of keeping and preserving attached property until after the judgment.

APPEAL from Superior Court, Lassen County; F. A. Kelley, Judge.

Action by Jules Alexander against T. W. Wilson, sheriff, and others. From a judgment for defendant Wilson for his costs only, disallowing a counterclaim, he appeals. Modified.

C. L. Claflin and H. D. Burroughs for appellant; Goodwin & Goodwin for respondent.

SMITH, C.—This is a suit brought by plaintiff against appellant, Wilson, and his surety, for the sum of $4,200, as damages for failure of said defendant, as sheriff, to sell under execution certain personal property held by him under attachment in the suit of plaintiff against Anderson & Berry. The defendants pleaded in justification an injunction issued from the district court of the United States for the northern district of California in bankruptcy proceedings there pending; and the defendant Wilson further pleaded by way of counterclaim that plaintiff was indebted to him in the sum of $568 for money paid by him as keeper's fees, at plaintiff's request, while in charge of the property. The findings were for defendant, except as to the counterclaim, as to which the court finds: That the defendant Wilson did employ keepers of the property in his charge, who remained in possession until after the judgment; that an order was made by the superior court in the case allowing him the sum of $284 as his necessary expenses of keeping and preserving the property under the attachment; and that the said sum has not been paid to the defendant. But the court gave him judgment for his costs only, disallowing the counterclaim. The defendant appeals from the judgment, and the relief demanded is that the judgment be modified so as to adjudge to the appellant the amount of his counterclaim, as found by the court. The judgment was affirmed by this court on the appeal of the plaintiff June 30, 1904, 144 Cal. 5, 77 Pac. 706. There is no brief on file for respondent. The counterclaim seems to be a just debt; and no reason suggests itself as to why it should not be allowed (Lane v. McElhany, 49 Cal. 421, Shumway v. Leakey, 73 Cal. 261, 14 Pac. 841, and Stats. 1869–70, p. 158, c. 144, therein cited), and we are of the opinion that it should be so ordered.

We advise that the judgment be modified as above indicated, and, as modified, that the same stand affirmed.

We concur: Gray, C.; Cooper, C.

For the reasons given in the foregoing opinion, the judgment appealed from is modified by adding thereto a clause to the effect that the defendant also recover of plaintiff the further sum of $284, with interest from September 24, 1901, and, as so modified, stands affirmed: Shaw, J.; Van Dyke, J.; Angellotti, J.

LAKE v. OWENS et al.

L. A. No. 1512; January 25, 1905.

79 Pac. 589.

Trustee.—The Pact That the Purchaser of an Interest in a Mine was acting in the relation of trustee of such interest for the seller did not affect the validity of the purchase, it being a fair and open transaction for full value.

Appeal—Conflicting Evidence.—The Findings of Fact by the Court on conflicting evidence will not be disturbed on review.

APPEAL from Superior Court, San Bernardino County; Frank F. Oster, Judge.

Action for the cancellation of an instrument by E. S. Lake against Phoebe Ann Owens, executrix of J. A. Owens, deceased, and another. From a judgment for defendants and an order denying a new trial plaintiff appeals. Affirmed.

T. W. Duckworth and Henry W. Nisbet for appellant; Chas. L. Allison and C. C. Haskell for respondents.

CHIPMAN, C.—Plaintiff brings the action to rescind a certain agreement to sell to defendant C. W. Owens an undivided sixteenth interest in the so-called "San Bernardino Iron Mines"; also to rescind the deed subsequently made thereto by plaintiff in pursuance of said agreement, and to cancel both said instruments. The cause was tried by the court sitting without a jury, and the findings and judgment were in favor of defendants that plaintiff take nothing by his action. Plaintiff appeals from the judgment and from the order denying his motion for a new trial.

Plaintiff alleged, and it was found, that he was the owner of an undivided sixteenth interest in the said mines, the testator of defendant Phoebe Owens being also at his death the owner of an undivided, but not the whole of the remaining, interest therein. Defendant Phoebe Owens, widow of deceased, duly qualified as executrix, and was by his will named as sole devisee of her husband's estate, and inventoried the said mines as property of the estate. Subsequently, to wit, December 18, 1901, defendant C. W. Owens, son of deceased and defendant Phoebe Owens, procured from plaintiff a written contract, by which plaintiff agreed to sell his said interest in said mines to said defendant C. W. Owens for $200, and later, to wit, on February 8, 1902, plaintiff conveyed his said interest to defendant Phoebe pursuant to the directions of defendant C. W. Owens, and upon receiving full payment as provided in said contract. Plaintiff alleges in his complaint that he was induced to enter into said contract through the false and fraudulent representations of said C. W. Owens; that he (plaintiff) was an old man, infirm in bodily health and strength, and an inmate of the county hospital; that he reposed confidence in said Owens, and believed the representations made by him, and acted wholly upon said representation, among others, that plaintiffs' interest in said mines was not of greater value than $200; that soon after he had executed and delivered said deed he discovered that the defendants had, previously to the making of said contract and the delivery of said deed, joined in a contract for the sale of said mines for a sum which (had the contract been carried out) would have yielded to plaintiff $1,200 for his share therein, which fact defendants well knew and purposely concealed from plaintiff; and thereupon plaintiff gave notice to defendants rescinding said contract and deed, and offered to restore to defendants everything of value received from them by plaintiff. Without stating fully the allegations of the complaint, it may be conceded that plaintiff sets forth facts which, had the court found them to be true, would have entitled him to relief. But the court found that the said contract of sale made by defendants was but an option, and that "there had not been paid to either of the defendants any sum of money therefor, or upon said contract, and there was no means of ascertaining whether the said company (the purchaser) would purchase the mines and pay therefor or not.'' The court found against the plaintiff on all his allegations of fraud, misrepresentations, concealment and claims of plaintiff, having reposed confidence in defendant C. W. Owens in making said contract, and found that the transaction was fair and open, that plaintiff was acting on the advice of a friend other than defendant Owens, and that the price paid ''was the fair market value'' of plaintiff's interest in the mines. In view of the findings, we cannot see that the case presents any questions for serious discussion. If by the circumstances that in his lifetime deceased, Owens, held plaintiff's title in his name, and managed plaintiff's interest in the mines, and for that reason became trustee, and if this trust relation in some degree survived in the executrix, as claimed by plaintiff, still she could make the purchase of plaintiff's interest by fair and open dealing free from fraud, and for full value, as the court found was the fact. It is not entirely clear from the evidence that defendant C. W. Owens was acting for his mother when he procured the agreement to purchase the mines from plaintiff. But as the deed was made to her, and the payment also made by her, it is fair to assume that her son was acting as her agent. Plaintiff's principal contention is that this agent should have informed plaintiff of the then outstanding option, above referred to, and that the concealment of the fact is of itself sufficient to require a rescission of the contract. The evidence is conflicting as to what occurred between C. W. Owens and plaintiff and plaintiff's friend, by whose advice plaintiff in fact made the contract. Defendant Owens explained on the witness-stand all the facts and circumstances and why he did not mention the fact of the option. The trial court must have accepted defendants' evidence, and we think it was sufficient to support the findings negativing plaintiff's claim that he was misled by defendants' fraudulent concealment of important facts, as also is the evidence sufficient to support the other findings which themselves support the judgment.

It is advised that the judgment and order be affirmed.

We concur: Gray, C.; Cooper, C.

For the reasons given in the foregoing opinion, the judgment and order are affirmed; Van Dyke, J.; Angellotti, J.

I concur in the judgment: Shaw, J.

RIDGLEY v. ABBOTT QUICKSILVER MINING COMPANY OF ILLINOIS.*

S. F. Nos. 3966, 3982; February 4, 1905.

79 Pac. 833.

Mortgage Foreclosure—Deficiency Judgment.—In a Foreclosure Suit, a finding that a certain sum was due and unpaid from defendant to plaintiff, which was not made a part of the judgment, and which was not accompanied by an order for a deficiency judgment, was not an adjudication of personal liability, gave the clerk no authority to docket a deficiency judgment, and confined plaintiff to the mortgaged property alone for the satisfaction of his judgment and costs.[1]

Mortgage Foreclosure — Deficiency Judgment — Appeal.—A defendant in a suit to foreclose a mortgage, which had sold all its interest in the property before the suit was brought, and against which no personal or deficiency judgment was rendered, was not aggrieved either by the judgment or by an order allowing plaintiff receiver's costs and fees, in such sense as to entitle it to appeal from either the judgment or the order.

APPEALS from Superior Court, Lake County; George W. Buck, Judge.

Action by Edward Ridgley against the Abbott Quicksilver Mining Company of Illinois. From a judgment for plaintiff, and from an order allowing certain costs and fees, defendant appeals. Dismissed.

Gavin McNab for appellant; William Denman, J. P. Langhorne, Haven & Haven, Page, McCutchen & Knight and E. S. Pillsbury for respondent; Frank M. Stone, pro se.

PER CURIAM.—This is an action to foreclose a mortgage. The defendant, the Abbott Quicksilver Mining Company of Illinois, failed to answer, and judgment by default was entered against it. It brings two appeals—one from the judgment of foreclosure, and one from a subsequent order

---

*Rehearing denied March 6, 1905.

[1] Cited with approval in First Nat. Bank of Nome v. Mahoney (N. D.), 135 N. W. 772, where the court says: "The clerk is without authority to include anything in the judgment which is not authorized by the conclusions and order."

allowing certain receiver's costs and fees. A motion is made to dismiss these appeals upon the ground that the appellant is not a party aggrieved.

We think the appeals should be dismissed upon the ground and for the reasons stated. It appears that the appellant had sold all its right, title and interest in the property upon which rested the foreclosed mortgage before the suit was brought. The judgment appealed from ordered a sale of the premises mortgaged, and that the proceeds be applied to the payment of the amounts found to be due from appellant to the plaintiff. There was no personal judgment against appellant, nor was there any order that a judgment be entered for any deficiency left after application of the proceeds of the sale to the debt. To be sure, it was found that a certain sum was due and unpaid from appellant to plaintiff; but this was only a finding, and no part of the subsequent decree or judgment, "and cannot be regarded as an adjudication of personal liability." Without this "adjudication of personal liability" the clerk had no authority to docket a deficiency judgment: Herd v. Tuohy, 133 Cal. 61, 65 Pac. 139, and cases therein cited.

It follows from the foregoing that, the appellant having no interest in the property to be sold and it being impossible to enter any valid deficiency judgment against it on the decree rendered by the court and here appealed from, the plaintiff must look to the mortgaged property alone for satisfaction of his judgment, as well as for the amount allowed him on the subsequent order, and that appellant cannot be held in any way or for any sum by either the judgment or order appealed from. It follows that appellant is in no way aggrieved by said judgment or by said order.

The appeals are dismissed.

SHAW, J.—I concur in the foregoing, and add the following: The code provides that, if the proceeds of the mortgaged property are insufficient to pay the amount due the plaintiff, "judgment must then be docketed by the clerk .... against the defendant or defendants personally liable for the debt, and it becomes a lien on the real estate of such judgment debtor, as in other cases in which execution may be issued": Code Civ. Proc., sec. 726. The docketing of a judgment is a proceeding, ministerial in character, which cannot occur until there is a judgment rendered. It is not the making or giving of a judgment. It is the act of a mere clerk, and it necessarily implies the pre-existence of the judgment to be docketed. In this state the docketing must not only await the rendition of the judgment, but, according to the dircetions of the code, it is to be done after the filing of the judgment-roll, which takes place after the judgment is entered: Code Civ. Proc., sec. 671. The direction in section 726 that a clerk must docket a judgment for the deficiency indicates that there must be an existing judgment of the court declaring, at least, the existence of a personal liability, the amount thereof, and the persons from whom and to whom the same is due. Neither findings, conclusions of law, nor recitals will suffice.

In re HOVEY.*

Cr. No. 1090; March 3, 1905.

80 Pac. 234.

Attorneys — Admission to Practice — Jurisdiction of Court.— Under act of February 15, 1905, vesting in the district courts of appeal created by constitution, article 6, as amended November 8, 1904, the exclusive power to admit persons to practice as attorneys and counselors in the several courts of the state, the supreme court has no original jurisdiction of an application for such admission; and a contested application originating in the supreme court will be transferred to the proper district court of appeal.[1]

Application of Frank W. Hovey to be admitted to practice as an attorney. Transferred to district court of appeal for second district.

PER CURIAM.—Whereas, heretofore, at a session of this court held on June 17, 1904, Frank W. Hovey made application to this court for an order admitting him to practice as an attorney and counselor in all the courts of this state,

---

*See opinion following, post, p. 203.

[1] Cited with approval in In re Application for License to Practice Law, 67 W. Va. 240, 67 S. E. 609, as to the conclusiveness, under an appropriate statute, of the report of a referee as to the moral qualifications of an applicant to practice law,

and was thereupon duly examined by this court as to his qualifications, and upon said examination was by this court found qualified, and there being opposition to his said application for admission to practice, this court thereupon proceeded to make inquiry as to the good moral character of said Frank W. Hovey, and, to that end, made an order referring that question to Hon. M. T. Allen, judge of the superior court of Los Angeles county, as referee, to take testimony, and therefrom report to this court his findings concerning the character of said applicant, and said referee having thereafter made and filed in this court his report and finding in regard to the moral character of said applicant, and the matter having been thereupon continued for argument and determination upon said report; and whereas, there has been no hearing or determination thereon, and by an act approved February 15, 1905, it has been provided that power to make orders admitting persons to practice as attorneys and counselors in all the courts of this state is now lodged exclusively in the several district courts of appeal created by the amendment adopted November 8, 1904, to article 6 of the constitution: Now, therefore, it is ordered by this court that the aforesaid application of Frank W. Hovey be transferred to the district court of appeal for the second district for hearing and determination upon the report of said referee, and that the clerk of this court, when said district court of appeal is organized, do forthwith send to said court all the papers on file in said proceeding, together with a copy of this order and all other orders made by this court therein.

In re HOVEY.

Court of Appeal, Second District; June 2, 1905.

81 Pac. 1019.

Attorneys—Admission to Bar.—The Finding of a Referee appointed to ascertain and report as to moral character of applicant for admission to the bar that the applicant was of good moral character prior to his arrival in the state, and that he was then guiltless of crime or improper conduct as an attorney, is conclusive.

Attorneys—Admission—Pendency of Disbarment Proceedings.— The failure of an attorney, in making application for admission to the bar, to disclose to the court, and the attorney through whom his application is made, the pendency of disbarment proceedings against him in the state of his former domicile, does not materially affect his moral character or his admissibility to the bar.

Attorneys—Admission.—The Mere Fact of Pendency of Disbarment proceedings in the state of the former domicile of an applicant for admission to the bar does not disqualify him.

In the matter of the application of Frank W. Hovey for admission to the bar. Transferred from supreme court, ante, p. 202, 80 Pac. 234. Application granted.

SMITH, J.—This matter came before us under an order of the supreme court of the state of date March 6, 1905, which is as follows: "By the Court: Whereas, heretofore, at a session of this court held on June 17, 1904, Frank W. Hovey made application to this court for an order admitting him to practice as an attorney and counselor in all the courts of this state, and was thereupon duly examined by this court as to his qualifications, and upon said examination was by this court found qualified, and there being opposition to his said application for admission to practice, this court thereupon proceeded to make inquiry as to the good moral character of said Frank W. Hovey, and, to that end, made an order referring that question to Hon. M. T. Allen, judge of the superior court of Los Angeles county, as referee, to take testimony, and therefrom report to this court his findings concerning the character of said applicant, and said referee having thereafter made and filed in this court his report and finding in regard to the moral character of said applicant, and the matter having been thereupon continued for argument and determination upon said report; and whereas, there has been no hearing or determination thereon, and by an act approved February 15, 1905, it has been provided that power to make orders admitting persons to practice as attorneys and counselors in all the courts of this state is now lodged exclusively in the several district courts of appeal created by the amendment adopted November 8, 1904, to article 6 of the constitution: Now, therefore, it is ordered by this court that the aforesaid application of Frank W. Hovey be transferred to the district court of appeal for the second district for hearing and determination upon the report of said referee, and that the clerk of this court, when said district court of appeal is organized, do forthwith send to said court all the papers on file in said proceeding, together with a copy of this order and all other orders made by this court therein.''

The report of the referee mentioned in the order is as follows:

"The undersigned, one of the superior judges of the state of California, in and for Los Angeles county, who was by your honorable court authorized and directed to take testimony and determine therefrom and to report as to the moral character of the applicant, would respectfully report that, after due notice to all parties interested, he gave a full and patient hearing touching all such matters as might be offered affecting the personal character of the applicant, and finds:

"That the applicant was born in the Dominion of Canada. That when a child his father removed with the family to the state of Maine. That the father, after his arrival in the state of Maine, exercised the right of franchise; claimed to be, and was recognized as, a citizen of the United States; represented to applicant, and applicant believed, that the father had been regularly and properly admitted to citizenship while the applicant was a minor under the age of eighteen years. That in truth the father never became a citizen of the United States. That applicant, assuming in good faith that he was a citizen, after he attained his majority was admitted to the bar of that state, was elected to and discharged the duties of various public offices of trust and profit, and had no information until shortly before April 14, 1902, of the fact that the father was not a citizen, at which date applicant made application to the proper court, and was admitted to citizenship. That in the early part of 1898, by reason of financial disasters, overwork, and because of the death of a favorite daughter, the applicant became and was for a long time insane. That he so far recovered his reason that in the latter part of that year he took up his residence at Biddeford, in the state of Maine, and in some degree the practice of his profession. That in spring of 1902 certain parties maliciously presented to the bar of York county (the same being the county in which Biddeford is situated) charges against the applicant, of unprofessional conduct, lack of good faith to clients, perjury, subornation of perjury, forgery, and extortion, which charges I find to have been untrue. A committee was appointed by the York

bar, which, acting in good faith, and believing these charges
to have some foundation, on the 21st of April, 1902, formulated and presented to the justices of the supreme judicial
court of York county, Maine, formal charges of such criminal and unprofessional acts, and on the 22d of April, 1902,
filed the same in said court; and on the same day, said court
issued a citation requiring the applicant to appear and show
cause why he should not be removed from the office of attorney at law.

"The threat to file these charges, and their nature and
character, was known by applicant for some weeks before
the same were filed, and while he was still a resident of Biddeford. At this time, however, and for a long time prior,
he was suffering physically, and was not strong mentally.
Applicant's wife and her father, with a view of preventing
the immediate filing of those charges, an investigation of
which they felt assured would have the effect to occasion a
return of previous insanity, retained as counsel for applicant, to prevent the filing of such charges, the lawyer who
was their principal author in the first instance. This employment applicant acquiesced in, and advanced the money
to pay this lawyer's fee of a hundred dollars, and was led
to believe, not only by this lawyer, but by others, who were
his friends, and interested in protecting his health and good
name, that no charges would be formally presented; and
thereupon applicant and his wife, shortly before the filing
of such charges, left the state of Maine and went to the
city of Boston, Massachusetts, that applicant might undergo
a surgical operation. Shortly after this surgical operation
was performed, and while applicant was weak physically,
and in such condition of mind that, in my opinion, he was
not capable of managing his affairs or protecting himself
in anywise, the citation above referred to was served upon
his brother, in the city of Boston; but the contents thereof,
in a general way, were made known to him. Applicant's
wife retained other counsel, by letter, to appear and resist
such charges, and brought applicant to the state of California; intending to take up their residence in Eureka, in
this state. Their route of travel carrying them through Los
Angeles, they stopped off in this city about the 2d of May,
1902. The day subsequent to their arrival in Los Angeles,
having letters of introduction to Judge Waldo M. York,

one of the superior judges of this county, applicant and his wife called upon Judge York, and the latter insisted that applicant should be admitted to the bar of Los Angeles county; and Judge York introduced a member of the bar to Mr. Hovey, and, upon the motion of said member of the bar, Judge York entered an order admitting him to practice. Judge York, being advised of applicant's intention to go to Eureka, advised applicant to stop on his way, and be admitted to the supreme court of the state, and, to that end, he gave him a letter of introduction to Shurtleff, a former partner of Judge York; and applicant did, upon his arrival in San Francisco, present such letter to Shurtleff, and, upon his motion, and upon production of his certificate theretofore issued by the supreme court of Maine, he was admitted to practice by your honorable court. I find that what might appear to be undue haste in relation to admission to practice should not be charged against applicant, in view of the insistence of those in whom he had confidence in relation thereto, and his weak mental and physical condition at the time. Your honors are familiar with all the proceedings leading up to and including the striking of applicant's name from the roster by your honorable court, and no further reference is necessary to be made thereto.

"Notwithstanding the employment by applicant of counsel in connection with the charges brought against him in the state of Maine, the attorneys who should have represented him permitted his default to be entered, and his name to be stricken from the rolls in the state of Maine. In 1903 applicant returned to the state of Maine, procured the order striking his name from the rolls to be vacated, and made complete and perfect arrangements, at a large expenditure, looking toward a defense against the charges so presented. After employing counsel and making such expenditure, and while applicant was present with his witnesses to refute and disprove the charges made against him, the bar association filed certain specifications in relation to such charges, and, among others, for the first time, presented the question of his alienage, which, being true and admitted, deprived the court in that state of jurisdiction to hear and determine the truth of the other charges; and on account of such alienage, and for no other reason, applicant's name was again stricken from the rolls of that state.

"Your honors are in possession of the record, which shows that on the 19th of October, 1903, applicant filed an answer in response to a petition for his disbarment in your honorable court, in which he denied under oath that he knew that such disbarment proceedings were pending in the supreme judicial court of Maine on the twelfth day of May, 1902, when he requested Shurtleff, an attorney, to move his admission to practice in your court, and in which answer he alleged that there had been withheld from him all information with respect to said charges. In view of the fact that the service of the citation was not personally made upon applicant, that he had been advised and believed that these charges would not be filed, and considering this weak mental condition, I find that he had no actual notice that the charges had been filed and were in fact pending at the time when in the answer he alleged such want of notice of filing; but I find that it is not true, as stated in that answer, that all information with relation to these charges and their character was withheld from him, but, on the contrary, that information as to their general nature and character was given him in the city of Boston shortly after the service of the citation upon the brother, and before his arrival in California. In addition, when called upon by the grievance committee of the bar association of Los Angeles county, early in 1903, to make explanation concerning these various charges, he was not frank and candid with such committee in his answers to their inquiries, and he did not state to Mr. Shurtleff or to your honorable court any fact in relation to the knowledge he did possess as to the threatened charges in the state of Maine. I further find that, pending the examination before your referee, certain of the testimony which applicant desired to submit to such referee was in the nature of affidavits; that, the bar committee being unwilling to permit such affidavits to be read, applicant caused questions and answers thereto (all, however, in perfect accord with such affidavits and written statements in his possession, signed by the parties whose depositions were intended to be taken) to be prepared here, and forwarded to the officers in Maine, that they might be read and subscribed by such witnesses. In each instance, however, such prepared questions and answers were accompanied by a letter of applicant, requesting them, if such answers were not in accord with their remembrance, to make changes and interlineations so that they might conform to the truth.

"As a summary, then, your referee would report to your honorable court that upon arrival of applicant, Frank W. Hovey, in the state of California on the 1st of May, 1902, he was a man of good moral character; that he was guiltless of crime or improper conduct as an attorney prior thereto. His subsequent conduct in relation to the answer filed in your honorable court, his want of frankness with the attorney moving his admission, his want of frankness with the grievance committee of the Los Angeles bar, are matters which I deem purely within the province of your honorable court to consider, without recommendation or finding on my part as to their effect on his moral character and fitness.

"An apology is due for the length of this instrument. The great volume of testimony the long years through which the matter progressed, renders it impossible for me to present in a more brief way the facts elicited upon the hearing. I retain in my possession a transcript of the oral testimony offered, together with all exhibits, depositions, and papers, which, if desired by your honors, I will cause to be forwarded."

The report of the referee disposes of the charges against Mr. Hovey as to the matters occurring prior to his arrival in California on May 1, 1902, at which time, it is found, "he was a man of good moral character [and] . . . . was guiltless of crime or improper conduct as an attorney prior thereto." We have, therefore, to consider only the subsequent conduct of Mr. Hovey, as affecting the question of his moral character and his admissibility to the bar. This, as reported by the referee, was, in effect, that he did not disclose to the attorney moving his admission or to the court that proceedings for his disbarment were pending in the state of Maine, and that in his answer to the petition filed in the supreme court for his disbarment, which was verified, he denied that he knew that such disbarment proceedings were pending at the time of his application, and further alleged that all information of such proceedings had been withheld from him by his friends on account of the severe illness under which he was suffering at the time of the service of notice of the proceedings on his brother.

14

The force of these charges obviously depends upon the assumption that, at the times referred to, Mr. Hovey in fact did know of the pendency of the disbarment proceedings, and that this knowledge was then present to his mind. On this point the referee finds, in effect, that Mr. Hovey had been informed of the pendency and general nature of the proceedings in Boston shortly after the service of notice upon his brother, but that, on account of his physical and mental condition, this information was not present to his mind when he filed his answer. The latter finding, we gather from the report, was not based upon specific evidence as to the fact, but upon the physical and mental condition of Mr. Hovey, and the presumption of good character always existing until the contrary appears, which in this case was supported by the very high certificates of character given to him by lawyers, judges, and others in the state of Maine, attached to his answer; and, at all events, as the case is presented to us, the finding cannot be questioned. It may be added that it would be only in a clear case of conscious and intentional perjury that we would be justified in regarding the character of a defendant, especially in a criminal or quasi criminal proceeding, as affected by the denials and allegations of his answer.

With regard to the failure of Mr. Hovey to disclose to the attorney moving his admission to the bar and to the court that proceedings for his disbarment were pending in the state of Maine, though there is no express finding upon the point, it may be presumed that the same considerations will apply; otherwise, while we think Mr. Hovey would have done better to have disclosed the pendency of proceedings against him, we are not prepared to say that his failure to do so can be regarded as materially affecting his moral character or his admissibility to the bar. If the matter suppressed had been a conviction of gross misconduct, or, as in Case of Lowenthal, 61 Cal. 122, an actual disbarment, the case would be otherwise. But the mere fact of the pendency of proceedings against him would not have the effect of disqualifying him; nor would the court, perhaps, be justified in refusing his admission on account of the charges against him, without inquiry into and proof of the facts charged. In this case the order of disbarment which had been rendered by the Maine court at the time the petition for disbarment was filed in the supreme court here has been set aside, and the case finally disposed of, on grounds not affecting the character of Mr. Hovey, and without passing upon the charges made against him; nor in the present proceedings is any attempt made to establish the truth of those charges.

We do not think it necessary to consider the charge that Mr. Hovey was not frank and candid in his answers to questions put to him by the grievance committee, as, in view of the adverse relations of the parties, we do not deem it material.

We are of the opinion that Mr. Hovey is entitled to admission to the bar, and it will be so ordered.

We concur: Gray, P. J.; Allen, J.

In re ANTOLDI'S ESTATE.*

S. F. No. 4206; May 31, 1905.

81 Pac. 278.

Appeal.—A Finding of Fact Which is not Attacked on the ground of insufficiency of evidence to sustain it is conclusive.

Will Contest—Appeal — Parties Aggrieved.—Will contestants who are not heirs at law of a testator, nor related to him, are not parties aggrieved by the denial of their motion for a new trial, within Code of Civil Procedure, section 938, providing that parties aggrieved may appeal.

APPEAL from Superior Court, City and County of San Francisco; J. V. Coffey, Judge.

In the matter of the estate of S. Antoldi, deceased. From an order denying a motion for a new-trial in a contest of the will of deceased, Carolina Antoldi Casagrande and other contestants appeal. Dismissed.

A. D. Splivalo, R. W. Hent and J. A. Spinetti for appellants; G. W. McEnerney for respondent.

PER CURIAM.—This is an appeal from an order denying a motion of contestants for a new trial in a contest of the

---

*Rehearing denied June 30, 1905.

will of deceased. The present matter before the court is a motion of respondents to dismiss the appeal of contestants upon the ground that neither said Caroline A. Casagrande nor either of the other contestants is a party interested in said estate, or aggrieved by the order appealed from. The motion must be granted on the grounds urged.

It affirmatively appears from the record that in the petition for the revocation of the will of deceased it was alleged by the contestants that they were the only blood relations and heirs at law of the testator. This was denied in the answer of the proponents of the will, and the court found directly in their favor—that contestants were not either heirs at law of the testator or related to him. Contestants gave notice of intention to move for a new trial, specifying as one of the grounds thereof the insufficiency of the evidence to sustain the findings. Subsequently they prepared and had settled a statement on motion for a new trial, and thereafter moved for a new trial, which was denied. In the specification of errors contained in the said statement there is no specification at all of any insufficiency of the evidence to justify the finding that contestants were not heirs at law or related to the testator. This finding, not being attacked, must stand as conclusively true, with the obvious legal result that, as the contestants are not any of them heirs at law of the testator, they are not parties interested in the estate, nor are they parties aggrieved, under section 938 of the Code of Civil Procedure, who alone are entitled to appeal.

The appeal for this reason is dismissed.

WHITE v. WISE et al.

Court of Appeal, Third District; May 29, 1905.

81 Pac. 664.

Appeal — Remand — Proceedings Below — Judgment.—Where a judgment for plaintiff was reversed on appeal, with directions to render judgment for defendant as prayed in the answer, which was that the prayer of the complaint be denied, and that plaintiff take nothing by the action, and that defendant have judgment against plaintiff for costs, a judgment rendered that the prayer of plaintiff be denied, that plaintiff take nothing by the action, and that defendant have judgment against plaintiff for costs, and is entitled to "appropriate process" to enforce the judgment, and every part thereof, was not objectionable, as granting more relief than demanded, in so far as it awarded process to enforce the judgment.

APPEAL from Superior Court, Mendocino County; M. S. Sayre, Judge.

Action by Frankie White against John H. Wise and others. From a judgment in favor of defendants, plaintiff appeals. Affirmed.

W. T. Baggett, W. H. Linforth, and J. T. White for appellant; W. H. Langford for respondents.

McLAUGHLIN, J.—Upon a former appeal in this case, the judgment in favor of the respondent there, the appellant here, was reversed by the supreme court, "with directions to the lower court to enter a judgment on the findings for the appellant as prayed for in this answer": White v. Wise, 134 Cal. 613, 66 Pac. 959. The appellant mentioned there was Wise, the respondent here, and the prayer of his answer was as follows: "That the prayer of said complaint may be denied, and that said plaintiff take nothing by this action, and that this defendant have judgment against plaintiff for his costs herein incurred." Upon the receipt of the remittitur the lower court, on motion, rendered judgment as follows: "Now, therefore, in pursuance of the premises, and in accordance with *judgment, decision* and *direction* of the said superior court, ... it is ordered, adjudged and decreed that the prayer of plaintiff herein be, and the same is hereby, denied; that the said plaintiff shall take nothing by this action; and that the defendant John H. Wise shall have and is hereby given judgment against said plaintiff Frankie White for his costs herein incurred, amounting to the sum of $153.80. *And said defendant is entitled to and shall have any appropriate process of this court to enforce said judgment hereby given, and each and every part thereof.*" It is conceded that, but for the concluding clause in said judgment, there could be no pretext for this appeal. Notwithstanding appellant's strenuous objections to the language italicized, we cannot refrain from saying that this is an

instance where "much ado about nothing" has operated to
vex an adverse litigant, and needlessly consume the time of
the court. The successful defendant would, under the law,
be entitled to appropriate process to "enforce said judgment,
and every part thereof," regardless of this clause, which
could give him no more.

This appeal is without merit, and hence the judgment is
affirmed, with $50 damages, and the superior court is di-
rected to include this sum of money in the judgment, in
addition to other costs.

We concur: Chipman, P. J.; Buckles, J.

BERENTZ v. KERN KING OIL AND DEVELOPMENT
COMPANY et al.*

Court of Appeal, Second District; June 17, 1905.

84 Pac. 45.

Process—Service by Constable.—Where a Return of Service of
summons by a constable was not verified as required by Code of Civil
Procedure, section 410, it was ineffective.

Mining Claims—Oil Wells—Liens for Labor.—Code of Civil
Procedure, section 1183, as amended by Statutes of 1899, page 34,
chapter 35, provides for a lien on the whole of a mining claim for
labor performed or for materials furnished to be used in the construction of any building, wharf, bridge, ditch, flume, aqueduct, well,
tunnel, etc., and for labor performed in any mining claim or claims
and the works owned and used by the owners for reducing ores, etc.;
and section 1185 declares that the land on which any building,
improvement, well or structure is constructed, together with a convenient space about the same, or so much as may be required for the
convenient use and occupation thereof, to be determined by the court
on rendering judgment, is also subject to the lien, etc. Held, that the
mining claims referred to were mines of ore, exclusive of oil wells, and
hence a claimant of a lien for the drilling of an oil well, etc., was
not entitled to foreclose the lien, except as against such land as was
necessary for the convenient use and occupation of the well.[1]

---

*For subsequent opinion in supreme court, see 148 Cal. 577, 84 Pac.
47.

[1] **Cited** in Berentz v. Belmont Oil Co., 148 Cal. 579, 113 Am. St. Rep.
308, 84 Pac. 47, as part of the history of the case.

APPEAL from Superior Court, Kern County; J. W. Mahon, Judge.

Suit by J. H. Berentz against the Kern King Oil and Development Company and others. From a judgment for plaintiff, defendants appeal. Reversed.

William P. Veuve and A. B. Bigler for appellants; E. B. Coil for respondent.

SMITH, J.—This suit was brought to foreclose several liens for work and labor performed in the construction of an oil well on a tract of eighty acres of land described in the complaint. The Belmont Oil Company was and is the owner of the land, of which the other defendant holds a lease, and the latter defendant is also the owner of the drilling apparatus, derrick, etc., now on the land, and used, it is alleged, "in the development and working of the said land and mining claim." The Belmont Oil Company suffered default. The other defendant filed demurrer and answer, but did not appear at the trial. The judgment is against the Kern King Oil and Development Company and contractors for the sums therein named, and it is further adjudged "that plaintiff is entitled to enforce the liens upon the mining claims and the improvements described in the complaint herein for the said sum found due him, and that said liens are superior and paramount to the interest and claim of all the defendants herein." The appeal was taken within sixty days of the entry of judgment.

The judgment against the Belmont Oil Company must be reversed, for the several reasons that there is no allegation in the complaint that it had any knowledge of the work done on the land, that the judgment goes beyond the prayer of the complaint, and that there was no competent proof of the service of summons.

With regard to the latter point, there is a return of one Bristol, a constable, that he had served the Belmont Oil Company in the county of San Bernardino, but this was not verified: Code Civ. Proc., sec. 410. It is, indeed, intimated in respondent's brief that the return of service was amended, but we are not cited to what part of the transcript this amendment is to be found, nor does it appear in the index, nor have we been able to find it.

The judgment against the other defendant must also, we think, be reversed. The judgment is for a lien upon the whole of the land described in the complaint; but there is no allegation in the complaint that the whole of the land was necessary for the convenient use and occupation of the well, nor was any evidence introduced with reference thereto, nor is there any finding upon the subject. It is also to be observed that the action of the court in this particular seems to have resulted from the statement of the plaintiff's attorney that it was not denied in the answer that the whole of said land was required for the convenient use and occupation of the well, by which, as the fact was not alleged in the complaint, the court was doubtless misled.

It is now urged by the respondent's attorney that, under the provisions of section 1183 of the code, the lien in this case extends to the whole of the mining claim, whether necessary for the convenient use and occupation of the well or otherwise; citing Williams v. Mountaineer Gold Min. Co., 102 Cal. 134, 34 Pac. 702, 36 Pac. 388. But that case, we think, has no application, or, rather, none that can be regarded as favorable to the respondent's case. There the property involved was a "mining claim" in the ordinary sense of the word; that is to say, a "portion of the public mineral lands which the miner, for mining purposes, takes up and holds in accordance with mining law": Morse v. De Ardo, 107 Cal. 622, 40 Pac. 1018, and cases cited. And it was held that under section 1183 the lien extended to the whole of the mining claim. But from the decisions it appears to have been the opinion of the court that the section in question provides for two separate classes or categories of liens, namely, for labor performed or for materials furnished to be used in the construction, etc., "of any building, wharf, bridge, ditch, flume, aqueduct, tunnel, fence, machinery, railroad wagon road, or other structure," and for labor performed "in any mining claim or claims and the works owned and used by the owners for reducing the ores," etc., which is very clearly the case; and from this it is to be inferred that the cases provided for in the two clauses are exclusive of each other. The question, then, is, to which of these categories is the case to be assigned, and upon this point we are of the opinion that it falls under the former category; that is to say, that it is a structure similar in character to the other structures specified, and that the lien will extend only to "a convenient space about the same, or so much as may be required for the convenient use and occupation thereof, to be determined by the court": Code Civ. Proc., sec. 1185. This is rendered clear by the language of the latter section, which refers to "any building, improvement, well, or structure," and also from the language of section 1183, as amended in 1899 (Stats., p. 34, c. 35), in which the word "well" is inserted between the words "aqueduct" and "tunnel," appearing in the first clause of the former act. In a later amendment, the second category is made to include, also, not only "any mining claim or claims," but also "any real property worked as a mine." But this has no application to the present case. It also seems apparent from the language of the second clause of the section, in all the forms it has assumed since the amendment of 1880, that the mining claims referred to, and also the mines included by the last amendment, refer to mines of ore, exclusively, and that it was never intended to have any reference to the sinking of oil or other wells. It need not be determined in the present case whether the term "mining claim" can be construed as in any case applying to land owned in fee simple: Williams v. Santa Clara Min. Assn., 66 Cal. 193, 5 Pac. 85; Bewick v. Muir, 83 Cal. 373, 23 Pac. 390; Morse v. De Ardo, 107 Cal. 622, 40 Pac. 1018.

Judgment appealed from is reversed.

We concur: Gray, P. J.; Allen, J.

HARRISON, Judge, v. COLGAN, State Controller.[*]

S. F. No. 4375; July 21, 1905.

81 Pac. 1010.

District Courts of Appeal—Salary of Justices.—The supreme court is the only tribunal empowered to determine the amount of the salary of the justices of the district courts of appeal.

Supreme Court—Salary of Justices.—Statutes of 1905, page 224, chapter 249, amending a statute fixing the salary of the justices of the supreme court at $6,000 a year, by providing that the annual

---
*For subsequent opinion in bank, see 148 Cal. 69, 82 Pac. 674.

salary of each justice of the supreme court shall be $8,000, and the annual salary of each justice of the district courts of appeal $7,000, has no application to any justice of the supreme court in office at the time of the adoption of the amendment; but such justices during their term are entitled only to the salary fixed by the earlier statute.

Petition for a writ of mandamus by Ralph C. Harrison against E. P. Colgan, to compel respondent, as state controller, to draw his warrant on the state treasury in favor of petitioner. Alternative writ issued.

Charles W. Slack for petitioner.

PER CURIAM.—While in form this is an application by Ralph C. Harrison, presiding justice of the district court of appeal for the first judicial district, for a writ of mandate to the controller, requiring him to draw his warrant upon the state treasury in favor of the petitioner for the sum of $666.66, in effect it is an effort by all of the justices of the district courts of appeal to have determined the amount of salary which they are entitled to draw. This tribunal is the only tribunal under the law to which they can appeal for the determination of this question. The statute under which it is contended that they are entitled to their salary reads as follows: "The annual salary of each justice of the supreme court is $8,000, and the annual salary of each justice of the several district courts of appeal is $7,000": Stats. 1905, p. 224, c. 249. This statute is an amendment to the earlier provision of the law which declared: "The annual salary of each justice of the supreme court is $6,000 a year." Our conviction is absolutely fixed that the amendment above quoted has no application to any justice of this supreme court now in office, during the term for which he has been elected, and that the salary of each of such justices is, and must continue to be, in the absence of a constitutional amendment, during his term of office, the sum of $6,000 a year. With this expression of our conviction upon this subject, in view of the fact that this is the only tribunal to which the district courts of appeal can turn, we believe an alternative writ should be granted for the hearing and determination of such other questions as may be presented.

Let the alternative writ issue as prayed for, returnable before this court on Monday, September 4, 1905, at 10 o'clock A. M.

McFARLAND, J.—I concur in the order directing an alternative writ to issue; but I think that all of the questions involved in the petition for the writ should be left open until after full argument on the final hearing.

ADAMS v. THORNTON.*

Court of Appeal, Third District; July 25, 1905.

82 Pac. 215.

Cropping Contract.—Where Plaintiff, the Owner of Certain Orchards, contracted to let defendant a house and furnish implements, horses, wagons, feed, spraying materials, boxes, and trays for curing and marketing the fruit, furnish new trees to replace missing ones, pay for one-half of boxing materials when shipped, and, when dried, to pay for the expenses of cutting, drying, and sacking his share, and in consideration of defendant's labor in raising, harvesting, shipping, and marketing the fruit, the latter was to have one-half of the crop, the contract was a mere cropping contract, and not a lease, and plaintiff and defendant were therefore tenants in common of the crop.

Cropping Contract—Replevin.—Where Plaintiff and Defendant were Tenants in Common of a crop raised by defendant under a cropping contract, plaintiff was not entitled to maintain replevin against defendant for a portion of the crop alleged to have been wrongfully taken from plaintiff's premises.

APPEAL from Superior Court, San Joaquin County; Frank H. Smith, Judge.

Action by W. H. Adams against Arthur Thornton. From a judgment for plaintiff, defendant appeals. Reversed.

Louttit & Middlecoff for appellant;-Nicol & Orr and J. M. C. Murphy for respondent.

BUCKLES, J.—The complaint in this action was claim and delivery. The defendant set up by way of answer a contract, and alleged that under it he and plaintiff were copartners in carrying on the business of fruit growing and dividing the profits between them, and asked for a dissolution and an accounting. Judgment was for the plaintiff and for the

---

*Rehearing denied August 23, 1905.

return to him of all the property mentioned in his complaint, and for four dollars, damage and costs. Numerous errors are alleged in the bill of exceptions in the ruling of the trial court in the introduction of evidence, but in the briefs of counsel before us these matters are not touched upon at all, and only two points are presented for our consideration, viz.: 1. Were the plaintiff and defendant cotenants in the fruit in controversy? And 2. If cotenants, could the plaintiff maintain replevin against the defendant for the common chattels?

For the better understanding of the matter it is necessary to set out the contract under which the parties were operating, or, at least, so much of it as will assist in determining the questions involved, and it is as follows:

"New Hope, Cal., Nov. 1, 1899.

"This indenture, made this 1st day of November, 1899, between Arthur Thornton, of New Hope, county of San Joaquin, and state of California, as party of the first part, and W. H. Adams, as party of the second part, witnesseth: That the said Arthur Thornton, party of the first part, for and in consideration of the covenants hereinafter stated, hath let, and by these presents doth grant, demise, and let, unto the said party of the second part, W. H. Adams, all that parcel or parcels of orchard lands situated in the county of San Joaquin, near New Hope, and described as follows: [Then follows the description of a 50-acre orchard and a 10-acre orchard]—for the term of one year from above date. The said party of the first part does agree with the party of the second part that he will let him a house, that he will furnish implements, horses, wagons, feed, also spraying materials, also boxes and trays necessary for the curing and marketing of the fruit. The party of the second part does agree with the party of the first part that he will in due season prune the trees of said orchard in a workmanlike manner; that he will remove all brush and replant all trees needed to fill vacancies (said Thornton to furnish trees); that he will thoroughly spray said trees and plow and cultivate said lands; that he will properly thin fruit, will pick and deliver to railroad or steamer landing when shipping to cannery, and share and share alike, or, if for eastern market, will pack all fruit for shipment, furnishing crates or boxes for same, the said party of the first part to pay for one-half of boxing materials and packing, and share and share alike, or, if dried, the party of the second part agrees to cure the fruit properly and to deliver one-half of the dried fruit to the party of the first part, the said party of the first part to pay for the expense of cutting, drying and sacks for his share of the fruit.'' Signed by both parties.

This contract was continued in force to November 1, 1902. A settlement had been made for the crop of each year up to November, 1902. There remained on hand of the crop of 1902, 373½ sacks of dried apricots, which were in the possession of the plaintiff. On October 9, 1902, during the absence of plaintiff, the defendant came and carried said dried apricots away, and the plaintiff now seeks by his suit to have them returned to him. While the agreement set out and under which the parties were operating is called therein a lease, yet under the authority of Bernal v. Hovius, 17 Cal. 542, 79 Am. Dec. 149, it must be deemed only a cropping contract, and the parties are cotenants in the fruits raised during the time of the contract, and each has an equal right with the other to the possession of the whole of said fruit, and, under the general rule, neither can maintain a suit against the other for the possession of the fruit. In Walls v. Preston, 25 Cal., at page 62, the court says: ''It is the general rule that, where a term is created, the possession given to the occupant, and the produce agreed to be paid is to be paid as rent, then the instrument is to be regarded as a lease. It is also a general rule that, where the occupant covenants to deliver to the owner a portion of the crops, the agreement is held to be a cropping contract—a letting upon shares—and the owner and occupant are tenants in common of the crop.''

Plaintiff relies upon Clarke v. Cobb, 121 Cal. 596, 54 Pac. 74, as furnishing a different doctrine. In that case Justice Garoutte, who wrote the opinion, says: ''The parties entered into contracts whereby one Cobb agreed to farm and cultivate certain lands to grapes and grain for a term of ten years. . . . . It was provided therein that the lands were demised and let to said Cobb, he agreeing to give annually for the use thereof a certain portion of the crops of grain and other products grown theeon.'' There was a mortgage on the land, which was foreclosed, and the land sold while Cobb's contracts were in force. The justice continues: ''Crops of various kinds were cultivated upon these lands by Cobb under his contracts during the cropping season of 1895–96; and subsequent to the aforesaid sales of the land, and during the period of time allowed by law for redemption, these crops were gathered and harvested by Cobb. As provided in his contract, he set aside the portion thereof to be given for the use of the land." The question in that case was as to whether the purchaser or redemptioner was entitled to these rents. Justice Garoutte further says: "That these contracts were leases, that the conventional relation of landlord and tenant existed between the parties, and that the grains and fruits to be delivered to the landlord when gathered and harvested were rent, we are entirely satisfied. . . . . The authorities of this state recognize that such conditions may exist," such as cropping contract and cotenancy in the crops raised. "When it is established that a certain contract is a lease, and that the relation of landlord and tenant exists between the parties, there must be some appropriate words in the contract to indicate that the crops raised on the lands are to be held in cotenancy, or such will not be the conclusion reached. If there is nothing in the language to indicate that intention, then the products to be delivered to the landlord after harvest, by the tenant, will be deemed the property of the tenant until that time, and treated as rent to be then paid."

The contract in this case is vastly different from a contract where the landlord is to furnish the land and do nothing more but receive a stipulated part of the crop as rent, as was the case in Clarke v. Cobb. In the case at bar, Arthur Thornton agrees that he will let Adams a house, that he will furnish implements, horses, wagons, feed, also spraying materials, also boxes and trays for the curing and marketing of the fruit, furnish new trees to replace missing ones, also to pay for one-half of boxing materials when shipping, and, when fruit is to be dried, to pay for the expense of cutting, drying, and sacks for his share. His labor, and his capital, other than the land, went into the crops in raising, harvesting, shipping, and marketing. It seems to me they could not have made a clearer cropping contract, even though they had used the words, "We hereby enter into a cropping contract." It appears very plainly what the intention of the parties was. Thornton put up his land, his materials, his feed, his horses, and furnishings against the labor and skill of Adams; and they were to "share and share alike." Fruit was shipped in boxes, marked "Thornton & Adams." I presume, when the fruit was shipped to the eastern market, they stood "share and share alike" on losses, which sometimes do happen. Under the view taken by us the motion for nonsuit should have been granted.

Judgment is reversed.

We concur: Chipman, P. J.; McLaughlin, J.

Ex parte PRINDLE.

Court of Appeal, Second District; July 29, 1905.

94 Pac. 871.

Game—Protection by Local Authorities.—Constitution, article 11, section 11, authorizing any county, city, or town to make and enforce within its limits such local police regulations as are not in conflict with general laws, delegated to the county supervisors, prior to the passage of constitution, amendment, article 4, section 25½, authorizing the legislature to divide the state into game districts, the power to legislate for the complete protection of wild game within the bounds of their respective counties.

Game—Construction of Constitution.—Constitution, amendment, article 4, section 25½, authorizing the legislature to provide for the division of the state into fish and game districts and enact appropriate laws for the protection of fish and game therein, is to be construed with other sections of the constitution relative to the uniform application of the laws and the delegation of police power, and in such construction the more specific provision controls the general, without regard to the comparative dates; the different sections operating together, and neither working the repeal of the other.

Game.—Constitution, Amendment, Article 4, section 25½, authorizing the legislature to provide for the division of the state into fish and game districts and to enact appropriate laws for the protection of fish and game therein, prevails over earlier conflicting provisions of the constitution; and, while laws previously in force continue in force until substituted by new legislation, legislation subsequently adopted must be in harmony with the amendment.

Game—Mandatory Provisions of Constitution—"May."—Constitution, article 4, section 25½, providing that the legislature "may" provide for the division of the state into fish and game districts and "may" enact appropriate legislation for the protection of fish and game therein, is mandatory, and commands the legislature to enact necessary legislation touching the care and custody of game with reference to local conditions, which require special legislation for particular localities.

Game—Powers of Supervisors.—Under constitution, amendment, article 4, section 25½, requiring the legislature to provide for the division of the state into fish and game districts and to enact appropriate legislation for the protection of fish and game therein, any previous authority existing in the legislature to delegate legislative power in reference to fish and game to counties is revoked, and, notwithstanding the failure of the legislature to obey the mandate of the constitution, a board of county supervisors is without authority to regulate, by ordinance passed after the adoption of such amendment, the hunting of game within the limits of the county.

Game—Unreasonable Legislation.—In View of the Provision of Penal Code, section 626a, making it a misdemeanor to hunt, kill or destroy doves between February 15th and July 1st of the same year, a county ordinance declaring it unlawful to hunt or destroy doves within the limits of the county between the thirtieth day of June and the fifteenth day of August of each year, and between the fifteenth day of August and the sixteenth day of February of the year next ensuing, and thus leaving but one day in the year open to hunt doves, is unreasonable.

Application by Lyman D. Prindle for a writ of habeas corpus. Prisoner discharged.

Lee, Scott, Bailey & Chase, Miller & Page and Robt. E. Ross for petitioner; J. D. Fredericks, district attorney, and Hartley Shaw, chief deputy district attorney, for respondent; Henry T. Gage and W. I. Foley, amici curiae.

ALLEN, J.—The defendant was arrested for the violation of ordinance No. 120 (new series), enacted on the sixteenth day of May, 1905, by the board of supervisors of Los Angeles county. Section 1 of the ordinance provides: "It shall be unlawful in the county of Los Angeles, between the thirtieth day of June and the fifteenth day of August of each year, and between the fifteenth day of August of each year and the sixteenth day of February of the year next ensuing, for any person to hunt, pursue, take, kill or destroy, or have in his possession, any dove or doves." Upon trial the defendant pleaded guilty, and was committed to the county jail upon default of payment of the fine imposed. This writ was issued upon his application, and the respondent, upon the return, justifies the imprisonment under such conviction.

The question presented is as to the validity of said ordinance. Section 626a of the Penal code makes it a misdemeanor "to hunt, kill, pursue, or destroy, or have in possession, any dove or doves, between the fifteenth day of February and the first day of July of the same year." It will be observed that, taking the ordinance and the section of the Penal Code last referred to together, there remains but one day in each year open for the hunting, pursuing or killing of doves, or for having the same in possession, within Los Angeles county. The authority of the board of supervisors to enact this ordinance is claimed under section 11, article 11, of the state constitution, which reads: "Any county, city, town, or township may make and enforce within its limits, all such local, police, sanitary and other regulations as are not in conflict with general laws." The county government act of 1897 provides that boards of supervisors shall have power to provide by ordinance, not in conflict with the general laws of the state, for the protection of fish and game, and may shorten the season for the taking and killing of fish or game within the dates fixed by the state laws, but shall not lengthen the same.

The respondent's contention is that the regulation as to the killing and protection of wild game is referable to the police power, is local in its character, and is by the constitution delegated to the boards of supervisors. The right of the state legislature to enact laws for the protection of wild game, which belongs to the people of the state in their collective capacity, is held by our supreme court, in Ex parte Maier, 103 Cal. 482, 42 Am. St. Rep. 129, 37 Pac. 402, to be founded upon the general power to legislate, where not restrained by express or implied provisions of the constitution, and for the reason that the protection and preservation of game has been secured by law in all civilized countries, and may be justified on many grounds, one of which is for the purpose of food. In the case last mentioned, the legislative authority prohibiting one to have in his possession wild game, wherever killed, is said to be referable to the police power. The phrase "police power," as employed in the constitution, is admitted to be found many precedents wherein it is declared that certain legislation is referable to such power, notably in the case of Thorpe v. Rutland & Burlington R. R. Co., 27 Vt. 149, 62 Am. Dec. 625, cited and approved in Ex parte Maier, 103 Cal. 485, 42 Am. St. Rep. 129, 37 Pac. 405, where, in referring to

15

the phrase "police power," it is said: "It extends to the protection of the lives, limbs, comfort, and quiet of all persons, and the protection of all property within the state according to the maxim 'Sic utere tuo ut alienum non laedas,' which being of universal application, it must, of course, be within the range of legislative action to define. the mode and manner in which everyone may so use his own as not to injure others." It being established that it applies to the use of private property under certain exigencies, no reason is apparent why it should not be extended so as to include the interest and property which each citizen may own and possess in the collective property of the people of the state; and where, as in California, the diversity of climatic conditions—the immensity of its territory—would indicate the impropriety of exercising this police power through a general law applicable to the entire state, the necessity for local legislation, in order that complete and effective control or protection may be afforded, becomes apparent.

Were anything else required to establish the necessity for such local legislation, the amendment to the constitution, designated as section 25½, article 4, adopted in 1902, certainly indicates that the people of this state in the adoption of such amendment recognized the local character of legislation necessarily appropriate for the preservation of fish and game. We are of opinion, therefore, that the delegation of police power in section 11, article 11, should be held to include the local legislation necessary, in the opinion of the supervisors, to completely protect the wild game within the bounds of the various counties of the state. What we have here said applies to conditions existing prior to the year 1902, when the amendment to the constitution, designated as section 25½, article 4, was adopted. This amendment provides as follows: "The legislature may provide for the division of the state into fish and game districts, and may enact such laws for the protection of fish and game therein as they may deem appropriate." This section and the other sections of the constitution relating to the uniform application of the laws and the delegation of police power must be read and construed together; and in such construction the more specific provisions control the general, without regard to their comparative dates—the two acts operating together, and neither working the repeal of the other. Cooley's Constitutional Limitations, and other authorities cited in Martin v. Election Commissioners, 126 Cal. 411, 58 Pac. 932, in which latter case it is said that, although a new section may conflict with other sections of the same article, it would still be valid as to the particular cases for which it is intended, for in such case the particular and general both stand together, and neither abrogates the other; the former furnishing the rule for the particular case, the latter for all other cases. This section 25½ is manifestly a scheme for the regulation and control of a specific subject; and, according to the well-established rules of construction obtaining in relation to statutes, the latter will prevail, and the earlier be held to have been superseded: Mack v. Jastro, 126 Cal. 132, 58 Pac. 372. And in Murdock v. Mayor, 20 Wall. 590, 22 L. Ed. 429, cited in Mack v. Jastro, supra, where a like question was presented in relation to statutes, it is said: "We are of opinion that it was their intention to make a new law so far as the present law differed from the former, and that the new law embraced all that was to be preserved of the old."

While it is true that an immediate repeal of one of the provisions of the constitution may not be effected under the rule thus laid down as to statutes, yet the effect is to supersede previous constitutional provisions when conflicting amendments have been adopted whenever appropriate legislation is enacted carrying the amendments into effect. "There is no express repeal of the former provisions of the constitution. They merely cease to exist by reason of new provisions upon the same subject being substituted for them. . . . . The old provisions will cease to have effect from time to time, as the substituted provisions commence to operate:" In the Matter of Oliverez, 21 Cal. 418. Under these authorities, then, the laws in force when section 25½ was adopted continue in force until substituted by new legislation under the later amendments; but legislation after the adoption of such amendment must of necessity be in harmony with the constitution existing at the time of its enactment. So that even the legislature is restricted in its power to legislate upon this subject of game in any manner conflicting with section 25½.

The provisions of this section are mandatory. While the word "may" is employed, the subject of the amendment is in relation to the power given to public officers; and in Supervisors v. United States, 4 Wall. 436, 18 L. Ed. 419, it is said: "The conclusion to be adduced from the authorities is that, where power is given to public officers, ... the language used, though permissive in form, is in fact peremptory. What they are empowered to do for a third person, the law requires shall be done. The power is given, not for their benefit, but for his. It is given as a remedy to those entitled to invoke its aid"—cited in Hayes v. Los Angeles County, 99 Cal. 80, 33 Pac. 766. The word "may" in section 25½ must therefore be read "must"; and ever since its adoption the express command has been upon the state legislature to enact such legislation touching the care and custody of wild game as is necessary for its effectual and full protection, and this with reference to local conditions, if any such there be, which would require special legislation for particular localities.

We are unable to see, however, any significance attaching to the manner in which the word "may" shall be read in this constitutional amendment, inasmuch as its obvious intent was to confer upon the state legislature alone authority to deal with the subject of fish and game, and in such legislation to relieve it from the necessity of enacting general laws applicable alike to the whole state, and the effect of which could only be to remove the necessity theretofore existing for delegation of power to local authorities. We are of opinion, therefore, that any authority reposing in the legislature to delegate legislative power to counties in reference to this subject was revoked by the amendment 25½; and the failure and neglect of the legislature to obey the plain mandate of the constitution does not empower the board of supervisors to assume this duty reposing in the state alone. This ordinance, therefore, having been adopted since the adoption of section 25½, and since authority to delegate power with reference to this subject has ceased to exist, it must be held to be invalid. Were it even a valid exercise of power, the ordinance upon its face is an unreasonable exercise thereof. The delegated power originally was with reference to shortening the season, which can only be held to be a period of time within which persons might exercise a natural right to hunt and kill the game belonging to the public, and not to enact an ordinance in its nature prohibitive.

The ordinance, therefore, being void, it follows that the prisoner should be discharged; and it is so ordered.

I concur: Gray, P. J.

SMITH, J.—I concur in the decision on the ground last stated.

SCHINDLER v. GREEN et al.*

Court of Appeal, Third District; August 14, 1905.

82 Pac. 341.

Agency—Liability of Agent.—A Contract With Plaintiff for an alteration of defendants' house was signed by defendants' daughters, who had no interest in the house, but lived there with defendants. Defendants had actual knowledge of the agreement between plaintiff and their daughters, knew that the work was being performed by plaintiff, and received the benefit thereof. Held, that defendants' daughters were only agents for defendants, and were not liable on the contract signed by them.

Building Contracts—Acceptance of Work.—Plaintiff contracted to build an addition to defendants' house. The plastering of the addition was to be done by another contractor. Plaintiff claimed that his work was completed, and thereupon the plasterer went ahead with his contract, and did the plastering. But it was not shown that defendants occupied the addition. Held, that the doing of the plastering did not constitute an acceptance of plaintiff's work by defendants, such as to excuse plaintiff from actually completing the contract if it was not in fact completed when he quit work.

Mechanics' Liens—Trivial Imperfections—Unworkmanlike Construction.—The unworkmanlike failure of a contractor to place the front windows in the basement story of a small house directly underneath the front windows of the upper portion of the house did not constitute a trivial imperfection within the meaning of Code of Civil Procedure, section 1187, declaring that a trivial imperfection shall not be deemed such a lack of completion of the work as to prevent the filing of a mechanic's lien, but was a substantial noncompliance with the contract, which precluded the enforcement of a lien by the contractor.

APPEAL from Superior Court, Sacramento County; Peter J. Shields, Judge.

---

*For subsequent opinions, see post, p. 233; 149 Cal. 752, 87 Pac. 626.

Action by C. Schindler against Thomas Green and another. From a judgment for plaintiff and from an order denying a new trial, defendants appeal. Modified.

J. D. Moynahan and C. A. Elliott for appellants; R. Platnauer for respondent.

BUCKLES, J.—This is an action to foreclose a mechanic's lien. The contract was made by plaintiff with Annie and Maggie Green, daughters of the defendants, and who lived on the premises with the parents, defendants. The work consisted of doing the carpenter work in making alterations and adding two rooms to the house in which the defendants lived—one room as basement, twelve by sixteen, and one room above, twelve by sixteen, and a front porch six by sixteen feet. The plastering was done under another contract, by another party, with which plaintiff had nothing to do. There were no regular plans and specifications, or specifications as to where the doors or windows should be placed, the contract providing that there should be not to exceed six doors and not to exceed ten windows, and the new structure to be built uniformly with the old, to which it was to be an addition; to be plain, at the cost of $403.50 for all material and carpenter work. There were two windows put in the basement part in front, but they were not set directly under the two windows in the front of the upper story. The plaintiff claimed to have finished his contract and done all that he was required to do thereunder. The defendants and Mr. Devine (the brother of the defendant Margaret Green, and who drew the contract, and who seemed to be acting for defendants) demanded that the windows be changed so as to be directly under the windows above. This the plaintiff refused to do, and defendants thereupon refused to pay the balance of the contract, viz., $303.50, or for the extra work, until plaintiff should change the windows. After plaintiff had finished the job, as he claimed—at least after he had done all the work that he did do, and furnished all the material he did furnish—the man employed by defendants went on and did the plastering. The plastering was partially completed, if not fully so, when defendants employed another carpenter to change the windows, setting them exactly under the windows above, at a cost to defendants of $7.50. At the trial the plaintiff had judgment, and the appeal is by these defendants from the judgment and from the order denying their motion for a new trial. In the transcript there are thirty-seven specifications of error in the court's rulings as to the admission of evidence. We have gone over all of these rulings carefully, and, finding no reversible error therein, deem it unnecessary to refer to them further.

The appellant demurred to the complaint on the ground, among others, that there was a misjoinder of parties defendant. The demurrer was overruled, and no exception taken. It is now claimed that no lien could attach to the property until plaintiff should find it impossible to collect his judgment against Annie Green and Maggie Green, who signed the contract. They are not shown to have had any interest whatever in the property. The facts were shown to be as follows: Annie and Maggie Green were the daughters of the defendants, and lived with their parents on the said premises in said house. Devine, who drew the contract and who supervised and superintended the work, was a brother of the defendant Margaret Green, and the other defendant, Thomas Green, could sign his name only with a mark; and that both defendants had actual knowledge of the agreement between plaintiff and Annie and Maggie Green as regards the original contract and also as to the extra work, and they, and each of them, at the time the work was being performed, had actual notice that the work was being performed, and that the plaintiff was performing it. The defendants, and not Annie and Maggie Green, have been the recipients of whatever benefit came from the work of plaintiff, and Annie and Maggie, under all the circumstances named, appear as, and were, only agents for the defendants, and are not, therefore, liable.

It is claimed, also, by respondent that, inasmuch as the defendants caused the rooms he had built to be plastered, they thereby took possession and thereby accepted his work. There is neither allegation, issue nor finding upon this point. The evidence shows that the defendants were residing in the old part of the house, and that the man who was employed to do the plastering went ahead with his work after the plaintiff had placed the windows as he left them, and after he had quit work thereon. The plaintiff alleged he completed his contract October 13, 1902, but the court found he completed it September 18, 1902. The claim of lien was filed October 15, 1902. We think the circumstances of this case do not warrant us in saying there was an occupation and acceptance on the part of the defendants so as to excuse the plaintiff from completing his contract. The doing of the plastering was not an occupation of the rooms so as to create an acceptance of plaintiff's work, so as to start the statute in motion as to time to file lien. This is a dwelling-house, and there is no evidence that the defendants have ever occupied these two rooms built by plaintiff as a habitation: Jones v. Kruse, 138 Cal. 616, 72 Pac. 146.

The greatest fault found with plaintiff's work seemed to be in the manner in which the windows were placed in the front of the building. There was no dispute as to the fact that the lower windows were not immediately under the ones above. There was no reason given by any of the witnesses tending to show why they should not or could not have been so placed. The evidence did show that to place the windows as the plaintiff did place them was unworkmanlike, and the court found (finding 10): "That the two windows placed by plaintiff in the front portion of the basement story of said house were not directly underneath the two front windows of the upper portion of said house, which upper portion consisted of the old house after the same had been raised, and that the placing of such windows in this manner was not workmanlike; and the court finds that the failure of plaintiff to place said windows in the basement in a direct line underneath the two windows of the upper portion of said house is a trivial imperfection." We do not think the evidence supports the finding "that the failure of plaintiff to place said windows in the basement in a direct line underneath the two windows of the upper portion of said house is a trivial imperfection." Under the provisions of the last clause of section 1187 of the Code of Civil Procedure, a trivial imperfection in the work will not prevent a lien; but under the peculiar circumstances in this case, and where the court is compelled to find, as it did, that the work complained of was not done in a workmanlike manner, we do not think it can be said the defect is of a trivial nature to the owner. It is true the defect was small, but the building was a small one, and the addition made by plaintiff was a small structure. Whether or not the defect is a "trivial imperfection" in any case depends upon the facts and circumstances of each particular case: Willamette etc. Co. v. Los Angeles College Co., 94 Cal. 238, 29 Pac. 629. The defendants were just as much entitled to have their little structure, their home, completed according to the contract, and in a workmanlike manner, as the man who builds a palatial residence is to have first-class work done thereon, and in principle we can see no difference. It was a serious matter with the defendants, and they begged the plaintiff to make the change, which cost but $7.50 to make; but he refused, and declared he could do better in a lawsuit. The plaintiff had not complied with his contract. The findings do not support the judgment so far as the same fixes a lien upon said premises.

The motion for a new trial should have been granted. But, inasmuch as the question of the extra work and the value thereof was fully litigated in these proceedings, and the amount found due therefor, and the defendants have caused the work to be completed, it would be useless to order a new trial now, it appearing that a modification of the judgment would secure justice between the parties.

It is therefore ordered that the lower court be directed to modify its said judgment by striking therefrom the decree for a lien on the premises and providing for sale thereunder and cost of lien and attorney's fee, and enter judgment for plaintiff against defendants for the sum of $326.85, being the balance found due on said contract and for extra work, after having deducted the $7.50 paid by defendants for completing the work.

We concur: Chipman, P. J.; McLaughlin, J.

SCHINDLER v. GREEN et al.[*]

Court of Appeal, Third District; November 16, 1905.

82 Pac. 631.

Building Contract—Workmanlike Construction.—Where there is no provision in a building contract as to how windows are to be placed, there is an implied agreement that they shall be placed in a workmanlike manner.

---

[*]For subsequent opinion, see 149 Cal. 752, 87 Pac. 626.

Building Contract—Failure Fully to Perform—Compensation.—
Where a contractor fails to complete his contract, even though such
failure is a trivial variance, he must have acted in good faith and
honestly have endeavored to complete his work properly before he can
recover therefor, if the trivial variance is such as to entitle the
other party to damages to complete the work or make it as it should
be.

Mechanics' Liens—Appeal—Modification of Judgment.—Where,
in a suit to enforce a mechanic's lien, the lower court found that
defendants owed plaintiff a certain sum and awarded him a lien
therefor, and defendants found no fault with the amount awarded
plaintiff, but appealed on the ground that plaintiff was not entitled
to a lien, and all the evidence and proceedings had on the trial were
brought before the appellate court for review, that court, on setting
aside the judgment for error in giving plaintiff a lien, would not
remand the case for a new trial, but would direct the lower court to
modify the judgment by striking therefrom the provisions for a lien
and to enter a personal judgment in plaintiff's favor for the sum
found due.

BUCKLES, J.—This application for rehearing in this case
pretends to be based upon the ground that this court in the
original opinion in the case, filed August 14, 1905 (ante,
p. 229, 82 Pac. 341), committed error in holding that the
placing of two windows in the basement story of the house
not immediately under the windows in the story above was
unworkmanlike and was not satisfactory to defendants, and
was not a trivial imperfection. These windows constituted
a part of the ornamentation of this little house, as well as of
its constituent parts. Ornamentation is as much a matter
of substance as any of the constituent parts, such as light
and ventilation. The testimony in the case showed, and the
court below found, "that the two windows placed by plaintiff in the front portion of the basement story of said house
were not directly underneath the two front windows of the
upper portion of said house, which upper portion consisted
of the old house after the same had been raised, and that
the placing of such windows in this manner was not workmanlike." The testimony supports the above finding; but
this court found, further, "that the failure of plaintiff to
place said windows in the basement in a direct line underneath the two windows of the upper portion of said house
is a trivial imperfection." There is no evidence whatever
to support this finding, and no inflexible rule of law commanding such deduction: Harlan v. Stufflebeem, 87 Cal. 511.

25 Pac. 686. The evidence is that, as soon as defendants noticed that the windows were not properly placed, the attention of the plaintiff was called to it. He was then and repeatedly thereafter requested to change the windows and place them immediately under the ones above, but he refused to do so. When told that another would be employed to change the positions of the windows and the cost thereof would be deducted from what was due plaintiff, he replied he could do better to go to court, as defendants would have to pay counsel fees and other expenses. The evidence shows the cost of changing the windows and placing them as they should be to exceed $10.

It is true there was no provision in the contract as to how these windows were to be placed, but there was impliedly in plaintiff's contract an agreement that his work should be done in a workmanlike manner, and these windows were not placed in a workmanlike manner, and the failure to place them properly seems to indicate a want of good faith. In a Pennsylvania case, decided in Gillespie Tool Co., 123 Pa. 26, 16 Atl. 37, it is said: "The equitable doctrine of substantial performance is intended for the protection and relief of those who have faithfully and honestly endeavored to perform their contracts in all material and substantial particulars, so that their right to compensation may not be forfeited by reason of mere technical, inadequate, or unimportant omissions or defects. It is incumbent on him who invokes its protection to present a case in which there has been no willful omission or departure from the terms of his contract." The spirit manifested by this plaintiff, when his attention was called to the unworkmanlike manner of setting the front windows would indicate a willfulness, and not an honest endeavor to complete his work in a workmanlike manner. In Harlan v. Stufflebeem, 87 Cal. 511, 25 Pac. 687, the court says: "If there has been no willful departure from its provisions, and no omission of any of its essential parts, and the contractor has in good faith performed all of its substantive terms, he will not be held to have forfeited his right to a recovery by reason of trivial defects or imperfections in the work performed. If the omission or imperfection is so slight that it cannot be regarded as an integral or substantive part of the original contract, and the other party can be compensated therefor by a recoupment for damages, the contractor does not lose his right of action"—citing numerous cases. That case was before the supreme court on the judgment-roll alone, where the court was unable to view the evidence before the lower court, and the court said: "In the absence of the testimony upon this point, we are bound to assume that it was sufficient to support the finding that the plaintiffs substantially completed their contract, as also the finding that the defendants would be fully compensated for any imperfection in the work by deducting $5 from the contract price." But in the case at bar the testimony is before us, and we do not believe it supports the finding "that the failure of the plaintiff to place said windows in the basement in a direct line underneath the two windows of the upper portion of said house is a trivial imperfection"; that is, if such can be considered a finding of fact. In Perry v. Quackenbush, 105 Cal. 307, 38 Pac. 742, the court said: "In such case there must be a substantial performance of every material covenant in the contract, and the failure must not have resulted from design or bad faith, and whether these facts exist is a matter to be determined by the jury, or the court sitting as a jury. Substantial performance must be found."

Carpenter v. Ibbetson, 1 Cal. App. 272, 81 Pac. 1114, cited by respondent, is a case where the contract price was $1,000 and to be paid before the work begun, and $900 was so paid. There was extra work amounting to $300. Payment was refused, and the contractor brought suit, alleging completion of the work, which was inside work. The answer denies the completion or performance of the contract and the amount due, and by way of cross-complaint specifies breaches of the contract. The lower court found the contract had not been completed and that the defendants were damaged in the sum of $382.52, which was the amount that plaintiff sued for. The appellate court held that this was not the true measure of damages, and that the case was one of substantial compliance with the contract, and also that the payment was to be made before the commencement of the work, and is to be regarded as an independent promise. Besides, there was no suggestion of a want of good faith on the part of the contractor, as in the case at bar. In the case of Van Clief et al. v. Van Vechten, 130 N. Y. 579, 29 N. E. 1019, cited by respondent, this language is used: "But when, as in this case, there is a willful refusal by the contractor to perform his contract, and he wholly abandons it, and after due notice refuses to have anything more to do with it, his right to recover depends upon performance of his contract, without any omission so substantial in its character as to call for an allowance of damages if he had acted in good faith. While slight and insignificant imperfections or deviations may be overlooked on the principle of 'de minimis non curat lex,' the contract in other respects must be performed according to its terms. When the refusal to proceed is willful, the difference between substantial and literal performance is bounded by the line of 'de minimis' ''—citing a long list of cases. So, in the case at bar, the difference was such that it required the payment of damages, small though they were, to make the change of windows to make them conform to the implied contract that they would stand in the building in a workmanlike manner, and the plaintiff having abandoned the work, showing a willful disregard for his contract and entire want of good faith. It is deemed useless to cite further authorities, for there seems to be a remarkable uniformity in all the cases, holding that, where a contractor has failed to complete his contract, even though the failure is a trivial variance, he must have acted in good faith and honestly endeavored to complete his work properly, before he can recover, if the trivial variance is such as to entitle the defendant to damages to complete or make it as it should be. Good faith and honest intention are prerequisites before relaxing the rule of strict performance to substantial performance. It will be borne in mind this was a small dwelling, being but sixteen by thirty-two feet, with but two windows in the front in each story, so that the misplacing of the windows in the basement story is not so small a matter, and these people, the defendants, are as much entitled to have the windows in their little home put in perfectly, and in a workmanlike manner as the owner of a more imposing structure. The imperfections complained of, while generally they would be considered small, in this instance, to these people, became a matter of great importance. The evidence shows that, had the plaintiff acted in good faith, with an honest endeavor to do the right thing, he could have had his money without suit.

For the reasons stated the plaintiff is not entitled to a lien; and, as we see no reason for changing the views ex-

pressed in our former opinion, the same are adhered to. In
that opinion we directed that a personal judgment be entered in favor of plaintiff for $326.85, being the amount
found due him in the lower court. In his brief on rehearing
plaintiff objects to this, on the ground that, if he is entitled
to a personal judgment, he is entitled to a lien. That he
is not entitled to a personal judgment any more than a lien
is true, viewed as an abstract proposition of law. But all
the evidence taken in the lower court, as well as all the proceedings had on the trial, are before us, and it is plain,
under the views we have expressed and a review of the evidence, there is no reason for remanding the case for a new
trial: Bianchi v. Hughs, 124 Cal. 24, 56 Pac. 610. And possibly this court would have been justified in simply remanding the case for a new trial, even though nothing but delay
and vexation to both sides could result from such a course.
But in the case at bar the defendants stood ready to pay the
balance due by deducting the amount which it would take
to reset the windows, and tendered what was claimed by
defendants to be due, and deposited the same in court, and
at no time have defendants claimed they would not pay. It
is true there was some difference as to extra work, but no
material difference as to the cost of changing the windows,
all of which was thoroughly gone into at the trial, and the
lower court found defendants owed plaintiff the sum of
$326.85. The defendants in their brief seem to be satisfied
with the amount found due, and say that no good result
could come to either litigant by sending the case back for
a new trial. Quoting from defendants' brief: "The case appears to have been fully and exhaustively tried in the lower
court upon its merits." Then it quotes the following rule:
"Where the court can see from the record what the rights of
the parties are, it will not remand the case, but will render
such a decree as ought to have been rendered below"—and
the close of said brief declares that substantial justice has
been done between the parties. It appears, therefore, that
any further litigation in this matter is for the sole purpose
of attorneys' fees for plaintiff and the costs of making and
filing a lien, which plaintiff cannot recover upon, under the
views here expressed.

    Upon these considerations and in the interest of justice, it
is therefore ordered that the lower court be directed to

modify its said judgment by striking therefrom its decree declaring a lien on the premises and providing for a sale thereunder and costs of lien and attorneys' fees, then enter a personal judgment against defendants and in favor of plaintiff for the sum of $326.85, and, as so modified, the judgment is affirmed.

We concur: Chipman, P. J.; McLaughlin, J.

ALBION LUMBER COMPANY v. CALIFORNIA BRIDGE AND CONSTRUCTION COMPANY et al.

Court of Appeal, First District; September 13, 1905.

82 Pac. 631.

Appeal—Conflicting Evidence.—Findings of the Trial Court on a question of fact, based on conflicting evidence, will not be disturbed on appeal.

APPEAL from Superior Court, City and County of San Francisco; J. M. Seawell, Judge.

Action by the Albion Lumber Company against the California Bridge and Construction Company and others. From an order denying defendant's motion for a new trial they appeal. Affirmed.

W. Lair Hill for appellants; Albert H. Elliot and Edward H. Stearns for respondent.

HALL, J.—Appeal from order denying defendant's motion for a new trial. The motion was made on the ground of insufficiency of the evidence to justify certain findings. The labor of the court in this case is very greatly reduced by the frank admission on the part of the counsel for appellant that upon all points save one there was a substantial conflict of testimony. The suit is to recover a balance of $486.04 alleged to be unpaid upon an account for lumber furnished defendant by plaintiff for certain work done by defendant at San Rafael. The defendant claims that the court should have allowed defendant a credit for $183.92, loss upon certain piles furnished defendant by plaintiff, through one Pierce, for a job done by defendant near Fresno.

Upon this point the testimony of A. W. Burrell was to the effect that plaintiff agreed to furnish for the Fresno job, among other things, piles; that before the piles were shipped defendant was to have been notified, so that the piles might be inspected at San Francisco; that defendant was so notified, save as to two carloads, twenty-four piles in number, and that after the shipment of these two carloads, and before delivery at Sanger (a point near Fresno), it was discovered that they were not according to the description of piles which were to be furnished, and thereupon he notified McIntyre (the representative of the plaintiff) and asked to have the piles returned and suitable piles put in their place; that McIntyre said it would not pay to ship them back there (San Francisco), and directed him to sell them to the best advantage he could, or make such use of them as the company could make, and the Albion Lumber Company would "stand the loss." The witness further testified as to what he did do with the piles in question, and to the effect that it resulted in a loss of $183.92. On this point, however, the testimony of McIntyre, who represented the plaintiff, is set forth as follows: "The lumber and piles sold to Pierce [referring to the lumber and piles furnished defendant for the Fresno job] were all shipped as ordered, and were all inspected in San Francisco before being shipped, and were all of the character ordered, and no objection was ever made thereto. The witness denied that he ever directed Mr. Burrell to sell or use any defective piles, or ever stated that the Albion Lumber Company would stand any loss for defective piles, and denied that A. W. Burrell, or the California Bridge & Construction Company, or C. C. Pierce ever made any claim for defective piles." There is thus a direct conflict between the testimony of Burrell and McIntyre upon the question at issue. We cannot interfere with the decision of the trial court upon a question of fact, where there is a substantial conflict in the evidence.

The order denying a motion for a new trial is affirmed.

We concur: Harrison, P. J.; Cooper, J.

PROUTY v. ADAMS et al.

Court of Appeal, Third District; October 4, 1905.

82 Pac. 1081.

Appeal—Law of the Case—Pleading—Amendment.—Where, on a prior appeal, it was held that defendants' rights were limited by a written contract of indemnity, and that no defense at variance with the terms of the indemnity could be interposed, and judgment was reversed, with directions to the court to strike out or otherwise refuse to entertain a special defense objected to, whereupon the court struck the amended answer "according to the directions of the supreme court" and granted leave to amend, such decision was the law of the case, and defendants were not entitled to file an amended answer merely omitting all mention of the written contract and pleading the defense so stricken.

APPEAL from Superior Court, San Joaquin County; W. B. Nutter, Judge.

Action by S. Prouty against Robert Adams and another. From an order granting plaintiff's motion to strike certain matter from an amended answer, defendants appeal. Affirmed.

A. C. White and C. H. Fairall for appellants; R. C. Minor for respondent.

BUCKLES, J.—This is the second appeal in this cause: Prouty v. Adams, 141 Cal. 304, 74 Pac. 845. The facts are fully stated in the decision upon such former appeal. It was there held that the rights of the defendants were limited by a written contract of indemnity executed contemporaneously with the execution of the note sued upon, and that no defense at variance with the terms of that indemnity could be interposed. The judgment and order denying a new trial were there reversed, "with directions to the trial court to strike out or otherwise refuse to entertain the special defense above adverted to." Upon the going down of the remittitur, the trial court made the following order: "On motion of Avery C. White, Esq., counsel for defendants, the court made an order striking out the amended answer of defendants herein, according to the directions of the supreme court, and granted defendants fifteen days in which to file an amended answer herein." Thereafter, and within the

16

time so granted, the defendants filed an answer wherein all
mention of the written contract of indemnity was omitted,
and the self-same special defense included in the order of
the supreme court, and mentioned and stricken out by the
order granting leave to amend, was again pleaded. The
plaintiff moved to strike said matter from the amended answer, and from the order granting said motion defendants
prosecute this appeal.

Appellants claim that additional matter by way of "novation" or "substitution" was included in the matter stricken
out, but an examination of the record shows that, no matter
what this alleged new matter may be called, it is within the
very letter of the decision upon the first appeal which became the law of the case. Appellants also contend that the
order of the trial court permitted the amendment made. We
do not think so. The supreme court directed the lower
court to strike out or otherwise refuse to entertain this very
defense, and the order of the court below, construed in the
light of this direction, could only mean an amendment in
accordance with the law of the case as laid down by the
supreme court. Such was the construction placed upon its
order by the court making it. An order directing that certain matter may be stricken from an answer can hardly be
distorted into an order permitting its reinsertion. It is said,
however, that the amendment avoids the law of the case laid
down on the first appeal, and that neither the lower court
nor this court can have knowledge of the fact that there was
a written indemnity. In answer to this it may be said that
the court below certainly was compelled to take cognizance
of the order expressly excluding the very matter here
pleaded, and no amount of sophistical pleading or reasoning
could destroy the force of that order or nullify the rule of
law applied to the facts which the defendant placed before
the court. The amendment, including matter stricken out
by the court below in accordance with the mandate of the
supreme court, was therefore unauthorized. The mere omission of reference to the written indemnity could not nullify
such order, and, if it could, such an amendment would be
so plainly sham that the court would strike it out anyway.
The law does not impute to a court such ignorance of its
own records and the decisions of the supreme court that
matter may be repleaded which has not only been eliminated

by express order, but which would be brought within the law of the case in any event, and thus neutralized and destroyed, by the mere introduction of the written indemnity at the trial. Nor are courts so impotent that chicanery cannot be frowned upon, or playing fast and loose with courts of justice prevented.

The order is affirmed.

We concur: Chipman, P. J.; McLaughlin, J.

In re TUCKER.

Court of Appeal, Third District; October 23, 1905.

83 Pac. 814.

Appeal—Subsequent Settlement—Dismissal.—Where, after the submission of an appeal, the subject matter of the action was settled by the parties, the appeal will be dismissed on respondent's motion suggesting such settlement.

Application by W. E. Tucker for mandamus against F. L. Caughey, as county auditor of Mendocino county. On motion to dismiss appeal. Granted.

McNabb & Hirsch for appellant; W. E. Tucker in pro. per.

CHIPMAN, P. J.—This cause was submitted when reached upon the calendar upon the written statement of attorneys for appellant that they understood that respondent was willing to submit the case upon the authority of Humiston v. Shaffer, 145 Cal. 195, 78 Pac. 651, and asked that it be so submitted.

The court ordered the case submitted upon that statement. Subsequently the respondent served and filed a motion for dismissal of the appeal, supported by an affidavit in which it appears that the subject matter of the action has been settled by the parties and that the respondent has been paid by the county auditor the amount involved in the controversy and the judgment therein satisfied. The order heretofore submitting the cause is vacated and the motion of respondent is granted.

The appeal is dismissed, each party to pay his own costs.

We concur: McLaughlin, J.; Buckles, J.

UNION COLLECTION COMPANY v. NATIONAL FER-
TILIZER COMPANY.

Court of Appeal, First District; October 24, 1905.

82 Pac. 1129.

Assignment—-Action by Assignee.—Where a Complaint Alleged
that defendant was indebted to plaintiff's assignor for services rendered
at defendant's special instance and request between certain dates;
that the services were reasonably worth $1,050, which had not been
paid, except the sum of $46; that the claim was assigned to plaintiff
on a certain day, two days before the services were fully performed;
and that the plaintiff ever since has been, and now is, the owner and
holder thereof—stated a cause of action; it being immaterial when
the assignment was made.

APPEAL from Superior Court, City and County of San
Francisco; Thomas F. Graham, Judge.

Action by the Union Collection Company against the
National Fertilizer Company. From a judgment in favor of
plaintiff, defendant appeals. Affirmed.

Kinley & Kinley for appellant; P. A. Bergerot for respondent.

COOPER, J.—This appeal is from the judgment on the
judgment-roll alone. The complaint states facts sufficient to
constitute a cause of action. It alleges that the defendant
became indebted to plaintiff's assignor for services rendered at defendant's special instance and request between
the first day of June, 1901, and the thirty-first day of July,
1902; that such services were of the reasonable value of
$1,050, and the same has not been paid, except the sum of
$46. The assignment to plaintiff is alleged to have been
made on the twenty-ninth day of July, 1902, two days before
the services were fully performed. The complaint states
that by reason of the assignment the plaintiff "ever since
has been, and now is, the owner and holder thereof." It
does not concern the defendant as to when the indebtedness
was assigned to plaintiff. The findings follow the complaint and are sufficient.

There is no merit in this appeal, and the judgment is
affirmed, with $100 damages to respondent.

We concur: Harrison, P. J.; Hall, J.

Ex parte OATES.

Court of Appeal, Third District; November 10, 1905.

83 Pac. 261.

Habeas Corpus—Inability of Justices to Agree.—Rule 33, providing that when the judges of a district court of appeal fail to agree on a judgment in any cause, and their opinions have been forwarded to the supreme court, that court will order such cause to be transferred to the supreme court or to another district court of appeal, to be there heard and determined, does not apply to habeas corpus proceedings; and where three of the justices fail to agree in such proceedings, as required by constitution, article 6, section 4, the writ must be dismissed.[1]

Application of W. W. Oates for a writ of habeas corpus. Writ dismissed.

W. W. Middenhoff for petitioner; E. J. Williams for respondent.

CHIPMAN, P. J.—The petition for the writ was ordered to be heard by the court. Under the provisions of the constitution the concurrence of three justices shall be necessary to pronounce a judgment. Article 6, section 4 of the Constitutional Rule 33 (78 Pac. xiii), provides that when the judges of a district court of appeal fail to agree on a judgment in any cause, and their opinions have been forwarded to the supreme court, that court will order such cause to be transferred to the supreme court or to another district court of appeal, to be there heard and determined. We do not think this rule applies to habeas corpus proceedings. In the matter now before us the three justices constituting the court are unable to agree upon the question as to whether or not the court before which the contempt proceedings were brought had jurisdiction.

The writ is therefore dismissed, and the petitioner remanded to the custody of the sheriff of San Joaquin county.

We concur: Buckles, J.; McLaughlin, J.

---

[1] Cited and followed in the similar case of In re Osborne, 13 Cal. App. 736, 110 Pac. 583.

Cited and followed in Ex parte Sauer, 3 Cal. App. 238, 84 Pac. 995, the court saying that "on the authority of the decision in the case of Ex parte Oates . . . . under article 6, section 4, of the constitution, the writ must be regarded as denied." The Sauer case was that of a person in custody under the extradition laws.

HEWLETT v. BEEDE et al.*

Sac. No. 1405; February 26, 1906.

83 Pac. 1089.

Court of Appeals—Transfer of Cause to Supreme Court.—A petition to transfer a cause from the court of appeal to the supreme court, filed more than ten days after the judgment in the former court became final, will be stricken from the files.

Action by Samuel Hewlett against W. M. S. Beede and others. Plaintiff petitions to transfer the cause from the court of appeal to the supreme court. Petition stricken from files.

PER CURIAM.—It appearing that on February 10, 1906, the clerk of this court inadvertently filed the petition of the appellant herein for an order transferring the cause for hearing from the third district court of appeal to the supreme court, and that said date was more than ten days after the judgment in the said district court of appeal became final therein, it is therefore now ordered that said petition be stricken from the files of this court.

———

DARLINGTON v. BUTLER (KOHN, Intervener.)*

Court of Appeal, Third District; March 1, 1906.

85 Pac. 931.

Appeal—Dismissal.—The Consideration of a Motion to Dismiss an appeal by an intervener, on the ground that he is not a party aggrieved, will be postponed, where some of the questions involved in the appeal will have to be considered in determining the motion.

APPEAL from Superior Court, El Dorado County; N. D. Arnot, Judge.

Action by Abe Darlington against Sarah Butler; Nathan L. Kohn, Intervener. From the judgment rendered, the in-

*See 2 Cal. App. 561, 83 Pac. 1086.

*For subsequent opinion, see 3 Cal. App. 448, 86 Pac. 194.

tervener appeals. Original application to dismiss appeal. Consideration postponed.

Wm. F. Bray for appellant; Chas. A. Swisler for respondent.

BUCKLES, J.—This is an original application to dismiss the appeal pending in this court, brought here by Nathan L. Kohn, the intervener in the court below. The motion is made by the respondent upon the ground that said intervener is not a party aggrieved by the judgment and order appealed from, and that he has no right to appeal. As some of the questions involved in the appeal would have to be considered in determining this motion, we think the further consideration of the motion should be postponed and be taken up with the appeal when it is presented.

It is therefore ordered that the determination of the motion to dismiss the appeal be postponed, to be taken up with the appeal when said appeal is presented and determined at that time.

We concur: Chipman, P. J.; McLaughlin, J.

MOODY v. PEIRANO.*

Court of Appeal, First District; March 1, 1906.

84 Pac. 783.

Sale of Seeds—Breach of Warranty.—The Measure of Damages for breach of a warranty as to the quality or variety of certain seeds sold to plaintiff is the difference of the value of the crop produced and the value of the crop that would have been produced had there been no breach of warranty.[1]

Sale of Seeds.—In an Action for Breach of Warranty of Variety of seed wheat sold, plaintiff alleged that defendant warranted the wheat to be "White Australian," but that it was actually wheat of another and inferior variety, and produced a crop of hay inferior to that which would have been grown had the wheat been of the variety warranted, and that by reason of the premises plaintiff had been dam-

---

*For subsequent opinion, see 4 Cal. App. 411, 88 Pac. 380.

[1] Cited in the note in 37 L. R. A., N. S., 86, on the liability of a vendor of seeds.

aged in the sum of $1,000. Held, that the complaint sufficiently al-
leged that the crop produced was of less value than the crop that
would have been produced if the wheat had been as warranted, and
was therefore not demurrable for failure to specially allege the damages sustained.

Sale of Seeds.—Where, in an Action for Breach of Warranty,
the court found the facts as alleged in the complaint as to the sale
of the seed wheat in question, the warranty, the breach, the planting
of the wheat, and that the crop produced was inferior to that which
would have been produced had there been no breach, and further
found that plaintiff had been damaged in the sum of $359.50, for
which sum, less a counterclaim, judgment was given, such findings
were sufficient to support the judgment, without a finding of the evidentiary facts showing such damage.

Sale of Seeds—Breach of Warranty—Evidence.—Where, in an
action for breach of warranty in the sale of seed wheat warranted
to be "White Australian," defendant testified that he sold to M.
wheat from the same lot from which he sold plaintiff, evidence of M.
that he bought wheat of defendant near the time when plaintiff
bought his wheat, and that, when the crop was grown, it proved to be
different wheat from "White Australian," was relevant and material
to show that the wheat sold to plaintiff was not of that variety.

Sale of Seeds—Evidence—Res Inter Alios Acta.—In an action
for breach of warranty of the variety of certain seed wheat sold,
testimony of a third person that defendant sold wheat to him in
the same season that the wheat was sold to plaintiff, and warranted
it to be of the variety warranted to plaintiff, was res inter alios acta,
and inadmissible.

Witnesses—Cross-examination — Collateral Matters.—Where a
witness is cross-examined as to collateral matters not testified to in
chief, the party conducting the cross-examination is bound by the
witness' answers as to such matters, and cannot contradict the same
by other evidence for the purpose of impeaching the witness.

APPEAL from Superior Court, Santa Clara County; A. L.
Rhodes, Judge.

Action by W. D. Moody against G. Peirano. From a judgment in favor of plaintiff, and from an order denying defendant's motion for a new trial, he appeals. Reversed.

Wm. P. Veuve for appellant; F. J. Hambly for respondent.

HALL, J.—Appeal from judgment for plaintiff and order
denying defendant's motion for a new trial.

The action is one for damages for breach of warranty as
to the variety of certain seed wheat sold by defendant to

plaintiff. It is alleged that plaintiff purchased of defendant 27,760 pounds of seed wheat for planting. That defendant warranted said seed wheat to be "white Australian." That plaintiff planted the same, and it produced a crop of 275 tons of hay. That said wheat was not "White Australian," but was another and inferior variety, and produced a crop of hay inferior to that which would have been grown had said wheat been of the variety known as "White Australian" seed wheat. That by reason of the premises the plaintiff has been damaged in the sum of $1,000. Defendant demurred for insufficiency of facts to constitute a cause of action, which demurrer was by the court overruled. In this the court did not err. The point relied on is that the damages are not specially alleged. The measure of damages for breach of warranty as to quality or variety of seeds sold for planting is the difference between the value of the crop produced and the value of the crop that would have been produced had there been no breach of warranty: Wolcott v. Mount, 36 N. J. L. 262, 13 Am. Rep. 438; Wolcott v. Mount, 38 N. J. L. 496, 20 Am. Rep. 425; 1 Sedgwick on Damages, sec. 191; Passinger v. Thorburn, 34 N. Y. 634, 90 Am. Dec. 753; White v. Miller, 71 N. Y. 118, 27 Am. Rep. 13; Van Wyck v. Allen, 69 N. Y. 61, 25 Am. Rep. 136. The complaint alleges a breach of the warranty, and in terms alleges that the seed wheat "produced a crop of hay inferior to that which would have been grown had said seed wheat been of the variety known as 'White Australian' seed wheat. That by reason of the premises the plaintiff has been damaged in the sum of $1,000." The word "inferior" is defined by Webster as meaning less important or less valuable. The allegation, therefore, that the wheat produced a crop of hay inferior to that which would have been grown had said seed wheat been of the variety known as "White Australian," is in substance an allegation that the crop produced was of less value than the crop that would have been produced if the wheat had been as warranted. This was followed by the allegation that by reason of the premises the plaintiff has been damaged in the sum of $1,000. Thus the complaint states the cause of the damage and the amount of the damage, and in the face of a general demurrer only certainly is sufficient. "Where, under the allegation of damages in the complaint or declaration, the plaintiff would be entitled to recover some amount, although nominal, the complaint is not demurrable": 5 Ency. of Pl. & Pr. 704; Cowley v. Davidson, 10 Minn. 392 (Gil. 314). See, also, 5 Ency. of Pl. & Pr. 738; Sunnyside Land Co. v. Willamette Bridge Co., 20 Or. 544, 26 Pac. 835; Colrick v. Swinburne, 105 N. Y. 503, 12 N. E. 427; McCarty v. Beach, 10 Cal. 462.

It is urged that the findings do not support the judgment. The facts as to the sale of seed wheat, the warranty, the breach, the planting of the wheat, and that the crop produced was inferior to what would have been produced had there been no breach of warranty, are found as alleged in the complaint, and that plaintiff has been damaged by the breach of said warranty in the sum of $379.50, for which sum, less a counterclaim found to be due defendant from plaintiff, judgment was given plaintiff. The facts found as above set forth fully cover the allegations of the complaint, and are sufficient to support the judgment. Under the pleadings it was not necessary for the court to find the various evidentiary facts that show that the amount of the damages did amount to $379.50. ·

The third point relied on by appellant for a reversal is that the court erred in overruling his objections to certain questions asked witnesses Myall and Main. Mayall testified, over the objection of defendant, to the effect that he bought wheat of defendant near to the time when plaintiff bought his wheat, and when the crop was grown it proved to be a different wheat from White Australian. Defendant testified in this connection that he sold Myall wheat from the same lot from which he sold plaintiff. It is thus apparent that this testimony of Myall, taken in connection with the testimony of the defendant, tended to show that the wheat sold plaintiff was not "White Australian," and was therefore material and relevant. The witness Myall was also permitted to testify, over the objection of defendant, that defendant represented to him that the wheat he was selling him was White Australian. And also, after plaintiff had rested his case in chief, and defendant had closed his case, plaintiff was allowed to prove by the witness Main, over the objection of defendant, that it was not rebuttal, and was incompetent, irrelevant and immaterial, that defendant had sold wheat to him (Main) in the same season when he sold to plaintiff, and had warranted it to be "White Australian." This was clearly error. Except where the knowledge, notice or intention of a party is a material fact in the case, the rule is that no evidence of similar transactions with third parties can be given. Such evidence is uniformly rejected: 1 Whar. Ev., sec. 29; Martinez v. Planel, 36 Cal. 578; King v. La Grange, 61 Cal. 221; Roberts v. Dixon, 50 Kan. 436, 31 Pac. 1083; Gill v. Staylor, 97 Md. 665, 55 Atl. 398; Davis v. Kneale, 97 Mich. 72, 56 N. W. 220; Roles v. Mintzner, 27 Minn. 31, 6 N. W. 378; McLoghlin v. Bank, 139 N. Y. 514, 34 N. E. 1095; Aiken v. Kennison, 58 Vt. 665, 5 Atl. 757; Repass v. Richmond, 99 Va. 508, 39 S. E. 160; Hartman v. Evans, 38 W. Va. 669, 18 S. E. 810; Kelly v. Schupp, 60 Wis. 76, 18 N. W. 725; Oliver v. Morawetz, 95 Wis. 1, 69 N. W. 977.

The evidence as to representations and warranties made to third parties was clearly res inter alios acta. Such evidence did not tend to prove that defendant warranted the wheat he sold to plaintiff. The fact that defendant, in answer to questions put by plaintiff, in cross-examination (also over defendant's objections), had testified that he had not warranted the wheat sold to Main to be White Australian, did not make such evidence admissible. When a witness is cross-examined as to collateral matters not testified to in chief, the party conducting the cross-examination is bound by the answers of the witness as to such matters, and cannot contradict such answers by other evidence for the purpose of impeaching the witness: Trabing v. Calif. etc. Imp. Co., 121 Cal. 137, 53 Pac. 644; Redington v. Pacific Postal Co., 107 Cal. 317, 48 Am. St. Rep. 132, 40 Pac. 432. The evidence as to warranties to third persons was inadmissible for any purpose, and the objection that it was immaterial and irrelevant was sufficiently definite: Morehouse v. Morehouse, 140 Cal. 88, 73 Pac. 738. In this case the main controversy was as to whether or not the defendant had warranted the wheat sold to plaintiff to be "White Australian," and the erroneous admission of the testimony above referred to was clearly prejudicial: Rulofson v. Billings, 140 Cal. 452, 74 Pac. 35; Estate of James, 124 Cal. 653, 57 Pac. 578, 1008; Helling v. Schindler, 145 Cal. 303, 78 Pac. 710.

The judgment and order must be reversed, and it is so ordered.

We concur: Harrison, P. J.; Cooper, J.

ARCHIBALD ESTATE v. MATTESON.*

Court of Appeal, Third District; March 5, 1906.

84 Pac. 840.

Nonsuit.—Where the Testimony of the Plaintiff Tends to prove all the material allegations of his complaint, defendant's motion for a nonsuit will not be granted.[1]

APPEAL from Superior Court, Madera County; W. M. Conley, Judge.

Action by the Archibald estate against A. H. Matteson. From a judgment for defendant, plaintiff appeals. Reversed.

R. L. Hargrove for appellant; R. E. Rhodes for respondent.

BUCKLES, J.—This action is to recover $1,050 as money had and received. The appeal is from an order granting a nonsuit and from an order denying a motion for a new trial. The appeal comes here on a bill of exceptions.

The appellant was duly organized under the laws of the state of California, a corporation by the name of Archibald Estate. On June 4, 1904, the board of directors organized and elected J. F. Archibald president, and on that day passed and recorded in the minutes of the board the following resolution: "Resolved, That the President of this corporation be and he is authorized, empowered and directed to draw from any bank or person or corporation in which may be deposited any of the money or funds of this corporation upon his own signature and request, and the signature of the secretary shall not be necessary to draw said money or funds."

The answer of defendant specifically denies owing the plaintiff anything and claimed upon the trial and argues in his brief that his transaction out of which he received the $1,050 was had with J. F. Archibald individually, and not with the appellant. It appears from the evidence that the property, real and personal, including money, and funds in

---

*For subsequent opinion, see 5 Cal. App. 441, 90 Pac. 723.

[1] Cited in Archibald v. Matteson, 5 Cal. App. 442, 448, 90 Pac. 723–726, as an element in the history of the case; the latter appeal being from the judgment upon retrial had following the reversal in the earlier.

bank of J. F. Archibald were by him transferred to the appellant corporation. The money received by the respondent was paid to him by two checks, which are in the following words and figures, to wit:

"Madera, Cal., September 1, 1904.

"Commercial Bank of Madera: Pay to the order of A. H. Mattison the amount, eight hundred dollars.

"$800.00.   J. F. ARCHIBALD, Pres."

"Madera, Cal., October 22nd, 1904.

"Commercial Bank of Madera: Pay to the order of A. H. Mattison, amount two hundred and fifty dollars.

"$250.00.   J. F. ARCHIBALD, Pres."

Both these checks were cashed by defendant and paid from the funds of appellant. The evidence offered by plaintiff at the trial tends to show that J. F. Archibald, the president of appellant corporation, died November, 1904. That defendant received the $1,050 as a loan from appellant and had not paid the same. The defendant was called by plaintiff as a witness and testified that the money was loaned him on an agreement that J. F. Archibald would furnish him all the money needed for his farming operations for the years 1904 and 1905, but did not testify as to the amount needed. There was some question as to whether the debt was due when the suit was commenced, but we think the testimony tends in some measure to show that it was due. When appellant rested a motion for nonsuit was granted. This was error. The well-settled rule in this state is that where the testimony of the plaintiff tends to prove all the material allegations of his complaint, a nonsuit will not be granted. A nonsuit is denied where there is any evidence tending to sustain the plaintiff's cause. Citing of authorities is unnecessary.

The judgment of nonsuit is reversed.

We concur: Chipman, P. J.; McLaughlin, J.

Ex parte GOLDMAN.

Court of Appeal, Third District; March 7, 1906.

88 Pac. 819.

Habeas Corpus.—A Person Imprisoned Under an Indictment which does not charge a public offense may obtain his discharge on an application for a writ of habeas corpus.[1]

Penal Code, Section 32, Defining Accessories as those who after knowledge of the commission of a felony conceal it from the magistrate or protect the person charged with the crime, states the common-law rule that a person must know that he is assisting a felon or else he cannot be charged as an accessory, and the mere neglect to inform the authorities that a felony has been committed is not sufficient, the word "conceal" in the statute including some affirmative act on the part of the person looking to the concealment of the felony.

Obstructing Justice—Concealing Evidence.—An Indictment alleging that accused after and with knowledge that a third person had stolen certain property concealed the property stolen and concealed from the magistrate the commission of the felony, states no offense under Penal Code, section 135, punishing concealment of evidence about to be introduced, because it fails to state the purpose of the act.

Indictment—Requisites.—Where an Act may Fall Within the definition of several offenses, according to the purpose with which it is done, it is essential to the statement of any offense that the purpose be set forth.

Receiving Stolen Goods.—An Indictment Alleging That Accused, after and with knowledge that a third person, had stolen certain property, concealed the property and concealed from the magistrate the

---

[1] Cited with approval by Chief Justice Potter, dissenting from the majority opinion, in McGinnis v. State, 16 Wyo. 105, 91 Pac. 948, which was an appeal from an order denying a motion in arrest of judgment on a charge of robbery. There the citation was, in connection with that of In re Myrtle, 2 Cal. App. 383, 84 Pac. 335, on the question of what was, and what was not, a sufficient allegation.

Cited and followed in Ex parte Rickey, 31 Nev. 89, 135 Am. St. Rep. 651, 100 Pac. 137. There one was detained as for embezzlement, and averred, on habeas corpus, that the indictment, which the state admitted to state the facts, did not allege an offense; and it was held that this threw it upon the court to inspect the indictment and, if finding this to be deficient as averred, to discharge the prisoner.

Cited and followed in Ex parte Shaw, 4 Okl. Cr. 425, 113 Pac. 1066, where the charge intended to be made against the person held was the statutory offense of defrauding an elector of his vote.

commission of the felony, states no offense under Penal Code, section 496, punishing the receiving of stolen property.

Accessories.—An Indictment Charging That Accused after and with knowledge of the commission of a felony concealed its commission from the magistrate does not charge accused with being an accessory within Penal Code, section 32, defining accessories as those who after knowledge of the commission of a felony conceal it from the magistrate, as it does not allege the acts constituting the offense.

Application of Edward Goldman for a writ of habeas corpus. Petitioner discharged.

F. G. Ostrander and Frank H. Farrar for petitioner; E. H. Hoar, district attorney, for respondent.

McLAUGHLIN, J.—The petitioner was indicted by the grand jury of the county of Merced for the crime of "being an accessory to the commission of a felony." The particular circumstances of the offense charged are set forth in the indictment as follows: "That said Edward Goldman on or about the 20th day of January, A. D. nineteen hundred and six, ... (after and with full knowledge that one Ross Dunn theretofore at, and in said county of Merced, and on or about the 18th day of January, A. D. 1906, had willfully, unlawfully, and feloniously taken, stolen, and carried away from the freight depot of the Southern Pacific Company in the city of Merced, ten sacks of alfalfa seed of the value of $227.50; . . . . and said alfalfa seed being at the time it was so taken, stolen, and carried away the personal property of one W. C. Dallas) did willfully, unlawfully, and feloniously conceal the property stolen as aforesaid, and did conceal from the magistrate the commission by said Ross Dunn of said felony."

It is contended in behalf of the petitioner that the indictment does not charge a public offense, and hence that his imprisonment is unlawful. In answer to this contention it is argued (1) that habeas corpus is not the proper proceeding for the determination of the question involved; (2) that the offense is charged in the language of section 32 of the Penal Code, and therefore the indictment is sufficient. It is the settled rule in this state that defects or irregularities in an indictment will only be reviewed on appeal from the judgment, but, if the facts alleged do not constitute a public offense, habeas corpus will lie: In Matter of Corryell, 22 Cal.

183; Ex parte Harrold, 47 Cal. 130; Ex parte Maier, 103 Cal. 479, 42 Am. St. Rep. 129, 37 Pac. 402; Ex parte Williams, 121 Cal. 331, 53 Pac. 706. Our inquiry in the present proceedings must, therefore, be confined to the single question whether the indictment charges the commission of a public offense. If the indictment only contained the general accusation that the petitioner had committed a felony "by being an accessory to the commission of a felony," it would, undoubtedly, be wholly insufficient and void. This proposition is too plain to require elaboration or citation of authorities. We must, therefore, examine the facts alleged, in order to determine whether the acts or facts detailed constitute the offense designated in the general charge. The attorneys for the people defend the indictment on the ground that it sufficiently appears therefrom that the petitioner concealed his knowledge of the commission of the offense of grand larceny from a magistrate. This defense is equivalent to an admission that the prisoner should be discharged. Knowledge of the commission of a felony is, and always has been, necessary to charge a person as an accessory. Intent is an essential element of all crimes, and a person could hardly intend to conceal the commission of a crime, or render assistance to a criminal, when he was wholly ignorant of the commission of an offense or the participation of the person assisted. Hence the language, "after full knowledge that a felony has been committed," found in section 32 of the Penal Code, is but the statement of an essential prerequisite to guilty concealment, protection, or assistance. In other words, it is but a reiteration of the common-law rule that a person must know that he is assisting a criminal, or else he cannot be charged as accessory. While the existence of such knowledge was an essential ingredient of the offense at common law, still the mere neglect to disclose it or inform the authorities that a felony had been committed did not constitute the person maintaining such silence an accessory: 1 Bishop's Criminal Law, sec. 694; 1 Am. & Eng. Ency. of Law, p. 268; Blackstone's Commentaries, p. 37, n. 25, 120. Section 32 of the Penal Code is but a codification of the common-law rule or definition, and hence the supreme court of this state has pointedly said: "The word 'conceal,' as here used, means more than a simple withholding of knowledge possessed by a party that a felony has been committed. This concealment necessarily includes the element of some affirmative act upon the part of the person tending to or looking toward the concealment of the felony. Mere silence after knowledge of its commission is not sufficient to constitute the party an accessory'': People v. Garnett, 129 Cal. 366, 61 Pac. 1115. An examination of the original record in that case shows that the information contained a statement of the particular affirmative acts constituting the concealment from the magistrate, but did not contain the name of the magistrate. This portion of the information was upheld, and the cause was remanded for a new trial upon that issue. It was in passing upon the sufficiency of the information in this regard that the language quoted was used; and hence the contention that it is obiter dicta cannot be sustained. Viewed as dictum, however, it is sustained by the overwhelming weight of authority in the United States and England, and commends itself to our reason as a correct statement of the law.

Upon first impression it seemed to me that the averment that petitioner concealed the property stolen, with knowledge of the theft, might be sufficient to charge him as an accessory. But this averment is so plainly separated from any charge of concealment that we cannot, even by inference, construe the indictment as charging that the concealment of the property was for that purpose or with the intent to conceal the commission of the crime from the magistrate. The decisions in this state and elsewhere seem to hold that receiving or concealing stolen property constitutes an entirely different offense: Pen. Code, sec. 496; People v. Hawkins, 34 Cal. 182; People v. Stakem, 40 Cal. 601; People v. Fagan, 98 Cal. 234, 33 Pac. 60; Bishop's Criminal Law, sec. 699; 24 Am. & Eng. Ency. of Law, p. 48. Then, too, such concealment might have been for the purpose denounced as criminal in section 135 of the Penal Code. Where an act mala prohibita may fall within the definition of several offenses, according to the purpose with which it is done, it is essential to the statement of any offense that the intent or purpose of the act be set forth. While it was not contended in argument that the indictment could be sustained on the ground just discussed, we have nevertheless examined the point, with the result above indicated. There was and could be no pretense that the petitioner was charged or could be convicted under section 496

17

of the Penal Code, and hence we pass to the consideration of
the vital and most difficult question involved.

The indictment charges that petitioner, after and with full
knowledge of the commission of the felony, did conceal its
commission from the magistrate, and the question arises
whether this bald statement is sufficient to charge petitioner as
an accessory. The argument before us clearly indicated that
the sole intention was to charge a concealment of the commission of the felony by mere silence or withholding of knowledge from a magistrate. While we would, perhaps, be justified
in accepting this construction, which must result in the discharge of the prisoner, we deem it our duty in this kind of a
proceeding to determine whether any construction placed
upon the language used would support a judgment against
the petitioner as accessory to the crime committed by the other
party named. In People v. Perales, 141 Cal. 583, 75 Pac.
171, the defendant was charged with an assault by means
likely to produce great bodily injury, and the court said:
"When, however, the words or terms used in the statute have
no technical or precise meaning which of themselves imply
the offense, or when the particular facts or acts which shall
constitute it are not specified, but from the general language
used many things may be done which may constitute an offense, it is then necessary in charging an offense claimed to
be embraced within the general language of the statute, to set
forth the particular things or acts charged to have been done
with reasonable certainty and distinctness, so that the court
may determine whether an offense within the statute is
charged, or one over which it has jurisdiction."

This rule thus clearly stated has obtained in California for
more than fifty years, and, even if we had the right, we would
have no inclination to change it: People v. Neil, 91 Cal. 468,
27 Pac. 760; People v. McKenna, 81 Cal. 160, 22 Pac. 488;
People v. Washington, 36 Cal. 674; People v. Schwartz, 32
Cal. 165; People v. Wallace, 9 Cal. 32. To charge a person
with murder, robbery, grand larceny or being accessory to the
commission of either crime would obviously be the statement of
a legal conclusion. And an averment that a party concealed
the commission of an offense is as obviously the statement of
a mere abstract legal proposition. The indictment must show
on its face the acts or facts from which the conclusion flows.
The concealment of a crime "necessarily includes the element

of some affirmative act,'' and the particular affirmative act constituting the offense must be stated in the indictment, to the end that the court and defendant may know, independently of the conclusion stated, that such act constitutes an offense against the law. If this were not so, then it would be sufficient in all cases to charge an offense in the naked language of the statute, and this has never been, is not now, and in reason never can be the law. The wisdom and justice of the rule concretely stated in People v. Perales, supra, could have no more complete vindication than is afforded by the case before us. The whole tenor of the argument for the people in this proceeding was that the concealment consisted of withholding knowledge of the commission of the felony from a magistrate, and we have seen that mere silence or failure to disclose such knowledge did not constitute one an accessory at common law and does not have that effect under the code.

It follows that the petitioner is entitled to be discharged from custody, and it is so ordered.

We concur: Chipman, P. J; Buckles, J.

SHEPARD v. F. A. ROBBINS PRESS WORKS.

S. F. No. 4489; April 11, 1906.

85 Pac. 307.

Appeal—Filing of Transcript—Granting New Trial—Conditional Order.—A motion for a new trial in an action to quiet title was denied upon condition that plaintiff consent to an amendment of the findings and judgment, and the order denying the motion stated that defendant's counsel should prepare an order specifying in detail the amendment to be made, and it was provided that, if plaintiff did not consent within ten days, a new trial should be granted. Some four months later an order was made reciting the pendency of the motion for a new trial, specifying the amendment to be made and stating that if plaintiff failed to consent to the amendment within ten days, a new trial would be granted. Plaintiff at no time consented to the amendment. Held, that ten days within which plaintiff might consent to the amendment and avoid the new trial did not begin to run until ·after the making of the second order, so that it was not until after the expiration of ten days from that time that the forty days allowed for the filing of a transcript on appeal began to run.

APPEAL from Superior Court, Marin County; Thomas J. Lennon, Judge.

Action by Elizabeth A. Shepard against F. A. Robbins Press Works, in which A. D. Shepard, as administrator, was substituted as plaintiff. From a judgment for plaintiff, defendant appeals. On motion to dismiss the appeal. Motion denied.

A. J. Treat for appellant; Thomas, Gerstle & Frick for respondent.

ANGELLOTTI, J.—This is a motion by plaintiff to dismiss an appeal from the judgment, on the ground that appellant has not filed in this court a transcript on appeal within the time allowed by law. It is conceded that the forty days within which such transcript must be filed did not begin to run until the motion for a new trial made by defendant was decided by the lower court (rule 2 of this court [78 Pac. vii]), and the question here is as to when the motion was decided, within the meaning of our rule. The notice of motion to dismiss was served on November 24, 1905, and filed November 25, 1905, at which times no transcript on appeal had been served or filed. The action was one to quiet title to certain land. On June 22, 1905, in the matter of defendant's motion for a new trial, which had previously been argued and submitted on a bill of exceptions, the trial court made the following order, viz.: "It is ordered that defendant's motion for a new trial be denied, but upon the condition, however, that plaintiff consent that the findings, judgment, and decree heretofore herein made be amended and modified so as to make the southerly side of the disputed fence the northerly boundary of the Shepard property. If consent be not given by plaintiff within ten days, then it is ordered that a new trial be granted. Defendant's counsel will prepare and present to the court an order to this effect specifying in detail the amendment to be made." No order specifying in detail the amendment to be made was presented to the court until November 1, 1905, on which last-named day the trial court made the following order, viz.: "This cause having been tried and findings filed and judgment rendered in favor of the plaintiff, and the defendant having filed its bill of exceptions on motion for a new trial, and the same having been allowed and certified, and the motion for a new trial having been argued and submitted; and it appearing to the court that the case was tried upon the theory that the plaintiff claimed that the south line of the fence referred to in her complaint was the dividing line between the respective properties of the parties in said action; and it further appearing that the plaintiff by her findings and by her judgment has erroneously been given a boundary on the north line of her property three-fourths of an inch to the north of the north side of the fence between the north line of plaintiff's property and the south line of defendant's property; and it further appearing to the court that the true northerly line of plaintiff's property is a straight line along the southerly line of the said fence, as said line is prolonged from east to west, and that the court inadvertently signed findings and judgment in favor of plaintiff establishing the northern boundary line of her property in a straight line from east to west five and three-fourths (5¾) inches north of the southerly line of said fence; and it further appearing to the court that the said southerly side of said fence was at the time of the erection of the barn herein referred to situated six (6) inches north of the outside face of the corner post of the barn located in the northwest corner of plaintiff's property, to wit, four and one-quarter (4¼) inches from the outer face of the corner board of said barn: Now therefore, it is ordered, that if plaintiff within 10 days after the service of a copy of this notice upon her attorneys signs and files a relinquishment to defendant of all land north of a point beginning four and one-quarter (4¼) inches from the north or outer face of the corner board of the barn on the northwest corner of the property of the plaintiff, said last-named point being originally the southerly side of the fence between the property of the parties, and running thence in a straight line from west to east along the southerly line of said fence, as the same existed during the trial of said cause, the motion for a new trial upon the part of the defendant shall be denied. Further ordered that if within said ten days plaintiff shall fail to sign the relinquishment herein referred to and directed, then the motion of the defendant for a new trial will be granted upon all the grounds of said motion." This order was served on the attorney for plaintiff on November 13, 1905, and plaintiff having failed to file the required relinquishment, the trial court on December 8,

1905, made an unconditional order purporting to grant defendant's motion for a new trial.

Plaintiff's claim is that the order of June 22, 1905, became, by reason of the failure of the plaintiff to consent to the required modification, an order granting a new trial absolutely, at the expiration of ten days from the making of such order: See Holtum v. Grief, 144 Cal. 521, 78 Pac. 11, and cases therein cited. If this claim be well founded, it is apparent that the time for filing the transcript expired long before the giving of the notice of motion to dismiss. We are of the opinion, however, that under the terms of the order in question, the time for plaintiff to comply with the expressed condition upon which a new trial would be denied could not commence to run until the subsequent order, to be prepared by defendant, should be made by the court, specifying in detail the particular modification to which the plaintiff should consent. It is plain from the meager record before us that there was some doubt as to where the line designated in the order as "the southerly side of the disputed fence" was, such fence not being at all points still in existence, and the order made clearly shows the intent of the court that a subsequent order, specifically showing the modification desired, should be made, that plaintiff should have ten days thereafter within which to consent thereto, and that if within such ten days she consented to the modification specified in such subsequent order, the motion for new trial should be denied. Under the terms of the order of June 22, 1905, the ten days within which plaintiff might comply with the specified condition could not commence to run until November 1, 1905, the date of the making of the second order. Her failure to comply with the condition could not be effectual to render the order one granting a new trial earlier than at the expiration of said ten days. Until that time, therefore, there was certainly no decision of the motion for a new trial, within the meaning of our rule. It is apparent, therefore, that the time for filing the transcript on the appeal from the judgment had not expired at the time of the service and filing of the notice of motion to dismiss the appeal. It is not necessary for the purposes of this motion to decide whether the failure of plaintiff to file her consent to the required modification rendered the order one granting a new trial at the expiration of ten days from November 1, 1905, and we do not decide that question. It is

enough here that there was no decision of the motion prior to
such last-mentioned time.

The motion to dismiss the appeal from the judgment is denied.

We concur: Shaw, J.; Sloss, J.

SHOWERS et al. v. ZANONE.

Court of Appeal, Third District; April 13, 1906.

85 Pac. 857.

Appeal—Conflicting Evidence.—Findings of a trial court based
on conflicting evidence will not be disturbed on appeal, if there is
any evidence in the record on which they might be properly based.

Drains—Liability for Expense.—In an Action to Recover one-
fifth of the cost of a drainage ditch, evidence held to support a finding
that defendant fully consented to the scheme and promised to defray
her part of the expense involved therein.

APPEAL from Superior Court, Humboldt County; E. W
Wilson, Judge.

Action by Jacob Showers and others against Madaline M.
Zanone. From a judgment in favor of plaintiffs, defendant
appeals. Affirmed.

Mahan & Mahan for appellant; Gillett & Cutler for respondents.

McLAUGHLIN, J.—This is an action to recover one-fifth of
the cost of a drainage ditch constructed by the plaintiffs. The
complaint contains two counts. In the first a cause of action
for money expended for the use and benefit of defendant at
her request is stated. In the second it is alleged that the
plaintiffs were duly authorized by defendant to make arrangements for and construct said ditch, she agreeing to pay her
pro rata share of the expense. In this connection it is stated
that she acted by and through an agent, who communicated
her authorization and consent to plaintiffs, and that by her
conduct preceding the commencement of the work, and dur-

ing its progress, she led plaintiffs to believe that she acquiesced in the plan proposed to her, and that said agent had
authority to speak and act for her in the premises. The court
found for plaintiffs, and judgment was entered accordingly,
The sole point urged on this appeal is that the findings are
not supported by the evidence.

It is a cardinal rule of appellate practice that the findings
will not be disturbed when the evidence is conflicting: Broder
v. Conklin, 121 Cal. 284, 53 Pac. 699; Rose v. Rose, 112 Cal.
343, 44 Pac. 658; Astill v. South Yuba W. Co., 146 Cal. 57, 79
Pac. 594. The weight and effect to be given the evidence was
for the trial court to determine, and even though it was demonstrated that the preponderance of evidence was against the
conclusion reached, we could not disturb that conclusion if
any evidence was found in the record upon which it might
properly be based. All doubts must be resolved, and all in-
tendments indulged in favor of the judgment, and we ''must
construe the testimony as favorably as possible for the respondents'': Carteri v. Roberts, 140 Cal. 165, 73 Pac. 818;
People v. Wong Suey, 110 Cal. 117, 42 Pac. 420; Taylor v.
Kelley, 103 Cal. 178, 37 Pac. 216; Olmstead v. Dauphiny, 104
Cal. 635, 38 Pac. 505; Meyer v. Great Western Ins. Co., 104
Cal. 381, 38 Pac. 82; People v. Un Dong, 106 Cal. 83, 39
Pac. 12.

Viewing the evidence in this case in the light of these well-
settled rules, it certainly cannot be said that the findings are
not supported by the evidence. The business relations between the defendant and her alleged agent prior to this transaction, her visit to the scene of the contemplated improvement in his company, their joint examination of the premises
and what was said and done by each at that time and subsequently, had a strong tendency not only to show his agency,
but her consent to and acquiescence in the plan which had
been proposed to her. Her inquiry upon the street in Eureka and her conduct when the claim of plaintiffs was presented to her were of potent significance. She knew, and so
did her agent, that the work was in progress, and the latter
at least must have known that the plaintiffs were counting on
her to pay a portion of the expense incurred. Both defendant and her agent were cognizant of the fact that the ditch
would be of great benefit to her land by securing it against
overflow, and the facts and circumstances surrounding its con-

struction were such as to warrant the finding and judgment that she was liable for one-fifth of the expense: Bergthold v. Porter Bros. Co., 114 Cal. 688, 46 Pac. 738; Puget Sound L. Co. v. Krug, 89 Cal. 243, 26 Pac. 902; Burnett v. Fisher, 57 Cal. 152; Anglo-Cal. Bank v. Cerf, 147 Cal. 399, 81 Pac. 1081; Mechem on Agency, 83; Donnelly v. San Francisco Bridge Co., 117 Cal. 422, 49 Pac. 559; Carpy v. Dowdell, 115 Cal. 687, 47 Pac. 695; Dolbeer v. Livingston, 100 Cal. 621, 35 Pac. 328; Scott v. Jackson, 89 Cal. 262, 26 Pac. 898. Indeed, her failure to disclaim liability, and the excuse she gave for failure to pay, coupled with her pertinent inquiry as to what was being done, and other facts incident to her visit to the scene would alone lend strong support to a finding that she had fully consented to the scheme and had promised to defray her portion of the expense it would involve.

True, all this testimony was flatly contradicted, and it may even be said that the evidence would support findings directly to the contrary, but we have pointed to the reasons which forbid our interference, and hence the judgment is affirmed.

We concur: Chipman, P. J.; Buckles, J.

SWEENEY v. DOYLE, County Auditor.

Court of Appeal, Third District; April 16, 1906.

86 Pac. 819.

Officers—Salary During Contest—Repeal of Statute.—Political Code, section 936, relative to payment of the salary of an office, title to which is contested by proceedings in court, is not repealed by the county government act, which contains no provision relating to the payment of the salary for the time of the contest.

McLAUGHLIN, J.—In his petition for rehearing appellant insists that section 936 of the Political Code was repealed by the provisions of the county government act subsequently enacted. This point was made in the briefs, but was not noticed in the opinion filed, and hence we deem it proper to say that there is nothing in the point then and now urged. The county government act contains no provision relating to the payment of salaries in cases where an action to determine the right to an office is pending, and, as repeals by implication are not favored, the existing law relating to this particular subject was not repealed thereby.

The petition for a rehearing is denied.

We concur: Chipman, P. J.; Buckles, J.

SAN GABRIEL VALLEY BANK v. LAKE VIEW TOWN COMPANY et al.*

Court of Appeal, Second District; April 28, 1906.

86 Pac. 727.

Mortgage—Construing With Note.—Where a note is secured by a mortgage, the note and mortgage are to be construed together as evidencing the intent and purpose of the parties.

Mortgage—Maturity of Debt.—A note and mortgage securing the same provided that the principal should be paid in five years, that the interest was to be paid semi-annually, and if not paid when due, it should be added to the principal and bear the like interest; but, if default was made in payment of interest for thirty days, then the "whole sum, principal, here promised, shall, at the option of the holder of the note, become immediately due, payable, and collectible." Held, that, where an action to foreclose was commenced thirty days. after default in payment of interest, the mortgage was subject to foreclosure at plaintiff's election for the whole amount thereof.

Mortgage—Notice of Election to Declare Due.—Where a mortgage provided that on default for thirty days in interest, the whole sum, principal and interest, should become payable at the option of the holder, the filing of a complaint, after thirty days' default in interest, seeking to recover the entire debt, constituted a sufficient notice of election by the mortgagee to claim the whole amount as due.

Mortgage—Foreclosure.—An Objection That a Complaint in a Suit to foreclose a mortgage was insufficient for want of facts in that no definite or separate amount was alleged to be due could be taken advantage of by special demurrer, and was waived by defendant's failure to so object thereto.

Mortgage—Foreclosure—Res Judicata—Conclusiveness.—Where, in a suit to foreclose a mortgage, it was alleged "on information and belief" that M. had an interest in the said "premises or property mentioned" in said mortgage, but that the same was subsequent and subject to the mortgage interest, and M. made default, such default

---

*For subsequent opinion, see 4 Cal. App. 630, 89 Pac. 360.

was tantamount to an admission that M.'s interest was subsequent to plaintiff's, so that after judgment it was too late for him to assert that his rights were not adjudicated.

APPEAL from Superior Court, Riverside County; J. S. Noyes, Judge.

Action by the San Gabriel Valley Bank against the Lake View Town Company and others. From a judgment for plaintiff, defendants appeal. Affirmed.

Cyrus F. McNutt and Joseph E. Hannon for appellants; Wright, Bell & Ward for respondent.

NOYES, Special Judge.—Plaintiff filed complaint for the foreclosure of a mortgage executed by the defendant, the Lake View Town Company. The mortgage was given to secure the payment of a promissory note, likewise made by the said defendant to plaintiff for the sum of $5,000. The mortgage lien covers various subdivisions of land belonging to defendant, together with "one thousand shares of the capital stock of Lakeview Water Company; the said capital stock being in fact, and also mortgaged as, appurtenant to said land, on the plan, of one share of the capital stock to each acre of said land." The stock was evidenced by certificate No. 475, which was owned by the corporation defendant and assigned to plaintiff as pledgee in pursuance of the mortgage contract. The note, or that part of it pertinent to the legal questions here raised, is as follows:

"$5,000.   Pasadena, Cal., April 10, 1901.

"Five years after date, excepting as herein otherwise stated, Lake View Town Company, ... promises to pay unto San Gabriel Valley Bank, ... the sum of five thousand dollars, with interest thereon at the rate of ten per cent. per annum, payable semiannually. If interest be not paid when due, it shall be added to, and become a part of, and thereafter bear like rate of interest with, the principal sum. If default be made in the payment of interest for a period of thirty days, then the whole sum, principal, here promised, shall, at the option of the holder of this note, become immediately due, payable, and collectible."

A copy of this note was inserted in the mortgage and made a part thereof, and the mortgage, in fixing the rights of the parties thereto, provided, inter alia, but with some particularity, that "the mortgagor will, during the life of this mortgage, promptly pay all taxes that may be assessed against said mortgaged property, excepting the taxes upon the interest hereby created, and will pay all assessments that may be levied upon said water stock; that it will keep said land, or a large portion thereof, in reasonable state of cultivation; that it will promptly defend all adverse claims of title to, or lien against, such property. If the mortgagor fails to perform the tax, assessment, or defense covenants above stated, the mortgagee may perform the same and pay the expense of it, and the amount so paid, with interest thereon at the same rate named in said promissory note, shall be due and payable by the mortgagor to the mortgagee at the next interest due date therefor according to said note and be secured by said mortgage. . . . . In case of default in making payments hereby secured, the mortgagee may cause the mortgage to be foreclosed and the mortgaged property sold in manner provided by law in foreclosure cases," etc.

The foregoing excerpts from the mortgage, together with the copy of the note, constitute that part of the record pertinent to the questions raised by the appellants. They pray for a reversal of the judgment on the following grounds: First, that the complaint does not state facts sufficient to constitute a cause of action, or, if the complaint is sufficient, to warrant a decree favorable to plaintiff; second, it is sufficient to entitle plaintiff to a judgment for overdue interest and costs only. In aid of these two points appellants cite the cases of Bank of San Luis Obispo v. Johnson, 53 Cal. 99, and the late case of Yoakam v. White, 97 Cal. 286, 32 Pac. 238. The language of the first case is as follows: "In case of default by the mortgagor in the payment of the said note or interest, or in the performance of any of the conditions hereof, then the mortgagee may, at its option, either commence legal proceedings to foreclose," etc. And in Yoakam v. White: "The mortgagor promises to pay said note according to the terms and conditions thereof, and . . . . in default of the payment of note by its terms, the mortgagees or their assignees may foreclose this mortgage," etc. That a note, and mortgage given in security therefor, are to be construed together as evidencing the intent and purposes of the parties thereto, must be held as settled in this state. Being, as they are, essentially the indivisible parts of a single contract, their joint purport and meaning must control. Being thus construed together in this action, the contract between the parties, as concerns the amount due, is to the effect that the principal is to be paid within five years after April 10, 1901, and the interest is to be paid semi-annually; that if not paid when due it shall be added to and become a part of the principal and bear the like rate of interest; but if default be made in payment of interest for thirty days, then the "whole sum, principal, here promised, shall, at the option of the holder of this note, become immediately due, payable, and collectible." This action was commenced more than thirty days after the default in interest, and under the well-considered cases of Sichler v. Look, 93 Cal. 600, 29 Pac. 220, and Bank of Commerce v. Scofield, 126 Cal. 156, 58 Pac. 451, no separate or definite act of election was necessary as a prerequisite to commencing the case. The filing of the complaint is, for all the purposes of the case, to be considered sufficient notice of the election, and of the amount claimed as due. It was notice to all adverse parties that whatever legal and equitable rights the plaintiff claimed he proposed to obtain them in his judgment, and right here the first cause for reversal advanced by appellants may be settled. It is that the complaint does not state facts sufficient for a cause of action in that no definite or separate amount is alleged as due, etc. This point is not determinative, for the reason that appellants might have taken advantage of the defect by special demurrer. The most extreme criticism of the complaint would be that in this respect it was uncertain and ambiguous, and appellants not having availed themselves of this advantage are deemed to have waived it: Reynolds v. Hosmer, 45 Cal. 630; Montgomery v. McLaury, 143 Cal. 83, 76 Pac. 964. Bank of San Luis Obispo v. Johnson and Yoakam v. White, supra, are not in point. The mortgage contract in both cases provides that the plaintiff may foreclose on the default of any of the conditions and terms thereof, and it was held that plaintiff in both cases was restricted to a foreclosure for only the sums and amounts thus defaulted, and that no option under such default, under the terms of the mortgage contract, could be exercised to declare the whole or any further amount due. The distinction, therefore, between the reported cases and the one under consideration, in this: The reported cases hold that judgment of foreclosure may be had only for the particular amount defaulted, the contract between the parties having thus restricted plaintiff's rights. In this case it is held that as the action was commenced thirty days after default, and as the contract between the parties permitted plaintiff to elect the "whole sum" as due after such default for thirty days, the filing of the complaint was tantamount to such election, and on trial thereof, no special demurrer having been filed alleging uncertainty, etc., plaintiff could legally demand the "whole sum" and interest, disbursements, and costs in making up his judgment.

The point made that the rights of defendant McNutt should not be concluded by the judgment is not good. It is not alleged that defendant McNutt has any particular interest in said real property, or in said stock. "On information and belief," it is alleged McNutt has an interest in said "premises or property mentioned in said mortgage," but that the same is "subsequent and subject" to said mortgage interest. The defendant McNutt by his default confesses such allegation, and it is now too late for said defendant to claim that any of his rights were invaded. He has been offered the opportunity provided by law to set up whatever interests he may have, if any, and to have them adjudicated. His failure is now a bar to further claim on his part. Before he can claim error on the part of the court he must, as the law requires, set up whatever rights he may have, and it is upon these rights that the superior court is to pass, if it does so, and if error is made, then the same may be corrected by the appellate court. As the judgment was in conformity to the allegations of the complaint and entirely within the powers of the court, we do not see how a defaulting defendant can now claim error: Hutchings v. Ebeler, 46 Cal. 557.

The judgment is therefore affirmed.

We concur: Gray, P. J.; Allen, J.

BILLINGS v. PEARSON.

Court of Appeal, Third District; May 15, 1906.

86 Pac. 825.

Ejectment—Nonsuit.—Where, in Ejectment, Plaintiff Introduced no evidence tending to show her right to the land, that she had been ousted of her possession by defendant, or that she had any right to eject defendant, a nonsuit was properly granted.

APPEAL from Superior Court, Sacramento County; J. W. Hughes, Judge.

Ejectment by Miranda S. Billings against James Pearson. From a judgment in favor of defendant, plaintiff appeals. Affirmed.

Howard & Wharton for appellant; J. Frank Brown for respondent.

BUCKLES, J.—This is an action in ejectment; the plaintiff seeking to eject defendant from a strip of swamp and overflowed land containing three and nineteen hundredths acres and lying along the bank of the Sacramento river in front of land conceded to belong to the defendant. Appellant introduced her testimony, and when she rested respondent moved a nonsuit, which was granted, and from the order and judgment of nonsuit this appeal is prosecuted.

The defendant's land is in two descriptions, having received it from Johnson by deed at two different times. The calls in the first deed dated April 23, 1867, are as follows: "Commencing at a stake on the east bank of the Sacramento river . . . . 150 feet north from the junction of the north bank of the old American river with said last bank of said Sacramento river." The line then runs thence east and thence north and "thence west" to the bank of the Sacramento river; "thence down Sacramento river with the meanderings of said river to the place of beginning, containing fifteen acres more or less." There can be no doubt but what the west boundary line of this fifteen-acre tract is the east bank of the Sacramento river, and the grantor, Johnson, owned no land west of that boundary line. Defendant bought the second piece of six acres from said Johnson June

17, 1867, and this is described in the deed as follows: "Commencing at the center of a large oak tree on the edge of the east bank of the Sacramento river about sixty-four rods north from the junction of the old American river and the Sacramento river; running thence easterly .... forty rods; thence south twenty-five rods to Pearson's north line; thence west .... to the bank of the Sacramento river; thence to the place of beginning." There is some controversy as to the point of commencement in this last description. The "large oak tree" mentioned as the point of beginning does not seem to have stood on the east bank of the Sacramento river at that time. But the grantor and grantee evidently believed it did, and so intended to include in this conveyance all the land up to the bank of the river. The west boundary of Johnson's land was the east bank of the Sacramento as it existed in the year 1867. From 1867 up to 1898 accretion had formed in front of these lands, and the bank of the river had receded sufficiently to form the land in controversy, as shown by the map introduced by plaintiff. The deed of said Johnson to the plaintiff, made April 16, 1885, contains exactly the same description of the land owned by Johnson prior to his deeds to Pearson, and excepts from such conveyance to plaintiff the land (fifteen and six acres) theretofore deeded to defendant Pearson, the west boundary line being fixed on the east bank of the Sacramento river. The map shows the three and nineteen hundredths acres in controversy to be located along the east bank of the Sacramento river as it now exists, and immediately in front of the fifteen and six acres of land of defendant, and is evidently accretions thereto as appears from said map. All these deeds were put in evidence by plaintiff.

The motion for nonsuit was made upon the following grounds: "(1) That the evidence, as introduced by plaintiff, does not show that the land in controversy has at any time ever been owned, or occupied or possessed by the plaintiff. (2) That the evidence does not show that defendant Pearson ever entered upon or ousted the plaintiff from the land in controversy. (3) That the evidence does not show that plaintiff is the owner or possessor, or entitled to the possession, of the land in controversy at the present time, or at the time of the commencement of this action." We do not think there was any testimony at all tending to show plaintiff's right to the land, that she had been ousted of her possession by the defendant, or that she has any right to eject the defendant. There being no testimony tending to show any of these essential matters, we think the nonsuit was properly granted.

The order and judgment are affirmed.

We concur: Chipman, P. J.; McLaughlin, J.

Petition for Rehearing; June 15, 1906.

BUCKLES, J.—We see no reason for disturbing our former opinion in this matter. We think it is clear the west boundary line of defendant's deeds was the Sacramento river, and the calls in his deeds can have no other reasonable construction or meaning.

Rehearing is denied.

We concur: Chipman, P. J.; McLaughlin, J.

PEOPLE v. COLLINS.

Cr. No. 1358; July 9, 1906.

86 Pac. 895.

Prisoner—Right to Visit Clerk's Office.—A Single Justice of the Supreme Court has no jurisdiction to grant the application of an attorney, convicted of perjury and confined in the county jail, to visit the clerk's office of the county in charge of an officer, for the purpose of examining the records in the case in order to enable him, while acting as his own attorney, to prepare an appeal to the appellate district court.

George D. Collins was convicted of perjury, and pending the taking of an appeal he applied to a single justice of the supreme court for permission to visit the office of the county clerk for the purpose of examining the papers and records. Application denied.

LORIGAN, J.—This is an application addressed to me, as one of the associate judges of the supreme court, for an order, directed to the sheriff of the city and county of San

Francisco, to permit petitioner, who is in his custody pending appeal from a judgment of conviction for perjury, to visit, in charge of a deputy sheriff, the office of the county clerk of said city for the purpose of examining certain papers and records therein.

The application sets forth that the petitioner was convicted and sentenced, and that he has appealed from the judgment to the district court of appeals for the first appellate district, where such appeal is now pending; that a bill of exceptions on said appeal was presented, settled, certified, and filed; that in settling the same the judge of the superior court before which he was tried refused to allow a large number of important and substantial exceptions to be incorporated therein in accordance with the facts; that petitioner desires to apply to the supreme court of this state, under section 1174 of the Penal Code, to prove said exceptions; that the original bill is on file in the county clerk's office, and that to prepare his petition to the supreme court it will be necessary for him (acting as his own attorney) to inspect the same and the other records and papers in the case; that he has applied to the trial judge for permission to visit the county clerk's office for that purpose, which was denied him; hence this application.

I am not advised of any provision of law which confers upon an associate justice of the supreme court any authority to entertain or grant an application of this character. If it exists it rests in the supreme court as a court, and is not reposed in the individual justices constituting that tribunal.

It may also be suggested in this connection that, as the appeal of petitioner from the judgment of conviction to which his bill of exception pertains is pending in the district court of appeal for the first appellate district, that tribunal would appear to be, at least in the first instance, after refusal by the trial judge, the proper one, as matter of procedure, in which to make this application. I do not pass at all upon the merits of the application of petitioner, concluding, as I do, that, as an associate justice, I have no authority to entertain the petition. For that reason, let it be dismissed.

CROCKER et al. v. GARLAND.

Court of Appeal, Second District; July 9, 1906.

87 Pac. 209.

Broker—Fraud in Sale.—Where, in an Action Against a Broker for fraud in the sale of plaintiff's land, the findings, which were in favor of the defendant, were either in express conflict with the allegations of defendant's answer or were in conflict with the testimony, and there was also evidence opposed to the general finding, it was proper for the court to grant plaintiff a new trial.[1]

Appeal—New Trial.—The Discretion of the Trial Court in Granting a new trial for insufficiency of the evidence will not be disturbed, except in cases of manifest abuse.

Pleading—Variance.—Where an Objection to the Sufficiency of the complaint to entitle plaintiffs to the profit made by defendant on a sale of certain property presented at most a mere question of variance, the court was authorized to disregard the same by Code of Civil Procedure, section 469.

APPEAL from Superior Court, Los Angeles County; N. P. Conrey, Judge.

Action by Henry J. Crocker and others against William M. Garland. From an order granting plaintiffs' motion for a new trial, defendant appeals. Affirmed.

Clarence A. Miller and George J. Denis for appellant; Hunsaker & Britt, Mastick, Van Fleet & Mastick and Edward F. Treadwell for respondents.

SMITH, J.—This is an appeal from an order granting the plaintiffs' motion for a new trial.

The suit was brought by the plaintiffs for damages for fraud of the defendant, committed by him while acting as their agent for the sale of the land described in the complaint. The nominal purchaser was one Schweppe, with whom the defendant, as plaintiffs' agent, had made a contract of sale August 21, 1901, for the sum of $25,000, and to whom a deed of conveyance, executed to him as grantee by the plaintiffs and placed in escrow for delivery on receipt of the purchase money, was delivered on the sixteenth day of Octo-

---

[1] Cited in the note in Ann. Cas. 1912D, 1226, on duty of trial court to set aside verdict as contrary to evidence.

ber. Schweppe had executed a prior unrecorded deed of the land to one Hinman, but the land was shortly afterward reconveyed to him, and by him conveyed to one Earl by deed of date November 12, 1891. It is alleged in the complaint that Schweppe was not the real purchaser; that he was an intimate associate and blood relation of the defendant and Hinman, who was his father in law, and by agreement with the defendant permitted him to use their names in the transaction, but that in truth they had no interest in the purchase, but took the deeds referred to for the use and benefit of the defendant; and that the defendant fraudulently represented to the plaintiffs that Schweppe was the real purchaser, which was believed by them. The answer of the defendant alleges, in effect, that the real purchaser of the property was the said Hinman, and that the deed was taken by Schweppe in trust for him and as his agent; that neither he nor anyone except Hinman had any beneficial interest in such sale; that the entire purchase money of $25,000 was paid by Hinman; that the defendant had no interest whatever in the said sale of the said property or any portion thereof; that the plaintiffs knew and had reason to believe that Schweppe was not in truth or in fact the real purchaser of the land, but knew that the real purchaser was some person living "at or near Dunkirk, the residence of Hinman"; and that Hinman was known to them as the real purchaser from and after October 14th. The sale to Earl, it appears from the defendant's evidence, included a lot adjoining the plaintiff's, standing in the name of Schweppe, but belonging to the defendant, who had paid therefor the sum of $14,000. The aggregate purchase money received for the two lots was $60,000, of which $30,000 was paid to Hinman and the balance retained by the defendant.

The case was tried by a jury, who rendered a general verdict for the defendant, with special findings on certain questions submitted to them, among which were the following: (1) That the defendant did not conceal from plaintiffs the name of the real purchaser of the property; (2) that prior to the closing of the sale the defendant had no agreement with Hinman to the effect that the defendant should have the profits which might be made upon a resale of the property over and above the sum of $5,000; (3) that the real purchaser of plaintiffs' property under the deed was

Schweppe; and (4) that the plaintiffs, prior to the closing of the sale did discover who was the real person to whom the property was being sold. On the motion for a new trial, these findings, as well as the general verdict, were attacked on the ground of insufficiency of the evidence to sustain them; and the motion for a new trial was granted on the grounds, so far as the sufficiency of the evidence is concerned, (1) that the evidence was insufficient to support the special findings enumerated, and (2) that by reason of the insufficiency of the evidence to sustain the special findings, it was insufficient also to sustain the general verdict; and the question is whether, on the record before us, these rulings of the court can be sustained.

With regard to the special findings, the first and third of the findings enumerated are in conflict with the express allegations of the answer; the fourth, if it can be construed as referring to Hinman, is without any evidence to sustain it; and the second is in direct conflict with the testimony of the defendant, who admits that he did have such agreement with Hinman prior to the closing of the sale. It is clear, therefore, that as to these findings, the ruling of the court cannot be disturbed. With regard to the general finding, it may be inferred from the special findings that it was based on the assumed fact that Schweppe was the real purchaser; and upon this, indeed, is based the principal argument of the appellant on this appeal, which is, in effect, that the functions of the defendant as agent of the plaintiffs ceased upon the execution of the contract made by him with Schweppe on August 21st. But this argument assumes, not only that the contract was thus made to Schweppe as the bona fide purchaser, but that Schweppe continued to be ready and willing to perform the contract, and that in fact the deed was made to him as the real purchaser. But not only is this in conflict with the repeated and explicit allegations of the answer, but the evidence at least tends to show that the contract was in fact abandoned by Schweppe almost immediately after it was made, and that the defendant, after that, proceeded as the agent, not of Schweppe, but of the plaintiff's availing himself of the contract with Schweppe merely for the purpose of gaining time to effect the sale at the price specified. The evidence may, indeed, be susceptible of a different construction; but, if it could be assumed that the issue was before the jury, a finding of the jury to the effect stated, approved by the court, would have been conclusive, and equally the action of the court in granting a new trial would be within its discretion. Here not only is the evidence bearing upon the question inconclusive, but the actual fact found by the jury and relied upon by the appellant is in conflict with the allegations of the answer. We do not doubt, therefore, that it was within the discretion of the lower court to set aside the general verdict on this ground. Nor upon a review of the evidence can we say, as matter of law, that the court was not justified in granting a new trial on other grounds. We are of the opinion, therefore, that the order of the lower court must be affirmed, not only upon the special grounds above stated, but on the general ground that the discretion of the lower court in granting a new trial for insufficiency of the evidence will not be disturbed, except in cases of manifest abuse.

An objection is made by the appellant to the sufficiency of the complaint to entitle the plaintiffs to the profit made by the defendant by the sale of the property to Earl. But this, at most, was a mere question of variance, which it was within the right of the court to disregard (Code Civ. Proc., sec. 469 et seq.), and which in fact it did disregard in its instructions.

Other objections are urged to the instructions; but, as the case is presented to us, we do not deem it necessary to consider them.

The order appealed from is affirmed.

We concur: Gray, P. J.; Allen, J.

PLYLER v. PACIFIC PORTLAND CEMENT COMPANY.*

Court of Appeal, Third District; July 16, 1906.

87 Pac. 395.

Trial—Special Issues—Discretion of Court.—Under Code of Civil Procedure, section 625, as amended by act of March 6, 1905 (Stats. 1905, p. 56, c. 62), requiring that the court, on request in writing, must direct the jury to find a special verdict on all or any of the issues, the court must submit the special issues formulated in writing by either party only when they are within the issues, and where, in an action for injuries, the plaintiff alleged that his fall from an elevated walk was caused by smoke and the absence of guards, special issues, limiting, respectively, the cause of the injury to the absence of the guards and to the smoke and not referring to the combination of the two dangers, were properly refused.[1]

Trial.—Where Special Issues were Requested as a Whole and some submitted issues not in the case, the court was not bound, without a special request, to direct the jury to find on any of them.

APPEAL from Superior Court, Solano County; L. G. Harrier, Judge.

Action by James Plyler against the Pacific Portland Cement Company. From a judgment for plaintiff, defendant appeals. Affirmed.

Paul C. Harlan and C. H. Wilson for appellant; Frank R. Devlin for respondent.

BUCKLES, J.—This is an action for personal injuries suffered by plaintiff while in defendant's employ. The case was tried with a jury, and a verdict rendered for plaintiff for the sum of $2,500. Judgment was rendered accordingly, and the appeal is from the judgment.

The appellant states at the beginning of his closing brief that "the only question presented on this appeal is: Does

---

*Opinion vacated and rehearing granted by supreme court September 13, 1906. For opinion in supreme court, see 152 Cal. 125, 92 Pac. 56.

[1] Cited and followed in Miller v. Fireman's Fund Ins. Co., 6 Cal. App. 401, 92 Pac. 334, where the defendant complained that the court did not submit special issues to the jury in the language proposed by him, contending that, under section 625 of the Code of Civil Procedure, the court had no discretion in the matter. It was held that the position involved an absurdity.

section 625 of the Code of Civil Procedure, as amended March 6, 1905 (Stats. 1905, p. 56, c. 62), and which requires a jury to give proper reasons for its verdict, impose a mandatory duty upon the trial judge to submit issues and questions of fact to the jury, whenever requested to do so by either party?" There are other errors alleged as having taken place at the trial, but as appellant relies only on the one that is the refusal of the court to direct the jury to find on certain special issues, we will consider no other.

The defendant owns and operates a large plant in Solano county for the manufacture of cement, and the plaintiff was a laborer employed in the buildings and about the said plant. On June 22, 1904, plaintiff was directed, as a part of his duty, to go to a certain elevated platform in the upper part of one of the buildings to perform certain work, the character of which he did not know until his arrival at said platform. "The only means of ascending to, and descending from, said platform was to pass over and across a plank walk about fifteen feet long and three feet wide, and extending and suspended over a cement floor nineteen feet below said walk, thence up a ladder standing perpendicularly, about ten feet long, to said platform; that said walk had no rails, guard, or protection of any kind on either side thereof." The complaint then alleges the unsafeness of said platform, walk, and means of ascending and descending, etc., and then continues: "And immediately after plaintiff had arrived at said platform, and before being informed of the exact character of the work he was to perform, and while plaintiff was in the exercise of all due care and skill, and without any negligence on his part, defendant carelessly and negligently caused and suffered a great quantity of dense smoke to arise and envelop the space in and about said plank walk and said ladder and platform and the space in and about which plaintiff was standing, the said smoke rendering said space . . . . dark and impenetrable to sight, and making it impossible for plaintiff to see, and causing partial suffocation of plaintiff and rendering it dangerous to his life to remain on said platform; that plaintiff, by reason of said darkness and danger occasioned by said smoke, endeavored to descend from said platform, and did descend said ladder and was in the act of stepping on said plank walk to escape said danger from said smoke,

when, by reason of said darkness and partial suffocation
. . . . and by reason of the absence of rails, guards, or other
protection on said walk, plaintiff fell . . . . to the said
cement floor beneath said walk, a distance of nineteen feet,''
and received the injury, to recover for which this suit was
brought.

Before the defendant offered any evidence, he handed to
the judge of the court the following: ''The court is hereby
respectfully requested to direct the jury to find a special
verdict in writing upon the following issues in this case, to
wit: First. Was the accident and injury complained of
caused by the failure of defendant to provide rails or guards
on the plank walk described in the pleadings and evidence?
Second. Was the accident and injury complained of caused
by a great volume and quantity of dense smoke arising and
enveloping the space in and about the plank walk and ladder described in the pleadings and evidence?   Third, if you
answer the last interrogatory in the affirmative, was the
smoke alone of such a character as to threaten plaintiff with
great bodily injury, or justify him in really believing that
he was threatened with such great bodily injury as to require prompt action on his part to escape such injury?
Fourth. Did plaintiff see, and know, when he first went
upon the plank walk described in the pleadings and evidence, that there were no rails or guards on said plank
walk?''   The record shows that, before making the request
of the judge, the defendant did not show said special findings to the attorney for plaintiff, Mr. Devlin; that five
minutes before the argument of the case to the jury, the
judge did show Mr. Devlin these special issues, and he thereupon objected to them being presented to the jury because
of their uncertainty and ambiguity, and because contradictory in form, and further because the jury could not render
a verdict on the general issues and find on the special issues
offered.   Mr. Wilson, counsel for defendant, then rose and
stated: ''We take exception to the action of the court in
submitting to counsel the special issues presented to the
court on behalf of defendant, and we assert that, under the
law, it is the duty of the court to submit to the jury all
special issues that may be presented, and we also object to
the action of counsel in presenting before the jury any
objections to the special interrogatories that have been pre-

sented to the court." The cause was then argued and the court instructed the jury, but refused to direct the jury to find special verdicts as requested by defendant.

Defendant made the request for these special findings under the provisions of section 625 of the Code of Civil Procedure, as amended in 1905. Prior to said amendment, the court might, or might not, direct the jury to find special verdicts, for the words "may direct" were used. By the amendment of 1905 the word "may" was changed to "must," and reads: "In all cases the court must, upon the request in writing of any of the parties, direct the jury to find a special verdict in writing upon all or any of the issues." It is contended by appellant that, as amended, the court has no discretion, but must direct the jury to find specially. The court is not bound to prepare such special issues, but "when requested in writing" must be taken to mean interrogatories prepared and set forth in such writing. But even then, I apprehend the other side would have a right to offer amendments to such special interrogatories or special issues, and it would be the duty of the court then to settle the same and make them conform in an intelligent way to the real issues in the case. Unless the questions the party desires the jury to answer as special verdict are questions and issues pertinent to the real issue in the case, he has no right to have the jury directed to answer them, and, as in all other questions submitted to the jury, it becomes the duty of the court to first determine whether it is pertinent to the issue the jury is called to try. Were it otherwise, and had the legislature intended to have taken away all discretion of the court of saying whether matters parties may ask to have submitted to the jury are legitimate and pertinent, then a defendant in a damage suit with no legitimate defense could have such matters submitted to the jury as would so befog the minds of the jurors as to make it impossible to have a verdict that would stand. The legislature never intended to take away such discretion. Under the section as it now stands, the court must submit the special issues formulated in writing by either party when the same are within the issues and subservient of the general issue in the case.

Now, as to the special issues asked in this case. The complaint alleges that the fall which caused the plaintiff's injury was caused by said smoke and by reason of the absence of rails, guards or other protection on said walk. The injury was caused by both the smoke and the fact that there were no guards on the walk. Just how much each contributed to the fall is beyond the power of man to tell. In the first place, having such a walk nineteen feet above the ground is an element of danger, but probably when the vision is in no wise blinded one might not fall. The smoke was only dangerous simply causing partial suffocation, but when it darkened the vision, the fact that defendant was standing on a plank walk nineteen feet high and only three feet wide, and with no guards and no protection from the danger of falling, it, in conjunction with the smoke and the smoke in conjunction with the said walk, made the danger so great that the plaintiff was precipitated to the floor and seriously injured.

The first question the jury was called upon to answer as a special verdict would seem to limit the cause of the injury to but one thing—that of the absence of guards on the plank walk, while, in fact, that was but a contributory cause. The same may be said of the second special issue. The case was brought, and the trial was had, upon the theory that both these things combined to cause the injury, and not either the one or the other solely. If to the first special verdict the jury should answer "Yes," the effect would be to say the smoke was no factor in causing the injury. Should the jury answer the first with "No," and the second with "Yes," the result would be to eliminate the condition of the plank walk entirely. Special finding No. 3, being based upon the answer the jury might give to No. 2, which is not responsible to any issue, becomes immaterial. Special verdict No. 4 is responsive to an issue made by the pleadings. But, as these special issues were asked as a whole and not all being issues in the case, the court was not bound to direct the jury to find on any of them, without being specially requested so to do. The special issues could have been easily framed so that they would have correctly stated the issues and not been misleading or confusing had the plaintiff been given an opportunity to offer amendments thereto.

We think the refusal of the court to direct the jury as requested was within its power and the power was properly exercised. Therefore, in answer to the issue before us, we are of the opinion the requirements of section 625 of the Code of Civil Procedure, commanding the court to submit special issues to the jury are mandatory, and such special issues, when embodying the real issues in the case and not subject to other legal objections, must be submitted to the jury. But the court must pass upon their pertinency, their materiality and legality, as it is the court's duty to pass upon all other matters submitted to the jury. If such issues are in every way proper, the court has no discretion to refuse them.

The judgment is affirmed.

McLAUGHLIN, J.—I concur in the order affirming the judgment. There can be no doubt that section 625 of the Code of Civil Procedure as amended in 1905 makes it the absolute duty of the court to direct the jury "to find a special verdict in writing upon all or any of the issues," and to instruct them, "if they render a general verdict, to find upon particular questions of fact," whenever a written request for such direction or instruction is made. But this is far from saying that the court in the case at bar was bound to direct the jury to fix upon some particular fact as the sole cause of the injury, or to find upon each evidentiary fact addressed to any of the several issues or questions of fact raised by the pleadings. The general issue, which might have been answered by a general verdict, involved the liability of defendant and the extent of such liability. And the several issues or particular questions of fact involved in this main inquiry, concerning which the court was bound to direct the jury to find specially, must be gleaned from an analysis of the pleadings, and not from a survey of the numerous incidental questions arising from conflicting evidence touching some auxiliary fact. Eliminating questions of law which are not properly a matter of pleading, the issues or questions of fact raised by the pleadings are: (1) Was the platform an unsafe, unsuitable or dangerous place for plaintiff to work? (2) Should the defendant, in the exercise of ordinary care, have known that it was an unsafe and dangerous place for an employee to work? (3) Was the means of ascending or descending from said platform unsafe and dangerous, and should defendant, in the exercise of ordinary care, have known of its dangerous and unsafe character? (4) Did the defendant, immediately after plaintiff went upon the platform, cause or suffer a dense volume of smoke to envelop the same, rendering the space in and about the plaintiff and the platform dark and impenetrable to sight? (5) Did plaintiff, by reason of such darkness, in endeavoring to escape from impending danger of suffocation through the absence of guard-rails on said platform, fall and receive the injuries complained of? (6) Was the plaintiff damaged thereby in the sum of $10,000 or any other sum? (7) Were these injuries caused in whole or in part by the negligence of plaintiff himself? (8) Did the injuries suffered by plaintiff grow out of the risks assumed by plaintiff in his contract of employment? Wherever these questions include two or more propositions of fact they might properly be subdivided, and each question be made to include only one averment of fact disputed in the answer. Aside from such subdivision, however, the eight questions above enumerated include all of the questions of fact or issues which it was the duty of the court to consider in determining the propriety of directions or instructions requested.

Instead of submitting a request for a special verdict or finding on any one or all of these issues or particular questions of fact, the defendant submitted requests which it was no part of the duty of the court to grant. The requests numbered 1 and 2 are palpable attempts to compel the jury to fix upon one particular fact as the cause of the plaintiff's injuries, and are confusing and misleading. The complaint clearly and specifically charges that the accident was due to a combination of both causes, and the court was not bound to split an issue which the parties had made single, and which could not be divided without danger of confusion leading to incongruous and untoward results. For instance, the jury might answer both of these questions in the negative and still find that the injuries were caused by defendant's negligence in causing a smoke to envelop a platform, safe under ordinary conditions, but dangerous under the circumstances narrated in the complaint. The third request is based on an affirmative answer to the second, and as the latter was improper, the request was properly refused. The fourth request is an attempt to compel the jury to find on an auxiliary evidentiary fact pertinent to one of the several issues or questions of fact, and was, for that reason, improper. Every law must receive a reasonable construction, and it certainly was never intended by the framers of this law that either party could by simple request compel a jury, through a direction of the court, to answer each collateral fact going to make up a single issue, or give a finding touching each disputed item of evidence. Such a practice would lead to intolerable confusion, not only in the minds of jurors, but in the trial of causes. The request must come within, and be confined to, the issues or questions of fact presented by the pleadings, and cannot be made to include a separate finding on every minor detail of an issue, and on every one of a series of facts going to establish or controvert averments from which these issues arise.

I concur: Chipman, P. J.

On Rehearing.

BUCKLES, J.—This is a petition for rehearing. We see no reason for granting it, and it is therefore denied.

I concur: McLaughlin, J.

CHIPMAN, P. J.—I concur in the order denying a rehearing. Upon a comparison of section 625 of the Code of Civil Procedure, as enacted in 1872, with the section as amended in 1905 (Stats. 1905, p. 56, c. 62), I see no substantial difference except that "upon the request in writing of any of the parties," if a general verdict is rendered, it is made mandatory upon the court to direct the jury "to find upon particular questions of fact"; whereas, the section formerly left it discretionary with the court. I cannot, therefore, see that the amendment has introduced any new practice aside from making it the duty of the court to do what it formerly had the discretion to decline to do. The scope and purpose of the section appear to be unchanged so far as they relate to the "particular questions of fact" upon which the jury must be directed to make written findings. I think it is the right of either party to submit any one single question material to the issue or any of the issues, whether or not he desires to submit other such questions of fact. He is not obliged, in other words, by his proposed questions of fact, to address questions to all the material issues of the case.

Counsel in their petition for rehearing claim that it is their right, under said section 625, "to interrogate the jury as to matters material to the issues, *yet not necessarily covering any of the issues.*" If counsel mean by the phrase italicized that the jury may be interrogated as to facts not related or pertinent to the issues of any of them, I cannot agree with them, and I agree with Justice McLaughlin in what I understand to be his view of the meaning of the section, that it is not the right of a party to submit questions for the jury upon every evidentiary fact, though material to the issue. A wise discretion must be exercised by the trial court in determining to what extent questions of fact pertinent to the issues should, for their elucidation, be submitted to the jury. It is not easy to draw the precise line of demarcation between questions of fact which it would be the duty of the court to submit to the jury, and such as the court may properly refuse to so submit. An examination of the cases will show a somewhat wide latitude allowed under this section: See Los Angeles C. Assn. v. Los Angeles, 103 Cal. 461, 37 Pac. 375; McAulay v. Moody, 128 Cal. 202, 60 Pac. 778.

I agree with counsel for defendant that it is their right to submit questions of fact to the court for the jury without first having submitted them to opposing counsel, and the responsibility is then put upon the court to determine whether or not to place them before the jury. I see no controlling analogy between the practice under this section and the practice as to instructions. The discretion rests with the court either to submit or refuse the questions as requested, for, if it be held that the court may change or modify the questions as propounded, it would cease to be a request of the party asking it, and the statute would be no longer mandatory. This discretion, of course, is subject to review by the appellate court, as is the exercise of discretion generally.

Upon further consideration of the case I agree with my associate, Justice Buckles, that the fourth question was responsive to an issue, and was a proper question of fact to be submitted to the jury. It was alleged in the complaint that the absence of rails guarding the walk in question was one of the causes leading to the injury, but the defendant submitted the series of questions and asked that they be submitted in their entirety, and, when the request as made, was refused, it was the duty of defendant, if it desired any one of the questions to be submitted separately, to so request the court. It would certainly be of advantage to the profession if a comprehensive statement could authoritatively be given as to the complete rights of the parties to an action as matter of practice under this section 625. When such an exposition is made, however, it would be perhaps better that it should come from the supreme court. Here the case does not seem to call for such statement.

GRAHAM v. BRYANT.

Court of Appeal, First District; July 24, 1906.

87 Pac. 232.

Appeal—Conflicting Evidence.—A Verdict Based on conflicting evidence and sustained by the trial court will not be reversed.[1]

APPEAL from Superior Court, City and County of San Francisco; M. C. Sloss, Judge.

Action by F. J. Graham against A. M. Bryant. From a judgment for defendant, plaintiff appeals. Affirmed.

George D. Collins and A. E. Ball for appellant; William Cannon for respondent.

HARRISON, P. J.—Action upon a promissory note. The cause was tried before a jury, and a verdict returned in favor of the defendant. Plaintiff moved for a new trial upon the grounds that the verdict was not sustained by the evidence, and that certain errors of law were committed at the trial. The motion was denied, and from this order the plaintiff has appealed.

---

[1] Cited and followed in McDonnell v. Minneapolis St. P. & S. S. M. Ry. Co., 17 N. D. 608, 118 N. W. 819, where, in a suit for injuries to the plaintiff's cattle, the jury had found that the defendant's servants had not exercised ordinary care after discovering the animals on the track. The court said that it would require a clear case of insufficiency of evidence to be shown before it would disturb the verdict.

The signing of the note by the defendant was conceded, and the only issue presented to the jury was the want of consideration for making the same. Upon this issue there was a direct conflict of testimony between the defendant and the witness for the plaintiff, with whom the defendant had the transaction in which the note was signed. It is unnecessary to recount this testimony, since the determination of the jury as to which of these witnesses was entitled to credit is conclusive. The jury were fully and clearly instructed as to the elements necessary to constitute a consideration for the note in view of the evidence before them, and no exception was taken to these instructions. The fact, moreover, that the trial court declined to set the verdict aside is an additional ground for us to hold that it was fully sustained by the evidence. The contract of the defendant in reference to the prosecution of her claim against the Adler estate was properly received in evidence as illustrative of the circumstances connected with her signing of the note sued upon. The exhibit shown to the witness for the plaintiff was offered solely for the purpose of affecting his credibility, and was admissible for that purpose.

The other errors relied upon do not require consideration. The order is affirmed.

We concur: Cooper, J.; Hall, J.

In re DOMINICI'S ESTATE.*

KOHLER et al. v. ARNDT et al.

Court of Appeal, Third District; July 23, 1906.

87 Pac. 389.

Appeal — Exclusion of Evidence — Presumptions.—Where the court reserved its ruling on testimony objected to, and the record is silent as to what the ruling was, it must be presumed that the court excluded it, and it cannot be considered on appeal.

Wills—Construction—Devisees.—Testator Gave His Property to his sister and his nephew, S., and "his sister, my niece," and on the

---

*Opinion vacated and rehearing granted by supreme court September 21, 1906. For subsequent opinion in supreme court, see 151 Cal. 181, 90 Pac. 448.

death of his sister added a codicil giving the share of his sister to "the other two residuary legatees therein named, S., and to his sister, my niece, whose name is Marie K., and whose residence is Salzwedel, Germany, share and share alike," and confirming his will save as it was inconsistent with his codicil. The evidence showed that S. had a sister living, but that her name was not Marie K., and that Marie K. was not his niece. Held, that the words referring to Marie K. were used to express the name and residence of testator's niece, and not having accomplished that, were to be disregarded as surplusage.

Will Contest — Compromise — Conclusiveness.—A person not a party to a will contest, nor to a compromise resulting therefrom, is not bound by it.

APPEAL from Superior Court, Stanislaus County; W. M. Conley, Judge.

Action by Marie Kohler and others against Christiane Arndt and others to determine the construction of the will of Joseph Dominici, deceased. From a judgment for defendant and an order denying their motion for a new trial, complainants and others appeal. Reversed.

W. H. Hatton and T. J. Maddux for appellant Kohler; W. O. Minor, J. M. Knox and Loewy & Gutsch for respondent Arndt.

BUCKLES, J.—This is an action to determine the proper construction of the last will and testament of Joseph Dominici. The appeal is by Marie Kohler and the heirs of William Dominici, deceased, and the heirs of Sophia Miller, deceased, from the judgment and from the order denying their motion for a new trial.

After making some specific devises, and appointing George W. Bates executor, the will provides: "Lastly, I give, bequeath and devise all the rest, residue and remainder of my property, real and personal, of whatsoever kind or character or wheresoever situated, share and share alike, unto my sister, Louise Jahnke, and unto my nephew Heinrich Schluther and his sister, my niece, all residing in Luckow, Hanover, Germany." This was dated November 22, 1897. On May 3, 1898, the following codicil was added, after recital of having made the will: "Now therefore I do make, publish and declare this to be a codicil to the same. I hereby ratify and confirm said will in every respect, save so far as any part thereof is inconsistent with this codicil. Whereas it has come to my knowledge that my sister, Louise Jahnke, one of the residuary legatees therein named, is dead, I hereby give, bequeath and devise the share of my said estate in said will given, bequeathed and devised to my said sister to the other two residuary legatees therein named, Heinrich Schluther and to his sister, my niece, whose name is Marie Kohler, and whose residence is Salzwedel, Altmark, Germany, share and share alike."

A contest of said will was filed by Sophia C. Ward, a daughter of Sophia Miller, a deceased sister of testator, and, as a result of said contest, the following stipulation in writing was entered into:

"It is hereby stipulated by and between the parties hereto that the contest of the probate of will heretobefore filed herein shall be dismissed, and that letters testamentary shall be issued to George W. Bates, the executor named in said will, and that the property of the said estate shall be distributed as follows, to wit: (1) The expenses of administration shall be paid. (2) There shall be distributed to Marie Kohler, the surviving legatee and devisee named in said will, one-half of the residue, less one hundred ($100.00) dollars. The remaining portion of said estate shall be distributed as follows: (a) The specific legacies of one hundred dollars each shall be paid to the daughter of Milton F. Dominici, and to the female children of E. B. Learch. (b) That part of said remaining portion of the said estate which, by the will, or the intestate law of California would have been distributed to Marie Kohler, which is by this stipulation waived by her, shall be divided among the heirs represented by the contestants of said will. (c) The remaining portion of the said estate shall be distributed according to the intestate laws of the state of California, save and except that no portion thereof shall be distributed to Marie Kohler, except the portion of said estate hereinbefore, by stipulation, agreed to be distributed to Marie Kohler, to wit, one-half, less one hundred dollars.

"W. H. HATTON,
"Attorney for Marie Kohler.
"L. J. MADDUX and
"L. W. FULKERTH,
"Attorneys for Contestants.
"L. L. DENNETT,
"Attorney for Petitioning Executor."

There were filed three petitions for distribution. One
by George W. Bates, the executor, and asks that the estate
be distributed according to said stipulation. A petition
for distribution by Christiane Arndt (formerly Christiane
Schluther), the sister of Heinrich Schluther. This petition
alleges the death of Heinrich Schluther. The petitioner is
the only sister of Heinrich Schluther, and is the party
named in said codicil as the sister of said Heinrich Schluther,
and niece of deceased, and who, by mistake, deceased called
"Marie Kohler," and by mistake stated to reside in Salzwedel, Altmark, Germany. That it was the intention of deceased to name Christiane Arndt in the codicil as the name
of the sister of Heinrich Schluther, and his intention to bequeath to her, and not to Marie Kohler, the bequest mentioned in said codicil as made to the sister of Heinrich
Schluther. That by the last bequest in said will the testator
intended to devise and bequeath the residue of his estate
to said Louise Jahnke, Heinrich Schluther, and his sister, as
a class, to wit, to his, testator's, sister, Louise Jahnke, and
the two children of his sister, Marie Schluther (formerly
Marie Dominici), now deceased. That it was the intention
of testator in making the bequest in said codicil to devise
and bequeath the share of his estate formerly devised and
bequeathed to Louise Jahnke, to said Heinrich Schluther and
to his sister, Christiane Arndt as a class, and that it was
not the intention of the testator, either in the will or codicil,
to give Marie Kohler anything, and that her name and place
of residence, to wit, Salzwedel, Altmark, Germany, were inserted in said codicil by mistake and inadvertence. That
this petitioner was not a party to the alleged compromise
and settlement of contest. The third petition, that of Marie
Kohler, after setting forth the jurisdictional facts, alleges
that she is one of the residuary legatees mentioned in said
will and codicil. That by mistake she is described as the
sister of Heinrich Schluther, and that it was the intention of
the testator to name the petitioner in said will and codicil
as one of the residuary legatees, and that he so expressed his
intention by expressly naming her and her residence. Ac-
knowledges the compromise and claims the distributive share
therein stated she should have.

The court found that the word "and" was inadvertently
and unintentionally omitted before the words "my niece,

whose name is Marie Kohler," etc., in said codicil at the time of the execution thereof. Inserting the word "and" the devise in the codicil is made to read as follows, "to the other two residuary legatees named, Heinrich Schluther and to his sister 'and' to my niece whose name is Marie Kohler." When the codicil was made, Heinrich Schluther was living. The codicil itself recites that there were but two residuary legatees after the death of the testator's sister, Louise Jahnke, and the purpose of the codicil seems to have been to dispose of the devise in the will to her. The inserting by the court of the word "and" there would still appear to be three residuary legatees. But in order to determine the true meaning, in this instance, of the testator, the will and the codicil must be read in the light of each other. The gentleman, Mr. Dennett, who drew the will, testified that Dominici did not remember the name of the niece, but was to return with it at a later date and then the name was to be inserted. The testator did return and gave the name "Marie Kohler," and whose residence is "Salzwedel, Altmark, Germany," and this Mr. Dennett supposed to be the name and address of Heinrich Schluther's sister. It did not occur to him that the testator had named in his will four residuary legatees, nor that he was adding another when the codicil was drawn. It seems to me the will provides but three residuary legatees, to wit: Louise Jahnke, Heinrich Schluther, and Heinrich Schluther's sister; "my niece" is but descriptive of "his sister," whose name was not then remembered by testator. When he did remember the name of this sister of Heinrich Schluther, as he doubtless supposed he did, he returned and made the codicil. He had then learned of the death of his sister, Louise Jahnke, and, in addition to having the name of Heinrich Schluther's sister inserted, he desired also to dispose of the devise made to his dead sister, and the scrivener, Mr. Dennett, proceeded to write the codicil, and, in disposing of the dead sister's devise, used the words "the other two residuary legatees," which of itself shows that there were but three residuary legatees in the will, and, as Dennett understood the testator, there would be but two residuary legatees in the codicil; and this is borne out by the phraseology "to the other two residuary legatees therein named, Heinrich Schluther and to his sister, my niece, whose name is," meaning thereby the sister of Heinrich Schluther. Now, let us see the probability of this having been the true intention of the testator. The testimony shows that he had been in correspondence with the Schluther family for years. He was a carpenter, and before leaving Germany, had helped to construct the house the Schluthers lived in, which had also been occupied by his parents. His son Solon had visited Germany and the Schluthers, and put in the most of his time with them, and they were his and his father's favorites. This son Solon had died after returning to this country, about November 13, 1897, a month before this will was made.

The testator had been heard to speak of this sister, Christiane Schluther, several times and had written her a letter, but was never heard to speak of Marie Kohler; and, when speaking of the Schluthers, it was always in terms of affection. To one witness, J. F. Beausange, in speaking of Christiane, he always spoke of her, not by name, but as Heinrich Schluther's sister. Maria Schluther was the mother of Christiane Arndt (Heinrich Schluther's sister), and during her lifetime the testator wrote to her once or twice a year. She died June 18, 1890, and after that he wrote one letter to Christiane, and had not written at all for the last few years. She had written one later to testator announcing the death of her mother, and probably another after the will was made announcing the death of his sister, Louise Jahnke. It appears also that the testator and his brother William, residing in La Grange, California, were not on good terms, and while the Schluthers were on friendly terms with Joseph, the testator, Marie Kohler was on friendly terms with William. The wife of the testator was the godmother of Christiane Arndt. On November 17, 1897, the testator wrote his sister, Louise Jahnke, and which was received after her death by Christiane Arndt, and is as follows:

"Dear Sister: Have not heard from you for a long time, sad news from me, Solon my last joy isn't any more. He died the 13th of this month. Requested me to send you all his last greeting. Write soon, also would like to hear from Henry Schluther and his sister."

The will was made November 22, 1897—five days later. There is no testimony indicating any further correspondence was received by testator from the Schluthers, though there was testimony showing that soon after Heinrich Schluther was married in November, 1898, he wrote to testator. The testimony of Mr. Dennett, though not clear upon the subject, would indicate that the testator brought to him a letter from Marie Kohler when he came to have the codicil drawn. This is what Mr. Dennett said: "When Mr. Dominici came down he gave me instructions for the will, and I asked for the names and explained to him that the personal data would be sufficient if it was perfectly clear, but that the names would be better. Subsequently he came down and at that time he told me that he had received a letter from Germany giving them, and had ascertained that Louise Jahnke was dead. And he then gave me, in accordance with our previous understanding, the name which he wished to go in the will or in the codicil, and I understood that to be the name of Henry Schluther's sister. He never suggested to me that he wanted to change from Henry Schluther's sister to anyone else. The idea and desire was simply to make clear the provision of the will. . . . . I don't remember particularly what part the letter played in what took place, with the exception of the fact that my attention was called to the fact that he had such a letter."

These, then, are the facts relied upon to support the claim the testator intended to and did make Christiane Arndt his third residuary legatee in his will, and did not intend by his codicil to make Marie Kohler a residuary legatee. There was some evidence that the testator had declared his intention of making the Schluther people his legatees, but this testimony was objected to and ruling reserved, and although the record is silent as to what the ruling was, it must be presumed the court excluded it when it came to consider the matter and render its decision, and, therefore, such evidence is not considered here: Civ. Code, secs. 1318, 1340. The evidence shows the intimacy of the testator with the Schluthers; that they were in his mind all the time, and that there was an absence of friendliness between himself and Marie Kohler and her parents; that just before making the codicil he had received a letter from Germany, whether from Christiane Arndt notifying him of the death of his sister Louise or from Marie Kohler, but probably from both. If from Marie, then, that is the only letter which appears to have been written by her to the testator. That there is a mistake in the codicil is patent on the face of it. The words in the will "to my sister

Louise Jahnke and unto my nephew Heinrich Schluther and his sister, my niece,'' indicate without any doubt or confusion that Louise Jahnke, Heinrich Schluther and Heinrich's sister, who was testator's niece, were the three persons and none others who were intended to be the residuary legatees. Now, when his sister dies or when he learns of her death he desires to dispose of the share she was to take and also to have the name of Heinrich's sister stated, and for these purposes, and for no other, makes the codicil. This view is borne out by the statement in the codicil—"to the other two residuary legatees therein named, Heinrich Schluther and to his sister," etc. Since it very clearly appears that the only intention of the testator in making the codicil, outside of disposing of his dead sister's share, was to have the name of Heinrich's sister, who was his niece, expressed, to show the names of all the persons who were his residuary legatees. Marie Kohler does not pretend to be Heinrich's sister, but there is no contention but what Christiane Arndt is his sister and the only sister living, the only other sister having died November 30, 1889, and of whose death the testator knew, as shown by his letter to Christiane written October 26, 1890. The sister of Heinrich was one of the residuary legatees in the will. The codicil says: "I hereby ratify and confirm said will in every respect, save so far as any part thereof is inconsistent with this codicil," and the codicil still making her a residuary legatee, it seems to me there can be no question that in the connection in which they are used the words "whose name is Marie Kohler and whose residence is Salzwedel, Altmark, Germany," were used to express the name and residence of Christiane Arndt, and as they do not accomplish that, are mere surplusage, which in the interpretation of the will and codicil are to be given no meaning at all. The testimony in the case and the wording of the will and of the codicil all show clearly that the inserting of the word "and" after "my niece" in the court's interpretation of the codicil, was unwarranted. Christiane Arndt was neither a party to the contest of the will nor to the compromise which resulted therefrom, and could not be bound by it. Marie Kohler, not being a legatee, cannot claim as such under the said compromise.

The order and decree of distribution and the order denying a new trial are reversed.

We concur: Chipman, P. J.; McLaughlin, J.

On Rehearing.

BUCKLES, J.—This is a petition on the part of Marie Kohler for a rehearing. The petition contains nothing new The case was fully gone into at the hearing and thoroughly considered in writing the opinion. We are therefore unable to see any reason for granting a rehearing.

The petition is denied.

We concur: Chipman, P. J.; McLaughlin, J.

NOBLE v. LEARNED et al.[*]

Court of Appeal, Third District; July 31, 1906.

87 Pac. 402.

Jury Trial—Legal or Equitable Actions or Issues.—A suit to determine title to stock in a building association, to cancel the certificate representing the stock, to restrain the payment of money on account of the certificate, and to require the issuance to plaintiff of a new certificate for the stock, is a suit in equity, and a jury trial is not demandable as of right under Code of Civil Procedure, section 592, providing that, in cases other than actions for the recovery of specific real or personal property, etc., issues of fact must be tried by the court, subject to its power to order issues to be tried by a jury.

Gifts—Assignments of Corporate Stock—Delivery.—An owner of stock in a building association gave to the secretary thereof a list of the persons to whom she wanted the stock assigned, and assignments were made on the back of the certificates. The secretary was given possession of the certificates subject to the owner's order, and told to hold them until the owner's death, and then deliver them to the assignees. A few months afterward the owner died. Held, that title did not vest in the assignees, but remained in the owner.

APPEAL from Superior Court, San Joaquin County; F. H. Smith, Judge.

Action by Arthur M. Noble, as executor of Deborah H. Lee, against D. A. Learned and others. From a judgment for plaintiff, defendants appeal. Affirmed.

---

[*] For subsequent opinion in supreme court, see 153 Cal. 245, 94 Pac. 1047.

A. H. Carpenter for appellant; Plummer & Dunlap for respondent; Budd & Thompson for building and loan association.

BUCKLES, J.—This action was prosecuted to determine
the title to certain stock in the San Joaquin Valley Building
and Loan Association, and for the delivery up and cancellation of the certificate representing the same, for an injunction restraining the payment of money on account of said
certificates, and for the issuance to plaintiff of certificates of
said stock. Judgment was for plaintiff, and the appeal is
from the judgment.

The first error assigned is that the court refused the defendants' demand for a jury. Whatever view may be taken
of the case as to other matters, it is an equity case, and there
was therefore no error in denying the defendants' demand
for a jury: Code Civ. Proc., sec. 592; Meek v. De La Tour,
2 Cal. App. 261, 83 Pac. 300; Ashton v. Heggerty, 130 Cal.
517, 62 Pac. 934. The complaint alleges that Deborah H.
Lee died intestate March 12, 1903, and at that time she was
the owner and entitled to forty shares of the capital stock of
the San Joaquin Valley Building and Loan Association, in a
certificate numbered 465, and that one Gennis H. Learned,
upon the death of said Deborah H. Lee, wrongfully and unlawfully took possession of said certificate of stock, had the
same canceled and a new certificate issued to her in her own
name for thirty-nine shares and received $100 in money for
the other shares. That said Gennis H. Learned died testate,
and the said certificate of stock is now held by D. A. Learned,
the executor of the last will of said Gennis H. Learned. Alleges demand made, and the value of the property to be
$4,000. The prayer is that the certificate of stock No. 559
be delivered up by said defendant, that it be canceled and
the San Joaquin Valley Building and Loan Association issue
to plaintiff certificates in due form evidencing the ownership
of plaintiff to said thirty-nine shares, and also the return of
the $100. The San Joaquin Valley Building and Loan Asso-
ciation answered by general denial. D. A. Learned answered
by denying specifically, admitting the death of Deborah H.
Lee and Gennis H. Learned and the proceedings taken to settle their respective estates, and, further answering, alleges
that on October 17, 1902, Deborah H. Lee duly assigned by

indorsement all said shares of stock to Gennis H. Learned, and then delivered the same so indorsed to A. M. Noble, to be held by him in trust for the said Gennis H. Learned as long as the said assignor should live, and at her death to be delivered to the said assignee; that said Noble accepted said trust; that the said trust was not revoked, and was in force when the said Deborah H. Lee died; that after her death, and on or about the 20th of March, 1903, Noble delivered said certificates of stock to Gennis H. Learned, and she then had said certificate for forty shares canceled and the new certificate No. 559 issued to her for thirty-nine shares in said association, receiving $100 in money. Prays that the said trust be declared valid, and defendant be adjudged the owner and entitled to the possession of said stock. The court found that Deborah H. Lee never made any gift of said shares of stock to Gennis H. Learned and ''never created any trust therein, and never parted with any title, ownership or control of said property during her lifetime, and the property and the whole thereof was, at the time of her death, the property of the said Deborah H. Lee, deceased, and at the date of her death constituted, and still constitutes, a part and parcel of the estate of said deceased.''

This finding is based upon the testimony of Arthur M. Noble, of whom she purchased the forty shares of the capital stock of the San Joaquin Valley Building and Loan Association. Mrs. Deborah H. Lee was sick, had about $1,600 which she wanted placed where she could have the income from it and use any part of the principal in case she needed it at any time. In negotiating the purchase of said shares of stock with the witness A. M. Noble, who was the secretary of the San Joaquin Valley Building and Loan Association, she informed him that this was the only money she had, and that she did not want to put it out of her control. This certificate of stock No. 465, with others, was issued to her with the assurance to her by Mr. Noble that she could retain control of them and draw money on them. The certificates were then issued in the name of Deborah H. Lee, and given to her. She assigned them to different persons, assigning No. 465 to Gennis H. Learned. They were then by Mrs. Lee returned to Mr. Noble, who testified in relation thereto as follows: ''I left them [certificates] at the house with her. Two or three days subsequent to that she sent for me and wanted me to take these certificates and pass-book and keep them for her, subject to her order—call. She said if she did not get well, and anything happened to her, to notify the people to whom these certificates had been assigned and send for them and deliver them to them. She said she would use more or less of it, and what was left at the time of her death was to be given to the people mentioned by her. In pursuance of that, I presume I took the certificates. I took certificate No. 465 which has been read in evidence. After this occurrence I had occasion to visit Mrs. Lee again. She sent for me, because she said she needed some money and wanted to surrender one of those certificates of stock she held. I took the certificate No. 480 for one share out with me.'' After this he went out to her house with said certificates as she desired to get money on them. He continues: ''After the cancellation of the last certificate, on the 28th day of February, 1903, the remainder of the certificates were handed back to me. Mrs. Lee told me to take and keep them the same as I had done before—to keep them for her. There were nineteen certificates of this stock, and all issued in the name of Deborah H. Lee. She afterward, but on the same day, gave me a list in writing of the persons to whom she wanted the stock assigned, and the assignments were made on the back of the certificates.''

It thus clearly appears that Deborah H. Lee did not and never intended to part with control of her title to said stock while she lived. On March 12, 1903, she died without having revoked said assignments, or any of them. The certificates were then in the safe in the possession of Noble, who afterward delivered certificate No. 465 to Gennis H. Learned, she being the one named therein as assignee. The finding is warranted by the evidence: Noble v. Garden, 146 Cal. 225, 2 Ann. Cas. 1001, 79 Pac. 883. This, then, disposes of the issue that Noble held the certificate as trustee, against the contention of appellant. A similar case to the one before us, and involving the same question as to delivery and title of others of these identical certificates of stock, was well considered and decided in Noble v. Garden, 146 Cal. 225, 2 Ann. Cas. 1001, 79 Pac. 883. The court there held under the same state of facts that Deborah H. Lee retained control and dominion of these certificates; and that the title did not vest in the parties to whom the assignments were made because she expressly stated it should remain in deceased. Upon the authority of Noble v.

Garden, supra, the judgment of the lower court must be upheld.

Judgment is affirmed.

We concur: Chipman, P. J.; McLaughlin, J.

Ex parte WILLIAMS.

Court of Appeal, Third District; July 31, 1906.

87 Pac. 565.

Gaming.—It is not a Crime, Under Penal Code, section 330, making it an offense to operate any banking or percentage game played with any device "for money, checks, credit or other representative of value," to set up and operate a slot machine on which games are played, unless played for money, checks, credits or other representative of value, and, if played for something not included in these words, it is not a crime.[1]

Gaming.—Penal Code, Section 330, Making It an Offense for anyone to operate any banking or percentage game played with any device for money, checks, credit, or other representative of value, adopted in 1872, prior to the existence of cigar slot machines, when considered in connection with section 331, prohibiting the use of any house for gambling, prohibited by section 330, and section 4, providing that the Penal Code is to be construed according to the fair import of its terms, does not make it an offense to operate a slot machine on which games are played for cigars.

Application by C. C. Williams for a writ of habeas corpus for his discharge from imprisonment on conviction of an alleged criminal offense. Petitioner discharged. Transferred to supreme court: See post, p. 309, 87 Pac. 568.

T. J. Butts, for petitioner; C. H. Pond, district attorney, for the people.

BUCKLES, J.—The petitioner was engaged in the saloon business, also selling cigars and tobacco in the city of Petaluma, and had therein a slot machine used by his customers in gambling for cigars. The complaint on which the petitioner was charged, arrested, tried, and convicted was as fol-

----

[1] Cited in the note in 121 Am. St. Rep. 693, on gambling games and devices.

lows: "On the 4th day of December, A. D. 1905 . . . . did willfully and unlawfully open, carry on, and conduct, at his saloon and place of business at 319 Main street, in the city of Petaluma, Sonoma county, state of California, a certain banking game, played by means of a slot machine, for money, checks, and other representatives of value, to wit, cigars and tobacco." While the complaint charges "for money, checks, etc.," there is no pretension that either money or checks were played. It does appear from the return and record in the case that the crime charged and intended to be charged was using the slot machine for "other representatives of value," and that such representatives of value were cigars and tobacco. The petitioner was sentenced to pay a fine of $100, and to be imprisoned until such fine be paid, etc. The fine was not paid, and the petitioner was imprisoned. This answer to the return made by the sheriff contains the following, to wit: "That the slot machine mentioned in said complaint is operated by dropping a nickle or slug in the slot in the right-hand side of said machine, and then pressing a lever, and, if the proper combination of cards showed upon the cylinder, the party putting the nickle in the slot was entitled to a certain number of cigars, according to the combination of cards. If a royal flush was made to show upon the cylinder, the party playing the machine was entitled to forty cigars; for four aces, fifteen cigars; for four kings, fourteen cigars; for four queens, thirteen cigars, and under queens, ten cigars; full hand, eight cigars; a flush, six cigars; for three queens, three cigars, and under queens, two cigars; and two pairs, jacks up, two cigars; and one pair, aces, kings, or queens, one cigar; and any other combination would not win anything. That said machine was played for cigars, and nothing else, and that these facts were established and proved at the trial of this case." These facts are not controverted, and are set forth with above particularity for the sole purpose of showing that the entire charge made and the crime complained of was running the slot machine, not for money, checks, or credits, but for "other representatives of value." The slot machine is a device or thing where the person who plays it must, of necessity, play at a chance game, the owner or operator thereof paying when the person who has put in his nickle wins, and taking the nickle when there is a loss, and it is thus a banking game: People v. Carroll, 80 Cal. 153,

22 Pac. 129. It is not a crime, under section 330 of the Penal
Code, to set up and run such a device as a slot machine described here, unless played "for money, checks, credits, or
other representatives of value." If played for something not
included in these, it is not a crime.

As it is here admitted that it was not played for either
money, checks or credit, but for cigars, we are therefore called
upon to determine what the legislature intended to include
within the words, "or other representative of value." The
respondent contends they can have but one meaning, and
that anything of value, and therefore includes all kind of
property having a value; while the petitioner claims they can
refer only to some similar thing—to money, checks or credit.
If the legislature was intending to prohibit all gambling with
banking devices or by banking games played with cards, dice
or any device, it seems to us there would have been no limitation as now to money, checks or credits, but the statement
would have been for anything of value or that represents
value. Gambling such as it is sought to prohibit by section
330 is carried on almost exclusively for money, or some obligation or promise which calls for money, and not other property. The very language of the section precludes any other
idea. Then, if this be so, we must keep this in view in try-
ing to determine to what the words "or other representative
of value" were intended to apply. There is a general rule
in construing statutes, either penal or otherwise, which forbids the adoption of any construction that will defeat the
purpose for which the statute was obviously intended, and
our code (Pen. Code, sec. 4) provides that all of the provisions of the Penal Code are to be construed according to the
fair import of their terms, with a view to effect its object and
to promote justice. These rules apply here. If we take into
consideration, as the people contend we must, the fact that
the chapter in which section 330 is found is headed "Gaming," we are furnished no aid, no light by which to arrive
at the meaning of the words "or other representative of
value," for there is no pretense that the section contains
a prohibition against all kinds of gaming, but is limited to
the kinds therein mentioned. Courts have no power to legislate, and if the legislature intended to simply prohibit banking and percentage games where played for money, checks,
credits and other things similar to money, checks and

credits, this court has no power to add a further prohibition, and say that it will be a crime if such banking or percentage game is for other kinds of property, such as grain,
fruit, horses, cattle, lumber, and all other things of whatever kind which may have a value. The rule seems to
be well established in the interpretation of statutes and
clauses like the one under consideration that where general
words follow particular ones, the former are construed as
applicable to persons or things of the same kind, class or
nature. The rule has been further stated as follows: "Where
a statute or other document enumerates several classes of
persons or things, and immediately following and classed with
such enumeration the class embraces 'other' persons or things,
the word 'other' will generally be read as 'other such like,'
so that the persons or things therein comprised may be read
as of the same kind, class, or nature, with and not of a quality superior to, or different from, those specifically enumerated": 21 Am. & Eng. Ency. of Law, 1012. In New York,
where a statute exempted from taxation every building
erected for the use of a college, incorporated academy, or
other seminary of learning, it was held, as all those enumerated were corporations, that the general words "or other
seminary" required that such institution should also be an incorporated one in order to have the benefit of the exemption;
Chegaray v. Mayor etc. of New York, 13 N. Y. 220. In the
Illinois Criminal Code the words "or other instrument of
writing" is held to include only instruments of the same kind
as those previously specified; that is, bills, notes, checks, etc.,
for the payment of money, and not to apply to the case of a
contract under which it was wholly uncertain whether the
money would ever become payable: Shirk v. People, 121 Ill.
61, 11 N. E. 888. So in Kentucky, where the statute read:
"Section 1. Whoever with or without compensation, shall set
up, carry on, or conduct, or shall aid and assist in setting up,
carrying on, or conducting, a keno bank, faro bank, or other
machine or contrivance used in betting whereby money or
other things may be won or lost, etc.," the indictment charged
that the defendant "unlawfully and feloniously set up, carry
on, and conduct a machine and contrivance used in betting,
to wit, a game of oontz played with dice and upon which
money was won and lost." It was held that other machine
or device must be of the same kind or nature with the keno

bank or faro bank, under the rule above stated. In that case the evidence showed that the game played was that commonly known as "craps" or "oontz," in which no machinery or implements are used save two ordinary dice: Commonwealth v. Kammerer (Ky.), 13 S. W. 108. Many other cases may be cited which uphold this rule, but we deem this sufficient. But the rule is not inflexible, for where it is plain from the whole act, document or subject matter that the real intent was different, then such manifest intent, and not the above rule, prevails. As in the definitions given in the code of degrees of murder: "All murder which is perpetrated by means of poison, or lying in wait, torture or by any other kind of willful, deliberate and premeditated killing . . . . is murder in the first degree." One who administers poison to another with intent to kill, and death results therefrom, is at once guilty of murder in the first degree, because the deliberation, premeditation, malice aforethought, and all have been established. So when the killing follows from lying in wait or from torture, but there are many other ways than these by which murder in the first degree may be committed: People v. Bealoba, 17 Cal. 389. The killing may be accomplished by pushing one from a high wall or into a deep well, or by any means which shows willful, deliberate and premeditated killing. Such statute needs no interpretation, for the intent of the lawmaker is seen at once. The betting on elections, on horseracing, and the gambling in stocks and in grain are kinds of gambling not included within section 330. The very language of the statute itself shows that the gambling which the legislature was attempting to prohibit was that sort of gambling usually carried on at a fixed place of business, where those seeking to play at games of chance could come, and where money is the thing usually wagered, or its representative, such as checks or anything which is a demand to be paid in money. It would hardly be considered reasonable that the legislature had in mind that the games and devices enumerated were played in the general markets where grain, animals and stocks are bought and sold. The intent of the legislature to legislate against games set up and carried on at a fixed place and in houses or rooms is shown by section 331 of the Penal Code, which attempts to prohibit the use of any house for the gambling prohibited in section 330. Neither is it plain that the legislature had in mind any kind of

20

property other than money, the thing most common for use
in such games, and its representative such as checks and demands for the payment of money. Neither would it be a
reasonable supposition that in 1872, when the act was passed,
any banking game would be set up or carried on in gambling
for anything but money and the instruments representing
money, and therefore the legislature could not have had in
mind the cigar slot machine, and could not have prohibited
its use. The ingenuity of man, however, has devised a banking game in the cigar slot machine by which gambling may
be carried on for property not included within "money,
checks, credits or other representatives of value." There is
nothing in section 330 which prohibits gambling for cigars.
It follows that the petitioner must be discharged. The prisoner is discharged.

McLAUGHLIN, J.—I concur. Section 330 of the Penal
Code provides that: "Every person who deals, plays, or carries on, opens, or causes to be opened, or who conducts, either
as owner or employee, whether for hire or not, any game of
faro, monte, roulette, lansquenet, rouge et noir, rondo, tan,
fan-tan, stud horse poker, seven-and-a-half, twenty-one, hokey-
pokey, or any banking or percentage game played with cards
or dice or any device, for money, checks, credit, or other
representative of value," is guilty of a misdemeanor. It is
clear from the language of this section that it is a misdemeanor to conduct or carry on a slot machine or any other
device played for money, checks, or credits, but we are here
called upon to determine whether a person who conducts or
carries on such a device played for cigars and tobacco is likewise guilty of an infraction of the law. Such acts as those
enumerated in this and similar statutes are crimes only because they are prohibited by law, and unless the act charged
against the petitioner is so prohibited, he is entitled to his
discharge. If it is forbidden by law at all, it must be because
cigars and tobacco are representatives of value, within the
meaning of the section quoted. The words "or other representative of value" found in the section must be construed in
connection with the preceding language in the same sentence,
for the word "other" is a correlative and specifying word,
meaning "different from that which has been specified; not
the same; not this or those; different": Hyatt v. Allen, 54

Cal. 357. In other words, the word "other" will "generally be read as 'other such like,' so that persons or things therein comprised may be read as ejusdem generis with, and not of a quality superior to or different from, those specifically enumerated": 21 Am. & Eng. Ency. of Law, p. 1012; Stroud's Judicial Dictionary, p. 1359 et seq.; Lewis' Sutherland on Statutory Construction, secs. 423–430. A study of the innumerable cases supporting this doctrine or dealing with the proposition under discussion, found in the notes in works above cited, will show that in nearly every instance where this rule was not followed the word was used in a different connection or sense from that apparent in the statute before us. In a recent case the supreme court of this state said that there was little, if any, controversy as to the rule in its application to the penal statutes: Matter of La Societe Francaise, 123 Cal. 531, 56 Pac. 458. Applying this rule, and adopting the meaning of the word "other" when used in exactly the same connection and sense as in section 330 of the Penal Code, declared in Hyatt v. Allen, supra, we cannot escape the conclusion that conducting a slot machine played for cigars and tobacco is not within the prohibition of that section of the Penal Code.

But, aside from this, there is another rule commanding that words not plainly used in a technical sense shall be taken in their ordinary, general sense, and if this applied to the word "representative," as used in the section, it seems quite clear to my mind that cigars or tobacco cannot be considered as representative of value. The word "representative" as used in the statute certainly means "typifying"; "presenting by means of something"; "standing in the place of"; "that which represents anything." Cigars and tobacco are things of value; they have a value. This is beyond cavil. But in my opinion it could hardly be said that they represent their own inherent or market value. A certain coin or check or bill will represent the value of any quantity of cigars or tobacco, and these in turn will be inherently worth the price obtainable for them. But it would hardly be contended that because they have a certain value, measured by current mediums of exchange, they represent the value of the coin or currency paid for them, any more than they represent any other commodity which might be exchanged for them in the course of trade. Every commodity has a value measured according to

fixed standards, but the various commodities sold and bought
in many markets and transactions do not represent the value
of the gold, silver or currency paid for them. On the contrary, the medium of exchange established by law or recognized in business dealings represents their value. Thus we
are led to the conclusion that the words "representative of
value" do not mean that cigars and tobacco or any other commodity represents its own intrinsic or market value. A similar statute was before the supreme court of Montana in a
recent case, and the decision of that court illustrates this distinction. There the statute read "for money, checks, credits
or any representative of value, or for any property or thing
whatever," and the court held that this language included
cigars and tobacco, and in so holding said: "The enumeration
includes every species of property of classes to which the particulars belong. 'Money' includes all money; 'checks' includes all kinds of articles embraced under that designation;
'credits' is a term of universal application to obligations due
and to become due; and when we consider the expression 'any
representative of value' there is nothing left of any of the
classes of property enumerated; and unless the words 'any
property or thing whatever' were designated to include merchandise such as cigars and similar articles, then it must be
rejected as of no import whatever": State v. Woodman, 26
Mont. 348, 67 Pac. 1120. It will be noted that the statute
there construed was much stronger than ours. It not only
contained the comprehensive language "any property or thing
whatever," but it was far more emphatic, in this, that it included "any representative of value," and hence the maxim
ejusdem generis could not apply. And yet no person reading
the decision can doubt that if the words "any property or
thing whatever" had been omitted, the decision would have
been the other way. And so it must be here, for had the legislature intended to place the ban of the law on slot machines
played for cigars or any other class of merchandise, the natural, ordinary common sense, and in fact the only way to do
so, would have been to use the phrase "anything of value,"
or some similar and equally comprehensive expression. Not
having done so, we cannot extend the scope of the statute by
giving it a construction at variance with rules of law and the
accepted and established meaning of words employed. If
the legislative department of the government desires to pro-

hibit this character of gaming, that result may easily be accomplished; but until they do so, every citizen is entitled to immunity from punishment for acts which are neither mala in se nor mala prohibita.

I concur: Chipman, **P. J.**

Ex parte WILLIAMS.

Cr. No. 1364; September 25, 1906.

87 Pac. 568.

Court of Appeals—Transfer of Cause to Supreme Court.—The constitutional provision with reference to the transfer of a case from the district court of appeal to the supreme court has no application in matters of habeas corpus.

Application by C. C. Williams for a writ of habeas corpus for his discharge from imprisonment on conviction of an alleged criminal offense. The district court of appeal discharged petitioner: Ante, p. 301, 87 Pac. 565. Application for an order transferring the cause to the supreme court for determination. Denied.

PER CURIAM.—The application for an order transferring the above-entitled cause from the district court of appeal to the supreme court for hearing and determination after judgment in the said district court of appeal is denied; a majority of the justices of this court being of the opinion that the constitutional provision with reference to the transfer of cases from the district court of appeal to the supreme court has no application in matters of habeas corpus.

PINNEY v. WILSON et al.

Court of Appeal, Third District; September 25, 1906.

87 Pac. 1111.

Broker.—In an Action for Compensation for the Sale of Mining Claims for $235,000, where plaintiff's witnesses testified that ten per cent was a reasonable compensation, and defendant testified that he offered $7,500, and that plaintiff offered in writing to take $10,000, but no such writing was introduced in evidence, and there was a verdict for plaintiff for $7,500, an award of a new trial to plaintiff was not an abuse of discretion.[1]

APPEAL from Superior Court, City and County of San Francisco; Carroll Cook, Judge.

Action by George M. Pinney against Homer Wilson and others. From an order granting plaintiff's motion for a new trial, defendant Homer Wilson appeals. Affirmed.

Gavin McNab for appellant; Geo. M. Pinney and Carter, Rickets & Dolph for respondent.

BUCKLES, J.—This was an action to recover the sum of $40,000 as a reasonable compensation for plaintiff's services rendered in procuring a purchaser for the defendant's mining claims, situated in Trinity County, known as the Chloride-Baily, Jenny Lind, and Maple group of mines. The action is based on a written promise, contained in a letter written by defendant to plaintiff, "to pay you a reasonable compensation for such service." In another part of the letter he says: "To pay you such compensation as in equity and good conscience you are entitled and the margin of profit therein will permit." The case was tried with a jury, which returned a verdict in favor of the plaintiff in the sum of $7,500, and judgment was given for that amount. Plaintiff moved for a new trial, which was granted, and defendants appeal from the order granting a new trial.

At the trial it was shown that plaintiff introduced to Wilson (defendant and appellant) one Charles Sweeny, who purchased of Wilson the said mines for $235,000. Every witness produced for the plaintiff testified that ten per cent on the amount for which mining property should sell was a reasonable compensation for the services in finding a purchaser. There was no testimony on the part of defendant, except that given by defendant himself. He testified that when he gave plaintiff the letter referred to, in which he promised a reasonable commission, he offered to give the sum of $7,500; that he considered it reasonable. Then, when the sale was made, he testified that plaintiff came to him and offered to take $10,000 for the services rendered. Defendant said this offer to take

---

[1] Cited in the note in Ann. Cas. 1912D, 1226, on duty of trial court to set aside verdict as contrary to evidence.

$10,000 was contained in writing brought to him by the plaintiff. No such writing was offered in evidence. We do not think there was any abuse of discretion in granting the new trial.

The order granting the new trial is affirmed.

We concur: Chipman, P. J.; McLaughlin, J.

E. P. VANDERCOOK CO. v. WILMANS CO.

Court of Appeal, First District; September 21, 1906.

87 Pac. 1116.

Broker.—In an Action for Compensation for the Sale of real estate, evidence held sufficient to sustain findings that the plaintiff procured a purchaser who was ready, able and willing to purchase, and thereby completed its services and earned its commission.

Broker—Right to Commissions—Necessity for Actual Sale.— Under a contract whereby the owner of land gave plaintiff exclusive authority to sell it and agreed to pay a commission on any amount for which the property should be sold, the plaintiff was entitled to his commission on procuring a purchaser able, ready and willing to purchase though the sale was not actually completed.

APPEAL from Superior Court, Alameda County; Henry A. Melvin, Judge.

Action by the E. P. Vandercook Company against the Wilmans Company. From an order denying defendant's motion for a new trial he appeals. Affirmed.

John S. Partridge for appellant; Snook & Church for respondent.

COOPER, J.—This action was brought to recover $791.87 as commissions for the sale of real estate under a written contract. The case was tried before the court, findings filed, and judgment ordered and entered for plaintiff. Defendant has appealed from the order denying its motion for a new trial. The court found that, pursuant to the authorization contained in the contract, the plaintiff procured a purchaser for the lands therein described who was ready, able and willing to purchase, and thereby completed its services and earned its commissions. The defendant contends that the evidence does not support the findings of the court in this regard. The findings are conclusive upon us if there is substantial evidence to support them, even though the evidence may be conflicting or may preponderate in favor of defendant.

The defendant was, at the times mentioned in the pleadings and findings, a corporation. Its capital stock was divided into three hundred shares, and was at the time the contract was made owned and held by J. M. Wilmans, F. W. Wilmans, Lillian W. Wilmans, Clara E. Wilmans, and Martha J. Wilmans. J. M. Wilmans was the secretary and managing agent, and owned two-thirds of the shares of the capital stock of the corporation. Its assets consisted of about fourteen hundred acres of land situate in Stanislaus county in this state. The managing agent of defendant, J. M. Wilmans, spoke of the defendant's property as his own land and as being mortgaged for $75,000, or, in his language: "I owed $75,000 on the whole property." There is evidence to the effect that on May 21, 1903, Merle, the agent of plaintiff, was in Stanislaus county with one Witcher, who was looking at lands with a view of purchasing, and Merle was showing Witcher different tracts of land. They saw the lands belonging to the defendant, and Witcher seemed to be pleased with them, and to desire to purchase them, or at least a part of the land owned by the defendant. Merle procured from defendant, through J. M. Wilmans, its agent, with admitted power to act, a contract in writing, authorizing the plaintiff, exclusively, to sell a tract of land described therein, containing three hundred and ten acres, at $100 per acre, and another lot containing two and one-quarter acres at $300 per acre. The contract contained the clause: "If said property is sold, or a purchaser is found by E. P. Vandercook Co., or through their agency, we agree to pay the said E. P. Vandercook Co. 2½ per cent. commission on any amount for which said property shall be sold." The contract was to continue for one month from date, May 21, 1903, and was continued by written extensions to July 20, 1903. It contained a clause that it should be irrevocable until withdrawn by written notice.

Merle testified that he showed the property to Witcher and "Witcher said he would take that particular piece of property described in the contract. He was to take three hundred and ten acres for $100 an acre and two and one-quarter acres at $300 an acre. . . . . Mr. Witcher said if everything was all right, the abstract of title was correct, he would take that amount of land. He made no other objection than that the abstract of title should be correct. We had been at the ranch a couple of hours driving around the premises. This particular three hundred acres was pointed out by Mr. Wilmans on the map and we drove down and saw the land. Mr. Witcher did not tell Mr. Wilmans at the ranch that he would take the land; he told him so at the hotel." Witcher testified that he was ready at the time the contract was made; that the purchase looked all right to him.

Now, after the plaintiff had procured for the defendant a purchaser for the land described in the contract who was able, ready and willing to take the land, there arose some question in the mind of Witcher as to whether or not the amount of land described in the contract would be sufficient for his purposes. Wilmans suggested that he would sell Witcher a half interest in the whole ranch. Merle testified that, while this proposition was pending, he went to Wilmans and asked him as to the plaintiff's commissions in case Witcher purchased half the ranch instead of that described in the contract, and that Wilmans replied: "I will stand by my agreement; will pay you your commission as I agreed on the purchase price, which was $31,000." Witcher testified that he heard this conversation, and that Wilmans said: "We will pay the commissions on the sum of $37,675 at the rate of two and one-half per cent, but that it was in reference to the three hundred and twelve and one-half acres in reference to the first deal." Wilmans testified in regard to this conversation with Merle: "Then he asked about the commission; I told him that if the trade went through, if he made any trade, that I would see that he got his commission of two and one-half per cent."

It therefore appears clear that the minds of the seller and purchaser were first brought together by the plaintiff on the sale of the lands described in the contract. It is admitted that Witcher was able to purchase. It is a significant fact that he gave Wilmans $2,400 while the contemplated sale under the contract was in progress. It is now claimed both by Wilmans and Witcher that this $2,400 was a loan and had nothing to do with the contract, but the claim that it was a loan seems to have been an afterthought. Witcher testified as to this payment: "This thing had been dragging along from May 23d to June 24th. Mr. Wilmans stated to me that he was in need of $2,400 to pay some money due in San Francisco. . . . . I said to Mr. Wilmans, 'I have some idle money, I will lend you that $2,400; if I ever buy anything from you it can be applied to the price. If I don't, it is an ordinary loan to be returned to me when the note becomes due.'" The witness could not remember the length of time of the note, nor whether it was given by the corporation or Wilmans. Wilmans testified that he "owed some money in the bank, and I was anxious to pay it. I asked him if he would advance it and take my note for it, and if there was nothing went of this I had to pay him back." Wilmans did not remember whether he gave his personal note or the note of the corporation. No security was asked or given. The note was not produced in evidence. Before the sale of the lands described in the contract was completed the arrangement was changed at the suggestion of Wilmans, and Witcher agreed to buy the shares of capital stock of defendant corporation belonging to the Wilmans. He took an option on them in August, 1903, bought half of them in September and the balance in October of the same year. Witcher testified: "I think the suggestion that I should buy the stock of the corporation came from Mr. Wilmans." Witcher was asked: "Q. Mr. Witcher, if you had not bought the stock of the corporation, would you have purchased any part of the ranch? A. Well, I probably would have in time, though I never did get around far enough to close up the deal." Wilmans testified on the same point: "I suggested that he take the five hundred acres, and he said he would entertain it about the first day of August. I suggested to him along about the 1st of August that he take stock in the company." It is a significant fact that, although the parties had been brought together by the plaintiff, and Witcher had given the defendant $2,400, after the suggestion of the sale of the stock to the contemplated purchaser, the sale of the stock was not made until the contract with the plaintiff had expired. The sale of the stock of the corporation to Witcher was, as to the owners of the stock, the equivalent of the sale of the ranch. The sale is spoken of by Wilmans as a sale of the land. He testified: "Some of that land is not worth any $100 an acre, while there is a portion of the property would be worth $110, and some down at $80. So in fixing it all up, in adjusting the value, I put it on that basis, $91.50 for the fourteen hundred acres.''

At the time the plaintiff was employed the Wilmans were the owners of all the stock of defendant and thus owned all that defendant owned. Defendant owned the ranch of fourteen hundred acres and nothing else. The Wilmans were, for the purposes of this case, the corporation, and they desired to sell the lands described in the contract and pay their debts. They did, in effect, sell the lands described in the contract, together with all the lands owned by the corporation. They sold to the purchaser found by plaintiff. The defendant promised to pay plaintiff the commissions when it made the contract, and it again promised when the contract was changed so as to include other lands. It has not paid the commission, and it is no defense that the sale was made by a different mode from that contemplated in the contract. The purchaser produced by plaintiff has, in fact, become the owner of the lands which defendant desired to sell. It is true that Witcher, who purchased the land by purchasing all the shares of the stock of defendant, was not a party to the contract, but he knew of it when he purchased the stock. He heard Wilmans promise to pay the commissions. He will not be allowed in this way to defeat the claim of plaintiff against defendant.

When the sale of the capital stock was completed Witcher retained $30,000 out of the amount to be paid by him ''as a guaranty that the company was not further obligated than what the books showed.'' The company was under the obligation to plaintiff to pay the commissions due it, whether the books showed it or not. The transaction must be stripped of all its intricacies and viewed in the light of common sense. It was, in substance, a sale of the ranch of the Wilmans to Witcher. The corporation was only the instrument by which the title was held for the owners of the capital stock, and by its duly authorized agent it agreed to pay plaintiff for its services. The services have been performed and the defendant must pay for them. If the corporation had sold the ranch to Witcher and made its deed under its corporate seal, and he had paid the money to the corporation, the title would have passed. The title is now in the corporate name of defendant, but as Witcher holds all the shares of the capital stock of defendant, he holds that which is equivalent to the title. We therefore conclude that the findings are supported by the evidence.

The contention of the appellant that the commissions were to be paid only out of the purchase money when an actual sale should be made is without merit. The agreement was to pay plaintiff "two and one-half per cent commission on any amount for which said property shall be sold." This does not make the commissions payable only out of a particular fund. When plaintiff procured a purchaser, able, ready and willing to purchase, defendant could not by its own act, in suggesting and carrying through a different scheme, take the benefit of the plaintiff's services without compensation. Courts will not readily lend their assistance to aid parties in escaping their just liabilities through technicalities.

The order is affirmed. ·

We concur: Harrison, P. J.; Hall, J.

JONES v. WATERMAN.*

Court of Appeal, Second District; August 17, 1906.

87 Pac. 469.

Appeal—Conflicting Evidence.—A Finding of a Trial court based on conflicting evidence will not be disturbed on appeal where there is sufficient evidence in the record to support it.

Agency—Evidence of Authority.—In an Action to Recover an Agreed rent for certain reamers used by a well driller in drilling a well under contract with defendant, the memorandum of agreement between defendant and the driller, and evidence of the oral agreement between them, by which the driller agreed to furnish all tools necessary for the work, was admissible to show that no authority could be implied from the transaction by which the driller was authorized to obtain the reamers on defendant's credit.

Agency—Unauthorized Acts — Ratification.—Where defendant employed a well driller to drill a well on his ranch and to furnish all required tools, the fact that one of the defendant's employées paid the expressage on certain reamers hired by the driller from plaintiff for use in drilling the well, and agreed to pay $30 toward such hire, without defendant's knowledge, was insufficient to establish that the driller had authority to contract for the reamers on defendant's behalf.

*Rehearing denied October 11, 1906.

APPEAL from Superior Court, Santa Barbara County; J. W. Taggart, Judge.

Action by Fred W. Jones against Isaac G. Waterman. From a judgment for defendant, plaintiff appeals. Affirmed.

Wm. Griffith for appellant; Canfield & Starbuck and H. C. Booth for respondent.

ALLEN, J.:—Action for money. Judgment for defendant, and a motion for new trial denied. Plaintiff appeals from the judgment and order.

The action was brought in the court below by plaintiff to recover a sum for the hire of two certain under-reamers, alleged to have been furnished by him to defendant for use in drilling a well. The complaint is based upon an express contract upon the part of defendant to pay for the reasonable value of such hire. The answer denies the contract and also the hire or the use by defendant of said tools. The court finds in favor of defendant upon all of the issues.

There is no evidence in the record tending to support the issue as to the express promise to pay for such hire, and were we to assume that under the issues evidence was admissible to show an implied agreement to pay therefor, the record discloses a conflict in such evidence, and that there is sufficient in the record to support each and every finding of the court below, and under the well-established rule such findings will not be disturbed.

There was no error in admitting in evidence the memorandum of agreement between defendant and the well driller, nor in admitting the oral agreement between the parties in reference to the driller's obligation to furnish all tools necessary in the prosecution of the work. It was competent as tending to show that no obligation rested upon defendant to furnish such tools, and that no authority could be implied from the transaction between defendant and the party who made the order. The order for such under-reamers was made by the driller, and he did not, in terms, represent that he was acting for defendant. He simply ordered the tools, and directed them to be shipped to defendant's ranch, where he was then employed, and defendant is not shown to have had any knowledge of such order, or to have acquiesced therein; and it was competent for him to show that he gave no authority for the order, but, on the contrary, that the tools were to be furnished by the driller, and the driller's use thereof in no wise established any implied promise on defendant's part to pay for the hire. The mere fact that one of defendant's employees paid the expressage, and had, without authority from defendant, agreed to pay $30 toward such hire, would not render defendant liable on account of such hire, he having no knowledge either of the payment of expressage nor of the arrangement between the driller and his employee.

We perceive no prejudicial error in the record, and the judgment and order are affirmed.

We concur: Gray, P. J.; Smith, J.

———————

MONETA CANNING AND PRESERVING COMPANY v. MARTIN et al.

Court of Appeal, Second District; November 9, 1906.

88 Pac. 369.

Trial.—Findings are not Necessary in Relation to separate defenses in support of which no evidence was offered.

APPEAL from Superior Court, Los Angeles County; Chas. Monroe, Judge.

Action by the Moneta Canning and Preserving Company against Samuel Martin and another. Judgment for plaintiff. Defendants appeal. Affirmed.

F. B. Woodruff for appellants; E. J. Fleming and Paul E. Ussher for respondent.

ALLEN, J.—Action to recover the agreed price of certain pea vines delivered to appellants by plaintiff under a written agreement. Judgment in favor of plaintiff, from which, and an order denying their motion for a new trial, defendants appeal.

The defendants answered separately, each denying the execution of the agreement or the receipt of the vines. The court found in favor of plaintiff upon these issues, and the evidence is uncontradicted in support of its findings. An attempt was made by defendants to plead a rescission of the contract upon the grounds of fraud in its procurement and a total failure of consideration. The answers were each insufficient to constitute a defense or to entitle the defendants to any relief. No facts were pleaded showing fraud upon plaintiff's part; neither was any fraudulent intent claimed, nor is it averred that defendants were ignorant as to the representations upon which they claimed to have relied.

It is argued by appellants that the vines not being existent when the contract was made, a warranty of their merchantable character and soundness failed under the provisions of section 1768 of the Civil Code. Were all this conceded, there is no evidence tending to show that the goods were either unsound or unmerchantable when delivered; but the contrary appears. There was no finding of the court in relation to the separate defenses, but, there being no evidence offered in support thereof, findings were unnecessary. A brief synopsis of the evidence is set out in the transcript, from which it appears that the judgment of the court could not have been otherwise than as rendered.

The judgment and order are affirmed.

We concur: Gray, P. J.; Smith, J.

HARRIS v. HARRIS et. al.

Court of Appeal, Third District; November 21, 1906.

88 Pac. 384.

Quieting Title—Issues and Proof.—Where, in an action to quiet title, plaintiff alleged that the lot in question was formerly owned by a certain association, and defendants established that they were the successors in interest of such association, defendants, in order to entitle themselves to recover, were not bound to prove title in such association.

APPEAL from Superior Court, City and County of San Francisco; J. B. Hebbard, Judge.

Action by Anna Harris against Michael G. Harris and others. From a judgment in favor of defendants, plaintiff appeals. Affirmed.

Marcus Rosenthal for appellant; M. G. Cobb and H. K. Wolff for respondents.

McLAUGHLIN, J.—Action to quiet title to a lot in the city of San Francisco. In her complaint the appellant alleged that the lot in question was formerly owned by the Central Park Homestead Association, and defendants, by competent evidence, established the fact that they are the successors in interest of said association. Notwithstanding the above-mentioned averment appellant contends that the evidence is insufficient to justify the findings in favor of respondents, because no evidence was introduced showing title in the said association. It is an elementary rule that the law neither does nor requires an idle act, and it would certainly be idle for defendants to consume time and energy in proving a fact alleged in the complaint and not denied in the answer. The finding that defendants are the owners of the lot in dispute is also assailed on the ground that the evidence shows that plaintiff had acquired title by adverse possession. There is nothing in this point. The evidence is ample to sustain the findings, and, as this is the only point presented for decision, the judgment is affirmed.

We concur: Chipman, P. J.; Buckles, J.

HIGUERA v. DEL PONTE et al.

Court of Appeal, First District; December 28, 1906.

88 Pac. 808.

Water Rights—Prescription.—In an Action to Quiet Title to certain land, evidence held sufficient to sustain a finding that defendants had acquired a prescriptive right to the use of waters of a spring located on plaintiff's land and flowing through a pipe to the land belonging to defendants.

APPEAL from Superior Court, Santa Clara County; M. H. Hyland, Judge.

Action by Bernardo Higuera against David Del Ponte and others. From a judgment in favor of defendants Del Ponte and another, and from an order denying plaintiff's motion for a new trial, he appeals. Affirmed.

Charles Clark for appellant; W. H. Johnson for respondents.

HALL, J.—Appeal from judgment in favor of defendants Del Ponte and Persico, and from the order denying plaintiff's motion for a new trial.

The action is in form an action to quiet title to a tract of land described as "lot seven (7) of the Higuera Rancho," but, as appears from the answer of defendants Del Ponte and Persico, and from the statement on motion for new trial, the only real controversy in the case was as to the ownership of certain water flowing from a spring on lot 7 of said rancho, through an iron pipe, to lot 4 of said rancho, and the right of way therefor. Defendants pleaded that they were the owners of said water, water right, and right of way, and specially pleaded "that for more than five years prior to the commencement of this action they and their grantors have been in the open, notorious, continuous, peaceful, uninterrupted use and occupation of all that part or portion of said water flowing from the said spring on said lot seven of said Higuera Rancho, and to the said lot four of said Higuera Rancho; that the said use and occupation of said water as aforesaid has been for all of said time hostile and adverse to any claim of all persons, and that the said water had been so used by the said defendants and their grantors with the full knowledge of-the said plaintiff." The court found the facts in accordance with the plea of the prescriptive right thus set up, and gave judgment accordingly. Appellant attacks the sufficiency of the evidence to sustain this finding.

This action was commenced July 21, 1903. The Higuera Rancho, prior to her death, belonged to the mother of plaintiff. In 1886 she caused a pipe to be laid from a spring situate on lot 7, now the property of plaintiff, to lot 4, now the property of defendants, for the purpose of conveying water to the family dwelling, which was situate on the portion of the rancho now known as "lot 4." From that time

21

until the commencement of this action it is perfectly clear
that the pipe has remained and water has run through it and
been used by the various and successive owners of that portion of the rancho (lot 4), for irrigating an orchard and the
usual domestic purposes. Mrs. Higuera died in 1889. October 8, 1891, as the result of a suit in partition, a decree
of partition was rendered by the superior court of Santa
Clara county, in which lot 7 of said rancho was awarded to
plaintiff herein, and lot 4 to Martin Higuera, a brother of
plaintiff, who died before the trial of this action. The only
reference to water rights in the said decree is in these words:
"And it was then and there in open court agreed by all the
parties having interests in said land and premises that said
Bernardo Higuera should have the ownership and exclusive
use of the two springs of water nearest his house on said
land."

Both parties introduced evidence to show whether or not
the spring that is the subject of this controversy was one of
the two springs referred to in this decree. While plaintiff
and several of his relatives testified that the spring from
which the iron pipe leads was one of two nearest Bernardo's
house, and was intended to be reserved to Bernardo, other
witnesses testified that there were at least two other springs
nearer said house than the one in controversy. Indeed,
counsel for appellant concedes that on this point the evidence is conflicting, but the point seems to be of little or
no importance as to the prescriptive right pleaded by defendants. The fact is, as abundantly appears from the record, that Martin Higuera and the successive owners of lot
4 continued to use the water flowing from said spring
through said pipe openly and with full knowledge of plaintiff and of all persons in interest. It is claimed, however,
that the use has not been uninterrupted, and has not been
adverse. But upon these points we think the evidence was
of such a nature as to warrant the court in finding that for
more than five years before the commencement of the action
the use had been continuous and adverse. While the evidence shows that there was a stop-cock in the pipe near the
spring, no witness was produced that ever turned off the
water, either by the stop-cock or by any other means. There
was no cock or other means of stopping the flow of the water
at the outlet of the pipe on lot 4. The plaintiff was himself

a witness, and his testimony as to any stopping of the flow of water through the pipe is not at all clear or satisfactory. He testified that the portion of lot 7 where the spring in question is situated has been in the actual possession of his tenant, Mrs. Mesa. On his direct examination he said that there is a stop-cock in the pipe near the spring, and it would stop the flow of the water when it was turned, but he did not say that it had ever been turned. He did say that Mrs. Mesa had been using the water to irrigate nine or ten acres of lot 7, but on his cross-examination he said that the water used by Mrs. Mesa for irrigation was the overflow, "the water used for irrigating lot seven is where Mrs. Mesa lives. It is an overflow when the pipe is full. Q. Just what escapes from the overflow when the spring is full? A. Yes, sir." Continuing, he said: "This water runs continuously, and has not been stopped off since the pipe was put in. Was used by my mother for the purpose of getting water for family use in the house." On redirect examination he modified what he had said about the water running through the pipe continuously, and said: "When Mrs. Mesa and I wanted water for that nine or ten acres we would stop it. We let the water run until we wanted to use it, and then would shut it off." But on recross-examination he said: "I did not stop the water off. My tenant, Mrs. Mesa, stopped it. Q. How do you know that Mrs. Mesa stopped it? A. Well, they told me they wanted the water there to irrigate." Mrs. Mesa was not called as a witness, nor was anyone else who ever stopped the flow of water through the pipe. One Flavio Sargarda was also a witness for plaintiff, and appears to have been on the premises (lot 4) and in charge thereof for the owners (Severances) for two years and over immediately preceding the purchase thereof by defendants. Although it appears that plaintiff once spoke to him about the water while the Severances owned the premises (lot 4) and wanted to stop the water, he did not stop it.

Evidence was also given by the defendants to the effect that after their purchase of lot 4 plaintiff applied to them to put in a faucet at the house on lot 4 so that so much water would not be wasted. He asked it as a favor to Mrs. Mesa. This seems inconsistent with his present claim that he had the right to shut off the water from lot 4 at his pleasure.

From the whole record we are of the opinion that there is sufficient evidence to support the finding of the facts supporting a prescriptive right in the owners of lot 4 to the use of the waters that flow through the pipe.

The decree does not award to defendants all the waters of the spring in question, but only such as flows through the pipe.

The judgment and order are affirmed.

We concur: Harrison, P. J.; Cooper, J.

TRACY v. CALIFORNIA ELECTRICAL WORKS.

Court of Appeal, First District; April 5, 1907.

90 Pac. 461.

Sales—Action for Price—Breach of Warranty.—In an action to recover the balance due on the contract price of an engine, where there was a defense of breach of contract and guaranty, and a cross-claim for damages, evidence considered, and held sufficient to sustain the finding of the court that certain knocking of the engine and flickering of the light produced by the electric plant run thereby were not caused by any defect of the engine, and that the engine was not defective.

Appeal—Refusal of New Trial.—The Appellate Court will not reverse an order of a trial court refusing a new trial for insufficiency of the evidence to support the findings of fact, if there is substantial evidence to support the findings of the trial court.

APPEAL from Superior Court, City and County of San Francisco; Frank H. Kerrigan, Judge.

Action by H. H. Tracy against the California Electrical Works. From a judgment for plaintiff, defendant appeals. Affirmed.

Frank M. Parcells for appellant; William S. Schooler for respondent.

HALL, J.—Appeal from order denying defendant's motion for a new trial.

Defendant entered into a contract in May, 1900, with A. C. Bilicki & Co., whereby defendant agreed to furnish and install an electric light plant in the basement of the Hollenbeck Hotel, in the city of Los Angeles; said electric light plant to consist of a dynamo of a specified description, and an engine known as a "Shepard cross-compound, vertical noncondensing engine." Defendant, in order to carry out its contract with Bilicki & Co., entered into a contract with the Tracy Engineering Company, a copartnership (assignor of plaintiff), whereby the Tracy Engineering Company agreed to furnish the engine, and install both the engine and dynamo, which was furnished by defendant, in the Hollenbeck Hotel for a stipulated price. The contract between the defendant and the Tracy Engineering Company contained various stipulations concerning the engine, and among other things the following guaranty, to wit: "The party of the second part guarantees the material and workmanship entering into the construction of engine for one year, and any defects or flaws developing within the said one year from date of acceptance will be made good by the party of the the second part, unless it is shown that such breakage, flaws or defects were caused by unskillful management of the machinery during the said one year." The engine was furnished and the plant installed by the engineering company, and the engine was accepted by defendant on the third day of November, 1900, as completed and having run six days successfully, conditionally, however, upon the results of a test to be thereafter made as to economy and regulation; any defects found during that test to be made good, according to the contract. The electric plant, however, proved to be unsatisfactory; and after efforts, both by the engineering company and defendant, to discover the cause and to correct its defects, extending over several months, defendant was obliged to remove the plant from the hotel, and to pay damages in the sum of $1,650 to Bilicki & Co. Plaintiff, as assignee of the Tracy Engineering Company, brought this action to recover of defendant the sum of $1,284, being the alleged balance due on the contract price of the engine. Defendant for a defense pleaded a breach of the guaranty concerning the engine, and also, by leave of court, set up, by way of cross-complaint against the Tracy Engineering Company (said company having been made by order of court a party to the action), a breach of its contract and guaranty concerning said engine, and damages resulting to defendant by reason thereof. Defendant claimed that the engine was defective, and that by reason thereof when in operation it caused a loud and continuous knock or pound, and also caused the lights generated to flicker. There is no dispute as to the fact that, after the acceptance of the engine, the lights generated by the electric plant did flicker, and that the engine, when operating the dynamo, did "knock" or "pound." Defendant claimed that the "knock" or "pound" was caused by defects in the engine, and that the flicker of the lights was caused by the "knock" or "pound," or, at any rate, by some defect in the engine; while the plaintiff and the Tracy Engineering Company claimed that the flicker of the lights was not caused by the "knock" or "pound," or by any defect of the engine, and that the "knock" or "pound" was not caused by any defect of the engine, but was caused by unskillful management of the engine. The court found against the contentions of defendant, and it is the action of the court in this regard that is attacked by this appeal.

Appellant urges with great earnestness that the evidence shows without conflict that both the flicker in the lights and the "knock" were caused by some defect in the engine. A careful examination of the record certainly discloses very persuasive evidence to the effect that both the "knock" and flicker of the lights were caused by some defect in the engine; but we also find substantial evidence supporting the conclusion that neither the "knock" nor the flicker were caused by any defect in the engine. Evidence was given on behalf of plaintiff that the engine was not defective when turned over to the engineer of the hotel, and was at that time working all right. Edward H. Minor, a mechanical engineer, who had charge of the work of installing the plant, testified that he ran the engine for about eleven days before turning it over to the engineer of the hotel. He first ran it five days, and then shut down to correct some trouble with the armature (a part of the dynamo), which caused some noise. After this was repaired, the engine was started again, and ran all right for six successive days, when it was turned over to the engineer of the hotel. During this time witness testified that there was not the slightest trouble or difficulty with the lights. The engine ran five days successfully, and then six days successfully, and everything ran correctly.

There was no unusual noise, and no flicker in the lights. "The material and workmanship which entered into the construction of that engine are first class. . . . . When I went away the engine was running all right. When I came back it was not, in my judgment. It had been misused or abused. . . . . I was conversant with the engine in its entirety, and knew it to be a first-class engine, and knew it was running in good order, and that everything was in first-class shape about it when I went away." H. N. Tracy, a member of the firm of the Tracy Engineering Company, and a mechanical engineer, testified that he first saw the engine in operation after it had been running five days. There was then a jar or bump, which he located in the armature shaft, and corrected. "When it started up there was no bump or knock discernible. It was started then again on the 28th of October. This engine was the quietest direct connection engine I had ever seen. It then ran all right for six days successfully, when we got the letter of acceptance on November 3d." He further testified that he returned in two or three weeks, when it was found that the lights flickered when the engine was examined, and subjected to certain tests by experts. He testified that he was convinced that the engine was all right, and that "I came to the conclusion that they had treated the engine shamefully. After a careful examination, lasting over quite a period of time, I am satisfied that the engine had nothing to do with the flicker of the lights." It was shown by certain tests that the revolutions of the shaft that imparted motion to the dynamo were uniform in speed. Edward S. Cobb, a consulting mechanical and hydraulic engineer, examined the plant in question as an expert, and testified that in his opinion there was no causal connection between the "knock" in the engine and the flicker in the lights; there was no rythmic connection between them. Other witnesses testified to this effect also. This witness also testified to certain alternating discolorations in the commutator bars in the dynamo, which always appeared after the dynamo had been run for a time, whereupon the flicker in the lights would appear. This witness gave his opinion that the flicker was caused by some fault in the dynamo. Clarence N. Cory, witness for plaintiff, professor of electrical engineering, and engaged also in the business of consulting electrical and mechanical engineering, was furnished with full data concerning the tests and estimates made by Mr. Cobb and Mr. H. N. Tracy, respecting the engine and dynamo in question, made mathematical calculations based upon that data, and reached the conclusion that the disturbing cause of flicker of lights was located in the dynamo. He further said: "I took up the question of the engine tests, and I am satisfied that the flicker was not caused by the knock or pound of the engine, and the knock might be caused by many things, but in this case the engine did not produce the flicker. . . . . I should say that the knock would be caused rather from improper handling than from any inherent defect in the engine." John Lafferty, a witness for defendant, and an expert engineer, employed as such by the Hollenbeck Hotel, had charge of the plant for some time, and testified that he did not think the knocking was responsible for the flicker, although in another part of his testimony he disclaimed all knowledge as to what did cause the flicker. J. W. Milstead, a witness for defendant, and an expert steam engineer, worked on the engine for twenty-four days for defendant, testified to knock in engine, but said in regard to the engine: "There was not anything erroneous in its construction. There was not any knocking whatever so far as I know when there was no electricity generated. . . . . I don't pretend to say that the knock or noise affected the lights." W. H. Hanscom, also a witness for defendant, and an expert engineer, who examined the plant, testified: "A knock or pound in an engine that was being run for the first time I should not consider of any importance. I could not see that the jarring or knocking was directly or immediately the cause of the flicker." He also said that if, after the dynamo started up, the flicker gradually appeared, it might be due to the engine, or it might be due to the generator. Other witnesses testified that the flicker did gradually appear in this way. He also testified to the alternating discolorations in the commutator bars, and that this showed defects in the commutator bars.

Other evidence was given of a similar character to that which we have above set forth; but we think we have specified enough to show that there is in the record sufficient evidence to support the findings of the court that the engine was not defective, and that neither the flicker in the lights nor the "knock" in the engine were caused by any defect in the engine. It is true, as we have before stated, that there is in the record much persuasive evidence supporting a contrary conclusion; but this court cannot reverse the order of the trial court for insufficiency of the evidence to support the findings of fact, if there be any substantial evidence supporting the findings made by the trial court.

No other point being suggested why the order should be reversed, the same is affirmed.

We concur: Cooper, P. J.; Kerrigan, J.

TRACY v. CALIFORNIA ELECTRICAL WORKS.

Court of Appeal, First District; April 5, 1907.

90 Pac. 463.

APPEAL from Superior Court, City and County of San Francisco; Frank H. Kerrigan, Judge.

Action by H. H. Tracy against the California Electrical Works. From a judgment for plaintiff, defendant appeals. Affirmed.

Frank M. Parcells for appellant; William H. Schooler for respondent.

HALL, J.—Appeal from order denying defendant's motion for a new trial.

In this action defendant pleaded as a counterclaim the same matters pleaded as a defense, and by way of cross-complaint, in the action of the same title, and numbered 205, this day decided by this court: Ante, p. 324, 90 Pac. 461. The two cases involved the same issues, and were tried upon the same testimony, and the same grounds are urged for a reversal of the order.

For the reasons set forth in the opinion this day filed in said action No. 205, the order appealed from is affirmed.

We concur: Cooper, P. J.; Kerrigan, J.

PRINE v. DUNCAN.

Court of Appeal, Third District; April 23, 1907.

90 Pac. 713.

Appeal—Time for—Order Denying New Trial.—Under the direct provisions of Code of Civil Procedure, section 939, subdivision 3, an appeal from an order dismissing proceedings for the settlement of a statement to be used on motion for new trial and all proceedings for a new trial may only be taken within sixty days after the order is entered.

APPEAL from Superior Court, Colusa County; W. M. Finch, Judge.

Action by David Prine against Margaret A. Duncan. Judgment for plaintiff, and from an order denying a new trial, defendant appeals. Motion to dismiss the appeal. Dismissed.

C. F. Purkitt and C. L. Donohoe for appellant; Thos. Rutledge for respondent.

CHIPMAN, P. J.—Motion to dismiss the appeal from the order denying motion for a new trial. This is the same case as No. 322, 5 Cal. App. 433, 90 Pac. 712.

It appeared that on November 17, 1906, the trial court made an order denying defendant's motion to be relieved from her default in the matter of presenting her statement on motion for a new trial and the proposed amendments of plaintiff thereto within the time required by law; and the court further ordered, on the motion of plaintiff, that all proceedings for the settlement of the defendant on motion for a new trial be dismissed. On January 17, 1907, defendant filed her notice of appeal from said order of November 17, 1906, and on the same day filed her undertaking on said appeal. No bill of exceptions or statement on appeal from said order has been settled or filed, and defendant has not requested the clerk to certify a correct transcript in said cause.

The ground of the motion is that the appeal was not taken, and the notice of the appeal was not filed with the clerk, within the time allowed by law. Appellant makes no an-

swer to the motion and has failed to appear. The appeal
was taken on the sixty-first day after the day on which the
order was entered, and was not taken in time: Code Civ.
Proc., sec. 939, subd. 3.

The appeal is dismissed.

We concur: Burnett, J.; Hart, J.

McPHERSON et al. v. GARBUTT et al.*

Court of Appeal, First District; March 13, 1907.

89 Pac. 991.

Quieting Title—Evidence—Sufficiency to Support Finding.—In
an action to determine the rights of the parties in certain land in
which plaintiff prayed that she be declared the equitable owner of a
one-sixth interest therein on certain payments being made by her,
evidence examined, and held sufficient to support the finding of the
court, except in regard to credit given plaintiff for a certain sum.

APPEAL from Superior Court, Santa Clara County; M. H.
Hyland, Judge.

Action by S. W. McPherson, as administratrix, and others,
against Frank A. Garbutt and others. From a judgment for
defendants, plaintiffs appeal. Modified and affirmed.

Houx & Barrett for appellants; J. L. Murphy for respondents.

KERRIGAN, J.—This is an action by which the plaintiff
in part prayed that the nature of the interest of the defendants in certain land be declared; that she be decreed the
equitable owner of an undivided one-sixth interest therein
upon certain payments being made by her at a time to be
fixed by the court; that the property be sold, and one-sixth of
the proceeds, less the amount due from her to Garbutt, be
paid to her. The case was tried by the court sitting without
a jury, and in accordance with the prayer of the answer it
was adjudged that the plaintiff had no interest whatever in
the land described in the complaint; that title to it was in

---

*Rehearing denied by supreme court May 9, 1907.

the Moody Gulch Oil Company (hereinafter called the M. G. Co.). The defendant Garbutt, in addition to other matters set forth in the answer, counterclaimed against the plaintiff for the amount due him on her three certain promissory notes, with interest, costs, and the sum of $12.81, an expense incurred by him for her; upon which claim judgment was rendered in his favor for $1,068.57. The appeal is from an order denying plaintiff's motion for a new trial upon the grounds that the decision is against law, insufficiency of the evidence, and errors of law. The principal ground relied upon is the insufficiency of the evidence to support the findings.

The facts of the case are somewhat involved. Briefly, they are as follows: Prior to April 16, 1900, the appellant's intestate, Mrs. Walker, and the defendant Sorey, owned a majority of the stock in the Golden Gate Oil and Development Company (hereinafter called the G. G. Co.), which company had a lease for ten years on two hundred acres of land in Santa Clara county owned by D. B. Moody. After some negotiations by Mrs. Walker, Sorey, and Garbutt, on April 16, 1900, they made an agreement which, in substance, was as follows: (1) It provided for the organization of a corporation known as the "Moody Gulch Oil Company," in which each was to subscribe for one-third of the capital stock. In payment for the stock, Mrs. Walker and Sorey were to transfer sixteen thousand six hundred and twenty-five shares of stock in the G. G. Co. fully paid, and Garbutt was to pay into the treasury of the new company $4,000 in cash. (2) Mrs. Walker and Sorey represented that the outstanding indebtedness of the G. G. Co. did not exceed $1,000. (3) Mrs. Walker was to obtain an option from Moody to purchase the Moody land at a price not to exceed $7,300; the option and purchase to be in the name of Garbutt. (4) At the completion of the organization of the M. G. Co., and on payment for the subscribed stock therein, as above mentioned, Garbutt was to purchase from Mrs. Walker one-half of her stock (one-sixth of the subscribed stock) in the M. G. Co., and to pay therefor $2,000. (5) Mrs. Walker was to buy a one-sixth interest from Garbutt in the Moody land for the sum of $1,216.66, plus one-sixth of the expense of making the purchase. Five hundred dollars was to be paid June 16, 1900; the balance in two equal payments at ninety and one hundred and twenty days, with interest on deferred payments at six per cent per annum. (6) Upon payment of these amounts by Mrs. Walker, she and Garbutt were to transfer their interests in the land to the M. G. Co., taking pay therefor either in money or stock in said company at its option; but, if Mrs. Walker defaulted in any of her payments, then Garbutt was to be released of all liability to convey any interest in the land to her or the company.

Another agreement was made April 18, 1900, by Mrs. Walker and Garbutt, which, after stating that Garbutt had agreed to purchase the Moody land for $8.000, provided substantially: (1) That by reason of certain desires Mrs. Walker was to make such payments, and rebates in her commission for making the sale, as would make the price paid by Garbutt for the land not to exceed $7,300. (2) That she was to purchase a one-sixth interest therein from Garbutt, paying therefor the sum specified in the agreement of April 16th (to which reference has been made above) at the times therein set forth. These amounts were to be evidenced by three promissory notes, and as security for the payment of these notes she was to give Garbutt her stock in the M. G. Co. (3) In case of default in the payment of any of her notes, Garbutt, at his option, might return her notes, together with the stock securing them, and terminate the interest of Mrs. Walker in the land. (4) If she carried out her contract, then, at the option of Garbutt, she was to join with him and others in transferring the land to the M. G. Co., taking payment for the same at cost price, either in cash or stock at the par value thereof at the company's option.

On April 16, 1900, Garbutt and Sorey made an agreement by which, upon payment of $1,216.66 (one-sixth of the cost of the land), they and others would transfer the land to the M. G. Co., on payment to them by the company of the cost of said land either in money or stock, etc. It is unnecessary to summarize the contents of this contract. April 23, 1900, Mrs Walker executed her notes to Garbutt, and thereafter delivered seventy shares of the M. G. Co. stock as security for the payment thereof. In May, 1900, the sale of the land from Moody to Garbutt was consummated. Moody received from Garbutt $7,300 in cash, a note from Mrs. Walker for $300 and a waiver by her of $400, which Moody had agreed to pay her as commission for making the sale. November 30th an option to purchase for $28,000 the

Moody land and other interests was given to C. C. Blair. The only payment made by Mrs. Walker was $250 on account of her note for $500, which became due June 16, 1900. After a number of requests for payment of the balance due from her, on December 3, 1900, Garbutt, through his agent, Neumaber, handed Mrs. Walker a letter dated November 30, 1900, signed by Garbutt, which purported to terminate any and all interest that she might have in the Moody land under their contract of April 18th. Together with this letter were her notes, her seventy shares of stock of the M. G. Co., and an unsigned document for her signature, which in effect was a receipt for the notes and stock, and a release of Garbutt from his obligations to her under the contract of April 18th. December 4, 1900, Mrs. Walker returned the notes, security, and the document unsigned to Neumaber, together with a letter offering to pay the amount remaining unpaid on her notes, and one-sixth of the expenses of making the purchase of the Moody land. On December 7th Garbutt replied to her letter of the 4th, saying: "I am willing, however, to forego my strict legal rights in the matter, provided you make the payments offered by you in your letter of December 4th and otherwise perform your portion of said agreement of April 18th, 1900, on or before 3 o'clock P. M. of Wednesday, December 12th. The amount of the expenses of purchase is $76.90, of which your one-sixth would be $12.81. You have the notes in your possession and can readily compute their present value. I am writing Mr. Neumaber today of 232 California street, your city, to accept these payments under the above conditions on my behalf, provided that, at the same time, you join with Moody Gulch Oil Company, in accordance with paragraph fourth of our agreement of April 18, 1900. On the execution of which deed the Moody Gulch Oil Company will make payment for said property as provided in the above contract." December 11th, in reply to this letter, she informed Garbutt that she had commenced this suit on December 8th, and, among other things, said: "When you present me a deed duly executed by you and your wife and all parties having an interest in said land .... necessary to convey me a good .... title to one-sixth of said land, or present a deed executed by you, your wife and other parties, sufficient to vest .... title in the M. G. Co., when I execute said deed I will concurrently pay the balance remaining unpaid on my said notes and one-sixth of expense of purchase, and concurrently join with you . . . . in transferring said land to the M. G. Co., taking payment for the same . . . . as provided in the contract of April 18, 1900.''

Subsequently, a deed conveying to the M. G. Co. the Moody land, signed by Garbutt and his wife, was handed to Mrs. Walker, with a request that she also sign the deed, and at the same time she was tendered twelve and three hundredths shares of stock in the M. G. Co. She refused to sign the deed, claiming that others held interests in the land, and until their signatures were obtained to the deed she would not execute it; and she also insisted that the land had cost her one-sixth of the $7,300 paid by Garbutt, to wit, $1,216.66, $12.81 expense of purchase, $40 interest, $300 paid to Moody, and $400 commission, making a total of $1,970, and that she was therefore entitled to nineteen and seven hundredths shares of stock in the company. On January 1, 1901, Garbutt, for himself and for Mrs. Walker, acting under the power given him in the contract of April 18th, executed a deed of the land in question to the M. G. Co. The court, after trial, upon evidence sufficient, found in part: That plaintiff had failed to perform the conditions of the agreement of April 18, 1900, on her part to be performed; that prior to the commencement of this action she was indebted to Garbutt in the sum of $1,068.75; that the purpose of the agreements of April 16 and 18, 1900, was not that plaintiff should have an undivided one-sixth interest in said land for her separate use and benefit, but it was the purpose of those agreements that the land when purchased should be conveyed to the M. G. Co.; that defendants Garbutt and Sorey, January 1, 1901, conveyed to the M. G. Co. the Moody land; that Garbutt executed the deed in his own name, and for and in the name of plaintiff as her attorney in fact; that he was empowered to so act for her by the contract of April 18th. The court further found that prior to that conveyance to the M. G. Co., and on or about December 4, 1900, the M. G. Co. demanded of plaintiff and Garbutt that they convey the land to it, and offered to pay to plaintiff one-sixth of the cost price of said land and one-sixth of the expenses incurred in obtaining it, in all amounting to $1,229.47, in fully paid-up stock of said company; that plaintiff refused to accept said stock; that plaintiff's offer on December 4th to perform her part of the contract was made in bad faith.

It would serve no useful purpose to take up and pass upon each of the points discussed in the briefs. Findings were made on all the material issues presented by the pleadings. Those just referred to meet nearly all of the contentions of appellant. Other points made are covered by other findings, and all the findings are based on ample evidence, except that the evidence does not disclose that plaintiff was given credit for $133.41 paid Garbutt by the G. G. Co. at her request. There is no other point made by appellant that requires notice.

The judgment in favor of Garbutt against appellant is directed modified by deducting therefrom $133.41. In all other respects the judgment and order appealed from are affirmed.

We concur: Cooper, P. J.; Hall, J.

HERBERT et al. v. SUPERIOR COURT OF FRESNO COUNTY.

S. F. No. 4810; May 21, 1907.

91 Pac. 800.

Counties—Division—Election.—The Provision of the Statute for Submission to the voters of the district affected by the question of detachment from a county, requiring the election to be held within sixty days after the organization of the special commission, is directory merely, so that, if the election within that time is prevented by injunction, it may be held at a reasonable time after the injunction is removed.

Certiorari.—The Right of Appeal from the Granting of an Injunction excludes the right to a writ of certiorari.

Prohibition—Remedy by Appeal.—Writ of Prohibition will not be granted, where, by appeal, which can be advanced to a speedy hearing, the whole case can be taken up and reasonably decided on the merits.

Application by J. W. Herbert and others for writ of prohibition to the superior court, Fresno county; Hon. H. Z. Austin, Judge. Writ denied.

Hannah & Miller and C. G. Lamberson for petitioners; Frank H. Short for respondent.

BEATTY, C. J.—The court has had this matter under advisement, and we are all of the opinion that the provision of the statute for submitting to the voters of the district affected by the question of detachment from Fresno county, requiring the election to be held within sixty days after the organization of the special commission, is directory merely; that it is not essential that the election should be held within sixty days; and that, if it is prevented by the injunction, it may be held afterward, at any reasonable time after the injunction is removed. We are satisfied also that it was an error on the part of this court to issue the writ of certiorari in this case; the fact being that there is an appeal from the injunction, and the right to appeal excluding the right to a writ of certiorari.

As to the writ of prohibition, we think that is unnecessary and inadvisable under the circumstances, because by an appeal from the order granting an injunction, which would be advanced to a speedy hearing by the court on the application of either party, we can take up the whole case and decide it on its merits before any election is held, and thus prevent any complications which are apprehended by reason of the holding of an election while the question is undetermined as to whether the act is constitutional or not. For these reasons we have decided to set aside the writ of certiorari granted in the case and to deny the writ of prohibition, suggesting to the parties that they bring the matter up by an appeal as speedily as they like, when the court will advance it to an early hearing, that it may be decided at once upon the merits, and the election held as soon afterward as the necessary arrangements can be made.

The order of the court is: The writ of certiorari be discharged, and writ of prohibition denied.

22

ROTHROCK v. BALDWIN.

Court of Appeal, Second District; August 20, 1907.

91 Pac. 1014.

Appeal—Record.—Where an Examination of the Record on ap-
peal suggests no error, and the attention of the court is called to none
by reason of the failure of appellant to file points and authorities, the
judgment will be affirmed.

APPEAL from Superior Court, Los Angeles County; W.
P. James, Judge.

Mandamus proceedings by A. B. Rothrock against Fred
P. Baldwin, as clerk, and another, as president of the board
of trustees of the city of Long Beach, to compel defendants
to issue and deliver a warrant for labor performed for the
city. From a judgment for plaintiff, defendants appeal.
Affirmed.

John E. Daly and Carl Monk for appellants; F. A. Knight
for respondent.

ALLEN, P. J.—This is a proceeding in mandamus commenced by plaintiff to obtain an order of the superior court
commanding defendant Downs, as president of the board
of trustees, and defendant Baldwin, as clerk of the city of
Long Beach, to draw, sign, countersign, and deliver a certain
warrant on account of labor done and performed by plaintiff
for said city at its request, which payment had not theretofore been made. A demurrer was interposed to the petition
and overruled. The cause was subsequently tried upon its
merits, findings of fact and conclusions of law filed and judgment entered in favor of plaintiff. From the judgment so
entered this appeal is taken.

The transcript on appeal was filed November 2, 1906.
Stipulations were filed for an extension of time within which
appellants should file points and authorities. This time expired in December, 1906, and no points or authorities have
ever been filed in the case.

An examination of the record suggests no error, and, our
attention being called to none, the judgment is ordered
affirmed.

We concur: Shaw, J.; Taggart, J.

PONET v. LOS ANGELES BREWING COMPANY.

Court of Appeal, Second District; September 23, 1907.

92 Pac. 400.

Appeal—Affirmance—Error not Shown.—Where, on an appeal, no brief is filed by either party, and no stipulation or order extending time to file briefs appear, and on call of the appeal there is no appearance by either party, no reason being advanced why the judgment should not be affirmed, and none appearing to the reviewing court, the judgment will be affirmed.

APPEAL from Superior Court, Los Angeles County; Walter Bordwell, Judge.

Action by Victor Ponet against the Los Angeles Brewing Company. Judgment for plaintiff and defendant appeals. Affirmed.

Wright, Bell & Ward for appellant; J. Wiseman McDonald for respondent.

TAGGART, J.—Appeal from judgment for plaintiff for two months' rent under lease. Defendant served and filed notice of appeal June 4, 1906, and transcript was filed in this court December 11, 1906. No brief of points and authorities has been filed by either party, and no stipulation of parties or order of the court extending time of either to file such briefs appears in the records of said cause in this court.

The appeal was placed upon the calendar for oral argument on the twenty-fourth day of July, 1907, and regularly called on that day, but no one appeared to represent either party thereto, whereupon the cause was ordered submitted. No reason being advanced why the judgment of the lower court should not be affirmed, and none appearing to this court, it is ordered that the judgment of the superior court in said cause be affirmed.

We concur: Allen, P. J.; Shaw, J.

LOS ANGELES NATIONAL BANK v. CHANDLER et al.

Court of Appeal, Second District; October 21, 1907.

92 Pac. 872.

Appeal—Record—Scope and Contents—Documentary Evidence.
Where the record purports to contain copies of an undertaking on appeal and of an affidavit alleging that the cause in which such undertaking was given had been affirmed, and asking judgment against the sureties on such undertaking, and the documents are not embodied in the bill of exceptions or otherwise authenticated, they cannot be considered on appeal.

APPEAL from Superior Court, Los Angeles County; W. H. Clark, Judge.

Action by the Los Angeles National Bank against Burdette Chandler and others. From a judgment for plaintiff, Thomas B. Clark and J. K. Skinner appeal. Judgment affirmed.

Del Valle & Munday for appellants; Flint & Barker and Gray, Barker & Bowen for respondent.

SHAW, J.—Appeal from judgment. The transcript in this case was filed August 15, 1898. No points have ever been filed by appellants, and the appeal is probably abandoned.

The record contains what purports to be copies of an undertaking on appeal and an affidavit, wherein it is averred that the cause in which such undertaking on appeal was given had been affirmed, and asking judgment against the sureties in said undertaking. These documents are not embodied in a bill of exceptions or otherwise authenticated, and therefore cannot be considered.

The record contains no other document, except the judgment, which is affirmed.

We concur: Allen, P. J.; Taggart, J.

HATCH v. NEVILLS et al.

L. A. No. 1756; October 22, 1907.

95 Pac. 43

Street Improvements — Validity of Contract.—A contract for street improvements providing that all loss or damage arising from the nature of the work to be done under the agreement, or from any unforeseen obstruction or difficulties which may be encountered in the prosecution of the work, etc., shall be sustained by the contractor, is void as tending to increase the cost of the work, and is therefore insufficient to support an assessment for work done thereunder.[1]

APPEAL from Superior Court, Los Angeles County; N. P. Conrey, Judge.

Action by P. E. Hatch against William A. Nevills and others. Judgment for defendants and plaintiff appeals. Affirmed.

E. C. Denio and A. B. McCutchen for appellant; R. W. Kemp for respondents, O. B. Carter amicus curiae.

SLOSS, J.—The plaintiff appeals from a judgment entered in favor of defendants in an action to foreclose a street assessment lien for work done in the city of San Pedro.

The various proceedings of the city board of trustees leading up to the contract itself provided that the work should be done in accordance with certain specifications on file in the office of the city clerk. These specifications included the following clause: *"All loss or damage arising from the nature of the work to be done under this agreement,* or from any unforeseen obstruction or difficulties which may be encountered in the prosecution of the same, or from the action of the elements, or from encumbrances on the lines of the work, or from any act or omission on the part of the contractor, or any person or agent employed by him, not authorized by this agreement, *shall be sustained by the contractor."* In the case of Blochman v. Spreckels, 135 Cal. 662, 57 L. R. A. 213, 67

---

[1] Cited, in Gay v. Engebretson, 158 Cal. 23, 139 Am. St. Rep. 67, 109 Pac. 877, on the question of the contractor holding the municipality harmless from suits by individuals growing out of the contractor's neglect to keep lights about the work during the night-time.

Pac. 1061, this court held that there could be no valid assessment for street work done under a contract which referred to and included specifications containing the following language: "All loss or damage arising from the nature of the work to be done under these specifications shall be sustained by the contractor." The italicized portion of the provision which we have quoted from the specifications in the present case is substantially the same as the clause considered in Blochman v. Spreckels, and, on the authority of that case, the contract and assessment here sued upon must be held to be invalid. It is unnecessary to consider any other point made by the respondents.

The judgment is affirmed.

We concur: Angellotti, J.; Henshaw, J.; McFarland, J.

We dissent, for the reasons given in the dissenting opinion in Woollacott v. Meekins, 151 Cal. 701, 91 Pac. 615; Shaw, J.; Lorigan, J.

BRYANT v. HAWLEY.

Court of Appeal, Second District; February 4, 1908.

94 Pac. 850.

Appeal—Record.—In an Action on a Note Given for an Option to purchase lots, matters of testimony or exhibits constituting title or showing some kind of an agreement, as to which there is no mention in the record, cannot be considered on appeal from the judgment.[1]

APPEAL from Superior Court, Los Angeles County; G. A. Gibbs, Judge.

Action by W. S. Bryant against C. O. Hawley. Judgment for defendant and plaintiff appeals. Affirmed.

Job Harriman, Harriman & Spring and M. E. C. Munday for appellant; Waterman & Wood for respondent.

---

[1] Cited with approval in People's Nat. Bank v. Board of Commissioners of Kingfisher Co., 24 Okl. 150, 104 Pac. 55, where it was said: "It being thus determined that the title to the assets of the bank remained in the bank and did not pass by the sale of its stock to the new set of stockholders, it becomes immaterial to discuss to what extent Seay, as a director, was chargeable with knowledge of what the books of the bank contained."

TAGGART, J.—Appeal from a judgment. The action was on a promissory note executed by defendant to plaintiff and two other parties, who assigned their interests to plaintiff. Defendant by his verified answer denies that there is anything due or payable on the note, and alleges that it was given in payment of an option to purchase certain particularly described lots of land, which option to purchase he was induced to enter into by false and fraudulent representations as to the property made to him by the plaintiff. The court finds that the note was given for the option, but upon all the other issues finds in favor of plaintiff, and gives judgment in his favor.

The only points presented by appellant on the appeal relate to some matters of testimony or exhibits constituting title or showing some kind of an agreement, as to which there is no mention in the record. No question which this court can consider upon an appeal from a judgment is urged.

Judgment affirmed.

We concur: Allen, P. J.; Shaw, J.

RICHMOND et al. v. HOUSER, Judge, et al.

Court of Appeal, Second District; May 29, 1908.

96 Pac. 908.

Certiorari—Return—Sufficiency.—Where No Objection is Urged to the sufficiency of a return on an application for certiorari to review the proceedings of the superior court, and all parties treat the same as a correct transcript, the court of appeal will so regard it.

Certiorari—Existence of Remedy by Appeal.—Certiorari lies to review an order of the superior court remanding an action in forcible detainer theretofore certified to the superior court by a justice of the peace, and such order is not reviewable only on appeal, since it is an improper divestiture of jurisdiction.

Certiorari—Parties.—On Certiorari to Review an Order of the superior court, it is necessary that it should be a party, and, in its absence, the writ being directed to the judge of such court, its order cannot be annulled.

Application by Emma Agnes Richmond and others for a writ of certiorari, directed to Frederick W. Houser, as judge of the superior court in and for Los Angeles county, and others. Application denied, without prejudice.

Wm. T. Blakely for petitioners; Tipton & Cailor for respondents.

ALLEN, P. J.—This is an application for a writ of certiorari to review the proceedings of the superior court of Los Angeles county remanding an action in forcible detainer theretofore certified to such court by a justice of the peace. The writ is not directed to the court, but to Frederick W. Houser, judge of said court. There is no return by the clerk of the superior court, and the transcript certified to this court is certified to by the justice of the peace; but therein is contained a certificate of the clerk of the superior court, showing the action and proceedings of the superior court. No objection is urged as to the sufficiency of this return, and all parties treat the same as a correct transcript, and we will so regard it.

The return shows that the action of the justice in certifying the case to the superior court was proper, and the order of remand unwarranted. It is insisted by respondents that such order is erroneous, and reviewable only on appeal. We are of the contrary opinion. The superior court had jurisdiction to hear and determine the case before it upon its merits, and the order of remand was an improper divestiture of its right of jurisdiction. "Where such is the case, the writ of certiorari is a proper proceeding to annul the order": Hall v. Superior Court, 71 Cal. 550, 12 Pac. 672; Levy v. Superior Court, 66 Cal. 292, 5 Pac. 353. This writ of certiorari, however, being sought to review the action of an inferior tribunal, it is necessary that such tribunal should be a party, that an effective review be had. This court cannot, in the absence of a proper party, make an order annulling the order of remand.

The application is therefore denied, without prejudice.

We concur: Shaw, J.; Taggart, J.

BARRON v. BARRON.

Civ. No. 432 and S. F. No. 4509; June 11, 1908.

96 Pac. 273.

Divorce—Interlocutory Decree—Vacation and Dismissal.—After six months prescribed by Civil Code, section 131, and Code of Civil Procedure, section 473, within which appeal may be taken from or attack by other means inaugurated against an interlocutory judgment of divorce by default, has expired, plaintiff cannot, on an ex parte application, have the same set aside and the suit dismissed before expiration of the year during which such judgment must be in existence, under section 131, preceding entry of final judgment.[1]

Divorce—Interlocutory Decree—Waiver of Right to Divorce.—An interlocutory judgment of divorce provided for by Civil Code, section 131, which becomes final by the lapse of six months from entry without appeal or motion to set it aside, merely establishes conclusively plaintiff's rights to a divorce, and it does not necessarily follow that he or she may not waive the exercise of such right and dismiss the action.

APPEAL from Superior Court, City and County of San Francisco; F. H. Kerrigan, Judge.

Action for divorce by Rita A. Barron against George H. Barron. From an order denying a motion by plaintiff to dismiss a motion by defendant to set aside and vacate an order on motion of plaintiff, setting aside and vacating an interlocutory judgment for plaintiff, and from an order granting the motion of defendant sought to be dismissed, plaintiff appeals. On affirmance by the district court of appeal, plaintiff appeals. Affirmed.

The following is the opinion of Hart, J. (concurred in by Chipman, P. J., and Burnett, J.), in the district court of appeal.

"The plaintiff commenced a suit against the defendant for a divorce, in the superior court of the city of San Francisco, by filing a verified complaint in the office of the clerk of said court on the first day of June, 1904. On the same day sum-

---

[1] Cited and followed in Reed v. Reed, 9 Cal. App. 754, 100 Pac. 897, holding that at the end of the year following the granting of the interlocutory judgment, the court has jurisdiction only to enter a final decree carrying the interlocutory judgment into effect.

mons was issued in said action, and on the sixth day of June, 1904, the same was served on the defendant in said city of San Francisco. The defendant did not answer the complaint within the time allowed him by law, and, accordingly, his default was entered on the twenty-third day of June, 1904. The cause was tried on the twenty-fifth day of June, 1904, the defendant not appearing at said trial, and, after hearing the proofs, the court granted an interlocutory judgment in favor of the plaintiff, as authorized by section 131 of the Civil Code. On the sixth day of April, 1905, something over nine months after the entry of the interlocutory judgment, plaintiff made an application to the court, in the form of a petition, in which all the proceedings theretofore had in the case were fully set out, for an order setting aside and vacating said interlocutory judgment. Said petition also alleged that it was the desire and intention of plaintiff, if said interlocutory judgment was set aside, to move for a dismissal of said action. No notice of this last-mentioned proceeding was served upon or given the defendant. 'On said sixth day of April, 1905, the said court read and heard said petition, and made an order and decree in said action vacating and setting aside the interlocutory judgment and decree made and entered on the twenty-fifth day of June, 1904, and dismissing the said action, and directing the clerk of said court to enter a dismissal thereof upon his docket.' This order of the court was entered on the sixth day of April, 1905. On the thirty-first day of May, 1905, the defendant, having by some means learned of the action of the court vacating the interlocutory judgment, gave notice of a motion for an order vacating and setting aside the said order of April 6, 1905, setting aside and vacating the interlocutory judgment made and entered on the twenty-fifth day of June, 1904. On the second day of June, 1905, the plaintiff filed a motion to dismiss the last-mentioned motion by the defendant for an order vacating and setting aside the said order of April 6, 1905. On September 25, 1905, defendant's motion to vacate the order made on the 6th of April, 1905, and the plaintiff's motion to dismiss said motion of defendant, were heard by the court, and an order made and entered denying the motion of plaintiff to dismiss the motion of defendant, and granting the motion of defendant to set aside and vacate the order made on the sixth day of April, 1905, setting aside and vacating the interlocutory judgment entered on the twenty-fifth day of June, 1904. The plaintiff prosecutes this appeal from the order denying her motion to dismiss the motion of the defendant and from the order granting the defendant's motion to set aside and vacate the order vacating and setting aside the interlocutory judgment.

"The appellant contends that the court was without jurisdiction to make the order upon defendant's motion, as heretofore explained, because the action had been dismissed and was no longer pending in said court. On the other hand, the respondent contends that the court exceeded its jurisdiction in making the order setting aside the interlocutory judgment and the subsequent order dismissing the action after the lapse of six months after the entry of said interlocutory judgment. Under the decisions of the supreme court having any bearing upon the question, as we understand them, the contention of the respondent must be sustained. Section 131 of the Civil Code reads: 'In actions for divorce the court must file its decision and conclusions of law as in other cases, and if it determines that no divorce shall be granted, final judgment must thereupon be entered accordingly. If it determines that the divorce ought to be granted, an interlocutory judgment must be entered, declaring that the party in whose favor the court decides is entitled to a divorce, and from such interlocutory judgment an appeal may be taken within six months after its entry, in the same manner and with like effect as if the judgment were final.' The exact question presented here is a new one in this state. By this we are to be understood as saying that whether a plaintiff who has obtained an interlocutory judgment by default in an action for divorce may, upon an ex parte application, have the same set aside and the suit dismissed at any time before the expiration of the year during which said interlocutory judgment must be in existence preceding the entry of final judgment, is a question upon which there are in this state no judicial precedents precisely in point.

"The policy of the law is not only to discourage divorces, but to encourage the reconciliation of married persons between whom some degree of estrangement has arisen which may likely or probably will lead to permanent separation and the restoration of the parties to the status of unmarried people through judicial determination. The institution of mar-

riage constitutes one of the essential and strongest of the
cornerstones of the social fabric. While in a restricted sense
it involves a contractual relation in which the immediate parties themselves are alone vitally interested, in a comprehensive sense it affects and permeates and is an indispensable
part of the whole social system, and in that view becomes a
question of vital public concern. Consequently, the public is
in fact, if not in name, a party to every action for the dissolution of the marriage relation. Therefore the legislative
policy has been, is, and always will be, so long as society is
supported by its present standard, against allowing divorces
for slight or trivial or capricious reasons, but strongly favors
a prevention of them where it can be done consistently with
the highest interests of the immediate parties and of society.
Our present law is the fruition of many years of legislative
effort to bring about the ends to which we have referred.
First, it was thought that the interdiction of the marriage of
the divorced parties within a year after the final decree would
discourage, to some extent, the desire for legal separation for
at least slight and capricious causes. This enactment proved
futile for the purpose intended to be achieved, for the courts
held that, while in this state a marriage contrary to the provisions of that law would be void, either party could avoid
the effect of the law by having the marriage ceremony sol-
emnized in another state at any time after the entry of the
decree. The facility with which such persons could cross the
California line, either into Nevada, Oregon or Arizona, soon
demonstrated the utter impotency of the enactment to accomplish its principal design. Then the legislature gave us the
present law, by the provisions of which a final judgment must
be predicated of an interlocutory judgment of one year's
existence. Many specific reasons could be given why the legislature has thus exercised such jealous solicitude over the
institution of marriage as evidenced by the restrictions which
it has thrown around the action for divorce. Among these
it has been suggested that the provision for the postponement
of a final decree of divorce for a specified time after the finding that a party was entitled thereto was founded upon the
consideration that the parties might be reconciled during such
time, and a final separation thus obviated: De Yoe v. Superior Court, 140 Cal. 484, 98 Am. St. Rep. 73, 74 Pac. 28, per
Mr. Justice Angellotti. And again, as is further suggested by

the learned writer of the opinion in the case just cited, 'it might be contended with much force that such legislation was justified upon the theory that the postponement of the giving of final judgment for a specified time removes to some extent the temptation to resort to collusion or fraud, in order to obtain a speedy divorce and contract a new marriage.'

"We have thus referred to some extent to the nature of the contract of marriage and its peculiar relation to the state and its effect upon society, in order to show that the policy of the law is to discourage divorces and encourage reconciliation between the parties where divorces seem imminent, thus showing the reasons impelling legislation regulating the subject of marriage and divorce. And it is upon the policy of the law against divorces that counsel for appellant builds almost the entire fabric of his argument in support of the principle for which he contends here, to wit: That the statute should be so construed as to sustain the action of the court in setting aside, on the motion of plaintiff, an interlocutory judgment in an action for divorce, at any time within the year during which such judgment must exist before the entry of a final judgment; that such a course would harmonize with the public policy upon the subject as expressed through the legislation thereon. But, the supreme court, in a very recent case, has used language which forbids such a construction of section 131 of the Civil Code as would authorize either party to a divorce suit, upon a mere ex parte application, to cause an interlocutory judgment therein to be set aside and vacated after the expiration of the time prescribed by said section within which an appeal may be taken from or an attack by any other means inaugurated against such interlocutory judgment. The statute provides, as will be observed, that an appeal may be taken from the interlocutory judgment in an action for divorce within six months after the entry of such judgment. Section 473 of the Code of Civil Procedure prescribes the same time limit within which proceedings under that section may be initiated. In the case at bar the motion to vacate the interlocutory judgment and to dismiss the action and the orders of the court to that effect were made over nine months after the entry of such judgment. In Claudius v. Melvin, 146 Cal. 260, 79 Pac. 897, the following plain, unambiguous and unqualified language is used by Mr. Justice Shaw, speaking for the court: 'The judgment entered on September 4, 1903, therefore, constituted a valid interlocutory judgment declaring the plaintiff entitled to a divorce. As such it was subject to be vacated on appeal, or on motion for a new trial, or by proceedings under section 473 of the Code of Civil Procedure. The time for all these proceedings having expired, and no such proceeding to vacate it having been instituted, *the court thereupon lost all power by any proceeding in the case to modify or vacate the judgment, in so far as it constituted an interlocutory judgment.'* (The italics are ours.) The foregoing language is, as already suggested, so clear and plain as to the meaning intended to be thereby conveyed that nothing can be added to make its meaning clearer. The proposition as thus declared is stated without qualification—that the time having expired within which proceedings to vacate such judgment could be instituted, and no authorized proceedings having been instituted within the time limited, the 'court thereupon lost all power by any proceeding in the case to modify or vacate the judgment, in so far as it constituted an interlocutory judgment.' Indeed, if this language cannot be clearly understood, then surely judicial opinions are of little force and practically of no use as precedents upon which nisi prius courts can rely to guide them to correct conclusions, or at least conclusions in harmony with the regularly authenticated views of the higher courts.

"But it will doubtless be argued that the proceedings authorized to be taken as against such interlocutory judgments are supposed to be initiated by the defendant in the action and not the plaintiff, and therefore the opinion of the supreme court from which we have quoted deals with the section as exclusively applying to and qualifying the rights of the defendant in such case, and that the opinion may be interpreted as having no application to a case, like the one here, where the plaintiff is merely attempting to recall her own act. The unequivocal language of the opinion, in no manner or degree or in any sense qualifying or attempting to qualify the proposition expressed thereby, will not, by even the most adroit or subtle interpretation, if indeed interpretation is necessary to gather its true meaning, support such a position. Besides, we think there are sound and unimpeachable reasons why the distinction suggested cannot be sustained. It is our opinion that when the six months have expired within which proceedings may be inaugurated, either by way of appeal or otherwise, against the interlocutory judgment, such judgment, if no such proceedings have been taken within the time prescribed, becomes a permanent interlocutory judgment and remains so until superseded by the final judgment, into which it finally merges. We think, therefore, the court's power over that judgment, under such circumstances, ceases to exist as clearly and conclusively as does the power of the court over a final judgment after the expiration of the time for an appeal therefrom. We are, of course, assuming the judgment in either case to be valid on its face. Has it ever been supposed for an instant that the court possesses the power to recall a final judgment, valid on its face, and vacate or modify it in any material respect, either upon its own motion or upon the application of one of the parties, after the time within which an appeal may be taken therefrom has elapsed, except where it appears that the judgment entered is not the judgment actually rendered, or some other clerical misprision affecting such judgment is apparent upon the face of the record? The very fact that the legislature has fixed a time within which an attack by any authorized means upon an interlocutory judgment in an action for divorce must be made, if at all, necessarily implies that after the expiration of the time so limited an interlocutory judgment, as such, is as strongly intrenched against disturbance from any cause or any source, except where both parties join in a motion to set it aside, as is a final judgment after the time for appeal therefrom has passed.

"Again, let it be supposed that the plaintiff in the case at bar had, in addition to the allegations declaring the grounds upon which she sought a divorce, alleged that there were certain community property rights, as to which she prayed for an adjustment by the court. Suppose, further, that the defendant defaulted, or failed to answer the complaint or to appear at the trial, and that the court awarded the plaintiff the full relief called for by the allegations of the complaint and as prayed for. In such case, is it possible that more than six months after the entry of the interlocutory judgment, valid on its face, none of the authorized proceedings having been instituted against said judgment within that time, the plaintiff could by any proceeding of her own cause said judgment to be modified or vacated merely because she had been convinced or had convinced herself after the entry of the judg-

ment that she had not, for some reason, thereby obtained a
fair adjustment of the community property rights? We think
no such contention would for a moment be made, and we
think the supposititious case contains not an extreme but a
conservative and fair illustration of the precariousness and
instability of an interlocutory judgment in an action for divorce if the plaintiff were permitted for any reason to cause
it to be set aside or modified after the time when the law contemplates that it is, for the purposes for which it is intended,
as formidable as a final judgment.

"The interlocutory judgment in a divorce case is the result
or crystallization in concrete form of all the material issues
tendered and tried, and presumptively covers and includes all
such issues, and, after the time has passed within which it
may be attacked, is, as such interlocutory judgment, if valid
on its face, as impregnable against attack as a final judgment
under similar circumstances.

"The final judgment in a divorce case is, practically and in
reality, in our opinion, only the judicial declaration authorized to be made in accordance with the expressed legislative
policy of the state against the marriage of married persons
already found to be entitled to a divorce within a year from
such finding that the interlocutory judgment shall become
active and effective, and that the parties may exercise all the
rights which such judgment declared them to be entitled to,
and which rights, while actually existing, were only dormant
because of the avowed policy of the law. These rights, we
should say, in other words, became vested rights from the
time of the entry of the interlocutory judgment, subject only
to be modified or set aside by appeal or by other appropriate
proceeding within the time prescribed, but their actual enjoyment postponed, for reasons of public policy, to a future
determinate time. · Laying aside a consideration of a right of
appeal from the final judgment, the legislature has in effect
said that 'the interlocutory judgment shall go into effect and
become final one year after its entry, unless an appeal within
time has been taken therefrom and the same undisposed of at
the expiration of the year.'

"If, for any reason, the contention of appellant were sustained, the result would be that, while the defendant could
not, after he had allowed the prescribed time to pass without
initiating any proceedings against the judgment, exercise any

power over such judgment, the plaintiff would be without any restraint in that respect until the final judgment was entered. It is impossible that the law contemplates any such absurd situation.

"The court below, in making the orders appealed from, no doubt did so upon the theory that it was without jurisdiction to make the order vacating and setting aside the interlocutory judgment and dismissing the action.

"As the action of the court as to the orders appealed from conforms to the views herein expressed, the said orders are affirmed."

F. A. Berlin for appellant; Lynch & Drury for respondent.

PER CURIAM.—In denying the petition for a rehearing of this cause we are not to be understood as approving that part of the opinion of the district court of appeal which implies that, after an interlocutory decree of divorce has become final by the lapse of six months from its entry without appeal or motion to set it aside, the plaintiff has not the right to dismiss his or her action at any time before the entry of a final decree. The interlocutory decree, when final, merely establishes conclusively the right of the plaintiff to a divorce. It does not necessarily follow that he or she may not waive the exercise of that right. Whether the plaintiff could have done so was not a question arising on this appeal, and it is not decided.

GIANELLA v. GRAY et al.*

Court of Appeal, Third District; April 25, 1908.

96 Pac. 329.

Injunction—Sufficiency of Allegations—General Demurrer.—A complaint alleged plaintiff's right to the exclusive use and occupation of land bordering on a navigable river and extending to low-water mark; that defendants had entered thereon, though prohibited to do so by plaintiff's agent, and had occupied the land above low-water mark, taken down fences, and had threatened to do so, and camped thereon, and had crossed over the land, leaving gates open, and made preparations to remain thereon, in violation of plaintiff's rights; that

---

*Rehearing denied by supreme court June 24, 1908.

owing to the great number of defendants, and their repeated acts of
trespass, the law furnished plaintiff no adequate protection, and that
he was compelled to resort to equity to avoid a multiplicity of actions.
Defendants' insolvency was alleged, and that, unless restrained by
injunction, they would enter upon and occupy the land in violation of
plaintiff's rights, causing irreparable injury to the lands, and compel
plaintiff to bring a multiplicity of actions. It was also rather vaguely
averred that the lowlands lying immediately along the river bank
overflow at times of high water, and are separated from the higher
land by fences, and that at such times plaintiff's stock would drown
unless removed to the higher land. Held, that, though the complaint
was not clear and distinct in its averments, from which the court
might determine whether the threatened injury complained of was
likely to be irreparable, or that an adequate remedy at law was not
available, it was good as against a general demurrer.

APPEAL from Superior Court, Butte County; John C.
Gray, Judge.

Action by V. Gianella against Charles Gray and others.
Judgment for plaintiff restraining defendants from committing alleged acts of trespass, and from an order denying
a motion to dissolve the injunction, defendants appeal.
Affirmed.

Joseph T. Matlock, Jr., for appellants; Guy R. Kennedy
for respondent.

CHIPMAN, P. J.—This is an action to restrain defendants
from trespassing upon plaintiff's land. The amended complaint alleges plaintiff's right to the exclusive use and occupation of certain land, particularly described in the complaint, bordering on the Sacramento river at a point where
the same is navigable, and that his said right extends to
low-water mark of said river; that defendants heretofore
"have entered upon the above-described land, though prohibited so to do by the agent and attorney of the plaintiff,
have taken down fences, and camped and occupied said land
above low-water mark of said Sacramento river, and that
they, and each of them, threaten to remain and use said land
and premises, in violation of the rights of the plaintiff, and
have built and are maintaining camp and camps thereon,
and have taken down fences thereon, and have threatened
so to do, and have taken a horse across said land, and have
said horse now on said land, above low-water mark of said

Sacramento river, and have crossed through and over, and have left gates open, and are maintaining and making preparations to remain on said above-described land above low-water mark of said Sacramento river, in violation of the rights of plaintiff herein; that owing to the great number of defendants, and their constant, continuous, and repeated acts of trespass, the law furnishes plaintiff no adequate protection through the ordinary process, and he is compelled to resort to equity for relief, so as to avoid the bringing of a multiplicity of actions." Insolvency of defendants is alleged, and it is alleged that, "unless restrained by injunction, the defendants will enter upon, use, and occupy said lands and premises in violation of the rights of plaintiff, causing irreparable injury to said lands, and to the property of the plaintiff used in connection with said lands, and compel plaintiff to bring a multiplicity of actions against said defendants, and each of said defendants." It also appears from the complaint, by rather vague averments, that the lowlands lying immediately along the river bank overflow in times of high water, and are separated from the higher land by fences, and that in times of high water plaintiff's stock would drown unless removed to said higher land. The court made and entered its order, restraining defendants from committing the alleged acts of trespass, on March 14, 1907, and on the same day entered its judgment to like effect. The amended complaint was filed April 11th, 1907, and on the 12th defendants filed a general demurrer thereto, and on the same day served and filed a notice of motion to dissolve said injunction on the grounds set forth in the demurrer. On April 15th the court overruled the demurrer, with twenty days' leave to answer, and on April 24th the court denied defendants' motion to dissolve the injunction. Defendants made no answer, and the appeal is from this latter order. Appellants cite Bishop v. Owens, 5 Cal. App. 83, 89 Pac. 844, and other cases in which the principles governing this class of cases are fully stated and applied; and it is claimed that, when these principles are properly considered, the complaint will be found to be wholly insufficient. It must be conceded that the complaint is not only inartificially drawn, but is not clear and distinct in its averments from which the court must determine whether the threatened injury complained of is likely to be irreparable, or that an adequate remedy at law is not available to plaintiff. A special demurrer pointing out the deficiencies in the complaint would doubtless have been sustained, but we cannot say that, upon general demurrer, it should be held to be wholly insufficient. For like reason we cannot say that the injunction is without support in the complaint.

The order denying the motion to dissolve the injunction is affirmed.

We concur: Hart, J.; Burnett, J.

STEWART v. BURBRIDGE et al.*

Court of Appeal, Second District; November 23, 1908.

101 Pac. 419.

Appeal.—Where No Undertaking has Been Filed to perfect an appeal from an order denying a motion for a new trial, the appeal will be dismissed.

Appeal—Notice and Undertaking.—Where a notice of appeal from a judgment was duly served on the adverse party, and the notice and an undertaking to perfect the appeal were on the same day filed in the trial court, the appeal was properly taken.

Action by C. P. Stewart against O. H. Burbridge and another. From a judgment for plaintiff, and an order denying a new trial, defendants appeal. On motion to dismiss. Appeal from order dismissed, and motion to dismiss appeal from judgment denied.

Samuel Barnes Smith for appellants; Woodruff & McClure for respondent.

PER CURIAM.—It appearing to the court that no undertaking has been filed to perfect the appeal taken from the order denying defendants' motion for a new trial in the above-entitled action, it is ordered that the said appeal be dismissed.

It further appearing to the court, from a duly certified copy thereof on file herein, that a notice of appeal from the

---

*For subsequent opinion, see 10 Cal. App. 623, 102 Pac. 962.

judgment was served on plaintiff and filed in the superior court, and an undertaking to perfect the same filed on the same day, to wit, on the seventeenth day of July, 1908, it is ordered that the motion to dismiss the appeal from the judgment is hereby denied.

PEOPLE v. GLASS.*

Court of Appeal, First District; November 25, 1908.

99 Pac. 553.

Appeal—Demurrer to Indictment.—On a Motion for Permission to file a certified copy of a demurrer to the indictment in the appellate court, on the ground that the demurrer should have been made a part of the record by virtue of Penal Code, section 1207, whether the demurrer is properly a part of the record will not be decided in advance of the hearing of the appeal, but the motion will be granted and the question decided on the hearing.

Louis Glass was convicted of crime and appeals. Motion in appellate court for permission to file a certified copy of a demurrer to the indictment. Motion granted.

D. M. Delmas, T. C. Coogan, H. C. McPike and C. W. Cross for appellant; U. S. Webb, attorney general, for respondent.

KERRIGAN, J.—Upon suggestion of diminution of the record the appellant moves for permission to file a certified copy of the demurrer to the indictment. He claims that under section 1207 of the Penal Code a copy of the demurrer should have been included by the clerk of the trial court in making up the record. Respondent, on the other hand, contends that the demurrer was properly omitted. It is unnecessary for us to pass upon this question at this time. We will permit the certified copy of the demurrer to be filed, subject to further consideration upon the determination of the appeal. If at that time it becomes necessary to pass upon the points raised by the demurrer, we will then con-

---

*For subsequent opinion in supreme court, see 158 Cal. 650, 112 Pac. 281.

sider and determine the question whether or not the demurrer to the indictment is a part of the judgment-roll; and, if
we determine that it is not, we will not consider it in this
case.

It is therefore ordered that the appellant may file with
the clerk of this court a certified copy of the demurrer to
the indictment.

We concur: Cooper, P. J.; Hall, J.

SOMERS v. McMORDIE et al.

L. A. No. 2151; January 7, 1909.

99 Pac. 482.

Boundaries—Government Plat — **Conclusiveness.**—There is no
provision in Revised Statutes of the United States, sections 2395, 2396,
2397 (U. S. Comp. Stats. 1901, pp. 1471–1473), relating to the rules to
be followed where corners have been lost, or in the circular of instructions approved by the Secretary of the Interior October 16, 1896 (23
Land Dec. Dep. Int. 361), relating to lost or obliterated corners, for
a proportionate measurement based on the deficiency in acreage of
adjoining parcels of land, and, where there is no question as to the
establishment of a lost corner, the exact boundaries as shown on the
government plat must prevail, and they will control a further description by quantity.

APPEAL from Superior Court, Los Angeles County; Chas.
Monroe, Judge.

Action by William F. Somers against J. G. McMordie and
others. From an order denying a motion for a new trial,
plaintiff appeals. Remanded, with instructions to grant the
motion.

H. W. Duncan and Wm. T. Blakely for appellant; Shank-
land & Chandler for respondents.

MELVIN, J.—Suit was commenced by William F. Somers
to quiet his title to the northeast quarter of the northeast
quarter of section 27, township 3 south, range 14 west, San
Bernardino meridian, containing, according to the allega-

tions of the complaint, forty acres. Mrs. McMordie, the respondent here, answered, admitting the title of Somers to all of said land, except a small portion thereof, and asked to have her title quieted as against Somers to lot 1, section 27, township 3 south, range 14 west, San Bernardino meridian, which was described also in her pleadings by metes and bounds. Before trial plaintiff dismissed as to the fictitious defendants.

There is a statement of stipulated facts wherein, among other things, it is agreed by these litigants that both parties derive title to their respective lands through patents issued by the state of California under indemnity lists duly approved and certified by the Secretary of the Interior; that the government plat of the survey of said lands shows Somers' land as containing forty acres and the McMordie lot as having an area of twenty-one and thirty-eight hundredths acres; that there is a shortage of four and forty-four hundredths acres in the two tracts; that this deficiency was imposed in the judgment upon the parties hereto according to their several proportions of the whole acreage embraced in the boundaries of the two tracts, the plaintiff Somers being given by this method thirty-six and ninety-one hundredths acres and the defendant McMordie twenty and three hundredths acres; and that the sole question on the appeal from the order denying the motion for a new trial is whether or not the court erred in apportioning said land as set forth in the judgment and decree. It is also agreed that the measurements of the exterior lines of the two tracts are as indicated upon a certain plat attached to the stipulation. Appellant asserts that the cause was decided by the learned judge of the superior court in an effort to comply with section 2395 of the United States Revised Statutes (6 Fed. Stats. Ann. 363; U. S. Comp. Stats. 1901, p. 1471), and the rule of "proportionate measurement" as used in the circular of instructions in relation to lost or obliterated corners, approved by the Secretary of the Interior October 16, 1896 (23 Land Dec. Dep. Int. 361), and respondent's brief contains an assertion that the court was governed by sections 2395, 2396, 2397 of the United States Revised Statutes (6 Fed. Stats. Ann. 363–369, U. S. Comp. Stats. of 1901, pp. 1471–1473), and the circular of the Secretary of the Interior mentioned above. These sections have reference to the rules to be followed where the corners have been lost and in originally locating corners and lines. The term "proportionate measurement," as used in the circular, is for the guidance of surveyors who follow the field-notes in the surveyor general's office in relocating lines and corners, and refers to a measurement "having the same ratio to that recorded in the original field-notes as the length of chain used in the new measurement has to the length of chain used in the original survey, assuming the original and new measurements have been correctly made." There is no provision, either in the cited sections or in the circular, for a "proportionate measurement" based upon the deficiency in acreage of adjoining parcels of land. It has been held that a deficiency in the contents of the section must as between a quarter-quarter section and a residuary fraction fall entirely upon the latter, and cannot be apportioned between them: Wharton v. Littlefield, 30 Ala. 245. But whether we conform to that doctrine or not, we find no warrant for the application of the principle here sought to be invoked, that the deficiency in acreage must be apportioned between the lands of Somers and McMordie. Here, there is no question as to the establishment of a lost corner. The section corner is shown on the plat, as is also the south line of plaintiff's property. The exact boundaries must prevail as shown on the government plat, and they will control a further description by quantity: Wadhams v. Swan, 109 Ill. 46.

The cause is remanded, with instructions that appellant's motion be granted.

We concur: Lorigan, J.; Henshaw, J.

PEDLEY v. WERDIN et al.

L. A. No. 2154; January 20, 1909.

99 Pac. 975.

Under Code of Civil Procedure, section 939, fixing the time within which to appeal from a judgment after the entry of judgment, the time to appeal begins to run from the moment of the actual entry of the judgment.

Appeal—Time.—An Appeal, Taken Before the Judgment is entered of record, as required by Code of Civil Procedure, section 668, is premature, and must be dismissed, though the judgment entered after the notice of appeal was entered nunc pro tunc as of a date prior thereto.

Appeal—Time.—Code of Civil Procedure, sections 941a–941c, as amended by Laws of 1907, page 753, chapter 410, providing for a new method of appeal, did not take effect, by reason of Political Code, section 323, until sixty days after the date of approval by the governor, and an appeal taken during the sixty days was not affected thereby.

APPEAL from Superior Court, Los Angeles County; W. P. James, Judge.

Action by W. H. Pedley, administrator of H. M. Praeb, deceased, against E. R. Werdin and others. From a judgment for defendant, the Pacific Electric Railway Company, rendered after sustaining a demurrer to the complaint, plaintiff appeals. Dismissed.

Wm. J. Danford for appellant; Bicknell, Gibson, Trask & Crutcher for respondent.

MELVIN, J.—Respondent has moved to dismiss the appeal herein on the ground that it was prematurely taken. The record shows that the demurrer of the Pacific Electric Railway Company (a corporation), the respondent here, was sustained on December 17, 1906; that upon plaintiff's declaration that he did not desire to amend, it was ordered that plaintiff take nothing as against said corporation; that plaintiff filed a notice of appeal on April 16, 1907; and that judgment was not entered until October 18, 1907. Appellant contends that the motion should be denied because the order of October 18, 1907, was entered nunc pro tunc as of December 17, 1906. The fact is of no importance in determining this motion. The time to appeal begins to run from the moment of the actual entry of the judgment: Code Civ. Proc., sec. 939; Coon v. United Order of Honor, 76 Cal. 354, 18 Pac. 384. In the case of the Home for the Care of Inebriates v. Kaplan, 84 Cal. 486, 24 Pac. 119, the following language was used: "This court has uniformly held that an appeal taken before the judgment is entered of record (see Code Civ. Proc., sec. 668) is premature and must be dismissed.'' The same rule is stated in McHugh v. Adkins, 117 Cal. 228, 49 Pac. 2, in Bell v. Staacke, 137 Cal. 307, 70 Pac. 171, and in More v. Miller, 6 Cal. Unrep. 78, 53 Pac. 1077, 54 Pac. 263, 6 Cal. Unrep. 110.

It is unnecessary to discuss the question whether or not sections 941a, 941b, and 941c of the Code of Civil Procedure, as amended by Laws of 1907, page 753, chapter 410, would apply to a motion like this, because those sections were not in effect on April 16, 1907, the date of the filing of the notice of appeal. Although these enactments providing for a new method of appeal had been approved by the governor on March 20, 1907, they did not become operative until sixty days after the date of approval: Pol. Code, sec. 323.

The motion to dismiss the appeal is granted.

We concur: Henshaw, J.; Lorigan, J.; Shaw, J.; Angellotti, J.

NOBLE v. CLELAND, Treasurer.

S. F. No. 4899; February 19, 1909.

100 Pac. 254.

Municipal Corporations—Officers—Offices—Creation—Executive Officer.—The city of Ukiah had power to create the office of "executive officer" by city ordinance, and to fix his salary.

APPEAL from Superior Court, Mendocino County; J. Q. White, Judge.

Action by J. H. Noble against T. M. Cleland, treasurer. Judgment for defendant and plaintiff appeals. Affirmed.

J. W. Preston for appellant; Arthur J. Thatcher for respondent.

PER CURIAM.—This is an action by a taxpayer to enjoin payment of a city warrant issued in payment of the monthly salary of one B. H. Miller as ''executive officer'' of said city of Ukiah. The office in question was created by an ordinance of the board of trustees of the city. Plaintiff claims that the board had no power to pass the ordinance creating the office, and hence that it is void. The court below held the ordinance valid, and gave judgment for the defendant. In the case of De Merritt v. Welden, 154 Cal. 545, 16 Ann. Cas. 955, 98 Pac. 537, 671, this court, in bank, considered this question, and declared the ordinance valid.

Upon the authority of that case, the judgment is affirmed.

LUCAS v. REA et al.*

Court of Appeal, Third District; March 9, 1909.

101 Pac. 537.

Mechanics' Liens.—A Complaint in an Action by a Materialman against the owner for materials furnished for a building, which alleges that the materialman agreed with the owner to furnish the materials, and that the owner agreed to pay a specified sum therefor on the completion of the work, followed by appropriate averments for the foreclosure of a materialman's lien, states a good cause of action.

Mechanics' Liens—Enforcement Where Contract With Owner Void.—Under Code of Civil Procedure, sections 1183, 1184, providing that, where the contract between the owner and contractor is void because not in writing and not recorded, materials furnished by materialmen shall be deemed to have been furnished at the personal instance of the owner, and they shall have a lien for the value thereof, etc., a materialman furnishing materials to a contractor may aver a direct agreement with the owner if the contract between the owner and contractor is void.

Mechanics' Liens—Enforcement—Appeal.—Where the Suit by a Materialman against the owner to establish and foreclose a lien for materials for the construction of a building was tried on the theory that the law made a contract between the materialman and the owner for the materials, the uncertainty in the complaint arising from the fact that it alleged that the contract was made with the owner, while the recital in the notice of lien showed that it was made with the contractor, did not justify a reversal.

Mechanics' Liens—Enforcement—Issues and Proof.—One seeking to establish and foreclose a lien for materials furnished for the construction of a building must prove the contract substantially as set out in his notice of lien, where the terms thereof are controverted.

Mechanics' Liens—Complaint—Proof—Variance.—The variance between the complaint in an action to foreclose a materialman's lien

---

*For opinion on rehearing, see 10 Cal. App. 641, 102 Pac. 822.

which alleges a demand for $780.70 and the proof showing a value of $859.67 and a payment of $60 is immaterial.

Mechanics' Liens — Foreclosure. — The Variance Between the Complaint in an action to foreclose a lien for materials which alleges a demand for $780.70, and the notice of lien demanding a lien for $19 more, is unimportant, in the absence of evidence of fraud.

Mechanics' Liens.—A Notice of a Lien by a Materialman for materials furnished in the construction of a building which alleged that the amount of the demand was $799.97 over and above legal set-offs, that the name of the person by whom claimant was employed and to whom he furnished the material was the contractor, and that the contractor agreed to pay a specified sum on completion of the work, showed an agreement to pay a definite sum for the materials.

Mechanics' Liens.—A Complaint in an Action to Establish and Foreclose a materialman's lien which averred, in reference to the notice of lien, "a copy of which is hereto attached marked 'Exhibit A,' and made a part of the complaint," that the claimant had in his verified notice of lien stated that the recitals therein were true, and where the contract to pay a specified sum for the materials set forth in the notice of lien was denied, evidence of an agreement to pay the correct price was insufficient to justify a recovery.

Appeal—Theory Below—Construction of Pleadings.—Where a party believed that evidence admitted without objection was within the issues, and there was an attempt to deny the contract sued on, the existence of the contract must be treated after trial as in issue.

APPEAL from Superior Court, Mendocino County; J. Q. White, Judge.

Action by R. R. Lucas against S. L. Rea and another. From a judgment for plaintiff, defendants appeal. Reversed.

McNab & Hirsch for appellants; J. W. Preston for respondent.

BURNETT, J.—The judgment in favor of plaintiff established and decreed the foreclosure of a lien for materials used in the construction of a residence belonging to defendant Rea, and which was mortgaged to the said Bank of Ukiah.

1. The complaint states facts sufficient to constitute a cause of action. The cases cited to the contrary by appellants are not in point. For instance, in Nason v. John, 1 Cal. App. 540, 82 Pac. 566, it is stated: "The action is by a materialman against the owner (appellant) for the value of material furnished the contractor for the painting of the

house of appellant. There is in the complaint no attempt to allege that at the time of filing the notice of lien or of bringing the action there was anything owing from the owner to the contractor, nor is any attempt made in the complaint to allege any fact, such as a premature payment by the owner to the contractor, or the like, that under section 1184 of the Code of Civil Procedure might be claimed to give the materialman a lien against the property of the owner for the value of his material.'' It was rightly held in line with many authorities that the complaint failed to state a cause of action. Here, however, it does not appear from the complaint that the material was furnished to the contractor. On the contrary, the allegation is: ''That on or about the sixth day of July, 1906, R. R. Lucas and T. A. Lucas, comprising the firm of Lucas Bros., entered into an agreement with the defendant S. L. Rea wherein and whereby the said R. R. Lucas and T. A. Lucas agreed to furnish, ... and the defendant pursuant to said contract agreed to pay to the said Lucas Bros. for the said material so furnished as aforesaid the sum of $780.70 upon the completion of said building.'' Thus it is seen that the complaint shows a contract directly between the materialman and the owner, and it presents an action in assumpsit with additional appropriate averments for the establishment and foreclosure of a materialman's lien. The material was actually furnished, however, to the contractor and under a contract with him, and not by virtue of any agreement between the Lucas Bros. and defendant Rea, the owner of the building. This appears from the evidence and also from the notice of lien, which recites: ''That the name of the person by whom claimants were employed and to whom they furnished the material, is A. S. Howell, the original contractor with S. L. Rea for the erection of said building, and said A. S. Howell agreed to pay said sum of seven hundred and ninety-nine and 97/100 dollars, etc. Wherefore appellants make the further contention that there is a variance between the proof and the allegations of the complaint, and that the complaint was rendered ambiguous and uncertain by reason of said notice of lien which was attached to and made a part of said complaint. The evidence, though, shows, further, that the contract between the owner and the contractor was and is void because, being for more than $1,000, it was not recorded until after the work was begun, and the plans and specifications, which were made a part of the contract, were not recorded at all: Code Civ. Proc., sec. 1183; Yancy v. Morton, 94 Cal. 558, 29 Pac. 1111; Barrett-Hicks Co. v. Glas, 9 Cal. App. 491, 99 Pac. 856. Therefore, the materials furnished as aforesaid are deemed to have been furnished at the personal instance of the owner, and a lien can be maintained therefor: Code Civ. Proc., sec. 1183. The result is that by operation of law the contract of the Lucas Bros. with the contractor is considered a contract with the owner, and the supreme court has held that it may be so alleged, although not in accordance with the actual transaction.

In Yancy v. Morton, supra, it is said: "The complaint in this case is upon a contract for the value of goods sold at the special instance and request of defendant (the owner). Sections 1183 and 1184 of the Code of Civil Procedure provide that when the contract between the parties, for any of the reasons therein enumerated, is void, materials shall be deemed to have been furnished at the special instance and request of the owner, and the building is subject to a lien for the same. In support of his complaint, plaintiff introduced the contract in evidence for the purpose of showing that it was void. The court found such to be the fact, and the evidence and findings were justified under the complaint. No substantial reason is suggested to us why the necessity existed for plaintiff to set out the contract and then allege its invalidity. Such matters were matters of evidence, and the completeness of the pleading did not demand it": See, also, Lumber Co. v. Gottschalk, 81 Cal. 646, 22 Pac. 860; Reed v. Norton, 90 Cal. 598, 26 Pac. 707, 27 Pac. 426; McClain v. Hutton, 131 Cal. 135, 61 Pac. 273, 63 Pac. 622. In the McClain case it is stated that "Mrs. Hutton [the owner] was properly named as the person by whom the claimant was employed, ... and there is no objection to the use of this form of statement." It seems to be the better practice to allege the facts as they occur, and leave the court to draw the conclusion that the property is subject to the lien; but it is settled that, where the original contract is void, plaintiff may pursue that course or aver a direct agreement with the owner.

This is conceded by appellants in their closing brief, but it is insisted that the notice of lien renders the complaint subject to the special demurrer for uncertainty and ambiguity. An allegation that the contract was made with the owner is certainly inconsistent with a recital that it was made with the contractor; but, admitting that the special demurrer should have been sustained on that ground, it is clear that appellants have not been prejudiced by the error. At the beginning of the trial, an objection was made to the evidence on the ground of variance between it and the complaint and of the uncertainty growing out of the recitals of the notice of lien, but the objection was overruled; the court justifying its ruling "on the theory the law makes the contract between the plaintiff and Rea." The case was tried upon that theory. No doubt counsel for appellants upon the argument of the demurrer were informed of plaintiff's contention in that regard, and it would be inexcusable now to reverse the case and impose the additional cost of a new trial simply because of the said apparent uncertainty.

2. If controverted, the terms of the contract must be proved by the claimant substantially as set out in his notice of lien. Appellants complain of a variance, inasmuch as while the notice states that the amount due over and above all setoffs is $799.97, and that Howell agreed to pay the same on completion, and there was no other condition, the proof shows that the amount of the bill was not the sum stated either in the complaint or in the notice, and that there never was an agreed sum to be paid nor any agreement as to the time of payment. It is true that the complaint alleges a demand for $780.70 and the proof shows a value of $859.67 and a payment of $60. We agree, however, with respondent, that there is no material difference between a statement of the amount due after deducting credits and the statement of the whole amount with the credits: Star Mill & Lumber Co. v. Porter, 4 Cal. App. 470, 88 Pac. 497. As there is no evidence of fraud, it is likewise unimportant that the complaint is for $19 less than the amount called for in the notice: Barber v. Reynolds, 44 Cal. 519; Malone v. Big Flat Gravel M. Co., 76 Cal. 578, 18 Pac. 772; Harmon v. San Francisco etc. R. R. Co., 86 Cal. 617, 25 Pac. 124.

The second point is more serious. Respondent answers that: "No agreed price is stated in the claim of lien at any place. 'The amount of claimant's demand is $799.97 over and above all legal setoffs.' Is this a statement of an

agreed price?'' Certainly not; but reading a little further
we find this in the said notice: ''That the name of the person
by whom claimants were employed and to whom they furnished the material is A. S. Howell, the original contractor
with S. L. Rea for the erection of said building, and said
A. S. Howell agreed to pay said sum of seven hundred and
ninety-nine and 97/100 dollars, so due, upon completion of
the work.'' The notice, therefore, sets forth an agreement
to pay a definite sum as clear as language can make it. The
evidence is equally clear that there was no agreement as to
the amount to be paid. The plaintiff himself testified that:
''I don't think that there was any terms. My recollection
is Mr. Howell would come down and want to know about
the prices of lumber; was nothing specified about any particular price. He left that to us to give him the correct
price of whatever he required of us.'' He further said that
there was no arrangement whatever as to price, and that
the firm charged Howell the market rate as the lumber went
out of the yard.

In Malone v. Big Flat Gravel M. Co., supra, it is said:
''As we understand the law, the plaintiff can recover only
upon the contracts stated in the notices of lien. We do not
mean to say that a difference in the amounts stated and the
amounts proved would be fatal; and it is possible that there
may be other differences which would not be material. But
we think in all essentials the contracts must be the same.''
In Reed v. Norton, supra, it is held that: ''A finding that a
notice of claim of lien filed by a materialman was 'in due
form as required by law' is not sustained by the evidence
when the notice stated that the materials were to be paid
for on the basis of what they were reasonably worth, and
the evidence shows that part of them were furnished at an
agreed price, and the remainder without any agreement as
to price, though it is testified that they were all reasonably
worth the amount charged; nor does such evidence sustain a
finding of an agreement to pay them all at what they were
reasonably worth.'' In Wagner v. Hansen, 103 Cal. 107, 37
Pac. 195, it is said: ''On the trial plaintiff testified that except as to one item, amounting to only $18, there was no
agreed price for any work done; that there was no agreement to pay for plaintiff's labor or for labor and materials
$163 or any other specific · sum. No other evidence was

given upon the subject. Defendants moved for a nonsuit on
the ground that there was a fatal variance between the evidence and the statement in the complaint and in the claim
of lien, in both of which it was stated that the work was
done under a contract by which he was employed to do specified work at a price agreed upon. The nonsuit should have
been granted. This was not only a variance, but it showed
that the statute had not been complied with, and that plaintiff had acquired no lien.'' In Wilson v. Hind, 113 Cal. 357,
45 Pac. 695, it was held to be a material variance where the
notice set forth a contract to pay what the goods were reasonably worth and the evidence disclosed that they were
bought at a fixed price. Wilson v. Nugent, 125 Cal. 280, 57
Pac. 1008, Buell v. Brown, 131 Cal. 158, 63 Pac. 167, and
Nofziger Bros. Lumber Co. v. Shafer, 2 Cal. App. 219, 83
Pac. 284, are to the same effect. In view of the foregoing
decisions, it is impossible to uphold the judgment here except upon the theory advanced by respondent that there
was no denial of the terms of the contract as set forth in
the complaint, and therefore the evidence cannot be considered. The contention is made upon the ground that ''the
complaint does not state in the body thereof the 'terms, time
given and conditions' of the contract, but refers to the
claim of lien attached to the complaint,'' and therefore it is
argued that this is equivalent to an averment of those terms,
and, since they are not specifically denied, no evidence is
admissible to contradict them.

But respondent has misconceived the significance of the
following averment in reference to the notice of lien: ''A
copy of which is hereto attached and marked 'Exhibit A'
and made a part of this complaint.'' This is not equivalent
to an allegation that the recitals therein are true, but it is
tantamount to an averment that claimant has in his verified
notice of lien stated them to be true. If the written instrument attached and made a part of the complaint had
been signed by the parties sought to be charged, and it was
the basis of the action, it might be sufficient to allege that
they executed it without averring specifically the verity of
the recitals therein contained, but no such case is presented.
In an action brought upon a promissory note, for instance,
if the note itself is made a part of the complaint, it is unnecessary to allege that defendant promised to pay, because

24

it follows from the allegation that he executed the note, which contains his promise. If in pursuance of the terms of the note a written demand were made upon the maker by the payee in which it was recited that a certain amount was due and this demand were made a part of the complaint, it would hardly be claimed that plaintiff is thereby released from the duty of alleging in his complaint that the amount is unpaid. With this obvious distinction in view, it is easy to understand the cases cited upon the subject. In City of Los Angeles v. Signoret, 50 Cal. 298, the notice of lien was annexed to the complaint and made a part thereof and the same contention was made as here, but the supreme court properly said: "Several matters of substance are lacking in the averments found in the complaint which are sought to be supplied only by reference to the recitals found in an exhibit annexed to the complaint, 'and to which for all particular allegations therein contained reference is hereby made,' etc. This is not sufficient in pleading." In Lambert v. Haskell, 80 Cal. 611, 22 Pac. 327, the action was based upon an undertaking executed by the parties sought to be charged. It was there declared that it was proper to set forth the instrument in full, but that this does not involve an assertion of preliminary or collateral matters recited in the instrument. "Whatever may be the effect of such recitals as evidence, they cannot serve as allegations in pleading. The facts of the case relied upon well illustrate this. The action (Los Angeles v. Signoret, supra) was upon a street assessment. The street law required certain preliminary steps to be taken to give the municipal authorities jurisdiction to make the assessment. The complaint was silent as to the taking of these steps. The only thing to show that they had been taken was the fact that they were recited in the assessment. This did not amount to an assertion by the pleading that the steps had not been taken. It was at most an assertion that the officer who made the assessment had asserted that they had been taken, which was clearly insufficient." Ward v. Clay, 82 Cal. 506, 23 Pac. 50, 227, an action upon a promissory note, cited with approval the foregoing cases. There is nothing inconsistent therewith in Georges v. Kessler, 131 Cal. 183, 63 Pac. 466. The point made there was that the complaint did not allege that the notice of lien described the property, nor the terms, time given, and conditions of the contract. But the notice was made a part of the complaint, as here, and it seems quite obvious that it is not necessary to allege what a written instrument contains when the instrument is set out in haec verba. The court, moreover, held that the complaint independent of the exhibit stated a cause of action.

Again, plaintiff, proceeding upon the theory, as we have seen, that the contract with Howell was equivalent to a contract with Rea, alleged in his complaint that the defendant Rea, "pursuant to said contract, agreed to pay to the said Lucas Bros. for the said material so furnished as aforesaid, the sum of $780.70 upon the completion of the said building." This is specifically denied in the answer of each appellant. There was only one contract referred to in the complaint and the notice of lien, and, although made with Howell by operation of law, since the original contract was invalid, he is deemed in the transaction to be the agent of the owner. Hence the issue suggested as to the agreement to pay a stipulated price is squarely presented, and the allegation of the complaint is not supported by the evidence.

Again, the evidence to which we have referred was admitted without objection on the part of respondent. Appellants undoubtedly believed that it was within the issues, and, since there was certainly an attempt to deny the contract, it should be treated after trial as though in issue.

We find no other error, but for the reason stated the judgment and order are reversed.

We concur: Chipman, P. J.; Hart, J.

In re SNOWBALL'S ESTATE.[*]

Sac. No. 1708; August 30, 1909.

104 Pac. 444.

Guardianship — Prior Proceedings—Res Judicata.—Determination of an issue as to the fitness of the mother of certain children to act as their guardian in a prior application for appointment is res judicata on a subsequent application between the same persons, except as to evidence of facts occurring since the former order.

---

*See 156 Cal. 235, 104 Pac. 446.

Guardianship.—Where Certain Facts Offered to Prove a Mother's alleged abandonment of her children, as a defense to her application for guardianship, were insufficient as a matter of law to establish abandonment, objectors to her appointment were not prejudiced by the exclusion of such evidence.

Parent and Child—Abandonment of Children.—In the absence of proof that a mother intended to bring about final separation from her minor children, evidence of mere temporary absences accompanied by statements not indicating an intent to surrender parental rights, and the fact that she placed the children in care of another while she was away, was insufficient to establish abandonment.

Guardianship — Testamentary Appointment — Consent.—Under Civil Code, section 241, declaring that a guardian of the person or estate of a child may be appointed by a will or deed if the child be legitimate by the father with the written consent of the mother, or by either parent if the other be dead or incapable of consent, a testamentary appointment by the father of a legitimate child having a surviving mother without the mother's consent is invalid.

Guardianship—Right to Appointment—Priority.—Code of Civil Procedure, section 1751, gives to the surviving mother of infants a primary right to be appointed their guardian, which should be recognized in the absence of proof compelling a finding of her unfitness.

APPEAL from Superior Court, Yolo County; E. E. Gaddis, Judge.

Petition by Leutie C. Snowball to be appointed guardian of the persons and estates of Aldanita Ann Snowball and Carmen Snowball, minors, to which Winnette Squires filed objections, and prayed that she be appointed guardian of their estate. From an order granting the petition of the mother, Leutie C. Snowball appeals. Affirmed.

R. H. Countryman for appellant; Arthur C. Huston and Harry L. Huston for respondent.

SLOSS, J.—Aldanita Ann Snowball and Carmen Snowball are minor children of Milton S. Snowball, now deceased, and of the respondent Winnette Squires, who, after having been divorced from Milton S. Snowball, was married to Lowell Squires. Each of the children is under fourteen years of age. Milton S. Snowball died in January, 1908, leaving a will, under the terms of which his children were named as beneficiaries. On June 15, 1908, Leutie C. Snowball (sister of Milton S.) filed her petition praying that she be appointed guardian of the persons and estates of the said minors. Mrs.

Squires, the mother of the children, filed a petition on her own behalf, in which she asked that she be appointed as guardian of the estate of each of the minors. Both petitions were set for hearing at the same time, and such hearing resulted in an order granting the petition of Winnette Squires and denying that of Leutie C. Snowball. From this order Leutie C. Snowball appeals.

In her pleading the appellant alleged that Winnette Squires was not a fit or proper or competent person to have the care or custody of either of said minor childen. The court found this allegation to be untrue. It appeared that on the 17th of February, 1908, some four months prior to the commencement of the present proceeding, Leutie C. Snowball, the petitioner herein, had filed in the superior court a petition asking that she be appointed guardian of the persons of the said minors. Opposition to this application was filed by Winnette Squires. The matter came on for hearing on the twenty-fourth day of February, 1908, at which time the petitioner amended her petition by inserting an allegation that "Winnette Squires, the mother of the said minors, is incompetent, and not a fit and proper person to act as their guardian." This allegation was denied by Mrs. Squires, and thereupon, evidence having been introduced, the court made findings to the effect, among other things, that the mother was competent and a fit and proper person to act as guardian of the children, and entered a judgment that the amended petition of Leutie C. Snowball be denied. The proceedings upon this former application having been offered in evidence and shown to the court upon the hearing of the petitions in this proceeding, the court, upon the objection of the respondent, excluded certain testimony offered by the petitioner for the purpose of showing unfitness on the part of the mother. If this ruling had gone so far as to preclude the petitioner from showing, by any character of testimony, the alleged unfitness of Mrs. Squires, it would undoubtedly have been erroneous. The doctrine of res adjudicata cannot apply to successive applications for guardianship of minors to the extent of precluding the court, upon the later application, from a consideration of such circumstances as may have occurred since the rendition of the prior order. If the person appointed guardian should, after appointment, develop or exhibit traits of character indicating an inability to properly perform the functions of guardianship, the changed conditions may, of course, be shown to the court with a view to invoking its power to make new provision for the custody or care of children: See Beyerle v. Beyerle, 155 Cal. 266, 100 Pac. 702. Here, however, the objection of respondent and the rulings of the court were carefully limited so as to preserve the right of appellant to prove Mrs. Squires' unfitness by any fact or circumstance which had not occurred or existed prior to the hearing of February, 1908. Her fitness to act as guardian at the time of that hearing had there been made an issue. That issue had been found in her favor, and the court had upon such finding denied the application of Miss Snowball for letters of guardianship. This was an adjudication of the rights of the parties (Ex parte Miller, 109 Cal. 643, 42 Pac. 428) at the time of the proceeding. That the order took the form of a denial of relief to. petitioner made it none the less a determination, upon the merits, of her claim, and an adjudication, binding in every subsequent litigation between the same parties, as to every fact necessarily found as the basis of the order: Estate of Harrington, 147 Cal. 124, 109 Am. St. Rep. 118, 81 Pac. 546. The order of February, 1908, denying appellant's petition, conclusively determined, therefore, as between the parties, the fitness and competency of the mother at that time. To hold otherwise would mean that a party defeated in an effort to establish a superior right to be appointed guardian of minors could, notwithstanding the adverse finding of the court on material issues, present the same issues and retry them in any number of subsequent proceedings. It may be that, where it is claimed that the circumstances have changed since the making of the first order, evidence of facts antedating that order may be admissible, in connection with later occurrences, as a basis for the contention that all of the facts, taken together, show unfitness. But no such question was presented here. The appellant offered to show on the issue of unfitness only matters which had taken place before the earlier hearing, and, in effect, to relitigate in this proceeding the very issue which had already been decided against her.

The first application was for guardianship of the persons only; the second, for guardianship of persons and estates. The court permitted the appellant to offer any testimony she had on the new issue presented; i. e., the fitness of respondent to act as guardian of the estates of the minors.

The appellant made an offer to prove certain facts which, as she claimed, tended to show that the respondent had abandoned the children, and had thereby forfeited her right to guardianship: Civ. Code, sec. 246, subd. 4. All of said facts occurred prior to the guardianship proceedings of February, 1908. An objection to the offer was sustained. Regardless of whether the appellant was precluded by the judgment in the earlier proceeding from showing matters which might have been there litigated (Rucker v. Langford, 138 Cal. 611, 71 Pac. 1123), we are satisfied that the appellant was not injured by the ruling for the reason that the facts alleged were not sufficient to show an abandonment. In order to constitute abandonment, "there must be an actual desertion, accompanied with an intention to entirely sever, so far as it is possible to do so, the parental relation and throw off all obligations growing out of the same": Gay v. State, 105 Ga. 599, 70 Am. St. Rep. 68, 31 S. E. 569; Shannon v. People, 5 Mich. 71. There must be more than a mere temporary absence or neglect of parental duty: State v. Davis, 70 Mo. 467. There was nothing in the offer here made which would justify the inference that the respondent ever intended to bring about a final separation from her children. At most, there was an offer to prove temporary absences, accompanied by statements, which do not in any way evidence an intent to surrender parental rights. While respondent was away from her children they were in the care of a Mrs. Chambers. In the absence of proof of the circumstances under which the children were placed with Mrs Chambers, the fact that the respondent allowed them to remain with her is not enough to establish an intent to throw off the obligations of a mother.

The court properly declined to consider the will of Milton S. Snowball, whereby he undertook to appoint the appellant as guardian of his children. Unsupported, as it was, by the written consent of the mother of the children, the attempted appointment was void: Civ. Code, sec. 241; In the Matter of Baker, 153 Cal. 537, 96 Pac. 12. In view of what we have said regarding the offer to prove abandonment, we need not discuss the appellant's position regarding the effect of abandonment by the mother on her right to control a testamentary appointment by the father.

The point that the evidence is insufficient to sustain the finding of fitness on the part of the respondent is without merit. There was testimony which fully authorized the conclusion reached. The mother had the primary right to be appointed (Code Civ. Proc., sec. 1751) and, in the absence of proof compelling a finding that she was not fit to act as guardian, this right was properly recognized: In re Campbell's Estate, 130 Cal. 381, 62 Pac. 613; Guardianship of Salter, 142 Cal. 412, 76 Pac. 51.

There was no substantial error in admitting or rejecting evidence.

The order appealed from is affirmed.

We concur: Shaw, J.; Angellotti, J.

In re STUDENTS OF HASTINGS COLLEGE OF LAW.

Court of Appeal, First District; June 1, 1910.

110 Pac. 341.

Attorney—Admission to Bar—Collateral Questions.—Whether Hastings College of Law in the University of California created by Statutes of 1877–78, chapter 351, as a matter of law, has affiliated with the university, as provided by such act, and whether the faculty of the university has granted diplomas to persons applying for admission to the bar thereon, cannot be tried collaterally on such application.

Attorney—Duty to License—Graduates of Hastings College.—Under Statutes of 1877–78, chapter 351, providing that the diploma granted students of Hastings College of the Law in the University of California shall entitle the student to a license to practice in all the courts of the state, subject to the right of the chief justice of the state to order an examination as in ordinary cases of applications without such diploma, it is the duty of the supreme court, on application of the students of such college, to license students holding such diplomas to practice as attorneys and counselors in all courts of the state.

In the matter of the application of students of the Hastings College of the Law for admission to practice. Granted.

Thomas I. Bergin for directors of college; Edward R. Taylor for students.

PER CURIAM.—Application has been made, on motion of Hon. Edward R. Taylor, dean of Hastings College of the Law, for an order admitting the following named persons to practice as attorneys and counselors at law in all the courts of this state, to wit: Stephen Cornelius Asbill, Gustave Louis Baraty, Edward Ignatius Barry, Absalom Francis Bray, Jr., Harry Alexander Davie, Harry Geballe, Gerald Hansen, Peter John Ihos, James Frederick Johnson, James Kelleher, Harold Louis Levin, Frank Bartholomew Lorigan, Greg Shobe McEvers, Frank Mitchell, Jr., George Franklin Owens, Albert Picard, Andrew Robert Shortky, Will Stephen Solari, Harry Ignatius Stafford, Adolph Tiscornia, Theodore Wittschen, Marcus David Wolff, Frederick Leslie Woodburn.

Under the act to create "Hastings College of the Law in the University of California" (Stats. 1877–78, p. 533), it is provided that the said college shall affiliate with the university of the state, and shall be the law department of the state university. The act provides: "Sec. 3. The faculty of the university shall grant diplomas to the students of the college, and the president shall sign and issue the diplomas. . . . . Ses. 6. The diploma of the students shall entitle the student to whom it is issued to a license to practice in all the courts of this state, subject to the right of the chief justice of the state to order an examination as in ordinary cases of applicants without such diploma."

Each of the above-named persons has a diploma signed by the president of the university. We must presume that official duty has been regularly performed, and that the faculty of the university has granted the diplomas in pursuance of the law. We must also presume that the said Hastings College of the Law has affiliated with the university of the state; in fact, the legislature, by its many appropriations, and by its appropriations for suitable buildings for the law department of said college, has time and time again recognized the Hastings College of the Law as a department of the university. The very title of the act is "to create Hastings College of the Law in the University of California." The questions as to whether or not the said college has, as matter of law, affiliated with the university, and as to whether or not the faculty of the university has granted the diplomas which the said persons hold, cannot be tried collaterally on this application.

It is our duty to grant a license to each of said persons entitling him to practice as an attorney and counselor at law in all courts of this state, and it is so ordered.

***

In re NAPHTALY.

No. 8025; December 30, 1881.

Attorney—Suspension for Violating Bankrupt Law.—An attorney, with knowledge of the facts, who advises and takes steps to assist in a violation of the bankrupt law of the United States, whereby one creditor unlawfully secures a preference, is subject to suspension.

Stanly, Cary & Baldwin for the prosecution; McAllister & Bergin for defendant.

MYRICK, J.—This is an application made to this court that Joseph Naphtaly, an attorney and counselor of this court, be removed. The information is laid and the prosecution made by a committee of the Bar Association of the city and county of San Francisco, appointed for that purpose. In proceedings had before the association for the purpose of determining whether it would institute measures for his removal, Mr. Naphtaly had leave to make such statement as he desired; and in pursuance thereof he made a statement in writing, which was introduced in evidence on the hearing of this matter, and from which we hereinafter copy.

The charges made against the respondent are:

"That the said Joseph Naphtaly has violated his duties as a member of the bar of this court and as an attorney and counselor at law as aforesaid, by employing, for the purpose of maintaining a cause confided to him, means which he knew were false and inconsistent with truth.

"The said Joseph Naphtaly has violated his duty as a member of the bar of this court and as an attorney and counselor as aforesaid, by his failure and neglect to support the laws of the United States and of this state.

"That the said Joseph Naphtaly has violated his duty as a member of the bar of this court and as an attorney and counselor as aforesaid, in counseling and maintaining an action and proceeding grossly unjust.

"That the said Joseph Naphtaly has violated his duties as a member of the bar of this court and as an attorney and counselor at law as aforesaid, in not maintaining the respect due to the courts of justice of the state of California."

The specifications accompanying the charges embrace the facts hereinafter stated, and relate to advice given and steps taken by the accused in and about certain matters of business intrusted to his care, conduct and management as an attorney and counselor at law.

First. By section 282 of the Code of Civil Procedure of this state it is made the duty of an attorney and counselor:

To counsel and maintain such actions, proceedings or defenses only as appear to him legal or just, except the defense of a person charged with a public offense; to employ, for the purpose of maintaining the causes confided to him, such means only as are consistent with truth, and never seek to mislead the judge or any judicial officer by an artifice or false statement; nor to encourage either the commencement or the continuance of an action or proceeding from any corrupt motive of interest.

The oath of an attorney and counselor is that he will support the constitution of the United States of this state, and that he will faithfully discharge the duties of an attorney and counselor at law to the best of his ability.

By section 287, Code of Civil Procedure, an attorney and counselor may be removed or suspended by this court for any violation of the oath taken by him or of his duties as such attorney and counselor.

Under the constitution of the United States, Congress has power to pass a general bankrupt law. Under that power a law was passed (see U. S. Rev. Stats., p. 969, amended June 22, 1874, Supp. Vol. 1, p. 71), which was in existence at the time of the transactions herein referred to. By section 5021 it was provided that if any person, being insolvent, shall procure his property to be taken on legal process, with intent to give a preference to one or more of his creditors, or with the intent by such disposition of his property to defeat or delay the operation of the act, or who, being a banker, broker, merchant, trader, manufacturer, or miner, has stopped, suspended, and not resumed payment of his commercial paper within a period of forty days, he shall be deemed to have committed an act of bankruptcy, and to have become liable to be adjudged a bankrupt, and the assignee may recover the property, and the creditor shall not be allowed to prove his debt in bankruptcy. The adjudication might be had on the petition of creditors, constituting one-fourth in number, with provable debts at least one-third in amount. It was also provided that the title to the property of a bankrupt shall vest in the assignee as of the commencement of the proceedings, although the same was then attached on mesne process, and any attachment made within four months next preceding the commencement of the proceedings should be dissolved.

Second. As to the facts. Schoenfeld, Cohn and Newman were partners in business, merchants, under the firm name of Schoenfeld, Cohn & Co., in the city and county of San Francisco. In 1874 one Lewis, as appears from the evidence, lent to said Newman, for the use of the firm, the sums of $5,000, $3,000, $2,000 and $8,000, in all $18,000, for which sums the notes of the firm were executed, payable on demand, to the order of Newman, which notes were indorsed by Newman and delivered to Lewis. In September, 1876, Newman became embarrassed by reason of stock speculations, and requested of Lewis the use of the notes to pledge with the London and San Francisco Bank, Limited, for his individual debt of $6,000, which request was complied with, and the notes were accordingly pledged. In December, 1876, Lewis demanded of Newman the delivery of the notes pledged, but Newman declared his inability to comply with the demand. It was then agreed that Lewis should be paid $1,000, and should have another note of the firm for $17,000, payable on demand. This $17,000 note was drawn by Schoenfeld, and was delivered to Lewis December 23, 1876, bearing date that day payable on demand, and is in this opinion denominated the "demand" note. The pledged notes remained with the bank as a pledge. About June 10, 1877, Lewis was informed by the partners that the firm was insolvent, and in a conversation had between them, it was agreed to save first all confidential claims, and then the California creditors; the danger of eastern creditors putting the firm into bankruptcy was discussed, and it was agreed between the parties, Lewis and the partners, that Mr. Naphtaly should be consulted with reference to the matter; and on the 27th of June, 1877, Lewis, Newman and Schoenfeld consulted with Mr. Naphtaly, and "he was retained to manage the affairs so that no proceedings in bankruptcy could be instituted, and if instituted, that they should not be sustained.'' The firm was at that time insolvent, and was indebted largely to California as well as eastern creditors, of which facts Mr. Naphtaly was informed. Another note was involved in the transaction, viz.: A Mrs. Alexander had placed $5,000 in the hands of Newman, to loan for her benefit, and the amount was taken by Schoenfeld, he giving his note and placing the money in the business of the firm. Mrs. Alexander did not have the custody of Schoenfeld's note, but had received monthly payments of interest from the firm.

Mr. Naphtaly, in the statement above referred to, says:

"He [Lewis] informed me that the firm, Schoenfeld, Cohn & Co., owed him $31,000, on the following notes: Note for $17,000, dated December, 1876, payable on demand, made by Schoenfeld, Cohn & Co.; note for $2,000, made by said firm; note for $8,000, made by S. Schoenfeld, payable to order of Schoenfeld, Cohn & Co., and by the payees duly indorsed; note for $4,000, payable to Mrs. Alexander's order and drawn by said firm. He requested me to sue on these notes and attach the store of the defendants, and if possible make the money. I expressed apprehension that the firm of Schoenfeld, Cohn & Co. would go into bankruptcy, and thus defeat him. He replied that the firm was anxious to save him the money, as it represented confidential debts. I then replied that if the defendants would not voluntarily go into bankruptcy, one great point was saved, for then only the firm's creditors holding the necessary quorum could put the concern into bankruptcy. On looking at the $17,000 note, I found it was payable on demand, and on inquiry I was informed that demand had been frequently made for its payment. I then stated that if I would sue on that note, interested parties would see from the complaint that as the note was forty days overdue, that a ground for bankruptcy proceedings would be furnished to hostile creditors. Being then asked what was the best to be done, I advised that inasmuch as the note was already six months overdue, that my client should procure from the firm of Schoenfeld, Cohn & Co. a note in exchange of this demand note, which would by its terms be payable six months after date. The firm of Schoenfeld, Cohn & Co. took up that demand note, gave Lewis a note bearing the same date, for the same sum, payable in six months.''

Before the commencement of the suit an agreement had been made between Lewis and the local creditors that Lewis would divide the proceeds of the property to be attached and sold on his debt pro rata among them and himself, and that the balance, if any, should be paid to members of the firm, to the exclusion of creditors abroad. The agreement for the pro rata division was known to Mr. Naphtaly before the commencement of the suit. The suit was commenced June 27, 1877, an attachment was issued, and the property of the firm seized. The property seized consisted of a large stock of toy goods. The complaint, stating that the note in suit was made in December, 1876, was verified by Lewis. Mr. Naphtaly states that he instructed his clerk to commence the suit and procure the attachment to be issued, but that he did not instruct him to have the complaint verified.

We further quote from Mr. Naphtaly's statement:

"I took these notes to my office and got my clerk to prepare the complaint. During its preparation I noticed that the $4,000 note of the firm, payable to the order of Mrs. Alexander, was not indorsed, and I returned the note to Mr. Lewis, stating that I could sue on that note in his name, for want of Mrs. Alexander's indorsement. I was then told that it would be a difficult matter to find Mrs. Alexander. As the note was a new note, I inquired concerning it. I was then told that the firm of Schoenfeld, Cohn & Co. did not directly borrow that money from Mrs. Alexander, a widow, but that Mrs. A., having $5,000, she gave it to Mr. Newman to lend it out on interest; that N. had loaned it to Schoenfeld, who had put that money in the firm of Schoenfeld, Cohn & Co., giving Newman his own note for it; that Newman held that note for Mrs. Alexander, and that Mrs. Alexander believed that the money was loaned to the firm, and that the widow collected her interest on that note in the store of the firm of Schoenfeld, Cohn & Co. That the firm had assumed the payment of that indebtedness, and that $1,000 had been paid on account of it, thus leaving $4,000 still due. On calling for her note it was produced. I asked when the firm assumed or became responsible to pay that debt. A date was given me, which I think was about the time when Mrs. Alexander received the payment on account. In order to protect that widow's money, and believing that the partnership had a legal and moral right to assume the payment of that debt, especially as every dollar went into the firm, I informed Messrs. Schoenfeld, Cohn & Co. that, as they had guaranteed the payment of the money due Mrs. Alexander, they ought to indorse that guaranty on the genuine note rather than give a new firm note for the amount due her. That was done.''

Referring to the subject of including the Mrs. Alexander note in the suit, Lewis says, in his affidavit, that ''Naphtaly inquired if a note had been given for the loan of $5,000, and where the note was; said Schoenfeld handed it to said attorney, who replied, in substance, that if there is a genuine note there is no use putting into this case a note that may burst the whole thing.''

If the proceedings, being instituted, were legal and just, there was no occasion to fear such a calamity.

We quote again from Mr. Naphtaly's statement:

''Not until several days after the suit was brought by me did I learn of the consideration of the $17,000 note. After the suit was brought, I learned that Mr. Lewis had agreed with them, Schoenfeld, Cohn & Co., that he would settle all the California indebtedness of the firm. I agreed to see that his promise would be carried out. Soon after that, and before judgment could be recovered, the parties came to my office, and then I was told the following in regard to the demand note for $17,000, viz.: That in the year 1876 the firm of Schoenfeld, Cohn & Co. had given to Mr. Newman, who was a member of the firm, its notes for $18,000 for money which Mr. Lewis loaned to the firm through Newman; that Newman became embarrassed through stock transactions; that to raise money Lewis had loaned Newman these $18,000 notes, which Newman then pledged with the London and San Francisco Bank for $6,000; that when Lewis was about to leave this state he asked Newman to procure for him these notes; that N. had not the money to redeem them; that Lewis threatened to redeem them and attach Schoenfeld, Cohn & Co.; that then it was agreed between that firm and Mr. Lewis and Newman that Lewis should be paid $1,000 on account, and that the firm of Schoenfeld, Cohn & Co. should give to Mr. Lewis a demand note for $17,000, but with the agreement that if Lewis ever enforced payment of this $17,000 note, that Lewis should take up from the London Bank these pledged notes, so that they should not be used against the firm. Mr. Lewis admitted that to be the agreement, and I assured Schoenfeld, Cohn & Co.

that I would see that the agreement was carried out. I was, of course, anxious to get the judgment entered before creditors could put the estate into bankruptcy. I could not tell the California creditors that it was understood that Schoenfeld, Cohn & Co. would not go into bankruptcy, or that Lewis had agreed to share with them in the proceeds of the judgment, as I would then have given to the parties adverse to my client's interests sufficient grounds for bankruptcy proceedings. To my surprise a demurrer to the complaint was filed on the last day when the answer was due; and on inquiry why such a course was taken, I was informed that the attorney who filed the demurrer desired to see me about the agreement Lewis had made to settle with the California creditors, and take up the pledged notes. I was delayed by that proceeding for seven days. In due course I took my judgment.''

The last sentence would indicate that the delay of seven days resulted to the satisfaction of the California creditors. At all events, the judgment was taken, Mr. Naphtaly acting as attorney for Lewis, execution was issued, and the property was seized and sold, Lewis being the purchaser.

It was agreed between Lewis and the firm, and some other local creditors, including one junior attaching creditor, that the property should be sold in large lots, in such manner that it would bring the smallest possible price.

Mr. Naphtaly says in his testimony: ''He [Lewis] wished me then to see that the sale is made in large parcels. I told him that it required the consent of the defendant and consent of the Anglo-California Bank, who were subsequent attaching creditors. He brought me the consent of the defendant, and Mr. Brandt [Mr. Naphtaly's clerk] procured the consent of the Anglo-California Bank. I was not at the sale.''

This arrangement was partly interfered with by one bidder, who, apparently, was not a party to the understanding, but it was so far successful that the property was bid in by Lewis for about $19,000 net, and was afterward sold by him in such manner that he received about $44,000. Out of this amount he paid $23,930 for expenses and for the California debts, including the $6,000 to the London and San Francisco Bank, $5,300 to the Anglo-California Bank, $4,750 in full of an $8,000 note included in the suit, and $4,000 to Mrs. Alexander. Mr. Naphtaly says he was not a participant in the conduct of the sale. He does say, however, that he assured the California creditors they should be paid pro rata out of the proceeds; and it appears that the result of the transaction was that his client received his debt in full—the object for which his services were secured and rendered.

After the rendition of the judgment, Schoenfeld, from some motive, moved to set it aside. Mr. Naphtaly resisting the motion on behalf of Lewis. The affidavits of Lewis and Mr. Naphtaly used in opposition to the motion are in evidence before us here, and from them and Mr. Naphtaly's statement above referred to, and his evidence in court on this hearing, we derive nearly all the facts stated by us. The court denied the motion to set aside the judgment, and that action is suggested as an adjudication by that court that no fraud was committed. That court would have been justified in denying the motion, no matter how fraudulent the transaction had been —for the motion was made by Schoenfeld, and if he was known to all the transactions, as was claimed by Lewis and Mr. Naphtaly, the court could well have refused the motion on that ground. The denying of the motion, then, would not have said there was no fraud, but, rather, there was fraud, and Schoenfeld was a party to it and was therefore in pari delicto, and ought not to be heard to make any such objection to the judgment.

It appears in this case that bankruptcy proceedings were instituted, and that the acts had upon the advice and with the assistance of Mr. Naphtaly were used in resistance of such proceedings.

The judgment of the federal court in a suit brought against Lewis by the assignee was offered in evidence in this court and objected to. We think it is admissible not to show, of itself, the truth of any charge against Mr. Naphtaly in this court, for, for such purpose, these proceedings may be said to be inter alios acta; but it is admissible as a fact, as a part of the history of the case (1 Greenl. Ev., secs. 527, 528, 538, 539; 2 Whar., sec. 823), to show that parties had to resort, as was intended they should if they obtained anything, to steps to set aside the proceedings which had been instituted, and to show that they were actually set aside for fraud. The judgment of that court was that the judgment obtained by Lewis against Schoenfeld, Cohn & Co. was obtained by fraud and

25

collusion, and was a fraud upon and against the creditors of the firm. The sale, also, was set aside for fraud in fact, and judgment was rendered against Lewis for $81,425.07 principal, and $17,091.26 interest.

Third. From the facts as above given, and considering the law applicable thereto, we are of opinion that Mr. Naphtaly violated his duty as an attorney, not for Lewis alone, but for Lewis and the members of the firm, to advise them how Lewis' claim could be secured, and a pro rata division be made among the California creditors in violation of the bankrupt law, and yet no act of bankruptcy be apparent, and to take the steps necessary to accomplish that object. He advised and caused Lewis to take a note from the firm, substituted for another, changing the date of payment, so that the time of payment should be different from that of the first, and so that it should appear that no act of bankruptcy had been committed, thus misleading other creditors, and attempting to defraud them of their rights—he having been informed at the time that an act of bankruptcy had been committed. The significance of the advice given as to the substitution of the six months' note for the demand note is apparent from the facts that the advice was given June 27, 1877; that the demand note was dated December 23, 1876, and was long overdue, and that the new note was dated December 23, 1876, and was made payable in six months, so that it might appear to have become due a few days only (less than forty days) before the commencement of the suit, and thus avoid the provision of the bankrupt law by which the stoppage of payment of commercial paper might be held to be an act of bankruptcy. He caused a suit to be commenced upon the fictitious note (fictitious as to time of payment and fictitious as to when made). The complaint was verified. Mr. Napthaly states that the verification was not by his instruction. The suit itself and the affidavit for attachment were commenced and made, the writ issued and property seized, at his instigation and by his direction.

In obtaining an attachment an affidavit is required to be made (Code Civ. Proc., sec. 538), that the defendant is indebted to the plaintiff (specifying the amount) upon a contract express or implied, and that the attachment is not sought, and the action is not prosecuted to hinder, delay or defraud any creditor of the defendant. Mr. Naphtaly knew that the object of having the six months' note (the one sued on) executed and the suit brought thereon, rather than on the demand note, was for the very purpose of hindering, delaying and defrauding other creditors—making the record show that no act of bankruptcy had been committed; compelling them to ascertain, if they could, that his proceedings were in fraud of the bankrupt law, and to have recourse to the courts to do away with the effect of his acts; and attempting to subject the property to the payment of a false claim. The firm of Schoenfeld, Cohn & Co. agreed that voluntary proceedings in bankruptcy should not be commenced; therefore, it became important to make the record appear as if no creditor had grounds for instituting proceedings in voluntary bankruptcy.

The making of the substituted note and the commencement of the suit upon it was for the purpose of misleading the court, in this: In case of a motion to dissolve the attachment, the court would have required evidence to show that the note was not in fact given as alleged.

Mr. Naphtaly in his statement says that "the firm of Schoenfeld, Cohn & Co. took up the demand note and gave Lewis a note bearing the same date, for the same sum, payable in six months." Referring to the complaint filed in the suit, we observe that it is therein averred that the $17,000 note sued on was executed on the twenty-third of December, 1876, payable to Isaac Newman, and was thereafter by him indorsed and delivered to the plaintiff Lewis. If the transaction was as stated by Lewis and Mr. Naphtaly, a plain business transaction between the firm and Lewis, what occasion was there for Newman to figure as payee as well as joint maker? The firm owed him nothing in regard to this matter. To say the least, it tended to show a false color on the transaction. However, we take the transaction as the parties have presented it to us.

He caused the firm, in furtherance of the same general object, to make a new contract with reference to the Mrs. Alexander note. That debt, as to Mrs. Alexander, was the debt of Schoenfeld; the firm had not guaranteed or assumed its payment. He, however, advised the firm to indorse its guaranty upon the note, thus assuming a liability not before existing in that form to the payee. The asserted reason for that was, that as Schoenfeld had put the money in the business and the firm had paid interest, it was practically the debt of the firm; the real reason was, Mrs. Alexander was out of the way, and without the guaranty the note could not have been included in the suit.

After being informed that the demand note was itself fictitious, having been given for an assumed indebtedness not existing, he prosecuted the suit to judgment. This action was had with knowledge that the real indebtedness was evidenced by the notes which had been pledged; that the interest of Lewis in the indebtedness was that part of it only which would remain after the payment of the $6,000 and interest to the bank; that at least $6,000 of it was property held by the bank; and that the note which he had advised should be surrendered and a new one substituted was itself simulated, and that in justice and in law Lewis should have relied upon his interest in the $18,000 notes; that not one dollar of the amount of the note sued on was owing by the firm to Lewis; that it was a sheer fabrication; that the full amount of the $18,000 notes would be provable by the bank in bankruptcy proceedings, and that the new note would swell the apparent indebtedness of the firm by the amount for which it was given, and would compel creditors to resort to legal proceedings to show its simulated character; yet with that knowledge, and as a part of a scheme to obtain unjust and illegal advantages over eastern creditors, as an imposition upon the court, and in fraud of the bankrupt law, he prosecuted to judgment the suit upon the note simulated for a fabricated note. In like furtherance of the general purpose, he gave advice as to the sale not warranted by the law. The statute concerning execution sales is (Code Civ. Proc. 694), that "when the sale is of personal property capable of manual delivery, it must be within view of those who attend the sale, and be sold in such parcels as are likely to bring the highest price."

The advice given was not in accordance with the section above referred to, but was in direct conflict with it. Not alone were Mr. Lewis and the members of the firm and the Anglo-California Bank interested, but the firm being insolvent, every creditor, California and eastern, was interested, in having the sale conducted according to law and in such manner as to bring the highest price. The command of the law is clear and express that when the sale is of personal property. capable of manual delivery, it must be made in such parcels as are likely to bring the highest price, the only privilege given

by the law to the judgment debtor, if present at the sale, being
to direct the order in which the articles of personal property
which can be sold to advantage separately shall be sold. This
section of the statute has been several times before this court
for construction, and its ruling has invariably been in accordance with what has been above stated.

This was done that the plaintiff Lewis might become the
purchaser of the property sold by the sheriff at greatly less
than its value; which was actually accomplished as stated
above. It was done, also, by a combination with the defendants that they might derive a profit from it, to the prejudice
of their creditors. There was thus a secret trust for the benefit of the debtors, one of the plainest and significant badges
of fraud. These proceedings were an actual fraud upon all
creditors not parties to the transaction or who were to be protected by Lewis.

In fact, the substituted note was made and suit was brought
upon it, judgment recovered, execution issued, and the property sold in a manner not warranted by law, with the intent
to hinder, delay and defraud the eastern creditors of Schoenfeld, Cohn & Co. The rights of such creditors being thus
affected by these proceedings, the question whether the substituted note was, as between the parties sustained by a consideration, becomes immaterial, and need not be considered.
The transaction was tainted with fraud, and the consequences
resulting therefrom attached to it though it had been sustained
by any amount of consideration. Such was the judgment in
Twyne's Case, 1 Smith's Lead. Cas. 33.

In that case, though the purchaser had paid full consideration for the property bought, yet inasmuch as the purchase
was made with the intent to hinder, delay and defraud creditors, it was adjudged null and void. In the case before us
the intent is acknowledged.

We notice the caution manifested in the course of the proceedings. In reference to the agreement to divide pro rata
with the California creditors, Mr. Naphtaly says: "I assured
Schoenfeld, Cohn & Co. that I would see that that agreement
was carried out. I was, of course, anxious to get the judgment entered before creditors could put the estate into bankruptcy. I could not tell the California creditors that it was
understood that Schoenfeld, Cohn & Co. would not go into
bankruptcy, or that Lewis had agreed to share with them in

the proceeds of the judgment, as I would then have given to the parties adverse to my client's interests sufficient grounds for bankruptcy proceedings.''

If the suit was an open business transaction, that of a delinquent creditor taking legal steps to gain priority, he being by law entitled to a gained priority, what was there to fear? It is said, too, that there is no evidence of any debt or claim held by eastern creditors. If California creditors were to share pro rata with Lewis, who were the ''parties adverse'' to Lewis' interests? Who were the ''hostile creditors,'' from whom knowledge must be kept? Why such care taken to conceal evidence of the real nature of the proceedings? If the property of a debtor is to be fairly and equally divided among all, there are no hostile creditors; all have a common object. The California creditors appear to have been paid in full out of the proceeds of the property, leaving a profit in the hands of Lewis. If, then, there were no other creditors than Lewis and those whom he agreed to protect, who was there to institute bankruptcy proceedings? What ground was there for such proceedings? Why apprehend bankruptcy proceedings at all? Why such anxious haste to procure the judgment ''before creditors could put the estate into bankruptcy''?

It seems to us beyond controversy that it was manifest to all—Mr. Naphtaly, Lewis, and the members of the firm—that the firm was hopelessly insolvent, and that a large amount of the indebtedness was held by eastern creditors, and the patent intent was to hinder, delay and defraud them, and that Mr. Naphtaly advised, aided and abetted it in every way, practiced imposition and deceit upon the court, and took no step backward. By such means the bankrupt laws were evaded and a fraud was practiced on their provisions. To counsel or maintain such actions and proceedings could not appear, and did not appear, to be legal or just. And the artifices resorted to misled and imposed on the court. The fraud in hindering and delaying creditors was attempted to be further carried out by a fraud on the provisions of the bankrupt law, one of the chief designs of which was to forbid and deprive of all force such proceedings. To carry out this design to defraud creditors steps were taken to conceal evidence which would have shown acts of bankruptcy. It was well known that proceedings in bankruptcy would have caused the whole plan to miscarry, and fail of its intended end and aim. To prevent this, evidence was covered up by an artifice based on falsehood; a note and contract were fabricated, on which suits should be brought and attachments sued out and property seized and sold by collusion with and procurement of the bankrupts, and the court was thus misled and imposed on. Such conduct was in clear violation of his duties as an attorney and counselor at law.

It is not proper to consider this piecemeal, but in its integrated mass. Considering the separate steps in the transaction, isolating one step from another, it might be ingeniously argued that innocence should be predicated of each one of them. But the just deduction is to be made from all the facts of the case. The intent which pervades them is thus clearly shown, and it becomes more apparent as one fact succeeds another. The force of the evidence is thus increased as the facts multiply in a ratio which it would be difficult to indicate in language. As one fact is added to another, the testimony which embraces the intent is multiplied in force. As is said by Starkie in his great work on Evidence, "Where each of a number of independent circumstances, or combination of circumstances, tends to the same conclusion, the probability of the truth of the fact is necessarily greatly increased, in proportion to the number of those independent circumstances": Starkie on Ev., 9th Am. ed., 852, and note illustrative of the text. The whole mass of facts thus considered prove the intent to defraud, as above pointed out.

The statute of this state authorizes us to either remove or suspend. This is the first case of this character which has been brought before this court. While, therefore, we are not at liberty, nor have the desire, to omit our duty in the premises, yet, in choosing between penalties, we take into consideration the heretofore good standing of the respondent, and give him credit for the suggestion that possibly he may have, for the moment, overlooked his duty as an officer of the law, in his eagerness to serve his client, and we propose to affix such penalty only as will indicate the estimate we attach to professional conduct.

The judgment of the court is that respondent be suspended as an attorney and counselor at law for the period of six months from this day.

I concur: McKee, J.

I concur in the judgment and the conclusions reached by Justice Myrick: Thornton, J.

ROSS, J.—I concur in the judgment. According to the testimony before us, when in June, 1877, Mr. Naphtaly's legal advice was sought, there were outstanding notes of the firm of Schoenfeld, Cohn & Co., aggregating $18,000, drawn in favor of Newman, by him indorsed to Lewis and by the latter permitted to be pledged to the London and San Francisco Bank, Limited, as collateral security for certain moneys advanced by the bank. These notes were payable on demand and evidenced all the indebtedness from Schoenfeld, Cohn & Co. to Lewis. There was also then (in June, 1877), in existence a simulated note for $17,000, dated December 23, 1876, executed by Schoenfeld, Cohn & Co., to Lewis. I say simulated, because this note purported to represent an indebtedness that did not exist—the true and only indebtedness to Lewis being evidenced by the notes then held by the London and San Francisco Bank, Limited, as collateral security for the moneys it had advanced on the faith of those securities. When Mr. Naphtaly's legal advice was sought, the firm of Schoenfeld, Cohn & Co. was insolvent, and he knew it. Extensive purchases of goods had been but recently made by the firm, which had not been paid for. A scheme was then concocted by Schoenfeld, Newman and Lewis looking to the application of these goods as well as the balance of the stock of the insolvent firm to the payment of the amount due Lewis and the local creditors, and to the securing of the remainder to the members of the firm. This purpose was palpably fraudulent. Whether, when first retained, Mr. Naphtaly was informed of the whole of the scheme is immaterial, for he admits that he advised the execution by the firm of a simulated note for $17,000, as of date December 23, 1876, and payable six months after its date, on which he proposed to bring, and did bring, an attachment suit in Lewis' name, by virtue of which the property was attached and subsequently sold. His purpose in thus advising and acting, as explained by himself, was to prevent any proceedings in bankruptcy on the part of those creditors not a party to the conspiracy. And according to his own statement, he was fully informed of the fraudulent nature of the scheme shortly after the commencement of the action, and, with that knowledge, he prosecuted the suit to judgment, and subsequently resisted, professionally and by his personal affidavit, a motion to vacate the judgment made on behalf of one of the partners who had, from some cause, become dissatisfied with the plan or its execution.

All this involved falsehood and deception on the part of the promoters and prosecutors of the scheme, fraud on the creditors not parties to it, and imposition on the court. When, in June, 1877, Schoenfeld, Cohn & Co., signed the note to Lewis, antedated December 23, 1876, and made payable six months after the fictitious date, Lewis was not entitled to any note from them, for there remained in existence the notes from them evidencing the amount due him, and which were still held by the bank as collateral security. Not only was Lewis not entitled to another note from the firm (the execution of which Mr. Naphtaly advised), but the note was made to speak falsehood after falsehood, for the unlawful and fraudulent purpose of deceiving those creditors of the firm not parties to the conspiracy; and it was this note that the court was made the innocent instrument in enforcing by one of its own officers. Mr. Naphtaly testified before us that in acting as he did he did not realize he was doing anything wrong, but thought he was justified in thus securing advantages to his clients. I am inclined to think he did not sufficiently reflect before advising and acting, and hence I am disposed to make the punishment reasonably light. But it would never do for the court to acquit him of blame in the face of such facts as are presented to us. Judicial sanction of such proceedings would, in my opinion, surely and justly bring the courts as well as the bar into disrepute and contempt.

We concur: McKinstry. J.; Morrison, C. J.

SHARPSTEIN, J.—I dissent. The evidence in this case, as I construe it, shows that in the month of June, 1877, one Lewis applied to the respondent to bring an action against Schoenfeld, Cohn & Co., upon certain promissory notes, of which said Lewis represented himself to be the indorsee. Among said notes was one for $17,000, dated December 23, 1876, payable on demand. The respondent ascertained from the indorsee that this note had been due more than forty days. Thereupon respondent informed said indorsee that the fact that the makers of said note had suffered the same to remain unpaid for a period of forty days after it had matured would of itself constitute an act of bankruptcy, and that a complaint filed upon that note would necessarily disclose that the makers of said note had committed an act of bankruptcy. To avoid that, the respondent suggested the execution of a new note, for the same sum, and of the same date as the old one, payable six months after date. That suggestion was followed, and an action was commenced on the new note by filing a complaint verified by the plaintiff in the usual form, and an attachment was sued out by filing an affidavit in the usual form.

It is urged that the allegation in the complaint that the note was made on the day of its date was false, and that the respondent knew it to be false when the complaint was verified. The evidence upon this point is that the respondent did not prepare the complaint, or direct that it should be verified, or know that there was any intention to have it verified, or that it had been verified, until after it had been filed. I do not think that he can be held criminally responsible for an act done by another without his advice or knowledge.

It is further urged that the affidavit upon which the attachment was obtained was false, because it was stated in said affidavit that the attachment was not sought and the action was not prosecuted to hinder, delay or defraud any creditor of the defendants.

I have always supposed that where an attachment was sought and an action prosecuted by a person for the purpose of securing the payment of his own demand, that he might safely make that affidavit, although the result of suing out such attachment might not only be to hinder and delay other creditors, but to render their claims against the defendant worthless. The object of the attaching creditor in such a case being to secure the payment of his own demand, without reference to how others might be thereby affected. And I do not understand that, in the absence of any bankrupt law, this would be disputed. And the bankrupt law did not forbid the security of a preference by one creditor over all others by attaching all the property of his debtor: Barbour v. Priest, 103 U. S. 295, 26 L. Ed. 480; Wilson v. City Bank, 17 Wall. 473, 21 L. Ed 723. The fact of the debtor's property might be all absorbed, in the payment of the attaching creditor's claim. It is therefore obvious that it was not the intention of the bankrupt act to deprive an attaching creditor of any advantage which he might secure over other creditors of a common debtor by being the first to attach the property of such debtor.

But it is said in reply that if this be so, the respondent, by advising the substitution of a note which would not show on its face that the makers had committed an act of bankruptcy for one that did show that they had, counseled the perpetration of a fraud. In other words, his client wished to obtain a preference over all other creditors of his debtors, and the respondent told him that if said debtors chose to go into bankruptcy, or if any creditor or creditors could find any good ground for throwing them into bankruptcy, he could not obtain any preference by being the first to sue and attach. The respondent was assured that the debtors would not voluntarily go into bankruptcy, but on an inspection of the $17,000 note he discovered that it had been due more than forty days, and he then informed his client that if one-fourth in number of creditors of the makers discovered that fact, they might throw them into bankruptcy, as that of itself constituted an act of bankruptcy. And to obviate that, he advised the surrender of that note to the makers and the execution of a new note by them which would not on its face show that they had committed an act of bankruptcy. It cannot be denied that as between the makers and payee of the note this transaction was perfectly legitimate. They had a perfect right to make and he to take a new note in the place of the old one. And as between themselves they had a right to antedate if they chose. But the objection which is made to this transaction is, that the object of making and taking a new note was to conceal from the creditors of the makers the fact that they had committed an act of bankruptcy. Not to disclose was to conceal. Was it the duty of the respondent on discovering that his client's debtors had committed an act of bankruptcy to advise that the fact be at once published? I presume that it will not be claimed that it was. On the other hand, I think that it will be admitted that it was his duty to conceal it. The law would not permit him, without the consent of his client, to disclose it. "An attorney cannot, without the consent of his client, be examined as to any communication made by the client to him, or his advice given thereon in the course of professional employment." (Code Civ. Proc., 1881.) His lips were sealed.

As before stated, the antedating of the note was not an illegal act. But it is claimed that the antedating of it for the purpose of concealing the fact that the makers of it were bankrupt was a gross wrong upon their creditors. In Gladwin v. Gladwin, 13 Cal. 330, the counsel for the intervener contended that "the antedating of the note sued on—the manufacture of a present cause of action out of debts not due —the agreement that plaintiff sue out attachment by way of securing the debt; these facts, appearing without explanation, were a fraud in law upon the other creditors." But the court held in effect that the note having been executed upon a sufficient consideration, its validity was not affected by the circumstances above stated. The court in that case cited Dana v. Stanfords, 10 Cal. 269, Little v. Little, 13 Pick. (Mass.) 426, Cushing v. Gore, 15 Mass. 73, Haseltine v. Guild, 11 N. H. 390, which seem to me to hold that a creditor of an insolvent debtor may secure a preference over other creditors quite as questionable as those which the respondent advised should be resorted to for the purpose of giving his client a preference over other creditors. And as the act which he counseled was not legal, it does not seem to me that the existence or nonexistence of a bankrupt law at the time is a material circumstance. The act was neither malum prohibitum or malum in se, and would therefore be quite as reprehensible when there was not as when there was a bankrupt law in force. Other creditors would be prejudiced just the same in either case. If, in the absence of a bankrupt law, an attorney would be justified in advising parties to do what was done in the cases above cited, for the purpose of giving one creditor a preference over all other creditors, I am unable to perceive why the respondent might not advise what he did without incurring the penalty of disbarment or suspension. It is not illegal for one creditor to obtain a preference over other creditors. Nor is it illegal to antedate a note. How, then, can it be a misdemeanor to advise the doing of two legal acts? Or the doing of a legal act for the purpose of accomplishing a strictly legal object?

Assuming, however, that the views which I have above expressed are erroneous, it seems to me that there is a total absence of proof to support the charge based upon the antedating of the $17,000 note. I have examined the evidence very carefully, without discovering anything in it which proves or tends to prove that any creditor of the makers of that note were prejudiced by the antedating of it. It is claimed that the object of antedating it was to defraud eastern and European creditors. But I am unable to find from the evidence before us that there are, or ever were, any such creditors. They are alluded to as if they did exist. The respondent, in his testimony, says he knew nothing of their existence until long after the suit was brought and attachment levied. But it is not stated who they were, how many there were, the amount or nature of their claims, or whether those claims were paid or not. For anything that appears to the contrary, they may have been satisfied with the course pursued by the parties here.

It appears by a decree which was offered in evidence that the firm which made the note has been adjudged bankrupt, not at the instance of any creditor of the firm, but upon the petition of a member of it. The respondent's responsibility is for the advice which he gave upon the facts which he knew or which had been communicated to him at or before the time when he gave it.

As I read the testimony, there is no evidence tending to prove that the respondent did, but there is evidence tending to prove that he did not, know before the commencement of the action upon said $17,000 note that the defendants in that action had any eastern or European creditors, or that there was a note in the Anglo-California Bank which had been given for the same loan that the note sued on was given for, or that there was an agreement between the plaintiff and defendants in that action that whatever surplus might remain of the amount realized on the sale of the property attached, after satisfying the plaintiff's judgment and the California creditors, should be turned over to the defendants, or that the notes sued on did not represent a bona fide indebtedness of said firm.

As to the selling of the goods in bulk instead of parcels, the respondent testifies that he did not advise that they should be so sold, and no one testifies that he did.

The measures taken to protect Mrs. Alexander appears to me to have been eminently proper. One of the partners had been acting as her agent, and it was his duty in her absence to protect her interest: Barbour v. Priest, supra.

It is quite evident that an impression prevails that the respondent's client and the firm of Schoenfeld, Cohn & Co. entered into a conspiracy to defraud the creditors of said firm, and that for that purpose an action against the firm was commenced and an attachment sued out with the intention of transferring the goods belonging to said firm to respondent's client, at a great sacrifice, so that he might resell the goods at private sale and realize a large profit thereon, to be divided between him and the members of said firm. Whether there is any evidence before us to support that theory I shall not now stop to inquire. The respondent swears that he did not know of any such arrangement, and he is not contradicted. He pleaded not guilty to the charges preferred against him, and the evidence mainly relied upon to support them consists of a communication written by him to the president of the Bar Association, supplemented by the testimony which he gave in open court on the hearing of this matter. The findings of this court upon the material issues arising upon the pleadings ought to be in accordance with the proof presented. The respondent should be held responsible for the advice which he gave upon the facts communicated to him or which were otherwise within his knowledge. For acts which he did not devise, and designs of which he was ignorant, he cannot justly be held responsible. The advice which a lawyer gives to his client must in nearly every case be based upon the statement of the client. "And it is not the saints of the world who chiefly give employment to our profession. It has essentially and habitually to do with all that is selfish and malicious, knavish and criminal, coarse and brutal, repulsive and obscene, in human life": In the Matter of Goodell, 39 Wis. 245, 20 Am. Rep. 42.

HIBERNIA SAVINGS AND LOAN SOCIETY, Respondent, v. DENNIS JORDAN, Appellant.*

No. 6215; November 29, 1880.

Executors and Administrators — Presentation of Mortgage Claims.—In an action of foreclosure on a mortgage against a decedent commenced in 1877, where the notice to creditors had been published in February, 1873, during which year the statute provided that a mortgage claim need not be presented, there is no necessity for a presentation, though at the time the mortgage was executed, and also during the last half of 1874, and all of 1875, the statute required presentation, and provided that no action could be maintained without it.

---

*For former opinion, see 2 Cal. Unrep. 79.

Executors and Administrators — Presentation of Mortgage Claims.—The amendments of 1874 of sections 1493 and 1500 of the Code of Civil Procedure, in the matter of presentation of mortgage claims against decedents' estates, did not have any retroactive operation.

APPEAL from the District Court of the Fourth Judicial District, City and County of San Francisco.

G. R. B. Hayes for appellant; Tobin & Tobin for respondent.

ROSS, J.—The mortgage, for the foreclosure of which this action was brought, was executed in March, 1872, and was made payable three years after its date. The mortgager died in December, 1872. Administration upon her estate was had. Notice to creditors was published in February, 1873. The claim in suit was never presented to the representative of the estate for allowance, but the plaintiff, in 1877, commenced the present action, and in the complaint expressly waived all recourse against any other property of the estate than that embraced in the mortgage.

According to the law in force at the time the mortgage was executed, presentation of all claims to the representative of the estate for allowance was necessary; but in January, 1873, it was provided by statute that a mortgage claim need not be presented where all recourse against all other than the mortgaged property is expressly waived in the complaint. Such was the law at the time the notice was given, and such it remained until July, 1874. According to the law, therefore, under which the notice was given, the plaintiff was not required to present its claim for allowance within the time mentioned in the notice, nor at all. In July, 1874, however, the law was again changed and the statute then made to read as follows:

"Section 1493. If a claim arising upon a contract heretofore made be not presented within the time limited in the notice, it is barred forever, except as follows: If it be not then due, or if it be contingent, it may be presented within one month after it becomes due or absolute, if it be made to appear by the affidavit of the claimant, to the satisfaction of the executor or administrator and the probate judge, that the claimant had no notice, as provided in this chapter, by reason of being out of the state, it may be presented at any time before a decree of distribution is entered. A claim for a deficiency remaining unpaid after a sale of property of the estate mortgaged or pledged, must be presented within one month after such deficiency is ascertained. All claims arising upon contracts hereafter made, whether the same be due, not due, or contingent, must be presented within the time limited in the notice, and any claim not so presented is barred forever; provided, however, that when it is made to appear by the affidavit of the claimant, to the satisfaction of the executor or administrator and the probate judge, that the claimant had no notice, as provided in this chapter, by reason of being out of the state, it may be presented at any time before a decree of distribution is entered.''

''Section 1500. No holder of any claim against an estate shall maintain any action thereon, unless the claim is first presented to the executor or administrator.''

Unless these sections are made by construction to retroact, we do not see what application they can have to the plaintiff's case. Not only is there nothing in the sections themselves to indicate an intention on the part of the legislature to give them such effect, but section 3 of the same code (Code Civ. Proc.) declares that ''no part of it is retroactive unless expressly so declared.''

To hold the plaintiff's claim barred by the statute would be to give an effect to the notice which it did not and could not have under the law under which it was published, and would require us to give to section 1493, above quoted, a retroactive effect when there is nothing in the section itself demanding such construction, and when there are other sections of the same code indicating that it could not be given. In our opinion, the judgment should be affirmed, and it is so ordered.

We concur: McKinstry, J.; Thornton, J.

I concur in the judgment: Myrick, J.

Morrison, C. J., not having heard the argument, took no part in the decision of this case.

McKee and Sharpstein, JJ., dissented.

PEOPLE v. NOBLE.

No. 7736; June 27, 1883.

Dedication.—Noble's Alley in San Francisco was not dedicated as a public street.

APPEAL from Superior Court, San Francisco.

L. Quint and J. W. Winans for appellant; E. J. Pringle for respondent.

By the COURT.—We are of the opinion that the proofs fail to sustain the allegation of the complaint and the finding of the court that the alleyway denominated Noble's Alley was a public street and highway, accepted as such by the city and county, in that they fail to show a dedication as such by the owner.

Judgment and order reversed and cause remanded for a new trial.

26

INDEX.

[References to volumes are in bold-face figures.]

ABANDONMENT.

Of appeal. See Appeal and Error, § 69.
Of work as affecting right to recover for services. See Contracts,
   § 13.
Of highway. See Dedication, § 5.
Of easement in matter of waters. See Easements, § 4.
Of highway. See Highways, § 4.
Of homestead. See Homestead, § 6.
By mortgagor. See Mortgages, § 16.
Of public work by contractor. See Municipal Corporations, § 29.
Of child. See Parent and Child, § 1.
By occupant of public land. See Public Lands, § 6.

ABATEMENT.

By pendency of another action. See Divorce, § 6.

ABSCONDING DEBTOR.

See Arrest, § 1.

ACCEPTANCE.

Of negotiable instrument. See Bills and Notes, § 4.
Of street or highway by public. See Dedication, § 4.

ACCOMMODATION PAPER.

In general. See Bills and Notes, § 6.

ACCOMPLICES AND ACCESSORIES.

§ 1. Concealment of crime.
§ 2. —— Indictment.
§ 3. Officers detecting crime.
§ 4. Corroboration and instructions relative thereto.
§ 5. In larceny—Evidence and corroboration.
§ 6. In robbery—Evidence and corroboration.
§ 7. In homicide—Corroboration and instructions.

Participant in burglary. See Burglary, § 1.
Corroboration of accomplice. See Receiving Stolen Goods, § 3.
In embezzlement. See Embezzlement, § 7.

§ 1. Concealment of Crime.

Penal Code, section 32, defining accessories as those who after
knowledge of the commission of a felony conceal it from the magistrate or protect the person charged with the crime, states the common-
law rule that a person must know that he is assisting a felon or else
he cannot be charged as an accessory, and the mere neglect to inform
the authorities that a felony has been committed is not sufficient,
the word "conceal" in the statute including some affirmative act on
the part of the person looking to the concealment of the felony.—Ex
parte Goldman, 7, 254.

§ 2. —— Indictment.

An indictment charging that accused after and with knowledge
of the commission of a felony concealed its commission from the

(403)

magistrate does not charge accused with being an accessory within Penal Code, section 32, defining accessories as those who after knowledge of the commission of a felony conceal it from the magistrate, as it does not allege the acts constituting the offense.—Ex parte Goldman, 7, 254.

§ 3. Officer Detecting Crime.

One who aids in the commission of a crime effected through violence cannot afterward escape responsibility as an accomplice by claiming he was a peace officer at the time, acting with a purpose to detect and convict the criminal.—People v. Scott, 1, 68.

Where evidence against a person charged with a crime is given by a police officer who aided in the act charged from a concealed motive of afterward giving such testimony, the defendant is entitled to have the court instruct the jury that the witness was an accomplice and his evidence, without corroborating proof to support it, insufficient to convict.—People v. Scott, 1, 68.

§ 4. Corroboration and Instructions Relative Thereto.

Where an accomplice has testified against the accused, the latter is entitled to have the judge instruct the jury that such evidence must be corroborated if it is to be believed.—People v. Lyons, 1, 63.

Under Penal Code, section 1111, requiring corroboration of the testimony of an accomplice, it is not necessary that corroborative evidence should go so far as to establish by itself, and without the aid of the testimony of the accomplice, that defendant in a prosecution for receiving stolen goods possessed the requisite guilty knowledge.—People v. Solomon, 6, 305.

It was also error to refuse to charge that, if the jury found such witness to be an accomplice, and did not believe the evidence of his wife, then there was no corroborating evidence of the accomplice, and it was their duty to acquit.—People v. Strybe, 4, 505.

One who could not have been proceeded against as other than a principal cannot be prejudiced by a refusal to grant instructions relating to accessories.—People v. Lockhard, 1, 219.

§ 5. In Larceny—Evidence and Corroboration.

One who has not aided in the theft but, with knowledge of it, accompanies the thief and aids in the care and management of the stolen property, is an accessory after the fact, and should be tried as such and not as a principal.—People v. Valenzuella, 2, 87.

On a prosecution for the larceny of $280 it appeared that the defendant knew of the money being in the pocket of the prosecuting witness, and that he, with others, drank with the defendant, and then went with him to a dance-hall, where the money was taken by a woman. On the prosecuting witness making complaint, defendant told him he would try to get back the money, and he got the witness out of town that night. When the prosecuting witness returned, and had the woman arrested, defendant gave him $40, and induced the witness to attempt to have the prosecution dismissed, which the witness did not succeed in doing, and defendant again sent witness out of town. Defendant then fled from the state, and when found was living under an assumed name. Held, that the circumstances were sufficient to corroborate the testimony of an accomplice as to defendant's guilt.—People v. Ardell, 6, 827.

On a prosecution for larceny, evidence as to a conversation between the prosecuting witness, defendant, and another in regard to having a prosecution against an alleged accomplice of defendant, growing out of the robbery, dismissed, was properly received to show the defendant's solicitude in settling the matter.—People v. Ardell, 6, 827.

§ .6. In Robbery—Evidence and Corroboration.

Where the only evidence to convict defendant of a robbery is that of an accomplice, who testifies that defendant planned the robbery and received part of the proceeds, and that of two witnesses, that they had seen defendant and the accomplice together on two occasions before the robbery, there is no such corroboration of the evidence of the accomplice, as required by Penal Code, section 1111, as to justify conviction.—People v. Larsen, 4, 286.

There is evidence to identify defendant as the person who committed the robbery, prosecuting witnesses testifying that he was one of the persons who robbed him, though defendant and his witnesses testified that he cut off his mustache a month before the robbery, and had not worn one since, and prosecuting witness, who testified that he had seen defendant after, as well as a year before, the robbery, said that when he "previously met" him he wore a mustache, the jury being at liberty to hold that the time thus referred to was when he met defendant a year before the robbery.—People v. Cappola, 6, 232.

Though Penal Code, section 31, makes accomplices principals, they are not "perpetrators," so that, on a prosecution for robbery of two of the five persons present when the crime was committed, a requested instruction that the jury must be satisfied of the identity of defendants as the perpetrators is properly refused, as misleading, in ignoring the fact that they may have been accomplices.—People v. Chin Yuen, 7, 188.

§ 7. In Homicide—Corroboration and Instructions.

On a murder trial, the court, on evidence fully authorizing it, submitted to the jury the question as to whether or not a certain witness for the state was an accomplice. The only corroborative evidence was given by the wife of such witness, who testified to certain oral confessions. Held, that it was error to refuse to charge that the testimony of an accomplice ought to be viewed with distrust, and the evidence of the oral admissions of defendants ought to be viewed with caution, under Code of Civil Procedure, section 2061, which directs such instructions to be given "on all proper occasions."—People v. Strybe, 4, 505.

ACCORD AND SATISFACTION.

§ 1. In General.

Payment of a part of a sum due is not satisfaction of the whole, even though the payment is made and received in pursuance of an agreement that it should be so regarded, since such an agreement would be without consideration.—Bull v. Eby, 1, 281.

A San Francisco merchant purchased coal from a dealer in New South Wales. The dealer drew a draft on the merchant for an amount less than the agreed price under the existing customs duties. Afterward the customs duties on the purchase were reduced, and later the cargo arrived. Held, that payment of the draft was on account, and not in full satisfaction.—Withers v. Moore, 7, 125.

§ 2. Pleading and Evidence.

An answer in an action on notes which denies that certain of the first four notes have not been paid, and alleges that they have been "satisfied and discharged," does not plead an accord and satisfaction. Hogan v. Burns, 4, 62.

In such action it appeared that after the date of such first four notes defendant gave plaintiff an order at the bottom of a stated account against him amounting to $70 less than the face of such notes on the attorney for the executor of a certain estate; that such attorney accepted the order, reciting in the acceptance that "certain moneys will in the future, in all probability, become due and payable to" defendant out of the income from certain real estate belonging to such estate, and that the order was payable only out of moneys coming from such estate, "and not claimed or affected by attachments or other claims." Held, that, though an accord and satisfaction was pleaded, it was not error to exclude such account, order, and acceptance from the evidence in the absence of any offer to show by other evidence that they were intended or accepted as satisfaction of either of the notes, or that either the account or order had been paid.—Hogan v. Burns, 4, 62.

ACCOUNTING.

By partners. See Partnership, §§ 11–15.
By trustee. See Trusts, § 21.

ACCOUNTS.

Of executor. See Executors and Administrators, § 33.
Of guardian. See Guardian and Ward, § 9.

ACCOUNT STATED.

§ 1. In General.

Upon an account stated a written promise by the debtor to pay at request in gold coin can be enforced, even though before gold could not have been demanded, the amount due being a sufficient consideration.—Dodge v. Mariposa Co., 1, 398.

ACKNOWLEDGMENT.

To toll statute of limitations. See Limitation of Actions, § 8.

§ 1. By Married Woman.

A deed by a married woman of her separate property must, in order to pass title, be acknowledged by her, and her acknowledgment certified, in the manner required by the statute.—Butler v. Welton, 1, 731.

ACTIONS.

§ 1. Right as dependent on values.
§ 2. Legal and equitable.
§ 3. Effect of mistaking remedy.
§ 4. Joinder and misjoinder.
§ 5. —— Legal and equitable.
§ 6. —— Ejectment.
§ 7. Consolidation of causes.

In case of husband and wife. See Husband and Wife, § 9.
On judgment. See Judgments, § 22.

§ 1. Right as Dependent on Values.

The right of a person to redress for an injury to property cannot depend upon the value of the property injured as contrasted with the value of another's business enterprise, in the promotion of which the injury came about.—Hill v. Weisler, 1, 724.

§ 2. Legal and Equitable.

Although both legal and equitable forms of relief may be obtained in the same forum, the same substantial differences between them exists now as of old, and to obtain the relief formerly administered by courts of equity one must establish the same facts as when relief was obtainable only in those courts.—Reed v. Union Copper Mining Co., 1, 587.

The old distinction between legal and equitable remedies will not prevent a California court, in a simple action to recover on a promissory note, from directing by its judgment a sale of property upon which it has been made to appear that such note was expressly secured.—Harden v. Ware, 2, 72.

§ 3. Effect of Mistaking Remedy.

A suit does not fail because of the plaintiff's happening to mistake the form of his remedy.—Harden v. Ware, 2, 72.

§ 4. Joinder and Misjoinder.

Misjoinder of causes of action in a complaint is a defect to be taken advantage of by demurrer only, and if not so taken advantage of is deemed to be waived.—Martin v. Wray, 1, 25.

The object of the sixty-fourth section of the Practice Act was to authorize parties to unite causes of action which already existed, and not to give additional causes of action. It was not contemplated therein that the right to an account should follow the recovery in ejectment.—Reed v. Union Copper Mining Co., 1, 587.

Error, if any, in overruling a demurrer to a complaint on the ground that it united with a cause of action for foreclosure of mortgage a cause of action on a guaranty is harmless, the court having found that the guaranty was without consideration.—Savings Bank of San Diego County v. Fisher, 5, 115.

§ 5. —— Legal and Equitable.

The Practice Act authorizes the joining of several causes of action, subject to certain restrictions, but contains no requirement that the causes of action thus united shall be either all of a legal or all of an equitable nature.—Reed v. Union Copper Mining Co., 1, 587.

§ 6. —— Ejectment.

Two causes of action are inconsistent, as set up in an action of ejectment, if the defendant is asked to be found virtually a trespasser under the one, while under the other he is alleged to have entered as the plaintiff's guardian to manage the estate for the plaintiff; such causes cannot properly be joined.—Reed v. Union Copper Mining Co., 1, 587.

§ 7. Consolidation of Causes.

Where two actions between the same parties were consolidated, and judgment rendered for plaintiff in one action, it is immaterial, on an appeal by defendant, that the complaint in the other action did not state facts constituting a cause of action.—Adams v. De Boom, 5, 1.

An action to enforce a contract to convey land in consideration of plaintiff's doing certain grading, and an action to recover for the grading in three counts—First, the reasonable value thereof; second, the price therefor under a written contract; and, third, the value of extra grading—were consolidated. The court found for defendant as to the first action, and for plaintiff as to the second, on the second count, and for $350 "in addition to said written contract." Held, that the finding of the additional sum related to and was supported by either the first or third count of the second action.—Adams v. De Boom, 5, 1.

On the entry of judgment on an order of plaintiff dismissing the action before an answer seeking affirmative relief has been filed, the court loses jurisdiction, and cannot thereafter vacate the judgment on application of defendants, and consolidate such action with another.—Wolters v. Rossi, 6, 266.

ADMINISTRATORS.

See Executors and Administrators.

ADMISSIONS.

Admissibility. See Evidence, §§ 10–15.
In pleading in ejectment. See Ejectment, § 10.
In pleadings. See Pleading, § 17.

ADVANCE BIDS.

At executor's sale. See Executors and Administrators, § 22.

ADVANCES.

Lien for on consignment for sale. See Factors, § 5.
Mortgage to secure. See Mortgages.

ADVERSE POSSESSION.

Under mistake. See Boundaries, § 2.
Estoppel to deny landlord's title. See Landlord and Tenant, § 8.
Acquisition of right of way by. See Railroads, § 1.
As between cotenants. See Tenancy in Common, § 2.
Prescriptive water rights. See Waters and Watercourses, § 7.

§ 1. In General.

To constitute a bar to the recovery on the legal title, adverse possession must be open, notorious and exclusive, and adverse not only to the plaintiff but to every person holding or claiming title.—Larue v. Chase, 1, 613.

Plaintiff's recovery cannot be defeated on the ground of defendants' adverse possession, where the evidence shows that before the statute had run the structures by which defendants held possession were carried away by flood, and rebuilt in a different place on plaintiff's land; for, as defendants were trespassers, their possession was adverse only to the extent of the land actually occupied by them.—Dietz v. Mission Transfer Co., 3, 354.

An owner of land, after conveying an undivided fraction, may hold the latter by adverse possession against the grantee, as being included in the term "the whole world."—Hartman v. Reed, 1, 858.

Where plaintiff in ejectment claims the west twenty-five feet of a certain lot on which a building is located, and the land in controversy consists of a certain number of feet off the east side of said strip of twenty-five feet, and the evidence shows that plaintiff and her grantors supposed they had located the building as far east as they claimed possession, and made no claim of possession to any land east of the building until after defendant inclosed the same, plaintiff cannot claim constructive adverse possession to the land east of said building.—Buckley v. Mohr, 6, 321.

Where in a suit to recover possession of land defendant claims title by prescription, but there is no evidence of an adverse claim, her user is, under Code of Civil Procedure, section 321, to be presumed in subordination of plaintiff's title. The presumption is not defeated by a deed to defendant which conveyed not an easement, but the title, taken in connection with circumstances tending to show the deed not bona fide.—Allen v. McKay & Co., 6, 993.

One may hold adverse possession of lands so as to acquire title, without having knowledge of the nature of the title of the real owner. Packard v. Johnson, 2, 365.

Defendant in a suit to recover possession of land claimed an easement, and the court instructed that the easement could only be sustained by proof of adverse possession for five years, and that, to have been adverse, it must have been asserted under a claim of title with knowledge and acquiescence of plaintiff. Held, that the instruction was not misleading in connection with the following instruction in which the court charged that it is not necessary to prove actual knowledge, but is sufficient if the adverse claim made and the facts were such that the plaintiffs ought to have known of their existence. Allen v. McKay & Co., 6, 993.

Where, in a suit to recover possession of land used by defendant's grantors, in connection with their mill, for booming purposes, the defendant claimed by adverse possession of the grantors, whose deed to defendant was of the mill and "appurtenances," it was not error to refuse to permit defendant to prove that mills are usually conducted with booms, and that their use is customary, there being no question as to the fact that the land in dispute was used with the mill in such a way that, assuming it to have been owned by the owners of the mill, or in their adverse possession, it would have been appurtenant thereto.—Allen v. McKay & Co., 6, 993.

§ 2.   Claim and Color of Title.

A decree adjudging that a party or his grantor was the owner or seised of some estate in the lands in controversy is a "decree or judgment of a competent court," so as to operate as color of title in favor of one who enters in good faith under such a decree and holds adversely for five years, and will entitle such person to the benefit of the statute of limitations.—Packard ·v. Johnson, 2, 365.

Code of Civil Procedure, section 321, provides that in every action for the recovery of real property the person establishing legal title is presumed to have been possessed thereof within the time required by law, and the occupation of the property by any other person is deemed to have been in subordination to the legal title, unless there has been adverse possession for five years. Held, that where, in a suit to recover realty claimed by defendant by adverse possession by herself and predecessors, there was evidence sufficient to overcome the presumption in favor of plaintiff raised by the statute, but one witness testified that one of defendant's predecessors, in answer to a direct question by plaintiff's attorney, stated he did not claim title, and accepted a license to use the land, and it appeared that another predecessor also disclaimed, the jury were justified in finding that defendant's predecessors held in subordination to plaintiff's title.—Allen v. McKay & Co., 6, 993.

§ 3.   —— Landlord and Tenant.

Code of Civil Procedure, section 326, provides that when the relation of landlord and tenant has existed the possession of the tenant is deemed the possession of the landlord until the expiration of five years from the time of the last payment of rent, though the tenant may have claimed to hold adversely. Held, that where one holding land jointly with others in subordination to the title of the owner secures a deed from the others of their interest, it will not be presumed that she then set up an adverse claim, or that the character of her possession was changed.—Allen v. McKay & Co., 6, 993.

§ 4. Notice to Owner.

In 1873 plaintiffs' grantor entered into possession of a number of lots, including the one in controversy, under a three-year lease, and retained possession of them till 1892. In 1882 he received a deed to the lot in question from a tax sale purchaser thereof, which was duly recorded, but he performed no act to change the character of his possession, and gave no notice that it was hostile. Before 1882 the lot was used by him as a cow pasture, in subordination to the owner's title. Held, that such possession did not constitute notice to the owner of said lot of the adverse character thereof.—Millett v. Lagomarsino, 4, 883.

The record of a deed from the owner of the tax title to one already in possession under permission of the owner does not affect the owner with notice that the possession of the grantee thereafter is adverse to his title.—Millett v. Lagomarsino, 4, 883.

§ 5. Payment of Taxes.

Where defendant claimed by adverse possession, but it appeared she had not paid taxes as required, refusal of instructions as to adverse possession were harmless.—Allen v. McKay & Co., 6, 993.

Code of Civil Procedure, section 325, provides that in no case shall title by adverse possession be considered established unless the party claiming such title shall have paid all taxes assessed against the land. Plaintiff and his grantor claimed title to a portion of a mining claim by adverse possession, and alleged payment of taxes by them for a period of thirteen years. Plaintiff's grantor testified that he furnished the money to his niece, and she paid the taxes. The niece and other witnesses denied that she received money from plaintiff's grantor, and stated that she paid the taxes with money belonging to her brother. The tax receipts offered in evidence confirmed the latter witnesses. Held, sufficient to sustain a finding that the taxes had not been paid by plaintiff or his grantor during the years claimed, and hence that they had not acquired title by adverse possession.—Williams v. Gross, 6, 477.

§ 6. Purchase by Occupant.

It is possible for a person in possession adversely to continue to hold adversely to an asserted title notwithstanding he has, while so in possession, purchased or attempted to purchase an interest in such title; but the fact of such purchase is admissible in evidence against him.—Cottle v. Henning, 1, 702.

§ 7. Tenants in Common.

A tenant in common does not, by merely occupying the premises, have the benefit of the statute of limitations against his cotenant, seeking by action to be admitted into the possession, unless it appears that he held adversely to the plaintiff.—Freer v. Tripp, 2, 91.

A claim of an interest in land as a cotenant is of no avail as against the person having possession of the land, who has held the same adversely under a claim of title for a period of twenty years prior to the commencement of the action.—Tully v. Tully, 2, 645.

Until the contrary appears, the possession of one tenant in common is deemed the possession of the other also; it is amicable to him until shown to be hostile, which showing must be, by acts and declarations of the person in possession, brought home to the other.—Hartman v. Reed, 1, 858.

When the statute of limitations is relied on by a tenant in possession as against his cotenant, it must, at the trial, be proved by the party so relying that his possession was hostile and not amicable, but in pleading it is sufficient to aver an open, notorious and exclusive possession as against the whole world.—Hartman v. Reed, 1, 858.

§ 8. Mexican Grant.

A person in continuous adverse possession of premises for more than five years may not be made to relinquish them to one asserting rights through an old Mexican claim who has no patent and no final confirmation of title.—Aurrecochea v. Hinckley, 1, 864.

When a plaintiff relies for recovery upon a final confirmation of title, the statute of limitations begins to run only at the issuance of the patent, and so bare possession for any time antecedent would not benefit his adversary; but, without actual issue of patent, a Mexican claim which such issue might make into a practical right cannot be recognized as a claim entitled to protection by the United States.—Aurrecochea v. Hinckley, 1, 864.

§ 9. Evidence.

A finding as to the length of an adverse possession, if made up by the court below on evidence substantially conflicting, is not to be disturbed on appeal.—Cottle v. Henning, 1, 702.

Findings reviewed, and held not supported by the evidence.—Cohen v. Mitchell, 2, 629.

On a review of the evidence, held, that the plaintiff had not acquired title by adverse possession to the whole of the premises in dispute, and judgment affirmed.—Bath v. Valdez, 2, 498.

A defendant in an action of ejectment, who had been for some twenty years in continued adverse possession of a strip of land adjoining his lot, successfully pleaded the statute of limitations against one who held the paper title to said strip, the defendant being permitted to prove by parol the continued occupation of the land in controversy by himself and the grantors of his lot.—Cook v. McKinney, 2, 711.

Where land was claimed by adverse possession, and the only evidence of actual adverse possession was testimony of defendant's superintendent that "we claimed title to the land in defendant," the evidence was insufficient.—Allen v. McKay & Co., 6, 993.

§ 10. Pleading Title by Adverse Possession.

Code of Civil Procedure, section 437, provides an answer must contain a denial of the allegations of the complaint and statement of any new matter constituting a defense or counterclaim. Held, that in a suit for possession of realty a claim of title by prescription, in order to be taken advantage of, should be pleaded.—Allen v. McKay & Co., 6, 993.

AFFIDAVIT.

For attachment. See Attachment, § 1.
For continuance. See Continuance, § 2.
On opening default. See Judgments, § 14.
On application for new trial. See New Trial, § 13.
Of service of summons. See Process, § 4.

AFFREIGHTMENT CONTRACTS.

See Shipping, § 2.

AGENCY.
See Principal and Agent.

ALIAS WRIT.
Of possession. See Ejectment, § 23.

ALIBI.
§ 1. In General.
Where the defense is alibi, it is not error to allow the people, in rebuttal, to contradict the witnesses who testified to the alibi, by disproving the collateral facts testified to by them on their direct examination as a means of fixing the time when they saw defendant at the place distant from the scene of the crime.—People v. Evans, 5, 125.

It is not error to permit the people to rebut the circumstances called out on cross examination of the witnesses to an alibi, though no foundation is laid for contradiction, where no objection is made on such ground.—People v. Evans, 5, 125.

Where the court instructed that, if the evidence tended to establish an alibi, to the extent that it raised a reasonable doubt as to defendant's guilt he should be acquitted, and gave other correct instructions on the subject, the refusal to instruct that, if the jury entertained a reasonable doubt as to the sufficiency of the evidence to establish an alibi, defendant should be acquitted, was not reversible error.—People v. Feliz, 6, 939.

ALIENS.
See Escheat.

ALIMONY.
See Divorce, §§ 9–13.

ALTERATIONS.
Of record. See Appeal and Error, § 62.
Of promissory note. See Bills and Notes, § 5.

AMENDMENT.
§ 1. Of pleading.
§ 2. —— Review on appeal.
§ 3. —— After remittitur.
§ 4. Of statement of case.
§ 5. Of judgment.
§ 6. Correction of minutes in criminal case.

Of transcript. See Appeal and Error, § 49.
Of indictment. See Indictment and Information, §§ 3–5.
Of charter. See Municipal Corporations, § 1.
Of notice of new trial. See New Trial, § 11.
Of instructions. See Trial, § 13.

§ 1. Of Pleading.
See, also, Pleading, §§ 12, 13.

In an action on a note given to settle a balance found due on a statement of accounts, the overruling of defendant's motion to amend his answer so as to attack the statement of accounts on the ground of fraud is not an abuse of discretion where the proposed amendment alleges the fraud only in general terms, without pointing out the facts which constitute it.—Clarkson v. Hoyt, 4, 547.

The point that it cannot be ascertained how the cause of action in an amended complaint is connected with the cause of action stated in the original complaint is not reached by demurrer to the amended complaint on the ground that it is "ambiguous, unintelligible, and uncertain"; it not appearing in the amended complaint what was alleged in the original.—Pottkamp v. Buss, 5, 462.

A complaint alleged that on April 1, 1891, defendant gave his note to plaintiff, and to secure payment thereof delivered a stock certificate which he had assigned to plaintiff on March 31, 1887. The prayer was for sale of the stock to apply on the overdue note, and for a personal judgment for any deficiency. An amended complaint alleged that on March 31, 1887, defendant gave his note to plaintiff, and delivered said certificate as security, and that on April 1, 1891, a new note was given in place of the old one, and the certificate redelivered to plaintiff as security for the new note. The prayer was the same, except that plaintiff waived judgment for deficiency. Held, that the amendment did not set up a different cause of action.—Malone v. Johnson, 5, 575.

§ 2. —— Review on Appeal.

The action of the court in allowing plaintiff to amend by inserting matters not set out in the notice of amendment served on defendants is not reversible error, where defendants were not injured thereby.—Wells v. Law et al., 4, 903.

Granting leave to amend pleadings at the trial will not be reversed except for abuse of discretion.—Ford v. Kenton, 5, 780.

It is not an abuse of discretion to refuse leave to amend a fourth amended complaint.—Smith v. Ferries etc. Ry. Co., 5, 889.

A cause will not be reversed by reason of a failure to allow the amendment of a pleading when no permission to amend is asked.—Butler v. Burt, 6, 917.

§ 3. —— After Remittitur.

Where the supreme court held it error to refuse permission to plaintiff to file his amended complaint, and remanded the cause "for a new trial, with leave to the parties to amend the pleadings," plaintiff may, after the remittitur goes down, file, without leave of the trial court, an amended complaint other than the one offered on the first trial.—Pottkamp v. Buss, 5, 462.

§ 4. Of Statement of Case.

After the statement of the case has been settled for an appeal, the court can allow additions to be made thereto, though the omissions arose from the negligence of the attorney.—Warner v. F. Thomas Parisian Dyeing & Cleaning Works, 4, 680.

§ 5. Of Judgment.
See, also, Judgments, § 8.

The supreme court will not amend its judgment directing a demurrer, to the complaint to be overruled, by adding thereto a direction that respondents be allowed to answer, as application for leave to answer can be made to the trial court.—Ashton v. Heydenfeldt, 6, 279.

§ 6. Correction of Minutes in Criminal Case.

In sustaining motion made by a district attorney, on the day to which a case has been continued, for the correction of the court's minutes of the day from which the continuance was had—which minutes show erroneously the granting of a new trial to the defendant—the court only exercises the ordinary power of courts to amend their records while the proceedings are in fieri, so as to make them correspond with the real facts and give a true history.—People **v.** Castro, 1, 284.

ANIMALS.

Mortgage of. See Chattel Mortgages, § 1.
Pasturage. See Landlord and Tenant, § 5.
Killing stock on railway. See Railroads, § 7. ·

§ 1. Liability for Pasturage.

Where one contracts to have cattle pastured, the fact that he does not own all of them does not affect his liability to pay for the pasturage.—Howard v. Low, 1, 82.

§ 2. Liability for Trespass.

The owner of cattle and horses is responsible for the willful **entry** therewith upon lands belonging to another and in his possession.—Martin v. Jacobs, 2, 282.

The rule as to notice to the owner, where a lien is asserted upon such cattle, etc., does not apply to this case.—Martin v. Jacobs, 2, 282.

A land owner being injured by the trespass of sheep in possession and care of defendant, the latter, under the evidence herein, is liable therefor. Testimony showing that by reason of the injury the plaintiff's stock had to be fed with hay goes only toward showing the extent of the injury, and is properly admitted.—Faber v. Cathrin, 2, 268.

Where a trespass is committed by the animals of several persons, those of one person cannot be sold to pay the damages caused by animals of others, he not having any control over them, and not having contributed to the cause of their trespassing, and no authority for such sale being given by act of March 7, 1878, concerning trespassing of animals.—Dooley v. Seventeen Thousand and Five Hundred Head of Sheep, 4, 479.

A finding that 7,000 sheep, marked with certain brands, trod down and depastured all of plaintiff's lands, being 9,460 acres, comprising ten whole and twenty fractional sections, is not supported by evidence only that they were seen on five different days and on three sections of the land, there being evidence that other sheep were seen on the lands, and it not being shown that 7,000 other sheep did not trespass on the lands as alleged in the complaint.—Dooley v. Seventeen Thousand and Five Hundred Head of Sheep, 4, 479.

ANNULMENT.

Of marriage. See Marriage, § 5.

ANSWER.

See Pleading.

APPEAL AND ERROR.

I. APPELLATE JURISDICTION.

§ 1. As Dependent upon Amount Involved.

That the supreme court may have jurisdiction of an appeal, the record must show the amount in controversy to be over $200.—Earl v. George, 1, 52.

Appeal does not lie in cases where the amount involved is less than $200.—Myers v. Liening, 1, 78.

An appeal cannot be considered where the amount in controversy, as shown by the ad damnum clause of the complaint, is less than the jurisdictional amount of the supreme court, and the "legality" of the license tax for which the action is brought is not questioned, but the contention is that a license already obtained covered the premises.—Santa Monica v. Eckert, 4, 92.

§ 2. In Case of Appeal from Justice's Court.

The supreme court has no jurisdiction over an appeal from a judgment of the superior court affirming a judgment in the justice's court for a sum within its jurisdiction.—Hackley v. Craig, 2, 289.

§ 3. In Case of Issuance of Execution.

The enforcement of a judgment by execution does not deprive defendant of the right to appeal.—Ramsbottom v. Fitzgerald, 6, 214.

§ 4. On Appeal from Order Granting New Trial.

On appeal from an order granting a new trial, the supreme court has no jurisdiction to reverse the judgment.—In re Bill's Estate, 7, 174.

27

II. APPEALABILITY OF ORDERS AND JUDGMENTS.

§ 5. In General.

Where a judgment is itself appealable, and no motion is made for a new trial, an appeal from a subsequent order refusing to set the judgment aside will not lie.—Gregory v. Gregory, 3, 836.

Under Code of Civil Procedure, section 963, allowing an appeal from a special order made after final judgment, an order denying a motion to correct a judgment or the file mark thereon is appealable, where an appeal from the judgment will not present all the facts on which the motion is based.—Tuffree v. Stearns Ranchos Co., 6, 129.

III. PARTIES.

Parties to be notified. See post, § 22.

§ 6. Persons Entitled to Appeal.

A judgment that cannot injure the appellant in any respect is not to be reviewed on appeal.—Burnett v. Tolles, 1, 519.

A person cannot appeal from a judgment who is not a party nor privy thereto, nor injured thereby.—Dunphy v. Potrero Co., 2, 408.

A party who is not injured by a judgment cannot be heard to complain on appeal from an order denying him a new trial.—Baker v. Varney, 6, 376.

§ 7. One Who has not Previously Appeared.

A person whom the record shows to be a party may appeal, though he has not previously appeared in the case.—In re Meade's Estate, 5, 678.

§ 8. Necessary Adverse Parties.

A defendant who held a second mortgage, conditioned that if the first mortgage was foreclosed his mortgage should not be foreclosed, by cross-complaint or otherwise, and who answered a foreclosure action, praying the application of surplus, if any, to his mortgage debt, and who was by the decree adjudged to hold a second mortgage, on which a certain amount of money was due, is a necessary adverse party, on whom notice must have been served of an appeal from such decree, though it merely directed the payment of the surplus into court to await a further order.—Porter v. Lassen County Land and Cattle Co., 6, 183.

IV. MAKING OBJECTIONS IN LOWER COURT AND SAVING EXCEPTIONS.

§ 9. Exceptions in General.

No exception can be regarded on appeal unless its relevance and materiality are disclosed by the record.—People v. Jenkins, 1, 77.

Exceptions taken on the ground that the findings are not supported by or are contrary to the evidence are not valid; if findings are open to such objection, the party should move for a new trial.—Hibberd v. Smith, 1, 554.

Error in granting nonsuits is an error in law which must be excepted to that it may be considered on appeal.—Nelmes v. Wilson, 4, 267.

§ 10. Objections to Testimony.

Objections to evidence as not being admissible under the allegations of the complaint cannot be raised for the first time on appeal.—Ellsworth v. Middleton, 1, 153.

If a ruling admitting an answer to a question over objection appears not to have been excepted to, it is presumed on appeal to have been acquiesced in.—Baird v. Duane, 1, 492.

The fact that a cause is tried by the court without a jury is no reason why objections to testimony should not be promptly determined and exception formally taken.—Brown v. Houser, 1, 578.

To make them matters of appeal, questions put to a witness by the trial court must be objected to at the time.—Hewlett v. Steele, 2, 157.

An objection not made to the introduction of evidence when it is offered is waived, and cannot be considered on appeal.—Yaeger v. Southern California Ry. Co., 5, 870.

§ 11. Exceptions to Instructions.

An appeal from instructions, given or refused, not appearing to have been excepted to, will not be entertained.—Native American Mining Co. v. Lockwood, 1, 5.

An exception to an oral charge will not be considered unless it was so specific as to point the trial court to any error in the charge, so that it might be corrected before the retiring of the jury.—Page v. Lynch, 2, 121.

Any error of the court as found in the charge to the jury as taken down by the court reporter is available on appeal without being excepted to or embodied in a bill of exceptions.—People v. Smith, 2, 215.

The judgment of a trial court will not be disturbed on the ground of erroneous instructions, because portions of the charge may be objectionable, if the charge itself, as a whole, fairly presents to the jury the law bearing on the evidence before them.—People v. Prather, 2, 447.

Alleged error in instructions given and in refusing other instructions cannot be considered in the absence of exceptions to the giving and refusal.—Taggart v. Bosch, 5, 690.

The appellate court will not consider an objection to oral instructions given by the trial court, where no exception was taken, nor the attention of the court called to anything objectionable therein.—Los Angeles County v. Reyes, 3, 775.

An objection to an instruction as not sufficiently explicit will not be considered, where no request was made to make it more explicit. Crowley v. Strouse, 4, 29.

An exception reading, "to said oral instructions, and each and every part thereof, and to the giving thereof by the court, the defendant then and there duly excepted," is too general.—Moore v. Moore, 4, 190.

An exception, "to which said charge, and the whole thereof, defendant then and there duly excepted," is not sufficiently specific.—Love v. Anchor Raisin Vineyard Co., 5, 425.

§ 12. Effect of Absence of Exception.

The admission of improper evidence is, on appeal, no ground for a new trial unless shown to have been objected to.—Berri v. Fitch, 1, 53.

Where there was no motion for a new trial in the court below, and the instructions, for alleged error in which the appeal has been taken, were not excepted to, the appeal is to be dismissed.—Myers v. Liening, 1, 78.

On appeal the court cannot notice rulings of the court below 'to which no exceptions have been taken.—Briggs **v.** Wangenheim, 1, 518.

§ 13. Right to Urge Questions not Raised Below.

The admission in evidence of a record which the plaintiff relied on to meet averments in the answer and ought, therefore, to have pleaded by way of replication, which he had failed to do, cannot be objected to for the first time on appeal.—Willson v. Truebody, 1, 156.

When it does not appear from the statement on motion for a new trial that the instruction complained of, as a ground for the motion, was excepted to at the trial, the exception cannot be taken for the first time on appeal from the order denying the motion.—Couldthirst v. Kelley, 1, 796.

An objection that the notice of motion for a new trial and the supporting statement came too late to be available cannot be raised for the first time on appeal.—Hill v. Gwinn, 1, 882.

A point urged on appeal, as to which point no exception was taken at the trial, will not be considered.—Hewlett v. Steele, 2, 157.

Where it is not objected, at the time a motion for a new trial was passed on, that notice of motion was not given, it will be presumed on appeal that the notice was given.—Gage v. Downey, 3, 7.

A judgment in an action by the assignee of an insolvent will not be reversed on the ground, raised for the first time on appeal, that the complaint contained no averment showing that in the proceedings for plaintiff's appointment a copy of the petition filed by creditors was served on the insolvent, as required by statute, the record being silent on the subject.—Stewart v. Dunlap, 4, 503.

Error in the admission of evidence will not be considered on appeal, where no exception is taken to the ruling admitting it.—McVey v. Beam, 4, 903.

Where questions, the determination of which is essential to the full adjustment of the equities between the parties, were not presented to the trial court for determination, and the findings of that court upon the issues submitted are supported by the evidence, its judgment, warranted by such findings, will not be reversed on appeal.—California Loan & Trust Co. v. Hammell, 5, 282.

An objection that the legal and equitable issues on a summary proceeding for unlawful detainer were tried together cannot be raised for the first time on appeal.—Diggs v. Porteus, 5, 753.

V. PROCEEDINGS TO PERFECT APPEAL AND TIME THEREFOR.

§ 14. Manner of Taking Appeal in General.

In order to have the court consider an appeal the appellant must bring it agreeably to the one hundred and ninety-fifth section of the Practice Act; gross irregularities in the manner of bringing the case up cannot be overlooked.—Black v. Goodin, 1, 155.

An appeal presented on documents of an irregular sort not in accord with the statutory requirements for bringing cases up on appeal will not be considered.—People v. Mellon, 1, 543.

§ 15. Time to Appeal in General.

The right of appeal from an order granting a new trial may not be kept alive by the court's vacating its order, once duly made, and thereafter virtually reinstating it.—Nichols v. Dunphy, 2, 143.

Where an appeal is taken before the determination of appellant's motion for a new trial on account of a statute requiring appeals to be taken within a certain time after the rendition of the judgment, and a new trial is afterward granted by the trial court, the appeal will be dismissed.—Blackburn v. Abila, 4, 982.

An appeal may be taken from an order denying a motion for new trial, when made within proper time after the denial, though the time limited for appeal from the final judgment has expired.—Houser & Haines Mfg. Co. v. Hargrove, 6, 384.

Under the direct provisions of Code of Civil Procedure, section 939, subdivision 3, an appeal from an order dismissing proceedings for the settlement of a statement to be used on motion for new trial and all proceedings for a new trial may only be taken within sixty days after the order is entered.—Prine v. Duncan, 7, 330.

Code of Civil Procedure, sections 941a–941c, as amended by Laws of 1907, page 753, chapter 410, providing for a new method of appeal, did not take effect, by reason of Political Code, section 323, until sixty days after the date of approval by the governor, and an appeal taken during the sixty days was not affected thereby.—Pedley v. Werdin, 7, 360.

§ 16. —— When Sufficiency of Evidence Questioned.

When an appeal is taken within sixty days after judgment, a bill of exceptions, containing the evidence, may, even though there is no motion for a new trial, be looked into to determine whether it is sufficient to support the verdict under Code of Civil Procedure, section 939, providing that such exceptions cannot be reviewed unless the appeal be taken within sixty days.—Perkins v. Cooper, 3, 279.

Under Code of Civil Procedure of California, section 939, providing that an exception to the decision or verdict because not supported by the evidence cannot be reviewed unless the appeal is taken within sixty days after the rendition of the judgment, an appeal from a decree settling an administrator's account, taken within the statutory time after the entry of the decree, but not within sixty days after the decision and the filing of the findings, is not in time to present the question of the insufficiency of the evidence.—In re Rose's Estate, 3, 50.

Under Code of Civil Procedure, section 939, permitting an appeal within a year of entry of judgment, but inhibiting consideration of an exception to the decision, as being unsupported by evidence, unless the appeal is within sixty days after rendition of judgment, the evidence cannot be considered on an appeal taken after the sixty days.—Nelmes v. Wilson, 4, 267.

Where no motion for a new trial is made, the question whether the judgment is supported by the evidence will not be considered on appeal unless the appeal is taken within sixty days after the rendition of the judgment on a bill of exceptions setting out the evidence.—Steen v. Henry, 4, 916.

Under Code of Civil Procedure, section 939, providing that an exception to the decision or verdict on the ground that it is not supported by the evidence cannot be reviewed unless the appeal from the judgment is taken within sixty days after its rendition, the judgment must be affirmed where only ground urged on an appeal not taken within sixty days is that the evidence was insufficient to sustain certain findings of fact.—Rhoads v. Gray, 5, 664.

Under Code of Civil Procedure, section 939, providing that "an exception to the decision on the ground that it is not supported by the evidence cannot be reviewed on appeal from the judgment unless the appeal is taken within sixty days after the rendition of the judgment," on an appeal taken in May from a judgment entered the preceding August the bill of exceptions cannot be examined for the purpose of reviewing the sufficiency of evidence.—People v. Jones, 7, 64.

§ 17. —— When Time Begins to Run.

An order entering judgment nunc pro tunc does not deprive a party of his right to appeal. The time for appeal dates from the actual entry of the judgment.—Noce v. Daveggio, 2, 354.

An appeal is taken under Code of Civil Procedure, section 940, when notice of appeal is served and filed, though the undertaking by which the appeal is perfected is not filed till afterward.—Perkins v. Cooper, 3, 279.

Time for appeal by interveners commences to run from time complaint in intervention is stricken out for want of interest, not from time of judgment between original parties.—More v. Miller, 6, 78.

Under Code of Civil Procedure, section 939, fixing the time within which to appeal from a judgment after the entry of judgment, the time to appeal begins to run from the moment of the actual entry of the judgment.—Pedley v. Werdin, 7, 360.

§ 18. —— Prematurity in Taking Appeal.

An appeal from a final judgment before its entry is premature, inasmuch as the time within which such appeal may be taken does not begin to run until the entry.—More v. Miller, 6, 110.

An appeal, taken before the judgment is entered of record, as required by Code of Civil Procedure, section 668, is premature, and must be dismissed, though the judgment entered after the notice of appeal was entered nunc pro tunc as of a date prior thereto.—Pedley v. Werdin, 7, 360.

§ 19. —— Expiration of Time, and Dismissal of Appeal.

An appeal taken from a judgment after one year from its rendition cannot be entertained.—Larue v. Chase, 1, 613.

An appeal from a judgment which is not taken within a year after the entry of the final judgment, as required by Code of Civil Procedure, section 939, will be dismissed.—Bunting v. Salz, 3, 193.

An appeal not taken within the time prescribed by law will be dismissed.—Childs et al. v. Kincaid, 3, 503.

An appeal from a judgment should be dismissed where it is not taken until more than two years after the entry thereof.—Hooper v. Patterson, 3, 811.

An appeal from an order denying a new trial, not taken within sixty days after the order is entered on the minutes of the court (Code Civ. Proc., sec. 939), will be dismissed.—Esrey v. Southern Pacific Co., 4, 402.

An appeal from a decree, not taken within a year from its entry, will be dismissed.—Raskin v. Robarts, 4, 465.

An appeal not filed within the time prescribed by court rules will be dismissed, no good cause for the delay being shown, though no notice of the motion to dismiss was served on appellant's assignee in insolvency, he having, however, knowledge of the notice served on appellant's attorneys.—Burr v. Navarro Mill Co., 4, 471.

An appeal, not having been taken within the statutory time, will be dismissed.—Fitzgerald v. Fitzgerald, 4, 664.

§ 20. Notice of Appeal in General.

The notice of appeal is a document of which the trial court has exclusive control, and the supreme court has no power to allow an amendment of either it or the admission of service having reference to it.—Brooks v. Lubbock, 1, 210.

The rule of the supreme court that "transcripts used on appeal must show that a notice of appeal has been duly served upon the other side" does not justify a respondent in raising the point of service after the appeal has been taken, for the first time then denying the fact, when the certificate of the clerk to the transcript establishes the existence of the original document on file in his office and the record shows the acknowledgment of service with the name of the respondent affixed.—Western Pacific R. R. Co. v. Reed, 1, 327.

When the original transcript does not show that the notice of appeal was served on plaintiff's attorney of record, and a motion to dismiss on that ground is made, such motion may be overruled if the defendant, upon leave, files a certificate of the clerk of the court below showing that proof of service of such notice is on file in the clerk's office.—Nissen v. Bendixsen, 2, 285.

The fact that one of the defendants in whose favor a judgment was rendered in an action in which he was sued as administrator was convicted of embezzlement is not cause for dismissing an appeal, as in such case the administrator does not become civiliter mortuus, so that no notice of appeal could be served on him or his attorney.— Brown v. Mann, 2, 627.

Where the affidavit of service on the adverse attorney of a notice of motion to dismiss an appeal does not show that any attempt was made to serve him at his office between the hours of 8 o'clock A. M. and 6 o'clock P. M. of the day when the notice was left at his residence, the motion to dismiss will be denied.—Sneath v. Waterman, 3, 483.

An appeal will be ineffectual where the notice of appeal was not signed by the attorney of record, or of counsel for appellant, or where no proof is shown of service of the notice of appeal upon the respondent.—Ellis v. Bennett, 2, 302.

An appeal will be dismissed where the record does not show service of the notice of appeal, required by Penal Code, section 1240, and no certificate of the clerk that there was service has been filed, though permission to file such certificate, on the ground that the failure of the record to show such service was due to an error of the printer, was asked several months before the dismissal.—People v. Swearinger, 4, 964.

When a notice of appeal is for "errors of law occurring at the trial," the appellate court will not consider irregularity in the proceedings of the court, the appeal being made from an order denying a new trial, and such questions not being presented to the trial court on the motion.—Yaeger v. Southern California Ry. Co., 5, 870.

Where there is no properly certified copy of the notice of appeal in the record of the appeal, the appellant, on motion, may be authorized to complete the record by supplying the defect.—Swortfiguer v. White, 6, 778.

§ 21. —— Time for Giving or Serving.

An appeal is not taken, in fact, unless the notice is served contemporaneously with or after the filing of it.—Lubbock v. Brooks, 1, 212.

By failing to file the notice of appeal before the lapse of the statutory time for filing it, a party who would appeal from a judgment loses the right.—Harper v. Minor, 1, 225.

As no appeal is instituted by the service of a notice of appeal after the time to appeal has expired, an order will not be made dismissing such an attempted appeal.—In re Walkerly's Estate, 4, 819.

An appeal will be dismissed where the notice thereof is not given within the statutory time.—Southern California R. Co. v. Slauson, 6, 874.

Where a notice of appeal from a judgment was duly served on the adverse party, and the notice and an undertaking to perfect the appeal were on the same day filed in the trial court, the appeal was properly taken.—Stewart v. Burbridge, 7, 356.

§ 22. —— Parties to be Notified.

A party not served with a notice of appeal is not before the appellate court so that the appellant's rights as against him may be considered.—McLeod v. Davis, 1, 763.

An appeal by lien claimants, who have obtained a personal judgment against the mortgagor's grantee, from an adjudication that their liens are invalid as against the lien of a prior mortgage, will be dismissed, where the notice of appeal has not been served on the mortgagor and his grantee.—Pacific Mut. Life Ins. Co. v. Fisher, 4, 980.

In an action to foreclose a mortgage, the owners of two-thirds of the property alleged that plaintiff, as mortgagee, had been in possession and received certain rents and profits, and prayed for an accounting. A demurrer to this answer having been sustained, judgment was rendered against such owners, and they appealed. The owner of the other third interest consented to judgment for plaintiff, the latter having waived a deficiency judgment. The mortgage debt bore interest at eight per cent, and the judgment at seven. Held, that notice of appeal must be served on the owner of the one-third interest, since he would be injuriously affected by a reversal of the judgment.—De Arnaz v. Jaynes, 4, 226.

An appeal will be dismissed, where notice was not served on all parties interested.—In re Walkerley's Estate, 5, 5.

Under Code of Civil Procedure, section 940, requiring notice of appeal to be served on the adverse party or his attorney, and section 1015, requiring the service of papers on the attorney, instead of the party, where he appears by attorney, notice of appeal must be served on appellee's attorney, if he have one.—Jones v. McGarvey, 6, 277.

Where, in an action concerning the separate property of a wife, whose husband defaulted, it appears that pending a motion for a new trial such wife died, whereupon all parties consented to the substitution of her administrator, and notice of appeal was served on him, a motion to dismiss the appeal on the ground that such husband and wife had not been served with notice of the appeal is of no avail.—Gardner v. Stare, 6, 777.

§ 23. Bond or Undertaking in General.

An undertaking on appeal filed more than a month before the notice of appeal is filed is no undertaking at all, and an appeal based thereon must be dismissed.—Iverson v. Jones, 2, 437.

Under Code of Civil Procedure, section 940, requiring an undertaking to be filed or waived within five days after service of notice of appeal, the waiver must be made within the five days, but it need not be filed within that time. Perkins v. Cooper, 25 Pac. 411, 87 Cal. 241, followed.—Newman v. Maldonado, 3, 540.

The provision of Code of Civil Procedure, section 953, that the clerk or attorneys shall certify that an undertaking on appeal in due form has been filed, is not complied with by a general certificate that the record is correct.—Jones v. Iverson, 3, 707.

A county officer, against whom suit has been brought, is not exempt from filing an undertaking on appeal by Code of Civil Procedure, section 1058, declaring that in any civil action wherein the state is plaintiff, or any state officer in his official capacity or on behalf of the state, or any county, city, or town, is plaintiff or defendant, no undertaking shall, as to such parties, be required.—Von Schmidt v. Widber, 3, 835.

Where a surety on an appeal bond disposes of his property pending the appeal, the court cannot require appellant to file a new bond in the absence of a statute authorizing it to do so.—Macomber v. Conradt, 4, 723.

Where no undertaking has been filed to perfect an appeal from an order denying a motion for a new trial, the appeal will be dismissed.—Stewart v. Burbridge, 7, 356.

§ 24. —— Sufficiency and Validity.

The act of 1861 (Laws of 1861, p. 589) prescribes the course to be pursued by appellants in order to avoid a dismissal for insufficiency of an undertaking on appeal, and an application to that end not in accordance with the statute will not be granted.—People v. Fannon, 1, 158.

The petition and bond for removal, and order thereon, are not a part of the judgment-roll, and the bond not being signed by the principal, it is insufficient. The judgment must therefore be affirmed. Rough v. Booth, 2, 270.

Where an appeal bond is signed by one Ball as surety, but by a clerical error the judgment is against Bell, and the record shows the error and contains the data necessary to correct it, the error should be corrected by the trial court on motion of any party to the judgment.—First Nat. Bank of Santa Monica v. Kowalsky, 3, 759.

Where an appeal is taken from the judgment, and also from the order denying a new trial, an undertaking which recites only that it was in consideration of the appeal from the judgment is ineffectual as to the appeal from the order.—Rhoads v. Gray, 5, 664.

Where the notice of appeal specifies that it is taken from the judgment, and from an order denying a new trial, and the undertaking is one on appeal from the judgment only, the appeal from the order will be dismissed.—McRae v. Argonaut Land & Dev. Co., 6, 145.

An appeal bond must conform to the notice of appeal.—Stockton School District v. Goodell, 6, 277.

§ 25. —— Corporation as Surety.

Under article 4, section 25, of the constitution of California, the act of legislature of March 12, 1885, is void, in so far as it attempts to authorize the acceptance of a corporation as sole and sufficient surety in an undertaking on appeal.—Cramer v. Tittle, 2, 715.

§ 26. —— Justification and Approval.

Upon exceptions being duly served on the appellant by the respondent to the sufficiency of the sureties executing the undertaking filed with the notice of appeal, it is not sufficient that the respondent be notified that the sureties will justify within two days thereafter, when the notice does not specify the officer before whom or the time of the day at which the sureties are to justify.—People ex rel. Scott v. Fannon, 1, 158.

The approval of an undertaking, on appeal to the supreme court, may be set aside by the superior court, and the power to set it aside is not taken away by the filing of a transcript in the supreme court.—Palmer v. Galvin, 2, 446.

§ 27. —— Liability of Sureties.

Liability on an appeal bond does not attach upon reversal of the judgment appealed from with directions to enter a different judgment.—Chase v. Ries, 1, 67.

A judgment against a surety on an appeal bond, rendered more than thirty days after the filing of a remittitur from the supreme court, is valid, though the surety had no notice of the motion therefor; since the undertaking, as prescribed by Code of Civil Procedure, section 942, is that "if the appellant does not make such payment within thirty days after the filing of the remittitur from the supreme court in the court from which the appeal is taken, judgment may be entered, on motion of the respondent, in his favor, against the sureties, for such amount together with interest." This is an express waiver of further notice.—Mowry v. Heney, 3, 277.

An action cannot be maintained on an appeal bond given to stay a judgment for the delivery of certain hay, or for $299, the value thereof, the bond being conditioned, under Code of Civil Procedure, section 978, to pay the judgment if the appeal be dismissed, unless it is shown that an execution has been issued since the dismissal of the appeal, or a demand for the property made, or that a delivery thereof cannot be had, since it was necessary that this should appear before the money judgment could be payable.—Pieper v. Peers et al., 3, 646.

VI. EFFECT OF APPEAL AND STAY OF PROCEEDINGS.

§ 28. Effect on Jurisdiction of Trial Court.

An appeal from an order does not devest the trial court of jurisdiction to make subsequent orders in the cause, but, at most, is only matter in abatement.—Gardner v. Stare, 6, 945.

§ 29. Order of Stay by Supreme Court.

The supreme court may order a stay of proceedings on a judgment appealed from on the filing of a sufficient bond for the protection of the respondent.—McClatchy v. Sperry, 6, 345.

§ 30. Effect of Undertaking as Stay.

Upon taking the appeal, the filing of the undertaking, for $300, required by section 941, Code of Civil Procedure of California, had the effect of staying execution of the judgment as to appellant. Motion to stay execution granted.—Cummings v. Cummings, 2, 744.

VII. RECORD, BILL OF EXCEPTIONS AND STATEMENT.

§ 31. Scope and Contents of Record.

An appeal from an order denying a continuance will not be considered when the affidavits upon which the application was made are not embodied in the statement or bill of exceptions.—Robles v. Robles, 1, 58.

A point urged on appeal, based upon the trial court's opinion which is no part of the record, will not be considered.—Hewlett v. Steele, 2, 157.

Where the record purports to contain copies of an undertaking on appeal and of an affidavit alleging that the cause in which such undertaking was given had been affirmed, and asking judgment against the sureties on such undertaking, and the documents are not embodied in the bill of exceptions or otherwise authenticated, they cannot be considered on appeal.—Los Angeles National Bank v Chandler, 7, 340.

§ 32. Judgment-roll.

An appeal brought up on a judgment-roll does not need a statement to be annexed to the judgment-roll.—Wright v. Treganza, 1, 325.

Exceptions taken at the trial and settled when taken, as prescribed by sections 188–190 of the Practice Act, are annexed to and become part of the judgment-roll, and on appeal the judgment-roll will be considered.—Wetherbee v. Davis, 1, 403.

On an appeal from the judgment alone, supported by a statement on appeal, the question as to whether the proper judgment was rendered cannot be looked into, unless there are written findings or an agreed statement of facts forming a part of the judgment-roll.—Semple v. Ware, 1, 657.

On an appeal on the judgment-roll alone, there being no statement or bill of exceptions annexed, where an appeal from an order denying a new trial has been abandoned, the judgment is to be affirmed if the evidence justifies the findings.—McLeod v. Davis, 1, 763.

On appeal from a judgment, brought up on the judgment-roll, if the complaint states facts sufficient to constitute a cause of action and the findings support the judgment, the latter is not to be disturbed.—Hayes v. Kinsman, 2, 168.

An appeal from a judgment, and from an order discharging a rule requiring plaintiff to show cause, etc., will be dismissed when the transcript does not contain a copy of the judgment-roll.—Dorland v. Bernal, 3, 75.

Where an appeal from an order denying a new trial is dismissed for want of an undertaking, only such questions can be considered as arise upon the judgment-roll.—Broker v. Taylor, 5, 250.

§ 33. Defect not Cured by Certificate.

The evidence stated in the record must be agreed on by the parties and signed by the trial judge, and a record defective in this regard is not made good by being certified by the judge to be correct.—Berri v. Fitch, 1, 53.

§ 34. What Should be Shown by Record.

An appeal from the overruling of an objection to testimony must show on what grounds the objection was based, whether the court ruled on it, and, if it did rule, that an exception was taken to the ruling.—Kellogg v. Crippen, 1, 161.

On appeal from an order disposing of a motion for a new trial the record should always show, either by a copy of the order or by direct statement, what the ruling was and what the appeal is from.—Watts v. Crawford, 1, 355.

An objection to the record on the ground that it does not show what was the ruling appealed from on the motion below for a new trial will not be considered if not taken in time under the rule.—Watts v. Crawford, 1, 355.

The record should show the action of the court below in admitting or rejecting matter of proof and the exceptions, if any, in each instance, so that an aggrieved party may, through the instrumentality of his exceptions, have the points of grievance considered on appeal. Brown v. Houser, 1, 578.

An appeal from a judgment cannot be considered if the record shows no entry of it.—Meysan v. Chabrie, 2, 508.

A judgment will not be reversed because of the failure of the trial court to find on issues the burden of proving which was on appellant, unless he shows by bill of exceptions or by statement that he offered evidence in support thereof, sufficient, in the absence of countervailing evidence, to justify a finding in his favor thereon.—Newman v. Maldonado, 3, 540.

Where error is predicated on the court's failure to give certain instructions, they must appear in the record.—Becker v. Feigenbaum, 5, 408.

§ 35. Matters not Shown by Record.

On appeal from an order of court granting a new trial, where no briefs are presented, and there is nothing to show upon what grounds the court granted the motion, the order will be affirmed.—Hughes v. Thompson, 2, 841.

On appeal from a judgment on the judgment-roll alone, which shows that the judgment was entered on default of defendant to answer or demur to an amended complaint, the objection that the amended complaint was not filed within the time provided in the order allowing the amendment, and that it does not affirmatively appear that the time was extended, will not be considered, as the order allowing the amendment is no part of the judgment-roll.—Carter v. Paige, 3, 64.

A finding by the court that the cause of action was barred by the statute of limitations will not be disturbed on appeal where the evidence is not brought up, and nothing appears in the record to the contrary.—Janes v. De Azevedo, 3, 556.

A contention on appeal that the court erred in matter of law in rejecting a part of appellant's counterclaim cannot be considered where there is no foundation for the point in record, either by exception or specification.—Young v. Donegan, 3, 486.

Where the transcript shows that the findings of fact cover all the issues raised by the pleadings, and the judgment follows and is in conformity with the findings and conclusions of law drawn therefrom, affidavits, though contained in the transcript, claiming that a litigant had been erroneously denied a jury trial by the court, will not be regarded on appeal, where it does not appear that the affidavits were served on the adverse party, or were filed in court or certified to as having been used at the hearing on a motion for a new trial.—Wilkes v. Tibbets, 3, 708.

A finding by the trial court that plaintiffs' causes of action are barred by limitation is conclusive on appeal, where no exceptions were taken to such finding, and where the appeal was not taken within sixty days after judgment rendered.—Richardson v. Dunne, 3, 728.

The denial of a motion for a new trial on the ground of insufficiency of evidence will not be reviewed where the bill of exceptions on which the motion was made contains no exception on that ground, and no specification of any particular in which it is claimed the evidence was insufficient.—Davis v. Lamb, 5, 765.

Where defendant demurred to the complaint, but the record did not show that the demurrer was passed on, or that any ruling thereon was called for, but defendant afterward answered, the demurrer must be deemed to have been waived on appeal.—Diamond Coal Co. v. Cook, 6, 446.

Complaint cannot be made on appeal that the court made no disposition of a demurrer, the record not showing it was presented to the court.—O'Neil v. McLennan, 7, 161.

In action on a note given for an option to purchase lots, matters of testimony or exhibits constituting title or showing some kind of an agreement, as to which there is no mention in the record, cannot be considered on appeal from the judgment.—Bryant v. Hawley, 7, 342.

§ 35½. Statement in General.

The power to grant new trials is conferred upon all the courts referred to in the Practice Act, and when an appeal lies to the supreme court from an order disposing of a motion for a new trial, it becomes the duty of the trial judge to settle a correct statement properly presented.—Grow v. Rosborough, 1, 258.

Under the Practice Act, when a statement on appeal is proposed, a copy must be served upon the respondent, who may thereafter prepare his amendments and serve them upon the appellant.—More v. Massini, 1, 655.

A motion on the minutes for a new trial having been overruled, the only statement that could then be pending is a statement on appeal, and the time for that having expired, and no transcript having been filed in the time limited, the appeal will be dismissed.—Buckley v. Althoff, 3, 282.

Code of Civil Procedure, section 950, provides: "On an appeal from a final judgment, the appellant must furnish the court with a copy of the notice of appeal, of the judgment-roll, and of any bill of exceptions or statement in the case on which the appellant relies. Any statement used on motion for a new trial, or settled after decision of such motion, when the motion is made upon the minutes of the court, as provided in section 661, or any bill of exceptions settled, as provided in sections 649 or 650, or used on motion for a new trial, may be used on appeal from a final judgment equally as upon appeal from the order granting or refusing the new trial." Held, not to give a party intending to appeal from a judgment an independent right to have settled a statement of the case for the use of such appeal, but to limit him to the use of such statements only as have been regularly and legally settled in the course of some proceeding on motion for a new trial.—Vinson v. Los Angeles Pacific R. R. Co., 7, 142.

§ 36. Certificate of Statement.

The only evidence the court may notice on appeal, in respect of the fact that the statement in the record is the engrossed statement on which the motion for a new trial was heard, is the certificate required in that connection by the statute.—Twiss v. Preuss, 1, 571.

On appeal from an order denying a motion for a new trial when the certificate by the trial court is to the effect that the statement is "settled by adding thereto the amendments," etc., and it does not appear that any amendments were added, and what is offered by way of statement in the transcript is not shown on its face to be the engrossed statement on motion for a new trial, the court cannot consider the appeal.—Twiss v. Preuss, 1, 571.

With an unauthenticated statement of a motion for a new trial and with no point made on the judgment-roll there is nothing before the court.—Hart v. Tibbetts, 2, 218.

A statement on motion for a new trial, when certified by the judge of the court in the manner provided by law, and filed with the clerk, becomes part of the record; and if the notice of motion for a new trial specifies that such motion will be based on a statement of the case, it will be presumed that such statement, prepared, settled and filed, was used on the hearing of the motion; and on appeal, if it is part of the record certified by the clerk, it will be considered, without further identification or proof, that it was used on the motion for a new trial.—Williams v. Southern Pac. R. Co., 2, 613.

§ 37.   Insufficiency of Statement.

Where the statement is so imperfect that it is impossible to ascertain the merits, the judgment will be affirmed.—Knowles v. Calderwood, 1, 80.

If the notice of a motion for a new trial designates as its ground the insufficiency of the evidence to justify the verdict, and the statement fails to specify the particulars in which such evidence lacks sufficiency, the statement is to be disregarded.—Quinn v. Kenyon, 1, 128.

The grounds for a notice of motion for a new trial, on which a party relies on appeal, should, so far as they relate to the matters appearing in the statement, be shown in some manner in such statement; however, unless objected to by the opposing party, the appeal will be heard as if they were so shown.—Doll v. McCumber, 1, 135.

No question as to the effect of a document introduced in evidence is presented by a statement that fails to show that at the trial such introduction was objected to, or what was the trial court's ruling, if any, in that connection.—People v. Parrott, 1, 412.

A statement that contains the evidence but no ruling excepted to on any part of it is insufficient on appeal from the judgment only. People v. Parrott, 1, 412.

In a statement on appeal it is not sufficient to have indicated what "the evidence tended to show," but the court must have the evidence itself submitted for the exercise of its own opinion as to the tendency. Valentine v. Jansen, 1, 525.

A mere proposed statement on motion for a new trial, or a statement not first agreed upon by counsel or certified by the trial court, will not be considered on appeal from an order denying the motion.—Bensley v. Lewis, 1, 633.

Where, on appeal from an order denying a new trial, the statement as certified by the trial judge contained a summary of the evidence, but made no mention of any exceptions to evidence or other errors of law alleged to have occurred at the trial, and excepted to by plaintiff, such exceptions and errors cannot be considered.—Springer v. Springer, 6, 662.

§ 38.   Necessity of Statement.

The only mode by which an order of court, not made upon affidavits alone, can be brought up on appeal, so as to merit consideration, is by a statement made subsequently to the trial, both parties participating in and settling it.—Wetherbee v. Davis, 1, 403.

Upon an appeal from an order which is not based solely on affidavits, review will not be had unless a statement on appeal is annexed to the order.—Rousset v. Boyle, 1, 768.

§ 39.   Absence of Statement.

Where there is neither statement nor bill of exceptions, the appeal will not be considered.—People v. Davis, 1, 45.

One appealing from a judgment may bring his appeal on the judgment-roll with or without a statement as he may desire, but if without, then nothing outside of the judgment-roll will be considered.—Wetherbee v. Davis, 1, 403.

Without regard to whether a stipulation to the effect that the foregoing so many pages constitute, etc., enumerating essential papers, precludes a respondent from denying the correctness of a bill of exceptions, etc., so referred to, such a stipulation does not dispense with the statement on appeal required by statute.—Wetherbee v. Davis, 1, 403.

No exception, save those annexed to the judgment-roll, will be considered on appeal, unless there is a statement in the preparation of which both parties were heard.—Wetherbee v. Davis, 1, 403.

Where, on appeal, there is neither a bill of exceptions nor a statement of the evidence, the findings of fact will be accepted as true.—In re Smith's Estate, 4, 919.

§ 40. Bill of Exceptions—Contents and Sufficiency.

Although all the testimony need not be embodied in the statement of the case or in a bill of exceptions, there should be enough of it there to disclose to the court the points in controversy.—Graham v. Gregory, 1, 13.

When the appeal is based solely on errors during the trial and instructions given the jury, and the bill sets out neither the evidence nor the instructions, judgment is to be affirmed.—People v. Godkins, 1, 61.

Evidence of facts relied on to overcome the statute of limitations, set up as a defense, must appear in the bill of exceptions in order to be considered on appeal.—McCracken v. Pacific Commercial Co., 2, 172.

On appeal from a judgment on the pleadings, the bill of exceptions must show that the appellant excepted to the order granting the motion for judgment, or that he was absent from court when the order was granted, in which case the order is deemed to have been excepted to: Code Civ. Proc., sec. 647.—Lamet v. Miller, 2, 679.

Under Code of Civil Procedure of California, section 648, providing that, where an exception to a decision is on the ground of the insufficiency of the evidence to justify it, the objection must be stated, with so much of the evidence or other matter as is necessary to explain it, a bill of exceptions which merely sets forth the other findings of fact, and that such facts are established by the evidence, is not properly a bill of exceptions, stating evidence in compliance with above statute.—Cox v. McLaughlin, 2, 858.

A paper in the transcript, denominated a "bill of exceptions," not certified by the clerk to be a correct copy of any bill of exceptions on file, and not containing any specific exceptions to any particular finding of the court, will not be considered by the supreme court.—Helsel v. Seeger, 4, 236.

§ 41. Presentation and Settlement of Bill.

A court may settle a bill of exceptions notwithstanding delay in presenting it for the purpose, when the delay has been the result of arrangement by the opposing attorneys from motives of accommodation.—Claffey v. Head, 2, 156.

Under Code of Civil Procedure, section 652, providing that, if a judge refuses to allow an exception in accordance with the facts, the party desiring the bill settled may apply by petition to the supreme court to prove the same, such an application will be granted where the petitioner alleges that a bill settled by the judge is not in accordance with the facts, pointing out the particulars in which it is incorrect, and the judge alleges that the bill is true.—Curran v. Kennedy, 3, 259.

Where the only defense to a motion to dismiss an appeal is that the trial court has refused to settle a bill of exceptions, and that mandamus is pending in the appellate court to compel such settlement, on the refusal of the writ of mandamus the appeal will be dismissed. Reid v. Kowalsky, 6, 823.

Where the failure to have a bill of exceptions, which an appellant has proposed to be used on an appeal, settled, was not caused by any fault or laches of such appellant, a motion to dismiss the appeal will not be granted.—Crooks v. Crooks, 6, 878.

§ 42. Certification of Bill.

Where there is no bill of exceptions, nor certificate of the judge that the papers printed in the transcript were used on the hearing of the motion which resulted in the making of the order appealed from, the order will not be reviewed.—Weiner v. Korn, 2, 342.

A petition for leave to prove a bill of exceptions, and to have the same certified as correct, in the supreme court, under section 652 of the California Code of Civil Procedure, sufficiently "sets forth the exceptions taken, and the evidence in support thereof," if it has annexed to it, and made a part of it, as an exhibit, a writing containing the evidence, rulings and exceptions taken on the hearing in the court below.—Estate of Hawes, 2, 656.

§ 43. Necessity for Bill of Exceptions.

Where the whole case appears on the record, no bill of exceptions is requisite, the purpose of the bill of exceptions being to place on the record that which, without it, would not appear.—In re Ling, 2, 490.

§ 44. Absence of Bill of Exceptions.

In the absence of a bill of exceptions the transcript is held as showing no error.—People v. Reynolds, 2, 186.

With no valid bill of exceptions before it, or valid statement of the evidence, the appellate court must presume correctness on the part of the court below in granting a new trial.—Garnier v. Grimaud, 2, 214.

In the absence of a bill of exceptions, the order denying defendant's motion for a new trial will not be reviewed on appeal.—Williams v. Benicia Water Co., 2, 342.

After the case was given to the jury, counsel for defendant said that he desired certain exceptions entered, to which the judge replied, "Have any exceptions entered that you. desire," and in answer to counsel's question, "Shall I have the clerk enter them?" the judge replied, "If you choose to do so." Counsel, however, never had any exception entered, either by the court or clerk, and never prepared or had settled any bill of exceptions. Held, that this did not entitle defendant to a review of the rulings.—Sukeforth v. Lord, 3, 238.

§ 45. Transcript—Time for Filing.

A transcript on appeal is filed within the time prescribed by rule 2 of the supreme court if filed on August 5, 1885, where the notice of appeal was filed on June 3d, of the same year, and the bill of exceptions settled on July 1st, and filed July 2d.—Horton v. Dominguez, 2, 548.

The filing of a transcript on appeal, within forty days after the bill of exceptions is settled, is a sufficient compliance with rule 2, supreme court of California, requiring the transcript to be filed within forty days after appeal taken.—Newman v. Bank of California, 2, 793.

An appeal was taken, and the appellant also brought a mandamus as to the same controversy; and the appellant was granted forty days after the decision of the mandamus proceeding in which to prepare, serve and file the printed transcript in the appeal case. The mandamus proceeding was in bank, and determined adversely to the appellant, but he presented no petition for a rehearing. Held, that the time to prepare and file the transcript commenced to run on the determination of the mandamus proceeding, instead of after the expiration of thirty days thereafter in which a rehearing could be granted.—Brunnings v. Townsend, 6, 647.

A motion for a new trial in an action to quiet title was denied upon condition that plaintiff consent to an amendment of the findings and judgment, and the order denying the motion stated that defendant's counsel should prepare an order specifying in detail the amendment to be made, and it was provided that, if plaintiff did not consent within ten days, a new trial should be granted. Some four months later an order was made reciting the pendency of the motion for a new trial, specifying the amendment to be made and stating that if plaintiff failed to consent to the amendment within ten days a new trial would be granted. Plaintiff at no time consented to the amendment. Held, that ten days within which plaintiff might consent to the amendment and avoid the new trial did not begin to run until after the making of the second order, so that it was not until after the expiration of ten days from that time that the forty days allowed for the filing of a transcript on appeal began to run.—Shepard v. F. A. Robbins Press Works, 7, 259.

§ 46. —— Extension of Time.

Supreme court rule provides: "The appellant in a civil action shall, within forty days after the appeal is perfected and the bill of exceptions and the statement (if there be any) are settled, serve and file the printed transcript of the record." Code of Civil Procedure, section 661, provides: "The judgment-roll and a statement to be subsequently prepared, with a copy of the order, shall constitute the record on appeal from the order granting or refusing a new trial. Such subsequent statement shall be proposed by the party appealing . . . . within ten days after the entry of the order . . . . but the statement shall only contain the grounds argued before the court for a new trial, and so much of the evidence or other matter as may be necessary to explain them." Held, that the pendency of proceedings to settle a statement on motion for a new trial after the time for appeal from the order denying a new trial had expired, no appeal having been taken from the order, did not operate to extend the time for the filing of the transcript on the appeal from the judgment, nor authorize the filing of such transcript more than forty days after the time of perfecting the appeal.—Vinson v. Los Angeles Pacific R. R. Co., 7, 142.

§ 47. —— Dismissal for Delay in Filing.

Where no transcript on appeal is filed within forty days, as required by the rule of the court, and no showing made to take the case out of that rule, the appeal will be dismissed on motion of respondent.—Vitoreno v. Corea, 3, 343.

An appeal will not be dismissed because of the failure to file a printed transcript of the record in time, where an application is pending to settle the bill of exceptions.—In re Walkerly's Estate, 4, 819.

Where a transcript is not filed within the time granted by the supreme court, but such failure is due to a mistake as to when such time expired, and is filed shortly thereafter, and no material delay is occasioned, and no costs are caused to respondent, the appeal will not be dismissed therefor.—Brunnings v. Townsend, 6, 647.

§ 48. —— Authentication.

Orders, stipulations and an oath and account of a receiver in the transcript, not being authenticated, cannot be considered on appeal, being no part of the judgment-roll.—O'Neil v. McLennan, 7, 161.

The sufficiency of testimony contained in a transcript on appeal, unaccompanied by a certificate that it was given or is correctly stated, will not be considered.—Hawkins v. Morehead, 4, 224.

§ 49. —— Amendment.

Where plaintiff took two appeals from the same judgment, and the printed transcript filed contained the second notice of appeal only, on the second appeal being dismissed leave should be granted to appellant to amend the transcript by inserting therein the first notice of appeal.—Swortfiguer v. White, 6, 779.

§ 50. —— Contents and Requisites.

The transcript should contain nothing beyond what is necessary to enable the court to consider the points it is asked to decide.— People v. Smith, 2, 59.

An appeal from points in a charge to a jury is not to be entertained upon a transcript containing no copy of the charge, but showing only that one had been given, an oral one, and having in it nothing to show any exceptions taken.—People v. Ward, 2, 205.

An order appealed from cannot be reviewed on a record which contained no copy of an undertaking on appeal, or showing that the same was filed, or that, instead thereof, a deposit in money had been made; no bill of exceptions; no showing what papers were used upon the hearing of the order to show cause upon which the order appealed from was made; and no certification of the transcript on appeal by the clerk of the court or the attorneys in the cause. The certificates of the presiding judge and clerk, made after the service and filing of the notice of motion to dismiss the appeal, will not supply the defects in the transcript.—Ellis v. Bennett, 2, 302.

Where respondent in his brief suggests imperfections in the transcript because of the absence of necessary papers and because the transcript is not properly certified, and appellant, at the hearing, files the requisite papers with the proper certificate, the motion to dismiss should be denied.—People v. Jacobs, 2, 672.

§ 51. —— Dismissal for Defects in Transcript.

An appeal assuming to be from an order made after final judgment, when the transcript contains no final judgment nor indicates that there has been one, will be dismissed.—Schaefer v. French Savings etc. Soc., 2, 108.

Where no index is prefixed to the transcript, the court, under the rule, is authorized to dismiss the appeal.—Donahue v. Mariposa Land & M. Co., 2, 389.

Where the transcript on appeal does not show that the findings of fact and conclusions of law set out in it were signed by the trial judge and filed with the clerk, and that judgment was entered upon such findings and conclusions, as required by Code of Civil Procedure, sections 632, 633, the appeal will be dismissed.—In re De Leon's Estate, 4, 388.

§ 52. —— Failure to File—Dismissal.

Appeal dismissed for want of transcript being filed.—Estate of Curtis, 2, 240.

Appeal will be dismissed, in pursuance of rules 3 and 4 of the California supreme court, for failure to file transcript, on clerk's certificate of that fact.—McAvoy v. Bothwell, 2, 717.

A motion to dismiss appeal on the ground that the transcript was not filed in time will be denied, where it appears that the question of the settlement of the bill of exceptions in the cause was not determined until the day of the motion.—Hyde v. Boyle, 3, 309.

A clerk of appellant's attorney, during the illness of his employer and against his directions, took the appeal, but failed to file a transcript. Appellant's attorney was first apprised that appeal had been taken by respondent's notice of motion to dismiss, when he served and filed a transcript. Held, that the appeal would not be dismissed.—Bates v. Schroeder, 3, 21.

An appeal will be dismissed after the time allowed for filing a transcript has elapsed, if no transcript has been filed, nor attempt made to prepare one, and no sufficient excuse is offered for failure to do so.—First National Bank of Santa Monica v. Kowalsky, 3, 432.

Subsequently to the taking of the appeal, one of the appellants, being ill, requested her attorney to desist from further proceedings, but, after receiving notice of a motion to dismiss the appeal for failure to file the transcript within the required time, said appellant directed the attorney to proceed with the cause. No action was taken toward the preparation of a transcript prior to appellant's first direction to her attorney, nor after the order to proceed with the appeal. Held, that the appeal would be dismissed.—Hart v. Kimberly, 5, 532.

An appeal will be dismissed for failure to file the transcript within the time limited by the rules of the court.—Johnson v. Goodyear Min. Co., 6, 274.

VIII. ASSIGNMENT OR SPECIFICATION OF ERRORS.

§ 53. In General.

Assignments of error not apparent in the record will not be considered.—Native American Mining Co. v. Lockwood, 1, 5.

On appeal from an order denying a motion for a new trial, the statement in the record must contain a specification of the grounds the motion was based on; a setting forth of the points in a general way in the motion itself will not suffice.—Harper v. Minor, 1, 225.

On appeal from an order denying a motion for a new trial the court will not consider a point as to which there is no specification in the statement on motion.—Franklin v. Le Roy, 1, 806.

An assignment of error that the findings do not support the judgment cannot be considered on appeal from an order denying a new trial; an appeal from the judgment is necessary.—Hayford v. Wallace, 5, 489.

Assignments of error, on a motion for a new trial in sustaining objections to and refusing to receive certain evidence, will be disregarded where they are not supported by the record, which shows that the court overruled all objections to and admitted such evidence.—Lower Kings River Reclamation Dist. v. Phillips, 5, 776.

Assignments of error, on motion for new trial, that the court erred in rendering judgment in favor of defendant, when the decision and judgment should have been for plaintiff, will be disregarded under Code of Civil Procedure, section 659, because of being a mere general objection to the final judgment.—Lower Kings River Reclamation Dist. v. Phillips, 5, 776.

An assignment of error not discussed in appellant's brief will not be reviewed.—Bassett v. Fairchild, 6, 458.

A specification of error in a notice of motion for a new trial, that the decision is against law for any reason appearing on the judgment·

roll, can only be considered on appeal from the judgment.—Swift v. Occidental Mining and Petroleum Co., 7, 23.

§ 54. As to Sufficiency of Evidence.

On appeal from an order denying a motion for a new trial, the order is to be affirmed in all cases where the statement contains no specification of the particulars in which it is claimed the evidence was insufficient to justify the decision, or of the alleged errors relied upon for a reversal.—Hendrick v. Hitchcock, 1, 347.

On an appeal from a judgment only, a specification that "the evidence did not justify or warrant the judgment" is insufficient.— People v. Parrott, 1, 412.

On appeal it is not necessary to specify that the evidence is insufficient to support a finding not embraced in the issues.—Fiske v. Casey, 4, 558.

An assignment of error, on motion for a new trial, that the "evidence is insufficient to justify the third finding of fact, in that there is no evidence to show that there is due and owing plaintiff" a certain sum, is insufficient to question on appeal the sufficiency of the evidence to sustain such finding that no part of the principal has been paid except a certain sum.—First Nat. Bank of South Bend v. Kelso, 5, 40.

A specification of insufficiency of evidence, "that the evidence clearly showed that the total amount due . . . . was not the sum of ———, but was the sum of ———, and no larger or greater sum whatever," is insufficient.—Love v. Anchor Raisin Vineyard Co., 5, 425.

An assignment that the court erred in finding that a certain sum was due from defendant to plaintiff is not a specification of the "particulars" in which the evidence is insufficient to sustain the finding.—Barnhart v. Edwards, 5, 558.

Where, on an appeal from an order denying a new trial, there are no specifications of insufficiency of evidence, the question whether the findings are supported by the evidence cannot be considered.— Pickering Light and Water Co. v. Savage, 6, 985.

Under Code of Civil Procedure, sections 657, 659, requiring assignments of error to point out the particulars in which the ruling objected to is erroneous, an assignment "that the evidence is insufficient to justify the court in finding," followed by the language of the finding, but containing no specification of any particular wherein the finding is unsupported, is insufficient.—Swift v. Occidental Mining and Petroleum Co., 7, 23.

Code of Civil Procedure, section 648, provides that when the exception is to the verdict or decision, upon the ground of the insufficiency of the evidence to justify it, the objection must specify the "particulars" in which such evidence is alleged to be insufficient. Held, that specifications in a bill of exceptions that the evidence "is insufficient to justify the finding" are defective.—Bell v. Staacke, 7, 28.

That a specification as to the insufficiency of evidence may avail, it must be directed to a material finding of fact and it must be clearly shown that there is no substantial testimony to sustain the finding. If there is, the credibility of witnesses, and the weight to be given their testimony, will not be considered.—Silveira v. Reese, 7, 112.

§ 55. As to Verdict.

An objection that the verdict is against the law is not sufficient to raise the point that plaintiff was guilty of contributory negligence.— Crowley v. Strouse, 4, 29.

§ 56. Effect of Delay in Filing.

Undue delay in filing assignments of error after sending up the record calls for a dismissal of the appeal for lack of prosecution.—People v. Buck, 1, 94.

Where an appellant fails to point out any error in the order or judgment appealed from, within the time allowed him to file briefs, the supreme court will not examine the record, but will affirm the decision of the trial court.—Dalmazzo v. Drysdale, 3, 84.

IX. BRIEFS, POINTS AND AUTHORITIES.

§ 57. Failure to File.

No brief having been filed, although fifty days had been allowed therefor after submission of the case, and the transcript having been withdrawn by one of the parties, the court is justified in affirming the judgment without considering the appeal.—Chapman v. Wade, 1, 158.

An appeal will be considered abandoned when the appellant fails to file his points prior to the day set for argument, as required by the rule, or to file a brief within the time allowed by the court.—Keating v. Edgar, 2, 226.

Where no points and authorities are filed within the time allowed, judgment will be affirmed.—People v. Lee Hung, 2, 248.

Appellant having failed to file points and authorities within the time allowed, judgment affirmed.—Hite Gold Quartz Co. v. Stermont Silver Min. Co., 2, 481.

Where appellant has filed no brief showing the particular ground on which he relies for reversal, and on examination of the record no error prejudicial to him is apparent, the judgment will be affirmed.—Romine v. Cralle, 3, 417.

Where there is no appearance by appellant and there are no points or authorities filed in his behalf, the judgment appealed from will be affirmed.—Scott v. Sowden, 2, 842.

Case to be submitted on briefs will be dismissed for failure to file briefs within time allowed.—Markham v. Fowler, 2, 853.

Where, on appeal from an order sustaining a demurrer, the respondent does not appear and does not file points or authorities, the court is left to reverse the order if the pleading demurred to seems sufficient on its face.—Funke v. Lyons, 2, 164.

Where appellant, long after the time granted by the court to file briefs, fails to file either briefs, points or authorities, the judgment appealed from will be affirmed.—Purdy v. Rahl, 3, 106.

When a case is submitted, without oral arguments, on briefs to be filed, and none are filed, the judgment will be affirmed without looking into the record.—Hanson et al. v. Voll, 3, 117.

Where appellant's failure to file a brief was due to a misunderstanding between two attorneys as to which was to act for her in the supreme court, and appellant, through her ignorance of English, was excusable for that misunderstanding, the appeal not being in the opinion of counsel without merit, respondent's motion to dismiss will be denied.—Santa Paula Waterworks v. Peralta, 5, 779.

Where appellant did not file his points and authorities in time, but they were on file at the time of hearing, a motion to dismiss the appeal will not be granted, no delay being caused.—In re Lakemeyer's Estate; Blizard v. Drinkhouse, 6, 695.

Where an examination of the record on appeal suggests no error, and the attention of the court is called to none by reason of the failure of appellant to file points and authorities, the judgment will be affirmed.—Rothrock v. Baldwin, 7, 338.

§ 58. Excuses for Failure to File.

That a case was set for the last day of the session of the supreme court, and the court for years past had never been able to finish the calendar, and that defendants' attorney did not expect the case to be reached, is not sufficient to justify setting aside a judgment of affirmance, made because there was no appearance, or points or authorities on file, for defendant.—Huggins v. Handy, 2, 854.

§ 59. Striking Out for Impropriety.

Respondent's brief after charging the commission of perjury by appellant in his answer, as to a fact alleged to be within his attorney's knowledge, continued: "When counsel can be permitted to draft pleadings and present them to their clients for verification; and the pleadings being drawn from facts within the knowledge of counsel, and the counsel causes his client to willfully commit perjury," etc. Held, a gross violation of professional ethics, and that the brief should be stricken out, with permission to file another within ten days, or the judgment would be reversed without an inspection of the record.—Cramer v. Tittel, 3, 80.

X. DISMISSAL OR ABANDONMENT OF APPEAL.

§ 60. In General.

Where the record bears no evidence that the nominal appellant actually took an appeal, and there is no brief filed by him nor any suggestion of a diminution of the record, the case is to be stricken from the files.—People v. Pico, 1, 711.

Although under the rules of the supreme court the transcript shall be filed within forty days after the appeal is perfected, and a motion to dismiss for failure in this respect must be accompanied with a certificate of the clerk of the court appealed from to show the fact and date of filing the bill of exceptions and the statement on appeal, such motion to dismiss must be held as prematurely made if the clerk's accompanying certificate is not definitely to the point. while by another certificate of his, filed by the other side. it appears that the appellant has proposed the bill and statement, and the respondent has proposed amendments, but that neither such bill nor such statement has been settled.—Gilmore v. American Fire Ins. Co., 2, 190.

Appeal dismissed as to defendants, who waived a right to appeal by stipulation in the lower court.—Oliver v. Blair, 2, 441.

Though an appeal appear totally destitute of merit, yet, if regularly taken, the court will be reluctant to dismiss it summarily.— Parker v. Bernal, 2, 507.

A motion to dismiss appeals involving an inquiry into the merits will not be considered.—In re Williams' Estate, 4, 511.

Where a motion to dismiss an appeal involves an examination into its merits, the motion will be denied, with leave to renew it on submission of the cause.—Ohlandt v. Joost, 6, 10.

§ 61. Grounds for Dismissal.

For failure to serve notice of appeal. See ante, § 20.
For defects in or failure to file transcript. See ante, § 51.
For failure to file points and authorities. See ante, § 57.

An appeal is dismissable for some irregularities in taking it, for failure to prosecute, for want of appearance, or on consent of par.

ties; but where it has been perfected according to law and the appellant appears, he is entitled to be heard upon any question of fact involved in the merits. Because the proposed statement on motion for a new trial was not served upon a certain one of the adverse parties is not ground for dismissal of the appeal.—Dore v. Dougherty, 2, 402.

Statement having been settled more than forty days before the transcript of record was served and filed, time to file the same not having been extended, and no transcript having been served or filed until notice to dismiss the appeal had been served and filed, appeal ordered dismissed.—Smith v. San Francisco, 2, 479.

A motion to dismiss an appeal on the ground that the transcript has not been filed within the time prescribed by the supreme court rules will be denied, where the certificate of the clerk of the trial court on which such motion is based does not conform to supreme court rule 4.—In re Sweet's Estate, 3, 485.

An appeal will be dismissed, it having been perfected and the bill of exceptions settled and filed in the clerk's office for eight months, said clerk not having been requested to certify to the correctness of any transcript on appeal, no such transcript having been filed in the supreme court, and no extension of time to file it having been granted.—Warren v. McGowan, 7, 190.

Where, after the submission of an appeal, the subject matter of the action was settled by the parties, the appeal will be dismissed on respondent's motion suggesting such settlement.—In re Tucker, 7, 243.

§ 62. —— Alteration of Record.

An appeal will not be dismissed because of interlineations in the transcript of the record.—White v. White, 3, 265.

Where, after numerous motions to supply the defects in a record in the supreme court, appellant's attorney makes alterations in the printed record, by underscoring various passages, and by marginal notes and interlineations in writing, for the purpose of directing attention to particular parts of the record, and, without leave of court, alters his reply brief by pasting therein numerous leaflets containing citations of authorities, and comments thereon, of which no service is made on opposing counsel, thus imposing upon the court more labor than would have been required to dispose of the case on its merits if presented in an orderly manner, and there appears to be no substantial merit in the appeal, it will be dismissed.—Clarke v. Mohr, 6, 378.

A motion to dismiss an appeal from an order denying a new trial because such motion was not served on all the parties who would have been adversely affected by the granting of the motion will not be considered, since it involves the merits of the appeal and an examination of the record.—Gardner v. Stare, 6, 777.

§ 63. —— Second or Other Appeal.

An appeal will be dismissed when previous appeal from same judgment has been perfected.—People v. Jordan, 2, 271.

Appeal dismissed on the ground that the court had jurisdiction of another appeal on the merits.—Guardian Fire & Life Assur. Co. v. Thompson, 2, 594.

Where two appeals are taken by the same party from the same judgment, and no question is raised as to the validity of the first appeal, the second appeal should be dismissed.—Swortfiguer v. White, 6, 778.

Pending appeal from an order denying defendant a change of venue, a demurrer to the complaint was sustained, and, after the complaint was amended, defendant again moved for change of venue, and appealed from the order denying the change. Held, that on determination of the first appeal the second presented merely a moot case and would be dismissed.—Read v. San Diego Union Co., 6, 845.

§ 64. Parties Concerned.

On appeal from an order denying a new trial, taken by one of several defendants (being dissatisfied with the adjustment effected by the findings as between him and his codefendants rather than as between him and plaintiff) a motion to dismiss made by plaintiff should be denied.—Williams v. Conroy, 2, 192.

Motion to dismiss appeal on the ground that appellants have no interest will not be sustained.—People v. Perris Irr. District, 6, 349.

§ 65. Notice of Motion.

An appeal may in all cases be dismissed, without a motion therefor first filed, where the appellant has no "case" on appeal, that is, no statement on appeal, and it is not claimed that there is error in the judgment-roll.—Havens v. Dale, 1, 237.

A motion to dismiss an appeal cannot be considered where it is uncertain to which of two notices of appeal it is directed.—De La Cuesta v. Calkins, 5, 163.

§ 66. Continuance of Motion.

Motion to dismiss appeal, involving an examination of the entire record, and incidentally a consideration of the merits, will be continued until the hearing of the merits.—Leonis v. Leffingwell, 6, 219.

The consideration of a motion to dismiss an appeal by an intervener, on the ground that he is not a party aggrieved, will be postponed, where some of the questions involved in the appeal will have to be considered in determining the motion.—Darlington v. Butler, 7, 246.

§ 67. Effect of Denial of Motion.

When a motion to dismiss an appeal is based upon two grounds, but only one is urged, the decision denying the motion is final as to both grounds.—Lang v. Specht, 2, 111.

§ 68. Effect of Dismissal by Consent.

When the court, by consent of the parties, dismisses an appeal as to the subject matter, it cannot at the same time let it stand as to fees and expenses allowed to referees in the cause, such being merely incidental to the appeal from the judgment or final decree.—Bernal v. Bernal, 1, 581.

§ 69. Abandonment of Appeal.

Where plaintiff in an action to enjoin the issuance of a tax deed appealed from a judgment against him rendered on his refusal to amend after a demurrer to the complaint was sustained, he abandoned his remedy by appeal by afterward redeeming the property by paying the taxes, etc., and the court will not determine the questions raised.—Dehail v. City of Los Angeles, 5, 866.

XI. HEARING AND REHEARING.

§ 71. Setting Aside Submission.

Where a justice has not heard the argument, and it is deemed important that all the justices should participate in the decision, the submission of the appeal will be set aside, with leave to counsel to stipulate to resubmit the case on the briefs and printed arguments already on file.—Fair v. Angus, 6, 283.

§ 72. Rehearing.

On appeal from a sentence of death, the supreme court will consider questions raised for the first time in a petition for rehearing.—People v. Bruggy, 3, 415.

A motion before one department of the supreme court, to set aside a sale of real property, will be dismissed, without prejudice to its renewal, where the judgment of that department on which it rests has been set aside, and a hearing in bank ordered.—Hewitt v. Dean, 3, 416.

A motion for rehearing made on account of the clerk's failure to record appellant's brief, so as to bring it to the attention of the court, will be denied, where an examination of the brief fails to disclose anything that would justify a reversal.—People v. Moran, 3, 740.

Where, on the hearing in the supreme court, there is no appearance for the appellant, and the judgment is affirmed, such judgment will not be vacated, for the purpose of another hearing, though a sufficient and good showing be made concerning such nonappearance, so as to authorize the court to do so, if it appears that it would be useless to do so for the reason that, upon another hearing, a like judgment must follow.—Bishop v. Glassen, 5, 744.

A reversal of a judgment on appeal will be set aside, on the ex parte application of the respondent for leave to remit a portion thereof, and for an affirmance of the remainder, to enable the court to consider such application on a rehearing, which will be limited to that proposition.—Fox v. Hale & Norcross Silver Min. Co., 5, 1005.

XII. FRIVOLOUS APPEALS AND PENALTY THEREFOR.

§ 73. In General.

On the dismissal of an appeal, damages will not be awarded in the respondent's favor on his ex parte affidavit that he has been informed and believes the appeal to be without merit.—Kirby v. Harrington, 2, 740.

Where an appeal appears to be frivolous, a mere oral assurance in argument that it was taken in good faith is insufficient to avoid the imposition of damages, but such assurance must find some support in the record.—Younglove v. Cunningham, 5, 281.

§ 74. When Appeal Regarded as Frivolous or for Delay.

An appeal by a defendant from a money judgment, where the answer controverted no fact set up in the complaint, and no evidence of payment was offered at the trial, is a frivolous appeal, warranting affirmance of the judgment and the adding of twenty per cent damages.—Flynn v. Travers, 1, 27.

An appeal taken for delay merely is to be disposed of by being affirmed with damages.—Stebbins v. Smiley, 1, 133.

After an appeal had been perfected and then allowed to rest for two terms unprosecuted, the judgment appealed from may, on motion by the respondent, be affirmed with damages as for an appeal frivolous and intended for delay only.—Dillon v. Kelly, 1, 251.

An appeal based on conduct of the trial court, invited by counsel for the purpose of providing points for appeal, and not in fact prejudicial to his client, is to be regarded as a frivolous appeal, and in such cases on respondent's motion damages should be awarded.—Dwyer v. California Steam Navigation Co., 1, 442.

An appeal from a judgment in an action on a bond, given to release an attachment, where a demurrer to the complaint, which complaint alleged each step in the former action, the judgment, refusal of the defendant to pay same, and that it was still unpaid, and prayed accordingly, was overruled, and, upon an answer being then filed presenting as the sole issue the recovery of the judgment, the court found for the plaintiff, is so plainly without merit that it must have been taken for delay only, wherefore the supreme court, while confirming the judgment appealed from, adds twenty per cent damages. Heney v. Alpers, 2, 164.

Where the finding in ejectment is that defendant did not "wrongfully or unlawfully enter upon or oust plaintiff" from the possession of the premises, an appeal on the ground that there was no finding upon the issue as to ouster is frivolous.—Dunphy v. Heinmann, 2, 851.

In view of the plain provisions of the Code of Civil Procedure, section 662, and numerous decisions of the supreme court, an appeal taken on the ground that trial courts have no authority to set aside verdicts is frivolous.—Foote v. Hayes, 4, 976.

§ 75. Imposition of Penalty or Damages.

An appeal on errors assigned, in no manner supported by the record, subjects the appellant to damages along with affirmation of the judgment.—De Wolf v. Bailey, 1, 37.

An appeal without merit calls for the imposition of damages.—Berri v. Minturn, 1, 50.

An appeal taken manifestly for delay calls for the imposition of damages.—Spencer v. Barney, 1, 56.

A frivolous appeal manifestly intended for delay only calls for an affirmation of the judgment, with damages.—Parburt v. Monroe, 1, 72.

It is not necessary to give damages because an appeal was taken without reason, when the appellant has only stayed his own judgment drawing ten per cent interest.—Howard v. Low, 1, 82.

While affirming a judgment, where satisfied that the appeal is destitute of merit, the court exacts damages of the appellant.—Wheeler v. Turner, 1, 798.

Defendant in ejectment, after pleading the general issue and possession for the statutory period, filed a disclaimer of any interest, but from a judgment for plaintiff, after a trial by the court, findings of fact being waived, he appealed. The record, however, contained no bill of exceptions or other showing of error, and defendant filed no brief or points and authorities. Held, that, the appeal being manifestly without merit, $100 damages would be directed for plaintiff as part of the costs on appeal.—De Pena v. Trujillo, 3, 504.

To a complaint in the ordinary form of ejectment a general denial and the statute of limitations were pleaded. Findings of fact were waived, and judgment was rendered for plaintiff. Defendant, on appeal, furnished no bill of exception or other record of error, and filed neither brief nor points and authorities. Held that, the appeal being manifestly without merit, .payment of $100 damages, as part of costs on appeal, would be directed for respondent.—Meyers v. Trujillo, 3, 505.

Where, in an action to recover personal property, it appears that an appeal by plaintiff is without merit, and was taken for delay, and that defendant has been deprived of the use of such property for more than a year, the latter will be awarded $200 damages in addition to his costs.—Boehm v. Gibson, 4, 483.

Where no circumstances showing peculiar hardship appear, damages for a frivolous appeal will not be awarded on a dismissal thereof.— Brite v. Briggs, 6, 922.

§ 76. —— Setting Aside.

Where, on failure of an appellant to appear when his cause is called, the judgment appealed from is affirmed, with damages for frivolous appeal, on motion of respondents, there being no brief on file, and it thereafter appears that failure to file a brief was due to appellant's ignorance that his cause was on the calendar, and an examination of the record shows that the appeal was not frivolous, that part of the judgment imposing damages for frivolous appeal will be set aside.— Emhoff v. McMann, 3, 243.

XIII. REVIEW AND AFFIRMANCE OR REVERSAL.

§ 77. In General.

A judgment by the court upon evidence submitted by the plaintiff in default of the defendant's appearance, such evidence not being made a part of the record, is conclusive on appeal.—Love v. Watts, 1, 24.

An order denying a motion, made too late for the court to have jurisdiction of it, cannot be inquired into upon appeal from an order involving the same subject matter.—Brigham v. Swift, 1, 31.

An appeal by an unsuccessful defendant whose answer put in issue no averment of the complaint except the general one of payment, and whose points urged to impeach the judgment are either frivolous or not sustained by the record, should result in affirmance if it appears that the trial court put the case fairly before the jury and the jury gave a just verdict.—Cravens v. Dewey, 1, 89.

A judgment on a verdict not unwarranted by the evidence is not to be disturbed.—Fay v. Lawler, 1, 294.

Where there is a failure to find on a material issue, judgment will be reversed.—Hawes v. Green, 2, 286.

On failure of the trial court to find on the issues made by the pleadings in an action, the judgment must be reversed on appeal, and the cause remanded for a new trial.—Conklin v. Stone, 2, 449.

Where the facts of the case are such that a judgment upon them other than that rendered would plainly be unjust, there ought not to be a reversal on such a ground as that the answer was not in proper form technically.—People v. San Francisco etc. R. R. Co., 1, 391.

A judgment based on findings wrongly arrived at will not be affirmed on the ground that on all the evidence offered and received the plaintiff ought to have recovered, since the defendant might show in a new trial that, notwithstanding such evidence, the plaintiff was not, for some reason, entitled to recover.—Madden v. Ashman, 1, 583.

Where, on appeal from a judgment in a cause tried by the court without a jury, the findings are not contradictory, and cover all the material issues presented therein, the judgment of the trial court must be affirmed.—Whittle v. Doty, 2, 702.

Where the court's findings support the judgment, and are on all material issues, the judgment will be affirmed.—German v. Brown, 3, 864.

A judgment cannot, on appeal, be reversed on the evidence, and judgment ordered for appellants, when the findings of fact support the judgment.—Oullahan v. Baldwin, 5, 423.

A county brought suit to restrain its treasurer from paying a certain warrant, and, upon the hearing, the court dissolved the preliminary injunction, and denied a perpetual injunction; and two days later the county gave notice of appeal, but did not perfect its appeal for over three years. Held, that as there was no appearance by respondent, and as the warrant was doubtless paid, the case would not be considered on its merits, and the judgment would be affirmed.—Modoc County v. Madden, 6, 10.

Where appellant insists that, on the findings of the lower court, he is entitled to a more favorable judgment, but waives all right to have the case remanded for a new trial, the court will rely entirely on the findings whether or not the evidence supports them.—Bryson v. McCone, 6, 35.

Where, on an appeal, no brief is filed by either party, and no stipulation or order extending time to file briefs appears, and on call of the appeal there is no appearance by either party, no reason being advanced why the judgment should not be affirmed, and none appearing to the reviewing court, the judgment will be affirmed.—Ponet v. Los Angeles Brewing Co., 7, 339.

§ 78. Divided Court.

When the appellate court is equally divided in opinion the judgment appealed from will be affirmed.—Kimball v. Semple, 1, 554.

Where one justice of the supreme court is disqualified, and the six remaining are equally divided in opinion, the judgment will be affirmed.—Smith v. Ferries etc. Ry. Co., 5, 889.

§ 79. Questions Reviewable.

Points not raised by the record or necessary to be considered in disposing of an appeal are to be disregarded.—Tibbetts v. City of San Francisco, 1, 23.

On appeal from the disposition of a motion for a new trial when the sole ground for the motion, as specified in the statement, is the insufficiency of the evidence to justify the findings, the court is precluded from considering other points urged by the appellant.—Ryer v. Hicks, 1, 234.

A question raised as to the judgment being inconsistent with the findings cannot be entertained by the supreme court except on appeal from the judgment.—Larue v. Chase, 1, 613.

On a second appeal of a case a party may not avail himself of a ruling made at the first while denying the truth of matter on which that ruling was based.—San Francisco v. Spring Valley Water Works, 1, 783.

An appeal on points disposed of in a previous appeal of the same case will not be entertained.—People v. Hurtado, 2, 206.

Questions which can be determined only from the evidence are not reviewable on an appeal taken upon the judgment-roll alone.—Haynes v. Backman, 3, 712.

An order of the court, of its own motion, setting aside a verdict is the equivalent of an order granting a new trial, and is reviewable upon a statement on appeal; but, being a matter within the legal discretion of the trial court, this court will not interfere with it unless abuse of discretion is shown.—Hynes v. Nelson, 5, 741.

A judgment in an action on a note for a sum larger than the principal and interest due on the note will be corrected on appeal therefrom, as the error is one that is apparent on the judgment-roll.—Davis v. Lamb, 5, 765.

Where the evidence as to later items in an account not claimed to be barred by limitation justified a verdict for the amount rendered, the question whether earlier items were barred will not be considered. Grant v. Dreyfus, 5, 970.

Error assigned to the introduction in evidence of a judgment-roll of another action can only be considered upon the review of the order denying a new trial.—Sprigg v. Barber, 6, 161.

On appeal from an order denying a motion for a new trial, the court will consider the sufficiency of the evidence, and the errors of law, if any, occurring during trial.—Houser & Haines Mfg. Co. v. Hargrove, 6, 384.

Under Code of Civil Procedure, sections 656, 657, defining a new trial as "a re-examination of an issue of fact in the same court after a trial and decision," the supreme court, on appeal from an order denying a motion for a new trial, may review questions as to the sufficiency of the evidence to support the findings and errors of law excepted to, occurring during the trial, but cannot consider the sufficiency of the complaint, nor whether or not the findings support the judgment.—Owen v. Pomona Land and Water Co., 6, 438.

On appeal from an order denying a motion for a new trial, where the judgment rendered is not appealed from, the sufficiency of findings to support such judgment will not be considered.—Strouse v. Sylvester, 6, 798.

On an appeal from an order denying a motion for a new trial, conclusions of law are not reviewable.—Strouse v. Sylvester, 6, 798.

§ 80. Matters of Pleading.

A party whose demurrer has been overruled at his own request will not be heard, on appeal from the judgment entered in the case, to question the correctness of the ruling.—Haley v. Nunan, 2, 189.

The insufficiency of a complaint cannot be considered on an appeal from an order granting a new trial.—Hook v. Hall, 2, 459.

Though a general demurrer to a complaint was overruled by consent, defendant may, on appeal from a default judgment after answer, question its sufficiency.—Jones v. Los Angeles & P. Ry. Co., 4, 755.

Where defendant answers over after demurrer to the complaint is overruled, and no appeal is taken, he cannot, on the appeal of plaintiff from a judgment in defendant's favor, insist upon affirmance upon the ground that his demurrer should have been sustained.—Bank of National City v. Johnston, 6, 418.

The sufficiency of the complaint, and whether findings of the court sustain the judgment, cannot be considered on appeal from an order denying a motion for a new trial.—Swift v. Occidental Mining and Petroleum Co., 7, 23.

§ 81. Admission or Rejection of Evidence.

The admission of inadmissible testimony, through misapprehension by the trial court of the bearing of a decision of the higher court, is error for which a judgment will be reversed.—Dopman v. Hoberlin, 1, 9.

To show that an irrelevant question was asked is not enough on appeal; it must appear that it was answered, and how it was answered, before it can be held that incompetent or irrelevant testimony was admitted; and it is by the record that this must be made to appear.— Baird v. Duane, 1, 492.

Judgment will not be reversed on the ground of erroneous admission of evidence, where such error resulted in a finding of nominal damages only, against the party claiming injury therefrom.—Hughes v. Parsons, 2, 451.

A reversal is not warranted, on appeal, by the exclusion of evidence on the ground of immateriality, if the materiality of the evidence offered is not apparent.—Hogan v. Tyler, 2, 489.

§ 82. Weight or Sufficiency of Evidence.

A judgment will not be reversed as being against the weight of the evidence when there is sufficient in the record to justify it.—Whitney v. Flint, 1, 8.

The finding of a jury, deciding on the weight of the evidence, will not, on appeal, be reversed unless impeached for fraud, misconduct or other improper influence.—Bernard v. Raglan, 1, 17.

Under the Practice Act the sufficiency of the evidence on which the trial court based its findings or the jury its verdict can be questioned only on a motion for a new trial; and these questions can be reviewed only on appeal from the order disposing of such motion.—Doll v. Mc-Cumber, 1, 135.

Where the testimony at the trial was amply sufficient to sustain the findings, the judgment is not to be disturbed.—Petree v. Harris, 1, 152.

The supreme court will not hold there was insufficient evidence at the trial to justify the findings, even though the findings seem to be contrary to the weight of the evidence.—Ogilvie v. Barry, 1, 254.

In the absence of distinct findings of fact and conclusions of law, the evidence will be looked into no further on appeal than to see that there was some evidence tending to support the judgment of the court below.—Larco v. Roeding, 1, 438.

A finding of the trial court will not be disturbed if supported by evidence deemed sufficient, even if the reviewing court regard the supporting evidence as not very satisfactory.—Hughes v. Desmond, 1, 684.

When no motion for a new trial was made before the court below, the question of whether the judgment was justified by the evidence will not be considered on appeal.—Himmelmann v. Sherman, 1, 803.

On appeal from an order denying a motion for a new trial the point of insufficiency of the evidence to support the judgment will not be considered if not specified first in the statement on the motion.—Mahon v. Simms, 1, 872.

The practice of the supreme court is to refrain from disturbing a finding of fact, made by the trial court and supported by evidence in the record, merely because the evidence on the point is contradicted by other evidence also appearing in the record.

Where the evidence is insufficient to support the findings the judgment will be reversed.—Wilson v. Baker, 2, 251.

Where there is no evidence to support the findings of the court below, the judgment will be reversed.—Crites v. Wilkinson, 2, 258.

Where the question is one of mere preponderance of evidence, the judgment of the lower court will not be disturbed.—People v. Burt, 2, 295.

Where, on appeal, there is no conflict in the evidence, but rather a question as to the correctness of the findings on the testimony introduced at the trial, and the testimony will allow a reasonable difference of opinion as to the facts to be deduced therefrom, the judgment of the lower court will not be disturbed.—Kelly v. Brown, 2, 536.

On an appeal from an order granting a new trial on the ground of insufficiency of the evidence to support the finding, where there is a conflict of evidence on material points, the order will not be set aside. Hogan v. Sanders, 2, 787.

Where, on appeal, the evidence is found sufficient to justify the findings of the trial court, the judgment of that court will not be disturbed.—Fisher v. Hopkins, 4, 8.

On appeal from an order denying a new trial, only rulings of the trial court assigned as error, and the sufficiency of the evidence to sustain the verdict, can be considered.—Andrews v. Wilbur, 5, 144.

The determination of a jury as to the credibility of testimony is not subject to review.—People v. Belardes, 5, 663.

A finding of the trial court based on conflicting evidence will not be reviewed on appeal.—Cannon v. McGrew, 5, 497.

The appellate court cannot decide on the weight of the evidence.— Downing v. Mulcahy, 6, 242.

A finding of fact which is not attacked on the ground of insufficiency of evidence to sustain it is conclusive.—In re Antoldi's Estate, 7, 211.

Where there is any evidence of negligence of defendant, a verdict for plaintiff will not be set aside for its insufficiency.—Donnolly v. Kelly, 6, 550.

§ 83. Verdict of Jury.

Where the case on trial is one in which the jury might have found either for the plaintiff or for the defendant, without becoming obnoxious to the charge of passion, prejudice, misconception or caprice, the verdict is not to be disturbed on appeal.—Hodges v. Cushing, 1, 450.

It is only when a strong case is presented that the appellate court is disposed to disturb the verdict of a jury or the findings of the court below on a question of fact.—Martin & Co. v. Levy, 1, 514.

Verdict by a jury on an issue as to whether an account-book on which plaintiff based his claim was one of original entry or a fraudulent fabrication is one of fact, and the verdict of a jury thereon will not be disturbed.—Grant v. Dreyfus, 5, 970.

§ 84. Findings of Court or Jury.

A finding of the court will be affirmed, where it cannot be said upon the record that the decision was erroneous.—Welsh v. Gould, 3, 72.

The question whether a conclusion of law is supported by the findings of facts cannot be considered on appeal from an order denying a new trial.—Raskin v. Robarts, 4, 465.

Findings of fact on issues not made in the pleadings cannot be considered for the purpose of supporting the judgment.—Fiske v. Casey, 4, 558.

Findings of fact by the trial court will not be reviewed on appeal. Monterey County v. Seigleken, 4, 613.

Where the findings of the trial court are sustained by sufficient evidence they will not be disturbed.—Dugan v. Adams & Co., 1, 52.

When on a particular point in a case the question of fact has been submitted to a jury, and the latter's finding thereupon is deemed, on appeal, as sufficiently supported by the evidence, such finding will not be disturbed.—Forster v. Pico, 1, 841.

The appellate court cannot review the evidence or findings of fact on an appeal from the judgment.—People v. Parrott, 1, 412.

Where a finding is on a material issue, and there is no evidence to sustain it, the judgment will be reversed and a new trial ordered. Jones v. Desmond, 2, 455.

Findings by the court will not be disturbed on appeal where there is evidence to justify them.—Adams v. Farnsworth, 4, 682.

A finding supported by evidence will not be disturbed on appeal.— Yore v. Seitz, 6, 293.

The supreme court will not disturb a finding of fact made by a trial court, if there is any substantial evidence to support it.— Blair v. Squire, 6, 350.

Where on appeal a question has been held to have been one for the jury, and on a second trial the jury, on the same and additional evidence in support of their prior finding, have found the same way as before, the finding cannot be questioned.—Allen v. McKay & Co., 6, 993.

§ 85. Conflicting Evidence—Verdict Based on.

A verdict found by a jury on conflicting evidence will not be disturbed on appeal.—Native American Mining Co. v. Lockwood, 1, 5; Lawson v. McGee, 1, 9; Rondel v. Fay, 1, 835; Castagnino v. Balletta, 3, 107; Weyers v. Espittalier, 3, 824; Ferguson v. McBean, 4, 429; Todd v. Martin, 4, 805; Andrews v. Wilbur, 5, 144; Fogel v. San Francisco etc. Ry. Co., 5, 194; McGee v. San Francisco etc. Ry. Co., 5, 285; Matthews v. Bull, 5, 592.

Where there was a substantial conflict of evidence at the trial, the verdict thereupon is not to be disturbed on appeal as not being justified by the evidence.—Couldthirst v. Kelley, 1, 796.

Where evidence is conflicting, the court will not interfere with the verdict, on appeal, on the ground of insufficiency of the evidence. Hogan v. Tyler, 2, 489.

A verdict rendered on conflicting evidence will not be disturbed on appeal, though the preponderance is apparently in favor of appellant.—In re Irvine's Estate, 4, 181.

Where the evidence is conflicting, and a motion for new trial was denied, the verdict will not be set aside.—Schwartz v. Wright, 6, 248.

Where the jury found for plaintiff, on conflicting evidence, and much of the evidence raising the conflict was in the shape of ex parte affidavits and depositions, made by citizens of a foreign country, the rule that a verdict on conflicting evidence will not be disturbed on appeal controls.—Meyerink v. Barton, 6, 551.

A verdict based on conflicting evidence and sustained by the trial court will not be reversed.—Graham v. Bryant, 7, 288.

A verdict found upon a substantial conflict of evidence is not to be disturbed.—Donaldson v. Neville, 1, 124.

§ 86. Conflicting Evidence—Findings Based on.

Where the evidence is conflicting the findings will not be disturbed, but the judgment affirmed.—Moore v. Moore, 2, 510; Peterson v. Doe, 2, 587; Springer v. Springer, 6, 662; Megginson v. Turner, 6, 208; Pattison v. Pratt, 6, 453; Patterson v. Mills, 6, 929.

When there is little conflict in evidence, the supreme court is disposed to reverse the trial court if the findings seem to be upon insufficient evidence.—Elias v. Verdugo, 1, 333.

Where there has been a substantial conflict of evidence the findings of the trial court will not be disturbed unless the evidence was insufficient to base them on.—Rodriguez v. Comstock, 1, 604.

On appeal from an order denying a motion for a new trial, where the ground for the motion was that the evidence did not support the findings, the findings are not to be disturbed, if there was a substantial conflict of evidence.—Clark v. Anthony, 1, 888.

Findings of fact cannot be reviewed on conflicting evidence.—Christensen v. McBride, 4, 542.

Where evidence is conflicting on a vital question of fact, the appellate court cannot pass on the question of preponderance of the evidence.—Grangers' Bank v. Shuey, 6, 190.

Findings on conflicting evidence will not be disturbed, though the appellate court differs with the trial court as to the weight of the evidence.—Stockton Ice Co. v. Argonaut Land & Dev. Co., 6, 275.

In order that findings and judgment on conflicting evidence may stand on appeal, such conflict must be one that is material.—Chapman v. Bent, 6, 740.

Where the evidence is conflicting, a finding will not be disturbed on appeal, though most of plaintiff's evidence is by depositions.—Rounthwaite v. Rounthwaite, 6, 878.

Findings of a trial court based on conflicting evidence will not be disturbed on appeal, if there is any evidence in the record on which they might be properly based.—Showers v. Zanone, 7, 263.

A finding of a trial court based on conflicting evidence will not be disturbed on appeal where there is sufficient evidence in the record to support it.—Jones v. Waterman, 7, 316.

Findings of a jury on material facts will not be disturbed where the evidence is conflicting.—Hughes v. Parsons, 2, 451; Carlson v. Mutual Relief Assn., 2, 452; Bayley v. Employers' Liability Assur. Corp., 6, 254.

The finding of the jury upon a substantial conflict of evidence will not be disturbed, though the evidence seems to preponderate in appellant's favor.—Ramsbottom v. Fitzgerald, 5, 941.

A finding by the trial court upon evidence substantially conflicting will not be disturbed on appeal.—Forster v. Pico, 1, 841; Ruffatt v. Cashman, 1, 449; Dorlan v. San Francisco etc. R. R. Co., 1, 457; Sharp v. Griffin, 1, 886; Charleton v. Reed, 1, 695; Burton v. Nichols, 2, 240; Partridge v. Owens, 2, 756; Morgans v. Adel, 2, 863; Wright v. Wright, 3, 343; Sullivan v. Hume, 4, 161; Johnson v. Greenberg, 4, 687; Woodbridge v. World Pub. Co., 5, 26; Welk v. Snow, 5, 150; Leverone v. Hildreth, 5, 192; Smith et al. v. Sabin, 5, 254; People's Ditch Co. v. 76 Land and Water Co., 5, 292; Oullahan v. Baldwin, 5, 423; McKenzie v. Joost, 5, 430; Skym v. Weske Consolidated Co., 5, 551; Ormsby v. De Borra, 5, 947; Hillman v. Griffin, 6, 354; Lake v. Owens, 7, 197; Albion Lumber Co. v. California Bridge and Construction Co., 7, 239.

On a question whether or not the defendant assumed the contract of a third person, the finding of the trial court, if had upon conflicting testimony, is not to be disturbed.—Murdock v. Ware, 1, 647.

The trial court's finding upon a substantial conflict of evidence as to the understanding of the transaction had by the parties is not to be disturbed.—Carroll v. Belden, 2, 205.

A finding by the trial court on evidence in which there is no substantial conflict will not, on appeal, be disturbed.—Haight v. Sexton, 5, 203.

Findings of the trial court, unsupported by any evidence, are cause for reversal.—Silberhorn Co. v. Wheaton, 5, 886.

Where the trial court finds for defendant on conflicting evidence, such finding will not be disturbed on appeal, though the evidence would have justified a verdict for plaintiff.—Schweikert v. Seavey, 6, 554.

Where there is no substantial conflict in the evidence, but it is all against the finding by the court, such finding will be set aside on appeal.—Leach v. California Safe Deposit and Trust Co., 6, 822.

§ 87. Conflicting Evidence—Judgment Based on.

A judgment following a verdict found upon a substantial conflict of evidence will not be disturbed.—Kellogg v. Crippen, 1, 161; Shipley v. Larrimore, 1, 297; Tompkins v. Bacon, 1, 836.

Where evidence is substantially conflicting, judgment will not be reversed on the ground of insufficiency of the evidence to justify it.

29

Whitesides v. Briggs, 2, 529; New Zealand Ins. Co. v. Bradbeer, 4, 275; Oakland Bank of Savings v. Applegarth, 2, 411; Farnsworth v. Wixom, 2, 435; Haley v. Shepherd, 2, 509; Patent Brick Co. v. Wissinger, 4, 915; Newell v. Steele, 5, 205; Connolly v. Wicks, 5, 867.

Where there has been a substantial conflict of evidence, a judgment is not to be disturbed on the ground that it was unsupported by the evidence.—Moultrie v. Brophy, 1, 536.

A judgment based on findings on the point of prior possession made on evidence substantially conflicting will be allowed to stand.—Penny v. Weiland, 1, 767.

An order for judgment, made without findings, where there had been a manifest conflict of evidence at the trial, is not to be disturbed. Wheeler v. Turner, 1, 793.

Where there is a material conflict in the evidence, the judgment of the lower court will not be disturbed on the ground that it was not justified by the evidence.—Jack v. Saunders, 2, 353.

Where there is a conflict in the evidence, the judgment will not be reversed on the ground that the findings are not supported by the evidence.—Cohen v. Mitchell, 2, 629.

Where the sole question is one of fact, and the evidence is sufficient to support the findings, the judgment will be affirmed.—Thornton v. Petersen, 3, 415.

An appellate court will not disturb the judgment of a trial court, where the plaintiff and defendant were the principal witnesses at the trial, and their testimony was conflicting.—Cross v. Reed, 3, 484.

Where plaintiff and defendant are the principal witnesses in the case, and their testimony is conflicting, a judgment for plaintiff will not be disturbed in the absence of any reason why the court should have believed defendant rather than plaintiff.—Hogan v. Burns, 4, 62.

A judgment for plaintiff will not be disturbed where there is a substantial conflict in the evidence, with a clear preponderance in plaintiff's favor.—Ontario Land & Imp. Co. v. Howard, 4, 734.

§ 88. Harmless Errors.

A judgment is not to be reversed for errors disclosed by the record when, from the whole facts legitimately proved, the verdict has as nearly accomplished strict justice as is ever attained in warmly contested litigation.—Stevenson v. Haskins, 1, 45.

Where manifestly the judgment is correct, even conceding error where alleged as made in course of the trial, it should not be disturbed.—Kimball v. Wilber, Kimball v. Raught, 1, 165.

The use of the word "defendant" instead of "defendants" in conclusions of law, when clearly a clerical misprision, is not entitled to any regard on appeal.—Doolan v. Cunningham, 2, 414.

Error, without injury, is not ground for reversal.—Quimby v. Butler, 2, 436.

Reversal will not be granted for errors in the admission of evidence, which do not affect the substantial rights of. the appellant.—Carlson v. Mutual Relief Assn., 2, 452.

Reversal is not warranted by variances between allegations and proof which are immaterial, if no one is misled thereby.—Ah Goon v. Tarpey, 2, 483.

Reversal is not warranted by error which is favorable to the appellant.—O'Connor v. Flynn, 2, 484.

Exceptions based upon the rulings of the trial court as to the admission of testimony will not be considered on appeal, in the absence of anything to show that the appellant was prejudiced thereby.—Cannon v. McGrew, 5, 497.

A reversal is not warranted by the admission without prejudice to the appellant of immaterial or incompetent evidence.—Damsguard v. Gunnoldson, 2, 512.

The admission of immaterial evidence, if it work no injury to the party complaining thereof, is error without injury, and not ground for a reversal.—Adair v. Crane, 2, 559.

A plaintiff cannot, on appeal, complain of the denial of a motion for nonsuit made by the defendant, the cause having thereafter been submitted on the merits and judgment rendered thereon.—Klumpke v. Ackerson, 2, 653.

Error in admitting evidence is not ground for reversal, unless it was prejudicial.—Graham v. Franke, 4, 839.

Error in admitting testimony is harmless where the party complaining testified to the same facts.—Steinhart v. Coleman, 5, 162.

Where plaintiff had already testified as to what he told his grantee certain lands conveyed by him "ought" to have been worth at the time, exclusion of his estimate of their value was harmless.—Peres v. Crocker, 5, 606.

Where the record shows that evidence offered by plaintiff was admitted subject to defendant's objections, plaintiff cannot complain of the subsequent failure of the court to rule on the objections.—Meserve v. Pomona Land and Water Co., 5, 759.

Where there is no fact not covered by the findings which, if found in favor of appellant, could affect the judgment, objections as to want of findings on certain issues are immaterial.—Schwannecke v. Goodenow, 5, 955.

The striking out of evidence is harmless where it would have authorized no other relief than that warranted by the evidence admitted. In re Walker's Estate, 6, 294.

A judgment supported by sufficient findings will not be reversed because of existence of immaterial findings not within the issues.—Wolfskill v. Douglass, 6, 396.

The rule that error, to work a reversal, must be prejudicial, applies to error in overruling demurrers to complaints on ground of ambiguity.—Warren v. Southern California Ry. Co., 6, 835.

A case having been tried on the theory that a particular issue was presented, a party cannot claim on appeal that there was no such issue, for the purpose of claiming as harmless error in admitting evidence thereon.—Ryan v. Pacific Axle Co., 6, 902.

§ 89. Presumptions and Intendments.

So far as the evidence below was conflicting, the presumptions are in favor of the findings of the trial court and the judgment thereupon. Miller v. Board of Education, 1, 607.

When there are no findings in writing, every fact within the issues presented by the pleadings which are necessary to support the judgment will be presumed, on appeal, to have been found in favor of the prevailing party.—Himmelmann v. Sherman, 1, 803.

The presumption is that the trial court ruled correctly on evidence when the evidence itself is not before the court appealed to.—Ellsworth v. Middleton, 1, 153.

On appeal no evidence can be considered not inserted in the statement, the presumption being that all the evidence on the specified points is in the transcript.—Madden v. Ashman, 1, 583.

On appeal from an order granting a new trial, made by a judge other than the one who presided at the trial of the cause, on the ground that the evidence was not sufficient to support one of the findings of fact, every intendment prevails in favor of the correctness of such order, and such intendment must be overcome by an affirmative showing of error, and an abuse of t. it sound legal discretion which the lower court was called upon to exercise in relation to the matter, in order to justify a reversal of such order by the appellate court.—Hammel v. Stone, 2, 785.

Where none of the pleadings or proceedings in the court below prior to judgment appear in the transcript, and the evidence is not brought up, the judgment must be presumed to be right.—Martin v. Splivalo, 3, 83.

A judgment will not be reversed for the want of a finding on an issue with respect to which there was no evidence; and on appeal on the judgment-roll alone it will not be presumed, against the correctness of the judgment, that there was evidence on a point as to which there was no finding.—Himmelman v. Henry, 3, 92.

As against respondents on appeal, the findings of the lower court must be presumed to be true. It will not be presumed that an error was the result of inadvertence.—Murdock v. Clarke, 3, 265.

On appeal from an order granting a new trial, where the motion was made on several grounds, including insufficiency of the evidence, and it does not appear on what ground it was granted, it will be presumed, in support of the order, where there was a conflict of evidence on a material point, that it was granted because of insufficiency of the evidence, and the order will not be reversed.—Austin v. Gagan, 3, 533.

Where, on appeal from a refusal to grant a motion for a new trial on the ground of newly discovered evidence, the record does not show the evidence given on the trial of the cause, so that it may be determined whether or not the newly discovered evidence is merely cumulative, it will be presumed that the lower court found that it was cumulative, and that the order refusing a new trial was correct.—Sirkus v. Central R. Co., 3, 535.

Where an appeal is taken from a j   ent which recites that the motion for judgment was made on afh.. it, and the record does not contain the affidavit, the supreme court will presume that it stated facts necessary to justify the judgment.—First Nat. Bank of Santa Monica v. Kowalsky, 3, 759.

Where findings are waived, every presumption in support of the judgment must be indulged, except such as are cut off by the specifications of error; and though there is nothing in the testimony, all of which is certified to be in the record on appeal, showing the date of the execution of a written instrument, the judgment cannot be attacked on appeal for the insufficiency of the evidence in this respect, where this particular ground of insufficiency was not called to the attention of the trial court in the specifications.—Petersen v. Taylor, 4, 335.

Where, on appeal, the record does not contain the evidence, and findings of fact were waived, it will be presumed that the allegations of the complaint were proven, and that the affirmative allegations in the answer were not.—Ullrich v. Santa Rosa Nat. Bank, 4, 741.

A reviewing court cannot add any fact to the findings of the trial court by presumption.—Kuschel v. Hunter, 5, 793.

Where the record purports to contain all the evidence taken at the trial of an action, the court on appeal will not presume that resort was had to evidence not disclosed by the record.—Metz v. Bell, 7, 41.

Where the order granting a new trial does not disclose the ground on which it is made, but it appears from the record that it might well have been made on the ground of the insufficiency of the evidence to sustain the verdict, the court on appeal may presume that it was made on that ground.—Harloe v. Berwick, 7, 58.

Where the court reserved its ruling on testimony objected to, and the record is silent as to what the ruling was, it must be presumed that the court excluded it, and it cannot be considered on appeal.— In re Dominici's Estate, 7, 289.

§ 90. Modification of Judgment.

On appeal from a judgment correct in respect to the findings in all except the amount due, which amount also is in excess of the demand in the complaint, the judgment is to be modified so as to accord with the demand as proved, and allowed to stand as modified.—People v. Hoag, 1, 326.

§ 91. Remand for Retrial or Further Proceedings.

A reversal of a judgment and remanding for further proceedings does not import that the trial court shall, from the facts originally found, enter judgment in favor of the party not favored before.— Haynes v. Meeks, 1, 79.

Where on appeal the facts appear in an agreed statement, and show a party to be entitled to a judgment, it is unnecessary to send the case back to the court below for a new trial.—Brunette v. Wolf, 1, 103.

In reversing a judgment in a cause submitted to the trial court on an agreed statement of facts, when the facts as stated are indefinite, and the record fails to show that the court relied on them alone, the appellate court cannot indicate the character of the judgment to be entered, but can only remand the cause for further proceedings.—Brown v. Houser, 1, 578.

On the first trial, evidence was taken of plaintiff's right to bring the action as a stockholder of a corporation, and the court found facts authorizing plaintiff to sue in behalf of the company. Defendants did not except to the sufficiency of such evidence, or present the question thereof on appeal. The case was affirmed on appeal as to a certain issue, and remanded for retrial as to another issue. Held, the findings being sufficient to show the right of plaintiff in that regard, that the issue as to the right of plaintiff to bring the action as a stockholder was not open for investigation in the second trial, either as to the issue on which a new trial was denied, or as to that on which a new trial was awarded.—Fox v. Hale & Norcross Silver Min. Co., 5, 980.

When, on appeal, the judgment of the lower court is affirmed as to one cause of action, and reversed and remanded for a new trial as to another cause of action, all the issues involved in the cause of action remanded must be retried, though the appellate court deems the evidence sufficient to sustain the judgment of the trial court on one of the issues.—Fox v. Hale & Norcross Silver Min. Co., 5, 980.

Where a judgment is affirmed as to certain issues and reversed and remanded for a new trial as to other issues, it is a modification of such judgment, and such action is within the province of the supreme court.—Fox v. Hale & Norcross Silver Min. Co., 5, 980.

Where a judgment for plaintiff was reversed on appeal, with directions to render judgment for defendant as prayed in the answer, which was that the prayer of the complaint be denied, and that plaintiff take nothing by the action, and that defendant have judgment against

plaintiff for costs, a judgment rendered that the prayer of plaintiff be denied, that plaintiff take nothing by the action, and that defendant have judgment against plaintiff for costs, and is entitled to "appropriate process" to enforce the judgment, and every part thereof, was not objectionable, as granting more relief than demanded, in so far as it awarded process to enforce the judgment.—White v. Wise, 7, 212.

§ 92. Remittitur.

By a rule of the supreme court no mandate or remittitur is allowed to issue to the court below before the expiration of ten days from the date of judgment.—Haight v. Kary, 1, 3.

An application made ten years after the issue of a remittitur for a withdrawal of such remittitur is to be denied, unless made upon good cause shown—San Francisco v. Calderwood, 2, 120.

A motion to recall a remittitur to enable an examination and correction of errors of the court below, since the remittitur went down, is not a proper way to reach such errors, and the motion will be denied. Dorland v. Bernal, 2, 529.

A remittitur will not be recalled where it conforms to the judgment as rendered, and it is too late to amend the judgment.—San Francisco Savings Union v. Long, 6, 278.

May 3d an appeal was dismissed. May 25th a remittitur was issued. June 9th the remittitur was filed in the lower court. August 11th notice of motion to recall remittitur was served. Affidavit of moving counsel stated that he left the city May 2d, and was absent nearly two months, and on his return one of the members of the firm associated with him in the case, and who had taken part in the appeal, was, and till the filing of the motion continued to be, absent from the city, and that he was unable to consult with him. Held, that excuse for not making the motion within the time fixed by law was not shown, so that the motion would be denied.—In re Sanford's Estate, 7, 159.

Under Statutes of 1895, page 269, chapter 207, and Code of Civil Procedure, section 1963, subdivisions 15 and 17, providing that it will be presumed that official duty has been performed, and that a judicial record, when not conclusive, still correctly determines or sets forth the rights of the parties, it will be presumed that failure to file the remittitur for four months after it was sent down was because the fee for filing had not been paid or tendered, or for some other sufficient reason.—Mabb v. Stewart, 7, 186.

§ 93. Effect of Reversal.

An order made by the court after judgment, and going to the same effect as the judgment in part, is reversed by a reversal of the judgment.—Hidden v. Jordan, 1, 216.

§ 94. Restitution by Losing Party.

Where, on appeal, a judgment is reversed, the appellate court will not compel restitution by the losing party of money which was not paid after, or in consequence of, the judgment appealed from, but was paid in consequence of an order made prior to the judgment, which order was not appealed from.—Reynolds v. Reynolds, 2, 547.

APPEARANCE.
See Attorney and Client, § 2.

§ 1. In General.

Irregular service of process is cured by the defendant subsequently appearing and putting in his answer.—Drake v. Duvenick, 1, 678.

APPROPRIATION.

To pay bonds. See Bonds, § 3.
To pay claims. See State, § 2.

ARBITRATION.

§ 1. Stay of Judgment.

On motion of one of the parties to an arbitration to vacate the award, the court below, concluding that the submission to arbitration was not a statutory submission, refused to entertain the motion, and ordered the judgment entered, and all proceedings under it to be perpetually stayed. Held, that the ruling was proper, it appearing that the judgment on the award was void.—In re Kreiss, 3, 475.

ARCHITECTS.

§ 1. Value of Services.

In an action by architects to recover for services, evidence of a rule of compensation of architects established by architects' institutes and associations is not admissible when not accompanied by any proof that the rule was known to defendant at the time of the alleged contract, or that it was so generally accepted by the public as to give it the standing of a custom, knowledge of which was to be imputed to him.—Laver v. Hotaling, 5, 534.

§ 2. Action Against County for Services.

An action was brought by an architect against a county to recover for the value of services rendered in making certain plans for a jail building, which plans had been accepted conditionally by the county board of supervisors, provided that a bid should be accepted from some reliable party for the building of the jail. The board of supervisors refused to open any of the bids received, and rejected plaintiff's plans, on the ground that he had been guilty of improper acts in getting his plans provisionally accepted. Held, that it was within the discretion of the board to refuse to open or accept any of the bids based upon plaintiff's plans, and that the condition upon which plaintiff was entitled to compensation never having happened, he could not recover.—Hall v. County of Los Angeles, 2, 754.

ARGUMENT.

Of counsel. See Trial, § 10.

ARREST.

Homicide in resisting. See Homicide, § 3.

§ 1. Absconding Debtor.

An affidavit for an order of arrest under section 479. Code of Civil Procedure of California, need not, in order to show that the defendant's proposed departure from the state is with intent to defraud his creditors, allege that he is about to remove any of his assets or property.—Ex parte Bernard, 2, 729.

ARREST OF JUDGMENT.

Motion in. See Criminal Law.

ARSON.

§ 1. Evidence.

On a trial for arson, where the evidence is circumstantial, and a witness for the state testifies that she was awakened during the night by the smell of burning rags, she may be asked on cross-examination whether there was not a great deal of rubbish in the back yard, near where the fire originated.—People v. Fournier, 5, 620.

Where the fire was seen in rubbish in a yard near the building burned, evidence that the rubbish was on fire in the same yard the day previous was admissible.—People v. Fournier, 5, 620.

Where a suspicious circumstance in the evidence against defendant was the removal of certain goods from the burned building the day before the fire, it was error to exclude evidence of defendant explaining the removal.—People v. Fournier, 5, 620.

Where a suspicious circumstance against defendant was that his building was insured, evidence that the building of a third person in which the fire started was also insured was admissible.—People v. Fournier, 5, 620.

§ 2. Instructions—Malice.

Instructions in prosecution for arson held sufficient.—People v. Lee Hung, 2, 226.

On a trial for arson an instruction that "malice, within the meaning of the law, includes not only anger, hatred and revenge, but every other unlawful and unjustifiable motive," is correct; Penal Code, section 7, subdivision 4, providing that "the words 'malice' and 'maliciously' import a wish to vex, annoy or injure another person, or an intent to do a wrongful act.—People v. Daniels, 4, 248.

ASSAULT AND BATTERY.

Removal of trespasser. See Trespass, § 5.

§ 1. Assault With Intent to Kill.

An assault with a knife, where prosecutor is cut on the head and neck, is not a simple assault.—People v. Davis, 4, 524.

On prosecution for assault with intent to murder, an instruction that the malice necessary to make a killing murder might be either express or implied, though technically correct, was inapplicable and erroneous, as the intent must be proved in such prosecution, and implied malice may show no actual intent.—People v. Mendenhall, 6, 631.

§ 2. Civil Action—Evidence and Instructions.

If a defendant admits that he struck the plaintiff with a fence pole, when he is charged with having struck him with a heavy club, the court is not unduly asserting judicial knowledge in instructing the jury that "the defendant admits that he struck the plaintiff substantially as charged."—Barker v. Hope, 1, 877.

In an action for personal injuries it appeared that plaintiff entered defendant's shop and was ordered out; that, as plaintiff stepped back to the door, defendant struck him several times on the head with a mallet and with his fist, which caused plaintiff to fall on a cutting machine, and injure his left arm so that it had to be amputated. Held, that a verdict for plaintiff was justified by the evidence.—Townsend v. Briggs, 3, 803.

In such action it was proper to charge that, "if the jury find from the evidence that defendant, from malicious motives, and a wrongful disregard of" plaintiff's rights, "assaulted him and beat him wrongfully," and plaintiff was injured, "directly or approximately, then plaintiff is entitled to recover all damages he has suffered thereby," and the amount of damages is for the jury alone to determine.—Townsend v. Briggs, 3, 803.

§ 3. Damages for Assault.

A judgment for $5,000 for an assault and battery is held excessive and reversed.—White v. Prader, 1, 54.

In an action for damages caused by a beating, a verdict of $1,300 will not be set aside as excessive.—May v. Steele, 2, 611.

In such action, a verdict of $9,000 was not so excessive as to show bias or prejudice.—Townsend v. Briggs, 3, 803.

ASSESSMENTS.

Of stock. See Corporations, § 24.
By irrigation district. See Irrigation, § 1.
Of swamp lands. See Swamp Lands, § 5.
In general. See Taxation, § 3.

ASSESSOR.

See Counties, § 2.

ASSIGNMENT.

§ 1. In general.
§ 2. Of contract to purchase land—Evidence.
§ 3. Of bank accounts—Change of possession
§ 4. Fraud.
§ 5. Suit for reassignment of life insurance.

Of error. See Appeal and Error, §§ 53–56.
Of guaranty to pay rent. See Guaranty, § 4.
Of lease. See Landlord and Tenant, § 4.
Of mortgage. See Mortgages, § 19½.
Of lien for special assessment. See Municipal Corporations, § 39.
Right of assignee of lease to have it reformed. See Reformation of
    Instruments, § 4.

§ 1. In General.

The obligor of a claim which apparently has been assigned is justified in treating with the assignee, if without knowledge or notice. that such is not the bona- fide owner of it.—Hendrickson v. Smith, 2, 187.

Upon the assignment of a secured debt, the creditor may also assign his security.—Chester v. Toklas, 2, 443.

In an action against the assignee of a paving contract for material furnished, it appeared that the assignment was absolute on its face; that, after the assignment, the assignees kept no account with the assignor; that they furnished all other materials not furnished by plaintiff, paid the bills, and received pay for the work, and stated in a verified complaint to collect an assessment for the work that they became and were, by assignment, contractors to perform the work. Held, that plaintiff could recover.—McCarty v. Owens, 5, 153.

Where a complaint alleged that defendant was indebted to plaintiff's assignor for services rendered at defendant's special instance and request between certain dates; that the services were reasonably worth $1,050, which had not been paid, except the sum of $46; that the claim was assigned to plaintiff on a certain day, two days before the services were fully performed; and that the plaintiff ever since has been, and now is, the owner and holder thereof—stated a cause of action, it being immaterial when the assignment was made.— Union Collection Co. v. National Fertilizer Co., 7, 244.

§ 2. Of Contract to Purchase Land—Evidence.

Plaintiff, having made a contract to purchase land from C., assigned it to defendant, who agreed to pay plaintiff a certain sum if he purchased the land from C. Held, in an action to recover such sum, that it was competent to show the circumstances attending the making of the contract of assignment, it being disputed whether C.'s sale of the land to defendant's stepson was under the contract between C. and plaintiff, and the relations between defendant and his stepson in regard to the entire transaction being a material issue raised by the pleadings.—Ferguson v. McBean, 4, 429.

It was proper to deny defendant's motion to strike out plaintiff's evidence as to conversations with a third person, not in the presence of defendant, and to retain such evidence till plaintiff's evidence was in, as other evidence might show that such third person was authorized to represent defendant.—Ferguson v. McBean, 4, 429.

Evidence that a third person agreed to pay plaintiff a part of the sum sued for was properly excluded, since defendant could not be relieved from his written obligation by such person's agreement to pay it, unless plaintiff released him.—Ferguson v. McBean, 4, 429.

Evidence that defendant's stepson told another person that he was representing defendant and was ready to consummate the trade was competent to show that the purchase was made under the contract assigned to defendant.—Ferguson v. McBean, 4, 429.

It was also competent to corroborate defendant's statement, after the sale, that he had purchased the property.—Ferguson v. McBean, 4, 429.

The possession and production by defendant's stepson, at the time of the transaction, of the assignment of the contract by plaintiff to defendant, were competent to show that he was defendant's agent.—Ferguson v. McBean, 4, 429.

The admission of testimony that plaintiff said defendant was represented by his stepson at the sale was not cause for reversal, when plaintiff had already testified to the circumstances connected with the assignment of the contract, and that the stepson was a party to the assignment, though it was not so stated therein.—Ferguson v. McBean, 4, 429.

Plaintiff having made the contract with C. personally, and having assigned it to defendant, evidence that plaintiff made the contract with C. at the request of one R. was properly excluded, as such fact would not alter defendant's liability.—Ferguson v. McBean, 4, 429.

§ 3. Of Book Accounts—Change of Possession.

"Book accounts and bills receivable, including all debts of every kind due (the assignor) from any person," are "things in action," and as such expressly exempt under Civil Code, section 3440, from the statutory rule requiring a valid transfer of personal property to be followed by immediate delivery and change of possession.—Kirk v. Roberts, 3, 671.

H., having transferred by assignment certain book accounts and bills receivable to plaintiff, in part payment of a debt and as security, retained possession thereof as agent to collect the same, and subsequently defendant was appointed his receiver and assignee in insolvency. Held, in an action for moneys collected by defendant on such accounts and notes assigned to plaintiff, where the complaint averred demand on defendant and refusal by him to pay, that it was not necessary to aver or prove nonpayment of plaintiff's claim, such fact being a matter of defense.—Kirk v. Roberts, 3, 671.

§ 4. Fraud.

The release from a past indebtedness due from the fraudulent assignee of a claim, who assumes to transfer the latter, is not a sufficient consideration as against the just owner, so as to insure rights in the transferee.—Hendrickson v. Smith, 2, 187.

One who purchases a claim from an assignee with notice of mala fides in the assignment cannot withhold the claim from the assignor. Hendrickson v. Smith, 2, 187.

Defendant having induced plaintiff to consent to an assignment of a lease by representations that the assignment provided for an annual rent of $800 to be paid plaintiff, it is unnecessary, in an action for fraudulent representations, that plaintiff prove that $800 could have been obtained, but if no more than $500, the amount actually provided for in the assignment, could have been obtained, this was a matter of defense.—Christensen v. Jessen, 5, 45.

§ 5. Suit for Reassignment of Life Insurance.

Where a plaintiff, while owner of a policy of life insurance, has assigned the same to the defendant, to secure advances made such defendant, and afterward sues for a reassignment of the policy in order to collect it from the insurance company, the court should not adjudge the plaintiff the owner of the policy and entitled to receive the whole amount from the company, for the interest of the plaintiff is only what remains after the advances have been satisfied. The defendant has the legal title, and cannot be made to surrender it until his advances have been paid.—Gilman v. Curtis, 2, 274

ASSIGNMENT FOR CREDITORS.

§ 1. In General.

An assignment by a dying debtor to his creditor may not after the death, if the estate proves to be insolvent, be allowed to benefit the taker up to the full amount of the thing assigned, but the taker is entitled to judgment for so much of it as will satisfy the debt.—Jamison v. King, 1, 833.

. An assignment for the benefit of creditors, that is shown not to include all of the debtor's property, will be held void, unless it is further shown that the omitted property is exempt from execution.—Aylesworth v. Dean, 2, 696.

Where an attorney, employed by an assignee to settle claims with the creditors, compromises the claims, giving his own notes in settlement at the rate of fifty cents on the dollar, with the understanding that the estate is to pay them when due, he cannot, on failure of the estate to do so, and after seeing that the estate is in fact solvent, have the claims assigned to a third person, who advanced to him the money to pay the notes, and collect the full amount of the claims for the benefit of such third person.—Sutliff v. Clunie, 4, 697.

Where, in such case, the attorney is the law partner of the assignee, the latter will be chargeable with constructive notice of all the facts in the transaction coming to the knowledge of the former, so as to render him liable for payments in excess of what the attorney paid for the claims.—Sutliff v. Clunie, 4, 697.

Where an assignee employs counsel to uphold the validity of an unjust claim against the estate, which he paid, he cannot, in case of defeat, charge the estate with the counsel fees.—Sutliff v. Clunie, 4, 697.

§ 2. Failure to Record.

Under Civil Code, section 3465, which declares an assignment for the benefit of creditors "void" as against nonassenting creditors, unless recorded as required by sections 3463, 3464, no preliminary suit is necessary by a nonassenting creditor to set aside an unrecorded assignment before he can maintain a creditors' bill to apply the assignor's property in the assignee's hands on a judgment against the assignor.—Watkins v. Willhoit, 4, 450.

The fact that an unrecorded assignment may be valid as between the parties does not render it merely voidable as against nonassenting creditors, since Civil Code, section 3465, expressly declares it "void" as against them.—Watkins v. Willhoit, 4, 540.

§ 3. Creditors' Bill to Set Aside.

The right to bring a creditors' bill to set aside an assignment for the benefit of creditors as in fraud of plaintiff's rights accrues when the execution on plaintiff's judgment against the assignor is returned unsatisfied, and not when the assignment was made.—Watkins v. Willhoit, 4, 450.

ASSISTANCE, WRIT OF.

In general. See Execution, § 13.
Prohibition against. See Prohibition, § 1.

ASSOCIATIONS.

Mutual life insurance. See Insurance, §§ 14, 15.

§ 1. To Defend Suits—Assessments.

Under a contract by which an association is formed to defend a suit for land, held in separate parcels by the associates, and directors are chosen to employ counsel, procure proofs, etc., with power in these directors to levy assessments on the associates according to their holdings, the assessments to be a lien on the land, which contract by its terms is to terminate when the suit does, no assessment can be made if after conclusion of the suit and payment of the costs the directors still have money of the associates in their hands.—Lowe v. Woodard, 1, 799.

§ 2. By-laws—Evidence.

An agreement by the stockholders of an association which recited that, "being desirous of having my oranges handled in the manner set forth in the by-laws" of the association, they individually appointed the association their agent, may be introduced in evidence, without the by-laws referred to, in an action by the association on a contract between it and a fruit company for the sale of fruit.—Tustin Fruit Assn. v. Earl Fruit Co., 6, 37.

Under Code of Civil Procedure, section 1854, providing that "when a detached act, declaration, conversation or writing is given in evidence, any other act, declaration, conversation or writing, which is necessary to make it understood, may also be given in evidence," defendant may introduce plaintiff's by-laws, where plaintiff introduced an agreement between its stockholders and plaintiff which stated that, "being desirous of having my oranges handled in the manner set forth in the by-laws" of plaintiff, they individually appointed plaintiff their agent.—Tustin Fruit Assn. v. Earl Fruit Co., 6, 37.

§ 3. Sick Benefits.

In an action against a benevolent association for the recovery of sick benefits, the burden of proof is on the plaintiff to establish a by-law, rule, or custom rendering the society liable for such sick benefits.—Mullally v. Irish-American Ben. Soc., 2, 440.

ASSUMPSIT.

See Pleading, §§ 2, 3.

ASSUMPTION.

Of mortgage by vendee. See Vendor and Vendee, § 4.

ASSUMPTION OF RISK.

By employee. See Master and Servant, §§ 5–11.

ASTRONOMICAL OBSERVATORY.

Trust for founding. See Trusts, § 5.

ATTACHMENT.

§ 1. In General.

Under the provision of Code of Civil Procedure, section 538, excluding from the debts on which an attachment may be obtained those secured "by any mortgage or lien upon real or personal property, or any pledge of personal property," the fact that a debt is secured by a bond executed by the debtor with sureties will not defeat an attachment thereon.—Slosson v. Glosser, 5, 460.

Evidence to impeach an affidavit of attachment is not admissible in a collateral proceeding by a stranger to the attachment suit to recover possession of the property.—Hilman v. Griffin, 6, 354.

A sheriff is entitled to an allowance of his necessary expenses of keeping and preserving attached property until after the judgment.—Alexander v. Wilson, 7, 195.

§ 2. Undertaking to Prevent Attachment.

In an action on an undertaking given to prevent the levy of a writ of attachment the plaintiff must allege and prove the consideration for which the undertaking was executed.—Preston v. Hood, 2, 148.

In an action on an undertaking given to prevent the levy of a writ of attachment judgment for the plaintiff is error when it appears by the pleadings and proof that actually a levy had been made and plaintiff had released it.—Preston v. Hood, 2, 148.

In a suit on an undertaking given to prevent a levy, where the complaint states that it was·given to release a levy, the variation is not material.—McNamara v. Hammerslag, 2, 259.

§ 3. Claim of Ownership—Mingled Goods.

The fact that goods of an attachment defendant are in the possession of a third person, who has mingled them with his own goods, and refuses to point them out, but claims ownership of all, does not warrant the seizure of goods, his title to which is unquestioned, and which are readily distinguishable from those of the attachment defendant.—Susskind v. Hall, 5, 304.

A notice to an officer of a claim of ownership of attached property is not vitiated by the statement therein that the claimant is the owner of all the property "except a portion owned by" another, who is not a party to the action.—Susskind v. Hall, 5, 304.

§ 4. Bond to Release Attachment.

In an action on a bond given to secure release of attached property, conditioned for liability in case judgment was rendered against defendant in attachment, a finding that a judgment was not rendered is not warranted where, in the record of the attachment suit subsequent to a judgment of nonsuit, appears a judgment for plaintiff therein, as to the legality of which there is no evidence, there being a presumption in its favor.—Moore v. Mott, 4, 269.

Plaintiff in an action on a note attached the property of one of the defendants, who gave an undertaking for the release of the attached property under the statute. Held, that, where plaintiff obtained a judgment on the note against the defendants, it fixed the liability of the sureties on the undertaking, given to release the attachment to the extent of the undertaking.—March v. Barnet, 5, 863.

In attachment against two defendants, the property of one only was seized, and an undertaking was executed to release the same. Judgment was recovered on the note sued on, and paid by one of the sureties on the attachment bond. Held, that under Civil Code, section 2848, providing that sureties on satisfying the obligation can enforce every remedy which the creditor then has against the principal, to the extent of reimbursing what he has expended, such surety could enforce the judgment on assignment to him against both of the parties, though the property of one only was attached.—March v. Barnet, 5, 863.

K. executed to plaintiff a redelivery bond, signed by defendants, to secure the release of an attachment; and, after the release, K. executed a mortgage on the property. Plaintiff, after obtaining judgment against K., issued an execution; but the sheriff released the levy and returned the execution unsatisfied, because the property was claimed by the mortgagor, whereupon plaintiff sued defendants on the redelivery bond. Held, that the levy of the execution by the sheriff constituted a sufficient demand by plaintiff for the return of the property to support an action against the sureties on the bond.—Mullaly v. Townsend, 6, 483.

Code of Civil Procedure, section 555, provides for the release of attached property on the giving of a bond for redelivery to the proper officer, if judgment be for plaintiff. Laws of 1880, chapter 87, section 17, makes an assignment within one month after the attachment operate as a dissolution thereof, and section 45 permits plaintiff who had a valid lien of attachment on property released under a redelivery bond to prosecute the case to final judgment in order to fix liability of sureties. Held, that section 45 does not apply to attachments within one month preceding the assignment, the sureties being released by dissolution of the attachment.—Rosenthal v. Perkins, 6, 21.

§ 5. Dissolution of Attachment.

An order refusing to dissolve an attachment will not be reversed on appeal where the evidence is conflicting.—Slosson v. Glosser, 5, 460.

Where, upon a motion to dissolve an attachment, the counter-affidavits of the defendant are fully answered by the affidavits produced in behalf of plaintiffs, the court has no right to disregard or discredit the showing on behalf of plaintiffs, and, on appeal, the order dissolving the attachment will be reversed.—Cahen v. Mahoney, 2, 709.

The undertaking in this case executed by the plaintiffs examined, and held to be sufficient.—Cahen v. Mahoney, 2, 709.

§ 6. Wrongful Attachment.

See, also, Sheriffs and Constables, § 4.

In an action for the alleged wrongful attachment and sale of plaintiff's wagon to satisfy another's debt, evidence of its cost price is admissible to aid in determining its value at the time of the alleged conversion.—Bunting v. Salz, 3, 193.

A question as to whether the debtor, subsequent to the sale and up to the time of the levy of the attachment, exercised any acts of ownership or control over the property, is not objectionable, as calling for opinion evidence.—Bunting v. Salz, 3, 193.

In an action of claim and delivery against an officer on account of a levy under an attachment against plaintiff's vendor, defendant may, under a denial of plaintiff's title, show that there was not an immediate delivery or continued change of possession as between plaintiff and his vendor, and he need not specially plead such facts.—Eaton v. Metz, 5, 59.

In an action against an officer for property levied on under an attachment against plaintiff's vendor, an averment by defendant that the sale to plaintiff was made with the design on his part, and on the part of his vendor, to delay and defraud the creditors of the grantor, and to prevent the application of the property to the satisfaction of their demands, does not authorize the admission of evidence of actual fraud.—Eaton v. Metz, 5, 59.

§ 7. —— Exemplary Damages.

Where a sheriff, in attaching property, was not guilty of any oppression, fraud or malice, within the meaning of Civil Code, section 3294, but acted fairly in all respects, and simply performed the duties required of him as a public officer, exemplary damages will not be allowed against him on dissolution of the attachment.—Spooner v. Cady, 5, 357.

ATTORNEY AND CLIENT.

Power of board of education to employ counsel. See Schools and School Districts, § 3.

Action by attorney for services, setoff. See Setoff and Counterclaim, § 1.

Argument and conduct of attorney. See Trial, § 10.

Counsel fees in trover. See Trover and Conversion, § 8.

Absence of attorney from trial. See Trial, § 9.

Counsel fees in suit involving will. See Wills, § 5.

§ 1. Duty of Attorney Toward Court.

Counsel should act in good faith toward the court, and in emergencies not remain silent in order to invite an inadvertence with a view, if possible, of torturing it into an error.—Dwyer v. California Steam Nav. Co., 1, 442.

§ 2. Authority of Attorney to Appeal or Bind Client.

A court cannot enter judgment upon a report of a referee to state the accounts between partners who are not parties to the proceeding, notwithstanding the agreement of attorneys to that effect.—Young v. Hoglan, 2, 46.

On appeal it will be presumed that appellant's attorney had authority to appear for him, from the mere fact that he assumes to do so.—In re Meade's Estate, 5, 678.

Where plaintiff's attorney entered into a stipulation with defendants solely on behalf of a coplaintiff, reserving all plaintiff's rights, the fact that the attorney was also attorney for plaintiff did not render the agreement binding on plaintiff.—Richardson v. Chicago Packing and Provision Co., 6, 606.

§ 3. —— As to Compromise.

Where the matter of a compromise was talked over between a client and his attorney, and the attorney did compromise on the terms which he supposed his client assented to, a finding is justified that the client authorized his attorney to compromise as he did.—Chaffey v. Dexter, 2, 397.

Whether an attorney correctly understood his client, regarding his desires as to a compromise, is a question dependent on the weight of evidence, and, the question being in doubt, the finding of the lower court will not be disturbed.—Chaffey v. Dexter, 2, 397.

§ 4. Duty and Liability of Attorney to Client.

A client cannot recover of his attorney damages on account of negligence, in the absence of any injury to the client caused by such negligence.—Hinckley v. Krug, 4, 208.

Money received by an attorney from his client, under a misapprehension on the part of the latter as to the purposes for which it is being paid, and under circumstances which require the attorney in good conscience to refund the same, may be recovered back.—Lutz v. Rothschild, 4, 888.

An attorney who buys his client's note at less than its face value, and then collects from the client its full value, is liable for interest, on the excess of the amount received by him over the amount paid, from the date of its receipt.—Andrews v. Wilbur, 5, 144.

§ 5. Employment and Compensation of Attorney.

In an action on an express contract for an attorney's compensation, the client is estopped to defend on the ground that the services contemplated by the contract were contra bonos mores.—Ballard v. Carr, 1, 704.

In an action by an attorney for compensation for services rendered in conducting a case, before the end of the trial of which his client had discharged him, an order for judgment for less than the fee as agreed upon in advance of such trial would not indicate, in the absence of written findings, that the court had found a failure on the plaintiff's part to perform the agreement.—Wheeler v. Turner, 1, 793.

Where the value of services sued for is found to be more than alleged in the complaint, the latter cannot be amended on appeal to conform to the findings.—Perkins v. West Coast Lumber Co., 4, 155.

Where an attorney renders services in various matters, and the client makes a partial payment "on account of fees for legal services," the attorney cannot credit the money on certain items of his account so as to place them beyond controversy.—Hinckley v. Krug, 4, 208.

The general employment of an attorney to defend a case is an entire contract, and, if he withdraws without cause, or is discharged for justifiable reasons, before the contract is completed, he cannot maintain an action for the value of his services.—Cahill v. Baird, 7, 61.

§ 6. Contingent Fees.

In an action for the recovery of attorney fees, the first count of the complaint was on a quantum meruit. The second count alleged that defendant promised to pay plaintiff an absolute fee of $500 for conducting certain litigation, and $1,000 in addition upon the contingency that plaintiff conducted said litigation successfully. The answer admitted that defendant promised to pay the absolute fee, but denied that he promised to pay any contingent fee. Held, that expert testimony was inadmissible to prove what would be a reasonable contingent fee, as the reasonableness of said fee was not in issue. The right to recover such fee depended entirely upon the proof of the alleged promise to pay it, and the performance by plaintiff of his part of the contract.—Ellis v. Woodburn, 3, 288.

The court instructed the jury that it was admitted that plaintiff did render some service, and "if you do not find that there was an express contract, as stated by either plaintiff or defendant, the services being admitted, and it being admitted that plaintiff has been paid $500 for his services, if you are satisfied that plaintiff's services were worth more than the $500 you will render a verdict for plaintiff for any amount above $500 that you find such services to be worth, not exceeding the sum of $1,000." Held, that the testimony having been as to what would have been a reasonable contingent fee under all the circumstances and as to what would be a reasonble attorney's fee in the case, taking into consideration not only the services actually rendered, but others which the plaintiff agreed to render, and there being no evidence as to what the services actually rendered were worth, it was error to give the instruction.—Ellis v. Woodburn, 3, 288.

An attorney to whom a cause is intrusted must, in order to become entitled to benefits promised him by his client in the event of success in his efforts, watch the progress of the action and keep himself in a position to perform any service which the exigency of the cause may demand.—Ballard v. Carr, 1, 704.

§ 7. Action to Recover Fees.

Attorneys' fees cannot be recovered where the agreement to pay them is not directly averred in the complaint, but is merely inferable from an exhibit annexed thereto.—Lee v. McCarthy, 4, 498.

A judgment for attorneys' fees in an amount in excess of that claimed in the complaint cannot be sustained.—Skym v. Weske Consolidated Co., 5, 551.

Under Code of Civil Procedure, section 1855, subdivision 5, providing that "there can be no evidence of the contents of writings other than the writing itself, except . . . . when the original consists of numerous documents, ... and the evidence sought from them is only the general result of the whole," it would not be necessary, in order to prove the character and value of the services rendered by an attorney in an action, to produce the record.—Cahill v. Baird, 7, 61.

§ 8. —— Negligence as Defense.

In an action for services as an attorney between certain dates, a finding of damages for defendant because of negligent advice given defendant at a time prior thereto must be disregarded, such negligence not having been pleaded.—Perkins v. West Coast Lumber Co., 4, 155.

In an action by an attorney to recover for professional services, defendant claimed damages for incompetency and negligence, and there was evidence that he employed plaintiff to prosecute certain actions to judgment for a fixed sum in each case, and that plaintiff was discharged before judgment for negligence and incompetency, in failing to file lis pendens in two foreclosure suits. Held, that evidence that plaintiff explained to defendant the effect of filing and failure to file such notices, and the probable expense, and that defendant said he did not want to spend the money for filing them, was admissible.—Hinckley v. Krug, 4, 208.

In such case it is not error to exclude evidence that part of the property covered by one of the mortgages plaintiff was employed to foreclose was conveyed by the mortgagor before, but the deeds were not recorded until after the foreclosure suit was commenced, where it appears that the remaining property sold for enough to satisfy defendant's judgment.—Hinckley v. Krug, 4, 208.

Where part of the services for which plaintiff seeks to recover consisted in examining the title to a lot, it is error to exclude evidence that, through the advice of plaintiff that the title was clear defendant purchased the lot, and was afterward compelled to redeem it from a prior tax lien.—Hinckley v. Krug, 4, 208.

§ 9. Admission to Practice.

Under act of February 15, 1905, vesting in the district courts of appeal created by constitution, article 6, as amended November 8, 1904, the exclusive power to admit persons to practice as attorneys and counselors in the several courts of the state, the supreme court has no original jurisdiction of an application for such admission; and a contested application originating in the supreme court will be transferred to the proper district court of appeal.—In re Hovey, 7, 202.

The finding of a referee appointed to ascertain and report as to moral character of applicant for admission to the bar that the applicant was of good moral character prior to his arrival in the state, and that he was then guiltless of crime or improper conduct as an attorney, is conclusive.—In re Hovey, 7, 203.

§ 10. —— Students of Hastings' College.

Whether Hastings' College of Law in the University of California created by Statutes of 1877-78, chapter 351, as a matter of law has affiliated with the university, as provided by such act, and whether the faculty of the university has granted diplomas to persons applying for admission to the bar thereon, cannot be tried collaterally on such application.—In re Students of Hastings' College of Law, 7, 376.

Under Statutes of 1877-78, chapter 351, providing that the diploma granted students of Hastings' College of the Law in the University of California shall entitle the student to a license to practice in all the courts of the state, subject to the right of the chief justice of the state to order an examination as in ordinary cases of applications without such diploma, it is the duty of the supreme court, on application of the students of such college, to license students holding such diplomas to practice as attorneys and counselors in all courts of the state.—In re Students of Hastings' College of Law, 7, 376.

§ 11. —— Pendency of Disbarment Proceedings.

The failure of an attorney, in making application for admission to the bar, to disclose to the court, and the attorney through whom his application is made, the pendency of disbarment proceedings against him in the state of his former domicile, does not materially affect his moral character or his admissibility to the bar.—In re Hovey, 7, 203.

The mere fact of pendency of disbarment proceedings in the state of the former domicile of an applicant for admission to the bar does not disqualify him.—In re Hovey, 7, 203.

§ 12. Unprofessional Conduct.

It is not unprofessional conduct on the part of an attorney to bring an action on a just claim against a nonresident, and serve summons by publication, when employed to do so, with the hope that possibly the defendant therein will pay the judgment obtained, on its being sent to the place where he resides, though such attorney knows such action cannot be maintained for want of jurisdiction.—Hinckley v. Krug, 4, 208.

But if the attorney advised his client, in such case, that the service by publication was good and a valid judgment could be obtained, such attorney cannot recover for services rendered therein.—Hinckley v. Krug, 4, 208.

§ 13. Disbarment and Removal.

Failure of testimony to sustain charges of misconduct preferred against an attorney entitles him to a dismissal of the proceedings.—People v. Redfield, 2, 120.

Proceedings to remove an attorney for professional misconduct are to be dismissed upon the filing of satisfactory affidavits in disproof and motion to dismiss made by the attorney accusing.—People v. Turner, 2, 123.

Evidence held insufficient to justify the defendant's removal or suspension from practice at the bar as an attorney and counselor.—In re Lowenthal, 2, 300.

Charges against an attorney at law, which, if proven, would not clearly constitute a cause for suspension or removal under the provisions of the code (Code Civ. Proc., sec. 287), will not be investigated on proceedings to remove him.—In re Treadwell, 2, 413.

Where the supreme court has, by its judgment, disbarred an attorney, a motion for a new trial will not be heard by it.—In re Tyler, 2, 740.

Charges against an attorney for the purpose of disbarring him held not sustained by the evidence.—In re Knapp, 2, 806.

An attorney, believing a certain paper to be a forgery, hired an expert to examine it. The expert expressed his doubt as to the forgery; and the attorney, supposing that the expert believed the paper a forgery, and only expressed doubt to extort money, offered him a large sum of money to testify in regard to the forgery. Held, that such conduct was subject to criticism but not sufficient ground for disbarment.—In re Barnes, 2, 847.

The respondent was charged with procuring one to steal a paper, but the only evidence against him was the testimony of the party who lost the paper that the person who stole it said that respondent had hired him to steal it. Held, that such statement was not evidence, and the respondent could not be disbarred on the charge.—In re Barnes, 2, 847.

Under Code of Civil Procedure, section 287, providing that an attorney may be disbarred for the reason, among others, that he has been convicted of a crime involving moral turpitude, the supreme court has no authority to proceed against a member of the bar upon a mere verified accusation of larceny, preferred by another attorney. In re Tilden, 3, 383.

The judge of department 9 of the superior court of San Francisco, who had directed a guardian not to pay out any of the trust fund except on order of the court, refused to grant an attorney an order allowing payment for services, because not properly itemized. This judge had, in fact, never had jurisdiction of the matter, and the attorney was so told by the judge of department 9, where the same was pending, and who promised to sign the order. The attorney thereupon, in good faith, obtained the money from the guardian, after telling him the facts. Held, no ground for disbarment.—In re Kowalsky, 4, 377.

An appeal by the accuser in a proceeding to remove one from his office of attorney and counselor is not contemplated by the law, and will therefore be dismissed.—In re Thompson, 5, 414.

Since the superior court has concurrent jurisdiction with the supreme court to disbar attorneys, an original application for disbarment will not be entertained by the supreme court unless the proceeding is instituted or supported by a bar association, or the misconduct is alleged to have direct connection with matters pending in the supreme court.—In re Delmas, 7, 146.

An application for the disbarment of an attorney on the ground that he had deprived prosecutor of certain money by fraud will not be entertained by the supreme court until prosecutor had established his cause of action against the attorney in the ordinary tribunals of the county in which the cause of action accrued by either criminal or civil process.—In re Delmas, 7, 146.

An attorney, with knowledge of the facts, who advises and takes steps to assist in a violation of the bankrupt law of the United States, whereby one creditor unlawfully secures a preference, is subject to suspension.—In re Naphtaly, 7, 378.

BAIL.

§ 1. Magistrate Having Jurisdiction.

Bail in a felony case is a matter for the consideration of the magistrate issuing the warrant, or of some other magistrate of the same county with him.—Ex parte Ah Fong Chi, 2, 70.

§ 2. Judgment on Bond.

The fact that judgment on a bail bond is rendered against the principal, who was not summoned and who did not appear, does not render it invalid as to the sureties, against whom judgment was also rendered, in accordance with the terms of the bond making each surety liable for the full amount thereof.—People v. Worth, 4, 121.

BAILMENT.
See Warehouse.

Embezzlement by bailee. See Embezzlement, § 6.

§ 1. Action Against Bailee—New Trial.

Where an action was brought to recover the value of certain goods left with a defendant for safekeeping, and the court rendered a judgment in favor of defendant, and afterward granted the plaintiff a new trial, held, upon the facts of the case, that there was no such abuse of the discretion vested in the trial court as would warrant a reversal of the order.—Daggett v. Vanderslice, 2, 745.

BALLOTS.
See Elections.

BANKRUPTCY.
See Insolvency.

§ 1. In General.

On the same day that a discharge in bankruptcy was granted to B., the maker of a note and mortgage, "from all debts and claims which are made provable against his estate," a stipulation was entered into between B. and C., the owner of the note, whereby it was agreed that the interest should be reduced, that the note should be extended, and that proceedings to enforce its payment should be dismissed. Held, that, as it did not appear that the agreement to pay the note was made after the discharge, the parties did not intend to make a new contract on which the bankrupt could be held, but only to extend the time and reduce the interest of the note and mortgage.—Chapman v. Pennie, 4, 970.

§ 2. State Insolvent Law.

Proceedings in insolvency under the state law for the relief of insolvent debtors and protection of creditors are not affected by the act of Congress of March 2, 1867, known as the Bankrupt Act.—Sedgwick v. Berry, 1, 482.

BANKS AND BANKING.

1. Collections and accounting therefor.
2. Overdraft—Mortgage as security.
§ 3. Authority of president as to land contract.
§ 4. Savings banks.

Deposits by partnership. See Partnership, § 8.

§ 1. Collections and Accounting Therefor.

Where a bank for collection, having a claim against a certain party, took certain of his notes from another party under an agreement to collect them, and, when collected, pay the proceeds thereof over to plaintiff, deducting costs and expenses of collection, and in pursuance of the agreement did so collect a portion of the notes by means of an action, judgment, and execution sale, if the proceeds were not sufficient to satisfy the demand of plaintiff, the owner of the notes, after payment of the bank's own debt and costs and expenses, neither the plaintiff nor the bank is entitled to payment in full out of the proceeds of the sale, but each is entitled to share in the proportion in which their claims against the debtor had paid the purchase price at the execution sale, and the plaintiff became entitled to his share thereof after sale upon demand.—Marks v. Bodie Bank, 2, 583.

§ 2. Overdraft—Mortgage as Security.

A bank took a mortgage as security for an overdraft, and later a note for the amount due on the draft, as a matter of bookkeeping, but with the agreement that it was not a payment of the account. The mortgage recited that it was to stand as security for whatever indebtedness to the bank might result from the account at any particular period. Held, to justify a finding that the note was not given in final judgment, and that the lien still subsisted.—Grangers' Bank v. Shuey, 6, 190.

§ 3. Authority of President as to Land Contract.

In the absence of authority by charter, resolution, or by-law, it will not be presumed that the president of a bank is authorized to waive conditions of a contract for the sale of land.—Chadbourne v. Stockton Sav. & Loan Soc., 4, 535.

§ 4. Savings Banks.

Act of April 11, 1862, section 10, providing that it shall be unlawful for a savings bank corporation or its directors to contract any debt or liability against the corporation for any purpose whatsoever, is to be construed in connection with the remainder of the act, which authorizes such corporation to purchase a lot and building for its business, and to employ and compensate help, and to incur other expenses, and in connection with the amendatory act of March 12, 1864, conferring on such corporations power to do a commercial banking business, buying bonds, securities, etc.; and hence the former act does not prevent the bank from incurring any liabilities whatsoever, but only those not authorized by the other legislation mentioned.—Laidlaw v. Pacific Bank, 6, 849.

Where there is a finding in an action against the bank by a creditor that a debt of the latter is for money expended by the creditor for the use and benefit of the bank and at its request, it will be presumed on appeal that the money was expended for purposes for which the bank could incur a liability.—Laidlaw v. Pacific Bank, 6, 849.

Where the debt of a creditor of a bank is for money expended for its benefit and at its request, it will not be heard, in an action by the creditor to recover the money, to deny liability on the ground that it could not legally be bound by a contract to pay.—Laidlaw v. Pacific Bank, 6, 849.

Act of April 11, 1862, section 10, providing that the assets and stock of a savings bank shall be security to depositors who are not stockholders, does not give priority to the claim of a depositor who is not a stockholder over the claim of a creditor of the bank who is also a stockholder thereof.—Laidlaw v. Pacific Bank, 6, 849.

BASTARDS.

Right to appointment as administrator. See Executors and Administrators, § 1.
Determination of heirship. See Executors and Administrators, § 37.

BENEFIT SOCIETIES.

See Associations.
Mutual life insurance. See Insurance, §§ 14, 15.

BIAS.

Of judge. See Justices of Peace, § 2.

BILL OF DISCOVERY.

See Discovery.

BILL OF EXCEPTIONS.

In general. See Appeal and Error, §§ 40–44.

BILL OF PARTICULARS.

See Pleading, § 14.

BILLS AND NOTES.

§ 1. Consideration.
§ 2. —— Want or failure of consideration.
§ 3. Delivery.
§ 4. Acceptance—Time of payment.
§ 5. Alteration by inserting interest clause.
§ 6. Accommodation paper.
§ 7. Joint and several obligation.
§ 8. Parol to explain note.
§ 9. Renewals—Consideration.
§ 10. Indorsement—Rights and liabilities of parties.
§ 11. Indorsement before delivery,
§ 12. Indorsement after maturity.
§ 13. Bona fide holders.
§ 14. Demand, presentation, notice and protest.
§ 15. Maturity and payment.
§ 16. Actions—Ownership to maintain.
§ 17. —— Pleading.
§ 18. —— Evidence.
§ 19. —— Defenses.
§ 20. —— Fraud as defense.
§ 21. —— Forgery as defense.
§ 22. —— Statute of limitations.
§ 23. —— Findings and judgment.
§ 24. —— Attorney fee.

Note given for broker's commission. See Brokers, § 8.
Execution of notes by corporate officers. See Corporations, §§ 15, 16.
Parol to vary indorsement. See Evidence, § 8.
Guaranty of payment of note. See Guaranty, § 2.
Agreement for indemnity. See Indemnity.
Disaffirmance by infant. See Infants, § 1.
Designation of parties. See Names, § 1.
In case of partnership. See Partnership, § 7.
Release from liability. See Release, § 1.
Replevin for note. See Replevin, § 2.
Cross-examination as to genuineness of note. See Witnesses, § 9.

§ 1. Consideration.

Money advanced by the plaintiff to the defendant on account of the latter's share of the capital in a business, which sum he was to invest and contribute to the business, is sufficient consideration to support a note given to secure such sum, and plaintiff may recover on such note, though the plaintiff and defendant were partners at the time of giving such note.—Talmadge v. Stretch, 2, 323.

In an action on a note for $625, the evidence was undisputed that, in consideration for the note, plaintiff transferred to defendant a one-half interest in a note for $2,500, on which the maker thereof agreed to pay $1,250 as a compromise. Held, that the fact that afterward, in an action thereon, the latter note was declared to have been made without consideration, does not affect the consideration for the note in suit, and plaintiff should recover.—Bean v. Proseus, 3, 558.

Where there is no evidence to show any consideration for a note, other than the circumstances disclosed in the statement of counsel, preceding a question asked by him as to whether there was any other consideration, permitting such question to be asked is not prejudicial. Eppinger v. Kendrick, 5, 295.

§ 2. —— Want or Failure of Consideration.

A promissory note given by defendant to plaintiff on the representation, innocently made, that the probate court had allowed plaintiff such sum for his services as guardian of defendant, when in reality no such sum had been allowed, is invalid for failure of consideration. Estudillo v. Aguirre, 2, 420.

In an action by a transferee of a note, where defendant sets up want of consideration, but does not produce any evidence that plaintiff's transferrer was a party to the fraud, or took the note with notice, or after maturity, a verdict for defendant should be set aside. Foote v. Hayes, 4, 976.

Where the makers of notes resisted payment on the ground of failure of consideration, evidence to vary the terms of the notes, which in no way related to consideration, was properly excluded.—Easton Packing Co. v. Kennedy, 6, 626.

Defendants executed two notes, for $385 each, in payment of a commission for selling land, and payable only in the event that the vendees of the land remained on it for one year, and made improvements equal in value to the notes. The vendees plowed one hundred acres, which increased its value $2.50 per acre, erected buildings, constructed drainage worth $75, and a levee worth $64, but with the consent of defendants, to whom they executed a reconveyance, abandoned the premises before the expiration of the year. Held, that a finding that there was not a failure of consideration for the notes was proper.—Easton Packing Co. v. Kennedy, 6, 626.

§ 3. Delivery.

A note placed in the keeping of a person, not named in it as a party, who was to deliver it only on a stated contingency, cannot be enforced by the payee's administrator who has got hold of it without the contingency taking place.—Hill v. Grigsby, 1, 720.

Where the payee of a check had notice of what was to be done by third parties before the check was to be delivered, evidence of negotiations with such third parties in the absence of the payee of the check is admissible to show nondelivery.—Schwartz v. Wright, 6, 248.

In an action on a check, defendants denied delivery, and in proof thereof introduced evidence showing that the check was made in payment of certain stock to be delivered, and entry of the other parties in the agreement into a pooling contract, and that the check was taken without consent by one of the parties, to whom it had been given for inspection. Held, that evidence of failure of the consideration for which the check was to be given was admissible as tending to show want of delivery.—Schwartz v. Wright, 6, 248.

Error in rejecting certain evidence as to the conditional delivery of a note was cured by the subsequent admission of all facts tending to show the real consideration for the note.—Easton Packing Co. v. Kennedy, 6, 626.

§ 4. Acceptance—Time of Payment.

Plaintiff furnished lumber for a building, and took an order to secure the purchase price, indorsed by defendant corporation: "Ac-

cepted, payable as follows: $375 upon completion of the house. . . . ."
Held, the acceptance was not conditional on the completion of the
building, but merely fixed a time of payment, and liability on the
acceptance matured on the destruction of the building by fire and the
determination of the owner not to rebuild.—Hogan v. Globe Mutual
Building etc. Assn., 7, 138.

§ 5. Alteration by Inserting Interest Clause.

In an action on a note a defense was that the note had been altered
by the insertion therein of writing calling for interest. The plaintiff in a verified complaint had alleged indorsement and transfer of
the note by the payee to another for value before maturity, and a
like indorsement by him to plaintiff. He testified that he had not
received payment. Held, that such testimony tended to establish
a prima facie case for plaintiff. On cross-examination of such witness defendant had a right to show by him facts which would dispute
his testimony that the payee assigned the note to him before maturity to show why he had not received payment, and to dispute that
the note had not been in his possession as testified by him.—Reese
v. Bell, 7, 73.

§ 6. Accommodation Paper.

In an action on a note, on the issue as to whether defendant signed
the note for the accommodation of the maker or for the accommodation of plaintiff, the payee, to enable him to use it as collateral,
the testimony of defendant and the agent who acted for plaintiff in
securing defendant's signature was directly contradictory. There was
evidence of subsequent circumstances which, on their face, appeared
contradictory of defendant's claim, but, as explained by him, did not
discredit his testimony. Held, that a verdict for defendant would
not be disturbed.—Eppinger v. Kendrick, 5, 295.

Where, in an action on a note, defendant claims that he signed
the note merely for the accommodation of plaintiff, to enable him
to use it as collateral, and has already testified as to the circumstances
of the transaction, as claimed by him, it is not prejudicial to plaintiff to permit defendant to be asked as to what was his understanding
as to the purpose of his signature.—Eppinger v. Kendrick, 5, 295.

§ 7. Joint and Several Obligation.

In an action on a note against one as surety, defendant denied
the suretyship, and alleged that he joined in the execution, for the
accommodation of plaintiff, and that, if he were liable as surety, the
principal maker had put in plaintiff's hands sufficient wheat to pay
the note, and directed that the proceeds thereof be applied thereon,
and that plaintiff did not so apply them. Held that, though the
defenses were not separately pleaded, the answer was sufficient, when
questioned, for the first time, on motion to exclude evidence offered
thereunder.—Eppinger v. Kendrick, 5, 295.

Civil Code, section 1659, relative to interpretation of contracts,
provides that where all the parties who unite in a promise receive
some benefit from the consideration, whether past or present, their
promise is presumed to be joint and several. Section 1431 provides
that an obligation imposed on several persons is presumed to be joint,
and not several, except in the cases mentioned in the title on the
"Interpretation of Contracts." Held, that, where a note was given
by two persons to obtain money for the benefit of one of them, the
obligation was joint as well as several.—Leonard v. Leonard, 7, 99.

§ 8. Parol to Explain Note.

If a note has been given with the understanding that it is to be
used in a particular way or with a particular qualification, parol evi

dence is admissible in an action between the original parties to prove the understanding.—Whiting v. Steen, 2, 175.

Where a receipt and a note are executed contemporaneously, the receipt is admissible in an action on the note, where there is evidence to show that both were part of one transaction; and oral testimony is admissible to apply the receipt to the note and to prove that it was the only consideration for the note.—Talmadge v. Stretch, 2, 323.

§ 9. Renewals—Consideration.

A widow is liable on her note given in renewal of prior notes to which her deceased husband was a party, though she gave it under misapprehension as to her liability for his debts, not induced by any misrepresentation by the payee.—Lyon v. Robertson, 6, 390.

The surrender of valid notes to one of the joint makers for cancellation is a good consideration for a new note given by him and the widow of the other maker in renewal thereof.—Lyon v. Robertson, 6, 390.

§ 10. · Indorsement—Rights and Liabilities of Parties.

One who takes by indorsement a fraudulent note, with knowledge of the fraud, cannot enforce it against the alleged maker.—Wells, Fargo & Co. v. William Mears Colman & Co., 1, 26.

The execution by an indorser of his own note, which is given and accepted in full payment of the note on which he is liable as indorser, constitutes a novation under Civil Code, section 1530, providing that "novation is the substitution of a new obligation for an existing one," and is made (section 1531) "by the substitution of a new obligation between the same parties with intent to extinguish the old obligation"; and the maker of the first note becomes liable to the indorser, though the holder, instead of canceling it, indorsed it without recourse to the indorser.—Stanley v. McElrath, 3, 163.

An indorsee of a note takes the same subject only to such defenses as would have been good against his indorser.—O'Conor v. Clarke, 5, 323.

Where a judgment is recovered against the maker and indorser of a note, and the property of the maker is attached, and the surety on the bond given to release the attachment pays the judgment recovered, and afterward collects the same from the indorser of the note, the only remedy of the indorser is against the maker of the note.—March v. Barnet, 5, 863.

§ 11. Indorsement Before Delivery.

A bill drawn payable to the drawer's order, and indorsed by him in blank, before maturity, is transferable by delivery merely.—O'Conor v. Clarke, 5, 323.

A person writing his name on a bill before maturity, to enable the drawer to whose order it was drawn to negotiate the same, is liable as an indorser.—O'Conor v. Clarke, 5, 323.

§ 12. Indorsement After Maturity.

Civil Code, section 3123, provides that an indorsee in due course is one who in the ordinary course of business and for value before its maturity, and without knowledge of the dishonor, acquires a negotiable instrument duly indorsed to him or indorsed generally. Held, that, where a note was not duly indorsed to plaintiff before its apparent maturity, in an action thereon by him the maker might set up any equitable defense.—Rees v. Bell, 7, 73.

Where a payee of a note made a mere equitable assignment thereof, and after maturity indorsed the same, the doctrine of relation would not apply to cut off the right of the makers to set up any defense good against the payee.—Reese v. Bell, 7, 73.

§ 13. Bona Fide Holders.

In an action on a note, indorsed in blank and transferred for value before maturity to the plaintiff, the maker cannot set up by way of counterclaim a claim against an intermediate holder of the note assigned to the defendant after the note came into the plaintiff's hands—Son v. Brophy, 1, 227.

A regularly authorized insurance agent to whom is forwarded by his company a policy to be delivered to the assured, together with the latter's note for collection or discount, and who discounts it without any knowledge of the soliciting agent's alleged fraudulent representations in procuring the policy, and who has no interest in the insurance or collection wi h the soliciting agent except an agreement that he will discount notes taken by the latter, is a bona fide holder of the note, and the soliciting agent's misrepresentations are not available as a defense against him.—McMahon v. Thomas, 4, 984.

An instruction that if the jury believe that there was known, at the time of the transfer of a note, facts sufficient to arouse the suspicions of an ordinarily prudent person, then the purchaser of the note cannot defeat the title of the true owner, is immaterial, where it appears, without conflict, that the parties so purchasing the note are not indorsees of the note, and therefore received no better title than the assignor had.—More v. Finger, 6, 326.

Receipts indorsed on a promissory note, and signed by the payee, do not make the holder of the note the indorsee thereof, within the meaning of Civil Code, section 3124, providing that the indorsee of a negotiable instrument, in due course, acquires an absolute title thereto.—More v. Finger, 6, 326.

§ 14. Demand, Presentation, Notice and Protest.

When all the circumstances go to prove that one who became the indorser of a note did so for the express purpose of having an extension given the maker for payment, that he knew the note would not be paid at maturity, which, counting the three days grace, would be four days after date, and that none of the parties contemplated a presentation formally on the day of maturity, there is shown by such circumstances that when indorsing the note the person concerned, by implication at least, waived presentation, notice and protest.— Pincus v. Aaron, 1, 468.

An indorser of a note who, after its maturity, has full notice that it has not been presented for payment, nor protested for nonpayment, and with such notice has promised to pay the note, is bound by the promise.—Pincus v. Aaron, 1, 468.

In an action on a promissory note payable on demand, no prior demand need be averred or proved.—Clauss v. Froment, 1, 690.

An indorser waives demand and notice if, immediately before the maturity of the note, he tells the payee to give himself no uneasiness in regard to payment, since he is collecting money for the maker and will see that the note is paid when due.—Bryant v. Feder, 1, 863.

An indorser of a note signed the following provision thereon: "I hereby guaranty the payment of the within note, ... and waive presentation, demand, notice of nonpayment and protest." Held that, as demand and notice of nonpayment need not be given a guarantor, the waiver was by the party as indorser.—Savings Bank of San Diego County v. Fisher, 5, 113.

Where a note secured by mortgage declares that, on failure to pay the annual interest when due, the whole sum of principal and interest shall become immediately due and payable at the option of the holder, demand after default is not necessary to support an action for the entire sum. Bringing the suit to foreclose is sufficient demand.—Hewett v. Dean, 3, 385.

A delay of three months after default in the interest is not a waiver of the right to exercise the option, when the delay is caused by reason of defendant's request to be allowed a few days additional in which to pay the interest.—Hewett v. Dean, 3, 385.

§ 15. Maturity and Payment.

A stipulation in a mortgage, making the principal of the note become due and recoverable at once upon default in the interest, is not necessarily invalid for repugnancy to the express terms of the note for payment on a day certain with annual interest.—McKissick v. Cannon, 2, 67.

A note expressly made payable after the maker should be released from an attachment then in force is not, before that event, subject to a demand for payment.—Henrickson v. Smith, 2, 187.

The payee of a note, in order to be able to have it discounted, induced another person to indorse it. An extension note, which was signed by the surety, but not by the maker, was paid, for the benefit of the surety by the payee of the original note; and both notes were marked "Paid," and delivered to him. Held, that such payment did not extinguish the original maker's liability, as it was not by a mere volunteer.—Dow v. Nason, 4, 865.

§ 16. Actions—Ownership to Maintain.

Possession of a note is sufficient to enable the holder to sue to enforce payment.—Berri v. Minturn, 1, 50.

Transfer of a note to a bank for collection gives it such ownership thereof that it can sue the maker thereon.—First Nat. Bank v. Hughes, 5, 454.

A finding that plaintiff bank was not the owner of the note sued on, which was in evidence, indorsed by the payee, cannot be sustained, as against the positive testimony of plaintiff's president and cashier that the note was bought by plaintiff of the payee before maturity, though plaintiff, on sending the note after maturity to another bank for collection, sent a new note to be executed by defendant, extending the credit for six months, which was made payable to the payee of the first note—plaintiff's president testifying that it was customary to have renewal notes so executed, and then indorsed by the payee—and though the cashier of another bank testified that it was customary to have notes discounted by a bank marked differently from the one in question.—First Nat. Bank v. Hughes, 5, 454.

§ 17. —— Pleading.

A complaint that does not show the plaintiff to be the holder or indorsee of a bill sued upon, made by defendant in favor of a third person and protested for nonpayment, is bad on demurrer.—Gatliff v. Cram, Rogers & Co., 1, 47.

In a simple action to enforce payment of a promissory note, allegations in the answer to the effect that the note was secured by mortgage does not constitute a good plea in either bar or abatement.—Harden v. Ware, 2, 72.

An answer in an action by one claiming to be a bona fide indorsee for value before maturity of a bill of exchange drawn on and accepted by defendants' testator, denying on information and belief that the drawer of the bill ever transferred it to plaintiff by indorsement or otherwise, as alleged in the complaint, that it was ever delivered to plaintiff, that he paid any value therefor, or that he was ever the bona fide holder or owner thereof, puts in issue plaintiff's title to the bill, and it is error to render judgment in his favor without proof of title.—Mair v. Forbes, 3, 81.

In an action on two notes the answer admitted the allegations in the complaint, but set out a contract for a deed to defendant from plaintiff, with the averment that the execution of the contract and the making of the notes were parts of the same transaction, and that the contract was the only consideration for the notes, and that no deed had been tendered by plaintiff. Held, that the complaint was defective, and presented no cause of action, in that it did not set out the contract, and allege performance by plaintiff of its conditions. Naftzger v. Gregg, 3, 520.

A complaint on a note alleging its date and execution, and promise to pay ninety days therefrom by defendant maker, and a transfer by indorsement to plaintiff, and nonpayment by defendant, states a sufficient cause of action.—Pilster v. Highton, 3, 632.

By failing to verify their answer, where a copy of the note was set out in the complaint, defendants admitted, not only the genuineness, but also the due execution, of the note.—San Bernardino Nat. Bank v. Andreson, 3, 771.

In an action on a note, the complaint need not specially aver a consideration.—Younglove v. Cunningham, 5, 281.

§ 18. —— Evidence.

In an action on a note, where the question is whether or not plaintiff is an innocent holder for value, interrogatories whose evident purpose is to show that plaintiff took the note with notice of a partial failure of consideration, it having been held on a former appeal of the case that such partial failure of consideration was a defense pro tanto, are allowable, although defendant is precluded from questioning plaintiff's ownership of the note by the fact that the pleadings admit that it was indorsed and delivered to him.—Braly v. Henry, 3, 3.

Where the answer to a complaint on a promissory note expressly admits its execution, it is unnecessary to introduce it in evidence.—Sheehy v. Chalmers, 4, 617.

In an action to hold one liable as an indorser, evidence that defendant was seventy-five years old, and unable to read or write; that he never authorized the indorsement, but only authorized his name to be written on an undertaking for a small amount, is sufficient to sustain a verdict that defendant did not indorse the note.—Ford v. Kenton, 5, 780.

Where, in a suit on a note, a witness testified that he had been attorney for the maker after the note was given and at the time certain indorsements were made by the payee, but that he was not the attorney for the payee, his testimony was not rendered incompetent because the payee subsequently testified that such witness was his attorney, the evidence being conflicting, and the court accepting that of the attorney.—Reese v. Bell, 7, 73.

Where one of the makers of a note who had paid it sued the other, on the ground that the note was for defendant's benefit and that it was agreed he would reimburse plaintiff if he paid it, and no objection was made to plaintiff's evidence because the note itself was not introduced in evidence or its absence accounted for, the absence of such evidence was no ground for a nonsuit.—Leonard v. Leonard, 7, 99.

§ 19. —— Defenses.

In an action against the maker of a note for the amount paid thereon by the indorser, it is no defense that the indorser paid it without proper demand and notice; for, as these are for the benefit of the indorser, he may waive any defects therein.—Stanley v. McElrath, 3, 163.

In an action on a note given for a balance found due on a settlement of accounts, where defendant failed to allege fraud in the account, his offer to show that plaintiff received money as his agent, for which he failed to account, was properly overruled.—Clarkson v. Hoyt, 4, 547.

§ 20. —— Fraud as Defense.

Fraudulent representations, to be defense to note, must be such as to cause defendant to execute the note.—Farmers and Merchants' Bank v. Richards, 6, 19.

No defense to note is shown by answer alleging that, by false representations of plaintiff's officers, defendant was induced to make the note in payment of others previously given for money borrowed by him from plaintiff, no damage being shown.—Farmers & Merchants' Bank v. Richards, 6, 19.

§ 21. —— Forgery as Defense.

The fact that nothing was heard of a defense that an indorsement on a note was a forgery until the maker had absconded does not estop the party from asserting it, especially where there was evidence that he did not know that he was held liable until suit was commenced.—Ford v. Kenton, 5, 780.

§ 22. —— Statute of Limitations.

Where plaintiff and defendant gave a note for the benefit of defendant the money being to pay an obligation of defendant's and defendant agreed to pay the note or repay plaintiff if he paid it, the transaction was not a loan by plaintiff, and his cause of action against defendant for the purpose of the statute of limitations did not arise until payment by him of the note.—Leonard v. Leonard, 7, 99.

§ 23. Findings and Judgment.

Under Code of Civil Procedure, section 667, providing that judgments in suits on contracts or obligations in writing for the direct payment of money may be made payable in the kind of money specified therein, a judgment payable in "U. S. gold coin" is not erroneous, when the note on which it is rendered is payable in "U. S. gold coin." Sheehy v. Chalmers, 4, 617.

Where defendant in an action on notes alleges the conveyance to plaintiff of property as security, and asks for an accounting, it is not error to render judgment dismissing the cross-complaint where the evidence shows that plaintiff holds the property, not as security, but as a naked trustee, and is ready to surrender the same.—Megginson v. Turner, 6, 208.

Where there was sufficient evidence of plaintiff's ownership of the notes in suit, and the court found against the defendants on the only defense set up by them, error of the court in finding that plaintiff came into possession of the notes without notice of equities in favor of defendants was harmless.—Easton Packing Co. v. Kennedy, 6, 626.

§ 24. —— Attorney Fee.

Where a stipulation in a note for an attorney's fee in case the note is sued on does not fix the amount of such fee, a reasonable sum therefor will be allowed.—Hildreth v. Williams, 4, 141.

BOARD OF EDUCATION.

Duty of city attorney to defend. See City Attorney.
Power to employ counsel. See Schools and School Districts, § 3.

BOARD OF EQUALIZATION.

See Taxation, § 12.

BOARD OF EXAMINERS.

See State Board of Examiners.

BONA FIDE HOLDERS.

Of negotiable paper. See Bills and Notes, § 13.

BONDS.

§ 1. Execution and delivery.
§ 2. Bond to secure note—Action on—Pleading.
§ 3. Appropriation to pay—Liability of state.
§ 4. Municipal bonds.
§ 5. —— Elections.
§ 6. —— Subsequent statute affecting purchases.
§ 7. —— Funding—Limitation of actions.

See Principal and Surety.

On appeal and liability of sureties. See Appeal and Error, §§ 23-27.
In attachment. See Attachment, §§ 2–4.
Assumption by corporation. See Corporations, § 17.
Issuance by corporation. See Corporations, § 18.
In case of injunction. See Injunctions, § 3.
On appeal to superior court. See Justices of Peace, § 7.
Failure to file. See Mechanics' Liens, § 3.
Of municipality. See Municipal Corporations, § 7.
For performance of public work. See Municipal Corporations, § 27.

§ 1. Execution and Delivery.

When the execution of a bond sued upon is not denied in the answer, the question of delivery is not before the court on appeal.—County of Merced v. Turner, 2, 216.

Where a bond is in form joint and several, the failure of all the parties named in the instrument as obligors to sign the bond does not render it void.—Stinson Mill Co. v. Riley, 5, 218.

§ 2. Bond to Secure Note—Action on—Pleading.

A complaint averred that defendant T. gave to plaintiff a note for $700; that, six months afterward, defendants D., as principal, and S. and C., as sureties, gave T. a $3,000 bond, which was set out, conditioned that whereas T. and T. J. C. (who was not made a party) "are now indebted to parties hereinafter named in the sums set opposite each name, and that the purpose of this obligation is to relieve the said T. from any and all liability on said indebtedness as follows, and we hereby agree to assume and pay the same, to wit, two promissory notes of $700 each, and the interest thereon: . . . . Now, if the said T. J. C., or any of the parties save and except the said T.," shall pay such sums, the bond shall be void, etc.; that T. was then indebted to plaintiff on two notes, one of which is the one sued on; and that the only indebtedness from T. to plaintiff was that evidenced by such notes. Held, that such complaint was not subject to a general demurrer, because the bond was to relieve T. from liability on a joint indebtedness of T. and T. J. C., while the debt sued on was T.'s only.—Nevin v. Thompson, 4, 390.

Nor was such complaint demurrable because T. J. C. was not a party, as he was not a necessary party.—Nevin v. Thompson, 4, 390.

Such complaint was not defective for uncertainty as to whether the suit was on the note or on the bond.—Nevin v. Thompson, 4, 390.

§ 3. Appropriation to Pay—Liability of State.

Act of May 3, 1852 (Stats. 1852, p. 59), provided for the issuance of bonds to pay the expense of military expeditions, such bonds to be payable out of funds appropriated for that purpose by Congress, with the condition that, if such appropriation was insufficient, the bonds would be a valid claim against the state. Congress, in 1845 (10 Stat. 576), appropriated an unapportioned amount intended to pay the military expenses of the state incurred under the act of May 3, 1852, and under prior acts, but such appropriation, while sufficient to cover the expense under the act referred to, was insufficient to pay the entire indebtedness for which it was appropriated, and interest coupons on such bonds held by plaintiff were unpaid. Held, that the liability of the state being conditioned on the failure of Congress to make an appropriation sufficient to pay the bonds issued under that act, such appropriation being sufficient for that purpose, the state was not liable, though the appropriation was insufficient to cover another and prior indebtedness not mentioned in the act.—Reis v. State, 6, 358.

§ 4. Municipal Bonds.

A city has no power to issue bonds payable in "gold coin of the United States" (in conformity with the ordinance submitting the matter to the voters, and the notice of election), instead of in "gold coin or lawful money of the United States," as required by act of March 1, 1893 (Stats. 1893, p. 61).—Murphy v. City of San Luis Obispo, 5, 665.

The term "five per cent per annum" in a municipal bond means that the interest is payable annually.—Murphy v. City of San Luis Obispo, 5, 665.

§ 5. —— Elections.

Under Statutes of 1889, page 399, section 2, authorizing a city to prescribe by ordinance the manner of holding a special election for the issuance of municipal bonds, an ordinance directing each voter to indicate his wish by "writing or causing to be written or printed 'Yes' or 'No' on the right-hand margin on his ticket, opposite the proposition on which he may desire to vote," is mandatory, and is not satisfied by stamping a cross opposite the word "Yes" or "No" printed after the proposition, as provided by the general election law, which the ordinance declares shall only be followed when not in conflict with said ordinance.—Murphy v. City of San Luis Obispo, 5, 665.

§ 6. —— Subsequent Statute Affecting Purchasers.

Act of March 26, 1851 (Stats. 1851, p. 391), incorporating the city of Sacramento, and investing it with authority to sue and be sued, and acts of April 26, 1853 (Stats. 1853, p. 117), and April 10, 1854 (Stats. 1854, p. 196), authorizing the issuance of bonds of the city, gave the purchaser of such bonds the right to sue the city if they were not paid when due; and this right could not be impaired by subsequent legislation.—Bates v. Gregory, 3, 170.

§ 7. —— Funding Limitation of Actions.

Act of March 22, 1864 (Stats. 1864, p. 217), entitled an "Act to provide for the liquidation of the indebtedness of the city of Sacramento which accrued prior to January 1, 1859," and empowering the board of trustees of the city to issue new bonds, in liquidation, to all holders of claims against the city, was passed merely for the purpose of completing the funding of the city's indebtedness, and did not withdraw claims, existing before the passage of the act, from the operation of the statute of limitations; and an action for mandamus to compel the board of trustees to issue bonds, as therein provided, in place of those issued by the city under acts of April 26, 1853, and April 10, 1854, cannot be maintained where such bonds have since the act of 1864 become barred by the statute of limitations.—Bates v. Gregory, 3, 170.

BOOKS OF ACCOUNT.

As evidence. See Evidence, § 29.

BOUNDARIES.

§ 1. Navigable stream.
§ 2. Possession under mistake as to line.
§ 3. Oral agreement concerning.
§ 4. Evidence as to location.
§ 5. Maps and plats.
§ 6. Conclusiveness of verdict or finding as to line.

Of counties, changing. See Counties, § 1.

§ 1. Navigable Stream.

Where a surveyor's straight and angular lines along a navigable stream are concerned in the map of a government survey, it is not to be supposed that the government meant to reserve the small and useless parcels between these and the banks. Where there is no natural boundary the line of survey will determine the boundary, but where the call is for a nevigable stream, the only necessity for a survey is for purposes of computation.—Madden v. Ashman, 1, 610.

§ 2. Possession Under Mistake as to Line.

Where coterminous proprietors are in possession of certain land under a mutual mistake as to the division line, such possession has no effect upon their legal rights, nor is it adverse or conclusive against the assertion of any existing rights based upon the true title.—Smith v. Robarts, 2, 604.

§ 3. Oral Agreement Concerning.

Adjoining proprietors may orally agree that the division line between their lands shall be a certain fence.—Adair v. Crane, 2, 559.

Where coterminous proprietors enter into a verbal agreement to have the true division line surveyed, and to abide by the line so established, such agreement is binding, and is not within the statute of frauds.—Smith v. Robarts, 2, 604.

§ 4. Evidence as to Location.

A one-time county surveyor may be called to explain in court a plat produced from the official records but made by him during his incumbency, and in explaining may use memoranda and field-notes found among his private papers from which he made the plat.—Valentine v. Jansen, 1, 525.

Parol evidence should not be received to prove a boundary line when the best evidence in point is procurable in the form of an express grant of the land.—Umbarger v. Chaboya, 1, 698.

On the question of the location of a point called for in a patent and survey, the court may consider the field-notes and description

31

in the patent of an adjoining tract, the boundaries of the two tracts being coincident for a distance of several miles, and both having been surveyed by the same surveyor at about the same time.—Adair v. White, 4, 261.

Statements of a former owner of land, and his acts in putting in stakes on an alleged boundary line, are unavailing to establish the boundary, where the adjoining owner was not present, nor had any knowledge of such acts.—Borchard v. Eastwood, 6, 736.

Where, in an action to determine a boundary line, a witness has testified to a survey, the admisssion in evidence of a map made by him explanatory of such survey is not error.—Pickering Light and Water Co. v. Savage, 6, 985.

The lines described in a patent must be located by the court according to the calls of the patent. Witnesses can testify only as to the existence and condition on the ground of what is called for in the writing; and it is error to admit their opinions, speculations, or conjectures as to the location of the lines.—Tognazzini v. Morganti, 3, 235.

§ 5. Maps and Plats.

Where plaintiff in ejectment claims land under the official map of a certain addition to a city, and defendant claims under the official map of an adjoining addition, and it is stipulated that the map under which defendant claims is the official map of that addition, and that under it defendant has shown title to the land in controversy, and the evidence shows that such map is the one under which both parties have acted, it will be considered as the controlling map by which to locate the line between the two additions.—Buckley v. Mohr, 6, 321.

There is no provision in Revised Statutes of the United States, sections 2395, 2396, 2397 (U. S. Comp. Stats. 1901, pp. 1471–1473), relating to the rules to be followed where corners have been lost, or in the circular of instructions approved by the Secretary of the Interior October 16, 1896 (23 Land Dec. Dep. Int. 361), relating to lost or obliterated corners, for a proportionate measurement based on the deficiency in acreage of adjoining parcels of land, and, where there is no question as to the establishment of a lost corner, the exact boundaries as shown on the government plat must prevail, and they will control a further description by quantity.—Somers v. McMordie, 7, 358.

§ 6. Conclusiveness of Verdict or Finding as to Line.

The verdict of a jury on the question of a boundary, when the deeds produced in evidence were conflicting in their descriptions, and the oral testimony bearing thereon also conflicting, is to be taken as final.—Valentine v. Jansen, 1, 525.

Where on appeal a point has reference to a boundary line indefinite in the statement, by reason of the absence of maps referred to in the evidence, the court deeming the evidence conflicting may on that ground refuse to disturb the judgment.—Madden v. Ashman, 1, 610.

On the question of the proper location of a point called for in a survey and patent, a finding by the court on conflicting evidence will not be disturbed on appeal.—Adair v. White, 4, 261.

The findings of the trial court as to the location of a division line will not be disturbed where the evidence is conflicting.—Ponet v. Wills, 5, 659.

BREACH OF PROMISE TO MARRY.

§ 1. Evidence.

Code of Civil Procedure, section 1845, provides that a witness can testify to those facts only which he knows of his own knowledge.

Held, that, in an action for breach of marriage promise, the admission of plaintiff's declarations to third parties, who were not invited to attend the wedding, and before any wedding day had been set, that plaintiff and defendant intended to marry, constituted prejudicial error.—Leibbrandt v. Sorg, 6, 687.

The fact that there was competent evidence to prove a contract of marriage in an action for breach of promise did not render the admission of declarations of plaintiff to third parties that plaintiff and defendant intended to marry harmless, where the court stated in the presence of the jury that such evidence was competent.—Leibbrandt v. Sorg, 6, 687.

Evidence to the effect that after an alleged promise by the defendant to marry the plaintiff the latter announced to several persons, in the defendant's absence, that she was engaged to him, is admissible to show that the promise had been accepted by the plaintiff, although not tending to prove the promise itself.—Reed v. Clark, 1, 95.

§ 2. Damages.

In an action for damages for breach of promise to marry, it is not error for the court to charge the jury that in assessing the damages it is their province to take into consideration the defendant's pecuniary condition.—Reed v. Clark, 1, 95.

In an action for breach of promise to marry, it is not error for the court to charge the jury that they may consider in aggravation of damages whether or not the defendant had come into court and wantonly attempted to show the plaintiff guilty of improper conduct with other men, of which she was innocent.—Reed v. Clark, 1, 95.

Where, in an action for breach of promise, the court charged that, if plaintiff and defendant entered into an agreement to marry, plaintiff was entitled to damages if defendant wrongfully violated the agreement, a further charge that the shock and injury to plaintiff's affections occasioned by defendant "having violated his promise" was a proper element of damages was not misleading.—Leibbrandt v. Sorg, 6, 687.

§ 3. New Trial.

A motion by the defendant for a new trial based upon newly discovered evidence in a suit for breach of promise to marry, is properly denied if such evidence goes merely to the question of the plaintiff's chastity and at the trial the defendant has introduced much evidence on that question.—Reed v. Clark, 1, 95.

BRIEFS.

On appeal, in general. See Appeal and Error, §§ 57-59.

BROKERS.

§ 1. Contract with Principal.

R. wrote a broker that, "if there is any possibility of selling both or either piece of property, see if you can make it this week. . . . .

Also V. told me S. told him he had a man who wanted Hoza Bernal's place. . . . . You had better see S., and get hold of the buyer, ... for if V. finds out who it is he is bound to spoil the sale. . . . . In case you make a sale of the 29½ acre piece," a certain mortgage can remain on the place for one year. "Also the Ratke place, there can be" a mortgage for one year or longer. Held, that such letter did not authorize such broker to sell real estate situate in the county of A. "generally known as the 'Jose Reyes Bernal Rancho,'" or any other real estate, and was inadmissible in an action by such broker against R. for services in selling such real estate, under Civil Code, section 1624, subdivision 6, which requires agreements authorizing or employing brokers to sell real estate for compensation to be in writing. Such letter was not rendered admissible by evidence by plaintiff which tended only to apply the description in the complaint to a particular one of Jose Bernal's several tracts, and did not show which one of such several tracts was intended by the expression "Hoza Bernal's place," in such letter.—Mendenhall v. Rose, 4, 81.

§ 2. Parol Agreement—Divisibility.

Though, under Civil Code, section 1624, a parol contract employing a broker to sell land is invalid, a broker employed to sell or exchange land, and the personalty thereon, under an agreement for a commission of five per cent on the price may, on bringing about an exchange, recover five per cent on a separate valuation placed on the personalty by the principal, though in the exchange, as between the parties thereto, there may have been no division of the consideration, as the contract, in such case, is divisible, and that part as to the land is not unlawful, but merely incapable of enforcement.—Porter v. Fisher, 4, 324.

It is immaterial whether the separate valuation was placed on the personal property by the principal before or after the exchange, or to whom he made the statement as to the valuation, since it is an admission that the personal property was exchanged at such valuation, so that its price can be separated from the gross sum involved in the exchange.—Porter v. Fisher, 4, 324.

§ 3. Agreement With One Executor.

Under Civil Code, section 1624, providing that an agreement authorizing an agent to sell real estate for a commission must be in writing, a real estate agent cannot recover from executors, as individuals, commissions for selling property, when the contract produced is contained in letters from one of the executors only, which show that he was acting as executor, and not individually.—Perkins v. Cooper, 3, 279.

§ 4. Acting for Both Parties.

Where the evidence shows that plaintiff in an action to recover commissions earned under a contract to find a purchaser for defendant's land was employed by the purchaser without defendant's knowledge to buy the land from defendant at a figure which would suit the purchaser's views, a finding that he was the purchaser's agent was proper, though he had no written agreement with the purchaser for compensation, but was to get his compensation from defendant; and, being the agent of both parties without defendant's knowledge, he cannot recover.—Berlin v. Farwell, 3, 634.

§ 5. Revocation of Authority.

On appeal from a judgment in favor of a broker for commissions for selling the defendant's real estate, the question of an alleged revocation before the sale of the plaintiff's authority to sell will be left as found by the trial court, if the evidence was conflicting.—Brown v. Pforr, 1, 632.

A person authorized by the owner of land to sell it gave a con· tract to a third person for the price named but "subject to perfect record title, thirty days allowed for examination of title." The owner of the land let such third person take the abstract to examine, but told him he could not have thirty days. Held that, as the agent had not produced a purchaser ready and willing to take the property on the terms embraced in the authority, the owner might, before such unconditional acceptance, revoke the authority of the agent.—Blumenthall v. Goodall, 3, 311.

§ 6. Compensation and Actions Therefor.

The plaintiff and defendant entered into a written agreement that if plaintiff should succeed in selling certain mining stock in defendant's possession, that plaintiff should receive all defendant's stock at twenty cents per share, and the shares held for third person at fifty cents per share. Plaintiff then went to T., one of the stockholders, and by inducing him to believe that all the stockholders had agreed to take twenty cents per share for their stock, procured an order on defendant authorizing him to sell all T.'s stock at twenty cents per share and deposited the said order with defendant. The next day T. revoked the order, but plaintiff received no notice thereof, and sold the mine at the price agreed on between himself and defendant. Defendant received all the money paid by the persons to whom plaintiff sold, and paid T. fifty cents per share for his stock. Plaintiff sued defendant for the difference between the price of the stock at twenty cents and fifty cents per share. Held, that defendant was not liable, not having received any money from the sale of the stock for the use of plaintiff.—Wallace v. Hopkins, 2, 873.

A real estate broker who makes a contract with a property owner can recover commissions only in accordance with such contract.—Quiggle v. Prouty, 5, 398.

In an action for compensation for the sale of mining claims for $235,000, where plaintiff's witnesses testified that ten per cent was a reasonable compensation, and defendant testified that he offered $7,500, and that plaintiff offered in writing to take $10,000, but no such writing was introduced in evidence, and there was a verdict for plaintiff for $7,500, an award of a new trial to plaintiff was not an abuse of discretion.—Pinney v. Wilson, 7, 309.

In an action for compensation for the sale of real estate, evidence held sufficient to sustain findings that the plaintiff procured a purchaser who was ready, able and willing to purchase and thereby completed its services and earned its commission.—E. P. Vandercook Co. v. Wilmans Co., 7, 311.

Under a contract whereby the owner of land gave plaintiff exclusive authority to sell it and agreed to pay a commission on any amount for which the property should be sold, the plaintiff was entitled to his commission on procuring a purchaser able, ready and willing to purchase though the sale was not actually completed.—E. P. Vandercook Co. v. Wilmans Co., 7, 311.

§ 7. —— Insufficiency of Evidence.

On January 17, 1891, plaintiff, at London, transmitted to decedent an offer from a corporation there to purchase certain land owned by him which he accepted on conditions, one of which was that £10,000 be advanced as security for performance. On April 25th plaintiff wrote, asking that the conditions be waived. No direct response was made, and decedent, on June 2d, wrote that, unless he received notice by July 1st that the matter was closed, he would withdraw about one-

half of the land from the pending proposals. No such notice was
sent, but plaintiff wrote that the letter was not clear, and that he
expected to hear from decedent that the proposition was satisfactory.
On December 5th plaintiff wrote that the corporation would be glad
to do business, and requested decedent to send some one to London to
complete the negotiations as outlined in their former propositions,
which letter was delivered by R. On January 15, 1892, decedent replied that he was sorry his last letter was not sufficiently clear, and
that he was willing to sell on the terms proposed in their letter of
January 17, 1891, or would divide the property into two portions, and,
if the matter was definitely settled, his son in law could go to London, provided £1,000 was paid for his expenses. On March 16th plaintiff wrote that the corporation was in liquidation, and he would try
to sell the land to others. R. testified that when he delivered the
letter of December 5, 1891, decedent said he knew satisfactory terms
had been made between himself and the corporation about June or
July, 1891, and that plaintiff had effected a sale with these parties,
and that he should have gone across, and closed up the matter on the
other side. Held, in an action to recover for services rendered in
procuring the purchaser for the land, that there never was such a
meeting of the minds of the negotiating parties as would authorize recovery.—Leszynsky v. Meyer, 6, 53.

§ 8. —— Notes Given for Commission.

Plaintiff brokers were engaged to sell certain property for a specified commission, one-half to be paid when the first installment of the
price was paid, and the other half on the payment of the second installment. A sale was effected, it being agreed that the purchaser
should be allowed one-half of the commissions. To settle the purchasers' claim that they were entitled to one-half of the entire commission on the payment of the first installment, plaintiffs allowed the
former to retain half the entire commission, and entered into an
agreement with them which recited that the purchasers had received
the full amount of their commission, and plaintiffs were to have all
the commission due on the second installment; and that certain non-
negotiable notes contemporaneously executed by the purchasers to
plaintiffs for plaintiffs' share of the commission on the first installment should be returned to the purchasers if the second payment
"was completed." The second installment was not paid, and plaintiffs
sued the purchasers on the notes. There was nothing to show that
plaintiffs had in any way prevented the payment of the second installment. Held, that, irrespective of whether there was a tender
of the second installment by the purchasers, and a wrongful refusal
of the sellers to accept it, which of itself would "earn" the commission, plaintiffs were entitled to recover on the notes, since they were
based on a valuable consideration, and the second payment was not
"completed."—Wallace v. Randol, 6, 150.

§ 9. Purchase and Sale of Stock by Broker.

In an action by a broker against a customer who, after an alleged
purchase of stock for him by such broker at his request, has repudiated the transaction, evidence that the plaintiff did not, when buying
the stock, name the defendant to the vendor as the real purchaser,
is immaterial.—Shipley v. Larrimore, 1, 297.

Buying stock in his own name without the consent, knowledge or
ratification of the particular customer for whom he buys is not a
conversion of the stock by the broker, and it is not a waiver of the
contract had with the customer to buy for him.—Shipley v. Larrimore, 1, 297.

In the trial of an action by a broker for the price of stock purchased for the defendant at his request, the defendant cannot, under an answer that denies he ever made such a request, introduce evidence to show that the plaintiff waived the request to buy for him and had bought for himself, or had converted the stock.—Shipley v. Larrimore, 1, 297.

The sale by a broker, under the rules or custom of the board of brokers, of stock in his hands for which the customer has not paid, the customer being given timely notice in contemplation of such sale, does not amount to a conversion.—Shipley v. Larrimore, 1, 297.

§ 10. Fraud of Broker—Liability to Principal.

A broker who fraudulently represented to the principal, whose money he was loaning, that the security was good, is liable, though the principal was in a position to have examined the security.—Rubens v. Mead, 6, 14.

The recovery in action by principal against broker, for fraudulently representing that the worthless property on which loan was made was good security, is not affected by the question whether he shared the money with, or delivered any part of it to, the pretended borrower.—Rubens v. Mead, 6, 14.

Where, in an action against a broker for fraud in the sale of plaintiff's land, the findings, which were in favor of the defendant, were either in express conflict with the allegations of defendant's answer or were in conflict with the testimony, and there was also evidence opposed to the general finding, it was proper for the court to grant plaintiff a new trial.—Crocker v. Garland, 7, 275.

BUILDING AND LOAN ASSOCIATION.

Liability on secretary's bond. See Principal and Surety, § 2.

§ 1. Actions Involving—Jury Trial.

A suit to determine title to stock in a building association, to cancel the certificate representing the stock, to restrain the payment of money on account of the certificate, and to require the issuance to plaintiff of a new certificate for the stock, is a suit in equity, and a jury trial is not demandable as of right under Code of Civil Procedure, section 592, providing that, in cases other than actions for the recovery of specific real or personal property, etc., issues of fact must be tried by the court, subject to its power to order issues to be tried by a jury.—Noble v. Learned, 7, 297.

BUILDING CONTRACT.

§ 1. Interpretation of contract.
§ 2. Failure to furnish bond.
§ 3. Payment to contractor or subcontractor.
§ 4. Failure to perform—Acceptance and compensation.
§ 5. Action to recover for work and materials.

See Mechanics' Liens, § 2.

§ 1. Interpretation of Contract.

A condition in a building contract that "should the contractor at any time during the progress of the work refuse or neglect to supply a sufficiency of material or workmen, the owner shall have power to provide materials or workmen, after one day's notice in writing being given to finish said work, and the expense shall be deducted from the amount of the contract," does not require that the owner shall, on default of the contractor, either finish the work in his place, or wait until the time has expired when the contract was to be finished under the agreement, and then proceed against the contractor for damages. The owner may, instead, enter into an independent contract for the completion of the work.—Dingley v. Greene, 2, 441.

Where there is no provision in a building contract as to how windows are to be placed, there is an implied agreement that they shall be placed in a workmanlike manner.—Schindler v. Green et al., 7, 233.

§ 2. Failure to Furnish Bond.

Where in an action for a breach of contract it appeared that defendant verbally accepted plaintiff's written offer to furnish stone for a building defendant had undertaken to build, and that plaintiff was required, as one of the conditions, to execute a bond for the performance of the work and to commence the work as soon as possible, the failure of plaintiff to furnish or tender the bond within eight or nine days precludes his right to recover prospective profits, when nothing has been done under the bid.—Flynn v. Dougherty, 3, 412.

§ 3. Payment to Contractor or Subcontractor.

In payment to a contractor for erecting a building, deduction cannot be made for money given, without his prior authority or subsequent ratification, to satisfy a demand by a subcontractor.—Miller v. Board of Education, 1, 607.

A payment made to a subcontractor and charged to the account of the contractor without authority by him first given is validated by a ratification by the contractor afterward.—Miller v. Board of Education, 1, 607.

If a person has furnished materials as a subcontractor, and other materials at the sole instance of the owner, any ratification by the contractor of a payment by such owner to such subcontractor, deducted from the contractor's account, is presumed to have applied no further than to the amount of what was due under the subcontract. Miller v. Board of Education, 1, 607.

§ 4. Failure to Perform—Acceptance and Compensation.

Plaintiff contracted to build an addition to defendants' house. The plastering of the addition was to be done by another contractor. Plaintiff claimed that his work was completed, and thereupon the plasterer went ahead with his contract, and did the plastering. But it was not shown that defendants occupied the addition. Held, that the doing of the plastering did not constitute an acceptance of plaintiff's work by defendants, such as to excuse plaintiff from actually completing the contract if it was not in fact completed when he quit work.—Schindler v. Green, 7, 229.

Where a contractor fails to complete his contract, even though such failure is a trivial variance, he must have acted in good faith and honestly have endeavored to complete his work properly before he can recover therefor, if the trivial variance is such as to entitle the other party to damages to complete the work or make it as it should be.—Schindler v. Green, 7, 233.

§ 5. Action to Recover for Work and Materials.

Assumpsit will lie to recover a balance due on a special contract to erect a building, and it is not necessary to allege the performance of all the conditions to be performed before payment was due.—Castagnino v. Balletta, 3, 107.

In an action for services for construction of a building, defendant, after testifying that plaintiff left the job uncompleted, and that he (defendant) thereafter superintended the work himself, and that it took up his time so that he could not attend to his business (which, it appears, was that of a merchant) for two months, was asked "the value of the time he lost" while personally superintending the work. Held, that the question was objectionable, as calling, not for the reasonable compensation of a superintendent, but for the value of his time.—Crawford v. Harris, 5, 403.

Allowing defendant, on cross-examination, in an action for construction of a building which he claimed he had to complete himself, to be asked if he had not told the brickman that he would not pay him, but that if he got anything he would have to get it out of plaintiff, even if error, is harmless, defendant's answer being "No."—Crawford v. Harris, 5, 403.

BUILDINGS.

Tools falling into street. See Negligence, § 4.

§ 1. Removal of Building—Suit for Recovery.

Under Code of Civil Procedure, section 442, providing that, when a defendant seeks affirmative relief relating to the transaction upon which the action is brought, he may file a cross-complaint, a cross-complaint in an action to recover buildings removed from plaintiff's land which alleged that plaintiff purchased the land and erected the buildings for defendants, agreeing to convey the premises to them when they could purchase the same; that defendant tendered him the purchase price therefor, but that he refused to give them a deed thereto, and which prayed judgment that plaintiff deed the property to defendants, was improperly stricken out.—Hall v. Cole, 4, 928.

In an action to recover buildings removed from plaintiff's land, wherein defendants admitted that plaintiff purchased the land and erected the buildings, but claimed to own the premises by reason of plaintiff's agreement to sell the same to them, and their tender to him of the purchase price, plaintiff testified that he agreed to sell the premises to defendants, and that they advanced him money to apply in purchasing the land and erecting the buildings, but that they withdrew all of the same soon after; that he let defendants go into possession of the premises without any further transaction; that thereafter defendants tendered him the purchase price of the land, only, and he told them merely that he could not give them a deed, but would have to see the man who then held the title to the property to secure a loan to plaintiff. Held, that ownership of the buildings not appearing in defendants, a nonsuit was improperly granted. Hall v. Cole, 4, 928.

BURGLARY.

§ 1. Participant in crime.
§ 2. Evidence.
§ 3. —— Possession of stolen' property.
§ 4. Verdict—Degree of guilt.
§ 5. Judgment.

§ 1. Participant in Crime.

The fact that a person was living with one guilty of burglary at the time the burglary was committed, and that he made untruthful statements as to where the guilty party obtained the property, is not sufficient evidence to warrant the conviction of such person as participating in the crime.—People v. Brady, 6, 719.

§ 2. Evidence.

Evidence held insufficient to justify the verdict.—People v. Carlton, 2, 381.

Defendant leased a house in which there was no furniture. A vacant house on another farm about nine miles distant contained household furniture, which was found in defendant's possession at the time of his arrest. One witness testified that the defendant had borrowed a team about the time the furniture was supposed to have been taken, and another witness testified as to seeing such a team going in the direction of the vacant house, and later return toward the defendant's place. Defendant made many contradictory statements as to where he obtained the furniture. Held, sufficient to warrant a conviction for burglary.—People v. Brady, 6, 719.

Where, on a prosecution for burglary, the defendant's wife had testified as to the purchase by her husband of the alleged stolen articles, it was proper cross-examination to ask her as to statements, inconsistent with her testimony, at the time of her husband's arrest. People v. Brady, 6, 719.

Defendant was found at night, less than an hour after a malt-car was burglarized, and less than two blocks from the car, with two other boys, each having on his shoulder a sack of the stolen malt. Defendant's companions escaped, but he was seized in the act of dropping the malt. He refused to explain to the officer what he was doing with the malt, and on his preliminary examination testified that he did not remember anything of his arrest, or that he had any conversation with the officer, or that he had any sack in his possession, or was in company with anyone at the time of his arrest. At the trial he testified that he was intoxicated on that evening; that he met three persons, who had four sacks of malt with them; and that he, at their request, assisted in carrying one of the sacks for them. Held, that defendant's conduct in refusing to answer the officer, and his failure of memory at the preliminary examination, followed by his recollection of an important fact in his favor on the trial, betrayed guilt, which, corroborated by the fact of the possession of the stolen property, was sufficient to support a conviction.—People v. Joy, 6, 824.

An officer accosted defendant at night with stolen malt in his possession, and asked him what he was doing with that; whereupon defendant replied that he was no chicken, and was not going to tell. Held, that such statement was a mere declaration of the defendant against interest, and not a confession, and was therefore admissible without a foundation showing that the statements were voluntary.—People v. Joy, 6, 824.

§ 3. —— Possession of Stolen Property.

In a burglary case it appeared that a Chinaman's trunk and pipe were stolen from the burglarized building. There was evidence that two persons carried a "China trunk" from the lot on which the building was situated about the time the crime was committed; that defendant and others were seen with such a trunk about that time; and that such Chinaman's trunk was found open two days afterward, a considerable distance from the building. There was no evidence that a "China trunk" is any different from any other trunk. The pipe was put in evidence, but there was no testimony as to where it was found. Held, that the evidence did not justify an instruction as to the effect of possession of property recently stolen.—People v. Abbott, 4, 276.

It is error to charge that the possession of stolen property soon after the taking, while not sufficient to justify a conviction, is a "guilty circumstance," and that defendant was bound to explain the possession in order to remove its effect.—People v. Abbott, 4, 276.

On a prosecution for burglary, it was not error to instruct that the possession of stolen property soon after the commission of the alleged offense by the person charged was a circumstance tending to prove their guilt, and that the jury should consider the proximity of the place where the property was found to the place of the alleged burglary, the lapse of time since the property was taken, the character and nature of the property taken, and whether the parties denied or admitted the possession, in determining how far the possession of the property by the accused tended to show his guilt.—People v. Brady, 6, 719.

§ 4. Verdict—Degree of Guilt.

Under the Penal Code, section 1157, providing that whenever a crime is distinguished into degrees, the jury, if they convict, must find the degree of which defendant is guilty, the jury are not excused from finding the degree though the indictment was for burglary, of which there are but two degrees, and the court instructed that if the jury found defendants guilty they could find them guilty of no higher offense than burglary in the second degree.—People v. Bannister, 4, 333.

Under Penal Code, section 1151, providing that a general verdict on a plea of not guilty is either "guilty" or "not guilty," which imports a conviction or acquittal of the offense charged in the indictment, the designation of the offense in a general verdict is mere surplusage, and a verdict finding defendant guilty of "burglary" is valid.—People v. Brady, 6, 719.

On a prosecution for burglary it was not error to leave it to the jury to formulate their own verdict on blank forms furnished, stating the degree of guilt of the defendants, if either of them were guilty, and that, if the jury needed further instruction as to framing a verdict, it should return to the courtroom for such instruction.—People v. Brady, 6, 719.

§ 5. Judgment.

Defendant pleaded guilty to a charge of burglary in the first degree, and the judgment recited that, "whereas defendant has been convicted of the crime of burglary in the first degree, ... it is ordered," etc. Held, that the judgment was valid, though the minutes of the court did not show that any evidence was heard to prove the degree of the crime of which defendant was found guilty, there being nothing in the minutes to contradict the recitals of the judgment.—Ex parte Woods, 5, 149.

BY-LAWS.

In general. See Associations, § 2.

CANCELLATION OF INSTRUMENTS.

Of lease procured by conspiracy. See Landlord and Tenant, § 2.
Of deed. See Mines and Minerals, § 9.

§ 1. Jurisdiction in General.

The doctrine of courts of equity with respect to setting aside deeds, securities and agreements is referable to the jurisdiction they exercise in favor of a party quia timet.—Keller v. Lewis, 2, 29.

§ 2. Grounds for Cancellation and Instruments Subject Thereto.

A court of equity will not direct to be delivered up or canceled an instrument illegal on its face, since there can be no danger that lapse of time will deprive of defense a party applying for the cancellation. Keller v. Lewis, 2, 29.

If an agreement having reference to land is valid on its face and might be made the foundation of and important evidence in an action, it operates as a cloud on the title, and the owner of the land has a right to have it set aside either as such cloud or as a probable subject of future litigation.—Keller v. Lewis, 2, 29.

If an instrument ought not to be used or enforced, it is against conscience for the party holding it to retain it, since his retaining it can only be for some sinister purpose.—Keller v. Lewis, 2, 29.

One who holds an instrument that menaces the title of another's land, and whose continuing so to hold can serve no just purpose of his own, cannot justify the retention of it by disallowing any intent to rely upon it and by claiming it was obtained by the other's fraud.—Keller v. Lewis, 2, 29.

If one holding a contract looking to the sale of land to him, which contract he has failed to live up to and has voluntarily abandoned, puts the land owner to the necessity of suing for a cancellation, the court has jurisdiction to bar him, by the terms of its decree, from asserting any claim to money paid by him on the contract.—Keller v. Lewis, 2, 29.

Mere inadequacy of price is insufficient to warrant setting aside a sale.—Barry v. St. Joseph's Hospital, 5, 625.

Plaintiff deeded a lot to her son, retaining a life estate therein. In an action by her to cancel the deed, the attorney drawing it testified that at the time of executing it her mind was sound. There was no evidence that she was of weak intellect, though she was old and in feeble health. Held, that a finding that she was of sound mind will not be reversed.—Springer v. Springer, 6, 662.

§ 3. Pleading and Practice.

A complaint to cancel a deed alleged that defendant, without plaintiff's consent, abstracted the deed from a safe where it had been deposited by plaintiff in escrow pending the completion of a proposed sale to defendant of land therein described; that defendant after thus obtaining the deed caused it to be recorded; that no money was ever paid for the land; and defendant refused to pay the consideration or reconvey to plaintiff. Held, that the complaint showed a good cause of action.—Rising v. Gibbs, 3, 506.

Where plaintiff conveyed a lot to her son, and he conveyed it to his wife, in an action by plaintiff to cancel her deed to the son findings that his deed to the wife was for a valuable consideration, and also for love and affection, were not prejudicial to plaintiff, the court having refused to cancel plaintiff's deed.—Springer v. Springer, 6, 662.

CARRIERS.

See Shipping.

§ 1. Carrier of Goods.

In the trial of a case against alleged bailees to recover for damage claimed to have happened to goods of the plaintiff intrusted to defendants for transit, a verdict for the plaintiff after he by his own testimony, as well as other evidence, has proved that the contract of shipment was made by him with the defendants as agents, he knowing them to be such at the time, cannot be sustained.—Muller v. Rogers, 1, 451.

§ 2. Connecting Carriers—Limitation of Liability.

Under Civil Code, section 2201, declaring that the liability of a carrier who accepts freight for a place beyond his route ceases on delivery to a connecting line, "unless he stipulates otherwise," a provision in a freight contract that the carrier's responsibility shall cease at the connecting point is not rendered ineffective by a further stipulation for through passenger train service.—Colfax Mountain Fruit Co. v. Southern Pac. Co., 5, 527.

There being no repugnancy between the provision limiting the carrier's liability to its own line and the stipulation for through passenger train service, the fact that the first is printed, while the last is in writing, is immaterial in construing the contract.—Colfax Mountain Fruit Co. v. Southern Pac. Co., 5, 527.

Where a railroad company receives freight for shipment under an agreement to forward it to its destination, and the stipulation that its liability as carrier shall cease on delivery of the goods to the first connecting line, the contract also providing for "passenger service through," the duty of the company as forwarding agent continues till the goods arrive at their ultimate destination, and it is therefore liable for any delay caused by its failure to notify each successive connecting road of the conditions of the contract in respect to the manner of transportation.—Colfax Mountain Fruit Co. v. Southern Pac. Co., 5, 527.

§ 3. —— Burden of Proof.

In an action by the shipper against the contracting carrier for damages caused by such delay, the burden is on defendant to show that it notified each successive connecting road of the conditions regarding the manner of transportation, or, if it did not, that the delay was not attributable to its default in this respect.—Colfax Mountain Fruit Co. v. Southern Pac. Co., 5, 527.

§ 4. Carrier of Passengers—Injury in Boarding Car.

Where a passenger goes on the side of the platform car opposite the platform, and not at the place arranged to receive passengers, and attempts to climb on the train from between the cars, and in so doing places his foot on the bumper, where it was injured by the engine moving up to couple the train, he is guilty of contributory negligence, and cannot recover.—Wardlaw v. California Ry. Co., 5, 225.

In an action against a railroad company for injuries received by a boy seventeen years old, while attempting to pass between the cars of a freight train to reach a passenger train which he intended taking, an instruction that no recovery could be had if the boy possessed mental capacity to realize the danger to which he was subjecting himself, because the law is that one going into a place of danger assumes the risk, without any restriction as to the qualified measure of care and caution required of one not of full age, was not objectionable, where such qualifications were repeatedly given, and specifically applied in other instructions.—Maglinchey v. Southern Pac. Co., 5, 363.

§ 5. —— Injury in Alighting from Street-car.

In an action against a cable-car company for injuries received in alighting from a car alleged to have been prematurely started, after instructing the jury that common carriers of passengers must use such vigilance and foresight as they can, under the circumstances, in view of the character and mode of conveyance adopted, to prevent accidents, it was not improper to instruct that "it was the defendant's business to know, before starting up the car, whether passengers getting off or on the car were in a position to be injured, and it would be negligence to start the car suddenly, under such circumstances, without exercising every precaution for the safety of those who might be getting off or on."—Tobin v. Omnibus Cable Co., 4, 214.

In an action against a street-car company for personal injuries, plaintiff claimed, and the evidence tended to prove, that a car was started while she was alighting therefrom, while defendant claimed, and gave evidence to show, that the car was started before plaintiff left her seat, and that she tried to get off while the car was in motion. Held, that an instruction making the defense of contributory negligence dependent on whether defendant could have guarded against such negligence was rendered harmless by subsequent instructions that the verdict must be for the defendant if the injuries were caused either solely by plaintiff's negligence, or, jointly and concurrently, by the negligence of plaintiff and defendant or its servants, and that if plaintiff, knowing the car was in motion, chose to run her chances, and get off by stepping directly out from the car, she must abide the risks she took.—Tobin v. Omnibus Cable Co., 4, 214.

§ 6. —— Injury While on Train.

If a law provides that in case a passenger on a railway train suffers injury "on the platform of a car or on any baggage, wood, gravel or freight car, in violation of the printed regulations of the company posted up at the time in a conspicuous place inside of its passenger cars then in the train . . . . such company shall not be liable for the injury, provided said company at the time furnished room inside its passenger cars sufficient for the accommodation of its passengers," it is immaterial that the law does not in express terms prohibit a recovery of a person so suffering an injury.—Cullen v. Southern Pac. R. R. Co., 2, 9.

In the trial of an action against a railroad company for injuries received by the plaintiff while riding on one of the defendant's cars, when in fact it was not a passenger car, and a law relieved a company observing certain conditions from liability for injuries received on other than passenger cars, an instruction asked by the defendant on the hypothesis virtually of the plaintiff being debarred from recovery under this law is not too broad merely for failing to state just what description of car it was the plaintiff was riding on.— Cullen v. Southern Pac. R. R. Co., 2, 9.

§ 7. —— Upsetting of Stage or Coach.

An instruction in effect that, it being admitted that defendant was a common carrier and that plaintiff on a day named was a passenger riding in a defendant's coach, and while so riding was upset and was injured thereby, plaintiff had made out a prima facie case, unless defendant proved the upsetting to have been the result of inevitable casualty, was not in conflict with another, in substance, "If you believe from the evidence in this case (that is, on both sides) that the upsetting was not occasioned by the negligence and carelessness of the defendant but by an act of God you should find for defendant."— Wiggin v. Ayres, 2, 184.

In an action by a passenger against a stage company for personal injuries received from the upsetting of a stage in coming down a mountain road, it appeared that one of the horses had been inclined to run away; that the road was muddy and slippery; that the horses were going at "a slow jog," when they were frightened by a landslide; that they ran one hundred yards before the driver regained control; that flying mud and slush made it hard for the driver to see, and tended to frighten the horses; and that the horses were going in a trot, when they were so frightened by another slide that the driver lost control, and they ran away and upset the stage. Held, that there was evidence for the jury as to whether defendant failed to provide suitable horses and driver.—Knight v. Pacific Coast Stage Co., 4, 358.

Where the only issues were as to the suitableness of the horses and driver, the court properly refused to instruct concerning latent defects in the stage and concerning the duty of the injured party to exercise proper care in endeavoring to recover from the injury.—Knight v. Pacific Coast Stage Co., 4, 353.

§ 8. —— Injury to Passenger by Captain of Boat.

Plaintiff was arrested by the captain of defendant's steamboat, and chained to a post on the lower deck, and ejected before he reached his destination. The court charged that plaintiff could recover only the actual damages suffered by him, unless defendant authorized the acts complained of, or participated therein or ratified them; and that the jury should not allow anything by way of punishing the defendant, unless it authorized the captain's acts or ratified them; and that, unless defendant participated in or authorized the captain's acts or ratified them, the measure of damages would be the amount which would compensate the plaintiff for all detriment proximately caused by the wrongful acts. Held, that the instructions were not erroneous as contradictory and too general.—Trabing v. California Nav. and Imp. Co., 6, 696.

§ 9. —— Evidence and Presumptions.

In an action for injury from being thrown from a car by its coming to a sudden stop, by reason of a defective switch, while being run at a high rate of speed, evidence that other persons than plaintiff were thrown from the car and injured is admissible to overcome the claim of defendant that plaintiff's injuries were caused by his negligence in jumping from the car when in motion.—Fogel v. San Francisco etc. Ry. Co., 5, 194.

In an action for injuries received in an accident due to a defective switch, evidence by a skilled switch-tender as to whether anything was not done that could have been done to have avoided the accident is inadmissible, as invading the province of the jury.—Fogel v. San Francisco etc. Ry. Co., 5, 194.

Where it is shown that an injury to a passenger was caused by the act of the carrier in operating the instrumentalities employed in his business, there is a presumption of negligence, which throws on the carrier the burden of showing that the injury was sustained without any negligence on his part; and hence a verdict for plaintiff for injuries against a street railroad will not be reversed because the evidence fails to show that the rate of speed of the car at the time of the accident was excessive, or that the excessive rate of speed or other negligence of defendant was the proximate cause of the injury, since it is sufficient that it fails to show that it was not so.—Bassett v. Los Angeles Traction Co., 6, 700.

The admission of evidence that defendant's cars had been running slower at the place where the accident occurred since it happened was harmless, if erroneous.—Bassett v. Los Angeles Traction Co., 6, 700.

In an action for injuries to a passenger from a railroad collision, it is presumed in the first instance that the collision was the result

of the carrier's negligence, to rebut which defendant must affirmatively show that the collision was the result of inevitable casualty,
or of some cause which human care and foresight could not prevent.
Sambuck v. Southern Pac. Co., 7, 104.

§ 10. —— Damages Recoverable by Passenger.

A charge that plaintiff was entitled to recover only the actual damages proven, as distinguished from mere imaginary or exemplary damages, was properly refused, as tending to mislead the jury as to the
character of proof necessary.—Trabing v. California Nav. and Imp.
Co., 6, 696.

A charge that plaintiff could not recover for his injured feelings
and mental anguish was properly refused.—Trabing v. California Nav.
and Imp. Co., 6, 696.

Where plaintiff, a boy of fourteen, was arrested by the captain of
defendant's vessel, and chained to a post, and was ejected at midnight, before reaching his destination, and was obliged to walk thirty
miles to reach home, a verdict of $1,500 was not excessive.—Trabing
v. California Nav. and Imp. Co., 6, 696.

In an action for injuries to a passenger, the carrier is liable for
the slightest negligence.—Sambuck v. Southern Pac. Co., 7, 104.

CERTIFICATE.

Of purchase. See Public Lands, § 14; State, § 2.

CERTIFICATION.

Of statement, bill of exceptions or record. See Appeal and Error,
§§ 33, 36, 42, 48.

CERTIORARI OR WRIT OF REVIEW.

§ 1. Scope and office of writ.
§ 2. Reaches only matters going to jurisdiction.
§ 3. Application for writ in particular instances.
§ 4. Petition, parties and return.

§ 1. Scope and Office of Writ.

The office of the writ of certiorari is to remove for review final
adjudications of inferior tribunals, etc., exercising judicial functions,
when such tribunals have exceeded their jurisdiction and the party
aggrieved has no appeal and no plain, speedy and appropriate remedy.
Central Pacific R. R. Co. v. Board of Equalization, 1, 460.

When it is conceded or shown that an inferior tribunal had power
to hear and determine the subject matter in controversy between the
parties before it, and that the determination was within the law as
to amount, time, place, etc., the only question that can arise upon
the proceedings is one of error, which question is not before the court
under the writ of certiorari.—Central Pacific R. R. Co. v. Board of
Equalization, 1, 460.

When it is found by the court issuing a writ of certiorari that the
inferior tribunal had jurisdiction of the subject matter and of the
parties, and that the adjudication was not in excess of the authority
conferred upon it by law, the adjudication will not be disturbed because error, either of law or of fact, intervened in the proceedings.—
Central Pacific R. R. Co. v. Board of Equalization, 1, 460.

When by the constitutional amendment of 1863 the power to issue
a certiorari was secured to the supreme court, the writ was not purely
the common-law writ of that name, but the statutory writ here when

the amendment passed or as it might be thereafter through statutory regulation.—Grogan v. County Court, 1, 617.

By its enactments in respect of the writ of certiorari, the legislature intended to permit this summary remedy for a usurpation of jurisdiction only in cases where there is no appeal allowed by law, whereby the error of the inferior court, officer or tribunal may be corrected, and where there is no other plain, speedy and adequate remedy. Grogan v. County Court, 1, 617.

In California the only office of the writ of certiorari is to ascertain and determine whether the inferior tribunal to which it is directed has exceeded its jurisdiction in the proceeding sought to be reviewed.—Hagar v. Supervisors of Yolo Co., 1, 770.

The right of appeal from the granting of an injunction excludes the right to a writ of certiorari.—Herbert v. Superior Court, 7, 336.

Certiorari lies to review an order of the superior court remanding an action in forcible detainer theretofore certified to the superior court by a justice of the peace, and such order is not reviewable only on appeal, since it is an improper divestiture of jurisdiction.—Richmond v. Houser, 7, 343.

§ 2. Reaches Only Matters Going to Jurisdiction.

Where a court has jurisdiction of the subject matter, and of the parties to an action, an order, though erroneous, if not in excess of jurisdiction, cannot be reviewed on certiorari.—Brown v. Superior Court, 2, 322.

Where the superior court has jurisdiction over the subject matter and the party, an application for a writ of certiorari or review will be denied.—Nunan v. Superior Court, 2, 346.

Certiorari cannot be used to review an error or irregularity committed in exercise of a court's jurisdiction. A rehearing after judgment, on a writ of review, cannot be had in the lower court. The question upon the return of the writ is whether the court, whose judgment is the subject matter of review, pursued its jurisdiction, and the judgment on that question is reviewable only on appeal.—Alexander v. Municipal Court of Appeals, 2, 390.

Errors in proceedings, not involving excess of jurisdiction, cannot be reviewed by certiorari.—Board of Supervisors v. Superior Court, 5, 797.

§ 3. Application for Writ in Particular Instances.

Actions on contract, commenced in the justice's court and appealed to the superior court, are within the jurisdiction of those courts, and therefore not subject to review on certiorari.—Alpers v. Superior Court, 2, 358.

Where an administrator's first annual account is settled, an order that such account should be again gone into, in connection with the second annual account of the administrator, cannot be reviewed on certiorari, as it involves no question of jurisdiction of the lower court. Hirschfeld v. Superior Court of Tulare Co., 2, 549.

In a suit to condemn land the plaintiff obtained, in March, 1887, leave to amend complaint and summons filed December, 1886, by inserting the name of the petitioner herein as defendant, and in April, 1887, having consolidated with other railroad companies, obtained an order to substitute the consolidated company as plaintiff. Petitioner applied for a writ of certiorari. Held, that it must be denied. In re Marshall, 2, 811.

Where a judgment has been entered for defendant, and, on plaintiff's motion, the court vacates the judgment, and restores the case

32

to the calendar for a new trial, a writ of review by the supreme court will not lie to a subsequent order, made on defendant's motion, setting aside the former order, and refusing a new trial.—Ryan v. Superior Court, 2, 871.

The petition for a writ of review to an order vacating a judgment for petitioner will be denied, where it appears that petitioner appealed from the same order, and the questions sought to be reviewed have been determined thereon.—Broder v. Superior Court of Mono County, 3, 886.

§ 4. Petition, Parties and Return.

Where the petition for a writ of review neither shows nor alleges want of excessive exercise of jurisdiction, the writ will be denied.—Brandon v. Superior Court, 2, 654.

Upon an application for a writ of review of a judgment of the superior court of California, dismissing an appeal taken on both law and fact from a justice's court, where no statement of the case on appeal had been made and filed as provided by section 975, Code of Civil Procedure of California, the application was denied on the ground that the petition did not set forth sufficient facts.—Simon v. Superior Court, 2, 747.

In a petition for a writ of review, the petitioner alleged, as cause therefor, that the judge of the superior court had rendered judgment against him, when neither he nor his counsel was present, in excess of its jurisdiction, and contrary to the rule of court regarding the notice to be given when the court calendar will be taken up. Held, that the petition was insufficient.—Merrick v. Superior Court, 2, 803.

Where no objection is urged to the sufficiency of a return on an application for certiorari to review the proceedings of the superior court, and all parties treat the same as a correct transcript, the court of appeal will so regard it.—Richmond v. Houser, 7, 343.

On certiorari to review an order of the superior court, it is necessary that it should be a party, and, in its absence, the writ being directed to the judge of such court, its order cannot be annulled.—Richmond v. Houser, 7, 343.

CHALLENGES.
To jurors. See Jury, § 5.

CHAMBERS.
Judgment at. See Forcible Entry and Detainer, § 8.

CHANCE VERDICT.
See Trial, § 17.

CHANGE OF POSSESSION.
Of goods sold. See Fraudulent Transfers, § 1.

CHANGE OF VENUE.
See Venue.

CHARACTER.
Of accused and deceased. See Criminal Law, § 12; Homicide, §§ 9, 10.

CHATTEL MORTGAGE.

§ 1. On Livestock—Registration.

Civil Code, section 2955, provides for chattel mortgages on certain property; and section 2957 provides that the record of such mortgages shall be constructive notice, and that mortgages not recorded shall be void as against subsequent creditors and purchasers. Held, that the act of March 9, 1893, amending section 2955, so as to authorize mortgages on sheep and neat cattle, does not entitle a mortgage on such stock, executed before the passage of such act, to be recorded, so as to render its record, made after the passage of the act, constructive notice.—Bank of Ukiah v. Gibson, 5, 11.

A chattel mortgage on property other than that authorized to be mortgaged by the Civil Code, section 2955, is, as a common-law mortgage, valid against all persons except subsequent creditors and bona fide purchasers of the mortgagor and bona fide purchasers.—Bank of Ukiah v. Gibson, 5, 11.

§ 2. On Crops—Prior Mortgage—Registration.

Plaintiff took a mortgage on certain crops as security for a loan, and subsequently defendant took a mortgage on the same crop for seed furnished, and to secure future advances. Plaintiff's mortgage was not recorded. Held, that a finding, on conflicting evidence, that defendant had notice of plaintiff's mortgage before making the advances on the second mortgage, would not be disturbed.—Fette v. Lane, 4, 813.

Where defendant's second mortgage for seed furnished was made before he had notice of plaintiff's prior unrecorded mortgage on the same crops, defendant has a prior lien to the extent of the seed furnished, but cannot enforce against the plaintiff liens for advances furnished the mortgagor after notice of the first mortgage.—Fette v. Lane, 4, 813.

In an action by the first mortgagee of crops to recover the amount of his lien from a second mortgagee, who had sold them, one of the mortgagors may testify as to a statement by plaintiff that it was understood that the crops should be sent to defendant subject to plaintiff's lien, in order to rebut an allegation that plaintiff had surrendered his lien.—Fette v. Lane, 4, 813.

A finding that barley subject to mortgages to plaintiff and defendant was to be stored by defendant in plaintiff's name, that he stored it in his own name, that plaintiff's demand of enough to secure his claim was not complied with, and that the barley was sold by defendant, and the proceeds retained by him, shows a conversion of the barley.—Fette v. Lane, 4, 813.

§ 3. Unrecorded Mortgage.

See two preceding sections.

An unrecorded mortgage of personal property is valid against a subsequent mortgagee with notice.—Fette v. Lane, 4, 813.

§ 4. Misnomer of Mortgagor.

Misnomer of the mortgagor of chattels (E. H. Wheeler for E. H. Walker) in the body of the affidavit is immaterial, where the mortgage purports to be made, and is signed, by E. H. Walker, as is the affidavit.—Sanborn v. Cunningham, 4, 95.

§ 5. Default in Installment—Election by Mortgagee.

When a mortgagor in default as to an installment tenders the amount due before the mortgagee elects to treat as due the entire debt, as the mortgage authorizes him to do on default, the right of election is lost.—Sykes v. Arne, 5, 601.

§ 6. Action by Mortgagee for Conversion.

In an action by a chattel mortgagee of growing crops, for conversion thereof, the defense being a justification as purchaser thereof, a finding that at the time of giving the mortgage the mortgagor was the owner and in possession of the crop authorized a judgment for plaintiff.—Wetzel v. Webb, 4, 129.

In an action by a mortgagee for conversion of the mortgaged chattels, there is no abuse of discretion in allowing defendant, at the trial, to amend his answer, and to aver that the mortgage was released before defendant took the property.—Irwin v. McDowell, 4, 329.

CHECKS.

See Banks and Banking; Bills and Notes.

CHIEF OF POLICE.

Certificate of election. See Elections, § 4.
Election of disqualified chief. See Officers, § 1.

CHINAMAN.

Testimony of will not convict. See Homicide, § 6.

CIRCUMSTANTIAL EVIDENCE.

Of conspiracy. See Conspiracy, § 1.

CITY ATTORNEY.

§ 1. Duty to Defend Board of Education.

The charter of San Francisco, in requiring the city attorney to prosecute and defend suits by or against the board of education, does not impose any "school function" on him, but his "function" remains that of an attorney.—Denman v. Webster, 7, 65.

Under the charter of San Francisco, authorizing the election of a city attorney, and in article 5, chapter 2, section 1, requiring him to prosecute and defend for the city and county all actions at law or in equity, and to give advice to all officers, boards and commissions, and in article 7, chapter 3, section 1, subdivision 3, authorizing the board of education to require the services of the city attorney in all actions, suits, and proceedings by or against it, it is the duty of the city attorney, when so required, to appear for and defend such board in all suits brought against it.—Denman v. Webster, 7, 65.

§ 2. —— Refusal to so Defend.

Under the charter of San Francisco, article 16, section 18, providing that any elected officer may be suspended by the mayor for cause, and that he "shall appoint some person to discharge the duties of the office during the period of such suspension," on the refusal of the city attorney to defend the board of education in a suit brought against it the board is not authorized to employ another attorney, but should notify the mayor of such refusal.—Denman v. Webster, 7, 65.

CLAIM AND DELIVERY.
See Replevin.

CLAIMS.
Against county. See Counties, § 8.
Against estate of decedent. See Executors and Administrators, §§ 14–19.
Against city and their payment. See Municipal Corporations, §§ 10, 11.
Against state. See State, § 1.

CLEANING.
Of streets. See Municipal Corporations, § 16.

CLOUD ON TITLE.
See Quieting Title.

COLLATERAL SECURITY.
See Pledge.

COLOR OF TITLE.
See Adverse Possession, § 2.

COMMISSION MERCHANTS.
See Factors.

COMMUNITY PROPERTY.
See Husband and Wife, §§ 7, 8.

COMPLAINT.
See Pleading.

COMPOSITION WITH CREDITORS.
§ 1. Validity.
A contract whereby a single creditor agrees with his debtor to compromise the debt cannot be enforced, but where various creditors have so contracted with a common debtor the case is different.—Pierson v. McCahill, 1, 276.

An agreement by a creditor with a debtor to accept payment of part of a debt in satisfaction of the whole is not the less invalid, as being without consideration, if the part, instead of being named in terms of money, is named as "property worth" that much money. Bull v. Eby, 1, 281.

COMPROMISE.
Authority of attorney. See Attorney and Client, § 3.

CONCEALING.
Evidence. See Obstructing Justice, § 1.

CONCURRING NEGLIGENCE.
See Negligence, § 1.

CONDEMNATION PROCEEDINGS.
See Eminent Domain.

CONDITIONS.

CONDONATION.

CONFESSIONS.

CONFIRMATION.

CONFISCATION.

CONFLICTING EVIDENCE.

CONSENT.

CONSIDERATION.

CONSOLIDATION.

CONSPIRACY.
§ 1. Circumstantial Evidence.

Circumstantial evidence tending to prove a conspiracy is properly admissible, with the qualification that if a conspiracy is not shown such evidence may be stricken out on motion.—More v. Finger, 6, 326.

CONSTABLES.

CONSTITUTIONAL LAW.
§ 1. Impairment of obligation—Change of remedy.
§ 2. Forfeiture and confiscation.
§ 3. —— Of fishing-tackle.
§ 4. Curative statutes.
§ 5. —— Taxes and assessments.
§ 6. Imposing judicial functions on surveyor general.
§ 7. Ex post facto law.
§ 8. Compensation of justices and constables.

§ 1. Impairment of Obligation—Change of Remedy.

A law directed at a remedy merely cannot be said to impair the obligation of contracts, when the effect is not to take away all redress.—Tully v. Tranor, 2, 43.

If the legislature changes the remedy in respect of a contract, it does not thereby necessarily impair the obligation.—Hibernia Savings and Loan Soc. v. Jordan, 2, 79.

A legislative act giving creditors recourse to law, whereas their sole recourse theretofore was to equity, in proceeding against a stockholder, does not impair the obligation of contracts.—Morrow v. Superior Court, 2, 124.

§ 2. Forfeiture and Confiscation.

Forfeiture of rights or property cannot be adjudged by legislative act, and confiscations without a judicial hearing and judgment after due notice are void, as being not due process of law.—Hey Sing Yeck v. Anderson, 2, 76.

§ 3. —— Of Fishing-tackle.

Section 636, chapter 1, title 15 of the Penal Code is unconstitutional and void in so far as it declares that all nets, seines, fishing-tackle, etc., used in violation of its provisions shall be forfeited, and may be seized by the peace officer and by him destroyed or sold.—Hey Sing Yeck v. Anderson, 2, 76.

§ 4. Curative Statutes.

In regard to curative acts the legislature has the same power over "easements," or taxes levied for the improvement of streets in cities and incorporated villages, which it has over taxes levied for the purpose of revenue.—Himmelman v. Janson, 1, 371.

§ 5. —— Taxes and Assessments.

Whenever the legislature has power to authorize an act to be done, it also has power to ratify and confirm it, if it has been done irregularly or not, in the mode previously prescribed.—Himmelman v. Janson, 1, 371.

§ 6. Imposing Judicial Functions on Surveyor General.

Section 3972 of the Political Code, making the validity of surveys depend upon the approval of the surveyor general, did not confer judicial functions upon that officer.—Borel v. Bogg, 2, 105.

§ 7. Ex Post Facto Law.

Penal Code, section 1217, provides that the warrant for the execution of a prisoner sentenced to death must appoint a day for the execution, "which must not be less than thirty or more than sixty days from the time of judgment." Section 1227 imposes on the sheriff the duty of executing criminals. Section 1229 directs that the execution must take place in the county where judgment is rendered. Laws of 1891, page 272, amended these sections by providing that the day of execution "must not be less than sixty or more than ninety days from the time of judgment," and that the warrant must also direct the sheriff to deliver the prisoner to the warden of one of the state prisons, on which officer is imposed the duty of executing criminals, and directing that the execution take place in the prison to which the criminal is delivered. Held ex post facto as regards prisoners awaiting execution, because imposing greater punishments by the confinement in the state's prison than the acts repealed.—People v. McNulty, 3, 441.

Where it is evident that the legislature in passing such statute intended it to apply the new punishment alike in all cases of murder, past as well as future, and would not have passed it except as an entirety, and that its partial enforcement would produce effects which the legislature would never have sanctioned, the whole act must be declared unconstitutional.—People v. McNulty, 3, 441.

§ 8. Compensation of Justices and Constables.

Act of March 28, 1895 (Stats. of 1895, p. 267), "to establish the fees of county, township and other officers," etc., in so far as it attempts to give the district attorney a supervisory control over fees of justices and constables in criminal cases, by providing that the boards of supervisors may reject all their bids in criminal cases in which he has not, in writing, approved the issuance of the warrant of arrest, conflicts with constitution, article 1, section 11, requiring all laws of a general nature to have a uniform operation. It is also in conflict with constitution, article 11, section 5, providing that the legislature shall regulate the -compensation of county and township officers in proportion to the duties they perform.—Westerfield v. Riverside County, 5, 855.

CONSTRUCTIVE SERVICE.
See Process, § 3.

CONTEMPT.

§ 1. Acts Constituting.

A tax collector enjoined against making a tax sale cannot be in contempt for disobeying the injunction when the sale was made before its issue.—Sacramento v. Burke, 1, 280.

A petition for rehearing stated that "how or why the honorable commissioner should have so effectually and substantially ignored and disregarded the uncontradicted testimony . . . . we do not know. . . . It sems that neither the transcript nor our briefs could have fallen under" the commissioner's observation. "There is not a scintilla of evidence to the contrary, and yet the honorable commissioner assumes," etc., and "in very euphuistic language says," etc. "A more disingenuous and misleading statement of the evidence could not well be made." "It is substantially . . . . untrue, and unwarranted." "The decision . . . . seems to us to be a travesty of the evidence." Held, that counsel drafting the petition was guilty of contempt committed in·the face of the court, notwithstanding a disavowal of disrespectful intention.—McCormick v. Sheridan, 3, 35.

An attorney for defendant, in an action in which judgment is rendered that defendant restore possession of premises, who thereupon notifies the sheriff that he is the owner, and in exclusive possession, of the premises, and that defendant is not in possession, and that he will, by all lawful ways, resist any attempt to take possession from him, is not thereby guilty of contempt, though his notice deters the sheriff from serving the writ.—De Witt v. Superior Court of Fresno, 5, 598.

§ 2. Proceedings for Punishment—Commitment.

Order to show cause discharged and proceedings dismissed.—In re Taylor, 2, 648.

A commitment for contempt of court, in disobeying an order requiring the person committed to restore to the administrator of an estate in process of settlement money which he had obtained, as attorney for such administrator, by false pretenses, is void, where the judgment on which the commitment issued fails to show that he was in fact such attorney.—Ex parte Carroll, 4, 295.

§ 3. Appeal.

No appeal lies from an order adjudging one guilty of contempt for violating a restraining order.—Natoma Water & Min. Co. v. Hancock, 4, 529.

Under Code of Civil Procedure, section 1222, a judgment in contempt proceedings is not appealable.—Mott v. Clarke, 6, 244.

CONTEST.

Of will. See Wills, §§ 9–13.

CONTINUANCE.

§ 1. Absence or sickness of parties, attorneys or witnesses.
§ 2. Affidavits.
§ 3. Diligence.
§ 4. Discretion and appeal.

Of divorce case. See Divorce, § 7.

§ 1. Absence or Sickness of Parties, Attorneys or Witnesses.

It is error, in a criminal trial, to refuse the defendant a continuance, asked for on the ground of absence of witnesses from the county, where, from the uncontradicted affidavit of the defendant, it appears that such witnesses were regularly subpoenaed; that the facts which defendant expected to prove by them, and which are stated in the affidavit, are material to the defense; that he could not prove the same facts by any other witnesses; and that he expected to be able to procure their attendance, if the trial was postponed.—People v. Lee, 2, 569.

Defendant and his witnesses were present at the time fixed for trial, but his attorney was absent from sickness. The court stated that the case would be continued on that account, and the defendant and his witnesses left without instructions as to future attendance. The next day the attorney was still sick, and the defendant and his witnesses did not appear. A motion for continuance was denied. Held, that the absence of defendant and his witnesses was excusable, and the continuance should have been granted.—Light v. Richardson, 3, 745.

A motion for a continuance on the ground of defendant's sickness was supported by a certificate signed "H. H. L." To the court's question as to who L. was, defendant's attorney answered that he did not know, and did not know whether L. was a physician or not. The motion was denied, and no exception was taken. The trial proceeded, and defendant's attorney's subsequent offers to prove that L. was a regular physician were denied. No offer of competent evidence to prove defendant's sickness was made, and no delay was asked for the purpose of an examination of defendant by a physician. Held, that the motion was properly denied.—Gainsley v. Gainsley, 5, 310.

There is no error in denying continuance because of defendant's sickness, there having been a previous continuance on this ground, on stipulation that there should be no further postponement on that ground, and it not appearing that defendant's presence would have been of any avail.—Rubens v. Mead, 6, 14.

§ 2. Affidavits.

Code of Civil Procedure, section 595, which provides that "the court may require the moving party, where application is made on account of the absence of a material witness, to state on affidavit the evidence which he expects to obtain," is not imperative, and should not be required of counsel when he cannot be aided in making the affidavit by his client, who is excusably absent.—Light v. Richardson, 3, 745.

§ 3. Diligence.

An application for a continuance should be denied on a showing that the applicant has been lacking in diligence.—Molle v. Jacob Kohlberg & Co., 1, 58.

§ 4. Discretion and Appeal.

The granting of a continuance is a matter largely within the discretion of the trial court.—Thornton v. Thompson, 1, 170.

Except on a showing of abuse of discretion on the part of the trial judge, his action in disposing of a motion for a continuance is not subject to interference on appeal.—People v. McDonald, 1, 437.

The granting of a motion for a continuance is very much within the discretion of the trial court.—Willson v. McDonald, 1, 516.

The granting of a continuance and dismissal of a complaint in intervention being, under the circumstances, discretionary with the court, held that, where there is no abuse of discretion, the order of the lower court refusing the same will not be interfered with on appeal.—Fleming v. Hawley, 2, 364.

CONTRACT.

§ 1. Consideration.

Judgment against plaintiff, and findings against sufficiency of consideration of written instrument, held, contrary to the evidence, as the uncontradicted evidence of defendant's witness, instead of overcoming the presumption in favor of the written instrument on which plaintiff based his claim, really showed a sufficient consideration in all respects as foundations for findings in plaintiff's favor.—Golden State & Miners' Iron Works v. Muir, 2, 588.

Cancellation of a pre-existing debt is a valuable consideration.— Kennedy v. Conroy, 5, 337.

§ 2. Execution and Acceptance.

It is possible for parties to a contract in writing to be bound by the instrument, although they have not signed it.—Lafouton v. Gaucheron, 1, 30.

When, under the terms of a contract, so many days are given by one party to the other in which to make up his mind whether he will accept, time is always of the essence.—Vassault v. Kirby, 1, 668.

Except when so expressed in the contract, acceptance of its terms, where time has been allowed to decide in, need not be by word of mouth, but the accepting party may apprise the other of his decision by a note left at his place of business within the time.—Vassault v. Kirby, 1, 668.

§ 3. Duress and Undue Influence.

A contract for sale of stock, which plaintiff owned and had pledged to a bank, was not obtained by "menace," within the definition of Civil Code, section 1570, "a threat of injury to the character," where defendant said that he would inform the bank that plaintiff was not the owner of the stock if plaintiff did not make the contract.—Bancroft v. Bancroft, 5, 31.

Nor can the contract be said to have been obtained by undue influence, plaintiff being a mature man, in the possession of all his faculties, who for several years had been manager of the corporation in which were the shares, though defendant, who was the owner of the majority of the corporation's stock, and plaintiff's uncle, had been accustomed in a great measure to direct plaintiff's action, and was a tyrannical and overbearing man.—Bancroft v. Bancroft, 5, 31.

§ 4. Interpretation and Consideration.

The construction by the lower court of the contract sued upon held erroneous, and judgment and order reversed, and cause remanded. Martin v. Hill, 2, 310.

The agreement mentioned in the opinion construed, and held, that the defendant was not bound to carry on the business therein provided for for any particular time.—Huntington v. Russell, 2, 558.

Upon a construction of the agreement which is the subject of the suit, judgment affirmed.—Martin v. Hill, 2, 403.

In construing a contract the intention of the parties is to be determined not from the facts as they actually were, but as the parties supposed them to be.—Parrish v. Rosebud Mining etc. Co., 7, 117.

§ 5. —— "Grape Vines."

Where a contract requires a party to plant "grape vines," and the word "vines" does not appear to have been used in any special or local sense, expert evidence is not admissible to show its meaning, but it will be held to mean indifferently either cuttings or rooted plants, according to common usage.—Remy v. Olds, 4, 240.

§ 6. —— "Copper Establishment."

A contract for services as superintendent of a "copper-smelting establishment," whereby plaintiff was to receive from defendant six thousand dollars a year salary and fifty cents in addition for every ton of ore smelted, would not, unless so expressed specifically, bind the defendant to have the "establishment" in constant activity in order to swell to the utmost the amount per ton so to be paid.—Desormaux v. Meader, 1, 400.

§ 7. —— Conditional Liability.

Under a contract whereby a certain sum is to be paid on a named day absolutely, another similar sum on a contingency and more thereafter, to make up in all a sum total promised to be paid, which contract, however, provides that "if the claim should fail to pay after testing the contract is to be null and void," nothing at all is due from the promisor after such failure is developed.—Isbell v. Owens, 1, 322.

One G. contracted: "On or before sixty days, I, G., do hereby agree to pay B., or order, out of the profits realized by me from my business of packing raisins at M. during the present season, the sum of $310 in gold coin of the United States of America." A few days thereafter G. sold his interest in the raisin business, and made no profits therefrom for that season. Held, that G. never became liable on the contract.—Bagley v. Cohen, 5, 783.

§ 8. Newspaper Notice—Implied Contract.

A newspaper notice by a keeper of a pasture that he wanted every horse taken out as soon as possible, and, if not, the owner would be charged a certain amount per day, is sufficient to charge one who read the notice, with the terms thereof, as under an implied contract. Grant v. Dreyfus, 5, 970.

§ 9. Modification or New Agreement.

After defendant had agreed to repay to plaintiff all moneys received under a contract in consideration of its annulment, a proposition by him to pay a certain amount was accepted by the latter, if he would agree in writing to do so, and defendant promised to send the agreement, but never did so. Held, that the new agreement was never perfected so as to change the defendant's liability under the agreement for the rescission of the contract.—Haines v. Stilwell, 5, 27.

Defendants, being indebted to plaintiff, executed their note to him for the amount, and pledged 520,000 gallons of wine to secure payment. A contract between the parties, made two days later, contained provisions inconsistent with the prior agreement. It provided for a division of profits of defendants' business between the parties, on a basis different from that contained in the first agreement. The wine was by it again delivered to plaintiff; and it fixed the conditions on which the wine might be sold by plaintiff, and the time of sale, and the price to be received, and entered into details of past, present and future dealings, and the manner in which they were to be carried out. Held, that the second agreement superseded the first. Bourn v. Dowdell, 5, 820.

§ 10. Performance or Nonperformance.

Where plaintiff, in an action for breach of contract, must show performance on his part before he can recover, nonperformance by him cannot be excused on the ground that it was caused by the act of God; and Civil Code, section 1511, providing that want of performance is excused "when it is prevented or delayed by irresistible superhuman cause," does not apply to such cases.—Remy v. Olds, 4, 240.

Where one of the issues in an action on a contract is as to whether there was such performance by plaintiff as would entitle him to recover. an instruction that, if the jury believe that defendants did not perform their part of the contract, they must find for plaintiff, is erroneous, as it takes from the jury the issue as to performance by plaintiff.—Remy v. Olds, 4, 240.

§ 11. Contract to Make Passenger Elevator—Warranty.

A warranty in a written contract to manufacture and put up a passenger elevator, that the contractor would furnish first-class work, and keep the elevator in repair for one year, does not include a warranty that the design submitted with the specifications would be suitable.—Bancroft v. San Francisco Tool Co., 5, 586.

The implied warranty created by Civil Code, section 1770, which provides that one who manufactures an article under an order for a particular purpose warrants that it is reasonably fit for such purpose, forms a part of a written contract to manufacture and put up a passenger elevator, so that an action for breach thereof is one on a written contract (Code Civ. Proc., sec. 337), for breach of which action may be brought within four years.—Bancroft v. San Francisco Tool Co., 5, 586.

A cause of action for a breach of warranty that the design of a passenger elevator would be suitable for the purpose for which it was intended accrues when the elevator is completed.—Bancroft v. San Francisco Tool Co., 5, 586.

§ 12. Contract to Put Down Well.

In an action on a well contract, where plaintiff alleged that he was prevented from finishing the well because of defendant furnishing unsuitable casing, which collapsed and stopped up the well, an allegation that plaintiff offered to dig another well without profit, at its actual cost, was unnecessary to the cause of action, and ineffectual as an offer to perform.—McPherson v. San Joaquin County, 6, 257.

Where a county having a well bored was to furnish the casing, the presumption that it should be suitable and of proper strength is not overcome by Civil Code, section 1654, providing that an uncertainty in a contract between a public body and a private person shall be presumed to be caused by the latter, and most strongly construed against him.—McPherson v. San Joaquin County, 6, 257.

Specifications for a well contract provided that all materials should be of the best quality and suitable. Held, that this applied to the casing to be furnished by the county having the well bored, as well as to the material furnished by the contractor.—McPherson v. San Joaquin County, 6, 257.

§ 13. —— Action on Account of.

In an action on a well contract, a count for extra work caused by and on account of improper casing furnished by defendant having the work done states a cause of action.—McPherson v. San Joaquin County, 6, 257.

Where, under a well contract, the owner could stop the work at any time, the contractor cannot recover damages for being prevented from completing the contract by the owner's furnishing defective materials, this not being done willfully.—McPherson v. San Joaquin County, 6, 257.

In an action against a county on a well contract, the petition alleged that the county entered into the contract, acted on it, and made payments under it; and the contract recited that the county made it through its duly authorized agent. Held, on demurrer, that the petition was not bad as not setting out the authority under which the agent acted.—McPherson v. San Joaquin County, 6, 257.

A county cannot escape liability under its contract to furnish suitable casings for a well being bored for it because of the neglect of duty of its officers in selecting the casings.—McPherson v. San Joaquin County, 6, 257.

On an issue of implied contract of a land owner to pay for a well, evidence of the capacity of the well, and of the amount of stock on the place, and of the fact that crops were being raised where none were raised before, is immaterial.—Brabury v. McHenry, 6, 294.

Evidence that a tenant did not think he was liable to pay for the boring of a well on the premises is not admissible against the landlord to show that he was liable therefor.—Bradbury v. McHenry, 6, 294.

In an action against a husband and wife to pay for boring a well on the wife's premises, which had been leased to a firm composed of the husband's brother and a third person, evidence as to whether the husband and his brother had ever been partners is immaterial.—Bradbury v. McHenry, 6, 294.

§ 14. —— Abandonment of Work.

In an action on a contract for boring a well on plaintiff's land it appeared that he agreed to furnish the casing, fuel, and board for defendant and his men "at his own expense," and pay a certain sum when the well was completed. Defendant agreed to continue boring the well, "barring bad weather or other unavoidable hindrances," till a certain depth was reached or impenetrable rock was encountered. When about half the agreed depth was reached, defendant's auger broke near the lower end, and became fastened in the well. Defendant claimed he could remove the broken piece, and, after striving unsuccessfully for three weeks, plaintiff refused to furnish further fuel and board, and defendant abandoned the work. Held, that plaintiff was not entitled to recover for the value of supplies furnished defendant to the date the work was abandoned, since by the contract he was not released from furnishing them while boring was prevented by "unavoidable hindrances."—Barrett v. Austin, 3, 551.

In such action defendant is not entitled to recover on a cross-complaint for the number of feet bored, at the contract price, since he was not prevented by plaintiff, nor by encountering impenetrable rock, from performing his contract.—Barrett v. Austin, 3, 551.

§ 15. Action for Breach—Pleading and Practice.

Where, by a stipulation in an agreement, the party agreed that, in building a certain mill, he would not let any sawdust or rubbish be put into the stream, so as to prevent the use of the stream by plaintiff's family, in an action for breach of such stipulation an allegation in the answer that the defendant prevented the sawdust and rubbish from being carried down by the stream, and that the waters thereof were not rendered impure, etc., by reason of such sawdust and rubbish, constitutes a valid defense.—Peterson v. Hubbard, 2, 607.

In an action for breach of contract it is not necessary to allege as part of the contract, which was for excavating and cutting ditches by machine, that the machine should be so employed as not to injure defendant's vines; stipulations necessary to make a contract reasonable are implied.—Biggerstaff v. Briggs, 2, 339.

Evidence of the expense of digging a ditch in a manner materially different from the mode provided as a test of value in the contract alleged by plaintiff was irrelevant, because he was not entitled to recover anything unless the actual contract was substantially the same as that by him alleged.—Biggerstaff v. Briggs, 2, 339.

Where plaintiff swore to an offer to commence work, he is entitled to prove facts tending to show how he was prevented from perform.

ing his contract, and for that purpose may testify to a message delivered to him by the foreman of defendant. The question of agency is for the jury.—Biggerstaff v. Briggs, 2, 339.

It is a question for the jury whether a notice to defendant was left at his residence with his wife, and whether it reached him.—Biggerstaff v. Briggs, 2, 339.

§ 16. —— Payment as Defense.

In an action for breach of contract, settlement and payment in full is a valid defense.—Peterson v. Hubbard, 2, 607.

CONTRIBUTION.

From cosurety. See Principal and Surety, § 5.

CONTRIBUTIONS.

For relief. See Money Received, § 1.

CONVERSION.

See Trover and Conversion.

CONVEYANCES.

See Deeds; Vendor and Vendee.

CONVICTS.

§ 1. Right to Visit County Clerk's Office.

A single justice of the supreme court has no jurisdiction to grant the application of an attorney, convicted of perjury and confined in the county jail, to visit the clerk's office of the county in charge of an officer, for the purpose of examining the records in the case in order to enable him, while acting as his own attorney, to prepare an appeal to the appellate district court.—People v. Collins, 7, 273.

§ 2. Contract for Convict Labor.

A board of directors of the state prison cannot make a contract for convict labor which shall extend beyond the limits of their term of office.—Porter v. Haight, 1, 715.

CORPORATIONS.

§ 1. Organization and charter.
§ 2. —— Pleading and evidence.
§ 3. Annulment of charter.
§ 4. De facto corporation.
§ 5. Meeting of directors—Notice.
§ 6. —— Quorum.
§ 7. Salaries and compensation of officers.
§ 8. Notice to officers.
§ 9. Contract between president and company.
§ 10. Purchase or sale of property.
§ 11. Purchasing own stock.
§ 12. Ratification of contract by corporation.
§ 13. Rescission and return of consideration.
§ 14. Borrowing money.
§ 15. Execution of note.
§ 16. —— Signatures.
§ 17. Assumption of debts and bonds.
§ 18. Issuance of bonds—Limitation on indebtedness.
§ 19. Right to become stockholder.

As surety on appeal bond. See Appeal and Error, § 25.
Banking corporations. See Banks and Banking.
Purchase and sale of stock by broker. See Brokers, § 9.
Admissions of officers. See Evidence, § 14.
Gift of stock. See Gifts, § 1.
Limitation of actions in case of fraud. See Limitation of Actions, § 4.
Service of process on agent. See Process, § 2½.
Pledge of stock. See Pledge.
Deed by corporation. See Vendor and Vendee, § 10.
Venue of action against. See Venue, § 2.

§ 1. Organization and Charter.

A corporation organized "under general laws" as provided in a then prevailing constitution, which provided in the same connection that "all general laws pursuant to this instrument may be altered from time to time or repealed," is subject to appropriate enactments thereafter both constitutional and legislative.—Morrow v. Superior Court, 2, 124.

§ 2. —— Pleading and Evidence.

An allegation in a pleading that a corporation was duly, regularly, and legally formed, and that it has continued to act as such, is a mere averment of a legal conclusion and raises no issue.—People v. Lowden, 2, 537.

Where the contract sued on describes plaintiff as a corporation, no further proof of its incorporation is necessary.—Tustin Fruit Association v. Earl Fruit Co., 6, 37.

§ 3. Annulment of Charter.

The complaint in an action to annul the charter of a corporation, for conducting a business in violation of the laws against lotteries and gambling, should clearly and distinctly allege its illegal acts.—People ex rel. Attorney General v. San Francisco Public Stock Exchange, 4, 85.

§ 4. De Facto Corporation.

A de facto corporation may sue and assert its corporate character as against the world, except in a direct proceeding by the attorney general to test its right to its franchise.—People's Ditch Co. v. 76 Land and Water Co., 5, 292.

§ 5. Meeting of Directors—Notice.

Where, in the absence of by-laws fixing the times for meetings of directors of a corporation, all of the directors, being duly assembled, agree to adjourn to a date and hour named, a meeting held by a majority of the directors at the time thus fixed is a legal meeting of the board, though no personal notice of the meeting is given to each

stock, which it had bought in for delinquent assessment, and had not authorized to be reissued.—Tulare Irrigation Dist. v. Kaweah Canal & Irrigation Co., 5, 330.

A stockholder of a corporation, which purchased a street railroad of another corporation and agreed to assume bonds issued by it, cannot raise the question of fraud in constructing the road, or attack the validity of the bonds.—Smith v. Ferries etc. Ry. Co., 5, 889.

A purchase by a corporation of all the property of another corporation is not void merely because the boards of directors of both corporations were the same.—Smith v. Ferries etc. Ry. Co., 5, 889.

Where plaintiff owned a certificate of purchase of state school lands, and the court found that plaintiff was a corporation, but there was no other proof, such certificate is admissible in evidence, as it will be presumed that the corporation had power to purchase and hold lands.—Diamond Coal Co. v. Cook, 6, 446.

§ 11. Purchasing Own Stock.

The purchase by a corporation of a part of its own stock, until it is reissued, in effect reduces its stock to that extent.—Tulare Irrigation Dist. v. Kaweah Canal & Irrigation Co., 5, 330.

§ 12. Ratification of Contract by Corporation.

A corporation may ratify a contract made by persons who, without authority, have assumed to represent it, and its power is, in that particular, coextensive with that of a natural person, unless by the charter the power is taken away or restricted to some particular formula or mode.—Martin v. Zellerbach, 1, 335.

A ratification need not in all cases be expressed; it may be implied, and the implication, which usually is based on conduct, may consist of acts or of omissions to act, or of both.—Martin v. Zellerbach, 1, 335.

After an unauthorized act of a corporation, in contracting to convey, has been ratified by the stockholders, a creditor, who has become such after the ratification, may not claim that the contract was fraudulent and void as to creditors, and hence not enforceable, unless he proves that the ratification was had with a fraudulent intent; he cannot put upon the defendant the burden of proving the honesty of the ratification.—Martin v. Zellerbach, 1, 335.

A plaintiff, whose contention rests on an act of corporation alleged by him to be unauthorized, may rebut evidence put in to sustain the defense of ratification by proof that the ratification was with fraudulent intent, and may do so without first replying specially to the defense in the pleadings.—Martin v. Zellerbach, 1, 335.

§ 13. Rescission and Return of Consideration.

Civil Code, section 1691, provides that one party cannot rescind a contract without the consent of the other party unless he restores to the latter everything of value which he has received from him thereunder. A corporation which owed $46,650 to its principal stockholder borrowed money from a bank, and, in consideration of his guaranteeing its note, paid its indebtedness to him before maturity. Held, in an action by other stockholders to compel repayment to the corporation, that the action could not be maintained without releasing the principal stockholder from his guaranty.—Wills v. Porter, 6, 492.

Civil Code, section 1691, provides that a party entitled to rescind a contract must do so promptly. A corporation which owed $46,650 to its principal stockholder borrowed money from a bank, and, in consideration of his guaranteeing its note, paid its indebtedness to him before maturity. Held, that an action brought by other stockholders two years thereafter to compel repayment to the corporation

could not be maintained, no excuse being shown for the delay.—
Wills v. Porter, 6, 492.

Where the complaint in an action to compel repayment of money
paid by a corporation to its principal stockholder alleged that complainants had no knowledge thereof at the time, but did not allege
when they obtained knowledge, it will be presumed on appeal that
they obtained knowledge at least by the day following the transaction.—Wills v. Porter, 6, 492.

Where a corporation pays a debt due its principal stockholder before
maturity, as a consideration for his guaranteeing its note, repayment
to the corporation will not be enforced by a court of equity at the
suit of other stockholders, without a showing that the corporation
or its stockholders were injured in some way.—Wills v. Porter, 6, 492.

§ 14. Borrowing Money.

A resolution of the board of directors authorizing the secretary to
borrow money for the corporation is sufficient, though not entered on
the minute-book, and, therefore, in an action against stockholders to
recover the money so borrowed, the admission in evidence of a resolution adopted by the board and entered on its minutes is immaterial.
Bank of Yolo v. Weaver, 3, 569.

§ 15. Execution of Note.

The fact that a resolution of the corporation, with the corporate
seal thereon, authorizing defendants to make the loan and execute
the note in the name of, and as the note of, the corporation, was
attached to the note, was without effect, as such attachment did not
make the resolution a part of the note.—San Bernardino Nat. Bank
v. Andreson, 3, 771.

§ 16. —— Signatures.

Where defendants sign a note with their individual names, adding
thereto "president" and "secretary," respectively, in which note they
promise to pay plaintiff bank a certain amount, and there is nothing
on the face of the note to indicate a principal back of them, they
are personally bound, and cannot set up a defense that they executed
the note as officers of a corporation, that the loan which the note
was given to secure was made to such corporation, and that the intention of both parties was that it should bind the corporation, and
not defendants.—San Bernardino Nat. Bank v. Andreson, 3, 771.

§ 17. Assumption of Debts and Bonds.

Where a president of a corporation agrees that the corporation shall
assume the debts of a person, it cannot be held liable by a creditor
of such person, no corporation action with relation to the contract
being shown, but it being claimed simply that money paid on the
contract came into possession of the corporation.—Hamilton v.
Bates, 4, 371.

It is not ultra vires for a corporation to assume the payment of
bonds that were issued by another corporation in violation of Civil
Code, section 309, prohibiting the contraction of debts beyond the
subscribed capital stock.—Smith v. Ferries etc. Ry. Co., 5, 889.

A corporation which, in payment for property, assumes the payment of bonds issued by another corporation, cannot retain the
property, and claim the bonds were invalid, as being overissued, in
violation of Civil Code, section 309, prohibiting the contraction of
debts beyond the subscribed capital stock.—Smith v. Ferries etc. Ry.
Co., 5, 889.

§ 18. Issuance of Bonds—Limitation on Indebtedness.

Prior to the statute of 1889, directors of a corporation had power to create an original bonded indebtedness.—Smith v. Ferries etc. Ry. Co., 5, 889.

A stockholder claiming that bonds issued by the directors were void, because issued without notice to the stockholders, must allege that the stockholders did not consent to the meeting at which the indebtedness was created, as Civil Code, section 317, provides that such consent abrogates the necessity of notice.—Smith v. Ferries etc. Ry. Co., 5, 889.

Bonds of a corporation issued in violation of Civil Code, section 309, prohibiting the contraction of debts beyond the subscribed capital stock, are not void.—Smith v. Ferries etc. Ry. Co., 5, 889.

The decision of the supreme court that bonds of a corporation, issued in violation of Civil Code, section 309, are not void, is a declaration of a rule of property, and will not be overruled.—Smith v. Ferries etc. Ry. Co., 5, 889.

Shares of stock delivered by a corporation to the stockholders of another corporation, as a part of the price of property purchased from it, are part of the former corporation's capital stock, within Civil Code, section 309, prohibiting the creation of debts by a corporation beyond its "subscribed capital stock."—Smith v. Ferries etc. Ry. Co., 5, 889.

§ 19. Right to Become Stockholder.

A person cannot compel a corporation, without having some agreement with it to that effect, to accept him as a member, or to receive his interest in the mining ground and issue stock to him in return.—Cornwall v. Burning Moscow Gold and Silver Min. Co., 1, 172.

§ 20. Ratification by Stockholders.

Stockholders may ratify the action of the board of directors in ratifying a payment to a director for services outside his duties as a director, and the fact that such director was present at the stockholders' meeting at which action thereon was taken did not invalidate it; a majority of the stockholders, independent of such interested stockholder, having voted in favor of the resolution.—Basset v. Fairchild, 6, 458.

The fact that such ratification was a ratification of all the acts of the directors since the preceding stockholders' meeting could not be urged against its validity as a ratification of such payment, where the objection was made to the adoption of the resolution at the meeting on the ground that it would cover such specific payment, since that phase of the question was thereby distinctly presented and voted on by the stockholders.—Bassett v. Fairchild, 6, 458.

§ 21. Ownership of Stock and Evidence Thereof.

Evidence that a person subscribed for stock is not sufficient proof that he actually owns the shares, when it does not appear that he bought them on credit, but rather that he was to pay for them at once, and it also appears that he did not pay or offer to pay for them, and that no certificate of them was ever issued to him.—Bank of Yolo v. Weaver, 3, 569.

One who purchases stock from a bailee who, by the indorsed assignment, is made the apparent owner thereof, will be protected as against the bailor, though the stock stood on the corporation books in the latter's name.—Krouse v. Woodward, 5, 230.

§ 22. Fictitious Issue of Stock.

Where directors of a corporation purchased of another corporation, of which they were the stockholders, property of the value of $1,200,000, and in payment therefor issued to themselves 24,750 shares of stock, of the par value of $2,475,000, and assumed an indebtedness of $1,050,000, a stockholder of the former corporation is not entitled to have such issue of stock declared void and fictitious, without setting aside the whole transaction.—Smith v. Ferries etc. Ry. Co., 5, 889.

Complainant alleged that a corporation purchased property of another corporation worth at least $1,200,000, and as the price assumed an indebtedness of $1,050,000, and issued to the latter corporation's stockholders twenty-four thousand seven hundred and fifty shares of stock, of the par value of $2,475,000. He did not allege that the former corporation had any property before such purchase. Held, that there was no fictitious issue of stock, within constitution, article 12, section 11, providing that all "fictitious" issues of stock shall be void.—Smith v. Ferries etc. Ry. Co., 5, 889.

§ 23. Subscriptions to Stock and Enforcement Thereof.

In an action by an opera-house company to recover a subscription to its capital stock, it appears that a "prospectus" recited in detail the objects of the intended corporation, the amount of stock, etc., and that the subscriptions were to be called in on installments; that defendant signed the prospectus for a certain number of shares; that four calls had been ordered by the board of directors, and payment demanded; and that defendant had failed to pay. Held, that plaintiff was entitled to recover.—Auburn Opera House etc. Assn. v. Hill, 3, 839.

Such prospectus stated that the building was "to be built by a corporation with a capital stock of $20,000, consisting of one thousand shares at twenty dollars per share." Held, that it was not a condition precedent to defendant's liability that $20,000 of plaintiff's stock should be first subscribed for.—Auburn Opera House etc. Assn. v. Hill, 3, 839.

It appeared that defendant was one of plaintiff's directors for two months, during which time he signed the articles of incorporation, was present at meetings of the board when the calls for the first two installments were ordered, and voted in favor of accepting the building lot, and that he served as a member of the building committee, prepared several plans for building, and consulted various architects and contractors about the same. Held, that, though the subscription for the full amount of stock mentioned in such contract was a condition precedent to defendant's liability, he had waived any objection on the ground that such amount was not subscribed.—Auburn Opera House etc. Assn. v. Hill, 3, 839.

A complaint on a stock subscription is not inconsistent because alleging that defendant, by his subscription, agreed to pay a certain amount "when and as it might be demanded," while this promise is not expressed, but merely implied, in the subscription set out as an exhibit.—Ventura etc. Ry. Co. v. Collins, 5, 469.

In a stock subscription, by which the subscribers agreed "to take the number of shares set opposite our names respectively, and thereon to pay the amount in cash named, to wit, ten per cent of the amount of stock by us subscribed, to B., treasurer of said corporation," opposite the name of each subscriber, under the words "Stock Subscribed," was written "$2,000," and under the words "Amount of Cash" was written "$200 pd." Held, that the obligation on the subscription was not limited to the $200, but this amount was to be paid contemporaneously with the subscription, and the balance on call.—Ventura etc. Ry. Co. v. Collins, 5, 469.

Where a subscriber for corporate stock sought to enforce subscriptions made under the same circumstances as his own, he could not repudiate his liability thereon under Civil Code, section 359, providing that no corporation shall issue stock except for money paid, labor done, or property received.—Richardson v. Chicago Packing and Provision Co., 6, 606.

Where stockholders ˙agreed that shares should be deemed fully paid by payment of a stated amount less than the par value, a creditor, who was also a stockholder, could not compel the payment of the par value of shares owned by other stockholders, the creditor being a party to the agreement.—Richardson v. Chicago Packing and Provision Co., 6, 606.

A judgment creditor of a corporation sued to enforce unpaid balances on stock subscriptions of fifteen stockholders. One of the defendants was also a judgment creditor of the corporation, but the action was dismissed as to him, and he became plaintiff by the court's order. The corporation owed no other debts. The original plaintiff's claim was paid by the fourteen remaining defendants, under a stipulation in which none of the other plaintiff's rights were relinquished, and the court gave the fourteen defendants a several judgment against such plaintiff by way of contribution, ignoring the fact that he was also a creditor of the corporation. Held, that such plaintiff was entitled to have the amount of his proportionate liability to the corporation on both claims deducted from his own claim, and the balance due him apportioned against the fourteen defendants.—Richardson v. Chicago Packing and Provision Co., 6, 606.

Where a creditor has the right to be subrogated to the rights of a corporation to claim unpaid balances due on shares, he does not lose that right by reason of the fact that he is a stockholder.—Richardson v. Chicago Packing and Provision Co., 6, 606.

§ 24.   Stock Assessments and Their Enforcement.

In an action to recover an assessment on corporate stock, evidence that the assessment was made on the same day that defendant purchased the stock is sufficient to show that it was made while defendant was the owner of the stock, as it will not be presumed that the assessment was made a fraction of a day before the purchase.—San Gabriel Valley Land etc. Co. v. Dennis, 4, 272.

A resolution by the board of directors "that the president and secretary are hereby ordered to commence suit for the collection of assessment" on stock sufficiently shows a waiver of further proceedings under the chapter for the collection of delinquent assessments.—San Gabriel Valley Land etc. Co. v. Dennis, 4, 272.

In the absence of any limitation imposed by statute or the articles of incorporation or by-laws of a corporation, requiring the object of a special meeting to be stated in the notice therefor, a board of directors, duly assembled at an adjourned meeting, may resolve to proceed by action for the collection of an assessment upon stock, as provided in Civil Code, section 349, where the resolution levying the assessment fixed a day when unpaid assessments would become delinquent, and the time for payment has expired.—Bank of National City v. Johnston, 6, 418.

§ 25.   —— Sale for Assessments.

An instrument intended to convey shares of stock of a person for nonpayment of assessments, but containing no allusion to him by name, not signed by him personally or for him by another under express power, and not consented to by him, is not good as a bill of sale.—Sayer v. McNulty, 1, 130.

Under a power, by virtue of merely the articles of agreement of a company, to sell shares of members for nonpayment of assessments, such articles not showing in that connection the manner of sale, one cannot sell shares validly at private sale and without notice to the owner.—Sayer v. McNulty, 1, 130.

§ 26. Transfer of Stock.

Under the statute controlling transfers of stock in incorporated companies (Stats. of 1853, p. 87, sec. 9), transfers not entered on the books of the company are valid against all the world except subsequent purchasers of the stock in good faith and without notice.—Mead v. Elmore, 1, 441.

§ 27. —— Conversion.

If the attorney in fact of a stockholder presents the certificate of stock, together with a power of attorney from the stockholder giving him full authority to deal with the stock, and the corporation's officers are ignorant of any intention on the part of the attorney to misappropriate the stock, the corporation will not be guilty of conversion simply by issuing another certificate in the name of the attorney, who appropriates the stock wrongfully.—Tafft v. Presidio and Ferries Ry. Co., 3, 152.

The fact that the attorney was also a director of the corporation does not warrant the presumption that the corporation had notice of his intention to convert the stock to his own use, as he assumed to act, not for the corporation, but for his principal.—Tafft v. Presidio and Ferries Ry. Co., 3, 152.

The lack of the owner's indorsement on the certificate was not inconsistent with the right of the attorney to cause the stock to be transferred to himself.—Tafft v. Presidio and Ferries Ry. Co., 3, 152.

The neglect of the officers to require an indorsement of the certificate is only nonfeasance, and is no evidence of conversion.—Tafft v. Presidio and Ferries Ry. Co., 3, 152.

It is not the duty of the officers of a corporation to inquire into the motives of an attorney in fact, having full power to transfer stock, for desiring it to be transferred to himself.—Tafft v. Presidio and Ferries Ry. Co., 3, 152.

§ 28. Stockholders' Liability.

On stock subscriptions. See ante, §§ 23, 24.

The constitution of 1849 needed the aid of the act of 1850 (section 32) and the act of 1853 (section 16) in order to subject each member of a corporation to the paying of the debts of the company. Morrow v. Superior Court, 2, 124.

Section 3 of article 12 of the present constitution (1882), that provides for subjecting each member of a corporation to the paying of the company's debts, is self-executing and needs no legislation to give it practical effect; and is, like all other provisions of the instrument, mandatory.—Morrow v. Superior Court, 2, 124.

Under Civil Code, section 1473, providing that performance of an obligation by one on behalf of the party whose duty it was to perform it, and with his assent, if accepted by the creditor, extinguishes it, an indorser of a corporation's note, who paid the same and took an assignment thereof from the payee, was not entitled to maintain an action thereon, since the debt was extinguished, and hence he could not enforce the statutory liability of stockholders for such debt. Yule v. Bishop, 6, 513.

§ 29. Stockholders' Suit—Parties and Pleading.

An averment that the plaintiffs were owners of the stock of the corporation before suit brought, and ever since 1881, sufficiently alleges ownership of the stock.—Moyle v. Landers, 3, 113.

Such suit may be brought by any one or any number of stockholders.—Moyle v. Landers, 3, 113.

The directors who are charged with having connived in such defaults are proper parties defendant in such action.—Moyle v. Landers, 3, 113.

A stockholder's allegation that certain directors furnished labor and material for the corporation, and charged large profits against it, "with the consent and connivance of" the other directors, is not sufficient to show liability of the latter directors.—Smith v. Ferries etc. Ry. Co., 5, 889.

An allegation that a corporation's stockholder "is informed and believes" that certain directors furnished labor and material for the corporation, and charged large profits against it, and that no accounting had been made, is insufficient on demurrer.—Smith v. Ferries etc. Ry. Co., 5, 889.

Where a corporation purchased all the property of another corporation, including a street railway, and all the property it might acquire, and all its rights, except its right to be a corporation, and assumed certain bonds that it had issued, the latter corporation is a necessary party defendant, where a stockholder of the former attacks the validity of the bonds, and charges that the railway was fraudulently constructed.—Smith v. Ferries etc. Ry. Co., 5, 889.

§ 30. —— Grounds for Action.

A dissatisfied stockholder alleged that the directors, in pursuance of a fraudulent scheme, had created a bonded indebtedness in excess of the capital stock, and had purchased certain property of another corporation, of which they were also directors, and in payment therefor had issued stock to its stockholders, and had assumed the payment of illegal bonds. Held, he was entitled to no relief that could not be granted to the corporation itself.—Smith v. Ferries etc. Ry. Co., 5, 889.

A stockholder alleged that the directors purchased property of another corporation worth at least $1,200,000, and in payment therefor issued shares of stock of the par value of $2,475,000, and assumed an indebtedness of $1,050,000. He did not allege that the corporation owned any property before such purchase. Held, he did not show that he was injured.—Smith v. Ferries etc. Ry. Co., 5, 889.

Where a stockholder of a corporation alleges that its bonds were invalid, as being an overissue, it will be presumed the bonds are in the hands of bona fide holders, in the absence of allegations to the contrary.—Smith v. Ferries etc. Ry. Co., 5, 889.

The allegation of a stockholder, assailing the issue of bonds by the directors, "that six per cent bonds, legally issued and properly secured, were worth much more than the face value, to wit, fifteen per cent more in the market," is not an allegation that the six per cent bonds issued by the corporation were worth fifteen per cent premium.—Smith v. Ferries etc. Ry. Co., 5, 889.

A transaction by directors that is voidable only will not be set aside at the instance of the stockholder, unless he shows that he sustained damage.—Smith v. Ferries etc. Ry. Co., 5, 889.

A suit to procure relief for the misappropriation of the funds of a corporation is properly brought by the stockholders, without any demand on the directors to bring such suit, where the complaint alleges that the corporation is under the control of the defaulting directors, and that such demand would be useless.—Moyle v. Landers, 3, 113.

§ 31. —— Limitation of Actions.

Such a suit is not barred by the statute of limitations where the defaults are said to have occurred between August 1, 1882, and May 1, 1885, and the suit is brought July 1, 1885, Code of Civil Procedure of California, section 338, providing that suits for relief on the ground of fraud shall be brought within three years of the discovery of the fraud.—Moyle v. Landers, 3, 113.

CORPUS DELICTI.

Proof of. See Criminal Law, § 15.

CORROBORATION.

Of accomplice. See Accomplices.

COSTS.

§ 1. In general.
§ 2. On appeal or in disposing of appeal.
§ 3. Filing memorandum.
§ 4. Judgment for costs.

On dismissal of mandamus. See Mandamus, § 5.
In suit to abate nuisance. See Nuisance, § 5.
In partition. See Partition, § 5.
Verdict for costs. See Trial, § 16.
In trover. See Trover and Conversion, § 8.

§ 1. In General.

Where the action involves the title of the land described in the pleadings, and the court decides that the plaintiff has no cause of action against the defendant, the defendant is entitled to his costs and disbursements in the action.—Lawrence v. Getchell, 2, 267.

Where the issue is found against the plaintiffs they are not entitled to recover any costs or disbursements incurred in the action.—Lawrence v. Getchel, 2, 359.

§ 2. On Appeal or in Disposing of Appeal.

In disposing of an appeal from a default judgment, given against other than parties named in the complaint, for a sum beyond that demanded in the complaint, and in a case where the sums mentioned in the summons and in the complaint differed in amount, the defendants are to be awarded costs.—Lamping v. Red Star Co., 1, 166.

In modifying the trial court's judgment, erroneous merely through an incorrect and excessive computation of interest, the respondent is made to pay the costs of appeal.—Charleton v. Reed, 1, 695.

No error appearing from the transcript on appeal, the order amending judgment as to costs is affirmed.—Estate of Crozier, 2, 334.

On appeal from a judgment and order denying a new trial, where the court orders the submission set aside as to the appeal from the judgment and the hearing thereon continued until further orders, but on the other appeal reverses the order denying new trial, appellant is entitled to his costs.—Dixon v. Pluns, 4, 502.

Costs on appeal from two improper judgments which, if enforced, would have cast heavy expense on the appellant, are properly chargeable to respondent.—Schaeffer v. Hofmann, 4, 839.

In such case appellant is entitled to costs on the appeal.—Blackburn v. Abila, 4, 982.

Where a transcript on appeal did not set out the orders from which the appeals were taken, and in the notice of appeal the appeals were stated to be "from the order and judgment of the court striking out petitioner's bill of cost and disallowing the same," etc., but the bill of exceptions did not contain any bill of costs, or make reference to any, or to any action of the court thereon, questions relative to the court's action concerning costs could not be reviewed.—In re Pina's Estate, 7, 101.

§ 3. Filing Memorandum.

A memorandum of costs filed three days after the filing of the remittitur is filed in due time.—Mabb v. Stewart, 7, 186.

§ 4. Judgment for Costs.

The court, by filling a blank left in a judgment for the insertion of costs, only performs a duty which would have devolved upon the clerk if the court had not so acted.—Moultrie v. Brophy, 1, 536.

A judgment for costs, without regard to whether it is or is not regular, cannot be attacked in a collateral proceeding.—Hihn v. Parkhurst, 1, 541.

COUNTERCLAIM.
See Setoff and Counterclaim.

COUNTIES.

§ 1. Boundaries and change thereof.
§ 2. County assessor.
§ 3. County treasurer—Payment of warrant.
§ 4. Supervisors as road commissioners—Compensation.
§ 5. Employment and discharge of physician.
§ 6. Purchase of land—Tax to pay.
§ 7. Subsidy to railroad.
§ 8. Expenses and claims.
§ 9. Presentation of claim.

Action against by county. See Architects, § 2.

§ 1. Boundaries and Change Thereof.

Taxes on land within a part of a county taken off for annexation to an adjacent county, levied and becoming a judgment against the owner of the land and a lien upon the latter before the passage of the act effecting the change in county lines, belong to the county from which the part was taken.—In re Corbett, 1, 314.

An act, in effect, to set off part of one county and annex it to another, is sufficiently expressed by a title so worded as to begin with "An act to amend an act," and to continue by a reference expressly to the original act organizing the county thus to be enlarged.—In re Corbett, 1, 314.

The line dividing the counties of Sonoma and Napa, as fixed by a survey approved by the surveyor general under authority of section 3972 of the Political Code, is conclusive.—Borel v. Bogg, 2, 105.

Act of March 11, 1893 (Stats. 1893, p. 158), erected a new county out of existing ones, and provided that commissioners should apportion the property and indebtedness of the old county and the new one. At that time certain railroad taxes were delinquent for each of eight years, and the railroad company paid the first six years' taxes, but left the taxes for 1886-87 unpaid. Under the reassessment act of March 23, 1893 (Stats. 1893, p. 290), the state board of equalization reassessed the latter taxes, and apportioned the valuation and taxes between the two counties according to the mileage in each. After the passage of the reassessment act, but before the reassessment, the commissioners apportioned the property of the old county, including taxes due, and fixed a ratio for the division of said taxes, excepting the taxes for 1886-87, and adjusted the indebtedness between the counties. The latter taxes were afterward paid into the treasuries of the old and new counties in the ratio established by the state board of equalization. Held, that, the commissioners having made no adjustment of the respective rights of the counties in them, an action by the old county to recover the amount of said taxes paid to the new county would not lie.—San Diego County v. Riverside County, 6, 170.

The provision of the statute for submission to the voters of the district affected by the question of detachment from a county, requring the election to be held within sixty days after the organization of the special commission, is directory merely, so that, if the election within that time is prevented by injunction, it may be held at a reasonable time after the injunction is removed.—Herbert v. Superior Court, 7, 336.

§ 2. County Assessor.

The California county government act of March 14, 1883, did not go into effect for the purpose of creating county offices until January 1, 1885, and therefore prior to that date there was no such office as county assessor of Alameda county.—Rosborough v. Boardman, 2, 456.

§ 3. County Treasurer—Payment of Warrant.

In an action to compel a county treasurer to pay a warrant, plaintiff alleged that under a contract with the county he had collected certain money due it, for which his compensation was to be fifty per cent; that he presented his claim to the supervisors, who allowed it; that the auditor drew a warrant, and that the treasurer refused to pay it. The answer denied any agreement with plaintiff except a certain written contract, substantially as alleged by plaintiff. The answer averred that such contract was ultra vires and void, denied that plaintiff rendered any services under the contract, and alleged that the county from which the money was collected had instituted an action to recover it back, and that the same was still pending. The contract with plaintiff did not, on its face, appear to be ultra vires or void. Held, that the pleadings made a prima facie case in favor of plaintiff, and the burden of proof was on defendant to show facts, if any existed, to defeat the case thus made.—Kelley v. Sersanous, 5, 485.

§ 4. Supervisors as Road Commissioners—Compensation.

By Political Code, sections 2641, 2645, as amended by Statutes of 1893, page 113, county supervisors are made ex-officio road commissioners in their respective districts, and their compensation for such services is therein fixed, "when not otherwise provided by law." By the county government act (Stats. 1891, p. 295, sec. 173, subsec. 15), the compensation of supervisors in counties of the eleventh class is fixed at six dollars per day for actual service, and certain mileage; and section 216 provides that the salaries and fees provided in the act shall be in full compensation for all services rendered, either as officers or ex-officio officers. Held, that the compensation of supervisors in counties of the eleventh class, while acting as road commissioners, is provided for by the county government act, and fixed at six dollars per day, and is therefore not affected by the provisions of code, section 2645.—Ellis v. Tulare County, 5, 327.

§ 5. Employment and Discharge of Physician.

In an action by a physician to recover damages for breach of contract made with him by the supervisors of a county, held, that defendant was not, on the facts recited in opinion, justified in discharging plaintiff previous to the expiration of the time for which he had been employed to perform the service.—Grindley v. Santa Cruz County, 2, 326.

§ 6. Purchase of Land—Tax to Pay.

When a statute provides, as a condition precedent to a valid purchase by county supervisors, a valuation of the property in manner specifically prescribed in the act, an alleged vendor to the county, who petitions for a mandamus to have a tax levied to pay him his price, must allege that the condition had been complied with before the sale.—People ex rel. Edgecomb v. Loomis, 1, 214.

§ 7. Subsidy to Railroad.

A subsidy, under act of the legislature, voted a railroad company by the people of a county and conditioned, by specific words in the act, upon the construction of the company's road through the county, may be withheld if the company, by an arrangement made privately with the supervisors, constructs the road, not through the county, but only part way; since in such case the supervisors are mere agents with powers measured by the terms of the act, and by departing from those terms, in their arrangements so made, act without authority and so fail to bind the county.—Santa Cruz R. R. Co. v. Board of Supervisors, 2, 99.

§ 8. Expenses and Claims.

In an action against a county, by a road overseer, to recover for services and money expended in the repair of county roads, testimony of the road commissioner that he had spoken to plaintiff in regard to working on the public roads, and had always directed him not to run in debt in excess of the funds appropriated for such work, and that he did not know anything about plaintiff's doing the work on which his claim was based until the bills therefor came in, is insufficient to show that the work in question was authorized by the commissioner, so as to authorize plaintiff to recover therefor.—Ludy v. Colusa County, 5, 381.

A member of the board of supervisors, who attended a supervisors' convention in another county as one of a committee of the whole, authorized and appointed by the board so to do, cannot recover compensation from the county for his expenses, since not within the duties of the board as authorized by law.—Shepherd v. Keagle, 6, 52.

§ 9. —— Presentation of Claim.

The presentation of a claim duly verified is an essential prerequisite to the maintenance of an action against a county, and unless the fact of such presentation appears in the complaint in any such action the complaint fails as insufficient.—Dorsey v. Tuolumne County, 1, 456.

Statutes of 1893, page 346, sections 43, 44, requiring a second presentation of claims allowed in part to the board of supervisors before bringing suit for the balance, do not apply to claims wholly rejected. San Diego County v. Riverside County, 6, 170.

COUNTS.
Pleading several. See Pleading, § 3.

COUNTY CLERK.
Failure to pay over to successor. See Officers, § 3.

COUNTY CLERK'S OFFICE.
Right of convict to visit. See Convicts, § 1.

COUNTY TREASURER.
Mandamus against. See Mandamus, § 1.

COURT COMMISSIONERS.
§ 1. In General.
An order was made transferring an action "to W., court commissioner of this court, for an accounting; said court commissioner to report back to this court the evidence taken, and the balance found due." Held, that this was a reference to the court commissioner officially, and not as referee.—Jackson v. Puget Sound Lumber Co., 5, 960.

The powers of court commissioners as prescribed by Code of Civil Procedure, section 259, cannot be enlarged by consent.—Jackson v. Puget Sound Lumber Co., 5, 966.

COURTS.

See Judges; Justices of Peace.

Mandamus against judge. See Mandamus, § 3.
Suspending rules. See Rules of Court, § 1.

§ 1. Probate Court.
The probate courts have no jurisdiction of the estates of persons who died previously to the time of the enactment of the probate laws of the state.—Paty v. Smith, 1, 727.

§ 2. Municipal Court of Appeals.
A dismissal of an appeal from the justice's court, taken on questions of law and fact, by the municipal court of appeals of the city and county of San Francisco, after the cause has been placed on the calendar by stipulation of the parties, if the appellant fails to appear at the trial, although no notice of a motion to dismiss has been given, though irregular, is not reviewable on certiorari.—Alexander v. Municipal Court of Appeals, 2, 390.

§ 3. Police Justice.
There is no such office as "police justice of the city of San Jose." and therefore such office cannot be usurped, intruded into, or unlawfully held or exercised.—People v. Veuve, 2, 313.

§ 4. Manner of Establishing Police and Inferior Courts.

Constitutional article 6, section 1, provides that "the judicial power of the state shall be vested in the senate sitting as a court of impeachment, in a supreme court, superior courts, justices of the peace, and such inferior courts as the legislature may establish in any incorporated city or town, or city and county." Section 13 provides that the legislature shall fix by law the jurisdiction of any inferior courts which may be established in pursuance of section 1, and shall fix by law the powers, duties and responsibilities of the judges thereof. Held, that an inferior court can be established only by the passage of an act of the legislature, and its approval by the governor, or its passage over his veto, in the same manner as any other law is enacted under constitutional article 4, sections 15, 16.— People v. Toal, 3, 227.

Laws of 1887, pages 88–90 (Constitutional 16th Amend., amending article 11, section 8), provides that any city of more than ten thousand, and not more than one hundred thousand inhabitants may frame a charter for its own government "consistent with and subject to the constitution and laws of the state," and, if ratified by a majority of the qualified voters of the city, it shall be submitted to the legislature for its approval or rejection as a whole and, if approved by a majority vote of the members elected to each house, it shall become the charter of such city, and the organic law thereof, and "shall supersede any existing charter, and any amendment thereof, and all special laws inconsistent with such charter." Held, that this does not dispense with the requirements of constitutional article 6, section 13, and that the provisions of a charter establishing a police or inferior court in such city which depend alone for their validity on a joint resolution of approval of the charter by a majority of the members of the legislature, but in no way submitted to or passed on by the governor, are unconstitutional, and the acts of such court are void.—People v. Toal, 3, 227.

§ 5. Jurisdiction of Superior Court.

The constitution clothes the superior courts with jurisdiction of all cases where breach of confidence is shown.—Cota v. Jones, 2, 131.

A superior court has no jurisdiction of an action to recover from each of several stockholders of a corporation his proportion of a debt contracted by the corporation, where the amount sued for is less than three hundred dollars, though the aggregate amount sought to be recovered from the several stockholders be more than three hundred dollars.—Evans v. Bailey, 2, 457.

Under constitution, article 6, section 5, giving the superior court jurisdiction in cases in which the demand, exclusive of interest, amounts to $300, the compounding of interest on a note for less than $300, pursuant to its terms, does not convert such interest into principal, and hence the superior court has no jurisdiction of an action on the note, although the amount of interest compounded renders the amount involved in excess of $300.—Howe v. Halsey, 6, 148.

§ 6. Judge Holding Court in Another County.

The request of the governor of the state of California to the judge of the superior court of one county to hold a superior court in another county is sufficient authority to entitle the latter to take jurisdiction of causes brought before him for trial in such county.—Pico v. Williams, 2, 671.

§ 7. Jurisdiction of Supreme Court.

The jurisdiction of the supreme court, for the purposes of a particular appeal, remains as of the time when the appeal was taken.—De Long v. Haines, 1, 120.

The jurisdiction given the supreme court where the validity of a tax is impeached does not go to the reviewing of a case where the question is, not the validity of the tax, but whether the court appealed from had the power to impose a penalty for not paying it.—De Long v. Haines, 1, 120.

· The supreme court, under the constitution of California, article 6, section 4, has appellate jurisdiction, in criminal cases prosecuted by indictment in a court of record, in questions of law only, and cannot set a verdict aside where the evidence is conflicting.—People v. Bowers, 2, 878.

The supreme court has no jurisdiction of an appeal from an order, made after final judgment, refusing to strike out plaintiff's cost bill, which amounts to less than $300.—Ertle v. Placer County, 5, 302.

§ 8. Court of Appeals—Transfer of Cause.

A petition to transfer a cause from the court of appeal to the supreme court, filed more than ten days after the judgment in the former court became final, will be stricken from the files.—Hewlett v. Beede, 7, 246.

The constitutional provision with reference to the transfer of a case from the district court of appeal to the supreme court has no application in matters of habeas corpus.—Ex parte Williams, 7, 309.

§ 9. Salary of Justices.

The supreme court is the only tribunal empowered to determine the amount of the salary of the justices of the district court of appeals.—Harrison v. Colgan, 7, 217.

Statutes of 1905, page 224, chapter 249, amending a statute fixing the salary of the justice of the supreme court at $6,000 a year, by providing that the annual salary of each justice of the supreme court shall be $8,000, and the annual salary of each justice of the district courts of appeal $7,000, has no application to any justice of the supreme court in office at the time of the adoption of the amendment; but such justices during their term are entitled only to the salary fixed by the earlier statute.—Harrison v. Colgan, 7, 217.

COVENANTS.

§ 1. Action for Breach—Pleading and Practice.

In an action for breach of covenant in a deed, the complaint alleged a certain money consideration, upon which issue was joined; the answer alleging the consideration to consist of certain contracts between the parties, which contracts plaintiff had violated. The findings of fact showed a contract resembling the one set up in the answer, and that plaintiff had violated it; but there was no finding whether the deed rested for its consideration on the payment of money as alleged by plaintiff, or on the contract set up in the answer, though there was evidence touching this issue. Held, that a judgment for defendant was not supported by the findings.—Holzheier v. Hayes, 5, 965.

CRIMINAL LAW.

§ 1. Intoxication as Defense.

Under Penal Code, section 22, providing that, whenever the existence of any particular motive is necessary to constitute any particular crime, the jury may consider the fact that the accused was intoxicated at the time in determining his motive, a jury is warranted in holding accused responsible for a robbery committed while intoxicated, which he confessed to when in full possession of his faculties. People v. Gilmore, 6, 57.

No prejudicial injury results from sustaining an objection to a proper question on cross-examination as to the manner of accused when intoxicated, where, by other questions to the same witness, the information sought is elicited, and the witness further testifies that accused was not intoxicated the day after the commission of the crime, when he confessed having committed it.—People v. Gilmore, 6, 57.

§ 2. Insanity as Defense.

In the absence of a plea of insanity, evidence that defendant had long ago been hit on the head and mentally and physically injured is immaterial.—People v. Davis, 4, 524.

§ 3. Plea of Former Jeopardy.

An appeal will not lie from a judgment upon a plea of former judgment of conviction, nor from an order denying a motion for a new trial.—People v. Majors, 2, 264.

Two men being murdered in furtherance of a conspiracy, each conspirator was guilty of the murder of each of the victims, and conviction of the killing of one is no bar to a prosecution for the killing of the other, even though both men were killed at the same time and place.—People v. Majors, 2, 264.

Deering's Penal Code of California, section 1017, provides that a plea must be entered upon the minutes of the court in substantially the following form: "(3) If he plead a former conviction or acquittal: 'The defendant pleads that he has already been convicted [or acquitted] of the offense charged by the judgment of the court of,'" etc. "(4) If he plead once in jeopardy: 'The defendant pleads that he has been once in jeopardy for the offense charged [specifying the time, place, and court].'" Defendant asked to have entered, as a plea of former acquittal: "Defendant pleads that he has already been acquitted of the offense charged by the judgment of this court, rendered at this courtroom on the fourteenth day of February, 1887, when defendant's demurrer to plaintiff's information was sustained by the court, and said court then and there or at any time failed to render its opinion that the objection to said demurrer could ever be cured by filing a new information." Held, a sufficient plea of former acquittal.—People v. O'Leary, 2, 843.

Defendant asked to have entered, as a plea of once in jeopardy: "Pleads, further, that he has been once in jeopardy, he having on the ——— day of January, 1887, been placed on trial for the offense now alleged in the information before the justice court of Cache Creek township and a jury, which court was a competent court, and which jury was a competent jury; and witnesses against defendant were sworn before said jury, and, before the final submission of said matter to said jury, the jury was discharged, against the objection of the defendant." Held, a sufficient plea of once in jeopardy.—People v. O'Leary, 2, 843.

The failure of the clerk to make the entry as fully as he ought to have done could not prejudice defendant.—People v. O'Leary, 2, 843.

Penal Code, section 1017, provides that pleas must be oral, and entered upon the minutes in substantially the following form, if defendant plead a former conviction or acquittal: "The defendant pleads that he has already been convicted [or acquitted] of the offense charged by the judgment of the court of," specifying the time, place, and court. If he plead once in jeopardy: "The defendant pleads that he has been once in jeopardy for the offense charged," specifying the time, place, and court. Defendant's pleas, as entered on the minutes (though his counsed offered written pleas which were much fuller), were: "First, defendant pleads not guilty of the offense charged; second, a former acquittal; third, once in jeopardy." Held, that the two latter pleas were insufficient.—People v. O'Leary, 3, 102.

Under Penal Code, section 1008, providing that the allowance of a demurrer to an indictment or information is a bar to another prosecution, unless the court, "being of the opinion that the objection on which the demurrer is allowed may be avoided in a new indictment or information, ... directs a new information to be filed," it is not necessary that the court actually render such opinion; it is sufficient if the court directs the district attorney to file a new information.—People v. O'Leary, 3, 102.

Former conviction of felony may be shown by the examination of the witness, or by record of the judgment, and questions asked of the defendant, when testifying on his own behalf, as to such fact, are proper.—People v. Abbott, 2, 383.

34

§ 5. Doctrine of Reasonable Doubt.

To be satisfied beyond all reasonable doubt, as under proper instructions of the court a jury must be in order to convict a defendant of crime, is not the same as to be entirely satisfied.—People v. Loomis, 1, 315.

An instruction concerning intent, as an element in the commission of crime, is not objectionable because it omits to state that a conclusion adverse to defendant must be one that does not admit of a reasonable doubt, where the jury were elsewhere fully instructed as to the doctrine of reasonable doubt.—People v. Gilmore, 6, 57.

In a criminal case, refusal to charge that the jury have a right to consider that innocent men have been convicted, and to consider the danger of convicting an innocent man in weighing the evidence whether there is reasonable doubt as to his guilt, is proper.—People v. Machado, 6, 600.

§ 6. Conduct of District Attorney.

Where the prosecuting attorney proposes to read to the jury-in his argument a paper not in evidence, and stated that it purported to be the record of defendant as furnished by a chief of police, while his course is reprehensible, it does not prejudice defendant when it is promptly rebuked by the court, who charges the jury that statements of counsel not in proof are not evidence, and to be disregarded.— People v. Bowers, 2, 878.

There is no objection to the district attorney's reading to the jury parts of the court's instructions, if the court permits.—People v. Davis, 4, 524.

§ 7. Misconduct of Judge.

Where a witness for the state, in a criminal case, is absent when wanted, and is brought in by an officer, it is error for the court, in the presence of the jury, to hold a colloquy with such witness, which tends to discredit defendant and his counsel, and lead the jury to believe that, if they were not guilty of a grave offense in procuring the absence of the witness, they were, in the opinion of the court, capable of committing it, and that such conduct on their part could only be induced by consciousness of defendant's guilt.—People v. Abbott, 4, 276.

§ 8. Misconduct of Jury.

The legal presumption is that jurors perform their duty, and that presumption is not overcome by proof of the mere fact that, during a trial which lasted over thirty days, two or three of the jurors, after the adjournment of the court for the day, drank a few glasses of liquor at the expense of the district attorney or that one of them took dinner at his house under circumstances rendering the act of invitation necessary, or took supper with counsel under similar circumstances. To set aside a verdict and grant a new trial on the ground of irregularities or misconduct of the jury, it must be either shown as a fact or presumed as a conclusion of law that injury resulted from such irregularity or misconduct, and where there has been no injury the verdict will not be disturbed.—People v. Lyle, 2, 393.

§ 9. Waiver of Rights by Accused.

There is, in criminal cases, no presumption to the effect that the defendant has waived a right; the record must show the waiver.— People v. O'Hara, 1, 71.

If the counsel for an accused person answers "no" to the court's inquiry as to whether he has any instructions he wishes to be given the jury, this is an express waiver, and not within the rule against inferences of waiver of rights in criminal cases.—People v. Lyons, 1, 63.

§ 10. Evidence and Examination of Witnesses.

A defendant may not open his own case by cross-examining witnesses for the prosecution because they happen to know facts pertinent to the defense; he must wait until the prosecution rests, and then call the witnesses as his own.—People v. Jones, 1, 544.

The conduct, acts and statements of a person under arrest for a crime which he is charged with having committed, are admissible in evidence, and such inference may be drawn from them as are warranted by the evidence; but an inference of guilt cannot be drawn from a statement evincive of innocence, nor from silence, where a person is not bound to speak, nor from refusal to answer unauthorized questions touching the charge against him.—People v. Elster, 2, 315.

The conduct, acts and expressions of a person accused of crime, at the time of his arrest, are admissible against him.—People v. Abbott, 2, 383.

A question of one witness as to declarations of another, who was not himself questioned in relation thereto, was properly stricken out. People v. Machado, 6, 600.

Where, on a criminal prosecution, the testimony of a witness was read to the jury at their request it was not error for the judge to have the last question re-read to him.—People v. Eaton, 6, 906.

§ 11. —— Confessions.

Evidence of confessions made by a defendant while under arrest are admissible, if voluntarily made, the fact that defendant was under arrest not necessarily proving that the declarations were involuntary.—People v. Abbott, 2, 383.

§ 12. —— Character of Accused.

In a criminal case the jury must take evidence of character into consideration for the purpose of determining whether it creates a reasonable doubt of guilt, and the consideration of such evidence by the jury is not confined to cases where the guilt of the accused is doubtful.—People v. Lee, 2, 569.

The cross-examination of witnesses who testified to defendant's general reputation for truth, honesty and integrity may take a wide scope.—People v. Garcia, 6, 367.

§ 13. —— Testimony Taken at Preliminary Examination.

Where a witness telegraphed and wrote to the district attorney from another state that, owing to business engagements in that state, he could not be present at the trial, which began about twelve days thereafter, and the return to a subpoena for such witness was that he could not be found within the county, there was a showing of such "due diligence" as justified the reading at the trial of his evidence taken at the preliminary examination before a committing magistrate, under Penal Code, section 686, providing for the reading of such evidence upon its being satisfactorily shown to the court that the witness "with due diligence cannot be found within the state."—People v. Munroe, 4, 66.

A subpoena for the prosecuting witness, a farm laborer, issued more than two weeks before the trial, and like writs sent and specially commended to the sheriffs of four adjoining counties, were all returned unserved. The county officer testified that inquiry had been

made of the farmers in the chief towns of the county, and all over
the county. Held, a predicate for a sworn stenographer's report of
his evidence in the preliminary examination.—People v. Davis, 4, 524.

On error assigned to the admission of the reporter's record of evidence on preliminary examination, the certificate, if not set out in the
record, is presumed to have been in proper form.—People v. Davis, 4,
524.

On a criminal prosecution parts of the testimony of a police officer,
given at the preliminary examination of the defendant as to a conversation between the officer and defendant, may be read to the officer
to refresh his memory.—People v. Joy, 6, 824.

An objection to the reading of the testimony of a police officer
given at the preliminary examination on the trial, to refresh his
memory, merely reciting that it is an objection to the testimony of
the lower court on the pretense that it is used to refresh the memory
of the witness or for any other purpose, without any objection to
the evidence as incompetent, secondary or hearsay, is insufficient.—
People v. Joy, 6, 824.

§ 14. —— Examination and Cross-examination of Defendant.

Where questions put to the defendant when on the witness-stand
elicited only favorable answers and no attempt was made to contradict him, he could not have been prejudiced by such examination.—
People v. Carleton, 2, 381.

To ask defendant on cross-examination the name of his father and
mother cannot prejudice him.—People v. Bowers, 2, 878.

Penal Code, section 688, provides that in a criminal action one cannot be compelled to testify against himself and section 1323 provides
that, if a defendant in a criminal action offer himself as a witness,
he may be cross-examined as to matters about which he was examined
in chief. Held, that, where defendant had merely denied that he
had advised another to draw money from a bank for the purpose of
embezzling it, and had denied all knowledge of intention of the other
so to do, it was error on cross-examination to allow him to be asked
questions relating to facts transpiring after the money was drawn.—
People v. Gallagher, 4, 113.

§ 15. Proof of Corpus Delicti.

Where proof of the corpus delicti has been had only through the
confession of the defendant, a conviction is error.—People v. Long,
1, 710.

§ 16. Instructions to Jury.

See, also, Forgery, § 26; Homicide, § 13; Rape, § 5.

The mere fact of refusing particular instructions asked by the defendant cannot prejudice the jury against him when the jury has not
heard them read and refused as read.—People v. Lockhard, 1, 219.

Requested instructions when in effect they have already been given
with equal fullness and greater accuracy are properly refused.—People
v. Jones, 1, 544.

Where the charge to the jury, considered as a whole, correctly
states the law, and no portion of it is calculated to mislead the jury,
the verdict should not be disturbed, although some part of the charge,
standing alone, may contain some inaccuracy of expression which
would be the subject of criticism.—People v. Biggins, 2, 303.

Where, at the request of a party, certain instructions are given, he
cannot thereafter complain of them.—People v. Biggins, 2, 303.

Instructions to a jury should be given with reference to the imminent facts in the case. If controverted, instructions upon them should

be hypothetical, leaving the supposed facts which the evidence tends to prove to the consideration of the jury. If uncontroverted, the court may assume them.—People v. Biggins, 2, 303.

Where the charge, taken as a whole, is as favorable as the circumstances required, the judgment will not be disturbed.—People v. Carleton, 2, 381.

Where the evidence warrants an instruction suggesting a theory not presented by any other instructions given, it is the duty of the court to give the same at the request of one of the parties.—People v. Wong Chow, 2, 382.

The refusal of a court to give instructions on the law of self-defense, and as to excusable homicide by accident or misfortune, in sudden combat, in a prosecution for murder, is not error if there is no evidence on which to rest such a defense.—People v. Munn, 2, 519.

It is not error to refuse to give an instruction if the same has already been given in other instructions.—People v. Sullivan, 2, 552.

Where the instructions given by the court are contradictory, the judgment will be reversed.—People v. Higgins, 2, 717.

Where the court, after charging in strong language as to the presumptions surrounding defendant and that certainty of proof required, calls the jury's attention to the fact that the law should be fearlessly administered, and that, if they were satisfied beyond a reasonable doubt of defendant's guilt, they should be derelict in duty if they failed to find so, it is not prejudicial, though not in good taste. People v. Bowers, 2, 878.

An instruction that, "where the evidence is entirely circumstantial, yet is not only consistent with the guilt of the defendant, but inconsistent with any other rational conclusion, the law makes it the duty of the jury to convict, notwithstanding such evidence may not be as satisfactory to their minds as the direct testimony of credible eye-witnesses would have been" is correct.—People v. Daniels, 4, 248.

Instructions telling the jury of their duty to convict if the evidence satisfies them of defendant's guilt, though not erroneous, are better omitted.—People v. Crowl, 4, 355.

An instruction that an intention is manifested by the circumstances connected with the offense and the sound mind and discretion of the accused does not assume any fact.—People v. Crowl, 4, 355.

It was harmless error to charge that "where weaker evidence is produced, when in the power of the party to produce higher, it is presumed that the higher evidence would be adverse, if it had not been produced," where the record did not show that defendant offered weaker evidence when it was in his power to produce higher.—People v. Dole, 5, 934.

Where the evidence was largely direct and positive, it was not prejudicial error to charge that, where the evidence is entirely circumstantial, yet it is not only consistent with the guilt of defendant, but inconsistent with any other rational conclusion, the jury must convict, notwithstanding such evidence may not be as satisfactory to their minds as the direct testimony of credible eye-witnesses would have been.—People v. Dole, 5, 934.

It is not error for the court to refuse to give an instruction, the substance of which he has given in a preceding one.—People v. Solomon, 6, 305.

There was no error in instructing the jury that the police officer was under no obligation to assist the defense of any of the parties to the crime by making any experiment.—People v. Eaton, 6, 906.

§ 17. —— Oral or Written Charge.

The defendant in criminal cases enjoys a right by statute to have the court's instructions in writing, to insure their preservation in authentic and accurate form.—People v. O'Hara, 1, 71.

Without the consent of the defendant, it is error for the court to give an oral instruction to the jury in a criminal case.—People v. Silva, 1, 283.

§ 18. —— Charge in Disjunctive.

The court should not charge in the disjunctive that a defendant is guilty if he "aided, abetted, or assisted" any other person to commit the crime.—People v. Dole, 5, 934.

Error in using the disjunctive in a charge that defendant was guilty if he "aided, abetted, or assisted" any other person to commit the crime was harmless.—People v. Dole, 5, 934.

§ 19. Verdict.
See, also, Burglary, § 4; Homicide, § 14.

When a prosecution is against more than one person, a verdict finding "the defendant guilty," etc., is void for uncertainty.—People v. Salazar, 2, 119.

A verdict of "guilty as charged," etc., is sufficient.—People v. Smith, 2, 215.

Defendant entered three pleas: First, not guilty; second, a former acquittal; third, once in jeopardy. The jury found only on the first. Held, that there could be no conviction without a verdict on each plea. People v. O'Leary, 2, 843.

Where the verdict fails to find the degree of the crime of which defendant is guilty, he is not entitled to a discharge, but merely to a new trial.—People v. Bannister, 4, 333.

§ 20. Sentence.
See, also, Habeas Corpus, § 1.

The imposing of sentence within two days after judgment of conviction is an irregularity and contrary to section 1191 of the Penal Code, but the question should be raised by direct appeal from the court's action, rather than by habeas corpus.—Ex parte Mess, 2, 217.

§ 21. Stay of Execution.

Where the court, at defendant's request, stayed execution of judgment of conviction until the judgment had become final by the expiration of more than a year after its entry without appeal, and without a motion for a new trial, defendant cannot object to an order vacating an order directing a commitment to issue; otherwise, the court would be powerless to carry the judgment into effect.—People v. Walker, 6, 472.

§ 21½. Motion in Arrest—Bill of Exceptions.

Under Penal Code, section 1185, providing that a motion in arrest of judgment may be "founded on any defects in the indictment or information mentioned in section 1004," a bill of exceptions, prepared for and used only upon a motion in arrest, cannot properly contain a written plea offered by defendant; and the contents of such writing cannot be looked to in this court to aid the pleas actually entered on the minutes.—People v. O'Leary, 3, 102.

§ 22. Appeal.

In a plain case of proven crime the appellate court is not disposed to reverse the judgment because of an instruction that is incorrect only from a technical standpoint.—People v. Taylor, 1, 19.

An appeal left unprosecuted after being brought up can be disposed of only by an affirmation of the judgment.—People v. Batierrez, 1, 726.

Where a verdict against the defendant is found contrary to the evidence and the court's instructions, the supreme court will reverse the judgment and remand the cause for a new trial.—People v. Dowd, 2, 68.

Where no objection is taken to irregularities on the trial, the matter cannot be raised on appeal.—People v. Lyle, 2, 393.

Where, in a criminal case, none of the evidence given on the trial appears in the record on appeal, the appellate court must presume that the instructions granted by the court at the instance of the prosecution, and its charge to the jury on its own motion, were proper, if such a state of the evidence therein is conceivable as may have rendered them correct.—People v. Johnson, 2, 573.

Where the record fails to show that defendant objected to numerous continuances, a denial of motion to dismiss, made on the ground that he had not been brought to trial within the time required by the Penal Code, will be affirmed.—People v. Bell, 4, 522.

Where no brief is filed, a conviction will be affirmed if it appears that the evidence sustains the verdict, and no exception was taken to any ruling of the court.—People v. Short, 5, 158.

Action of the trial court in granting a new trial in a criminal case on the ground that the verdict was not supported by the evidence, which, though ample, was conflicting, will not be disturbed.—People v. Fugitt, 5, 496.

Where the record on appeal discloses sufficient evidence to uphold a conviction, the judgment will not be disturbed.—People v. Bennett, 5, 824.

Under Penal Code, section 1237, permitting an appeal from a final judgment of conviction or from an order denying a new trial, and from an order made after judgment affecting the substantial rights of the party, and section 1259, providing that, on appeal by a defendant from a judgment, the court may review any intermediate order or ruling involving the merits, or which may have affected the judgment, an appeal will not lie from an order denying a motion in arrest of judgment, since it may be reviewed on appeal from final judgment.—People v. Walker, 6, 472.

Where on appeal an order of the police court denying petitioner a new trial was reversed, and a new trial had in the superior court, resulting in a conviction, as to the appeal from the order denying the new trial there was a finality as to petitioner's rights.—Wilson v. Superior Court, 6, 713.

Defendant, being convicted in police court, appealed to the superior court from an order denying a new trial, which order was reversed, and on new trial in the superior court defendant was convicted. Thereafter the superior court, by mistake, owing to the papers on appeal bearing a different number, rendered a decision reversing the judgment of the police court. On the attention of the court being called thereto, it set aside the order wherein the judgment was reversed. Held, that the judgment rendered on appeal reversing the order denying a new trial, and the conviction of appellant on such new trial in the superior court, was final, and there was, therefore, in fact no appeal in the case pending, in which the second judgment was rendered reversing the judgment below.—Wilson v. Superior Court, 6, 713.

Under Penal Code, section 1253, providing that a judgment may be affirmed if the appellant fail to appear, but can be reversed only after argument, though the respondent fail to appear, a judgment of conviction could only be affirmed where defendant filed no brief, made no appearance, and submitted the case on the record without argument.—People v. Gehrig, 7, 149.

§ 23. —— When Lies.

A defendant has no appeal from an order granting him a new trial.—People v. Ah Choy, 2, 106.

An appeal will not lie from an order overruling a motion to discharge from imprisonment, nor from an order denying a motion to vacate the judgment of conviction, since the judgment of conviction was appealable, and all objections could have been reviewed on appeal from it.—People v. Walker, 6, 472.

An appeal will not lie from an order overruling a motion to correct the minutes of the court as to arraignment of defendant, under Code of Civil Procedure, section 963, allowing an appeal from a special order made after final judgment.—People v. Walker, 6, 472.

§ 24. —— Time for Taking.

Under Penal Code, section 1239, requiring an appeal from a judgment to be taken within a year, an appeal from a conviction in a criminal case, taken more than one year after rendition of judgment, cannot be considered.—People v. Walker, 6, 472.

An appeal from an order fixing the day for the execution of a sentence of death will be dismissed where it appears that the day so fixed has long since passed.—People v. Thompson, 5, 533.

Under Penal Code of California, section 1246, requiring the clerk with whom the notice of appeal is filed, within ten days thereafter, or within ten days after the settlement of the bill of exceptions, to transmit to the clerk of the appellate court a copy of the record, an appeal will be dismissed on a showing by certificate of the clerk below that four years have elapsed since the taking of the appeal; that defendant has never requested the clerk to make up a transcript; that the bill of exceptions has never been filed, though settled; and that no transcript has been sent to the supreme court.—People v. Frink, 2, 736.

§ 25. —— Exceptions and Record.
See, also, ante, § 21½.

A certificate by a clerk of court to the effect that the district attorney agreed to the statement is extra-official and without sanction.—People v. Davis, 1, 45.

An appeal from the overruling of a demurrer to an information is not entitled to be considered, in the absence of a record showing what the order was. Here, nevertheless, the court examined the information and sustained it as good in substance.—People v. Clarke, 2, 110.

Where the record in a murder trial recites that the court read to the jury "instructions asked by the respective parties, and allowed by the court, and those given by the court of its own motion," but does not contain those given by the court of its own motion, or requested by the people, the appellate court will not determine whether or not the trial court erred in refusing to give an instruction asked by defendant, but will set aside a submission of the cause, and restore it to the calendar, to be heard when all the instructions are incorporated into the record.—People v. Vital, 4, 320.

The people and defendant consented that the preliminary evidence as to the admissibility of an alleged written confession by defendant and a fellow-prisoner, and the argument on defendant's objections, should be heard in the absence of the jury. Held, that the action of the court in proceeding in accordance with such arrangement would not be reviewed, in the absence of objection and exception in the trial court.—People v. Evans, 5, 125.

Where the court, of its own motion, gives an instruction based on a contention which it states was made on the trial, it cannot be presumed on appeal, in the absence of such fact being affirmatively shown by a bill of exceptions, that the contention was not made.—People v. Gonzales, 6, 263.

On a motion for permission to file a certified copy of a demurrer to the indictment in the appellate court, on the ground that the demurrer should have been made a part of the record by virtue of Penal Code, section 1207, whether the demurrer is properly a part of the record will not be decided in advance of the hearing of the appeal, but the motion will be granted and the question decided on the hearing.—People v. Glass, 7, 357.

CROPS.

Mortgage on. See Chattel Mortgage, § 2.
Levy on cotenant's share. See Execution, § 1.
Pledge for rent. See Pledge, § 2.

§ 1. Farming on Shares.

Of persons working a farm on shares the claim of one for his share of the profits against the other who has absorbed them all may be put into suit without a preliminary demand.—Silva v. Dobble, 2, 107.

§ 2. Cropping Contracts.

Where plaintiff, the owner of certain orchards, contracted to let defendant a house and furnish implements, horses, wagons, feed, spraying materials, boxes, and trays for curing and marketing the fruit, furnish new trees to replace missing ones, pay for one-half of boxing materials when shipped, and, when dried, to pay for the expenses of cutting, drying and sacking his share, and in consideration of defendant's labor in raising, harvesting, shipping and marketing the fruit, the latter was to have one-half of the crop, the contract was a mere cropping contract, and not a lease, and plaintiff and defendant were therefore tenants in common of the crop.—Adams v. Thornton, 7, 219.

Where plaintiff and defendant were tenants in common of a crop raised by defendant under a cropping contract, plaintiff was not entitled to maintain replevin against defendant for a portion of the crop alleged to have been wrongfully taken from plaintiff's premises. Adams v. Thornton, 7, 219.

§ 3. Conflicting Liens.

The lien of a mortgage of a crop, taken with notice that a creditor of the owners has already been given possession of it to gather and apply upon his debt, is inferior to his lien.—Lavensohn v. Ward, 1, 764.

CROSS-COMPLAINT.

See Pleading, § 10.

CROSS-EXAMINATION.

In general. See Witness, § 8.

CROSSINGS.

Injuries at. See Railroads, § 10.

CRUELTY.

As ground for divorce. See Divorce, § 2.

CURATIVE STATUTES.

See Constitutional Law, § 4.

CUSTOM DUTIES.

See Sales, § 15.

CUSTOMS AND USAGES.

§ 1. Admissibility as Evidence.

Where, in an action against a mining company, the court made a finding of fact, which was not reviewable, that plaintiff acquiesced in and consented to the use of certain oil for fuel, error, if any, in the introduction of evidence of a custom in the community to permit lessees of land for prospecting purposes to burn oil found to run their engines and pumps, was harmless.—Swift v. Occidental Mining and Petroleum Co., 7, 23.

Where the court holds that a contract has not been made with reference to a custom, evidence as to the existence of the custom is properly struck out as immaterial.—Withers v. Moore, 7, 125.

Code of Civil Procedure, section 1870, subdivision 12, provides that evidence of usage may be given to explain the true character of an act, contract or instrument, where such true character is not otherwise plain, but usage is never admissible except as in an instrument of interpretation. A San Francisco merchant cabled to a coal dealer in New South Wales, "Offer subject to immediate reply twenty-four shillings cost freight and insurance exchange duty paid two cargoes." The coal dealer replied, "Ultimatum twenty-four shillings and three pence." The merchant responded by letter confirming his cable acceptance, and saying, "We beg to confirm having purchased from you [stating kind of coal and price] 'cost' 'freight,' 'insurance,' 'exchange,' 'duty paid,'" etc. Held, that the contract of sale thus evidenced was free from ambiguity, so that extrinsic evidence of a custom of the port of San Francisco giving to the purchaser of imported goods the advantage of a reduction of customs duties was inadmissible.—Withers v. Moore, 7, 125.

Proof of custom is not admissible to oppose or alter a rule of law, or to change the legal rights and liabilities of parties as fixed by law.—Hill v. Weisler, 1, 724.

DAMAGES.

In replevin. See Replevin, § 7.
For breach of contract of sale. See Sales.
For trespass. See Trespass, § 3.
For conversion. See Trover and Conversion, § 6.
For diversion of waters. See Waters and Watercourses, § 9.

§ 1. For Personal Injuries—Evidence.

In the trial of an action founded on the alleged breach of a contract, an instruction that sets forth the measure of damages in unintelligible language is error.—Winans v. Sierra Lumber Co., 2, 222.

It was proper to allow plaintiff to testify that he had formerly lost two fingers on his right hand, and to show his hand to the jury, since they should know to what extent the loss of his left arm had deprived him of his earning power.—Townsend v. Briggs, 3, 803.

It was proper for plaintiff's physician to testify that he told plaintiff of his condition, and that it was necessary to amputate his arm, since the mental suffering resulting therefrom was attributable to defendant, if he was the cause of the injury.—Townsend v. Briggs, 3, 803.

§ 2. —— Examination of Plaintiff's Person.

Where, in an action for injuries, plaintiff's physician testified that on examination there were no objective signs of injury on his body, and no bruises, and that his injuries were subjective, rather than objective, and defendant's physician had thoroughly examined plaintiff, and fully detailed his condition, as a witness, defendant was not prejudiced by the court's refusal to compel plaintiff to submit to an examination of his person at the trial.—Sambuck v. Southern Pac. Co., 7, 104.

§ 3. Liquidated Damages.

Under Civil Code, sections 3387, 3389, which provide that a contract otherwise proper may be specifically enforced, though a penalty is imposed, or the damages are liquidated for its breach, as it is presumed that the breach of an agreement to transfer real property cannot be adequately relieved by pecuniary compensation, the parties may agree to stipulated damages in contracts for the purchase of land.—Aikman v. Sanborn, 5, 961.

§ 4. Pleading Special Damages.

If special damages are claimed, the facts establishing such special damages must be stated with particularity, in order that the defendant may be enabled to meet the charge if it be false, and, if not so stated, cannot be given in evidence.—Montgomery v. Locke, 2, 693.

In ordinary actions of tort, it is unnecessary to state specifically, and in amounts, the different statements or items which go to make up the sum total of the damages; it is enough to state the facts constituting the cause of action, and claim as much in gross, as damage for the wrong done.—Montgomery v. Locke, 2, 693.

§ 5. Verdict Calling for "Gold Coin."

A verdict requiring the damages found to be paid in gold coin is bad if the action was not on a contract for money expressly so payable, or there was not an understanding between the parties that it was to be so payable, or the money was not received by the defendant in a fiduciary capacity.—Finger v. Diel, 1, 889.

§ 6. Measure of Recovery—New Trial and Appeal.

Where a defendant conceives damages to be excessive, he should, on motion for a new trial, have his statement specify in what respect the evidence was insufficient to support this portion of the finding, and wherein and for what reason the damages were excessive.—Chiarini v. Rochon, 1, 540.

The appellate tribunal will not go beyond the strict rules of law to increase plaintiff's allowance of damages for loss of profits.—Bryson v. McCone, 6, 35.

Finding of damages in excess of amount averred in complaint established damages to amount claimed, so that judgment for the excessive amount need not be reversed, but merely modified.—Kerry v. Pacific Marine Supply Co., 6, 118.

DAMS.

Liability for injuring. See Waters and Watercourses, § 10½.
Negligence in repairing. See Waters and Watercourses, § 11.

DANGEROUS PREMISES.

See Negligence, §§ 3, 4.

DEATH.

Of one of plaintiffs. See Judgments, § 6.
Of judge. See New Trial, § 11.
Of partner and rights of survivor. See Partnership, § 14.
As revocation of power of attorney. See Power of Attorney, § 3.
Of entryman. See Public Lands, § 15.
Of trustee. See Trusts, § 18.

§ 1. Damages for Death of Married Woman.

In an action for the death of a married woman, her husband and children were entitled to recover as damages all pecuniary loss suffered by them from the loss of society and protection of the deceased. Green v. Southern California Ry. Co., 6, 843.

DECEASED WITNESS.

Testimony of. See Evidence, § 4.

DECEDENT.

Witnesses in claim against. See Wills, § 4.

DECLARATIONS.

Admissibility. See Evidence, §§ 10–15.

DECREES.

See Judgments.

DEDICATION.

§ 1. Of land for public use in general.
§ 2. What constitutes dedication for street or highway.
§ 3. —— Filing map of plat.
§ 4. Acceptance by public.
§ 5. Abandonment of highway.
§ 6. Revocation by land owner.

See Easements; Highways.

§ 1. Of Land for Public Use in General.

When more than six years have run, from the beginning of a public user of land up to the bringing of suit by the owner, the court is justified in inferring a dedication on the day such user began.—Rice v. Boyd, 2, 196.

The finding that the defendants neither have nor had any title to the land is sustained by the evidence, and, this being so, it is immaterial to them who the owners were who dedicated it for a street, and they cannot object that there is no finding by the court as to who such owners were.—People v. Blake, 2, 272.

The fact that, twelve years after the city had caused Union street to be graded, it took steps to declare Union street a public street, and to procure the legal title thereto, cannot operate as an estoppel in pais to defeat a recovery for work done by the contractor who graded the street.—Spaulding v. Wesson, 5, 399.

§ 2. What Constitutes Dedication for Street or Highway.

In an action to quiet title to a strip of land, it appeared that plaintiff company filed for record a map of its land, platted as a cemetery, on which map the strip in question, forty feet wide along the west side of the tract, was left blank, with an entrance indicated therefrom into the cemetery. Subsequently, in cutting the land up into cemetery lots, the company left another strip, twenty feet wide, adjoining the former strip, and the whole was known as "E. Avenue," which was used by the public for three years without objection. Held, that the facts showed an intention to dedicate the strip to the public for street purposes.—Los Angeles Cemetery Association v. City of Los Angeles, 3, 783.

In an action for trespass, where defendant alleges that the land entered on was a public highway, it appeared that the line of the road for nearly its whole length had been changed from time to time by the owner of the land; that during all the time the public had been permitted to use the road it had been barred by several gates, to be opened and closed by persons passing over it; that for twelve years no work had been done or public money expended thereon by the road overseers; and it did not appear that there had been before that time. Held, that the road had not become a highway by dedication.—Hibberd v. Mellville, 3, 879.

A question, "For the last ten or fifteen years, how many people have used that road or traveled it?"—was properly excluded, since its answer would not have shown an intention of the owners to dedicate the road/to the public.—Hibberd v. Mellville, 3, 879.

Defendant, for the purpose of changing the course of a highway, opened a road through his land, fenced it on both sides, allowed it to be used by the public, and to be worked and controlled by the public authorities. Held, that the road was dedicated to the public. McKenzie v. Gilmore, 3, 886.

A county highway terminated at the western boundary of certain land, the terminal being marked by stone monuments sixty feet apart. The owner of the land employed a surveyor, who surveyed a strip sixty feet in width from the terminal of the highway to the eastern boundary of the land, and there placed a post at the northern and southern boundaries of the strip; and a map was made, showing the strip surveyed, with the eastern end closed, and filed for record in the county. At the time of the survey the owner of the land informed the surveyor and his children that his purpose was that a map might be made of the road, in order that, in dividing his land among his children, reference might be made to the map, to insure certainty of description, and that the county could not have the strip as a highway unless it paid for it. He told the children to farm up to the center of the road, which they did. The strip surveyed was never recorded or platted as a county road, and no highway connected the strip on the east. Held, that there was no dedication of it for use as a highway.—Smith v. Glenn, 6, 519.

§ 3. —— Filing Map of Plat.

The filing in the recorder's office by a tract owner of a map of the tract, divided into blocks, bearing a memorandum written and signed by him requesting such filing to be made and stating the map to be a plan according to which he would make sales and conveyances, is a dedication to the public of the streets marked on the map, which dedication on being accepted becomes irrevocable.—Bigley v. Nunan, 1, 852.

Where a plat of land is recorded, and land appears thereon not numbered as a lot, nor corresponding in size or shape to one, but bounded by lines clearly intended to represent the lines of a street, and lots are sold as being bounded on such street, such land is dedicated for a public street, though not named as such on the plat.— San Francisco v. Burr, 4, 634.

§ 4. Acceptance by Public.

Acceptance by the public of a street dedicated through the filing in the recorder's office of a map of a tract is sufficiently shown by the fact of a public user of one side of the street bed, although the other side is obstructed by sand so as to render it impossible for travel.—Bigley v. Nunan, 1, 852.

The conveyance of a tract of land within the corporate limits of a town, by deed describing the tract as bounded by the lines of certain designated streets, if projected, and as being the northwest quarter of a certain designated block, as laid down on the official map of said town, together with five years' use of the projected streets by the public, constitutes a complete dedication of such streets to public use, without a formal acceptance by the town.—City of Eureka v. Croghan, 3, 24.

User by the public of a strip of land as a street for four years is sufficient to show acceptance of a previous offer to dedicate the land for street purposes.—Los Angeles Cemetery Association v. City of Los Angeles, 3, 783.

It appeared that in 1855 and 1856, under certain ordinances, a land owner had a tract subdivided into blocks and lots, with streets delineated thereon, among which was Union street, and a map was made and approved, showing such survey. In 1861 the then owner of defendant's lot made a declaration of homestead upon it, showing it to be bounded on the north by Union street. The conveyance of said lot to defendant, and a declaration of homestead and mortgage executed by him, all described the lot in a similar manner. When Union street was graded, defendant made no objection thereto. After the grading was finished the fences were adjusted to Union street as thus laid out, the street was sewered and paved, and a street railroad was placed thereon, without objection by defendant. Held, that Union street was dedicated to public use as a street, and accepted as such.—Spaulding v. Wesson, 5, 399.

§ 5. Abandonment of Highway.

A petition asking that a highway be vacated was presented to a board of supervisors. Viewers were appointed, and in their report they recommended that the highway be made a private road, and that the owners of the land over which the road passed give a deed to the county for the private road. The board made an order adopting the report, but no deeds of the land were ever made. Held, that the order of the supervisors was not an abandonment of the highway.—McKenzie v. Gilmore, 3, 886.

§ 6. Revocation by Land Owner.

Neither the owner of land nor anyone claiming under him can recall a dedication once made and accepted, so long as the land remains in the use to which it was dedicated, although, subject to the user, the owner has the fee notwithstanding the dedication.—Rice v. Boyd, 2, 196.

In 1862 the owner of a tract of land caused the same to be surveyed and platted. Part of one of the streets marked on the plat was never opened or used as a public street, and for a period of more than twenty years the owner had a barn and shed on said part, inclosed by a substantial fence. There was no acceptance of said street until the passage of a city ordinance, in 1884, directing the street commissioners to demand the possession of the part the street so occupied. Held, that there was no sufficient dedication or acceptance, and that, if there had been a dedication, it was revoked before acceptance.—People v. Reed, 3, 40.

Where a person dedicates land for a public highway he cannot afterward reclaim the same by showing that he was induced to make such dedication by the promise of a neighbor to give him the use of other lands, and that he had ceased to use such lands.—McKenzie v. Gilmore, 3, 886.

DEED ABSOLUTE.

As mortgage. See Mortgages, § 12.

DEED OF TRUST.

See Trusts; Mortgages.

DEEDS.

§ 1. In General.

There is no rule, either by statute or in equity, whereby an un-recorded deed, made by a mortgagor after executing the mortgage and before suit to foreclose it is begun, shall be treated as made pendente lite.—Brooks v. Tichner, 1, 104.

Bare right of possession, without claim or color of title, cannot be transferred by deed, nor otherwise than by the former possessor yielding up or abandoning the possession, and permitting a new pos-session to be taken by another.—Daubenbiss v. White, 3, 590.

§ 2. Quitclaim.

A quitclaim deed is as effectual to transfer title as a grant, or bar-gain and sale.—Packard v. Johnson, 2, 365.

§ 3. Validity—Fraud and Undue Influence.

A part owner who, through the fraud of his co-owner by the medium of a deed pretending to effect an exchange of properties, believes he owns the whole of a tract and so conveys a half interest to a third party, also not knowing of the fraud, whereby he has noth-ing left, cannot, if on learning of the fraud he makes no effort to have the deed set aside but chooses rather to accept large compensation for the fraud, make a subsequent deed to a fourth party of whatever interest may remain in him, which last deed passes anything at all.—Peres v. Sunol, 1, 647.

Deed untainted by fraud is not impeachable for fraud committed afterward in the obtaining of another deed between the same parties for different premises.—Gutierrez v. Brinkerhoff, 2, 232.

Where a deed of gift was executed upon consideration of love and affection, and afterward suit was brought by the grantor to cancel the deed, charging the grantee with using undue influence over the grantor in procuring the execution of the deed, in the absence of proof of such undue influence, or of any decree of turpitude on the part of the grantee in receiving and recording the deed, held, that the deed was valid.—Richards v. Donner, 2, 675.

§ 4. Ratification by Person Recovering from Illness.

Where a person sick in the hospital makes a deed to it for a cer-tain sum paid and an agreement for further care, and recovers, and for several weeks is able to transact business, and up to the day of his death is satisfied with the transaction, it amounts to a ratification thereof.—Barry v. St. Joseph's Hospital, 5, 625.

§ 5. Date of Execution.

The date mentioned in a deed as the date of its execution is only presumptively the true date, when there is no evidence that it was really executed at a different time.—Merle v. Meagher, 1, 644.

By statute the certificate of acknowledgment is prima facie evi-dence of the genuineness of the deed, that is, that it had been executed at the time the certificate was made; as to what time that was, the date on the face of the certificate is itself prima facie evidence.—Merle v. Meagher, 1, 644.

§ 6. Volunteer Joining in Deed.

By joining in a deed unnecessarily, unasked and as a volunteer only, a person creates no relations with the grantee or, a fortiori, with his assign whereby he may make the latter account to him in any way with reference to the transaction.—Morenhout v. Brown, 1, 139.

§ 7. Delivery.

The delivery of a deed to a stranger for the use of the grantee is a valid delivery, and takes effect from the time of the act by relation, provided the deed is afterward accepted by the grantee and the grantor intended it to take effect as a conveyance.—Hibberd v. Smith, 1, 554.

A husband signed and acknowledged a deed conveying land to his wife, stating to the notary before whom he acknowledged it that he wished to give the property to her. The wife testified that her husband put the deed on the table, told her what it was, and directed her to put it away, saying that it could be recorded at any time. She stated that she put the deed in the trunk, and at another time said her husband did so. Their daughter corroborated her mother, and stated that her father said he would put it away for her mother, and that she could record it any time. An inmate of the house stated that she was in position to have heard any such conversation, if it had occurred, but that she neither saw nor heard anything of the deed, but her testimony was vague as to the continuousness of her presence. Held, that the deed was delivered.—McGrath et al. v. Hyde, 3, 98.

Proof that the consideration for a deed was not paid is not alone sufficient to rebut the presumption under Civil Code, section 1055, that a grant duly executed is delivered at its date.—Gerke v. Cameron et al., 5, 798.

§ 8. —— To Take Effect After Death.

Deeds executed by husband and wife, conveying each to the other their separate properties, and delivered to a third person, with direction to record that of the person dying first, are not testamentary or revocable.—Kenney v. Parks, 6, 111.

§ 9. Consideration—Love and Affection.

Love and affection is a good consideration for a conveyance of land by a husband to his wife, and will support the conveyance.—Springer v. Springer, 6, 662.

§ 10. —— Care and Support.

In a suit to set aside a sale made in consideration of a promissory note and board and care, plaintiff cannot recover unless she offers to return the note, and pay for the board and the care.—Barry v. St. Joseph's Hospital, 5, 625.

§ 11. —— Marriage.

A conveyance by the owner of mortgaged premises, in consideration of marriage and money received, of his interest in the premises, to his intended wife, is valid.—Klauber v. Vigneron, 3, 795.

Where such mortgagor, after marriage, substitutes for the previous mortgage, which is canceled, one of larger amount, the last-named mortgage is void.—Klauber v. Vigneron, 3, 795.

If the mortgagee is entitled to any relief, he should declare on the previous mortgage, and ask to have the satisfaction set aside on the ground that it was made through mistake, accident or fraud.—Klauber v. Vigneron, 3, 795.

§ 12. —— Presumption.

Where the evidence was clear and unequivocal that a deed was made on or within a day or two of October 15, 1883, and there was no evidence to show that the property conveyed had at the time a market value in excess of the amount paid, and there was no evi-

35

dence of fraud, held, that a finding of fact to the contrary, based upon presumptions, could not be sustained.—Frankel v. Deidesheimer, 2, 768.

Under Code of Civil Procedure, sections 1614, 1963, subdivision 39, providing that a written instrument is presumptive evidence of a consideration, the introduction of a deed in evidence places the burden of showing want of consideration on the party alleging it, and carries with it a presumption that it was given for a valuable consideration.—Blair v. Squire, 6, 350.

§ 13. Description of Grantee.

A deed to Henry Stull & Co. vests the legal title in Henry Stull alone, and his deed will give to his grantee a good and valid title.—Ketchum v. Barber, 2, 698.

§ 14. Description of Land.

A deed in which the description of the land errs in respect of locating the point of beginning, whereby confusion results from the subsequent courses given, is sufficiently explained by words following the description, such as "it being the same land described in," etc., thus subrogating the grantee to the ownership of the grantor under the deed by which the latter acquired title.—Huber v. Clarke, 1, 475.

In construing deeds with inconsistent calls, when it is obvious that one of them must of necessity be a false call, evidence aliunde is admissible to explain the error, unless it is explained by other portions of the deed.—Huber v. Clarke, 1, 475.

A deed offered in evidence is not to be rejected because of alleged uncertainty in describing the land granted, since it is for the jury to decide from this and all other evidence produced at the trial what the true description is.—Valentine v. Jansen, 1, 525.

A jury may be charged by the court that if they believe a grantee was aware of the contents of the deed on its being delivered, then his accepting and recording it is competent evidence tending to show what land he claimed as his; provided it is charged at the same time that such acceptance would not estop him to claim that the true description of the land is other than that given in the deed.—Valentine v. Jansen, 1, 525.

A description in part "bounded on the east by the lands or ranchos of," etc., written in a deed, means the lands or ranchos mentioned as they were understood by the parties to the deed at the time the latter was made.—Umbarger v. Chaboya, 1, 765.

A description in a conveyance is not too vague if it gives the contents of the land and its local situation and designates it as lot No. 62 on the official map of the outside lands of the town of Santa Barbara.—Thompson v. Thompson, 2, 32.

Under a deed purporting to convey a certain number of feet along a street commencing at a certain point, only that number of feet passed by the deed, and therefore evidence that the grantor, in measuring off the land granted, measured more than that number of feet, is incompetent to show that more than the number of feet stated passed by the deed.—Hogins v. Boggs, 4, 322.

Where, in a deed, land is described as commencing at the corner of certain sections "in the Chapman tract in the Rancho Santiago de Santa Ana in the county of Orange," the description is sufficient, though the township and range are not stated.—Borchard v. Eastwood, 6, 736.

Where the description in a deed is all "the lands owned by the grantor" in a certain county, with certain exceptions, it is sufficient to convey all his lands in such county not included within the exceptions.—Borchard v. Eastwood, 6, 736.

§ 15. —— Mistake.

Where, in a deed, the land is fully and correctly described, except the number of the township is given as "45" instead of "4," and the land can be identified by the rest of the description, such mistake will not vitiate the conveyance.—Borchard v. Eastwood, 6, 736.

§ 16. Interpretation and Effect.

When one yields a large consideration in rents, damages and costs for the purpose of clearing up his title, the deed, in the transaction, from the recipient of the consideration is not to be regarded as ineffective for the purpose merely because the subject matter is described as "a claim against the lot."—Willson v. Truebody, 1, 238.

An instrument in terms a deed of warranty, but given on an express promise by the grantee to redeem at any time within one year therefrom on request by the grantor and a tender back of the consideration, is, in default of such request and tender within six years, to be regarded as a conveyance of the fee.—Elze v. Ohm, 1, 252.

Deed construed, and held not to impose on defendant water company the obligation to complete a certain canal named therein.—State v. Folsom Water Co., 2, 704.

The alienating force of a deed, which by plain terms purports to pass the grantor's entire interest, is not restricted by the fact that it contains an allusion to an executory contract which the grantor has with a third party respecting the land, and from whom he is to get a quitclaim deed, when the allusion is made simply for the purpose of describing more particularly the premises conveyed.—Grant v. De Lamori, 2, 770.

The recital in an instrument of sale that there was conveyed "that certain store, and all the stock and goods therein, and the bakery attached thereto, and the tools and fixtures of said bakery," will be construed as conveying the land on which the store and the bakery attachment stand, and so much as may be necessary for their ordinary use.—Pottkamp v. Buss, 3, 694.

§ 17. —— Construction by Acts of Parties.

Defendant conveyed part of a tract of land, and a fence was constructed by him and a subsequent grantee so as to include the land described in the conveyance and an additional piece belonging to him, and the land was subsequently conveyed to plaintiff by a description following the line of the fence. Defendant claimed that after the fence was constructed he discovered that it included too much land, and so notified the owner, but took no steps to have it moved, and allowed it to remain for twenty years, and in conveying an adjoining piece had it surveyed, and used a description corresponding to the line of the fence. Held, in an action to quiet title to the additional piece on the ground that it should have been included in the original conveyance by defendant, that the subsequent acts of the parties had established plaintiff's title.—California Mortgage & Savings Bank v. Hampton, 6, 301.

§ 18. Parol to Explain.

When, of many tenants in common, among whom are a father and daughter, the former makes, for a nominal consideration, a deed to another absolute on its face and presenting no patent ambiguity, and on the same day this person makes, for the same consideration, a like deed to the daughter, parol evidence is not admissible years afterward to prove this second deed to have been intended as a mere confirmation to the daughter of the interest already held by her when such deed was made.—Reed v. Union Copper Min. Co., 1, 587.

§ 19. Conveyance Subject to Easement for Street.

After a conveyance in fee of a strip of land known as a certain avenue, subject only to an easement in the public for road purposes, the grantor has no interest therein which he can convey to a subsequent grantee.—Southern California Ry. Co. v. Southern Pac. R. R. Co., 5, 288.

§ 20. Reservations.

The reservation of land for a particular use imposes upon the owner no obligation to put it to that use, but he may devote it to any lawful use that may suit him, or may at his pleasure dispose of it.—Belknap v. Byington, 1, 374.

§ 21. —— Of Oil and Minerals.

The owners of land conveyed a part of it to plaintiff, with a reservation to them and their assigns of "the exclusive right to all oils, petroleum, asphaltum, and other kindred mineral substances," and the right to do whatever was necessary to obtain and transport such minerals, including the erection of proper machinery, and the laying of pipes. The rest of the original tract was conveyed in parcels to other persons, with the same reservation, and finally the reserved rights and interests in the whole were granted to defendants. Held, that defendants have no right to the possession of plaintiff's land further than is necessary to the exercise of the rights reserved in that tract alone.—Dietz v. Mission Transfer Co., 3, 354.

Plaintiff's deed to defendants of all structures erected by him on the land, for the purpose of exploring for, obtaining, and transporting such mineral, will not estop him to claim title to, and the right of possession of, the land on which such structures stand.—Dietz v. Mission Transfer Co., 3, 354.

Where, in ejectment, it is shown that defendants have taken possession of a part of plaintiff's land, to enable them to exercise the rights reserved in the rest of the original tract by their grantors, and that they are not seeking the minerals in question on plaintiff's land, and that none exists there, plaintiff is entitled to recover the possession of the land occupied by them.—Dietz v. Mission Transfer Co., 3, 354.

A judgment in a former action determining that a lease to plaintiff, granted before he obtained his deed, of the right to take such minerals in the entire tract had expired and enjoining him from interference with defendants' right to take such minerals, they having purchased it from his grantors, is no bar to such action of ejectment.—Dietz v. Mission Transfer Co., 3, 354.

DE FACTO.

Corporation. See Corporations, § 4.

DEFAULT.

Judgments by and their opening. See Judgments, §§ 12–14.
In action to enforce tax. See Taxation, § 18.

DEFICIENCY JUDGMENT.

See Mortgages, § 26.

DEGREE OF CRIME.

In burglary. See Burglary, § 4.

DELIVERY.

Of negotiable instrument. See Bills and Notes, § 3.
Of deeds. See Deeds, §§ 7, 8.
Of mortgage. See Mortgage, § 6.

DEMAND.

In case of negotiable paper. See Bills and Notes, § 14.
Necessity for in ejectment. See Ejectment, § 7.
For return of money. See Embezzlement, § 2.
Necessity in replevin. See Replevin, § 3.
Necessity for. See Specific Performance, § 3.
Necessity for in trover. See Trover and Conversion, § 2.

§ 1. For Excessive Sum.

In an action on a contract demand may not be made for a sum exceeding what the contract calls for.—Dyer v. Ryan, 2, 173.

§ 2. Before Suit by Administrator.

An administrator seeking to recover personal property of deceased, held by a transferee under color of title by gift, need not make a demand therefor before instituting suit.—Knight v. Tripp, 5, 735.

DEMURRER.

See Pleading.

DENTISTS.

See Physicians and Dentists.

DEPOSITIONS.

§ 1. Admissibility in Evidence.

Where neither parties nor the issues in two different actions are identical, depositions taken in one are inadmissible in the other.—Wolters v. Rossi, 6, 266.

Depositions taken in one action are inadmissible in another as against a party who had no opportunity to cross-examine the witnesses.—Wolters v. Rossi, 6, 266.

DEPUTY SHERIFF.

Liability for acts of. See Sheriffs and Constables, § 5.

DESCENT AND DISTRIBUTION.

See Executors and Administrators, §§ 37–40.
Succession by surviving spouse. See Husband and Wife, § 8.

DESCRIPTION.

In deed. See Deeds, §§ 13–15.
Of property in judgment. See Judgments, § 7.
Of premises. See Mortgage, § 7.

DESERTION.

As ground for divorce. See Divorce, § 1.

DEVISES.
See Wills.

DICTUM.
See Obiter Dictum.

DISBARMENT.
Of attorney. See Attorney and Client, §§ 11, 13.

DISCLAIMER.
By defendant as to part. See Quieting Title, § 5.

DISCOVERY.

§ 1. Bill of Discovery in Ejectment.

In ejectment the plaintiff cannot, under California practice, require a bill of discovery in aid of his action, since under that practice he may probe the defendant's conscience by requiring an answer under oath or may call the defendant to the stand as a witness.—Reed v. Union Copper Mining Co., 1, 587.

DISEASED TREES.
Sale of. See Sales, § 10.

DISJUNCTIVE.
Instruction in. See Criminal Law, § 18.

DISMISSAL.
Of appeal. See Appeal and Error, §§ 61–69.
Of proceedings for new trial. See New Trial, § 24.

DISMISSAL AND NONSUIT.

§ 1. Dismissal in general.
§ 2. —— For want of prosecution.
§ 3. —— For failure to enter judgment.
§ 4. Fraud in procuring dismissal.
§ 5. Motion to vacate dismissal.
§ 6. Nonsuit and judgment therefor.

In suit to quiet title. See Quieting Title, § 9.

§ 1. Dismissal in General.

In the absence of any showing to the contrary, the reason had by the trial court for dismissing an action must be presumed good and legal.—Brown v. Vidal, 1, 15.

It is error to dismiss an action without giving the plaintiff an opportunity to show cause why it should not be dismissed.—Saville v. Frisbie, 2, 181.

Where defendant in his answer sought affirmative relief, an attempted dismissal of the action by plaintiffs, on the day before the case was to be called for trial, was a nullity.—Thompson v. Spray, 2, 346.

Where the evidence warrants a finding that the attorney who brings a suit for a corporation against one of the stockholders was not authorized by the corporation to do so, it is proper for the court, on motion of defendant, to enter a judgment dismissing the action.—Magnolia v. Healdsburg Fruit Cannery v. Guerne, 3, 589.

A direction by plaintiff to the clerk, though sufficient to authorize him to enter a judgment of dismissal in a pending action, did not effect a dismissal, where such judgment was never entered; and the court therefore retained jurisdiction over the cause and the parties.—Truett v. Onderdonk, 5, 785.

§ 2. For Want of Prosecution.

Where the summons was not issued till nearly a year after the action was begun, and had not been served at the time of a motion to dismiss three years and eight months after its issuance, plaintiff explaining that he forebore to serve the summons for the reason that certain persons represented that defendant would abide the event of a test case, but not showing their authority to make the representations, and defendant denying it, held, that there was no abuse of discretion in granting the motion to dismiss.—Pacific Bridge Co. v. Jacobus, 2, 749.

A case was tried before the court, who announced that his opinion was for defendants, but notice of decision was not given, or finding of facts filed or waived. After some delay, plaintiff applied to the clerk to enter judgment, that he might appeal, and, being refused, moved for a new trial, which motion was dismissed, whereupon he moved to place the case on the calendar for trial, pending which defendants moved to dismiss the case for want of prosecution. Held, not proper case for dismissal.—Pardy v. Montgomery, 2, 869.

It is within the sound discretion of the lower court to dismiss an action for inexcusable delay in failing, for two years after the commencement of the action, to serve defendant with process.—Castro v. San Francisco, 4, 500.

§ 3. —— For Failure to Enter Judgment.

Code of Civil Procedure, section 581, provides that an action may be dismissed, or judgment of nonsuit entered, "when, after verdict or final submission, the party entitled to judgment neglects to demand and have the same entered for more than six months." Held, that where defendant, on receiving a verdict, prepared a draft of judgment, and requested the clerk to make the entry, the verdict should not be dismissed, though the clerk neglected for more than six months to enter the same.—Jones v. Chalfant, 3, 585.

A motion to dismiss an action tried to the court, on the ground that plaintiff has neglected to have judgment entered for more than six months after decision, is not authorized by Code of Civil Procedure, section 581, where neither party is entitled to judgment at the time, because written findings have not been prepared and approved by the judge, or waived by the parties.—Neihaus v. Morgan, 5, 391.

§ 4. Fraud in Procuring Dismissal.

After the commencement of an equitable action for a partnership accounting, the parties submitted to arbitration, and, on payment of the amount awarded to him, plaintiff executed to defendant a full release, and to the clerk a direction to enter a dismissal of the action; but no judgment of dismissal was ever entered. Plaintiff, on discovering, long afterward, that defendant had been guilty of a fraudulent suppression and misrepresentation of facts in effecting said settlement, filed a retraction of such authority to dismiss, and a motion for an order authorizing same, supported by affidavits setting out the fraudulent acts, none of which were controverted, and showing defendant's absence from the state. Defendant appeared by counsel, and filed a counter-motion for the entry of judgment of dismissal, pursuant to the previous authorization. Held, that an order refusing to vacate plaintiff's direction, and ordering the entry of judgment of dismissal, was erroneous, though such dismissal was without prejudice, where there was no showing that defendant would ever return to the state.—Truett v. Onderdonk, 5, 785.

§ 5. Motion to Vacate Dismissal.

Where an attorney appears in court five minutes after the dismissal of the cause and rendition of judgment against his client because of the absence of both attorney and client when the case was called for trial, it is not an abuse of discretion for the court, on motion supported by a sufficient affidavit, to vacate the order of dismissal and judgment, and restore the cause to the calendar.—Ashton v. Dashaway Association, 4, 27.

§ 6. Nonsuit and Judgment Therefor.

A nonsuit in a cause in which the defendant had filed no answer may properly be set aside, and there should be a new trial awarded the plaintiff.—Schwartz v. De Wit, 1, 40.

If a defendant, after denial of his motion for a nonsuit, proceeds with his evidence and thereupon the supposed defects are cured, the denial is not good matter for an appeal.—Madden v. Ashman, 1, 610.

A judgment against plaintiff at the close of his evidence on the ground that he has not made out his case is a judgment of nonsuit, though part of the evidence introduced by him was a stipulation with defendant which provided that it could be used as evidence by either party.—Cleary v. Folger, 4, 76.

It is error to grant a nonsuit where the plaintiff gives evidence tending to sustain the issues presented in the complaint.—Craven v. Nolan, 2, 551.

Where the evidence given on a trial tends to sustain the allegations of the complaint concerning the acts complained of it is error to grant a nonsuit.—Heilbron v. Last Chance W. D. Co., 2, 633.

A judgment of nonsuit is not final, and determines nothing, and the admission of such a judgment as evidence to establish title to land is error.—Gates v. McLean, 2, 636.

Where there is evidence to sustain a material issue for plaintiff, a motion for a nonsuit is properly denied.—Wells v. Snow, 5, 150.

Where, in an action on a promise made in a letter written by defendant's intestate, the court struck out the testimony of the intestate's wife that the letter was the writing of her husband, and there was no other evidence in the record showing that he wrote it, the refusal to grant a nonsuit was erroneous.—Metz v. Bell, 7, 41.

Where the testimony of the plaintiff tends to prove all the material allegations of his complaint, defendant's motion for a nonsuit will not be granted.—Archibald Estate v. Matteson, 7, 252.

DISQUALIFICATION.

Of judge. See Justices of Peace, § 2.

DISSOLUTION.

Of partnership. See Partnership, § 11.

DISTRICT ATTORNEY.

§ 1. Assistance by Other Attorneys.

The statute prescribing the duties of the district attorney does not, either expressly or by implication, prohibit the court from allow-

ing other attorneys to assist that officer in prosecuting persons charged
with crime.—People **v.** Lynch, 1, 444.

DISTRICT COURT OF APPEALS.
Transfer of cause. See Courts, § 8.

DITCH.
Liability for injury to or destruction of. See Waters and Water.
courses, § 12.

DIVIDED COURT.
Decision by. See Appeal and Error, § 78.

DIVORCE.

Annulment of marriage. See Marriage, § 5.

§ 1. Grounds—Desertion.
In an action for divorce for desertion, evidence held insufficient
to support a finding that the separation between plaintiff and defendant was voluntary, and with defendant's consent.—McMullin v.
McMullin, 7, 93.

Where a husband deserted his wife against her consent, he could not,
eighteen years thereafter, cure such desertion by an offer to return,
so as to entitle him to a divorce for desertion on the wife's refusal
of his offer.—McMullin v. McMullin, 7, 93.

§ 2. —— Cruelty.
It would be difficult, if not impossible, to state in advance what
facts, lying near the borders of legal cruelty, would fill the definition of the term.—Lord v. Lord, 1, 417.

A charge by a husband, in a cross-bill filed by him for divorce,
that his wife was pregnant by some one other than himself when
he married her, and that she concealed the fact from him, tends to
cause the wife "grievous mental suffering," and is a sufficient ground
to sustain a subsequent bill by the wife, where it appears that the
charge was false and malicious, and that the husband's bill was dismissed.—Haley v. Haley, 2, 761.

The provision of Civil Code of California, section 130, that "no
divorce can be granted upon the uncorroborated . . . . testimony of
the parties," has no application to a case where the wife seeks a
divorce on the ground of a false and malicious charge against her

by the husband of concealed pregnancy by another man at marriage, although she is the only witness who gave testimony as to what her feelings about the charge were. Where the court finds that the charge was false, and there is nothing in the record to negative the fact that the wife is a pure and virtuous woman, the presumption is that such a charge had its natural effect on such a woman, and caused her "grievous mental suffering."—Haley v. Haley, 2, 761.

Plaintiff's physician testified, inter alia, that her nose had been flattened by a blow that defendant admitted having struck her, but said he did not mean to, and seemed ashamed. Their son swore that he had heard his father call his mother insulting names as long as she lived with him. Since the assault, plaintiff had been generally sick in bed, and her husband's language seemed to make her worse. Held, sufficient proof of "extreme cruelty," consisting of a blow and abusive language, to the injury of plaintiff's health.—Johnson v. Johnson, 4, 446.

In divorce plaintiff testified that defendant often, in the presence of others, accused her of being intimate with other men; that he had a venereal disease, and accused her of giving it to him; that he many times threatened to take the minor child away from plaintiff, and on one occasion took the child away for about two weeks and would not tell plaintiff where it was; that he called her a prostitute, and left her often without means of support; that she had to support herself; and that the conduct of defendant caused her mental suffering and bodily injury. Held, that such testimony sustained a finding of extreme cruelty.—Bryan v. Bryan, 7, 19.

§ 3. Pleading.

In divorce the court found that the allegations of the complaint and cross-complaint as to the date of marriage were true, but that the allegations of the supplemental cross-complaint were untrue. The supplemental cross-complaint set up a charge of adultery, and "re-alleged every allegation in the cross-complaint." Defendant contended the findings were inconsistent. Held, that the contention was of no merit, there being no issue as to the date of marriage, nor necessity for a finding thereon.—Bryan v. Bryan, 7, 19.

A complaint alleging extreme cruelty, in that "about three years ago" defendant, without cause, struck plaintiff, and since has continually, whenever they have been together, used vile language to her, is not demurrable as failing to specify the acts relied on.—Johnson v. Johnson, 4, 446.

A sworn complaint by a female for divorce from M., filed after her marriage to H., alleging her marriage to M., prior to the time of her marriage to H., and that she and M. "ever since have been and now are husband and wife," is, in the absence of explanation, conclusive, in an action against her by H. to annul his marriage with her, that she and M. were married in due form at the time alleged, and that M. was living, and was her lawful husband, when she married H.—Hunter v. Milam, 5, 107.

An allegation in a complaint for divorce that plaintiff is possessed of "considerable property, both real and personal, situate and being in the state of California," plaintiff's separate property, is sufficient to admit of evidence of a definite description, there being no special demurrer, but a default.—Mini v. Mini, 5, 432.

§ 4. Joinder of Causes and Parties.

With a suit for divorce, plaintiff also joined an action for the division of community property, uniting Ketchum, Simpson and the Bank of Watsonville as defendants. The complaint alleged that, during the coverture of plaintiff and defendant Cummings, the latter acquired, by the joint efforts of himself and wife, a quantity of real estate, which was community property, and part of which, without the knowledge or consent of plaintiff, he attempted to convey to defendant Ketchum; that this was done with the purpose and intent on the part of both parties to the conveyance to defraud plaintiff of her rights in the property; that the conveyance was without consideration; that the Bank of Watsonville claims some interest in the property by reason of a mortgage thereon, given by Ketchum, but that the mortgage was taken with knowledge of the fraud of the above-named defendants, and for the purpose of assisting in carrying it out; that said Simpson claims an interest in the land, but that his interest or claim is subordinate to plaintiff's interest therein. Defendants Ketchum and the Bank of Watsonville demurred, on the grounds (1) that several causes of action were improperly united; (2) that there was a misjoinder of parties defendant. Held, that the demurrers should have been sustained.—Cummings v. Cummings, 2, 774.

§ 5. Estoppel of Former Decree.

A decree dismissing a bill filed by the wife for divorce, and also dismissing the husband's cross-bill, because the charges of neither party had been sustained, does not operate as an estoppel upon the wife to bring another bill against the husband on the ground that the charges in his cross-bill, which the court had found to be false, amounted to cruel and inhuman treatment.—Haley v. Haley, 2, 761.

§ 6. Abatement by Pendency of Another Suit.

The pendency of an action by the husband to annul the marriage on the ground that it was contracted under duress does not prevent an action by the wife for divorce on the ground of nonsupport.—Simpson v. Simpson, 5, 139.

§ 7. Continuance.

In an action for divorce the affidavit for a continuance stated that defendant, a material witness, was in another state, and too poor to attend the trial, and that his deposition could not be obtained within a month; that the evidence in an action pending in another state by defendant against plaintiff to annul the marriage could not be obtained by the day set for trial. Plaintiff stipulated that the uncertified copy of the evidence in the other action might be used as though duly certified, and waived alimony. Held, a continuance was properly refused.—Simpson v. Simpson, 5, 139.

§ 8. Change of Venue.

A motion by defendant in divorce to change the place of trial to a county other than that in which the action was brought, on the ground that defendant resides in the former county, should be granted, where the affidavit of plaintiff creates no substantial conflict with defendant's, as to his residence.—Usher v. Usher, 4, 521.

§ 9. Alimony and Counsel Fees.

The enforcement of a provision in a judgment of divorce requiring defendant to pay counsel fees to plaintiff's attorneys cannot be restrained by a writ of prohibition, although the judgment was one of dismissal entered by consent of the parties.—Reynolds v. Superior Court, 2, 455.

Under a judgment in a divorce proceeding, requiring "all costs, expenses, and disbursements provided for and contemplated in this decree or judgment" to be paid by the plaintiff exclusively out of his separate property, defendant has no right to include in her cost bills items not taxable as costs.—White v. White, 4, 15.

Motions in a divorce proceeding for the payment to defendant of her costs and disbursements, and for permission to plaintiff to mortgage his property in order to pay alimony, counsel fees, and other expenses of the litigation, are addressed to the discretion of the court. White v. White, 4, 15.

An order by the judge who tried a divorce case, granting $100 printer's fees and $250 counsel fee on a pending appeal from a judgment in favor of the wife, and a contemplated appeal from an order denying a new trial, will not be reversed as excessive.—Wolff v. Wolff, 4, 820.

In an action for divorce, an order granting a counsel fee for an appeal from an order denying a new trial, made before such appeal is taken, will not be reversed as premature where, on the hearing of the appeal from the order granting such allowance, it appears that an appeal from the order denying a new trial is pending.—Wolff v. Wolff, 4, 820.

Where, on rendering a decree of divorce, the question of alimony is reserved, a subsequent order awarding alimony is not void.—Ex parte O'Brien, 5, 625.

§ 10. —— Evidence of Marriage.

Plaintiff and defendant in an action for divorce had never been regularly married. There was evidence that defendant furnished plaintiff a house for her residence, and lived with her there for about twenty-five years, and supplied her with necessaries of life, and that a child was born to them; that they were known as husband and wife, and held themselves out as such; and that he treated her son by another man as his stepson. These facts were corroborated by the stepson's affidavit. Counter-affidavits by neighbors denied them, and attacked the reputation for veracity and credibility of the affiants to those facts. Held, a sufficient prima facie showing of marriage to support an order of the court below for payment of alimony and counsel fees.—Hite v. Hite, 6, 216.

§ 11. —— Enforcement of Decree.

In a suit for divorce an interlocutory decree was entered, granting respondent a divorce from her husband, and enjoining the latter from disposing of his property before final decree. Thereafter a receiver was appointed to take charge of all of his property. In the final decree it was provided that the wife, "do have and recover the sum of one hundred thousand dollars," and that the receiver be continued and directed to take all necessary steps to collect the said sum. An order was made directing him to sell certain property, which the husband had leased after the injunction, but before the receiver's appointment, and in accordance therewith the property was sold to respondent. Held, on petition for writ of assistance to gain possession, that, though the judgment was not expressly made a charge on the husband's land, the court had jurisdiction to direct the sale, since the property was under its control by virtue of the receivership.—White v. White, 6, 499.

Respondent was granted a divorce from her husband, and awarded $100,000 alimony. Certain land which the husband had leased to his nephew was sold to her in part satisfaction of the said sum. Before the expiration of the lease she petitioned for a writ of assistance to gain possession, but the order granting the writ was not made until after the lease had expired. Held, on the nephew's appeal from the order, that it would not be disturbed by a court of equity, since he had no further right of possession, and therefore could not have suf. fered injury.—White v. White, 6, 499.

Respondent was granted a divorce from her husband, and awarded $100,000 alimony. Certain land, which the husband had leased to his nephew, was sold to her in part satisfaction of the said sum. She petitioned for a writ of assistance to gain possession, and after ex- piration of the lease the nephew asked leave to file an amendment to his answer, setting out a declaration of homestead filed by re- spondent, for the benefit of herself and husband, upon land covered by the lease. He did not allege that he had acquired any interest in the homestead after the expiration of the lease. Held, that leave should be denied, since the nephew's relation to the property would not authorize him to litigate the question of respondent's title.— White v. White, 6, 499.

§ 12. Adjustment of Property Rights.

Where the court, upon decreeing a divorce in favor of the wife, finds that there is a judgment outstanding against her in favor of the husband, and that the judgment, which was wrongfully rendered, was for money which he had given her in consideration of the relin- quishment by her of her rights in the homestead, so that he might sell it, the court may order the judgment to be assigned to her.— Haley v. Haley, 2, 761.

In an action for a divorce it is not an abuse of discretion for the trial court to set off to plaintiff the homestead and a small amount of personalty from the community property, leaving to defendant all other community property, section 146, subdivision 1, Civil Code, pro- viding: " . . . . The community property shall be assigned to the respective parties in such proportion as the court, from all the facts of the case and the condition of the parties, may deem just."—Boyd v. Boyd, 3, 748.

Plaintiff being an invalid and defendant more than able to make his living, it was proper for the court, while allowing no permanent alimony, to give plaintiff, besides most of the household furniture, the whole community house and lot, which was worth only $3,000, and was subject to a mortgage of $2,500.—Johnson v. Johnson, 4, 446.

§ 13. Support of Children.

Plaintiff, by a decree of divorce in 1885, obtained the custody of the child, with a monthly allowance of $5 from defendant for its sup- port. In 1891, plaintiff applied to the court for an increased allow- ance, and made affidavit that $30 per month was required, and that defendant's income was $250 per month, all of which defendant denied by his affidavit. Held, that an allowance by the court of $20 per month was not excessive.—Rogers v. Rogers, 3, 559.

Where, in such case, defendant's affidavit contained impertinent and scandalous matter reflecting on the character of plaintiff, such matter was properly stricken out.—Rogers v. Rogers, 3, 559.

An order was made in a divorce suit requiring the husband to pay to his wife (defendant) alimony pendente lite, $125 per month, and $200 counsel fees. There was one son, aged twelve years, who lived with his mother. Defendant's father had conveyed to her a house and lot worth at present $30,000, and yielding a rental of $135 per month. Two weeks after the suit was commenced, she conveyed it back to her father, without consideration, by deed which was not recorded. The rents thereof were still paid to her. Plaintiff's net earnings were $275 per month; his personal expenses $150 per month. He owed $600, which he was paying in installments. Held, that the monthly allowance should be reduced to $50 per month, to include the support and education of the son.—Meyer v. Meyer, 5, 944.

§ 14. Interlocutory Decree.

An interlocutory judgment of divorce provided for by Civil Code, section 131, which becomes final by the lapse of six months from entry without appeal or motion to set it aside, merely establishes conclusively plaintiff's rights to a divorce, and it does not necessarily follow that he or she may not waive the exercise of such right and dismiss the action.—Barron v. Barron, 7, 345.

After six months prescribed by Civil Code, section 131, and Code of Civil Procedure, section 473, within which appeal may be taken from or attack by other means inaugurated against an interlocutory judgment of divorce by default, has expired, plaintiff cannot, on an ex parte application, have the same set aside and the suit dismissed before expiration of the year during which such judgment must be in existence, under section 131, preceding entry of final judgment.— Barron v. Barron, 7, 345.

§ 15. Final Decree—Collateral Attack.

The question whether a judgment in a divorce suit was erroneous or regular, or whether the relief granted was within the power of the court to grant, cannot be raised in a separate proceeding, especially after the divorce judgment has been affirmed on appeal.—Gimmy v. Liese, 1, 353.

§ 16. New Trial and Appeal.

In a suit for divorce where there has been imputed to the defendant extreme cruelty, in considering a motion for a new trial the court is justified in being influenced by the thought that through the findings from the testimony at the trial the defendant's character may suffer irreparable injury of a most painful kind.—Lord v. Lord, 1, 417.

Under Code of Civil Procedure, section 939, allowing an appeal from a final judgment within six months from entry, where judgment was entered January 15, 1901, and notice of appeal served October 17, 1901, the appeal cannot be considered.—Bryan v. Bryan, 7, 19.

The statute provides that when the notice of the motion for a new trial designates, as the ground of the motion, the insufficiency of the evidence to justify the decision, the statement shall specify the particular insufficiency. In divorce defendant, in his answer and cross-complaint, alleged acts of adultery with five men, and with others unknown to defendant, and the court found against defendant as to each charge. Defendant assigned that the evidence did not sustain the findings that plaintiff was entitled to a divorce, for defendant had pleaded and proved recrimination under Civil Code, section 122, and that a divorce should have been denied plaintiff for that reason. Held, that the assignment was insufficient to raise any question as to the sufficiency of the evidence.—Bryan v. Bryan, 7, 19.

Where the testimony is conflicting, findings of fact thereon cannot be disturbed on appeal.—Bryan v. Bryan, 7, 19.

§ 17. —— Matters Appealable and Reviewable.

An order allowing alimony is appealable.—White v. White, 3, 265.

The question whether a judgment is the legal conclusion from the facts found cannot be considered on appeal from an order denying a new trial, but only on an appeal from the judgment.—Bryan v. Bryan, 7, 19.

On appeal from an order denying a new trial in divorce the supreme court has no power to modify the provision of the decree providing for the support of a minor child until its majority.—Bryan v. Bryan, 7, 19.

DOMICILE.
See Residence.

DRAINS.
§ 1. Liability for Expense.
In an action to recover one-fifth of the cost of a drainage ditch, evidence held to support a finding that defendant fully consented to the scheme and promised to defray her part of the expense involved therein.—Showers v. Zanone, 7, 263.

DUPLICITY.
In indictment. See Indictment and Information, § 3.

DURESS.
As affecting validity of contract. See Contracts, § 3.

DYING DECLARATIONS.
See Homicide, § 12.

EASEMENTS.
§ 1. By prescription.
§ 2. Right of way over land.
§ 3. In matter of water rights.
§ 4. —— Evidence of abandonment.
§ 5. Injunction to protect rights.

See Dedication; Highways.

Conveyance subject to. See Deeds, § 19.

§ 1. By Prescription.
To establish a prescriptive right to an easement, the user must have been continuous, adverse, under claim of title, and with the knowledge and acquiescence of the owner of the servient estate.—Richard v. Hupp, 4, 824.

§ 2. Right of Way Over Land.
The fact that a strip of land, over which a private right of way had been granted by the owner to two other land owners, to enable them to reach a highway from their land, is used, without objection, by others, going to and from their own lands, or the places of the two grantees, does not establish a dedication to the public.—Silva v. Spangler, 5, 277.

A deed conveying "a road and right of way over and across" land, "to be forever appurtenant to" adjoining land of the grantee, and providing that neither party shall, "nor shall his successors in interest, grant or give to any other person a right of way over said road," conveys only an easement for a right of way, and not a fee simple title.—Peterson v. Machado, 5, 273.

§ 3. In Matter of Water Rights.
Plaintiff, with defendant's consent, conducted water to a tank on his lot from a spring on defendant's lot. Thereupon he took possession of another lot, owned by defendant, and conducted water to the latter

lot from the tank. Having used the water about eight years, he surrendered possession of the lot to which he had no title, and about a year thereafter purchased the same with its appurtenances, and sold the lot on which was the tank. In the conveyance to plaintiff no mention was made of the right to use the spring, but there was evidence that it was understood that he might use it so long as defendant did not need it. Held, that plaintiff had no water rights in the spring appurtenant to the lot.—Bell v. Sausalito Land and Ferry Co., 4, 53.

The court having found for plaintiff in an action to enjoin the cutting off of the water, an assignment of error that there was no evidence to show any grant of the use of the waters of the spring to plaintiff was sufficient.—Bell v. Sausalito Land and Ferry Co., 4, 53.

And so of an assignment that there was no evidence that an easement had been created in favor of the premises deeded to plaintiff, or that a servitude had attached to the land where the spring was located.—Bell v. Sausalito Land and Ferry Co., 4, 53.

An assignment that there was no evidence to show the existence of an easement at any time in favor of plaintiff's land to the spring was likewise sufficient.—Bell v. Sausalito Land and Ferry Co., 4, 53.

§ 4. —— Evidence of Abandonment.

Plaintiff constructed a flume five hundred and sixty-four feet long in the bed of a stream to convey the water from his mine. The flume extended four hundred feet on land below, owned by defendant. Eighteen years later, defendant built a dam across the stream, causing the water to flow back, but not farther than the limit of his land. Held, in an action to abate the dam as a nuisance, there being evidence that the flume was built as an adjunct to plaintiff's quartz-mill, that evidence that the mill was no longer in operation, and that its condition for many years had been such that it could not be used, was admissible to show an abandonment of any prescriptive easement which plaintiff may have had over defendant's land — Richard v. Hupp, 4, 824.

§ 5. Injunction to Protect Rights.

An injunction to enjoin a grantee of an easement for a right of way from interfering with the grantor's laying pipes beneath the right of way, to connect with a ram placed in a gulch which encroached on the right of way, should be granted, where the grantor offers to widen the right of way by moving his fence, or by changing the location of the ram, and filing up the gulch.—Peterson v. Machado, 5, 273.

EJECTMENT.

See Public Lands, § 3.

Joinder of causes of action. See Actions, § 6.
Bill of discovery in. See Discovery, § 1.
Intervention in. See Intervention, § 3.
Parties in real action. See Parties, § 1.
Prohibition against action for realty. See Prohibition, § 1.

§ 1. Nature of Action and Right to Maintain.

In a suit of ejectment, denial of judgment to plaintiff on the ground of his not having the possession of the property shows the court to be unaware of the nature of the action.—Palmer v. Cook, 1, 25.

A person who, though asserting some sort of claim to land, has never occupied it or used it for any purpose, has no such possession as to warrant one assuming to hold through him to maintain eject-ment.—King v. Louderback, 1, 386.

The plaintiff in ejectment must show that he has a right to the possession.—Brigham v. Mullin, 1, 821.

In ejectment the plaintiff, in order to recover, must show he was entitled to the possession at the time his action was brought.—Sheldon v. Murray, 1, 891.

Actions other than those technically of ejectment can be brought for the recovery of the possession of real estate.—Heinlen v. Martin, 2, 20.

The legal title being opposed only by a mere naked possession, the holder of such title is entitled to the possession.—Shaeffer v. Matzen, 2, 271.

Ejectment will not lie against one not in possession of the land sought to be recovered.—Partridge v. Shepard, 2, 723.

In an action of ejectment, plaintiff can attack the patent from the United States, under which defendant claims, on the ground that the land officer had no power to issue a patent for the lands embraced therein.—United Land Assn. v. Knight, 3, 211.

A grantee of a deed absolute on its face cannot maintain ejectment thereon, where his grantor merely held the title as security for a debt which the grantee paid, and at the same time executed a bond to the original mortgagor in which he agreed to convey if the amount expended by him was repaid, with interest, by a specified time, since the instrument was a mortgage.—Meeker v. Shuster, 5, 578.

§ 2. Property for Which Action Lies.

Ejectment is maintainable for only corporeal hereditaments, and when the subject matter is land used as a turnpike, rather than the right of way, and there has been no dedication by the plaintiff or persons he has succeeded as title holder, it is the proper remedy.—Mahon v. Simms, 1, 872.

36

Plaintiff who has obtained a valid title to land by foreclosure, and is in possession of a portion of it, can bring ejectment for the balance, and is not compelled to rely on a writ of assistance.—Trope v. Kerns, 3, 47.

A city cannot maintain ejectment for recovery of possession of a street dedicated to the public by user, without showing ownership in the fee.—San Francisco v. Grote, 5, 612.

§ 3. Homestead Premises.

Where the complaint alleges that the land in controversy was set off as a homestead to the widow of a deceased owner, it must state whether the land was set off in fee or for life, since an assignment of a homestead to a widow in fee out of her deceased husband's estate, though erroneous, is conclusive unless appealed from.—Hutchinson v. McNally, 3, 209.

In ejectment by a widow against her husband's administrator for premises which had been set apart by order of court as a homestead to plaintiff and her minor children, absolutely, it appeared that, from the time of defendant's appointment as administrator till the homestead was set apart, defendant collected the rents of the premises, and paid taxes; that two months thereafter plaintiff demanded possession of him, which, she testified, he refused to give; that in his verified statement to the tax collector he included this homestead property; and that he leased part thereof to another. Held, that the evidence justified a verdict that defendant was in possession when the action was commenced.—Moore v. Moore, 4, 190.

§ 4. Defenses.

Claim through one who has abandoned premises. In ejectment the defense must show something more than a deed—of premises not really including those in suit—from one who had abandoned possession two years before the plaintiff's entry.—Hawkins v. Hancock, 1, 160.

In ejectment it is not a good plea "that the title of said plaintiff, if any he has, to said premises, did not accrue within five years prior to the commencement of this suit, and that he has not been in possession thereof within five years prior to this suit."—McKay v. Petaluma Lodge No. 77, F. A. M., 1, 278.

In an action of ejectment the defendant cannot withhold the possession by proof of a mortgage to him, proceedings in foreclosure, judgment not yet enforced by sale, and his holding under a stipulation so to hold for a year, delaying the sale for so long to eke out the debt from the profits, if possible, when the year has expired long since and the statute of limitations intervened, and the plaintiff is not the mortgagor.—Franklin v. Le Roy, 1, 806.

An agreement by plaintiff to transfer part of the land sued for, when recovered, to his attorneys, for their services, is not a defense to such action, even if within the prohibition of the statute forbidding attorneys to buy anything in action.—Gage v. Downey, 3, 7.

Where the defense of outstanding title in a third person is made to an action of ejectment, it is essential to show that the title was outstanding at the time of trial.—Robinson v. Thornton, 3, 741.

Where, in ejectment, the defense is possession under contract of purchase, indebtedness of plaintiff to defendant for salary and money paid in excess of the payments required may be considered as a performance of the contract, under Code of Civil Procedure, section 440, which provides that, where cross-demands have existed between persons under such circumstances that, if one sued the other, a counterclaim could have been set up, the two demands shall be deemed compensated so far as they equal each other.—Jacob v. Carter, 4, 543.

§ 5. Parties.

Where a defendant in ejectment is in possession of any part of the premises as tenant of another, it is proper to join the latter as party defendant.—Moore v. Moore, 4, 190.

§ 6. Intervention.

The effect of an intervention is to add new parties for the purpose of determining all conflicting claims to the matter in controversy, and does not affect the nature of the action at all, or interfere with the trial thereof; and therefore, where the plaintiff, in an action of ejectment, desires a jury trial, the filing of an intervention praying equitable relief will not affect such right, and a denial of a jury is error.—Reay v. Butler, 2, 501.

A person who does not claim to have derived title from both plaintiff and defendant in ejectment, and does assert title in himself paramount to both, cannot intervene in such action. Whether intervention applicable to ejectment at all, quaere.—Reay v. Butler, 2, 501.

Where an intervener in an action prays for only part of the demanded premises, it is error for the court to render judgment in his favor for the whole of the same, and to enjoin the plaintiff from prosecuting or maintaining an action therefor.—Reay v. Butler, 2, 501.

§ 7. Demand as Condition Precedent.

A demand is not necessary before bringing suit to recover land, where defendants deny plaintiff's title, and set up title in themselves. Webb v. Winter, 6, 768.

One acquiring title to real property who is not in possession is entitled to be let into possession on demand, and, until such demand, he cannot maintain an action to obtain possession against a person who is lawfully in possession.—McNally v. Connolly, 2, 621.

§ 8. Pleading—Complaint.

A complaint in ejectment that alleges prior possession by the plaintiff and ouster by the defendant is sufficient.—Booth v. Stone, 1, 88.

In ejectment it is not sufficient for the complaint to aver possession by the plaintiff on a certain day, naming the day, and allege ouster as of that day, without further averment of title, seisin or right to the possession; the complaint must show that the plaintiff was entitled to the possession when bringing the suit.—Slaughter v. Fowler, 1, 850.

In an action of ejectment, a complaint that alleges ownership in fee in plaintiff, and an ouster by defendant on a day named, before commencement of the action, is sufficient, without further alleging that plaintiff was the owner in fee at the commencement of the action.—Allen v. Holt, 2, 485.

Where a complaint in an action of ejectment brought by a vendor against a vendee avers ownership of the property in the plaintiff, the making of a contract for the sale thereof to defendant, the payment of a part of the contract price by defendant, his entry into possession, the tender of a deed, demand and refusal of payment, notice of rescission of contract by plaintiff, tender to the defendant of the money paid, with interest, and demand of possession, which was refused, it is sufficient.—Gates v. McLean, 2, 636.

Where the complaint in ejectment simply sets forth a deraignment of title, and then alleges that "while plaintiff was the owner, and entitled to the possession, as hereinbefore mentioned and set forth, the defendant entered," the allegation as to ownership will be disregarded, as stating a mere conclusion.—Hutchinson v. McNally, 3, 209.

Recovery cannot be had in ejectment for land not specified in the complaint.—Scott v. Rhodes, 5, 131.

Where, in ejectment to recover a storeroom under a lease of the entire building from one of defendants, the complaint alleged a conspiracy between defendants to withhold the property from plaintiff, a finding that the lease gave plaintiff the right of possession of the entire building except such storeroom, which was occupied by the other defendant, negatived the issue of conspiracy.—Schwannecke v. Goodenow, 5, 955.

§ 9. —— Answer.

An answer in ejectment setting up a perfect title in fee in a person from whom the defendant claims, the death and intestacy of this person, a forged will by the person from whom the plaintiff claims, his fraudulent acquisition thereby, and notice of the fraud had by the plaintiff and his grantors, cannot successfully be demurred to, since the demurrer admits these allegations to be true.—Chipman v. Hastings, 1, 817.

Where, in ejectment, the complaint merely alleges plaintiff's ownership and right to possession, and that defendant is in possession, and refuses to surrender the same, and the answer denies the ownership and right to possession, defendant may prove any facts showing that plaintiff had no right of entry or possession when the action was commenced.—Jacob v. Carter, 4, 543.

§ 10. —— Admissions in.

In ejectment an answer that denies entry by the defendant upon the land described in the complaint "except two hundred and fifty feet lying," etc., by this exception admits an entry which the plaintiff is at liberty to treat as an ouster.—Ryan v. Smith, 1, 751.

In ejectment for two and twelve hundredths acres of land plaintiffs alleged they were owners, and that defendant excluded them from possession. Defendant's answer denied every allegation "except as hereinafter stated," and then admitted defendant was in possession of one and sixty-five hundredths acres, and that he withheld the same from plaintiffs, but denied the possession or withholding of the remainder. Held, that the answer did not admit that plaintiffs owned forty-seven hundredths of an acre of land.—Stites v. Gater, 5, 389.

In ejectment, if the defendant in his answer admits acts amounting to an ouster, but denies plaintiff's title or right to possession, plaintiff is not bound to prove ouster, and, if he prove title and right to possession in himself, is entitled to recover.—Ketchum v. Barber, 2, 698.

§ 11. Evidence.

In an action of ejectment where the controversy rests on the plaintiff being able to locate premises described in his muniments of title, such location must be proved by better evidence than a map purporting on its face to be a copy, not in any way authenticated, and not shown ever to have been adopted by competent authority as a map of the city in which the premises are alleged to lie.—Whitcomb v. Hensley, 1, 483.

In ejectment, where defendant claims that plaintiff agreed to convey him the land in exchange for other land, the judgment-roll in a creditors' action against defendant to have a deed by him of his land declared void is admissible to show that defendant is unable to convey his land.—Royal v. Dennison, 4, 851.

Upon an issue that plaintiff's grantor had taken title for the joint benefit of himself and defendants, and that plaintiff took title from him with notice of defendants' rights, it is competent to show the circumstances of the purchase by such grantor, and his declarations at that time, as tending to show defendants' interest.—Lord v. Thomas, 5, 769.

§ 12. —— Of Possession.

The mere fact that a person at some time indefinite erected a "fence" around a piece of land, regardless of whether the structure was a substantial barrier or only a fence by assertion, is in itself no evidence of possession, so that one claiming title through such person can maintain ejectment.—King v. Louderback, 1, 386.

In ejectment for a strip of land a few inches in width between adjoining lots, where it appeared that defendant had been for about twenty-five years in possession of the strip, which was by a survey included in his deed, when another survey was made, showing the strip to belong to plaintiff's lot, defendant's testimony that his occupancy was under a claim of right to hold the same adversely to plaintiff and the whole world is sufficient to support a finding for defendant as by prescription, though it also appeared that after the latter survey defendant offered to surrender the strip if plaintiff would pay the expense of moving the house which extended onto it.—Miller v. Bensinger, 3, 704.

In an action in the nature of ejectment, where the evidence tends to prove that defendants were in possession of the premises when the action was commenced, an answer denying plaintiff's title and right of possession is sufficient evidence of ouster.—Moore v. Moore, 4, 190.

§ 13. —— Sufficiency of Proof.

A verdict, the effect of which is to deprive a party of his actual possession, ought to be found only from evidence affirmative and squarely to the point.—Weyle v. Center, 1, 310.

When parties rely for a recovery upon technical defects in the transfer of title to deprive others, who have purchased land in good faith and long improved and enjoyed it under the belief that they owned it, they cannot complain if they are required to make by proofs a strict technical title.—Wakelee v. Goodrum, 1, 358.

In an action of ejectment, where the plaintiff gives in evidence a judgment-roll showing a judgment in his favor and against defendants, an execution duly issued thereon, a sale of the demanded premises to plaintiff, an attachment and sheriff's return showing a levy which has never been released, and evidence of possession subsequent to the levy and prior to the judgment in the first suit, and defendants offer no evidence, a finding thereon for the plaintiff is amply supported by the evidence, and judgment must be affirmed.—Royon v. Guillee, 2, 301.

In ejectment, in which the answer denied ouster and the possession and withholding by defendants, it appeared that the land in dispute is a strip six feet wide, on which a water ditch is located. The evidence showed that defendants frequently put a pressure board in the ditch, which cut off plaintiff's water and diverted it into a flume made by them. Held, that the evidence established a trespass merely, and did not justify a judgment for plaintiff.—Tibbets v. Bakewell, 4, 477.

§ 14. —— Former Adjudication.

In the trial of a suit of ejectment a judgment-roll, writ of possession and return showing that in a former suit between the plaintiff's grantor and another not the present defendant, involving the same land, such grantor was given the possession, may be put in evidence, but only to prove the existence of such a judgment as tending to show the plaintiff's color of right.—Valentine v. Jansen, 1, 525.

§ 15. Prima Facie Case.

In an action of ejectment a plaintiff who has in his complaint made all the necessary averments may, at the trial, rest after putting in his proof of title, if the defendant has in his answer first denied everything contained in the complaint and then admitted possession, but not as a distinct defense.—Megerle v. Ashe, 1, 659.

In an action for the possession of land, failure by the plaintiff to prove actual possession by him of all the land described in the complaint does not call for a nonsuit if he has proved possession of a part.—Rathbun v. Alexander, 1, 664.

§ 16. Nonsuit.

It is not error to nonsuit a plaintiff in ejectment upon the opening statement of his counsel, where, according to such statement, the plaintiff has neither title nor prior possession.—Hoffman v. Felt, 1, 369.

In ejectment, defendant's motion for a nonsuit is properly denied where it appears that plaintiffs bought the property from its owner, and took a bond for deed, under which they entered into and held possession of the property, claiming title thereto for more than two years before defendants entered and ousted them.—Stephens v. Hambleton, 5, 543.

Where, in ejectment, plaintiff introduced no evidence tending to show her right to the land, that she had been ousted of her possession by defendant, or that she had any right to eject defendant, a nonsuit was properly granted.—Billings v. Pearson, 7, 271.

§ 17. Instructions.

In ejectment, plaintiff showed title by patent from the government, and defendant's title was a sheriff's deed on foreclosure of a mortgage given by plaintiff prior to receiving his patent. Plaintiff did not attack the foreclosure proceedings, nor object to their admission in evidence. In instructing the jury, after stating the evidence, the court directed a verdict for defendant, "if these facts all appear" as stated. Held, that by thus instructing the jury there was no violation of the constitution, article 6, section 19, which provides that "judges shall not charge juries with respect to matters of fact, but may state the testimony and declare the law."—Jones v. Chalfant, 3, 585.

§ 18. Recovery on Strength of Plaintiff's Title.

A plaintiff in ejectment must recover, if at all, only on the strength of his own title; and if he fails to show a right of possession in himself, it matters not whether the defendant has title or not.—Willson v. Truebody, 1, 238.

Plaintiff in ejectment must recover on the strength of his own title; and if both parties claim under a common grantor, a prior deed to plaintiff cannot be enlarged by a subsequent deed to the defendant.—Cox v. Hayes, 2, 520.

§ 19. Findings.

In ejectment against the lessor and another lessee, a finding that plaintiff lessee had no right of possession need not dispose of the relative rights and liabilities of defendants in the property in controversy.—Schwannecke v. Goodenow, 5, 955.

Findings that the original owner of land conveyed the same to her daughter, reserving in such conveyance an estate for life, and that later the same grantor conveyed the same premises by deed of gift to another daughter, are not conflicting, since the latter conveyance should be understood to mean a conveyance of the life estate, only, then remaining in possession of the grantor.—Reavis v. Gardner, 6, 427.

That findings of fact do not determine the ultimate fact of ownership of property in controversy is not material, where successive conveyances from the source of title to the plaintiff are found.—Reavis v. Gardner, 6, 427.

§ 20. Judgment and Relief.

The gravamen of the action of ejectment is the wrongful withholding of the possession of the premises from the plaintiff from the time of the alleged entry up to the commencement of the action; and the plaintiff, upon showing title, is entitled to recover the possession together with damages for the wrongful withholding of the possession, and the value of the rents and profits while the possession was so withheld.—Donner v. Palmer, 1, 392.

It is not usual, if indeed proper, for a judgment in ejectment to be accompanied with a perpetual injunction against trespassers.—Ryan v. Smith, 1, 751.

Where in ejectment there is coupled with a judgment for defendant an order that a certain sum be paid plaintiff, the leaving of this sum by defendant with plaintiff's attorney, which he refuses to accept, is not a satisfaction of the judgment so as to prevent an appeal by plaintiff.—Alexander v. Jackson, 3, 344.

§ 21. Confirmation Decree.

A valid confirmation by decree concludes all persons except such as claim under adverse grants, as defined by section 15 of the act of March 3, 1851.—Umbarger v. Chaboya, 1, 698.

A confirmation of title by decree of the United States court could have no effect to change the boundaries of a tract of land to the detriment of one, not a party to the proceeding, owning land adjacent to that as to which the decree was made.—Umbarger v. Chaboya, 1, 765.

§ 22. Sale Pending Action.

Where suit has been brought for the recovery of real estate, a purchaser from the defendant before any trial has been had cannot let the suit go undefended and after judgment for the plaintiff seek in equity to have the judgment annulled on the ground of surprise.—Board of Education v. Thorpe, 1, 254.

Where suit has been brought for the recovery of real estate, a purchaser from the defendant before any trial is had has no right to look to the vendor to continue the defense of the suit, since by the purchase such defense has become his own concern.—Board of Education v. Thorpe, 1, 254.

Where suit has been brought for the recovery of real estate, and a person purchases from the defendant before any trial is had, counsel employed by such defendant to defend the suit have a right to assume that they have been discharged by the sale.—Board of Education v. Thorpe, 1, 254.

Where suit has been brought for the recovery of real estate and a person purchases from the defendant before trial is had, if, innocently relying on his vendor to continue defending the suit, such purchaser allows the plaintiff to take judgment, his remedy, provided he has any at all, is by motion for a new trial made within statutory time after the judgment.—Board of Education v. Thorpe, 1, 254.

A person who, pending an action of ejectment, acquires the plaintiff's title by purchase may, in a subsequent action in which the parties are reversed, rely upon the recovery in the first action together with averments connecting himself with the title of the plaintiff therein; and allegations of the issuing and serving of the writ of possession are immaterial.—Murray v. Green, 2, 62.

§ 23. Writ of Possession—Alias Writ.

Plaintiff having obtained judgment in ejectment, a writ of possession was issued and executed in 1882 against defendants and one M., who was not a party to the suit, and a few months later M. re-entered, and remained thereafter in exclusive possession. In 1889, plaintiff moved for an alias writ of possession against defendants and M. Held, that M. could show on such motion that he was not a member of defendants' family, and that his possession was open and notorious, and that he was the owner of the premises in dispute, and was not a party to the ejectment suit.—Rousset v. Reay, 3, 717.

Where M.'s possession was adverse for more than six years from the time of his re-entry, and ripened into a new title, it could not be affected by the former judgment.—Rousset v. Reay, 3, 717.

A motion for an alias writ of possession should not be entertained where the lapse of time after re-entry is sufficient to create a title in an adverse possessor, and bar an action of ejectment.—Rousset v. Reay, 3, 717.

Where judgment for plaintiff in ejectment is fully executed by putting plaintiff in possession, an alias writ of possession cannot issue except upon an adjudication that the person against whom the writ is to run is guilty of a contempt. Huerstal v. Muir, 64 Cal. 450, 2 Pac. 33, followed.—Rousset v. Reay, 3, 717.

§ 24. Writ of Restitution.

A writ of execution issued on a judgment in ejectment for a restitution of the land and for rents and profits need not (the writ of restitution having been already executed) recite the judgment further than to identify it.—Hibberd v. Smith, 1, 554.

§ 25. New Trial and Appeal.

A verdict in ejectment awarding the plaintiff possession is not to be disturbed when based on substantially sufficient evidence.—Mayne v. Jones, 1, 296.

On appeal from a judgment in an action involving title to land, where at the trial two patents were admitted in evidence and the deed to the plaintiff, and no motion was made to exclude the patents as not embracing land described in the deed, it is presumed, if there are no findings of fact and the record contains neither of the patents, that a part of the land so described was included in one of the patents and the rest of it in the other.—Frisbie v. Whitney, 1, 447.

Where, in an action of ejectment, it was clearly established that plaintiff had possessory title, and that the withholding by defendants was unlawful, and judgment went for defendants, it is a proper case for granting a new trial, and the court in doing so does not abuse its discretion.—Johnson v. Hancock, 2, 401.

Where, in an action of ejectment, there is a decided conflict as to the facts going to show plaintiff's legal possession prior to defendant's entry, and as to the character of defendant's entry, an order refusing a new trial will be affirmed on appeal.—Goodwin v. Burney, 2, 786.

In an action in the nature of ejectment, a specification of error that "the evidence showed that defendant M. was not in possession of said premises, or of any part thereof, at the time of the commencement of this action," is insufficient.—Moore v. Moore, 4, 190.

Where, in an action to recover land held by defendant under a contract of purchase, he did not question the finding that he had failed to perform conditions, for breach of which the contract was to be void, and which were of the essence of the contract, on a motion for a new trial such motion was properly denied.—Frank v. Chatfield, 6, 414.

Though the pleadings and findings of a trial court do not support a judgment for rent of demanded premises, such question cannot be raised on an appeal from its order denying a new trial.—Frank v. Chatfield, 6, 414.

ELECTIONS.

§ 1. Residence of Voter.

A wood-chopper, who had no home, but who made a particular place in a ward his home whenever in town or out of work for five years past, and who was sent there when sick, and who never voted in any other place for eleven years, is a legal voter in such ward.—Smith v. Thomas, 5, 976.

§ 2. Votes and Ballots—Legality—Marks.

Testimony by the inspector of elections and the ballot clerk that they did not see a mark of identification on a ballot when they were counting them is sufficient to support a finding that such mark was placed thereon after it came out of the ballot-box.—Smith v. Thomas, 5, 976.

Under Code of Civil Procedure, section 1116, prohibiting the introduction of testimony of illegal votes in an election contest unless the contestant deliver to the defendant, at least three days before trial, a written list of the votes which he intends to prove were illegal, evidence as to the illegality of a vote is properly excluded which did not appear on the list served on the defendant, although it did appear on a list served by the defendant on the contestant.—Smith v. Thomas, 5, 976.

The legality of a vote in an election contest will not be determined where it was not claimed to have been cast for plaintiff, and it was not counted for defendant.—Smith v. Thomas, 5, 976.

Under Political Code, section 1211, providing that, if a voter marks more names than there are persons to be elected to an office, his ballot shall not be counted for such office, a ballot so marked can be rejected only as to such office.—Salcido v. Roberts, 6, 656.

A mark made opposite a name by an instrument so full of ink as to practically make a round spot or blot instead of a cross, but in which the cross can be seen, is a sufficient mark.—Salcido v. Roberts, 6, 656.

Writing a name in the wrong column does not invalidate the ballot as a whole, though the written name cannot be counted.—Salcido v. Roberts, 6, 856.

A ballot containing the name of a candidate written under the appropriate heading, but across the horizontal line between the title of the office and next below, or else below such line, is good.—Salcido v. Roberts, 6, 856.

A ballot marked with a cross opposite the "Yes" and "No" to proposed constitutional amendments is valid in other respects, and must be counted for the candidates properly voted for.—Salcido v. Roberts, 6, 856.

A mark on a ballot made by folding it before the ink on it had dried does not render the ballot void.—Salcido v. Roberts, 6, 856.

A ballot containing the written words "Blac Colu" in the blank column under the title "Justice of the Peace," together with a cross opposite the printed name of a candidate for that office, is valid in other respects, and must be counted for the candidates for other offices properly voted for, the court presuming that the voter intended to vote for a person named "Blac Colu."—Salcido v. Roberts, 6, 856.

§ 3. Contest of Election.

The act relating to elections (Hitt. Dig., art. 5, p. 2471) does not require the defendant, in order to meet the complaint of one contesting his election, to put in an answer, all the allegations of the complaint being understood by law to be denied.—Fleming v. Ingalls, 1, 344.

§ 4. Certificate of Election of Chief of Police.

As a condition precedent to the issuance of a certificate of election to a chief of police of San Francisco, it is required that the board of election commissioners declare that such election has been had.—People v. Tharp, 2, 123.

ELEVATORS.

Contract to make elevator. See Contracts, § 10.

EMBEZZLEMENT.

§ 1. What constitutes—Defense.
§ 2. Demand for return.
§ 3. Of horse.
§ 4. Of check.
§ 5. In drawing funds from bank by corporate officer.
§ 6. By bailee.
§ 7. Aiding and abetting.
§ 8. Information, evidence and instructions.
§ 9. New trial.

§ 1. What Constitutes—Defense.

The fact that an appropriation of an employer's money was made without attempt at concealment is no defense to a charge of embezzlement.—People v. Connelly, 4, 858.

§ 2. Demand for Return.

Where, on trial for embezzlement, admissions made by the defendant show a fraudulent and felonious taking of the money, which he is charged with having embezzled, evidence of an independent demand for its return is unnecessary.—People v. Coxe, 6, 820.

§ 3. Of Horse.

Section 514 of the Penal Code is not to be construed so as to make the embezzlement of a horse or mare punishable as less than grand larceny.—People v. Leehey, 2, 56.

§ 4. Of Check.

In a prosecution for embezzlement of a check, the evidence showed that one T. employed defendant as a broker to obtain a loan for him; that defendant went to complainant, who agreed to make the loan, and defendant was directed by her to attend to the matter of looking after the title to the land, and taking of a mortgage thereon; that defendant found the title satisfactory; that T. made the mortgage and gave it to defendant, to be delivered to complainant on receipt of the money; that afterward she drew the check in question for the balance in favor of defendant, who cashed it, and with the proceeds paid certain of T.'s obligations; and that defendant refused to deliver to complainant the mortgage until she settled with him for his services in the matter, and for certain other services which he claimed to have rendered her. Held, that ·the evidence was insufficient to sustain a conviction.—People v. Van Sciever, 5, 178.

§ 5. In Drawing Funds from Bank by Corporate Officer.

The president of a corporation, to pay an indebtedness of the corporation, the exact amount of which he did not know, signed, as president, a blank check, payable to the secretary, which was given to him, with directions to fill in the amount, and pay the debt. He filled it in for a larger amount, and on having it paid to him appropriated the entire sum. Held, that the money paid him was the money of the corporation, and not that of the bank.—People v. Gallagher, 4, 113.

It being within the course of the secretary's employment to draw, on like checks, the money of the corporation from the bank, and to pay its debts, he is estopped to claim that the money did not come into his control by virtue of his employment, because he filled in the check for a larger amount than he was authorized.—People v. Gallagher, 4, 113.

§ 6. By Bailee.

A defendant cannot be convicted of the embezzlement of money as bailee under Penal Code, section 507, upon evidence which shows without contradiction that he received the money from the complaining witness to be invested for her in stocks, and that he so invested it, and that if he was guilty of any offense it was the conversion of the stocks, the relation between the parties as to the money being one of agency, and not of bailment,—People v. Leipsic, 6, 536.

Penal Code, section 507, makes it embezzlement for one to convert property intrusted to him as bailee. Section 511 provides that, on any indictment for embezzlement, it is a sufficient defense that the property was appropriated openly and under a bona fide claim of title, though such claim is untenable. On a prosecution for the embezzlement of a mare sold by defendant while in his possession, prosecutor testified that he intrusted her to defendant to have her for her keep until demanded; that prosecutor stated a price that he would sell the mare for, but that in answer to a statement by defendant that he might buy the mare, prosecutor said that that would be "an after consideration." Defendant testified that prosecutor stated that he might buy the mare at any time for $55. Defendant did not inform prosecutor of the sale of the mare, or remit any of the alleged price. Held, that the evidence was sufficient to sustain a conviction.—People v. Klee, 6, 957.

On a prosecution under Penal Code, section 507, making it embezzlement for one to convert property intrusted to him as a bailee, the question whether it was error to fail to instruct that defendant must have "feloniously" intended to appropriate the property was immaterial on appeal; the jury having been instructed that the test to be applied for determining the guilt or innocence of defendant was whether he intended to permanently deprive prosecutor of his property. People v. Klee, 6, 957.

On a prosecution under Penal Code, section 507, for the embezzlement of property by a bailee, the court instructed substantially in the language of Civil Code. section 1572. which defines "fraud." Held, that though the section defines "fraud" within the meaning of the chapter relative to contracts, and had no application, there was no prejudice to defendant, the instruction being followed by one stating that the question was whether defendant intended permanently to deprive the owner of his property.—People v. Klee, 6, 957.

§ 7. Aiding and Abetting.

By previous appointment defendant went to a saloon near a bank, while the secretary drew the funds. They immediately went to another city, where defendant registered under a fictitious name, procured currency for part of the coin, took most of the funds, in a valise, to a railroad station, where he obtained two tickets, paying therefor from the appropriated funds. Defendant carried the funds part of the way, and when arrested had some of them on his person. Held, that the evidence warranted a conviction of defendant for aiding and abetting in the embezzlement.—People v. Gallagher, 4, 113.

§ 8. Information, Evidence and Instructions.

Verdict held sustained by the evidence.—People v. Jones, 2, 563.

On trial for embezzling $550 received by defendant on a certain state warrant, it is not error to cross-examine him as to whether he had received money on other state warrants.—People v. McCarthy, 3, 5.

On a prosecution for embezzlement, evidence that defendant, two months after the offense charged in the information, embezzled another sum of money from defendant, is not admissible to show his intention in taking the first sum.—People v. Hill, 4, 349.

On a trial for embezzlement, where no request is made to limit evidence of similar embezzlements by defendant to proof of criminal intent, a voluntary instruction that defendant is not on trial for embezzling any other sum than that charged in the information is not prejudicial because it fails to make such a limitation.—People v. Connolly, 4, 858.

When an information for embezzlement aptly charges the defendant with having received the money of another, and willfully and feloniously appropriated it to his own use, additional averments describing the check or instrument upon which he obtained the money are immaterial, and a discrepancy between such description and the proof does not constitute a variance.—People v. Allen, 6, 532.

§ 9. New Trial.

Defendant was convicted of embezzlement, his identity being established by four witnesses, three of whom testified that he had a beard of about two weeks' growth at the time of the crime. Defendant asked a new trial, based on newly discovered evidence, tending to show that he had no beard, and filed several affidavits. In one of these affiant stated that another told him before the trial that he had committed the crime. Affiant did not make this alleged fact known until after defendant's conviction. This affidavit also seriously contradicted statements made upon defendant's preliminary examination. Held, that the affidavits contained nothing which rendered it probable that on a retrial of the case a different result would be reached.—People v. Woodruff, 6, 346.

EMINENT DOMAIN.

Changing stream as taking land for public use. See Waters and Watercourses, § 14.

§ 1. Matters of Procedure.

When a railroad company invokes the exercise of the right of eminent domain for the purpose of devesting titles, it must pursue the statute substantially, not in some only, but in all its provisions.—Central Pacific R. R. Co. v. Pearson, 1, 790.

In an act giving the right to parties to condemnation proceedings, dissatisfied with the report, to move for a setting aside of the latter and for a new trial "upon good cause shown," the word "good" is to be understood as meaning sufficient.—Western Pacific R. R. Co. v. Reed, 1, 327.

On a motion for setting aside the report of commissioners under an act for condemnation, which act, or the order of court thereunder, contains no requirement that the evidence be reported, it is not sufficient for the statement to embody the minutes of the testimony which the commissioners happen to have taken and filed with their report.—Western Pacific R. R. Co. v. Reed, 1, 327.

The averments herein show sufficiently that the defendant was properly named, and was not the known owner and claimant of the land sought to be condemned. A demurrer, therefore, on the ground that these facts did not appear, as required, was properly overruled.—California Southern R. Co. v. Colton Land & Water Co., 2, 244.

§ 2. Proceedings for Highway or Private Road.

Provided it shows it has fully complied with the requirements of the statute under which private property may be taken for public uses, a county may institute proceedings to condemn land for purposes of a highway.—Butte County v. Boydstun, 2, 151.

Where defendant, through whose land a private road was surveyed, refused to accept the compensation awarded, and the case was tried by a jury, he cannot complain of the jury's action in assessing damages on the ground that the evidence is insufficient to justify the verdict, as the burden of proving damages rests on defendant.—Los Angeles County v. Reyes, 3, 775.

Political Code, section 2692, provides that a private road may be opened for the convenience of one or more residents or freeholders in the same manner as public roads are opened, except that only one petitioner shall be necessary. Held, that while the principal use of such private road may be for the petitioner, as a means of egress from his farm, it is also for the use of the public, in deriving the benefit of his products, and in going to his place, and the legislature has the power to declare it a public use, for which the right of eminent domain may be exercised.—Los Angeles County v. Reyes, 3, 775.

§ 3. Damages and Compensation.

Private property cannot be taken from its owner even for a public use unless he is given just compensation; and this consists of the whole value of the land taken and the damage resulting to the rest of the land, injuriously affected by the taking, less the amount of benefits accruing to the owner by reason of the improvement.—Butte County v. Boydstun, 2, 151.

In assessing damage to land, not taken but off which land is taken, in condemnation proceedings for a highway, one of the matters to be considered is increased necessary outlay for building fences; and it is error to exclude evidence bearing upon that consideration.—Butte County v. Boydstun, 2, 151.

§ 4. —— Time of Which Ascertained.

A person whose land is appropriated to a public use by the exercise of the right of eminent domain is entitled to be paid the value of the land as at the time when so taken, and not the value as at the time it was applied for.—Central Pac. R. R. Co. v. Pearson, 1, 790.

The compensation for land taken under condemnation proceedings is the value of it at the time of trial, and not at the date of the summons, as prescribed in section 1249, Code of Civil Procedure.—California Southern R. Co. v. Colton Land and Water Co., 2, 244.

EMPLOYER'S LIABILITY.
See Master and Servant.

ENDOWMENT BENEFITS.
See Insurance, § 14.

EQUITY.
§ 1. Jurisdiction and subjects of relief.
§ 2. Distinction between law and equity.
§ 3. Relief under general prayer.
§ 4. Demand for jury.
§ 5. Evidence.
§ 6. Verdict of jury.

See Actions; Cancellation of Instruments; Reformation of Instruments; Relation.

§ 1. Jurisdiction and Subjects of Relief.

A court of equity is not open to a party who has a remedy at law.—White v. Harris, 1, 40.

The equity jurisdiction with which our district courts are invested under the constitution is that administered in the high court of chancery in England. They are not, like the English exchequer, charged with the collection of debts due the state, nor with the collection of the public revenues; nor are they organized with any special reference to the recovery or protection of state lands, whether above or below the level of tide water.—People v. Dennis, 1, 262.

In order to invoke equity, under the Practice Act, the same circumstances must be made to appear as under the old system showing the inadequacy of the remedy at law, or some other ground of equitable interference.—Reed v. Union Copper Mining Co., 1, 587.

Equity has no jurisdiction of an action for damages merely unless under peculiar circumstances, where the party injured cannot maintain his action at law.—Reed v. Union Copper Mining Co., 1, 587.

A court of equity will interfere to prevent the fraudulent use of a paper for a purpose not contemplated by the parties at the time it was executed.—Whiting v. Steen, 2, 175.

§ 2. Distinction Between Law and Equity.

One of the main distinctions between law and equity is that at law a party usually receives compensation in damages, while equity gives a more specific remedy according to the circumstances of the case, and generally only in those cases in which compensation in damages would not be complete and an adequate remedy.—Reed v. Union Copper Mining Co., 1, 587.

§ 3. Relief Under General Prayer.

In courts of equity, if the specific relief asked cannot be granted, such relief as the case stated in the bill authorizes may be had under a prayer for general relief; but under such prayer no relief can be granted beyond that which is authorized by the facts stated in the bill.—Oliver v. Blair, 2, 564.

§ 4. Demand for Jury.

Where defendant's answer raises issues of fact on which he is entitled to a jury, but the principal features of his defense are equitable, a demand for a jury must relate to the specific issues on which he is entitled to the same.—Bates v. Escot, 6, 380.

§ 5. Evidence.

Where in an equity case, if tried alone by the court, the evidence would be required to be clear and convincing, the same rule must apply to the jury as to evidence submitted to them in the same case. A mere preponderance of testimony will not be sufficient.—Sweetser v. Dobbins, 2, 277.

§ 6. Verdict of Jury.

In a suit in equity, the court may order a jury, though the party is not entitled thereto; but, in such case, the verdict of the jury on the issues submitted by the court is advisory only, and it may be adopted or rejected by the court. A general verdict is insufficient, and a refusal to instruct a jury in such cases to find a general verdict is not error.—Evans v. Ross, 2, 543.

In cases at law the verdict of a jury is final, unless set aside; but in equity it is merely advisory, and may be adopted or not, as the court sees proper.—Sweetser v. Dobbins, 2, 277.

There is no error in regard to the admission of the evidence herein, and it does not appear that the judge assumed that he was conclusively bound by the verdict of the jury, though he arrived at the same conclusion.—Sweetser v. Dobbins, 2, 277.

ESCHEAT.

§ 1. Aliens—Act Removing Disability.

A proceeding instituted by the attorney general to have lands of a deceased person escheat by reason of alienage of the heirs is extinguished by a special act of the legislature, passed during its process, removing the disability.—People v. Atterbury, 1, 760.

ESTATES OF DECEDENT.

See Executors and Administrators; Wills.

ESTOPPEL.

By judgment. See Judgments, § 15.
To deny landlord's title. See Landlord and Tenant, § 8.
To rely on statute of limitations. See Limitation of Actions, § 11.
Of mortgagor. See Mortgages, § 16.
Of principal to deny agency. See Principal and Agent, § 3.
To plead setoff of note. See Setoff and Counterclaim, § 3.
To interfere with irrigation pipe. See Waters and Watercourses, § 10.

§ 1. By Record.

One claiming under a grant by a certain name is conclusively bound by a judicial determination and definition of what land was meant by that name.—Scott v. Rhodes, 5, 131.

§ 2. In Pais.

In an action against C. and her son for conversion of farming implements on a certain ranch, it appeared that C. and her husband sold such ranch, and all farming implements on it, to one H.; that afterward H. sold all the personal property to plaintiff; that, before the sale to H., the son bought all the implements on the ranch, and farmed the land as a tenant; that H.'s foreman, in company with the agent of C. and husband, made an inventory of the implements on the ranch; that the son did not point them out; that before the transfer of the personal property the son told H.'s agent that the implements were his, and the agent knew he was using them; and that, at the time, defendants were living in one of the houses on the ranch, the son being a tenant of H. There was no claim that the son had in any manner misled H. as to the ownership of the implements. Held, that the son was not estopped from asserting his ownership as against H. or plaintiff.—Warren v. Connor, 5, 537.

Evidence that a subsequent purchaser of real estate acquired the legal title with knowledge of the claim of a prior purchaser, who had not obtained the legal title, but who acquired his interest in the lands from the same source of title, and that the prior purchaser had made improvements on the land, and that the subsequent purchaser allowed him to continue making such improvements, and to use the land for a period of eight or nine years, without notifying defendant of any claim to the land or warning her not to improve the same, is sufficient to estop the subsequent purchaser from recovering the property.—Pacific Imp. Co. v. Carriger, 6, 884.

EVIDENCE.

§ 1. Admissibility in General.

To disprove title in the defendant's grantor, a deed executed long after his entry, and the record of a suit begun long after also, to which suit such grantor or the defendant was not a party or privy to a party, are not admissible.—Owen v. Mustard, 1, 119.

Evidence as to the number of boxes witness could pack in a given time is not admissible to show how many defendant could pack.— People v. Miller, 7, 192.

§ 2. —— Cumulative Testimony.

The refusal to permit the introduction of testimony on a point already established to the full by other testimony, and when there was no evidence at all to the contrary, is not error.—Houck v. Carolan, 1, 692.

§ 3. —— Testimony at Former Trial.

When a witness is disabled by sickness from attending a trial, his deposition, taken previously in another case after due notice to the opposing side, may, if otherwise competent and material, be read at such trial; if in the other case, even though it was entitled as be-

37

of plaintiff was positive that there was no such contract between the parties as that alleged in the cross-complaint, and defendant merely testified that the cross-complaint was true.—Haight v. Tryon, 5, 761.

§ 7. Judicial Notice.

Courts in California will take judicial notice of the legal distances from place to place in the state of California, as established by the Political Code in sections 150 to 202, inclusive, for the purpose of computing the time within which notice of intention to move for a new trial must be served.—Hegard v. California Ins. Co., 2, 663.

Code of Civil Procedure, section 1875, subdivision 3, providing that courts may take judicial notice of "public and private official acts of the . . . . judicial department of this state," does not authorize a court to dispense with formal proof of its judgment in another cause. Stanley v. McElrath, 3, 163.

Under Code of Civil Procedure, section 1875, subdivision 3, which permits courts to take judicial notice of the acts of the judicial department of the state, the supreme court will judicially notice the vacation of a decree confirming a Mexican grant.—Ohm v. San Francisco, 3, 314.

The courts will take judicial notice that the city of Los Angeles is a municipal corporation, by virtue of the several statutes organizing it into such corporation, and extending its limits, and adding to and changing the powers of its officers.—Bituminous Lime Rock Paving etc. Co. v. Fulton, 4, 151.

Under Code of Civil Procedure, section 1875, subdivision 8, authorizing courts to take judicial notice of the laws of nature, the court judicially knows the rules of mensuration by which the cubic contents of an irregular prismoidal body are ascertained.—Scanlan v. San Francisco and San Joaquin Valley Ry. Co., 6, 210.

§ 8. Parol to Vary or Explain Writing.

Parol to explain note. See Bills and Notes, § 8.
Parol to explain deed. See Deeds, § 18.
Parol to explain judgment. See Judgments, § 2.

In an action to foreclose a mortgage given by defendant to secure a note for money loaned to him by plaintiff, defendant may show by parol evidence that at the time of executing the note and mortgage it was agreed, as part of the same transaction, that defendant should pay all taxes levied on the money loaned, or on the mortgage, but that the agreement was purposely omitted from the mortgage, in order to evade constitution, article 13, section 5, which provides that imposing such an obligation on a borrower shall avoid the contract, as to any interest specified therein. as such parol evidence tends to "establish illegality" of the contract, within Code of Civil Procedure, section 1856, prescribing when such evidence is admissible to affect a writing.—Daw v. Niles, 4, 144.

The defendant may not introduce at the trial oral testimony to vary or contradict the terms of a written contract sued upon, when his answer contains no averment of mistake, etc., in that connection; but if, by leave of the court, he so amends the answer as to make it show the contract as he claims its terms really were, alleging that a material term had been omitted in the writing, and also to make it ask for a reformation in that respect and that the contract as reformed as asked be enforced in his favor, then such testimony is admissible.—Pierson v. McCahill, 1, 276.

An answer setting up a parol modification of the written contract sued upon is good if the modification is alleged in it as having been made subsequently to the making of the contract.—Wright v. Treganza, 1, 325.

Oral testimony is not admissible to vary the terms of a written agreement, or of an indorsement on the instrument extending the time of payment of money becoming due under the agreement, so as to make such agreement or indorsement cover a promissory note in no manner referred to in either.—Kelly v. Frisbie, 1, 408.

Oral testimony of the contents of a letter may be stricken out.—Hewlett v. Steele, 2, 157.

Where a contract has been interpreted on an appeal to this court, such contract is not ambiguous or uncertain, and on a new trial parol evidence cannot be introduced to show the intention of the parties, under Civil Code, section 1649, and Code of Civil Procedure, section 1864, authorizing parol evidence in cases of doubtful and ambiguous contracts; for these sections do not apply when the courts are able to declare the true intent of the parties.—San Diego Flume Co. v. Chase, 3, 792.

A receipt may always be explained by parol.—Lacrabere v. Wise, 7, 107.

§ 9. Hearsay Testimony.

The admission below of hearsay testimony cannot justify a reversal, where the admission could have in no way injured the party appealing.—Houck v. Carolan, 1, 692.

Evidence of a conversation had in a room where plaintiff was at the time need not be excluded as hearsay, if it is left to the jury to determine whether the plaintiff heard it.—Hewlett v. Steele, 2, 157.

§ 10. Admissions and Declarations.

In pleadings. See Pleadings, § 17.
Of one wrongdoer. See Trespass, § 2.

Conversation occurring five or six years before the trial and overheard by witnesses not interested in the subject is likely to have been misunderstood and inaccurately remembered. Such evidence is not to be depended upon.—Houck v. Carolan, 1, 692.

Declarations of decedent, not against interest, relative to a transaction with defendant, are not, in an action by her administrator, admissible in his favor.—Bedell v. Scoggins, 5, 66.

In an action of damages for injury to a child by a railroad train, the declarations of the engineer concerning the accident, made from three to five minutes after the casuality happened, are admissible against the principal as part of the res gestae.—Durkee v. Central Pac. R. Co., 2, 599.

§ 11. Respecting Title.

Declarations of parties in possession explanatory of the possession are always admissible, unless for some cause they are incompetent witnesses.—Baird v. Duane, 1, 492.

A plaintiff claiming title through commissioners, acting for a town to which lands have been confirmed, cannot rest on an admission by the defendant at the trial that such lands had been so granted, if virtually there was an exception in the grant; but he must show that the exception did not affect the property he was given title to.—Holloway v. Galliac, 1, 522.

Evidence, with respect to his title, of declarations made by a party after he had disposed of his interest in the property, is not admissible. Packard v. Johnson, 2, 365.

Declarations of an owner of land in disparagement of his title are admissible in evidence against him, and all claiming under him, while the legal title remains in him; but such declarations are inadmissible where made by him after he has parted with his title.—Frink v. Roe, 2, 491.

Where there were in evidence declarations of the owner of the land, while in possession, and at the time the survey was being made, that the same was made merely for convenience of reference, if it was erroneous to admit declarations of the owner to the same effect made after the survey, the plaintiff suffered no substantial injury by their admission, where the fact was not brought out as to how long afterward declarations were made, and, so far as appeared, they may have been made immediately afterward.—Smith v. Glenn, 6, 519.

A general objection to evidence of a certain conversation as not had in the presence of one of the parties to the suit was insufficient as affecting certain offensive words used in the conversation, where there was no motion made to strike them out, and they were thereafter repeated to such party in person.—Schwartz v. Wright, 6, 248.

§ 12. —— Of Counsel.

In an action for damages for personal injuries, defendant's counsel on the trial admitted that "the allegations in the complaint in respect to the amount of damages sustained by plaintiff were not denied by the answer," upon which admission the court sustained an objection to questions in relation to the amount of such damages. As a matter of fact the answer did put in issue such allegations, and the questions were therefore proper and admissible.—Payne v. Kripp, 2, 348.

§ 13. —— Of Agent.

Declarations by an agent or servant employed to perform a certain duty are not admissible against the principal, unless they are part of the facts and circumstances of some act happening within the scope of the servant's or agent's employment.—Durkee v. Central Pac. R. Co., 2, 599.

If intended to prove that the wood was in condition to be measured, it was improper, because the declaration of an agent under such circumstances cannot bind his principal.—Mutter v. I. X. L. Lime Co., 5, 211.

§ 14. —— Of Officer of Corporation.

The president and managing agent of a corporation have authority to make admissions in regard to the fulfillment of contracts which will be evidence against the corporation.—Bullock v. Consumers' Lumber Co., 3, 609.

In an action by the assignee of a note given by a corporation to its president, declarations of the president as to the amount due at the time of the transfer are not admissible against the corporation.—Love v. Anchor Raisin Vineyard Co., 5, 425.

§ 15. —— In Pleadings.

A plaintiff need not prove at the trial matter admitted in the answer. Charleton v. Reed, 1, 695.

Matters set up in the complaint and not denied in the answer are deemed admitted.—San Francisco v. Spring Valley Water Works, 1, 783.

A matter alleged in the complaint and not denied in the answer is not subject to disproof by evidence at the trial.—Tusch v. Cummings, 1, 782.

§ 16. Possession as Evidence of Title.

Possession is prima facie evidence of title, and raises a presumption, if unexplained, that the possessor is the owner.—Bigley v. Nunan, 1, 852.

§ 17. Evidence of Value and Quality.

Testimony as to the quality of old wire rope sold by sample, that the outer wires were broken into short pieces; that the rope was "rotten, and a little broken, instead of being as the sample"; that much of it was "broken, rusty and rotten"—relates to facts open to common observation and not requiring expert knowledge.—Gruwald v. Freese, 4, 182.

Merchants and clerks of merchants in a foreign country who deal in a certain article are competent to testify as to the market value of the article in such foreign country.—Gruwald v. Freese, 4, 182.

Where a witness testifies that he has been in the dairy business for seven years, and is familiar with the value of cattle for that business, his testimony as to the value of the cattle in suit is admissible, although he has not seen them for a year previous to the execution.—Paden v. Goldbaum, 4, 767.

Where witnesses as to the value of land were qualified to give an opinion, the question what was the value of the land as "between a party who wished to buy and one who wished to sell" was not objectionable as to form.—Fowler v. Carne, 6, 668.

Where a lawyer engaged for twenty years as an examiner of titles and as attorney for leading loaning companies in a city testifies that he is acquainted with the value of certain lots therein, he should be permitted to testify as to such value.—Norris v. Crandall, 6, 706.

§ 18. Expert Testimony—Qualification of Witness.

See, also, Libel and Slander, § 4; Forgery, § 4.

One who has been a civil and hydraulic engineer for several years is qualified to testify as an expert in matters touching civil and hydraulic engineering.—Egger v. Rhodes, 4, 850.

In an action to recover for personal services in nursing and caring for defendant's testator, plaintiff introduced as an expert witness as to the value of the services a woman of experience in the same kind of work, and who had seen the nature of plaintiff's services on the ranch where they were performed. In answer to the question, "From your experience, and what you saw on the ranch, are you able to say what such services are reasonably worth?" she replied, "Well, I am able to tell what I think." Held, that the court erred in excluding the testimony on the ground that witness had admitted her incompetency. Cowdery v. McChesney, 6, 315.

§ 19. —— Physicians and Their Opinions.

In homicide cases. See Homicide, § 11.

The opinion of a physician as an expert may not be asked as to a point it requires no scientific knowledge to determine.—People v. Smith, 2, 59.

Upon trial of an indictment for preparing a false affidavit, held proper to ask medical experts whether the person making the affidavit, who was ill at the date thereof, was at the time able to make such a statement as appeared in the affidavit.—People v. Brown, 2, 701.

Where a witness shown to be a physician has been "examined at length" as to plaintiff's injuries, it will be assumed that a proper foundation has been laid to enable him to testify as a medical expert. Fogel v. San Francisco etc. Ry. Co., 5, 194.

In an action for personal injuries, where plaintiff had testified to the fracture of the tenth rib, two inches from the spine, by the accident, it was proper for defendant to show by a medical expert the necessary force to produce such injury, and that it could not have been caused by the accident.—Yaeger v. Southern California Ry. Co., 5, 870.

Where plaintiff's evidence tended to show that one of his ribs had been fractured by the accident, and that inflammation of the nerves was the result, defendant's theory that fractured ribs could not have been caused by the accident, and that the condition of the nerves came from alcoholism, exposure, or another accident, did not present a case for hypothetical questions.—Yaeger v. Southern California Ry. Co., 5, 870.

§ 21.   Documentary Proofs.

In support of a complaint in which a description of land occurs, a deed may be introduced wherein the description does not correspond with the other description, provided evidence aliunde is forthcoming to show that both descriptions apply to the same land.—Baird v. Duane, 1, 492.

A withdrawn cross-complaint is not admissible in evidence.—Ruddock Co. v. Johnson, 6, 846.

§ 22.   —— Copies of Record.

A statute making copies of record to be evidence like in effect to the originals if produced does not dispense with the necessity of producing the original record when obtainable.—Macy v. Wheeler, 1, 49.

§ 23.   —— Record of Conviction.

The record of conviction of murder is admissible as evidence of the fact that the person convicted was implicated in said murder.—Harris v. More, 2, 421.

§ 24.   —— Resolution of Board of Directors.

A resolution of a board of directors, or of stockholders, to reimburse a named person for the amount expended by him in developing a mine may be an admission of indebtedness, but it is not sufficient to support a count in a complaint "for money loaned" the company.—Borel v. Fellows Quartz Min. Co., 1, 229.

A resolution of a board of directors, or of stockholders, appropriating a sum "not exceeding thirty thousand dollars" "from the proceeds of the Fellows Mine" to reimburse, etc., is not evidence to be relied on by the person to be reimbursed in a suit by him, or his representatives, against the company to prove any particular sum to be due or the time when any money became due.—Borel v. Fellows Quartz Min. Co., 1, 229.

§ 25.   —— Judgment Book or Roll.

A nonsuit judgment-roll establishes no facts, and, if offered as evidence in a subsequent case between the parties, may properly be objected to as irrelevant and immaterial.—Page v. Lynch, 2, 121.

Plaintiff cannot complain that a judgment-book introduced by defendant did not prove the judgment, if he himself introduced evidence of the judgment by introduction of the judgment-roll, although he introduced such judgment-roll for another purpose only.—Packard v. Johnson, 2, 365.

§ 26.   —— Letters.

A letter from a vendor's land agent to the vendee, written after the sale, is not evidence against an outside person in an action by him against the vendee's assign.—Brown v. Hambleton, 2, 65.

Plaintiff testified that he had written certain letters to defendants; that the postage was prepaid and the letters put in the mail box at his store; that said box was emptied daily; that it was the business of W., an employee, to take the letters, and mail them in the postoffice. W. testified that he was such employee at the time in question; that it was his duty to take the mail to the office, and that he did so; that if any letter was addressed and put in the box, he took and mailed it. Held, sufficient proof of mailing to support secondary evidence of the contents of the letters.—Sanborn v. Cunningham, 4, 95.

Where a party was notified to produce a letter sent him, a longhand copy thereof, shown to be such, is admissible, although not a fac-simile. Grant v. Dreyfus, 5, 970.

§ 27. —— Book of Registered Letters.

Petitioner introduced evidence tending to show that she received at Buffalo a letter signed C. K. (testatrix's name), containing a railroad ticket and five dollars. It was shown that the address of C. K. was at 616½ N. street, and that at about that time she borrowed five dollars to send, as she said, to her sister at Buffalo. Held, that petitioner might introduce from the book of registered letters of the San Francisco postoffice an entry reciting the receipt of a letter from C. K., 616½ N. street. addressed to M. R. (petitioner), Buffalo.—In re Kennedy's Estate, 4, 671.

§ 28. —— Absence of Revenue Stamp.

The fact that the record of a deed executed in 1872 does not show that any United States revenue stamps were placed thereon does not render such record incompetent evidence.—Bennett v. Morris, 4, 834.

§ 29. Books of Account.

The books of account of one party to an action are not evidence when the entries do not specifically connect the other party with the transactions they refer to.—Rogers v. Graves, 1, 21.

In an action to recover money due on contract, where one furnishes material and another does work under an agreement to divide the profits, the original books of entry of the parties are proper evidence to show the amount of work done.—Morgans v. Adel, 2, 863.

An entry in plaintiff's ledger, which the bookkeeper swears to be an original entry, if competent for nothing else, yet may be admitted to show with whom plaintiffs understood that they had dealt, and to whom they looked for payment.—Sanborn v. Cunningham, 4, 95.

On appeal by plaintiff from an order vacating an order for the inspection of books of account, and from an order denying a motion to strike out defendant's answer, no error is shown where the record states that final judgment was rendered for plaintiff several months before the order for inspection was made, and before the motion to strike out, and the purpose of the order and motion at such a time is not disclosed.—Clarke v. Baird, 4, 339.

S.'s clerk, Y., took an assignment of mortgage from him, foreclosed it, and took the property in his own name. S. having died, Y. contended, as against his widow, that he had bought the mortgage, and foreclosed it for himself. The widow asserted that she had bought it from her husband, and had it assigned to Y. for foreclosure. On direct examination, Mrs. S. was asked whether at the time in question Y. was her agent for collecting rents. Y.'s accounts were put in evidence, showing large credits for rents collected for her, and charges for the notary's fee on the assignment of the mortgage, for taxes on the same, and expenses of foreclosure and sale. Held, that the question was proper as an introduction of the accounts.—Hunt v. Swyney, 4, 108.

The account-books of a judgment creditor are original evidence to establish claims against the debtor, and should be introduced as part of the case, and it is proper to exclude them when offered in rebuttal. Paden v. Goldbaum, 4, 767.

On an issue whether a written contract was drawn up between plaintiff and defendant, where there was the positive evidence of two witnesses that such a contract was drawn, a refusal to permit defendant to show that a book containing a record of such transactions, kept by him, did not show an entry of a certain date of the drawing of such contract, was not reversible error, it appearing that defendant did not offer to prove that the book contained no entry in regard to the contract.—McRae v. Argonaut Land & Dev. Co., 6, 145.

EXAMINERS, STATE BOARD OF.

See State Board of Examiners.

EXCEPTIONS.

Necessity of taking and saving. See Appeal and Error, §§ 9–13.
Bill of, in general. See Appeal and Error, §§ 40–44.
In criminal case. See Criminal Law, § 25.

EXCHANGE.

§ 1. Of Real Properties.

Where, in a contract for the exchange of land, the values of the respective parcels have been fixed, a party to the contract, who had no title to the land he contracted to convey, and who has placed himself in such a position that he cannot acquire title, cannot object to the tender of the deed by the other party because made on condition that he pay the amount fixed by the contract as the value of the land to be conveyed by him.—Royal v. Dennison, 4, 851.

§ 2. Rescission of Transaction.

Where, in an action to rescind an exchange, the court found that defendant represented his property as worth $4,000, and believed it worth that, while it was worth only $2,000, the exchange should not be rescinded when the representation was made and relied on as an opinion, and not as a statement of fact.—Norris v. Crandall, 6, 706.

Where plaintiff sought to rescind an exchange of property on the ground of fraud, and the court finds there was no fraud, a failure to find as to all the facts alleged in the complaint is not error.—Norris v. Crandall, 6, 706.

Where, in an action to rescind an exchange of property, the parties treated the value of the properties exchanged as material, and evidence thereof is admitted over plaintiff's objection, the judgment should not be reversed, since, if immaterial, it could not prejudice plaintiff.—Norris v. Crandall, 6, 706.

EXECUTION.

As affecting appeal. See Appeal and Error, § 3.
Against husband, wife's property. See Husband and Wife, § 5.
Restraining sale. See Injunctions, § 9.
Recovering money paid to sheriff. See Payment, § 4.
Supplemental proceedings. See Supplementary Proceedings.
Liability of officer. See Sheriffs and Constables, § 4.

§ 1. Property Subject to Levy.

Things in action are property so as to be subject to levy in execution.—Johnson v. Reynolds, 1, 60.

On appeal from a judgment for the recovery from the sheriff of goods claimed as those actually of the plaintiff, though nominally belonging to the judgment debtor at the time of the levy, a reversal is proper where the proof is that a large part of the goods so recovered had never been the property of the plaintiff.—Jewett v. Adkinson, 1, 197.

The statute (Laws 1850, p. 444, sec. 184), referring to the lien of a judgment, is not to be construed so as to limit property leviable to that owned by the judgment debtor at the time of the filing of the transcript, thus excluding subsequently acquired property.—Belknap v. Byington, 1, 374.

The undivided share of one cutting hay on shares cannot be levied upon to satisfy the debt of his cosharer.—McDermott v. Apgar, 1, 149.

One to whom an offer for the sale of land is made—the offer to be kept open only on certain conditions—has not, in the absence both of a compliance with such conditions and an acceptance of the offer, an interest in the land, which is subject to sale on execution.—Chadbourne v. Stockton Sav. & Loan Soc., 4, 535.

§ 2. Exemptions.

Evidence as to indorsements on a sheriff's writ of execution, whereby part of the property seized thereunder was surrendered as exempt, was properly excluded on the ground that its ownership was not in issue.—Paden v. Goldbaum, 4, 767.

§ 3. Issuance of Writ and Return.

An execution signed by a deputy clerk for a clerk of the court, whose term expired several months prior to the issuance of the execution, is void, under Code of Civil Procedure, section 682, declaring that an execution shall be sealed with the seal of the court and subscribed by the clerk; and a purchaser at a sale had under a levy based on such execution acquires no title to the property, so as to enable him to question a conveyance thereof by the judgment debtor, as fraudulent.—O'Donnell v. Merguire, 6, 423.

Where it appeared by the sheriff's return on an execution that a levy under it was not made until after the expiration of the life of the execution, such levy by a sheriff is without jurisdiction.—Tower v. McDowell, 3, 714.

§ 4. Description of Property.

A levy in execution and the subsequent proceedings, inclusive of the sheriff's deed, are not invalid because no lot of land existed having technically the designation contained in such execution, etc., if the designation was preceded by the words "known as," and it can be shown that at the time of such proceedings the premises so designated were so known and are susceptible of identification.—Belknap v. Byington, 1, 374.

A description introduced by the phrase "known as" is not vitiated by the subsequent phrase "marked on the official map," when the latter is a description false in fact.—Belknap v. Byington, 1, 374.

§ 5. Bond of Indemnity to Sheriff.

Code of Civil Procedure, section 689, as amended by Laws of 1891, page 20, provides that, if one claiming property seized on execution serves on the sheriff a sworn claim setting out his title and his right to possession, the sheriff need not keep the property, unless the execution plaintiff gives a bond of indemnity to him against such claim. Held, that proof of the service on the sheriff of such claim is admissible against the sheriff in an action by a claimant for the wrongful seizure of property, though it is not pleaded in the complaint, since the statute is for the benefit of the sheriff, and is matter of defense.—Paden v. Goldbaum, 4, 767.

§ 6. Expiration of Sheriff's Term of Office.

On a writ of fieri facias coming into the hands of the sheriff of the then district of San Francisco, in 1850, another sheriff, newly elected and qualified as sheriff of the county of San Francisco, could not make a valid sale so as to vest the purchaser, or the grantee in the subsequent deed referring to such sale, with title to the property sold.—Clark v. Sawyer, 1, 573.

§ 7. Sale.

In order to establish a title through judicial proceedings and subsequent execution of the judgment, one must be held to show a judgment not subject to be impeached for lack of jurisdiction, a proper writ of fieri facias issued on the judgment, and a sufficient conveyance on a sale made under the writ by the officer designated by law to make it.—Clark v. Sawyer, 1, 573.

§ 8. —— Purchase by Executor.

The executor of an estate has no authority to bid for or purchase for the estate, at an execution sale, property sold to satisfy an execution on a judgment in favor of the estate, and, such sale being void, gives no cause of action against the estate for damages by reason of such sale.—Sedgwick v. Sedgwick, 2, 363.

§ 9. —— Sheriff's Certificate.

No title passes by the sheriff's certificate; it requires the deed to vest title in a purchaser at a sheriff's sale. The purpose of having the certificate filed is, that the judgment debtor and the redemptioners shall have information necessary for them to have in coming in to redeem.—Brooks v. Tichner, 1, 104.

§ 10. ―― Sheriff's Deed.

Where land is sold under execution in an attachment suit, the sheriff's deed takes effect as of the date of the levy of the attachment, and a conveyance by the attachment debtor after the attachment was levied, and before judgment, vests no title in his grantee. Robinson v. Thornton, 3, 741.

Where judgments are rendered foreclosing liens for labor, the liens relate back to the time when the labor for which they were claimed commenced, and the deeds executed in pursuance thereto take effect by relation to the time the liens attached.—Purser v. Cady, 5, 707.

§ 11. ―― Effect of Reversal of Judgment.

Plaintiff claimed title to certain land under execution sale and sheriff's deed to his grantors. After such sale the judgment was reversed in the supreme court as far as it awarded counsel fees, but was in all other respects affirmed. Held, that, since no order for the restitution of the property sold was ever made, as provided by Code of Civil Procedure, section 957, plaintiff's title acquired by the execution sale was not affected by such reversal.—Purser v. Cady, 5, 707.

§ 12. ―― Limitation of Actions.

The statute of limitations does not begin to run against the purchaser of land at a sheriff's sale, or his grantees, until delivery of the sheriff's deed.—Robinson v. Thornton, 3, 741.

§ 13. Writ of Assistance and Possession.

An order restoring one to possession of land, which is in accordance with the law as applied to the facts found by the court below, will not be disturbed on appeal.—Judson v. Molloy, 1, 504.

A judgment upon a writ of assistance awarding to the purchaser, at a sale for delinquent taxes, so much of the lot as the sheriff ought to have deeded when erroneously deeding the whole, will be, in the absence of specific findings, presumed to have been supported by necessary facts.—People v. Doe, 1, 538.

In order to recover possession of property purchased at execution sale, it is necessary to introduce in evidence the judgment as a basis of the execution.—Purser v. Cady, 5, 707.

On petition for a writ of assistance to gain possession of land, the tenant in possession cannot question the petitioner's title.—White v. White, 6, 499.

§ 14. Venditioni Exponas.

It is impolitic to disturb sales made by sheriffs under warrant of the ancient writ of venditioni exponas during the early days of the state.—Belknap v. Byington, 1, 374.

§ 15. Wrongful Sale—Remedy.

The right of action of a person aggrieved by the sale of his goods in execution of a judgment against another is not against the attaching officer alone; he may sue the purchaser for conversion.—Briggs v. Wangenheim, 1, 518.

If by the misconduct of the officer property levied upon was sold at a sacrifice, the owner's remedy is against the officer for damages, not against the purchaser to recover the property.—Foster v. Coronel, 1, 402.

Where, in trover against a sheriff, who claimed to hold by virtue of a levy under an execution, plaintiff introduced in evidence the execution under which defendant justified the taking, and his return thereon, showing the levy and sale and amount received from such sale, the exclusion of oral testimony as to what the property sold for is not harmful to the defendant.—Tower v. McDowell, 3, 714.

EXECUTORS AND ADMINISTRATORS.

§ 1. Appointment—Application and jurisdiction.
§ 2. Failure to give security.
§ 3. Revocation of appointment.
§ 4. Grounds and proceedings for removal.
§ 5. Special administrators.
§ 6. Inventory and appraisement.
§ 7. Money paid testator as security.
§ 8. Collection and management of estate—Delay and neglect.
§ 9. Conveyance for individual debt—Conversion.
§ 10. Dealing with estate.
§ 11. Liability of joint executors.
§ 12. Compensation and commissions.
§ 13. Family allowance.
§ 14. Claims against estate—Services.
§ 15. —— Presentation and allowance.
§ 16. —— Administrator's claim.
§ 17. —— Judgment claim.
§ 18. —— Mortgage claim—Homestead.
§ 19. Mortgage to pay debts.
§ 20. Sale of property.
§ 21. —— Petition for sale.
§ 22. —— Advance bids.
§ 23. —— Bar against heirs.
§ 24. —— Collateral attack.
§ 25. —— Appeal.
§ 26. Action by administrator.
§ 27. —— Foreign executor.
§ 28. Action against administrator—Rejected claims.
§ 29. —— For services or compensation.
§ 30. —— Witnesses and evidence.
§ 31. —— Attorneys and their fees.
§ 32. —— Judgment.
§ 33. Accounts and accounting—Items allowable.
§ 34. —— Absence of vouchers.
§ 35. —— Settlement and proceedings therefor.
§ 36. —— Appeal and review.
§ 37. Determination of heirship—Illegitimates.
§ 38. Distribution of estate.
§ 39. —— Payment of taxes.
§ 40. —— Setting aside and appeal.
See Public Administrator.

Contract of broker with one executor. See Brokers, § 3.
Review of administrator's account. See Certiorari, § 2.
Demand by administrator before suing. See Demand, § 2.
Purchase at execution sale. See Execution, § 8.
Probate homestead. See Homestead, §§ 4–10.
Attorney fees in action on injunction bond. See Injunctions, § 3.
Actions on life insurance policy. See Insurance, § 18.
Patent to executor on death of entryman. See Public Lands, § 16.
Claim against estate in case of death pending reference. See Reference, § 2.
Witness in enforcing claim against decedent. See Witnesses, § 4.

§ 1. Appointment—Application and Jurisdiction.

That the probate court may have jurisdiction to appoint an administrator, when the words in the petition lack precision as to where the deceased resided, the court may satisfy itself of the fact of residence otherwise than from the petition.—Lightstone v. Scull, 1, 226.

When it appears from an order of the probate court appointing an administrator, even though not by direct statement, that the residence of the deceased at the time he died had been proved to be in the county, residence is sufficiently shown as a jurisdictional fact.—Lightstone v. Scull, 1, 226.

Where an order refusing to permit an heir to withdraw a request for the appointment of another as administrator of an estate is based on conflicting testimony, it will not be reversed on appeal.—In re Selvar's Estate, 5, 494.

An appeal by a public administrator from an order denying his petition for letters on decedent's estate, and granting those of guardians of decedent's children, is frivolous, it not being contended that the guardians were not entitled to administer if the children were legitimate, and his petition having alleged that they were decedent's children and "heirs at law," and there being no evidence in the record of illegitimacy.—Clough v. Borello, 5, 657.

Under Civil Code, section 230, providing that the father of an illegitimate child, by publicly acknowledging it as his own and receiving it into his family, adopts it and makes it, for all purposes, legitimate from the time of its birth, the acknowledging of an illegitimate child by a father without receiving it into his family is not sufficient for its adoption, and such child can confer no right to administer her father's estate.—Garner v. Judd, 6, 675.

Where an application for letters of administration was supported by a petition stating that petitioner was a brother of deceased, and as such entitled to administer on his estate, and requesting that applicant be appointed in his stead, but the petition was not verified—merely having attached thereto a certificate in the form of an acknowledgment for a conveyance of real estate—and no evidence was offered that petitioner was a brother of deceased, or in any way related to him, the petition was properly excluded. There being no other evidence in support of the application, it was properly refused. In re Pina's Estate, 7, 101.

§ 2. Failure to Give Security.

Under Code of Civil Procedure, section 1395, which provides that, if sufficient security is not given within the time fixed, the right of an administrator to the administration shall cease, etc., where an administratrix fails to comply with the order, and obtains no further time, she is not entitled to notice of an order revoking her letters after the limitation has expired.—Barrett v. Superior Court of Placer County, 5, 569.

Where there has been a failure to comply with an order for an administratrix to give additional security, an order "that the right of the administratrix to the administration of this estate cease" cuts off her powers, and ousts her from office.—Barrett v. Superior Court of Placer County, 5, 569.

§ 3. Revocation of Appointment.

Code of Civil Procedure, section 1383, providing that when letters of administration have been granted to any other than the surviving wife, child, etc., of the intestate, any one of them may obtain the revocation of the letters, and become entitled to the administration, does not apply to letters of administration with the will annexed.—In re Li Po Tai's Estate, 4, 966.

Code of Civil Procedure, section 1379, having authorized a court to appoint a stranger as administrator of an estate upon the written request of one who would himself be entitled to letters of administration, where such request and a renunciation have been filed by a petitioner, and proceedings for his appointment have been instituted, the heir will not be permitted to revoke it without reason.—In re Silvar's Estate, 5, 494.

§ 4. Grounds and Proceedings for Removal.

Civil Code, section 2230, declares that neither a trustee nor any of his agents may take part in any transaction concerning the trust in which he or anyone for whom he acts as agent has an interest adverse to that of his beneficiary, and section 2233 stipulates that, if a trustee acquires any interest, or becomes charged with any duty, adverse to the interest of his beneficiary in the subject of the trust, he may at once be removed. Held, that an administrator who acquiesced in the conduct of his attorneys in accepting a retainer by one of the heirs who claimed the entire estate had violated the duties of his trust, and should be removed, the attorneys, as his agents, occupying confidential relations to the heirs.—In re Healy's Estate, 6, 780.

Under Code of Civil Procedure, section 1438, providing that in proceedings for the removal of an administrator the petition and answer must be in writing, a record on appeal is properly authenticated, though the petition, answer and order are not incorporated in the bill of exceptions, where the same were in the record certified to by the clerk.—In re Healy's Estate, 6, 780.

§ 5. Special Administrators.

The bringing of an action against adverse occupants of the land of a deceased person by a special administrator, to conserve the rights of the estate, is within not only the right but the duty of such administrator, and it is proper for the probate court to give him express authority to bring the action.—Belknap v. Byington, 1, 374.

The rights conserved by a special administrator in bringing an action against adverse occupants of the land of the deceased inures to successors to the right, title and interest of the deceased in the land.—Belknap v. Byington, 1, 374.

§ 6. Inventory and Appraisement.

Where land belongs to a wife, the fact that she, as administratrix of her husband, returned said land as assets of his estate is immaterial, and does not estop her to claim it as her own.—Whelan v. Brickell, 4, 47.

Claims due an estate and reported as worthless by the appraisers must be deemed to be of no value until the contrary appears.—In re Williams, 1, 467.

§ 7. Money Paid Testator as Security.

Plaintiff leased property of R., and gave him $500 as security for the lease, he agreeing to pay it back on the expiration of the lease. R. died before the expiration of the lease, and H., who was appointed his executrix, filed an inventory, which recited: "Moneys belonging to said deceased which has come to the hands of the executrix . . . . $500, held as security for lease from" plaintiff. H. died after the termination of the lease. Held, that it was not necessary to present a claim for the $500 against the estate of R., but that an action might be maintained therefor against the estate of H.—Reiter **v.** Rothschild, 4, 103.

In view of the sworn statement of H., the finding of the court that she had in her possession the money deposited by plaintiff is supported by the evidence, though her executor testified that he made such statement, and that as a matter of fact it was not true, but was made because they felt she was morally liable for the money.—Reiter v. Rothschild, 4, 103.

§ 8. Collection and Management of Estate—Delay and Neglect.

If an executor delays to take steps for the collection of a debt until after the same is outlawed, and the delay is not in consequence of any mistake of law, or of advice given by his attorney, he will be liable to the estate for the loss occasioned by his negligence.—Estate of Sanderson, 2, 750.

The fact that an administration has not been completed, though fourteen years have elapsed since the appointment of the administrator, is prima facie evidence of neglect of duty on his part, and, in the absence of satisfactory explanation of the delay, supports a finding that the administrator has wrongfully and willfully neglected the estate, and has unnecessarily, willfully and wrongfully prolonged its administration, to its great detriment, and justifies his removal, and the revocation of his letters of administration.—In re Moore's Estate, 3, 162.

§ 9. Conveyance for Individual Debt—Conversion.

One to whom an executrix conveys property of the estate, in payment of her individual debt, before distribution, and without authority of the probate court, is, on refusal to return, liable to the estate for conversion, though the executrix was the sole legatee, and the property was the community property, and executrix was testator's widow. In order to maintain such action, it is not necessary to prove an indebtedness against the estate and necessity of obtaining the property to satisfy it.—Horton v. Jack, 4, 758.

Though the person to whom an executrix conveys property belonging to the estate does, as he agrees, have it applied on the claim of a bank against her individually, the bank is not jointly liable with him to the estate for the conversion of the property, it not being shown that he was acting for the bank in such manner as to bind it. Horton v. Jack, 4, 758.

§ 10. Dealing With Estate.

Code of Civil Procedure, section 1963, subdivisions 19, 20, providing that the law presumes "that private transactions have been fair and regular," and "that the ordinary course of business has been followed," are not applicable to the dealings of an administrator with an estate and its funds.—Sanguinetti v. Gianelli, 6, 489.

§ 11. Liability of Joint Executors.

Each executor of an estate is responsible severally for his own acts, and for money or property which has come to his own hands.— Estate of Sanderson, 2, 750.

§ 12. Compensation and Commissions.

The court below is to be sustained in reducing, to figures deemed by it reasonable, the charges of an administrator and his attorney in the settlement of an estate.—Matter of the Estate of Kent, 1, 28.

Where, during the settlement of an estate, the property was occupied by the family, including the executor, he should not be allowed extra compensation for his services in excess of his commissions.—In re Coursen's Estate, 6, 756.

In fixing the commissions of an executor, the inventory value of the property is not conclusive, but the actual market value may be shown, and used as the basis.—In re Coursen's Estate, 6, 756.

Where a small sum of money left by testatrix was received and used by appellant's coexecutor for the benefit of the estate, it was not error to exclude such sum from the computation in fixing appellant's commissions.—In re Coursen's Estate, 6, 756.

Where an executor acts also as attorney for the estate, such services do not necessarily entitle him to extra compensation.—In re Coursen's Estate, 6, 756.

§ 13. Family Allowance.

On appeal by an administrator from an order directing him to pay the widow of decedent a certain amount per month, as a family allowance, it will be presumed, in the absence of the evidence before the court below, that the condition of the estate was such as to authorize the allowance of the sum fixed in the order.—In re Carriger's Estate, 5, 129.

§ 14. Claims Against Estate—Services.

Action on rejected claims. See post, § 28.

Evidence showing that services were rendered by one as nurse to deceased is sufficient to charge the estate therefor, without proof of an express request by deceased.—Todd v. Martin, 4, 805.

Where plaintiff, after the death of deceased, continued in his former work of taking care of the latter's stables and stock without any authority from the administratrix, such services form a charge of necessity on the estate.—Todd v. Martin, 4, 805.

§ 15. —— Presentation and Allowance.

Where all the assets have been taken possession of by the administrator of a deceased partner, under section 1493 of the Code of Civil Procedure, the surviving partner cannot bring suit against such administrator for his interest in such assets without first presenting his claim to such administrator.—McKay v. Joy, 2, 639.

Where there was no proof of the signature of the executor to the rejection of a claim against an estate, held, that there was no proof of the presentation of the claim.—Bank of Chico v. Spect, 2, 675.

An appeal cannot be taken to the supreme court from an order dismissing the petition, under Code of Civil Procedure, section 963, subdivision 3, which provides for an appeal from a judgment or order refusing, allowing or directing the payment of a debt or claim against an estate. In such case plaintiff's remedy is in an action against the executor individually.—In re Williams' Estate, 3, 788.

A finding that a claim was not allowed by an administratrix is improper where the only evidence on that issue was the testimony of the attorney of said administratrix, read from a transcript taken on a former trial before another judge, and was to the effect that he signed the allowance at her request and in her presence.—Wise v. Williams, 5, 197.

§ 16. —— Administrator's Claim.

The statutory requirement that in the settlement of estates the claim of an administrator, not growing out of his official position, must be presented to the probate judge for allowance, was intended

38

merely as a protection and authentic voucher for the administrator on his settlement.—Cavert v. Alderman, 1, 73.

An administrator is not precluded from his credit, in respect of any claim he may have unofficially against the estate, by his failure to have the claim allowed in the first instance by the judge of probate; but may show the existence and justice of the claim when settling his accounts, being prepared with his proofs in case he is challenged by the distributees.—Cavert v. Alderman, 1, 73.

§ 17. —— Judgment Claim.

The Probate Act, requiring a judgment creditor of the decedent to present his judgment to the administrator as a claim, defeats the provision of the Civil Practice Act, whereby on leave first had from the probate court, if a debtor has died after the recovery of judgment on the debt, execution may issue against the estate.—Hartman v. Reed, 1, 858.

§ 18. —— Mortgage Claim—Homestead.

The law in force in 1872 required a mortgage claim, like other claims, to be presented to the administrator for allowance. In 1873 the requirement was done away with, in 1874 it was restored, and in 1876 it was done away with finally.—Hibernia Savings and Loan Soc. v. Jordan, 2, 79.

Where the homestead, upon which the foreclosure of a mortgage is sought after the death of one of the mortgagors, has been released from the lien of the mortgage by the failure of the mortgagee to present his claim against the estate within the time limited for that purpose, the foreclosure proceedings cannot be sustained on the ground of an abandonment by the attempt of the survivor to get a homestead on other property after the expiration of the time for the presentation of claims.—Bull v. Coe, 2, 807.

Under Code of Civil Procedure, section 1475, providing that claims secured by liens or encumbrances "on the homestead" must be presented and allowed as other claims against the estate, a deed absolute, intended as a mortgage, executed by a husband and wife upon the wife's separate property, which had been declared a homestead, to secure the debt of the husband, cannot be foreclosed after the death of the husband, no claim having been presented against the estate.—Bull v. Coe, 2, 807.

In an action of foreclosure on a mortgage against a decedent commenced in 1877, where the notice to creditors had been published in February, 1873, during which year the statute provided that a mortgage claim need not be presented, there is no necessity for a presentation, though at the time the mortgage was executed, and also during the last half of 1874, and all of 1875, the statute required presentation, and provided that no action could be maintained without it.—Hibernia Savings and Loan Soc. v. Jordan, 7, 398.

The amendments of 1874 of sections 1493 and 1500 of the Code of Civil Procedure, in the matter of presentation of mortgage claims against decedents' estates, did not have any retroactive operation.—Hibernia Savings and Loan Soc. v. Jordan, 7, 398.

§ 19. Mortgage to Pay Debts.

Where there are several claims against a solvent estate, some of which are being pressed for immediate payment, and the property cannot be sold at once without great sacrifice, the probate court has jurisdiction to authorize a mortgage to pay off the pressing demands, the requirements of Code of Civil Procedure, sections 1643, 1645, that claims be paid in a certain order, as therein specified, having application to insolvent estates only.—Stambach v. Emerson, 6, 986.

In an action to foreclose a "probate mortgage," the order of the probate court authorizing the mortgage cannot be questioned, where the court had jurisdiction to make such order.—Stambach v. Emerson. 6, 986.

§ 20. Sale of Property.

Where a sale of real property is authorized in the settlement of an estate, the property is to be sold as a whole if it is evident it cannot be sold in parcels without detriment to the estate.—In re Williams, 1, 467.

A sale, under an order of a probate court, on the 4th of October, 1851, of lands of a person dying on the 14th of February, 1850, could be of no valid effect.—Paty v. Smith, 1, 727.

The curative act of April 2, 1866, "in relation to probate sales," by the use of the words "defects of form, omissions or errors," cannot be construed as embracing such matters as the want of power in the person assuming to act as an administrator or the absence of jurisdiction in the court which ordered the sale.—Pryor v. Downey, 1, 836.

An executor has no authority, without an order of the probate court, to sell currency belonging to the estate for coin, and it rests in the discretion of the court to approve or disapprove the sale.—Estate of Sanderson, 2, 750.

A contention that certain allegations in a petition to sell a testator's land were not proved cannot be sustained where they were matters which appeared from the papers on file in the case, to which the attention of the court was called.—In re Brannan's Estate, 5, 882.

Where testator's land was leased for a certain period, an executrix cannot object to a sale thereof before the expiration of the lease, to pay debts and legacies, on the ground that it would cause a loss of the rents, if they would not greatly exceed the interest on such debts and legacies.—In re Brannan's Estate, 5, 882.

An objection that, on account of the depreciated value of testator's property, a sale thereof would be to the damage of the residuary legatees, cannot be interposed against a petition for an order directing the executrix to sell, as the objection can be considered, under Code of Civil Procedure, section 1552 et seq., only when the sale comes up for confirmation.—In re Brannan's Estate, 5, 882.

An executrix may be directed to sell testator's property, subject to an existing lease for a term of years, giving the lessee an option to purchase at the end of the term, where the lease does not prohibit a sale during the term.—In re Brannan's Estate, 5, 882.

§ 21. —— Petition for Sale.

Where an order of probate sale of realty recites that at the hearing thereon the court "heard, understood, and fully considered the law and the premises," it will be assumed that it heard evidence as to the value of the property sold, and the sale will not, on collateral attack, be set aside because of the absence in the petition for sale of an allegation of the value of said property.—Burris v. Kennedy, 4, 936.

Where a petition in the probate court for the sale of realty recited that the petitioner "duly made and returned to said court . . . . a true inventory and appraisement of all the estate" of deceased, as "will more fully appear by reference to the papers on file in the clerk's office," it will be assumed, on a collateral attack on the sale, that the realty was inventoried and appraised as required by statute, and its actual cash value there stated, so as to supply an omission in the petition to state the value of the property.—Burris v. Kennedy, 4, 936.

Legatees presenting a verified petition for the sale of testator's land need not prove the allegations of the same, where they are not denied by answer.—In re Brannan's Estate, 5, 882.

§ 22. —— Advance Bids.

An executor, as devisee in trust, acting under the provisions of the will, sold property of the estate, and applied to the probate court for a confirmation. Plaintiff filed an advanced bid with the court, whereupon the executor conveyed the property to the first bidder. The court denied confirmation, and ordered and confirmed a sale to plaintiff, he paying the amount of his bid to the executor. The first bidder appealed from the order of confirmation, which was reversed. Plaintiff then filed a petition to compel the return from the estate to him of the money paid to the executor. Held, that plaintiff held no debt or claim against the estate.—In re Williams' Estate, 3, 788.

§ 23. —— Bar Against Heirs.

The statutory bar against an action by an heir, or other person claiming under a testator or intestate, to recover real estate sold by an executor or administrator more than three years before, applies to sales void for want of jurisdiction, as distinguished from sales voidable merely for some defect of procedure.—Meeks v. Kirby, 1, 711.

The statutory exception of "minors or others under legal disability to sue" from the operation of the bar against an action by an heir, or other person claiming under a testator or intestate, to recover real estate sold by an executor or administrator more than three years before, has reference to a disability personal to the party, and not to the mere condition of his title.—Meeks v. Kirby, 1, 711.

§ 24. —— Collateral Attack.

A probate sale of realty, when collaterally attacked by the grantee of a distributee under the final decree, who raised no objection to the validity of the sale, will not be set aside for mere irregularities.—Burris v. Kennedy, 4, 936.

§ 25. —— Appeal.

An appeal from an order of the probate court confirming a sale of real estate will not be considered on its appearing that the appellant is interested in the matter only as a creditor of the husband of the deceased, whose estate is in process of settlement, and the property sold was separate property.—In re Stokes, 1, 585.

§ 26. Action by Administrator.

In a suit by an administrator accounts filed by creditors, and allowed as just, may be shown in order to prove that such claims were filed against the estate.—Jamison v. King, 1, 833.

It is no defense to an action by an administrator upon a note due his decedent that pending the settlement of the estate the note was deposited with a trust company by order of court, and was produced therefrom only for the purpose of the action.—Cornwall v. McElrath, 4, 979.

§ 27. —— Foreign Executor.

A foreign executrix cannot maintain an action in the courts of California without first obtaining ancillary letters of administration or testamentary.—Lewis v. Adams, 2, 516.

§ 28. Action Against Administrator—Rejected Claims.

In an action by a creditor of a deceased person to establish a claim against the estate, rejected in the probate proceedings, an announcement by the court that the plaintiff's testimony, although admitted without objection, was not to be given the same weight as if the suit had been during the debtor's lifetime, is no ground for reversal, even if erroneous, in case the judgment is a proper one on the principal question.—Larco v. Roeding, 1, 438.

§ 29. —— For Services or Compensation.

There can be no recovery on a complaint against an administrator, alleging that a demand was made for services as an "expert nurse and medical attendant," when in fact the claim presented was for "medical attendance on deceased during his lifetime."—Roberts v. Levy, 3, 653.

There was no error in refusing to allow plaintiff to state that the paper introduced by him was in his possession at decedent's death, he having already been permitted to testify that the paper had been in his possession ever since decedent's death, which was, in effect, the same thing.—Robinson v. Dugan, 4, 472.

In an action against an administrator for compensation for services performed for testator, evidence that testator had expressed himself as not wishing to go away owing any man anything is immaterial.—Watson v. Miller, 6, 316.

In an action against an administrator for compensation for services performed for testator, a partner of plaintiff testified that plaintiff told him that he was attending to testator's affairs. Testator was not present when this statement was made. Defendant's counsel objected to the evidence, and questioned the witness with the object of showing that he was an interested party, following it by an objection to the testimony, which the court sustained. The testimony already given was not stricken out, nor did plaintiff's counsel offer any further testimony by this witness. Held, that the appellate court will not reverse, even though the objection was erroneously sustained. as the evidence of the witness was retained, and it cannot be assumed that any further facts would have been proven by him.—Watson v. Miller, 6, 316.

In an action against an administrator, it is not reversible error to overrule a demurrer by plaintiff to the complaint of intervening heirs, when the issues presented are the same as those raised by the answer of the administrator, and judgment must be the same as though the demurrer had been sustained.—Watson v. Miller, 6, 316.

In a suit for $30,000 against an administrator for services performed for testator, a finding that plaintiff performed work, the value of which did not exceed $500; that the deceased did not promise to pay for the services, but they were understood to be gratuitous; and that plaintiff was paid and received the sum of $500 in full payment, is sufficient to suppose a judgment against plaintiff.—Watson v. Miller, 6, 316.

In an action against an administrator for services performed for deceased, where the complaint alleges that deceased promised to pay for such services, and the answer denies the promise, a finding that deceased did not promise is not outside the issues.—Watson v. Miller, 6, 316.

§ 30. —— Witnesses and Evidence.

Under Code of Civil Procedure, section 1880, subdivision 3, forbidding a party to an action on a claim against a decedent's estate to testify to facts occurring before decedent's death, plaintiff cannot testify that a paper showing a debt from decedent to him was unpaid at decedent's death.—Robinson v. Dugan, 4, 472.

A witness who had stated that plaintiff on several occasions said that decedent owed no debts was properly allowed to state that in those conversations plaintiff made no exception in favor of himself.—Robinson v. Dugan, 4, 472.

In an action against the estate of the decedent, a brother of plaintiff, there was in evidence a paper in the handwriting of decedent, headed "S. R. [plaintiff] in Acct. with W. R. [decedent,] Cr.," reciting by cash a certain amount and by certain articles certain other amounts. A witness testified that he saw decedent hand plaintiff a paper like that in evidence, plaintiff having just before asked decedent what plaintiff had to show that decedent owed him. A witness testified that, on several occasions before and after decedent's death, plaintiff said that decedent did not owe anything. Held, that a finding that decedent was not, at the time of his death, indebted to plaintiff was justified by the evidence.—Robinson v. Dugan, 4, 472.

Code of Civil Procedure, section 2049, provides that the party producing a witness shall not impeach his credit by evidence of bad character, but may contradict him by other evidence, and show former inconsistent statements. Held, that the plaintiff in an action against an administratrix, having called her to testify in his behalf, is not necessarily bound by her answer.—Todd v. Martin, 4, 805.

In an action against an administratrix for services as nurse to deceased, one who served in the same capacity alternately with plaintiff may testify as to the nature and amount of the services.—Todd v. Martin, 4, 805.

In an action, tried before the court, on a note guaranteed by defendant's intestate, error cannot be predicated on the consideration of the note as evidence, on the ground that it had been altered after intestate's death, where no objection was offered to its admission on such ground, and the court found the note in the form in which it was made.—Davis v. Lamb, 5, 765.

In an action, tried before the court against an administrator on a note guaranteed by his intestate, the court's refusal to open the case after taking it under advisement, to permit the administrator to show that he demanded the production of the original note when the claim was presented to him, is a proper exercise of discretion when it does not appear that the claim was rejected because of the nonproduction of the original.—Davis v. Lamb, 5, 765.

In an action against an administrator, a former administrator of the same state was introduced as a witness. In cross-examination the decree of revocation of his letters of administration was introduced, and objected to as not being proper cross-examination and as irrelevant and immaterial. No part of the evidence in chief was set out, and the bill of exceptions did not set out the decree of revocation. Held, that the appellate court cannot pass upon this exception.—Watson v. Miller, 6, 316.

§ 31. —— Attorneys and Their Fees.

In an action to recover attorneys' fees for services rendered in an action in which defendant was named as defendant both individually and as executrix, though not a necessary party thereto, it appeared that she made no claim in such prior action in her individual capacity, and she testified that she employed plaintiff merely as attorney for the estate, but this plaintiff denied. The property received by defendant in settlement of the prior action was applied to the benefit of the estate of which she was executrix, and plaintiff received an allowance from the estate for his services, under order of court. Held, that a finding that plaintiff was not employed by defendant in her individual capacity was proper.—Malville v. Kappeler, 4, 843,

In such an action the inventory filed by the executrix, who was the wife of the testator, would not determine whether certain premises were separate or community property, and was therefore inadmissible for that purpose.—Malville v. Kappeler, 4, 843.

Code of Civil Procedure, sections 1597–1599, provides that, when a person who is bound by contract in writing to convey any real estate dies before making the conveyance, the court, after a hearing in which all interested parties may appear, may decree that his executor or administrator convey such realty to the person entitled thereto; and section 1664 declares that in all estates any person claiming to be an heir to the deceased may file a petition in the estate to ascertain and declare the rights of all persons to the estate, in which petition the name of the administrator shall be set forth, and a notice served on him. In the settlement of an estate, a nephew of the deceased claimed the entire estate by virtue of a promise made by the deceased to leave the claimant the property in consideration of certain services. Held, that the administrator was a proper, if not necessary, party, under either theory of the action, and hence the attorneys for the estate could not act as the attorneys for the claimant.—In re Healy's Estate, 6, 780.

Where an administrator knew that his attorneys had been retained by one of the heirs to prosecute a claim for the entire estate under promise of the deceased, and did not intervene in the action, or discharge his attorneys, he will be deemed to have acquiesced in the conduct of his attorneys.—In re Healy's Estate, 6, 780.

§ 32. —— Judgment.

A judgment in an action against an administrator that is entered against him personally will be corrected on appeal therefrom, as the error is one that is apparent on the judgment-roll.—Davis v. Lamb, 5, 765.

A judgment in an action against an administrator that is made immediately enforceable will be corrected on appeal therefrom so as to make it payable "in due course of administration," as required by Code of Civil Procedure, section 1504, as the error is one that is apparent on the judgment-roll.—Davis v. Lamb, 5, 765.

Judgment against one as administrator is invalid, he having been removed after submission of the cause, but before judgment, notwithstanding pendency of his appeal from order of removal. It may, however, be entered against him nunc pro tunc, as of the date of submission.—More v. Miller, 6, 78.

§ 33. Accounts and Accounting—Items Allowable.

Expenses incurred by the widow before she was appointed administratrix, and not apparently for the benefit of the estate, are not chargeable against it.—Todd v. Martin, 4, 805.

Where an executor stated in his petition for the probate of the will that a part of the estate consisted of a sum of money in his hands, and he died without rendering an account, a finding that such sum came into his hands while acting as executor is justified.—Raskin v. Robarts, 4, 465.

§ 34. —— Absence of Vouchers.

Where, on the settlement of an administrator's account, items aggregating more than $1,500 are allowed, for which no vouchers are produced, and as to which no testimony is given when, where or to whom the payments were made, held to be error.—Estate of Van Tassel, 2, 435.

Where an executor, in his final account, stated that all the money of deceased went into the hands of his coexecutor, and was used in settlement of the estate, and all the legatees interested stipulate that the account of the latter is correct, it is not error to allow the latter's account without vouchers.—In re Coursen's Estate, 6, 756.

§ 35. —— Settlement of Proceedings Therefor.

If an executor gives notice of the filing of his final account and of a day fixed for its settlement, this would mean filed for final settlement, and would mislead nobody; so too a notice given that with such final account a petition for distribution is filed; this would mean for final distribution.—Dean v. Superior Court, 2, 146.

A probate court has the power, in the settlement of an executor's account, to allow or disallow any items in the account, even though there is no contest; and, where it is brought to the knowledge of the court that the executor has failed to charge himself with money or property belonging to the estate, it is the duty of the court to examine the matter of its own motion.—Estate of Sanderson, 2, 750.

Evidence held insufficient to justify the decision and findings.—Estate of Feeley, 2, 314.

An administrator, in settling his accounts, presented a voucher signed by deceased's widow for payments alleged to have been made her in pursuance of an order granting her a certain amount as a family allowance. Held, that a creditor of the estate could not object to the allowance of the voucher as a credit on the ground that the amount covered by it had not been actually paid the widow.—In re Fisher's Estate, 5, 168.

An order in probate court settling the first annual account of executors, which strikes out certain items for sums paid to experts and detectives in investigating an alleged fraudulent claim against the estate, on the ground that the court is unable to examine such items because the executors object to disclosing the particulars for fear of defeating their object, is not erroneous, where leave is given to restate such items in some future account.—Murdock's Estate, 6, 70.

§ 36. —— Appeal and Review.

The action of the superior court in declaring void a decree of settlement of account, distribution and discharge, and in setting aside the decree, is not subject to appeal but writ of review.—Dean v. Superior Court, 2, 146.

An appeal cannot be taken from an order of the probate court refusing to postpone the final decree.—In re Burdick's Estate, 5, 6.

An executor, who has appealed from all of a decree made in the final settlement and distribution of the estate, except that part settling such executor's account with the estate, cannot, on such appeal, object that the funds in his hands were found to be community property, and distributed accordingly.—In re Burdick's Estate, 5, 6.

Persons claiming to be trustees of a devised estate, but who are neither heirs, devisees nor legatees, and who have presented no claim against the estate, cannot appeal from a decree rendered in the final settlement of the estate.—In re Burdick's Estate, 5, 6.

Where, in an action for an accounting, brought by a widow against the administrator of the estate of plaintiff's husband, the evidence is conflicting as to whether defendant paid certain claims with his own money, or out of the funds of the estate of plaintiff's husband, a judgment disallowing defendant's claim will not be disturbed.—Sanguinetti v. Gianelli, 6, 489.

Where the evidence warrants a finding that an executor did not pay certain taxes charged in his account, and for which he produced receipts, the order disallowing such charges should not be reversed.—In re Coursen's Estate, 6, 756.

It is only necessary for an executor to serve notice of appeal from an order settling his account on the persons who appeared and contested the account.—In re Scott's Estate, 7, 187.

§ 37. Determination of Heirship—Illegitimates.

On an issue whether petitioner was testatrix's illegitimate daughter, the exclusion of evidence that testatrix had never mentioned having any daughter was not prejudicial where petitioner not only made no claim that testatrix had ever recognized her as her daughter, but produced evidence that she had not.—In re Kennedy's Estate, 4, 671.

§ 38. Distribution of Estate.

Where a decree of the probate court distributed to certain trustees the legal title to an undivided one-third of certain property, "that is to say, ... one-third of the aggregated value of all the six items hereinafter specified," and contained a statement of such items, together with the amounts thereof, the values of the various items were thereby fixed.—Hinckley v. Stebbins, 3, 478.

A distribution of a part of a devised estate to trustees, at the special request of the sole devisee, will not be declared void on appeal because the record fails to show that such trustees established a legal claim to the property.—In re Burdick's Estate, 5, 6.

The probate court has jurisdiction to declare certain property devised to testator's son to be community property, and to distribute it to the wife, who is not a legatee or devisee.—In re Burdick's Estate, 5, 6.

A decree of the superior court, in a probate proceeding, making division of the property of a testator in accordance with a petition and stipulation of the widow and residuary devisee, filed with the final account of the executors, and without notice to other parties in interest, does not affect the rights of a prior grantee of the widow, by deed conveying her interest in community property, who was not a party to the proceedings, though such decree set off the property in severalty to other devisees. Such a decree can, in any event, extend only to the succession or testamentary rights in the property.—William Hill Co. v. Lawler, 5, 410.

Under Code of Civil Procedure, section 1665, providing that on the final settlement of the accounts of the executor, or at any subsequent time, the court may proceed to distribute the residue of the estate, the court has not jurisdiction to decree distribution of the estate on a petition filed after the final account was filed, but before it was settled; nor is such decree authorized by section 1663, which relates only to partial distribution.—In re Coursen's Estate, 6, 756.

Where testatrix devised to her son all her interest in the estate owned by his father, her first husband, and the remainder of her property to her second husband and his children, a final decree distributing certain specific property to the latter "and any other property not now known or discovered which may belong to said estate, or in which it may be interested," is erroneous, since such provision might carry any after-discovered property belonging to her first husband.—In re Coursen's Estate, 6, 756.

A legatee is not prejudiced because property in which he has no interest is improperly distributed by the final decree.—In re Coursen's Estate, 6, 756.

§ 39. —— Payment of Taxes.

Political Code, section 3752, providing that decree of distribution of an estate shall not be made until the taxes are paid, is to protect the revenues of the state, and has no application where the tax has in fact been paid, though the one who made the payment has a tax title to the property therefor.—In re Coursen's Estate, 6, 756.

§ 40. —— Setting Aside and Appeal.

An executor cannot appeal from a final decree on the ground that the property is improperly distributed.—In re Coursen's Estate, 6, 756.

If in an action to set aside a decree in distribution the court, after finding that the defendant procured the decree without notice to the plaintiff and without any appearance or knowledge on his part, finds that a named person "assumed to represent plaintiff at said hearing and making of said decree of distribution," and finds again that plaintiff was not represented at the hearing, the findings are too contradictory to base a judgment upon.—Baker v. Riordan, 2, 179.

EXEMPTION.
See Execution, § 2.

EXPERT TESTIMONY.
See Evidence, § 18.

EXPLOSION.
§ 1. Liability of Corporation for Act of Employee.

A corporation keeping five thousand pounds of gunpowder in a magazine is liable for the damages occasioned to near-by dwellings by an employee maliciously setting fire to the gunpowder, the maintenance of the magazine being a nuisance.—Kleebauer v. Western Fuse and Explosives Co., 6, 933.

EX POST FACTO LAW.
See Constitutional Law, § 7.

EXTRADITION.
§ 1. In General.

Where, from the return to a writ of habeas corpus on behalf of a prisoner held under requisition proceedings, it appears that the proceedings are regular, and that the act of Congress concerning fugitives from justice has been substantially complied with, the prisoner will be remanded.—Ex parte Bailey, 2, 248.

FACTORS.
§ 1. Contract of association with fruit company.
§ 2. Liability in case of sale under guaranty.
§ 3. Repudiation by purchaser because of absence of guaranty.
§ 4. Lien—Conversion.
§ 5. Lien for advances.

§ 1. Contract of Association With Fruit Company.

An association contracted with a fruit company to deliver No. 1 fruit f. o. b., and the company was to guarantee the sale. The association also agreed to deliver to the company No. 2 fruit f. o. b., the sale of which the company did not guarantee. The fruit was picked, graded, culled and packed under the supervision of the company's agent, who receipted for it as "Sold f. o. b."; and the company's president testified that, at the time of shipment, account sales were rendered the association by the company on the assumption that the fruit was No. 1 except where "otherwise stated." Held, that a certain consignment, not shown to be within the exception. was accepted by the company as No. 1 fruit.—Tustin Fruit Assn. v. Earl Fruit Co., 6, 37.

A fruit company contracted with an association to take from it No. 1 fruit, "guaranteeing original sales and collections; it being understood that all responsibility" of the association "ceases when said fruit is accepted" by the company on board cars. Held, that the company, having accepted fruit as No. 1 without any representations of the association touching its quality, was bound to account for that quality of the fruit, although, through a latent defect, the fruit proved to be inferior.—Tustin Fruit Assn. v. Earl Fruit Co., 6, 37.

Plaintiff sued on a contract by which defendant agreed to sell plaintiff's fruit, and guarantee sales, alleging that plaintiff "sold and delivered" at a certain place a stated amount of fruit, which was picked, packed and loaded "by plaintiff under the inspection and approval of the defendant, and was received, accepted, and receipted for by defendant at the prices mutually agreed upon by plaintiff and defendant for said fruit," and setting forth the amount unpaid from defendant to plaintiff for said fruit. Held, that the allegation, taken in connection with the contract, showed a sale by defendant, as a factor, for plaintiff, for which it was liable under its contract of guaranty.—Tustin Fruit Association v. Earl Fruit Co., 6, 37.

A fruit company agreed with an association not to handle the fruit of those who were not members of the association, without its consent. The association, in an action against the company, alleged that under that provision in the contract the company had agreed to pay plaintiff a certain price for each box belonging to a certain fruit-raiser, stating the number thereof; that defendant had begun to buy or ship the same; and that plaintiff was entitled to recover of defendant, "by reason of the agreement relating to the handling" of said fruit, a stated amount. Held, that the allegation was sufficient against a general demurrer, though it was not alleged that such fruit-raiser was not a member of the association, or that defendant in fact "handled" his crop.—Tustin Fruit Assn. v. Earl Fruit Co., 6, 37.

§ 2. Liability in Case of Sale Under Guaranty.

Under Civil Code, section 2029, providing that "a factor who charges his principal with a guaranty commission upon a sale, thereby assumes absolutely to pay the price when it falls due, as if it were a debt of his own," and section 1794, providing that the obligation of a factor who undertakes, for a commission, to sell merchandise and guarantee the sale is original, and need not be in writing, a factor selling under a guaranty of sales becomes liable absolutely for the price, and a finding that it was the purchaser is immaterial error.—Tustin Fruit Assn. v. Earl Fruit Co., 6, 37.

§ 3. Repudiation by Purchaser Because of Absence of Guaranty.

Where merchandise brokers present to purchasers a memorandum of the sale, or "bought note," which is accepted by them, the latter cannot repudiate the sale seven days after part of the goods are shipped, and two days after they receive invoices of such shipment, because the sellers did not give a certain guaranty required by the purchaser's contract with the brokers.—Numsen v. Levi, 4, 631.

§ 4. Lien—Conversion.

Defendant agreed to sell plaintiff's wine at a certain net price, the excess to be divided equally between them. After receiving a part thereof, and making advances to plaintiff thereon, and paying freight, in accordance with the agreement between them, defendant refused to receive any more; and, before any of the wine had been sold, plaintiff demanded a return of that which defendant had re-

ceived, without offering to pay back the money which defendant had
advanced and expended for freight. Held that under Civil Code,
sections 2026, 3051, 3053, defining a factor, and giving him a lien
on the property placed in his hands for money advanced and expended, defendant was a factor, and had a lien on the wine, and a
right to retain it, so that his refusal to comply with the demand did
not constitute a conversion.—Lehmann v. Schmidt, 3, 187.

§ 5. Lien for Advances.

Recovery for property consigned to defendant for sale cannot be
defeated on the ground that he had a lien thereon for advances and
expenses, where, before action, plaintiff tendered the amount of
these. Civil Code, section 2905, declaring that redemption from a lien
is made by offering to do that for which the property is a security.—
Miller v. Price, 4, 983.

Commissions cannot be had for making a sale which the person
was not authorized to make, and which the owner rescinded.—Miller
v. Price, 4, 983.

FALSE PRETENSES.
§ 1. In General.

Penal Code, section 1110, provides that if a false pretense was expressed in language, unaccompanied by a false token or writing, or
by some note or memorandum thereof in writing subscribed by the
defendant, there can be no conviction, unless the pretense is proved
by the testimony of two witnesses. The information charged that
defendant falsely represented that he owned the goods and fixtures
in his place of business, and that he was not indebted to any person,
and by means thereof obtained the goods in question. Held, that
as but one witness testified to the pretense, and there was no token
or writing given or shown, there could be no conviction.—People v.
Chrones, 7, 183.

FALSE TELEGRAM.
Offense of sending. See Telegraph Companies, § 2.

FAMILY ALLOWANCE.
See Executors and Administrators, § 13.
Is a "claim or demand" against estate. See Wills, § 4.

FARMING ON SHARES.
See Crops, §§ 1, 2.

FAST DRIVING.
Liability therefor. See Negligence, §§ 5, 6.

FELLOW-SERVANTS.
See Master and Servant, § 10.

FENCES.
Injunction against removal. See Injunctions, § 6.
Bond to build along railway. See Railroads, § 6.
Absence of along railway. See Railroads, § 7.

FERRIES.
§ 1. Franchise—Nonuser and Forfeiture.

Under an act granting a ferry franchise and providing for forfeiture in default of the establishing of the ferry by the grantee

within a time named, a failure to establish the ferry within that time would ipso facto operate as a forfeiture and needs no judicial proceeding to declare the fact and effect.—Upham v. Hosking, 2, 134.

§ 2. Breach of Covenant to Operate.

A covenant in a lease that premises should be used in good faith, continuously, during the existence of the lease, for the usual and ordinary business of a ferry (a boat having theretofore made regular daily trips therefrom), held to be broken by failure to operate the ferry during a period of twenty-nine days.—Heywood v. Berkeley Land & Town Imp. Assn., 2, 658.

FICTITIOUS.

Issue of stock. See Corporations, § 22.

FICTITIOUS NAME.

Judgment against person by. See Judgments, § 5.
Action against parties in. See Parties, § 2.

FINDINGS.

In general. See Trial, §§ 20–29.

FIRE INSURANCE.

See Insurance.

FIRES.

Liability of railway for starting. See Railroads, § 13.

§ 1. Treble Damages.

Since Political Code, section 3344, providing for treble damages to the party injured by the negligent setting out of fires, is silent as to whether the jury shall find such damages, or whether they shall find the actual damage, and the court shall enter judgment for three times such amount, it is immaterial which course is pursued, provided absolute certainty is attained, and this can be secured by preparing the form of verdict.—Galvin v. Gualala Mill Co., 3, 869.

FISHING TACKLE.

Seizure and destruction. See Constitutional Law, § 3.

FIXTURES.

Removal of buildings. See Buildings, § 1; Improvements.

§ 1. Engine and Machinery.

Where a tenant of real property, with the permission of the owner, erects an engine and boiler on a foundation made of brick and of timbers sunk into the ground, and attaches such engine and boiler and machinery to a building which is part of the realty by means of bolts and screws which are easily removed, quaere, whether such boiler and engine constitute real or personal property.—McNally v. Connolly, 2, 621.

§ 2. Houses and Buildings.

Houses built on mud-sills resting upon the soil, which is not disturbed, are affixed to the land within the terms of Civil Code, section 660, declaring that "a thing is deemed to be affixed to the land when it is .... permanently resting upon it, as in the case of buildings."—Miller v. Waddingham, 3, 375.

Such houses built by a contractor for a vendee in possession, who has paid part of the price for the land, and who, being unable to pay for the houses, turns them over to the contractor, cannot be removed from the freehold by the latter. Distinguishing Hendy v. Dinkerhoff, 57 Cal. 3.—Miller v. Waddingham, 3, 375.

A vendee who has not paid the entire purchase price cannot claim the right to remove houses built by him on the land on the principle that, since equity regards that as done which ought to be done, he should be deemed the trustee of the purchase money for the vendor, and the equitable owner of the land, with the right to deal with it as he pleases.—Miller v. Waddingham, 3, 375.

A vendee who, while in possession under an executory contract of purchase, has built houses on the land before paying the entire purchase price, may be enjoined by the vendor from removing them.— Miller v. Waddingham, 3, 375.

FORCIBLE ENTRY AND DETAINER.

§ 1. In General.

Forcible entry and detainer is a proceeding highly penal in character, and must be confined to cases specified in the statute.—Frisbie v. Whitney, 1, 129.

Forcible entry and detainer may not be resorted to upon facts sufficient to justify the institution of an action of ejectment.—Frisbie v. Whitney, 1, 129.

The law will not permit a person to take forcible possession of land, even though his own, in the peaceable possession of another.— Davis v. Mitchell, 1, 206.

In an action of forcible entry and detainer the title to the land is not in question.—Davis v. Mitchell, 1, 206.

§ 2. What Constitutes.

If A attempts to build a dwelling for himself on land occupied and cultivated by B, and responds to the remonstrances of B with such words as, "I intend to stay and defend my property and will defend it by force, if necessary," and interferes with B's plowing the land, declaring his teams shall not pass unless over his body, and strikes B's mules over the nose and waves his hat in front of them to stop their progress, the facts are sufficient to justify proceedings by B against A, within the statute, for forcible detainer.— Bailey v. Weymouth, 1, 745.

In forcible detainer, it appeared that plaintiff claimed under a lease of the stubble; that he kept sheep three days on twenty acres not in grain; that fifteen days afterward he put three watering troughs on the land; that fifty-three days thereafter he returned and demanded possession of defendant, who had taken possession; and that at such time the grain was cut, but on the ground unthreshed. Held, that plaintiff did not have such possession as entitled him to recover, under Code of Civil Procedure, section 1160, subdivision 2, which provides that a person is guilty of forcible detainer who, during the absence of the "occupant" of any lands, unlawfully enters thereon, and that "occupant" means one who, within five days preceding such unlawful entry, was in peaceable possession.—Saulque v. Durralde, 4, 126.

A lease provided that on failure of the lessee to perform certain covenants the lessor might recover possession without notice or demand. After the lessee had been in peaceable possession for several months, the lessor, claiming a violation of the lessee's covenants, ordered him to leave the premises, but did not give the written notice required by Code of Civil Procedure, sections 1161, 1162. On the lessee's refusal to leave, the lessor had him arrested on a warrant charging a public offense, and during his absence took possession, without the consent of the employee in charge, and refused to surrender possession to the lessee for more than five days after demand therefor. Code of Civil Procedure, section 1160, provides that a person who, during the absence of the occupant, unlawfully enters on real property which for more than five days prior thereto has been in the peaceable possession of such occupant, and refuses to surrender for five days after demand therefor, is guilty of forcible detainer. Held, that defendant was liable under said act.—Lasserot v. Gamble, 5, 510.

In an action against said lessor by the lessee for forcible detainer it was competent to show that plaintiff was arrested at defendant's instance, for the purpose of getting away from the premises, so that defendant might enter and take possession thereof.—Lasserot v. Gamble, 5, 510.

§ 3. Jurisdiction of Superior Court.

In an action by a landlord against his tenant for $183 rent due under a lease, and, as a second cause of action, for the restitution of the same premises, which were alleged to have been unlawfully detained after the expiration of a subsequent lease thereof, with damages for such unlawful detention, judgment was rendered for the rent demanded ($183), but restitution of the premises was denied. Held, that the superior court had jurisdiction to render the judgment in question, though it was for less than the jurisdictional amount ($300) of such court, since the relief demanded in prayer of judgment was within the jurisdiction of the court.—Lord v. Thomas, 3, 424.

§ 4. Jurisdiction of Equity.

A court of equity cannot relieve a person from the consequences of a forcible and unlawful attempt to redress his own wrongs.—Davis v. Mitchell, 1, 206.

§ 5. Pleading and Parties.

In a proceeding for forcible entry and detainer by a landlord to recover possession, a complaint that fails to show the nature and duration of the tenancy under the original letting, while showing the fact of the letting, that afterward the defendant entered, that defendant holds under the person who was the tenant of the plaintiff, that demand was made in writing on the defendant on the —— day of, etc., for possession of the premises so held as aforesaid, and the defendant neglected and refused, etc., shows a possession neither tortious at the time of the demand nor made tortious afterward by the demand.—Uridias v. Morrill, 1, 125.

A complaint in an action of forcible entry and detainer is not obnoxious to a demurrer as not stating facts sufficient to constitute a cause of action which sets up the plaintiff's ownership of certain described premises, his possession thereof on a day named, the unlawful entry of the defendants thereon on that day, and their forcible detainer thereof up to the time of bringing the action. Nor is it demurrable for joining the wife of the principal defendant as a party defendant, nor because it sets out one cause of action in several distinct counts, and only describes the premises in the first one.—Porter v. Murray, 2, 687.

§ 6. Service of Process.

Under Code of Civil Procedure, section 410, providing that, when a summons in unlawful detainer is served by a person other than the sheriff, it must be returned with an affidavit of service by such person, it is not necessary that it should appear that the party making the service did so at the request of the plaintiff or his attorneys.—Block v. Kearney, 6, 660.

§ 7. Evidence, Instructions and Findings.

In forcible entry and detainer the admission in evidence of an irrelevant record affecting title is not reversible error if subsequently the court so instructs the jury as substantially to withdraw the record from their consideration.—Quinn v. Kenyon, 1, 169.

In a proceeding for forcible entry and detainer the plaintiff need not prove that he has inclosed the premises, if he can prove that he has kept them continuously under cultivation.—Bailey v. Weymouth, 1, 745.

Findings held sustained by the evidence.—Alemany v. Ortega, 2, 323.

In an action of forcible entry and detainer, where the testimony for plaintiff tends to show that on a certain day the plaintiff's agent received notice that plaintiff's tenant would vacate the premises on the following day; that on that day at 8:30 A. M., the agent was on hand to take charge of the premises, and was told by the tenant's wife that the tenant would not go out until 1:30 P. M. of that day; that at 12:30 P. M. the agent returned and found one of the defendants in the house, with the windows and doors barricaded, and threatening to shoot the agent if he attempted to enter—a motion for a nonsuit was properly denied.—Porter v. Murray, 2, 687.

Where, in such an action, the findings show that, on the day mentioned in the complaint, the plaintiff was in the peaceable possession of the premises; that on that day the defendants wrongfully entered thereon, and have ever since forcibly detained possession thereof from the plaintiff; and the facts thus found, together with the admissions contained in defendants' answer, make out a cause of action alleged in favor of the plaintiff—it is no cause of complaint on the part of defendants that the court did not find the facts in as many ways as they were set out in the complaint.—Porter v. Murray, 2, 687.

In forcible detainer, under Code of Civil Procedure, section 1160, evidence of title in defendant is inadmissible.—Lesserot v. Gamble, 5, 510.

§ 8. Judgment in Chambers.

Where a judgment in unlawful detainer purports to have been rendered in open court, it cannot be attacked by an affidavit of counsel that it was in fact rendered in the judge's chambers, adjoining the courtroom, the door being open between the rooms.—Block v. Kearney, **6**, 660.

§ 9. Setting Aside Judgment.

Under Code of Civil Procedure, section 475, providing that the court must disregard any error or defect which does not affect the substantial rights of the parties, the fact that a summons in unlawful detainer alleges that plaintiff seeks to recover the amount claimed "in U. S. gold coin," while the complaint prays only for an ordinary money judgment, is not ground for setting aside a judgment entered in accordance with the prayer of the complaint, since the error is immaterial and could not harm the defendant.—Block v. Kearney, **6**, 660.

§ 10. Appeal and Review.

Where, in a case of forcible entry and unlawful detainer the court below has made findings which the evidence is sufficient to support, the findings will not be disturbed.—Gregory v. Haynes, **1**, 83.

Where in an action of unlawful detainer, plaintiff has recovered by way of penalty three times the amount of rent due, it would not be proper to also allow him damages for a frivolous appeal.—Block v. Kearney, **6**, 660.

On appeal from a judgment for plaintiff in a forcible entry and detainer case, the judgment should be affirmed if the evidence is considered to have been sufficient to sustain the court's findings of peaceable possession by the plaintiff, forcible entry by the defendant during plaintiff's temporary absence, breaking in by the defendant of the doors and windows of the building on the premises, expulsion of the plaintiff from the latter by the defendant that defendant continued to withhold the premises from the plaintiff by means of threats, etc., and that the defendant's entry was without color of right.—Ewing v. Anderson, **1**, 454.

FOREIGN EXECUTOR.

Action by. See Executors and Administrators, § 27.

FOREIGN TRUSTEE.

Action by. See Trusts, § 23.

FORFEITURE.

See Constitutional Law, § 2.

Of franchise. See Ferries, § 1.
Of mining claims. See Mines and Minerals, § 4.
By vendee. See Vendor and Vendee, § 24.

§ 1. Of Right of Way.

A complaint for forfeiture of a right of way granted on condition of the construction of the road on the line designated, continuous operation of the road when constructed, establishment of stations at points to be designated by plaintiff, and maintenance of the road in good condition, which alleges that the stations were not established, that the road on its completion was not operated continuously or at all, and that it has long since ceased to be operated, and has not been kept in good condition, but has been allowed to become wholly out of repair, and that there has been a total failure to comply with the conditions, sufficiently states, as against a general demurrer, the completion of the road and breaches of the conditions.—Jones v. Los Angeles & P. Ry. Co., **4**, 755.

39

FORGERY.

§ 1. What Constitutes.

Since the assignment by a public school teacher of salary not yet earned is void, the false making of such an instrument does not constitute forgery. But if the instrument containing such intended assignment contain likewise a guaranty of payment of the sum assigned, and a provision that, if the sum is not collected by a certain time, it will be paid by the assignee, it is valid in part, and hence is a subject for forgery.—People v. Munroe, 4, 66.

§ 2. Indictment or Information.

Where an information for uttering a forged check failed to charge that such uttering was with intent to defraud any person, or that defendant at the time knew that the check was false and forged, it was insufficient to sustain a conviction.—People v. Elphis, 7, 150.

The information charged defendant with forging a note purporting to have been executed to L. by M., and also with forging L.'s indorsement, and with uttering such forged instrument. At the trial the court withdrew the charges as to the indorsement and uttering, and instructed the jury to consider only the charge of forging the note itself. Held, that, the first charge being sufficient in itself, the contention of defendant on demurrer that the information was fatally defective by the insufficiency of the other charges was without merit.—People v. Lapique, 6, 830.

§ 3. Evidence.

In a prosecution for forgery for having feloniously issued and passed to one E. a counterfeit writing as a genuine promissory note of one F., with intent to damage and defraud said E., it is not error to admit evidence of the fact that by reason of the passing of the paper E. was damaged by being induced to make a journey, and to go to expense therefor.—People v. Phillips, 2, 624.

Where defendant, in prosecution for forgery, testified in his examination in chief that he had won the check in question at a game of cards, and also testified to his arrest, it was proper, on cross-examination, to ask him if he had admitted such fact to the arresting officers or to the jail officers.—People v. Dole, 5, 934.

On a trial of forgery, testimony that witness knew of a certain fluid which would remove ink marks from white paper was competent. If such evidence was irrelevant, the admission of it was harmless.—People v. Dole, 5, 934.

On a prosecution for forgery, evidence that the party whose name was alleged to have been forged had money in bank and a house free from encumbrances, and that defendant knew him to be a man of means, is admissible to show the motive for the forgery.—People v. Lapique, 6, 830.

§ 4. Expert Testimony as to Handwriting.

Where experts testified that a check defendant was charged with forging was signed by the name charged in the indictment, and the jury so found, a conviction will not be reversed on appeal on the ground of variance, though the name appearing thereon might be deciphered slightly differently.—People v. Oubridge, 6, 241.

On a prosecution for forgery, wherein genuine specimens of the handwriting of defendant and of prosecuting witness were introduced, an expert on handwriting compared these exhibits, in the presence of the jury, with the signature to the note alleged to have been forged, and illustrated by drawings on a blackboard and by photographs the points of similarity and dissimilarity between them, and gave his opinion that the signature to the note was copied from the genuine signature of the prosecutor. There was evidence that defendant had had an opportunity to make such copy. Held, that, the genuineness of the signature being a question for the jury, the appellate court, not having the various examples of handwriting, blackboard illustrations, and photographs before them, would not say that the evidence did not justify the jury in finding defendant guilty of forging the signature.—People v. Lapique, 6, 830.

§ 5. Refreshing Memory of Witness.

On a prosecution for forgery, a witness testifying as to the forged instrument cannot refresh his memory by reference to the copy contained in the information, which he does not, of his own knowledge, know to be correct.—People v. Munroe, 4, 66.

On a prosecution for forgery, where the prosecuting witness states that he was present when the complaint was drawn by the district attorney, that they compared the copy therein of the instrument alleged to have been forged with the original, and that such copy was correct, it is proper, if the original is in defendant's possession, and he refuses to produce it after notice so to do, to allow the witness to refresh his memory as to the original by reference to the copy in the complaint.—People v. Munroe, 4, 66.

§ 6. Variance.

Where an information for forgery sets out the forged instrument as an order addressed to a city, the fact that it was in reality addressed to the auditor of the city does not constitute a variance.—People v. Munroe, 4, 66.

§ 7. Instructions.

An instruction to the jury in a prosecution for forgery that, "if the prosecution does not show or establish by proof sufficient to convince you beyond a reasonable doubt that the defendant had no authority to sign the name" of the prosecutor, "then you must acquit the defendant," taken in connection with other instructions implying that the jury must also be satisfied as to the false character of the signature and that it was made by defendant, is not erroneous, as assuming that defendant made the signature in question.—People v. Lapique, 6, 830.

On a prosecution for forgery, under an information containing three separate charges, the first of which was sufficient, the court instructed the jury to disregard the second two charges, and to consider only the first. Held, that the jury was presumed to have obeyed the instruction of the court, and their verdict of "guilty as charged in the information" was sufficient.—People v. Lapique, 6, 830.

§ 8. New Trial and Appeal.

On a prosecution for forgery, wherein the prosecutor testified that he did not sign the note in question, and two other witnesses testified that he had admitted the signature to be genuine, newly discovered evidence that the prosecutor had admitted that the signature to the note had been placed there by himself is not ground for a new trial, since it was merely cumulative and impeaching.—People v. Lapique, 6, 830.

It was harmless error to charge that defendant was guilty of forgery, if he abetted in the commission of the crime, where there was no evidence that he had done so.—People v. Dole, 5, 934.

By the withdrawal of the alleged defective charges, and the instruction given to the jury that they should consider only the charge admitted to be sufficient, any error which may have been made in overruling the demurrer to the information was rendered harmless.—People v. Lapique, 6, 830.

Under Penal Code, section 1262, providing that, if a judgment against a defendant is reversed without ordering a new trial, the appellate court must, if he is in custody, direct him to be discharged therefrom, on the reversal of a conviction for uttering a forged check, for insufficiency in the indictment, the defendant, who was in custody, was entitled to be discharged.—People v. Elphis, 7, 150.

FORMER JEOPARDY.

Plea of. See Criminal Law, § 3.

FORMER TRIAL.

Evidence at. See Evidence, § 3.

FRANCHISE.

Of ferry. See Ferries, § 1.
And forfeiture thereof. See Street Railways, §§ 1, 2.

§ 1. Right to Avoid.

The right to avoid a public grant for failure to perform a condition subsequent is confined to the government.—Santa Rosa City R. Co. v. Central St. Ry. Co., 4, 950.

A public grant cannot be avoided for failure to perform a condition subsequent, except through a court's judgment, or a legislative declaration of forfeiture, unless the statute creating the condition expressly declares that a failure to perform it will, ipso facto, avoid the grant.—Santa Rosa City R. Co. v. Central St. Ry. Co., 4, 950.

FRAUD.

§ 1. Laches in seeking relief.
§ 2. Pleading.
§ 3. Evidence.
§ 4. Presumptions and burden of proof.

In assignments. See Assignment, § 4.
As defense to action on note. See Bills and Notes, § 20.
Of broker. See Brokers, § 10.
As invalidating deed. See Deeds, § 3.
In procuring dismissal of action. See Dismissal and Nonsuit, § 4.
Limitation of actions in case of. See Limitation of Actions, § 3.
In partnership matters. See Partnership, § 12.
On part of agent. See Principal and Agent, § 8.
Representations by vendor. See Vendor and Vendee, § 14.

§ 1. Laches in Seeking Relief.

There is no stale claim disclosed and the statute of limitations is no bar if a plaintiff, in an action for relief from a fraud practiced upon her, discovered the fraud only within two months of bringing suit.—Cota v. Jones, 2, 131.

In a complaint setting out fraud and objected to as revealing delay in bringing the action, it is sufficient to refer to investigation by counsel as the means whereby the fraud was unearthed, when the plaintiff is unused to business, ignorant, and unacquainted with the language.—Cota v. Jones, 2, 131.

Equity will not entertain a cause of action seeking relief from an alleged fraud, where complainants could have informed themselves of the facts by the exercise of reasonable diligence, but delayed bringing suit for over ten years, and until after the death of all the participants in the transactions.—Burling v. Newlands, 4, 940.

§ 2. Pleading.

In a suit by a cestui que trust against a trustee, a complaint that sets out fraud and asks accordingly for a restoration of property as the relief states facts sufficient to constitute a cause of action.—Cota v. Jones, 2, 131.

In charging fraud, a complaint must state the facts constituting the fraud—at least, in a general way; and such facts must be alleged with sufficient distinctness to enable the adverse party to come prepared with evidence on the general questions of fraud which will be raised.—Fox v. Hale & Norcross Silver Min. Co., 5, 980.

§ 3. Evidence.

In such case, if the representations made by defendant were false, he cannot show that plaintiff did not rely on them by evidence that plaintiff investigated the matter for herself, and expressed herself as fully satisfied, when such investigations consisted merely in asking information from persons to whom she was referred by defendant, and who knew and could know nothing of the process, except what they were told of it by him.—Kelley v. Owens, 3, 507.

Where fraud in the purchase or sale of property is in issue, evidence of other frauds of like character, committed by the same parties, at or near the same time, is admissible.—Kelley v. Owens, 3, 507.

Fraud cannot be conjectured from the fact that defendants have been guilty of other independent frauds. The evidence must be satisfactory, within the rule stated in Code of Civil Procedure, section 1833, defining "prima facie evidence" as that which suffices for the proof of a particular fact until contradicted and overcome by other evidence.—Fox v. Hale & Norcross Silver Min. Co., 5, 980.

The admissions of questions and answers of witnesses in evidence, which assumed that certain samples of ore were fair samples, and that assays thereof were fair assays, without proof that such was the case, when the question at issue was whether they were fair samples, and whether they were properly assayed, is error.—Fox v. Hale & Norcross Silver Min. Co., 5, 980.

Evidence of the intrinsic value of stock is not admissible in an action for false representations as to value thereof, it having a well-known and fixed market value, and the inquiry having been as to this.—Price v. Spencer, Layson v. Same, 6, 72.

§ 4. Presumptions and Burden of Proof.

Plaintiff asked that an agreement made by her to convey land to defendant for stock in an iron and steel company be canceled, alleging that defendant induced her to make the contract by representing that a new method had been discovered for the cheap manufacture, at a great profit, of a superior quality of fine steel and iron, for which invention a caveat had been filed and that this company had been formed for the manufacture of steel under this process, which representations plaintiff alleged to be false, and known by defendant so to be. Held, that, as these were negative allegations but little was necessary to shift the burden of proof to the party having the best opportunities for knowledge of the facts, and that testimony of an expert that the process, as given in the caveat, would not produce steel, was sufficient to place on defendant the burden of proving the truth of the representations made by him.—Kelley v. Owens, 3, 507.

When defendants are charged with a fraudulent conspiracy for two purposes, and it is proved for one purpose, the presumptions are still in favor of the innocence of defendants of conspiring for the other purpose.—Fox v. Hale & Norcross Silver Min. Co., 5, 980.

FRAUDS, STATUTE OF.

§ 1. In general.
§ 2. Memorandum and signature.
§ 3. Part performance.
§ 4. Pleading.

Assignment of book accounts. See Assignment, § 3.
Oral agreement as to boundary. See Boundaries, § 3.
Contract of broker. See Brokers, §§ 1, 2.
Necessity of change of possession of goods sold. See Fraudulent Transfers, § 1.

§ 1. In General.

An agreement to create a lien on real estate will be void unless made in writing, subscribed by the party to be charged. It is not necessary to allege, in an action to enforce such lien, that the agreement was in writing.—Marshall v. Livermore Spring Water Co., 2, 417.

A promissory note, such as, under Civil Code, section 2309, must be in writing, is a commercial note, not a mere non-negotiable promise to pay, and the latter may be ratified orally.—Goetz v. Goldbaum, 4, 749.

Where defendant had cut wood on plaintiff's property at the instance of a third person, and claimed a payment from plaintiff by virtue of a promise to pay, made after the cutting, but defendant had stated that he would hold the wood until he received payment, and that he did not care whether plaintiff or the third party paid, such promise was within Civil Code, section 1624, subdivision 2, declaring contracts to answer for the debt of another invalid unless in writing; and such promise is not valid under section 2794, subdivision 3, providing that such promise is good where the party receiving it cancels the antecedent obligation, and accepts the new promise as a substitute.—Diamond Coal Co. v. Cook, 6, 446.

§ 2. Memorandum and Signature.

A memorandum of a contract made by the secretary of a board of directors is a sufficient memorandum in writing to satisfy the statute of frauds.—McDonald v. Noyes, 1, 866.

The fact that a contract for the sale of chattels is reduced to writing does not, under the statute of frauds, render necessary the signature of the party to be charged, where the requirement of a writing was obviated by an immediate delivery of the goods sold.—Dupuy v. Macleod, 4, 147.

§ 3. Part Performance.

Under a verbal contract for the sale of land, payment of the pur-chase money is not, of itself, a sufficient part performance to take the case out of the statute of frauds; but there must be a showing that the purchaser's continued possession was due to or influenced by the verbal contract, or that but for it he would have abandoned the premises.—Reanda v. Fulton, 1, 844.

In an action brought in 1890 for specific performance of an oral contract to convey land, made in 1886, the court found that plaintiff was in possession, and took crops off the land, during 1886 and 1887, with defendant's knowledge, and that during such time, and ever since, plaintiff claimed title under the contract; but it was not al-leged or found that plaintiff continued in possession after 1887. She never paid anything on the contract price, though she tendered the whole of it "prior to the commencement of this action." Held, that there was no such part performance as would take the con-tract out of the statute of frauds.—Eshleman v. Henrietta Vineyard Co., 4, 584.

§ 4. Pleading.

In an action on a contract, required by the statute of frauds to be in writing, the complaint need not allege that it was in writing.— Morrow v. Norton, 4, 934.

A mere reference in a plea in bar to Civil Code, section 1624 (the statute of frauds), is insufficient as a plea of such statute.—Wolfskill v. Douglas, 6, 396.

FRAUDULENT TRANSFERS.

§ 1. Necessity of change of possession of goods sold.
§ 2. —— In case of livestock.
§ 3. —— In case of transfers between relatives or partners.
§ 4. Fraudulent conveyance of realty.
§ 5. —— As between parent and child.
§ 6. —— As between husband and wife.
§ 7. —— Proceedings to set aside.

§ 1. Necessity of Change of Possession of Goods Sold.

To make a valid sale, as against creditors of the seller, it is neces-sary under the statute of frauds that there shall be an immediate and continued change of possession. If the buyer allows the seller to have the goods in his keeping after the sale and perform acts as to them and upon them consistent only with ownership, a levy upon them for the seller's debt will be sustained.—McDermott v. Apgar, 1, 149.

A sale, in order that its subject may not be open to seizure for the debts of the seller, must be followed by a change of possession.— Decker v. Cain, 1, 832.

In case of conflicting evidence as to change of possession the find-ings of the trial court will not be inquired into on appeal if there was sufficient evidence to support them.—Lawrence v. Nunan, 2, 221.

A sale of chattels not accompanied by an immediate delivery, and actual and continued change of possession, is void as against credi-tors, and the chattels, the subject of the sale, may be seized on process by the sheriff.—James v. Fulkerth, 2, 524.

Where a sale is not accompanied by an immediate delivery and continued change of possession, it is void as against the vendor's creditors.—Harter v. Donahoe, 2, 633.

In an action against a sheriff for the recovery of property attached by him as that of one C., where it is claimed that C. sold the property to plaintiff before the attachment, testimony of plaintiff and C. to the effect that on a day named prior to the attachment C. sold the property to plaintiff, taking his promissory note in payment, and gave him a bill of sale of the property, viz., saloon furniture and stock; that C. delivered to plaintiff the keys of the safe and the saloon, took his account-book, and left, and has had nothing to do with the business since, and that plaintiff has continued to own the property, and carry on the business, up to the time of the levy of the attachment; that there was but one advertisement in any paper authorized by C., and that was changed on the day of the sale by the insertion of plaintiff's name in the place of that of C.; that the advertisements that appeared in various other papers were not changed; that the sale was made in good faith; that the plaintiff was C.'s bar-tender at the time of the sale, and the business was conducted after the transfer just as it had been before, plaintiff continuing to tend bar; held, insufficient evidence of an immediate delivery and continued change of possession of the property in controversy.— Cook v. Rochford, 2, 682.

Where negotiations for a sale by an employer to his employee of certain property, including safes, were made in March, but the sale was not consummated until April 1st, upon which day the vendor was sued by a creditor, and, after the sale, the property remained in the same building as before, but the vendee's name appeared on the sign as successor to the vendor, held, that the sale was not followed by immediate delivery, and an actual and continued change of possession, as required by Civil Code of California, section 3440, and execution obtained by the vendor's creditor could be levied on the safes.— Young v. Poole, 2, 748.

The plaintiff's theory was that no change of possession was necessary if the property, at the time it was sold, was in the possession of a third party, who held it as plaintiff's agent by agreement of both parties. Defendant contended that the debtor, who was the agent's husband, had never transferred his possession as required by Civil Code, section 3440. Held, that instructions on the law applicable, if the jury should find the evidence to sustain the theory of either party, were not contradictory.—Bunting v. Salz, 3, 193.

Where there is evidence that the wagon was sold to plaintiff through her agents, it is competent to show that delivery to and possession by one agent, for plaintiff, immediately followed the sale. Bunting v. Salz, 3, 193.

Defendant purchased of a debtor a number of raisin trays in payment of a debt. The trays were not removed from the shed on the debtor's farm where they were stored, but defendant wrote his name on a large number of them, and kept a man continuously at the debtor's house to look after the trays. Held, that there was no such open and continuous change of possession as would render the alleged purchase valid as against execution creditors of the vendor.—Byxbee v. Dewey, 5, 544.

Civil Code, section 3442, makes a question of fraudulent intent one of fact. Act of 1895 makes a voluntary transfer without consideration by one insolvent, or in contemplation of insolvency, fraudulent as to creditors. Held, that the rule under section 3442 of the Civil Code was not changed by act of 1895, except in transfers of the kind specially mentioned in the act.—Roberts v. Burr, 6, 154.

As against one claiming goods under a purchase from an insolvent firm, a statement of the firm to a mercantile agency long before the sale is not admissible in behalf of attaching creditors, if no actual fraud is alleged, and the only question is whether there was an actual and continued change of possession in the purchaser.—Roberts v. Burr, 6, 154.

Civil Code, section 3440, providing that transfers of personal property by a person in possession or control thereof, unaccompanied by an actual and continued change of possession, shall be conclusively presumed to be fraudulent against the seller's creditors, does not apply to a transfer of property after the same is in possession of the sheriff under an attachment against the seller.—Lilienthal v. Ballou, 6, 179.

§ 2. —— In Case of Livestock.

In an action of claim and delivery against a sheriff for seven horses taken on attachment against plaintiff's vendor, it appeared that the sale to plaintiff was bona fide, and that there was an "immediate delivery." The evidence showed that soon after the delivery plaintiff employed a man who had been in the service of his vendor, and put him in charge of the horses; that with six of them in a team he and said vendor, with a like team, did a large amount of plowing for a third person; that while doing the plowing one of the horses of plaintiff's team was exchanged, for convenience in working, for one of the horses of his vendor's team. Held, that the evidence supported the finding that there was an "actual and continued change of possession" following the sale of the property to plaintiff.—Freeman v. Hensley, 3, 536.

In such case, evidence as to whom credit was given for the plowing done by plaintiff's team is immaterial, in the absence of an offer to show that the credit was given by his direction.—Freeman v. Hensley, 3, 536.

In such case, a witness having testified in chief that he never heard the vendor, during a certain time, make any statement as to the ownership of the property, it was proper to ask him, on cross-examination, if the vendor did not, in a particular conversation during that time, tell him the horses belonged to plaintiff.—Freeman v. Hensley, 3, 536.

Plaintiff bought from M. a mare, then pasturing on the land of one W., five miles distant. He went to take possession of the mare, but W. was not at home. On his return he met W., and then arranged with him to remove the mare a few days later, and on the day specified he placed her on another ranch, under an agreement with the manager thereof, who received and held her for plaintiff. Held, that there was a sufficient compliance with Civil Code, section 3440, providing that every transfer of personal property will be deemed to be fraudulent as to creditors, unless accompanied by an immediate delivery, and followed by an actual and continued change of possession, of the things transferred.—Cameron v. Calberg, 3, 637.

In an action to recover certain mares and colts seized on an execution against plaintiff's husband, plaintiff testified that her husband sold her sixteen mares in satisfaction of a debt. The mares were pastured on the husband's land prior to the sale, and were branded with his brand, but at the time of the sale they were brought to the corral, vented with the husband's brand, and then branded with plaintiff's brand. A bill of sale was also given, and they were then turned back on the range where they had been before, and cared for, at seasons requiring care, by men hired and paid by plaintiff. Held, that there was sufficient delivery and change of possession of the property.—Asbill v. Standley, 3, 665.

A stepfather delivered to his stepson, who had been living with him on his ranch, a lease thereof, reserving two rooms in the house thereon for himself, and at the same time gave him, for value, a bill of sale of sheep and hogs running on the ranch. The lease was never recorded, and they continued to live together on the ranch without any change in their relations or in the possession being manifest to the world. Held, that the bill of sale was void, under Civil Code, section 3440, declaring all sales of personal property void as to creditors where there is not actual and continued change of possession.—Kennedy v. Conroy, 5, 337.

§ 3. —— In Case of Transfers Between Relatives or Partners.

Where plaintiff's son in law gave to her a bill of sale of articles on his ranch, which remained there and were used by him, there was no delivery and change of possession that would defeat an attachment of the property in an action against the son in law, though, with the bill of sale, there was given to plaintiff a deed of an undivided half of the ranch, and, before the attachment, plaintiff visited her son in law.—Dorman v. Soto, 4, 621.

One partner transferred to a creditor of the partnership their stock of merchandise without the knowledge of his partner, who for a month previous had not had anything to do with the affairs of the firm. After the transferring partner had shown the new delivery boy the delivery route, he left the store, leaving it in charge of the purchaser's agent, who had been employed there for a month previous. Held, that under Civil Code, section 3440, making transfers of personal property unaccompanied by an immediate delivery, and not followed by continued change of possession, fraudulent as to creditors, the evidence was sufficient to show an actual and continued change of possession.—Stratton v. Burr, 6, 141.

A firm composed of father and son sold to the wife and mother jewelry, which was delivered to her and kept for three months in her house, where she resided with her husband and son, except when she intrusted a part of it to them to sell to obtain necessaries for the family, they returning it on failing to find a purchaser. Held, that there was an actual and continued change of possession, as against creditors.—Roberts v. Burr, 6, 154.

A mother purchased jewelry from a firm composed of her son and another, and, after keeping the property three months, delivered it to plaintiff, to be sold on commission. Held, that the employment of the son by plaintiff to assist him in his business, under a contract to which the mother was not a party, did not indicate that there had been no actual and continued change of possession in the mother, as against creditors.—Roberts v. Burr, 6, 154.

A firm sold its stock to a creditor, after which plaintiff purchased it from him, and published a newspaper notice stating that a member of the firm was his manager. Held, that as against firm creditors, who attached property of plaintiff as belonging to the firm, the notice was admissible to show the partner's connection with plaintiff's business.—Roberts v. Burr, 6, 154.

A recorded bill of sale from husband to wife of cattle, possession of which remained as before on a ranch occupied by husband and wife, but leased to him alone, is within Civil Code, section 3440, providing that a transfer of personalty, made by one having the possession or control thereof, and not accompanied by delivery and followed by change of possession, is void against the seller's creditors. Riebli v. Husler, 7, 1.

§ 4. Fraudulent Conveyance of Realty.

The transfer of a debt by a creditor to a third person, to whom the debtor afterward makes a part payment, and executes a note for the balance, constitutes the transferee the "successor in interest" of the creditor, within the meaning of Civil Code, section 3439, which renders all conveyances by a debtor, made with the intent of defrauding any creditor, void as against all creditors and their "successors in interest."—Windhaus v. Bootz, 3, 351.

A preference of creditors by an insolvent is valid.—Kennedy v. Conroy, 5, 337.

On the issue as to the solvency of the grantor at the time of a voluntary conveyance, there was evidence that he was a member of a firm whose books showed assets considerably in excess of liabilities, but that the firm shortly afterward assigned for the benefit of creditors, and that the assignee, after seven years, had been unable to reimburse himself for money advanced to pay firm debts; that judgment was rendered against the grantor on an individual debt, which he compromised for fifty per cent; that he owed several thousand dollars in individual debts, and that he owned an interest in a land speculation, the value of which was placed by witnesses at between $20,000 and $30,000, but which proved worthless. Held, that a finding that the grantor was insolvent was warranted.—Hayford v Wallace, 5, 489.

§ 5. —— As Between Parent and Child.

A gift of land by a father to his son is not void as against creditors of the father, unless the latter had not, at the time of the gift, sufficient property subject to execution to satisfy his debts.—Windhaus v. Bootz, 3, 351.

The return of an execution nulla bona five years after the making of the gift is not sufficient to establish the father's insolvency when the gift was made.—Windhaus v. Bootz, 3, 351.

Land conveyed to a father in trust for his minor son, who pays the consideration with money earned by himself, or given to him by the father, who is then solvent, is not subject to the lien of subsequent judgment against the father, so as to render his voluntary conveyance of the land, after becoming insolvent, fraudulent as to his creditors.—Hayford v. Wallace, 5, 476.

§ 6. —— As Between Husband and Wife.

Where, in an action to set aside a conveyance from a husband to his wife as fraudulent as to plaintiff, a creditor of the husband, the evidence plainly supports a finding that the conveyance was not made with such intent, a judgment for defendants, based on such finding, will not be disturbed.—Clark v. Olsen, 3, 890.

It was not error to exclude certain letters written by defendants to plaintiff, offered to show the financial condition of defendant husband, where the complaint alleged the husband's insolvency, and the answer did not deny it.—Clark v. Olesen, 3, 890.

Knowledge of the wife as to her husband's intention to defraud creditors on transferring his property to her is immaterial where she parted with no valuable consideration.—Threlkel v. Scott, 4, 346.

The fact that the wife, on receipt of the deed, promised to pay all her husband's debts, does not preclude a finding that the conveyance was fraudulent as against his creditors, since it may have been intended to give her an advantage as to the time of making payment, and thus hinder and delay creditors.—Threlkel v. Scott, 4, 346.

The fact that one conveys a large portion of his property, without valuable consideration, to his wife, knowing at the time that his debts cannot be paid without recourse to such property, tends strongly to prove that the conveyance was made with intent to defraud creditors.—Threlkel v. Scott, 4, 346.

In such an action, statements made by the grantor shortly before executing the conveyance, showing his knowledge of his indebtedness, are admissible on the question of his intention in conveying away his property.—Threlkel v. Scott, 4, 346.

A transfer of property by an insolvent judgment debtor to his wife without consideration, made after an order for his examination in supplementary proceedings had been served, and on the day before that set for the hearing, is fraudulent.—Wolters v. Rossi, 6, 266.

The day before the one set for his examination in supplementary proceedings, which was the last day in February, a judgment debtor gave money to his wife, who deposited it in a bank, which issued to her a negotiable certificate of deposit. Several days thereafter the creditor commenced an action to set aside the transfer of the money, and on the trial a witness testified that about February or March the debtor had given witness the certificate, and thereafter the latter had turned it over to another. Held, that a finding was justified that the certificate was transferred before commencement of the action.—Wolters v. Rossi, 6, 266.

§ 7. —— Proceedings to Set Aside.

In a contest between the seller of goods and attaching creditors of the buyer, if the proof is that the representations under which the goods were bought were grossly false and fraudulent and that the buyer had no intention ever to pay for them, the findings ought to favor the seller.—Martin & Co. v. Levy, 1, 514.

A conveyance fraudulently obtained, in deference to which the probate court has distributed the grantor's share of the estate to the grantee, does not estop the grantor, proceeding without undue delay, to sue for a restoration, setting out the fraud in his complaint.—Cota v. Jones, 2, 131.

Evidence held sufficient to justify a finding that plaintiff's title was derived under a fraudulent sale, and void as to creditors.—Wideman v. Franks, 2, 288.

In an action to set aside fraudulent conveyances, a complaint which does not sufficiently state the facts constituting the fraud, and does not show that plaintiff would have been injured thereby, is demurrable.—Fox v. Dyer et al., 3, 139.

In an action for the conversion of merchandise levied on under an execution on a judgment against S., the answer alleged "that the defendant is informed and believes, and, upon such information and belief, so avers the fact to be, that, ... while said S. was so as aforesaid engaged in business, and while he was so as aforesaid indebted, he, said S. and the plaintiff, who is his brother, conspired together for the purpose, and with the intent, to hinder, delay, and defraud the creditors of said S. out of their just debts and demands against him, said S.; and with such purpose and intent said S. made a pretended false and fraudulent sale of the property mentioned in plaintiff's complaint . . . . to the plaintiff; and with such purpose and intent the said plaintiff received said pretended false and fraudulent conveyance; and thereupon said plaintiff took possession of said property, and so held the same, and not otherwise." Held, that defendant could not prove fraud, under the answer, as it merely alleged a conclusion.—Sukeforth v. Lord, 3, 238.

In an action to set aside a conveyance as in fraud of creditors, an allegation in the complaint that the grantor was insolvent when the conveyance was made, and that it was done with intent to defraud creditors, is sufficient, without specifically stating the manner in which the fraud was accomplished, and the conduct and acts in reference to it.—Threlkel v. Scott, 4, 346.

The mere fact that the parties to a conveyance contradict each other in some particulars will not warrant a reversal of the trial court's finding that the conveyance was not fraudulent.—Smith v. Ellis, 4, 469.

Where the controlling issue was whether or not a certain conveyance was fraudulent as to creditors of the grantor, and there was abundant evidence to support the findings of the court, the conclusion drawn therefrom was not open to review, on appeal from an order denying a new trial and from a judgment in accord with such findings.—Fitzgibbon v. Laumeister, 5, 935.

In an action to restrain the sheriff from selling certain real estate on execution against plaintiff's grantor, the court did not err in denying a nonsuit, where plaintiff rested on the introduction in evidence of the deed to him, and it appeared that the execution creditor made no claim to the property, except such as was derived from such grantor subsequent to the date of such deed.—Fitzgibbon v. Laumeister, 5, 935.

FRIVOLOUS.

Appeals. See Appeal and Error, §§ 73-76.

FRUIT.

Sale of. See Sales, §§ 11, 13, 16.

FUND COMMISSIONERS.

§ 1. Salary.

The provision in statutes of 1861, section 1, page 554, making the salaries of fund commissioners "full compensation for all official services required of them by law," refers to services of such persons as officers of the city government, and not as fund commissioners.—Paxson v. Hale, 1, 471.

Unless the provision in Statutes of 1861, section 1, page 554, making the salaries of fund commissioners "full compensation for all official services required of them by law" refers to services not merely ex officio, there is no authority for these commissioners to be paid at all.—Paxson v. Hale, 1, 472.

FUTURE ADVANCES.

Mortgage to secure. See Mortgages, § 4.

GAME.

Destruction of fishing tackle. See Constitutional Law, § 3.

§ 1. Regulations for Protection.

Constitution, article 11, section 11, authorizing any county, city, or town to make and enforce within its limits such local police regulations as are not in conflict with general laws, delegated to the county supervisors, prior to the passage of constitution, amendment, article 4, section 25½, authorizing the legislature to divide the state into game districts, the power to legislate for the complete protection of wild game within the bounds of their respective counties.— Ex parte Prindle, 7, 223.

Constitution, amendment, article 4, section 25½, authorizing the legislature to provide for the division of the state into fish and

INDEX.

game districts and enact appropriate laws for the protection of fish
and game therein, is to be construed with other sections of the constitution relative to the uniform application of the laws and the
delegation of police power, and in such construction the more specific
provision controls the general, without regard to the comparative
dates, the different sections operating together, and neither working
the repeal of the other.—Ex parte Prindle, 7, 223.

Constitution, amendment, article 4, section 25½, authorizing the
legislature to provide for the division of the state into fish and game
districts and to enact appropriate laws for the protection of fish
and game therein, prevails over earlier conflicting provisions of the
constitution; and, while laws previously in force continue in force
until substituted by new legislation, legislation subsequently adopted
must be in harmony with the amendment.—Ex parte Prindle, 7, 223.

Constitution, article 4, section 25½, providing that the legislature
"may" provide for the division of the state into fish and game districts and "may" enact appropriate legislation for the protection of
fish and game therein, is mandatory, and commands the legislature to
enact necessary legislation touching the care and custody of game
with reference to local conditions, which require special legislation
for particular localities.—Ex parte Prindle, 7, 223.

Under constitution, amendment, article 4, section 25½, requiring
the legislature to provide for the division of the state into fish and
game districts and to enact appropriate legislation for the protection
of fish and game therein, any previous authority existing in the legislature to delegate legislative power in reference to fish and game to
counties is revoked, and, notwithstanding the failure of the legislature to obey the mandate of the constitution, a board of county
supervisors is without authority to regulate, by ordinance passed
after the adoption of such amendment, the hunting of game within
the limits of the county.—Ex parte Prindle, 7, 223.

In view of the provision of Penal Code, section 626a, making it
a misdemeanor to hunt, kill or destroy doves between February 15th
and July 1st of the same year, a county ordinance declaring it
unlawful to hunt or destroy doves within the limits of the county
between the thirtieth day of June and the fifteenth day of August
of each year, and between the fifteenth day of August and the sixteenth day of February of the year next ensuing, and thus leaving
but one day in the year open to hunt doves, is unreasonable.—Ex
parte Prindle, 7, 223.

GAMING.

§ 1. Gambling Games and Devices.

It is not a crime, under Penal Code, section 330, making it an
offense to operate any banking or percentage game played with any
device "for money, checks, credit or other representative of value,"
to set up and operate a slot machine on which games are played,
unless played for money, checks, credits or other representative of
value, and, if played for something not included in these words, it
is not a crime.—Ex parte Williams, 7, 301.

Penal Code, section 330, making it an offense for anyone to operate
any banking or percentage game played with any device for money,
checks, credit or other representative of value, adopted in 1872,
prior to the existence of cigar slot machines, when considered in
connection with section 331, prohibiting the use of any house for
gambling, prohibited by section 330, and section 4, providing that
the Penal Code is to be construed according to the fair import of its
terms, does not make it an offense to operate a slot machine on which
games are played for cigars.—Ex parte Williams, 7, 301.

GARNISHMENT.

§ 1. Of Board of Education.

A board of education is not subject to garnishment.—Board of Education v. Blake, 4, 891.

GAS BILLS.

Liability of tenant. See Landlord and Tenant, § 6.

GAS PLANT.

§ 1. Action to Recover for Installing.

In an action to recover the contract price for installing apparatus in gasworks, it was not necessary to prove any demand, since the bringing of the action was a sufficient demand.—Sims v. Petaluma Gaslight Co., 6, 540.

Where the contract set out in the complaint, in an action for placing apparatus for the manufacture of gas in a gasworks, did not show a stipulation that the cost of materials for the manufacture of gas should not exceed a certain sum, and the answer did not deny that the contract was as alleged, a finding that the plant was completed according to the contract would not be reversed on appeal, on the ground that the evidence failed to show that the plant would produce gas at the agreed cost.—Sims v. Petaluma Gaslight Co., 6, 540.

Where, in an action for installing a gas plant, the contract having required the apparatus to produce three thousand feet of gas per hour of a certain candle-power, the evidence was conflicting, a finding for plaintiff would not be reversed on appeal.—Sims v. Petaluma Gaslight Co., 6, 540.

In an action to recover for installing apparatus for the manufacture of gas in a gasworks, evidence as to whether the plant added anything to the value of the original plant was immaterial.—Sims v. Petaluma Gaslight Co., 6, 540.

GIFTS.

§ 1. In General.

A voluntary promise on the part of a husband to assign a life insurance policy to his wife, without delivery of possession of the policy, does not constitute a gift to the wife, so as to serve as a valuable consideration for a note subsequently given by the husband to the wife for the proceeds of the policy, which were collected and used by him.—Hayford v. Wallace, 5, 489.

A person about to undergo a surgical operation, the result of which was uncertain, transferred all her property to defendant, the real estate being conveyed by deed in due form, and the personal property, consisting of furniture, notes, clothing, etc., being transferred by a bill of sale, but no physical change in possession taking place. The intention was that the property should be used for the donor's benefit, and remain in her possession during her life, and, in the event of her death from the operation, defendant was to distribute it according to the directions of an unsigned written memorandum. Held, the donor having retained possession, and the right to expend as much of the personalty as she might need during her life, that the transaction was void as a gift.—Knight v. Tripp, 5, 735.

An owner of stock in a building association gave to the secretary thereof a list of the persons to whom she wanted the stock assigned, and assignments were made on the back of the certificates. The secretary was given possession of the certificates subject to the owner's order, and told to hold them until the owner's death, and then deliver them to the assignees. A few months afterward the owner died. Held, that title did not vest in the assignees, but remained in the owner.—Noble v. Learned, 7, 297.

§ 2. Undue Influence and Incompetency.

Where an attempt is made to avoid a gift on the ground of mental incompetency and undue influence, a finding that there was no incompetency or undue influence is sufficient, without finding as to the donor's physical condition or other facts stated as inducement to the ultimate facts.—Wheelock v. Godfrey, 4, 399.

GOODWILL.

§ 1. Sale and Action for Breach.

Defendant sold to plaintiff the goodwill of his "saddlery, harness, and carriage trimming business," and agreed not to enter a like business in the same place while plaintiff, or anyone deriving title to the goodwill from him, was engaged in such business. Later he engaged in a general merchandise business in that place, and, among other things, sold horse blankets, buggy robes and dusters, whips, and collar pads. Held, in an action for breach of contract, that evidence showing that such articles did not belong to the saddlery and harness business, but were articles of general merchandise, was admissible to prove there was no breach of contract.—Prior v. Diggs, 3, 565.

GRAND JURY.

See Indictment and Information.

§ 1. Residence of Juror.

Where, on a showing that a grand juror had a dwelling in San Francisco and lived in it during the winter, also a country seat in an outside county, where he lived during the summer and where he voted, the trial court's ruling that he was competent to be a grand juror in San Francisco will not be disturbed.—People v. Chang Wang, 1, 272.

§ 2. Legality of Jury.

An indictment is not bad because one member of the grand jury was lacking from the members of the body considering the case, he having been challenged by the person charged, and the challenge having been allowed by the court, but not so that he became no longer a member of the whole body, thus necessitating the appointment of a new member in his place.—People v. Phelan, 1, 723.

GUARANTY.

§ 1. Consideration.
§ 2. Of payment of note.
§ 3. In case of pledged wine.
§ 4. To pay rent—Assignment.

§ 1. Consideration.

A guaranty is without consideration where founded on an alleged agreement executed by officers of a corporation, when they have no authority to execute it.—Granger v. Bourn, 2, 518.

In an action by an assignee on a guaranty executed to plaintiff's husband for rent under a lease of his property making rents payable to her, plaintiff and her husband testified that the guaranty, the date of which was blank, was executed before the delivery of the lease, and as part of the same transaction. The guarantor admitted that when he signed the guaranty he did not know whether the lease had been delivered, or whether the lessee was in possession of the premises. Held, that the guaranty was good under Civil Code, section 2792, providing that, where an original obligation is entered into in consideration of a guaranty, no other consideration is necessary for the guaranty.—Cunningham v. Norton, 5, 35.

An objection of no consideration for a guaranty cannot be made where the complaint thereon alleges that it was made for a good consideration, and this is not denied in the answer.—Cunningham v. Norton, 5, 35.

§ 2. Of Payment of Note.

A guaranty of the above contract read: "I, E., do hereby guaranty the payment of the foregoing note in accordance with the conditions thereof. [Signed] E. J." Held, that the guarantors were not liable on the guaranty, as the principal's liability had never attached.— Bagley v. Cohen, 5, 783.

B. agreed in writing with R. to pay a note of R. and G. out of the proceeds of sheep mortgaged to B. by G. B. telephoned the payee that he had agreed to pay the note, and asked for thirty days' extension, which was granted on consideration of his promise. He sold the sheep, and shortly after "guaranteed full payment," and asked for another extension, and subsequently paid some interest. The sheep were attached in an action against G., and, to secure the release, B. paid the attachment debt, after deducting which, and expenses, the proceeds of the sheep were insufficient to pay the note. Held, that B. had obligated himself unconditionally to pay the note in full and had not limited his liability to the proceeds remaining after all claims against the principal were satisfied.—Bank of Lemoore v. Gulart, 6, 165.

Where a person who agreed to pay another's note, which was payable to a bank, telephoned the cashier that he had agreed to pay it, and thereby secured an extension, the bank's acceptance of the new agreement is inferred.—Bank of Lemoore v. Gulart, 6, 165.

An agreement of the maker of a note, restricting the liability of one who had promised to pay it, is ineffectual, as against the payee, where it was made after the payee had accepted the promise.—Bank of Lemoore v. Gulart, 6, 165.

§ 3, In Case of Pledged Wine.

Where wine was pledged with power in the pledgee to sell upon guaranty to the pledgors of a profit for them of $4,000, the guaranty was supported by a sufficient consideration.—Bourn v. Dowdell, 5, 820.

A contract provided "that B. should have the privilege at any time hereafter of selling the wine belonging to or hypothecated by D., at a price not less than thirteen cents per gallon." A subsequent clause provided that "the wine may be sold by B. at any price after March 1, 1893, provided that B. guarantees a profit to D. of $4,000." Held, that B. might sell before said date at not less than thirteen cents per gallon, and after said date at any price, upon guaranty of $4,000 profit to D.—Bourn v. Dowdell, 5, 820.

The guaranty was absolute, and not upon condition that the pledgee should be fully paid.—Bourn v. Dowdell, 5, 821.

40

Breach of the guaranty was not a mere offset pro tanto to a note secured by the pledge, but was a complete defense.—Bourn v. Dowdell, 5, 820.

§ 4. To Pay Rent—Assignment.

No notice of the assignment of a guaranty for rent is necessary before suit by the assignee, where the guarantor has not made any payment of rent to the assignor.—Cunningham v. Norton, 5, 35.

The assent of the guarantor to the assignment of a guaranty for rent is not necessary.—Cunningham v. Norton, 5, 35.

In an action on a guaranty to pay rent "which remains due and unpaid," it is immaterial whether the lessee could have paid the rent or not.—Cunningham v. Norton, 5, 35.

GUARDIAN AD LITEM.

§ 1. Appeal.

Where a guardian ad litem, after taking an appeal, failed to file a bill of exceptions or statement on appeal, and did not request the clerk of the trial court to certify any transcript of the record on appeal, and none was filed, the appeal will be dismissed.—In re Moss, 7, 172.

GUARDIAN AND WARD.

§ 1. Jurisdiction of probate court.
§ 2. Appointment of guardian.
§ 3. —— Appeal.
§ 5. Testamentary appointment.
§ 6. Loan of money by guardian.
§ 7. Sale or mortgage by guardian.
§ 8. Execution of lease of guardian.
§ 9. Action by guardian.
§ 10. Guardian's account—Board and care of ward.
§ 11. Release of surety on bond of guardian.

§ 1. Jurisdiction of Probate Court.

Under the judicial system in California, jurisdiction of the person and property of an infant is conferred upon the probate court.—Paty v. Smith, 1, 830.

The probate court, after having appointed an infant's guardian, has sole jurisdiction of proceedings either to settle the past or to insure the future maintenance and education of the infant. The district court has no jurisdiction to order a mortgage of the real estate of the infant.—McHenry v. Keithley, 2, 66.

§ 2. Appointment of Guardian.

The constitution of California gives the legislature of the state no power to appoint a guardian for an infant.—Paty v. Smith, 1, 830.

Determination of an issue as to the fitness of the mother of certain children to act as their guardian in a prior application for appointment is res judicata on a subsequent application between the same persons, except as to evidence of facts occurring since the former order.—In re Snowball's Estate, 7, 371.

Where certain facts offered to prove a mother's alleged abandonment of her children, as a defense to her application for guardianship, were insufficient as a matter of law to establish abandonment, objectors to her appointment were not prejudiced by the exclusion of such evidence.—In re Snowball's Estate, 7, 371.

Code of Civil Procedure, section 1751, gives to the surviving mother of infants a primary right to be appointed their guardian, which should be recognized in the absence of proof compelling a finding of her unfitness.—In re Snowball's Estate, 7, 371.

§ 3. —— Appeal.

Where an appeal in a proceeding to appoint a guardian for an incompetent, tried by his guardian ad litem, was taken by the incompetent himself, it was subject to dismissal on his application, on notice to his attorneys.—In re Moss, 7, 172.

§ 5. Testamentary Appointment.

Under Civil Code, section 241, declaring that a guardian of the person or estate of a child may be appointed by a will or deed if the child be legitimate by the father with the written consent of the mother, or by either parent if the other be dead or incapable of consent, a testamentary appointment by the father of a legitimate child having a surviving mother without the mother's consent is invalid.—In re Snowball's Estate, 7, 371.

§ 6. Loan of Money by Guardian.

Where a guardian loans the money of his ward on the sole credit of the borrower, it devolves on him to show that he acted in good faith and with due prudence, since, in the absence of such evidence, the presumption is otherwise.—In re Averill's Estate, 6, 774.

§ 7. Sale or Mortgage by Guardian.

A special act of the legislature intending to empower the mother, and as such the natural guardian, of an infant to sell the interest of such infant in his deceased father's estate, would not bestow the power intended.—Paty v. Smith, 1, 727.

Where a petition to mortgage property of minor heirs to raise a certain sum of money sets forth the items for which the money is wanted, such petition is not void on its face, though part of the items only are charges against the estate; hence a collateral attack on the validity of the petition on such ground, in a suit to foreclose the mortgage, is unavailing.—Howard v. Bryan, 6, 547.

Where an order of court authorizing a guardian to mortgage the property of minor heirs is susceptible of two constructions, one of which makes the interest of each minor liable only for his share of the entire debt, and the other makes the share of each liable for the whole debt, and the court can reasonably construe it to bind the interest of each for his share only, such construction will be given, and the order will be held valid.—Howard v. Bryan, 6, 547.

Under Code of Civil Procedure, section 1578, as amended, declaring that a mere error or irregularity in mortgaging the property of minor heirs under order of court shall not invalidate the mortgage where the mortgage is attacked in a collateral proceeding, a mortgage given without delivery of a note to the mortgagee is valid, as failure to give a note is a mere irregularity.—Howard v. Bryan, 6, 547.

§ 8. Execution of Lease by Guardian.

Where a mother was appointed guardian of the person and estate of her minor son, and on the same day presented her bond, which was approved, a lease made by her of the ward's property on the following day was held valid, though no letters of guardianship had been issued to her, and she had not taken the oath of office.—Whyler v. Van Tiger, 2, 800.

A lease purporting to be made by one tenant in common in her own right, and as the guardian of the estate of her cotenant and ward, is valid, although signed and delivered as her individual deed.—Whyler v. Van Tiger, 2, 800.

§ 9. Action by Guardian.

Though the code provides that a guardian must sue in the name of his ward, a payee of a note who is described as "guardian" may sue in his own name, in the absence of evidence of a ward or trust estate.—Sainsevain v. Luce, 4, 496.

§ 10. Guardian's Account—Board and Care of Ward.

The administrator of the estate of a deceased incompetent may contest the final account of the guardian of such incompetent.—In re Averill's Estate, 6, 774.

In proceedings to settle a guardian's account express findings are not necessary, since all facts necessary to sustain the judgment of the trial court will be presumed.—In re Averill's Estate, 6, 774.

The matter of allowance to be made to a guardian for the board and care of his ward is in the discretion of the court, and its award should not be set aside, when apparently sufficient, though there is uncontradicted testimony favoring a larger amount.—In re Averill's Estate, 6, 774.

§ 11. Release of Surety on Bond of Guardian.

Where the defendant became a surety in place of a surety on the former bond of a guardian, he and the other sureties on the former bond became joint obligors, though their contracts were contained in different instruments; and under the law, as it existed in California in 1871, a release of one of the joint obligors released all the co-obligors, and therefore, under an order releasing all the obligors on the former bond, but not including the defendant in the release, his liability ceased at the time of such release, and he cannot be held liable for any subsequent defalcation.—Spencer v. Houghton, 2, 464.

HABEAS CORPUS.

Attack on legal existence of court. See Justices of Peace, § 3.
In case of commitment in supplemental proceedings. See Supplement-
    ary Proceedings.

§ 1. In General.

The passing of sentence within two days after conviction does not entitle the convicted person to discharge on habeas corpus.—Ex parte Mess, 2, 217.

A prisoner will not be discharged on habeas corpus where, from the return of the officer having him in custody, it appears that he is held under an information in due form charging him with forgery. Ex parte Finley, 2, 389.

On application for discharge on habeas corpus, asked on the ground that petitioner was committed for obtaining money under false pretenses, without probable cause, in that the false pretenses were not proven by corroborating circumstances in addition to the testimony of one witness, as required by Penal Code, section 1110, the evidence must be taken as establishing all that it tends to prove.—Ex parte Chatfield, 4, 663.

When in habeas corpus the sheriff returns that he hold the pris-oner by virtue of a commitment to the house of correction for three years, and the commitment bears a date more than three years old, the court cannot consider an unauthenticated statement of dates when the prisoner escaped and was recaptured, and of the date when his term will end, the same being pinned to the sheriff's return, as proof that the prisoner has not in fact served his term.—Ex parte Murphy, 4, 733.

A person committed on a charge of murder will not be discharged on habeas corpus where the evidence points to him, and induces a belief that he may be guilty.—Ex parte Winthrop, 5, 56.

Habeas corpus cannot be resorted to, to obtain a speedy decision as to the validity of an ordinance, where petitioner is not in fact suffering imprisonment, or where the imprisonment terminates on the day of the hearing.—Ex parte Henion, 6, 182.

A petition for habeas corpus on the ground that the petitioner has been committed without reasonable cause, which does not set forth the evidence taken at the preliminary examination, is insufficient.—Ex parte Lapique, 7, 157.

A person imprisoned under an indictment which does not charge a public offense may obtain his discharge on an application for a writ of habeas corpus.—Ex parte Goldman, 7, 254.

§ 2. Delay in Bringing to Trial.

Though defendant is entitled to have the information filed against him dismissed under Penal Code, section 1382, which provides for such dismissal "if a defendant, whose trial has not been postponed on his application, is not brought to trial within sixty days after the finding of the indictment or filing of the information," he is not entitled to a discharge on habeas corpus until the information is dismissed.—Ex parte Strong, 3, 706.

A prisoner not brought to trial within sixty days after commitment will be discharged on habeas corpus.—Ex parte Vinton, 5, 624.

§ 3. Hearing in Supreme or Appellate Court.

Petitioner was arrested on the charge of kidnaping, and examined, and committed by the justice. He applied to the supreme court to be released on habeas corpus, pending the decision of which an information was filed against him for the same offense for which he had been committed. On the hearing of the habeas corpus before the court in bank (five justices present), evidence offered to show that the commitment was ordered by the justice on no other evidence than that petitioner had arrested a person by virtue of a warrant, and that, therefore, the commitment was "without reasonable or probable cause," was excluded (four justices concurring), on the ground that the filing of the information was conclusive as to probable cause. The case was subsequently submitted on briefs, but when it was taken up for decision it was found that, on account of the retirement of the chief justice, "the concurrence of four justices present at the hearing," required by the constitution of California, article 6, section 2, could not be had, and a rehearing was ordered, and the case resubmitted upon the original briefs. Held, that the ruling excluding the evidence was a final disposition of the question involved, and that petitioner must be remanded.—Ex parte Sternes, 3, 117.

Rule 33, providing that when the judges of a district court of appeal fail to agree on a judgment in any cause, and their opinions have been forwarded to the supreme court, that court will order such cause to be transferred to the supreme court or to another district court of appeal, to be there heard and determined, does not apply to habeas corpus proceedings; and where three of the justices fail to agree in such proceedings, as required by constitution, article 6, section 4, the writ must be dismissed.—Ex parte Oates, 7, 245.

HANDWRITING.

Expert testimony. See Forgery, § 4.
Evidence concerning. See Libel and Slander, § 4.

HARBOR COMMISSIONERS.

§ 1. Regulations in General.

Under Political Code, section 2524, authorizing the state harbor commissioners to make "reasonable" regulations concerning the management of the property intrusted to them, and to assign suitable wharves for the exclusive use of vessels, the courts may review the regulation of said commissioners, and declare them invalid, if unreasonable.—Union Transp. Co. v. Bassett, 5, 498.

Whether a regulation of the board of state harbor commissioners changing the docking place of a steamboat company, and requiring it to land its passengers and freight at a different wharf from that to which it had previously been assigned, is unreasonable, is a conclusion of law, to be deduced by the court from the facts proved.—Union Transp. Co. v. Bassett, 5, 498.

§ 2. Restraining Regulations and Resolutions.

In an action to enjoin the state harbor commissioners from enforcing a resolution requiring plaintiff steamboat company to change its landing place from the C. wharf to the M. wharf, four hundred yards distant, it appeared that nearly all the freight carried by plaintiff and its competitors consisted of wheat and flour, which the shippers generally required should be delivered at the B. and C. wharves, near which the market for produce of this kind had been established for more than ten years; that, as there was no sale for such produce at or near the M. wharf, carriers could not procure it as freight to be delivered there; that there was active competition for freight between plaintiff and another carrier, which had a landing place at the B. wharf; that said order, if executed, would discriminate against plaintiff, to its great detriment, and compel it to suspend business as a carrier of freight on that route; and that, though the C. wharf was overcrowded, there were boats, other than plaintiff's, which might be removed without prejudice to their interests. Held, that the resolution was unreasonable, and its execution would be enjoined.—Union Transp. Co. v. Bassett, 5, 498.

In an action to restrain the state harbor commissioners from enforcing a resolution requiring plaintiff steamboat company to change its landing place, the testimony of plaintiff's secretary as to a conversation with one K., in which the latter suggested that he could, for a consideration, effect a compromise, was inadmissible, there being nothing to show that K. was in any way connected with defendants, or that they authorized or knew of his proposal to plaintiff.—Union Transp. Co. v. Bassett, 5, 498.

In an action to restrain the state harbor commissioners from enforcing an order requiring plaintiff steamboat company to change its landing place, the admission of hearsay evidence tending to impugn defendants' good faith in passing the order of removal is harmless, if the court finds that the order is unreasonable, since such finding warrants the relief sought, irrespective of the motives of defendants. Union Transp. Co. v. Bassett, 5, 498.

HARMLESS ERROR.

See Appeal and Error, § 88.

HASTINGS COLLEGE.
Admission of students to practice. See Attorney and Client, § 10.

HEALTH.
Liability for tenant's. See Landlord and Tenant, § 9.

HEARSAY TESTIMONY.
See Evidence, § 9.

HEIRSHIP.
Determination of. See Executors and Administrators, § 37.

HIGHWAYS.
§ 1. Establishing by user or prescription.
§ 2. Overseers and supervisors—Work and repairs.
§ 3. Obstruction of culvert.
§ 4. Abandonment and reversion of fee.

Claim for repairs. See Counties, § 8.
Supervisors as road commissioners. See Counties, § 4.
Dedication of streets and highways. See Dedication.
Ejectment to recover. See Ejectment, § 2.
Condemnation proceedings. See Eminent Domain.
Negligent driving in street. See Negligence, §§ 5, 6.

§ 1. Establishing by User or Prescription.
Occasional travel on a road across government land, which has never been laid out, recorded or worked as a public road, will not constitute it a highway.—Sutton v. Nicolaisen, 5, 348.

The provision of Political Code, 1876, section 2619, as originally enacted, that "all roads used as such for a period of five years are highways," was repealed by act of March 30, 1874, as to all counties, though the amendment was in terms made applicable to certain counties only.—Sutton v. Nicolaisen, 5, 348.

Use by the public generally of a road for fifteen years, to the knowledge and with the acquiescence of the owner of the land on which it is located, does not show a dedication.—Hartley v. Vermillion, 7, 15.

A permissive use of a road without anything to show the owner an adverse claim, will not give a right by prescription.—Hartley v. Vermillion, 7, 15.

§ 2. Overseers and Supervisors—Work and Repairs.
Where the question of the necessity of taking land for a road was settled by a board of supervisors, it is not a question for the court to pass on.—Butte Co. v. Boydstun, 2, 699.

Under Political Code, section 2645, providing that road overseers, under the direction and supervision of the road commissioners, and pursuant to orders of the board of supervisors, must take charge of the highways in their districts, and shall employ the necessary help and keep the highways in good repair, the order of the road commissioner of a district is sufficient authority for the overseer to have repairs done on the road and material furnished therefor.—Ludy v. Colusa County, 5, 99.

A road overseer has sufficient authority to make repairs on roads and obtain material therefor, he having kept within the directions of the road commissioner, who, speaking to him in reference to work on the roads, told him not to work in excess of the funds of the district.—Ludy v. Colusa County, 5, 99.

§ 3. Obstruction of Culvert.

Where owners of land adjacent to a highway construct a system of artificial ditches, converging at a culvert crossing such highway, so as to discharge an unnatural quantity of water on the lower lands on the opposite side of such highway, the owner of such lower lands cannot dam the culvert on the highway for the purpose of protecting her lands from such overflow.—Myers v. Nelson, 5, 344.

§ 4. Abandonment and Reversion of Fee.

When land conveyed is bounded by a highway, the conveyance carries the fee to the center of the road, so that when the right of way or easement ceases, the soil becomes the absolute property of the grantee or his assigns.—Moody v. Palmer, 1, 777.

HOMESTEAD.

See Public Lands.

Action in ejectment. See Ejectment, § 3.

§ 1. In General.

If a declaration of homestead has been duly filed within the time required by statute, although after a levy in attachment, on premises occupied as their homestead by the owner and his wife from the time of their acquisition, such premises do not pass under a sheriff's deed sought to be made by virtue of the judgment and levy in the attachment proceedings.—Brunette v. Wolf, 1, 103.

Under the Civil Code, sections 1237 and 1238, subject only to the limitations mentioned in section 1239, the homestead right may be impressed upon land irrespective of the question whether it is owned exclusively, or in common, or in joint tenancy.—Hihn v. Shelby, 2, 96.

A homestead consists of the dwelling-house in which the claimant resides, and the land on which the same is situated, selected as provided by the statute (Civil Code, sec. 1237).—Grange v. Gough, 2, 410.

Where the family of an insolvent consisted of eleven persons, and his house on one lot contained three bedrooms, and on another lot was his well, cow-house, and other out-buildings, and also a building containing a wagon shop, rented out by the insolvent, and a blacksmith shop used by him, and in the unfinished upper part of the building some of his family slept, and which, when able, he intended to finish to use with his house, both lots were properly set off as a homestead.—In re Allen, 2, 834.

Where a homestead declaration contains no estimate of the cash value of the property, as required by Civil Code of California, section 1263, it is void.—Knock v. Bunnell, 3, 105.

A married man bought certain lots, terms part cash, balance on time, deed to be given on payment of balance, lots to be forfeited on failure to meet payments. He then built a house on the lots and moved into it with his family. The payments on the lots and the house were made with the community property. The wife executed and filed a declaration of homestead on the lots. Before final payments on the lots had been made, the husband assigned the contract and sold the house to plaintiff, who had knowledge of the homestead declaration, and who paid the balance of the purchase money and received a deed of the lots. Prior to the assignment to plaintiff, the wife offered to pay the vendor the amount due on the lots on condition that he would convey them to her or to her and her husband jointly. Held, that as at the time the declaration of homestead was filed the title was in the vendor, the wife acquired no rights in the property.—Alexander v. Jackson, 3, 344.

§ 2. Residence and Occupancy.

To constitute a homestead there must be actual occupancy, with intent to devote the property to the purpose of a family residence.—Meyer v. Adler, 1, 56.

A married woman owned two houses and a lot, and, while residing in one of the houses, prepared a declaration of homestead, and went into another county to visit for four months. Her husband, during her absence, occupied lodgings in a house, not on the property. While she was away, the declaration of homestead was filed. Defendant obtained judgment against·the plaintiffs, and levied on a portion of the lot, and sold it. Held, in an action by the husband and wife to quiet their title to the lot, that, as the claimants were not residing on the lot when the declaration was filed, it was not valid.—Maloney v. Hefer, 2, 819.

§ 3. Conveyance by Husband to Wife.

Code of Civil Procedure, section 1474, provides that if the homestead selected by the husband and wife be selected from community property, it vests absolutely in the survivor on the death of either spouse. A homestead selected from community property was deeded to the wife by a deed signed by the husband alone, and the wife alone deeded it to a third party. Held, that the deed from the husband did not destroy the homestead, nor the husband's right of survivorship, and on the death of the wife the husband, and not the wife's grantee, was entitled to the property.—Pryal v. Pryal, 7, 134.

§ 4. Mortgage of Property.

See post, § 9.

When the wife does not join with the husband in the execution of the instrument, a mortgage by him of the homestead is a nullity.—Morse v. McCarty, 1, 59.

Where husband and wife declare a homestead on mortgaged premises, an agreement by the payee of the secured note with the husband alone to extend the time of payment will not keep the mortgage on foot as against the homestead. That can be accomplished only by an instrument executed by both husband and wife.—Wells v. Harter, 2, 52.

§ 5. —— Foreclosure—Estate of Decedent.

The provision of Code of Civil Procedure, section 1500, that an action may be brought to enforce a mortgage or lien against the property of a deceased person where all recourse against any other property of the estate is expressly waived in the complaint, has no application to a mortgage upon a homestead, whether a probate homestead or one selected and recorded before the death of decedent.—Bull v. Coe, 2, 807.

Where a homestead has been released from the lien of a mortgage by the failure of the mortgagee to present his claim against the estate of one of the deceased mortgagors, if the right to enforce it as to any excess above $5,000 remains, the burden of proof is upon the mortgagee to show the existence of such excess.—Bull v. Coe, 2, 807.

§ 6. Abandonment.

By Civil Code, section 1243, a homestead can be abandoned only by a declaration of abandonment or a grant thereof; and the execution of a deed of the homestead absolute in form, but intended as a mortgage, is not an abandonment.—Bull v. Coe, 2, 807.

§ 7. Probate Homestead.

Code of Civil Procedure, section 1465, requires the court, if no homestead has been declared in decedent's life, to set one apart out of the common property for the use of the surviving spouse and the minor children. Section 1468 provides that such homestead is the property of the survivor, if there be no minor children; otherwise, it belongs half to such survivor, and half to such children. Held, that an order setting apart such homestead, made without notice to the minor children, cannot vest title in the widow alone, so devesting the children's interest both in the homestead use and in the inheritable fee.—Hoppe v. Hoppe, 4, 569.

Though the proceeding is in rem, the widow, as administratrix, cannot represent the children, further than to withdraw the premises from administration.—Hoppe v. Hoppe, 4, 569.

The judgment setting apart a homestead to the widow, though it recite the names of the children, does not necessarily imply that these, or any of them, are minors, nor adjudicate their interests in the premises.—Hoppe v. Hoppe, 4, 569.

If the effect of the order were to vest the fee in the widow, still she would be estopped to deny her trusteeship, as to the minors' half interest.—Hoppe v. Hoppe, 4, 569.

§ 8. —— Conveyance by Widow.

Code of Civil Procedure, section 1468, provides that, if deceased left also a minor child or children, one-half the real estate of which deceased died seised shall "belong" to his widow and the remainder to the child or children. Section 1485 provides that persons succeeding to the title of "successors to homesteads" have all the rights of the persons whose interests they acquire. Held, that a wife, having minor children by a former, deceased husband, could convey to her second husband a certain sixty acres of one hundred and seventy-five acres of land which were set apart to her and her children as a homestead out of the lands of her deceased husband.—McHarry v. Stewart, 4, 408.

§ 9. —— Mortgage.
Foreclosure. See ante, § 5.
Presenting as claim against decedent. See Executors and Administrators, § 18.

A widow's mortgage of a homestead set apart to her by the probate court for the use of the family is not void, as such homestead involves a joint use merely. Such mortgage attaches to the widow's interest, subject to the homestead use; and there being minor children entitled, with her, to such use, as well as to an undivided half of the fee, foreclosure is postponed till partition may be had, viz., when the youngest comes of age, and meantime the homestead use includes both possession and the rents and profits.—Hoppe v. Hoppe, 4, 569.

§ 10. —— Partition.

A homestead set apart by the probate court under Code of Civil Procedure, section 1465, for the benefit of the widow and minor children, will not be partitioned until the youngest child comes of age, unless the interests of the minors clearly demand it. That the minor joins in the petition, and is represented by a guardian ad litem, makes no difference, as the court will interpose sua sponte.—Hoppe v. Hoppe, 4, 569.

HOMICIDE.

Accomplices in. See Accomplices and Accessories, § 7.
Assault to kill. See Assault and Battery, § 1.

§ 1. Manner of Causing.

Where, by the evidence, it was shown that deceased while drunk had assaulted defendant, who thereupon knocked him down, and, while lying helpless on the ground, jumped with both feet on his face, from which act death ensued, held, that the killing was unlawful and felonious; that there were none of the elements of involuntary manslaughter in such act; and that the charge of the court to that effect was correct.—People v. Biggins, 2, 303.

Where one shoots a person through criminal negligence, his ignorance of the law can form no basis for acquittal.—People v. Kilvington, 4, 512.

Deceased, who was drunk, approached accused, a stranger, in a saloon, making an insulting remark, which the latter took to be addressed to himself, and, after pushing deceased away, on his second approach struck him with his fist—once in the face, and several times over the heart. Deceased was unarmed, but accused testified he had his right hand closed, and accused struck him to protect himself, though there was no showing that deceased's manner was menacing, nor that accused's violence was justifiable. Deceased died in two hours of heart rupture, which the evidence showed the blows were sufficient to cause. Held, that the killing was manslaughter, under Penal Code, section 192, making killing as the result of an unlawful act, committed without due caution and circumspection, such offense. People v. Denomme, 6, 227.

§ 2. Use of Poison.

On a trial for an attempt to poison, an instruction that such an attempt, in order to merit conviction, must be by some act independent of mingling the poison with medicine is properly refused, when it has been proved that the poison was not only so mingled but was maliciously exposed under such circumstances that the party it evidently was intended for would be likely to take it.—People v. Van Riper, 1, 352.

Where the stomach and intestines of deceased are set aside for analysis, but not sealed, and the physician who had them in charge is certain they have not been tampered with, it is for the jury to decide whether there is a doubt as to that fact; and an objection to the sufficiency of the identification, not made until after the testimony for the people is all in, comes too late.—People v. Bowers, 2, 878.

Where a druggist testifies that he had sold defendant, a physician, who is on trial for murdering his wife by poisoning with phosphorus, medicine during the illness of his wife, and says he would not put up phosphorus in overdoses for anyone but a physician, and is asked if he would then, and answers, not until he had spoken to the physician, the answer cannot prejudice defendant, as it is not proof of a general custom, nor is it claimed that he had sold phosphorus to defendant.—People v. Bowers, 2, 878.

§ 3. Shooting by Peace Officer.

The fact that the person whom defendant (a police officer) shot was being pursued by a person shouting "Stop thief," did not raise an implication that a felony had been committed, by reason of which he might shoot him to effect his arrest.—People v. Kilvington, 4, 512.

On a prosecution of a police officer for shooting deceased, who was running from a person who was shouting "Stop thief," defendant having testified that he intended to shoot over him, an instruction that act and evil intent must combine to constitute crime is properly refused, the question being whether there was criminal negligence.— People v. Kilvington, 4, 512.

Where the defense to homicide is that defendant, a constable, was attempting to arrest deceased, an instruction, "If the jury believe that defendant, when he fired the fatal shot, was lawfully attempting to arrest deceased, and intended to shoot over his head, they will find defendant not guilty," was properly modified to read, "If the jury believe that defendant had reasonable cause to believe, and did believe, that the deceased had committed a felony, and was attempting to arrest deceased, and fired the fatal shot intending to shoot over the defendant's head."—People v. Matthews, 6, 341.

An instruction that, "if the jury had any doubt about the lawfulness of the means adopted by defendant to arrest deceased, they should acquit defendant," is properly refused, as being indefinite.— People v. Matthews, 6, 341.

§ 4. Justification or Excuse.

When an act is proved to have been done by the accused, if it be an act in itself unlawful, the law in the first instance presumes it to have been intended, and the proof of justification or excuse lies on the defendant to overcome this presumption.—People v. Abbott, 2, 383.

§ 5. Right of Self-defense.

An instruction may be wrong in omitting to inform the jury under what circumstances an apparent necessity for self-defense would have justified the defendant in the killing, but if this omission is so fully cured, in the instructions given at the defendant's instance, that the jury cannot possibly have been misled to the defendant's prejudice, the error is not a reversible one.—People v. Anderson, 1, 697.

To establish plea of self-defense, and entitle defendant to acquittal, it is not necessary that the fact of danger to life and limb should be shown by the evidence beyond a reasonable doubt, and to charge the jury that such proof is necessary is error.—People v. Lee, 2, 569.

An instruction that if defendant killed deceased in resisting an attempt on the part of deceased to "murder" defendant, or an attempt to do defendant great bodily harm, then the killing was justifiable, is not fatally erroneous, as it does not tend to lead the jury to understand that an attempt to kill defendant not constituting murder would not justify the killing by defendant.—People v. Bruggy, 3, 406.

An instruction that if defendant drew his pistol with a deliberate intent to kill deceased, and that deceased saw the pistol, and, believing himself in danger of defendant, ran away, and that defendant, with intent to willfully and deliberately kill deceased, followed for the purpose of overtaking or meeting and killing him, and did meet him, unarmed, and showing no disposition to kill defendant, and defendant then and there, without believing himself in danger of losing his own life, fired, and killed deceased, then the evidence showed no self-defense, cannot be objected to on the ground that it omits the hypothesis of defendant's being in danger, or believing himself in danger, of receiving great bodily harm.—People v. Bruggy, 3, 406.

Penal Code, section 197, provides that to constitute justifiable homicide, if defendant was the assailant in a mortal combat, he must in good faith have endeavored to decline any further struggle before the homicide was committed. Held, that where one accused of murder commenced the combat, but in good faith tried to withdraw before the homicide, and was followed by deceased, who continued the combat, the fact that deceased, by reason of injuries sustained at defendant's hands, was unable to realize that defendant sought to withdraw, does not limit the right of defendant to claim that the killing was done in self-defense.—People v. Button, 4, 876.

If it was defendant's purpose in good faith to withdraw from the combat, and he endeavored to do so, it is not necessary to his justification that the conflict should have actually ceased, or that there should have been such an interval as would divide it into two different combats.—People v. Button, 4, 876.

On a trial for murder, the opinions of witnesses at the inquest that the defendant committed the homicide in necessary self-defense were not competent as direct evidence.—People v. Reed, 5, 957.

Where a defendant charged with murder was guilty of the first assault upon decedent, though the same was not felonious, it was incumbent on him in good faith to decline further struggle before he could invoke the right of self-defense to excuse the killing.—People v. Reed, 5, 957.

Where it appears that the defendant, who made the first assault, received a knife wound and retreated from the deceased, the question whether he then in good faith abandoned the combat, or whether he continued desirous to renew it on the first opportunity, was material in determining his right of self-defense, and where the evidence shows he continued ready and renewed it on the first opportunity, when the deceased was killed, it is sufficient to sustain conviction for manslaughter.—People v. Reed, 5, 957.

§ 6. Evidence.

On a trial for murder it is not error to admit testimony bearing upon the relations between the defendant and the deceased, even though at the time of the offer all the testimony connecting the defendant with the homicide may not yet have been put in.—People v. Thompson, 1, 416.

The evidence of a Chinaman cannot be admitted to prove a white man guilty of manslaughter.—People v. Harrington, 1, 768.

It is not error to allow a witness for the prosecution to testify after defendant has opened his case, when the reasons given by the court for so doing show there has been no abuse of the discretion given by Penal Code, section 1094.—People v. Bowers, 2, 878.

In a homicide case where defendant, a police officer, shot at—intending to frighten—deceased, who was running away from a person who was shouting "Stop thief!" the admission of evidence that deceased had gone to the place for a lawful purpose, though improper, is harmless, the real question being whether defendant acted with criminal negligence.—People v. Kilvington, 4, 512.

On a prosecution of a police officer for killing deceased, who was being pursued by a person shouting "Stop thief!" such person, having testified for defendant, may be impeached by evidence that, a few days before, he had a quarrel with deceased, he having testified that he never saw him before the time of the shooting.—People v. Kilvington, 4, 512.

Where it appears deceased was shot, and there is evidence that defendant, when arrested, said he could not shoot a rifle, or had not shot a gun for a long time, it is proper to admit evidence that he is an expert with the rifle.—People v. Evans, 5, 125.

Testimony to the effect that witness, on the night of the homicide, passed a young man on the road; that afterward she heard a wagon coming rapidly up behind, and soon after the sound ceased, and she heard a pistol shot; that she passed the place next morning, and saw a pool of blood; and that she had recognized a body at the morgue as the body of the young man she had passed on the road, is material, and properly admitted.—People v. Matthews, 6, 341.

§ 7. —— Sufficiency to Support Conviction.

If a physician, immediately after a stabbing affray, has examined the victim, though not thoroughly, and testified that one of the wounds was dangerous and there was a probability of its being fatal, this, together with the fact that the victim died within four days after receiving the wounds, would justify a jury in concluding that these wounds caused the death.—People v. Ah Coon, 2, 207.

Verdict of the jury, finding defendant guilty of the crime of murder, held justified by the law and evidence given in the case. Instructions held full and correct.—People v. Silvas, 2, 425.

The external marks and bruises about deceased, who was an old woman, living alone, and the condition of her clothing and person, showed she was strangled in resisting a rape. The circumstantial evidence against accused showed his presence at deceased's home; and a witness stated that accused, who had been drinking, said repeatedly that he proposed to sleep with deceased that night, or choke her to death, and on leaving witness he went in the direction of her house. Accused relied on his uncorroborated evidence, with testimony to discredit such witness. Held, sufficient to justify a conviction for the murder of deceased.—People v. Wheelock, 6, 914.

§ 8. —— Threats.

On trial for the murder of T., it was not error to admit evidence that, some time before the murder, defendant, referring to the killing of a certain girl, said that the man who killed her did not intend to kill her; that he was very sorry for killing the girl; that he meant to kill T., and would have him yet before he stopped.—People v. Evans, 5, 125.

§ 9. —— Character of Accused.

Where the question as to what the witness in a murder case had heard against the defendant was not limited to a period prior to the homicide, it was properly ruled out.—People v. McSweeney, 4, 924.

Where a witness in a murder case on his direct examination did not testify that he knew the defendant's reputation at any time, and on cross-examination his testimony tended to show that his knowledge of such reputation prior to the homicide was insufficient to quality him to testify regarding it, it was not error to refuse to allow him to further testify on the subject of his redirect examination.—People v. McSweeney, 4, 924.

Rebutting evidence showing defendant's bad reputation for truth is competent, where he testified in his own behalf.—People v. Reed, 5, 957.

Evidence showing that at the time of the murder defendant was sober is not prejudicial to defendant where he and others have testified to the same effect.—People v. Matthews, 6, 341.

§ 10. —— Character of Deceased.

A charge on a murder trial that evidence of the character of deceased, tending to show that he was a violent, quarrelsome and dangerous man, was not admitted as tending "in any way" to justify his slaying by accused, was not improper when qualified by the rest of the instruction, to the effect that the evidence of bad character was to be considered only as a circumstance illustrating the facts of the homicide,· and indicating the aggressor and the nature of the aggression.—People v. Young, 6, 634.

In a prosecution for murder, evidence is not admissible on the part of defendant as to the character of deceased for peace and quietness. People v. Munn, 2, 519.

§ 11. —— Expert Testimony.

Where the proof is that the ball from defendant's pistol entered a named spot in the victim's body, and reached without deflection another named spot, a physician, produced as an expert, should not be asked his opinion as to the relative positions of the parties when the shooting was done.—People v. Smith, 2, 59.

When it is possible for a described wound to have been made with any one of innumerable weapons, the opinion of a witness should not be asked as to which one of three weapons named to him the wound was made with.—People v. Smith, 2, 59.

In prosecution for murder, where the theory of the prosecution is that a blow struck by defendant with his fist caused the death, testimony of the medical expert is admissible as to whether, in his opinion, a blow from a man's fist could have produced the fracture which caused the death of deceased.—People v. Munn, 2, 519.

A witness who testifies that he has had experience with wounds, and is able to tell from seeing them what they were made with, though not a professional expert, may testify as to whether, in his opinion, a wound was inflicted with a dull or sharp instrument.—People v. Sullivan, 2, 552.

In a trial for murder, where the state claims the death was caused by poisoning, it is admissible to ask expert witnesses the cause of the death, when there is some evidence to support the facts hypothetically stated in the questions.—People v. Bowers, 2, 878.

It is proper to propound a hypothetical question to an expert, based on any facts of which there is evidence, though the weight of evidence may be strongly against the truth of the facts assumed, and it is for the jury to disregard the opinion if the evidence fails to establish the facts thus assumed.—People v. Bowers, 2, 878.

§ 12. —— Dying Declarations.

Where dying declarations have been admitted as evidence, the question of their credibility comes within the province of the jury, and they are to give to them such credit as, on the whole they may think them entitled to.—People v. Abbott, 2, 383.

Declarations made by deceased held to have been made under a sense of impending death, and therefore admissible as dying declarations.—People v. Abbott, 2, 383.

In a prosecution for murder, the admission of declarations of deceased, made after receiving the injury, will not warrant a reversal if they are not calculated to prejudice the defendant, although they are not properly dying declarations, nor part of the res gestae.—People v. Sullivan, 2, 552.

§ 13. Instructions.

An incorrect definition of manslaughter given by a court in charging a jury is not such an error as will avail a defendant against whom the jury subsequently in the case brought in a verdict of murder.—People v. Wise, 1, 33.

Instructions on the law of murder and malice, in the language of sections 187, 188 of the Penal Code, are sufficient.—People v. Abbott, 2, 383.

An instruction isolating a single item of evidence, and telling the jury that the fact alone of its admission was insufficient to enable it to draw conclusions in connection with other facts as to the facts it tended to establish, was error.—People v. Reed, 5, 957.

An instruction is properly refused which is based upon a state of facts of which there is no evidence.—People v. Matthews, 6, 341.

§ 14. Verdict.

A verdict of "guilty of murder in the first degree as charged" is valid.—People v. Hurtado, 2, 206.

§ 15. New Trial and Appeal.

Where, after defendant appeals from a conviction for murder, a third person confesses that he committed the crime, and that defendant is innocent, these matters not being in the record, and there being no law by which they can be for the first time presented to the supreme court, cannot be considered by it.—People v. Bowers, 2, 878.

An appeal from a judgment in a capital case will not be affirmed merely because no counsel has appeared to support the appeal by brief or oral argument.—People v. Morasco, 4, 889.

Where, in a murder case, the only dispute is as to the identity of the murderer, and there is a sharp conflict in the evidence, the supreme court will not disturb the verdict because not entirely satisfactory.—People v. Evans, 5, 125.

A verdict of guilty will not be set aside because of the erroneous admission of evidence which is not injurious to defendant.—People v. Evans, 5, 125.

The admission of evidence not affecting substantial rights of defendant and not prejudicial to the merits of his defense is not ground for reversal.—People v. Matthews, 6, 341.

The court properly granted a new trial in a prosecution for murder where the only direct testimony against defendant was that of an accomplice, and the corroborating testimony was insufficient to connect him with the commission of the offense so as to justify a conviction, even assuming that the accomplice's testimony, if true, was sufficient for that purpose.—People v. Kennedy, 7, 184.

HUSBAND AND WIFE.

§ 1. Sole Traders.

The act of April 12, 1872, did not make it essential to publish the declaration to carry on business as a sole trader.—Bernard v. Heynemann, 2, 166.

§ 2. Liability for Necessaries Furnished Wife.

In an action against a husband for necessaries furnished his wife, the complaint must allege that the goods were sold and delivered to defendant and an averment of the furnishing of such goods to the wife is not sufficient. Although a demurrer to the complaint was filed, an absence of such necessary averment may be taken advantage of on appeal.—Nissen v. Bendixsen, 2, 609.

§ 3. Maintenance of Wife—Condonation.

The act of a wife, in allowing the husband to return and cohabit with her, after she has obtained a decree for separate maintenance on the ground of desertion, amounts to condonation, although done under the impression that her refusal would furnish ground for divorce; and the maintenance, therefore, must be discontinued.—Wade v. Wade, 3, 576.

§ 4. Liability of Wife for Support of Husband.

Under Civil Code, section 155, providing that husband and wife contract toward each other mutual obligations of support, and section 176, providing that the wife must support the husband when he is unable to do so from infirmity, the wife may be required to contribute to the support of her infirm husband out of her separate estate.—Livingston v. Conant, 5, 933.

§ 5. Execution Against Husband—Wife's Property.

The testimony of a witness in regard to a conversation with the judgment creditor prior to the execution, wherein he offered to take a new note from the husband if the wife would sign it, was admissible to show that the creditor had knowledge that the property levied on was the property of the wife.—Paden v. Goldbaum, 4, 767.

In an action by a wife to recover for cattle alleged to be her separate property, but sold on execution by a judgment creditor of

41

her husband, although the evidence shows that her husband returned the stock for taxation in his name, and had the use thereof for dairy purposes, and represented to the judgment creditor that he was the owner thereof, if it appears that the stock was bought by the wife with money earned before marriage, and its increase was reserved as her property, a finding that the stock was in fact hers will not be disturbed.—Paden v. Goldbaum, 4, 767.

An inventory of a wife's separate property, filed with the recorder, is admissible in evidence, against a judgment creditor of her husband, in an action to recover her separate property seized by him on execution, though the husband's debt to him was contracted before such filing, if the levy of execution was made subsequent thereto.—Paden v. Goldbaum, 4, 767.

Where a husband pastures his wife's cattle in return for their use for dairy purposes, she reserving the increase, such use by the husband, accompanied by a representation on his part that they were his, cannot, in the absence of any such representation on her part, or any act tending to mislead one holding a judgment against her husband as to the ownership of the stock, estop the wife from setting up ownership to defeat an execution levied on the stock under such judgment.—Paden v. Goldbaum, 4, 767.

A finding that the allegations in the answer are untrue is justified when the only allegations therein are that the plaintiff, by her conduct, held out her husband as the owner of her separate stock seized on execution against him, and that, on faith thereof, credit was given the husband, and such allegations are contradicted by evidence showing that the creditor ordered the sheriff to seize the property in question, and gave a bond indemnifying such sheriff against the claim of the wife, and had constructive notice of such claim by a previously recorded statement of her separate property, including the stock seized.—Paden v. Goldbaum, 4, 767.

§ 6. Separate Property of Wife.

In an action for the possession of land, brought by a woman both in her own right and as executrix of her husband, judgment is not to be given vesting the title in her alone as her separate estate if not in accord with the documentary proof at the trial.—Harper v. Hamer, 1, 801.

Where property purchased with community funds is conveyed to the wife by direction of the husband, and with the intent that it shall become separate property, that conveyance will operate as a gift from him to her.—Wright v. Wright, 5, 119.

Where a complaint alleges the making of deeds to certain property in the wife's name, and that the property was paid for with community funds, and is community property, and the answer admits the making of the deeds, but alleges that the property was paid for with the wife's separate funds, and is her separate and individual property, there is no reversible error in a finding that the deeds were so executed by the instruction of the husband, for the purpose of vesting title in the wife, as her separate and individual property, and not as belonging to the community.—Wright v. Wright, 5, 119.

In an action by a husband to have set aside conveyances of certain realty to his wife, and to have the property declared community property, the complaint also alleging desertion of him by the defendant, judgment will not be reversed for want of a finding on that particular issue, the court having found that the property was the wife's separate estate.—Wright v. Wright, 5, 119.

The presumption that property conveyed to a married woman becomes her separate estate is not conclusive.—Santa Cruz Rock Paving Co. v. Lyons, 5, 260.

§ 7. Community Property.

Disposal by will, power of sale. See Wills, §§ 6, 7.

A husband and wife occupied a tract of land belonging to the United States from 1847 until 1856, when the wife died. The husband continued to occupy the land until 1871, when he received a deed to it from the town of Santa Cruz under act of Congress of July 23, 1866. Held, that the occupation by the husband and wife during her life did not operate to render the land community property, or vest the wife with any ownership whatever. Following Labish v. Hardy, 19 Pac. 531.—Labish v. Hardy, 3, 202.

In an action by a daughter of the first marriage against a second wife, to whom the land had been deeded, to recover the interest claimed by plaintiff as heir of her deceased mother, the deed will not be vacated on the ground that it was a gift, and the husband was indebted to plaintiff, and did not have sufficient property to pay her.—Labish v. Hardy, 3, 202.

Where property is sold on foreclosure of a mortgage executed by a widow, who owned one-half thereof as community property and the other half for life under her husband's will, of which she was executrix, the remainder being devised to their children, the purchaser at such sale cannot acquire title to the interest of the children by adverse possession, pending administration of their father's estate, or without giving notice that he claimed absolute title to the whole property.—Webb v. Winter, 6, 768.

The presumption that cattle bought by the husband during the marriage were community property is not overcome by the wife's mere testimony that it was bought with her money, and that she had a certain amount of money in banks and loaned when she was married, three years before the purchase, they having been placed on a ranch occupied by them under a lease to the husband alone, and treated as his property by his afterward giving her, when he was insolvent, a bill of sale thereof.—Riebli v. Husler, 7, 1.

Act of March, 1897, amending Civil Code, section 164, so as to make a conveyance to a married woman by instrument in writing presumptive evidence that title is thereby vested in her, provides that in cases where married women have conveyed real property which they acquired prior to May 19, 1889, "the husbands or their heirs or assigns, of such married women," shall be barred from maintaining any action to show that the real property was community property, unless begun within one year from the date of taking effect of the act. Code of Civil Procedure, section 434, declares that if no objection be taken to the complaint, either by demurrer or answer, defendant must be deemed to have waived the same, except, etc. Held, that where the wife's grantees failed to object to an action by the husband's heirs to recover alleged community property conveyed by her to them was not brought within the time prescribed by the act of 1897, they could not raise that objection on appeal.—Pryal v. Pryal, 7, 134.

§ 8. Right of Surviving Spouse.

The additional right, acquired in community property by either the husband or the wife upon the death of the other is acquired by inheritance.—In re Burdick's Estate, 5, 6.

A surviving wife cannot be deprived of her rights in community property by an act of the husband subjecting such property to the control of trustees for the use of others.—In re Burdick's Estate, 5, 6.

Property acquired by either spouse during the marriage, under a deed of bargain and sale reciting a valuable consideration, is prima facie community property, and is assets in the hands of the executor or administrator of the husband for the payment of debts.—Harper v. Hamer, 1, 801.

§ 9. Actions—Parties.

See ante, §§ 6, 7.

A married woman may sue without her husband joining as a plaintiff, in an action concerning her separate property.—Frisbie v. Whitney, 1, 447.

§ 10. —— To Set Aside Conveyance.

In the trial of an action to set aside a deed by plaintiff to a married woman on the ground that a mortgage and note for an unpaid balance of the purchase money was not joined in by the husband, and that at the time of the sale both husband and wife had represented that she was a sole trader with full power to contract in her individual name, the plaintiff rests prematurely if proving only thus far, not proving a repudiation of the instruments by the maker or a claim by either her or her husband that she was not a sole trader.—Robinson v. Vail, 1, 329.

An action to set aside the conveyance of community property made by a husband, on the ground of fraud, cannot be maintained by the wife while the marriage bond exists.—Cummings v. Cummings, 2, 774.

IMPAIRMENT.

Of obligation. See Constitutional Law, § 1.

IMPEACHMENT.

Of witnesses. See Witnesses, § 10.

IMPROVEMENTS.

See Fixtures.

Recovery for by vendee. See Vendor and Vendee, § 21.

§ 1. When Voluntary and Gratuitous.

Improvements put on land by one having notice of equities in the land enjoyed by another are, unless made at this other's request, voluntary and gratuitous.—Rand v. Hastings, 1, 307.

INDECENT EXPOSURE.

§ 1. Complaint or Indictment.

A complaint under Penal Code of California, section 311, which declares it an offense to "willfully and lewdly procure, counsel or assist" anyone to make an indecent exposure of the person, charged that defendant "willfully, unlawfully, and lewdly solicited" an indecent exposure. Held, that a conviction on such complaint will be sustained, on an application for discharge on habeas corpus.—Ex parte Hutchings, 2, 822.

INDEMNITY.

§ 1. For Payment of Note—Consideration—Constitution.

An agreement by certain signers of a note to assume responsibility for its payment, and to indemnify the other signers for any loss or damages they may sustain on account of it, stands on the same footing, as concerns consideration, as a release.—Rogers v. Kimball, 5, 725.

A signer of a note, who has been released from liability thereon by the other signers, who also agree to indemnify him for any loss or damage he may in any manner sustain on account of the note, can, on paying judgment rendered against him on the note, recover therefor of the others, though they had paid the note before judgment was rendered against him, and though they had no notice of the action against him; there being no defense which he was informed of and neglected to interpose.—Rogers v. Kimball, 5, 725.

The release of one of the signers of a note by the others from liability thereon, and their agreement to indemnify him for any damages on account of the note, being joint, he can recover against them all, though judgment is rendered against him on the note for only the balance thereof remaining after one of them had paid his proportion thereof.—Rogers v. Kimball, 5, 725.

INDEPENDENT CONTRACTOR.

§ 1. Liability for Negligence.

Where a person obtains from a city, by ordinance, license to lay pipes along its streets, he will be liable for injuries resulting from the negligent manner in which such work is done, even though the work is not done by himself, but by an independent contractor employed by him for that purpose.—Colegrove v. Smith, 3, 874.

INDICTMENT AND INFORMATION.

§ 1. In general.
§ 2. Sufficiency and requisites.
§ 3. Duplicity.
§ 4. Correction or amendment.
§ 5. Demurrer—Effect of sustaining or overruling.
§ 6. Objections and motion to quash.

See Grand Jury.

Of accomplice. See Accomplices and Accessories, § 2.
For embezzlement. See Embezzlement, § 8.
For forgery. See Forgery, § 2.
For larceny. See Larceny, § 5.
For concealing evidence. See Obstructing Justice, § 1.
For failure of officer to pay over to successor. See Officers, § 3.
For rape. See Rape, § 1.
For receiving stolen goods. See Receiving Stolen Goods, § 1.

§ 1. In General.

Prosecution upon information, instead of upon indictment, does not violate the constitution of the United States.—People v. Hurtado, 2, 206.

The names of witnesses examined before the committing magistrate need not be inserted at the foot of or indorsed on the information filed in court against defendant after he had been examined before such magistrate, though Penal Code, section 943, provides that when an indictment is found the names of the witnesses before the grand jury must be so indorsed.—People v. Sherman, 3, 851.

Where the grand jury submitting an indictment had no authority in the matter, the court is without jurisdiction.—Terrill v. Superior Court, 6, 398.

§ 2. Sufficiency and Requisites.

An information is sufficient, on demurrer, which complies substantially with the provisions of the statute.—People v. Biggins, 2, 303.

An indictment states the offense sufficiently when it follows the language of the statute describing the act which it makes a criminal one.—People v. Eveart, 1, 217.

An indictment against one for destroying a dam sufficiently locates the dam as within the county where the indictment is found when it charges that the act charged was committed within that county.—People v. Eveart, 1, 217.

An indictment for crime must conform substantially to the requirements of sections 237 and 238 of the Criminal Practice Act, and must state the facts constituting the offense in ordinary and concise language.—People v. De la Guerra, 1, 345.

An information inartificially drawn and more verbose than necessary is to be sustained if good in substance.—People v. Clarke, 2, 109.

Where an act may fall within the definition of several offenses, according to the purpose with which it is done, it is essential to the statement of any offense that the purpose be set forth.—Ex parte Goldman, 7, 254.

§ 3. Duplicity.

An information which charges two offenses is demurrable, and cannot be amended after the taking of defendant's plea, without a new arraignment and plea to the amended information.—People v. Clement, 4, 493.

A defendant who has demurred to an information as charging two offenses does not waive his right to move in arrest of judgment by moving for a new trial.—People v. Clement, 4, 493.

§ 4. Correction or Amendment.
See ante, § 3, post, § 5.

Where it is apparent that a defendant has had a fair and full examination before an examining magistrate, and has been held to appear and answer on a criminal charge, and an information against him has been set aside for some technical error or irregularity, not going to the merits—such as failure to certify the depositions in a homicide case—the court may permit a correction to be made, and a new information filed, without a further examination before a committing magistrate.—People v. Kilvington, 4, 512.

§ 5. Demurrer—Effect of Sustaining or Overruling.

Penal Code, section 1008, declares that if a demurrer to an information or indictment is allowed, the judgment is final, and a bar to another prosecution, unless the court directs the case to be submitted to "another grand jury." Prior to 1880 the act read, "the same or another grand jury." Held, the words were omitted ex industria, and a submission to the same grand jury was error.—Terrill v. Superior Court, 6, 417.

Where a demurrer to an information is overruled, and a plea of not guilty is entered, the court may set aside the order overruling such demurrer, and allow counsel for the people to confess the demurrer, and file a new information, and such order will be equivalent to an allowance of the demurrer.—People v. Biggins, 2, 303.

Under Penal Code, section 1008, declaring that the judgment allowing a demurrer to an indictment is final, and a bar to another prosecution for the same offense, unless the court, being of the opinion that the objection may be avoided in a new indictment, directs the case to be submitted to "another grand jury," where a demurrer to the indictment was sustained, but the indictment was resubmitted to the same grand jury, which found another indictment, charging defendant with the same offense, founded on the same facts, such indictment was void.—Terrill v. Superior Court, 6, 398.

§ 6. Objections and Motion to Quash.

A defendant should present his objections to the indictment before he pleads to it.—People v. Taylor, 1, 19.

After pleading to an indictment it is too late to move to quash it. People v. Sellers, 1, 34.

INDORSEMENT.

Of negotiable paper. See Bills and Notes, §§ 10-13.

INFANTS.

§ 1. Disaffirmance of Promissory Note.

An infant over the age of eighteen years executing a promissory note, the consideration of which he receives, and which note is paid by an indorser, cannot disaffirm his contract with the indorser without refunding the amount paid in taking up the note.—Combs v. Hawes, 2, 555.

§ 2. Time When must Assert Rights.

The time within which a minor may assert his rights, or commence an action for an interest in real property, is five years from the time of attaining his majority. The time of his minority is calculated from the first minute of the day on which he is born to the first minute of the day corresponding which completes the period of minority; and, in calculating the time within which he may thereafter bring such action, as he attains majority on the first minute of a day, the whole of that day is to be calculated as the first day of the five years within which he may bring the action.—Ganahl v. Soher, 2, 415.

INFORMATION.

See Indictment and Information.

INFORMATION AND BELIEF.

Denials on. See Pleading, § 9.

INJUNCTION.

§   1.   In general.
§   2.   Pleading and evidence.
§   3.   Bond—Action on, attorney fees.
§   4.   Against trespass.
§   5.   Against waste—Cutting timber.
§   6.   Against removal of fence.
§   7.   Against repair of public work.
§   8.   Against breach of trade agreement.
§   9.   Against execution sale.
§ 10.   In cases involving waters.
§ 11.   Dissolution of injunction.

To protect easement. See Easement, § 5.
Against regulations of harbor commissioners. See Harbor Commissioners, § 2.
Against obstruction of lake. See Navigable Waters, § 1.
Against use of wall. See Party-walls, § 2.
Against railway using street. See Railroads, § 4.
Against tax collector. See Taxation, § 14.
Against diversion of water. See Waters and Watercourses, § 8.

§ 1. In General.

If a tenant in common of land, the usufruct of which belongs to him and his cotenant jointly as partners or otherwise, wrongfully excludes the cotenant of all beneficial use of any share, he cannot complain that an injunction to restrain him in this connection interferes with his beneficial enjoyment of his own share.—Thompson v. Gibb, 1, 173.

An injunction filed after the actual doing of the act enjoined fails for want of subject matter.—Sacramento v. Burke et al., 1, 280.

§ 2. Pleading and Evidence.

An averment in a complaint that defendants are lawless and irresponsible does not import necessarily that they are insolvent.—Gates v. Teague, 1, 46.

The pleadings of a party to whom relief is granted must be sufficient to warrant the relief. Where plaintiff, therefore, does not allege that defendant asserts any claim to his property, he is not entitled to a judgment restraining defendant from asserting such a claim.—Lawrence v. Getchel, 2, 359.

Injunction held not warranted by facts stated in complaint.—Crescent City Mill and Transp. Co. v. Hayes, 2, 458.

In an action to restrain certain acts of a corporation arising from constructing a dam, where an officer of the corporation was asked on the trial: "Unless there is an injunction issued in this case forbidding the corporation, through its agents, from doing this act, you, as long as you are agent of the corporation, will continue to do it when you think it necessary to do it, and to the advantage of the corporation" —the refusal of the court to allow such question is error.—Heilbron v. Last Chance W. D. Co., 2, 633.

§ 3. Bond—Action on, Attorneys' Fees.

The filing of a bond after the expiration of the time named in an order dissolving an injunction unless a bond be filed within such time cannot keep the injunction alive.—Jennings (Dowling) v. Polack, 1, 202.

In an injunction suit an undertaking was given for a temporary restraining order, valid to a certain date. On that date another undertaking was filed for a continuance of the injunction, with different sureties. Held, on a suit against the second sureties, that under the recitals the second undertaking was not given in place of the first one, and that the sureties sued were not liable for the damages caused during the time covered by the first undertaking.—California Ins. Co. v. Schindler, 2, 228.

In an action by an administrator on an injunction bond, the amount of attorneys' fees paid by the intestate in procuring a dissolution of the injunction cannot be recovered, when such fees have not been paid, and no claim for them had been filed against the estate, at the time of filing the complaint.—Hooper v. Patterson, 3, 811.

In such action, it is error to allow interest on the damages from the date of filing the complaint, as such damages are unliquidated and uncertain until settled by process of law, or by the parties.— Hooper v. Patterson, 3, 811.

A complaint on an injunction bond, conditioned that plaintiff will pay to the parties enjoined such damages as they may sustain by reason of the injunction, which fails to allege that plaintiff in the injunction suit has not paid the damages, does not state a cause of action.—Curtiss v. Bachman, 5, 56.

§ 4. Against Trespass.

An injunction will not be granted to restrain a trespass except where the injury threatened would be irremediable.—California Steam Nav. Co. v. Brown, 1, 22.

In cases of trespass an injunction is granted only when irremediable injury is imminent.—Gates v. Teague, 1, 46.

A complaint by a corporation operating a sawmill, which alleges that plaintiff, the owner in fee of certain land, commenced the construction of a logging road thereon to convey timber to the mill; that defendants entered on the land, and obstructed the men employed by plaintiff in continuing the work, threatening to use violence should they persist, whereby the work was stopped; that such interruption was repeated when an attempt was again made to construct the road, and that defendants threaten such interruption whenever the work is attempted; that the road is necessary for the operation of the sawmill; and that defendants are insolvent—warrants the granting of a preliminary injunction.—Sisson, Crocker & Co. v. Johnson, 4, 265.

§ 5. Against Waste—Cutting Timber.

A mortgagee under a mortgage given by one of several land owners may have an injunction to stay waste as to only the land of the mortgagor.—Ross v. Parvin, 1, 285.

A bill filed to restrain the cutting of wood on mortgaged premises is to that extent without subject matter, if the wood has already been cut.—Ross v. Parvin, 1, 285.

A purchaser of standing timber who, as to the land itself, acquires no greater right than that of entry and way for the purpose of cutting and removing the timber, has an adequate remedy at law for the destruction or conversion of the timber, and is not entitled to an injunction if the wrongdoers are responsible for their acts.—Hendy v. Duncan, 1, 289.

§ 6. Against Removal of Fence.

In an action to enjoin a road overseer from removing a fence, where defendant does not deny plaintiff's allegation of possession, but relies on an easement in the public as justifying him, plaintiff need not prove title, possession being sufficient upon which to maintain his action.—Cramer v. Kester, 4, 603.

§ 7. Against Repair of Public Work.

An injunction to restrain the repairing of a public work is not to be granted on grounds amounting to no more than the petitioner's opinion as to the probable efficiency of the work when done.—Hoke v. Perdue, 2, 116.

§ 8. Against Breach of Trade Agreement.

A complaint alleged that plaintiffs and defendants were each engaged in the butcher business, and had agreed not to handle trading stamps, vegetables, or to give premiums as "inducements tending to draw trade" from one to the other, but that, to the "irreparable injury of plaintiffs," defendants did handle and give trading stamps, vegetables, etc., and an injunction was prayed. Held, that in the absence of averments that defendants were giving the stamps to draw trade, or giving them to persons trading with the parties, or that defendants were insolvent, or the damages not ascertainable, the complaint was insufficient.—Schmidt v. Bitzer, 7, 115.

§ 9. Against Execution Sale.

In an action to restrain the sale of land under execution against plaintiff's grantor the court should continue the restraining order pending final determination, and it is an abuse of discretion to dissolve it upon the filing of an answer denying the allegations of the bill.—Chace v. Jennings, 3, 474.

§ 10. In Cases Involving Waters.

In an action for equitable relief by way of injunction to restrain defendant from draining the waters of a certain lake into the ocean, the complaint averring, in substance, that plaintiff was a corporation engaged in the manufacturing, transportation and sale of lumber; that its mills were located on the banks of said lake, and that it was necessary that a certain depth of water in such lake, which now exists there, should be maintained, the same being essential to the conduct of plaintiff's business; and that a decrease of its depth, or destruction of its navigability, would result in great and irreparable injury to plaintiff. Defendant, in answer to the complaint, denied that plaintiff owned or possessed the mill mentioned in the complaint; that the mill was situate upon said lake; that the lake was navigable; or that the destruction of its navigability would injure plaintiff; or that the defendant intended to obstruct or impair plaintiff's alleged rights therein. Held, that the answer raised issues entitling defendant to a trial on the merits, and that a demurrer thereto should not be sustained.—Crescent City Mill and Transp. Co. v. Hayes, 2, 657.

A bill to restrain public officers from filling up a ditch along the side of a road, which fails to show whether the road is public or private, whether the ditch or watercourse is artificial or natural, or occupied a part of the road or was outside of it, is insufficient.— Grimes v. Linscott, 5, 38.

A complaint alleged plaintiff's right to the exclusive use and occupation of land bordering on a navigable river and extending to low-water mark; that defendants had entered thereon, though prohibited to do so by plaintiff's agent, and had occupied the land above low-water mark, taken down fences, and had threatened to do so, and camped thereon, and had crossed over the land, leaving gates open, and made preparations to remain thereon, in violation of plaintiff's rights; that owing to the great number of defendants, and their repeated acts of trespass, the law furnished plaintiff no adequate protection, and that he was compelled to resort to equity to avoid a multiplicity of actions. Defendants' insolvency was alleged, and that, unless restrained by injunction, they would enter upon and occupy the land in violation of plaintiff's rights, causing irreparable injury to the lands, and compel plaintiff to bring a multiplicity of actions. It was also rather vaguely averred that the lowlands lying immediately along the river bank overflow at times of high water, and are separated from the higher land by fences, and that at such times plaintiff's stock would drown unless removed to the higher land. Held, that, though the complaint was not clear and distinct in its averments, from which the court might determine whether the threatened injury complained of was likely to be irreparable, or that an adequate remedy at law was not available, it was good as against a general demurrer.—Gianella v. Gray, 7, 353.

§ 11. Dissolution of Injunction.

Where the charges set out in a bill for a permanent injunction are fully denied by the answer and accompanying affidavits, the denials being as circumstantial and positive as the charges, the injunction should be dissolved.—Baker v. Scannell, 1, 72.

Where there is nothing in the record to show upon what the court acted in dissolving an injunction, the presumption is that it was dissolved upon good cause shown. Moreover, the retention or dissolution of an injunction is within the sound discretion of the court, with which this court will not interfere unless the record shows abuse of discretion.—Fowler v. Heinrath, 2, 249.

Under Code of Civil Procedure, section 437, authorizing denials upon information and belief, such denials, while sufficient to raise an issue, will not justify the dissolution of a temporary injunction on the ground that the bill is fully denied by the answer.—Chace v. Jennings, 3, 474.

When it is not clear that a reversal of an order dissolving a temporary injunction would have no legal effect, a motion to dismiss an appeal therefrom on that ground will not be sustained.—Fox v. Grayson, 6, 72.

Where an injunction is granted on a verified complaint, the court, in its discretion, may refuse a dissolution, provided the complaint states facts sufficient to authorize the granting of the injunction in the first instance.—Schmidt v. Bitzer, 7, 115.

INSANE PERSONS.

§ 1. Competency as Witness—Restoration to Sanity.

The discharge of a person from an insane asylum by the resident physician and secretary, though the certificate does not state that she is restored to reason, is prima facie evidence that she is so restored, or that she was improperly committed, and is therefore a competent witness, these being the only grounds for her discharge under the statute.—Clements v. McGinn, 4, 163.

Under Code of Civil Procedure, section 1880, declaring that persons "who are of unsound mind at the time of their production for examination" cannot be witnesses, the fact that a person has been committed to an asylum as insane does not render her an incompetent witness, but the question of competency is for the court, and her testimony is properly received, in the absence of anything to show her of unsound mind.—Clements v. McGinn, 4, 163.

INSANITY.

As defense to crime. See Criminal Law, § 2.

INSOLVENCY.

§ 1. In general.
§ 2. Jurisdiction—Foreign corporations.
§ 3. Assignee—Appointment.
§ 4. —— Rights and liabilities.
§ 5. Schedules.
§ 6. Sale of property.
§ 7. Discharge.
§ 8. —— Setting aside.

See Bankruptcy; Composition With Creditors.

§ 1. In General.

In insolvency the proceedings setting the jurisdiction of the county courts in motion are not intended to be summary or hurried, since the point of importance is, as in other cases, not so much the avoidance of delay as the promotion of substantial justice.—Grow v. Rosborough, 1, 258.

Petition in insolvency held sufficient.—Campbell v. Judd, 2, 522.

On a contest of a claim against an insolvent's estate, it appeared that the insolvent had become indebted to claimant's assignor, B., for the price of certain land and merchandise, and gave him the notes constituting the claim in question. As part of the same transaction, B. gave a bond conditioned to convey the land to the insolvent on payment of the amount of the notes. Held, that the title to the land was reserved to secure the entire debt, and that the claim was properly rejected where claimant attempted to prove the full amount of the notes, without either deducting the value of the land, as required by section 44 of the insolvency act, or conveying his interest in it to the assignee.—In re Harvey, 3, 832.

Costs incurred in wrongful attachment against the estate of an insolvent cannot be recovered, under section 65 of the insolvency act, as said section applies only to costs which would have been a legal charge.—In re Harvey, 3, 832.

Evidence that a debtor, when called on to pay his notes when due, replied that he was unable to pay them; that he had tried to raise the money, but could not—warrants a finding that he was insolvent.— Clarke v. Mott, 4, 80.

Under insolvent act of 1880 (Append. Code Civ. Proc.), sec. 2, which provides that one owing over $300 may file a petition for discharge from his debts in a county where he has resided the six months preceding the filing, and provides that, in the petition, the petitioner shall "set forth his place of residence," a petition need not allege that the petitioner resided in the county where the petition was filed the six months preceding the filing thereof.—In re Thomas, 5, 303.

In replevin, where defendant, as assignee of an insolvent debtor, alleges that the property was fraudulently transferred to plaintiff by the insolvent in order to defeat his creditors, special findings that plaintiff knew the debtor was insolvent at the time of the transfer, and that the transfer was made to prevent the property from coming into the hands of the assignee, and from being distributed among the creditors with a view to defeat the object of the California insolvent act of 1880, plaintiff having reasonable cause so to believe, but that the transfer was not made to give preference to any creditor, are sufficient to support a general verdict for the defendant under act of April 16, 1880, section 55, relating to transfers by insolvent debtors. Salisbury v. Burr, 5, 314.

Where, prior to insolvency proceedings against a firm, the wife of a member, who was also a creditor, received a draft belonging to the firm in good faith, without intending to defraud other creditors, but to keep the money from being wasted by attachments, her surrender of the principal part of the money to the assignee after an action was brought by him against her therefor, but before judgment, was in time to entitle her to share in the dividends, as a creditor free from fraud, though she contested the assignee's right to the balance of the proceeds of the draft, which she had used for family purposes. In re Doyle & Son's Estate, 6, 392.

§ 2. Jurisdiction—Foreign Corporations.

The effect of the constitutional amendments is that the jurisdiction of the county courts in insolvency proceedings—contrary to what it was prior to 1863—rests upon the same basis as the general jurisdiction of the district courts and of the supreme court, both appellate and original, such proceedings being no longer "special cases" as then known.—Grow v. Rosborough, 1, 258.

Under the insolvency act of 1880, which provides, in section 8, that the petition shall be filed in the county where the debtor resides, or has his place of business, and, in section 21, makes certain provisions in case of a nonresident debtor, the California courts have jurisdiction of proceedings in involuntary insolvency against a foreign corporation which has property and a place of business in the state.— In re Castle Dome Mining and Smelting Co., 3, 1.

§ 3. Assignee—Appointment.

In a case of involuntary insolvency there is no provision for serving any notice on the creditors who are the moving parties in the proceeding, and jurisdiction to appoint the assignee is acquired by the service upon the debtor of the creditors' petition and order of the court.—Ohleyer v. Bunce, 2, 252.

§ 4. —— Rights and Liabilities.

An assignee in insolvency takes the property of the insolvent subject to all the rights and equities of third persons attached to it in the hands of the insolvent.—Kirk v. Roberts, 3, 671.

Where, in an action by an assignee in insolvency for possession of property, defendant claims under a bill of sale, a finding that defendant procured it by fraud is proper as a fact bearing on defendant's right to possession, though the issue of fraud is not raised by the pleadings.—Haight v. Sexton, 5, 203.

An assignee of an insolvent cannot be charged with the difference between what the property brought and what the court held it would have brought if sold in parcels, if he acted in good faith and reasonable care.—In re Nichols' Estate, 5, 856.

An assignee of an insolvent who has acted in good faith and with reasonable care will not be held liable for mistakes of judgment.—In re Nichols' Estate, 5, 856.

§ 5. Schedules.

On an issue of fraud the question whether property described in the schedule of an insolvent as "interest in land bought of ——" was not intended by such insolvent to indicate "The —— tract," the names being identical, the burden is on the party asserting the fraud.—Thomas v. Creditors, 1, 164.

The rule that, except where there has been an abuse of discretion, the supreme court will not disturb an order of the court below granting or denying leave to amend in civil proceedings, applies to the petition and schedules of an insolvent.—Hamlin v. His Creditors, 2, 203.

§ 6. Sale of Property.

The proper remedy, where personal property is sold by an assignee of an insolvent en masse, and would have brought a larger price if sold in parcels, is to move the court to set aside the sale.—In re Nichols' Estate, 5, 856.

In an action by an assignee in insolvency to enforce the payment of an amount bid for property of the insolvent at a constable's sale defendant may set off his claim for money borrowed from him by the insolvent, which had been filed and proved against the insolvent's estate.—Meherin v. Saunders, 6, 279.

The fact that a creditor of an insolvent had filed and proved his claim against the estate, and accepted a dividend based on the entire amount, does not estop him from setting off such claim, in an action by the assignee to enforce payment of a bid for property of the insolvent sold at constable's sale.—Meherin v. Saunders, 6, 279.

§ 7. Discharge of Debtor.

The rights of a creditor are not affected by the discharge in insolvency of his debtor, where neither the creditor himself nor his debt were within the jurisdiction of the court in which the proceedings in insolvency were had.—Stone v. Hammell, 3, 128.

The discharge in insolvency of a debtor does not affect the rights of his surety on a note who subsequently contributes to the payment thereof.—Stone v. Hammell, 3, 128.

§ 8. —— Setting Aside.

The disposition of a motion to set aside a decree of final discharge in insolvency rests largely on the discretion of the nisi prius court, and will not be reviewed except in case of an abuse of that discretion.—Longnecker v. His Creditors, 2, 852.

Where a person has been discharged in insolvency, the court has no jurisdiction to hear a petition by his assignee to annul the certificate of discharge, since, under insolvent act of 1880, section 53, providing that "any creditor" of an insolvent debtor who has obtained such discharge may contest its validity on the ground that it was fraudulently obtained, such a proceeding can only be commenced by a creditor.—Wagner v. Superior Court of Los Angeles County, 4, 310.

In an action by an assignee in insolvency to recover the value of property transferred by an insolvent debtor to defendants, findings that defendants neither knew nor believed, nor had reasonable cause to believe, that the debtor was insolvent, or made the deed in contemplation of insolvency, are sufficient to support a judgment for defendants.—Smith v. Fratt, 4, 821.

INSTRUCTIONS.

In civil cases generally. See Trial, §§ 12, 14.
In criminal cases. See Criminal Law and Crime in Question.

INSURANCE.

§ 1. Construction of Policy.

Parol evidence is not admissible as to what is meant by the words "barroom fixtures" as used in insurance policy.—Hegard v. California Ins. Co., 2, 663.

An instruction submitting to the jury, as a question of fact, the inquiry whether "there was a reserve on the policy" of a certain amount "calculated as provided in said statute," the substance of the statute having been given them, was error, since it is not within the province of the jury to determine a question depending upon purely mathematical calculation and the construction of a statute.—Nielsen v. Provident Savings Life Assur. Soc., 6, 804.

§ 2. Warranties—Misrepresentations.

Findings in an action on an insurance policy that plaintiff had not misrepresented his ownership of the property insured, nor its value, held sustained by the evidence.—Hegard v. California Ins. Co., 2, 663.

The objection of immateriality cannot be urged against a warranty in a policy so as to avoid the effect of a breach thereof.—Bayley v. Employers' Liability Assur. Corp., 6, 254.

§ 3. —— Insertion of False Answers by Agent.

Where an insurance company's agent inserted false answers in an application for a fire policy after full information as to the facts had been given him by insured's manager, such answers constituted no defense to an action on the policy though the answers were declared to constitute warranties.—Parrish v. Rosebud Mining etc. Co., 7, 117.

The falsity of such answers constituted a valid defense to a policy issued by another company, not represented by such agent, on the same property, based on such application.—Parrish v. Rosebud Mining etc. Co., 7, 117.

§ 4. Delivery of Policy and Payment of Premiums.

A policy dated July 30th, calling for quarterly premiums, provided that it should not be binding until delivered and its first premium paid. It was not delivered, nor the first premium paid, until September 3d, and insured died in November following. Held, that the policy did not begin to run until September 3d, and was in force for three months thereafter, and hence was not forfeited for failure of assured to pay the quarterly premium, which would have been due October 30th, had the policy taken effect on the day of its date.—Methvin v. Fidelity Mutual Life Assn., 6, 332.

Where an insurance policy provided that the insurer should not be liable while any note for premiums remained past due and unpaid, and the notes executed in payment of premiums contained a similar provision, and the property was destroyed while the first premium note was due and unpaid, the provision was valid, and the insured, by tendering the amount of the note, could not hold the insurer liable for the loss.—Palmer v. Continental Ins. Co., 6, 455.

Civil Code, section 2598, enacting that an acknowledgment in a policy of the receipt of a premium is conclusive evidence of its payment, so far as to make it binding, notwithstanding a stipulation that it shall not be binding until the premium is actually paid, applies only to a policy containing a stipulation that it shall not be binding until the premium is actually paid.—Palmer v. Continental Ins. Co., 6, 455.

§ 5. Nonpayment of Premium—Application of Reserve.

A notice, in writing, stating the number of the policy, amount of premium, place at which and person to whom it was payable, and which was inclosed in a securely closed envelope, addressed to the insured at his residence in California, and deposited, postage prepaid, in the postoffice in New York, thirty days prior to the day on which the premium fell due, was a sufficient notice, under the laws of New York, requiring notice of insurance premiums to be given at least fifteen, and not more than forty-five, days before such premiums become due.—Nielsen v. Provident Savings Life Assur. Soc., 6, 804.

Under the New York statute, providing that, when an insurance policy has lapsed for nonpayment of premiums, the net reserve on such policy shall, on demand made, with surrender of the policy within six months after such lapse, be taken as a single premium, etc., and shall be applied "as shall have been agreed in the application and policy, either to continue the insurance of the policy in force at its full amount so long as such single premium will purchase temporary insurance for that amount, or to purchase upon the same life" paid-up insurance, a policy on which two annual premiums have been paid, providing that its reserve fund shall be "used toward offsetting any increase in the premiums" on such policy, is not self-perpetuating after nonpayment of premiums, although its reserve fund is more than sufficient to buy temporary insurance up to the death of the insured, since the statute requires an election to be made by the insured, and the policy makes no provision for the application of such reserve to continue insurance.—Nielsen v. Provident Savings Life Assur. Soc., 6, 804.

§ 6. Survey of Premises.

Where a fire insurance policy refers to a survey of the insured premises and the application as a warranty on the part of the insured, the right of the company to rely on such application and survey is not defeated by the fact that they were not furnished until after the policy was delivered, and that they were written on blanks prepared for the use of another insurance company.—Rankin v. Amazon Ins. Co., 3, 330.

§ 7. Keeping Watchman.

In an action on a policy, evidence that the insured premises were idle for two months, during which time the insured employed only one watchman, who habitually slept in a building three hundred feet away, with the approval of the insured, shows a failure on the part of the insured to comply with a condition of the policy requiring him to employ a watchman "to be in and about the premises by day and night" during the time that they are idle, and not merely negligence on the part of the watchman in performing his duty, and is a good defense to the action.—Rankin v. Amazon Ins. Co., 3, 330.

§ 8. Interest of Insured.

The purchaser of mortgaged property did not record her deed until after suit brought to foreclose the mortgage. Before expiration of the time of redemption, an insurance policy was issued to her, which stated her interest in the premises as being her building, and provided that, unless her interest was not truly stated therein, it should be void, and that it was to be void if such interest was not unconditional and sole ownership. Held, that, in view of Civil Code, section 2888, which provides that a lien on property transfers no title, the policy correctly stated insured's interest, her failure to record the conveyance only affecting her title as against a purchaser at the foreclosure sale, if there should be no redemption.—Breedlove v. Norwich Union Fire Ins. Soc., 6, 94.

§ 9. Change in Title.

To put a lessee in possession of insured property under a contract that he shall buy the property on the termination of the lease, or, at his option, at any time during its continuance, is a breach of a condition of the policy that it shall become void if any change takes place in the title or possession.—Smith v. Phenix Ins. Co., 3, 244.

Notice to the insurance company, before the destruction of the property by fire, of the lease and change of possession, but not of the agreement to convey contained in the lease, cannot affect the company's right to afterward insist on the enforcement of such stipulation.—Smith v. Phenix Ins. Co., 3, 244.

A notice of a change of title may be given to the person who signed the policy as insurer's agent when the policy was issued, where the insured had no knowledge that such person had ceased to be the insurer's agent.—Whitney v. American Ins. Co., 6, 220.

Under a clause in a policy insuring a mortgagee, providing that the insurance should not be invalidated by the mortgagor's neglect, provided the mortgagee notified insurer of any change of ownership coming to his knowledge, and had permission for such change indorsed on the policy, a change of ownership to the mortgagee's knowledge does not invalidate the policy, if the change did not increase the risk, though he gave insurer no notice thereof, the provision respecting the giving of notice by him being merely directory. Whitney v. American Ins. Co., 6, 220.

§ 10. Other Insurance.

Evidence held to show a waiver of notice of other insurance or any act working an estoppel from asserting want of such notice, on defendants' part.—Locey v. American Central Ins. Co., 2, 708.

Evidence held to fail to show a waiver of notice of other insurance, or any act working an estoppel from asserting want of such notice, on defendants' part.—Locey v. American Cent. Ins. Co., 2, 712.

§ 11. Voluntary Exposure to Danger.

Deceased was overtaken by a policeman while driving, and, in an altercation which ensued, the policeman shot and killed him. After deceased was shot, he fired his pistol at the policeman, but there was no positive evidence that he took the pistol from his pocket until he was shot. His pistol had a white handle, and one witness testified that before the shooting he saw deceased take something from his pocket and threaten to kill the policeman, while another testified that deceased went toward the policeman, unbuttoning his overcoat with his left hand, and that he raised his right when close to him, saying, "You will not stop my horse," and had nothing in his hand that witness could see; that after deceased was shot, and had fired at the policeman, witness saw something white in his hand. Held, that it was not an abuse of the trial court's discretion to refuse to set aside a verdict finding that deceased had not voluntarily exposed himself to unnecessary danger, within the exception of a policy.—De Greayer v. Fidelity and Casualty Co., 6, 335.

In an action on a policy excepting from its operation death by voluntary exposure to unnecessary danger, an instruction that whether the assured so exposed himself did not depend on his having exercised reasonable care or caution, or that he had been guilty of negligence or unlawful acts, but whether he voluntarily exposed himself to unnecessary danger, and death resulted in consequence thereof, is not erroneous, as misleading or confusing.—De Greayer v. Fidelity and Casualty Co., 6, 335.

§ 12. Waiver by Insurer.

A provision in a benefit certificate, that it shall be payable only on its surrender is waived where the benefit society refuses to pay solely on the grounds of nonpayment of assessments, and that another

42

beneficiary had been substituted.—Himmelein v. Supreme Council A. L. of H., 4, 173.

The fact that an accident insurer had waived a false statement that the insured had never before received compensation for any accident, in so far as it had paid him therefor in 1892, and knew of certain other like payments by third persons in 1892, does not waive the falsity of the statement in that prior compensations for accidents had been paid the insured in 1886, of which the insurer had no knowledge.—Bayley v. Employers' Liability Assurance Corp., 6, 254.

A life insurance policy provided for an annual renewal, without medical re-examination, upon payment of a certain premium on a certain day, and that failure to pay such premium on the day specified should terminate the policy; but it was the custom of the company to reinstate policies upon the insured's paying the premium and furnishing a health certificate within thirty days from such lapse. The insured failed to pay the third annual premium, but within thirty days sent a money order to the company, but without a health certificate. Notices of this premium had been accompanied by a blank health certificate, and requests for its execution in connection with the remittance. The company receipted for the money order, expressly stating that they could not accept it as payment unless the health certificates were sent within thirty days. Insured died without sending the certificate, and the money order was returned. Held, that, the policy having lapsed and the health certificate being a prerequisite to its reinstatement, the evidence was not sufficient to show a waiver of the forfeiture on the part of the company.—Nielsen v. Provident Savings Life Assur. Soc., 6, 804.

§ 13. Reinsurance.

A contract of a company to pay losses under policies issued by another company as promptly as losses under its own policies is not a contract of reinsurance, under Civil Code, section 2646 et seq., and hence the company is directly liable to the insured.—Whitney v. American Ins. Co., 6, 220.

§ 14. Endowment Benefit.

A mutual endowment society, by alleging in its answer to an action to recover an endowment that the conditions of the contract, made by its law conditions predecent to recovery, have been fulfilled by the assured, "except as hereinafter set forth," assumes the burden of alleging and proving nonperformance of such conditions by the assured.—Osterman v. District Grand Lodge No. 4, I. O. B. B., 5, 237.

Where the laws of a mutual endowment association make suspension for nonpayment of dues a forfeiture of membership benefits, and provide a formal method for suspension in such case, nonpayment of dues will not, ipso facto, work a forfeiture, though the assured was secretary of the society, and formal proceedings for suspension have not been had because he failed, as required, to report his own delinquency.—Osterman v. District Grand Lodge No. 4, I. O. B. B., 5, 237.

In an action by a wife against a grand lodge—whose laws made membership in a subordinate lodge, and an election as member of the endowment fund, conditions precedent to a right to participate therein—to recover an endowment on her husband's membership, it appeared that, on report of the husband's death to the grand by the subordinate lodge, the grand lodge sent the amount due to the subordinate lodge, to be paid, "through the trustees," to plaintiff; that the trustees, prior to its receipt, obtained from her an order to deduct from the amount due sufficient to make good defalcations of her husband, which, as one of them testified, they told her, would amount to at least $1,000. The wife testified that they said it would be about $500. The trustees subsequently obtained her receipt for the whole amount, on representations that it was necessary to procure the money from the defendant. Plaintiff, failing to receive the money, demanded it from defendant, and defendant, then first learning that plaintiff's husband was not in good standing at his death, directed the trustees of the subordinate lodge to return the amount sent to it. There was no evidence what became of this money, except that it was deposited in the bank by the trustees to whom it was delivered. Held, that a finding against defendant's plea of payment was warranted.—Osterman v. District Grand Lodge No. 4, I. O. B. B., 5, 237.

Under the above facts, the grand lodge, and not the subordinate lodge, was the proper party to be sued.—Osterman v. District Grand Lodge No. 4, I. O. B. B., 5, 237.

In an action for an endowment benefit, where defendant alleges in defense that plaintiff consented that the money due should be applied in paying a sum embezzled by the assured, and that it was so applied, an instruction placing the burden of proving such issue on defendant is proper.—Osterman v. District Grand Lodge No. 4, I. O. B. B., 5, 237.

§ 15. Mutual Life Insurance.

Under Statutes of 1891, page 126, section 2, compelling mutual assessment life insurance companies to deposit a fund for the protection of policy holders, and section 4, providing that the beneficiaries shall have a lien on all property of the corporation, with priority over all indebtedness thereafter incurred, one who was entitled to payment of a death benefit at the time the statute became effective had a lien on such deposit as soon as it was made, the protection of the lien being not restricted to after-incurred debts.—San Francisco Savings Union v. Long, 6, 60.

Where the holder of a deposit created under Statutes of 1891, page 126, section 2, providing that assessment life insurance corporations shall deposit a certain sum for the protection of policy-holders, had brought an action to interplead various claimants to such fund, it was proper to permit a party who claimed the right to enforce a beneficiary's lien on such fund to assert such lien in the same action, and not to relegate him to a creditors' bill or a writ of execution.—San Francisco Savings Union v. Long, 6, 60.

Allegations that a judgment out of which defendant's claim grew was based on a certificate of life insurance issued by a named life association to one L. M. on May 1, 1896, and in favor of M. M., who was then the wife of said L. M.; that said certificate was for the sum of $6,000; that on a certain date said M. died, and at the time the said certificate was in full force and effect, and by reason of his death, there became due and payable, etc., in the absence of demurrer or objections to their sufficiency below, sufficiently plead such policy, performance of conditions thereof, and accrual of the right of action thereon.—San Francisco Savings Union v. Long, 6, 60.

Where a lien on a fund created to secure payment of death benefits under Statutes of 1891, page 126, sections 2, 4, relating to assessment life insurance corporations, attached pending an action on a policy, the establishment of such indebtedness by final judgment gave the right to enforce such lien, and it attached to the judgment, and continued until same was satisfied; and hence such lien did not, by virtue of Civil Code, section 2911, providing that liens shall be extinguished on the expiration of the time within which an action may be brought on the principal obligation, become extinguished on the lapse of such period of limitation from the time the lien attached.—San Francisco Savings Union v Long, 6, 60.

Where a lien on a fund created to secure payment of death benefits under Statutes of 1891, page 126, sections 2, 4, relating to assessment life insurance corporations, attached pending an action on a policy, the establishment of such indebtedness by final judgment gave the right to enforce such lien; and, such enforcement being sought in an action begun thereafter within the time prescribed for bringing an action on the policy, the claim of the lien was not barred by limitation, though more than the period of such limitation had elapsed since the lien attached.—San Francisco Savings Union v. Long, 6, 60.

§ 16. Proofs of Loss or Death.

An insured may make proofs of loss to one who had assumed insurer's liabilities, where insurer had authorized him to receive them, and had withdrawn all its own agencies from the state.—Whitney v. American Ins. Co., 6, 220.

Where a policy required proof of death to be made on blank forms furnished by the company, and declared that no action should be brought on it after one year from the date of insured's death, without reference to the time of furnishing the proofs of the death, such requirements must be construed together, and, if failure to bring the action within one year was occasioned by the company's refusal to furnish the blanks required, it is not entitled to urge the limitation to defeat plaintiff's recovery.—Methvin v. Fidelity Mutual Life Assn., 6, 332.

Where a policy declared that proof of death should be made on blanks furnished by the company, and that no action should be begun after one year from assured's death, without reference to the time of furnishing such proofs, the words in the limitation clause, "without reference to the time of furnishing proofs of death," refer only to the time when proofs are furnished, and do not apply to a case where the making of proofs of death was prevented by the company's refusal to furnish blanks.—Methvin v. Fidelity Mutual Life Assn., 6, 332.

§ 17. Action on Policy.

Action on benefit certificate. See post, § 22.

If, in an action on an insurance policy covering several classes of property, the complaint states the amounts of the losses upon the various kinds of property insured separately, and demand for judgment for the aggregate sum of such losses is made, this will be sufficient for the purpose of informing the defendant how much, and on what account, the plaintiff claims to recover it.—Hegard v. California Ins. Co., 2, 663.

The fact that a policy of insurance declared the measure of recovery for loss sustained on an insurance policy must be "in no case greater than the actual damage to or cash value of the property at the time of the fire," only established a rule as to the proof necessary to be made in order to show the damage or loss sustained, and it is unnecessary to allege in the pleading the actual cash value of the premises, this being a matter of evidence.—Hegard v. California Ins. Co., 2, 663.

Where a plaintiff in his complaint fails to state material facts, as, in an action on an insurance policy, failing to set out or attach and make a part of the complaint the application for insurance, so that no cause of action is stated, if these facts are supplied by the averments of the answer, the omission is immaterial, and the defect is cured.—Hegard v. California Ins. Co., 2, 663.

§ 18. By Administrator.

The administrator is the proper person to sue for the recovery of an insurance policy on the decedent's life made out in favor of the insured himself.—Jamison v. King, 1, 833.

An administrator suing on an insurance policy assigned by the decedent on his deathbed may, if his complaint is based on a fraudulent assignment, amend the same so as to have it charge donation in expectation of immediate death.—Jamison v. King, 1, 833.

§ 19. —— Time for Bringing.

Where an insurance policy contains a clause that any suit or action thereon should be commenced within twelve months after the loss, the action thereon must be brought within the time limited, and held, that the evidence in the present action did not sustain a finding that the delay in bringing the suit was caused by defendant's conduct.—Garido v. American Cent. Ins. Co., 2, 560.

§ 20. —— Amount of Recovery.

Where an insurance policy provides that in no case shall the recovery be greater than the actual damage or cash value of the property, a finding that the loss sustained on account of the destruction of a building by fire was a certain sum, the amount insured for, is sufficient, and the court need not state the evidential fact that the cash value of the property when destroyed was a certain sum.—Hegard v. California Ins. Co., 2, 663.

Under an insurance policy providing that "the cash value of property destroyed or damaged by fire shall in no case exceed what would be the cost to the assured, at the time of the fire, of replacing the same, and in case of the depreciation of such property, from use or otherwise, a suitable deduction from the cash cost of replacing the same shall be made to ascertain the actual cash value," the court does not err in refusing to allow the defendant to prove depreciation in the value of the building which occurred anterior to the time of its being insured.—Hegard v. California Ins. Co., 2, 663.

§ 21. —— Payment During Litigation, Bond for Repayment.

Where, pending a controversy as to the liability of several insurance companies for a loss, the L. Co. paid insured ninety-five per cent of the face of its policy, and took from insured a bond for repayment in case a judgment should be rendered adverse to insured in any of the actions contemplated against the other insurance companies, such bond was a guaranty, and not a contract of suretyship, and no recovery could be had thereon if the principal obligation was void for any cause other than the personal disability of the principal obligor.—Parrish v. Rosebud Mining etc. Co., 7, 117.

Pending a controversy as to the liability of insurers for a loss, one of them paid ninety-five per cent of its liability, and took a bond from insured, obligating it to repay such amount in the event that in any of the actions contemplated by insured against any of the other companies named, which had concurrent insurance on the property, a final judgment should be rendered in favor of the "defendant herein." Held, that the word "herein" could not be stricken out, and the word "therein" substituted, since the term "defendant herein" was not improperly applied to the obligee as being defendant in one of the cases enumerated, or as expressing an intention that the "adverse judgment" should be on grounds favorable to such obligee.—Parrish v. Rosebud Mining etc. Co., 7, 117.

Pending a controversy between insured and several insurance companies concerning the latter's liability for a loss, the L. Co. compro-

mised the claim against it, and took a bond from insured, by which
the latter agreed that, in the event that in any of the actions contemplated against the other insurers named, a final judgment should
be rendered in favor of the "defendant herein," then insured should
repay to the L. Co. the amount so paid. Held, that the intention of
the parties was to make such repayment contingent on a judgment
adverse to insured on the merits in a case involving the same questions as were involved in the controversy with the obligee, and hence
a judgment against insured in one of such actions on a defense not
available to the obligee did not justify a recovery on the bond.—Parrish v. Rosebud Mining etc. Co., 7, 117.

Where insured gave a bond obligating it to repay the proceeds of
a policy in the event an adverse judgment should be rendered in suits
against other insurers, a recovery could not be had in an action on
the bond against an obligor other than insured in an action to which
insured was not a party.—Parrish v. Rosebud Mining etc. Co., 7, 117.

§ 22. Action on Benefit Certificate.

In an action on a benefit certificate, by the terms of which the
claim was not due until proof of death was furnished, interest will
be allowed only from the commencement of the action, where the
complaint merely states that proof of death had been made, without
showing when, and the findings only show that the proof was made
"before the commencement of this action."—Himmelein v. Supreme
Council A. L. of H., 4, 173.

An application for membership in a benefit society, and statements
of the applicant to the medical examiner, both of which are on file in
the office of the secretary of the society, and are referred to in the
benefit certificate, and made part of the contract, need not be set out
in the complaint in an action on the certificate.—Himmelein v. Supreme Council A. L. of H., 4, 173.

In an action on a benefit certificate, by which defendant promised
"to pay out of its benefit fund to [plaintiff] a sum not exceeding
$500," the complaint after setting out the certificate alleged that "by
the terms and conditions of the said contract the said defendant promised to pay to the plaintiff, out of its benefit fund, the sum of
$5,000"; that the member had performed all the conditions of the
contract; "and that said sum of $5,000 is now due and owing from
the said defendant to this plaintiff." Held, that the complaint sufficiently stated a cause of action for $5,000.—Himmelein v. Supreme
Council A. L. of H., 4, 173.

INTEREST.

Inserting interest clause in note. See Bills and Notes, § 5.
In action on injunction bond. See Injunctions, § 3.
Default in payment. See Mortgages, § 18.
As disqualifying witness. See Witnesses, § 2.

§ 1. In General.

Where, in an action on an undertaking on appeal, given to secure
rents and profits of certain real estate pending an appeal to the
supreme court, under Code of Civil Procedure, section 945, if the
judgment is affirmed, but not as rendered by the court below, the
plaintiff is not entitled to recover anything of defendants, and therefore a ruling of the lower court adverse to his claim of interest, in
this action on the judgment appealed from, is not erroneous.—Heinlen v. Beans, 2, 719.

Defendant, after having agreed, in consideration of the rescission
of a contract, to repay plaintiff all moneys received thereunder, refused to do so. Held, that he was liable for interest on the money

received from the date of the later agreement.—Haines v. Stilwell, 5, 27.

In an action to recover money given under an agreement that the person who received it would do certain things, where such person has refused to perform his agreement he is chargeable with interest on the sum received from the time of such refusal.—Link v. Jarvis, 5, 750.

§ 2. Rate—Compound Interest.

When interest on a note is payable at a certain rate monthly in advance, "and, if said principal or interest is not paid as it becomes due, it shall thereafter bear interest at" a higher rate, acceptance of interest from time to time, for two years after maturity, at the former rate, waives the latter, though this be in no wise a penalty.—Thompson v. Gorner, 4, 606.

Where defendant, in California, executed her promissory notes payable in thirty days, with interest thereon at the rate of four per cent a month, interest to be paid monthly in advance, and, if not so paid, to become a part of the principal, and bear thereafter the same rate of interest, compounding monthly in advance, the court may properly, in calculating the interest due to plaintiff, allow interest on compound interest, or "interest on interest on interest."—Fisk v. Lee, 2, 720.

INTERPLEADER.

In suit to foreclose lien. See Mechanics' Liens, § 17.

§ 1. Payment of Judgment.

Where a defendant has disclaimed interest except as stakeholder, and prayed interpleader, and judgment is given against it in accordance with his own prayer, with costs against the defeated claimant, it may safely pay the judgment, in spite of irregularities in the interpleader suit which are uncomplained of by said claimant.—Wheelock v. Godfrey, 4, 396.

INTERVENTION.

In ejectment. See Ejectment, § 6.
In suit to foreclose lien. See Mechanics' Liens, § 16.

§ 1. In General.

A plaintiff's demurrer to an intervention should have been sustained when the intervention did not allege facts showing that the judgment was unjust, or facts showing that the defendant in the case had a defense to that action.—Chielovich v. Krauss, 2, 700.

Under section 659 of the Practice Act a person is permitted to intervene: 1st. When he has an interest in the success of the plaintiff; 2d. When he has an interest in the success of the defendant; and 3d. When he has an interest against both.—Donner v. Palmer, 1, 392.

§ 2. By One Tenant in Common.

When one tenant in common sues to recover the possession of the premises, and the damages sustained by the ouster, and the rents and profits to which he is entitled, the case is not one where his cotenant can intervene, for the cotenant is not interested.—Donner v. Palmer, 1, 392.

§ 3. In Ejectment.

Where the ownership, as claimed by the plaintiff, is of three undivided fourths, and this is the subject matter of his ejectment suit, one who would intervene does not show a right to do so by alleging that he is "the owner in fee simple and entitled to the possession of the undivided one-fourth part" of the premises, "being the one undivided one-fourth part of the said premises mentioned in the plaintiff's complaint; that is, the undivided one-third of the undivided three-fourths thereof, as mentioned therein."—Donner v. Palmer, 1, 392.

One should not intervene, in a suit for land, whose claim rests upon a transaction in no wise connected with issues in the suit and cannot possibly be concluded by any judgment therein.—Donner v. Palmer, 1, 623.

If one seeking to intervene in an ejectment suit does not allege, in his petition, that he had title before the commencement of the action the omission is fatal; and he does not cure it by alleging that he "is the owner and entitled to the possession," etc.—Donner v. Palmer, 1, 392.

It is doubtful if one tenant in common can, under the provisions of the statute, intervene in an action of ejectment brought by his cotenant; since tenants in common are such as hold by several and distinct titles, even though also by unity of possession, while a plaintiff in ejectment can recover only on the strength of his own title.—Donner v. Palmer, 1, 392.

INTOXICATING LIQUORS.

§ 1. Regulating Sale.

Judgment reversed and cause remanded, on the authority of Ex parte Walters, 3 Pac. 894, holding that boards of supervisors have power to regulate the sale of spirituous liquors within their counties by imposing a license on the sale of such liquors at retail.—People v. Dwyer, 2, 351.

The taxing clause of a county ordinance provided that every person who should sell intoxicating liquors in quantities less than one quart should obtain a license, and pay therefor $100 per year. Held, that since this clause did not impose a license for carrying on the business of selling liquor, as authorized by Statutes of 1893, page 358, but imposed it for the simple act of selling, and applied to each sale before it was made, it could not be changed by implication from the wording of other sections of the ordinance, which suggested an intention to tax the business itself.—Colusa County v. Seube, 6, 32.

A city ordinance providing that it shall be a misdemeanor for any person to sell or give away any spirituous liquors, within the city, except a licensed druggist selling on the prescription of a regularly licensed physician, which does not conflict with any general law of the state, is valid, though it prohibits a single act of selling or giving away malt and spirituous liquors by one not engaged in the liquor traffic.—Ex parte Fedderwitz, 6, 562.

Where a city ordinance provides that it shall be a misdemeanor for any person to sell or give away any malt or spirituous liquors within the city except a licensed druggist selling on the prescription of a regularly licensed physician, a complaint charging a violation of such ordinance need not allege that defendant was not a licensed druggist, since that is a matter of defense.—Ex parte Fedderwitz, 6, 562.

§ 2. Refusal of License to Sell.

Where a board of supervisors refuses a liquor license, and, after a peremptory writ of mandate, approves the bond filed by the applicants, and orders the license to issue, it cannot appeal from the judgment of mandate.—Leet v. Board of Supervisors, 5, 573.

An appeal by supervisors from a judgment of mandate requiring it to issue a liquor license, when the hearing is after the license has expired, will be dismissed.—Leet v. Board of Supervisors, 5, 573.

INTOXICATION.

As defense to crime. See Criminal Law, § 1.

INVENTORY AND APPRAISEMENT.

Of estate of decedent. See Executors and Administrators, § 6.

IRRIGATION.

See Waters and Watercourses.

§ 1. Assessments.

A complaint to recover money paid on a public assessment must show the nature of the proceedings to collect it, the threat of which constituted the compulsion.—Decker v. Perry, 4, 488.

Where thirty-three days must have elapsed, after plaintiff paid the assessment, before the three weeks' advertisement of sale of his land therefor could have begun (Stats. 1891, p. 245), and he does not allege that any sale had been already advertised or otherwise threatened when he paid, he fails to show any intention to sell it such as would make his payment involuntary.—Decker v. Perry, 4, 488.

§ 2. Complaint Against District Officer.

A complaint against an irrigation district officer alleged that such proceedings had been had before the board of supervisors that said board declared the district duly organized. Held, no averment that the district was incorporated, as provided by act of March 7, 1887, since it did not show the jurisdiction of the board, or an election held, or that its declaration "was duly given or made," or that a copy of the order had been filed for record.—Decker v. Perry, 4, 488.

§ 3. Deprivation of Rights by Corporation.

Where a land owner is entitled to an undisputed right and easement in and to a certain proportion of water, which an association was entitled to take from a stream to supply its irrigating plant connected with his land, on payment of his proportionate share of the expenses of maintaining the plant, a corporation succeeding to the rights of the association and the rights of other individual owners takes its property subject to his easement, and cannot deprive him thereof, though it improves and extends the system, and changes open ditches to pipe-lines.—Beck v. Pasadena Lake Vineyard Land and Water Co., 6, 363.

JAIL.

Injury to. See Malicious Mischief, § 1.

JOINDER.

Of causes. See Actions, § 4.
Of causes and parties in divorce. See Divorce, § 4.
Of actions in trover. See Trover and Conversion, § 4.
Of local and transitory actions. See Venue, § 3.

JOINT EXECUTOR.

Liability of. See Executors and Administrators, § 11.

JOINT LIABILITY.

On note. See Bills and Notes, § 7.

JUDGES.

§ 1. Attorney sitting by consent of parties.
§ 2. Disqualification and proceedings thereupon.
§ 3. Liability for acts.
§ 4. Payment of salaries.

In general. See Courts; Justices of Peace.
Testimony of as to decision. See Evidence, § 5.
Mandamus against. See Mandamus, § 3.
Death of judge. See New Trial, § 11.

§ 1. Attorney Sitting by Consent of Parties.

A trial before an attorney, acting as judge under no authority other than the consent of the parties, is a nullity.—Thompson v. Danforth, 1, 28.

§ 2. Disqualification and Proceedings Thereupon.

An order dismissing an action, made by a judge akin to the defendant within the third degree of relationship, is void.—Burton v. Covarrubias, 1, 209.

Bias or prejudice on the part of a trial judge constitutes no legal incapacity to sit on the trial of a cause.—McDowell v. Levy, 2, 590.

Where a case is transferred, because of the disqualification of the judge, to an adjoining judicial district, such court acquires jurisdiction, the judge having had authority under the statute to make the transfer, though the county was not the nearest one to which the case might have been transferred; and its judgment cannot be collaterally attacked.—Gage v. Downey, 3, 7.

Under Code of Civil Procedure, section 170, disqualifying judges to act who are interested in the controversy, where three parties are adversely claiming to be the owners of a certain tract of land, one of whom is the judge, and the other two adverse litigants before him, asking him to determine which of them is the owner of the land which he claims to own, and to appoint a receiver .for said land, a writ of prohibition will issue to prevent him from acting further in said cause.—Heilbron v. Campbell, 3, 204.

Code of Civil Procedure, section 398, requiring a judge who is disqualified from acting in a cause to transfer it, if pending before him, to some other court, is not satisfied by calling to the court of the disqualified judge a judge who is not disqualified.—Remy v. Olds, 5, 182.

The answer of a judge to a petition to restrain him from further acting as judge in a case pending before him admitted that he claimed to be the owner of certain land. The petitioner, who was a party to such pending action, claimed in his petition that said land was involved in the said action pending before the judge. Held, that a prohibitory order would issue to such judge, though by his answer he declared that, his attention having been called to the fact that the land claimed by him was claimed to be involved in the suit, he would not further act in it.—Heilbron v. Campbell, 5, 748.

§ 3. Liability for Acts.

An act of any sort by a judicial officer, provided it is judicial in character, is not a thing the officer can be made to answer for in an action by the person conceiving himself aggrieved.—Den v. Fernald, 1, 70.

§ 4. Payment of Salaries.

See Courts.

The words "as in other cases," occurring in the act of February 27, 1865 (Stats. 1865, p. 123), directing the county treasurers of Alpine county to pay the warrants issued to the county judges for their salaries and by the judges presented to such treasurers for payment, justify the payment of such warrants with other warrants according to the order in which all are registered.—Eno v. Carlson, 1, 354.

The fifteenth section of the constitution requiring the salaries of county judges to be paid "at stated times" does not execute itself, but is directory to the legislature merely; and the legislature in carrying out such direction passed the act of February 27, 1865, making the salary of the county judge of Alpine county payable monthly by warrant from the auditor, which warrant the treasurer is to honor on presentment of the same "as in other cases."—Eno v. Carlson, 1, 354.

JUDGMENTS.

§ 1. Construction and interpretation.
§ 2. —— Parol to explain.
§ 3. Findings and conclusions.
§ 4. Parties.
§ 5. —— Name, Christian or fictitious.
§ 6. —— Death of one plaintiff.
§ 7. Validity and propriety in general.
§ 8. Amendment and modification.
§ 9. Relief in excess of demand in complaint.
§ 10. On pleadings.
§ 11. Entry by consent.
§ 12. Default judgment.
§ 13. —— Opening or setting aside.
§ 14. —— Affidavits.
§ 15. Res judicata.
§ 16. Collateral attack.
§ 17. Setting aside or vacating.
§ 18. —— For defective service of process.
§ 19. —— Appeal from order.
§ 21. Payment and satisfaction.
§ 22. Action on—Statute of limitations.

Amendment of. See Amendments.
On bail bond. See Bail, § 2.
In action on note. See Bills and Notes, § 23.
Dismissal for failure to enter. See Dismissal and Nonsuit, § 3.
In ejectment. See Ejectment, § 20.
Confirmation decree. See Ejectment, § 21.
As evidence. See Evidence, §§ 22–25.
Claim against decedent. See Executors and Administrators, § 17.
In action against executor. See Executors and Administrators, § 32.
On foreclosure of lien. See Mechanics' Liens, § 21.
In foreclosure proceedings. See Mortgages, §§ 25, 26.
Conclusiveness and effect of partition. See Partition, § 4.
In suit to quiet title. See Quieting Title, § 11.
In replevin. See Replevin, § 6.
In action to enforce tax. See Taxation, § 18.

§ 1. Construction and Interpretation.

A sum is not the less included in a judgment if, instead of being named there in figures, it is referred to in apt words to indicate money then on deposit in court.—Pierson v. McCahill, 1, 276.

one of these, and the substitution of his executors, may be corrected, and are not ground for reversal.—Sanborn v. Cunningham, 4, 95.

§ 7. Validity and Propriety in General.

A verdict for simply the recovery of property does not warrant a judgment for damages in addition.—Peck v. Powell, 1, 48.

After a new trial, had agreeably to stipulation between the parties, a judgment that the first judgment "shall stand," the court thus adopting the findings upon which that judgment was rendered, is good.—Dermitt v. Delessert, Cordier & Co., 1, 12.

A money judgment on a verdict erroneous only in respect of its requiring payment to be made in gold coin cannot be modified on appeal. The judgment must conform to the verdict; hence the defendant is entitled to a new trial.—Finger v. Diel, 1, 889.

When the substantive fact upon which depends the cause of action, as stated in the complaint, is found against the plaintiff on sufficient evidence, the defendant should have judgment.—Warren v. Mould, 2, 163.

A case having been regularly set for trial, of which plaintiffs had notice, it was their duty to have attended at the time appointed, and a judgment in their absence is not error.—Thompson v. Spray, 2, 346.

An order denying a motion to vacate a void order does not validate such void order.—Smith v. Los Angeles etc. R. R. Co., 4, 237.

It being an admitted fact that the Geyser springs and hotel improvements are located on the N. E. ¼ of section 13 (the property in controversy), there was no impropriety in adding to the description of the property in the judgment the words "the same being known as the 'Geyser Hotel property.'"—Chapman v. Polack, 2, 424.

Where a complaint alleges that certain defendants were the owners of stock, and that they transferred the same for certain purposes to another, who, in turn, in fraud and violation of the agreement under which he received the stock, transferred the same to the appellant, who, having full knowledge of the facts, threatened to sell such stock, a decree as to him, enjoining the sale or the offering for sale of such stock, and directing that he return and deliver the same in specified amounts to persons named, is justified by the allegations of the complaint.—Oliver v. Blair, 2, 472.

Where a judgment contained the recital that it "duly appeared" to the courts that the prayer should be granted, the presumption is that the court had sufficient evidence to justify the judgment.—Cahill v. Colgan, 3, 622.

§ 8. Amendment and Modification.

See, also, Amendments, § 5.

A court has the power to amend the judgment entered in order to make the latter conform to the order directing it to be entered, and conform to the findings.—Mayo v. Sacramento, 1, 646.

When an issuable fact, in an action for the payment of money, is the payment in gold coin, and, the jury having rendered a general verdict for the plaintiff for a certain sum, judgment is entered accordingly, the trial court may amend the judgment by making it payable in gold.—Merritt v. Wilcox, 1, 884.

Where the complaint contains two counts, one of which does not constitute a cause of action, and the error in rendering a judgment thereon can be cured by a modification of the judgment, the verdicts on each count having been returned separately, a new trial will not be ordered.—Castle v. Smith, 4, 561.

§ 9. Relief in Excess of Demand in Complaint.

A judgment may not be given for relief beyond that demanded in the complaint or for a sum in excess of the sum demanded.—Lamping v. Red Star Co., 1, 166.

On its being shown that a judgment by default has been taken for a sum greater than that asked for in the complaint and against more and other persons than named in the summons and complaint, and that the demand in the summons was beyond that in the complaint, the court on appeal may order the plaintiffs to file their written consent to a modification of the judgment within a time named, in default of which consent the judgment must be reversed.—Lamping v. Red Star Co., 1, 166.

§ 10. On Pleadings.

A motion by the plaintiff for judgment on the pleadings can be allowed only where the answer wholly fails to deny any material allegation of the complaint.—Willson v. McDonald, 1, 516.

A judgment on the pleadings, on a motion therefor, can be rendered only on averments of the pleadings, admitted or not denied, justifying a judgment on one side or the other as the case may be.—Vassault v. Kirby, 1, 668.

Where action is brought under contract to pay certain tolls, and the answer does not deny the contract, but alleges that such tolls are illegal, and the plaintiff offers evidence in support of the complaint, and no evidence is introduced by the defendant the plaintiff is entitled to judgment on the admissions in the answer.—Frantz v. Harper, 6, 560.

§ 11. Entry by Consent.

A judgment record reciting that the same was ordered upon the written stipulation of defendant, consenting thereto, is conclusive of its correctness on appeal by defendants, in the absence of any bill of exceptions or other contradiction by the record.—Hibernia Savings & Loan Soc. v. Russell, 6, 404.

§ 12. Default Judgment.

A judgment given the plaintiff must not be for anything more than what the complaint and summons inform the defendant will be asked of the court.—Hanson v. Smith, 1, 261.

Where a default has been entered against one of two defendants, for failure to answer the original complaint, the failure to serve amended complaints on such defendant will not be ground for reversal of the judgment, where the record does not show that such amended complaints were not served.—Heinlen v. Erlanger, 2, 257.

Where plaintiff sues on a judgment, joining as defendants persons claiming adverse rights therein, demanding, in addition to the recovery on the judgment, a determination that the adverse claimants have no interest therein, and judgment is rendered against him on the latter contention, he is not entitled to judgment against the judgment debtor who is in default, under Code of Civil Procedure, section 585, allowing judgment by default in actions arising on contract for the recovery of money only.—McDonald v. Mayor etc. of City of Placerville, 6, 192.

§ 13. —— Opening or Setting Aside.

A judgment by default will not be opened when it appears to have come about through the defendant's gross neglect only.—Whipley v. Flower, 1, 35.

A judgment for the plaintiff, entered upon the failure of the defendant to appear at the trial, is not to be set aside on a showing by defendant that his nonappearance was by reason of his being "extremely and necessarily busy on his ranch taking care of his cattle."—Del Valle v. More, 1, 66.

In refusing to open a default judgment, taken only after several months have passed since the lapse of the statutory time for answering, the court will be deemed not to have overstepped the bounds of sound discretion.—People v. Seale, 1, 321.

Where a defendant has failed to answer through an excusable misunderstanding between his attorney and himself, rather than through either inattention or indifference, and he really thought he had a good defense and intended to have it made, a default judgment against him should be set aside.—Sweet v. McGlynn, 1, 773.

An order setting aside a judgment by default will not be disturbed on appeal, unless there is a showing made of an abuse of discretion.—Southern Pac. R. R. Co. v. White, 2, 151.

Where defendant answers, but, failing to appear at the trial, judgment was rendered for plaintiff, there was no abuse of discretion on the part of the court below in granting defendant's motion to vacate the judgment and award a new trial, on the grounds of accident and surprise.—Heinlen v. Centerville etc. Irr. Ditch Co., 2, 347.

To set aside a judgment by default on motion and affidavits showing that defendant's attorney had suddenly died, and that defendant himself had no knowledge of the case, is not an abuse of the court's discretion.—Boyle v. Solstien, 2, 846.

An order setting aside a default and permitting a defendant to plead after the time allowed by law has elapsed will not be set aside unless the court abused its discretion.—Clarke v. Wittram, 4, 65.

Where, in ejectment, default and judgment were taken and rendered against a tenant without the knowledge of his landlord, a motion to set aside the default and vacate the judgment was properly granted.—Mowry v. Nunez, 4, 162.

While a motion to open a default is addressed largely to the discretion of the court, all doubts should be resolved in favor of the application; and, where the circumstances lead the court to hesitate as to the merits of the application, an order denying such a motion will be reversed on appeal.—Vermont Marble Co. v. Black, 4, 901.

An order setting aside a judgment by default is largely discretionary, and, where moved for at once and granted upon terms, will not be disturbed on appeal, though the showing made is not strong.—Goodrich v. Loupe, 5, 453.

Where there is a conflict of evidence submitted on a motion to set aside a default, the determination of the court denying the motion will not be reviewed on appeal.—Bank of Ukiah v. Reed, 6, 604.

Where a written memorandum of an agreement between the parties to a suit is executed, in which is expressed the consent of defendants that their defaults be entered, and an agreement on the part of plaintiff not to take judgment until a certain time, the burden of proof is on defendants to show that they were entitled to a further notice, and to additional time beyond the date expressed in the memorandum, before judgment could properly be entered against them by default.—Bank of Ukiah v. Reed, 6, 604.

§ 14. —— Affidavits.

An affidavit to set aside a judgment by default is not sufficient where it shows that defendants served notice of appearance on plaintiff's attorneys, but does not show that they agreed to extend defendants' time to answer, or that defendants supposed their time had been extended.—Jenkins v. Gamewell Fire-alarm Tel. Co., 3, 655.

An affidavit of merits, stating facts on information and belief, is insufficient, as being hearsay.—Jenkins v. Gamewell Fire-alarm Tel. Co., 3, 655.

§ 15. Res Judicata and Estoppel.

Former judgment in ejectment. See Ejectment, § 14.

Where there are two judgments in different suits, commenced at different times, between the same parties, involving the same subject matter, and determining the same points in different ways, the party prevailing in the first suit will be estopped by the judgment in the last; this judgment can operate as an estoppel, however, only upon those matters which were necessarily determined.—Willson v. Truebody, 1, 238.

A decision of one question of law presented by stipulation does not imply a waiver of all other questions in the case, nor does the decision of that question imply that other questions that might have been determined upon the record as presented were in fact decided.—Donner v. Palmer, 1, 392.

If an inferior court of limited jurisdiction has been passed upon the necessary jurisdictional facts and decided them to be sufficiently proved, the parties and their privies are estopped to litigate them again in a collateral action.—People v. Hager, 2, 13.

Each claim presented to and rejected by a board of supervisors constitutes a distinct and separate cause of action, and a judgment obtained on one will constitute no bar to an action for the recovery of the others.—Hughes v. Mendocino County, 2, 333.

A judgment against a city in a former action, declaring that no dedication of certain land had been made, is a bar to a subsequent action by the city against the same parties to obtain possession of the land under the same claim of alleged dedication.—People v. Holladay, 2, 438.

Plaintiff alleged, in an action against her husband's administrator for certain land, that her husband, who owned no property, acquired title to the land in question under a mortgage which he took to secure a loan of her money. It appeared that he acquired title to part of the land under the mortgage, and to the remainder by deed. Held, that a decree in plaintiff's favor for the entire tract is conclusive of her right thereto as against her husband's estate.—Gage v. Downey, 3, 7.

In an action to enjoin the diversion of "any water" from a river, and the obstruction thereof by "any" dam, defendant claimed a right, by adverse user, to divert "14,400 inches per second, under a four-inch pressure." It was adjudged that plaintiff's cause of action was barred, the court finding specially that defendant had adversely diverted "one hundred cubic feet per second, under a four-inch pressure." Held, in a subsequent action by plaintiff to enjoin the diversion of a greater quantity of water than "14,400 cubic inches per second," that defendant was not estopped by the first judgment to claim that it had acquired the right to divert more than that quantity, since the special finding in the first action should be construed to mean that it had a right to one hundred miners' feet, equal to fourteen thousand four hundred miners' inches, per second, under a four-inch pressure, the amount intended to be claimed in the answer; and judgment was properly rendered that defendant was entitled to an equivalent quantity, "450 cubic feet of water per second," under the evidence, which showed, in addition to the rate at which the water would flow under such pressure through an aperture of one hundred square feet, that defendant, when taking steps to appropriate the water under Civil Code, section 1415, after posting notices claiming fourteen thousand four hundred cubic inches per second under a four-inch pressure, constructed a ditch of sufficient capacity to carry off seven hundred and seventy-seven thousand six hundred cubic inches, equal to four hundred and fifty cubic feet, per second, rather than fourteen thousand four hundred cubic inches only.—Lillis v. People's Ditch Co., 3, 494.

Where a judgment for defendant has been rendered in an action on notes because the complaint did not set out the contract under which the notes were given, and allege performance of its conditions, which performance was necessary for a recovery upon the notes, and where there is no issue tendered in the complaint or answer as to the performance of this condition, this judgment is no bar to an action on the notes and the contract.—Naftzger v. Gregg, 3, 520.

A judgment cannot be pleaded in bar during the time for appeal therefrom and while a motion for a new trial is pending.—Fresno Milling Co. v. Fresno Canal & Irr. Co., 4, 592.

A judgment rendered in an action for an unlawful entry of certain lands has no effect upon a subsequent action between the same parties to quiet title to said lands.—Millett v. Lagomarsino, 4, 883.

In ejectment against several defendants a judgment in a former action between plaintiff and one of the defendants, offered generally against all, is inadmissible, unless they are privy in estate and bound by such judgment.—Lord v. Thomas, 5, 769.

A prior judgment is conclusive upon parties only as to matters actually and necessarily decided therein.—Lord v. Thomas, 5, 769.

In a former action brought by defendants against plaintiff to quiet title, the judgment quieted title in defendants, with a proviso that nothing in the decree should impair the rights reserved in the Van Ness Ordinance to the plaintiff, over lands that had "then been occupied or set apart" for public use. The opinion of the supreme court deciding that case held that all the rights which the plaintiff had, and which could be conveyed by said ordinance, had passed to defendant's grantor at a time shortly after the passage of such ordinance. Held, that the expression "then occupied or set apart," as used in the judgment, had reference to the date of the passage of the ordinance, and not to the date of the commencement of the action to quiet title, or the decree therein.—City and County of San Francisco v. Center, 6, 595.

§ 16. Collateral Attack.

A judgment is good until reversed, and therefore is not to be questioned for the first time in an action on an alleged wrongful sale in execution of it.—Foster v. Coronel, 1, 402.

A void order may be attacked in any proceeding.—Smith v. Los Angeles etc. R. R. Co., 4, 237.

43

§ 17. Setting Aside or Vacating.

A party aggrieved by a judgment obtained by fraud may seek relief by appeal or by bill in equity, but the trial judge is without jurisdiction to set the judgment aside.—People v. Talmage, 1, 36.

After the expiration of the term during which a judgment is made the trial court is without jurisdiction to set it aside, except in a case where the defendant was not served with process.—White v. Williams, 1, 51.

No surprise on the part of defendants being shown from the facts, and no new evidence being produced, the orders denying a motion to vacate judgment on the ground of surprise, and denying a motion for a new trial on the ground of newly discovered evidence, were properly made, and are affirmed.—Cox v. O'Neil, 2, 352.

A judgment regular on its face cannot be set aside on motion attacking its validity.—Tuffree v. Stearns Rancho Co., 6, 129.

Where on a motion to set aside a judgment there is no affidavit of merits, the ground of mistake and excusable neglect cannot be considered.—Block v. Kearney, 6, 660.

A judgment void for want of jurisdiction may be set aside on motion made on notice, though more than a year has elapsed since entry of the judgment.—Hanson v. Hanson, 3, 66.

§ 18. —— For Defective Service of Process.

Judgment may not be had against a defendant not served with process and who has not appeared in the action.—Megerle v. Ashe, 1, 659.

A judgment rendered in a suit begun by an irregular service of the summons and complaint, or of either, may not be attacked in a collateral action as void for want of jurisdiction.—Drake v. Duvenick, 1, 678.

Judgment may not be had against a defendant not served with process and who has not appeared in the action.—Megerle v. Ashe, 1, 659.

Acquiescence in a judgment for ten years, the rights of third persons having supervened, estops a defendant to question it on the ground of defective proof of service of process, even though the ground might have been good on motion to quash before judgment rendered.—Drake v. Duvenick, 1, 678.

Where a judgment is vacated because the defendants had not been served with summons, nor had appeared in the action, a refusal to make an order that the respondent should answer the complaint is not error.—Merced Co. v. Hicks, 2, 483.

The trial court has no power to review its own order setting aside a judgment for want of service of summons, where the order was regularly made after hearing and consideration.—Hanson v. Hanson, 3, 66.

§ 19. —— Appeal from Order.

Under Code of Civil Procedure, section 939 (3), authorizing an appeal from a special order made after judgment, an appeal lies from an order refusing to vacate a judgment.—Hibernia Savings & Loan Soc. v. Cochran, 6, 821.

Where on appeal from the denial of defendant's motion to vacate the judgment, respondent moves to dismiss on the ground that the order is not appealable, because the judgment is itself appealable, the motion will be denied, since whether the grounds relied on for the appeal would have been available on an appeal from the judgment involves an examination of the record.—Hibernia Savings & Loan Soc. v. Cochran, 6, 821.

§ 21. Payment and Satisfaction.

A judgment satisfied of record by order of court is no longer an actionable claim against the person named therein as the judgment debtor.—Strathern v. Rock Island G. & S. M. Co., 2, 71.

M. held a judgment against G., which he agreed to release if G. would deliver him a deed to certain property, which he did. Prior to such agreement, G. had made an assignment of all his property for the benefit of his creditors. M. knew that G. had made an assignment, but denied knowing that it included the specified property. G. made no attempt to conceal any fact. Held, that an order directing the entry of satisfaction of the judgment was proper.— Musser v. Gray, 3, 639.

Where judgment is rendered against a savings bank for a deposit with accrued dividends, the creditor having leave to apply for any relief needed to fix the amount and enforce payment, and later a decree is entered fixing the amount due to date at a certain sum, for which judgment is rendered against the bank, the first judgment is interlocutory, and payment of the second discharges both.— Wheelock v. Godfrey, 4, 396.

§ 22. Action on—Statute of Limitations.

The plea of nul tiel record is a good defense to an action on a judgment.—Reynolds v. Robertson, 2, 414.

Under Code of Civil Procedure, section 336, limiting the time within which an action on a judgment or decree must be brought to five years, no recovery could be had in an action on a judgment brought more than five, but less than six years after judgment was entered, Code of Civil Procedure, section 1049, providing that an action is pending from its commencement until its final determination on appeal, or until the time for appeal has passed, unless the judgment is sooner satisfied, not giving additional life to the judgment.— Feeney v. Hinckley, 6, 666.

JUDGMENT-ROLL.

See Appeal and Error, § 32.

JUDICIAL NOTICE.

In general. See Evidence, § 7.

JUDICIAL SALES.

See Execution, §§ 7–12; Executors and Administrators, § 20; Mortgages, § 27.

§ 1. Rights and Title of Purchasers.

The title of a purchaser of real estate at a sheriff's sale does not depend on and is not affected by the advertisement or the return of the officer to the writ, but rather on the judgment, execution, sale and deed.—Hibberd v. Smith, 1, 554.

D., against whom plaintiff held a judgment, succeeded, on his wife's death, to one-third of her lands, and conveyed his interest to defendant in trust to be leased, and one-half of the profits applied to his support during his life, and at his death the whole to go to his children. After the execution of the trust deed, plaintiff levied an execution on D.'s interest in the land, and at the sale bid it in, taking a sheriff's deed. Afterward, plaintiff received the balance due on the judgment, and entered a satisfaction in full. Held, that at the time of the sale under execution the legal title was in defendant, and plaintiff, under the sheriff's deed, took nothing but D.'s equitable interest therein, which ceased on D.'s death.—Judson v. Lyford, 3, 199.

Whatever may have been plaintiff's right, as a creditor, to set aside the deed of trust because given to hinder and defraud creditors, it was lost by his purchasing the "right, title, and interest of D." in the property, and accepting the balance due on the judgment, and acknowledging satisfaction thereof, and he thereafter had no other standing than that of a purchaser at an execution sale, subject to the rule of caveat emptor.—Judson v. Lyford, 3, 199.

§ 2. When Will be Set Aside.

In a proceeding by a judgment defendant to set aside a sheriff's sale it appeared that 600,000 feet of lumber belonging to the execution defendant were sold to claimant for $700, and that the sale was made in lump for a grossly inadequate sum. Held, that the sale was properly set aside.—Georgeson v. Consumers' Lumber Co., 3, 584.

JURISDICTION.

See Venue.

On appeal. See Appeal and Error, §§ 1–3.
In general. See Courts.
Of justice. See Justices of Peace, § 1.

§ 1. Finding of Lack of Jurisdiction—Effect.

After a finding against the plaintiff for lack of jurisdiction of the court, the right remains in him to proceed in a court that has jurisdiction, and pleadings framed so as to prejudice this right are bad.—Fairbanks v. Bear, 1, 39.

JURY.

§ 1. Right to jury trial—Waiver.
§ 2. Calling by court.
§ 3. Summoning new panel.
§ 4. Qualification and competency.
§ 5. Challenges.
§ 6. Jury fees—Certificate for payment.

Trial by jury in building and loan case. See Building and Loan Associations, § 1.
Misconduct of. See Criminal Law, § 8.
In equity cases. See Equity, §§ 4–6.
Misconduct or prejudice as ground for new trial. See New Trial, §§ 4, 5.

§ 1. Right to Jury Trial—Waiver.

By failure to file, within six days of the beginning of the term, a notice that a jury will be required a party waives a jury.—Thornton v. Thompson, 1, 170.

Plaintiff brought an action under Code of Civil Procedure, section 1050, alleging that defendant was making a claim against him for money upon a pretended promissory note; that the exact nature of the claim was unknown to plaintiff; and praying that defendant be compelled to set forth the nature and extent thereof, in order that the court might determine it to be invalid. Defendant answered in the form of an ordinary complaint on a promissory note, and to this plaintiff filed a reply, alleging fraud in procuring the note, mistake, and want of consideration. Held, the action being purely statutory and equitable in form, the reply to plaintiff's answer was unnecessary to the relief sought, and he was not entitled to a jury trial upon the issue thereby raised.—Taylor v. Ford, 3, 297.

§ 2. Calling by Court.

Though both parties to an action which Code of Civil Procedure, section 592, provides must be tried by jury, unless a jury trial is waived, waive the trial by jury, the court has the right to call a jury for the trial of the cause.—Bullock v. Consumers' Lumber Co., 3, 609.

§ 3. Summoning New Panel.

In the absence of direct proof to the contrary, the trial court is supposed to have acted properly in ordering the sheriff to summon a new panel.—People v. Wise, 1, 33.

§ 4. Qualification and Competency.

By expressly waiving a juryman's incompetency, as being nonresident of the county, a person under trial for crime would be conferring jurisdiction by consent, which cannot be done.—People v. March, 1, 6.

An opinion as to guilt or innocence, based on rumor or purported facts in the case, not fixed and settled but which would require evidence to remove, does not subject a proposed juror to challenge for implied bias.—People v. Jones, 1, 544.

A juror on his voir dire was asked by the defense if he had any special prejudice against offenses "committed during Sunday broils." The district attorney, objecting, remarked that no one broiled but defendant. The juror was accepted without challenge. Held, no prejudice.—People v. Davis, 4, 524.

When a juror understands English "pretty well," but will not say that he could always understand what anyone might say in English, it is for the court to decide whether he, is competent to comprehend all that might be said in his hearing.—People v. Davis, 4, 524.

§ 5. Challenges.

Error in refusing to allow a challenge for cause is not prejudicial if the party, although forced thereby to use a peremptory challenge, has a peremptory challenge to spare when the jury is completed.—Baird v. Duane, 1, 492.

To sustain the refusing of a peremptory challenge on the ground that the juror had already been accepted by the challenging party, the statement in the bill of exceptions must show that this juror had been sworn before so challenged; the fact may not be left to be inferred.—People v. Melville, 1, 508.

No exception can be taken to the decision of a court allowing a challenge. A person summoned as a juror, who entertains conscientious scruples against finding a man guilty of a crime for which he would be hung must neither be permitted nor compelled to serve as a juror.—People v. Abbott, 2, 383.

No exception lies to a ruling denying a challenge to a juror for actual cause.—People v. Brown, 2, 701.

§ 6. Jury Fees—Certificate for Payment.

Where a party to a suit is ordered to pay the jury fees, the court has not the power to order the clerk to issue certificates for their payment out of the county treasury, upon the mere neglect, failure, or refusal of the party to comply with the order by paying as required.—Ex parte Makinney, 2, 283.

JUSTICES OF THE PEACE.

§ 1. Jurisdiction of justice.
§ 2. Existence of office.
§ 3. —— Attack upon by habeas corpus.
§ 4. Vacancies in office.
§ 5. Fees to be paid by litigants.
§ 6. Appeal to superior court.
§ 7. —— Notice and bond.

Compensation of. See Constitutional Law, § 8.

§ 1. Jurisdiction of Justice.

The exercise by a justice of the peace of jurisdiction outside of that conferred by the constitution is not the exercise of an office, and the result thereof would be to render acts done outside of such jurisdiction void.—People v. Veuve, 2, 313.

A justice of the peace has no jurisdiction of the crime of embezzlement committed in another county.—Ex parte Cooke, 4, 969.

§ 2. Existence of Office.

Code of Civil Procedure, section 103, as amended by Statutes of 1899, page 88, provides that in every city or town of the fourth class there shall be one justice of the peace. Statutes of 1883, page 24, as amended by Statutes of 1899, page 141, provides that all municipal corporations having a population of 10,000 and not exceeding 15,000 constitute the fourth class, and that there may be a speial enumeration to determine the population of a city, which when made shall be deemed the number of inhabitants of such city for the purpose of legislation affecting municipalities. Statutes of 1895, page 409, in the preamble to a resolution ratifying the freeholders' charter of a town, recited that such town had a population of more than 10,000. Held, that the office of justice of the peace for such town had a legal existence, and could be legally filled.—Ex parte Fedderwitz, 6, 562.

§ 3. —— Attack upon by Habeas Corpus.

Where the office of justice of the peace in a city has a legal existence, the title of the incumbent cannot be attacked in habeas corpus proceedings by a party convicted before such justice of violation of a municipal ordinance.—Ex parte Fedderwitz, 6, 562.

§ 4. Vacancies in Office.

City justices of the peace are not township or county officers, and the board of supervisors has no authority to fill vacancies therein.—People v. Sands, 4, 424.

Although inferior court in incorporated cities can be established only by the constitution (article 6, section 1), and their jurisdictions, powers and duties must be fixed by the legislature (Constitution, article 6, section 13) still a valid provision for filling vacancies may be made by charter.—People v. Sands, 4, 424.

Under a charter providing that the mayor shall appoint suitable persons to fill vacancies in office, he is empowered to fill vacancies in the offices of city justices of the peace.—People v. Sands, 4, 424.

§ 5. Fees to be Paid by Litigants.

After payment of the sum of two dollars to a justice of the peace, required to be paid by a party on beginning an action in his court, an additional sum of three dollars is to be paid him only in the event of there being an actual trial of the case.—People v. Pennie, 1, 348.

§ 6. Appeal to Superior Court.

On an appeal from a justice's court to a superior court, where all the papers in the case have been transferred except a copy of the justice's docket, the superior court has jurisdiction to order the transfer of a copy of the justice's docket under Code of Civil Procedure of California, section 975.—Burgess v. Superior Court, 2, 741.

A judgment entered by consent in the justice's court is not appealable, and the superior court is authorized to dismiss such an appeal of its own motion.—Yeazell v. Superior Court, 2, 355.

On appeal from a default judgment of a justice of the peace, whether on questions of law or of law and fact, there cannot be a trial de novo.—Maxson v. Superior Court of Madera County, 6, 124.

On appeal from a justice court, the superior court has no jurisdiction, on reversing, to remand the case to the justice, the effect of an order vacating a justice's judgment being to dismiss the action without prejudice.—Maxson v. Superior Court of Madera County, 6, 124.

§ 7. —— Notice and Bond.

An appeal will not be dismissed because the bond was not filed within thirty days after the rendition of the judgment by a justice of the peace, if the bond was delivered and left at the office of the justice, but was not received or marked "Filed" by him until two days after the thirty days.—Perkins v. Superior Court of Fresno County, 4, 788.

The marking of the filing of a notice of appeal by a justice is not the only competent evidence of the filing of the paper and the absence of an entry in the justice's docket is not conclusive proof of the fact that it had not been filed.—Williams v. Superior Court of Lassen Co., 5, 598.

JUSTIFICATION.

Of sureties on appeal bond. See Appeal and Error, § 26.

LACHES.

In seeking relief from fraud. See Fraud, § 1.
In enforcing resulting trusts. See Trusts, § 7.
As barring right to specific performance. See Specific Performance, § 4.

LANDLORD AND TENANT.

§ 1. Lease and construction thereof.
§ 2. —— Cancellation because obtained by conspiracy.
§ 3. Extension, repudiation or rescission.
§ 4. Assignment of lease or sale of leasehold.
§ 5. Pasturage of stock.
§ 6. Gas and water bills.
§ 7. Rent and actions to recover.
§ 7a. Notice to quit.
§ 8. Estoppel to deny landlord's title.
§ 9. Liability for tenant's health.
See Forcible Entry and Detainer; Unlawful Detainer.

Possession of tenant. See Adverse Possession, § 3.
Lease by guardian. See Guardian and Ward, § 8.

§ 1. Lease and Construction Thereof.

A contract of lease and an amendment thereof provided for the payment of rental as follows: A rental of $30 per month; $4,000 to a bank (the amount being secured by mortgage on the premises), together with $26.65 per month as interest thereon; also $900, which is "now a lien on the premises," as follows: $200 in one year, $200 in two and one-half years, and $350 "at the expiration of the lease," or whenever the lessee purchases the premises, under an option. The lease was to run for twenty years, unless sooner terminated. Thereafter the lessee surrendered possession, a part of the monthly rental and interest, and also the first installment of the $900, having accrued. Held, that the lessee could not object to a construction of the lease which merely made her liable for the sums mentioned, and released her from liability for the $4,000 and the two installments of the $900 which had not matured, etc.—Hobson v. Silva, 7, 31.

A lease provided that the lessee's liability should not commence until a certain suit is "finally adjudicated and determined in favor of G." It was admitted that the suit was adjudicated in favor of G. by a judgment rendered on September 3d, as alleged in the complaint. After said date an amended lease was made, making no mention of the lawsuit. Defendant from the very first paid rent, regardless of the provision. Held, that, even if the allegation of the complaint was not as broad as the language used in the lease, it might be assumed that the provision was regarded as fully complied with.—Hobson v. Silva, 7, 31.

§ 2. —— Cancellation Because Obtained by Conspiracy.

Where a complaint averred that defendants had conspired to cheat and defraud the plaintiff by inducing him to lease to one of them certain lands, and that they had carried out such conspiracy by fraudulent representations to plaintiff to his injury, and that he had suffered damage thereby, the complaint was held to state a good cause of action entitling him to a cancellation of the lease.—Davis v. McGrew, 2, 561.

§ 3. Extension, Repudiation or Rescission.

A tenant who has repudiated his lease and set up title in himself cannot complain if he is made to pay damages as a trespasser.—Hibbard v. Chipman, 1, 16.

Plaintiff leased land to defendant for a certain period, before the expiration of which plaintiff told defendant that he could have the land for another like period, the defendant agreeing to cut plaintiff's crops as a part consideration for the extension; and subsequently plaintiff said that he would not go back on his word, and that, as the ground was low, and not in shape for planting, defendant "could summer-fallow it." Part only of the land was summer-fallowed by defendant before the expiration of the original lease. Held, that the summer-fallowing of the ground was not a condition precedent to the extension of the lease, since it was a mere suggestion by plaintiff, and a matter of no concern to him, since he was not to be paid a crop rental.—Schweikert v. Seavey, 6, 554.

Civil Code, section 1689, provides that contracts may be rescinded only in cases where the consent of the party rescinding is obtained by fraud, duress or undue influence; or failure of consideration through fault of party as to whom the contract is rescinded; or on such consideration becoming entirely void from any cause; or if the consideration, before it is rendered, fails in a material respect; or by consent of all the parties. Section 1691 declares that the rescinding party must restore or offer to restore the value he has received under the contract. Plaintiff leased certain land to defendant for a certain period, before the expiration of which he told defendant he might have it for another like period, and subsequently acknowledged to plaintiff that he told him he might have the land, but that his word was worthless, and that he could not have it. Held, that this did not amount to a rescission of the contract, but was a mere repudiation.—Schweikert v. Seavey, 6, 554.

§ 4. Assignment of Lease on Sale of Leasehold.

The denial of a new trial, after a finding that an assignment of a lease was procured by fraud, is to be sustained if ordered upon any supporting evidence.—Linehan v. Joost, 2, 171.

A lessor sued defendant for a conversion of crops grown on a leasehold purchased by defendant under execution against the lessee. The lease provided that crops grown on the premises should be the lessor's property until the lessee performed certain conditions. Held, that as the conditions had not been performed, the purchaser acquired no right to the crop, and the judgment-roll and execution were properly excluded from evidence, as immaterial and irrelevant.—Farnum v. Hefner, 2, 831.

In the absence of an agreement to the contrary, a tenant who assigns his lease for the whole term remains liable thereon to the landlord, as surety for the assignee.—Dietz v. Kucks, 5, 406.

§ 5. Pasturage of Stock.

Where a lessee denied that he agreed before making the lease to pasture horses belonging to the lessor's son free in consideration of their use, and the evidence tended to show that all the conditions of the lease were entered into prior to its execution, in an action by the lessee for pasturage, an instruction that an agreement reduced to writing is conclusively presumed to contain all its terms, in the absence of fraud or mistake, was applicable.—Grant v. Dreyfus, 5, 970.

In an action by a lessee on an account for pasturing stock belonging to lessor's son, evidence of the removal from the premises, and sale by him of certain materials, which evidence related to the breach of a covenant of the lease, was inadmissible, there being no issue concerning any breach.—Grant v. Dreyfus, 5, 970.

§ 6. Gas and Water Bills.

A lessee who makes a lease, knowing that other tenants are in possession, who are to attorn to her, cannot recover from the landlord for gas and water bills overdue when she takes possession, where it does not appear that they are not the personal bills of the other tenants.—Hobson v. Silva, 7, 31.

§ 7. Rent and Actions to Recover.

The complaint in an action for rent alleged that, after plaintiff had commenced a suit to foreclose a mortgage on the leased premises, defendant entered into possession under an agreement requiring him to pay a portion of the rent to plaintiff and a portion to the mortgagor. The answer set out a lease with the mortgagor alone, under which defendant claimed that he took possession of the property; but it required the payment to plaintiff of the same portion of the rent as alleged in the complaint. The answer also set out a guaranty of possession to defendants, which had been executed by plaintiff. Held, not such a variance as to the manner of leasing the property as would preclude judgment on the pleadings in plaintiff's favor. Butler v. Burt, 6, 917.

Where a tenant enters into possession of the leased premises under a lease reciting a decree of mortgage foreclosure and order for the sale of the property, and requiring the tenant to pay a portion of the rent to the mortgagee if he purchases the property at the foreclosure sale, the fact that the mortgagee has the decree and order of sale set aside does not preclude him from recovering such rent, after he has purchased the property at a sale under a subsequent decree in the same suit.—Butler v. Burt, 6, 917.

The defendant in an action for rent alleged the surrender of possession and the payment of $140 to plaintiff on the day when the latter commenced an unlawful detainer suit. The claim in the action for rent was to a certain date, and the rent from that time till the surrender of the premises would amount to $140 at the rate at which the property was rented. It was also alleged that such payment and surrender of possession was under the agreement that it was not to be taken as an admission by defendant that plaintiff had any claim against defendant for rent. Held, that it was not error, in rendering judgment for plaintiff on the pleadings, which did not. show any defense, to refuse to give defendant credit for the $140.—Butler v. Burt, 6, 917.

§ 7a. Notice to Quit.

A notice to quit, requiring the tenants to pay their rent, amounting to $100, "being the amount now owing from me to you," or deliver possession, was good, and entitled the landlord to maintain unlawful detainer, notwithstanding the mistake in the phrase "me to you."—Lacrabee v. Wise, 7, 107.

§ 8. Estoppel to Deny Landlord's Title.

Where plaintiff had such title under a deed of trust as enabled him to execute a valid lease for a term not exceeding the life of the beneficiary named therein, and defendant entered under said lease, and has never been disturbed in possession, and no one except plaintiff has claimed any right to the rents, he cannot deny plaintiff's title in an action to recover the rents accruing after the death of the beneficiary, though such title ceased on the death of such beneficiary. Ashton v. Golden Gate Lumber Co., 6, 307.

Under Code of Civil Procedure, section 1962, subdivision 4, providing what presumptions shall be deemed conclusive, declaring that a tenant is not permitted to deny the title of his landlord at the time of the. commencement of the relation, the conclusive presumption of the landlord's title having attached, it continues until in some mode recognized by the law it may be rebutted.—Ashton v. Golden Gate Lumber Co., 6, 307.

A lease given to a person in possession of land by a person out of possession, and accepted by the first person under threat of being ousted in case of his rejecting it, does not estop the lessee to deny the title of the lessor.—Holloway v. Galliac, 1, 522.

A tenant is estopped to deny his landlord's title, and such estoppel continues, not to the end of his term merely, but to the end of his possession; or, where there has been a repudiation of the tenancy, and a consequent adverse holding by the tenant, until the statute of limitations has run in his favor; and such an adverse possession cannot be set up without a surrender of possession as tenant.—Sawyer v. Sargent, 2, 480.

§ 9. Liability for Tenant's Health.

Civil Code, section 1941, requiring the lessor to put buildings intended for human occupation in a condition fit for occupancy, does not create such an implied warranty that a tenement is fit for human occupation as to render the lessor liable to the tenant for injury to his health resulting from a defective sewer, where the lessor had no notice of the defect.—Angevine v. Knox-Goodrich, 3, 648.

LARCENY.

Accomplices in. See Accomplices and Accessories, § 5.

§ 1. What Constitutes.

The crime of larceny is complete when the felonious taking or asportation is consummated.—People v. Valenzuella, 2, 87.

In a prosecution for grand larceny, if the act of taking the property is admitted, but a felonious intent denied, the question of intent is one for the jury.—People v. Grider, 2, 285.

§ 2. Grand Larceny.

In fixing $50 as the value test of property stolen, in order to make the charge grand larceny, the legislature is not presumed to have contemplated national legislation thereafter making a new sort of money legal tender.—People v. Welch, 1, 221.

Under section 487 of the Penal Code, larceny of a horse or mare is grand larceny, though the value of the animal is less than $50.—People v. Leehey, 2, 56.

The stealing a watch from the person of another is grand larceny, though the value of the watch is less than $50.—People v. Sherman, 3, 851.

Evidence examined, and held to sustain defendant's conviction for grand larceny.—People v. Taylor, 6, 942.

§ 3. Jurisdiction of Superior Court.

Where a defendant is convicted in the superior court of petit larceny, on an information which charges him with grand larceny, he may be confined in the county jail under such conviction, though the superior court has no jurisdiction of petit larceny, since the charge of grand larceny gave the court jurisdiction, and Penal Code, section 1159, authorizes a conviction of petit larceny when grand larceny is charged.—Ex parte Bell, 4, 309.

§ 4. Venue of Crime.

Section 786 of the Penal Code, authorizing a trial in the county into which the property has been brought, contemplates property "taken by larceny" in another county and a completed offense in that other county.—People v. Valenzuella, 2, 87.

A fresh larceny cannot be imputed to the thief in every county into which he leads or carries the stolen property, as the effect of the law authorizing his being tried in a county into which he has brought such property.—People v. Valenzuella, 2, 87.

§ 5. Indictment or Information.

Defendant, on a day and in a county named, "did unlawfully and feloniously take, steal and carry away one horse, of the persona!

goods and chattels of one ——," naming the owner, etc., is sufficient. People v. Salazar, 2, 90.

A demurrer to an information on the ground that it was indefinite was properly overruled, as that is not one of the grounds for demurrer enumerated by Penal Code, section 1004.—People v. Garcia, 6, 367.

As Penal Code, section 487, declares that grand larceny is committed when the value of the property taken exceeds $50, an information is within the statute whether it alleges that the stealing of property of such value was from the person or not.—People v. Garcia, 6, 367.

An indictment sufficiently describes the stolen property as "one cow, the same being the property then and there of H."—People v. Machado, 6, 600.

§ 6. Evidence in General.

It was not error for the court to permit a witness to describe the trunk found with the one that had been stolen, such evidence not being given to show that such trunk had been stolen or lost.—People v. Nicolosi, 4, 341.

Defendant and one F. were jointly indicted for grand larceny. On the trial there was evidence that wheat stolen by F. was stored in an outbuilding of defendant, but there was nothing to connect him with F., nor was it shown that defendant was acquainted with him. Held, that the verdict against defendant was not sustained by the evidence.—People v. Curran, 3, 643.

Where the evidence tended to show that an alleged larceny took place in a certain room, evidence that defendant lived therein was admissible, though it appeared that a woman jointly accused with him of the same offense lived in the same room, and the circumstance was possibly unfortunate to defendant, with the jury.—People v. Garcia, 6, 367.

The evidence in a prosecution for larceny of money tended to show that the money was taken from an intoxicated person, to whom defendant afterward introduced a hack driver as his coachman, and directed the driver where to go and throw him out. Held, that, if it was error to admit evidence of what was thereafter done by the driver and defendant's victim in his absence, it was entirely harmless. People v. Garcia, 6, 367.

Admission of testimony as to statements of a third person to one accused of a crime, though not accompanied with proof of the conduct of accused, was not error, where accused did not move to strike out.—People v. Machado, 6, 600.

In a larceny prosecution, a witness testifying that the stolen property belonged to one person cannot be impeached by showing that in another case he had testified that it belonged to another.—People v. Machado, 6, 600.

In a prosecution for grand larceny of a watch, evidence that defendant, within two minutes after he had been seen with the prosecutor, also had his cane, was admissible as tending to show that the parties were together, and not objectionable as tending to prove another crime.—People v. Taylor, 6, 942.

In a prosecution for grand larceny, testimony by the officer arresting defendant that he had a conversation with a party who had seen defendant and the prosecutor together, even if material, was not prejudicial, the contents of the conversation not being given.—People v. Taylor, 6, 942.

§ 7. —— Of Horse or Cattle Stealing.

Identification of a horse by its owner and the latter's testimony that it was stolen from him at the time and place stated in the indict. ment, together with testimony of one subsequently finding the horse in the prisoner's hands that he did so find it, that the prisoner claimed its ownership and to have raised it, and so effected a sale or exchange of it with witness, is sufficient evidence on which to base a verdict of "guilty as charged," etc., in a prosecution for grand larceny.—People v. Salazar, 2, 90.

In a prosecution for larceny of a cow a witness had testified to finding on the premises of accused a "slunk" calf—that is, one that had been taken from its mother—and that it had been taken from the stolen cow, to which no objection nor motion to strike out was made. Held, that a question asking for the appearance of the calf as to when it had been taken from its mother, and his answer giving the facts on which his conclusion was based, were not objectionable as assuming that the calf had been taken from "a" cow; not "the" cow—that is, from the stolen cow.—People v. Machado, 6, 600.

Where a witness in a prosecution for the larceny of a cow had testified in reference to a hide found on the premises of accused, but had not testified that any part of a brand on it was indistinguishable, a question, on cross-examination, asking what part of the brand was indistinguishable, was properly excluded.—People v. Machado, 6, 600.

A question to a witness, "Now, when you went to the butcher-shop or slaughter-house for the first time, you didn't go in?" was properly excluded for uncertainty, as it could not be understood whether it referred to the butcher-shop or the slaughter-house.—People v. Machado, 6, 600.

Where, in a prosecution for the larceny of a cow, a witness testified, without objection, to the finding of the carcasses of two calves in a certain locality in question calling for their condition, and the answer to the effect that they were very much decomposed, which was favorable to accused as showing that they could not have come from the stolen cow, were properly admitted.—People v. Machado, 6, 600.

§ 8. —— Similar Transactions.

In a prosecution for larceny where, under the case as made out, the prosecuting witness had transferred money to the defendant, it was error to admit evidence of transactions of a similar nature had by the defendant with other persons, which might tend to show this to be a familiar dishonest method with him but could not show that the understanding of the parties in this particular transaction was not that the property should pass as well as the possession.—People v. Wood, 2, 208.

§ 9. —— Possession of Stolen Goods.

When a man in whose possession stolen property is found gives an account of how he came by it, as by telling the name of the person from whom he received it, it is incumbent on the prosecution to show that the account is false, unless the account given be unreasonable or improbable on the face of it.—People v. Elster, 2, 315.

While it would be proper, in a case in which there is any evidence tending to prove inculpatory facts and circumstances in connection with the possession of property recently stolen, for a court to instruct the jury that they will be justified in finding the defendant guilty of the theft, it would be improper and erroneous to give such instructions if there were no evidence in the case to warrant the inference of such circumstances.—People v. Elster, 2, 315.

A trunk alleged to have been stolen by defendant was found in a shanty which had been occupied by defendant and another for several weeks. The officer searching for it found it, with another trunk, under defendant's bed, covered over with old clothing; and defendant, when asked what it was, replied that it was nothing. When ordered to open it, he said he did not have the key, but when the trunk was examined the lock was found to be broken, and a letter was found in it, addressed to defendant's brother. Being asked whose name it was, and how it came there, defendant said it was his name, and that he put the letter in the trunk himself. Defendant said that the trunk had been left there two weeks before by a man whom he did not know, and who promised to pay him for keeping it. It was shown that the trunk had been stolen about two weeks before it was found in defendant's possession. Held, sufficient to warrant a finding that defendant stole the trunk.—People v. Nicolosi, 4, 341.

As the evidence clearly proved that the trunk was found either in the sole possession of defendant, or the joint possession of defendant and the person occupying the room with him, the court properly refused to charge that if the trunk was only found in a house which defendant occupied jointly with another, equally capable of having committed the theft, then no definite presumption of guilt could be made, the instruction not being applicable to the facts.— People v. Nicolosi, 4, 341.

§ 10. —— Res Gestae.

In a prosecution for grand larceny of a watch, where a witness testified that, as he passed defendant and prosecutor, he noticed the prosecutor's watch and chain, and that two minutes later he saw defendant leave the prosecutor, his further testimony that he then noticed prosecutor's vest was unbuttoned, and the watch and chain was gone, was admissible as part of the res gestae.—People v. Taylor, 6, 942.

§ 11. View by Jury.

On a prosecution for the larceny of cattle, it is error for the court, jury, counsel and officers of the court to go to a neighboring corral to examine the brands on certain cattle, when such examination is not conducted as a part of the regular trial—neither the cattle nor the brands being offered in evidence, nor defendant given an opportunity to object—since Penal Code, section 1119, authorizing the court to order the jury to be conducted to the place in which the offense was committed, or other material fact occurred, does not apply to such case.—People v. Fagan, 4, 87.

§ 12. Instructions.

When a charge to the jury defines grand larceny correctly as "the felonious stealing, taking, carrying away," etc., and in the next sentence tells the jury that if they find the defendant "did steal, take, carry away," etc., the property, naming it and its owner and stating its value as of fifty dollars or more, the omission of the word "feloniously" in the latter sentence is not reversible error, since "felonious" in the preceding sentence prevented the jury from being led astray.—People v. McDonald, 1, 437.

Where the contention of the prosecuting witness was that a transfer of money by him to defendant was intended to be a deposit, while that of the defendant was that it was intended to be a loan, the defendant was entitled to have the court instruct the jury to the effect that they should acquit him if they believed the understanding of both parties at the time of the transaction was that he was to use the money in his business.—People v. Wood, 2, 159.

In a prosecution for larceny it is error to give an instruction based on a hypothesis which assumes facts, so far as they go, like those proved at the trial, particularly when an instruction preceding contained such words as "this whole case turns upon the intent to steal at the time the money was paid."—People v. Wood, 2, 208.

Where, on a prosecution for grand larceny, there was evidence connecting defendant with the commission of the crime other than the mere fact of his presence and failure to interfere with the commission thereof, the refusal to instruct that the mere fact that one is present when a larceny is committed, and makes no attempt to prevent it, does not render him guilty of the crime, was not prejudicial error.—People v. Feliz, 6, 939.

On a prosecution for grand larceny, an instruction that if defendant was not present when the alleged crime was committed he was not guilty, was properly refused, as aiding and abetting the crime would have rendered defendant guilty as a principal.—People v. Feliz, 6, 939.

§ 13. Assessment of Punishment.

A jury has no power, upon convicting a person for grand larceny to assess the punishment, except where in their discretion death is deemed to be the only adequate one.—People v. Buelna, 1, 32.

§ 14. New Trial and Appeal.

On trial for larceny, where there was some evidence tending to show defendant's guilt, a verdict of guilty will not be disturbed on the ground of the insufficiency thereof.—People v. Nagle, 3, 488.

Where there is evidence before the convicting magistrate that a watch was taken from one B. when he was asleep, and when defendant and one F. were present, and it was afterward found concealed on the person of F., so as to indicate that it must have been taken feloniously, a finding by the trial court that defendant had been legally committed by the magistrate will not be disturbed on appeal. People v. Sherman, 3, 851.

A conviction of larceny of a horse and cart will not, after denial of a new trial, be disturbed, where there was evidence that the property was stolen; that defendant, when seen, shortly afterward, traveling away with it from the scene of the larceny, tried to evade identification, and when arrested with the property, a few hours afterward, twenty-three miles away, made false statements in explanation of his possession.—People v. St. Clair, 5, 294.

LAW BOOKS.

Reading to jury. See Trial, § 11.

LAW OF CASE.

§ 1. In Civil Cases.

A judgment in accordance with the principles of a past decision on appeal of the same case is to be affirmed.—Dabovich v. Emeric, 1, 90.

An appeal from a final judgment does not bring up the finality of a former judgment in the cause, the vacating of which might have been appealed from at the time but was not.—Hamlin v. His Creditors, 2, 203.

The result of a former appeal in a suit involving the title to land claimed through a United States patent to a railroad company, where the judgment was reversed because the court below rejected evidence to the effect that, at the time the grant from Congress to the railroad company took effect, the land was within the limits of a Mexican grant, then sub judice, is that if, at the time, the land was within the limits of a Mexican grant then sub judice, the patent was void, and could be attacked collaterally, and, the decision never having been appealed from, is not now subject to review.—Carr v. Quigley, 2, 823.

Where, after the reversal of a judgment in a mechanic's lien suit, the case is remanded for a new trial, and the plaintiff amends his complaint and sues in assumpsit, the law of the decision on the appeal is no longer the law applicable to the pleadings.—Castagnino v. Balletta, 3, 107.

The fact that on an appeal from a judgment of nonsuit the court treats certain facts as established does not make these facts the law of the case, so that defendant cannot on a new trial prove a different state of facts.—Cleary v. Folger, 4, 76.

On an appeal on the judgment-roll by plaintiff from a judgment for defendant, the supreme court reversed and directed the court below to enter a judgment on the findings for plaintiff in accordance with the prayer of the complaint. The court did so, and defendant excepted and appealed. Held, that the question whether the complaint stated a cause of action was decided on the former appeal, whether the demurrer was in the record or not.—Klauber v. San Diego Street-car Co., 4, 289.

Where, on the retrial of an action after a judgment of reversal by the supreme court, the conclusion of the trial court, based on the same facts established on the first trial, is in accordance with the decision on such appeal, such conclusion will not be reviewed on a second appeal.—Smith v. City of San Luis Obispo, 4, 344.

Where part of the defendants have previously appealed, and the question has been decided adversely to them, such decision will not be disturbed upon appeal of other defendants, prosecuted on the same grounds.—Hunter v. Hubert, 4, 978.

On a second appeal the decision on a former appeal as to the law of the case will not be re-examined.—Woodside v. Tynan, 5, 807.

Where, on a prior appeal, it was held that defendants' rights were limited by a written contract of indemnity, and that no defense at variance with the terms of the indemnity could be interposed, and judgment was reversed, with directions to the court to strike out or otherwise refuse to entertain a special defense objected to, whereupon the court struck the amended answer "according to the directions of the supreme court" and granted leave to amend, such decision was the law of the case, and defendants were not entitled to file an amended answer merely omitting all mention of the written contract and pleading the defense so stricken.—Prouty v. Adams, 7, 241.

§ 2. In Criminal Case.

Under a charge of assault with intent to commit murder, defendant was convicted of the lesser offense of assault with a deadly weapon, and a new trial was granted him, for insufficient evidence. On a second trial he was convicted of the higher offense, and on his motion a new trial was granted on the sole ground that he had been twice put in jeopardy for the same offense. On appeal by the people the judgment was reversed because he did not plead former jeopardy. The trial court, on return of remittitur, pronounced judgment on the verdict. Held, that the supreme court could not, on appeal by defendant from such judgment, review its former decision.—People v. Bennett, 5, 824.

LEASES.
See Landlord and Tenant.

LEGACIES.
See Wills.

LEGAL TENDER ACT.
See Payment, § 1.

LEGISLATIVE ASSEMBLY.
See San Francisco.

LEGISLATURE.
See State; Statutes.

LETTERS.
As evidence. See Evidence, § 26.

LETTERS OF ADMINISTRATION.
See Executors and Administrators.

LEVEES.
See Swamp Lands.

Clause in contract for construction of levee. See Vendor and Vendee, § 2.

§ 1. Districts and Their Organization.

A levee district was organized under act of March 25, 1868 (Stats. 1867-68, p. 316), providing a method for the organization of such districts, and, such act being declared void as to the method of organization, the legislature, by act of March 30, 1872 (Stats. 1871-72, p. 734), recognized the existence of such district. Held, that such legislative recognition gave legal existence to such district, though it was irregularly created, since the legislature, having power to create such districts, on the law under which it was created being held invalid could give it legal existence by positive recognition.—People v. Levee Dist. No. 6 of Sutter County, 6, 615.

Act of March 31, 1891 (Stats. 1891, p. 235), providing a new form of government for a certain levee district, is not violative of constitution, article 11, section 6, and article 12, section 1, declaring that neither municipal nor private corporations shall be created by special laws, since such levee districts are neither municipal nor private corporations, but are mere governmental agencies having certain of the attributes and functions of corporations.—People v. Levee Dist. No. 6 of Sutter County, 6, 615.

Act of March 31, 1891 (Stats. 1891, p. 235), providing a new form of government for a levee district, does not contravene constitution, article 4, section 25, subdivision 3, forbidding the enactment of local or special laws if a general law can be made applicable, since it was a question for the legislature whether a general law was applicable, and its determination of the necessity for a special law will not be interfered with.—People v. Levee Dist. No. 6 of Sutter County, 6, 615.

44

LIBEL AND SLANDER.

§ 1. Publication of Slanderous Words.

Communication by a husband to his wife of slanderous words in regard to a woman is a publication.—Sesler v. Montgomery, 3, 27.

§ 2. Privileged Communications.

Under Civil Code of California, section 47, providing that a privileged communication is one made without malice to a person interested therein, by one who is also interested, or by one who stands in such a relation to the person interested as to afford a reasonable ground for supposing the motive for the communication innocent, and section 48, providing that malice is not to be inferred from the mere fact of publication, a finding of the jury that a communication from a husband to his wife, with whom he was on bad terms, slanderous of a female acquaintance of hers, who had testified for her in divorce proceedings between her and her husband, was made with malice, and was not privileged, cannot be disturbed.—Sesler v. Montgomery, 3, 27.

§ 3. Pleading and Evidence.

In a suit for libel, if the complaint contains solely and verbatim one part of the publication as the grievance, an offer in evidence of the whole is no variance although the other part is libelous also.—Seiders v. Post Publishing Co., 2, 58.

Where in a suit for libel the plaintiff has set out in his complaint only one part of the publication, and at the trial offers in evidence the whole, whereby, in fact, other libels might appear, defendant should shape his objection as for the exclusion of the libels not so set out.—Seiders v. Post Publishing Co., 2, 58.

In an action for slander it is not a sufficient averment of the speaking of slanderous words to allege that at a certain time, in the presence of certain persons, "as the plaintiffs are informed and believe," the defendants spoke the words complained of; and the defect in the complaint arising therefrom goes to the sufficiency of the facts stated, and not to the manner of stating them, and may be taken advantage of by a general demurrer.—McKinney v. Roberts, 2, 532.

In an action for slander, where it is shown that defendant accused plaintiff of perjury and want of chastity, in a room where his wife was, in a voice loud enough to be heard outside, there is sufficient evidence that she heard and understood the words.—Sesler v. Montgomery, 3, 27.

In an action for slander in charging plaintiff with associating with another in a theft of certain cattle, declarations made by such other after the alleged transaction was completed are inadmissible to show that plaintiff was associated with him.—Barkly v. Copeland, 3, 350.

In an action for slander, for calling plaintiff "valhaca," plaintiff and several witnesses (all illiterate Portuguese) testified that the word was in common use among the Portuguese, and meant "whore." Defendant's witnesses, some of whom were educated Portuguese, testified that the term "valhaca" did not mean "unchastity," but that it meant "knave, rogue, crafty," and that the word "puta" was in common use, meaning "whore." Held, sufficient to support a verdict that defendant intended to impute unchastity to plaintiff.—Matts v. Borba, 4, 691.

After defendant had examined his witnesses, and rested, plaintiff gave evidence that the word "valhaca" meant "whore." Held, that, if the evidence was improperly admitted, defendant was not prejudiced, there being already sufficient evidence to support the verdict. Matts v. Borba, 4, 691.

§ 4. —— Expert and Opinion Evidence.

In a prosecution for libel, evidence that a witness knew that the defendant was innocent, and that she did not write the letter complained of, is incompetent, as mere opinion.—People v. Storke, 6, 405.

In a prosecution for libel, it is not error to strike out and refuse to submit to the jury specimens of the handwriting of a person other than defendant who has admitted his authorship of the writing stricken out, where an expert has testified that the writing in the libelous article does not resemble such writings, and there is no evidence to connect the author thereof with the writing of the libelous matter.—People v. Storke, 6, 405.

Where testimony of experts in regard to the authorship of a libelous letter was introduced in a criminal prosecution, it was not error to refuse to instruct that the testimony of experts should be received and weighed with great caution, and that the evidence of a witness who is brought on the stand to support a theory by his opinion is testimony exposed to a reasonable degree of suspicion, which there is great reason to believe is in any instance the result of employment, and his bias arising out of it.—People v. Storke, 6, 405.

§ 5. —— Impeachment of Witness.

Where a witness in a prosecution for libel testified that he gained access to defendant's room by climbing through a transom over the door, the testimony of one who had charge of the room and the keys thereof, as to whether or not anyone ever applied to him for access to the room, was incompetent to impeach the former witness.—People v. Storke, 6, 405.

Where a witness, on cross-examination in a prosecution for libel, testified that he went to a certain town and inquired of M. who the woman in the town was who would have been likely to have written the letters complained of as libelous, and M. answered that he knew of but one woman, testimony of M. that he did not make the statement ascribed to him by witness is inadmissible to impeach the latter, as such statement related to an immaterial and collateral matter.—People v. Storke, 6, 405.

§ 6. Counsel Fees.

Counsel fees are not recoverable in an action of slander by a defendant in whose favor a judgment is rendered, unless such fees are included in his memorandum of costs.—McKinney v. Roberts, 2, 532.

§ 7. Appeal and Review.

The supreme court will not reverse a conviction for libel, for refusal to give an alleged requested instruction, where the record does not show that defendant requested the court to give the instruction. People v. Storke, 6, 405.

LICENSE.

To sell liquor. See Intoxicating Liquors.
To marry. See Marriage, § 1.

Of physicians and dentists. See Physicians and Dentists, §§ 1–3.
Water right based on. See Waters and Watercourses, § 6.

§ 1. Mandamus to Issue Barber License.

Where. an action was brought against the State Board of Barber
Examiners to compel the issuance of a license to plaintiff, and during
the pendency of the suit the act creating such board was repealed,
and no successor in interest or obligation was provided for, the action abated.—Porco v. State Board of Barber Examiners, 7, 158.

§ 2. License to Enter on Land.

A license, as contradistinguished from an easement, furnishes no
defense to a bill filed by the property holder to restrain the defendant as to an act in the future under the license.—Walkup v. Evans,
1, 231.

§ 3. —— Revocation of Parol License.

A land owner orally granted B a license to construct a reservoir
and lay pipes on his land to convey water from a certain spring, in
consideration that B would give him the right to use such water in
case of fire, and would so construct the reservoir as to enable him to
take water therefrom in case of fire. There was no agreement as to
the time they should be maintained. B afterward expended $1,500
in improvements, which were used by him and such land owner.
Held, that the land owner, or his grantees with actual notice, could
revoke such license only on condition that the licensee should be permitted to remove his improvements, if it could be accomplished without material loss, or, if not, that the licensor should make just compensation therefor.—Flick v. Bell, 5, 206.

LICENSEE.
Injury to on railway right of way. See Railroads, § 11.

LIENS.
Conflicting liens. See Crops, § 3.
Of factor. See Factors, § 3.
For labor or materials. See Mechanics' Liens; Mines and Minerals,
   § 10.
Of pledgee. See Pledge, § 3.
Of vendor. See Vendor and Vendee, § 26.

LIFE INSURANCE.
See Insurance.

LIMITATIONS OF ACTIONS.
§ 1. In general.
§ 2. When statute begins to run.
§ 3. Fraud and mistake.
§ 4. —— Corporate transactions.
§ 5. Denial of trust.
§ 6. In case of sales and conveyances.
§ 7. Effect of amended complaint.
§ 8. Acknowledgment or new promise.
§ 9. Pleading statute.
§ 10. Evidence and findings.
§ 11. Waiver and estoppel.
§ 12. Raising defense on appeal.
      See Adverse Possession.
Action on note. See Bills and Notes, § 22.

In case of bonds. See Bonds, § 7.
Stockholders' suit. See Corporations, § 31.
Concerning execution sales. See Execution, § 12.
Time when minor must assert rights. See Infants, § 2.
Action on judgment. See Judgments, § 22.
To enforce lien. See Mechanics' Liens, § 15.
Foreclosure proceedings. See Mortgage, § 21.
On treasurer's bond. See Principal and Surety, § 3.
In trover. See Trover and Conversion, § 3.
In case of trust. See Trusts, § 17.
In case of misrepresentations by vendor. See Vendor and Vendee, § 15.

§ 1. In General.

The term "final confirmation by the government of the United States," as used in the proviso of the act of 1855 amending the statute of limitations, includes the issuance of the patent, and when title is derived from the Mexican or Spanish government, the statute, in actions for the recovery of real estate, does not begin to run until the patent issues.—Hibberd v. Smith, 1, 554.

The act of March 5, 1864, sometimes called "The Hawes Limitation Act," is not repugnant to the constitution of the state.—Moody v. Palmer, 1, 777.

Code of Civil Procedure, section 360, relative to limitations, provides that no acknowledgment is sufficient evidence of a new contract by which to take a case out of the statute unless the same is in writing. Civil Code, section 1697, enacts: "A contract not in writing may be altered in any respect by consent of the parties, in writing, without a new consideration, and is extinguished thereby to the extent of a new alteration." One orally agreed to give another a certain sum in consideration of his moving off certain land, and thereafter the promisor stated to the promisee that he would pay the money as soon as convenient or as soon as he could get the money from a certain source, to which the promisee acquiesced, and there was nothing to indicate that the promisee was pressing payment. Held, that the agreement as to payment from a certain source was not a mere forbearance, and therefore not within section 360, but was either a new or continuing contract within section 360, or a material alteration within section 1697; and being oral did not prevent limitations from running against the promisee from the time of his removal.—Morehouse v. Morehouse, 6, 966.

§ 2. When Statute Begins to Run.

Where a sum of money is to be paid by the debtor "when my circumstances hereafter may permit me," the statute of limitations runs from the time the debtor has money to pay with, rather than from the time he can pay without inconvenience to his business.—Larco v. Roeding, 1, 438.

Where money is given under an agreement that the person who receives it will do certain things, and he fails to perform his agreement, the statute of limitations will not commence to run against the claim of the person who gave money until there is a refusal to perform the contract.—Link v. Jarvis, 5, 750.

§ 3. Fraud and Mistake.

Under Code of Civil Procedure, section 338, providing that an action for relief on the ground of fraud or mistake must be commenced within three years after the cause of action accrued, such cause of action not to be deemed to have accrued until the discovery of the mistake by the aggrieved party, a complaint for relief on the ground of a mistake which occurred thirty years previous, and which is silent as to the time when such mistake was first discovered, is bad on demurrer.—Smith v. Irving, 3, 121.

A cause of action for fraud is not taken out of the operation of the statute of limitations by the Code of Civil Procedure, section 338, subdivision 4, which provides that the statute does not begin to run until discovery of the fraud, where it appears that the slightest examination of the public records would have put plaintiffs in possession of the facts, and that they acquired their information on which the action was based by inquiry of their friends and acquaintances—a course open to them before the statute had run.—Burling v. Newlands, 4, 940.

Code of Civil Procedure, section 338, subdivision 4, limiting to three years "an action for relief on the ground of fraud or mistake," applies to an action at law, as well as in equity.—Christensen v. Jessen, 5, 45.

A complaint states a cause of action, not for recovery of real estate, but for relief on the ground of fraud, which, by Code of Civil Procedure, section 338, subdivision 4, is barred in three years, it being by a daughter of C., deceased, against his second wife, and alleging that C. being addicted to drink, so as to partially disqualify him from business and render him the prey of designing persons, defendant resolved to get possession of his property, and for this purpose married him, and shortly thereafter, in pursuance of this purpose, while from drinking he was not able to intelligently transact business, she, by influence of her superior will, got him to deed property to her, and title to property which he bought was taken in her name at her instance and dictation, he being compelled thereto and overpowered by her will; and the prayer being that it be adjudged that the conveyance was obtained by fraud and undue influence, and that it be set aside, and that the title to the second lot was taken in her name through fraud and undue influence, and that she holds it in trust.—Murphy v. Crowley, 7, 49.

§ 4. —— Corporate Transactions.

Code of Civil Procedure, section 338, provides that actions for relief on the ground of fraud must be commenced within three years after discovery thereof. A complaint in a suit commenced in 1898 alleged that a corporation's directors conspired to defraud plaintiff, and accordingly sold him considerable capital stock; that in 1888 they levied an assessment on the stock without necessity, and sold his stock in payment thereof; that in 1889 plaintiff commenced an action to set aside the assessment and sale thereunder, which suit was afterward compromised. Held, that the action was barred, since eight years had expired since the fraud was discovered.—Marks v. Evans, 6, 505.

The fact that a complainant in a suit against a corporation's directors for fraudulently selling capital stock alleged that the directors afterward appropriated the corporation's property did not prevent the statute of limitations from running from the time that the sale was discovered, since the sale was the gravamen of the action.—Marks v. Evans, 6, 505.

Where plaintiff knew that a corporation's directors had fraudulently assessed his stock, and sold the same under the assessment, his failure to discover other frauds perpetrated by them, without seeking to inspect the corporation's books, did not delay the running of limitations, since he would be presumed to know all that reasonable diligence would have disclosed to him.—Marks v. Evans, 6, 505.

§ 5. Denial of Trust.

Where, in an action to compel defendant to account for money belonging to plaintiff, placed in his hands, and invested by him in a lot without authority, the evidence was that, when plaintiff went to defendant for a settlement, he began to talk about the lot, but, on plaintiff telling him she did not come to talk about the lot, but for a settlement, defendant began to talk about the imprisonment of his brother, whereupon plaintiff left his office, there was not shown a sufficient denial of the trust by defendant to put in operation the statute of limitations against plaintiff's claim.—Spencer v. Duncan, 5, 41.

§ 6. In Case of Sales and Conveyances.

Where a seller of stocks fails to deliver them, limitations against his implied promise to refund the purchase money begin to run from the date of his notice to the purchaser of inability to deliver.—Rose v. Foord, 3, 438.

An action by a vendee against the vendor to recover the purchase price paid for land on failure of the vendor to convey as required by the written contract of sale is an action founded upon an instrument in writing, within Code of Civil Procedure, section 337, and must be brought within four years.—Thomas v. Pacific Beach Co., 5, 319.

Where the contract of sale requires a conveyance by the vendor "on demand," the statute does not begin to run against an action by the vendee for breach thereof by the vendor until after demand by the vendee for a conveyance.—Thomas v. Pacific Beach Co., 5, 319.

§ 7. Effect of Amended Complaint.

Where an amended complaint is filed which does not state a new cause of action, nor bring in new parties, it relates back to the filing of the original complaint, and the statute of limitations ceases to run against plaintiff's claim at the date of filing the original complaint.—Link v. Jarvis, 5, 750.

§ 8. Acknowledgment or New Promise.

After such notice, verbal promises to deliver the stocks when he could will not take the case out of the statute of limitations, by reason of Code of Civil Procedure, section 360, which provides that no promise is sufficient for such purpose, unless in writing, signed by the party to be charged thereby.—Rose v. Foord, 3, 438.

In an action for money loaned, written acknowledgment of which is claimed to have been made within four years, as required by Code of Civil Procedure, section 360, a finding that defendant did not acknowledge any indebtedness to plaintiff in writing is sustained, where the indebtedness claimed by plaintiff to have been acknowledged was of a debt due to her husband.—Rounthwaite v. Rounthwaite, 6, 878.

Defendant's promise, if made to plaintiff, being without any consideration, is unenforceable.—Rounthwaite v. Rounthwaite, 6, 878.

Where an account, after it is barred by limitations, is sent to the debtor, with a blank indorsement, acknowledging its correctness and a promise to pay, which he declines to sign, his silence as to its correctness cannot remove the bar of Code of Civil Procedure, section 360, providing that no acknowledgment is sufficient evidence of a new contract, unless in writing and signed by the party charged.—Rounthwaite v. Rounthwaite, 6, 878.

An estoppel in pais cannot be urged as against the requirements of the code that the promise must be evidenced by writing to remove the bar.—Rounthwaite v. Rounthwaite, 6, 878.

§ 9. Pleading Statute.

The statute of limitations, in order to be availed of as a defense, must have been pleaded.—Pharris v. Downing, 1, 769.

Under the California practice, when all the facts that defendant would be required to prove to sustain his plea of the statute of limitations appear on the face of the complaint, defendant may take advantage thereof by demurrer; but, to uphold a demurrer, the complaint must show, not that the cause of action may be barred, but that it is barred.—Palmtag v. Roadhouse, 4, 205.

The statute of limitations, to be availed of, must be pleaded.— Bixby v. Crafts, 6, 12.

Under Code of Civil Procedure, section 458, providing that, "in pleading the statute of limitations, it is not necessary to state the facts showing the defense, but it may be stated, generally, that the cause of action is barred by the provisions of section (giving the number of the section and subdivision thereof, if it is so divided, relied upon)," a plea of the statute of limitations, alleging that a cause of action is barred by Code of Civil Procedure, section 339, is insufficient, since such statute contains several subdivisions.— Wolters v. Thomas, 3, 843.

The objection to the answer need not be taken by special demurrer for uncertainty.—Wolters v. Thomas, 3, 843.

The statute of limitations is sufficiently pleaded by reference in the answer to the sections of the code.—Packard v. Johnson, 2, 365.

§ 10. Evidence and Findings.

The plea of the statute of limitations or any mere matter of avoidance is not in the nature of a cross-complaint, to be met by further pleadings. The plaintiff may, on the pleadings as they stand, introduce any evidence which will avoid the effect of the new matter.— Madden v. Ashman, 1, 610.

Where the statute of limitations is set up as a defense, a finding that "all the allegations of plaintiff's complaint are true" is not a finding as to the issue of the statute of limitations.—Lewis v. Adams, 2, 516.

Failure to find upon the issue of the statute of limitations is ground for reversal of the judgment.—Porteous v. Reed, 2, 707.

Evidence held to sustain defense of statute of limitations, and judgment affirmed.—Greer v. Tripp, 2, 727.

Where a complaint for money had and received, filed July 1, 1895, alleged that the cause of action arose "on or about January, 1894," a finding that all the allegations therein are true is an adverse finding on defendant's plea of limitations.—Wolfskill v. Douglas, 6, 396.

§ 11. Waiver and Estoppel.

In an action on promissory notes, where the bar of the statute of limitations is set up and issue is joined thereon, the plaintiff relying upon a writing signed by the defendant waiving the benefit of the statute of limitations, parol evidence is admissible of the circumstances under which such writing was executed as part of the res gestae.—Cross v. Zellerbach, 2, 578.

The fact that a mortgagor was the general attorney of the mortgagee in other matters does not make the position of the mortgagor a fiduciary one, or render it anything but adverse to the mortgagor's interest, as far as the mortgage is concerned, so as to estop him to set up the statute of limitations to an action of foreclosure.—Palmtag v. Roadhouse, 4, 205.

§ 12. Raising Defense on Appeal.

Where there is no express showing that the filing of an amended answer after the complete running of the statute of limitations was done without leave of court asked and obtained, but so far as the record discloses without objection by plaintiffs, objection cannot be made for the first time on appeal.—Chipman v. Hastings, 1, 817.

LIQUIDATED DAMAGES.

See Damages, § 3.

LIQUORS.

See Intoxicating Liquors.

LIS PENDENS.

Sale pending ejectment. See Ejectment, § 22.

§ 1. Effect of Statute.

The statute has not declared the effect of a notice of lis pendens, but merely says that "from the time of filing only shall the pendency of the action be constructive notice to a purchaser or encumbrancer of the property affected thereby."—Brooks v. Tichner, 1, 104.

§ 2. Retrospective Operation of Notice.

The notice of lis pendens is not made to reach back, by relation, from the time of its being filed, so that a person who acquired an interest in the property subjected to litigation before the suit was begun shall be affected by such filing with notice of the suit.—Brooks v. Tichner, 1, 104.

LOCATION.

Of mining claims. See Mines and Minerals, § 3.

LOGS AND LOGGING.

§ 1. Contracts—Construction and performance.
§ 2. Lien for labor on logs.
§ 3. Conflicting rights of purchasers of timber.
§ 4. Recovery for value of logs—Possession of land.

§ 1. Contracts—Construction and Performance.

Where a contract provides that the logs shall be scaled by a licensed scaler, an officer authorized to pass on the merchantable character of logs, both parties, in the absence of fraud, are bound by his decision.—Bullock v. Consumers' Lumber Co., 3, 609.

Even if the purchaser was not bound by the inspection and decision of the scaler, yet if the defects which rendered the logs unmerchantable were plain and readily seen on ordinary observation, and there was no fraud on the part of the seller, and the purchaser, having full opportunity to observe the defects, made no objection, he would be bound by his acceptance.—Bullock v. Consumers' Lumber Co., 3, 609.

In an action on a contract for saw-logs sold and delivered the controversy was as to the meaning of a clause in the contract which stated that the logs were "to be scaled by licensed scalers by the quarter scale, with ten per cent deducted for waste." It was claimed that the terms "by the quarter scale" and "for waste" were technical terms, having a particular meaning in the locality where the timber was sold, and testimony of the licensed scalers was introduced to show their meaning. Held, that testimony of the one who made the contract on behalf of defendant, as to what he understood by the terms at the time he made the contract, was inadmissible.—Bullock v. Consumers' Lumber Co., 3, 609.

Defendant offered to prove by the same witness that by reason of his belief as to the terms of the contract he agreed to pay one dollar per thousand more for the logs than he would otherwise have paid, and also offered to show from the "mill tally" the quantity of merchantable lumber obtained from the logs. Held, that this evidence was properly excluded, the price as well as the mode of ascertaining the quantity of lumber being fixed by the contract.—Bullock v. Consumers' Lumber Co., 3, 609.

Defendant offered to prove that the words "for waste" in the contract were understood by both parties to mean the cut of the saw after the logs had been squared by the quarter scale, with all deductions for rot, rotten knots, sap and shakes. Held, that the evidence was not admissible, unless defendant could show that those terms in the agreement have a technical meaning, and apply simply to the cut of the saw.—Bullock v. Consumers' Lumber Co., 3, 609.

Under a contract to furnish logs to a mill, to be floated to the mill the next spring, if practicable, and, if not, then the spring following, where it is found that delivery the first spring was not practicable, a delivery the second fulfills the contract; and no damages are recoverable for the delay, or for the depreciation in value of the logs during the year.—Irish v. Pauley, 5, 651.

§ 2. Lien for Labor on Logs.

A mechanic having a lien on logs cut by him does not lose it because of advancements made on the property by another, under a contract of purchase, but he is entitled to enforce his lien against such property.—Shuffleton v. Hill, 2, 473.

§ 3. Conflicting Rights of Purchasers of Timber.

If a land owner, after making a sufficient conveyance of a millsite and mill rights, with the right to enough timber on the land to supply the mill, gives a license to another person, who has knowledge of the conveyance, to cut timber on the same land and carry it away, when there is on the land only timber sufficient to supply one mill, the mill owner may sue both the land owner and the licensee for such damage as he can show as the result of performance under the license.—Hendy v. Duncan, 1, 291.

§ 4. Recovery for Value of Logs—Possession of Land.

In order to recover the value of sawlogs, alleged to have been wrongfully cut and removed by the defendant from the land of the plaintiff, the plaintiff must show actual possession in himself of the land from which the logs were cut.—Bassett v. Hollenbeck, 1, 500.

LOST INSTRUMENT.

Loss of summons. See Process, § 6.

§ 1. Proof of Contents of Power of Attorney.

The contents of a lost power of attorney cannot be proved by secondary evidence without requisite proof first having been had of the loss of the instrument.—Tong v. Richmond, 1, 809.

MAINTENANCE.

Action for by wife. See Husband and Wife, § 3.

MALICIOUS MISCHIEF.

§ 1. To County Jail.

Conviction for malicious mischief, in breaking the doors and otherwise injuring the jail of Tulare county, sustained.—People v. Vincent, 1, 681.

MALICIOUS PROSECUTION.

§ 1. What Constitutes.

A complaint against a flume company alleging incorporation of defendant; that defendant maliciously had plaintiff arrested and imprisoned, necessitating bail, and tried, on a charge of interfering with its flume meters without authority; that he was tried and duly acquitted; that by these acts he was injured in reputation, and suffered great anxiety, to his damage in a certain sum—sufficiently states a cause of action for malicious prosecution.—Runk v. San Diego Flume Co., 5, 251.

Where a civil action was instituted three times, but dismissed without trial, no action for malicious prosecution thereof would lie, as a judgment on the merits in defendant's favor is an essential element of the evidence of want of probable cause.—Hurgren v. Mutual Life Ins. Co., 6, 964.

§ 2. Probable Cause.

Where the uncontradicted evidence in a suit for malicious prosecution tends to show probable cause, and the verdict of the jury is against the instructions of the court, we cannot hold that there was an abuse of discretion in setting it aside.—Hynes v. Nelson, 5, 741.

When a prosecution, under Penal Code, sections 701–714, authorizing the arrest of a person charged with having threatened to commit an offense, results, after a hearing, in an order requiring the accused to give an undertaking to keep the peace, the order, unless it is shown to have been procured by fraud, is conclusive evidence of probable cause.—Holliday v. Holliday, 6, 1.

A defendant in an action for malicious prosecution, who relies on the defense of probable cause by showing that he in good faith acted on the advice of counsel, after having disclosed to him all the material facts within his knowledge relating to the offense and the accusation, need not show that he also disclosed all the material facts bearing on the case which he could have ascertained by reasonable diligence, the other disclosures being sufficient.—Holliday v. Holliday, 6, 1.

§ 3. Termination of Action.

In an action for malicious prosecution, it appears that, in one of the prosecutions on which the action was based, the plaintiff was discharged on a writ of habeas corpus, on the ground of the insufficiency of the commitment, and a possible defect in the warrant; and, in the other, upon the statement that she could not give a bond and assurances that she would not harm defendants, who were seeking to compel her to give an undertaking to keep the peace, she was discharged on motion of the district attorney, on her own recognizance. Held, that an instruction that plaintiff's release upon the habeas corpus proceedings and the dismissal on the motion of the district attorney were each a sufficient termination of the prosecution, for the purposes of this action, going to show a want of probable cause, is error.—Holliday v. Holliday, 6, 1.

An allegation, in an action for malicious prosecution, that the prose-cution on which the action is based had been finally determined in plaintiff's favor, is sufficient, without alleging, in addition, the means, as by writ of habeas corpus, by which that end was accomplished.— Holliday v. Holliday, 6, 1.

MALPRACTICE.

Liability of physicians. See Physicians and Dentists, § 4.

MANDAMUS.

§ 1. When will issue.
§ 2. In case of teacher's salary.
§ 3. To judge or court.
§ 4. In supreme court.
§ 5. Matters of practice.

To issue license to dentist. See Physicians and Dentists, § 1.

To issue patent to land. See Public Lands, § 20.
To levy tax. See Taxation, § 13.
To locate toll gates. See Turnpike Companies, § 2.
To supply water. See Waters and Watercourses, § 19.

§ 1. When will Issue.

A court's mandate to the board of supervisors of a county direct-ing it to proceed to audit certain claims is not to be taken as directing an audit that must be favorable to the petitioner.—People ex rel. San Francisco Gas Co. v. Board of Supervisors of San Fran-cisco, 1, 68.

A mandamus to direct an officer to execute a writ of possession against an occupant, unsuccessful as defendant in ejectment, will not be granted if, since the judgment in ejectment, the occupant has been given judgment in a suit to quiet title, although it is claimed in the petition that an appeal from the latter judgment has been taken and its operation thereby suspended. The burden is on the relator to prove the appeal as a fact.—People v. Davis, 1, 317.

Under Statutes of 1891, chapter 216, section 25, subdivision 23, providing that the board of supervisors shall fix the price of all county advertising, mandamus will not lie to compel such board to contract for such advertising by giving public notice calling for pro-posals. Such statute repeals Political Code, section 3766, providing that county advertising must be contracted for with the lowest bid-der.—Maxwell v. Board of Supervisors, 3, 782.

A petition to the supreme court for a writ of mandate showed that, after the death of plaintiff's intestate, she, as administratrix, applied for and received from the county auditor warrants for salary due deceased as sheriff; that, upon presentation to the county treas-urer, he refused to pay said warrants; that the judge of the superior court of the county was disqualified to act; and that no other judge in said county was qualified. Held, to be sufficient grounds for issu-ance of the writ to compel the treasurer to pay the warrants.—Ward v. Forkner, 5, 806.

The writ of mandate will not issue where there is a plain, speedy and adequate remedy in the ordinary course of law.—Williams v. Bagnelle, 7, 55.

§ 2. In Case of Teacher's Salary.

Mandamus will not lie to compel school trustees, who have wrong-fully dismissed a teacher before the completion of her contract, to issue an order for the full amount of her salary, where no demand was made on them.—Shirley v. Board of Trustees of Cottonwood School District, 3, 605.

Political Code, title 3, article 12, section 1699, provides that any teacher whose salary is withheld may appeal to the superintendent of public instruction, who shall require the superintendent of schools to investigate the matter, and that the judgment of the superintendent of instruction shall be final, and that on receiving it the superintendent of schools, if it is in favor of the teacher, shall, if the trustees refuse to issue an order for such salary, issue his requisition in favor of such teacher. The salary of a teacher was withheld by the superintendent of schools, and she applied for a peremptory writ of mandate directing him to draw a requisition in favor of petitioner. Held, that the writ would not issue, plaintiff not having pursued the remedy under the statute, which applied to a case where the salary was withheld by such superintendent, as well as where withheld by the trustees.—Williams v. Bagnelle, 7, 55.

Code of Civil Procedure, section 1085, provides that the writ of mandate may be issued to compel the performance of an official act required to be done by law. Political Code, section 1543, requires the county superintendent of schools to draw requisitions on the county auditor against the school fund of the district, and provides that no such requisition shall be drawn unless the order states the monthly salary of teacher, and names the months for which it is due. An order drawn by trustees in favor of a teacher was "on account of balance on yearly contract for $1,000 from ———— to ———— during the present school year. . . . . Monthly salary . . . . $————." Held, that the writ of mandate would not issue to compel the superintendent to issue a requisition for the teacher's salary, as the superintendent was' not authorized to draw a requisition, the monthly salary not being mentioned in the order, nor the month for which it was due.—Williams v. Bagnelle, 7, 55.

§ 3. To Judge or Court.

Mandamus to compel the superior court to place a cause on appeal from a justice's court on the calendar, and proceed with the trial thereof, issued on authority of Ward v. Superior Court, 58 Cal. 519. Beatty v. Superior Court, 2, 159.

Mandamus will not lie to compel the sustaining of a motion for judgment made by petitioner in an action in the trial court, and to permit him to prove certain allegations of his complaint, appeal being the proper remedy, if such rulings be erroneous.—Tibbetts v. Campbell, 3, 430.

Mandamus will not lie to compel a judge to hear a matter notwithstanding an appeal, on the ground that the appeal is invalid, where the order appealed from is an appealable one.—Davis v. Wallace, 4, 949.

§ 4. In Supreme Court.

Where, on an application for a writ of mandate before the supreme court, no reason is shown why the application was not made in the first instance to the superior court, the application will be denied. Smith v. Dunn, 2, 473.

Application for mandamus denied on the ground that the petition fails to state sufficient reasons for not applying to the superior court in the first instance.—Sankey v. Society of California Pioneers, 2, 635.

An application for a writ of mandate will not be entertained by
the supreme court until the petitioner has exhausted his remedy in
the superior court, unless special cause be shown therefor. The fact
that the petitioner, a candidate for the office of supervisor, was defeated in a contest for such office in the superior court is not sufficient
cause for an application in the supreme court for a writ to compel
the board of supervisors to allow him to exercise the office of supervisor, where, subsequent to the decision of the election contest, there
was a change of the judge of such superior court.—Snow v. Supervisors of Stanislaus County, 2, 445.

§ 5. Matters of Practice.

Neither under the Practice Act nor by any rule or usage of the
profession need a mandamus proceeding be given a title or the parties be particularly designated.—Myers v. Mayor and Common Council of Placerville, 1, 565.

Findings held to support the judgment.—Keating v. Edgar, 2, 289.

Where the resolution of a board of supervisors, to enforce which
an alternative writ of mandate has been issued, is afterward repealed, the writ must be dismissed.—People v. Bartlett, 2, 437.

On a motion to quash a writ of mandamus compelling a state
officer to redeem certain bonds in accordance with a state law, an
affidavit which states, in substance, that the validity of the bonds
had been passed on in the United States court is insufficient.—Kahn
v. Bauer, 2, 728.

Alternative mandamus was issued by the chief justice, returnable
before department 2 of this court. On application to the court in
bank for a peremptory writ, the record showed no evidence of service
on respondent, and no return by him. Held, that the application
must be denied.—Wilson v. Hunt, 2, 831.

Where, on an application for a writ of mandate against a city
treasurer, the surpeme court, after the cause is submitted, concludes
that the constitutionality of certain acts must be determined, which
questions have not been argued, the submission will be set aside, and
an opportunity for argument thereof will be afforded.—Home for Care
of Inebriates v. Reis, 3, 426.

Where a petition for a writ of mandate, and the answer of the
court, are submitted without evidence, the answer must be taken as
true.—Sherer v. Superior Court, 3, 680.

Where, pending an appeal by a city treasurer from an order directing him to pay certain coupons out of certain moneys paid in under
protest, the action by the property owners, who paid in the money,
to recover the same, is determined against them, the defense, to the
issuance of the writ, of the pendency of such action, is unavailable.
Livingston v. Widber, 5, 557.

A citizen is not "beneficially interested" (Code Civ. Proc., sec. 1086)
in the appointment of police commissioners for the city and county
of San Francisco, so as to entitle him to sue, without permission of
the attorney general, for a writ of mandate to compel the governor
to make such appointment.—People ex rel. Wirt v. Budd, 5, 572.

Where, after submission of an application to compel a judge to
settle a bill of exceptions, he signs it, the application will be dismissed, without costs.—In re Donnolly, 7, 172.

MANSLAUGHTER.

See Homicide.

MAPS.

As showing boundary. See Boundaries, § 5.
Filing in dedication of street or highway. See Dedication, § 3.

MARKETABLE TITLE.

See Vendor and Vendee, § 9.

MARKS.

On ballots. See Elections, § 2.

MARRIAGE.

§ 1. License.
§ 2. Want of authority to perform.
§ 3. Woman under age.
§ 4. Evidence and presumptions.
§ 5. Annulment of marriage.

Breach of promise. See Breach of Promise to Marry.
Conveyance in consideration of. See Deeds, § 11.

§ 1. License.

Phior to act of April 9, 1863, a license was not a prerequisite to marriage.—Hunter v. Milam, 5, 107.

§ 2. Want of Authority to Perform.

The fact that the person performing a marriage ceremony in California in 1858 was not authorized to perform such ceremonies would not invalidate the marriage, if assented to by the parties and consummated by cohabitation as husband and wife.—Hunter v. Milam, 5, 107.

§ 3. Woman Under Age.

Under Statutes of 1850, page 424, making fourteen years the age of consent, and declaring guilty of a misdemeanor one who joins in marriage a female under eighteen years of age without consent of her parent, the marriage is not void, though consent of the parent is not obtained, the female being over fourteen years old.—Hunter v. Milam, 5, 107.

§ 4. Evidence and Presumptions.

The findings of the court below as to a contract of marriage in the present are not to be disturbed when made up on evidence substantially conflicting.—McCausland v. McCausland, 2, 11.

It cannot be conclusively presumed that a woman was married in 1889, at the time of receiving a grant of land, from proof of coverture in 1891, 1893 and 1897, and that in 1897 a son of the same name as her supposed husband commenced a suit, and was presumably of full age.—Reavis v. Gardner, 6, 427.

§ 5. Annulment of Marriage.

Where a man marries a woman whom he has debauched before marriage, and whom he knew to be pregnant at the time of marriage, he cannot have the marriage annulled on the ground that he was deceived by the false assurances of the wife that he was the father of the child, and that she had been chaste to all others, under Civil Code, section 82, providing for annulling marriages where the consent of either party was obtained by fraud.—Franke v. Franke, 3, 656.

The fact that the woman was pregnant at the time of her marriage is not ground for setting the marriage aside under Civil Code, sections 58, 82, for physical incapacity.—Franke v. Franke, **3, 656.**

MARRIED WOMEN.
See Husband and Wife.

MARSHAL.
Fees for serving process. See Process, § 5.

MASTER AND SERVANT.

§ 1. Contract of employment—Wages.
§ 2. —— Employee not a tenant.
§ 3. Action for employer's breach of contract.
§ 4. —— By traveling salesman.
§ 5. Presumption of risk and contributory negligence.
§ 6. Railway employees.
§ 7. —— Employee in sawmill.
§ 8. Defective appliances.
§ 9. Negligence in giving signals.
§ 10. Fellow-servants.
§ 11. —— Selecting and retaining employees.

See Independent Contractor; Work and Labor.

§ 1. Contract of Employment—Wages.

Plaintiffs, by letter, offered their services to defendant for $5,000 a year. Defendant replied that plaintiffs' "names shall appear on the pay-roll at the rate of $416.66 per month." Later, defendant's president inquired if the salary was satisfactory, and plaintiffs replied that they did not know whether they were employed by the month or year, that they would accept no employment except by the year, to which defendant's president consented. Held, that the employment was by the year, at $5,000, payable monthly.—Luce v. San Diego Land & Town Co., **4, 726.**

Civil Code, section 2011, declares that, "in the absence of any agreement" as to the term of service, time of payment, or rate of wages, a servant is presumed to be hired by the month, at a monthly rate of wages, to be paid when the service is performed. Held, that where the evidence is not before the supreme court, it will not presume that there was no agreement as to the time a servant's wages were to be paid, in order to render available the presumption authorized by such provision of the code.—Kuschel v. Hunter, **5, 793.**

§ 2. —— Employee not a Tenant.

One who takes charge of another's ranch, with the understanding that he is to receive for his services a certain sum per month, and, after paying from the gross proceeds the operating expenses, including his own salary, and deducting what was due for supplies and equipments furnished by him, to return the balance to the owner, and who does not agree to bear a part of any loss which may occur, is merely a hired man, and not a tenant. A verbal understanding that he was to remain in possession of the property, and have a lien thereon till he was paid, is no defense to the owner's action for recovery of possession.—Todhunter v. Armstrong, **6, 27.**

§ 3. Action for Employer's Breach of Contract.

In an action for breach of a written contract of employment, plaintiff may amend the complaint to show that her discharge before the time agreed on therein had caused a loss of certain profits, which, by a collateral oral agreement with defendant, she was entitled to receive from each customer, such loss being in the nature of consequential damages.—Wells v. Law, 4, 903.

§ 4. —— By Traveling Salesman.

A written proposition by defendant to plaintiff recited that "we will pay you a commission of seven and one-half per cent on all orders taken by you and shipped by us between this date and October 31, 1887. You are not to pay out any money or contract any obligation of whatever nature for us, nor represent us in any legal proceeding of any kind or in any place, unless specially authorized in writing so to do. Your duty to us is to take orders for our goods. We reserve the right to decline such orders as we may not want to fill"; and the same was orally accepted by plaintiff. Held, in an action by plaintiff for a wrongful discharge, that oral evidence was inadmissible to change or enlarge the terms of the contract thus made, except as to matters necessarily implied in it or necessary to its performance.—Wiley v. California Hosiery Co., 3, 814.

In such action plaintiff is not entitled to recover the specified commission on the amount of goods sold by other salesmen for defendant in territory in which plaintiff claimed the exclusive right to sell for it, since he had not such privilege under the contract.—Wiley v. California Hosiery Co., 3, 814.

The fact that plaintiff, for three years preceding such contract, had solicited orders for defendant in such territory, would not entitle him to such privilege, and evidence of such fact is inadmissible.—Wiley v. California Hosiery Co., 3, 814.

In such action plaintiff admitted that he took orders at prices below those given to him by defendant, and without its express permission, and that, when he told defendant's secretary that he could not get such prices of certain persons, he said, "You have got to get these prices for the goods, or else not sell them, and the goods have to bring that price this year." The evidence showed that defendant wrote plaintiff several times protesting against his taking orders at cut prices, and finally wrote him that "we will have no man working for us in any manner who will not take our instructions. Because you have been with us a long time, we again give you your choice of doing as we want you to do, or return our samples and reference book"; and that plaintiff replied that "you have been the only violators of the contract, and I defy you to show a point wherein I have not fulfilled it to the letter. In your letter of July 7th, you state I may consider myself no longer in the employ of your company. I consider a full discharge." Held, that plaintiff voluntarily quit defendant's employ, rather than comply with reasonable instructions, and the evidence did not support a verdict for plaintiff.—Wiley v. California Hosiery Co., 3, 814.

An instruction in such case that, if the jury found for plaintiff, they should find the amount of defendant's goods plaintiff would have sold during the remainder of his term of employment, and allow seven and one-half per cent thereon, is erroneous, since it fails to take into account plaintiff's expenses, which should be deducted therefrom.—Wiley v. California Hosiery Co., 3, 814.

In such action plaintiff testified that he told defendant's secretary that he could not sell their goods alone for less than ten per cent and the former promised him a side line of flannels; that "I said that is just what I wanted, and on the strength of that we entered into this contract. I told him I was to have a line of gloves in con-

nection with defendant's goods." Held, that plaintiff was not entitled to recover for commissions that he would have made on the
sale of gloves during the remainder of his term of employment, in
the absence of any other evidence of a contract with defendant in
relation thereto.—Wiley v. California Hosiery Co., 3, 814.

In such action evidence of a usage by which plaintiff was allowed,
in his discretion, to make reductions within certain limits from the
price list, in so far as the same was inconsistent with the written
agreement and positive instructions of defendant, was inadmissible.
Wiley v. California Hosiery Co., 3, 814.

In such case the rule for estimating the amount of sales plaintiff
would have made during the remainder of his term of employment
should be based on the sales made during the part of the term which
had expired at the time of the discharge, modified by the facts as
to whether the sales would be greater or less during the early or
later period.—Wiley v. California Hosiery Co., 3, 814.

§ 5. Assumption of Risk and Contributory Negligence.

Plaintiff had been for seven years in charge of stills for distilling
petroleum, and inspected the bottoms, and notified defendant, the
owner, when they were to be replaced. The life of a bottom was
about five and a half months, and at the end of four months he would
begin inspections, making them after every run. He knew the danger
of the bottoms giving way, and whether they had been regularly
inspected. A crack being discovered in a bottom, plaintiff and the
superintendent knelt down and looked at it, neither thinking of any
danger. At the superintendent's suggestion, plaintiff then proceeded
to remove a burner to prevent the oil in it being caked, and while
standing in front of the still the bottom gave way, and a quantity
of asphaltum ran out, burning plaintiff. Held, that the injury was
caused by an unforeseen accident, resulting from the inevitable impairment of the still, of which plaintiff had equal means of knowing
with defendant, and he could not recover.—Wright v. Pacific Coast
Oil Co., 6, 84.

§ 6. —— Railway Employees.

Where, on the trial of an action for damages against a railroad
company brought for the death of a train conductor in defendant's
employ, it appears that such conductor was in absolute control of a
long freight train; that there were three brakemen who were under
him, and whose positions, respectively, were on the front, middle
and rear of the train; that the middle brakeman, when the train was
leaving the last station at which it stopped before the accident, was
about to go to his position, when he was stopped by the conductor
to assist him in checking way-bills, and remained in the baggage-
car after such checking was finished, and until the accident happened, there is evidence of negligence in the conductor; but the verdict for plaintiff may be sustained, where the instructions of the
judge are clear, on the theory that the jury considered that the
negligence of the conductor did not contribute proximately to produce the accident.—Brown v. Central Pac. R. Co., 2, 730.

In an action by a brakeman against a railroad company for injuries received in a collision with an ox which was on the track
through defendant's negligence in not keeping up proper fences, it
appeared that it was apparent to anyone who looked at them that
the fences were insufficient to turn stock; and it was known that
cattle had frequently broken through them while plaintiff was in
defendant's employment, when the train would be stopped, and the
cattle driven off the track; and at least once plaintiff had assisted

in driving them off. Plaintiff, a man of intelligence, had, as brakeman, ridden over the road along which the fences ran for some months. The court charged that if plaintiff knew the condition of the fences, or, as a prudent, reasonable man, should have known it, the verdict should be for defendant. Held, that a verdict for plaintiff could not be sustained, though he testified that he did not know the condition of the fences.—Magee v. North Pacific Coast R. Co., 3, 43.

§ 7. —— Employee in Sawmill.

Plaintiff, an adult, had worked about defendant's sawmill for about four years, and for nearly a year as helper to the sawyer at an "edger," consisting of eight circular saws arranged upon a table four feet high. Under the table, six inches below the saws was a revolving shaft, with a collar upon it fastened by a projecting set-screw. Plaintiff testified that on several occasions he had run the edger himself, by direction of his employer, after telling him that he did not understand machinery; that the saws were stopped and started at will by pulling, respectively, two ropes which hung near; that the morning of the accident was quite dark, but there were no lights; that he had been directed to run the machine, and while doing so, a sliver dropped upon the shaft which he attempted to remove, as he had seen the sawyer do, without stopping the saw, and while doing so his sleeve was caught by the set-screw, of whose existence he was ignorant, and his hand cut off. Held, that there was no evidence of negligence, and that he was guilty of contributory negligence.—Ingerman v. Moore, 3, 336.

§ 8. Defective Appliances.

In an action by a servant against the master for injuries caused by the breaking of the hook of the upper block on a derrick used in moving stone, there was evidence that the hook, which was of wrought iron, broke because of crystallization. The derrick, block and hook had been in use but a few months. Defendant's expert testified that, if the iron had been flawless, the hook could have been safely used for about five years in lifting from seven to ten tons, while plaintiff's expert testified that if the hook was new it would support six tons, which was the weight of the stone being raised when the hook broke. Held, that the evidence was insufficient to charge defendant with negligence.—Lyons v. Knowles, 3, 846.

§ 9. Negligence in Giving Signals.

Where an employee is injured by the dropping of a hammer of a pile-driver, at a signal by the foreman, before he was signaled by the employee putting a ring on the pile, the employer is liable if the foreman negligently gave the signal.—Matthews v. Bull, 5, 592.

§ 10. Fellow-servants.

The slingman of a stevedore's crew employed to load a vessel, whose duty it is to stand on the wharf and attach the hoisting tackle to the articles to be loaded, is a fellow-servant of the riggers, whose duty it is to set up and rig the hoisting apparatus to the vessel.—Burns v. Sennett, 5, 370.

§ 11. —— Selecting and Retaining Employees.

Under Civil Code, section 1971, providing that "an employer must in all cases indemnify his employee for losses caused by the former's want of ordinary care," the employer is responsible for an injury caused to one employee by the negligence of another, whom he has retained with knowledge of his incompetence.—Matthews v. Bull, **5,** 592.

A master cannot devest himself of responsibility for the selection and retention of competent servants by delegating the duty to another.—Matthews v. Bull, 5, 592.

MECHANICS' LIENS.

§ 1. Constitutional Questions.

The constitution of 1879 (art. 20, sec. 15), as to mechanics' liens, was intended to be merely declaratory of the law in that regard theretofore in force as construed by decisions of the supreme court then extant.—Latson v. Nelson, 2, 199.

The mechanics' lien law in force at the time of the enactment of the constitution of 1879, as construed by decisions of the supreme court extant at the time, gave no warrant to laborers and materialmen to charge the building with liens exceeding in amount the balance of the contract price remaining unpaid when the notice of lien was given.—Latson v. Nelson, 2, 199.

The legislature, in amending section 1183, Code of Civil Procedure, as to mechanics' liens in assumed compliance with the mandate of the constitution of 1879, could not validly extend the law beyond what the constitution intended.—Latson v. Nelson, 2, 199.

§ 2. Building Contract.

See Building Contracts.

Failure of the contract for erecting a building to comply substantially with Code of Civil Procedure, sections 1183, 1184, relating to mechanics' liens, does not render the contract void.—Dunlop v. Kennedy, 4, 196.

A contract for erecting a building, which provides that twenty-five per cent of the sum to be paid shall remain unpaid until thirty-five days after completion of the building, and the remainder be paid in partial payments equal to seventy-five per cent of the value of the work and material done and furnished at the time of such payments, sufficiently complies with Code of Civil Procedure, section 1184, providing that the contract price shall, by the terms of the contract, be made payable in installments at specified times after commencement of the work, and on the completion of the work, provided that at least twenty-five per cent of the whole contract price shall be made payable at least thirty-five days after final completion of the contract.—Dunlop v. Kennedy, 4, 196.

Under Code of Civil Procedure, section 1184, requiring the contract for erecting a building to specify times when payments are to be made, and requiring twenty-five per cent of the price to be retained until thirty-five days after completion, partial payments, however they are specified as to time, may be safely made, provided no notice of their subcontracts is given by materialmen, in the absence of which they must rely on the responsibility of the contractor, and the twenty-five per cent required to be retained; and in such case they are not injured by any uncertainty as to the times of payment specified nor by payments in advance of the specified time.—Dunlop v. Kennedy, 4, 196.

All that materialmen can require, in such case, is that at the time they serve written notice upon the owner, or, if no notice is served, at the time their lien is filed, there shall be in his hands the amount required by the contract and said section.—Dunlop v. Kennedy, 4, 196.

The mechanic's lien statute does not require that the contract for erecting a building shall be signed by the owner, and it is sufficient if it be signed by the reputed owner.—Dunlop v. Kennedy, 4, 196.

A contract for erecting a building, and also for improvements on an adjoining lot running "westerly," is not avoided by the fact that the recorded memorandum of the contract erroneously uses the word "easterly" nor is the sufficiency of the memorandum destroyed.—Dunlop v. Kennedy, 4, 196.

A memorandum of a contract for a building costing over $1,000, filed in the recorder's office, in which the only description of the property and of the work to be done is that "the building is to be a frame building," is fatally defective.—Blyth v. Torre, 4, 912.

§ 3. Failure to File Bond.

Under Code of Civil Procedure, section 1203, requiring a bond, in case of a building contract, it by its terms to inure to the benefit of persons performing labor and furnishing materials for the con-tractor, one given to "T. [the owner], legal representatives or as-signees," and not in terms inuring to the benefit of anyone else, is insufficient.—Gibbs v. Tally, 6, 621.

Under Code of Civil Procedure, section 1203, requiring a bond, in case of a building contract, in an amount equal to at least twenty-five per cent of the contract price, inuring to the benefit of persons performing labor and furnishing materials for the contractor, and providing as limit of damages, in case of a bond, the value of labor and materials furnished, not exceeding the amount of the bond, and declaring that any failure to comply with the provisions of the sec-tion shall render the owner and contractor liable to materialmen and laborers entitled to liens on the property, the measure of damages, in the absence of a bond, is the amount of the claim for labor or mate-rial, not exceeding twenty-five per cent of the contract price.—Gibbs v. Tally, 6, 621.

Under Code of Civil Procedure, section 1203, giving action for damages "to any and all materialmen, laborers and subcontractors entitled to a lien," if bond is not filed where there is a building contract, the claimant who sues first and obtains judgment is entitled to recover up to the limit of the owner's liability, unless other claimants intervene, or, having brought actions, have them consolidated with his.—Gibbs v. Tally, 6, 621.

Though a materialman, suing the owner of a building for failure to have a bond of the contractor filed, alleges nonpayment of the claim for materials furnished, it is enough for him to prove the debt, and defendant has the burden of proving payment.—Gibbs v. Tally, 6, 621.

Under Code of Civil Procedure, section 1203, giving action for damages to a laborer or materialman against the owner of the property who, in case of a contract to build thereon, does not take a bond for their benefit, and providing that action on the bond, if one is taken, shall not affect the laborer's lien nor any action to foreclose it, except that there shall be but one satisfaction of the claim, action for failure to take bond is not affected by the bringing of an action to foreclose the lien.—Gibbs v. Tally, 6, 621.

A claim under Code of Civil Procedure, section 1203, for damages by a laborer against the owner of property who, in case of contract to build thereon, does not take a bond from the contractor, is within Civil Code, section 1458, declaring "a right arising out of an obligation is the property of the person to whom it is due, and may be transferred as such."—Gibbs v. Tally, 6, 621.

§ 4. Payments.

In consolidated actions to establish mechanics' liens by P., a subcontractor, against the contractor and owner, and by M., a materialman, against P. and such contractor and owner, the complaints both alleged that P. was the subcontractor and performed the work, and that M. furnished the materials to P. These allegations were not denied. The court found that P. & Co., a copartnership, made and performed the subcontract; that M. furnished the materials; and that the contractor paid P. & Co., who in turn paid M. Held, that a judgment for defendants in the consolidated case was not erroneous, on the ground that such findings were contrary to the admissions of the pleadings, since the acceptance of payment by such firm implies P.'s consent, and must be considered as payment to him.—Petersen v. Shain, 4, 122.

The owner of a building who, out of the contract price, has paid laborers who were entitled to file liens, and would have filed them but for such payment, and who has also retained out of the contract price the twenty-five per cent required by Code of Civil Procedure, section 1184, to be retained until thirty-five days after completion of the contract, is entitled to credit for such payment; and materialmen are not entitled to have the amount of such payment considered as part of the fund available for their claims, on the ground that there could be no privity between the owner and such laborers until they have filed their liens, so as to entitle him to pay them.—Dunlop v. Kennedy, 4, 196.

It appeared that the contractor delivered to M. certain checks, payable to the order of P. & Co., to enable him to get his pay, and that they indorsed the checks to him, but the latter applied the money to payment of other indebtedness due him from such firm. Held, that a finding that M. was paid was proper, and not inconsistent with other findings.—Petersen v. Shain, 4, 122.

The fact that the building contract, in providing for the payments, retains, until thirty-five days after the completion of the work, slightly less than the twenty-five per cent of the contract price required by statute, does not render the owner personally liable for all labor and materials furnished, especially when more than twenty-five per cent was in fact actually retained.—Stimson Mill Co. v. Riley, 5, 218.

When the building contract provides for payments as the work progresses, payments made when the work has been substantially finished to the required stages cannot be considered premature, so as to subject the owner to liability to materialmen to the additional extent of the payments so made.—Stimson Mill Co. v. Riley, 5, 218.

§ 5. Right to Lien in General.

When materials are furnished or work done, free from any contract to give credit, and a debt in personam is thereby created against the owner of the premises, there is no reason why the materialman or laborer may not proceed at once, both to record his lien upon the property under the statute and immediately to enforce it by action.— Bender v. Palmer, 1, 601.

A materialman is not estopped from enforcing his lien because he is on the contractor's bond to the owner to secure him from loss on account of the default or negligence of the contractor.—Blyth v. Torre, 4, 912.

It does not prejudice persons furnishing a contractor material for erecting a building that the owner of the land purchased material from a firm of which he was a member, and furnished it to the contractor as a partial payment of the contract price, which partial payment he had a right to make.—Dunlop v. Kennedy, 4, 196.

The unworkmanlike failure of a contractor to place the front windows in the basement story of a small house directly underneath the front windows of the upper portion of the house did not constitute a trivial imperfection within the meaning of Code of Civil Procedure, section 1187, declaring that a trivial imperfection shall not be deemed such a lack of completion of the work as to prevent the filing of a mechanic's lien but was a substantial noncompliance with the contract, which precluded the enforcement of a lien by the contractor.— Schindler v. Green, 7, 229.

§ 6. Building on Government Land.

A mechanic's lien right, accruing against a building on government land to which the person in possession, for whom the building was constructed, had not yet acquired full title, is not lost by transfer of the possession of the land; but those entering successively under such person are concluded, even the final taker to whom the complete title is granted.—Bender v. Palmer, 1, 601.

§ 7. House on Another's Lot.

A went into possession of certain lots, then owned by B, under a contract of purchase, built and paid for a house thereon, and afterward removed the house onto the land of C, as a temporary resting place, without B's permission, and after default in the payments on the lots. Held, that it cannot be implied that B furnished the material with which the house was built, nor that A acted at the time of constructing the house as the agent of C, so as to subject C's lot to a lien under sections 1183, 1185, 1192, Code of Civil Procedure.— Fresno Loan & Savings Bank v. Husted, 5, 715.

C was not required to post written notice upon this building within three days after it was moved on his lots, under section 1192, supra, in order to escape liability, as the house, by agreement, was to remain on the lots in question but a few days, and was therefore personal property while it rested there.—Fresno Loan & Savings Bank v. Husted, 5, 715.

§ 8. Notice and Claim of Lien.

Under Code of Civil Procedure, section 1184, requiring the owner of a building to retain sufficient funds to pay a claim for materials, furnished by a materialman who has given notice of his claim to such owner, a materialman who serves the required notice acquires a prior right to the fund in the hands of the owner, due the contractor, though the contractor subsequently abandons the contract.— Russ Lumber & Mill Co. v. Roggenkamp, 4, 462.

Under Code of Civil Procedure, section 1184, providing, in regard to mechanics' liens, that the owner shall retain a certain percentage of the contract price for thirty-five days after the completion of the work, and that the materialmen, etc., may at any time serve notice on the owner of their claim for material furnished or labor performed, whereupon the owner shall retain sufficient of the money due or to become due the contractor to satisfy such claims, the notices may be served after the expiration of the thirty-five days, provided there are funds due the contractor still in the hands of the owner.—Board of Education v. Blake, 4, 891.

Where the owner of a lot gives permission to his tenant to erect a building thereon of a certain character, and the tenant does so, he had such knowledge of the intended construction of the building as to render a notice posted by him after the lien was filed, on visiting the premises, too late, under Code of Civil Procedure, section 1192, providing that buildings constructed on lands with the owner's knowledge shall be held to be constructed at his instance, and liable for a lien, unless, within three days after knowledge of the construction, he post notices thereon.—Santa Monica Lumber & Mill Co. v. Hege, 5, 628.

A notice of a lien by a materialman for materials furnished in the construction of a building which alleged that the amount of the demand was $799.97 over and above legal setoffs, that the name of the person by whom claimant was employed and to whom he furnished the material was the contractor, and that the contractor agreed to pay a specified sum on completion of the work showed an agreement to pay a definite sum for the materials.—Lucas v. Rea, 7, 363.

§ 9. —— Sufficiency and Requisites of Statement.

A claim of lien, filed by a materialman giving the names of several persons to whom different portions of the material were furnished at different times, without any designation as to what portion was furnished to each severally, does not sufficiently comply with Code of Civil Procedure of California, section 1187, requiring the claim to state "the name of the person by whom he was employed, or to whom he furnished the materials."—Gordon Hardware Co. v. San Francisco etc. R. R. Co., 3, 140.

A description of the materials furnished as "nails, spikes, iron, steel, picks, shovels, and other like material, is too indefinite and uncertain to sustain the lien.—Gordon Hardware Co. v. San Francisco etc. R. R. Co., 3, 140.

The fact that a claim of lien, filed by a materialman, included more than was due him, if the error was without fraud, will not defeat his right to recover.—Harmon v. San Francisco etc. R. R. Co., 3, 144.

The claimant of a lien for materials furnished set out in its notice that the claimant undertook to furnish to a certain mining company explosives in such quantities as it might require, each parcel to be paid for at delivery, or as soon thereafter as might be, with interest upon such payments in case of delay. Held, that this notice was in substantial compliance with Code of Civil Procedure, section 1187, requiring such claimant to state the terms, time given, and conditions of his contract, wherein the words "time given" mean the time of payment for the materials furnished.—California Powder Works v. Blue Tent Consolidated etc. Mines, 3, 145.

A claim of lien filed by a materialman against a railway company for materials furnished a contractor and his assignee, who assumed all liabilities, although it omits to show the proportion of materials furnished to each, is sufficient, under Code of Civil Procedure, section 1187, requiring that the claim state the name of the person to whom the materials were furnished.—Harmon v. San Francisco etc. R. R. Co., 3, 256.

The fact that a claim of lien filed by a materialman includes more than is due him, if the error is without fraud, will not defeat his right to recover.—Harmon v. San Francisco etc. R. R. Co., 3, 256.

Where a mechanic's lien notice describes the property as a dwelling-house, situate upon a certain lot, and it turns out to be situated partly on that lot and partly on another, the lien cannot be enforced, as there is no lien on that part of the house not situated on the lot named, and it would work great injury to the owner to allow the lien to be enforced against a part only of the house.—Willamette Steam etc. Lumber Co. v. Kremer, 3, 300.

Where the materials were furnished at the same time for two buildings of the same owner, while it is not necessary to file separate claims on each building, the subcontractors are not entitled to a joint lien on both buildings for the entire amount claimed.—Booth v. Pendola, 3, 283.

Code of Civil Procedure, section 1187, prescribing what facts must be stated in the recorded claim of a mechanic's lien, inter alia, requires a statement of claimant's "demand after deducting all just credits and offsets," but does not require a statement that the materials furnished and used were furnished "to be" used in the buildings. Held, that the claim of lien need not contain such statement.—Neihaus v. Morgan, 5, 391.

A claim of lien on two buildings stated that the reasonable value of the materials furnished by plaintiffs for each house was $182.70, no part of which had been paid, and that the sum of $365.40, "in gold coin of the United States," was still due on such buildings, after deducting all just credits and offsets. Held, that the claim was not open to the objection that it did not state the amount of plaintiffs' demand after deducting all just credits and offsets, because of the quoted words.—Neihaus v. Morgan, 5, 391.

The fact that a contract, as to one item, is improperly set forth in the notice of a mechanic's lien, will not render the lien void as to the other items, concerning which the contract was correctly stated, but recovery can be had for all such items as are correctly stated.—Linck v. Johnson, 6, 817.

§ 10. —— Time for Filing.

A mechanic's lien is not acquired upon a building by a subcontractor who has furnished materials to be used thereon, by filing his claim prior to the completion of the building: Code Civ. Proc., sec. 1187.—Perry v. Brainard, 2, 591.

Code of Civil Procedure, section 1187, which provides that the notice of such claim must be filed within thirty days after the completion of the improvement, alteration, etc., does not refer to the operation of the mine, which may be continuous in its nature, as the thing to be completed.—California Powder Works v. Blue Tent Consolidated etc. Mines, 3, 145.

As the right to a lien does not attach until the materials have been used, plaintiff does not lose such right by a failure to file its claim within thirty days after the materials were furnished.—California Powder Works v. Blue Tent Consolidated etc. Mines, 3, 145.

Code of Civil Procedure, section 1187, provides that any trivial imperfection in the construction of any building shall not be deemed such a lack of completion as to prevent the filing of any lien. Held, that where a building was erected at a cost of $4,700 and was completed on March 7, 1889, with the exception of about $7 worth of alteration, which was done on April 6, 1889, the building was completed on March 7th, within the meaning of the statute, and a lien for materials furnished, filed more than thirty days after March 7th, was not in time.—Santa Clara Valley Mill etc. Co. v. Williams, 3, 700.

A contractor agreed to excavate a cellar, and to erect walls of concrete and steps to the streets, and plaintiff did work thereon for said contractor. The work was accepted by the owner, as complete, July 26th; but in August a carpenter employed by the owner placed a frame in the cellar door, and plaintiff, at the owner's request, filled a small hole outside of the cellar. Held, that the lack of this additional work was a "trivial imperfection," within the meaning of Code of Civil Procedure, section 1187, which provides that such imperfection shall not prevent the filing of the lien claim, and hence the filing of the claim August 29th was not within the statutory time of thirty days from the completion of the work.—Lippert v. Lasar et al., 4, 74.

Where there was evidence that buildings were, in effect, completed before the claim of lien was filed, a finding to that effect will not be disturbed, though there was evidence of trifling imperfections remedied after such time.—Santa Monica Lumber & Mill Co. v. Hege, 5, 628.

§ 11. Attachment and Mortgage Liens.

The lien of a materialman under a contract to deliver lumber from time to time as wanted and paid for is superior to a mortgage on the premises only in respect of lumber delivered and not paid for at the time of the recording of the mortgage.—Spencer v. Barney, 1, 56.

In a proceeding to establish mechanics' and other liens, an attachment lien claim on the fund, set up for the first time at the trial before the referee and not mentioned in any petition by claimant in the cause, is properly rejected.—Blythe v. Hammond, 1, 455.

§ 12. Reputed Owner.

A claim of lien sufficient in form is properly admitted, as against objection that it does not correctly state the names of either the owners or reputed owners of the premises, there being at the time no evidence before the court to contradict its terms.—Kelly v. Lemberger, 5, 433.

Though one states, in his claim of lien, that a certain person is owner and reputed owner of the premises, his lien is not impaired by proof that such person was the reputed owner only.—Kelly v. Lemberger, 5, 433.

A finding that one was the reputed owner of premises, as alleged in a claim of mechanic's lien, is not impaired by the fact that conveyances to other persons were on record.—Kelly v. Lemberger, 5, 433.

§ 13. Personal Liability of Owner.

Code of Civil Procedure, section 1183, providing that a building contract shall be void if not filed with plans and specifications, and that in such case the labor done and materials furnished by all persons except the contractor shall be deemed to have been done and furnished "at the personal instance of the owner," and that the persons furnishing them shall have a lien for their value, does not create a contractual relation between the owner and subcontractor, whereby the owner can be held personally liable for such work and materials, but merely affords an opportunity for a lien by complying with the statute.—Gnekow v. Confer, 5, 654.

§ 14. Trivial Imperfections—Completion of Work.

Under Code of Civil Procedure, section 1187, as amended by Stats. and Amend. 1887, page 154, providing that every person, save the original contractor, claiming a lien, must, within thirty days after the "completion" of the building, file his lien, but that any "trivial imperfection" in the construction shall not be deemed such a lack of completion as to prevent the filing of the lien, a lien filed before the doors of a house were hung, the plumbing finished, the closets and bathroom completed, ventilators placed, and moldings put in, is premature, and cannot be enforced, as such things are not "trivial imperfections," but are necessary to be done to effect a "completion" of the building.—Schallert-Ganahl Lumber Co. v. Sheldon, 3, 779.

§ 15. Enforcement and Foreclosure—Statute of Limitations.

In a suit to enforce a merchanic's lien, it is not the service of process upon the defendant that marks the beginning of the proceedings, but the filing of the complaint; and this filing, if within the ninety days, saves the limitation for each defendant lienholder named in it, since the court has jurisdiction of him by virtue of the filing of the complaint.—Phelps v. Davidson, 1, 653.

§ 16. Intervention by Other Lienholders.

In a proceeding to establish mechanics' and other liens, an attachment lien claim set up by an intervener's petition cannot be considered on appeal, if the evidence, as found in the record, fails to show any writ of attachment ever to have been issued or served in such a manner as to create a lien on the fund.—Blythe v. Hammond, 1, 455.

Lienholders, properly made defendants by the complaint in a suit to enforce a mechanic's lien, should not come in as interveners. But their petitions in intervention should be, on motion, allowed to stand as their answers, if containing all the allegations necessary to enable them to have their claims enforced as liens and to participate in the proceeds of the sale of the premises.—Phelps v. Davidson, 1, 653.

§ 17. —— Interpleader.

A county deposited money due a contractor in court, and two creditors of the contractor, one only of whom had a lien on the fund, together with the contractor, were ordered to interplead for the same. The contractor failed to set up any claim to the fund. Held, that the balance of the fund left after satisfying the creditor's lien should be paid to the other creditor to satisfy a judgment held by him against the contractor, instead of to the contractor.—Board of Education v. Blake, 4, 891.

§ 18. —— Pleading.

The objection that the causes of action of respective lienholders, made defendants by the complaint, for the enforcement of their liens, have been barred by the statute, can be taken only by answer or demurrer.—Phelps v. Davidson, 1, 653.

One seeking to establish a lien under act of March 31, 1891 (Stats. 1891, p. 195), requiring corporations to pay laborers and mechanics wages due weekly or monthly on such day as shall be selected by the corporation, and giving said laborers a lien for wages not so paid, must show that his wages were payable weekly or monthly.—Kuschel v. Hunter, 5, 793.

An allegation that claimant "agreed to do work by the month" at the "agreed rate of $100 per month" is not an allegation that the corporation agreed to pay him monthly.—Kuschel v. Hunter, 5, 793.

A finding of the court that the corporation "promised" claimant "the sum of $100 per month," and that it did not pay "its employees" the wages earned by them "weekly or monthly on a pay day in each week or month selected by said company," is not equivalent to a finding that the corporation agreed to pay claimant monthly.—Kuschel v. Hunter, 5, 793.

In an action to foreclose a mechanic's lien, a mistake in the complaint in regard to the terms of the contract, as to time of payment, where the contract, the notice of lien, and the findings show the facts, is immaterial.—Webb v. Kuns, 6, 97.

In an action to foreclose a mechanic's lien, the complaint alleged the date of the completion of the building, and that the lien was filed on April 6, 1894, within thirty days thereafter. The answer denied "that within thirty days from and after the completion of said building, to wit, upon the sixth day of April, 1894, or at any other time, or at all," plaintiffs filed their claim of lien, containing a statement of their demand. Held, that the answer was but a denial of the time of filing the notice of lien, and of its sufficiency, and admitted the allegation of the time when the building was completed. Lingard v. Beta Theta Pi Hall Assn., 6, 226.

A complaint in an action by a materialman against the owner for materials furnished for a building, which alleges that the materialman agreed with the owner to furnish the materials, and that the owner agreed to pay a specified sum therefor on the completion of the work, followed by appropriate averments for the foreclosure of a materialman's lien, states a good cause of action.—Lucas v. Rea, 7, 363.

Under Code of Civil Procedure, sections 1183, 1184, providing that, where the contract between the owner and contractor is void because not in writing and not recorded, materials furnished by materialmen shall be deemed to have been furnished at the personal instance of the owner, and they shall have a lien for the value thereof, etc., a materialman furnishing materials to a contractor may aver a direct agreement with the owner if the contract between the owner and contractor is void.—Lucas v. Rea, 7, 363.

A complaint in an action to establish and foreclose a materialman's lien which averred, in reference to the notice of lien, "a copy of which is hereto attached marked 'Exhibit A,' and made a part of the complaint," that the claimant had in his verified notice of lien stated that the recitals therein were true, and where the contract to pay a specified sum for the materials set forth in the notice of lien was denied, evidence of an agreement to pay the correct price was insufficient to justify a recovery.—Lucas v. Rea, 7, 363.

In an action for the foreclosure of a mechanic's lien, the complaint should aver the amount due under the contract to the contractor from the owner of the building on which the work was done.—Doggett v. Bellows, 2, 454.

§ 19. —— Issues, Proof and Variance.

Where the claim of mechanic's lien, and the complaint in an action to foreclose the lien, alleged a contract to pay plaintiff $3.50 per day, and a contract to pay the reasonable value of his services was proved, and such value was shown to be $2.84 per day, the variance is fatal. Jones v. Shuey, 5, 17.

In an action to enforce a materialman's lien, plaintiff can recover only for the materials furnished between the dates stated in the claim of lien, though the proof shows that materials were furnished on other dates.—Santa Monica Lumber & Mill Co. v. Hege, 5, 628.

Where, in an action to foreclose a mechanic's lien, it is stipulated that defendant was at all times represented by her father as her agent in all the matters in controversy, that proof of such agency is unnecessary, and that her father attended to all business with plaintiff, evidence that such father told witness, when he wanted materials, to order them, and that when materials were wanted the father either ordered them or directed the witness to do so, is admissible to show authority for supplying extra materials.—Linck v. Johnson, 6, 817.

One seeking to establish and foreclose a lien for materials furnished for the construction of a building must prove the contract substantially as set out in his notice of lien, where the terms thereof are controverted.—Lucas v. Rea, 7, 363.

The variance between the complaint in an action to foreclose a materialman's lien which alleges a demand for $780.70 and the proof showing a value of $859.67 and a payment of $60 is immaterial.—Lucas v. Rea, 7, 363.

The variance between the complaint in an action to foreclose a lien for materials which alleges a demand for $780.70, and the notice of lien demanding a lien for $19 more, is unimportant, in the absence of evidence of fraud.—Lucas v. Rea, 7, 363.

§ 20. —— Costs and Attorney Fees.

An allowance of attorneys' fees in an action to enforce mechanics' liens will not be set aside as insufficient unless clearly unreasonable. Stimson Mill Co. v. Riley, 5, 218.

Under Code of Civil Procedure, section 1195, providing that the court must allow, as a part of the costs on foreclosure of a mechanic's lien, the money paid for filing and recording the lien, and reasonable attorneys' fees—such costs and fees to be allowed to lien claimants whose liens are established—a party establishing a claim is properly allowed such fees and costs where defendant makes no tender of the amount due, or offer to allow judgment for any sum.—Linck v. Johnson, 6, 817.

§ 21. —— Judgment.

In an action by subcontractors to enforce a lien for materials furnished in the erection of a building, the contract for which, between the owner and contractor, was never filed for record, a judgment for plaintiffs cannot be supported where the complaint does not allege the reasonable value of the materials, and there is no finding as to such value, though the complaint does allege the amount agreed to be paid by the contractor.—Booth v. Pendola, 3, 283.

Code of Civil Procedure, section 1183, provides that the contract for building a house shall be in writing, and, before the work is begun, shall be filed with the recorder, otherwise to be void, and no recovery had thereon; and that labor done and material furnished by others than the contractor shall be deemed furnished at the instance of the owner, and be deemed a lien. Held, that when the original contractor had not filed his contract, and the materialman had not filed any lien under the statute, the latter is not entitled to a personal judgment against the owners of the building for material furnished the contractor.—Santa Clara Valley Mill etc. Co. v. Williams, 3, 700.

In an action to enforce a mechanic's lien on two buildings, the decree was that plaintiffs have a valid lien on the houses and lot for the sums found due them; that the sheriff sell the property, and from the proceeds of the sale pay plaintiffs the sums found due them, viz., $365.49 on account of their claim, $50 for attorneys' fees, and $45.60 for their costs; and that he bring the surplus money, if any, into court, to abide its further order. Held, that the decree was not open to the objection that it was unintelligible, and incapable of being executed by the sheriff.—Neihaus v. Morgan, 5, 391.

§ 22. Appeal and Modification or Reversal.

Where, in a suit to enforce a mechanic's lien, the lower court found that defendants owed plaintiff a certain sum and awarded him a lien therefor, and defendants found no fault with the amount awarded plaintiff, but appealed on the ground that plaintiff was not entitled to a lien, and all the evidence and proceedings had on the trial were brought before the appellate court for review, that court, on setting aside the judgment for error in giving plaintiff a lien, would not remand the case for a new trial, but would direct the lower court to modify the judgment by striking therefrom the provisions for a lien and to enter a personal judgment in plaintiff's favor for the sum found due.—Schindler v. Green, 7, 233.

Where the suit by a materialman against the owner to establish and foreclose a lien for materials for the construction of a building was tried on the theory that the law made a contract between the materialman and the owner for the materials, the uncertainty in the complaint arising from the fact that it alleged that the contract was made with the owner, while the recital in the notice of lien showed that it was made with the contractor, did not justify a reversal.—Lucas v. Rea, 7, 363.

MEDICAL BOOKS.

Reading to jury. See Trial, § 11.

MEXICAN GRANTS.

See Adverse Possession, § 8; Public Lands, § 2.

§ 1. In General.

A Mexican grant of eight hundred varas square, "at a place called Rincon, embraced within the limitation of Yerba Buena," is so vague and uncertain that nothing passes by force of the grant alone, nor will it be helped out by possession taken under it by the grantee, as the Mexican law, then in force, required possession to be given "by judicial authority, with the citation of all those bounded upon him."—Ohm v. San Francisco, 3, 314.

Such grant is also fatally defective, where the original application, to which it attached each successive paper or certificate up to and including the final grant, fails to show on its face that the grant was made with the approval of the pueblo, of the governor, and of the departmental assembly, and that a record of such fact was made in the public archives, as required by the laws of Mexico then in force.—Ohm v. San Francisco, 3, 314.

In ejectment, plaintiffs claimed under a Mexican grant that had been confirmed by the federal district court in 1857, and had been patented to plaintiffs by the United States in 1858, in accordance with the decree of confirmation which described the land by specified boundaries, giving lines and monuments. The survey made by the surveyor general in carrying out the decree of confirmation conformed to the exterior boundaries, as described in the decree, which mentioned no reservation within the limits of these exterior boundaries. There was a clause in the certificate of survey which read: "Excepting, reserving, and excluding from the tract, as thus surveyed, that portion thereof covered by the navigable waters of the inner bay of San Pedro, and which are included within the following described lines." The land in controversy was an island lying within these lines." This island, together with other land lying within the inner survey, was patented to defendant by the United States in 1881. Held, that the Mexican grant, as confirmed and patented by the United States to plaintiff, included the whole space lying within its exterior boundaries, and that defendant had acquired no title under his patent.—De Guyer v. Banning, 3, 321.

§ 2. Limitation of Actions.

One who alleges that he has a perfect title to land under a Mexican grant, not barred by the statute of limitations, may maintain a legal action for the possession, and there is no necessity for the interference of a court of equity to enable him to assert his rights.—Ohm v. San Francisco, 3, 314.

Since the passage of Statutes of 1863, page 327, which gives five years "from the date of its passage" in which one claiming title to land under a Spanish or Mexican grant may commence an action for its enforcement, the want of confirmation, patent, or survey of such a grant by the United States government has not operated to interrupt the running of the statute.—Ohm v. San Francisco, 3, 314.

MIGRATORY LIVESTOCK.
See Taxation, § 10.

MILITIA.
§ 1. Allowance Under Statute of 1863.

The allowance of money, under Laws of 1863, page 445, to duly uniformed military companies, payable to their several commanding officers, was intended to defray necessary company expenses and not for the benefit of the members as individuals.—Davison v. Board of Examiners, 1, 446.

The law of 1863 allowing $300 to each uniformed company, payable to its captain or commanding officer, cannot be availed of, after its repeal, by a captain of a company long disbanded.—Davison v. Board of Examiners, 1, 446.

MINES AND MINERALS.

§ 1. In General.

The words "lead" and "vein" are to be taken as the equivalents of "lode" and "ledge."—Inimitable Copper Min. Co. v. Union Copper Min. Co., 1, 599.

One in actual possession of mining ground, although without title, may proceed against a mere intruder having no superior right to entry.—Rathbun v. Alexander, 1, 664.

§ 2. Rules of District.

The owners of a mining claim, having consistently with mining usages at the time of locating, posted at each end of the claim notices: "We, the undersigned, do claim 1950 feet in this lead or lode, it being the Reed lead, with all dips, spurs, angles and cross-leads"— cannot be affected by any by-laws or mining rules of the district, subsequently made, so as to have their claim, thus published, rendered a less one.—Inimitable Copper Min. Co. v. Union Copper Min. Co., 1, 599.

§ 3. Location of Claims.

The "sixty days" mentioned in the mining laws, securing rights, etc., to persons locating claims, are to be computed from the time of the location.—McClelland v. King Solomon Gold etc. Quartz Min. Co., 1, 205.

If one first discovering a vein or lode does not make a valid location thereon, another may make such location.—Willeford v. Bell, 5, 679.

Location of a mining claim is invalid if not "distinctly marked on the ground, so that its boundaries can be readily traced," as required by Revised Statutes of the United States, section 2320.—Willeford v. Bell, 5, 679.

It being provided by Revised Statutes of the United States, section 2324, only what "all records of mining claims . . . . shall contain," it is not necessary, in the absence of local rules or customs, for one asserting a location to prove the notice posted on the claim, but merely the recorded notice, which he may do by a copy.—Willeford v. Bell, 5, 679.

§ 4. Forfeitures.

Mining laws introduced in evidence are to be construed by the court, and the question whether by virtue of them a forfeiture has accrued is a question of law.—Fairbanks v. Bear, 1, 39.

§ 5. Cotenancy or Partnership in Property.

Under an instrument by which the lessee of a mine transfers for value a fractional interest in the latter and agrees to conduct the business of the mine, for the transferee as well as himself, and be sole agent irrevocably for the transferee in all matters in that regard, the parties become, as to the mine, tenants in common of the lease-hold estate and, as to the business, partners.—Thompson v. Gibb, 1, 173.

§ 6. —— Contribution.

A sale by a constable for mining assessments, under the act "concerning partnerships for mining purposes" (Laws 1866, page 828), is not valid unless the owner of the stock was not notified of the assessment as required by sections 2 and 4 of the act.—Sayer v. Donahue, 1, 410.

§ 6½. —— Sales for Assessments.

One tenant in common of a mining claim is bound to contribute his proportion of the value of the yearly work required to be done thereon to perfect title, and performed by his cotenant, unless he abandons his interest in the unpatented claim, or offers to perform the work.—Holbrooke v. Harrington, 4, 554.

§ 7. Contracts or Options to Purchase.

A contract giving an option to purchase a mine, wherein the vendors covenant to sink a shaft of at least one hundred feet, imposes on them the absolute duty of sinking the shaft to the agreed depth, though they find no evidence that the mine contains enough valuable ore to justify them in purchasing it.—Davis v. Eames, 4, 436.

Where a contract granting an option to purchase a mine was signed by two of three co-owners, and an action to enforce it was brought against the signers, the burden was on them to show, as claimed, that the contract was not to be operative unless signed also by the other owner, who was named therein.—Stanton v. Singleton, 6, 129.

An allegation that defendants "made and entered into" the agreement sufficiently imports delivery as against a general demurrer, in an action for specific performance.—Stanton v. Singleton, 6, 129.

A contract whereby plaintiff was given an option to purchase an interest in a mine for a certain price on performing certain conditions is not void for want of mutuality, so that it cannot be specifically enforced, where plaintiff notified the other parties thereto of his election to perform his part thereof.—Stanton v. Singleton, 6, 129.

§ 8. Partition of Claim.

Where, in partition by one tenant in common of a mining claim, on an accounting for money spent upon the land in excess of her share no personal judgment is rendered against the other tenant, but the property is ordered to be sold, plaintiff should be allowed the full amount of the sums properly paid out, instead of only one-half, before the residue is divided.—Holbrooke v. Harrington, 4, 554.

Where, in such an action, the amount allowed is less than plaintiff is entitled to, being for one-half the amount paid out, error in allowing improper credits is harmless.—Holbrooke v. Harrington, 4, 554.

§ 9. Quieting Title and Canceling Deed.

An amended complaint in an action to quiet title to an interest in a certain mining claim was filed several months after the filing of the original complaint, and alleged that plaintiff then was, and at all times therein mentioned had been, the owner of such interest, there being no other time mentioned in the pleadings, and no demurrer thereto. There was a finding that defendant conveyed the interest by deed of a date prior to the filing of the original complaint, and that plaintiff practiced no fraud in obtaining such deed, which finding was not questioned on appeal. Held, that the finding sustained an averment of ownership prior to the time the complaints were filed.—Downing v. Rademacher, 6, 582.

Action was brought to quiet title to an undivided two-thirds interest in a certain mine, the claim being founded on a contract whereby plaintiff was to have such interest, and was to deliver one-third of the output to defendants. The decree adjudged plaintiff the owner in fee of a thirty-two sixtieth interest, and that defendants had no title thereto, and enjoined the latter from setting up any claim to such interest adverse to plaintiff, similar provisions being decreed as to the interests of defendants. Held, that the decree did

46

not cut off defendants from claiming one-third of the minerals under the contract, since the interests as adjudged were undivided, the owners becoming tenants thereof in common.—Downing v. Rademacher, 6, 582.

Where an undivided interest in a mining claim is conveyed in consideration of the grantee's agreement to work the mine and deliver one-third of the minerals to defendant, and do certain other acts in the future, their performance not being made a condition subsequent, a mere failure to perform on the part of the grantee does not constitute a failure of consideration, so as to warrant cancellation of the deed.—Downing v. Rademacher, 6, 582.

Where an action is brought to quiet title to an undivided interest in a mining claim, such interest having been conveyed in consideration of a certain contract, whereby plaintiff was to work the mine as he saw fit, and deliver one-third of the output to defendant, plaintiff cannot be required to work the mine, as a condition on which his title will be quieted, since his contract is incapable of being specifically enforced.—Downing v. Rademacher, 6, 582.

Where the plaintiffs in a suit to quiet title to mining claim had been in actual possession for a number of years, a defense that a claim prior to plaintiff's had never been abandoned cannot be urged, the defendant not claiming title under such prior claimant, Civil Code, section 1000, providing that occupancy for any period confers title except as to those claiming by prescription, transfer, will or succession.—Ramus v. Humphreys, 6, 730.

§ 10. Lien for Labor.

A contract for labor on a mine provided that the laborers should receive certain supplies in part payment, and that, after those supplies were paid for, the balance of income remaining should be divided pro rata to the extent of each laborer's wages at three dollars per day. In case of failure of profits, the personal property of the mine should be sold to pay the wages due. Held, that in the absence of anything to show a profit, an action would not lie to enforce a lien for wages unless it were alleged and proved that there had been a request for a sale of the personal property, and a refusal on the part of the owner.—Skym v. Weske Consolidated Co., 5, 551.

The contract not being restricted in application to the labor performed after it was signed, the actual time of signing is immaterial. Skym v. Weske Consolidated Co., 5, 551.

The date when the contract purported to be signed by plaintiff is conclusive evidence that the labor performed after that date was done subject to its terms.—Skym v. Weske Consolidated Co., 5, 551.

Evidence that a contract purporting to have been made by plaintiff was read to him, he being unable to read or write, with comments thereon representing that it meant something very different from its true meaning, and that thereupon he assented to it, and authorized his name to be signed thereto, is sufficient to justify a finding that plaintiff did not make the contract.—Skym v. Weske Consolidated Co., 5, 551.

Plaintiff alleged that between June 1 and December 27, 1893, he performed one hundred and seventy days' labor on the mine of defendant corporation, that said services were worth $200 per month, and that a balance of $1,200 was due him. A second count alleged that about March 1, 1893, he was employed by defendant at $200 per month; that from said date until December 27, 1893, he labored on defendant's mine nine and one-half months; and that he had received $700, leaving a balance of $1,200. A third count was on a claim assigned to him for services performed by one D., and alleged that such services were reasonably worth $3 per day. The court found that plaintiff's services were reasonably worth $150 per month, and that D.'s services were reasonably worth $3 per day. Held, that plaintiff was not entitled to a lien under Statutes of 1891, page 195, providing for the payment of wages of laborers employed by certain corporations, and creating a lien therefor that can be enforced only when plaintiff shows that the wages were payable weekly or monthly. Spaulding v. Mammoth Spring Min. Co., 5, 712.

§ 11. —— In Case of Oil Wells.

Code of Civil Procedure, section 1183, as amended by Statutes of 1899, page 34, chapter 35, provides for a lien on the whole of a mining claim for labor performed or for materials furnished to be used in the construction of any building, wharf, bridge, ditch, flume, aqueduct, well, tunnel, etc., and for labor performed in any mining claim or claims and the works owned and used by the owners for reducing ores, etc.; and section 1185 declares that the land on which any building, improvement, well or structure is constructed, together with a convenient space about the same, or so much as may be required for the convenient use and occupation thereof, to be determined by the court on rendering judgment, is also subject to the lien, etc. Held, that the mining claims referred to were mines of ore, exclusive of oil wells, and hence a claimant of a lien for the drilling of an oil well, etc., was not entitled to foreclose the lien, except as against such land as was necessary for the convenient use and occupation of the well.—Berentz v. Kern King Oil and Dev. Co., 7, 214.

§ 12. —— Sufficiency of Statement.

Under Code of Civil Procedure, section 1187, which requires the claimant of a lien for labor performed on a mining claim to file for record his claim, containing a statement, among other things, of "the name of the owner or reputed owner, if known, and also the name of the person by whom he was employed," a lien claim which fails to state by whom the claimant was employed is fatally defective.—Ascha et al. v. Fitch, 5, 481.

A claim for lien, after describing the mining claim, stated that F was the owner of the claim, "the said lien being held and claimed for and on account of work and labor performed by me as a miner for said F. on said mining claim" for a period definitely stated, "under an agreement with said F.," etc. Held, that such claim stated by whom the claimant was employed, as required by Code of Civil Procedure, section 1187.—Ascha v. Fitch, 5, 481.

Such claim of lien contained sufficient statement of the "terms, time given, and conditions of the contract," as required by statute.—Ascha v. Fitch, 5, 481.

Where the precise words of the statute have not been used by the claimant of a lien for labor done on a mining claim, but substantially equivalent expressions have been resorted to, it is sufficient compliance with the statute.—Ascha v. Fitch, 5, 481.

In an action to enforce a lien for labor done on a mining claim, where it appears that the claim for lien is insufficient because it fails to state by whom the claimant was employed, the claimant is entitled to a personal judgment against defendant for the amount due him, and it is error to grant a motion for nonsuit.—Ascha v. Fitch, 5, 481.

MINORS.

See Infants.

MINUTES.

Correction of. See Amendments, § 6.

MISCONDUCT OF JURY.

As ground for new trial. See Criminal Law, § 8; New Trial, § 5.

MISJOINDER.

Of causes. See Actions, § 4.
Of parties. See Parties, § 3.
Of actions in trespass. See Trespass, § 2.
Of actions in trover. See Trover and Conversion, § 4.

MISTAKE.

Effect of mistaking remedy. See Actions, § 3.
Possession under. See Boundaries, § 2.
In description of land. See Deeds, § 15.
Limitation of actions in case of. See Limitation of Actions, § 3.
As ground for reforming instrument. See Reformation of Instruments, § 2.
In contract of sale. See Sales, § 3.
In name in taxation. See Taxation, §§ 5, 16.
By parties to contract to sell land. See Vendor and Vendee, § 7.

§ 1. Action for Relief.

A complaint claiming relief on the ground of mistake must aver not only the fact of the mistake, but also the circumstances under which the mistake occurred, so far as necessary to bring the case within the rules for giving equitable relief.—Hurtado v. Shafter, 1, 843.

In an action to amend a mortgage on the ground of mistake, and to foreclose the mortgage as amended, a judgment for defendant upon a finding that no mistake occurred, will not be disturbed on the ground that evidence did not support the finding when the evidence on the material points of the case is conflicting.—Straus v. Williamson, 2, 870.

MOBS.

Liability for the destruction of property. See Riots and Mobs, § 1.

MONEY.

In what kind of money payment to be made. See Payment.

MONEY LOANED.

§ 1. Action to Recover—Evidence and Finding.

In an action to recover money loaned, a finding that the money was loaned defendant and another jointly, and that defendant promised to repay the same, is not inconsistent, so far as to be insufficient to support a judgment for plaintiff.—Bacome v. Black, 7, 34.

In an action for money loaned, it was contended by defendant that the credit was given and the money loaned another. Plaintiff showed the loan was brought about by the other, but that defendant got the money to assist him in purchasing a newspaper route. Held, not prejudicial error to admit testimony that on the following day plaintiff loaned defendant a sum to make up the amount necessary to purchase the route.—Bacome v. Black, 7, 34.

§ 2. —— In Case Involving Bank.

G., plaintiff's vice-president, being at the C. Hotel in defendant's town, was asked by the latter's president for a loan on collateral, $25,000 to $40,000, and agreed to make it on proper security. N., who was present, writing G. about a note which said president proposed to send, "to obtain this loan, as I understand it," gave his opinion about certain notes, defendant's stock, etc. A note for $25,000 was made to G., vice-president, by four of defendant's directors and its cashier. The president, in sending the collaterals, wrote G. that he believed they were in substance, "about what was spoken of at the C. Hotel when Mr. N. was with us." On receipt of the collaterals, plaintiff credited defendant with $25,000, less discount, and paid it on defendant's orders. Held, that a finding that plaintiff lent defendant $25,000 was justified.—First Nat. Bank v. California Nat. Bank, 4, 403.

In an action by one bank against another on a note, and for money loaned, where defendant asserts that plaintiff bought the note, proof of the negotiations for the loan and that defendant received its proceeds is not incompetent as varying the written instrument.—First Nat. Bank v. California Nat. Bank, 4, 403.

In an action by one bank against another for money loaned, and on a note representing the balance due, the loan and balance being established, it is immaterial whether the note was authorized by the directors.—First Nat. Bank v. California Nat. Bank, 4, 403.

MONEY RECEIVED.

§ 1. Relief Contributions.

Where defendant, the publisher of a newspaper, received a sum of money in response to solicitations in his paper for contributions for the relief of families of three firemen who lost their lives in the performance of their duty, plaintiff, as heir of one of the firemen, cannot maintain an action to recover his part of the amount collected, as money had and received, since the transaction created no legal right in plaintiff to any part of the money.—Hallinan v. Hearst, 6, 592.

§ 2. Action to Recover—Jurisdiction and Pleading.

In an action for money received it is not essential to jurisdiction of the parties or of the subject of the action to allege where the cause of action accrued.—Downing v. Mulcahy, 6, 242.

It is not essential to a complaint in an action for money received that it recite every detail out of which the cause of action arises, since, under Code of Civil Procedure, section 454, defendant can demand a bill of particulars if the complaint is too general.—Downing v. Mulcahy, 6, 242.

MOOT CASE.

Not passed upon in habeas corpus. See Habeas Corpus, § 1.

MORTGAGES.

§ 1. In General.

The evidence supports the finding that the mortgage herein is not affected by the heretofore unknown rights of the interveners.— Chalmers v. Chalmers, 2, 277.

Equity will give to the grantee in a deed, construed to be a mortgage, a lien on the land to the extent of payments or other mortgages on the land, which he has been obliged to protect for his own security. Combs v. Hawes, 2, 555.

§ 2. —— Mortgageable Interest.

J. and R. entered into an agreement to sell A. certain lots, the consideration to be paid part in cash, and the balance in installments

at one and two years. By the contract it was provided that if A.
failed to pay either installment when due, J. and R. would be released
from performance on their part, time being of the essence of the contract; but in such case it was the duty of J. and R. to sell the lots
at auction to the highest bidder. and out of the money received to
pay off the amount still due on the contract, and expenses. A. went
into possession of the lots, built a house thereon, and occupied them
for over a year. Some months before the first installment became
due, A. mortgaged the lots to H. The mortgage was duly recorded.
About five months after the execution of the mortgage, A. gave possession of the lots to D., and requested J. to make the deed for them
to D., which he did. In an action by H. to foreclose his mortgage,
held, that A. had a mortgageable interest in the lots, and that D. took
them subject to the mortgage, J. and R., by conveying to him on A.'s
request, having waived any breach of the contract.—Houghton v.
Allen, 2, 780.

§ 3. —— Priority of Liens.

Title to land in suit was in B., who agreed to convey to H. on payment of balance of price, and H. agreed to convey to plaintiff on
same condition, and gave her possession. Plaintiff agreed to sell to
P. for $5,500, and to convey on payment of $3,200, but was to retain
possession until full payment. P. applied to defendant for $3,200—
$2,700 to pay balance to B., and $300 to pay plaintiff, of whom he
informed defendant he was purchasing. Defendant procured an abstract to the land which showed the agreements to convey between
B. and H., and H. and plaintiff, and was informed by counsel that
plaintiff should convey to P. in order to perfect the latter's title; and
he sent men to inspect the premises, who found plaintiff's husband
in "apparent" possession, cultivating the land as an employee of P.
Thereafter, and on the day before the deeds were executed to P. by B
and plaintiff, defendant loaned P. the money as requested, and took
a mortgage of the land. Held, that defendant was not a mortgagee
without notice of plaintiff's lien for the unpaid price.—Austin v.
Pulschen, 4, 988.

§ 4. To Secure Future Advances—Trust Deed.

A deed of trust to secure $20,000, and also all further indebtedness
of the grantor to the third party that might be contracted during the
continuance of the trust, not exceeding $35,000, provided that on pay-
ment the trustees should reconvey to the grantor, his heirs or assigns,
and contained a power of sale on default. Held, that where such
grantor afterward made an absolute conveyance to B., and paid the
original debt secured, such deed of trust afforded no security for other
sums advanced by such third party to the grantor for the purposes
stated therein, with actual notice of such conveyance, and that a purchaser at the trustee's sale made on default in payment of such advances held the title in trust for B.—Savings & Loan Society v.
Burnett, 4, 701.

In an action by such purchaser to quiet title, the court found that
the grantor was seised in fee originally, that he executed the deed of
trust, and that default was made, and the property sold to plaintiff.
Held, that such findings did not establish a full fee-simple title in
plaintiff, where it appeared that such default in payment was of sums
not secured by the deed of trust.—Savings & Loan Society v. Burnett,
4, 701.

Even if $2,000 of the original debt secured was unpaid, a sale of the
property regarded by plaintiff as sufficient security for $35,000 did
not give an absolute legal title to the purchaser having knowledge
of all the facts.—Savings & Loan Society v. Burnett, 4, 701.

A mortgage given to secure advances up to a certain sum, if duly recorded, takes precedence of a subsequent attachment, to the extent of any balance due on such advances up to said sum.—Bank of Oroville v. Lawrence, 4, 845.

Where a conveyance was made as security for certain money advanced, parol evidence is inadmissible to show that, by agreement with the attorney of the grantor, the effect of the instrument was changed so as to also secure future advances.—Barnhart v. Edwards, 5, 558.

An instrument by which land was conveyed to secure advances which provided for the repayment of all taxes upon the lands conveyed did not invalidate the agreement under constitution, article 13, section 5, providing that contracts for payment of taxes upon the "money loaned" should be void.—Barnhart v. Edwards, 5, 558.

§ 5. Nature of Mortgage.

The mortgage is simply a lien, a mere incident to the debt it is intended to secure; and the interest of the mortgagor, under former systems an equitable interest denominated an equity of redemption, is under our system regarded as the legal title in every sense and for every purpose.—Brooks v. Tichner, 1, 104.

The security follows the note secured; hence the holder of a mortgage note has the rights of a mortgagee, although there may have been no actual assignment of the mortgage.—Berri v. Minturn, 1, 50.

An instrument signed by a creditor and delivered to the debtor cannot be deemed a mortgage.—Rand v. Hastings, 1, 307.

§ 6. Execution—Signing and Delivery.

In the case of a purchase money mortgage the interest of the wife in the premises is bound, although she does not join the husband in the execution.—DeWolf v. Bailey, 1, 37.

A deed left by a mortgagor as an escrow, to be delivered upon default in payment by him of a sum fixed upon in satisfaction of all indebtedness, does not become operative until default, and creates no lien on the land.—McDonald v. Huff, 2, 860.

§ 7. Description of Premises.

In order to identify premises as being those described in a mortgage deed by a tract name, although respect must be had first to the description in the deed, the premises are to be located as within the limits of the tract as known when the instrument was delivered, rather than as ascertained by a subsequent survey because adjudicated upon by the United States court, and parol evidence is admissible for this purpose.—Gill v. O'Connell, 1, 825.

A mortgage of specifically described land, together with all the lands, mines and minerals of every kind belonging to the mortgagor in a designated county, covers all mineral lands in that county shown by proper evidence dehors the mortgage to have belonged to the mortgagor at the time of its execution.—Staples v. May, 3, 250.

§ 8. Consideration.

Under Civil Code, section 1605, providing that any prejudice suffered by a promisee shall constitute a good consideration, the execution of a deed is sufficient consideration to support an agreement by the grantee to return the deed on the payment of a debt.—Kyle v. Hamilton, 6, 893.

§ 9. —— Unlawful Consideration.

On a mortgage foreclosure the evidence showed that, at the time the note and mortgage were given, there was pending, in insolvency proceedings against defendants' father, the latter's petition for discharge and plaintiff's opposition thereto; that the consideration of the note, though not expressed therein, was an assignment to defendants by plaintiff of his claim against the insolvent, which was of the same amount as the note, and that the estimated value of the claim was one-sixth of its face; that by agreement plaintiff's claim against the insolvent assigned to defendant was to be held by plaintiff's attorney, and, when paid, to be applied on the note; that, after the giving of the note and mortgage, plaintiff's opposition to the discharge of the insolvent was withdrawn. Held, that the mortgage and note were void as against public policy.—Benicia Agricultural Works v. Estes, 3, 855.

The fact that a mortgage was given as security for the performance of an unlawful contract may be shown by oral testimony in an action for foreclosure, though no infirmity appears on the face of the mortgage.—Benicia Agricultural Works v. Estes, 3, 855.

§ 10. Construction and Interpretation.

Where a note is secured by a mortgage, the note and mortgage are to be construed together as evidencing the intent and purpose of the parties.—San Gabriel Valley Bank v. Lake View Town Co., 7, 266.

A finding that a mortgage was not intended to secure a note executed by the mortgage prior to the mortgage is not sustained by the evidence where it appears that the mortgage was executed to secure a running account, that the amount of said note was charged to the account, that the note was surrendered and a statement of his indebtedness rendered to the mortgagor without objection, that at the time the mortgage was executed the mortgagees had for sale merchandise of the mortgagor of almost equal value with his then indebtedness, and the only testimony of an opposite tendency was that of the mortgagee's bookkeeper, who stated that the "mortgage was not given to secure any special indebtedness," and that said note "was evidently surrendered and a new note taken."—Wise v. Williams, 5, 197.

§ 11. —— Conditional Sale.

Foreclosure proceedings were dismissed, and the mortgagor executed a deed to the mortgagee, pursuant to an agreement whereby the mortgagee was to satisfy the mortgage of record, and the mortgagor was to have the privilege of selling the land within six months thereafter, and retain all moneys which he might receive therefor over and above a specified sum, which he was to pay to the mortgagee. Held, that, in view of the facts that the mortgagor made no promise to pay any sum to the mortgagee, that the sum to be paid the mortgagee in case of a resale was several thousand dollars less than the mortgage debt, that no interest was to be paid by the mortgagor, and that the mortgagee at once took possession of the premises, the transaction must be construed, not as a mortgage, but as a conditional sale, to become absolute on the mortgagor's failure to sell the land within the time specified.—Fletcher v. Northcross, 3, 799.

§ 12. Deed Absolute as Mortgage.

Plaintiff's intestate owed defendant and others large amounts of money which he was unable to pay, and in consideration of the re-

lease of defendant's and payment of other debts conveyed a ranch
to him, defendant surrendering intestate's notes, and taking possession of the land. Intestate remained on the land, boarding with
the tenants, until his death, four years after; collected rents, sold
crops, and cultivated a portion for one year himself. There was
evidence that the intestate was agent and tenant of defendant, and
did not claim ownership of the land. Defendant testified that the
sale was absolute, but that shortly afterward he agreed, in writing
that if intestate could within a year find a purchaser, he would
convey the land, taking the amount of the debts and interest, and
allowing intestate to retain the residue. Admissions of defendant
of facts from which a mortgage, instead of a sale, might be inferred,
were explained. Some other circumstances were proved for and
against the theory that the transaction was intended only as security
for a debt. Held, that the finding of the trial court, that the intention of the parties was to make an absolute sale, should not be disturbed.—Pendergrass v. Burris, 3, 22.

Defendant's mother owed her, and defendant was surety for her
mother for more than the value of the mother's interest in land conveyed to defendant by absolute deed, in consideration of full satisfaction of the mother's indebtedness. Defendant took possession of
the land, collected rents, and paid interest on other liens assumed
by her. She did not surrender her mother's notes, but did not keep
them with any idea of collecting them, and at the time of the execution of the deed, defendant took a continuing mortgage from her
mother on the land in renewal of a previous mortgage for the same
amount, to preserve her priority over other liens. Held, that the
evidence was sufficient to support a finding that the deed was an
absolute conveyance, and not a mortgage.—Blair v. Squire, 6, 350.

Where a deed is executed by the parties, as a substitute for an
existing mortgage, under a mutual mistaken idea that no foreclosure
will be necessary, and may be rescinded by reason of such mistake,
under Civil Code, sections 1566, 1578, providing that a consent which
is not free may be rescinded, and that mutual mistake of law constitutes mistake, within the meaning of the article, but it is not
so rescinded, an agreement that the deed shall be returned on the
payment of a debt is binding.—Kyle v. Hamilton, 6, 893.

Where a deed is executed contemporaneously with a contract by
the grantee to return the deed on the judgment of a debt by the
grantor, the delivery is strong evidence that the contract was also
delivered.—Kyle v. Hamilton, 6, 893.

A deed, and contract by the grantee to return the deed on the
payment of a debt, were executed at the same time, and evidence that
both instruments were delivered to H. for the parties entitled thereto
was uncontradicted, and the agreement was shown to have been recognized by grantee prior to the suit. The contract was delivered
by H. to the grantee, but the former testified that it was by mistake. Held, sufficient to show the delivery of the contract.—Kyle
v. Hamilton, 6, 893.

Where a deed, and contract requiring the grantee to return the
deed on a payment of a debt, are made at the same time, and the
contract imposes no obligation on the grantor, and the delivery is
not conditioned on his signing it, it is not invalid because his signature is not attached thereto.—Kyle v. Hamilton, 6, 893.

Plaintiff's grantor borrowed money at a bank, stating that defendants had applied to him for a loan to pay off two mortgages and
that they would deed him the property. The mortgages were taken
up, and assignments of them made to plaintiff's grantor, defendants

deeding him the premises. Subsequently plaintiff's grantor presented defendants with a paper which showed the amount of the interest due on the alleged loan, and defendants paid him a fee for the services of the person who computed the interest. After execution of the deed, defendants continued in possession of the premises, paying no rent or leasing the premises, and continuing to make improvements. Held, that the deed was a mortgage.—De Carrion v. De Aguayo, 6, 716.

Where plaintiff's land was conveyed to M. as security for a loan, to be conveyed by the latter to W., or his order, on repayment of the amount—the agreement being for plaintiff's benefit—evidence held not to support a finding that the reconveyance was conditioned on plaintiff's paying W. a certain additional sum.—McCaughey v. McDuffie, 7, 175.

§ 13. —— Action to Declare or Foreclosure.

A deed given to secure the payment of money advanced by the grantee is in effect a mortgage, and must be foreclosed in accordance with the statute: Code Civ. Proc., sec. 726.—Combs v. Hawes, 2, 555.

In proceedings for redemption from a mortgage, where the question at issue is whether a deed absolute in form with an agreement for reconveyance was intended as a mortgage or not, a book of account cannot be introduced in evidence to show that defendant credited plaintiff with the alleged purchase price of the lot in controversy.—Ross v. Brusie, 2, 647.

In an action to declare a deed absolute in form a mortgage, and sell the property conveyed thereby to satisfy certain notes described in the complaint, where the complaint states that the notes were made payable to parties named, and that a subsequent deed of trust reciting the former deed was made to secure the payment of the amount thereof, and the deed, which is set out in the complaint, states that it was given to secure the payment thereof, the allegations as to the making and delivery of the notes are sufficient to sustain a decree of foreclosure and sale.—Arnot v. Baird, 2, 692.

A decree deciding that a deed absolute on its face is not a mortgage will not be disturbed, on appeal, where the evidence is conflicting.—Harris v. Sutherland, 3, 34.

In an action to declare a deed absolute on its face a mortgage, and to foreclose same, a finding by the court that, prior to its maturity, plaintiff had claimed such mortgage to be an absolute conveyance, and refused performance of the obligation, and that such refusal stopped the running of interest after maturity, is error, when no such issue is presented.—Fiske v. Casey, 4, 558.

In an action to declare a deed absolute in form a mortgage, a judgment for defendant cannot be set aside where, in confirmation of the presumption of the deed, there was evidence from the conduct of the grantor, and from his pecuniary condition at the time of its execution, and his declarations before and after, that the deed was in fact absolute.—Peres v. Crocker, 5, 606.

A judgment declared an instrument in form a deed absolute to be a mortgage, and provided that it should be foreclosed, and that each party should pay his own costs and one-half of the jury fee. The jury fee had been paid by plaintiff, the mortgagor. The mortgagee appealed, whereupon the decree was modified by denying a foreclosure because not prayed for, and by directing that the decree fix a reasonable time within which the mortgagor should pay the balance due, and that, in default of such payment, the action should be dismissed. An "amended" judgment was then entered in the lower court, in accordance with the mandate, but it made no reference to costs or jury fees. Held, that the original judgment, in so far as it referred to the costs or jury fees, was not affected.—Cline v. Robbins, 6, 176.

A judgment declaring a deed to be a mortgage, and ordering a foreclosure of it, found the amount due the mortgagee, and directed that "the commissioner . . . . pay to plaintiff [the mortgagor] or his attorney, out of said proceeds [of the foreclosure sale], the sum of thirty-six dollars, jury fees, of this suit." Held, that the cost should be deducted from the amount due the mortgagee, and not from the proceeds of the sale.—Cline v. Robbins, 6, 176.

A judgment declared a deed a mortgage, and ordered defendant, the grantee, to reconvey on payment of a certain sum, and directed that, unless the payment was made within a certain time, the action should be dismissed. Held, that it was no ground for dismissing the action that prior to a tender the grantor conveyed the property in fraud of creditors.—Cline v. Robbins, 6, 176.

Where a conveyance of land, absolute in form, is intended as a mortgage to secure a loan, a decree of strict foreclosure, vesting a title in the grantee upon nonpayment within a specified time, and without a foreclosure sale, will not be made.—McCaughey v. McDuffie, 7, 175.

§ 14. Mortgagee in Possession.

Although a mortgagee can have legal possession only after foreclosure, after actual possession for over seven years he may not be dispossessed by a mere order of court.—Hidden v. Jordan, 1, 216.

A conveyance of land to secure the payment of money, though the grantee is put in possession under an agreement for an accounting for the rents and profits, is only a mortgage, and does not pass the legal title.—Murdock v. Clarke, 3, 265.

By an agreement between a mortgagor and mortgagees, the latter were to have the sole right to the possession of the land mortgaged, accounting for the rents and profits, and were to select a person to manage the property. At an accounting against the mortgagees, the latter testified that they were to send a man to take possession, in order to take care of the personal property security, and that everything was to be run in their name. They also spoke of the man selected, both in their testimony and in the pleadings, as their agent. Held that, for the purposes of possession and accounting, such person must be considered as the agent of the mortgagees only, although his selection was approved by the mortgagor, and his salary was paid as a part of the running expenses. In such case the mortgagees are held to the exercise of reasonable diligence in the management of the property mortgaged.—Murdock v. Clarke, 3, 265.

Where both the agent and the defendants kept their own cattle on the mortgaged land, along with the cattle of the mortgagor, the wrong done was satisfied by charging defendants with a proportion of the running expenses, and with the value of the use of the land.—Murdock v. Clarke, 3, 265.

Nothing was chargeable to defendants on account of horses which they sent to the land, and which were needed and used for farm work. Murdock v. Clarke, 3, 265.

One of the notes given by the mortgagor providing for compound interest if not paid when due, the net receipts were properly applied first to the payment of the interest on such note.—Murdock v. Clarke, 3, 265.

Sums advanced to the wife of the mortgagor without any order from him were not chargeable against his estate.—Murdock v. Clarke, 3, 265.

Certain land was transferred to plaintiff to secure a loan. At the time of the transfer, it was under a lease which the lessee subsequently assigned to plaintiff. Held, by thus getting possession, plaintiff became the mortgagee in possession, and was liable to defendants only for the income and profits received from the land.—Barnhart v. Edwards, 5, 558.

§ 15. Payment of Taxes.

A mortgage, given to secure a contemporaneous note bearing twelve and one-half per cent interest, provided that "all payments made by the mortgagee for taxes and assessments on said premises, excepting taxes on the interest of the mortgagee therein," might be included in the decree of foreclosure. The mortgagee signed a separate agreement to credit the mortgagor with two and one-half per cent interest on the note if the latter presented receipts showing that he had paid "all taxes against the property covered by the mortgage." Held, that this was not an agreement by the mortgagor to pay taxes on the money loaned, nor could parol evidence be given that such was the intention, for the purpose of avoiding the entire interest, under constitution, article 13, section 5, declaring any contract by which a debtor agrees to pay taxes on the money loaned shall be void as to any interest specified therein.—Hewett v. Dean, 3, 385.

The provisions in the mortgage that the mortgagor shall pay taxes "on said premises, other than taxes on this mortgage or the money hereby secured," does not oblige the mortgagor to pay taxes on the mortgage itself.—Cortelyou v. Jones, 6, 475.

§ 16. Estoppel and Abandonment.

A mortgage cannot be satisfied or extinguished by an abandonment on the part of the mortgagor.—Rand v. Hastings, 1, 307.

A mortgagor is estopped by the terms of his deed to deny that his estate was other than an estate in fee, and the terms of a mortgage, importing a conveyance of the fee, are equivalent to a general warranty running with the land.—Trope v. Kerns, 3, 47.

Where the vendee in an unrecorded deed, acting as attorney in fact for the vendor, procures a mortgage for the latter on the property, and represents that the vendor is the owner, he is estopped thereafter to set up title to the land except in subordination to the mortgage.—Filipini v. Trobock, 6, 589.

Where the vendee in an unrecorded deed, acting as attorney in fact for the vendor, procures a mortgage on the latter's property, and represents that the vendor is its owner, one succeeding to his interest as a mere volunteer is equally estopped to set up title except in subordination to the mortgage.—Filipini v. Trobock, 6, 589.

§ 17. Maturity of Debt—Election to Declare Due.

When an overdraft account with a bank is secured by a note and mortgages payable on or before three years, and interest as due is charged in the account, the rules against parol evidence (Civ. Code, sec. 1625; Code Civ. Proc., sec. 1856) forbid proof of an oral agreement that the debt should be due at any time within the three years, at the bank's option.—Bullion & Exchange Bank v. Spooner, 4, 531.

A note and mortgage securing the same provided that the principal should be paid in five years, that the interest was to be paid semi-annually, and if not paid when due, it should be added to the principal and bear like interest; but, if default was made in payment of interest for thirty days, then the "whole sum, principal, here promised, shall, at the option of the holder of the note, become immediately due, payable, and collectible." Held, that, where an action to foreclose was commenced thirty days after default in payment of interest, the mortgage was subject to foreclosure at plaintiff's election for the whole amount thereof.—San Gabriel Valley Bank v. Lake View Town Co., 7, 266.

Where a mortgage provided that on default for thirty days in interest, the whole sum, principal and interest, should become payable at the option of the holder, the filing of a complaint, after thirty days' default in interest, seeking to recover the entire debt, constituted a sufficient notice of election by the mortgagee to claim the whole amount as due.—San Gabriel Valley Bank v. Lake View Town Co., 7, 266.

§ 18. Default in Interest—Forfeiture.

A mortgage given to plaintiff by defendant association provided that there should be quarterly payments of interest, and that, on failure to so pay, the whole sum, at plaintiff's election, should become due. After the papers had passed defendant's officers agreed that plaintiff could have the payments monthly, by calling for them, to which plaintiff assented, and for several months thereafter called and received her interest. Later, she failed to call, the interest was not paid, and plaintiff sought to have the whole debt declared due. Held, that, after plaintiff's promise to call for the interest, defendant was excused from seeking her, to make payment, and, since the failure to pay was caused by her own act, she could not exact a penalty for such failure.—Foerst v. Masonic Hall Assn., 3, 720.

The fact that plaintiff called for the interest once, when defendant's president, who always paid her, was not in does not aid her claim of forfeiture, when it does not appear that she demanded the interest from anyone else, nor that, at the time she called, any interest was due.—Foerst v. Masonic Hall Assn., 3, 720.

A finding that plaintiff authorized an agent to collect the interest, and that he demanded it from defendant's president, who refused to pay unless he brought a written order from plaintiff, is contrary to the evidence, when the only testimony on the subject is that of the agent, who stated that he called on defendant's president, and asked him about the interest, and the president said that the money was ready for plaintiff, but that he would like to have an order before paying it, to which request the agent made no objection.— Foerst v. Masonic Hall Assn., 3, 720.

A finding that plaintiff's attorney, both before and after October 1st, which was more than three months after the last payment, demanded payment of the interest, and that such payment was refused unless he had written authority, if true, would not be conclusive of a default; for the question would still be open as to whether defendant had reasonable ground to doubt the attorney's authority.— Foerst v. Masonic Hall Assn., 3, 720.

Where plaintiff knew that defendant's agents were looking for her, to pay the interest, but she did not inform them where she was, or that she had authorized an agent to receive the money, failure of defendant to pay the interest within the prescribed time does not constitute a default.—Foerst v. Masonic Hall Assn., 3, 720.

§ 18½. Tender and Payment.

The tender of the amount due on a debt which is secured by mortgage, after due, will not release the mortgage lien.—Chielovich v. Krauss, 2, 643.

Where one who is obligated, as between himself and a mortgagor, to pay a portion only of the mortgage debt, pays such portion, and afterward pays the balance due, the payment does not extinguish the mortgage as to such balance.—Ingham v. Weed, 5, 645.

§ 19. —— Insurance, Agency.

Defendants executed a mortgage to plaintiff, the insurance on the building being made payable to her. The building burned, and the person who had acted as agent for defendants in negotiating the loan wrote her for the mortgage, to use in adjusting and collecting the insurance. She refused to send the mortgage to him, but sent it to N.—one of the defendants. After the insurance was adjusted, N. wrote her that the company had the money, which could not be turned over to anyone but herself, and sent her a sum sufficient, with such insurance money, to pay the mortgage. She answered, acknowledging receipt of the money sent, and that she would soon go to the city to receive the insurance money. When she went, N.'s wife stated that he was absent, and referred plaintiff to such former agent. When she went to him, he took her to a bank, and directed a transfer from his account to hers of a sum $200 less than the insurance money, and, on her objecting to the amount, stated that the balance would be paid in a few days. She thought she was dealing with the agent of defendants, and made no inquiry as to how he came by the money, and did not know that, pretending to act as her agent, he had surrendered the policy, received and receipted for the check in her name, and forged her indorsement thereto. Civil Code, section 1478, provides that "performance of an obligation for the delivery of money only is called payment." Held, that the insurance money was simply additional security for the debt, and that there had been no payment of the debt, except as to the money actually received by plaintiff.—Ballard v. Nye, 6, 947.

The receipt, without inquiry, of a part of the insurance money from the one who had pretended to act as plaintiff's agent, and without notice or knowledge that he had so acted, was not a ratification of his acts.—Ballard v. Nye, 6, 947.

Defendants were familiar with such pretended agent's disposition to keep things which did not belong to him, and having placed the policy and mortgage in his hands after the mortgage was sent to them by plaintiff, and thereby enabled him to get control of the money, should be the sufferers, rather than plaintiff, under Civil Code, section 3543, providing that, when one of two innocent persons must suffer by the act of a third, he by whose negligence it happened must be the sufferer.—Ballard v. Nye, 6, 947.

§ 19½. Assignment of Mortgage and Rights of Assignee.

The assignee of a mortgage, by an assignment absolute on its face, may maintain an action to foreclose in his own name, though, by a collateral agreement, he may be bound to account for the proceeds to another.—Ingham v. Weed, 5, 645.

Though an assignment of notes secured by a mortgage declares certain express trusts, the assignees may sue to foreclose the mortgage without joining the beneficiaries.—Cortelyou v. Jones, 6, 475.

An assignment of "those certain mortgages and credits more particularly described as follows," followed by a description of the mortgage in suit, which sets forth the notes sued on, and declares that it is made to secure them, after which the assignment includes "all other moneys now due to me from any source whatever," is a sufficient assignment of the debts secured to support an action by the assignees, though the assignment is not of the notes themselves. Cortelyou v. Jones, 6, 475.

§ 20. Foreclosure of Mortgage.

Action to enforce deed absolute as mortgage. See ante, § 13.

There can be but one action for the recovery of any debt secured by mortgage.—Harden v. Ware, 2, 72.

Tender by a defendant in an action to foreclose a mortgage needs to be of a sum no greater than the complaint expressly calls for.—Goodwin v. Rickabaugh, 2, 160.

The object of a foreclosure suit, so far as concerns the land, is to subject that to sale for the satisfaction of the debt and to bar the parties brought before the court from all right to redeem it, except as allowed by statute, from the sale under the decree.—Brooks v. Tichner, 1, 104.

Strict foreclosure is not known to our law, but under our system the court decrees that the mortgagor's interest in the land, held by him when executing the mortgage or acquired by him subsequently, be sold in satisfaction of the debt.—Brooks v. Tichner, 1, 104.

The only object or effect of the statute relative to foreclosures of mortgage is to afford a protection to a subsequent purchaser for a valuable consideration and without notice.—Brooks v. Tichner, 1, 104.

Under a mortgage of land, "together with . . . . the rents, issues, and profits thereof," the right of the mortgagor to dispose of the crops growing thereon is not devested by foreclosure proceedings until sale under the decree.—Bank of Woodland v. Christie, 6, 545.

Error in admitting secondary evidence to prove a note in a suit to foreclose a mortgage given as security is waived by failure to object at the time.—Filipini v. Trobock, 6, 589.

§ 20½. —— Sale Under Trust Deed.

A deed of trust to secure a debt, with power of sale to be exercised after breach of the obligation for which it is given to secure is, in effect, only a mortgage with power of sale, such as is authorized by Civil Code, section 2932, and is within the policy of Code of Civil Procedure, section 726, providing that only one action can be maintained to enforce any debt or right secured by a mortgage, and that such action shall be the one therein prescribed, which contemplates a sale and exhausting of the security before any personal judgment can be rendered.—Herbert Craft Co. v. Brian, 6, 923.

The trustees in a deed of trust to secure a debt, who were apparently not interested in the debt at the time of the execution of the deed, subsequently, without the knowledge or consent of the grantors, became shareholders and directors in a corporation which thereafter purchased the debt. The corporation then had the property sold by the trustees, bought it in, and sold it again at a profit. Held, that the sale was voidable at the mere instance of the grantor, or, if affirmed by him, he was entitled to an accounting for the profits of the resale, and to credit therefor as of the time of the resale.—Herbert Craft Co. v. Brian, 6, 923.

The assignee of a note secured by a deed of trust, who purchases the property at a sale under the deed of trust, cannot deny that the payee of the note, his assignor, accepted the deed of trust as security for such note.—Herbert Craft Co. v. Brian, 6, 923.

In an action to determine the rights to property under a deed of trust, the court must follow the provisions of the trust, and, where such trust provides for the sale of the whole of such property, the court is not authorized to order a sale of a part thereof.—Reynolds v. Weston, 2, 343.

In an action to foreclose a trust deed, where the answer set up that the property conveyed was the separate property of the wife; that her husband had been arrested on a criminal charge, and ob. tained bail; that he became financially embarrassed; and that the wife signed the trust deed upon the representations made to her by her husband and the plaintiff, who was a creditor of the husband and one of his bondsmen, that unless she signed the deed the bondsmen would withdraw, and her husband would have to go to jail, and would probably be convicted, and go to the penitentiary, and that by signing the deed she would not lose anything, and that the deed would not devest her of her homestead; held, that a demurrer to such answer was properly sustained.—Levy v. Burkle, 2, 778.

In an action to recover the balance due on a note after sale under a trust deed securing it, a claim set up in defendant's answer that the trust sale was void, and that no suit could be maintained on the note until the security was exhausted conflicted with a claim, also set up in such answer, that defendant was entitled to the profits realized from a resale of the property which defendant had purchased at the trust sale; and the granting of relief based on one of such claims would exclude the granting of that based on the other.—Herbert Craft Co. v. Brian, 6, 923.

§ 21. —— Limitation of Actions.

Where the trial court finds facts showing that a suit to foreclose a mortgage is not barred, failure to find expressly that the suit is not barred is immaterial.—Filipini v. Trobock, 6, 589.

A foreclosure suit was based on the liability specified in the mortgage, and not on a new promise to pay the debt, made before it became barred by the limitation, and before a judgment lien on the premises was created. A demurrer by the judgment creditor was sustained on the ground that the debt was barred; and, plaintiff declining to amend, judgment dismissing the action was entered, after which the creditor, relying on the allegations of the complaint, purchased the property on execution sale under the judgment, without notice of any renewal. Held, in a subsequent suit to foreclose the mortgage, in which plaintiff relied on a new promise, that he was estopped from maintaining the action.—Newhall v. Hatch, 6, 653.

§ 22. —— Parties.

Foreclosure by assignee. See ante, § 19¼.

The owner of the legal title is a necessary party to a suit for the foreclosure of a mortgage.—Brooks v. Tichner, 1, 104.

If a plaintiff in foreclosure is mistaken as to or ignorant of the actual ownership of the property when bringing his suit, his course is, upon learning who is the true owner, to bring the latter before the court during the proceedings, or else after the proceedings have his interest subjected to the decree.—Brooks v. Tichner, 1, 104.

One who has transferred all his interest in mortgaged property is not a necessary party to an action to foreclose.—Ingham v. Weed, 5, 645.

§ 23. —— Pleading.

In a suit to foreclose a mortgage the description of the premises may be either contained in a schedule attached to, or incorporated in, the body of the complaint.—Berri v. Minturn, 1, 50.

47

Demurrer to a complaint in foreclosure is not a proper way to test whether the property set out as the mortgaged property is sufficiently described, since the decree in foreclosure gives the plaintiff only what the mortgage calls for. When, after the foreclosure, the mortgagee takes possession, his right to the particular property can be tested by bringing an action against him.—Coddington v. Hopkins, 1, 199.

To uphold a demurrer to a complaint in foreclosure on the ground of indefinite description of the premises it must appear that the description is so vague that no part of the land may be located by reference to it.—Coddington v. Hopkins, 1, 199.

An allegation that a purchaser of mortgaged property covenanted and agreed to pay the mortgage debt and discharge the mortgage lien is sufficient to sustain the judgment of foreclosure and sale.—Pellier v. Gillespie, 2, 407.

In foreclosure, after a demurrer to the petition had been overruled, defendants were granted fifteen days to answer, and on their motion were given five days more. They filed an answer May 2, 1895, which plaintiff moved to strike out because unverified. Defendants confessed the motion, and asked leave to file an amended answer, purporting to have been verified April 3, 1895, by a defendant, who claimed no interest in the premises. There was no showing why the verified answer, which stated no defense, was not filed in the first instance, it being an exact copy of the other. Held, that the court did not err in denying leave to file the amended answer.—Tulare Building & Loan Assn. v. Coleman, 5, 334.

An instrument conveyed certain lands to secure, among other matters, a loan of $2,500, secured by a pledge of certain wheat. Held, in an action to foreclose the lien, that, as the note was expressly named as one of the debts secured, it was incumbent on defendant, if he would avoid liability therefor, to plead the facts by virtue of which the land had been exonerated from this liability.—Barnhart v. Edwards, 5, 558.

Where to a bill to foreclose a mortgage is attached a copy of the mortgage, which contains a recital that it "draws eight per cent net, as security for the payment of a promissory note, of which the following is a true copy," whereupon follow copies of the notes set out in the complaint, and this is not denied by the answer, the title of plaintiffs, who are assignees of the mortgage only, to the notes, is so far admitted as to sustain a judgment in their favor thereon.—Cortelyou v. Jones, 6, 475.

An allegation, in an answer to a mortgage foreclosure suit, that the mortgage was annulled by a subsequent mortgage between the parties, is to be construed as an allegation that there was a novation of the new mortgage for the old.—Kyle v. Hamilton, 6, 893.

An objection that a complaint in a suit to foreclose a mortgage was insufficient for want of facts in that no definite or separate amount was alleged to be due could be taken advantage of by special demurrer, and was waived by defendant's failure to so object thereto. San Gabriel Valley Bank v. Lake View Town Co., 7, 266.

§ 24. —— Receivership.

Where a mining company operates its various mines under one system, and the proceeds of the ore extracted from each are used indiscriminately, for the common benefit of all, a receiver appointed on the foreclosure of mortgages covering a part only of the company's property, with power to take possession of the mortgaged premises and to carry on the mines, who is permitted by the company to take possession of its entire property, and to work all its mines, rendering them more valuable and more capable of paying creditors, cannot be considered a trespasser, and is not personally liable to a general creditor of the company for sums realized by him from a mine not covered by the mortgage.—Staples v. May, 3, 250.

Where a complaint to foreclose a mortgage prays a receiver to take and hold the premises, and collect and apply the rents and profits, third persons may intervene to assert an adverse title to the possession, and an interest in the rents.—Hoppe v. Hoppe, 4, 569.

§ 25. —— Decree, Validity and Effect.

Where a mortgage provides that the percentage be allowed on the sum due and the judgment in foreclosure so allows it, rather than on the value of the property, there is no error.—Berri v. Minturn, 1, 50.

Where, in an action of foreclosure of mortgage, a cross-complaint is filed, charging plaintiff and others with fraud and conspiracy regarding the execution of the mortgage, and the lower court finds against the defendant as to such fraud, the plaintiff is entitled to his judgment of foreclosure, however fraudulent the conduct of the other parties (joined in such cross-complaint) may be.—Thatcher v. Edsall, 2, 331.

A decree in a mortgage foreclosure case precluding a person from asserting any right acquired from the mortgagors after the execution of the mortgage would not devest him of any rights held paramount to the title of the mortgagor.—Hitchcock v. Clarke, 2, 37.

Whenever it appears by the pleadings or proof in a case that the plaintiff is entitled to recover judgment upon a debt secured by mortgage, the court may by its judgment direct the sale of the mortgaged property, even though such relief has not been specifically demanded in the complaint.—Harden v. Ware, 2, 72.

On appeal from a judgment of foreclosure after all the defendants had made default, where the case is presented on the judgment-roll simply, and the point urged is the excessive amount of the judgment, it must be presumed that the trial court, having had the evidence before it, was correct in its findings, until error is shown in the manner provided by law.—Savings and Loan Soc. v. Horton, 2, 137.

In an action to foreclose a mortgage plaintiff cannot have the judgment include taxes he has paid on the mortgaged property unless his complaint contains appropriate averments.—Goodwin v. Rickabaugh, 2, 160.

A foreclosure decree must not direct a sale of a greater interest than that mortgaged; it cannot embrace property of the mortgagor acquired subsequently to the execution of the mortgage.—Marshall v. Livermore Spring Water Co., 2, 417.

In an action to foreclose a mortgage the record owner of the mortgaged property cannot complain if, after he by his answer has virtually invited the true owner to contest his title, the court determines the ownership.—Odd Fellows' Savings Bank v. Noonan, 2, 162.

A judgment in a foreclosure suit does not fail for not directing the docketing of judgment for a deficiency.—MacNeil v. Ward, 2, 174.

A judgment in a foreclosure suit does not fail for not adjudging expressly the defendant's personal liability to the plaintiff, if such an adjudging is to be inferred from it.—MacNeil v. Ward, 2, 174.

A decree in foreclosure cannot be attacked in ejectment brought to recover the land sold under the decree.—Trope v. Kerns, 3, 47.

In a proceeding to set aside a foreclosure sale on a showing promptly made, it appeared that the property had brought a very inadequate price; that the deputy having the matter in charge had been asked to bid for the mortgagee in the latter's absence, but had neglected to do so; that the mortgagee's intention to bid was known to the purchaser; and that the mortgagee could not collect any of the deficiency from the mortgagor. Held, that the court might properly set aside the sale.—Haynes v. Backman, 3, 710.

Where, in a suit to foreclose a mortgage, it was alleged "on information and belief" that M. had an interest in the said "premises or property mentioned" in said mortgage, but that the same was subsequent and subject to the mortgage interest, and M. made default, such default was tantamount to an admission that M.'s interest was subsequent to plaintiff's so that after judgment it was too late for him to assert that his rights were not adjudicated.—San Gabriel Valley Bank v. Lake View Town Co., 7, 266.

§ 26. —— Deficiency Judgment.

The docketing of a judgment of foreclosure does not create a lien for the deficiency on the property of the judgment debtor, but to establish such a lien the deficiency, when ascertained, must be docketed as a personal judgment. From the time of so docketing only does such lien commence.—Hibberd v. Smith, 1, 554.

An action cannot be maintained against an administrator for a deficiency judgment on foreclosure, where the decedent, the mortgagor, was a nonresident at the time of commencement of the action to foreclose, remained away from the state until after the sale thereunder, and never appeared in the action.—Chapman v. Pennie, 4, 970.

Plaintiffs, having executed a note and mortgage to defendant, conveyed the mortgaged property to another, who assumed the payment of said note and mortgage, but he having defaulted thereon, defendant agreed with plaintiffs to purchase the land at the foreclosure sale for the full amount of his claim, and not to take a personal judgment against plaintiffs, and the latter, relying on such promise, allowed default to be entered, and refrained from attending the sale. Held, that there was a sufficient consideration for such agreement. Such agreement was not void as altering the terms of the note and mortgage. Nor was it void as an agreement to prevent bidding at the sale.—Heim v. Butin, 5, 19.

The complaint, in a suit to enjoin the enforcement of a deficiency judgment, obtained against plaintiffs in such foreclosure suit, alleged that plaintiffs, relying on defendant's promise, failed to appear in the suit, or to be present at the sale, or make any bid thereat, though they were able to purchase the property and protect themselves. Held, that the complaint showed that plaintiffs were damaged by their reliance on defendant's promise, they having a right to demand that the deficiency judgment be entered also against the owners of the property.—Heim v. Butin, 5, 19.

Where, on foreclosure of a mortgage, a deficiency judgment was entered in favor of a junior mortgagee, but prior to his judgment a portion of the mortgaged lands not included in his mortgage had been conveyed by receiver's deed, he was not entitled to redeem such lands, under Code of Civil Procedure, section 701, giving a right of redemption to creditors having a lien.—White v. Costigan, 6, 641.

In a foreclosure suit, a finding that a certain sum was due and unpaid from defendant to plaintiff, which was not made a part of the judgment, and which was not accompanied by an order for a deficiency judgment, was not an adjudication of personal liability, gave the clerk no authority to docket a deficiency judgment, and confined plaintiff to the mortgaged property alone for the satisfaction of his judgment and costs.—Ridgley v. Abbott Quicksilver Min. Co., 7, 200.

A defendant in a suit to foreclose a mortgage, which had sold all its interest in the property before the suit was brought, and against which no personal or deficiency judgment was rendered, was not aggrieved either by the judgment or by an order allowing plaintiff receiver's costs and fees, in such sense as to entitle it to appeal from either the judgment or the order.—Ridgley v. Abbott Quicksilver Min. Co., 7, 200.

§ 27. —— Sale and Rights and Liabilities Arising Therefrom.

The grantee of an unrecorded deed to the mortgaged property, made after the execution of the mortgage, is not, after the mortgage has been foreclosed, estopped to claim such property as against the purchaser at the foreclosure sale by his having been aware of the proceedings while they were going on, and even though he acted as attorney for the defendants in those proceedings, the mortgagee and such purchaser not knowing of his interest.—Brooks v. Tichner, 1, 104.

An order for the sale of mortgaged premises, after proceedings had to foreclose the mortgage, may be applied for only in the court which rendered the decree of foreclosure.—Franklin v. Le Roy, 1, 806.

A sheriff's deed on foreclosure relates back to the delivery of the mortgage and things affixed to the mortgaged premises by the mortgagor during the interval pass with that deed.—Hill v. Gwinn, 1, 882.

In ejectment by a mortgagee to recover the premises after due foreclosure proceedings, the mortgagor cannot defend his withholding possession on the ground of equities now set up for the first time.—Ingraham v. Burton, 2, 195.

A complaint in an action by a mortgagor to recover, under Code of Civil Procedure, section 957, the proceeds of a foreclosure sale set aside on appeal, alleged that foreclosure proceedings were commenced against plaintiff, in which defendant, a second mortgagee, was joined as a party, and filed a cross-complaint asking a foreclosure of his mortgage; that an order of sale on the judgment foreclosing both mortgages "was duly issued by the clerk, ... and was thereupon delivered to the sheriff," who sold the land to defendant, and after paying the first mortgage "there remained the sum of $3,080." Held, that the complaint was demurrable, as it did not show that the sheriff had applied any part of the proceeds of such sale to the satisfaction of defendant's debt.—Patton v. Thompson, 3, 871.

In such case H.'s title is unaffected by any knowledge or want of knowledge by him of the contents of the deed from the trustees to his grantor, the mortgagee, or of the trust agreement.—Corcoran v. Hinkel, 4, 360.

Where a receiver was appointed in a suit to foreclose a mortgage, and the mortgagee purchased the mortgaged premises at the foreclosure sale for the full amount of his debt and costs, the rents and profits of the mortgaged premises in the hands of the receiver at the time of the sale belonged to the mortgagor and not to the mortgagee.—Pacific Mutual Life Ins. Co. v. Beck, 4, 393.

The mortgagee did not become owner by purchasing at the foreclosure sale, so as to entitle him to rents payable ten days after the sale, since his title was not changed thereby, except that the amount of his debt was fixed, and his right to a deed or to a sum paid to redeem within six months became absolute.—Pacific Mutual Life Ins. Co. v. Beck, 4, 393.

Where the commissioner's deed and demand for the premises had been presented to the general guardian of an incompetent, who was the owner of the premises, the demand was sufficient, without being made on the incompetent, and a writ of assistance will not be set aside for improper service.—Taylor v. Ellenberger, 6, 725.

In an action to foreclose a mortgage given by the owner of an undivided half of the premises and life estate in the other half, the owners of the remainder after expiration of the life estate were made parties defendant and defaulted. Held, that the foreclosure sale conveyed only the interest of the mortgagor, and did not affect the title of the other parties.—Webb v. Winter, 6, 768.

§ 28. —— Counsel Fees.

The note provided that, if suit was commenced to enforce its payment, the maker would pay five per cent on the principal as an attorney's fee, and the mortgage provided for the payment of "a reasonable counsel fee" upon foreclosure. The complaint alleged "that the sum of $300 is a reasonable attorney's fee or counsel fee for the foreclosure of said mortgage." Held, that this was sufficient to support a judgment for an attorney's fee without averring that plaintiff had actually incurred expense for that purpose. But plaintiff was not entitled to recover as counsel fee more than five per cent on the principal, as provided in the note.—Hewett v. Dean, 3, 385.

On appeal from a judgment foreclosing a mortgage which provides for the allowance of reasonable attorney's fees on foreclosure, the allowance will not be disturbed if the appeal is brought up on the judgment-roll alone, without exceptions, and there is nothing in the record to show that the court abused its discretion in making the allowance.—Ogden v. Packard, 4, 463.

Where a mortgage secures in terms only the principal and interest of a note a lien cannot be had for attorneys' fees, though the note provides for them.—Sainsevain v. Luce, 4, 496.

A lien for attorneys' fees cannot be obtained in a suit to foreclose a mortgage which contains a provision that, should suit be commenced, or an attorney employed, the mortgagors agree to pay an additional sum of ten per cent on principal and accrued interest as attorneys' fees, since the mortgage does not purport to secure such fees.—Lee v. McCarthy, 4, 498.

Where an attorney's fee on foreclosure is taxable "in the bill of costs," an appeal from a judgment allowing costs, taxed at $22.90, and plaintiff's attorney's fee, of $100, is frivolous.—Grogan v. Nolan, 4, 600.

A mortgage expressly stating that it is given "as security for the payment of" the principal sum of the note, "with interest thereon according to the terms of the note," does not secure counsel fees provided by the note in case of suit being brought against the maker Rafferty v. High, 5, 113.

Where a mortgage provides that the mortgagee may include in its foreclosure a reasonable attorney's fee, and a copy of the mortgage is attached to and made a part of the complaint in foreclosure which alleges that plaintiffs have employed an attorney and become liable to him for a reasonable fee, "which fee is secured by said mortgage," there is a sufficient allegation as to attorneys' fees to support a judgment therefor in plaintiffs' favor.—Cortelyou v. Jones, 6, 475.

Where a mortgage foreclosure suit is based on a mortgage which has been superseded by a deed given as security for the debt by reason of a mutual mistaken idea that it will obviate a foreclosure, and the mortgage contains an attorney fee clause which is not in the deed, a judgment foreclosing the mortgage and allowing an attorney fee cannot be sustained, as a decree allowing an attorney fee is not authorized by the deed.—Kyle v. Hamilton, 6, 893.

§ 29. —— Appeal.

Where, in a foreclosure case, the court orders the sale of exempt property, the error, if any, is to be corrected by appeal.—Luce v. Superior Court, 2, 167.

The undertaking in regard to a deficiency, where the judgment appealed from is for the sale of mortgaged premises, is required only in the case of an appellant in possession of the premises adjudged to be sold.—Home Loan Assn. v. Wilkins, 2, 171.

From a decree of foreclosure defendants appealed. Respondent moved to dismiss the appeal, and in support thereof filed affidavits as follows: That appellants had threatened, in case of foreclosure sale, to resist the issuing of a writ of assistance to place the purchaser in possession thereof; that the property was insufficient security for the debt, its value decreasing, with danger, by reason of noninsurance, of further loss; that appellants were insolvent, and had stated their appeal to be for purposes of delay and vexation; that the amount of the undertaking on the appeal was insufficient to cover the probable deficiency that would arise from the foreclosure sale, and was fixed by a judge other than that of the trial court, in chambers, without notice to or knowledge of respondents; that the trial court refused to set aside said undertaking, or increase the amount thereof, because the supreme court alone had jurisdiction after the appeal was taken; and that appellants had deposited no money in court to perfect their appeal. Held, that this showing was insufficient to support such motion.—Gregory v. Keating, 2, 865.

In such case the facts alleged are insufficient to support a motion to issue an execution or grant an order of sale pending the appeal.—Gregory v. Keating, 2, 865.

In such case a motion to advance the hearing of the cause will be denied.—Gregory v. Keating, 2, 865.

A judgment of the supreme court reversing a judgment in a mortgage foreclosure for $1,200 and costs and attorney's fees, and directing a judgment for the principal and interest stipulated in a note, less interest paid—defendant to have costs of appeal—does not deny plaintiff the counsel fees and costs of the trial court, no question of such counsel fees or costs being considered on the appeal.—Walsh v. Hyland, 6, 108.

Where the supreme court ordered a judgment modified, a contention that the judgment, as modified, was erroneous, in that the trial court did not amend the findings, is without merit, since the supreme court cannot modify a judgment if it is necessary to amend the findings to support it, the findings not being in the control of such tribunal.—Taylor v. Ellenberger, 6, 725.

A contention that an order of sale directed to be executed by the sheriff was void where performed by a commissioner will not be considered on appeal, the question not having been raised in the lower court.—Taylor v. Ellenberger, 6, 725.

Under Code of Civil Procedure, section 726, as amended in 1893, providing that a commissioner, when appointed to conduct a foreclosure sale, shall possess the powers and be subject to the duties of sheriffs in like cases, a sale conducted by a commissioner is not vitiated by the fact that the order of sale was directed to the sheriff, the direction to the sheriff being a harmless irregularity.—Taylor v. Ellenberger, 6, 725.

§ 30. —— Modification of Judgment.

Code of Civil Procedure, section 957, provides that when a judgment is reversed or modified the appellate court may make restitution of all property lost by the erroneous judgment or order, so far as such restitution is consistent with the protection of a purchaser of property at a sale ordered by the judgment. The supreme court directed a superior court to modify a judgment of foreclosure for the sale of personalty and realty by ordering a separate sale of each, which modified decree was entered after the real estate had been sold. Held that, the direction for the restitution of the property being discretionary, such sale would not be set aside, in the absence of any showing that the mortgagors had been injured by the sale, and that the proceeds were insufficient to pay the real-estate mortgage.— Taylor v. Ellenberger, 6, 725.

Where a defendant in a mortgage foreclosure claims an interest in the property adverse and superior to that of the mortgagee, and the findings by the trial court do not determine such claim, the judgment, which bars only the right, title and equity of redemption of such defendant, will be modified so as to preserve, unaffected and unprejudiced, the adverse right so claimed.—Gregory v. Keating, 3, 208.

§ 31. Redemption.

The omission in a decree of foreclosure to provide for a redemption of the property does not of itself prevent a redemption being made.—De Wolf v. Bailey, 1, 37.

In a suit by the grantee named in a deed of trust to recover the possession of the granted premises from purchasers under an execution, in which suit the defendants have answered by a cross-bill construable as an offer to redeem, if the court, by its findings and conclusions and its referring the matter to a court commissioner to be reported upon, has virtually sustained the answer, there should be, after the commissioner's having reported, a decree that the defendants pay or tender to the plaintiff within a reasonable fixed time the amount found to be due him, naming it, together with the costs of the suit, and that the plaintiff, upon receipt of this, execute and deliver a good and sufficient deed to the defendants, but that in default of so paying or tendering these be debarred from all further claim or right to redeem.—Tyler v. Granger, 1, 634.

Under the Civil Code, an offer to pay by one who seeks to redeem from a mortgage must be made with intent to extinguish the obligation.—Chielovich v. Krauss, 2, 700.

A court has no authority to order a sale of property without the right of redemption given by statute; and it makes no difference whether the security under which the sale is ordered is a mortgage or a trust deed.—Levy v. Burkle, 2, 778.

Where a purchaser at mortgage sale made a quitclaim deed of the land to the owner, such deed operated as a redemption, and perfected the owner's title.—White v. Costigan, 6, 641.

By Code of Civil Procedure, section 703, a redemption from a mortgagee is followed by a sheriff's deed, and section 705 requires a redemptioner to serve, with his notice of redemption to the sheriff, a copy of any assignment necessary to establish his claim. Held, that where, after mortgage foreclosure, the purchaser on mortgage sale gave a deed of the premises to the owner, and prior thereto, and with the knowledge of the owner, one who was unauthorized to redeem attempted to do so, and paid the redemption money to the sheriff, under section 703 the redemption was virtually an assignment of the purchaser's interest, though the sheriff was not authorized to make the deed under section 705, and hence should be regarded as the assignee of the purchaser, and the owner entitled to have her title quieted only on condition of paying the redemption money to the redemptioner.—White v. Costigan, 6, 641.

Where the purchaser at mortgage sale gave a deed of the premises to the owner, and prior thereto one not entitled to redeem had paid the redemption money to the sheriff, the redemptioner's right to be regarded as the assignee of the purchaser's interest, being purely one in equity, did not extend to the forfeiture of the owner's title for nonredemption, she not being affected by the transaction between the purchaser and the redemptioner, and the deed from the purchaser being, in effect, a redemption.—White v. Costigan, 6, 641.

Where one who was not authorized to redeem from a mortgage sale paid the redemption money to the sheriff, such redemptioner had a right to have his equitable title perfected by a conveyance from the owner, to whom the purchaser thereafter conveyed the land.—White v. Costigan, 6, 641.

Where one who was not authorized to redeem from a mortgage sale paid the redemption money to the sheriff, his right to be repaid his money, or to have a conveyance from the owner of the lands, being an equitable one merely, he should be allowed legal interest only on the amount paid by him from the date of payment.—White v. Costigan, 6, 641.

§ 32. —— Junior and Senior Mortgagees.

In a suit brought by a junior mortgagee for the purpose of being allowed to redeem from a sale made in foreclosure of the senior mortgage, the complaint should not be dismissed merely because not strictly in form to reach the end aimed at, provided it is susceptible of being put into proper form by amendment.—Carpentier v. Brenham, 1, 812.

If a mortgage is made upon land on which an earlier mortgage is already due, and subsequently the junior mortgagee would enforce his lien, the land having been sold meantime in foreclosure of the senior mortgage, the latter will be kept alive and deemed to be still in force, with the same effect as though the mortgagor still held the legal title.—Carpentier v. Brenham, 1, 812.

If the mortgagee, under a mortgage made after another mortgage on the same land has become due, would redeem from a sale in foreclosure of the senior mortgagee, he must exercise the right to do so within the same period the mortgagor might have exercised it, since his right can be no greater in respect of time than that which the mortgagor himself possessed.—Carpentier v. Brenham, 1, 812.

§ 33. —— Waiver of Redemption.

Defendant in a mortgage foreclosure suit made a compromise agreement with plaintiff, whereby the latter agreed to accept a part of the amount claimed if paid within sixteen months, the purpose of the parties being stated to be a sale of the mortgaged premises after a reasonable time to extinguish the debt as fixed by the contract and to save expenses of foreclosure sale. The contract provided that the land be conveyed to trustees and be by them reconveyed in case defendant paid plaintiff within twelve months; that defendant might sell any part by having the price paid to plaintiff; that after twelve and before sixteen months plaintiff might sell the remainder at auction; that a decree should be entered for the full amount claimed, and proceedings stayed until the expiration of the sixteen months, at the end of which time the trustees should convey the unsold land to plaintiff, who might sell it under the decree, in which case the agreement fixing the amount due should be void. Defendant conveyed the land to the trustees, and then negotiated a sale to H., but defects in the title delayed the closing of the sale until after the sixteen months during which the trustees had power to convey to a purchaser, and it was necessary to convey to plaintiff in order to give H. a good title. Plaintiff, with defendant's consent, conveyed the land to H. at the agreed price. Held, that Civil Code, section 2889, which provides that "all contracts for the forfeiture of property subject to lien, in satisfaction of a lien secured thereby, and all contracts in restraint of the right of redemption from a lien, are void," had no application to such transaction.—Corcoran v. Hinkel, 4, 360.

In such action to redeem it was competent for H. to show by parol that the conveyance by the trustees to the mortgagee was made, not as a forfeiture, but to consummate a sale made by the mortgagor to a third party.—Corcoran v. Hinkel, 4, 360.

The fact that plaintiff did not formally cancel the indebtedness against such defendant did not entitle the latter's administratrix to redeem the land from the sale to H. when it appeared that such plaintiff never asserted the existence of any such indebtedness after the conveyance of the land to it by the trustees, and that it actually received such conveyance in full satisfaction.—Corcoran v. Hinkel, 4, 360.

A finding that the mortgagee granted, bargained and sold the land to H. is not inconsistent with the finding of the circumstances attending the sale, which show that the conveyance was made in fulfillment of the arrangement between deceased (the mortgagor) and H., by which the mortgagee became the conduit through which the title passed.—Corcoran v. Hinkel, 4, 360.

It appeared that defendant authorized the trustees to sell the land at a price named, and "to pay commissions" out of the proceeds. They then authorized certain brokers to sell, and the latter negotiated a sale at the price named by defendant. On the title being found defective, defendant directed the trustees to decrease the price agreed on through such brokers by the amount necessary to perfect the title, which they did. Held, that the brokers were the agents, not of the trustees, but of defendant.—Corcoran v. Hinkel, 4, 360.

MOTIONS.

§ 1. Time for Consideration.

A motion to strike from the records a certain order and findings will not be considered until final hearing.—In re Williams' Estate, 4, 511.

MUNICIPAL CORPORATIONS.

§ 1. Freeholders' Charter—Amendment.

Constitution, article 11, section 8, providing that a freeholders' charter of a city may be changed by amendment submitted by the legislative authority of the city to be voted on at an election held.

under the California homestead act of 1862, by which the homestead estate, on the death of either, vested absolutely in the survivor. Thereafter, the city deeded the land to the widow, she having complied with the various ordinances and legislative acts relative thereto. Held, that as she had bona fide, actual possession at the passage of the act, no trust arose, under the conveyance to her, in favor of said children.—Wheelan v. Brickell, 4, 830.

§ 3. Creation of Executive Office.

The city of Ukiah had power to create the office of "executive officer" by city ordinance and to fix his salary.—Noble v. Cleland, 7, 362.

§ 4. City Council—Right of Members to Office.

The district court has no jurisdiction of the question of the right of a person to hold the office of common councilman of the city of Los Angeles, since the law devolves the duty and confers the power of decision in that regard upon the body of the common council.—People v. Metzker, 1, 676.

Chapter 5 of the Practice Act does not repeal by implication section 10 of the act of March 11, 1850, to the extent of devesting the common council of a city, organized under the provisions of the act, of the exclusive jurisdiction conferred thereby over the question of a person's right to hold office as a member.—People v. Metzker, 1, 676.

§ 5. —— Notice of Special Meeting.

Where all the members of the council were present at a special meeting, except one, and a resolution was adopted unanimously, there is no error in admitting testimony of the clerk of the council that he served a proper notice of the meeting on all the members, the notice not having been entered of record.—Gill v. Dunham, 4, 229.

§ 6. Ordinances—Adoption and Publication.

Where for fourteen years after the passage of an ordinance the city recognized its existence and validity, and treated it as duly adopted and published, it will be presumed to have been approved by the mayor and published as required by the city's charter.—Santa Rosa City R. Co. v. Central St. Ry. Co., 4, 950.

Testimony of a city clerk that after search he was unable to find among the city records any orders for the publication of certain ordinances is admissible to show the nonexistence of those orders.—Santa Rosa City R. Co. v. Central St. Ry. Co., 4, 950.

Where a city charter requires that ordinances shall be published only by order of the council, and that the city clerk shall keep a book into which he shall copy each ordinance, with a certificate annexed to the copy stating, among other things, that it was published according to law, the certificate of the clerk that the ordinance was published is sufficient evidence that the order for publication was made.—Santa Rosa City R. Co. v. Central St. Ry. Co., 4, 950.

§ 7. Fiscal Affairs—Contracts and Bonds.

In an act empowering a municipality to make a particular contract, a provision allowing its common council an option to declare the contract void on a certain contingency does not make the happening of the contingency ipso facto a nullification of the contract.—Myers v. Mayor and Common Council of Placerville, 1, 565.

After issuing bonds before satisfying conditions made precedent, under the law conferring the power to issue them, a municipality is estopped to say that it issued the bonds in violation of law.—Myers v. Mayor and Common Council of Placerville, 1, 565.

A denial that a municipality failed or refused to pay interest on its bonds, coupled with an averment that there was no means for payment in the treasury, is an admission of nonpayment.—Myers v. Mayor and Common Council of Placerville, 1, 565.

§ 8. —— Subscription to Railroad Stock.

After subscribing to capital stock of a railroad company under a special act empowering it to do so, municipality stands in the same relation to the company as any other stockholder except as expressly provided in the act.—Myers v. Mayor and Common Council of Placerville, 1, 565.

After subscribing to stock of a railroad company, under a law regulating the preliminaries while conferring the power, a city is estopped to evade responsibility for its act by asserting that a step in such preliminaries by it was taken invalidly.—Myers v. Mayor and Common Council of Placerville, 1, 565.

In the act authorizing the city of Placerville to subscribe for the capital stock of the Placerville and Sacramento Valley Railroad Company, the condition limiting the city's liability for the company's debts to the amount of the subscription so authorized did not contemplate its being itself annexed to the subscription on the company's books, but that the limitation was to attach ipso facto by the act of subscribing.—Myers v. Mayor and Common Council of Placerville, 1, 565.

§ 9. —— Order for Money.

An order drawn directly on a city, instead of on the auditor thereof, is not void on its face.—People v. Munroe, 4, 66.

§ 10. —— Allowance and Payment of Claims.

The auditor of San Francisco must, before allowing a claim, satisfy himself not only that "the money is legally due and remains unpaid," but also that "the payment thereof from the treasury of the city and county is authorized by law, and out of what fund."—Paxson v. Hale, 1, 472.

Where a decree of a court having jurisdiction directed a city treasurer to pay a certain claim against the city, such decree was a complete defense to an action to charge him with official misconduct in having paid the claim.—Fresno Canal & Irr. Co. v. McKenzie, 6, 691.

Where judgment had been rendered for plaintiff in an action against a city treasurer and board of trustees to compel payment of a claim against the city, such judgment was sufficient to justify the treasurer in paying the claim, though the trustees refused to approve it, or issue a warrant thereon.—Fresno Canal & Irr. Co. v. McKenzie, 6, 691.

Where a city treasurer, acting under a judgment, paid a claim against the city, such judgment was admissible in evidence as justification in an action charging him with official misconduct in having paid the claim.—Fresno Canal & Irr. Co. v. McKenzie, 6, 691.

§ 11. —— For Maintaining Nuisance.

Under act of March 13, 1883, chapter 49, subchapter 7, section 864, providing that all demands against a city or town shall be presented to and audited by the board of trustees in accordance with such regulations as they may prescribe by ordinance, where plaintiff sued defendant city for damages for maintaining a nuisance, his failure to make a demand on the city prior to the suit was fatal to his cause of action, since the term "demands," as used in the statute, includes claims for damages for torts as well as on contract.—Adams v. City of Modesto, 6, 486.

Where plaintiff sued defendant city for damages for maintaining a nuisance, without making a demand prior to the suit, and defendant demurred to the complaint as not stating facts sufficient to constitute a cause of action, it did not waive its right to raise the objection of plaintiff's failure to make a demand, required by act of March 13, 1883, chapter 49, subchapter 7, section 864, on appeal.—Adams v. City of Modesto, 6, 486.

Under act of March 13, 1883, chapter 49, subchapter 7, section 864, providing that all demands against a city shall be presented to and audited by the board of trustees in accordance with such regulations as they may by ordinance prescribe, where plaintiff sued defendant city for damages, without making a demand prior to the suit, and the petition contained no averment that the city had not passed any ordinance prescribing in what manner such demands should be presented, plaintiff cannot excuse his noncompliance with the statute on the ground of the city's failure to pass such ordinance. Adams v. City of Modesto, 6, 486.

§ 12. Streets—Olive Avenue and Noble's Alley.

A reservation of land for public use, made by city ordinance, is within the act of Congress of 1866, relinquishing the title of the United States to land in the western addition of San Francisco "except such portions thereof as may be reserved and set apart by ordinance of said city for public use," although the reservation was made before the passage of such act; and if a street so reserved, such as Olive avenue, is definitely outlined and located on the map, it is not material that it is not designated by name.—Bigley v. Nunan, 1, 855.

Noble's alley, in San Francisco, was not dedicated as a public street. People v. Noble, 7, 400.

§ 13. —— Obstruction of Street and Remedy of Individual.

If the obstruction of a public street renders access to a lot less convenient than it otherwise would be, the owner of the lot can maintain an action to abate the nuisance and recover special damages.—Bigley v. Nunan, 1, 855.

Where the obstruction of a public street furnishes a continually recurring cause of action to a lot owner, a court of law cannot afford him adequate relief. Injunction is his remedy.—Bigley v. Nunan, 1, 855.

§ 14. —— Vacation of Alley.

Where a public alley is vacated, the right of an abutting owner to the portion adjoining his land is not, as against an abutting owner on the opposite side of the alley, affected by the fact that the vacation was unlawful.—Bigelow v. Ballerino, 5, 101.

§ 15. —— Extension and Widening of Street.

Any person aggrieved by the report of the commissioners appointed by the county court under the act of 1864, authorizing the board of supervisors to extend streets, might appeal to the supreme court; and the court thus appealed to might then review the report, or the proceedings of the commissioners or of the court, or any or all of them, upon matters of law, or confirm, correct, modify or set aside the report.—Grogan v. County Court, 1, 617.

In the act (Stats. 1867–68, 555) repealing the act of 1864, the proviso that nothing therein should affect "any proceedings taken, or to be taken, to widen Kearny and Third streets or to the extension of Montgomery street," etc., included the whole proceeding relating to the extension of Montgomery and Connecticut streets, which was but one proceeding; and it is not to be presumed that the legislature intended to preserve a part of the proceeding and to defeat the remainder.—Grogan v. County Court, 1, 617.

Statutes of 1889, page 70, sections 10–15, regulating the procedure for widening streets, provide that the commissioners must file with the clerk of the board of supervisors a report specifying each lot, etc., assessed for the improvement with the name of the owner and a plat of the assessment district; that the clerk must give notice requiring persons interested to show cause, at a time named, why such report should not be confirmed, etc. Held, that a lot owner who failed to object to an assessment, and to proceed as provided by such statute, could not maintain an action to declare the assessment void, and enjoin the execution of a deed pursuant to a sale of the assessed property to pay the assessment.—Mietzsch v. Berkhout, 4, 419.

§ 16. Street Cleaning.

The power of the board of supervisors to cleanse the streets of San Francisco is subject to legislative control, both as to the extent of the work to be done and the mode in which the power is to be exercised.—Weed v. Maynard, 2, 34.

The principal purpose of the act of April 3, 1876, looking to the regulation of street cleaning in San Francisco, was to limit the authority of the board of supervisors in respect of both their power to regulate and the mode of its exercise, and the scope of the act in this respect is not to be defeated by mere reference to its title, "An act to confer additional powers upon the board of supervisors of the city and county of San Francisco."—Weed v. Maynard, 2, 34.

An act of the legislature limiting the powers of a board of supervisors in respect of street cleaning does not impair the obligation of a contract already made with a private person by such board if the contract is by its express terms to continue "during the pleasure of the board."—Weed v. Maynard, 2, 34.

"The pleasure of the board," as expressed in a contract between a board of supervisors of a city and a private person for the cleansing of streets, during which "pleasure" only the contract was to continue, would be determined ipso facto by the enactment of a law limiting the powers of the board in that connection.—Weed v. Maynard, 2, 34.

§ 17. Opening in Sidewalk—Liability of Tenant.

A city ordinance provided that no person should obstruct any sidewalk so as to interfere with its convenient use, and that everyone should keep around every flight of stairs descending from the sidewalk to the basement a fence or railing at least two feet high. Held, that where the owner of a building had made an opening in the sidewalk, with stairs running to the cellar, the opening being provided with iron doors that constituted part of the sidewalk when closed, a use by the tenant of the opening and doors so as to violate the ordinance rendered only the tenant liable, and not the landlord.—Morrison v. McAvoy, 7, 37.

An opening in a sidewalk with stairs leading to the cellar, the doors forming part of the sidewalk when closed, and the sides of the doors affording a protection when open, was not a violation of the ordinance.—Morrison v. McAvoy, 7, 37.

§ 18. Liability—Where Horse Frightened by Steam Roller.

A city hired from an improvement company the use of a steam roller and engineer. The city had full control over the movements of the steam roller, and directed its engineer where to operate it. The company paid the salary of the engineer, and had the power to discharge him. The roller, being directed to operate where the ground was too soft to hold it up, sank in the mud, and the engineer, in a proper exercise of his duties, put on full steam, and extricated the roller from the mud. The steam then escaped with a loud noise, and frightened the horse of a traveler, who was permitted by the city's superintendent to approach without warning, injuring him. Held, that the city was liable therefor, and not the company.—Stewart v. California Imp. Company, 6, 432.

§ 19. Street Improvements.

The power of a board of supervisors to award a contract for macadamizing can be exercised only in such a manner as may not deprive the property owners of their statutory right to do the work themselves, the enjoyment of which right would be impossible if such award should be made before completion of the grading.—Dyer v. Hudson, 2, 149.

In a proceeding in relation to a street improvement the fact that in some instances names, other than those of the parties named in the petition, who therein avow themselves to be owners of the lots platted on the diagram accompanying the petition, appear marked as owners of the lots on the diagram itself, should not disprove allegations of the petition as to ownership.—Sloan v. Bluxome, 2, 161.

Where the matter was not at issue, and neither party introduced any evidence thereon, it was erroneous for the court to find that such street work was ordered without the recommendation of the superintendent of streets.—Dyer v. Heydenfeldt, 2, 409.

Where a city supervisor is required to sign a certificate as to a public improvement, it cannot be signed by his clerk, who had no specific directions from him to sign it.—Dowling v. Adams, 5, 115.

§ 20. —— Authority of Committee of Council.

The charter of Stockton, by authorizing the common council of the city to cause streets to be graded and to let contracts in that connection, conferred no such authority upon a committee of that body.— City of Stockton v. Creanor, 1, 774.

Such an irregularity as the assuming by a committee of the common council of Stockton of the functions of the whole body under the charter, in causing streets to be graded and letting contracts for the grading, is not cured by the act of 1870 reincorporating the city.— City of Stockton v. Creanor, 1, 774.

§ 21. —— Resolution of Intention.

A resolution of intent to grade a street passed by the board of supervisors of San Francisco, prior to the act of April 25, 1862 (Stats. 391), must be presented to the president of the board in order to justify a subsequent lien for street assessments against an adjacent property holder.—Creighton v. Lawrence, 1, 295.

A resolution to pave and curb a street required the city engineer to furnish the council with estimates. The estimates, in addition to the items of paving and curbing, stated, under the head of "grad-

48

ing," that sixty-six cubic yards of excavation and forty-two cubic yards of embankment would be required. The grading, if taken from the entire surface of the street, would involve the removal of one and five-sevenths inches in depth. Held, that it would be assumed, from the small amount of the so-called "grading" required, that the street had been graded, and that the grading mentioned in the estimates was merely the removal of small inequalities in the surface, and therefore an assessment for the paving and curbing was not invalid on the ground that it required grading, which was not mentioned in the resolution.—Williams v. Bisagno, 4, 305.

A resolution to pave a street, which refers by number to certain ordinances for the manner in which the work is to be done, is sufficient, without reciting the provisions of the ordinance.—Williams v. Bisagno, 4, 305.

Act of March 14, 1889, amending act of March 18, 1885, in relation to improvement of streets, provides (section 3) that before ordering improvements the council shall pass a resolution of intention, which shall be "published and posted for two days in the manner prescribed by section 34." The latter section provides that resolutions required to be published shall be published in a newspaper, etc.; provided, however, that in case there is no newspaper, they shall be posted and kept posted for the same time as required for publication. Held, that a resolution which is published need not also be posted.—Gill v. Dunham, 4, 229.

§ 22. —— Notice of Intention or Improvement.

The statute of 1872 authorized the board of supervisors of the city and county of San Francisco, on recommendation of the street superintendent, to give notice of their intention to order that Broadway, from the west line of Buchanan to the west line of Webster street, be graded, when two blocks on each side of said portion of Broadway had been graded, without any petition for such order.—Dyer v. Heydenfeldt, 2, 409.

A recital in the record on appeal by defendant, in an action to enforce a street assessment, that plaintiff produced two witnesses who testified that the notice of the improvement "was posted at the time and in the manner required by law, both as to the number of said notices, the place of posting, and the time during which the same remained posted," sufficiently shows that the law as to posting the notice was complied with.—Williams v. Bisagno, 4, 305.

Street improvement act, section 3, requires that the notice of the passage of the resolution of intention to make street improvements shall be posted along the line of work, after it has been posted for two days on the door of the council chamber. Held, that the posting of such notice on the council chamber door on the sixth day of the month was completed on the seventh, and hence a posting thereof along the line of work on the eighth was proper.—Greenwood v. Hassett, 6, 430.

§ 23. —— Objections to Improvement.

Within ten days after the expiration of the time for the publication and posting of the resolution of intention to order a street improvement, the owners of a majority of the property abutting on the proposed work made their written objection to the same, and delivered it to the clerk of the board of supervisors, who indorsed thereon the date of its reception. No other resolution or action of the board was taken, but after six months from the filing of such protest it passed a resolution ordering the work to be done. Held, that the board of supervisors had no jurisdiction to order the work.—Pacific Paving Co. v. Reynolds, 6, 535.

The street improvement act requires (Stats. 1891, p. 196, sec. 3) that a written objection, intended to delay proceedings for an improvement, and required to be made within a specified time, "shall be delivered to the clerk of the city council who shall indorse thereon the date of its reception by him." Held, that the efficacy of such objection was dependent as much on the indorsement authenticated by the clerk's signature as on the delivery thereof, and that mere delivery was not enough.—City Street Improvement Co. v. Babcock, 6, 910.

§ 24. —— Contract, Signing, Validity, Time of Awarding.

Evidence that a husband signed a contract for street work in front of a lot the record title to which was in the wife, and stated to the contractors that the lot was community property, will sustain a finding that he was the "reputed owner," within Code of Civil Procedure, section 1191, as amended, providing that any person performing work on a street in front of a lot at the request of the "reputed owner" shall have a lien on the lot for work and materials.—Santa Cruz Rock Paving Co. v. Lyons, 5, 260.

The power of a board of supervisors to award a contract for macadamizing is largely controlled by local conditions at the time; it follows that such a contract cannot be awarded before completion of the grading.—Dyer v. Hudson, 2, 149.

A contract for street improvements providing that all loss or damage arising from the nature of the work to be done under the agreement, or from any unforeseen obstruction or difficulties which may be encountered in the prosecution of the work, etc., shall be sustained by the contractor, is void as tending to increase the cost of the work, and is therefore insufficient to support an assessment for work done thereunder.—Hatch v. Nevills, 7, 341.

§ 25. —— Notice of Award of Contract.

The statute controlling the award of contracts for the improvement of streets does not provide who shall cause the notice of the award to be published.—San Francisco v. Chambers, 1, 840.

The statute controlling the award of contracts for the improvement of streets requires that "notice of such award shall be published for three days," etc. Publication for two days only does not satisfy the statute.—San Francisco v. Chambers, 1, 840.

§ 26. —— Plans and Specifications.

Under Acts of 1889, page 159, relating to public improvements, and providing that plans and specifications shall be furnished to the city council, if required by it, by the city engineer, but not specifying the mode of requiring them, the fact that they were prepared by the engineer, and were on file, and approved by the council, is sufficient evidence of their authenticity.—Gill v. Dunham, 4, 229.

§ 27. —— Bond for Performance of Contract.

Where a bond given for the faithful performance of a contract for public work recites that it is of "even date with the contract," the fact that it is dated one day earlier is not sufficient to prove, in an action to enjoin an assessment levied therefor, that the bond was in fact executed a day earlier than the contract.—Byrne v. Leining Co., 4, 895.

The fact that such a bond provides that the superintendent of streets shall not be liable for any delinquency on his part does not vitiate the entire bond, though such provision be against public policy. Byrne v. Leining Co., 4, 895.

§ 28. —— Time for Commencing and Completing Work.

Under Statutes of 1885, page 151, section 6, which authorizes a superintendent of streets to enter into a written contract for grading or other street work, and requires him to fix the time for the commencement and for the completion of the work under all contracts, a fixing of the time for the commencement of work under a contract at "within fifteen days from the date thereof," and for its completion at one hundred and eighty days "thereafter," makes the time for the completion dependent on the time of actual commencement, and is not such a compliance with the statute as entitles the contractor to enforce assessments for the work.—Palmer v. Burnham, 5, 583.

Under Vrooman act, section 6 (Stats. 1885, p. 151), requiring that the superintendent of streets "shall fix the time for the commencement, ... and for the completion of the work under all contracts entered into by him," it is not necessary that the time be fixed in the contract itself, but only that the superintendent shall in writing, authenticated with his official signature, fix the time.—Buckman v. Hatch, 7, 11.

§ 29. —— Abandonment by Contractor.

Where a contractor for street improvements, who is to be paid by assessments of benefits, abandons the contract before it is completed, because the assessments made were illegal, he is not entitled to any warrant or assessment thereunder.—Connolly v. San Francisco, 4, 134.

§ 30. —— Establishing or Changing Grade.

The grade of Vallejo street, in the city of San Francisco, between Montgomery and Kearny streets has been legally established.—Fanning v. Leviston, 2, 182.

Under constitution of 1879, article 1, section 14, providing that private property shall not be taken "or damaged" for public use without just compensation having been first made, damages peculiar to property of an abutting owner may be recovered of one who fills earth into a street to conform to a new grade to which it had been lawfully changed, though he is duly authorized to do so.—De Long v. Warren, 4, 677.

§ 31. —— Sewer Contract, Extras.

A contract with a city for constructing a sewer provided that the city should withhold a certain sum from the contract price for six months after the completion of the work, to make any repairs necessary, and at the end of such period should pay the contractors said sum, or so much thereof as had not been paid, for the repairs. Part of said sum was expended for repairs, made before the expiration of the six months, and the additional expenditures for repairs within the succeeding two months exceeded the sum retained. The city began the work of repairs well within the six months, and the good faith of its acts was in no way questioned. Held, that the contractor could not recover the balance in excess of the cost of repairs expended at the end of the six months, within the rule that particular clauses of a contract are subordinate to its general intent: Civ. Code, sec. 1650.—Griffith Co. v. City of Los Angeles, 6, 119.

A contract with a city for constructing a sewer provided that no extras were to be allowed, except in case of a change in the route or appliances, and then only when the valuation of the changes should be agreed on between the parties, and indorsed on the contract, or, if unable to agree, when the valuation fixed by the city engineer should be indorsed on the contract. On the request of the city engineer, steel bands were used for the pipe, which constituted a change in the contract. The city council had no knowledge of the change until after the pipe was laid, and no indorsement respecting the bands or the price was made on the contract. The contract did not give the city engineer authority to act for the city in making the agreement. Statutes of 1889, page 506, provides that the city shall not be liable on a contract, unless in writing, and by order of the council. Held, that the contractor could not recover the value of the bands.—J. M. Griffith Co. v. City of Los Angeles, 6, 119.

The city was not impliedly liable as on a quantum meruit, since it had no opportunity to elect whether or not to accept the sewer with the bands, it being imbedded below the surface of the earth at the time payment for the extras was demanded.—J. M. Griffith Co. v. City of Los Angeles, 6, 119.

§ 32. —— Action to Recover for Work.

In an action to recover on a paving contract, where plaintiff had read in evidence a written contract, under the terms of which plaintiff agreed to pave the street in front of defendant's premises to the satisfaction of the superintendent of streets, a resolution of the board of supervisors stating that the work had been constructed to the satisfaction of the superintendent, and accepting the same, was competent evidence.—Thomason v. Richards, 6, 863.

Evidence as to the character of concrete work in the street after the date when the work had been accepted by the street superintendent was incompetent, especially when there was nothing to show that it related to any of the work for which plaintiff sought to recover.—Thomason v. Richards, 6, 863.

§ 33. —— When No Assessment Possible.

Where a contractor for street improvements is to be paid by assessment of benefits, and he agrees to exempt the city from any liability under his contract, he cannot recover of such city for the improvements, because no legal assessment can be made to pay him therefor. Connolly v. San Francisco, 4, 134.

Where a contractor is to be paid for street improvements by assessment of benefits, and the supreme court decides that no legal assessment can be made under the act authorizing the same and the improvements, the personal liability of the city, if any, becomes fixed, and the statute of limitations begins to run not later than the date of such decision, and an action against the city to recover therefor, commenced more than nine years after such decision, is barred.—Connolly v. San Francisco, 4, 134.

§ 34. Special Assessments.

A street assessment, levied and collected under the taxing power, is essentially a tax as to the property assessed, and the act authorizing the enforcement of its payment is constitutional.—Dougherty v. McAlpine, 1, 370.

It is no valid objection to the assessment list that the dollar mark does not precede the sum placed opposite the lots named as assessed; if that mark is placed before the amount in the footing of the several assessments of the different lots, it is equally significant.—Himmelmann v. Reay, 1, 505.

The dollar mark placed before the amount in the footing of the assessment-roll sufficiently indicates the character of the figures of the several sums in the column above, if those sums appear with no such mark preceding them.—Himmelmann v. Reay, 1, 615.

Where the board of supervisors declare their intention that sidewalks on a street be reconstructed, and one lot with a frontage of eighty-six feet is charged in the assessment for new sidewalks with only thirty-nine feet, there being nothing in the assessment or diagram indicating which particular thirty-nine feet is made subject to assessment or that such thirty-nine feet are separately assessed, the description is insufficient.—Gately v. Bateman, 2, 113.

The superintendent of streets has no power to charge each separate lot with the work done in front of it; if sidewalks between certain termini are ordered reconstructed, all the lots fronting on the street are to be treated as benefited in the proportion that each bears to the whole frontage.—Gately v. Bateman, 2, 113.

The superintendent of streets has no power to make separate assessments on lots for old and new sidewalks, but the assessment must be to each lot for a share of the whole expense of reconstruction in the proportion its frontage bears to the whole.—Gately v. Bateman, 2, 113.

Though acts which the statute requires to be performed before making a public improvement are conditions precedent to the power to levy a tax on the property owners, only a substantial compliance with the statute is required; and the assessment is not vitiated by want of technicality of expression, or precision of statement as to the work, which does not affect the essential object in view.—Gill v. Dunham, 4, 229.

§ 35. —— Second Assessment.

The street improvement act (section 9), authorizing a second assessment where an action to foreclose a lien for street work is defeated by reason of a defective assessment, does not authorize a second assessment where such an action is defeated for want of an engineer's certificate.—Ede v. Cuneo, 6, 185.

Section 9, authorizing a second assessment where a suit to foreclose a lien for street work has been defeated by some defect in the prior assessment, does not apply when such a suit is defeated by any defects other than in making the assessment.—Gray v. Richardson, 6, 200.

§ 36. —— Appeal to Supervisors or Council.

A property owner is not bound to appeal to the board of supervisors to have a void assessment annulled.—Gately v. Bateman, 2, 113.

Act of March 18, 1885, page 147, section 11, provides for an appeal to the city council from an act of determination of the superintendent of streets as to the legality of any assessment; that on such appeal the city council may "confirm, amend, set aside, alter, modify, or correct" the assessment, as it may deem just; that all decisions of the council shall be conclusive, on all persons entitled to such an appeal, as to all errors and irregularities which the council might have remedied. Held, that an appeal on the ground that an assessment for paving a cul-de-sac failed to assess the land at the end of the same presented a question which the city council had power to determine, and therefore their decision was conclusive.—Dowling v. Altschul, 4, 58.

Under Statutes of 1885, page 156, section 11, providing that an appeal from an assessment shall be taken to the board of supervisors "within thirty days after the day of the warrant," the petition on appeal must show that a warrant was in fact issued, and the order of the board of supervisors that a warrant be set aside is insufficient to supply the deficiency.—Williams v. Bergin, 6, 299.

§ 37. —— Payment Under Protest.

Political Code, section 3819 (Laws 1893, p. 32), authorizing actions against counties to recover taxes paid under protest, does not apply to special assessments levied by the city and county of San Francisco, for a specific purpose, in a designated district, to be collected in proportion to benefits, and, when collected, placed in a special fund, over which the city and county have no control, and which can only be used in payment of the principal and interest of bonds for which the city and county are not liable.—Easterbrook v. San Francisco, 5, 341.

§ 38. —— Demand on Unknown Owners.

Under the street law for San Francisco (Statutes of 1863, section 11, pages 529 and 530), when the lots upon which it is sought to establish a lien were assessed to unknown owners, the only demand necessary to be made, under the warrant of assessment, is a public demand on the premises assessed.—Himmelmann v. Reay, 1, 615.

Under the street law for San Francisco (Statutes of 1863, section 11, pages 529 and 530) the contractor is not required to seek an owner, or his agent, for the purpose of making a demand when "the name of the owner is stated as unknown" on the assessment.—Himmelmann v. Reay, 1, 505.

§ 39. —— Assignment of Lien and Action Thereafter.

The lien of an assessment for a public improvement is merely an incident of the demand, and passes with an assignment thereof.—Gill v. Dunham, 4, 229.

In an action by an assignee to enforce an assessment for a public improvement, which was against a certain lot, but to an unknown owner, the fact that the assignment, which describes the lot, also states that the assessment was to a certain person as owner, does not render it inadmissible, as the name of the alleged owner may be rejected as surplusage.—Gill v. Dunham, 4, 229.

§ 40. Action to Enforce Assessment or Lien.

A street assessment lien cannot be enforced against less than all of the property owners liable therefor.—Tobelmann v. Roper, 2, 116.

Where a city lot is assessed only $2.50 for a street improvement, and sold for nonpayment, and the owner could redeem from the sale by paying $3.90, the maxim, "De minimis non curat lex," applies, and a court of equity will not restrain the execution of a deed pursuant to such sale, if invalid.—Mietzsch v. Berkhout, 4, 419.

In an action on a street assessment, the court found that the board of supervisors did not duly pass a resolution ordering the work to be done, instead of finding the facts from which it might appear that the resolution was not duly passed. Held, sufficient.—City Street Improvement Co. v. Babcock, 6, 910.

§ 41. —— Pleading.

Under the provisions of the statutes, as applied to actions to enforce street assessments, the assessment lists do not prove even prima facie that the city council "has caused a survey and estimate to be prepared of proposed work, to be filed with the city clerk," or "fixed a time for the hearing upon such proposition," or ordered work or improvements to be done; nor are the lists evidence of a publication of notice soliciting bids, or of the awarding of a contract, or of any of the acts of officers of the municipality which precede, at least, the doing of the work. None of these acts separately, or all of them together, constitute the levy of an assessment, yet all of them must be averred, and, if they are denied, must be proved by competent evidence.—City of Stockton v. Dahl, 2, 337.

Code of Civil Procedure, section 456, provides that in pleading the determination of a board or officer the facts conferring junisdiction need not be stated, but such determination may be stated to have been duly given or made. Held, that, in an action to enforce the lien of a street-paving assessment, an averment "that all the several acts required to be done by said city council, said superintendent of streets, and this plaintiff have been duly done, made, and performed by it and them, in the manner and at the times and in the form required by law," is sufficient on general demurrer.—Bituminous Lime Rock Paving etc. Co. v. Fulton, 4, 151.

An averment that "the city council of the city of Los Angeles . . . . passed a resolution of intention . . . . that New High street, in said city, ... be paved," is a sufficient averment that such street is an open public street, Statutes of 1885, page 147, section 1, providing that "all streets . . . . in the municipalities of this state now opened or dedicated, or which may hereafter be opened or dedicated, shall be deemed and held to be open public streets, ... and the city council of each municipality is hereby . . . . invested with jurisdiction to order to be done thereon any of the work mentioned in" the act.—Bituminous Lime Rock Paving etc. Co. v. Fulton, 4, 151.

In an action to enforce an assessment for street improvements, a complaint which, after alleging that the work was to be done according to specifications to be provided by the city, alleges general performance of the requirements, without specially setting out the specifications, is not subject to general demurrer.—Byrne v. Luning Co., 4, 895.

A demurrer to a complaint to foreclose a lien for street work, alleging that a second assessment had been made under the street improvement act (section 9), for the reason that the prior assessment and engineer's certificate were "never duly or properly or legally recorded," should be sustained for uncertainty, as the statement as to the defects in the first assessment is merely a legal conclusion.—Ede v. Cuneo, 6, 185.

A complaint in an action to foreclose a street assessment lien is sufficient though it fails to set forth the specifications attached to and forming a part of the contract for the work.—Greenwood v. Hassett, 6, 430.

In pleading the determination of a board of supervisors as to certain public improvements, it is not necessary to state the facts conferring jurisdiction, but the determination may be pleaded as duly given or made.—Buckman v. Hatch, 7, 11.

In an action to foreclose a street assessment, where no objection is taken to the complaint by demurrer, and the proceedings on the trial do not appear in the record, the court on appeal must presume that evidence was given to uphold every allegation of the complaint, whether defectively stated or not, and, to this end, that the original resolution of intention describing the work was put in evidence, and that the resolution contained a full description of the work as required by statute, including a specific description of the materials of which cesspools and culverts were to be constructed.—Buckman v. Hatch, 7, 11.

§ 42. —— Evidence.

In an action to enforce a street assessment evidence in support of an averment of the answer that the owners of the major part of the frontage duly undertook to do the work at the contract price but were prevented by the superintendent, is material and should be admitted.—Himmelmann v. Reay, 1, 615.

Where plaintiff, in an action to collect a street assessment, has made prima facie proof of the regularity of the proceedings, under act of March 18, 1885 (Stats. 1885, p. 147), and thereafter introduces, without objection, certain parol proof, a refusal to strike this out, if error, is without injury, as such proof was unnecessary.—Manning v. Deu, 3, 309.

§ 43. —— Dismissal as to Some Defendants.

A dismissal, in a street assessment suit, as to defendants not having any interest in the land assessed, is not error prejudicial to other defendants.—Dyer v. Heydenfeldt, 2, 409.

§ 44. —— Judgment Without Notice to Owner.

A judgment had without notice to the owner of property affected by it, in an action for an assessment for the construction of a sewer, will not bind his interest, and a sale in pursuance of such judgment will not pass his title.—Porter v. Garrissino, 2, 6.

MUNICIPAL COURT.

Of appeals. See Courts, § 2.

MURDER.

See Homicide.

MUTUAL LIFE INSURANCE.

See Insurance, § 15.

NAME.

Misnomer of mortgagor. See Chattel Mortgage, § 4.
Rendition and entry of judgment. See Judgment, § 5.

§ 1. Designation in Note.

It is immaterial by what name persons are described in a note, if the note was made, executed and delivered to them, and they are in fact the persons intended to be designated as payees.—Clauss v. Froment, 1, 690.

NAVIGABLE WATERS.

As boundaries. See Boundaries, § 1.

§ 1. Obstruction—Injunction.

In an action to enjoin defendants from interfering with the navigability of Lake Earl, which was declared by the legislature to be navigable, the complaint shows special injury to the plaintiff where it avers that plaintiff is the owner and in possession of a mill situated on Lake Earl; that it has been such owner and so possessed of this mill for thirteen years next last past; that plaintiff's business is the manufacture of lumber for sale at this mill; that it is necessary that plaintiff should use said lake in transporting the saw-logs cut from its lands to said mill; and that what defendants threaten to do will destroy the navigation of said lake, so that the logs cannot be transported to said mill.—Crescent Mill & Transportation Co. v. Hayes, 2, 577.

NECESSARIES.

Liability of husband. See Husband and Wife, § 2.

NEGLIGENCE.

See Damages; Death; Explosions; Master and Servant; Railroads. Homicide through. See Homicide, § 1.

§ 1. Concurring Negligence.

Negligence on plaintiff's part, amounting to absence of ordinary care, which, concurrently with the negligence of defendant, proximately contributes to the injury, is a good defense, whether or not defendant, with ordinary or extraordinary care, could have guarded against it.—Tobin v. Omnibus Cable Co., 4, 214.

§ 2. Contributory Negligence.

In an action for damages for personal injuries suffered by the plaintiff through the falling upon her of the defendant's lumber, alleged to have been negligently piled, the fact that at the time of the accident the plaintiff was sitting on other lumber would not show such contributory negligence as ought to bar a recovery.—Kelly v. Frazer, 1, 737.

One who by his ordinary negligence or willful wrong, has proximately contributed to an injury caused by the mere negligence of another, cannot recover compensation therefor, if but for his concurring and co-operating fault the injury would not have happened, unless the more proximate cause of the injury is the omission of the other party, after becoming aware of the danger to which the former is exposed, to avoid the injury by the use of a proper degree of care. Williams v. Southern Pac. R. Co., 2, 613.

The question of contributory negligence, when left in doubt by the evidence, should be submitted to the jury, under proper instructions; but when the evidence is clear as to the facts, the question is one of law for the court.—Williams v. Southern Pac. R. Co., 2, 613.

One is guilty of contributory negligence if he is guilty of want of ordinary care, and the want of extraordinary care merely is no defense.—Tobin v. Omnibus Cable Co., 4, 214.

§ 3. Dangerous Premises.

A complaint alleged that defendants were the owners of a certain lot in San Francisco; that on or about a certain day they did unlawfully, wrongfully, and negligently maintain thereon, and about ten feet from a public traveled street, a privy-vault, filled to the surface with the contents thereof, and of the depth of ten feet, without any guard or protection, and without any inclosure to separate it from the public street; that prior thereto they did unlawfully and negligently remove the fences inclosing the privy-vault, and all the covering around the same, and removed the building adjoining same, and prior thereto had commenced grading said lot and removing the earth therefrom, the premises being then open and accessible for teams and workmen; that by reason of their negligent acts in leaving the vault thus exposed and unprotected, without any fence or inclosure separating it from the street, plaintiff's minor child, three years of age, without any fault of plaintiff, fell into the same, and was drowned; wherefore he prayed damages. Held, that it stated a cause of action.—Malloy v. Hibernia Savings & Loan Society, 3, 76.

§ 4. Tool Falling from Building.

While plaintiff was walking on the sidewalk of a public street, an employee of defendant, who was repairing a building overhead, let fall a chisel, which struck plaintiff on the head, inflicting a serious injury. Held, that this established a prima facie case of negligence on the part of defendant, and a nonsuit was properly denied.—Dixon v. Pluns, 3, 735.

§ 5. Drivers and Pedestrians in Street.

Whether a driver of a wagon at a street crossing could resume his course after checking his horse to allow a foot passenger to get out of the way, without negligence, is for the jury.—Crowley v. Strouse, 4, 29.

That a person, in crossing a street, fails to use the best course to avoid the danger of being run over, does not show contributory negligence.—Crowley v. Strouse, 4, 29.

§ 6. Fast Driving.

Plaintiff was run over at a street crossing by a wagon driven at great speed by defendant's servant. Plaintiff saw the wagon when it was about a block away, but, thinking that it would not be turned toward the side street where he was standing, because of the high speed, paid no further attention. Held, that the question of contributory negligence was properly left to the jury.—Johnson v. Thomas, 5, 256.

In an action for injuries due to fast driving, a city ordinance prohibiting fast driving is admissible to show negligence.—Johnson v. Thomas, 5, 256.

§ 7. Pleading, Proof and Practice.

Upon a judgment found against a defendant in an action for damages for personal injuries suffered by the plaintiff through the defendant's default, the law presumes that every fact necessary to sustain the judgment was found against the defendant.—Kelly v. Frazier, 1, 737.

Where the facts are undisputed and the inference of negligence is irresistible, the question is one of law for the court.—Wardlaw v. California Ry. Co., 5, 225.

In an action for personal injuries, plaintiff need not allege that he was not negligent.—Matthews v. Bull, 5, 592.

NEGOTIABLE INSTRUMENTS.
See Bills and Notes.

NEW PROMISE.
To toll statute of limitations. See Limitation of Actions, § 8.

NEW TRIAL.

§ 1. Grounds and Occasions in General.

Questions arising upon rulings of the court during the trial and not excepted to at the time cannot be raised as grounds for a motion for a new trial.—People v. Guiterez, 1, 148.

Where, on a motion by the defendant for a new trial, the court so modifies the judgment as to accomplish for the moving party virtually all that a new trial could bring him, he has no cause for complaint if the motion as made is denied.—Moultrie v. Brophy, 1, 536.

A certain finding by the court that there was consideration for the note sued upon is no argument against a new trial ordered by the court after one resulting in plaintiff's favor, when the record discloses that the finding on the question of consideration was not sustained by the evidence.—Whiting v. Steen, 2, 175.

Where the defendants do not actually question the acts of the plaintiff and are satisfied with the findings so far as they concern him (the dissatisfaction being rather so far only as those findings concern the defendants inter se), they cannot justly ask for a new trial, in which, necesssarily, plaintiff must be a party, in order to secure a different adjustment.—Williams v. Conroy, 2, 192.

Where material issues in a case are not disposed of by the verdict of a jury, or the findings of a court, there must be a new trial.—West v. Girard, 2, 360.

A new trial must be granted where the findings of the jury do not determine all the material issues made by the pleadings.—Millard v. Supreme Council American Legion of Honor, 3, 96.

The trial court has a right to reconsider the evidence before it, and to grant the new trial for the reason that the findings as to limitations rested only on certain evidence, whereas there was other material evidence which showed the findings to be without foundation.—Morehouse v. Morehouse, 6, 966.

§ 2. —— Surprise.

Surprise is no ground for a new trial when based on testimony which, although disconcerting to the applicant, was that of a notoriously adverse witness well known as such before the trial, and when the precise point upon which such testimony bore was distinctly raised by the pleading.—Donaldson v. Neville, 1, 124.

§ 3. —— Fraud or Improvidence.

The trial court having found actual fraud from the evidence which was conflicting, its order thereafter for a new trial ought not to be disturbed, since the fraud imputed might, on reconsideration, turn out to have been mere improvidence.—De Gutierrez v. Brinkerhoff, 2, 141.

§ 4. —— Prejudice of Juror.

Where a new trial was asked for because two of the jurors were prejudiced against defendant, and affidavits are read as to statements made by the jurors showing their prejudice, which statements are denied by the jurors in counter-affidavits, the action of the court in denying the new trial will not be disturbed.—Townsend v. Briggs, 3, 803.

§ 5. —— Misconduct of Jury.

The presumption being that jurors have faithfully performed their duty, a new trial is properly denied where the affidavits charging misconduct of jurors are fully met by counter-affidavits of the jurors. Crawford v. Harris, 5, 403.

§ 6. —— Insufficiency of Evidence.

A new trial asked for on the ground of insufficiency of the evidence to sustain the verdict, will be refused if the evidence is conflicting on every material point.—Shumway v. Leakey, 2, 690.

A motion for a new trial, made on the ground of the insufficiency of the evidence to sustain the decision and judgment, is addressed to the sound discretion of the court, and an order on such a motion granting a new trial will not be reversed unless there has been a manifest abuse of that discretion.—Kerr v. Kerr, 2, 753.

An order granting a new trial, applied for on the ground that the evidence was insufficient to justify the verdict, will not be reversed unless a manifest abuse of discretion appears.—Haas v. Whittier, 3, 83.

A motion for a new trial on the ground that the evidence does not sustain the verdict, is addressed to the discretion of the court, and its judgment thereon will not be disturbed unless clearly abused.—Gollin v. Lyle, 3, 621.

A new trial should not be awarded on the ground of newly discovered evidence which is only hearsay.—Lawson v. McGee, 1, 19.

§ 7. —— Newly Discovered Evidence.

A motion for a new trial, based on alleged newly discovered evidence, is properly denied when from the accompanying affidavits it appears that the evidence newly discovered is only cumulative.—Ah Mouie v. Burns, 1, 763.

Newly discovered evidence is a ground for a new trial.—People v. Carty, 2, 294.

The refusal of a new trial on the ground of newly discovered evidence will only be reversed for abuse of discretion.—O'Conor v. Clarke, 5, 323.

Alleged newly discovered evidence of a fact known at the trial as to a matter about which one of the witnesses testified is no ground for a new trial.—People v. Lyle, 2, 393.

If alleged newly discovered evidence is merely cumulative, and every material fact is contradicted by counter-affidavits, and an appellate court cannot clearly say that the court below erred in refusing it, the order refusing it will not be reversed.—Kelleher v. Kenney, 2, 406.

Where a motion is made for a new trial on the ground of newly discovered evidence, if it was in the power of the person so moving to have produced the evidence on the first trial, the motion is properly denied.—People v. Jones, 2, 563.

The application for a new trial because of the newly discovered evidence of three witnesses showed that the materiality of their testimony appeared from the testimony of plaintiff, who testified in the morning of the first day of the trial, and that the trial closed at 1:30 on the second day; that a messenger was sent for one of the witnesses on the morning of the second day, but witness was away from home. No subpoena was issued for any of these witnesses, and no application was made for time to procure the attendance. Held, that the application failed to show reasonable diligence.—Weinburg v. Somps, 4, 10.

Newly discovered evidence, which is merely cumulative, is no ground for a new trial.—Christensen v. McBride, 4, 542.

The granting a new trial on the ground of newly discovered evidence is discretionary with the trial court.—Gruss v. Robertson, 4, 787.

Where, on appeal, no affidavit to support a motion for a new trial on the ground of newly discovered evidence is identified as used on the hearing of the motion, and the affidavits in the transcript show that the alleged new evidence is merely cumulative, and would not probably effect a different result on a new trial, the denial of such motion will be affirmed.—Silva v. Silva, 4, 870.

In an action against two defendants for work and labor, one defendant admitted that the work was performed at his request, and plaintiff and another witness testified that the other defendant also requested the performance of the work. On motion for a new trial on the ground of newly discovered evidence it was claimed that the defendant last mentioned was not at the place where this request was claimed to have been made on the date at which it was claimed to have b^en made; but no witnesses other than those present at the trial were mentioned as able to testify to this effect. No excuse for not calling these witnesses was produced, except the statement in the affidavit of the defendant who requested the services that the fact of the other defendant's absence at the time of the alleged interview had not occurred to defendants until after the trial. Held, that as the new evidence would not affect the liability of affiant, and as he was not qualified to speak for the other defendant, a new trial was properly refused.—Mazor v. Springer, 7, 194.

§ 8. Notice of Decision—Waiver.

Where a losing party files and serves a notice of intention to move for a new trial, he is presumed to have waived notice of the decision. Girdner v. Beswick, 2, 535.

§ 9. Notice of Intention to Move.

An order of the trial court denying a motion for new trial, which forms part of the record on appeal, and recites that notice of such motion was given, sufficiently shows that there was such notice.—Braly v. Henry, 3, 3.

A notice of motion for a new trial, directed against the "findings" rather than against the "decision" of the court, is sufficient, as under Code of Civil Procedure, sections 632, 633, the findings constitute the decision.—Haight v. Tryon, 5, 761.

The notice of motion for a new trial constitutes no part of the statement on appeal, without being referred to in the statement as such.—Sprigg v. Barber, 6, 161.

§ 10. —— Time for Notice.

It is required of one intending to move for a new trial that he give notice of that intention within ten days after the service upon him of notice of the decision of the court.—Bensley v. Lewis, 1, 633.

In jury cases, notice of intention to move for a new trial must be filed and served on the adverse party within ten days after verdict, and the trial court or judge has no power to extend the time for filing such notice.—Hook v. Hall, 2, 457.

A notice of intention to move for a new trial must be filed within the time limited by statute (Code Civ. Proc., sec. 659) or it will be unavailing.—Girdner v. Beswick, 2, 535.

As to time of moving for new trial, notice of intention, filed after judgment entered on a remittitur from the supreme court, may be given in reference to such judgment, rather than the original judgment.—Tuffree v. Stearns Ranchos Co., 6, 129.

§ 11. —— Amendment of Notice.

Code of Civil Procedure, section 659, subdivision 4, provides that where a motion for a new trial is made on the minutes of the court, and errors of law are relied on, the notice of motion must specify the errors relied on, and "if the notice do not contain the specifications . . . . the motion must be denied." Held, that, where the notice does not contain the required specification, it is radically defective, and cannot be amended by adding new specifications after the time for filing it has expired, and if it is so amended, by leave of the trial court, after such time has expired, the specifications will not be considered on appeal.—Packer v. Doray, 4, 297.

§ 12. Change in Personnel of Bench.

Where the record is not definite in respect to the facts, and the disposition of the motion for a new trial has been made by a judge other than the trial judge, then dead, the court on appeal is not justified in overruling the discretion of the court below.—Louderback v. Duffy, 1, 137.

A motion for a new trial on the ground of insufficiency of evidence is addressed to the discretion of the court, and will not be reversed unless a manifest abuse of discretion is shown. The fact that there was a change in the incumbency of the bench between the trial and the determination of the motion for a new trial does not change the rule.—Gutierrez v. Brinkerhoff, 2, 232.

An order granting a new trial, when the evidence is conflicting, will not be reversed because the judge who made the order was not the one who presided at the trial.—Austin v. Gagan, 3, 533.

Where the evidence is conflicting on all the material issues an order granting a new trial by a judge who did not preside at the trial will not be disturbed, unless there is a clear abuse of discretion.— De Camp v. Bryson, 5, 3.

§ 13. Affidavits.

Where a refusal of a continuance, asked on the ground of the absence of a material witness, is made the basis of a motion for a new trial, an affidavit of such witness must be produced, if obtainable, and if it is not obtainable this should be shown.—Thornton v. Thompson, 1, 170.

Under the Practice Act a party who intends to move for a new trial must file with the clerk of the trial court a statement or affidavit within the required time, the statement being "a proposed case."—More v. Massini, 1, 655.

Where the affidavits are conflicting as to the question of surprise, made the ground of a motion for a new trial, the court below cannot be said to have acted without the exercise of a proper discretion.— Symons v. Bunnell, 3, 69.

§ 14. Statement in General.

The court has no power to settle a proposed case not previously filed with the clerk, except by stipulation by the parties.—More v. Massini, 1, 655.

A statement on motion for a new trial, if neither signed nor certified by the judge of the court below, will, on appeal, be stricken out. Martin v. Vanderhoof, 2, 485.

On appeal from an order denying a new trial, the clerk cannot, by certificate, supply what is required to appear in the statement.— Sprigg v. Barber, 6, 161.

Where the statement on a motion for a new trial certified by the judge contained a summary of the evidence, but made no mention of any exceptions to evidence or other errors of law alleged to have occurred at the trial, and excepted to by plaintiff, plaintiff's remedy is not by motion to the trial court to amend the statement, but by petition to the appellate court.—Springer v. Springer, 6, 662.

§ 15. —— Specification of Grounds.

A specification of the errors relied on for the granting of a new trial must be contained in both the motion and the statement.—Stebbins v. Smiley, 1, 133.

Under the law of 1861 (Stats. 1861, p. 590) the grounds for a motion for a new trial shall be specifically set forth, and the statement shall contain only so much of the evidence, or such reference to the evidence, as may be necessary to explain them.—Stebbins v. Smiley, 1, 133.

The statement accompanying a motion for a new trial must specify the grounds on which the motion rests.—Kerr v. McCloskey, 1, 288.

A party moving for a new trial on the ground that the evidence was insufficient to support the findings must specify in his statement the respects in which the evidence failed of sufficiency.—Rodriguez v. Comstock, 1, 604.

Where a motion for a new trial was made on a statement of the case, no alleged error of law can be considered unless it is specified in the statement.—Carter v. Allen, 2, 399.

Code of Civil Procedure, section 659, subdivision 3, provides that, if a notice of motion for a new trial designates that the motion will be made upon a statement of the case, on the grounds of insufficient evidence and errors of law, the statement must specify wherein the evidence is insufficient, and the particular errors relied upon, otherwise it must be disregarded on the hearing of the motion. Held, that if the statement on which such a motion was made does not make the specification required, the motion should be denied.—Millan v. Hood, 3, 548.

Where there is no specification in the statement on motion for a new trial that a finding of fact is not justified by the evidence, and counsel do not make that point, the question whether it is justified cannot be considered on appeal from an order denying a new trial.—Raskin v. Robarts, 4, 465.

An order denying a new trial cannot be reviewed where the statement contains no specification of errors or the particular reasons relied on for the new trial.—Sprigg v. Barber, 6, 161.

Under Code of Civil Procedure, section 659, subdivision 3, providing that on motions for new trial for insufficiency of the evidence the notice shall specify the particulars in which the evidence is alleged to be insufficient, where a statement which does not contain all the evidence is stipulated to be correct, and is certified by the judge to have been settled and allowed, it will be inferred that only so much of the evidence has been inserted as is necessary to explain the grounds specified in the notice.—Cahill v. Baird, 7, 61.

§ 16. —— Time for Filing.

A motion to strike the statement, on motion for a new trial, from the transcript as not having been filed within the statutory time after notice to the appellant of the decision of the judge, should be sustained.—Spangel v. Dellinger, 1, 331.

On a motion for a new trial the court or commissioner is authorized by statute to extend the time for filing the statement twenty days in addition to the five days allowed the applicant as a right.—Carrillo v. Smith, 1, 481.

The fact that counsel consented to the first extension of time in which to serve the statement on a motion for a new trial did not authorize the court to further extend the time thirty days, under the code, exclusive of the first extension.—Desmond v. Faus, 4, 6.

§ 17. Motion—Necessity and Requisites.

When it does not appear that there was a motion made for the new trial ordered by the trial court, nor an agreed or settled statement on such motion nor any affidavits, the order is to be reversed.—Budd v. Drais, 1, 637.

Under Code of Civil Procedure of California, section 659, relating to motions for new trial and their contents, it is not necessary, in a motion for new trial for failure to pass on all such issues, to set out in the statement such failure as a ground for the motion.—Millard v. Supreme Council American Legion of Honor, 3, 96.

§ 18. —— Time for Motion.

Under the statute the ten days within which a party may move for a new trial are to be computed from the day of his being given notice of the filing of the findings.—Garvitt v. Armstrong, 1, 213.

§ 19. —— Motion by Both Parties.

The granting of a new trial on motion of both parties is not an abuse of discretion so as to justify reversal.—Tibbetts v. City of San Francisco, 1, 23.

49

§ 20. Granting or Denying Motion.

Where, on appeal, a new trial is ordered without limitation for a special reason, the new trial should not be limited to the one issue discussed.—Jacobs v. Walker, 3, 865.

A new trial may be granted as to the issues raised by a cross-complaint without granting one as to those raised by the complaint and answer.—Jacob v. Carter, 4, 543.

Where one of the grounds of the motion for a new trial is insufficiency of evidence to justify the verdict, and the order granting the new trial is general in its terms, it must be affirmed.—Ben Lomond Wine Co. v. Sladky, 7, 110.

§ 21. —— Discretion of Court.

The exercise of discretion by the trial court in granting a new trial will not be too closely scrutinized, particularly when the granting has been conditional upon payment of costs by the party favored.—Dollarhide v. Thorne, 1, 2.

An order granting a new trial will be sustained on appeal in all cases where an abuse of discretion by the trial court is not shown.—Thurn v. Swain, 1, 94.

An order for a new trial after findings based on testimony reported by a referee, where therefore the court has not seen the witnesses and heard them testify, is not to be deemed as granted through the court's exceeding the bounds of sound judicial discretion.—Lord v. Lord, 1, 417.

All presumptions are in favor of an order granting a new trial.—Whiting v. Steen, 2, 175.

When the discretion of the judge who presided at the hearing of the motion for a new trial appears to have been fairly exercised, the supreme court will not condemn his action.—Doty v. Whittle, 2, 690.

A motion for a new trial is addressed to the sound discretion of the trial court, and where that discretion has not been abused the order upon that motion will not be disturbed.—Garnier v. Grimaud, 2, 214.

The rule that an appellate court will not disturb a verdict where there is evidence to sustain it does not apply with equal force to the trial judge, who saw and heard the witnesses, and an order granting a new trial will not be reversed unless there has been an abuse of discretion.—Scrivani v. Dondero, 5, 371.

The discretion of the trial court in granting a new trial for insufficiency of the evidence will not be disturbed, except in cases of manifest abuse.—Crocker v. Garland, 7, 275.

§ 22. —— Imposing Conditions.

A condition imposed by the court in granting a new trial, that the moving party pay the costs, becomes an integral part of the order and binding on the parties, and the court has no power to dispense with the condition, since that would be substantially to dispose of the motion anew.—Emerson v. Barron, 1, 879.

When an order is made granting a new trial on condition that the moving party pay the costs accrued, payment, or tender of payment, of the costs becomes a condition precedent.—Emerson v. Barron, 1, 879.

A new trial may be granted conditionally upon failure of one of the parties to perform certain conditions, as the payment of costs and expenses.—Reynolds v. Scott, 2, 334.

§ 23. Setting Aside Order by Trial Court.

If a motion for a new trial is realized as having been granted inadvertently or prematurely the trial court may set aside its order, but not otherwise.—Nichols v. Dunphy, 2, 143.

§ 24. Dismissal or Abandonment of Proceedings.

A failure to prosecute a motion for a new trial is to be regarded as an abandonment of it, and an order, made upon application of the opposing party in such a case, refusing the new trial, is to be upheld. Green v. Doane, 1, 86.

An order both denying and dismissing a motion for new trial, though somewhat inconsistent, must be considered as a dismissal, and proper, where, through inexcusable neglect of the moving party, the motion has not been brought into condition for hearing.—Descalso v. Duane, 3, 893.

The fact that such a motion can be brought to hearing, under Code of Civil Procedure, section 660, either by the moving or opposite party, after notice or affidavits, etc., does not prevent the opposite party applying for dismissal, where, through inexcusable neglect, the motion has not been brought into condition for hearing.—Descalso v. Duane, 3, 893.

An order denying a motion for a new trial is properly made on the hearing of a motion to dismiss the same for failure to prosecute with due diligence.—Desmond v. Faus, 4, 6.

§ 25. Review of Order Granting or Denying.

On appeal the court will not consider a motion for a new trial as if denied, when no order to that effect was made, but rather one refusing the applicant leave to file a statement out of time and then dismissing the motion for lack of prosecution.—Miller v. Beveridge, 1, 332.

Appellate courts will set aside an order for a new trial in those cases only where the order has been clearly erroneous.—Lord v. Lord, 1, 417.

The action of the court in granting a new trial must be affirmed where the grounds for granting the same are not stated.—Warner v. F. Thomas Parisian Dyeing and Cleaning Works, 4, 680.

Where there is any evidence to support a verdict, and a motion for a new trial is denied by the court, its judgment will not be reversed on appeal.—Dietz v. Kucks, 5, 406.

Where the order granting a new trial was general in its terms, the supreme court, on appeal therefrom, was not limited to a consideration of the reasons given therefor by the lower court in an opinion filed by it at the time.—Ben Lomond Wine Co. v. Sladky, 7, 110.

§ 26. —— Sufficiency or Insufficiency of Evidence.

The appellate court is reluctant to reverse the denial of a motion for a new trial made on the ground that the findings were contrary to the evidence.—Easterling v. Power, 1, 62.

An order denying a motion for a new trial, where the evidence below was without material conflict and the findings by the court were contrary to the weight of it, is not to be sustained.—Easterling v. Power, 1, 62.

The supreme court will not interfere with a judgment and an order denying a motion for a new trial, when the sole ground is that the verdict was contrary to the evidence.—Macomber v. Yancy, 1, 517.

When the trial court determines it has erred in its findings and orders a new trial accordingly, the order is not to be disturbed if the error was the finding of a material fact without sufficient evidence, or contrary to evidence, or on a conflict of evidence.—Savage v. Sweeney, 2, 138.

An order granting a new trial for insufficiency of evidence to sustain the verdict is not reviewable on appeal if there is any appreciable conflict in the evidence.—Harloe v. Berwick, 7, 58.

The appellate court will not reverse an order of a trial court refusing a new trial for insufficiency of the evidence to support the findings of fact, if there is substantial evidence to support the findings of the trial court.—Tracy v. California Electrical Works, 7, 324.

§ 27. —— Conflicting Evidence.

Affidavits of counsel filed with a motion for a new trial and the counter-affidavits filed by the opposing counsel may go. to make up conflicting testimony, within the rule against disturbing the trial court's order, disposing of such a motion, when based upon conflicting testimony.—Love v. Watts, 1, 24.

On appeal from an order granting a new trial, based partly on the ground that the verdict was against the evidence, the action of the trial court will not be interfered with even although there was a substantial conflict of evidence at the trial.—Soule v. Berry, 1, 761.

The appellate court should not reverse an order for a new trial if there was before the trial court a substantial conflict of evidence on any material issue.—De Gutierrez v. Brinkerhoff, 2, 141.

In a case where the evidence was conflicting an order for a new trial is not to be disturbed.—Ellis v. Judson, 2, 169.

An order granting a new trial, where the evidence was substantially conflicting will not be disturbed on appeal.—Nelson v. Floyd, 2, 325.

Where the evidence is conflicting, the order granting a new trial will not be disturbed.—Reynolds v. Scott, 2, 334.

In case of a conflict of evidence the appellate court will not interfere with the order of the court below granting a new trial.—Herzog v. Julien, 2, 356.

Where the evidence is conflicting, an order granting a new trial will not be disturbed on appeal.—Kellogg v. Colgan, 3, 250.

Where the evidence is dubious and conflicting, the court on appeal will not, although it may differ in opinion with the lower court, revise the action of the court below in granting or refusing a new trial, unless an abuse of discretion is shown.—Kellenberger v. Market Street Cable Ry. Co., 3, 862.

Where there is a substantial conflict in the evidence an order denying a new trial will not be disturbed.—Steinhart v. Coleman, 5, 162.

An order denying a new trial for insufficiency of the evidence will not be disturbed where there is a material conflict in the evidence.—Taggart v. Bosch, 5, 690.

§ 28. —— Presumption in Favor of Order.

In the absence of an affirmative showing of error, it must be presumed that in disposing of a motion for a new trial the trial court, which had all the evidence before it and best could judge of its effect, ruled correctly.—Page v. O'Brien, 1, 316.

Every intendment is in favor of an order granting a new trial, and it must appear on appeal from the order that prejudicial error or abuse of discretion has been committed, or the order must be affirmed.—Lewis v. Adams, 2, 516.

Where a new trial is ordered by a court, every intendment is in favor of the order, and the legal presumption is that it was made on the ground of insufficiency of the evidence to justify the decision; and, in the absence of all proof of abuse of discretion in the trial judge, such order is not reversible.—Craig v. Allen, 2, 634.

NEWLY DISCOVERED EVIDENCE.
As ground for new trial. See New Trial, §§ 7–11.

NEWSPAPER NOTICE.
As implied contract. See Contracts, § 8.

NONSUIT.
See Dismissal and Nonsuit.

NOTICE.
To owner of adverse possession. See Adverse Possession, § 4.
Of appeal. See Appeal and Error; §§ 20–22.
Of motion to dismiss appeal. See Appeal and Error, § 65.
And demand. See Bills and Notes, § 14.
Published in paper as implied contract. See Contracts, § 8.
Of directors' meeting. See Corporations, § 5.
To officers as notice to corporation. See Corporations, § 8.
Of appeal to superior court. See Justices of Peace, § 7.
To quit. See Landlord and Tenant, § 7.
Of claim of lien. See Mechanics' Liens, § 8.
Of public improvements. See Municipal Corporations, § 22.
Of award of contract. See Municipal Corporations, § 25.
Of special meeting of council. See Municipal Corporations, § 5.
On motion for new trial. See New Trial, §§ 8, 9.
Of intent to appropriate water. See Waters and Watercourses, § 4.

§ 1. Possession of Premises.

The mortgagee of land occupied exclusively by a person other than the mortgagor must, in order to disprove notice of a claim, show that he sought with the utmost diligence to be informed of the rights of such person to the land, but vainly.—Hellman v. Arpin, 2, 86.

To put the mortgagee on inquiry, the possession of a person other than the mortgagor must be open, visible, exclusive and unambiguous. Hellman v. Arpin, 2, 86.

After a positive finding to the effect that the plaintiff took and recorded his mortgage, without notice of the occupant's claim, it will not be inquired into on appeal whether the evidence did not tend most strongly to favor the occupant.—Hellman v. Arpin, 2, 86.

Where, in an action by a grantor against the grantee to set aside a deed for fraud, the findings are for the defendant, the question whether possession by the grantor operated as notice to subsequent purchasers is immaterial.—Whitmore v. Ainsworth, 4, 870.

NOVATION.
In case of partnership. See Partnership, § 11.

§ 1. What Constitutes.

S., being indebted to plaintiff, gave him a written order on defendant, who was indebted to S., and plaintiff presented the order to defendant's foreman, who accepted it. Defendant afterward denied the foreman's authority to accept it, but, on being shown it, and told

the circumstances, agreed to pay plaintiff whatever should be due
S. from him. Held to constitute a novation.—Wolters v. Thomas,
3, 843.

Under Civil Code, section 1530 et seq., in reference to novation,
and defining it as the substitution of a new debt for an old, the execution and interchange of a deed and a contract to return the deed
on the payment of a debt, intended to take the place of a mortgage
securing the debt, is a novation of the mortgage.—Kyle v. Hamilton,
6, 893.

NUISANCE.

§ 1. Prescriptive right to maintain.
§ 2. Powder magazine.
§ 3. Liability of grantee—Fence in highway.
§ 4. Remedies—Pleading and practice.
§ 5. —— Costs.

Claim against city for maintaining. See Municipal Corporations, § 11.

§ 1. Prescriptive Right to Maintain.

The rule that a right to maintain a nuisance cannot be acquired by
prescription applies only to public, and not to private, nuisances.—
Drew v. Hicks, 4, 440.

Where evidence showing a prescriptive right to maintain a private
nuisance has been admitted without objection that it is not within
the issues made by the pleadings, it is an abuse of discretion to refuse to allow defendant to amend his answer so as to allege the right.
Drew v. Hicks, 4, 440.

§ 2. Powder Magazine.

The maintenance of a powder magazine wherein was kept five thousand pounds of gunpowder within two hundred and fifty yards of
numerous dwellings was a nuisance per se.—Kleebauer v. Western
Fuse Explosives, 6, 933.

§ 3. Liability of Grantee—Fence in Highway.

In an action against the grantee of land for the continuance of a
nuisance erected by his grantor, notice to defendant that the erection
was a nuisance is essential to plaintiff's cause of action, and it is
not for defendant to show want of such notice. Such notice is not
dispensed with by Civil Code, section 3483, making a grantee liable
"in the same manner as the one who first created the nuisance," as
the liability of the creator is based on the presumption that he has
notice that it is a nuisance, which presumption does not arise against
the grantee.—Castle v. Smith, 4, 561.

There is no presumption that a grantee knows that a dam erected
by his grantor on the land was erected without the consent of others
affected thereby.—Castle v. Smith, 4, 561.

Where in an action against a grantee of the owner to abate a
nuisance consisting of a fence erected by her on the strip, on the
ground that the strip had been dedicated by her grantor as a highway, the defense was that there was no dedication, but that the survey and map were made merely that the map might be referred to
in conveyances, to insure certainty of description, and the court
found that the strip was not a highway, findings that the strip was
not a continuance of the county road, and that it was not dedicated
to the public by the owner, and not abandoned to the public, were
not necessary.—Smith v. Glenn, 6, 519.

In an action against a grantee of the owner to abate a nuisance
consisting of a fence erected by her on the strip, it was not error

to exclude the field-notes and memorandum-books of the surveyor, where it appeared that they were never shown to defendant's grantor and were not recorded, and the evidence showed that the map was made from the field-notes, and it did not appear that the notes, if admitted, would throw any additional light on the map, or the grantor's intention in having it made, and the surveyor used the field-notes in testifying, and it was not restrained from stating any facts relating to the survey found in them.—Smith v. Glenn, 6, 519.

In an action against the grantee of the owner to abate a nuisance, declarations of the owner of the land, while in possession, and at the time he was having the survey made, to the effect that the same was being made merely for convenience of reference in making conveyances, were admissible.—Smith v. Glenn, 6, 519.

§ 4. Remedies—Pleading and Practice.

A private person cannot recover damages resulting from a public nuisance suffered by him in common with the public, yet if he sustain a peculiar injury which is a special damage to him, in addition to the damage to the public, an action will lie.—Bigley v. Nunan, 1, 852.

An action for nuisance imputed to the defendant in obstructing a public street in front of his premises is not one involving title to real estate, so as to be beyond the jurisdiction of the county court.—Bigley v. Nunan, 1, 852.

In an action for damages caused by the erection of a nuisance, and to compel defendant to abate the same, plaintiff may waive the equitable relief, and thereby render a finding of facts by the court unnecessary.—Castle v. Smith, 4, 561.

In an action to abate an embankment, thereby throwing surface water over plaintiff's right of way, where there is no allegation that the right of way was a public one, it is unnecessary to allege any special injury differing from that resulting to the public.—Silva v. Spangler, 5, 277.

Under Code of Civil Procedure, section 430, the failure of a complaint, in an action to abate an embankment, to allege any damage to plaintiff different or peculiar from that resulting to the common public, is not a ground of demurrer, though, in a proper case, the objection may be urged, under a demurrer, on the ground that the complaint does not state facts sufficient to constitute a cause of action.—Silva v. Spangler, 5, 277.

On an issue whether an irrigation ditch which plaintiff had authorized defendant to construct on his land had been materially enlarged by defendant at a later date, and without authority, so as to entitle plaintiff to damages, and to a judgment abating it as a nuisance, where the evidence was conflicting the finding of the trial judge that the ditch had not been materially enlarged was conclusive on appeal. Smith v. Fresno Canal & Irr. Co., 6, 900.

§ 5. —— Costs.

In a suit in equity for the abatement of a nuisance, the allowance of costs is within the discretion of the court.—Couldthirst v. Kelley, 1, 796.

OBITER DICTUM.

§ 1. Of Supreme Court in Reversing Case.

The supreme court, in its opinion reversing a case for lack of a certain and unambiguous finding on a material question of fact, added that, if the finding could be construed as in favor of respondent, it was enough to say that in the court's opinion it was not supported

by the evidence. Held, that said remark was clearly obiter, and did
not preclude the trial court from finding for respondent on substantially the same evidence, strengthening its conclusion by other new
findings, based on the evidence, and probative of the main finding.—
Luco v. De Toro, 4, 291.

OBSTRUCTING JUSTICE.

§ 1. Concealing Evidence—Indictment.

Indictment alleging that accused after and with knowledge that a
third person had stolen certain property concealed the property stolen
and concealed from the magistrate the commission of the felony,
states no offense under Penal Code, section 135, punishing concealment of evidence about to be introduced, because it fails to state
the purpose of the act.—Ex parte Goldman, 7, 254.

OFFICERS.

§ 1. Election of disqualified chief of police.
§ 2. Salary during contest.
§ 3. Failure to pay over to successor.
§ 4. Duration of liability on bond.

§ 1. Election of Disqualified Chief of Police.

Where one, without ·the qualification of being a citizen of the
United States, has been elected to the office of chief of police of a
city, the election will be annulled and his certificate canceled.—Drew
v. Rogers, 4, 369.

§ 2. Salary During Contest.

Political Code, section 936, relative to payment of the salary of an
office, title to which is contested by proceedings in court, is not repealed by the county government act, which contains no provision
relating to the payment of the salary for the time of the contest.—
Sweeney v. Doyle, 7, 265.

§ 3. Failure to Pay Over to Successor.

Penal Code, section 950, provides that an information must contain
"a statement of the acts constituting the offense, in ordinary and concise language, and in such manner as to enable a person of common
understanding to know what is intended." Held, that an information, which alleged that defendant, "having theretofore" been a
county clerk, and "charged with the receipt, safekeeping, transfer,
and disbursement of public moneys, in his official capacity as such
clerk and officer, and his official term . . . . having expired, ...
and there then and there remaining in his hands certain public moneys theretofore received by him in his official capacity as such clerk,"
he willfully omitted to pay them over to his successor, the demand
therefor "having then and there been made of" defendant by his
successor, sufficiently charged that defendant, as county clerk, received money as such officer, and failed to pay it over to his successor; and the use of the participle instead of the past tense of the
verb did not make the allegations mere recitals.—People v. Hamilton,
3, 825.

Penal Code, section 426, declares that the phrase "public moneys"
includes all money received or held by county officers in their official
capacity. Held, that an allegation that moneys were received by
defendant "in his official capacity" was the allegation of a fact
which fixed their character as "public moneys."—People v. Hamilton,
3, 825.

The allegation that defendant received the money in his official capacity was sufficient, without referring to the statute under which the information was drawn, or to any statute which created a duty, the antecedent existence of which constituted a factor connected with the offense, the general conclusion of the information, "contra formam statuti," being sufficient.—People v. Hamilton, 3, 825.

§ 4. Duration of Liability on Bond.

The fact that no term of office was ever fixed or put an end to by any by-law, order or resolution, does not affect the liability of the sureties, the bond being conditioned that he should perform his duties "so long as he shall continue and be continued in said office." No want of consideration being shown, the sureties could bind themselves for an unlimited period.—Humboldt Savings etc. Co. v. Wennerhold, 3, 52.

OIL.

Reservation in deed. See Deeds, § 21.

OIL WELL.

Lien for labor. See Mines and Minerals, § 11.

OPINION EVIDENCE.

In general. See Evidence, §§ 18–20.
In libel case. See Libel and Slander, § 4.

OPTIONS.

Purchase of stock by broker. See Brokers, § 9.
To purchase mining property. See Mines and Minerals, § 7.

§ 1. Acceptance or Election to Exercise.

A contract may be so made as to be optional on one of the parties and obligatory on the other, or obligatory at the election of one of the parties; but if as so made the option or election is to be exercised within a time named, after that time it cannot be claimed as a right.—Decker v. Hughes, 1, 193.

Defendant gave plaintiff a written option to purchase stock for $3,100 cash and the balance on time. On the last day of the option plaintiff said he would take the stock "according to the terms of the writing," but defendant, desiring time to get a portion thereof from one to whom it was pledged, indorsed an extension of eleven days on the agreement. After such extension, plaintiff let defendant have $3,100 to get the pledged stock, but he failed to do so, and, after the expiration of the option, demanded the return of the $3,100. Held, that there was no binding acceptance of the option.—Buttner v. Smith, 4, 627.

Plaintiff is entitled to interest on the sum sought to be recovered from the date of his demand for its return.—Buttner v. Smith, 4, 627.

There is no contract authorizing action for damages by one given option to buy within certain time, where he does not give notice of acceptance of offer, though the offer is withdrawn before expiration of the time.—Abbott v. '76 Land & Water Co., 6, 25.

§ 2. Complaint in Action for Breach.

A complaint for the breach of the following contract, "received of A. Gerberding one hundred dollars, for which I allow him the privilege of delivering me, at any time within thirty days from date, five hundred tons S/87 wheat, at one dollar and eighty cents per cental," signed, "E. H. K.," which is set out in haec verba, is sufficient on demurrer, although it does not allege that defendant executed the same.—Berry v. Kowalsky, 3, 418.

The fact that the abbreviation "S/87" is used as descriptive of the wheat to be delivered under the contract does not make the complaint unintelligible and uncertain, as oral evidence may be introduced to explain the customary meaning, and need not be pleaded.—Berry v. Kowalsky, 3, 418.

Where the contract sued upon was written on a sheet, with rules of the produce exchange printed at the head, and plaintiff testified that it was no part of the contract, and that the contract had no connection with the exchange, it was error to exclude evidence tending to show that it was an exchange contract, as well as the exchange rules governing such contracts.—Berry v. Kowalsky, 3, 418.

ORAL EVIDENCE.
See Evidence, § 8.

ORDER OF EXAMINATION.
See Supplementary Proceedings.

ORDER OF PROOF.
See Trial, § 1.

ORDINANCES.
Adoption and publication. See Municipal Corporations, § 6.

OVERDRAFT.
See Banks and Banking, § 2.

OVERSEERS.
Of road. See Highways, § 2.

PANDERING.
See Prostitution.

PARENT AND CHILD.
See Infants.

Fraudulent transfers as between. See Fraudulent Transfers, §§ 3, 5.

§ 1. Abandonment of Children.

In the absence of proof that a mother intended to bring about final separation from her minor children, evidence of mere temporary absences accompanied by statements not indicating an intent to surrender parental rights, and the fact that she placed the children in care of another while she was away, was insufficient to establish abandonment.—In re Snowball's Estate, 7, 371.

PARI DELICTO.
§ 1. When Rule not Available.

The rule of in pari delicto is not to be invoked in a case arising out of carelessness or indifference on the part of persons dealing with each other as it would be in a case arising out of their common fraud. Rogers v. Graves, 1, 21.

PAROL EVIDENCE.
See Evidence, § 8.

PART PERFORMANCE.

See Frauds, Statute of, § 3.

PARTIES.

§ 1. In General.

In an action affecting real estate it is proper to make persons parties defendant, who claim to have been in possession, and if they put in no proof at the trial to maintain the claim, it is proper for the court to conclude them by its judgment.—Garrioch v. Stanner, 1, 490.

In an action to recover money deposited by plaintiff with defendant under an agreement that it is to be paid to a third person on condition that the latter deliver a deed to plaintiff within a certain time, such person is not a necessary party.—Ullrich v. Santa Rosa Nat. Bank, 4, 741.

Under Code of Civil Procedure, section 369, the party in whose name a written contract is made, though partly for the benefit of another, may sue thereon without joining the latter.—Graham v. Franke, 4, 899.

§ 2. Fictitious Names.

Some of defendants were sued by fictitious names, but the summons was personally served on them. The complaint was afterward amended so as to properly name defendants. Held, that defendants were made parties, within the statute of limitations, when the summons was served.—Fox v. Hale & Norcross Silver Min. Co., 5, 980.

§ 3. Misjoinder of Parties.

Where it does not appear upon the face of the complaint that there is a misjoinder of parties defendant, objection on that ground must be taken by answer, under Code of Civil Procedure, section 433, providing that objections to a complaint, not appearing on the face thereof, shall be taken by answer.—Moody v. Newmark, 5, 850.

Where a complaint does not show that a party is improperly joined as a defendant, his remedy is by answer, and not by a demurrer for misjoinder of parties.—Lothrop v. Golden, 6, 284.

§ 4. Bringing in New Parties.

Where complete equity cannot be done to all parties before the court without the presence of other parties, the court will order these others to be brought in or dismiss the suit, the plaintiff not consenting to their being brought in, even though the point of defect of parties may not have been raised by the defendant by demurrer or answer.—Huber v. Clarke, 1, 419.

Under the Code of Civil Procedure, sections 379, 389, providing that one having an interest in the controversy, or whose presence is necessary to a final determination of it, may be brought into an action as defendant, the court may order one who purchased rights in the property in controversy after issue joined on the original complaint to be made defendant by an amended complaint.—People's Ditch Co. v. '76 Land and Water Co., 5, 292.

PARTITION.

§ 1. In general.
§ 2. Objections and exceptions.
§ 3. Sale—Referee's report and deed.
§ 4. Conclusiveness and effect on title.
§ 5. Costs—Compensation of referees.
§ 6. Notice of appeal.

Of probate homestead. See Homestead, § 10.
Of mining claim. See Mines and Minerals, § 8.
In violation of trust. See Trusts, § 12.

§ 1. In General.

The action of the commissioners under an interlocutory judgment in a partition proceeding is to be presumed to have been in accordance with the rules laid down in such judgment, if no error appears on the face of their report or those objecting to their actions do not make error therein affirmatively to appear.—Seale v. Greer, 1, 423.

When an interlocutory judgment has required the commissioners to set off the tracts in such manner that the tract allotted to each party shall include all his improvements, in order to have the report of the commissioners set aside, a party may not show that this course was not pursued in one instance unless he also shows how it could have been pursued without doing injury to the rights or interests of others.—Seale v. Greer, 1, 423.

A conveyance to plaintiff, vesting in him an undivided interest in land, and making him a tenant in common with defendant, entitled him to a partition; and the fact that he had never been in occupancy of the land, and that his grantors and the defendant were copartners in the crops raised on the land, did not affect his right to partition.—Noce v. Daveggio, 2, 354.

In an action for partition, where plaintiffs allege title in themselves to the undivided one-half of the premises and in defendants to the other undivided one-half, and defendants deny plaintiffs' title, allege title in themselves to the whole, and plead the statute of limitations, on the trial, after defendants have proved the entry of their grantor under one H., it is competent for the plaintiffs to show that H. acquired his title from B., who had been joint owner with plaintiffs' predecessor in interest, to the end that it might be determined whether the acts of defendants and their grantors had been sufficient to bar the plaintiffs' right of recovery.—Hardy v. Sexton, 2, 423.

In an action for partition of real estate, with the buildings and personal property thereon, it is proper to order partition of the real property separate and apart from the personal property, where it does not appear that such course will greatly prejudice the owners.—Woodward v. Raum, 3, 734.

§ 2. Objections and Exceptions.

A party is not entitled to except to the report of the commissioners in partition, on behalf of others who have not complained.—Seale v. Greer, 1, 423.

An objection by a party to a partition, that the part allotted to him is taken up to some extent by a road, must show that he would have been entitled to a further amount, equal in area to the road, had the latter been excluded.—Seale v. Greer, 1, 423.

§ 3. Sale—Referee's Report and Deed.

After a sale in partition of devised land, the bidder refused to pay his bid, whereupon, as agreed between plaintiff devisee and the other devisees, a deed was executed by the referee to said bidder, who conveyed the property to plaintiff and certain devisees, accepting the same in lieu of money from the estate, and devisees who received no part of the land were paid so much more money. Held, that plaintiff was estopped to impeach the transactions on the ground that the referee had no authority to make the deed without the receipt of the amount of the bid.—Gerke v. Cameron, 5, 798.

And where plaintiff thereafter obtained conveyances from all the devisees except defendant, without any additional consideration, the referee's deed, if invalid, could not be assailed on a subsequent partition suit by plaintiff, unless she tendered to defendant the money which he would have received from the estate, and in lieu of which he had accepted an additional interest in said land.—Gerke v. Cameron, 5, 798.

Where in an action to charge defendant for the difference between the price bid for land by him at a partition sale and the price obtained on a resale after his refusal to accept the land, he introduced evidence which would have sustained a finding that there had been a material variance between the terms of the sales, and, after finding to the contrary, the trial court ordered a new trial generally, such order will not be reversed on appeal, since it nowhere appeared that it was not granted because such finding was contrary to the evidence. Hammond v. Cailleaud, 6, 412.

Though the recitals of a referee's receipt given for a sale of land at public auction on partition are not conclusive of the terms and conditions of such sale in an action against the purchaser to recover the difference between the price bid by him and the price at which the property was subsequently sold on his refusal to complete the purchase, they are admissible as tending to show the true terms and conditions thereof.—Hammond v. Cailleaud, 6, 412.

§ 4. Conclusiveness and Effect on Title.

A partition of land the title to which has been in controversy between the parties concludes them as to that title in the particular partition.—Seale v. Greer, 1, 423.

A party in an action for partition, who acquires an independent title by deed pending the suit and before decree, and who does not assert such title in that action, will be concluded by the judgment therein from setting up such title in a subsequent action for the partition of the same property.—Phillips v. Winter, 4, 684.

§ 5. Costs—Compensation of Referees.

Section 308 of the Practice Act, providing that in partition suits the costs shall be paid by the respective parties proportionately and may be included and specified in the judgment, and proceeding then to provide for their becoming a lien on the shares in certain cases, contemplates that their so becoming a lien depends upon how the owner of the share may elect, and the solution of the question depends upon whether they are included and specified in the judgment of partition.—Hihn v. Parkhurst, 1, 541.

If both the plaintiffs and defendants in a partition suit are dissatisfied with the compensation awarded by order to referees, and if they themselves are the only parties necessary to an appeal from the order, reversal can be had in the court above by confessing error in that respect, provided the order is an appealable one.—Bernal v. Bernal, 1, 581.

§ 6. Notice of Appeal.

The notice of appeal, in the case of a partition suit, is to be served on each one of the parties concerned, since in such suits each party is adverse to the other.—Bernal v. Bernal, 1, 581.

Unless notice of an appeal from an interlocutory decree in partition is served upon all the adverse parties the appeal will be dismissed.—Luco v. Commercial Bank of San Diego, 2, 549.

PARTNERSHIP.

§ 1. Rights of Partners in Property.

While a partnership still is in existence and its affairs unsettled, the undivided assets of the firm cannot be said in law to be the individual private property of any one of the partners.—McKenzie v. Dickinson, 1, 426.

§ 2. —— Lien for Payment of Firm Debts.

Plaintiff, having leased a farm, and taken S. as a partner, agreed that the lessor might sell enough of the future crop to pay the rent; whereupon the latter bargained nineteen tons to third persons, but nothing was paid, nor any delivery made to them or to the lessor. Subsequently the whole crop, amounting to less than nineteen tons, which constituted the entire partnership assets, was attached as the property of S., and purchased at execution sale by the attaching creditor. Held, that under Civil Code, section 2405, giving each partner a lien on the assets for the payment of firm debts, and for any general balance due him, plaintiff was entitled to recover his share from the creditor.—Leedom v. Ham, 5, 633.

Plaintiff was not estopped, though he had, through mistake of law, notified the officer at the time of the attachment that he owned one-half the crop, "less nineteen tons belonging to" the lessor.—Leedom v. Ham, 5, 633.

§ 3. The Relation in General.

A promise to share a road, followed by a refusal to execute the promise, discloses no evidence of a partnership.—Miles v. Thorne, 1, 235.

One person, or an association of persons, may do business under a firm name entirely distinct from the name or names of the person or persons composing the firm.—Shain v. Du Jarlin, 4, 905.

The loaning of money by a partner to the firm does not change the original contract of partnership.—Silveira v. Reese, 7, 112.

§ 4. Remedy for Breach of Agreement to Form.

Where two persons agreed to form a partnership for doing certain work before any contract for doing the work was obtained, and the partnership was never launched, and one of the parties carries on the work alone, the only remedy of the one excluded is an action at law for breach of contract.—Thomason v. De Greayer, 3, 651.

§ 5. Assumption of Antecedent Debts of Members.

Civil Code, section 2395, provides that "a partnership is the association of two or more persons for the purpose of carrying on business together, and dividing its profits between them." Held, that a partnership was formed where a contractor, on assigning his contract to others, made a written agreement with them, which agreement provided that the contractor was to do the work, that the parties taking the contract were to furnish the money to carry it on, and receive the payments made as the work progressed, but that the profits were to be equally divided between them.—Kennedy & Shaw Lumber Co. v. Taylor, 3, 697.

Material was sold and delivered to the contractor before the agreement of partnership was made, and was afterward used in the work. Held, that a finding that the partnership assumed payment thereof was justified.—Kennedy & Shaw Lumber Co. v. Taylor, 3, 697.

§ 6. Power of Partner as Affected by Absence of Copartner.

The fact that one member of a partnership leaves the state to reside out of it does not operate to dissolve the partnership carried on within the state, and, in such absence of his copartner, the remaining one may make an assignment of any part of the partnership property to a creditor, and such assignment will have precedence over a subsequent sale by the absent partner.—Bernheim v. Porter, 2, 349.

§ 7. Promissory Notes.

When partners do business under the name specifically of one of them, and that one makes a note which, to the knowledge of the payee, is an individual note, such note cannot be enforced against the partnership.—Honeycult & Co. v. Hogan, 1, 122.

A promissory note made to two persons, copartners, for a partnership demand, and assigned by one of them in the name of both, may be recovered upon a suit of the assignee or of his assignee.—Tusch v. Cummings, 1, 782.

§ 8. Bank Receiving Deposits for Firm.

A bank receiving deposits from A. B. P. & Co. is put on inquiry as to whether the depositor is not a partnership, rather than the individual A. B. P.—Willey v. Crocker-Woolworth Nat. Bank, 7, 152.

A bank receiving deposits from, and doing business with, a partnership consisting of an individual and a corporation, is estopped to deny the validity of the partnership, when sued by it for a deposit. Willey v. Crocker-Woolworth Nat. Bank, 7, 152.

§ 9. Sales to or Purchases by Partner.

A partnership is not liable for goods sold and delivered to one partner in his individual capacity, though the items be charged in the partnership account.—Burt v. Collins, 2, 256.

Plaintiffs, having taken a crop of barley under a mortgage of $1,045, accepted the offer of C., one of defendants' firm, to take the crop, and pay them $750 the following week. Soon after, plaintiffs received a check for $500, drawn in favor of, and indorsed by, defendants. In a suit for the balance of the $750, one of the plaintiffs testified that he told his partner to ship the barley to defendants; but it appeared that the warehouseman billed it to C., as he often did shipments from plaintiffs to defendants. Plaintiffs had charged defendants the $750, and it appeared that the $500 was the firm's money, and was charged to C. on their books. Defendants asserted that it was C.'s personal affair, and that he had bought the crop from the grower, who had directed him to pay plaintiffs the $750 to release it. Held, that there was enough evidence to support a verdict against defendants for goods sold and delivered.—Sanborn v. Cunningham, 4, 95.

Defendants insisting that the transaction was the personal affair of one partner, a question by plaintiffs whether such transaction was in defendant's general line of business was proper.—Sanborn v. Cunningham, 4, 95.

Plaintiff's testimony that, in answer to his inquiry at the bank for a check which he wished to use as evidence, the cashier told him that he did not think plaintiff could get it, was competent, and there was no need to call the cashier to prove that fact.—Sanborn v. Cunningham, 4, 95.

§ 10. Actions—Pleading and Judgment.

In an action against many named persons jointly as partners to enforce a promissory note made by three of them, describing themselves in the body of the note as "we as trustees of," etc., a judgment may be given against the signers alone if no proof is produced at the trial that they acted under authority of the others.—Blanchard v. Kaull, 1, 665.

Although in a suit against many persons to enforce a note signed by three of them, describing themselves in the body of the instrument as trustees, the complaint sets up that all are partners, and the answer that they comprise a corporation, judgment may be taken against the signers as individuals, provided there is a failure at the trial to prove either partnership or corporation, or that the three had signed by the authority of the others.—Blanchard v. Kaull, 1, 665.

In an action by the payees of a promissory note drawn in favor of a firm, it is not indispensable that the complaint expressly set up the partnership if it contains a copy of the note and avers that the defendant thereby "undertook and promised to pay these plaintiffs," that the note is long past due and "payable from defendants to them"; particularly if the answer fails to deny these averments.—Clauss v. Froment, 1, 690.

Under Code of Civil Procedure, section 578, declaring that judgment may be given against one of several defendants, two persons being sued on an alleged partnership debt, and it being found that they are not partners, but that the debt is the individual debt of one of them, judgment may be rendered against him.—Morgan v. Righetti, 5, 397.

§ 11. Dissolution and Accounting.

If a partner, without the consent of his partner, sells his interest to a third person, the sale dissolves the partnership.—Blood v. Fairbanks, 1, 762.

If a partner sells his interest in the firm to an outside person, the remedy of a nonassenting copartner is not against the purchaser but the seller, who may be made to respond in a suit in equity for an accounting.—Blood v. Fairbanks, 1, 762.

A settlement of partnership accounts cannot be made in a collateral action in which the partners are not made parties.—Young v. Hoglan, 2, 46.

A lumber firm agreed with two of its members to sell them sawed lumber at a certain price. The two members formed a new firm, and one of them sold his interest in the contract to the other, and the latter sold interests therein to two strangers. The old firm continued to sell to the purchasing concern under the agreement, and to receive payment therefrom, without regard to its personnel, the bills being in all instances made out in the name of the purchasing concern. There was no evidence of any agreement to release the original contractors. Held, that there was no novation, and the lumber firm could sue one of the purchasing members for an accounting without joining his new associates in the purchasing contract.—Chapin v. Brown, 4, 300.

One partner advanced money to the firm, and permitted his copartner to withdraw it for his individual use. The latter died without having returned the money. Thereafter, an action was brought by his personal representatives against the surviving partner for an accounting. Held, that the claim need not be presented for allowance against the estate of the deceased partner, but would be adjusted by charging plaintiffs therewith on the partnership accounting.—Painter v. Painter, 4, 637.

Where, in an action for a partnership accounting, books offered in evidence were objected to as not showing the transactions between the parties, the action of the trial court in rejecting the books will not be disturbed on appeal unless on the trial the party offering the books pointed out wherein they were relevant, and the record shows what he proposed to prove thereby.—Harper v. Anderson, 4, 831.

One who buys out a retiring partner, and forms a partnership with the other member of the firm, is not a proper party to a suit by such member against the retiring partner for an accounting, the complaint alleging merely that he has funds of the new partnership in his hands, which were collected by the procurement of the retiring partner.—Harper v. Anderson, 4, 831.

§ 12. —— Fraud or Good Faith.

Under Civil Code, sections 2410, 2411, partners are bound to act in the highest good faith toward each other, and this continues and extends to the dissolution and liquidation of the partnership affairs.—Wiester v. Wiester, 5, 686.

Where, on settlement of a partition, the withdrawing partner accepted certain land in payment of his interest at $70 per acre, the deed will not be set aside, on the ground of fraud in the settlement, where it was evident that both parties believed the land to be of such value, that it was located at a distance, at a town in which there was at the time a "land boom," and similar property was then selling at from $100 to $150 per acre.—Wiester v. Wiester, 5, 686.

§ 13. —— Firm Hiring Laborers for Railway Construction.

S., W. & Co. made a business of hiring Chinese laborers to railroad and construction companies. No direct compensation was paid for this service, but the understanding was that S., W. & Co. were to have the right to furnish supplies to whatever men they obtained for the companies, which supplies were to be retained out of the men's wages. There being a scarcity of labor, S. proposed the importation of men direct from China. Not meeting with encouragement from the other partners, he took the matter to the president of the S. P. Co., and an agreement was perfected, under which importations were afterward made. The secretary of the construction company, one of the parties signing the contract, testified that certain advances were to be made under the contract by his own company and by S., W. & Co., to cover the cost of importation; that, according to his recollection, S., W. & Co. signed the contract, and that the last he saw of it it was in the hands of W. The person who was to go to China to secure the importation was to act ostensibly for the S. P. Co., as that company was better known than the construction companies. Directions were sent by the S. P. officials to the steamship agent in China to make the advances and draw on S., W. & Co. for the entire amount. The clerk to whom the draft was presented at S., W. & Co.'s office, in their absence, claimed that they were not to pay it. The secretary of the construction company testified that he then had some conversation with the clerk concerning payment, in which reference was made to the contract. The contract itself was not produced. A large number of Chinese were imported, and worked for the construction company. Held, that there was not merely a privilege to furnish supplies, but a contract to which S., W. & Co. was a party, and which, at least by force of usage, gave them the right to furnish supplies to the men obtained thereunder, and on the death of one of the partners his estate was entitled to a share of the profits arising therefrom.—Wallace v. Sisson, 4, 34.

The rescission of a partnership settlement effected through fraud, and return of property received thereunder by the estate of a deceased partner, is not necessary to the maintenance of a suit for further accounting by the representatives of deceased.—Wallace v. Sisson, 4, 34.

§ 14. —— Death of Partner and Rights and Liabilities of Surviving Partner.

The right of the surviving partner to settle the affairs of the firm results wholly from the joint interest whereby he might claim to hold the assets as if he were the owner; no such right inheres in one who has sold his entire interest to his copartner, even though he may not yet have received the purchase money.—Cavert v. Alderman, 1, 73.

It is competent for a surviving partner, closing up the affairs of the firm, to extend an outstanding contract made with the partnership, where such extension seems to him for the interest of the business so being closed up.—Sargent v. Fragg, 1, 118.

In the absence of an intention to the contrary expressed in the clearest and most unambiguous terms in the instrument establishing the relation of partners, the death of a partner dissolves the partnership, and the surviving partner becomes clothed with authority to close up the business.—Thompson v. Gibb, 1, 173.

Under section 1585, Code of Civil Procedure, where a partnership is dissolved by the death of one of the partners the surviving partner is entitled to all the assets of the firm and to settle up the business.— McKay v. Joy, 2, 639.

Upon the death of one partner the business was carried on for a number of years by the survivor. In a suit for an accounting and the appointment of a receiver, it appeared that the books contained many errors and erasures. Many of these errors compensated each other. The same method of bookkeeping was pursued, and the same irregularities were found, both before and after the deceased partner's death. Many of the more serious irregularities were explained. The books had been kept continuously by the same bookkeeper, who testified that he had never made a fraudulent entry. Held, not to sustain a finding of fraud.—Painter v. Painter, 4, 636.

Where a surviving partner has conducted the business for six years to the advantage of all parties concerned, a decree declaring all the assets to belong to the old firm, and refusing to allow such partner any compensation for his services, or even credit for amounts paid a manager of the business, is erroneous.—Painter v. Painter, 4, 636.

In a suit against a surviving partner for an accounting, a credit to him on account of real estate appeared in the ledger, written over an erasure under date of February 28, 1882. An expert witness surmised that the entry was made in 1883, after the death of plaintiff's decedent, and fraudulently antedated, as he saw nothing on the face of the books to justify the entry. Defendant's account-book, kept as one of the books of the firm, contained entries justifying the credit, and the item appeared properly entered in the journal between entries unquestionably made in 1882. Defendant testified, corroborated by vouchers and his account-book, that he took land in his name for the firm; that the payments were made by the firm, though charged to him, and the credit was made by the consent of his partner to balance his account. Held, insufficient to sustain a finding that the entry was fraudulent and void.—Painter v. Painter, 4, 637.

Where a surviving partner carried on the firm business with the firm assets until it was terminated by the appointment of a receiver, an accounting should be as of the date of the appointment of the receiver, and a personal judgment against the surviving partner, which merely fixed his liabilities as of the date of the deceased partner's death, was erroneous.—Painter's Exrs. v. Painter, 6, 677.

Where the assets of a partnership dissolved by the death of one of its members were used by a new firm formed by the surviving partner, the old partnership was entitled to a share in the profits of the new firm proportionate to the value of the assets of the old firm used, as compared with the value of the property or services contributed by the new firm; but all the property of the new firm should not be regarded as assets of the old.—Painter's Exrs. v. Painter, 6, 677.

Code of Civil Procedure, section 1585, gives a surviving partner the right to continue in possession of the partnership, and to settle its business and account with the executor or administrator, and to pay over such balances to him as may be payable to him in the right of the decedent. Held, that, as the right of a corporate surviving partner to close up the partnership business after the death of its individual partner was not affected by the question of the legality of a partnership between a corporation and an individual, the estoppel of a bank receiving deposits from and doing business with such partnership to deny its legality was not terminated by the individual partner's death.—Willey v. Crocker-Woolworth Nat. Bank, 7, 152.

§ 15. —— Receivership.

The control of firm assets and business should not be wrested from the surviving partner, by the appointment of a receiver, without a clear showing of mismanagement or improper conduct, and of danger of ultimate loss to the estate of the deceased partner.—Painter v. Painter, 4, 637.

Refusal to appoint a receiver in an action for dissolution of a partnership and an accounting is in the sound discretion of the trial court.—Silveira v. Reese, 7, 112.

PARTY-WALLS.

§ 1. Consent to Erection—Estoppel.

Where a board of directors consented to allow defendants to use a wall of the corporation's building as a party-wall, and the defendants erected a building with the knowledge and acquiescence of said directors, the corporation will be estopped to assert that defendants have no interest in the wall; but its remedy, if any, is an action for the recovery of a proportionate part of the cost of said wall.—Bank of Escondido v. Thomas, 5, 94.

§ 2. Injunction Against Use of Wall.

In an action to enjoin defendants from using a certain wall as a party-wall, the answer alleged that said wall rested in part on defendants' land. Held, that the issue as to whether plaintiff's building extended over the dividing line was sufficiently raised by the pleadings.—Bank of Escondido v. Thomas, 5, 94.

Where plaintiff's wall projects over defendants' land, equity will not enjoin defendants' use thereof as a party-wall.—Bank of Escondido v. Thomas, 5, 94.

PASSENGERS.

See Carriers, §§ 4–10.

PASTURAGE.

Liability for. See Animals, § 1.
Of stock. See Landlord and Tenant, § 5.

PATENT.

To land. See Public Lands, § 19.
Canceling patent to swamp land. See Swamp Lands, § 7.

PAYMENT.

§ 1. National legal tender act.
§ 2. Kind of money to be made in.
§ 3. —— Debt contracted in foreign country.
§ 4. Recovering money paid to sheriff.

See Accord and Satisfaction; Tender.

Of bills and notes. See Bills and Notes, §§ 4, 15.
As defense to action for breach of contract. See Contracts, § 15.
Of judgment. See Judgments, § 21.
On building contracts. See Mechanics' Liens, § 4.
Of special assessment under protest. See Municipal Corporations, § 37.
Allegation of nonpayment. See Pleading, § 2.

§ 1. National Legal Tender Act.

A judgment on a contract entered into before the passing of the national legal tender acts is payable in such treasury notes as are specified in such acts, unless the contract expressly provided for payment in gold.—McKeown v. Beatty, 1, 190.

A judgment on a contract entered into before the passage of the national legal tender acts is payable in such treasury notes as are specified in such acts, unless the contract expressly provided for payment in gold.—Gryff v. Rohrer, 1, 192.

A fine is not a "debt" under the act of Congress making treasury notes a legal tender in payment of debts.—In re Whipple, 1, 274.

§ 2. Kind of Money to be Made in.

Payment in gold coin is not obligatory unless made so by the terms of the contract calling for money to be paid.—Rand v. Hastings, 1, 307.

An allegation in a complaint for the payment of money that the understanding between the parties was that payment was to be made in a particular sort of money, presents an issuable and material fact which, if denied by the answer, must be proven.—Merritt v. Wilcox, 1, 884.

§ 3. —— Debt Contracted in Foreign Country.

A debt contracted in a foreign country is payable in the currency of that country, and therefore, where the creditor sues in the United States, he is entitled to recover such sum in money of the United States as equals the debt in the foreign country, when it was payable. Grunwald v. Freese, 4, 182.

§ 4. Recovering Money Paid to Sheriff.

Money paid under protest to a sheriff upon an execution cannot be recovered back if the judgment on which the execution rested was irregular merely and not void.—Witcher v. Jansen, 1, 85.

PECUNIARY CONDITION.

Of defendant. See Breach of Promise to Marry, § 2.

PENALTY.

For frivolous appeal. See Appeal and Error, §§ 73-76.

PERJURY.

§ 1. What Constitutes.

On an examination for perjury it appeared that defendant, on his voir dire as a trial juror, stated, when asked if he knew the proprietor of a certain gambling place, that he had nothing to do with "such places"; that at the place referred to gambling prohibited by statute was carried on; that defendant visited places where gambling not prohibited by statute was carried on. Held, that he was not guilty of perjury.—Ex parte Meyer, 5, 64.

PHYSICAL EXAMINATION.

Of plaintiff. See Damages.

PHYSICIANS AND DENTISTS.

§ 1. Refusal of dental examiners to indorse diploma—Mandamus.
§ 2. Action for compensation.
§ 3. —— Absence of license.
§ 4. Malpractice or abandonment of case.

Employment and discharge by county. See Counties, § 5.
Opinions as evidence. See Evidence, § 19.

§ 1. Refusal of Dental Examiners to Indorse Diploma—Mandamus.

Act of March 12, 1885 (Stats. 1885, p. 110), relating to the practice of dentistry, creates a board of examiners, and provides (section 5) that, if the examination "prove satisfactory," the board shall issue to qualified persons certificates, and shall indorse as satisfactory diplomas from any "reputable" dental college, "when satisfied of the character of such institution," on the holder furnishing "evidence satisfactory to the board" of his or her right to the same. Held, that the duties of such board are judicial, and its action in finding an examination unsatisfactory, or refusing to indorse "as satisfactory" a diploma from a dental college, is final.—Van Vleck v. Board of Dental Examiners, 5, 636.

A petition for a writ of mandate to the state board of dental examiners alleged that petitioner presented to the board a diploma issued to him by a certain dental college; that such college then, and when the diploma was issued, "was a reputable college, and there existed sufficient evidence of such fact"; that he furnished "evidence satisfactory" that he was the person named in the diploma, and that it was issued to him; that the board refused to indorse it; and that at the time the board "were satisfied" that such college was a reputable college. Held, that such allegations were not the legal equivalent of allegations that the board found that petitioner furnished evidence satisfactory to the board that he was the person named in the diploma, and that the board was satisfied of the character of the institution issuing it.—Van Vleck v. Board of Dental Examiners, 5, 636.

§ 2. Action for Compensation.

In determining what is a reasonable compensation for surgical and medical services in a given case, the skill and learning of the operator and the character and circumstances of the subject to which he devotes his services must be considered, and the rule that compensation is determined by "the usual price at the time and place of performance" does not necessarily apply.—Heintz v. Cooper, 5, 564.

Where plaintiff sues for services as physician, and defendant, by a cross-complaint, seeks damages for alleged negligent treatment, and plaintiff, in answer, alleges that defendant's suffering was aggravated by his own negligence and failure to follow plaintiff's directions, a finding that all the facts alleged in the cross-complaint, except that of plaintiff's employment, "are untrue," renders the issue of defendant's negligence immaterial, and a finding as to it is not required.—Heintz v. Cooper, 5, 564.

§ 3. —— Absence of License.

A party cannot recover for services rendered as physician and surgeon unless he has a certificate to practice medicine and surgery, as required by statute.—Roberts v. Levy, 3, 653.

§ 4. Malpractice or Abandonment of Case.

Before a witness can testify on the issue of a physician's neglect and unskillful practice, his competency must be shown.—Heintz v. Cooper, 5, 564.

Defendant was employed to attend plaintiff during her first confinement. He assumed charge of the case, visiting plaintiff at intervals, until he deemed it the proper time to employ instruments to aid in the delivery of the child, whereon the plaintiff shrank back and screamed, compelling the defendant to let go the instruments. Defendant threatened the plaintiff that if she did not quit screaming he would quit the case, and on the failure of a second or third attempt to use the instruments he abruptly left the house. This was at midnight, and it was an hour or more before another physician could be obtained, who, on examination, found that plaintiff's condition was not such as to require the use of instruments just then. Held, that a verdict of $2,000 was not excessive for the unwarranted abandonment of the case and the mental suffering occasioned plaintiff thereby. Lathrope v. Flood, 6, 637.

PLATS.

As showing boundaries. See Boundaries, § 5.
Filing in dedicating street or highway. See Dedication, § 3.

PLEADING.

§ 1. Verification.

That there is matter in the answer that vitally calls for verification, and the answer is not verified by some defendant concerned particularly in that matter, is no cause for judgment on the pleadings, if the answer would be good, even were that matter stricken out, the defendant who did verify being conversant with the remaining matter.—Houck v. Carolan, 1, 692.

Section 447 of the Code of Civil Procedure, in relation to pleadings, does not make invalid an unverified answer denying the genuineness and due execution of an assignment, but rather of an instrument that may be assigned.—Forbes v. County of El Dorado, 2, 219.

Under section 447 of the Code of Civil Procedure it is not essential that a defendant swear to his denial of the genuineness and due execution of the assignment of an instrument when the complaint contains no copy of the instrument and the assignment.—Forbes v. County of El Dorado, 2, 219.

Code of Civil Procedure, section 437, provides that "where the complaint is not verified a general denial is sufficient." Held, that where an unverified complaint alleges the value of property converted and the answer is a general denial, the value is put in issue --Paden v. Goldbaum, 4, 767.

§ 2. Complaint or Petition.

The purpose of a complaint is that the defendant shall be advised of the facts relied upon by the plaintiff to support his action.—Berri v. Minturn, 1, 50.

The allegations of a complaint are to be construed most strongly against the plaintiff, since it is to be presumed that a pleader will set out the aspect of the case most favorable to himself.—Morenhout v. Brown, 1, 139.

On a complaint, in an action on a contract, setting out the contract in haec verba and performance by the plaintiff's assignor, except as excused by the defendant, and claiming the contract price throughout and payment in gold according to the terms of the contract, recovery cannot be asked as for a quantum meruit et valebat.—Schumacher v. Adler, 1, 372.

A party must recover, if at all, according to the allegations of his pleadings, whatever the evidence introduced may be.—McKenzie v. Dickinson, 1, 426.

To constitute a cause of action, it is sufficient to allege the facts simply, without setting out matter tending to prove them.—Lorenz v. Jacobs, 2, 296.

Where a pleader, in his complaint, alleges a fact, and then sets out the written evidence on which he relies for proof of the fact, the complaint will be held good for only what the evidence proves.— Ohm v. San Francisco, 3, 314.

A complaint alleging that plaintiff demanded payment of a specified sum, that defendant refused payment, and that the sum is due and unpaid, sufficiently alleges nonpayment of the sum alleged to be due. Ferguson v. McBean, 4, 429.

Where an instrument which is in legal effect a mortgage and not a deed of trust is set out in full in the complaint, the fact that it is there designated a "trust deed so being and operating as a mortgage" does not create an ambiguity in the pleading.—Bank of Oroville v. Lawrence, 4, 845.

A complaint which sets out that defendant received plaintiff's money under an agreement which he afterward refused to perform, and asks damages for the breach, does not state a cause of action sounding in tort.—Link v. Jarvis, 5, 750.

In action against two, a complaint alleging that plaintiff and defendant, on a certain date, entered into a written agreement, and setting out the agreement, was sufficient as an averment that a certain one of the defendants entered into such agreement.—Diamond Coal Co. v. Cook, 6, 446.

§ 3. —— Several Counts.

A complaint containing several counts setting forth separate causes of action is sufficient if any one of the counts so contained is good.—Wilbur v. Sanderson, 1, 663.

A cause of action may be stated in different counts in order to meet any possible phase of the evidence, and the pleader will not be required to elect on which count he will proceed.—Remy v. Olds, 4, 240.

§ 4. —— Defects, Objections, Waiver and Cure.

When from the facts stated in a petition it does not appear that the petitioner is entitled to what he asks, the petition is to be considered as substantially defective.—People v. Loomis, 1, 214.

The point that the complaint does not state facts sufficient to constitute a cause of action is not waived by a failure to demur, but it may be made at any time.—Donner v. Palmer, 1, 392.

A complaint alleging that a certain note has not been paid, but omitting the alternative "or any part thereof," no special demurrer being interposed, is good after judgment.—Regensberger v. Quinn, 4, 986.

Under Code of Civil Procedure, section 434, providing that if objections to a complaint are not taken, either by demurrer or answer, the defendant must be deemed to have waived the same (with certain exceptions), the objection that a complaint is ambiguous or uncertain, that being a specific ground of demurrer, is waived, if not raised by demurrer.—Silva v. Spangler, 5, 277.

The fact that defendant's promise, in the action on a contract, is alleged in the complaint, merely by way of recital, is not ground for reversing a judgment for plaintiff, where the complaint is attacked for the first time on appeal, and where defendant specially denied the promise.—Haines v. Stilwell, 5, 27.

Judgment will not be reversed because of a defective allegation which did not mislead the opposite party, and which was not objected to by demurrer, and under which evidence was admitted without objection.—Christensen v. Jessen, 5, 45.

A judgment will not be reversed for alleged ambiguity in the complaint where it appears from defendant's answer that he was not thereby misled to his prejudice.—Lothrop v. Golden, 6, 284.

§ 5. Failure of Plaintiff to Deny Execution of Writing.

In an action for money had and received, the complaint alleged that defendant had on July 2, 1884, executed a written instrument certifying that he held $655 until certain disputes should be settled between two named claimants of the fund, and that both of the claimants had three years later assigned the certificate to plaintiff. The answer alleged that the dispute was settled on July 8, 1884, six days after the date of the certificate, and that both the claimants had on that day executed to defendant a written release of all their rights to the money, a copy of which was set out in the answer. Held, that plaintiff's failure to deny the execution of the release by affidavit filed with the clerk of court, as required by Code of Civil

Procedure, section 448, admitted the genuineness and due execution of the release, and it must be taken to be what it appears to be on its face.—Petersen v. Taylor, 4, 335.

A copy of a decree of discharge in insolvency is not a "written instrument," within Code of Civil Procedure, section 448, providing that "when the defense to an action is founded on a written instrument, and a copy thereof is contained in the answer, the genuineness and due execution are deemed admitted, unless the plaintiff file an affidavit denying the same."—Castle v. Hickman, 5, 159.

§ 6. Demurrer.

Amendment after demurrer. See post, § 13.

A demurrer to a complaint that is good in part should not be sustained, a cause of action being shown by such part irrespective of others that may be had.—Thomas v. Creditors, 1, 164.

The sustaining of a demurrer to a complaint containing three counts is error if one of the counts is good as set out.—Steiner v. American Falls Min. Co., 1, 189.

To interpose a meaningless demurrer is the same as to interpose none at all.—Hawkins v. Kingston, 1, 413.

If plaintiffs have a clear legal right in the subject matter of an action, and that right is being materially injured by wrongful acts complained of, the sufficiency of such a cause of action cannot be attacked by general demurrer for imperfect averment. Such errors can only be reached by a special demurrer.—Lorenz v. Jacobs, 2, 296.

Where no demurrer appears in the transcript, the overruling of the demurrer to the complaint, specified as error, will not be considered on appeal.—Damsguard v. Gunnoldson, 2, 512.

A complaint alleging that defendant's intestate was indebted to plaintiff's intestate in the sum of $5,000, for legal services rendered by plaintiff's intestate in prosecuting and defending numerous suits, drawing various instruments, consulting and advising with defendant's intestate about his business, at his request, which services are alleged to have been rendered between January 1, 1870, and October 11, 1883, is demurrable for uncertainty in not specifying the various items and the times of the rendition of such services.—Wise v. Hogan, 2, 893.

Where a general demurrer is filed to a complaint containing two counts, on the ground that the causes of action are barred by the statute of limitations, the demurrer must be overruled, if a good cause of action is stated in either county.—Moyle v. Landers, 3, 113.

The overruling of a demurrer to a cross-complaint, which makes the issue identical with that raised by the original pleadings, does not prejudice the party demurring.—Millan v. Hood, 3, 548.

The question whether a pleading is ambiguous and uncertain cannot be raised by a general demurrer.—Bennett v. Morris, 4, 834.

A complainant cannot, on appeal, first complain of error in sustaining a demurrer without leave to amend.—Smith v. Ferries etc. Ry. Co., 5, 889.

§ 7. Answer.

A motion for the allowance of more time to a defendant for the filing of his answer, on the ground of his being absent, is properly denied when it appears that he was personally served with the complaint in ample time and the affidavit accompanying the motion is insufficient as an affidavit of merits.—Coddington v. Hopkins, 1, 199.

An answer that makes mere negative averments instead of direct denials may sometimes be upheld, since the form of the denial is not material provided it traverses the allegation it was intended to meet.—Chamon v. San Francisco, 1, 509.

Averments of matters of law in a complaint call for no denial, and if denied present no issue.—Myers v. Mayor and Common Council of Placerville, 1, 565.

When a defense apparently good in substance is defectively pleaded, the appropriate remedy is by demurrer; a motion for judgment on the pleadings is the appropriate remedy when the pleading is fatally defective in substance.—Houck v. Carolan, 1, 692.

§ 8. —— Setting Up New Matter.

It is incumbent on a defendant to prove at the trial the new matter set up in his answer, and in default of his doing so the allegations of new matter go for nothing.—Thompson v. Thompson, 2, 32.

§ 9. —— Denial on Information and Belief.

A denial on information and belief is not good when the reference is to matters of which the defendant must have knowledge, but the court cannot assume a knowledge on the part of the defendant that at the time of the institution of the action the plaintiff was owner of the instrument sued upon.—Forbes v. County of El Dorado, 2, 219.

An answer denying the allegations of the complaint "as this defendant is informed and believes" does not constitute a sufficient denial thereof.—Shain v. Du Jardin, 4, 905.

§ 10. Cross-complaint.

A person who answers a complaint, in an action against him, and then files a cross-complaint, cannot, after a judgment has been given in both suits, raise the point that he should not have been made a party to the action in the first place.—Burnett v. Tolles, 1, 519.

A cross-complaint is unknown to the Code of Civil Procedure and new matter found in the answer is denied by force of the statute.—Thompson v. Thompson, 2, 32.

A cross-complaint in an action must be as distinct and separate from the answer therein as any other independent pleading in the cause, and each must rest on its own merits.—Harrison v. McCormick, 2, 612.

Where an answer and cross-complaint are both joined in the same pleading, an objection thereto is deemed waived if the plaintiff consented in writing to allow such pleading to be filed and stand as defendant's answer and cross-complaint.—Harrison v. McCormick, 2, 612.

In an action for partnership accounting defendant filed a "cross-complaint" which related to the partnership transaction set forth in the complaint, alleged the partnership contract in somewhat different terms, and contained only matters in avoidance, or constituting a defense or counterclaim. Held, the averments of the cross-complaint were not admitted by failure of plaintiff to answer, as the cross-complaint was really an answer to the complaint, and therefore its averments were deemed controverted under Code of Civil Procedure, section 462.—Haight v. Tryon, 5, 761.

§ 11. Supplemental Pleadings.

Under leave to file amendments to his answer a defendant may file an amended and supplemental answer, unless the opposing party shows that he is prejudiced thereby.—Dole v. McCumber, 1, 135.

If a defendant would avail himself of a law passed since the joinder of issue in the case, he must file a supplemental answer.—Baird v. Duane, 1, 492.

Where a supplemental complaint filed in 1879 sets forth a cause of action founded upon a verbal loan for one year, made in 1869, and secured by a deed, such action is barred by the statute of limitations.—Brown v. Mann, 2, 627.

§ 12. Amendment of Pleadings.

See, also, Amendments, §§ 1–3.

Court may, in the exercise of its discretion, refuse a second postponement of a trial, or may refuse an amendment to the answer asked for at the trial.—Levy v. Baldwin, 2, 509.

The fact that the amended complaint was filed after the time prescribed is an irregularity merely, and can be reviewed only on a motion to set aside the judgment, and on an appeal from the order denying the motion.—Carter v. Paige, 3, 64.

The refusal of a motion to amend the complaint, made after the decision in the case was rendered, to conform with evidence that the erection of the dam by defendant obstructed the flow of debris and tailings from mines above plaintiff's land, was within the discretion of the trial court.—Richard v. Hupp, 4, 824.

A pleading may be amended without leave of court under Code of Civil Procedure, section 472, providing that any pleading may be amended once as of course and without costs.—Spooner v. Cady, 4, 539.

An amended pleading which is stricken out on motion does not supersede the original.—Spooner v. Cady, 4, 539.

Where the complaint in an action for conversion describes plaintiffs as heirs of one B., which is merely matter of inducement, an amendment will not be allowed, after trial, so as to count on plaintiffs' rights, as heirs of B., whose estate had not been administered on or distributed, to sue for conversion of property of which they had never been in possession, and which defendant had received under a contract to which plaintiffs were not parties, as such amendment would raise new issues, which would probably require a new trial.—Bradley v. Parker, 4, 250.

Applications to amend pleadings are addressed to the discretion of the trial court, and should be allowed at any stage of the trial, when necessary for the purposes of justice.—Link v. Jarvis, 5, 750.

When the complaint is amended in any material respect, so as to present new questions, on which issues may be taken, defendant may answer as of course; and in such case the court cannot limit the defenses which may be interposed.—Fox v. Hale & Norcross Silver Min. Co., 5, 980.

§ 13. —— After Demurrer.

Judgment is properly rendered against the plaintiff who has failed to amend his complaint after a demurrer to it has been sustained.—Strathern v. Rock Island G. & S. M. Co., 2, 71.

A dismissal of the cross-complaint rightly follows a defendant standing on his answer and declining to amend after a demurrer to the latter has been sustained.—Becker v. Ferrier, 2, 225.

If a demurrer to the complaint is sustained, the plaintiff is entitled to leave to amend, unless the complaint is so defective that it cannot be made good by any amendment.—Ridgway v. Bogan, 2, 718.

§ 14. Items of Account and Bill of Particulars.

It not being necessary, under Code of Civil Procedure, section 454, to give an itemized account in pleading, the findings need not give the items of the account.—Murdock v. Clarke, 3, 265.

A bill of particulars, served by plaintiff in response to a demand therefor, becomes a part of the complaint.—Chapman v. Bent, 6, 740.

§ 15. Surplusage and Sham or Irrelevant Parts.

Words in a complaint putting a false construction upon a power of attorney copied at length in the same complaint are to be treated as surplusage.—Heinlen v. Martin, 2, 20.

It was not reversible error to refuse to strike out certain parts of the answer as "sham, irrelevant and redundant," where they could have no effect upon, and were not necessary to support, the judgment. Clark v. Olsen, 3, 890.

The fact that the complaint in an action by an assignee of an account for goods sold against copartners, after alleging the incurring of the liability by defendants, also alleges that one of the defendants promised to pay the same, does not render it demurrable, as the latter allegation may be treated as surplusage.—Morrow v. Norton, 4, 934.

§ 16. Variance.

When the complaint sets up that a sale was induced by the fraud of a named person aided by another, and the proof is that such person perpetrated the fraud alone, this is no variance.—Jewett v. Adkinson, 1, 197.

Calling sums of money "money advanced and expended," etc., in a counterclaim and calling them a "book account" in the answer, does not render the latter ambiguous, and evidence of a "book account" produced at the trial in proof is no variance.—Dennis v. Belt, 1, 275.

Under Code of Civil Procedure, section 469, providing that no variance between the allegation in a pleading and the proof is to be deemed material unless it has misled the adverse party, where a complaint by a judgment creditor of a corporation against a stockholder alleges that the debt was contracted on June 1st, proof that it was contracted on August 20th is not a fatal variance.—Cockins v. Cook, 5, 103.

Where an objection to the sufficiency of the complaint to entitle plaintiffs to the profit made by defendant on a sale of certain property presented at most a mere question of variance, the court was authorized to disregard the same by Code of Civil Procedure, section 469.—Crocker v. Garland, 7, 275.

§ 17. Admissions in Pleading.

See, also, Evidence, § 15.

An averment of a complaint which the answer, not denying expressly, by its language leaves it merely to be inferred to be denied is, under the rules of pleading, admitted.—Vassault v. Kirby, 1, 668.

A party in one action is not bound by allegations in a complaint in another action to which he is not party.—Mellus v. Mellus, 2, 530.

Where inconsistent defenses are pleaded, neither can be used as an admission to destroy the other.—Eppinger v. Kendrick, 5, 295.

An admission in plaintiff's answer that pledged property was sold after a certain date cures a cross-complaint defective in not so stating.—Bourn v. Dowdell, 5, 820.

PLEDGE.

§ 1. In general.
§ 2. Pledge of crops for rent—Creditors of lessee.
§ 3. Loss or divestiture of lien.
§ 4. Enforcement and foreclosure.
§ 5. —— Attorney fee.

Guaranty in case of pledged wine. See Guaranty, § 3.

§ 1. In General.

Where, on the question of an alleged fraudulent pledge made by the president and secretary of a corporation for the benefit of certain creditors, the court below directs the jury that said president and secretary had power to make the pledge, and the jury find the same to be fraudulent, a judgment affirming such verdict will not be disturbed, the question of fraud being for the jury, and their verdict not necessarily contrary to the direction of the court.—Caswell v. Harris, 2, 742.

Where wheat pledged is taken from the possession of the pledgee in attachment against the pledgor, and the litigation in relation thereto is conducted by the attorneys of the pledgor, the pledgee cannot be charged with conversion when the attachment is sustained.—Barnhart v. Edwards, 5, 558.

A pledge of corporate stock by indorsement and delivery of the certificate is valid as between the parties.—Malone v. Johnson, 5, 575.

An order to the pledge-holder of notes already indorsed, to hold them for the payment of another debt, constitutes a pledge without further delivery.—Ormsby v. De Borra, 5, 947.

An instrument termed a "bill of sale," executed by C., authorizing I. to take and sell the articles therein specified till C.'s debt to I. is satisfied, when the residue shall be returned to C., and reciting that it is given as security for the debt, is a contract for a pledge, within Civil Code, section 2987, providing that every contract by which the possession of personal property is transferred as security only is a pledge.—Irwin v. McDowell, 4, 329.

Though such instrument, by reciting that it is given in lieu of a certain chattel mortgage, shows an intention that it shall take the place of the chattel mortgage, it does not, in the absence of the delivery of the articles thereby agreed to be pledged, release the chattel mortgage, Civil Code, section 2988, providing that no pledge is valid till the property is delivered to the pledgee.—Irwin v. McDowell, 4, 329.

§ 2. Pledge of Crops for Rent—Creditors of Lessee.

An oral agreement between landlord and tenant that title to crops raised during the term should remain in the landlord, and that the crop was to be put in warehouse in the landlord's name, and that from a sale thereof the landlord was to retain as rent an amount equal to the rent reserved in the lease, and turn over the balance to the tenant, is merely an agreement that, after the crop was harvested and stored, it should become a pledge for payment of the rent, and does not create a lien which would support an action of conversion against a sheriff for levying on the crop while growing, and seizing it under attachment against the tenant as soon as harvested. Stockton Savings & Loan Soc. v. Purvis, 5, 164.

§ 3. Loss or Divestiture of Lien.

The delivery by the payee of a note, to the maker thereof, of a life insurance policy held by him as security for the payment of the note, which delivery was conditioned on the return of a paid-up policy to be thereafter issued, does not devest such payee of his lien on the security.—Castle v. Hickman, 5, 159.

A pledgee of stock, even if he converts it, by depositing it in escrow under an agreement to convey it to one on exercise of his option of purchase on all the corporation's property, does not thereby lose his lien, under Civil Code, section 2910, the pledgor having waived the tort by electing to treat the pledgee's contract as authorized.— Bixby v. Crafts, 6, 12.

§ 4. Enforcement and Foreclosure.

In an action to foreclose a pledge of notes placed with a bank as pledge-holder, the pledgee is entitled to their possession, and have them remain in the custody of the bank.—Ormsby v. De Borra, 5, 947.

One having no interest in the property pledged is not aggrieved by, and cannot complain of, the sufficiency of the judgment against the pledge-holder, in an action to foreclose the pledge.—Ormsby v. De Borra, 5, 947.

Both an order directing a pledgee to hold notes to secure payment of plaintiff's debt and the notes referred to are proper evidence in an action to foreclose the pledge.—Ormsby v. De Borra, 5, 947.

§ 5. —— Attorney Fee.

Statutes of 1873-74, page 707, providing that "in all cases of foreclosure of mortgage the attorney's fee shall be fixed by the court, . . . ,. any stipulation in said mortgage to the contrary notwithstanding," relates only to mortgage foreclosures, and does not apply to an action to enforce a pledge.—Hildreth v. Williams, 4, 141.

POINTS AND AUTHORITIES.

On appeal. See Appeal and Error, §§ 57–59.

POISON.

Killing by. See Homicide.

POLICE COURTS.

Establishment and jurisdiction. See Courts, §§ 3–5.

§ 1. Appeal to Superior Court.

Where an appeal from a judgment of the police court to the superior court had been taken, and papers filed in the superior court many months, the fact that the court decided the appeal without having first made an order submitting it to decision does not render the judgment void.—Wilson v. Superior Court, 6, 766.

Where the superior court inadvertently rendered judgment on an appeal from the police court, without first making an order submitting the appeal for decision, the judgment may be set aside on motion, but cannot be treated as void, and a second review and decision of the same question be compelled by mandate.—Wilson v. Superior Court, 6, 766.

POLICE JUSTICE.

In San Jose. See Courts, § 3.

POSSESSION.

Of stolen goods as evidence. See Evidence, § 9.
As evidence of title. See Evidence, § 16.

Necessity of change of on sale of goods. See Fraudulent Transfers,
§ 1.

As notice. See Notice, § 1.

§ 1. Actual Possession—Necessity of Inclosure.

If land is subjected to the exclusive dominion and control of the
possessor, whatever the means used for that purpose may be, there
is actual possession; and an inclosure is not indispensaole.—Tong v.
Richmond, 1, 809.

POSSESSION, WRIT OF.

See Ejectment, § 23; Execution, § 13.

POWDER MAGAZINE.

As a nuisance. See Nuisance, § 2.

POWER OF ATTORNEY.

§ 1. Of married woman to sell land.
§ 2. Conveyance under power—Extent of authority.
§ 3. Revocation by death.
§ 4. Execution and record in foreign country—Proof.

Evidence of contents of lost power. See Lost Instruments, § 1.

§ 1. Of Married Woman to Sell Land.

A power of attorney to sign, seal and deliver deeds of real estate
in California owned by a married woman is without legal effect if
not executed and acknowledged by her according to the laws of the
state prevailing at the time of its date.—Heinlen v. Martin, 2, 20.

§ 2. Conveyance Under Power—Extent of Authority.

Where the intention in executing a power of attorney was to give
the attorney control of the property for his own benefit, he may
convey the same in payment of his own debts.—Frink v. Roe, 2, 491.

Where a deed executed by an agent acting under a power of attorney is in excess of the power granted, the deed is void.—Alcorn
v. Batterman, 6, 776.

§ 3. Revocation by Death.

A power of attorney to convey becomes extinct by the death of
the constituent, although the power be irrevocable, and no title passes
by a deed subsequently made by the attorney.—Frink v. Roe, 2, 491.

§ 4. Execution and Record in Foreign Country—Proof.

When an original power of attorney is a foreign record in a foreign
country, an exemplified or sworn copy is admissible in evidence.—
Heinlen v. Martin, 2, 20.

When under the laws of a foreign country the constituting of one
person to be the attorney in fact of another is effected, not by the
execution of a paper and the manual transfer of it by the first person, but rather by a declaration by him to a notary in words which
the notary then writes in his presence into a book of public record,
he subscribing the writing, a copy of which is thereupon given the
attorney thus made, any objection that there is indicated here no
delivery from the donor to the donee is met by the fact that the document becomes by the executing it beyond its signer's control. which
fact is to be taken with that of the delivery to the notary and the
plain intention implied from all the circumstances that the parties regarded the transaction as complete.—Heinlen v. Martin, 2, 20.

POWER OF SALE.

In will. See Wills, §§ 7, 8.

PRE-EMPTION.

See Public Lands.

PRELIMINARY EXAMINATION.

Testimony taken at. See Criminal Law, § 13.

PREMIUMS.

On insurance policies. See Insurance.

PRESCRIPTION.

See Adverse Possession; Limitation of Actions.
Easement by. See Easements, § 1.
Establishing highway by. See Highways, § 1.

PRESENTATION.

Of negotiable paper. See Bills and Notes, § 14.

PRESUMPTIONS AND BURDEN OF PROOF.

On appeal. See Appeal and Error, § 89.
In actions against carriers. See Carriers, §§ 3, 9.
As to consideration of deed. See Deeds, § 12.
As to fraud. See Fraud, § 4.
In favor of order granting or denying new trial. See New Trial, § 28.

PRETERMITTED CHILDREN.

See Wills, § 8.

PRINCIPAL AND AGENT.

§ 1. Agency in general.
§ 2. Evidence of authority of agent.
§ 3. Ostensible agency or estoppel of principal to deny authority.
§ 4. Ratification by principal.
§ 5. Delegation of duties by agent.
§ 6. Lien of agent for commissions—Receiver.
§ 7. Purchase of principal's land by agent.
§ 8. Fraud and deceit of agent.
§ 9. Liability in contract made by agent.
§ 10. Suit by agent in own name.
§ 11. Pleading authority of agent.
§ 12. Revocation of authority.

See Brokers; Factors.

Admissions of agent. See Evidence, § 13.
Letter of attorney. See Power of Attorney.
Sale of land and payment therefor. See Vendor and Vendee, § 5.

§ 1. Agency in General.

When it is said that a person assumed to represent another, the meaning is that he took upon himself to represent that other and did not represent him; in which case it cannot be said that the other was not represented.—Baker v. Riordan, 2, 179.

51

Plaintiff was to act as purchasing agent for defendant, but was to assume no responsibility for the satisfactory working of the apparatus purchased. The contract contemplated that plaintiff should pay for the apparatus, and be repaid by defendant in a lump sum, which was to include all supplies. The apparatus proved defective, and defendant notified plaintiff not to pay therefor until an adjustment was reached, stating that it had claims on other purchases against the seller almost equalling the entire cost, to which plaintiff's agent agreed, and unsuccessful attempts were made to adjust defendant's claims extending over several months, and until after the insolvency of the seller. In an action for the price, plaintiff's treasurer and the seller testified that plaintiff paid for the apparatus soon after delivery, and before the notice of defect. Held, that the agreement to withhold payment by plaintiff's agent, who did not know payment had already been made, did not prevent recovery, since it was without consideration.—Thomson-Houston Electric Co. v. Central Electric Ry. Co., 6, 202.

§ 2. Evidence of Authority of Agent.

The complaint stated that the "parties hereto entered into a contract," etc., and that "defendant agreed with said plaintiffs to pay them the prices stated," etc. Held, that evidence of either an express or ostensible agency in the person who made the contract with plaintiffs was admissible.—Bibb v. Bancroft, 3, 151.

Declarations of one that he is agent of another are not admissible to prove the agency, nor to bind the alleged principal, until proof of the agency has first been made.—Santa Cruz Butchers' Union v. I X L Lime Co., 5, 495.

Testimony that witness acted as agent for another in a given transaction is competent proof of the fact.—McRae v. Argonaut Land & Dev. Co., 6, 145.

In an action to recover an agreed rent for certain reamers used by a well driller in drilling a well under contract with defendant, the memorandum of agreement between defendant and the driller, and evidence of the oral agreement between them, by which the driller agreed to furnish all tools necessary for the work, was admissible to show that no authority could be implied from the transaction by which the driller was authorized to obtain the reamers on defendant's credit.—Jones v. Waterman, 7, 316.

§ 3. Ostensible Agency or Estoppel of Principal to Deny Authority.

In an action for breach of a contract by which plaintiff was to remove debris for defendant, the evidence showed that plaintiff, when seeking the contract, was referred by defendant to one C., and was told that anything he would do with him would be all right. On the question of agency, the court instructed as to the law of ostensible agency. Held, that the instruction was not irrelevant on the ground that an express agency only was shown by the evidence.—Bibb v. Bancroft, 3, 151.

A bond given to the owner of a boat, conditioned to pay for all goods delivered to F., as steward of the boat, was executed by the sureties' bookkeeper without authority. In an action thereon by one who had furnished goods to F., it appeared that the bond was executed June 15th; that plaintiff had commenced furnishing goods June 1st, on F. agreeing to pay on the 15th of each month, and had furnished goods to the value of $100 before the bond was executed; that on June 30th, when $237 was due, and F. refused to pay, plaintiff declined to furnish more goods, but afterward, when F. showed him the bond, he continued to let F. have goods, but made no inquiry of the sureties as to the genuineness of the bond until after the goods sought to be recovered for were furnished. Held, that plaintiff did not deliver the goods to F., relying on the bond, "in good faith, and without ordinary negligence," within the meaning of Civil Code, section 2334, providing that only in such case is "a principal bound by the acts of his agent under a merely ostensible authority."—Malic v. Fox, 4, 19.

W., a merchant, and partner with plaintiff in a livery, failed, and transferred his property to his brother S., through whom he settled with most of his creditors, as he swore, with his own money. Business was done in S.'s name, but W. borrowed money from plaintiff for the business, bought out his interest in the stable, and gave him a note for the whole, signed, "S., per W." Plaintiff asked S. about the note, and S. said he would go and see about it, and went and talked to W., but said nothing to plaintiff. Later he proposed to plaintiff to go into partnership with him and W., putting in the note as capital; and then he took over the business and property from W., paying him some cash, and assuming the debts, among which, at the time, he mentioned this. Held, that he was estopped to say that W. did not sign the note as his agent, and that he had not ratified it.—Goetz v. Goldbaum, 4, 749.

Plaintiff purchased from defendant's son in law certain stock, part of which belonged to him and defendant and part to defendant and his son, and all of which were running on the same ranch, and credited the amount on the son in law's account with him. Defendant, being told of the sale, gave other stock to his son, to satisfy him, but did not say anything to plaintiff, who had previously purchased stock from the son in law under similar circumstances, as was known to defendant. Defendant took an assignment from his son in law of all his interest in the stock on the ranch, and made several payments on what he himself owed plaintiff, and for which he had given his note, and also told him that his son in law had plenty of property to pay his debt, and at last gave him a mortgage two years after the sale to secure a balance he owed plaintiff. Held, that defendant, who had become the assignee of his son's interest, could not deny the son in law's authority to sell the stock belonging to defendant and his son.—Kraft v. Wilson, 4, 794.

In an action for damages for an alleged breach of a written contract to purchase peaches from plaintiff, the contract price being for more than $200, and the agent, who was claimed to have executed the contract for defendants, not having been authorized in writing, plaintiff contended that defendants were estopped to deny the agency, and to plead the statute of frauds, because of a holding out of the agent as such in previous similar transactions. The evidence showed that previous sales of fruit were made by plaintiff to other parties than defendants, and defendants' agent testified that he told plaintiff's agent that the fruit in question was for the same purpose as formerly. It was shown that defendants were the agents of certain fruit dealers, and that the agent whom it was claimed had bound them was their subagent to purchase fruit for defendants' principals. Held, that no estoppel was shown, ostensible authority as a subagent not conferring authority to bind defendants as principals.—Ruddock Co. v. Johnson, 6, 846.

Evidence in an action for labor done in street paving that defendant told plaintiff, who was negotiating with her to do street paving for her, that all street work was arranged by A, and the fact that A executed another contract with plaintiff, as defendant's agent, for such kind of work, which she recognized, justifies a finding that A, in making and modifying such a contract, had ostensible agency, defined by Civil Code, section 2300, to be when the principal causes a third person to believe another to be his agent.—Union Paving and Contract Co. v. Mowry, 7, 6.

§ 4. Ratification by Principal.

If lumber is accepted by a carpenter for, and put by him into, the construction of a boat, and the facts are at the time within the knowledge of the boat's owner, the latter, although he has given the carpenter no authority to buy for him, is to be regarded as having ratified the acts of the carpenter as those of his agent, and he is responsible for the price of the lumber.—Soule v. Steamboat Pike, 1, 4.

As the ratification of an agent's act is equivalent to a prior command, a finding that an agent had authority to do an act is sustained by evidence that his principal ratified such act.—Kraft v. Wilson, 4, 794.

The question of ratification of an unauthorized act of an agent is a question of fact.—Kraft v. Wilson, 4, 794.

Ratification need not be expressly pleaded.—Goetz v. Goldbaum, 4, 749.

Plaintiff consigned goods to defendants, with instructions not to sell below a certain price without first advising him. Defendants sold at a price lower than that named and without consulting plaintiff, but notified him immediately after the sale. Plaintiff was absent from home when defendants' letter arrived, but, after his return, made no objection to the sale, until several months had elapsed. Held, that plaintiff's failure to disavow defendants' acts immediately on the learning of the facts of the sale was a ratification precluding recovery of damages therefor.—Kendall v. Earl, 5, 351.

Where defendant employed a well driller to drill a well on his ranch and to furnish all required tools, the fact that one of the defendant's employees paid the expressage on certain reamers hired by the driller from plaintiff for use in drilling the well, and agreed to pay $30 toward such hire, without defendant's knowledge, was insufficient to establish that the driller had authority to contract for the reamers on defendant's behalf.—Jones v. Waterman, 7, 316.

§ 5. Delegation of Duties by Agent.

The agreement by the manager of an enterprise of great magnitude to be his cotenant's agent in that connection does not contemplate his devoting always his own personal service to the carrying out of the agency; he may delegate the performance of local services, since his own presence often may be needed elsewhere for the good of all.—Thompson v. Gibb, 1, 173.

§ 6. Lien of Agent for Commissions—Receiver.

The petitioner was employed to superintend a canvass for subscriptions to a publication, and held the subscriptions as security for wages and commissions due to the solicitors and himself; but it appeared that all wages were in fact paid, and that the commissions were not to be paid to the solicitors until the publication was issued. Held, that the petitioner had no right to hold such contracts as against the receiver.—Ex parte Corran, 5, 92.

§ 7. Purchase of Principal's Land by Agent.

An agent, having charge of certain property for an absent firm, was directed to sell it for about $5,000, and, wishing to purchase for himself, reported his acceptance, subject to approval of an offer of $4,500 net, and sent a deed of the property with the grantee's name omitted. The owner executed the deed, and, returning it to the agent through the firm, accepted the agent's check for $4,500, which was the full value of the land. The agent did not understand himself to be in the owner's employ, nor that a selling agent's name could not be written in a deed as grantee without the grantor's consent, but, intending no fraud, entered into possession. Held, that the heirs of the grantor could not set up fraudulent concealment as a ground for ejectment. In any event, the grantee's possession could not be attacked without tendering back the purchase money.—Burke v. Bours, 3, 393.

§ 8. Fraud and Deceit of Agent.

Plaintiff authorized defendant to buy for him land from one B. for $2,750, agreeing to pay one-third cash, one-third in six months, and the balance in a year. Thereafter defendant represented that B. would not sell except for one-half cash and the balance in a year; that he had taken a deed to himself on those terms, and would convey to plaintiff on the terms agreed on between them. He then forwarded a contract of sale to plaintiff and drew on him for $916.66. Plaintiff executed the contract and paid the draft. Defendant's representation as to his purchase of the land from B. was false, B. having agreed to sell it to another for $1,375. Held, that plaintiff could recover the amount paid on the draft.—Ritchey v. McMichael, 4, 384.

In such case the relation of principal and agent existed between plaintiff and defendant, and the latter was accountable for the money paid him by plaintiff to carry out the purposes of the agency.—Ritchey v. McMichael, 4, 384.

§ 9. Liability on Contract Made by Agent.

A contract by an agent cannot bind the principal if it does not show on its face that someone other than the signer is intended to be bound by it.—Sayer v. McNulty, 1, 130.

A contract with plaintiff for an alteration of defendant's house was signed by defendants' daughters, who had no interest in the house, but lived there with defendants. Defendants had actual knowledge of the agreement between plaintiff and their daughters, knew that the work was being performed by plaintiff, and received the benefit thereof. Held, that defendants' daughters were only agents for defendants, and were not liable on the contract signed by them.—Schindler v. Green, 7, 229.

§ 10. Suit by Agent in Own Name.

Where an agent contracts directly as a principal, he may sue on the contract in his own name, regardless of whether the other party knew of his agency.—Tustin Fruit Assn. v. Earl Fruit Co., 6, 37.

§ 11. Pleading Authority of Agent.

A complaint on a contract executed by an agent may, without more, aver its execution by defendant, the principal; and, the agency appearing from the copy of the note set out, authority to execute it is implied, and need not be expressly alleged.—Goetz v. Goldbaum, 4, 749.

§ 12. Revocation of Authority.

Liabilities incurred by an agent on behalf of his principal after the termination of the agency, in favor of one having no notice of the revocation of the agency, are binding on the principal, though he never ratified the agent's act.—Stockton Ice Co. v. Argonaut Land Dev. Co., 6, 275.

PRINCIPAL AND SURETY.

§ 1. Suretyship in General.

Where A and B, owners in common, join in a conveyance to C by way of collateral for B's sole debt, A becomes a surety; and if thereafter full tender of the secured debt is made, C in the meantime having taken a sheriff's certificate in execution of a judgment in his favor against B for another debt, the rights of the several parties cannot be adjudicated, in the absence of evidence tending to show whose money was tendered; since, if it was A's, A would be subrogated to C's position against B in respect to the first transaction and have a lien on B's interest in the land superior to C's lien under the execution sale.—Pierce v. Hyde, 2, 145.

Where a surety on a note holds security for the payment thereof, the creditor is not bound to require the application of such security to the payment before he can sue the sureties.—Stone v. Hammell, 3, 128.

In an action against sureties for violation of a bond by the principals it is not necessary to allege any violation on the part of the sureties.—Farley v. Moran, 3, 572.

§ 2. Liability on Bond of Secretary of Building Association.

A secretary of a building association executed a bond to well and truly perform and discharge all his official duties, and do all things required by the by-laws, and to perform faithfully all duties required of him, and obey all orders given him by the board of directors. The secretary was confided with the general superintendence of the association's funds, received, cared for. and paid them out, and the performance of these duties by this officer had become the established usage of the association. Held, that his sureties on the bond were liable for moneys of depositors which he had received and entered in their pass-books, but not in the company's books, and converted to his own use; also for moneys taken by him, which had been deposited in the safe for persons who had borrowed the same; and also for moneys taken from the association and converted, he forging a receipt for the same in the name of a third person.—Humboldt Savings etc. Soc. v. Wennerhold, 3, 52.

§ 3. Liability on Treasurer's Bond—Limitation of Actions.

Defendant H. gave a bond as city treasurer for the faithful discharge of official duties then or thereafter imposed on him. As such treasurer he received money arising from the sale of certain street bonds, under Statutes of 1875-76, page 443, authorizing the widening of a certain street and providing (section 11) that the treasurer "shall receive and safely keep the same as moneys belonging to said city and county are kept," and designating a separate fund therefor. A warrant—No. 92—on an award for damages to a certain lot was issued to one A. as owner, without knowledge of plaintiff's claim of interest therein, but on the discovery of such claim another warrant—No. 114—was issued to the owner or owners of said lot, and notice thereof given to defendant H. The money was illegally paid by defendant's deputy on warrant No. 92; and the fund was sufficient to pay only a part of plaintiff's share under warrant No. 114. Held, that the sureties on the bond were liable for the residue.—Priet v. De La Montanya, 3, 122.

Where the evidence showed that at the end of the official term for which the bond sued on was given the principal had on hand $24,962.91 in the fund, against which there were no legal demands prior to warrant No. 114 for $10,932, a finding that there was a balance of $1,800 in said fund is against the evidence, if it relates to the first term of the treasurer, and if it relates to the end of his second term, it is beyond the issues pleaded.—Priet v. De La Montanya, 3, 122.

Where plaintiffs, whose cause of action depended on warrant No. 114, payment of which could not be enforced until the conflicting claims between them and the lot owner were finally determined, commenced their action within seven months after such determination, though more than four years after the illegal payment by the treasurer, their right of action was not barred by Code of Civil Procedure, section 337, providing that actions upon any contract, obligation, or liability founded upon an instrument in writing shall be commenced within four years.—Priet v. De La Montanya, 3, 122.

In an emergency to meet a pay-roll of $1,878, a corporation's treasurer obtained $600 of its funds from one of its officers, and paid it to the secretary, the disbursing agent, receiving his receipt therefor, and its president paid $600 of his own money direct to the same agent. Subsequently the board of directors, upon the account of the pay-roll, ordered warrants drawn for a check of $600 to repay the president, and one of $1,278 for cash, which warrants were presented by the secretary, and were honored by the treasurer, as he was in duty bound to do. In the books the treasurer charged himself with the $600 received from the officer, and credited himself with the amount disbursed on the pay-roll. He did not charge himself with the money received from the president, which did not come into his hands, but credited himself with the check of $600, to repay the president, and the check of $1,278. Held, not to show any shortage on the part of the treasurer.—Mechanics' Institute v. Firth, 5, 721.

§ 4. Action Against Principal by Surety.

Where the maker of a note, gives his sureties a mortgage to secure its payment, and the property is sold and the proceeds applied on the note, the maker cannot dispute the satisfaction of such mortgage in an action against him by a surety who has paid part of the note.—Stone v. Hammell, 3, 128.

The records of a probate court, showing the insolvency of a deceased surety who had not contributed to the payment of the note, are admissible in evidence in an action by a cosurety against the principal.—Stone v. Hammell, 3, 128.

Under Civil Code, section 2848, providing that a surety, upon paying the principal's debt, is entitled to enforce all the creditor's rights of action against the principal for the amount so expended, and to require his cosureties to contribute thereto, a cosurety, having so contributed by giving his own note to the paying surety, is entitled to reimbursement from the principal precisely as if he had paid the money to the creditor.—Stone v. Hammell, 3, 128.

§ 5. Contribution from Cosurety—Limitations.

A surety who has paid a note and received contribution from a cosurety is not a necessary party to a suit by the latter against the principal for the amount contributed.—Stone v. Hammell, 3, 128.

Code of Civil Procedure, section 339, provides that an action on a contract not in writing must be brought within two years. Section 351 provides that when the right of action against a party accrues during his absence from the state, the action may be brought within the time limited after his return. Held, that the surety's right of action for contribution against a cosurety who was absent from the state when the note was paid, accrued on his return, and the cosurety's right of action against the prinicpal accrued on his giving his note for the amount of such contribution within two years after returning.—Stone v. Hammell, 3, 128.

§ 6. Release of Surety.

A surety is released if, without notice to him, the creditor gives the principal debtor an extension.—Donlan v. Parrott, 1, 37.

A surety is not discharged by the acceptance by the creditor of a security merely cumulative to that he had before, although the consent of the surety may not have been received beforehand.—Post v. Eaton, 1, 287.

PRISONERS.

See Convicts.

PRIVATE ROADS.

Laying out and establishing. See Eminent Domain, § 2.

PROBABLE CAUSE.

See Malicious Prosecution, § 2.

PROBATE HOMESTEAD.

See Homestead, §§ 4, 7.

PROBATE LAW.

See Executors and Administrators; Guardian and Ward; Wills.

PROCESS.

§ 1. Requisites of summons and service thereof.
§ 2. —— Service on one defendant.
§ 2½. —— Service on corporation.
§ 3. Constructive service or publication of summons—Affidavit.
§ 4. Return or affidavit of service.
§ 5. Fees for serving—City marshal.
§ 6. Loss of original summons.

Service in forcible detainer. See Forcible Entry and Detainer, § 6.
Vacating judgment because of defective service. See Judgments, § 18.
Service by officer after term of office. See Sheriffs and Constables, § 3.
Service in action to enforce tax. See Taxation, § 17.

§ 1. Requisites of Summons and Service Thereof.

A summons directed to a man, naming him, and to his wife, she being identified in it by her given name only and the words "his wife" following, is a good summons, though the complaint in the action does not aver that the woman thus named is the wife of the man;

and service of it upon the woman secures jurisdiction of her person.—Pacific Mutual Life Ins. Co. v. Bugbey, 1, 871.

If a woman whose Christian name is Henrietta is sued under the initial H. and the sheriff returns the summons as served "by delivering to Harriet .... one of the defendants sued as H. ....," and it does not appear that Henrietta was served at all, judgment thereupon will not affect the latter or her property.—Porter v. Garrissino, 2, 6.

§ 2. —— Service on One Defendant.

Irregular service of process upon a defendant does not relieve a codefendant, regularly served, from the judgment in the case rendered subsequently.—Drake v. Duvenick, 1, 678.

Under the practice prevailing by statute in 1856, if several defendants resided within three miles of the county seat of the county in which suit was brought, service of the complaint upon one of them was service upon all.—Drake v. Duvenick, 1, 678.

§ 2½. —— Service on Corporation.

The statute which provides that process against a corporation may be served upon "an agent," in this state, of such corporation, is satisfied by a return making it appear that the service was made upon "the managing agent of the defendant."—Dodge v. Mariposa Co., 1, 398.

§ 3. Constructive Service or Publication of Summons—Affidavit.

When a mode of service of process, other than personal service, is adopted, a strict compliance with the conditions imposed by the statute must be shown, or the service will be bad.—In re Bowen, 1, 293.

A proof of service by mail that fails to state that the party for whom the service was to be made resides in the place of the mailing, and that the party upon whom the service was to be made resides in the place of the address, is defective under the statute.—In re Bowen, 1, 293.

It cannot, on appeal, be said that the court erred in construing its order for publication of summons in the "San Diego Union" as referring to the "San Diego Union and Daily Bee," in which it was published.—People v. McFadden, 7, 191.

The requirement in an order for publication of summons that it be published for two months must yield to Political Code, section 3549, making four weeks' publication sufficient; so that it is enough that it was published four weeks.—People v. McFadden, 7, 191.

Where an affidavit for the service of summons by publication stated that the summons had been placed in the hands of the sheriff of the county for service, that the sheriff had returned the same with his return indorsed thereon to the effect that he could not find the defendant within the county, and that affiant did not know the residence of defendant, etc., it was sufficient to justify the court in ordering service by publication.—Weis v. Cain, 7, 168.

§ 4. Return or Affidavit of Service.

See, also, ante, § 3.

An affidavit of service of summons by a person other than the sheriff should state that such person was over the age of eighteen years at the time of the service, else a judgment rendered thereon by default will be reversed on appeal.—Weill v. Bent, 2, 141.

An affidavit of service of summons is not fatally defective because it does not state that the parties on whom it was served were resi-

dents of the county where served. If it states that they were served
in that county, it will be presumed, nothing to the contrary appearing, that they resided in the county in which they were served
with process.—Pellier v. Gillespie, 2, 407.

Where a return of service of summons by a constable was not verified as required by Code of Civil Procedure, section 410, it was ineffective.—Berentz v. Kern King Oil & Dev. Co., 7, 214.

§ 5. Fees for Serving—City Marshal.

Act of March 13, 1883, section 790 (Stats. 1883, p. 261), as amended
by Statutes of 1893, page 299, provides, with reference to municipal
corporations of the fifth class, that the city marshal shall execute
and return all process issued and directed to him by any legal
authority; that he shall, for service of any process, receive the same
fees as constables, and shall receive from the city such compensation
as shall be fixed by ordinance, in addition to the fees and mileage
received for service of process in the state courts. Penal Code,
section 817, makes marshals peace officers, and section 814 provides
that warrants of arrest shall run "to any marshal," among other
officers. Held, that fees earned by a marshal in serving a process
issuing out of a justice's court for the township in which the city
is situated are chargeable to the county.—Carlisle v. Tulare County,
5, 701.

Section 790 contains the condition that the marshal shall receive
a compensation from the city in addition to the fees and mileage
received "for service of process of the courts of this state, other
than the recorder's court of such city." Under the municipal corporation act the recorder may be a justice of the peace as to some
matters, and a recorder as to others. When acting as a justice in
criminal matters coming before him under the Penal Code, his fees
are chargeable to the county. Held, that, where the recorder is
acting as justice of the peace, the marshal's fees for service of process issuing out of the recorder's court in misdemeanor cases under
the statutes of the state are chargeable to the county.—Carlisle v.
Tulare County, 5, 701.

§ 6. Loss of Original Summons.

If a summons has in fact been served, jurisdiction of the person
of the defendant has been secured even though the original is lost
after service.—Pacific Mutual Life Ins. Co. v. Bugbey, 1, 871.

If, after the service of a summons, the original has been lost, it
is competent to show the contents of the summons by secondary
evidence.—Pacific Mutual Life Ins. Co. v. Bugbey, 1, 871.

PROHIBITION.

§ 1. When Available as Remedy.

The enforcement of a writ of assistance, as against one not a party
to the action, cannot be restrained by a writ of prohibition, as there
is in such case an adequate remedy at law by appeal from the order
granting writ.—Childs v. Edmunds, 2, 649.

Writ of prohibition denied in contempt case.—Kelly v. Wilson, 2,
655,

Under the constitutional provision that actions for the recovery of real estate shall be commenced in the county in which it is situated, a writ of prohibition will issue to a court entertaining such an action, for real estate outside the county, though an accounting is also asked as to the rents and profits, and though various proceedings had been had in the action, without any question as to the jurisdiction of the court.—Grangers' Bank of California v..Superior Court, 4, 130.

§ 2. —— In Criminal Cases.

Where defendant had been tried and convicted on an indictment that was void, a writ of prohibition will issue to prevent the trial judge from pronouncing sentence of further proceeding in the case, under Code of Civil Procedure, section 1103, providing that such writ may issue where there is no speedy and adequate remedy at law.— Terrill v. Superior Court, 6, 398.

Where a judgment in a criminal case was reversed, and the case remanded for new trial, a writ of prohibition will not issue to prohibit such retrial on the ground that it appeared from the record that the jury before whom defendant was once tried was discharged without a verdict, without his consent and without necessity, and that consequently he had once been in jeopardy, since the remanding of the case for new trial was the final law on appeal, and defendant could make his defense of former jeopardy by plea on the trial.— Arnett v. Superior Court, 6, 416.

§ 3. —— Remedy by Appeal.

A writ of prohibition does not lie in a case open to appeal.—Luce v. Superior Court, 2, 167.

Writ of prohibition denied on the ground that the proper remedy is by appeal.—Mancello v. Bellrude, 2, 662.

Writ of prohibition will not be granted, where, by appeal, which can be advanced to a speedy hearing, the whole case can be taken up and reasonably decided on the merits.—Herbert v. Superior Court, 7, 336.

§ 4. Matters of Practice.

Where respondent to petition for writ of prohibition filed a demurrer and answer, and the demurrer was overruled, and judgment absolute given against respondent on the insufficiency of his answer, when, in the absence of a motion for judgment on the pleadings, he expected that only the demurrer would be passed on, a motion to vacate the decision on the ground of surprise, and to allow an amended answer, will be granted.—Heilbron v. Campbell, 5, 745.

§ 5. Effect of Refusal of Writ.

Where a writ of prohibition is asked to restrain a court from proceeding on the ground that it has no jurisdiction, the denial of the writ, without any decision on such question, does not take away the right to have it considered on writ of review.—Santa Monica v. Eckert, 4, 92.

PROMISSORY NOTES.
See Bills and Notes.

PROSECUTING ATTORNEY.
See District Attorney.

PROSTITUTION.

§ 1. Sufficiency of Evidence.

Judgment held not sustained by the evidence.—People v. Murray, 2, 356.

Conviction of enticement of female held not sustained by the evidence.—People v. Powellson, 2, 474.

PROTEST.

Of negotiable paper. See Bills and Notes, § 14.

PUBLIC ADMINISTRATOR.

§ 1. Compensation.

When a next kin appears and takes an estate out of the hands of the public administrator, the latter is to receive compensation as in any other case where an administrator has been removed and another appointed after a partial administration of estate.—Estate of Simmons, 1, 682.

§ 2. Bar of Statute of Limitations.

The bar of the statute of limitations, as to lands in the hands of a public administrator, is not complete against one with a right of entry until two years after their passing out of his hands.—Simmons v. Hollub, 1, 829.

PUBLIC IMPROVEMENTS.

See Municipal Corporations, §§ 19, 44.

PUBLIC LANDS.

§ 1. In general.
§ 2. Mexican grants—Conflicting titles—Quieting title.
§ 3. Possession—Ejectment.
§ 4. Townsite—Construction of statutes.
§ 5. —— Payment and deed—Quieting title.
§ 6. Ouster and abandonment.
§ 7. Locating on unsurveyed lands.
§ 8. Lands patentable by state.
§ 9. Declaratory statement—Failure to file.
§ 10. Applications to purchase.
§ 11. —— Curative statute of 1868.
§ 12. Necessity of residence by pre-emptor.
§ 13. Contests and determination of rights.
§ 14. Certificate of purchase.
§ 15. Death of entryman.
§ 16. —— Patent to executor.
§ 17. Conveyance or contract therefor before patent obtained.
§ 18. Conveyance subject to mortgage.
§ 19. Patent—Conditions precedent to issuance.
§ 20. —— Mandamus to governor to issue.
§ 21. —— Authority to issue.

See State Lands.

School lands. See Schools and School Districts, § 1.

§ 1. In General.

In actions involving rights of holders under the United States land laws, the transmission of the plat to the register by the surveyor general on a day named and its reception by the register on the succeeding day, together with the publication by the register and receiver in a public journal of a notice to settlers, requiring them to file their declaratory statements, are facts sufficient for a jury finding fixing the time when the plat was officially filed.—Megerle v. Ashe, 1, 659.

If it is proved that a plaintiff had all qualifications of a pre-emption claimant, had filed his declaratory statement within three months after the official filing of the plat, had taken the other necessary steps to pre-empt the premises, and had procured the issue of a patent to himself, it is immaterial whether warrants for school lands in the defendant's name were properly located or not, or whether the patent was duly issued.—Megerle v. Ashe, 1, 659.

The records of the state land office furnish the data for ascertaining with accuracy what lands have been sold and what unsold within any particular district, and in seeking to establish a new district this statutory requirement ought to be so complied with as to need no aid of presumption to supply deficiencies in the averments of the petition.—Hagar v. Supervisors of Yolo Co., 1, 770.

Unless affected by some valid pre-emption right, the title to land included within a sixteenth section vested in the state, upon approval of the survey of the township, under the act of Congress granting sixteenth and thirty-sixth sections.—Morrow v. Kingsbury, 1, 884.

Code of Civil Procedure, section 764, provides that when it appears, in an action of partition, that one or more of the tenants in common has conveyed in fee to another person a specific part of the common land, the land so conveyed shall be allotted in partition to such purchaser, etc., if such tract can be so allotted without material injury to the other cotenants. Held, that such purchaser's right to file upon an "adjoining farm homestead" under Revised Statutes of the United States, sections 2289, 2290, cannot be defeated by the possibility that, on the partition, other land adjoining that filed upon may be allotted him, instead of the specific part conveyed to him.—McHarry v. Stewart, 4, 408.

§ 2.   Mexican Grants—Conflicting Titles—Quieting Title.

See, also, Mexican Grants.

A decree of the United States circuit court, confirming a Mexican grant of lands, described them as a tract lying above high-water mark, bounded on three sides by the sea, and on the other by a direct line to be so run as to include the required quantity. The patent, issued by virtue of the authority of the decree and in pursuance thereof, granted a tract of land described by courses and distances which, if followed, would include a large tract lying below high-water mark, to which the state claimed title by virtue of act of Congress of September 28, 1850. Held, in an action by the state to quiet its title, that the patent was not conclusive, but that the decree, by virtue of which it was issued, was entitled to be read in connection therewith in determining what lands were conveyed, and that the natural boundaries called for in the decree would overrule the courses and distances of the patent.—People v. San Francisco, 2, 812.

In an action to determine an adverse claim to certain lands wherein the state was plaintiff, the complaint alleged that the lands were below high-water mark, and consequently belonged to the plaintiff as swamp lands, by virtue of act of Congress of September 28, 1850; that the defendant, as successor in interest to a Mexican citizen, obtained a decree from the United States circuit court, confirming its title to a tract of land described as included between certain boundaries, and as lying above high-water mark. The patent, issued by virtue of this decree, described a tract of land by courses and distances which, if followed, would include the lands in dispute. Held, that the complaint stated a good cause of action, in that if the allegations were true the plaintiff would be entitled to a decree, and a demurrer thereto should be overruled.—People v. San Francisco, 2, 812.

The Mexican government granted a certain described tract of land, known as "Las Positas," in 1839, which afterward became a part of the state of California, "containing in all two square leagues." A survey of it was made by the surveyor general, which showed that ten leagues were included within the description. This survey was set aside by the Secretary of the Interior, on the ground that it contained more land than was called for in the grant, and a new survey was made, and approved by the Secretary of the Interior in 1871, and a patent for the two leagues issued upon this last survey in 1872. Held, that the grant was sub judice until the final survey was approved by the Secretary of the Interior, and a title to land contained within the exterior limits of the Mexican grant, claimed through a United States patent to a railroad company in 1862, was void.—Carr v. Quigley, 2, 823.

The Mexican government granted a certain described tract of land, which afterward became a part of the state of California, "containing in all two leagues," and it actually contained ten leagues. The survey of the two leagues was made, and approved by the Secretary of the Interior in 1871, and a patent issued in 1872. Upon an action in ejectment by a person who claimed title to land within the limits of the grant, through a patent from Congress to a railroad company in 1862, held, that the defendant was not affected by opinions of the commissioner and the Secretary of the Interior, in proceedings in the land office to which he was not a party, to the effect that a preliminary survey made in 1854, but never approved by the Secretary of the Interior, established the exterior limits of the Mexican grant.—Carr v. Quigley, 2, 823.

§ 3. Possession in Ejectment.

Public lands of the United States, in the actual occupation and exclusive possession of one party, are not subject to pre-emption or homestead settlement by another.—Bishop v. Glassen, 5, 744.

A judicial decree, followed by possession under a bona fide claim, is color of title, within the meaning of act of Congress of February 25, 1885, prohibiting inclosures of public lands unless under "claim or color of title made or acquired in good faith," and, such possession having lasted for twenty-five years, the holder can maintain ejectment against persons assuming to enter on the premises as being "public lands of the United States."—Los Angeles Farming etc. Co. v. Hoff, 4, 294.

In ejectment to recover possession of public land, plaintiff claimed under a deed from D., who occupied the land without color or claim of title. There was no evidence of any act of possession on plaintiff's part, and several witnesses testified that defendants were in possession of the land in July, 1889. Held, that the evidence did not support a finding that D. sold and delivered possession to plaintiff in August.—Daubenbiss v. White, 3, 590.

§ 4. Townsite—Construction of Statutes.

Revised Statutes of the United States, section 2322 (U. S. Comp. Stats. 1901, p. 1425), confers on the locator of a mining claim a possessory title. Section 2324 (U. S. Comp. Stats. 1901, p. 1426) requires such locator to do a certain amount of work annually. Section 2386 (U. S. Comp. Stats. 1901, p. 1457) subjects townsite titles to whatever possessory right in the locator is recognized by local authority, as does also Statutes of 1867–68, page 696, section 10, so long as the locator shall comply with the laws. Section 2392 (U. S. Comp. Stats. 1901, p. 1459) provides that no town lot title shall be acquired "to any mine of gold, silver, cinnabar or copper, or to any valid mining claim or possession held under existing laws." Section

2387 (U. S. Comp. Stats. 1901, p. 1457) authorizes townsite lands to
be conveyed to occupants, and the balance to be sold, or otherwise
disposed of. Held that, construing section 2392 (U. S. Comp. Stats.
1901, p. 1459) in the light of previous legislation which it embodies
(Acts March 2, 1867, 14 Stat. 541 (U. S. Comp. Stats. 1901, p. 1460),
and June 8, 1868 (15 Stat. 67), showing that the intent was merely
to confer on mining titles acquired from the United States the same
superior quality given by section 2386, enacted March 2, 1865 (U. S.
Comp. Stats. 1901, p. 1457), to those recognized by local authority,
and construing it also in view of section 2387 (U. S. Comp. Stats.
1901, p. 1457), showing an intent that the entire townsite be disposed of, and also in view of its own wording, the clause, "or to any
valid mining claim or possession held under existing laws," must be
taken to refer to the possessory title conferred by section 2322 (U.
S. Comp. Stats. 1901, p. 1426), and not to any mine subject to a
valid claim or possession; and hence locators, whose claim had been
patented as a townsite, and who afterward failed to do the work
required by section 2324 (U. S. Comp. Stats. 1901, p. 1426), thereby
lost, under section 2386 (U. S. Comp. Stats., p. 1457), and Statutes
of 1867–68, page 696, section 10, their paramount title.—Callahan v.
James, 7, 82.

Even if the clause, "or to any valid mining claim or possession,"
be construed as applying to any mine subject to such claim or possession, the effect would be the same, since, construing it in connection with the previous clause, "to any mine of gold, silver," etc.,
"any valid claim or possession," must be a valuable mine, and not
a mere worthless claim, as, for aught that appeared, the one in suit
was.—Callahan v. James, 7, 82.

§ 5. —— Payment and Deed—Quieting Title.

In a suit to quiet title it was found that the trustee of a townsite platted on public lands of the United States executed deeds to
persons whose names appeared on the official map as being entitled
thereto, who had not previously obtained conveyances, and, among
others, to defendant's predecessor; and that the trustee left "all of
said deeds so executed" with one T. Held, that this was sufficient
to show delivery, since, if not to be regarded as express finding
thereof, delivery was to be inferred therefrom.—Callahan v. James,
7, 82.

In a suit to quiet title, the omission of a finding that defendant's
predecessor paid the purchase money for a town lot to the trustee of
a townsite is immaterial, it appearing from the evidence that the
money was paid by another for him.—Callahan v. James, 7, 82.

Statutes of 1867–68, page 696, section 24, relating to conveyances
of townsite lots platted on public lands, provides that every certifi
cate or deed granted to any person pursuant to the act shall be taken
as conclusive evidence that all preliminary proceedings have been
correctly performed. Held, that the payment of the purchase money
would be presumed from the fact of conveyance, and hence the omission of a finding thereof in a suit to quiet title was immaterial.—Callahan v. James, 7, 82.

Civil Code, section 870, provides that, when a trust in relation to
real property is expressed in the instrument creating the estate, a
deed in contravention of the trust is void. Statutes of 1867–68, page
696, section 15, relating to the conveyance of the lots of a townsite
platted on public lands, provides for the sale of unoccupied or vacant
land to possessors of adjoining lands or other citizens of the town,
and, if any lands remain unsold at the end of six months after filing
the plat, they are to be sold at auction. A federal statute provides that
any act of the townsite trustees not in conformity to the regulations

prescribed by the legislative authority of the state shall be void. Held, that the trustee's deed was sufficient to convey the legal title, though made to one who is not an occupant of the land.—Callahan v. James, 7, 82.

Statutes of 1867–68, page 696, section 15, authorizes conveyances of the lots of a townsite platted on public land, being unoccupied, to possessors of adjoining land, or other citizens of the town. Held, that it could not be inferred from findings in a suit to quiet title that defendant's predecessor was never "in possession of any part or portion" of the lot in controversy, that he was not an occupant, or otherwise qualified to receive a conveyance.—Callahan v. James, 7, 82.

§ 6. Ouster and Abandonment.

An occupant of public land who is ousted by a stranger will not be presumed to have abandoned his right to possession, where, after a contest for a year, he ceases to contend against a superior force maintaining an armed resistance.—Daubenbiss v. White, 3, 590.

§ 7. Locating on Unsurveyed Lands.

A purchaser under a certificate of purchase acquires no rights by the certificate when the lands described in the latter have not, at the date of its issue, been as yet surveyed.—Flint v. Bell, 1, 650.

If one locating upon unsurveyed lands and not entering upon them fails, within three months after the filing of the township map with the register, to present his claim to the lands, he loses all rights, as against a person who has in the meantime entered upon the lands and duly filed his declaratory statement as a pre-emption claimant.— Flint v. Bell, 1, 650.

§ 8. Lands Patentable by State.

The law gives the state no authority to issue patents for lands to which it has not acquired title from the United States, and a patent by it issued for any such lands is void.—Avery v. Black Diamond Coal Min. Co., 1, 873.

Land selected by the state in lieu of a sixteenth section reversed from the operation of the United States law granting it school lands is patentable by it only after being first listed or certified over to it by the general government.—Avery v. Black Diamond Coal Min. Co., 1, 873.

§ 9. Declaratory Statement—Failure to File.

The failure by a pre-emptor, having the requisite qualifications as such and living on the land, to file his declaratory statement in season would not, where there is no rival claimant to the land, disable him from becoming a pre-emptor de novo.—Megerle v. Ashe, 1, 756.

§ 10. Applications to Purchase.

An application for the purchase of lands from the state, under the act of 1868, was required to state that there were at the time no improvements on the land applied for other than such as were owned by the applicant.—Copp v. Harrington, 1, 753.

The facts required to be stated, on application for a certificate of purchase of state lands under the act of 1868, the law intended should be stated under oath.—Copp v. Harrington, 1, 753.

An application to purchase public land must be filed with the register, and, if the aim is to purchase by private entry, the application must be in writing; to this that official appends his certificate that the tract is subject to such entry, and his specification of the price, after which it is by the applicant, when making payment, delivered to the receiver, who then gives duplicate receipts, one of which is returned to the register, who next transmits it to the commissioner of the general land office, after first issuing a certificate of purchase to the applicant; the other duplicate is retained by the applicant, to be surrendered on his receiving his patent thereafter.—Figg v. Handley, 2, 23.

In applications to purchase public lands under the pre-emption laws, the declaratory statement must be filed with the register, but the proof must be made to the satisfaction of both him and the receiver, the latter then issuing duplicate receipts, one of which is retained by the applicant and the other delivered to the register, as in the case of a private entry. After this, however, the proofs and the decision thereon of the two officials are, with the duplicate receipt held by the register, forwarded to the commissioner of the general land office, and he, on approving the decision mentioned, issues the patent to the applicant on surrender of the duplicate retained by him.—Figg v. Handley, 2, 23.

§ 11. —— Curative Statute of 1868.

Where an application for the purchase of land from the state, under the act of 1868, was defective in failing to state that no improvements other than those of the applicant were on the land and also in failing to have all its statements made under oath, it became valid nevertheless by the curative act of 1870 in all cases where there were not two or more claimants to the land and where there was no conflict between claimants.—Copp v. Harrington, 1, 753.

The act of 1870, curing defects in applications for the purchase of state lands under the law of 1868, did not make the application any better or give it any higher grade or character than it would have possessed had it conformed to the law at the time it was filed.—Copp v. Harrington, 1, 753.

There is a clerical error in the act of 1868 where it is said, "Whenever any resident of the state desires to purchase any of the other lands mentioned in section 52 of this act," the mention being intended to be in section 51.—Copp v. Harrington, 1, 753.

§ 12. Necessity of Residence by Pre-emptor.

The pre-emption laws require a personal residence on the land; consequently a removal by the claimant to and his residing on other lands is presumptively a forfeiture of the claim.—Farley v. Gleason, 1, 878.

To withhold his pre-emption claim from forfeiture because of his failure to reside actually on the land, an appellant cannot raise the question of justifiable or excusable absence when the record shows the absence to have been voluntary.—Farley v. Gleason, 1, 878.

§ 13. Contests and Determination of Rights.

The act of 1868, regulating the proceedings necessary in the purchase of state lands, does not place a purchaser beyond reach of a contest after being given his certificate of purchase.—Copp v. Harrington, 1, 753.

The statute of 1868, regulating the proceedings necessary in acquiring lands from the state, does not contemplate that a contest may be brought before the surveyor general or register by any person who may choose to interfere, but provides for a contest between conflicting claimants of the land or of the right to purchase and to acquire the title.—Copp v. Harrington, 1, 753.

When one comes before the surveyor general, having himself a defective application for the purchase of lands under the law of 1868, for the purpose of contesting the claim of another to the same lands,

52

such application should not be recognized as raising a contest.—Copp v. Harrington, 1, 753.

Revised Statutes of the United States, section 2273, provides that all questions as to the right of pre-emption, arising between different settlers, shall be determined by the register and receiver of the district within which the land is situated, and for "appeals from the decision of the district officers." Held, that, in the absence of any statute limiting the power of the commissioner of the land office and Secretary of Interior on appeal, the power will not be denied to the commissioner and secretary to decide questions arising on evidence, which were not decided by such district officers.—McHarry v. Stewart, 4, 408.

Where the Secretary of the Interior, in a land contest, decided on the evidence that the residence of a claimant of land as an "adjoining farm homestead," under Revised Statutes of the United States, sections 2289, 2290, on his own land adjoining the tract claimed, was not such as to entitle him to such tract, the supreme court of California has no jurisdiction to review such question in ejectment against such claimant by one claiming the same land under the pre-emption laws of the United States.—McHarry v. Stewart, 4, 408.

§ 14. Certificate of Purchase.

Where, under the act of 1858, a certificate of purchase of certain lands is issued to a person by the state, and it recites that payment in full has been made, such person thus acquires a perfect equity as against the state, and entitles him to the benefit of the statute of limitations from the date of the certificate.—Packard v. Johnson, 2, 365.

The holder of a certificate of purchase from the United States and in possession of the land for fourteen years under claim of right has a title that may not be inquired into in a suit in a state court for an injunction to stay waste.—Ross v. Parvin, 1, 285.

By neither state law, act of Congress, nor regulation of the land office is a "certificate of purchase" defined, nor is it prescribed by either in what cases, under what conditions or by what officer it shall issue; the method in this connection rests upon a custom that has become established.—Figg v. Handley, 2, 23.

In the case of land taken under the pre-emption laws the receiver's duplicate must be held to be a "certificate of purchase, and is in all respects as satisfactory evidence that the proofs were sufficient, and that the applicant has purchased and paid for the land, as though it had been made by the register, and comes fully within the spirit of the statute declaring that certificates of purchase shall be prima facie evidence of title.—Figg v. Handley, 2, 23.

§ 15. Death of Entryman.

20 Stat. 113, relating to patents to timber culture claims, provides that no final certificate or patent shall be issued unless, at the expiration of eight years from the date of entry, the person making such entry, or, if he be dead, his heirs or representatives, shall prove that for not less than eight years they have cultivated such trees as aforesaid. Held, that one who died within two years after entry had an equitable interest in the land, capable of devise, and the title, when perfected, inured to him in whom the equitable title vested at the date of the issue of the patent.—Cooper v. Wilder, 5, 77.

Where a land patent is issued to the heirs of a person who made the entry, the courts should decide to whose benefit it should inure.—Cooper v. Wilder, 5, 77.

§ 16. —— Patent to Executor.

By a confirmation duly had or a patent duly issued to a person as executor or administrator, the legal title vests in him rather than in the equitable owners by reason of inheritance or devise from the decedent.—Sheldon v. Murray, 1, 891.

§ 17. Conveyance or Contract Therefor Before Patent Obtained.

A person in possession of public land may freely make a conveyance of his possession or right, so far as it goes, and the conveyance is as valid as would be one in fee simple; it is sufficient to transfer to his grantee the right of possession as against anyone not connecting himself with the title of the United States.—Slaughter v. Fowler, 1, 850.

A contract for the conveyance of land within a certain time, if the vendor within that time obtain title thereto by patent from the government, for an agreed price—money paid on the purchase price to be repaid to the vendee, without interest, if the vendor fail to obtain a patent—is not void for lack of mutuality or consideration.—Southern Pac. R. Co. v. Allen, 5, 51.

Plaintiff agreed to convey to defendant certain lands, within five years, if he obtained, within that time, title by patent from the government, for one-fifth cash, and the balance secured by mortgage, with interest. If plaintiff failed to obtain title, he was to repay the money paid by defendant, without interest. Pending suit by plaintiff for the interest due on the mortgage, the five years expired without his having obtained patent. Held, that judgment must be rendered determining the rights of the parties as of the time of the expiration of the contract period, and not as of the time of the commencement of the action.—Southern Pac. R. Co. v. Allen, 5, 51.

In an action to recover purchase money paid on contracts for the sale of lands claimed by defendant under grants from the United States, which contracts provided that the money was to be returned in case "it shall finally be determined" that patents shall not issue to the defendant, a finding that neither the supreme court of the United States, nor any court had determined that patents should not issue to the defendants for the land in question was a finding of fact, and not a conclusion of law; the complaint alleging that a contrary finding had been made by the United States supreme court, which allegation was denied.—Anderson v. Southern Pac. R. R. Co., 6, 731.

§ 18. Conveyance Subject to Mortgage.

A pre-emption claimant, before final proof and payment, mortgaged the claim to secure the repayment of money borrowed to perfect her title. After she had entered upon and paid for the land, and had received her certificate of purchase, she conveyed a part of the claim to one H. Held that, as the title acquired by the pre-emptioner from the United States inured to the benefit of the mortgagee when acquired, the conveyance to H. was subject to the mortgage.—Stewart v. Powers, 4, 33.

§ 19. Patent—Conditions Precedent to Issuance.

Before the governor may issue a patent for lands of the state, received from and confirmed by the United States, he must proceed to determine whether the land designated in the certificate of purchase from the register of the state land office, or a part of that land, belongs to the state and has been so confirmed to it, and whether the whole purchase money with interest thereon, as mentioned in the certificate, has been paid.—Lux v. Haight, 1, 622.

§ 20. —— Mandamus to Governor to Issue.

A petition for a peremptory mandate requiring the governor to issue a patent for lands, confirmed to the state by the United States, must allege as fact that the governor has found all the statutory prerequisites for his authority to issue the patent.—Lux v. Haight, 1, 622.

§ 21. —— Authority to Issue.

A patent for land issued without authority is open to collateral attack in an action of ejectment.—Connelly v. Mon Chung, 1, 748.

Act of Congress of 1864, section 7 (13 U. S. Stats. at Large, 334), provides that "it shall be the duty of the surveyor general of California, in making surveys of private land claims finally confirmed, to follow the decree of confirmation as closely as practicable, whenever such decree designates the specific boundaries of the claim; but when such decree designates only the outboundaries within which the quantity confirmed is to be taken, the location shall be made as near as practicable in one tract, and in a compact form, ... and it shall be the duty of the commissioner of the general land office to require a substantial compliance with the directions of this section before approving any plat and survey forwarded to him." Act of Congress of 1851, section 13 (9 U. S. Stats. at Large, 631) provides that "the patent shall issue to the claimant on his presenting to the general land office an authentic certificate of confirmation, and a plot or survey of said land duly certified and approved by the surveyor general, whose duty it shall be to cause all private land claims which shall be finally confirmed to be accurately surveyed and furnish plots of the same." The decree confirming defendant's land claim described the land as "a tract situated within the county of San Francisco, and embracing so much of the extreme upper portion of the peninsula above ordinary high-water mark, ... on which the city of San Francisco is situated, as will contain an area of four square leagues. Said tract being bounded on the north and east by the bay of San Francisco, on the west by the Pacific Ocean, and on the south by a due east and west line drawn so as to include the area aforesaid." The survey made under this decree included by metes and bounds land below the line of ordinary high tide. The patent following the survey described the lands by metes and bounds, but recited the decree of confirmation. Held, in ejectment for the lands below high tide, that the north, east and west boundary lines given in the decree and recited in the patent would prevail over those given in the survey and the granting clause of the patent, as there was no power by which land could be included in the survey and patent, the claim to which had not been confirmed by the decree.—United Land Assn. v. Knight, 3, 211.

PUBLIC OFFICERS.
See Officers.

PUBLICATION.
Of summons. See Process, § 3.

PUEBLO LANDS.
See Municipal Corporations, § 2.

QUANTUM MERUIT.
Complaint in action on. See Pleading, § 2.

QUIETING TITLE.

To mining claim. See Mines and Minerals, § 9.

§ 1. Right to Maintain Action.

In a suit under the statute to determine an adverse claim to real estate the plaintiff must show such a possession as would enable him to maintain the suit, which possession is an actual occupation by himself or tenant so far sufficient that without the aid of a deraignment of paper title he might by an action validly eject a mere intruder from the premises.—Sepulveda v. Haley, 1, 548.

Where in an action to quiet title to land it appears that the title of plaintiff is derived through a fraudulent judgment, it must be made to appear that the parties defrauded, where they had notice of such fraudulent judgment, took proper steps to avoid the consequence of such judgment by filing a motion under section 473, Code of Civil Procedure, to have the fraudulent judgment set aside.—Chielovich v. Krauss, 2, 643.

A bill to quiet title to an undivided interest in land will not lie, as against the grantee of one who has advanced money to clear the property, and taken a deed in the nature of a mortgage as a security for the loan, without payment or tender of the proportionate part of the money loaned.—Tripp v. Duane, 2, 757.

Mere possession of land within the limits of a grant to a railroad company, which had complied with the terms of the grant, but had not received a patent from the United States, will not enable such person to maintain an action to quiet title against the railroad company, where he does not show that he was qualified to take land under the pre-emption or homestead laws, or that he settled on it with the intention of filing a pre-emption or homestead claim.—Charlton v. Southern Pacific R. Co., 4, 157.

Land which had been conveyed in trust for the sole use of the minor son of one of the trustees was, after the minor reached his majority, conveyed by the joint deed of the father and son to the mother, in consideration of love and affection, the second trustee not joining in the conveyance. Held, that, as the purpose of the trust had ceased on the son's becoming of age, his equitable title passed to the grantee, so far as to enable her to maintain suit to quiet title against all persons except the holders of the legal title.—Hayford v. Wallace, 5, 476.

§ 2. Venue of Action.

The answer, as well as the complaint, may be looked to, to determine whether the action is one to quiet title—that is, to determine the right to an easement—within constitution, article 6, section 5, requiring actions to quiet title to real estate to be brought in the county in which the land is situated.—Miller v. Kern County Land Co., 7, 9.

§ 3. Parties.

If one conveys land to another by deed of bargain and sale, then conveys it—or assumes to do so—to another who has notice of the former conveyance and who then conveys to still another, having similar knowledge, he is neither a necessary nor a proper party to a suit to quiet title brought subsequently by the grantee named in the first conveyance.—Ellis v. Judson, 2, 169.

§ 4. Pleading.

Where defendant does not raise the objection that plaintiff has not legal capacity to sue, a finding that plaintiff was under twenty-three years of age at the time of commencing the action is not objectionable on the ground that he may have been under twenty-one years of age, and is sufficient.—Ybarra v. Sylvany, 3, 749.

The complaint in an action to quiet title alleged that the grantor was holding the property against his own deed, and that plaintiff was seised of and holds all the estate, right, title and interest, at law or in equity, which such grantor ever had or could acquire. The answer specifically denied such allegations and alleged the execution of a deed to one B., but asked no affirmative relief. Held, that the pleadings warrant findings and sustain a judgment for defendants.—Savings and Loan Soc. v. Burnett, 4, 701.

It is not necessary for plaintiff in an action to quiet title to certain lands to allege the source of such title, although his title was acquired by adverse possession.—Millett v. Lagomarsino, 4, 883.

In an action to quiet title and for other relief, the complaint is sufficient to support a judgment canceling and setting aside a certificate of redemption issued to defendant where it is alleged that the realty in controversy was never redeemed by anybody from the sale made by the sheriff to plaintiff's grantor, and that defendant was not the successor in interest of the judgment debtor, and not entitled to redeem.—Neale v. Bardue, 5, 413.

§ 5. Disclaimer as to Part of Land.

Where defendant in an action to quiet title disclaims as to part of the land, it is not error for the court to dismiss the action as to such part, instead of giving plaintiff judgment therefor, as such judgment would be merely formal, under Code of Civil Procedure, section 739, which provides that "if the defendant in such action disclaims in his answer any interest or estate in the property . . . . the plaintiff cannot recover costs."—Packer v. Doray, 4, 297.

§ 6. Defenses to Action.

To maintain his title against the grantee of A, B, who with knowledge accepts afterward a deed from A of the same property, cannot set up a failure by the first grantee to pay A the price agreed.—Ellis v. Judson, 2, 169.

A defendant in a suit to quiet title sufficiently connects his title with that of his predecessor, on which he relies, by showing that the predecessor's estate was assigned to his widow, who, with two of the children, conveyed to defendant, though the third child was a minor, and the order assigning the property to the widow might have been in excess of the court's jurisdiction in view of her remarriage, as the title of the two adult heirs vested in defendant, which was sufficient for purposes of defense.—Callahan v. James, 7, 82.

§ 7. Issues and Proof.

In an action to quiet title, where defendant set up that the deed of plaintiff was made to defraud the grantor's creditors, among whom was defendant, an offer by defendant to prove by the grantor, on cross-examination, that while the latter was insolvent he sold certain other land to another person for a nominal consideration, with a view of defrauding his creditors, was properly refused as not legitimate cross-examination.—Hayford v. Wallace, 5, 476.

In an action to determine the rights of the parties in certain land in which plaintiff prayed that she be declared the equitable owner of a one-sixth interest therein on certain payments being made by her, evidence examined, and held sufficient to support the finding of the court, except in regard to credit given plaintiff for a certain sum. McPherson v. Garbutt, 7, 331.

Where, in an action to quiet title, plaintiff alleged that the lot in question was formerly owned by a certain association, and defendants established that they were the successors in interest of such association, defendants, in order to entitle themselves to recover, were not bound to prove title in such association.—Harris v. Harris, 7, 319.

§ 8. —— Presumption of Title.

M. took possession of land in 1861, claimed it as his own, cultivated it regularly, and paid all the taxes. After eleven years he sold to his brother, who took possession, improved the property, and paid the taxes. After five years he conveyed to plaintiff's testator, who took possession, exercised acts of ownership, and held possession till 1881. M. knew of his brother's possession, and knew that he sold to plaintiff's testator, and that the latter was in possession and improving the property, and made no claim to the land, or any protest, till about 1880, when he discovered there was no deed on record of the original conveyances by himself. He then gave a deed of the land to defendant. Held, that there was a presumption of title in M.'s brother, which was not rebutted by the fact that he originally entered under an oral contract of purchase, or by the fact that there was no deed on record conveying to him.—Bryan v. Tormey, 3, 85.

In view of such presumption, it is immaterial that declarations of M. that he had conveyed to his brother were erroneously admitted in evidence.—Bryan v. Tormey, 3, 85.

§ 9. —— Nonsuiting Plaintiff.

In an action to quiet title, plaintiff described the land in question as "the west eighty acres of Pueblo lot numbered 1258, according to the Pasco map of the city of San Diego." As evidence of her title, plaintiff introduced a deed from the city, from which both parties claimed, wherein was conveyed to her a lot described as "being that lot of land containing eighty acres, and situate north of and immediately adjoining the eighty-acre lot granted to P." Plaintiff attempted to prove the location of the lot granted to P., but the only evidence of such grant was an entry in the official books of the city, showing that her petition for a lot had been filed, and the maps put in evidence were such that only a hazardous guess could be arrived at as to the location of the lands she had petitioned for. Plaintiff also put in evidence, in proof of a subsequent grant which it was claimed was made to amend the description of the land in the former deed, a resolution of the city's trustees that eighty acres of land out of the western part of Pueblo lot No. 1258 be deeded to plaintiff, the same having been sold her by a former board, and a deed given without a proper description of the land. The resolution was signed by one of the trustees and the secretary of the board, and the trustee testified that he signed and acknowledged a deed pursuant to the resolution, but did not deliver it, as others were to sign it, and he did not know what became of it. It appeared that the deed was never delivered directly to plaintiff, and that neither she, nor her husband ever saw it or had actual possession of it. No offer was made to prove its contents except by the resolution of the trustees. Plaintiff was never in possession of the lot which she claimed, and never improved it. Held, that she was properly nonsuited.—Israel v. Collins, 3, 753.

§ 10. Findings.

Where defendant pleads that the action is barred by certain specified sections of the Code of Civil Procedure, a finding that plaintiff, at the time of commencing the action, was under the age of twenty-three years, and his cause of action is not barred by either of the sections pleaded, is sufficiently specific.—Ybarra v. Sylvany, 3, 749.

In an action to quiet title, a finding that plaintiff is the owner in fee and entitled to the possession of the described parcel of land is a finding of an ultimate fact, and not a conclusion of law.—Ybarra v. Sylvany, 3, 749.

Where, in a suit to quiet title, plaintiff claimed title by prescription, and it was found that plaintiff had no title, the findings were not open to the criticism because of no express findings as to limitations, inasmuch as the finding of the ultimate fact as to the title included the whole controversy.—Southern California R. Co. v. Slauson, 6, 874.

The pleadings having alleged that plaintiff was the owner in fee of the property, a finding that he was the owner in fee is sufficient to show that fact, though there are probative facts stated tending to show the contrary, but which are not necessarily inconsistent with the fact of plaintiff's ownership, especially where the findings further state that defendant never had any title or interest in or to said land. Bryan v. Tormey, 3, 85.

§ 11. Judgment and Relief.

A judgment in a suit to quiet title has equal efficacy with one in ejectment to establish the rights of the parties.—People v. Davis, 1, 317.

Where defendant claims under a void guardian's deed, and sets up no claim for repayment of money paid, and it does not appear that he paid any for the land, a judgment quieting the title in plaintiff is not erroneous, though no tender of repayment is made.—Ybarra v. Sylvany, 3, 749.

Plaintiff, by a verbal contract with defendant, agreed to convey certain lands to him within five years on the payment of a certain sum. Defendant went into possession, and made improvements. Held, in an action to quiet title, that equity would require plaintiff to convey on payment of the amount due within a specified time, in default of which his title would be quieted.—Schaeffer v. Hofmann, 4, 839.

In an action to quiet title to lands, where no mortgage lien is claimed, and where the answer pleads possession under a contract of sale, and offers payment of the amount due, a judgment declaring the amount due to be a mortgage on the land will be reversed as not warranted by the pleadings.—Schaeffer v. Hofmann, 4, 839.

Where, for twenty-three years previous to an action to quiet title, defendant had maintained a dam across a stream at a point where it intersected the line between his land and the land in controversy, thereby backing the water over a part of the land involved so as to divert it into his ditch, and in the action, while alleging title to the land, he fails to allege a right to flow it, merely alleging riparian rights in the stream, he cannot complain that the judgment declaring that he had no interest in the land, but allowing him to maintain the dam, does not also give him the right to divert the water, and flow plaintiff's land.—California Mortgage & Savings Bank v. Hampton, 6, 301.

§ 12. Appeal and Review.

A judgment in a suit to quiet title in favor of the unsuccessful defendant in a preceding action of ejectment between the same parties is suspended in its operation by an appeal.—People v. Davis, 1, 317.

Findings of the trial court discrediting pretenses advanced to defend the occupancy of land, are not to be disturbed when justified by the evidence.—Forster v. Pico, 1, 841.

Where the decisive question in an action to quiet title is whether a note given for the purchase of the land was intended as an absolute payment, or as an evidence of debt, and the evidence is conflicting, a finding that it was merely evidence of debt will not be disturbed.—Frankish v. Smith, 3, 33.

A complaint to quiet title alleged that plaintiff was the owner and in possession of the property. The findings were that plaintiff was the owner, but that defendant was in possession, and judgment was rendered that plaintiff's title be quieted, and that defendant be removed from possession. Under Code of Civil Procedure, section 380, the action may be maintained by one not in possession. Held, that though the judgment was in direct contradiction to the complaint, it would be modified on appeal so as to omit the part relating to possession, and would be thus affirmed, without costs to either party.—Bryan v. Tormey, 3, 85.

Whether the findings in a suit to quiet title sustain a judgment giving defendant restitution of possession cannot be examined on an appeal from an order denying a motion for a new trial.—Southern California R. Co. v. Slauson, 6, 874.

Where, in a suit to quiet title, plaintiff and his grantor claimed title by adverse possession, and there was an irreconcilable conflict in the evidence as to whether plaintiff's grantor had furnished the money with which the property was bought, the findings of the lower court on such question will not be disturbed on appeal.—Williams v. Gross, 6, 477.

QUITCLAIM DEED.

In general. See Deeds, § 2.

QUO WARRANTO.   •

See Franchises.

Annulment of corporate charter. See Corporations, § 3.

§ 1. Pleading and Proof.

In quo warranto proceedings for usurpation of a corporation franchise, if the verified complaint alleges facts showing the illegality of the pretended corporation, such facts must be specifically denied by the answer, and a denial of the legal conclusions drawn from the facts merely is not sufficient.—People v. Lowden, 2, 537.

In a proceeding for usurpation of franchise of a corporation, the burden of proof is on the defendants to show that the corporation was legally formed, and that its existence is legal, and in such proceeding the answer should set forth the facts showing the same.— People v. Lowden, 2, 537.

§ 2. Estoppel to Maintain.

The fact that the person on whose relation the proceeding of quo warranto, for usurpation of a corporate franchise, was instituted was at one time acting as an officer of the alleged corporation, will not operate as an estoppel against the maintenance of the action by the attorney general.—People v. Lowden, 2, 537.

§ 3. Prior Proceedings as Bar.

Proceedings brought by the attorney general to determine the rights of defendants to exercise a franchise as a corporation are not barred by a prior application for a writ of mandate to compel a board of supervisors to fix rates of toll to be taken on a road claimed by the alleged corporation.—People v. Lowden, 2, 537.

QUORUM.

Of directors. See Corporations, § 6.

RAILROADS.

§ 1. Acquisition of right of way—Adverse possession.
§ 2. —— Interpretation of conveyance of land for right of way.
§ 3. Contract for railway construction.
§ 4. Unauthorized construction—Injunction.
§ 5. Construction and damages arising therefrom.
§ 6. Bond to build fence.
§ 7. Killing stock—Fences.
§ 8. Speed of trains—Ordinance limiting.
§ 9. Signals on approaching crossings.
§ 10. Injury to persons at crossings—Contributory negligence.
§ 11. Injury to persons on right of way—Licenses.
§ 12. Injury to person lying on track.
§ 13. Liability for fires—Pleading and proof.
See Carriers; Street Railways.

Subsidy to. See Counties, § 7.
Forfeiture of right of way. See Forfeiture, § 1.
Injury to employees. See Master and Servant, § 6.
Subscription to railroad stock by city. See Municipal Corporations, § 8.
Double taxation. See Taxation, § 2.

§ 1. Acquisition of Right of Way—Adverse Possession.

On an issue whether a railroad has acquired title to land by adverse possession, evidence that the person whom it had authorized to obtain rights of way for its road had an interview with the land owner, at which the latter agreed that the railroad might enter the land and lay its tracks thereon, provided it put in a station, and that on such performance the owner would make a deed of the right of way, was admissible, although there was no written contract to show that the railroad entered the land under the owner's permission, and not hostilely.—Southern California R. Co. v. Slauson, 6, 874.

A railroad company and a land owner agreed that, if the former would lay its tracks over the land, and put in a station, the owner would make a deed of the right of way; and thereafter the road was built and operated, but no station was built, nor did trains stop on the land. Held, that, the railroad having gone into possession under permission and in consonance with the owner's title, which it was not to have until the performance of conditions which had not been performed, the possession of the railroad was not adverse to the owner. Southern California R. Co. v. Slauson, 6, 874.

§ 2. —— Interpretation of Conveyance of Land for Right of Way.

A conveyance to a railroad company of the right of way for its road, as located, constructed and operated on the highway in front of the grantor's premises, to wit, on Third street, "for the full length and frontage of lots 23 and 24 in block 25," of a certain survey, and also the right to use "such street" for railroad purposes, with an acknowledgment of payment for "all damages sustained by me by reason of the construction of said railroad upon said street, and by reason of the operation thereof, and particularly . . . . for damages for any injury caused by the construction of said railroad in front of my property hereinbefore described," is a grant only of the right of way in front of the two lots; and the damages for which satisfaction is acknowledged are limited to those which had been sustained by construction and operation of the road in front of such lots, and do not apply to· damages afterward sustained by reason of a defective bridge on the road, not in front of the lots.—McDonald v. Southern California Ry. Co., 5, 142.

§ 3. Contract for Railway Construction. .

A contract for railroad construction is not to be interpreted in such a way as to make the contractor receive for the most difficult and expensive part of the work less pay than for the less expensive part.— McGlynn v. Central R. R. Co., 1, 464.

Where a contract for constructing a railroad embankment provided that additional dirt, not exceeding a certain quantity, should be added for shrinkage, the exact percentage to be specified by the company's engineer, and that payment for such embankment should be made by measurement of the material in the embankment, excluding that added for shrinkage, the amount designated by the engineer to be added for such shrinkage up to the limit specified is conclusive, even though the shrinkage be less.—Scanlan v. San Francisco & San Joaquin Valley Ry. Co., 6, 210.

Where the construction of a railroad embankment was to be paid for by an actual measurement of the cubic contents of the embankment, and the contractor completed it without making a survey or objecting to the one made by the company's engineer, his neglect to make such survey before the surface of the ground, which was one of the necessary data for the measurement, was covered, was an admission that the company's survey was correct.—Scanlan v. San Francisco & San Joaquin Valley Ry. Co., 6, 210.

In an action to recover for services by plaintiff in constructing an electric railroad for defendant, and for damages by reason of defendant's failure to perform its part of the contract, defendant set up by way of counterclaim that plaintiff had abandoned the contract before completing the road, and it appeared that the road had been sold in an uncompleted state. Held, that evidence of the price for which it was sold was inadmissible, since such evidence would not affect the amount of damages defendant would be entitled to by reason of plaintiff's failure to complete the road.—Electric Imp. Co. v. San Jose etc. R. R. Co., 3, 618.

§ 4. Unauthorized Construction—Injunction.

An ordinance granting a railroad company the right to enter upon and construct a track through a public street does not operate to justify wrongful acts of such company as trespassers prior to the passage of such ordinance.—Southern California Ry. Co. v. Southern Pac. R. R. Co., 5, 288.

Where defendant railroad corporation has been perpetually enjoined from entering upon and constructing its road over private lands, such injunction must be modified so far as it prohibits the exercise of rights subsequently acquired by defendant under right of eminent domain.—Southern California Ry. Co. v. Southern Pac. R. R. Co., 5, 288.

§ 5. Construction and Damages Arising Therefrom.

The right of a railroad company to erect an embankment along its line is coupled by law with the condition that it shall take reasonable precautions against doing an unnecessary damage to adjoining property holders.—Dorlan v. San Francisco etc. R. R. Co., 1, 457.

The fact that one who grades a street under a contract with a city, and a railroad under a contract with the company, keeps the same men and the same teams working on both jobs, does not render the railroad company liable for damages sustained by a property holder by reason of the street work, even though the railroad and the street are side by side.—Shaw v. Central Pac. R. R. Co., 1, 503.

§ 6. Bond to Build Fence.

In proceedings to condemn land for a railroad, the complaint prayed the court to ascertain, in accordance with Code of Civil Procedure, section 1248, the cost of fences along the line of the road, and of cattle-guards where necessary, and a bond for the construction of the fences was given, with the sureties required by section 1251. Held, in an action to recover from the sureties for violation of the bond, that, since the principals had taken possession of the land and built their railroad, sufficient consideration had passed to support the contract in the bond, even if the bond given was not a statutory one.—Farley v. Moran, 3, 572.

Where a company violates a bond to construct a fence along its railroad through plaintiff's land, plaintiff need not construct the fences before bringing an action on the bond.—Farley v. Moran, 3, 572.

In an action for violation of such a bond it need not be alleged or proved that the fences agreed to be built are necessary.—Farley v. Moran, 3, 572.

§ 7. Killing Stock—Fences.

The fact that a herder, after having rounded up his sheep a mile and a quarter from a railroad track, and after some of them have lain down as if for the night, takes his dog and goes home, is not such contributory negligence as will relieve the railroad company from liability if the sheep afterward stray on the track and are negligently killed; and the admission of incompetent evidence as to the custom of rounding up and herding sheep is not prejudicial to the company. McCoy v. Southern Pac. Co., 3, 398.

In an action against a railroad company for negligently killing stock, an allegation that the damage was caused by defendant's failure to maintain a good and sufficient fence will include any defect in the fence without more particular reference to it.—McCoy v. Southern Pac. Co., 3, 398.

One who has only a right to pasture his stock on another's land, adjacent to a railroad, is entitled to the protection of the statute requiring railroad companies to maintain a fence.—McCoy v. Southern Pac. Co., 3, 398.

§ 8. Speed of Trains—Ordinance Limiting.

Plaintiff set out an ordinance limiting the speed of railway trains, and then alleged that a train running at a great rate of speed by reason of said negligence struck plaintiff. A special demurrer to the complaint as ambiguous in not stating whether the negligence charged was a violation of the ordinance was overruled. Held, that, if error, it was not prejudicial, as the general allegation of negligence supported the cause of action, and would permit evidence of a violation of the ordinance.—Warren v. Southern California Ry. Co., 6, 835.

§ 9. Signals on Approaching Crossings.

A law requiring signals in case of a moving train approaching a street crossing has no reference to the management of cars in the making up of freight trains and loading them between crossings.—Hopkins v. Central Pac. R. R. Co., 2, 8.

§ 10. Injury to Persons at Crossings—Contributory Negligence.

In an action against a railroad company to recover for the death of a boy between five and six years of age, where the evidence tended to show that he was killed at a public crossing in a town of between two thousand and three thousand people, by being run over by defendant's passenger train, which was running from fifteen to forty miles an hour, the questions of the company's negligence and the contributory negligence of the boy and his parents are for the jury.—Bygum v. Southern Pac. Co., 4, 625.

Plaintiff was in a wagon, which another was driving. When within two hundred or three hundred feet of the crossing, the driver took the whip in her hand and slowed the horse to a walk, looking to the east, in which direction the view was unobstructed for one thousand feet. Thereafter the view in that direction became obstructed until a point twenty-five feet distant from the track, and at this point they looked to the west, and then, turning to the east, saw a train approaching, by which time the horse was but a few feet from the track, and the driver attempted to hurry across, but the wagon was struck, and plaintiff injured. Held, that the question of contributory negligence was for the jury.—Warren v. Southern California Ry. Co., 6, 835.

The horse being afraid of the cars, and the question whether to attempt to cross or to turn down the embankment being one to be decided on the instant, the attempt to cross, even though a mistake, did not establish contributory negligence.—Warren v. Southern California Ry. Co., 6, 835.

A general verdict for plaintiff being supported by evidence, a finding on a special issue that the horse was not under control immediately prior to the accident, though without support in the evidence, was not in substantial conflict with the general verdict.—Warren v. Southern California Ry. Co., 6, 835.

Deceased, when within thirty feet of the railroad, stopped, looked up the track, and found it clear for a space of eight hundred feet. She then, without again stopping or looking up or down the track, proceeded to cross, and was struck by a train running between twenty-five and thirty miles an hour. Held, that deceased was not guilty of contributory negligence as a matter of law.—Green v. Los Angeles Terminal Ry. Co., 6, 953.

In an action against a railroad for an accident causing death, a finding that there was no contributory negligence on the part of deceased will not be set aside unless such negligence affirmatively appears as a conclusion of law from the undisputed facts.—Green v. Los Angeles Terminal Ry. Co., 6, 953.

§ 11. Injury to Persons on Right of Way—Licensees.

In an action against a railroad company for the wrongful death of an employee of one of its contractors, it appeared that deceased, with the knowledge and consent of the company, was walking to his work on the right of way, in a narrow place between a bluff and the sea traversed by two parallel tracks, with knowledge that two locomotives, one on each track, would shortly follow him in the same direction; that he received warning by the bell of one, and then perceived that they were approaching at such relative rates of speed as would probably bring them together at the moment of passing him; that he at first took refuge between the tracks where there was barely room to escape unharmed, but a moment later attempted to cross the track toward the bluff, where there was ample room, and was struck and killed while so doing. Held, he was guilty of contributory negligence, and a nonsuit was properly directed.—Noyes v. Southern Pacific R. R. Co., 3, 293.

A complaint for injuries sustained by falling into an excavation between the tracks of defendant's road alleged that the right of way was an easement in a public highway. On trial, plaintiff admitted that the fee of the right of way was in defendant. Without any amendment, and without objection from defendant for variance, the trial proceeded on the theory that plaintiff could recover as a licensee, and that the excavation was in a path in general use by the public, to the knowledge and acquiescence of the defendant. Held, reversible error to exclude evidence that the path had been used constantly by the public, without objection from defendant, on an objection that it was "immaterial, irrelevant, and incompetent," since the objection was insufficient to raise the point of variance.—Davey v. Southern Pac. Co., 5, 386.

§ 12. Injury to Person Lying on Track.

A person is guilty of gross negligence who, in a state of intoxication, lies down upon a railroad track; and the company is not liable if he is injured by a passing train, unless, in the exercise of reasonable care after the person is discovered in his exposed position, it could have avoided the injury.—Williams v. Southern Pac. R. Co., 2, 613.

It is the duty of a railroad company and its employees, when a person is discovered asleep or helpless upon its track, to use all reasonable care by stopping its train so as to prevent injury; and failing in this duty, it becomes liable for injury to such persons, though they may have been guilty of contributory negligence, the injury being in such cases due to the willful or wanton act of the company as the proximate cause, and not to the negligence of the injured party. No presumption arises from the absence of care to watch for trespassers upon a track; and, in order to recover, a trespasser who is injured, being himself negligent, must show, not merely that he might have been seen, but that he was in fact seen in time, and under such circumstances as to render it the duty of the company to check the progress of its train.—Williams v. Southern Pac. R. Co., 2, 613.

When one goes upon a railroad, and lies down and goes to sleep in such a position as to be injured by a passing train, and is unseen by the officers in charge of the train, although they exercised ordinary care and diligence, held, that the railroad company is not liable.—Williams v. Southern Pac. R. Co., 2, 712.

§ 13. Liability for Fires—Pleading and Proof.

A railroad company is not liable for damages caused by fire escaping from its engines, if such engines are in good order, properly constructed, and supplied with the best appliances in use to prevent the escape of fire, unless the fire escaped through the negligence of the servants of said railroad company in managing such engines.—Smyth v. Stockton etc. R. Co., 2, 358.

Where the complaint in an action against a railroad company alleges the destruction of the plaintiff's property by a fire kindled on his premises by sparks which proceeded directly from defendant's locomotive to plaintiff's land, but the proof is that such property was destroyed by a fire kindled on the adjoining land by sparks from the same source, which fire moved onto plaintiff's land, this does not constitute a material variance between the proof and the allegation.— Butcher v. Vaca Valley & C. L. R. Co., 2, 427.

It is not erroneous to permit proof that prior and subsequent to the fire which produced the injury complained of, other fires had been kindled by defendant's engines.—Butcher v. Vaca Valley & C. L. R. Co., 2, 427.

Evidence of repairs made on the smokestack of the locomotive, which it is alleged caused the fire complained of, is properly admissible.—Butcher v. Vaca Valley & C. L. R. Co., 2, 427.

Whether the preponderance of evidence was on the one side or the other of a question of fact is a matter for the jury alone to determine. Butcher v. Vaca Valley & C. L. R. Co., 2, 427.

An instruction to a jury that if they "find that the fire complained of was kindled by defendants under circumstances incompatible with the idea that the engine was of approved construction and properly managed," they shall find for plaintiff, implies that there was evidence sufficient to justify such a finding, and is erroneous.—Butcher v. Vaca Valley & C. L. R. Co., 2, 427.

RAISINS.
Sale of crop. See Sales, § 11.

RAPE.
§ 1. Indictment.
§ 2. Evidence—Testimony of physician.
§ 3. Cross-examination as to previous offenses.
§ 4. Cross-examination of prosecutrix.
§ 5. Instructions.
§ 6. New trial for newly discovered evidence.

§ 1. Indictment.

An indictment alleging that defendant on a certain day had intercourse with H., a female under sixteen years of age, "and not the wife of defendant," unequivocally alleges that the female was not the wife of defendant at the time of the commission of the offense.— People v. Miller, 7, 192.

§ 2. Evidence—Testimony of Physician.

On a prosecution for rape, a physician who testified for the prosecution that penetration would produce the condition of the parts discovered by his examination could be cross-examined as to whether all such conditions could not have been caused by other things, though he had stated that a certain instrument would cause certain of the conditions.—People v. Knight, 5, 231.

On a trial for rape of one who lived with defendant and his wife, where a physician who examined prosecutrix twelve days after the offense, testified that the hymen was entirely absorbed, and that, from indications, it might have disappeared long before, and prosecutrix testified that her only excuse for not making immediate complaint was her fear of defendant, prosecutrix could be cross-examined as to whether any person had intercourse with her before defendant, especially where defendant claimed that the charge was concocted by his wife.—People v. Knight, 5, 231.

Where, on a prosecution for rape, defendant claims that the charge was concocted by his wife, it is error to exclude circumstantial evidence to support that claim.—People v. Knight, 5, 231.

§ 3. Cross-examination as to Previous Offenses.

In a prosecution for rape it was error to compel defendant on cross-examination to testify to the fact of his having had sexual intercourse with the prosecutrix on two prior occasions, one of which was more than a year before the crime charged was alleged to have been committed, and at a time when the prosecutrix was under the age of consent, such evidence not having been touched upon in the direct examination.—People v. Keith, 6, 916.

§ 4. Cross-examination of Prosecutrix.

Where, on a prosecution for rape, prosecutrix testified that she was seven years of age when she came to the state, and that at the time of trial she was ten years of age, and on cross-examination stated that she did not know when she came to the state, she could be asked by defendant what she gave as her age to her school teacher after coming to the state.—People v. Knight, 5, 231.

Where, on a prosecution for rape of one who lived with defendant and his wife, prosecutrix testified that the reason she did not complain until several days after the offense was committed was because defendant had made her afraid of him by throwing things at her and scolding her, questions put to her by defendant to determine when this treatment commenced should have been allowed. In such case she could be cross-examined as to whether defendant ever said anything to her about having intercourse with her.—People v. Knight, 5, 231.

In such a case, prosecutrix having testified that the wife went out and left her alone in the house with defendant, and that she was afraid of him, she could be asked on cross-examination why she did not go out with the wife.—People v. Knight, 5, 231.

On a trial for rape, under an indictment alleging several acts of intercourse with one who lived with defendant and his wife, after prosecutrix testified that she was compelled by threats of the wife to tell her of the offenses, and that the wife suspected it from finding her trembling, she could be cross-examined as to whether the wife saw her trembling after the first offense or after the last, or how many times she saw her thus.—People v. Knight, 5, 231.

Where, on a prosecution for rape, the prosecuting witness had already testified that she had agreed to go with a certain party to the dance from which she was returning when the crime was committed, but that she did not intend to keep the engagement, and did not expect to meet him when she left her home that evening, there was no error in excluding further questions as to whether she had agreed to go to the dance with him, and whether she knew when she left her home that she was going to meet him.—People v. Eaton, 6, 906.

Where, on a prosecution for rape, the prosecuting witness testified that defendant and his participants in the crime struck her "with the fist," and then described the injuries inflicted, in such a way as to show that the blows must have been powerful and solid, there was no error in excluding a question as to whether the blows were "powerful, solid blows with the fist."—People v. Eaton, 6, 906.

§ 5. Instructions.

An instruction, in a prosecution for assault with intent to commit rape, that a presumption is a deduction which the law expressly directs to be made from particular facts, and unless this is controverted by other facts the presumption will control, and that among such presumptions is one that an unlawful act was done with an unlawful intent, is proper, the instruction not relating to deductions of fact to be drawn by the jury.—People v. Crowl, 4, 355.

On a prosecution for rape of a ten year old child, an instruction asked by defendant on the question whether the child made any outcry at the time of the commission of the crime is properly refused.—People v. Knight, 5, 231.

§ 6. New Trial for Newly Discovered Evidence.

Defendant, being convicted of an offense, filed, in a motion for a new trial, the affidavits of himself and two others to the effect that he was in a certain saloon when the alleged offense was committed, that another person had admitted that he did the act, and that defendant did not know of such evidence until after the trial. Held, that a new trial was improperly refused.—People v. Kelleher, 2, 821.

RATIFICATION.

Of contract by corporation. See Corporations, § 12.
By stockholders. See Corporations, § 20.
Of deed. See Deeds, § 4.
Of agent's acts. See Principal and Agent, § 4.

REAL ACTIONS.
See Ejectment.

REASONABLE DOUBT.
Doctrine of. See Criminal Law, § 5.

RECEIPTS.
Parol to explain. See Evidence, § 8.
Bona fide purchaser of warehouse receipts. See Warehouses, § 2.

RECEIVERS.
§ 1. Appointment—Effect of void order of.
§ 2. Sale of land by receiver.
§ 3. Complaint in action by receiver.
§ 4. Appeal and review.

In mortgage foreclosure. See Mortgages, § 24.
For partnership. See Partnership, § 15.
Replevin by. See Replevin, § 5.

§ 1. Appointment—Effect of Void Order of.

A prayer for a receiver, as to wood cut on mortgaged premises, in a bill for an injunction to stay waste, is to be denied when it has not been shown that the defendants are insolvent.—Ross v. Parvin. 1, 285.

Where an order appointing a receiver of a corporation is void, a judgment creditor of the corporation does not, by intervening in the action for the purpose of enforcing his judgment, waive all objections to the order, and thereby lose the right to levy on the corporate property.—Smith v. Los Angeles etc. R. R. Co., 4, 237.

53

§ 2. Sale of Land by Receiver.

Though a receiver's sale of land had been held to be unauthorized on appeal in another suit, the facts affecting the validity of the sale not appearing from the record in the case at bar, and it having been expressly found in the trial court that the sale was properly made, it would be assumed, for the purposes of the case, that the sale was valid.—White v. Costigan, 6, 641.

§ 3. Complaint in Action by Receiver.

The complaint in an action by a receiver as such, for the conversion of property during his receivership, must allege that his insolvent was the owner or entitled to possession of the property.—Daggett v. Gray, 5, 74.

A complaint in an action by a receiver, as such, which alleges that the plaintiff was, on a certain date, by order of court in a certain suit against his insolvent, appointed receiver of the insolvent's property, with the right to take possession of and to sue for and demand the same, sufficiently avers plaintiff's appointment as receiver, and his right to sue.—Daggett v. Gray, 5, 74.

§ 4. Appeal and Review.

In the absence of a bill of exceptions and statement in the record, the contentions that the court never duly appointed a receiver and did not acquire jurisdiction to order a sale cannot be considered.—O'Neil v. McLennan, 7, 161.

RECEIVING STOLEN GOODS.

§ 1. Indictment.

An indictment alleging that accused, after and with knowledge that a third person had stolen certain property, concealed the property and concealed from the magistrate the commission of the felony, states no offense under Penal Code, section 496, punishing the receiving of stolen property.—Ex parte Goldman, 7, 254.

§ 2. Instructions.

In a prosecution for receiving stolen goods it is not error for the court to refuse to instruct that the fact that defendant did not attempt to prevent the owner from recovering his goods is evidence that he did not know that they were stolen.—People v. Solomon, 6, 305.

§ 3. Corroboration of Accomplice.

Under Penal Code, section 1111, requiring corroboration of the testimony of an accomplice, evidence in a prosecution for receiving stolen goods that defendant placed the goods in the back room of a saloon, saying that he had loaned money on them, and offering no explanation why they were put there, is sufficient to corroborate the testimony of the accomplice.—People v. Solomon, 6, 305.

RECLAMATION DISTRICTS.
See Swamp Lands.

RECOGNIZANCE.
See Bail.

RECORDS.

Amendment or correction. See Amendments, §§ 5, 6.
On appeal. See Appeal and Error, §§ 31–52.

Of assignment for creditors. See Assignment for Creditors, § 2.
Of chattel mortgage. See Chattel Mortgage, §§ 1–3.
On appeal in criminal case. See Criminal Law, § 25.
As evidence. See Evidence, §§ 22–25.

§ 1. What Constitutes Recording of Instrument.

Civil Code, section 1170, which provides that an instrument is
deemed to be recorded when deposited in the recorder's office for record, must be read in connection with section 1213, which requires the
instrument to be "recorded as prescribed by law" before subsequent
purchasers are charged with constructive notice of its contents; and
hence no notice is imparted until the instrument is actually placed
on record in the proper book, and then it relates back to the date of
deposit for record.—Watkins v. Wilhoit, 4, 450.

§ 2. Recording in Wrong Book.

The negligence of the recorder in recording a conveyance in the
wrong book cannot affect third persons, but the injury must fall on
the parties to the conveyance, since they are the "parties aggrieved,"
within the meaning of the county government act (section 133), making the recorder liable to the parties aggrieved in three times the
amount of damages occasioned by his negligence.—Watkins v. Wilhoit,
4, 450.

REDEMPTION.

In case of mortgages. See Mortgages, §§ 31–33.

REFERENCE.

§ 1. In General.

When, under an appropriate stipulation, an order of reference is
made with authority to the referee to try the issues and report a
judgment, and the referee thereupon overrules a demurrer to the complaint and promptly reports a judgment for the plaintiff which the
clerk of court enters on the same day, and subsequently execution is
issued, it is proper for the court, upon motion and affidavits and the
papers in the case, to set aside the judgment and execution and to
grant to the defendant, he having moved with due diligence under the
stipulation, leave to file his answer to the complaint.—Willson v. Cummings, 1, 83.

In an action on a note given for services for managing defendant's
cattle ranch, where plaintiff simply introduced his note and rested his
case, defendant's motion thereupon to have the court appoint a referee under Code of Civil Procedure, section 639, subsection 1, providing
that, when an issue of fact requires the examination of a long account, the court may appoint a referee to decide the issue, was properly denied, the note implying a settlement of the account between
the parties, and it not then appearing that the examination of a long
account was necessary.—Clarkson v. Hoyt, 4, 547.

§ 2. Death of Party—Claim Against Estate.

Pending a reference, defendant died, and his executor was substituted in his stead. On the hearing before the referee the executor objected to the taking of any testimony, because plaintiff had not filed
his claim with him. Held, that the objection being made before there
was any evidence as to whether the claim had been presented to the

executor, it was premature, and the referee rightly proceeded with the hearing.—Steen v. Hendy, 4, 916.

§ 3. Report of Referee.

A referee must, in his report, state the facts found and the conclusions of law.—Tryon v. Stratton, 1, 14.

§ 4. Appeal and New Trial.

A judgment on a report of a referee made upon conflicting testimony will not be disturbed on the ground that it is against the weight of the evidence.—Fierro v. Graves, 1, 18.

In the absence of a statement of facts, a judgment on a referee's report which contains a finding in the alternative, leaving the court to determine the amount of the judgment, must be sustained.—Head v. Barney, 1, 78.

A judgment upon a report of a referee, where no motion has been made to set it aside or for a new trial, will not be reviewed on appeal. Inches v. Van Valkenburgh, 1, 81.

Where a referee, who has had the witnesses before him and heard them testify, files his report, and the district court refuses to set this aside, such refusal is to be upheld.—Valentine v. Doane, 1, 91.

A judgment upon the report of a referee, where the evidence was sufficient to support the findings in such report, is to be affirmed.—Dick v. Le Count, 1, 91.

The findings of a referee are not to be disturbed if there was sufficient evidence in the case to sustain them.—Lomax v. Cooper, 1, 147.

Where a cause has been referred to a referee, who returns his decision and judgment to the court, the date of their filing is to legal intent the date of their rendering, and they have not until then a legal existence upon which a motion for a new trial might be based. Stipulated statements, notices or other proceedings, had before the date of such filing, are wholly insufficient as a basis of a motion for a new trial.—Harris v. Careaga, 2, 242.

REFORMATION OF INSTRUMENTS.

§ 1. In General.

To reform or alter the terms of a written contract for mistake, etc., is within the jurisdiction of courts of equity.—Luning v. Brooks, 1, 29.

The grantee of land is entitled to a deed precise and accurate in its terms, and, although the uncertainty be such as a court of law is able to overcome by resort to the technical rules of construction, equity will not deny relief in a case before it.—Huber v. Clarke, 1, 419.

Under the rule that a court of equity will not deal with a case piecemeal, when the case is one principally for the rectification of a deed, the court may decree as thus prayed, and at the same time decree, if it is asked, possession; and this is so particularly where, as in California, the jurisdictions of law and equity are blended.—Huber v. Clarke, 1, 419.

A cross-complaint setting up the facts in regard to the execution of the note, and praying that the corporation be made defendant, and that the note be reformed so as to make it the note of the corporation, could not be sustained; for, if a proceeding for reformation could be maintained by plaintiff, it could not by defendants, whose only interest in reforming the contract was to relieve themselves from liability thereon, and to show it was not their contract, but that of the corporation, which they cannot be allowed to do.—San Bernardino Nat. Bank v. Andreson, 3, 771.

§ 2. On Ground of Mistake.

The mistake as to which the terms of a written contract may be reformed on application to a court of equity must be proved to such court by competent evidence.—Luning v. Brooks, 1, 29.

A settler on public lands gave a wrong description of the land in his application for a patent, owing to a mistake of the government surveyor in marking the stakes, and a patent for the land issued containing such wrong description. The property, after several conveyances, was conveyed to plaintiff, but the original patentee remained in possession under an agreement with plaintiff by which he was to have the privilege to repurchase the land by a certain time. After the mistake in the description was discovered, plaintiff conveyed the land to the government, and received a patent in the name of the original patentee for the land as actually settled by the patentee. Held, that plaintiff was entitled to a reformation of the deeds from his grantor, and to the possession of the land taken in by the reformation.—Ross v. Williams, 2, 803.

§ 3. Readiness of Plaintiff to Do Equity.

If by mistake, as averred in the complaint, a deed through which the defendant claims included land not intended, and excluded land intended, to be conveyed, and so likewise the deed through which the plaintiff claims, wherefore the latter asks for a rectification of his deed by the defendant, while so asking the plaintiff must aver that he is ready and willing on his part to rectify the defendant's deed.— Huber v. Clarke, 1, 419.

In a suit for the ratification of a deed, where the error, strictly construed, reverses the ownership of the parties as to their respective tracts, the plaintiff must aver readiness and willingness to deed to the defendant as the facts call for upon the defendant's so deeding to him.—Huber v. Clarke, 1, 475.

§ 4. Right of Assignee of Lease to Reformation.

The assignment of a lease does not carry with it the lessee's right to have a court of equity reform the lease for cause shown.—Hibbard v. Chipman, 1, 10.

§ 5. Parties.

To a suit for the rectification of a deed to the plaintiff's grantor, made by the defendant's grantor, the plaintiff's grantor is not in all cases an indispensable party.—Huber v. Clarke, 1, 475.

The attorney who is alleged to have committed the fraud of making a deed conveying only a life estate, instead of a fee, is not a necessary party to an action to reform it.—Kenney v. Parks, 6, 111.

The executors in possession of the property of deceased, as well as the legatees and devisees claiming it under his will, are properly parties to an action to reform his deed to make it convey a fee, instead of a life estate.—Kenney v. Parks, 6, 111.

§ 6. Pleading.

In a suit between owners of contiguous parcels of land for the correction of the deed to the plaintiff's grantor, who took from a common source with the defendant, and has not been made a party to the suit, it is unnecessary to aver in the complaint either that by means of the erroneous deed such grantor acquired legal title to no land outside of that intended to be conveyed, or that, if he did so erroneously acquire the legal title, the plaintiff was, through the subsequent conveyance to him, put into a position to restore it to the defendant; since, if the complaint describes the land, the error and the circumstances of the transaction, such an averment would be a conclusion of law.—Huber v. Clarke, 1, 475.

In an action to have his name inserted as one of the parties to a contract between defendant D. and defendant corporation, plaintiff alleged that his name was omitted through the fraud practiced by D. on the corporation and on plaintiff. Held, that the allegations were insufficient to sustain the action, since no facts constituting the fraud were set up.—Thomason v. De Greayer, 3, 651.

There is no ambiguity prejudicial to defendants in a complaint to reform a deed so as to convey a fee, instead of a life estate, in that in one place a mutual mistake is alleged, as though both parties were misled by the reading of the deed by the attorney, while in another place it is charged that the attorney and grantor, knowing that the grantee believed the deed to convey a fee, did not disclose the fact that it did not.—Kenney v. Parks, 6, 111.

§ 7. Appeal and Review.
The discretion of the trial court in granting the reformation of a deed will not be reviewed, except in a very plain case.—Monterey County v. Seegleken, 4, 613.

REGISTERED LETTERS.
Book of as evidence. See Evidence, § 27.

REHEARING.
In general. See Appeal and Error, § 72.
Acts of contempt. See Contempt, § 1.

RELATION.
§ 1. Title by Relation.
A title by relation cannot override an intervening conveyance or encumbrance acquired in good faith.—Hibberd v. Smith, 1, 554.

RELEASE.
See Accord and Satisfaction.
Of surety. See Principal and Surety, § 6.

§ 1. Validity and Consideration.
Release of T. and L., two of the signers of a note, by the other signers, in consideration of the agreement of L. to make a conveyance to such other signers, is not invalidated, as to T., at least, by failure of L. to make the conveyance.—Rogers v. Kimball, 5, 725.

A release in writing of certain signers of a note by the other signers need have no consideration, Civil Code, section 1541, providing, "An obligation is extinguished by a release therefrom given by the creditor . . . . in writing with or without new consideration."—Rogers v. Kimball, 5, 725.

§ 2. Necessity of Pleading.
A release of a cause of action is not available unless it is specially pleaded.—Grunwald v. Freese, 4, 182.

RELIEF CONTRIBUTIONS.
See Money Received, § 1.

REMARKS OF COURT.
See Trial, § 8.

REMEDY.
Change of. See Constitutional Law, § 1.
Mistaking remedy. See Actions, § 3.

REMITTITUR.
In general. See Appeal and Error, § 92.

REMOVAL.
Of administrator. See Executors and Administrators, § 4.

RENEWALS.
Of notes. See Bills and Notes, § 9.

RENT.
Guaranty to pay. See Guaranty, § 4.
In general. See Landlord and Tenant.
Pledge of crops for. See Pledge, § 2.

REPEAL.
Of statute. See Statutes, § 4.

REPLEVIN.
§ 1. Right to maintain.
§ 2. —— For negotiable paper.
§ 3. Necessity of demand.
§ 4. Pleading.
§ 5. Action by receiver.
§ 6. Verdict, finding and judgment.
§ 7. Damages allowable.
§ 8. Appeal and review.

§ 1. Rights to Maintain.
Defendant seized in attachment certain stock which plaintiff claimed to have purchased from the defendant in attachment. Plaintiff's statement that he purchased the stock and had been in continued possession for some years prior to the attachment was uncontradicted. Held, he was entitled to recover such stock, although it happened to be, at the time of the levy of attachment, on the ranch of defendant in attachment.—Hillman v. Griffin, 6, 354.

Plaintiff purchased defendant's property at execution sale, which defendant refused to deliver, claiming that he furnished plaintiff the money to purchase the property for him. Plaintiff's testimony showed that she never had a conversation with defendant about purchasing the property, and that she obtained the money from her daughter, who borrowed it for the purpose, and that defendant held the property after the sale under a lease from plaintiff. Held, the evidence was sufficient to support a finding that plaintiff was the owner and entitled to the possession.—Moran v. Lennon, 6, 382.

§ 2. —— For Negotiable Paper.

Where defendants obtained possession of a note from one whom they knew had parted with his title thereto, plaintiff is entitled to recover possession thereof, without restoring to defendants any amount which they may have paid the pledgee of the note in order that they might fraudulently gain possession of same.—More v. Finger, 6, 326.

Evidence that defendants were mutually engaged in the accomplishment of the common purpose of obtaining possession of a note, and did obtain possession of it by a deal made with plaintiff's husband, who they knew had parted with all title to the note, and while he was intoxicated, is sufficient to support a verdict in favor of plaintiff.—More v. Finger, 6, 326.

§ 3. Necessity of Demand.

In an action to recover personal property, or its value, where it appears that the property came lawfully into the possession of the defendant, a demand and refusal to deliver must be shown; but if the original possession of the property was acquired by tort, no demand previous to the institution of the suit is necessary.—McNally v. Connolly, 2, 621.

§ 4. Pleading.

In replevin the subject matter of the action is confined to specific property mentioned in the complaint, and the defendant may not introduce in his answer another subject matter referring to other property, even if thereby it appears that he has a right to recover such other property in a separate action.—Lavensohn v. Ward, 1, 764.

In replevin, upon the introduction of plaintiff's evidence as to the quantity and value of the coal alleged to be withheld, there was no abuse of discretion in permitting an amendment of the complaint so as to allege the detention of a larger quantity of coal, of greater value, and correspondingly increased damages.—Cain v. Cody, 3, 489.

A complaint in replevin, which fails to state that plaintiff is the owner or is entitled to the possession of the property at the commencement of the action, is defective.—Masterson v. Clark, 5, 146.

A complaint alleged that plaintiff was the owner and entitled to the possession of certain personal property taken by defendant. The answer denied that plaintiff was "the owner in possession and entitled to the possession" of the property, and alleged that defendant was, and had been for a long time, the owner and in the possession of the property. Held, that the affirmative averment was sufficient to negative the allegation that plaintiff was entitled to the possession.—Byxbee v. Dewey, 5, 544.

§ 5. Action by Receiver.

In replevin, plaintiffs alleged that they had been duly appointed and qualified as receivers of a railroad company in another state, which thereupon delivered all its property to plaintiffs, and that the property in question had been wrongfully taken from them by defendant in this state. The answer admitted the appointment and qualification of plaintiffs as receivers, but denied that the company had delivered to them its property, and specifically denied the delivery of the property in question, which defendant claimed to hold as sheriff under an attachment issued against the company. Held, that the issues demanded a finding that the property had been delivered to plaintiffs as receivers before it came into this state, and that a finding that plaintiffs were entitled to its possession when taken from them by defendant was insufficient, it being but a conclusion of law.—Humphreys v. Hopkins, 3, 56.

§ 6. Verdict, Finding and Judgment.

Where, in an action for the recovery of personal property, the property is not delivered to the plaintiff, he is entitled, if he recover, to a judgment for the property or its value, the value being the value as of the day of trial.—Phillips v. Sutherland, 2, 241.

In an action of claim and delivery, the verdict and judgment must be in the alternative, as provided by section 667 of the California Code of Civil Procedure.—Holmberg v. Hendy, 2, 650.

In an action to recover possession of certain charcoal, and damages for its detention, the verdict was as follows: "We, the jury, : . . . find judgment for plaintiff in the following amount, to wit: Value of coal, $546; damages in pursuit of recovery of property, $384; total, $930." Held, that the verdict was a general finding that plaintiff was entitled to a return of the property, and a special finding as to value and damages.—Cain v. Cody, 3, 489.

The court's finding, in an action to recover the possession of goods, "that defendants unlawfully and wrongfully detain" the property in question, is a finding on the affirmative defense that the property was not in their possession at the commencement of the suit, and is a finding that defendants were in unlawful possession at the commencement of the action, and is sufficient, in the absence of any evidence to support the affirmative defense.—Williamson v. Strong, 6, 898.

§ 7. Damages Allowable.

It was proper to allow damages as compensation for the time and money expended in pursuit of the property.—Cain v. Cody, 3, 489.

§ 8. Appeal and Review.

In an action to recover the possession or value of personal property, the finding of the trial court will be affirmed when there is evidence to support it, though the evidence is conflicting.—Affierbach v. McGovern, 4, 660.

REPORTERS.
See Shorthand Reporters.

RESCISSION.
See Cancellation of Instruments.

Return of consideration. See Corporations, § 13.
Of exchange. See Exchange, § 2.
Of lease. See Landlord and Tenant, § 3.
By buyer of goods. See Sales, § 17.
Of contract for sale of land. See Vendor and Vendee, §§ 16–19.

§ 1. Pleading in Action to Rescind.

On the principle that he who seeks equity must do equity the plaintiff, in an action to compel the reconveyance of land, must aver his willingness to restore to the defendant the consideration paid by him.—Potter v. Roeth, 2, 523.

RESERVATION.
In deed. See Deeds, §§ 20, 21.

RES GESTAE.
In larceny. See Larceny, § 10.

RES JUDICATA.
In general. See Judgments, § 15.

RESIDENCE.

Of voter. See Elections, § 1.
As affecting homestead. See Homestead, § 2.
Of grand juror. See Grand Jury, § 1.
Of pre-emptor. See Public Lands, § 12.

RESIGNATION.

Of cotrustee. See Trusts, § 19.

RESISTING ARREST.

Homicide in. See Homicide, § 3.

RESOLUTION OF DIRECTORS.

As evidence. See Evidence, § 24.

RESTITUTION, WRIT OF.

See Ejectment, § 24.

RESULTING TRUST.

Parol to establish. See Trusts, § 6.

RETURN.

On certiorari. See Certiorari or Writ of Review, § 3.
Of service of summons. See Process, § 4.

REVENUE STAMP.

Absence of as affecting admissibility of document. See Evidence,
§ 28.

REVERSAL ON APPEAL.

Effect of. See Appeal and Error, § 93; Execution, § 11.

REVIEW, WRIT OF.

See Certiorari or Writ of Review.

REVOCATION.

Of administrator's appointment. See Executors and Administrators,
§ 3.
Of agent's authority. See Principal and Agent, § 12.

RIGHT OF WAY.

See Easements.
Forfeiture of. See Forfeiture, § 1.

RIOTS OR MOBS.

§ 1. Action for Destruction of Property.

Where the complaint in an action to recover for property destroyed
by riots or mobs alleges a specific sum as the amount of the destruction and demands that sum accordingly, and the answer merely "avers
that said plaintiff, by reason of that which is mentioned in said plaintiff's complaint, has not sustained or suffered any damages whatever
to exceed the sum of ————," mentioning a sum less than that alleged in the complaint, the value of the property destroyed or the

amount of the damages, so far as it exceeds the lesser sum, is put in issue.—Chamon v. San Francisco, 1, 509.

Where, in an action to recover for property destroyed the defendant does not deny the fact of the destruction but only the amount it is assessed at in the complaint, an offer by the plaintiff at the trial to prove the amount of interest due on the amount so assessed is properly rejected.—Chamon v. San Francisco, 1, 509.

The statute of 1868, providing compensation for the destruction of property by riots and mobs, merely gives a right of action against the municipality, without prescribing any rules by which the amount of damages is to be assessed. The common law must be looked to for the measure of damages.—Chamon v. San Francisco, 1, 509.

ROAD COMMISSIONERS.
Supervisors as. See Counties, § 4.

ROADS.
See Highways.

ROBBERY.
Accomplices in. See Accomplices and Accessories, § 6.

§ 1. Evidence of Crime.
On a trial for robbery, the testimony showed that defendant and a confederate, late at night, found the prosecuting witness intoxicated in a saloon; that, under the pretext of escorting him to his hotel, they took him along the street till they came to a blind alley; that, while one of them choked the witness, the other rifled his pockets; that they had been seen by an officer to enter the alley, and when he came upon them, defendant was stooping over the witness, and his confederate was standing near by; that a small amount of coin was found on the confederate, and a spectacle case belonging to the witness was found near where the confederate was standing. The accomplices claimed that the witness was their friend and shipmate, and that they were taking him home, but in fact they were strangers to the witness. Held, that a verdict of guilty was sustained by the evidence.—People v. McDonald, 5, 415.

In a prosecution for robbery, the owner of the property testified that defendant knocked him down, rendering him insensible, and that on recovering consciousness his purse and watch were missing. Another witness testified that he saw defendant holding the owner of the property on the ground. No one distinctly saw defendant rifle the latter's pockets, nor was the property found in defendant's possession. Held, that a conviction was justified.—People v. Gonzales, 6, 263.

§ 2. —— Statements of Confederate.
Where defendant, in the presence of witness, by arrangement with his partner in crime, agreed that witness should accompany his partner, who should tell witness where the stolen property was, and that witness should get it, and turn it over to defendant's partner, statements made to witness by such partner, in defendant's absence, as to where the property may be found, are admissible against defendant.—People v. Brady, 4, 661.

§ 3. Variance.
A variance between the name of the owner of the property, as given in an information for robbery and as shown in evidence, is immaterial.—People v. Gonzales, 6, 263.

RULES OF COURT.

§ 1. Suspension or Setting Aside.

A rule of the trial court established for the promotion of justice may, in the discretion of the court, and to meet the ends of justice, be set aside.—Chielovich v. Krauss, 2, 643.

Rules of court are but a means to accomplish the ends of justice, and it is always in the power of the court to suspend its own rules, or to except a particular case from their operation, whenever the purposes of justice require it.—Symons v. Bunnell, 3, 69.

SALES.

§   1.   In general.
§   2.   Meeting of minds.
§   3.   Mutual mistake—Estoppel.
§   4.   Bill of sale—Estoppel from accepting.
§   5.   Merchantable quality—Warranty—Damages for breach.
§   6.   Of horses—Warranty of stallion.
§   7.   Of harvester—Retention of title.
§   8.   Of cigars by sample.
§   9.   Of seeds—Breach of warranty.
§ 10.   Of diseased trees.
§ 11.   Of crop of raisins—Construction of contract.
§ 12.   —— Action for price.
§ 13.   Measurement of fruit sold—Action for price.
§ 14.   Of goods to arrive by ship—Charges.
§ 15.   Of coal to be imported—Construction of contract—Custom duties.
§ 16.   Refusal of buyer to accept perishables.
§ 17.   Rescission by buyer.
§ 18.   Action for price—Evidence—Defenses.

§ 1. In General.

Necessity of change of possession. See Fraudulent Transfers, § 1.

Defendant S., son of plaintiff, engaged with defendants M. and N. in working a mine, plaintiff agreeing to back his son for his share, and to send him either money or provisions to put in for his share, and, pursuant thereto, sent him provisions. Held, that there was no sale to the others, so as to make them liable therefor.—Snow v. Mastick, 7, 103.

A contract for the manufacture and delivery of "girders" of the best quality of pig iron, "to be put in place within forty-six days," must, considering the time limit, be held to mean the best quality to be found in the state, rather than in all the world.—Savage v. Sweeney, 2, 138.

For contradictory instruction as to the effect of the sale of personal property which was not in vendor's possession, and not accompanied by change of possession, judgment reversed.—Agnew v. Kimball, 2, 598.

§ 2. Meeting of Minds.

Where, in a proposed sale of personalty, the seller thinks to transfer property of one description while the buyer thinks to receive property of another and a more valuable description, there is no meeting of minds and hence no sale results, even though the seller's agent ignorantly transfers the more valuable property and gives a bill of sale for it.—Chiarini v. Rochon, 1, 540.

§ 3. Mutual Mistake—Estoppel.

Under the law of sales the effect of a mutual mistake as to either terms or subject matter is that neither party is bound; if, though, the contract by its terms admits the two constructions and one party proceeds with it, not correcting the other, whom he knows labors innocently under the wrong impression of it, he is bound by the contract as the other party conceived it to be.—McDonald v. Noyes, 1, 866.

§ 4. Bill of Sale—Estoppel from Accepting.

A memorandum given as a bill of sale of a "4-horse Concord" wagon, executed by the debtor to plaintiff, is competent evidence on the question of the sale, by the debtor to plaintiff, of the Concord wagon in dispute.—Bunting v. Salz, 193.

One who accepts a bill of sale purporting to transfer a certain number of cattle is not estopped thereby from denying that he actually received that number.—Murdock v. Clarke, 3, 265.

§ 5. Merchantable Quality—Warranty—Damages for Breach.

The fact that part of a lot of potatoes contracted for as "merchantable" have "sprouted a little" does not necessarily show that they are unmerchantable, but, there being evidence that the lot in question were salable for table use or shipment, the question whether the purchaser was justified in refusing to receive them is for the jury.—Marshall v. Keefe, 4, 188.

The damages sustained where defendants purchased from plaintiff, under a contract of sale, subject to the warranties declared under Civil Code, sections 1768–1771, two carloads of hams, which proved unmerchantable, and which defendants were compelled to sell at reduced prices, would be, where the contract price was not all paid, the difference between the amount the hams should have sold for if up to the standard agreed upon and the price actually realized, less the balance due on the contract price together with the cost of freight and smoking, which charges defendants were to pay.—Silberhorn Co. v. Wheaton, 5, 886.

§ 6. Of Horses—Warranty of Stallion.

Evidence as to whether plaintiff in 1889 gave in to the assessor the ranch as her property could not affect the validity of her purchase of the mares in question in the preceding July, and did not tend to show fraud in the transaction, and was therefore properly excluded.—Asbill v. Standley, 3, 665.

Plaintiff, while his mare was on the ranch of defendant's decedent, entered into negotiations for its sale to decedent, through an agent authorized to sell only the mare. Subsequently, after the mare had given birth to a colt, the agent testified that he sold both to decedent, the communications between the parties being by telegraph. Plaintiff permitted decedent to retain possession of the colt for twelve years, during the first three of which the colt developed as a wonderful trotter, and, during the time, asked decedent to give him an additional sum as a gratuity, on account of his good luck in the purchase. Held, that a finding that plaintiff sold both the mare and colt to decedent would not be disturbed.—Loose v. Stanford, 5, 366.

A bill of sale of a stallion merely guaranteeing him to be a breeder excludes a guaranty of his being pure bred.—First Nat. Bank v. Hughes, 5, 454.

A promise by the seller, in a bill of sale of a stallion guaranteeing him to be a breeder, that, on satisfactory proof that he is not a

breeder, the seller will give another in exchange for him, on his being
delivered at a certain place, limits the buyer's remedy, in the absence
of a refusal of the seller to comply with such agreement.—First
Nat. Bank ๆ. Hughes, 5, 454.

§ 7. Of Harvester—Retention of Title.

Plaintiff delivered a harvester to R. under contract that it did
not part with title until notes given therefor were fully paid, and in
case of default it was, if it wished, to take possession of the harvester, and all payments thereon were to be retained as compensation
for its use prior to the default. After default in payment, R. sold
the harvester to defendant for a valuable consideration. Held, that
R. having no title, but only a right to secure title, could convey none
to defendant, and that plaintiff was the owner, and entitled to possession.—Houser & Haines Mfg. Co. v. Hargrove, 6, 384.

Plaintiff delivered a harvester to R., retaining title until payment
made. The tax thereon, together with the tax on several other items
of personal property belonging to R. alone, was assessed to "R. and
wife and H." (the plaintiff), and the harvester was sold to defendant
for delinquent taxes. Held, that, under Political Code, sections 3628,
3636, providing that the assessor shall ascertain the name of the
owner, and assess the property to him, and, if unable to ascertain
the name, shall assess it to the "unknown owner," the assessment
was invalid.—Houser & Haines Mfg. Co. v. Hargrove, 6, 384.

§ 8. Of Cigars by Sample.

Unequivocal testimony of purchaser's agent that cigars shipped were
greatly inferior to samples, thus breaking contract, is not contradicted by testimony of defendant's agent that samples used were
honestly selected by him, without intention to defraud, and of persons
claiming to be experts that cigars of the same brand shown in court
were good cigars, and of a former salesman of the manufacturer that
it made only one class of cigars, and all of the same quality.—
Barkley-Gray Grocer Co. v. Kelley Cigar Co., 6, 990.

§ 9. Of Seeds—Breach of Warranty.

The measure of damages for breach of a warranty as to the quality
or variety of certain seeds sold to plaintiff is the difference of the
value of the crop produced and the value of the crop that would have
been produced had there been no breach of warranty.—Moody v.
Peirano, 7, 247.

In an action for breach of warranty of variety of seed wheat sold,
plaintiff alleged that defendant warranted the wheat to be "White
Australian," but that it was actually wheat of another and inferior
variety, and produced a crop of hay inferior to that which would
have been grown had the wheat been of the variety warranted, and
that by reason of the premises plaintiff had been damaged in the sum
of $1,000. Held, that the complaint sufficiently alleged that the
crop produced was of less value than the crop that would have been
produced if the wheat had been as warranted, and was therefore
not demurrable for failure to specially allege the damages sustained.
Moody v. Peirano, 7, 247.

Where, in an action for breach of warranty, the court found the
facts as alleged in the complaint as to the sale of the seed wheat
in question, the warranty, the breach, the planting of the wheat,
and that the crop produced was inferior to that which would have
been produced, had there been no breach, and further found that
plaintiff had been damaged in the sum of $359.50, for which sum,
less a counterclaim, judgment was given, such findings were sufficient

to support the judgment, without a finding of the evidentiary facts showing such damage.—Moody v. Peirano, 7, 247.

Where, in an action for breach of warranty in the sale of seed wheat warranted to be "White Australian," defendant testified that he sold to M. wheat from the same lot from which he sold plaintiff, evidence of M. that he bought wheat of defendant near the time when plaintiff bought his wheat, and that, when the crop was grown, it proved to be different wheat from "White Australian," was relevant and material to show that the wheat sold to plaintiff was not of that variety.—Moody v. Peirano, 7, 247.

In an action for breach of warranty of the variety of certain seed wheat sold, testimony of a third person that defendant sold wheat to him in the same season that the wheat was sold to plaintiff, and warranted it to be of the variety warranted to plaintiff, was res inter alios acta, and inadmissible.—Moody v. Peirano, 7, 247.

§ 10. Of Diseased Trees.

Plaintiff sold to defendant certain trees. It was provided that, on account of a disease with which the trees were affected, a certain percentage should be excepted. Defendant selected the trees and they were shipped to him in another county. On account of an ordinance of the county to which the trees were shipped, adopted after the sale, defendant was prohibited from planting therein any of the trees which were diseased, and returned the same to plaintiff, who refused to receive them. Held, that plaintiff could recover for all of the trees selected by and shipped to defendant.—Gray v. Long, 4, 724.

The fact that an ordinance of a county to which trees are shipped prohibits the planting of any diseased trees therein does not invalidate a sale of trees as to any diseased ones included therein, where the sale was made in another county before the ordinance was adopted.—Gray v. Long, 4, 724.

§ 11. Of Crop of Raisins—Construction of Contract.

Defendant, in writing, authorized plaintiff to sell all his crop of raisins at specified prices and terms. Shortly after, plaintiff notified him by letter that sale had been so made, repeating the prices and terms and asking confirmation. Defendant answered that he wished to confirm sale to plaintiff of his entire crop at the prices and terms specified. Plaintiff answered, accepting the modification, making it the purchaser, and inquiring when the raisins would be ready for inspection and shipment. At the time defendant said the crop would be ready, plaintiff sent its agent, who inspected and accepted all except a few boxes, which he claimed were marked a grade too high; but said he would accept them at the grade they actually inspected. Afterward defendant refused to deliver any of the raisins. Held, that there was a contract binding on defendant to sell all his crop to plaintiff at the prices and terms specified.—Johnson-Locke Mercantile Co. v. Howard, 6, 748.

Where, on a contract for the purchase of raisins, plaintiff tendered its check for the proper amount in payment, and no objection was made to the amount or form of the tender, defendant cannot afterward object that the tender was not in money.—Johnson-Locke Mercantile Co. v. Howard, 6, 748.

Where defendant contracted to sell his entire crop of raisins to be Fresno grade, he could not invalidate the contract by marking boxes of a higher quality than the raisins would grade, but plaintiff was entitled to the crop at the actual grades by the standard agreed on in the contract.—Johnson-Locke Mercantile Co. v. Howard, 6, 748.

The parties executed an agreement by which defendant agreed to
buy plaintiff's "partial crop as they may select crop of raisins from
vineyard . . . . M. (product of 1897), to be delivered in sweat-boxes
at buyer's packing-house in good, merchantable condition, on the following terms: . . . . Muscat and Malaga delivery not later than October 15, 1897. Price per pound, 2½c.; [defendants] to pick and cure
and put in sweat-boxes. Muscats to be graded from trays and sweat-
boxes into two grades . . . . 'London Layers' and 'Loose Muscatels.' "
Held, that as under this contract the grapes were to be picked and
cured by defendant, and such as were of merchantable quality then
became his property, and he was to put them in sweat-boxes, and
plaintiff could not deliver them until this was done, and the grading
from trays and sweat-boxes was the work of defendant, who could
not defeat the contract by neglecting or refusing to perform such
acts, plaintiff, in an action for the contract price, was not bound
to allege the performance of the acts necessary by the defendant,
and a complaint alleging that defendant had picked and dried a certain amount, a part of which plaintiff had delivered, and the balance
of which he was ready to deliver, and that a certain amount of the
contract price remained unpaid, was sufficient.—Malter v. Cutting
Fruit Packing Co., 6, 789.

§ 12. —— Action for Price.

Plaintiff brought an action for the price of raisins sold under a
contract by which the defendant was to select and cure the raisins
and place them in sweat-boxes, in which they were to be delivered
by the defendant. There was evidence that defendant picked a certain amount of grapes, a certain portion of which was hauled by
plaintiff's teamsters and delivered by them, after which defendant
refused to allow any more to be hauled; that the price had gone
down, and defendant claimed that he could not handle any more at
the contract price; that the balance of the raisins was on trays or
in boxes; that from half to two-thirds of those undelivered were of
as good quality as those delivered; that subsequently they were damaged or their value destroyed by rains. Held, that the evidence was
sufficient to sustain a verdict for the plaintiff.—Malter v. Cutting
Fruit Packing Co., 6, 789.

In an action for the contract price of raisins, a part of which
the defendant had refused to receive, it was not error to refuse
to permit a question to be asked plaintiff's witness on cross-examination, as to whether there had not been some complaint about the
condition of the raisins, as the question was not confined to complaints by persons connected with the transaction. The error, if any,
in refusing such question, was rendered harmless by allowing the
witness, in reply to subsequent questions, to fully explain the condition of the raisins.—Malter v. Cutting Fruit Packing Co., 6, 789.

In an action for the contract price of raisins which defendant had
picked and cured in plaintiff's vineyard, and a part of which he subsequently refused to receive, alleging that they were damaged by rain,
the error in allowing plaintiff to give evidence as to whether defendant did anything to prevent the raisins from being damaged,
there being no issue as to defendant's negligence, was not prejudicial,
as plaintiff claimed to recover only for such raisins as were merchantable, and the court instructed that his recovery must be so limited.—Malter v. Cutting Fruit Packing Co., 6, 789.

In an action for the contract price of raisins which defendant
had picked and cured in plaintiff's vineyard, but the delivery of part
of which he subsequently refused on the ground that they had been
damaged by rains, this part having been used by plaintiff in his

winery, the introduction of evidence by him that they were of no
value at the time they were so used, though such evidence was immaterial, was harmless error, in view of the fact that defendant had
abandoned such portion before their use, and that plaintiff only
claimed to recover for such as were of good, merchantable quality.—
Malter v. Cutting Fruit Packing Co., 6, 789.

Where, in an action for the contract price of fruit sold, defendant
wished to show that a certain payment was made to M., as a step
toward proving her to be the plaintiff's agent, and such evidence was
refused, but the witness testified as to what M. did and said in the
course of employment, the error in rejecting the evidence was not
reversible.—Malter v. Cutting Fruit Packing Co., 6, 789.

§ 13. Measurement of Fruit Sold—Action for Price.

In an action for the price of peaches sold on a contract fixing the
price per pound for each of several sizes of fruit "per box packed,"
where no method of measurement is provided, evidence of prior negotiations between the parties, out of which the contract grew, is admissible. In such action, where defendant contended that the size
and weight of the boxes determined the size and weight of the fruit,
an experienced fruit raiser and packer, who saw plaintiff's fruit
packed, could testify that peaches could not be graded in that way,
as they were packed in "break joints," by placing the upper layer
in the space between the fruit in the lower layer; and he could
also testify as to the average size of plaintiff's fruit, and the average
weight of the several sizes as packed.—Thresher v. Gregory, 5, 185.

In an action for the price of fruit sold on a contract which merely
fixed the price per pound for each of several sizes of fruit packed,
correspondence subsequent to the contract, showing that the method
of measuring the fruit had not been agreed on, is admissible on the
issue as to measurement. Where, in such a case, defendant testifies
that the contract with plaintiff is his usual form of contract, he may
be asked on cross-examination to write out a contract in his usual
form, and such contract may be put in evidence.—Thresher v.
Gregory, 5, 185.

Where, in an action for the price of peaches under a contract fixing
the price according to the size and weight of the fruit, there is a disagreement as to the method of measurement, and defendant testifies
that measuring-boards like those used by plaintiff injured the fruit,
and rendered it unfit for shipping, plaintiff may, in rebuttal, testify
that he had seen defendant and others use such boards, and then use
the fruit.—Thresher v. Gregory, 5, 185.

§ 14. Of Goods to Arrive by Ship—Charges.

Where plaintiff sold to defendant iron, to arrive by a certain ship,
then on her way—the iron to be delivered at defendant's wharf,
and received by him, as discharged—defendant is liable to plaintiff
for the necessary charges paid by him for the use of the ship and
wharfage while awaiting, after arrival, opportunity to discharge,
defendant's wharf being occupied by other vessels.—Blanchard v.
Pacific Rolling-mill Co., 4, 619.

§ 15. Of Coal to be Imported—Construction of Contract—Custom Duties.

A San Francisco merchant cabled to a coal dealer in New South
Wales an offer to purchase two cargoes of coal, which read: "Offer
subject to immediate reply twenty-four shillings cost freight and insurance exchange duty paid two cargoes," etc. The coal dealer re-

plied, "Ultimatim twenty-four shillings and three pence." The merchant cabled accepting this offer, and later wrote the coal dealer, "We beg to confirm having purchased from you [stating kind of coal and price] 'cost,' 'freight,' 'insurance,' 'exchange,' 'duty paid,'" etc. Held, that the contract would be construed to mean that the coal should be delivered at its destination with all enumerated charges, including customs duties, paid by the seller, whatever they might happen to be at the time of delivery, the purchaser having no advantage of an intermediate reduction in customs duties.—Withers v. Moore, 7, 125.

The purchaser's first cablegram contained the words, "Our usual form of charter-party," and in writing to the seller, confirming the contract, the purchaser said, "The vessels to be chartered under our usual form of charter-party as per copy previously sent you, and to contain all the clauses contained therein." He also stated that he forwarded by that mail a few originals and copies of the charter-party. The charter-party taken by the seller provided that, "being so loaded shall therewith proceed to San Francisco Harbor and deliver the said full and complete cargo in the usual and customary manner"; and again, "All port charges, pilotages, wharfage dues, and charges at port of discharge," etc., "to be paid by the ship as customary." Held, that if the purchaser had contemplated an advantage to him from a reduction of custom duties, as a feature of his form of charter-party, it should have been specifically mentioned, failing which he could not rely on the charter-party as conferring on him that advantage, in obedience to a claimed custom of the port.—Withers v. Moore, 7, 125.

A San Francisco merchant purchased coal from a dealer in New South Wales, stipulating that his form of charter-party should be used by the dealer. In violation of this stipulation, the charter-party actually employed omitted a clause providing that, if the vessel should be free from wharfage during discharge, the freight was to be reduced 4½d. per ton. Held, that this breach of contract would not justify the purchaser in rejecting the cargo, it being his duty to perform his part of the contract, and seek compensation in damages. Withers v. Moore, 7, 125.

§ 16. Refusal of Buyer to Accept Perishables.

Where a buyer refuses to accept perishable property under a contract, it is the right of the seller to sell it forthwith, so as to reduce his damages.—Tustin Fruit Assn. v. Earl Fruit Co., 6, 37.

Civil Code, section 3353, provides that in estimating damages the value of property to a seller is the price which he could have obtained in the market nearest to the place where the buyer should have accepted it, as soon after the breach of the contract as the buyer could, with reasonable diligence, have effected a resale. Held, that the value to a seller of fruit which a buyer refused to take is its value in the condition it was in when the owner could have sold it after the repudiation of the contract.—Tustin Fruit Assn. v. Earl Fruit Co., 6, 37.

§ 17. Rescission by Buyer.

After consummation of a sale, the buyer cannot rescind it for breach of a warranty not intended to operate as a condition, though a note for the balance of purchase money has not been paid, his remedy being for damages suffered from the breach.—First Nat. Bank v. Hughes, 5, 454.

A seller of stationary engines will not be relieved from his agreement to rescind the sale, and accept their return, by the mere fact that the purchaser returned one more engine than specified in the agreement, without, however, requiring its acceptance by the seller as a condition to the return of the others.—Willard v. Tatum, 3, 730.

A delay of eight months in shipping the engines after it was agreed that they should be returned to the purchasers from San Francisco to the sellers at Chicago, by a shipment via Cape Horn, is not so unreasonable, as matter of law, as will relieve the seller from his obligation to accept them, where it appears that they had been paid for by the purchasers; that the seller had the use of the money during all this time; that no loss was suffered by the delay; that the refusal to accept them was based on a claim that a change in the pattern of the engines rendered those returned less valuable than formerly; that some of the returned engines were in a branch house of the purchasers at Portland, Oregon, and had to be brought to San Francisco for shipment; and that the engines were in fact shipped by the first vessel carrying a miscellaneous cargo.—Willard v. Tatum, 3, 730.

§ 18. Action for Price—Evidence—Defenses.

See, also, ante, §§ 12, 13.

In an action for an agreed price, evidence of the value of the goods is irrelevant.—Sanborn v. Cunningham, 4, 95.

In an action by the assignee of R. & Co. for the price of goods sold by such firm to defendant, a witness stated that he was manager for R. & Co.; that he knew and had interviews and correspondence with defendant; that such firm sold him goods; that he was a customer of the firm before the witness became manager, and, without consulting the books, could not tell the extent of his purchases; that the balance due June, 1892, was $547; that he and defendant agreed on a balance of $497.30, which defendant agreed to pay in monthly payments; and that he afterward paid $57. Plaintiff proved an assignment to him by F. under a power of attorney from R. & Co. to F., executed by Y., who was shown to be the sole partner of such firm. Held, that the evidence supported a judgment for $440.30 for plaintiff.—Shain v. Du Jardin, 4, 905.

Where in an action for the purchase price of certain fixtures, defendant denied the purchase as alleged, and the evidence on such issue was squarely in conflict, a verdict in favor of defendant will not be reversed on appeal.—McCormick v. Gross, 6, 425.

Where on trial of an action for the purchase price of fixtures, defendant denied the sale, and testified that he made no claim to the property, and that plaintiff could have it at any time, the fact that, after verdict in his favor, defendant refused to deliver the property, except on onerous conditions, did not entitle plaintiff to a new trial on the ground that defendant's evidence was a gross irregularity in the proceedings, and that his refusal to deliver was a surprise justifying a new trial.—McCormick v. Gross, 6, 425.

The fact that a buyer paid part of the price did not preclude him from relief, in an action for the balance, on account of the worthlessness of part of the goods, where at the time of payment he had no knowledge of the defects.—Bowers Rubber Co. v. Blasdel, 5, 604.

In an action to recover the balance due on the contract price of an engine, where there was a defense of breach of contract and guaranty, and a cross-claim for damages, evidence considered, and held sufficient to sustain the finding of the court that certain knocking of the engine and flickering of the light produced by the electric plant run thereby were not caused by any defect of the engine, and that the engine was not defective.—Tracy v. California Electrical Works, 7, 324.

SAMPLE.

Sale of cigars by. See Sales, § 8.

SAN FRANCISCO.

§ 1. Supervisor, First Board.

The office of "supervisor, first board," does not exist in the city and county of San Francisco.—People v. Board of Election Commissioners, 2, 287.

§ 2. Legislative Assembly of District.

The so-called "legislative assembly of the district of San Francisco" and the ayuntamiento of San Francisco had no valid powers whereby the former could make a grant and the latter confirm it.— People v. Central Wharf Joint Stock Co., 1, 319.

§ 3. Compromise of Claims to Realty.

The purpose of the legislative "Act to authorize the commissioners of the funded debt of the city of San Francisco to compromise claims to real estate and to convey such real estate pursuant thereto" was to make good certain doubtful titles, and it was to have effect only in favor of persons who, by themselves, their tenants, or their grantors, had held actual possession of the parcels of land claimed by them from a time prior to the first day of January, 1855.—Blair v. Sherry, 1, 738.

A person invoking the benefit of the legislative "Act to authorize the commissioners of the funded debt of the city of San Francisco to compromise claims to real estate and to convey such real estate pursuant thereto" was required to state the fact of his possession in his petition and establish it by testimony before the commissioners, and it was recited in the deed, after which the deed became prima facie evidence of the truth of the recitals in it.—Blair v. Sherry, 1, 738.

The prima facie character, as evidence, of a deed from the commissioners under the legislative "Act to authorize the commissioners of the funded debt of the city of San Francisco to compromise claims to real estate and to convey such real estate pursuant thereto," may be met and overcome by testimony.—Blair v. Sherry, 1, 738.

SATISFACTION.

See Judgments, § 21.

SAVINGS BANKS.

In general. See Banks and Banking, § 4.
Taxation of. See Taxation, § 6.

SCHOOLS AND SCHOOL DISTRICTS.

Mandamus to pay teacher's salary. See Mandamus, § 2.

§ 1. School Lands—Application to Purchase.

Section 3495 of the Political Code, referring to applications for the purchase of school lands, is mandatory in requiring the applicant to state "that there is no occupation of such lands adverse to any he has"; or, in case there is such an occupant, in requiring the affidavit to show that the township has been sectionalized three months, and that the adverse occupant has been in occupation more than sixty days.—Oakley v. Stuart, 2, 1.

§ 2. Employment of Teacher.

The employment, by the board of education of the city and county of San Francisco, of inspecting teachers, whose duty it is to visit the schools and ascertain, by frequent oral examinations, the condition of the classes, and to give advice to teachers and principals when necessary, is within the power to "employ teachers" conferred on the board by Worley's Consolidation Act, page 171, section 1, subdivision 3 (Stats. 1871–72).—Barry v. Goad, 3, 302.

A contract of a school board employing plaintiff as a teacher for the ensuing year at a salary of $1,100 is proved by minutes of the board showing she was elected teacher for the ensuing year, a letter from one of the members to her informing her of her election, a letter from her to him accepting the employment, and proof that for several years previously she had been employed by the board at a salary of $1,100, and that, in pursuance of the employment for the year in question, she entered on her duties and taught for the first four months, receiving the due proportion of the salary at that rate.—Polk v. Board of Education, 7, 170.

§ 3. Power of Board of Education to Employ Counsel.

Under the charter of San Francisco, requiring the city attorney to defend the board of education in suits brought against it, and authorizing the mayor to suspend such attorney if he refuses to act, and appoint someone to act in his place, such board has no implied power to employ private counsel either in place of or to assist the city attorney to defend the board in a suit.—Denman v. Webster, 7, 65.

Political Code, section 1617, subdivision 7, authorizing boards of education and trustees of school districts to employ teachers, "janitors, and other employees of the schools," and subdivision 20, relating to the powers of trustees only, do not authorize a board of education to employ counsel to defend an action brought against it.—Denman v. Webster, 7, 65.

SEEDS.

Sale and warranty. See Sales, § 9.

SELF-DEFENSE.

Law of. See Homicide, § 5.

SENTENCE.

For burglary. See Burglary, § 5.
In general. See Criminal Law, § 20.

SEPARATE PROPERTY.

Of wife. See Husband and Wife, § 6.

SERVICE OF PROCESS.

In general. See Process.

SERVICES.

And compensation therefor. See Master and Servant; Work and Labor.

SETOFF AND COUNTERCLAIM.

§ 1. In Action by Attorney to Recover for Services.

Defendant claimed damages from negligent advice given by plaintiff before the contract was made, and not given in the performance of the services sued for. Held, that defendant's claim, being for un-liquidated damages, should be pleaded, to be available, even though treated as a cross-demand, within Code of Civil Procedure, section 440, providing that "when cross-demands have existed between persons under such circumstances that, if one had brought an action against the other, a counterclaim could have been set up, the two demands shall be deemed compensated, so far as they equal each other, and neither can be deprived of the benefit thereof by the assignment or death of the other."—Perkins v. West Coast Lumber Co., 5, 674.

Not having been pleaded in the original answer, limitations ran against defendant's claim, till set up in an amended answer.—Perkins v. West Coast Lumber Co., 5, 674.

The trial court's failure to find on issues presented by a counterclaim against which limitations have run is immaterial, where findings upon such issues could not have defeated the bar of limitations.—Perkins v. West Coast Lumber Co., 5, 674.

§ 2. Pleading and Evidence.

In an action for goods sold and delivered, the allegation of a counterclaim of $1,700 for 171,000 bricks sold and delivered by defendant to plaintiff, no part of which has been paid, states sufficient facts to support a judgment for defendant.—Valley Lumber Co. v. Wood, 4, 1.

In an action to which defendant pleaded a counterclaim for brick alleged to have been delivered to plaintiff corporation, the evidence was undisputed that the bricks mentioned in the answer were to be used in a certain building in which plaintiff had no interest. The contractor for the erection of the building testified that he ordered the bricks from defendant, while defendant testified that they were ordered by a member of an agency who were managing agents for plaintiff corporation, but there was no evidence to connect plaintiff with this transaction through the agency. Held, that the evidence did not justify a verdict for defendant on the counterclaim.—Valley Lumber Co. v. Wood, 4, 1.

§ 3. Estoppel to Plead Setoff of Note.

An equitable estoppel to plead a setoff of a note in an action on an account against defendant, which had been assigned to plaintiff by the maker of the note, did not arise out of the assignor's direction to defendant, after the assignment, to pay the amount of the account to plaintiff, and defendant's silence as to his possession of said note, it not appearing that plaintiff had knowledge of such request.—Randol v. Rowe, 5, 379.

SEWER CONTRACT.

Compensation for extras. See Municipal Corporations, § 31.

SHAM PLEADING.

See Pleading, § 15.

SHARES.

Farming on. See Crops, §§ 1, 2.

SHEEP.

In general. See Animals.

SHERIFFS AND CONSTABLES.

§ 1. Election of constables in San Francisco.
§ 2. Fees and compensation of constable.
§ 3. Expiration or abolition of office—Service of process.
§ 4. Liability of sheriff—Wrongful levy or seizure.
§ 5. Liability for acts of deputy—Exemplary damages.

Wrongful attachment. See Attachment, § 6.
Compensation of. See Constitutional Law, § 8.
Bond of indemnity to. See Execution, § 5.
Expiration of term of office. See Execution, § 6.
Deed and certificate of sale. See Execution, §§ 9, 10.
Wrongful execution sale. See Execution, § 15.

§ 1. Election of Constables in San Francisco.

The election for constables in San Francisco in the year 1866 **was** held without authority.—People v. Supervisors San Francisco County, 1, 386.

§ 2. Fees and Compensation of Constable.

Under act of March 5, 1870, providing that constables shall receive mileage for "every mile necessarily traveled, in going only, in executing any warrant of arrest, subpoena, or venire, bringing up a prisoner on habeas corpus, taking prisoners before a magistrate or to prison," a constable is entitled to mileage both for the distance traveled in going to make an arrest, and for that traveled in bringing his prisoner from the place of arrest to the magistrate or to prison. Allen v. Napa County, 23 Pac. 43, 82 Cal. 187, followed.—Monahan v. San Diego County, 3, 487.

Statutes of 1893, page 310, section 7, providing that, in counties of the class to which K. county belongs, constables shall receive "such fees as are now or may hereafter be allowed by law," does not make any change in the existing law relating to fees of constables in that county.—Orr v. Kern County, 4, 754.

The compensation of a constable is regulated by the provisions of the county government act (Stats. 1893, p. 390); and the provision limiting the amount of compensation he shall receive is valid.—Johnston v. County of Los Angeles, 5, 568.

Statutes of 1893, page 452, section 184, subdivision 17, which declares that subdivision 14 of the act (fixing the fees of the constables) shall apply to present incumbents, applies to a constable of Placer county holding office at the time of the passage of the act.—Fleckenstein v. Placer Co., 5, 774.

Statutes of 1893, page 452, section 184, subdivision 14, providing that the fees allowed constables for services in criminal actions other than felonies shall not exceed $75 for any one quarter, is not in conflict with constitution, article 11, section 5, which makes it the duty of the legislature to regulate the fees of officers in proportion to their duties. Nor does such provision conflict with constitution, article 4, section 25, prohibiting local and special legislation affecting the fees of any officer.—Fleckenstein v. Placer Co., 5, 774.

§ 3. Expiration or Abolition of Office—Service of Process.

A sheriff who has commenced the execution of process in his hands is bound to complete it, though he may, in the meantime, have been succeeded in his office by another incumbent.—Clark v. Sawyer, 1, 573.

The statute which abolished the office of sheriff of the district of San Francisco provided that quoad process then in hand the office should still exist, and that its incumbent should have power to, and remain charged with the duty to, complete the enforcement of such process.—Clark v. Sawyer, 1, 573.

§ 4. Liability of Sheriff—Wrongful Levy or Seizure.

The owner of property in the hands of one restrained by injunction from delivering it to him, in anticipation of a judgment of forfeiture, has, after such judgment, no action against the sheriff for levying on the property while in such hands.—Kent v. Solomon, 1, 13.

In an action to recover damages from a sheriff for levying upon the plaintiff's alleged property in execution of a judgment against a third person, the jury may find upon the validity of a sale of the property to the plaintiff by the judgment debtor on the day of the levy.—Keys v. Brockman, 1, 34.

In an action against a sheriff for the recovery of goods of the plaintiff, seized by him as being the goods of another person in an attachment proceeding against that person, the plaintiff has made out a prima facie case when he has proved possession at the time of the seizure.—Sack v. Ellis, 1, 346.

In an action against a sheriff for the recovery of goods of the plaintiff seized by him as the goods of another, the plaintiff, having rested after proving possession at the time of the seizure, may introduce evidence of the bona fides of such possession in rebuttal if the defendant meantime has put in testimony tending to show fraud.—Such evidence would not be cumulative.—Sack v. Ellis, 1, 346.

§ 5. Liability for Acts of Deputy—Exemplary Damages.

A sheriff, though liable for injuries done by his deputy, cannot be charged in exemplary damages for misconduct of such deputy as though he had personally committed the acts.—Nixon v. Rauer, 6, 788.

SHIPPING.

Liability to passengers. See Carriers, § 8.

§ 1. Wharfage Charges—Discrimination.

Wharfage charges imposed by the board of harbor commissioners on the owner of a barge and lighter, which were kept within a slip constructed, repaired and dredged by the board, are valid, and not in violation of the constitution of the United States, article 1, section 10, which prohibits a state from levying duty on tonnage without the consent of Congress.—People v. Roberts, 3, 372.

Where a lighter actually received the support of a wharf in discharging into and loading from a vessel tied to the wharf, the fact that the vessel lay between the wharf and the lighter, and that the owner of the vessel had paid regular wharfage rates, does not affect the right of the board of harbor commissioners to collect wharfage rates from the owner of the lighter.—People v. Roberts, 3, 372.

While act of March 17, 1880, which amends act of March 15, 1878, so as to exempt vessels engaged solely in domestic commerce from the wharfage tax, to which vessels engaged in interstate commerce still continue subject, may be invalid, in so far as it discriminates against vessels engaged in interstate commerce, yet the board of harbor commissioners, which is the agent of the state, with only such powers as are conferred on it by the legislature, cannot disregard the amendment, and collect wharfage taxes from vessels engaged solely in domestic commerce.—People v. Roberts, 3, 372.

§ 2. Liability on Contracts of Affreightment.

A person who charters a vessel, and by the terms of his contract as well as in fact assumed the exclusive possession, command and navigation of the vessel, whether for a particular voyage or an indefinite time, is the owner pro hac vice, and alone responsible upon contracts of affreightment.—Oakland Cotton Mfg. Co. v. Jennings, 1, 717.

In the respect of responsibility upon contracts of affreightment, after the owner of a vessel has let the latter to the master, the same law governs as would govern in the case of a letting to a stranger.—Oakland Cotton Mfg. Co. v. Jennings, 1, 717.

The exemption from liability enjoyed by the owner of a vessel for acts or omissions of a charterer, by which a bailor is aggrieved, or of a master assuming a relation to the owner similar to that of a charterer, is not lessened by the fact that under their contract the owner is to bear the expense of the vessel's repairs.—Oakland Cotton Mfg. Co. v. Jennings, 1, 717.

SHORTHAND REPORTERS.

§ 1. Constitutionality of Statute.

California act of March 21, 1885, relative to compensation of official shorthand reporters, considered, and held that the act was not unconstitutional, nor a delegation of power to the judiciary of legislating in regard to the matter, nor in violation of the county government bill, requiring a uniformity in county governments, nor in violation of article 11, section 6 of the constitution.—Smith v. Strother, 2, 525.

SICK BENEFITS.

See Associations, § 3.

SIGNALS.

On train approaching crossing. See Railroads, § 9.

SIGNATURE.

Of officers of corporation to note. See Corporations, § 16.

SIMILAR TRANSACTIONS.

Evidence of. See Larceny, § 8.

SLANDER.

See Libel and Slander.

SOLE TRADERS.

See Husband and Wife, § 1.

SPANISH GRANTS.

§ 1. Claimants Under.

One claiming title under a Spanish grant, who would avail himself of the proviso giving him five years after confirmation by the United States in which to bring suit, must both allege and prove the facts which bring him within the terms of the proviso.—Larue v. Chase, 1, 613.

SPECIAL ASSESSMENTS.

For street improvements. See Municipal Corporations, §§ 34–44.

SPECIAL FINDINGS.
See Trial, § 27.

SPECIAL VERDICT.
See Trial, § 18.

SPECIFICATION.
Of error. See Appeal and Error, §§ 53–56.

SPECIFIC PERFORMANCE.
§ 1. In general.
§ 2. Conditions precedent.
§ 3. —— Demand and tender.
§ 4. Laches of vendee.
§ 5. Parties.
§ 6. Pleading—Amendment.

§ 1. In General.

The action to enforce specific performance of a contract is an equitable remedy.—Martin v. Wray, 1, 25.

After failure to perform what he has bound himself to do under an agreement, a party cannot compel performance by the other parties of their part.—Connelly v. Eddy, 1, 86.

A naked claim that a person had taken possession of government land before it became subject to pre-emption, and had surrendered it to another at the latter's request and on his verbal promise to take all the steps necessary for the acquisition of a lawful title from the government, after which the second person was to execute a note to the first for a sum of money and a mortgage on the land to secure the note, is not sufficient to enable such first person to have a court of equity decree, in a suit for specific performance, that the second person execute the note and mortgage, such second person having acquired the lawful title from the government.—Saviers v. Barnett, 1, 452.

A decree for specific performance is always more or less within the discretion of the court. It may either be refused, it being deemed inequitable or against good conscience to enforce the contract, or it may be granted on such terms and subject to such conditions as may be just.—Ballard v. Carr, 1, 704.

§ 2. Conditions Precedent.

A covenant in a contract to convey land to a county for a highway and bridge, binding the county to furnish a cattle-way to the river, need not be performed in advance as a condition to a conveyance.—Monterey County v. Seegleken, 4, 613.

When a man has obligated himself by contract to execute a deed to another, it is not essential to a demand upon him preliminary to instituting suit on the contract that this other present, for him to execute, a deed of the precise nature he had contemplated giving or could be made to give.—Stone v. Garnett, 1, 804.

§ 3. —— Demand and Tender.

Under Civil Code, section 1440, allowing a party to an obligation which the other party repudiates before a default has occurred to enforce the obligation without performing or offering to perform the conditions in favor of the other, the refusal to allow a party to an option contract to perform the conditions of it, together with a repudiation of the contract prior to the expiration of the option, releases the holder of the option from tendering the price to be paid under it prior to suing for specific performance.—Stanton v. Singleton, 6, 129.

Defendant contracted to convey land to plaintiff free of encumbrance on payment of the purchase price on or before a certain day. Plaintiff had the money, and offered to pay the price before the day named, and demanded a·conveyance; but defendant had not removed the encumbrances, and on the day after the date named conveyed to another. Held, that an actual tender by plaintiff was not necessary to enable him to maintain an action for specific performance, since defendant was then unable to perform.—Luchetti v. Frost, 6, 763.

§ 4. Laches of Vendee.

Where a vendee of land delays more than four years after she accepts a deed, before suing to compel a conveyance of land which she alleges was wrongfully reserved in the deed to the grantor, she is not entitled to relief, though she did not discover the error until within three years of the suit, in the absence of fraud or deception which prevented her from sooner discovering it.—Eshleman v. Henrietta Vineyard Co., 4, 584.

Where it is not found that plaintiff did not discover the error thirty-five months before the commencement of such action, and before she tendered payment and demanded a deed, she is not entitled to specific performance, even if her negligence in not discovering the error sooner than she did was excusable.—Eshleman v. Henrietta Vineyard Co., 4, 584.

§ 5. Parties.

A mine owner who did not sign an option contract executed by his two co-owners is not a necessary party to an action to enforce the contract, where there is nothing to show that he is not willing to carry out the agreement, and no relief is sought against him.—Stanton v. Singleton, 6, 129.

§ 6. Pleading—Amendment.

In a suit for the specific performance of a contract between an attorney and his client whereby the former was to have land conveyed him by the latter in return for future services successfully performed, the defendant should be allowed to amend his answer so as to have it show omissions by the attorney putting the defendant to expense, the reimbursing him for which ought to be attached as a condition to any decree the plaintiff might be given.—Ballard v. Carr, 1, 704.

In an action to specifically enforce a contract for the sale of land, the allegations of performance by the vendee in the complaint held sufficient.—Alpers v. Knight, 2, 550.

The withdrawal of defendant's cross-bill for specific performance would not estop him to claim damages under the prayer of his answer. Cleary v. Folger, 4, 76.

SPEEDY TRIAL.

Right to. See Habeas Corpus, § 2.

STAGE.

Liability to passengers. See Carriers, § 7.

STAGE MANAGER OF THEATER.

Contract for employment of. See Work and Labor, § 3.

STALLION.

Warranty on sale of. See Sales, § 6.

STARE DECISIS.

See Law of Case.

STATE.

Liability as to bonds. See Bonds, § 3.

§ 1. Approval of Claims.

Where the state board of examiners have approved a claim, a subsequent change in the members of the board will not necessitate an approval by the new board to make the claim effective, the board being, in contemplation of law, the same board.—Cahill v. Colgan, 3, 622.

The approval of a claim by the board of examiners, and an appropriation of money to pay it by the legislature, is conclusive as to the validity of the claim as against the controller.—Cahill v. Colgan, 3, 622.

§ 2. Warrants and Appropriation to Pay Claims.

Political Code, section 672, provides that the state controller shall not draw his warrant for any claim unless it has been approved by the board of examiners, or has been "exempted" from the operation of this section. Held, that when a claim has been approved by the board, no exemption from the operation of this section need be shown to authorize the controller to draw his warrant for it.—Cahill v. Colgan, 3, 622.

Where a petition recites that a claim was presented to the board of examiners, approved as chargeable to the state for expenses in a suit in which the state was a party in interest, transmitted with such approval to the legislature, and that the legislature appropriated money "to pay said claim" under an act entitled "An act making an appropriation to pay costs and expenses of suits in which the state is a party in interest," and authorized the controller to draw his warrant for the amount appropriated, such a recital sufficiently identifies the claim as the one for which the appropriation was made.—Cahill v. Colgan, 3, 622.

§ 3. Action to Enforce Claims.

Where, in a petition for a claim which has been approved by the board of examiners, the petition states that the amount and "value" of such services was $504, the word "value" is surplusage, and requires no proof.—Cahill v. Colgan, 3, 622.

STATE BOARD OF EXAMINERS.

§ 1. Powers—Appointment of Expert.

Under constitution, article 4, section 32, forbidding the legislature to pay, or to authorize the payment of, any claim made under a contract "not expressly authorized by the law," the appropriation in act of March 28, 1895 (Stats. 1895, p. 280), "for salary of expert to board of examiners," is unavailable for that purpose, there being no express antecedent authority in the board to appoint such expert.—Lewis v. Colgan, 5, 373.

The performance of quasi-judicial acts by the state board of examiners in auditing claims does not make such board a judicial body, with implied power to appoint an expert and other necessary assistants at the expense of the state.—Lewis v. Colgan, 5, 373.

The several members of the state board of examiners, which consists of the governor, the Secretary of State, and the attorney general, do not, by virtue of their appointment on such board, carry with them, for exercise therein, the power conferred on them as executive officers, but have only such authority as relates to them as members of the board.—Lewis v. Colgan, 5, 373.

Act of March 28, 1895 (Stats. 1895, p. 280), entitled "An act making appropriations for the support of the government," etc., among which is an appropriation "for salary of expert to board of examiners," cannot be construed as creating the office of expert to such board, since the act would to that extent be unconstitutional, as embracing a subject not expressed in the title.—Lewis v. Colgan, 5, 373.

STATE LANDS.
See Public Lands.

§ 1. Application to Purchase—Contests.

The district court has no jurisdiction of a contest set on foot in the state land office by a party seeking to purchase lands of the state, as against another party to whom a patent for the lands has been issued by the state before the filing of his application by the contestant.—Somo v. Oliver, 2, 12.

The fact that plaintiff's application to purchase state land, of some portion of which he is in possession, has been adjudged invalid, and that it has been determined that he has no right to purchase, makes him none the less a proper party to proceedings to determine a contest inaugurated by a protest in the surveyor general's office against the purchase of the land by defendant. Garfield v. Wilson, 15 Pac. 620, 74 Cal. 175, and Perri v. Beaumont, 27 Pac. 534, 91 Cal. 30, followed.—Jacobs v. Walker, 3, 865.

The amendatory act of 1885 which does not require an application to purchase state land, not suitable for cultivation, to state that the applicant is an actual settler, does not cover applications made before its enactment, and render unnecessary proof that one previously applying is an actual settler, as required by the old statute.— Jacobs v. Walker, 3, 865.

§ 2. Certificate of Purchase.

A certificate of purchase issued to one of two applicants for certain state lands is not conclusive (in a contest to determine the right of the applicants to acquire title from the state to such land) of the right of the holder of such certificate to purchase as against the other applicant, who is in adverse possession of the land; each party to such contest must prove the right which he asserts and claims, and he has no enforceable claim in absence of proof of the facts upon which such right depends.—Gilson v. Robinson, 2, 486.

A certificate for the purchase of state lands is void if issued before the plat of survey of the township has been approved by the government officer or filed in the proper office.—Gilson v. Robinson, 2, 486.

§ 3. Two Mile Limit.

One attempting to defeat a patent on the ground that the land was within two miles of a town must show by affirmative evidence that at the time of the issue there was a town within the two miles. Upham v. Hosking, 2, 134.

In regard to lands purchased from the state prior to 1872, the objection that they were within two miles of town would, provided the requirements of law were complied with in other respects, have no force, in view of the curative act of March 27th of that year.—Upham v. Hosking, 2, 134.

STATEMENT.

Of case on appeal. See Appeal and Error, §§ 35–39.
Of claim for lien. See Mechanics' Liens, § 9.
On motion for new trial. See New Trial, §§ 14–17.

STATEMENT OF CASE.

Amendment of. See Amendments, § 4.

STATUTE OF FRAUDS.

See Frauds, Statute of.

STATUTE OF LIMITATIONS.

See Limitation of Actions.

STATUTES.

§ 1. Reading bills in legislature.
§ 2. Title of act—Amendatory statute.
§ 3. Repugnant acts.
§ 4. Effect of repeal.
See Constitutional Law.

§ 1. Reading Bills in Legislature.

Under the provision of the California constitution, article 4, section 15, which requires that every bill shall be read on three several days in each house, it is not required that the bill shall be read on three several days after an amendment thereto.—People v. Thompson, 2, 481.

§ 2. Title of Act—Amendatory Statute.

Under constitution of California, section 24, article 4, providing that "Every act shall embrace but one subject, which subject shall be expressed in its title," the act of 1880, entitled "An act to amend section 3481 of the Political Code," is constitutional, as a statute to be amended may be the "subject" of an amending act.—People v. Parvin, 2, 788.

§ 3. Repugnant Acts.

When two legislative acts are plainly repugnant, not susceptible of being reconciled, the one of the more recent enactment prevails.—Hartman v. Reed, 1, 858.

§ 4. Effect of Repeal.

A claim once barred through neglect by its owner to observe a requirement of a law then in force is not revived by the repeal subsequently of that feature of the law.—Hibernia Savings & Loan Soc. v. Jordan, 2, 79.

STAY.

Of proceedings. See Appeal and Error, § 29.
Of judgment. See Arbitration, § 1.
Of execution in criminal case. See Criminal Law, § 21.

STEALING.

See Larceny.

STEAMSHIP.

See Shipping.

STENOGRAPHERS.

See Shorthand Reporters.

STIPULATIONS.

§ 1. To Abide Result of Another Action.

A stipulation duly entered into by a plaintiff and defendant as to the issues in their action, to abide by the decision on similar issues in another action, is to be enforced by the supreme court on appeal.—Glenn v. Lackey, 2, 98.

A stipulation duly entered into by a plaintiff and a defendant as to the issues in their action, to abide by the decision on similar issues in another action, is to be enforced by the supreme court on appeal.—Shuggart v. Faneuil Hall Ins. Co., 2, 95.

§ 2. As to Pleadings and Evidence.

A stipulation agreeing to proposed evidence and expressly "permitting" either party to "add to it" such documentary evidence "as he may see proper" must be construed to mean, as to this added evidence, documents pertinent to the case and existing when the stipulation was made.—Donner v. Palmer, 1, 623.

If, after an intervener files his petition, all the parties, plaintiff and defendant stipulate with him to the dispensing with further pleadings, as if those already in met formally all questions on all sides, it cannot be objected to a judgment in his favor that it was not supported by his petition.—Donner v. Palmer, 1, 623.

§ 3. As to Rival Claims Founded on Execution Sales.

When a controversy was as to which is superior, between rival claims founded on sales in execution of different judgments against the one debtor, and by stipulation this naked controversy had been submitted to the court for its decision, after judgment the unsuccessful party cannot be heard to question the debtor's title to the property sold.—Donner v. Palmer, 1, 623.

STOCK AND STOCKHOLDERS.

See Corporations.

STOLEN GOODS.

Possession as evidence. See Burglary, § 3.
Possession of as evidence. See Larceny, § 9.

STREET RAILWAYS.

Liability to passengers. See Carriers, §§ 4–10.

§ 1. Organization and Franchise.

Where a street railroad franchise was granted to two persons, and they thereupon organized a corporation for the express purpose of constructing and operating a railroad under the franchise, and so declared in the articles of incorporation, an assignment of the franchise by said persons to the corporation was not necessary to vest the latter with any right relating thereto.—Santa Rosa City R. Co. v. Central St. Ry. Co., 4, 950.

§ 2. Forfeiture of Franchise.

Under the Civil Code (section 502), providing that, where a franchise has been granted to a street railroad, work on the road must be commenced within one year from the date of the grant of right of way, and finished within three years thereafter, and that a failure to comply with such provision "works a forfeiture" of the right of way as well as of the franchise, when a street railroad fails to comply with that provision, its right of way and franchise continue to exist until declared forfeited by a court or by legislative authority, said section not being self-executing.—Santa Rosa City R. Ry. Co., 4, 950.

When a city railroad's franchise is liable to forfeiture for a breach of condition subsequent, forfeiture thereof is not effected by the city's granting the same rights to another company.—Santa Rosa City R. Co. v. Central St. Ry. Co., 4, 950.

Where a city granted a street railroad franchise to two persons, who organized a corporation to operate a railroad thereunder, and thereafter the franchise became liable to forfeiture because the road was not constructed on certain streets within the specified time, but for eleven years after the breach, with full knowledge thereof, the city, in dealing with the company, by resolutions, orders, and ordinances, recognized the franchise as valid and in force, and took legal steps to enforce the obligations assumed by the company thereunder, and the company in consequence incurred expense in paving the streets on which its tracks were laid, and in paying taxes, the city and the public are estopped to claim a forfeiture of the franchise or deny the company's ownership thereof.—Santa Rosa City R. Co. v. Central St. Ry. Co., 4, 950.

§ 3. Injunction Against Another Company.

In an action by a street railroad company, operating its road under a franchise, to enjoin another railroad company, claiming the right to construct a road on the same street under a subsequent franchise, from tearing up plaintiff's tracks, plaintiff need not show ownership of the franchise under which it operates, its actual possession of the street being sufficient as against defendant.—Santa Rosa City R. Co. v. Central St. Ry. Co., 4, 950.

Where a street railroad company, claiming the right to construct its road over a street under a franchise, tears up the tracks and interferes with the operation of the road of another company already operating on said street under a prior franchise, the latter may bring an action to enjoin said acts, and recover its actual damages on account of them.—Santa Rosa City R. Co. v. Central St. Ry. Co., 4, 950.

In an action by the company to enjoin the tearing up of its tracks, an ordinance passed after its franchise became liable to forfeiture, granting plaintiff the right to construct a switch, which right should "extend until the expiration of the term of the franchise" first granted, was admissible, as tending to show both the original existence of the franchise and a waiver of the forfeiture.— Santa Rosa City R. Co. v. Central St. Ry. Co., 4, 950.

STREETS.

In general. See Municipal Corporations.
Negligent driving. See Negligence, §§ 5, 6.

SUBROGATION.

§ 1. In Cases of Suretyship in General.

The right of sureties to be subrogated to a lien on their principal's property may be assigned.—San Francisco Savings Union v. Long, 6, 60.

Where sureties had paid part of a judgment against the principal, which had paid the balance itself, and were entitled to be subrogated to a lien against the principal, the enforcement by their assignee of such lien to the amount paid by them is a single demand, and not obnoxious to the rule against splitting demands.—San Francisco Savings Union v. Long, 6, 60.

A surety who has not contributed to the payment of the principal's judgment debt is not a necessary party to the determination of a right of lien claimed by the assignee of his cosureties by subrogation to the rights of the judgment creditor.—San Francisco Savings Union v. Long, 6, 60.

§ 2. In Case of Insurance.

Where sureties for a life insurance company were obliged to pay a death benefit, they are entitled to be subrogated to a lien in favor of the beneficiary on a fund created for the protection of policyholders.—San Francisco Savings Union v. Long, 6, 60.

SUBSCRIPTIONS.

For relief of families. See Money Received, § 1.

SUBSIDY.

To railroad. See Counties, § 7.

SUCCESSION.

See Executors and Administrators, §§ 37–40.
To property by surviving spouse. See Husband and Wife, § 8.

SUMMONS.

See Process.

SUPERIOR COURT.

Jurisdiction. See Courts, § 5.

SUPPLEMENTAL PLEADINGS.

See Pleading, § 11.

SUPPLEMENTARY PROCEEDINGS.

§ 1. In General.

As proceedings supplementary to execution are purely statutory, the mode of procedure thereon provided for by statute must be followed; and a failure to comply with the statute will vitiate the proceedings.—Bryant v. Bank of California, 2, 475.

A judgment creditor, in a supplementary proceeding against a garnishee, brought in pursuance of an order made under the statute (Code Civ. Proc., sec. 720), must aver and prove the existence of the order and of the proceedings by which the order was founded. The record of such proceedings, to be admissible in such action, must be filed with the clerk of the court, and must come, either as an original or authenticated copy, from the hands of the officer in whose custody it is kept.—Bryant v. Bank of California, 2, 475.·

The law purporting to authorize a judge, by order, to permit the judgment creditor to institute and maintain an action against the debtor of the judgment debtor (viz., Code of Civil Procedure, section 720), is unconstitutional and void, as no notice of such proceeding to the judgment debtor is provided for.—Bryant v. Bank of California, 2, 567.

§ 2. Habeas Corpus in Case of Commitment.

Where, in proceedings supplementary to execution, defendant pleads a previous discharge in insolvency, and refuses to answer questions as to her property, and is committed for contempt, her remedy is by appeal, and not by habeas corpus.—Ex parte McDonald, 2, 853.

SUPPORT OF GRANTOR.

Deed for. See Deeds, § 10.

SUPREME COURT.

Jurisdiction. See Courts, § 7.
Salary of justices. See Courts, § 9.

SURETYSHIP.

See Principal and Surety.

SURFACE WATERS.

See Waters and Watercourses, § 16.

SURPLUSAGE.

In pleading. See Pleading, § 15.

SURPRISE.

As ground for new trial. See Trial, § 2.

SURVEYOR GENERAL.

Imposing judicial functions on. See Constitutional Law, § 6.

SURVEYS.

In general. See Boundaries.

SWAMP LANDS.

§ 1. In general.
§ 2. Reclamation districts.
§ 3. Reclamation funds—Assignment—Sale of Land.
§ 4. Construction and repair of works—Damages.
§ 5. Assessments.
§ 6. Application and proceedings for purchase.
§ 7. Cancellation of patent.

§ 1. In General.

It is questionable whether, under existing statutes, lands held under Mexican grants can be included in swamp land reclamation districts, particularly if the land sought to be so included be not itself swamp land.—Hagar v. Supervisors of Yolo Co., 1, 770.

In the organization of swamp land reclamation districts the powers of boards of supervisors are determined in each case by the board's own record of the case, which record cannot be enlarged or aided by proof aliunde.—Hagar v. Supervisors of Yolo Co., 1, 770.

The legislature of the state has power to grant swamp and overflowed lands to private persons, and such lands are taken subject to state legislation in regard to the reclamation thereof.—Packard v. Johnson, 2, 365.

Constitution, article 17, section 3, providing that state lands which are "suitable for cultivation" shall be granted only to actual settlers, applies to swamp lands granted to the state when such lands are suitable for cultivation, and can be reclaimed and cultivated by an actual settler.—Marsh v. Hendy, 3, 431.

§ 2. Reclamation Districts.

A reclamation district established under the act of March 25, 1868, is legally established if organized by the board of supervisors by virtue of that act, and its corporate existence cannot be attacked collaterally.—Hoke v. Perdue, 2, 116.

Political Code of California, section 3481, provides that the requisite number of owners of "lands within any reclamation or swamp land district, and in which the lands have not been reclaimed, may have said body of lands set off from such district." Held, that this did not repeal the prior laws, or affect the assessment proceedings thereunder, and applied to all future cases, whether the existing district was organized under the code or not.—People v. Parvin, 2, 788.

§ 3. Reclamation Funds—Assignment—Sale of Land.

Since Political Code, section 3477, requiring the county treasurer to pay amounts due on reclamation of swamp land to the original purchaser or his assigns, contemplates payment only to the owner or assignee of the indebtedness, mandamus will not lie to compel such a payment to one who is not shown to be the assignee of the claim on the fund of an original purchaser who became entitled thereto, though he claims as a successor in interest of such original purchaser, by virtue of a purchase of the land.—Miller & Lux v. Batz, 6, 481.

§ 4. Construction and Repair of Works—Damages.

That a levee has been constructed without due regard to the law warranting the construction is no reason in law for refraining from repairing it afterward when it needs repairs.—Hoke v. Perdue, 2, 116.

In projects for local improvements, such as reclamation works, the fact that the land of some one taxpayer will be injured rather than benefited does not make out a case of taking for the public use without a just compensation in violation of the constitution.—Hoke v. Perdue, 2, 27.

The omission of land within the district from the burden of taxation, however it might serve as a ground for injunction to restrain the collection of the tax, is no ground where the thing to be restrained is the reconstruction or repair of a levee.—Hoke v. Perdue, 2, 116.

§ 5. Assessments.

In an action by a swamp land reclamation district to enforce the payment of a swamp land assessment, plaintiff offered in evidence an order appearing in the "minute-book" of the board of supervisors, in which, by Political Code, sections 4029–4031, all orders of the board are required to be recorded; and it was conceded that, without the direction of the board, the order had been altered by B., who at the time of the entry, but not at the time of the alteration, was ex-officio clerk of the board. B. testified, against objection, that he made the alteration to correct what appeared to him, on examination, to be a clerical error of his deputy, now deceased, the then acting clerk of the board. The "rough minute-book," containing the original entry from which the record was made, and to which the altered record conformed, was also admitted against objection. Held, that it was error for the court to admit the order in evidence. Swamp Land Reclamation Dist. v. Wilcox, 2, 794.

Held, further, that the order was a record which B. had no right to alter or amend, and that parol proof was inadmissible to correct or change the record.—Swamp Land Reclamation Dist. v. Wilcox, 2, 794.

Under Political Code, section 3461, requiring certain assessment lists to contain "a description, by legal subdivisions, swamp land surveys, or natural boundaries," a description, naming the adjoining proprietors on the respective boundaries, is sufficient.—Swamp Land Reclamation Dist. v. Wilcox, 2, 794.

Political Code, section 3456, provides that assessments for swamp land improvements shall be proportionate to the resulting benefit, and section 3461 provides, among other requisites, that the list must contain "the amount of the charge assessed against each tract." The list in question conformed to the requirements of section 3461. Held, that the commissioners were not required to report that, in making the assessment, they had complied with section 3456, and that in the absence of evidence to the contrary, they must be presumed to have regularly performed their official duty.—Swamp Land Reclamation Dist. v. Wilcox, 2, 794.

In an action to enforce the payment of a swamp land assessment, it appeared that, in the assessment list, there was no dollar-mark before the figures opposite defendant's name, under the heading "Amount of charges assessed." In a number of assessments the dollar-mark preceded the figures under that heading, and in others the mark did not appear. Held, that the figures must be construed to represent dollars.—Swamp Land Reclamation Dist. v. Wilcox, 2, 794.

The commissioners of swamp land assessments were verbally sworn before viewing the land, but it did not appear that they subscribed their oath and filed it in the county clerk's office, as required of all "officers" by Political Code, sections 904, 909. Held, that whether the commissioners were or were not "officers," within the meaning of those sections, a failure of strict compliance with their requirements would not avoid official acts fully performed.—Swamp Land Reclamation Dist. v. Wilcox, 2, 794.

§ 6. Application and Proceedings for Purchase.

The taking of a single step, of many required, by one who would succeed as an applicant for the purchase of swamp lands under the statute, is not sufficient as evidence that such applicant was successful.—Tucker v. Cooper, 1, 744.

An appeal may not be taken, on the point of sufficiency of evidence, directly from an adjudication by the court to which the surveyor general referred rival applications to purchase swamp land, but, just as in other cases, only from an order of court upon a motion made on that ground for a new trial.—Tucker v. Cooper, 1, 744.

The foundation of the jurisdiction of boards of supervisors in the matter of the organization of swamp land reclamation districts is a sufficient petition, the requisites of which are prescribed by statute. Hagar v. Supervisors of Yolo Co., 1, 770.

When it affirmatively appears that a board of supervisors in the course of proceedings resulting in an assessment found, in the manner required by law, that the statements in a petition for the organization of a reclamation district were true and that no land was improperly included in the district, such statements cannot again be litigated in a collateral action by one who was a party to the reclamation proceedings.—People v. Hager, 2, 13.

The swamp lands granted to the state are not subject to application for purchase until they have been segregated to the state by a United States survey, and an application filed prior to such segregation confers no rights on the applicant.—Marsh v. Hendy, 3, 431.

§ 7. Cancellation of Patent.

When a suit is instituted in the name of the state, by the permission of the attorney general, upon the relation of the real party in interest, seeking the cancellation of the patent for state swamp lands, and the state has no direct interest in the event of suit, the attorney general is not authorized to move to dismiss, or to withdraw his consent to the use of the name of the people to the prejudice of the relator.—People v. Jacobs, 2, 672.

TAX DEED.
See Taxation, § 22.

TAXATION.

§ 1. In General.

The legislature in California has no constitutional power to tax the people to pay a void debt. So held, where, after the courts had declared unconstitutional and void the act of April 23, 1880, entitled

"An act to promote drainage," the legislature attempted to pass another act on March 10, 1885, providing for the payment of indebtedness incurred under said act of April 23, 1880.—Miller v. Dunn, 2, 673.

Taxes do not draw interest unless by some express statutory provision to that effect, and there is no difference in this respect between general taxation and the species known as assessments.—Dougherty v. McAlpine, 1, 370.

A provision, in an act to reincorporate a municipality, making two per cent the maximum tax rate unless otherwise determined by a vote of the people or by special act of legislature, has reference to taxes to be levied for defraying usual municipal expenses, and not to such as may be necessary to pay obligations already incurred by the municipality.—Myers v. Mayor and Common Council of Placerville, 1, 565.

§ 2. Double Taxation—Railroads.

When a railroad company, empowered by charter to build its road between termini in different counties, lays its tracks at one terminus on a wharf, and the whole railroad is assessed by the state board of equalization, pursuant to constitution, article 13, section 10, providing that the roadbed, rails, and rolling stock of all railroads operated in more than one county shall be assessed by that board, an assessment of the wharf by the county tax collector does not constitute double taxation, since the wharf is not a necessary part of the railroad, and brings in a separate income.—Pacific Coast Ry. Co. v. Ramage, 4, 743.

§ 3. Assessments.

A tax founded on a special supplemental assessment, made in the year 1880–81 by the assessor in the city and county of San Francisco, of certain personal property, did not become a lien on the property of the person assessed, as such assessment was levied.—Bowman v. Dewey, 2, 566.

Where the validity of an assessment is put in issue by the pleadings in an action, any fact or facts going to show that no valid assessment was ever levied, are within the issues and properly included in the findings.—Doane v. Barber, 2, 597.

A blank form of the statement under oath, required of owners of property by Political Code, section 3629, unsigned by them, on which is written an unsigned memorandum containing a description of the property, and under the head of "Value of Real Estate" the figures "20,000," and under that of "Value of Improvements" the figures "800," the dollar-mark not appearing, did not constitute an assessment of the property, which could be effected only by the insertion in due form in the completed assessment-book, and the certification of the latter by the assessor, as required by section 3652.—Allen v. McKay & Co., 6, 993.

§ 4. —— Description of Land.

Political Code, section 3650, relative to taxation, provides land shall be described in the assessment-book by township. range, section or fractional section, and when not a congressional division or subdivision, by metes and bounds, or other identifying description. Held, that a description by township, range and section, in connection with official surveys and plats, was sufficient.—Allen v. McKay & Co., 6, 993.

§ 5.—— Mistake in Name.

Political Code, section 3628, providing that a mistake in the name of the owner of real property shall not invalidate the assessment for

taxes, has no application to an assessment of personal property, and
hence an assessment of H.'s personal property to "R. and wife and
H." cannot be held valid thereunder.—Houser & Haines Mfg. Co. v.
Hargrove, 6, 384.

A sale of the personal property of H. for taxes due, not by him
alone, nor upon the property alone, but for taxes on property not
owned by H., and given to the assessor as the property of R., is void,
under Political Code, sections 3820, 3821, providing for a collection of
the personal property tax by seizure and sale of any personalty
owned by the person against whom the tax is assessed.—Houser &
Haines Mfg. Co. v. Hargrove, 6, 384.

§ 6. Omission of Property.

See, also, post, § 12.

An order of the board of equalization finding that a bank has
omitted property from the list of its taxable property, and should be
assessed thereon, and directing the assessor to add such property to
its assessment, is not an attempt by the board to add property to the
list, and exercise assessorial powers, but is a direction that the assessor makes such addition, though the order specifies the value of
the property to be added, and is authorized by Political Code, section
3681, requiring the assessor, at the request of the board, to list and
assess property which he has failed to assess.—Security Savings Bank
& Trust Co. v. Board of Supervisors, 4, 222.

Political Code, section 3681, under which the assessor is required,
at the request of the board of equalization, to list and assess property which he has failed to assess, which. section the city charter
of Los Angeles makes applicable to the common council, sitting as a
board of equalization, does not conflict with the constitutional provisions which define the powers and duties of state and county
boards of equalization, and which do not give the power to cause
property to be added to the assessment list, since it merely extends
the power and duty of the assessor.—Security Savings Bank & Trust
Co. v. Board of Supervisors, 4, 222.

§ 7. Savings Banks.

The fact that a corporation is engaged in a general banking business, in addition to a savings bank business, does not exempt that
part of its business done as a savings bank from taxation under the
laws applying to other savings banks.—Main St. Sav. Bank & Trust
Co. v. Hinton, 3, 757.

§ 8. Mortgages.

Neglect or refusal of a land owner to return a mortgage on his
land for taxation does not authorize the assessor to arbitrarily assess
it to him, since Political Code, section 3629, requires the land owner
to return only property belonging to himself; and section 3633,
authorizing arbitrary assessment on refusal of the owner to make a
statement, applies only to property belonging to him; and section
3650, subdivision 15, requires the assessor to deduct mortgages and
assess them to their owner.—Henne v. Los Angeles County, 6, 370.

Where the assessor fails to enter the value of the mortgages on
land assessed, in the proper column, and deduct the same, as required by Political Code, section 3650, subdivision 15, it cannot be
presumed that he made the proper deductions, but failed to so state
on the assessment-roll.—Henne v. Los Angeles County, 6, 370.

§ 9. Imported Goods Exposed for Sale.

Imported goods exposed for sale in the store of a merchant constitute a portion of the wealth of the state, for purposes of taxation,

as much as do domestic goods similarly situated; and it is immaterial whether the importer is also the merchant who sells or whether the goods are in the original packages and at the time owned abroad.—Low & Co. v. Austin, 1, 638.

§ 10. Migratory Livestock.

The act of March 16, 1874, "to regulate the assessment of migratory stock," imposes the duty upon the assessor, when making such assessment, to demand that the owner state if during the year the stock is to be taken out of the county; in default of such demand there is no duty on the owner so to state, regardless of whether he has the removal of them in mind at the time or resolves upon it thereafter.—People v. Thomason, 2, 69.

§ 11. Public Lands.

For the purposes of taxation there is no presumption of law that land occupied by private persons, assessed in due form by the proper officers as private property and sold for taxes, is a part of the public domain and not subject to taxation.—Rider v. Miller, 1, 222.

It is insufficient merely to claim land as United States government land, and hence exempt from taxation; the person concerned must show the fact.—Rider v. Miller, 1, 222.

Public lands are not subject to taxation, and an act of the legislature, intended to cure an ineffective assessment of them, is in itself ineffective.—People v. Mac, 1, 224.

§ 12. Board of Equalization.

A notice to a bank to appear before the board of equalization, and show cause why its "assessment on the solvent credits should not be increased from $2,774 to $275,000," sufficiently informs it that it is proposed to add property to the assessment.—Security Savings Bank & Trust Co. v. Board of Supervisors, 4, 222.

A person appearing before the board of equalization in response to a notice, and submitting to the action of the board, waives any defect in the notice.—Security Savings Bank & Trust Co. v. Board of Supervisors, 4, 222.

A finding by the board of equalization that a person has omitted taxable property from his list to a certain amount is conclusive on the courts on writ of review, since Code of Civil Procedure, section 1074, provides that the review on such writ cannot be extended further than to determine whether the inferior tribunal or board has regularly pursued its authority.—Security Savings Bank & Trust Co. v. Board of Supervisors, 4, 222.

Even if the fact that the property has been so omitted is necessary to give the board jurisdiction, the court cannot review the evidence to determine whether there was evidence to show such fact, since the fact is one to be determined by the board.—Security Savings Bank & Trust Co. v. Board of Supervisors, 4, 222.

The board of equalization has authority, upon a proper application or petition, to increase or diminish the valuation of the property listed and returned by the assessor.—Central Pacific R. R. Co. v. Board of Equalization, 1, 460.

In ascertaining and determining the proper valuation of property for purposes of taxation, the board of equalization acts in a judicial capacity.—Central Pacific R. R. Co. v. Board of Equalization, 1, 460.

§ 13. Compelling Municipality to Levy Tax.

A valid demand upon a municipality for the levying of a tax to pay interest on bonds, payable under a special act, must be made upon the mayor and common council as a body assembled; a demand each at his separate place of private business will not suffice.—Myers v. Mayor and Common Council of Placerville, 1, 565.

In a mandamus proceeding to compel municipality to levy a tax to pay interest on bonds previously issued by it, a denial in the answer that any demand in the premises was ever made upon the municipality presents a material issue.—Myers v. Mayor and Common Council of Placerville, 1, 565.

§ 14. Injunction Against Tax Collector.

If a judgment in an action against the tax collector of a county, which adjudges an assessment void, and enjoins him and his successors in office from proceeding under the assessment, is binding on him—which it is not unless the county is bound thereby—he has a right to proceed by suit or otherwise to set it aside, as preventing his performing his duties.—Sheehan v. Osborne, 6, 979.

An order dismissing a suit to set aside a judgment adjudging an assessment void, and enjoining the county tax collector from proceeding under it, though entered by the plaintiff tax collector's attorney with his consent, will be opened for mistake on showing that he gave consent in ignorance of his obligation to other parties interested, and that their interests would be prejudiced.—Sheehan v. Osborne, 6, 979.

§ 15. Actions to Enforce Tax—Pleading and Practice.

There can arise against a taxpayer no cause of action for delinquency in a case where there has been no valid assessment.—People v. San Francisco etc. R. R. Co., 1, 391.

In an action to collect delinquent taxes, an averment in the complaint, that "the tax collector had failed to collect the delinquent tax aforesaid by reason of his inability to find, seize or sell property of the delinquents," is a material averment, so that an answer denying it is neither irrelevant nor frivolous.—People v. Waterman, 1, 190.

In an action to collect delinquent taxes an answer denying an averment in the complaint that "the tax collector had failed to collect the delinquent tax aforesaid by reason of his inability to find, seize or sell property of the delinquents," is not contrary to the act of 1861, page 471, which provides that the defendant in such cases shall not be allowed to show any informality in the levy or assessment as a defense.—People v. Waterman, 1, 190.

In an action to collect delinquent taxes an answer denying an averment in the complaint that "the tax collector had failed to collect the delinquent tax aforesaid by reason of his inability to find, seize or sell property of the delinquents," indicates a defense on the ground, not that the defendants were not liable to pay the taxes sued for, but that the suit had been brought prematurely.—People v. Waterman, 1, 190.

In a case where, although there are several parcels of land of one owner severally assessed, there has been but one assessment and the cause of action is the failure to pay this, the assessment may be enforced in one action.—People v. Hager, 2, 13.

The act providing for the management and sale of lands belonging to the state requires that holders of such lands by purchase from the state shall be proceeded against for delinquent taxes in the same manner as provided by law for the collection of state and county taxes, which latter proceedings are brought in the name of the people. People v. Hager, 2, 13.

District attorneys are not authorized to commence and prosecute actions for the recovery of delinquent taxes. Any county may do so in its own name, and its action is to be directed by the board of supervisors of such county. The district attorney having brought this action without their direction or ratification, no attorney's fees can be recovered of the defendant, nor costs against the plaintiff.—San Diego Co. v. C. S. R. Co., 2, 238.

Though the term of office of tax collector terminates pending a suit by him, it may be prosecuted without substitution of his successor; Code of Civil Procedure, section 385, after giving the rule in case of death of a party, providing that in case of any other transfer of interest the action may be continued in the name of the original party.—Sheehan v. Osborne, 6, 979.

§ 16. —— Misnomer and Misdescription.

In an action for the collection of delinquent taxes, a defense based on misdescription of the land in the assessment is not good if claimed merely because of a defect in metes and bounds set forth, provided it is accurate as to the location and township where the land is situate, the number of acres, and the description by common designation or name.—People v. Williamson, 1, 742.

A judgment in a tax suit wherein the plaintiff is named as "The Mayor and Common Council of San Jose," instead of "The City of San Jose," is not void because of the misnomer.—Reanda v. Fulton, 1, 844.

§ 17. —— Service of Summons.

In an action for the collection of delinquent taxes, the judgment for the plaintiff will not affect both the personal defendant and the real estate assessed unless the summons has been served upon both.—People v. Williamson, 1, 742.

§ 18. —— Judgment—Default.

Where a default judgment is given for, among other things, taxes levied without authority, the supreme court will remand the case.—People ex rel. Bunnell v. Hager, 1, 92.

In an action for the recovery of taxes, where the summons does not contain the notice that "the plaintiff will apply to the court for the relief demanded" in the complaint, a judgment by default must be reversed.—People v. Mariposa Company, 1, 631.

A judgment in a tax suit which subjects the real estate to sale for the whole tax due instead of enforcing the lien upon each parcel, as asked in the complaint, would be susceptible to appeal for error but cannot be attacked collaterally.—Reanda v. Fulton, 1, 844.

§ 19. Payment by One as Payment for Others.

It may well happen that several persons may be assessed for a possession of, interest in, or claim to the same land, and when such is the case the payment by one would not operate as a payment for another.—People v. Williamson, 1, 742.

§ 20. Sale for Taxes.

A sale by the sheriff in execution of a tax judgment must be conducted according to the directions in such judgment.—Reanda v. Fulton, 1, 844.

§ 21. Purchase by State—Notice of Intention to Apply for Deed.

Where the state is the purchaser of land at tax sale, the controller and the attorney general have no authority to give notice for the state of an intention to apply for a deed.—San Francisco & Fresno Land Co. v. Banbury, 4, 789.

There being no statutory provision for the disposition of a fee for notice of intention to apply for a deed of lands sold to the state for taxes, it must be taken as the legislative intent that no such fee should be charged.—San Francisco & Fresno Land Co. v. Banbury, 4, 789.

§ 22. Tax Deed.

A tax deed is made by statute prima facie evidence of title in the grantee.—Rider v. Miller, 1, 222.

A tax deed describing the property conveyed as "an undivided interest in the," etc., is not bad for misdescription if otherwise it identifies the property, mentioning the record owner, whose interest was an undivided one, and the assessment to him.—People v. Hicks, 1, 236.

TEACHERS.

See Schools and School Districts.

TELEGRAPH COMPANIES.

§ 1. Limitation of Liability.

A stipulation purporting to exempt a telegraph corporation from all liability for mistakes or delays in the transmission or delivery, or for nondelivery, of any unrepeated message, whether happening by the negligence of its servants or otherwise, beyond the amount received for sending the same, is void for want of consideration to support it.—Hart v. Western Union Tel. Co., 2, 373.

It is not competent for telegraph companies to stipulate against or limit their liability for mistakes happening in consequence of their own fault, such as want of proper skill or ordinary care on the part of their operators, or the use of defective instruments. They are exempt only for errors arising from causes beyond their control; and whether such error was caused by negligence or was beyond their control is a question for the jury, the presumption being that it occurred through negligence.—Hart v. Western Union Tel. Co., 2, 373.

§ 2. Offense of Sending False Message.

A conviction of the crime of sending a false telegram is erroneous, and cannot be sustained, if from the evidence it appears that the defendant had not the slightest idea that he was deceiving the person to whom the message was sent, and that the person to whom the message was sent was not deceived.—People v. Devon, 2, 542.

TENANCY IN COMMON.

See Partition.

Ouster and adverse holding. See Adverse Possession, § 7.
Levy on undivided share of crop. See Execution, § 1.
Homestead on land held in common. See Homestead, § 1.
Intervention by cotenant. See Intervention, § 2.
In mining property. See Mines and Minerals, § 5.

§ 1. In General.

One tenant in common of personal property has no authority to sell the interest of his co-owner.—McGarry v. Proffitt, 1, 517.

A tenant in common cannot, as against his cotenant, give a license to a third person to enter on the land held in common.—Moore v. Moore, 4, 190.

§ 2. Ouster and Adverse Possession.

Under the rule that if one of several tenants in common labors under a disability which preserves his rights under the statute of limitations, this will not inure to the benefit of his cotenants against whom the statute has fully run, if the tenant under disability brings his action against the disseizor for the possession, he can recover only his undivided interest.—Chipman v. Hastings, 1, 817.

Tenants in common of land subject to a mortgage have such a community of interest as precludes one from acquiring an adverse title as to the other through such mortgage or the payment of it without affording the co-owner an opportunity of paying his proportionate share and enjoying the benefit.—Hitchcock v. Clarke, 2, 37.

A refusal by a tenant in common in possession to admit his cotenant into the possession is itself an ouster, and dispenses with further proof on that point.—Freer v. Tripp, 2, 91.

In an action by a tenant in common against his cotenant for admittance into the possession, a denial in the answer that the plaintiff has title and right of entry is an ouster.—Freer v. Tripp, 2, 91.

TENDER.

In specific performance. See Specific Performance, § 3.

§ 1. In General.

A tender, to be valid, must be unconditional.—Jones v. Shuey, 5, 17.

A tender of money under the United States Legal Tender Act of February 25, 1862, is good in this state.—Gann v. Bond, 1, 151.

§ 2. Waiver of Objections.

By the statute (Code Civ. Proc., sec. 2076), it is provided that the person to whom a tender is made must, at the time, specify any objection he may have to the money, instrument or property, or he must be deemed to have waived it; and if the objection be to the amount of money, the amount or the kind of property, he must specify the amount, terms or kind which he requires, or be precluded from objecting afterward.—Oakland Bank of Savings v. Applegarth, 2, 411.

THEATER.

Employment of stage manager. See Work and Labor, § 3.

THEFT.

See Larceny.

THREATS.

Evidence of. See Homicide, § 8.

TIDE LAND.

§ 1. Reclamation and Patent.

A patent for land, although purporting to have been issued under the state act of April 21, 1858, for the sale and reclamation of swamp and overflowed lands, was, whether made before or after the act of May 14, 1861, which refers to reclaimable tide lands, ineffectual to pass any title if the subject of the patent was tide land incapable of reclamation.—Connelly v. Mon Chung, 1, 748.

TIMBER.

Injunction against cutting. See Injunction, § 5.

TIME.

For appeal. See Appeal and Error, §§ 15–19.
For filing transcript. See Appeal and Error, §§ 45–47.

TITLE.

Declarations and admissions respecting. See Evidence, § 11.
Marketable title. See Vendor and Vendee, § 9.

TITLE OF STATUTE.

See Statutes, § 2.

TOLL ROADS AND GATES.

See Turnpike Company, § 2.

TOOLS.

Falling from building into street. See Negligence, § 4.

TOWN SITES.

See Public Lands, § 4.

TRADE AGREEMENT.

Restraining breach of. See Injunction, § 8.

TRADE MARKS AND NAMES.

§ 1. What Will be Protected as Such.

Under Civil Code, section 991, one may have a property in a trade-mark on cigar boxes, provided the mark does not relate only to the name, quality or description of them, or the place where they are produced or the business carried on.—Shaefer v. Korbel, 2, 166.

Where labels used on bottles containing medicine manufactured by defendants in no respect resemble labels used by plaintiffs on bottles containing similar medicine put up by them, except that both labels have thereon the words "Sarsaparilla and Iron," plaintiffs are not entitled to an injunction or to damages.—Schmidt v. Welch, 4, 417.

Defendant, the owner of land known as "Milbrae Station," formed a copartnership with plaintiffs to keep cows on said land, and sell the milk therefrom under the trade name of "Milbrae Dairy." Afterward the partnership was dissolved, plaintiffs taking the milk routes and business of selling milk, and defendant, who remained the owner of the land, agreeing to supply them with milk therefrom. Later plaintiffs terminated the contract with defendant, and took no more of his milk, but still conducted a milk business under the name of the "Milbrae Dairy," and formed a corporation under the name of the "Milbrae Company," to carry on the business. Held, that plaintiffs could not ask for an injunction to restrain defendant from using the name "Milbrae" in a competing business, since their own use of the name was a fraud on the public.—Milbrae Co. v. Taylor, 4, 714.

TRANSCRIPT.

On appeal. See Appeal and Error, §§ 45, 52.

TRAVELING SALESMAN.
Action for wrongful discharge. See Master and Servant, § 4.

TREASURER.
See Counties, § 3.

Failure to pay over to successor. See Officers, § 3.

Liability on bond of treasurer. See Principal and Surety, § 3.

§ 1. Payment of Auditor's Drafts.
County treasurers are not required to pay auditor's drafts unless the consideration upon which they were issued is stated and vouched for by the auditor on the face of the paper.—Conley v. Price, 1, 355.

TREES.
Sale of diseased trees. See Sales, § 10.

TRESPASS.
    § 1. Right to maintain action for.
    § 2. Actions for trespass—Matters of practice.
    § 3. Damages—Pleading.
    § 4. Prosecution for removing quartz.
    § 5. Removal of trespasser.

By animals. See Animals, § 2.

Injunction against. See Injunctions, § 4.

§ 1. Right to Maintain Action for.
Certified transcripts of several recorded deeds, the first purporting to convey "a portion" of certain land, but not designating any particular portion, the second a "further portion," and the third the "remaining portion," offered without any showing of title in the grantors or that the grantee had entered claiming under the said deeds, are not sufficient evidence of title to enable the grantee to maintain an action for trespass on the land.—Odd Fellows' Sav. Bank v. Turman, 3, 546.

Evidence of the survey of land, made for the purpose of locating a certain lake, an advertisement of the land for sale or rent, and a notification to a certain stockman to keep his stock off of "that land," is not sufficient, as to actual possession, to enable the alleged owner to maintain an action for trespass on the land.—Odd Fellows' Sav. Bank v. Turman, 3, 546.

Owner of land who leases it with understanding that the lessee, if he cannot keep stock of strangers off, shall charge them with the use thereof, cannot maintain trespass against one who, on his cattle intruding thereon, arranges with the lessee to use the land for his stock for the season for a certain amount; and it is immaterial whether the money so collected belonged to the tenant or land owner. Stufflebeem v. Hickman, 6, 17.

§ 2. Actions for Trespass—Matters of Practice.
In cases where joint trespassers are concerned, one action at law is sufficient.—Gates v. Teagus, 1, 46.

Although the plaintiff, in prior possession, is himself a trespasser, the defendants are not permitted to show the fact to justify the later trespass imputed to them.—Baird v. Duane, 1, 492.

On the question of a trespass all persons entering under any certain one are concluded by his declarations and statements, and these should go to the jury with appropriate instructions.—Baird v. Duane, 1, 492.

Findings held justified by the evidence.—Smith v. Idaho Quartz Min. Co., 2, 681.

A complaint in trespass, alleging that defendants entered plaintiff's close, and diverted the waters of his well, and frightened his wife is not objectionable as presenting a misjoinder of causes of action.—Razzo v. Varni, 3, 94.

In such action, where plaintiff shows peaceable possession under a paper title for several years, if defendants have any right of entry, it must be pleaded in justification.—Razzo v. Varni, 3, 94.

The fact that defendant, in an action for trespass on land, makes the defense that the land was not fenced, does not estop him afterward from denying plaintiff's ownership of land.—Odd Fellows' Savings Bank v. Turman, 3, 546.

§ 3. Damages—Pleading.

In such case, evidence by plaintiff that his loss was four dollars per day, estimated on the loss of profits on 'his crop of vegetables, is incompetent, as being the conclusion of the witness, and not the facts on which an estimate could be made.—Razzo v. Varni, 3, 94.

Such damages were special, and, if recoverable at all, must be pleaded.—Razzo v. Varni, 3, 94.

The evidence of plaintiff in trespass as to the extent of damages resulting therefrom is sufficient to support a finding of a less sum as the damages sustained.—Durkee v. Moulton, 6, 699.

§ 4. Prosecution for Removing Quartz.

Naked trespassers, without right and insolvent, removing goldbearing earth are subject to criminal prosecution.—Gates v. Teague, 1, 46.

§ 5. Removal of Trespasser.

In removing an intruder at the request of the owner of the property, the latter's agent has a lawful purpose in view, and he may carry out this purpose provided he use no more force than necessary.—Page v. Lynch, 2, 121.

TRIAL.

§ 1. Order of Proof.

A question as to the order of proof at the trial is one solely within the discretion of the trial court.—Hawkins v. Kingston, 1, 413.

The order in which testimony is to be received is a thing entirely within the discretion of the trial court to determine.—Baird v. Duane, 1, 492.

§ 2. Introduction of Testimony.

Testimony proper intrinsically may be improper prima facie, in which case counsel, when seeking to introduce it, may explain the purpose to the court. If by neglecting to do this he allows the court to rule it out ignorantly he cannot complain afterward.—Baird v. Duane, 1, 492.

The fact that evidence is introduced to contradict a fact alleged in the complaint is immaterial, where the fact is not denied in the answer, as there is no issue on the question.—Gill v. Dunham, 4, 229.

When a witness answers after objection to the question, the objection is not available, in the absence of a motion to strike the answer out.—Yaeger v. Southern California Ry. Co., 5, 870.

In a trial to the court, plaintiff was permitted to detail a conversation with one of several defendants, the court remarking that it would take care that the evidence harmed no one else. Held, that there was no error.—Tuffree v. Stearns Rancho Co., 6, 129.

Where a party believed that evidence admitted without objection was within the issues, and there was an attempt to deny the contract sued on, the existence of the contract must be treated after trial as in issue.—Lucas v. Rea, 7, 363.

§ 3. Objection to Testimony and Waiver Thereof.

An objection to testimony made by a defendant appearing himself to have no real interest in whether the testimony is admitted or not is to be overruled, although the objection might be good if made by some other defendant in the same cause.—Morse v. McCarty, 1, 59.

An objection to the mere form of testimony, in order to sustain an erroneous ruling of the trial court excluding the testimony on its merits, will not be considered when raised for the first time on appeal.—Gill v. O'Connell, 1, 825.

An objection to an offer to prove certain negative conclusions is properly sustained where there is no offer of the evidence from which the conclusions are to be drawn.—Manning v. Den, 3, 309.

Where plaintiff testified on the direct examination as to an alleged custom, defendant did not waive his objections to such evidence by cross-examining plaintiff thereon, or calling witnesses to disprove it.—Laver v. Hotaling, 5, 534.

Objection that evidence was inadmissible, not having been made when it was offered, is waived.—Willeford v. Bell, 5, 679.

Where, on objection to testimony, counsel introducing it explains that it is part of a conversation introduced by opposing counsel, and the court admits it, and it subsequently turns out to be immaterial, if no motion to strike it out is interposed the prejudiced party cannot complain.—Watson v. Miller, 6, 316.

Where an objection to testimony, which is admissible for some purposes, is general, the court's failure to limit it is not error if counsel do not ask that it be limited.—Baker v. Varney, 6, 376.

§ 4. Passing or Ruling upon Admissibility.

It is not error for the court, in passing on the admissibility of evidence, to assume pro hac vice that a necessary preliminary fact had been established by prima facie proof.—Reed v. Clark, 1, 95.

It is error for the court, in making up its findings, to consider a deposition which was objected to when offered, and with respect to which objection the court did not decide at the time, but reserved its ruling.—Tripp v. Duane, 2, 757.

Where testimony is objected to when offered, the party objecting has a right to have a ruling upon the point; and where the ruling is reserved, and the court, when making up its finding, wrongly considers the testimony, the error is not cured by tendering the objecting party a ruling upon the matter, when the statement on motion for new trial is presented for settlement.—Tripp v. Duane, 2, 757.

§ 5. Exclusion of Evidence.

Where, in an action against a railroad company for personal injuries, the jury found that plaintiff had suffered no injury for which he was entitled to redress, he was not injured by the exclusion of evidence to prove certain special damages.—Yaeger v. Southern California Ry. Co., 5, 870.

Possible error in the exclusion of evidence, on an issue which could not have affected the judgment, is harmless.—Heintz v. Cooper, 5, 564.

The rejection of immaterial evidence does not constitute error.—Moore v. Moore, 2, 510.

§ 6. Curing Error in Rejecting Evidence.

Where a witness is called in rebuttal, and then fully cross-examined as to a matter to which an objection was sustained when witness was first called, the error, if any, in sustaining the objection, is cured.—Weinburg v. Somps, 4, 10.

Error in refusing to permit the maker of a note to testify on cross-examination as to the circumstances under which he signed the note—the witness having been called by plaintiff for the purpose simply of proving his signature—is cured by his testifying in his own behalf in regard thereto.—Adams v. Farnsworth, 4, 682.

Error in rejecting evidence is cured by its subsequent admission.—Hayford v. Wallace, 5, 476.

§ 7. Striking Out Evidence.

A refusal to strike out evidence on the ground of incompetency and immateriality is not erroneous, if such evidence was admitted without any objection being taken on these grounds.—Marks v. Bodie Bank, 2, 583.

The reception of inadmissible evidence over appellant's objection is not reversible error where it was afterward stricken out on appellant's motion.—Ford v. Kenton, 5, 780.

Where plaintiff objected to testimony, and the court reserved decision, and, on re-examination in chief, the evidence was given without objection, it was within the discretion of the court to allow a motion to strike out the evidence without a restatement of the grounds of

objection, it being regarded as a renewal of the first objection.—
Diamond Coal Co. v. Cook, 6, 446.

§ 8. Remarks by Court.

A remark made by the court in rejecting evidence offered by plaintiffs, that he could see the dilemma plaintiffs were in, and wished
to give them all the latitude possible, but did not see the materiality
of the testimony offered, was not reversible error, as in effect telling the jury that plaintiffs had no case.—Bradbury v. McHenry,
6, 294.

§ 9. Absence of Attorney.

The court waited several hours for plaintiff's attorney to conclude
the trial of another case in another department of the same court,
with the understanding that the trial of the case against defendant
would then proceed. At the conclusion of such trial such attorney
did not appear, but engaged in the trial of habeas corpus proceedings, which he commenced two days before, and treated a notice by
defendant that the trial of his case would proceed with profane contempt. Held, that a trial of such case in the absence of such attorney was proper, plaintiff being present and offered an opportunity
to introduce his evidence.—Boehm v. Gibson, 4, 483.

§ 10. Argument and Conduct of Counsel.

Under Code of Civil Procedure of California, section 2061, subdivision 6, providing that evidence is to be estimated, not only by its
own intrinsic weight, but also according to the evidence which it is
in the power of one side to produce and the other to contradict,
comment to the jury upon the failure of the defendant to introduce
his wife to corroborate his own testimony is proper.—Lesler v. Montgomery, 3, 27.

It was agreed that the cause should be submitted without argument,
but plaintiff's attorney said: "I want to make this statement to the
jury: That plaintiffs have commenced this case in the superior court,
cannot recover any costs unless they recover $300 damages." And
the court said, "You must not make those statements." Held, that, if
defendant thought the court had not sufficiently informed the jury
not to consider the remarks, he should have asked for an instruction
to that effect, and that a new trial would not be granted on account
of such remarks.—Matts v. Borba, 4, 691.

The fact that plaintiff's counsel, in an action against a railroad
company passing through a city for personal injuries, said that
"there is no road in the city . . . . that has caused so many accidents
as this road, as is well known," is not ground for reversal where it
was casual, and did not evidently influence the jury.—Fogel v. San
Francisco etc. Ry. Co., 5, 194.

Remarks of counsel, which the jury were instructed to disregard,
are no ground for reversal.—Allen v. McKay & Co., 6, 993.

§ 11. —— Reading Books to or in Presence of Jury.

For counsel to read to the jury passages from a medical work is
or is not error according to what are the passages and for what purpose read.—People v. Gordon, 1, 459.

There is no error in calling the attention of counsel in the jury's
presence to the impropriety of reading law reports to the jury.—
People v. Anderson, 1, 697.

It is within the court's discretion to allow the presence of the jury
while counsel, in the course of argument, reads from the books.—
Sanborn v. Cunningham, 4, 95.

§ 12. Instructions in General.

Inaccuracy or want of precision in instructions to a jury is not reversible error unless thereby the party complaining was actually prejudiced.—People v. Lockhard, 1, 219.

A criticism upon a passage of the court's charge, selected from the whole, has no force when the entire instruction, taken together, is plainly not subject to criticism.—People v. Thompson, 1, 416.

An objection to any point in the judge's charge to the jury must have been excepted to at the trial in order to be given consideration on appeal.—People v. Tompson, 1, 416.

Counsel who make no effort at the trial to have the jury given full instructions, and subsequently claim on appeal that the court prejudiced the case and misled the jury by charging as to one branch of the case at the expense of another, indulge in a reprehensible practice.—Dwyer v. California Steam Nav. Co., 1, 442.

An instruction may not have such material words severed from it as "in pursuance of such design," and urged then in the mutilated form as error.—People v. Gordon, 1, 459.

Where the statute provides that the failure to file written findings shall not be cause for reversal when such filing was not requested by the appellant at the submission of the cause and the request entered on the court minutes, a failure in this regard is not ground for reversal if the request was made after the court announced its decision but before any judgment was entered.—Tong v. Richmond, 1, 809.

Some especial point in a charge cannot aggrieve a party, when the jury is told that they are the sole judges of the facts and the value of the testimony.—People v. Smith, 2, 204.

An appeal from a selected portion of a charge to the jury, when the charge as a whole corrects any possible error in particular parts, is not tenable.—People v. Smith, 2, 204.

Where there are conflicting instructions on material issues in a case, the judgment will be reversed.—Monroe v. Cooper, 2, 449.

An instruction to the jury that, if the air-brake was properly used to avoid a collision occasioned by the negligence of defendant, and plaintiff was injured by the sudden stoppage of the train, through the application of the air-brake, and not otherwise, they should find for defendant, is a proper instruction, there being evidence to support such a state of facts.—Yaeger v. Southern California Ry. Co., 5, 870.

An instruction to the jury, given at the request of the defendant "that when weaker or less satisfactory evidence is offered, when it appears that stronger and more satisfactory evidence was within the power of the party, and not offered, the evidence offered should be reviewed with distrust," was objected to by plaintiff, because not applicable to the case. Held, that if such instruction was not warranted by plaintiff's evidence, but was applicable to the defendant's evidence, it was not error.—Yaeger v. Southern California Ry. Co., 5, 870.

Plaintiff, being under contract to pasture defendant's stock for an indeterminate period, notified him to remove his horses, or he would be charged a certain amount. Plaintiff's account charged both for horses and cows, but the former charges were more than the verdict rendered in an action on the account. Held, that an instruction that defendant was notified to remove his stock, though too broad, was not injurious.—Grant v. Dreyfus, 5, 970.

Under Code of Civil Procedure, section 1963, declaring a presumption that a letter duly directed and mailed was received in the regular course of mail, an instruction in the latter language is not objectionable as meaning that the jury were to accept as a fact that the letter had been received.—Grant v. Dreyfus, 5, 970.

Where an affirmative defense is pleaded in an action, and the defendant fails to introduce any evidence, he cannot complain, on appeal, that the court did not make a finding on such defense.—Frantz v. Harper, 6, 560.

§ 13. —— Adding to or Amending.

It is not necessarily error for the court to add to an instruction, given at the request of a party, an explanation of its own.—Quinn v. Kenyon, 1, 169.

The court has a right to amend imperfect instructions submitted.—People v. Sherman, 3, 851.

§ 14. —— Refusal of Instructions.

Judgment will not be reversed for error in refusing a particular instruction, when the charge given embraced such instruction in substance.—People v. Fehely, 1, 38.

Where instructions given embrace substantially the points of those refused, the refusal is no error.—Doran v. Walker, 1, 62.

The refusal of particular instructions asked is not reversible error, even though properly they might have been granted, in a case where the court has put the substance of these instructions into the charge it actually gave.—People v. Lockhard, 1, 219.

An instruction on a point not raised by the pleadings and as to which no evidence has been put in should be refused, even though good law in the abstract.—Brown v. Pforr, 1, 632.

Instructions are properly refused when the charge of the court covers all the points in the case, including those found in the instructions requested.—Castagnino v. Balletta, 3, 107.

It is not error to refuse an instruction which has been already substantially given.—Kahn v. Brilliant, 4, 415.

The mere failure to instruct the jury on a point cannot be assigned as a refusal so to do where there was no request for such instruction.—Weinburg v. Somps, 4, 10.

Where the matter included in requested instructions was covered by the charge of the court, it was not error to refuse them.—Trabing v. California Nav. & Imp. Co., 6, 696.

§ 15. Verdict in General.

Specification of error as to verdict. See Appeal and Error, § 55.
Review of verdict. See Appeal and Error, § 83.
Verdict in criminal case. See Criminal Law, § 19.
Verdict calling for gold coin. See Damages, § 5.
Verdict of jury in equity. See Equity, § 6.
Verdict in replevin. See Replevin, § 6.

A verdict for defendant, who has offered no evidence, in an action in which the plaintiff has proved plainly a prima facie case cannot be sustained.—Deney v. Corey, 1, 98.

A general verdict that the plaintiff recover a certain sum of money may be construed as a finding in favor of the plaintiff upon all the issuable acts stated in the complaint.—Merritt v. Wilcox, 1, 884.

When the evidence has been conflicting, the verdict of the jury is allowed to stand as correct.—Pincus v. Aaron, 1, 468.

Considered in the light that a verdict must receive a reasonable interpretation and is to be construed in reference to only the controversy before the jury, a verdict in ejectment is not necessarily bad for being in such words as "We find for the plaintiff according to the patent and assess the damages at five cents per acre per year."—Black v. Sprague, 2, 54.

A verdict, if justified by the evidence, is not contrary to law.—Carlson v. Mutual Relief Assn., 2, 452.

A verdict will not be set aside on the ground that it is so uncertain that the judgment thereon cannot be executed, when such objection is presented on the judgment-roll alone, and there is no bill of exceptions presenting the facts sustaining the contention of the uncertainty of the verdict, and when the answer of defendant sheriff also shows a familiarity with the property referred to in the verdict.—Asbill v. Standley, 3, 665.

A verdict on conflicting evidence is conclusive.—Nash v. Kreling, 6, 233.

§ 16. ——— For Costs.

Code of Civil Procedure, section 626, provides that where a defendant establishes a claim for the recovery of money, in an action for the recovery of money, greater than the claim established by plaintiff, the jury must find the amount of the recovery. Held, that a verdict for defendant "for its costs" is not within the meaning of the statute, because such a verdict is for costs only, and there is no recovery by either party.—Electric Imp. Co. v. San Jose etc. R. R. Co., 3, 618.

§ 17. ——— Chance Verdict.

A verdict arrived at by adding together the amounts thought by each juror to be a just verdict, and dividing the sum by twelve, will be set aside.—Dixon v. Pluns, 3, 735.

Where the jury agree that each shall write out the sum he thinks plaintiff is entitled to recover, and then divide the aggregate of such sums by twelve, and that the quotient shall be the amount of the verdict, such verdict is determined by chance, within the meaning of Code of Civil Procedure, section 657, subdivision 2, providing that such misconduct of the jury may be shown by the affidavit of any of the jurors.—Weinburg v. Somps, 4, 10.

§ 18. ——— Special Verdict.

Where a complaint sets up a contract whereby the plaintiff was to release a debt due from defendant and give him an acceptance for more money, in consideration for which defendant was to deliver certain merchandise to him, and alleges then that afterward the parties changed the contract to the extent that the payment of $1,600 by defendant to plaintiff was substituted for the delivery of the merchandise, and the jury at the trial brought in a special verdict to the effect that the contract as set up in the complaint was the contract of the parties, the verdict is not bad as leaving questions of fact for the court to find.—Whitney v. Flint, 1, 8.

A judgment correct in substance will not be reversed because of an erroneous special verdict.—Lafonton v. Gaucheron, 1, 30.

In regard to the sufficiency of a special verdict, when the question submitted is whether one in employing another acted for himself or as an agent, the rule is that enough must be found, when the verdict is relied on as the basis of a judgment, to show in and of itself a legal conclusion of liability.—Garfield v. Knights Ferry & Table Mountain Water Co. No. 1, 1, 93.

When, on the trial of an action for damages, the jury are instructed that they may return either a general or a special verdict, but, if a general verdict is returned, they must also make written findings on the particular findings of fact submitted to them in writing, and the jury return a general verdict for the plaintiff, without passing on the special facts submitted, which is received and entered by the court without objection by counsel, the defendant cannot object to the verdict, on appeal, as irregular, as the reception and entry of the verdict by the court amounted to a waiver of the request for the special findings.—Brown v. Central Pac. R. Co., 2, 730.

Answers to special questions not disposing of all the issues in a case do not constitute a special verdict within Code of Civil Procedure, section 624, defining a special verdict to be that by which the jury find the facts; and such special findings, unaccompanied by a general verdict, are of no effect, since by section 625 the special findings only control when they are inconsistent with the general verdict.—Montgomery v. Sayre, 3, 365.

Under Code of Civil Procedure, section 625, as amended by act of March 6, 1905 (Stats. 1905, p. 56, c. 62), requiring that the court, on request in writing, must direct the jury to find a special verdict on all or any of the issues, the court must submit the special issues formulated in writing by either party only when they are within the issues, and where, in an action for injuries, the plaintiff alleged that his fall from an elevated walk was caused by smoke and the absence of guards, special issues, limiting, respectively, the cause of the injury to the absence of the guards and to the smoke and not referring to the combination of the two dangers, were properly refused.—Plyler v. Pacific Portland Cement Co., 7, 279.

Where special issues were requested as a whole and some submitted issues not in the case, the court was not bound, without a special request, to direct the jury to find on any of them.—Plyler v. Pacific Portland Cement Co., 7, 279.

§ 19. —— Impeachment of Verdict.

An affidavit by a juror that he is over sixty years of age is inadmissible to impeach his verdict.—People v. Sellers, 1, 34.

§ 20. Findings in General.

Review of findings. See Appeal and Error, §§ 84, 85.
Findings in action on note. See Bills and Notes, § 23.
Finding as to boundary. See Boundaries, § 6.
Findings in ejectment. See Ejectment, § 19.
Findings when statute of limitations set up. See Limitation of Actions, § 10.
Findings in suit to quiet title. See Quieting Title, § 10.
Findings in replevin. See Replevin, § 6.

The written opinion of the trial court is not a "finding."—Grim v. Manning, 1, 65.

After a finding "that the plaintiff was the owner in possession of the property on the day that the defendant seized upon it and removed it from her possession, custody and control," it is not necessary for the court to make a further finding, so as to dispose of any issue raised by the answer as to ownership of the property by some third person.—Haley v. Nunan, 2, 189.

Where, in an action concerning real property, there are but two deeds in the case considered, and they are referred to, in the findings and statement on motion for a new trial, as the "short deed" and "long deed," and the findings, evidence and decree clearly show what property was described in the one known as the "short deed," and that the other deed, called the "long deed," contained a description of the residue of the property in controversy, the reference to them by such names is sufficiently certain.—Boyd v. Slayback, 2, 421.

Findings held inconsistent with each other, and with the averments in the complaint, and judgment reversed.—Southmayd v. Berry, 2, 322.

Findings are not necessary in a case submitted on an agreed statement of facts.—Hamill v. Littner, 2, 511.

Findings reviewed and held to cover all the issues made by the pleadings, and to be sufficient.—Brown v. Mann, 2, 627.

In an action to recover money alleged to have been received by the defendant as the agent of the plaintiff on the sale of certain property of plaintiff, the latter alleging that the agent had falsely represented the amount received, and had thereby induced him to settle for a sum much less than he was entitled to, findings that the agent had agreed with the plaintiff on the amount due him, that no false representations had been made, and that the amount agreed upon had been paid, are sufficient to support a judgment for defendant.—Stover v. Baker, 3, 73.

Where the sole issue is the truth of the allegations of the answer, a finding "that the allegations of the separate defense contained in the answer of the defendant G. are untrue" is sufficient.—Paden v. Goldbaum, 4, 767.

A finding "that the plaintiff did not on the eighteenth day of November, 1892, lend the said defendant the sum of eight hundred dollars in U. S. gold coin," is insufficient on an issue framed by a complaint which states that "within two years last past, and on or about" that day, plaintiff loaned defendant "eight hundred dollars in gold coin of the United States."—Garbe v. Wilks, 4, 910.

A finding of an ultimate fact cannot be impeached by an immaterial finding of a mere probative fact.—Fairbanks v. Rollins, 6, 99.

Plaintiff alleged an agreement whereby third parties were to summer-fallow land for defendant, and that defendant should pay plaintiff the reasonable value thereof; that, after said plowing had been completed, said third parties directed defendant to pay plaintiff, and defendant agreed so to do. Defendant alleged execution of a two-years lease to such third parties in payment of said agreement, and that plaintiff and such third parties accepted the same in full satisfaction of the claim. Held, to require a finding as to whether, after the plowing was done, defendant, for a valuable consideration, promised to pay plaintiff therefor, as alleged in the complaint.—Bank of Orland v. Finnell, 6, 245.

§ 21. —— Outside of Issues.

The judgment will not be reversed where there are findings on all the issues because of findings on probative matters outside of the issues.—Whitesides v. Briggs, 2, 529.

A reversal of a judgment cannot be had because a finding was made on an issue outside the pleadings, where other findings in the cause are sufficient to support it.—Haight v. Sexton, 5, 203.

A finding of a fact clearly without the issue, and not required to support the judgment, is harmless error.—Livingston v. Conant, 5, 933.

§ 22. —— Necessity of Findings on All Issues.

The trial court must find upon all the material issues raised by the pleadings, and when this rule is not observed the judgment will be reversed.—Duane v. Neumann, 2, 255.

Where in an action judgment is rendered for defendant, a finding upon an affirmative defense not supported by proof is unnecessary.—Peterson v. Hubbard, 2, 607.

Findings are not necessary in relation to separate defenses in support of which no evidence was offered.—Moneta Canning and Preserving Co. v. Martin, 7, 318.

§ 23. —— Failure to Find on Some Issues.

Where a finding on one of the issues involved is determinative of the case against plaintiffs, the failure of the court to find on defendant's plea of the statute of limitations as to one of the plaintiffs is not prejudicial to such plaintiff.—Bradley v. Parker, 4, 250.

Where an answer contains two separate defenses, viz., a denial of the allegations of the complaint and a justification of the acts complained of, a finding for the plaintiff on the first defense renders a failure to find on the second immaterial.—Paden v. Goldbaum, 4, 767.

Failure to find on certain issues raised by the pleadings, and making findings outside the issues, is harmless error, where the findings made on material issues warrant the judgment whatever the findings on the other issues.—Roberts v. Ball, 4, 933.

Where counts for money loaned, money had and received, and on a special contract, which is especially set out, are joined, and the complaint shows that they are all on the same cause of action, the failure to find the issues under the first and second counts is not reversible error, the issues under the third count being found, as the latter include the former.—Haines v. Stilwell, 5, 27.

Failure of the court to make a finding is not reversible error, in the absence of a showing that there was evidence to justify a finding. Castle v. Hickman, 5, 159.

§ 24. —— Definiteness of Finding.

Where, in an action to quiet title, involving the question whether a conveyance to plaintiff was with intent to delay or defraud creditors (declared in such case by Civil Code, section 3439, to be void), the jury returned answers to interrogatories, which the court adopted, subject to its findings of fact, such findings to govern in case of conflict with the answers, and the jury found that plaintiff's husband conveyed the property to her to prevent defendant from satisfying his claim against him, that plaintiff knew her husband was insolvent, and that he made the deed to plaintiff with intent to hinder and delay, but not to defraud, defendant; and the court found that the deed to plaintiff was not executed "with a view to conceal his property from defendant or his other creditors, nor improperly to hinder or delay them"—the findings will be held too indefinite to support a judgment for plaintiff.—Sharp v. Frank, 5, 155.

§ 25. —— That Allegations are True.

A finding that all the averments of a complaint, down to and including a certain averment, are true, is sufficiently explicit.—Wheelock v. Godfrey, 4, 399.

A finding that all the allegations of the complaint are true, and all the allegations of the answer untrue, is sufficient.—Healey v. Norton, 5, 171.

A finding that all the allegations in the complaint not specifically found on are true, and the allegations in defendant's answer not specifically found on are untrue, does not require a reversal, where it appears that specific findings, on the allegations not directly found upon, would have necessarily been adverse to appellant.—O'Conor v. Clarke, 5, 323

A finding "that the matters and facts alleged in defendant's special defense and cross-complaint on file herein, except the allegations of plaintiff's employment, and agreements under such employment, are untrue in substance and in fact," supports a judgment for plaintiff, where the answer and cross-complaint both allege that defendant employed plaintiff as a physician and surgeon, for a reward, and that plaintiff undertook the service, whereby defendant was damaged by plaintiff's negligence and incompetency.—Heintz v. Cooper, 5, 564.

A concluding finding that "all other averments in the pleadings herein and in issue, not comprised and passed upon in these findings, are not true," is improper, but is not reversible error, where the preceding findings are so full and specific, and so clearly cover all the material issues, as to rebut the suggestion of uncertainty.—Perkins v. West Coast Lumber Co., 5, 674.

A finding that all the allegations of the complaint are true is sufficient to support a judgment, where the complaint states a good cause of action.—Wolfskill v. Douglas, 6, 396.

§ 26. —— Stating Facts and Law Separately.

Where the statement of facts found is distinctly separate from the conclusions of law, though both are written on one piece of paper, there is a substantial compliance with Code of Civil Procedure, section 633, requiring that "the facts found and the conclusions of law must be separately stated."—Gainsley v. Gainsley, 5, 310.

§ 27. —— Special Findings.

Where one special finding is conclusive of the whole case, findings on other issues are unnecessary.—Trope v. Kerns, 3, 47.

The findings of a jury on special issues are merely advisory to the court, and, if adopted, are the findings of the court. If a general verdict be rendered by the jury, the court can set it aside and find the facts and render judgment on the testimony taken, and in case of a general verdict must, notwithstanding the verdict, find the facts.—Sweetser v. Dobbins, 2, 277.

Where the record shows that two special questions were submitted to the jury which they answered, but gave no general verdict, and that these questions did not cover all the issues in the case; that the trial proceeded, and both parties introduced evidence; and that the case was submitted to the "court for decision and judgment," which was rendered against defendant—the right to trial by jury was waived by defendant under Code of Civil Procedure, section 631, providing that jury trial may be waived by oral consent in open court entered in the minutes or by failure to appear at the trial.—Montgomery v. Sayre, 3, 365.

If a discrepancy exists between the general finding and the more specific findings of particular facts, the latter must control.—Bank of Oroville v. Lawrence, 4, 845.

§ 28. —— Evidence to Support.

Evidence held sufficient to justify the findings.—Grange v. Gough, 2, 410.

Findings held supported by the evidence.—Cross v. Zellerbach, 2, 578.

Findings held sustained by the evidence.—Toomey v. Reilly, 2, 586.

Findings held supported by the evidence.—Peterson v. Doe, 2, 587.

§ 29. —— Refusal of Court to Adopt.

It being the duty of the court to find on all issues without any request, refusal to adopt a requested finding prepared by counsel is not error, the only thing necessary being that the findings cover all the issues and be sufficient.—Ricks v. Lindsay, 3, 578.

TROVER AND CONVERSION.

Action by mortgagee for conversion. See Chattel Mortgage, § 6.
Of stock. See Corporations, § 27.
In case of trust. See Trusts, § 15.

§ 1. In General.

In an action of trover the plaintiff must prove himself to be entitled to the immediate possession of the goods alleged to have been converted.—Greene v. Meyer, 2, 41.

Evidence held to support the findings in action for conversion.—Collins v. Frost, 2, 293.

A leasehold estate is not the subject of an action for conversion.—Goldschmidt v. Maier, 7, 162.

§ 2. Necessity of Demand.

In an action for conversion of property by unlawful detention, where the original possession was lawful, the complaint must allege a demand and refusal.—Daggett v. Gray, 5, 74.

In conversion, where plaintiff alleges that she placed in the hands of defendant, as her agent, a sum of money to be loaned on security, and defendant denies the agency, plaintiff need not allege or prove a demand on him for the money before suit.—Becker v. Feigenbaum, 5, 408.

§ 3. Limitation of Actions.

In a civil action for embezzling or converting personal property, where the time of the alleged grievance does not appear by the pleadings or testimony, a nonsuit based on the statute of limitations is not to be sustained.—Norton v. Zellerbach, 2, 181.

An action for conversion is within Code of Civil Procedure, section 338, subdivision 3, prescribing the limitation of an action for taking, detaining or injuring goods or chattels.—Horton v. Jack, 4, 758.

§ 4. Joinder of Actions.

Where, in an action for conversion, plaintiff claims damages for malicious acts of defendants in tearing down fences and buildings where the property was situated, there is not a misjoinder of causes of action, complainant's intention being to bring the case within Civil

Code, section 3294, allowing exemplary damages where defendant has been guilty of oppression and malice.—Lothrop v. Golden, 6, 284.

Plaintiff in an action for the conversion of grain alleged that a part had been returned prior to the suit, but sought, under Civil Code, section 3336, to recover compensation for the time and money expended in its pursuit. Held, that the actions were not improperly joined, since all the grain converted was taken at the same time, and the acts complained of constituted one and the same wrong.—Lothrop v. Golden, 6, 284.

§ 5. Instructions.

Where suit was brought for the conversion of goods sold to defendant, but which plaintiff claimed had previously been sold to him, and the evidence, instead of showing a sale to plaintiff, tended only to show an agreement to sell, and that the goods should remain with the seller until a certain time, and be paid for on or before delivery, an instruction giving the essentials of a contract of sale is improper, as the belief might thus be induced that, under such a contract, plaintiff would have sufficient title to maintain the suit.—Darden v. Callaghan, 3, 581.

Error, in an action for conversion, where plaintiff claimed damages for malicious acts of defendant in tearing down his fences to obtain access to the property, in an instruction that if defendants did such acts they were trespassers, and were liable therefor to plaintiff, is harmless, where the special verdict awarded no damages for trespass. Lothrop v. Golden, 6, 284.

In an action for conversion, it is not error to deny defendant an instruction as to the doctrine of commingling of goods, where there was no evidence thereof.—Lothrop v. Golden, 6, 284.

In an action for the conversion of grain, a part of which plaintiff alleged to have been recovered, and as to which he sought relief only for money expended in pursuit, an instruction that the jury, in estimating the damages, should find the value of the grain at the time of the taking, is not erroneous, as misleading them into believing that damages for the value of the grain returned could be recovered.—Lothrop v. Golden, 6, 284.

§ 6. Damages.

The amendment to section 3336 of the Civil Code, whereby one suing with reasonable diligence for the wrongful conversion of personal property could no longer assess the detriment presumable as at the highest market value between the conversion and the verdict, was intended to be retrospective.—Tully v. Tranor, 2, 43.

The amendment to section 3336 of the Civil Code, whereby one suing with reasonable diligence for the wrongful conversion of personal property could no longer assess the detriment presumable as at the highest market value between the conversion and the verdict, does not impair the obligation of contracts within the inhibition of the constitution of the United States.—Tully v. Tranor 2, 43.

A law changing a rule of presumption as to the measure of detriment to be claimed in an action for wrongful conversion does not deprive a plaintiff of a vested right.—Tully v. Tranor, 2, 43.

In an action for the conversion of grain, there was evidence that it was forcibly taken in the absence of the owner, and over the protest of his wife; that defendants were twice arrested to prevent their taking it, but they obtained their release and returned to the premises. Held, that a verdict allowing plaintiff damages for grain taken, for time and money expended in pursuit thereof, and for the malicious taking, was proper, there being sufficient evidence as to the amounts of such damages given.—Lothrop v. Golden, 6, 284.

§ 7. —— Exemplary Damages.

In an action for conversion, an erroneous instruction authorizing the jury to award exemplary damages if the taking was unlawful is not reversible error where the jury specially found damages for the malicious taking of the property.—Lothrop v. Golden, 6, 284.

§ 8. —— Costs and Counsel Fees.

Where the only evidence of money properly expended in the pursuit of personal property which has been wrongfully converted (made a measure of damages under Civil Code, section 3336) is that plaintiff made a note for a gross sum to an attorney, in full payment of all expenses of the proposed suit, from its commencement to its determination, and it does not appear what, if any, expenses were incurred, except that at the end of the controversy plaintiff had judgment for her costs, the money paid by plaintiff to her attorney cannot be properly taken into account, in estimating her damages.—Spooner v. Cady, 5, 357.

TRUST DEED.
See Trusts; Mortgages.

TRUSTEES.
See Trusts.

TRUSTS.

Limitation of actions, denial of trust. See Limitation of Actions, § 5.
Suit by trustee for construction of will. See Wills, § 4.

§ 1. In General.

A debtor agreed to transfer his property to his two creditors, who agreed to take possession and sell the same, and turn over to the debtor any balance after the payment of the debts and expenses. The property was transferred to one of the creditors, who accepted the same as trustee for himself and the other creditor, and sold the property for a sum insufficient to reimburse himself for expenses and to pay any part of the claim of the other creditor. Held, that the other creditor, as beneficiary under the trust, could not maintain an action in trover for damages, his remedy being in equity for an accounting.—Goldschmidt v. Maier, 7, 162.

The fact that the purchaser of an interest in a mine was acting in the relation of trustee of such interest for the seller did not affect the validity of the purchase, it being a fair and open transaction for full value.—Lake v. Owens, 7, 197.

§ 2. Effect of Trust Deed.

Under a deed of trust to secure a note to a third person, not yet due, the legal title to the land concerned is in the trustee.—Larue v. Chase, 1, 613.

The grantee of a trustee under a valid deed of trust made with the consent of creditors takes the granted premises relieved of the trust and is not accountable to such creditors afterward.—Campbell v. Sheldon, 1, 546.

§ 3. Declaration or Creation of Trust.

Under Civil Code, section 852, subdivision 1, providing that no trust in relation to real property is valid unless created and declared "by a written instrument subscribed by the trustee," such a trust is sufficiently declared by a deposition of the trustee, made in an action wherein the question of the creation of such trust was involved, and by which it appears that he so held the property in question.—Baker v. Baker, 3, 597.

Defendant gave deceased a note, for money which he owed her, by which he promised to pay $400 for her funeral expenses or to return it to her on demand. During her last sickness, deceased handed the note to defendant, saying, "Here is something for you." Held, that an express trust, to expend the money, after her death, for her funeral expenses, was created.—Bedell v. Scoggins, 5, 66.

§ 4. Revocation of Trust by Will.

Where a trust deed contained a reservation of power to revoke or modify the same by a deed of the grantor to be recorded in a certain city recorder's office under Civil Code, section 2280, providing that a power of revocation reserved in a trust should be strictly pursued, the trust could not be revoked by the grantor's will.—Carpenter v. Cook, 6, 410.

§ 5. Founding Astronomical Observatory.

See, also, post, § 8.

A trust for the founding of an astronomical observatory in connection with a university, "to be owned, controlled, and managed by said university," will not be construed as a trust for a private corporation, and therefore void, in the absence of anything to show whether the beneficiary is an educational institution for the benefit of the public, or conducted for mere private ends.—Spence v. Widney, 5, 516.

Nor will the trust be declared void as creating a perpetuity unless it appear that the beneficiary is a mere private enterprise and not a public charity.—Spence v. Widney, 5, 516.

§ 6. Resulting Trust—Parol Establishment.

Plaintiff made a deed to her son of real property, with an understanding that he should satisfy her debts, and reconvey the remainder to her. In effecting a compromise with certain parties, the son, in consideration of a deed of certain other of plaintiff's property, procured the property in dispute to be conveyed to him. Civil Code of California, section 852, enacts that no trust of real property is valid unless created by writing or operation of law. In an action to have the heirs of the son declared trustees, held, that parol evidence was admissible to show the nature of the dealings between plaintiff and her son, and to establish a trust in her favor.—Mallagh v. Mallagh, 2, 837.

Y., who had been the clerk of S., deceased, and Mrs. S.'s rent collector, took an assignment of mortgage from S., foreclosed it, and took title to the land in his own name. Mrs. S. therefore claimed the land as having bought the mortgage from her husband, and had it assigned to Y. to foreclose. Y. maintained that he had bought and foreclosed the mortgage for. himself. The record of the foreclosure case showed that Y., cross-examined, had admitted his agency for Mrs. S. in the matter, and that the price of the mortgage was applied on a debt due from S. to his wife. Held, that the court was justified in finding him a trustee who could have no possession adverse to Mrs. S.—Hunt v. Swyney, 4, 108.

§ 7. —— Laches in Asserting.

Plaintiff had owned the beneficial interest in property, and had been in possession thereof since 1879, and was in possession in 1883, when she brought action to have defendants, who held the naked legal title, declared trustees for her. Held, that the plaintiff was not guilty of laches in asserting her rights.—Mallagh v. Mallagh, 2, 837.

§ 8. Execution of Trust—Delay—Abandonment.

Where deceased gave money to defendant in trust to expend, after her death, for her funeral, and he thus expended it, her administrator cannot recover such sum from him, where all preferred claims have been paid, and it does not appear that the probate court has disapproved of the payments made by him, even admitting that claims against a decedent's estate cannot properly be paid without the sanction of the probate court.—Bedell v. Scoggins, 5, 66.

Plaintiff's testator granted land in trust to six trustees, the fund derived therefrom to be used in founding an astronomical observatory in connection with a university. Lenses were ordered, but it was found that the income was insufficient to pay for them. With the consent of the grantor the lenses were sold, and it was decided to wait until prices could be realized for the lands which would enable the trust to be accomplished. Held, that under the circumstances a delay of three years in taking further steps to carry out the trust was not unreasonable.—Spence v. Widney, 5, 516.

In such case the deed provided that the observatory should be located on Wilson's Peak, or some other suitable site on the Sierra Madre range, to be selected by the consent and approval of the grantor, who was also one of the trustees. Held, that the death of the grantor before any selection was made did not defeat the execution of the trust.—Spence v. Widney, 5, 516.

The sale of the lenses and the delay in selecting a site for the observatory cannot, in the absence of any express declaration to that effect, be construed as an abandonment of the trust.—Spence v. Widney, 5, 516.

§ 9. Execution of Trust by One of Two Trustees.

Where a trust deed provides among other things that one of the two joint trustees shall be competent to hold and act in case the other resigns the trust, the execution by one of them of a resignation and its delivery by him to his cotrustee, who is also his copartner in business and general attorney in fact, and who deposits the instrument immediately in the office safe among the firm papers, in which depository it is discovered after his death, are facts not sufficient to validate a deed of the trust property executed by only the trustee to whom the delivery was made, but in the body of which both persons are named as trustees.—Butler v. Welton, 1, 731.

The condition expressed in a deed of trust to two persons jointly that if one resigns the other shall hold and act alone unless, by some appropriate instrument in writing, the cestui que trust appoints another cotrustee, is not satisfied if, after a resignation by one of the trustees, the other alone executes a deed of the trust property, such deed not showing on its face, or it not being shown otherwise, that the cestui que trust was aware of the resignation before the execution of the deed.—Butler v. Welton, 1, 731.

§ 10. Conveyance by Trustee.

A transfer of all his interest by one who had advanced money to pay the state's charges for a deed to salt marsh and tide lands, and who, as security for the loan, had taken a conveyance to himself of the land in trust to reconvey upon payment, and with power, upon default, to sell after notice by advertisement, is valid as a conveyance of his equitable interest, although made without such notice, and is not in contravention of Civil Code of California, section 870, providing that, "where a trust in relation to real property is expressed in the instrument creating the estate, every transfer or other act of the trustee in contravention of the trust is absolutely void."—Tripp v. Duane, 2, 757.

§ 11. Ratification by Beneficiaries of Conveyance.

In an action to quiet title to an undivided interest in land, it appeared that defendant's grantor, as owner of a tract of land, after contracting to convey undivided interests in it to several persons, of whom plaintiff was one, and receiving part of the purchase price, by agreement with them dated March 1, 1888, conveyed the land to a trustee, a party to the agreement, with plenary power to sell and convey; that this agreement required the trustee to distribute the proceeds among the respective grantees in proportion to the interests held by each, deducting from the share of each the amount due from him on the purchase price, and pay the same to the grantor, less the amount of a mortgage which he had agreed to pay; that the trustee never sold the land, but, November 1, 1892, conveyed to each of the beneficiaries his undivided interest; that an interest of twenty-five fortieths was conveyed to the grantor, who recorded the deed thereof; that the grantor subsequently acquired an eight-fortieths interest conveyed to others by the trustee at the same time, and January 30, 1893, conveyed his entire interest (thirty-three fortieths) to defendant. There was no evidence that any of the parties to the agreement objected to the conveyances by the trustee, or that defendant did till filing its answer in this action, November 12, 1894. Held, that a finding that all the beneficiaries to the trust consented to and acquiesced in the conveyances by the trustee was warranted. Witter v. McCarthy Co., 5, 267.

§ 12. Partition in Violation of Trust.

Where a mother conveys real estate to her son, in trust, the rents and profits thereof to be used for her support, and on her death the estate to be equally divided among her heirs, and the son and other heirs voluntarily partition the same among themselves, before the mother's death, such son or his wife should not afterward be allowed to complain of such partition on the ground that it was made in violation of the trust.—Baker v. Baker, 3, 597.

In an action by the son's wife to set aside one of the partition deeds, on the ground that she did not join therein, there is no prejudicial error in refusing to allow her to introduce the judgment-roll of an action by the mother against the son, his wife, and the other heirs, to set aside the partition and enforce the trust, and wherein it was decided that the property was not held in trust, but that defendants therein, as against the mother, were the owners of the parts partitioned to them.—Baker v. Baker, 3, 597.

§ 13. Action to Establish Trust.

Where, in an action to establish a trust in lands, there is a substantial conflict in the evidence as to whether or not a certain person, one of defendants, in making a purchase of the lands, was the agent of plaintiff, a finding that he was not such agent will not be disturbed.—Tuffree v. Brock, 3, 761.

In such action a witness testified that after the purchase by such defendant the latter said he had paid a certain sum to bind the sale, and asked witness if he and a friend did not wish to take a part in it; that the next day they met at plaintiff's room, and heard that both made a claim to the land, and gave the idea up; that such defendant claimed the property for himself; and that afterward plaintiff claimed the property. Held, that it was not error to exclude evidence by such witness that he and his friend went to plaintiff's room for the purpose of acquiring an interest in the land from plaintiff on the assumption that he had an interest therein.—Tuffree v. Brock, 3, 761.

§ 14. Action for Trust Funds—Sufficiency of Evidence.

Plaintiff alleged that defendant collected money belonging to another, and agreed to hold it till a dispute as to its ownership was settled, giving a written acknowledgment that he so held it; that such dispute was settled; and the assignment of claimants' rights to plaintiff. Defendant's answer admitted receipt of the money, but denied plaintiff's other averments. Defendant also pleaded a former judgment on the same cause of action. Plaintiff put in evidence defendant's written acknowledgment and the assignments to himself, and one of his assignors testified that defendant had not paid the money. Defendant did not put in evidence any memorandum of settlement, nor the judgment pleaded by him. He admitted his signature to the acknowledgment, but said that he had no memory of the matter, and he failed to contradict any of plaintiff's testimony. Held, that a verdict for defendant was not justified.—Peterson v. Taylor, 4, 49.

Where, in an action to establish a trust, the findings controvert plaintiff's claims at all points, and there is evidence to support the findings, a decree for defendant will not be set aside except on the most satisfactory and convincing grounds.—Hamlin v. Philips, 4, 4.

§ 15. Trover by Beneficiary Against Trustee.

Where, in trover by a beneficiary against the trustee under a trust authorizing a sale for the benefit of creditors, the court properly decided that trover could not be maintained, the admission of testimony of witnesses as to their failure to conduct the assigning debtor's business at a profit was not prejudicial error.—Goldschmidt v. Maier, 7, 162.

A finding that a creditor had made a written demand on another creditor, who had accepted the possession of the debtor's property as trustee for the creditors, to share pro rata in the distribution of the proceeds of any sale, and to be consulted as to the management of the property, and that the trustee did not comply with the demand, sufficiently covers an allegation in the former creditor's complaint that the trustee "refused to recognize the rights" of the former creditor, "and took exclusive possession of the property."—Goldschmidt v. Maier, 7, 162.

§ 16. Right to Charge Trust or Hold Trustee Personally.

For the convenience of certain lenders and borrowers of money, who did their business through a bank, a firm of stockbrokers were in the habit of giving their promissory notes, and securing themselves by bank stock and other collaterals delivered to them by the president of the bank. Subsequently the bank failed, and the president conveyed all his property to a trustee, to be applied by him to "such purposes and uses as he may deem best for our joint and several interests." By fraudulent representations that the stock and collateral paid by the stockbrokers were worthless, the trustee induced them to pay to him $200,000, in consideration of his promise to pay all their outstanding notes, which promise he performed. Held, that the fraudulent representations by the trustee gave the stockbrokers only a personal right of action against him, and that they could not charge the trust estate in his hands for such sum, since they were not creditors of the bank president, who created the trust.—Burling v. Newlands, 4, 940.

§ 17. Limitation of Actions.

A certificate that the maker thereof holds certain money to abide settlement of disputes as to its ownership creates an express trust, with no definite time fixed for its termination by payment, and hence limitations will not run against a claim on such certificate until the true owner has been ascertained, and a demand made by one showing a right to the money.—Petersen v. Taylor, 4, 49.

§ 18. Death of Trustee.
See, also, ante, § 8.

Plaintiff's testator granted lands in trust to six trustees, to be sold, etc., with the approval of any four of them, and the fund derived therefrom to be used for founding an astronomical observatory. Before anything had been done to carry out the trust, three of the trustees died. Held, that under Civil Code, sections 2288, 2289, providing that on the death of one of several cotrustees the trust survives to the others, and that the superior court in the county in which the property is situated may appoint other trustees of the trust, the trust did not terminate as impossible of fulfillment.—Spence v. Widney, 5, 516.

§ 19. Resignation of Cotrustee.

A writing by a cestui que trust, uncalled for in law or by the terms of the trust deed, giving permission to a trustee to resign, is, in case the trustee thereupon executes a resignation and delivers it to his cotrustee who immediately deposits it in their office safe (the two being partners in business), no evidence that the cestui que trust was informed of the resignation so that she could appoint a successor, if under the deed of trust she was empowered so to appoint in case of a resignation.—Butler v. Welton, 1, 731.

Where a deed of trust does not provide that a joint trust is to be made an individual one simply by the delivery of his written

57

resignation by one trustee to his cotrustee, it requires other formalities to bring such a purpose into effect.—Butler v. Welton, 1, 731.

To be valid, the delivery of a written instrument intended to effect his resignation by a trustee must, as in the case of the delivery of other written instruments, be such as to put the instrument beyond the power of the person executing it.—Butler v. Welton, 1, 731.

§ 20. Action Against Cotrustee.

A trustee cannot maintain an action to recover possession of the trust property from his cotrustee, nor can he maintain an action for conversion on the sale of the trust property by the cotrustee when the trustees are authorized to sell the property.—Goldschmidt v. Maier, 7, 162.

§ 21. Accounting by Trustee.

An action against a trustee, under a secret trust, by the cestui que trust for an accounting is not to be dismissed as against public policy because at the time the trust was made the secret trustee was a pretended complaining creditor—there being other creditors at the time—and assumed to attach and hold the property for his individual debt; provided the real intention had by the cestui que trust and the effect of the transaction were to pay off all the creditors.—Metzger v. Childs, 1, 875.

An appeal, in a proceeding against a trustee to compel an accounting, from an order relating to the account before a certain date, does not preclude the trial court from making an order in reference to the trustee's accounts subsequent to such date.—Gardner v. Stare, 6, 945.

Where the record on appeal from an order sustaining objections to a trustee's account does not show the evidence on which it was based, the decision will be affirmed, as all presumptions are in favor of the action of the trial court.—Gardner v. Stare, 6, 945.

§ 22. —— In Probate Proceedings.

In a probate proceeding it appeared that by a decree of distribution made under a will Z. received, in trust for the grandchildren of testatrix, money to be paid when the oldest attained her majority. On the same date as the will the same testatrix conveyed to Z. a lot of land in trust for A., F., and O., grandchildren of testatrix to be conveyed when the eldest became of age. There were living at date of will and conveyance five grandchildren—M., A., F., C., and A., but no O., as mentioned in the conveyance. After M., the eldest, attained her majority, Z. conveyed the lot held by him in trust to the four grandchildren mentioned in the deed of trust, including O., who never existed, and on the same day deposited in a bank in his own name, as trustee for the five grandchildren, a part of the money held by him in trust, as M., the eldest, desired Z. to retain her share, and the other children had no guardian. Subsequently Z. filed his account, charging himself six per cent interest on the trust fund down to the time of deposit, and seven per cent on the amount retained by him after the deposit, and credited himself out of the whole fund with taxes paid, street assessments, and costs of conveyancing on the lot owned by only three of the grandchildren, and also credited himself with the amount in bank. Held, that Z. should be charged with the amount received by the decree of distribution, with interest at seven per cent until the deposit in the bank; after which time with the interest earned in the bank, and with the amount deposited in the bank. The amount paid by him for taxes, street assessments, and conveyancing should be credited him, and taken out of the shares distributed to the three grandchildren who own the lot, and in whose interest these sums were expended.—In re Hensing's Estate, 3, 685.

§ 23. Foreign Trustee—Actions.

A trustee appointed by a court is thereby vested with no authority to maintain an action outside the jurisdiction of his appointment, and such authority will rarely be recognized by a foreign court, in absence of a statute expressly authorizing it.—Iowa and California Land Co. v. Hoag, 6, 528.

Where an action was commenced by a foreign trustee who was without capacity to sue in the jurisdiction where it was brought, and whose appointment was also subsequently held void by the court which made it, no substitution of parties plaintiff can render the action maintainable.—Iowa and California Land Co. v. Hoag, 6, 528.

TURNPIKE COMPANY.

§ 1. Franchise.

The question whether an alleged road franchise is good, or whether the road, through dedication or user, possession and claim of right, belongs to the public, is for the jury.—Deer Creek & French Corral Turnpike Co. v. Oague, 1, 41.

§ 2. Toll Road and Gates.

The fixing by the board of supervisors of the number of toll-gates, and of where they were to be located, was a condition precedent to the right of the Waterloo Turnpike Road Company to collect tolls, under an act which in incorporating that company provided, in part, "such gates and tolls to be fixed and prescribed by such board of supervisors, as aforesaid, from year to year."—Waterloo Turnpike Road Co. v. Cole, 1, 869.

Where an application is made to a superior court for a writ of mandate to compel the board of supervisors of a county to locate toll-gates and to fix rates of toll on a certain road which it is claimed in the petition the corporation petitioner had a right to collect tolls upon, the superior court is in error if it sustains a demurrer to such petition on the ground that it does not appear therefrom that the petitioner had or owned any road, or right of way for a road, as such a petition states sufficient to entitle the petitioner to relief.—Santa Cruz Gap Turnpike Joint Stock Co. v. Board of Supervisors, 2, 650.

§ 3. Action on Contract to Pay Tolls.

Where an action is brought on a contract to pay certain tolls, and the answer does not deny the contract, but alleges that such tolls are illegal, the burden of establishing the illegality thereof is on the defendant.—Frantz v. Harper, 6, 560.

UNDUE INFLUENCE.

As invalidating contract. See Contracts, § 3.
As invalidating deed. See Deeds, § 3.
As invalidating gift. See Gifts, § 2.

UNIVERSITY OF CALIFORNIA.

§ 1. Instructions as to Sale of Land.

Instructions to the land agent of the University of California, directing him to receive applications for surveyed land, in accord-

ance with a designated plan, whether they emanate from the board
of regents or not, if subsequently recognized and enforced by them,
will be held to be the instructions of the board.—White v. Douglass,
2, 574.

§ 2. Disbursement of Funds.

Funds and securities deposited by the regents of the University of
California in the state treasury may be drawn therefrom in the
manner provided by statute, namely, on a resolution of the said regents, indorsed by the governor of the state, demanding the same, and
section 22, article 4, of the California constitution (providing how
money may be drawn from the treasury in other cases) does not apply
to such funds and securities, and the warrant of the controller is
therefore not an essential prerequisite to the disbursement of such
funds by the treasurer.—Regents v. Dunn, 2, 448.

UNKNOWN OWNERS.

Street assessments against. See Municipal Corporations, § 38.

UNLAWFUL DETAINER.
See Forcible Entry and Detainer.

§ 1. Evidence and Examination of Witnesses.

Evidence introduced by defendant held sufficient to justify verdict.—Howland v. Kreter, 5, 105.

Where, in an action for unlawful detainer of land, defendant answers that he holds over under an oral agreement by which he was
to do certain work as part consideration for extension of the lease,
the value of which was to be applied to the second year's rental,
there is no prejudicial error in overruling an objection to the question, "Have you been paid for this work?" asked of defendant by
his counsel, though it is not within any issue.—Schweikert v. Seavey,
6, 554.

In an action for unlawful detainer of land, defendant answered
that he held over under an oral agreement entered into before the
expiration of the original period, by the terms of which he was
to hold for another like period; and he was asked whether he held
the premises at that time under the original lease or the subsequent
agreement. Held, that, though the question asked for a conclusion
rather than a fact, error in admitting it was harmless, since it was
evident that defendant claimed to hold under the verbal agreement.
Schweikert v. Seavey, 6, 554.

Evidence in an action for unlawful detainer examined, and held
to sustain a finding that defendants had agreed to pay $50 a month
rent for the leased premises.—Lacrabere v. Wise, 7, 107.

§ 2. Definiteness of Verdict.

In an action for unlawful detainer, a verdict that "we, the jury,"
find for plaintiff "that he is entitled to the possession of the premises in controversy, and assess his damages at $———, and entitled
to the sum of $30 as rent per month," is not sufficiently definite to
support a judgment for rent at the rate of $30 per month from
April 1st, the date of the termination of the lease under the notice
which was conceded to have been given, to July 16th, the date the
verdict was rendered.—Diggs v. Porteus, 5, 753.

§ 3. Failure to Find on Certain Issues.

Where plaintiff in an action for unlawful detainer alleges that
the term for which the lands were demised had expired, which alle-

gation is denied, but the real issue is whether the lease had not been extended, in the absence of a showing or of a plain inference that a failure to find on the allegation of the termination of the lease was injurious, such action will not be reversed on appeal.—Schweikert v. Seavey, 6, 554.

Where defendant in an action for unlawful detainer answers that he held over under an oral agreement by which he was to do certain work for plaintiff as a part consideration for the renewal of the lease, which work he had performed, and which was of a certain value, failure to find the value of the work is not error, since the action was not for an adjustment of mutual accounts, and hence the value of the work was immaterial.—Schweikert v. Seavey, 6, 554.

VACANCIES.

In office. See Justices of Peace, § 4.

VACATION.

Of alley. See Municipal Corporations, § 14.

VALUE.

Evidence of. See Evidence, § 17.

VAN NESS ORDINANCE.

§ 1. In General.

The design of the Van Ness ordinance was to graft a city title upon a possession, not merely vague, indeterminate and floating, but actual, bona fide and exclusive, evidenced by acts clearly showing a segregation of the land and a subjection of it to the will and dominion of the claimant.—Weyle v. Center, 1, 310.

As against one entering under sale in foreclosure of a valid mortgage to him and for over six years in adverse possession as to the grantee of a deed subsequent to the mortgage, such grantee cannot maintain title under the Van Ness ordinance, if up to the introduction of the ordinance into the council the only occupancy claimed by him was through there being a pile of lumber left on the premises by his grantors, and not included in the deed, which lumber he had agreed to take care of, the premises not being cultivated by him or substantially fenced.—Wakelee v. Goodrum, 1, 358.

VARIANCE.

In action to enforce lien. See Mechanics' Liens, § 19.
Between pleading and proof. See Pleading, § 16.
In robbery prosecution. See Robbery, § 3.

VENDITIONI EXPONAS.

See Execution, § 14.

VENDOR AND VENDEE.

§ 1. Contract to Convey.

Where one party has promised to convey land to another upon payment of the price, together with taxes, interest, etc., but there is nothing to show that this other has, on his part, promised to pay accordingly, there is no mutuality apparent in the transaction and no right of action accrues to this last party as for the enforcement of a contract.—Rand v. Hastings, 1, 307.

In a negotiation, by means of letters and telegrams, for a purchase of lands, the words, "but in case you desire both I shall assent," from a vendor reluctant to dispose of but one of two parcels, followed by the words, "let me know at once," comprise an offer of both parcels, and, if accepted immediately, there is completed a contract for selling the two.—Polhemus v. Ashley, 1, 823.

On authority of Kerns v. McKean, 65 Cal. 411, 4 Pac. 404, judgment reversed, and cause remanded for a new trial.—Kerns v. Dean, 2, 460.

Under a contract for the sale of land a deed from the vendee transfers the equitable title to the grantee, and entitles him to demand a conveyance from the vendor or from subsequent purchasers without notice.—Alpers v. Knight, 2, 550.

A mortgagor agreed in writing to execute a deed to the mortgagee, and leave it in escrow, to be delivered upon default by him in paying an agreed sum less than the amount due, provided the mortgagee gave a receipt in full. The deed was accordingly left as an escrow. Default was made, but, before the mortgagee accepted the deed, the mortgagor demanded it back, and conveyed to another. Held that, as the mortgagee had not signed the agreement, and therefore could never have been compelled to accept the deed, the mortgagor was at liberty to withdraw it at any time before it was accepted; nor did the contract become an executed one from the mere fact that the mortgagee forbore suit upon the mortgage until it was barred by the statute of limitations.—McDonald v. Huff, 2, 860.

§ 2. —— Provision for Construction of Levee.

In an action to rescind a contract for the sale of land, which provided that the grantor was to build a levee along a river, whether the levee was completed within a reasonable time is a question for the court sitting as a jury; and, in the absence of any proof of damages to the grantee from failure to complete the same, a finding that it was completed within a reasonable time will not be disturbed, though the work was not completed for four years.—Quill v. Jacoby, 4, 736.

Where a contract for the conveyance of land facing on a street provides that a levee shall be constructed on the "west side of the said tract," which side faces a street, the construction of the levee in the center of the street is a compliance with the provision.—Quill v. Jacoby, 4, 736.

§ 3. Consideration for Contract.

The vendor and the vendee adversely claimed land in the former's possession worth $9,000, the vendee claiming under an attachment for $1,300. Held, that the vendee's agreement to purchase the vendor's interest for $4,750 was supported by a valuable consideration, though it afterward appeared that the vendee's title was the better one.—Ward v. Yorba, 6, 101.

§ 4. Assumption of Mortgage.

If A owns land subject in part to a mortgage and contracts to sell this land to B, reserving a number of acres indefinitely as having been contracted to be conveyed to C, and subsequently deeds are made to C and B successively, B assuming the mortgage in his, there has been here no contract between B and C so that B must save C's land from being foreclosed upon.—Morenhout v. Brown, 1, 139.

§ 5. Transactions With Agent.

Where an agent for the sale of land, intrusted with a deed thereof, through the negligence of the vendee, who knew that he was authorized to deliver the deed only after a purchase money note and mortgage were executed to the vendor, fraudulently took the note and mortgage in his own name, there was no valid delivery, and the vendor was entitled to a lien for the price, as against an innocent purchaser of the mortgage.—Raymond v. Glover, 4, 780.

Plaintiffs contracted to sell certain land to two of defendants, payment to be made at a specified time, and, if not so made, the contract to be void, at plaintiffs' option. It was also agreed that certain tracts should be conveyed on payment of the agreed price therefor, and that, if the vendees sold any of the land, they might retain one-fourth of the purchase price, and securities for the remainder should be deposited in bank to secure the performance of their contract with plaintiffs. The appellants purchased certain tracts of the vendees, paying them in part therefor, and tendered the balance to plaintiffs. Held, that plaintiffs were not bound by any payments made to their vendees, since such contract did not make them agents, or authorize them to receive any money for plaintiffs.—Green v. Grider, 6, 734.

§ 6. —— Husband and Wife.

Where a husband and wife sue to compel a conveyance of land to the wife, and hè alleges in the complaint that he has no interest in the land, defendant cannot object that he was bound to convey to the husband, who had not in writing authorized a conveyance to the wife, as the complaint is a sufficient authorization.—Foulke v. De Witt, 5, 942.

A husband contracted to buy land, and thereafter the wife tendered the amount due, and then sued to compel a conveyance to her. In the meantime an intervener had bought the land under an execution in his favor against the husband, and received a certificate of sale. Held, that the intervener could not complain of a decree requiring the wife to deposit with the clerk the amount of such execution, costs, interest, etc., to be paid to him upon his discharging his certificate, as a condition precedent to a conveyance to her by defendant.—Foulke v. De Witt, 5, 942.

§ 7. Mistake of Parties.

A contract to convey by good title was made between persons, both of whom claimed the premises by paramount title; but at the time of making the contract the vendee, acting on the advice of counsel, conceded the vendor's title to be the better one. The vendor testified that he agreed to cònvey only his interest, which was corroborated by another, and not denied by the vendee. Held, that a finding that the provision requiring a good title was inserted by mistake was justified. Ward v. Yorba, 6, 101.

The vendor and the vendee each claimed the premises by paramount title, and the vendee's counsel erroneously advised him that his title was inferior. The vendee knew all the facts on which this advice was based, and thereupon contracted to buy the vendor's interest. Held, that he was not entitled to be relieved from the contract on the ground of mistake, under Civil Code, section 1577, defining a mistake as an unconscious ignorance or forgetfulness of a material fact, or a belief in the existence of a material thing which does not or did not exist.—Ward v. Yorba, 6, 101.

§ 8. Possession of Property.

The grantee under a conveyance meant to take effect only on payment of the consideration takes no right of possession in the meantime.—Hawkins v. Kingston, 1, 413.

A paper executed by defendant, authorizing his agent to take possession of certain premises, is admissible to prove defendant's attempt to take possession thereof.—Whitmore v. Ainsworth, 4, 870.

§ 9. Title—Sufficiency and Marketability.

By act of Congress of July 27, 1866, land was granted to a railroad company, and by act of Congress of March 3, 1871, the same land was granted to a different railroad company. By decisions of the supreme court, the railroad company claiming under the prior grant was held to be the owner of the land. Held, that a grantee of the company claiming under the subsequent grant obtained no title, and a purchaser from it was entitled to rescind a contract of sale, irrespective of acts of Congress attempting to cure title in such company. Owen v. Pomona Land and Water Co., 6, 438.

One to whom a person has agreed to convey land is entitled to a deed from such person, and need not accept a deed from a stranger to the contract.—Royal v. Dennison, 4, 851.

Where a purchase contract gives the vendee thirty days for examination of title, provides for a deposit, and its return if title proves invalid, without specifying the time within which the conveyance is to be made, an unrecorded contract for sale of lands, of which the vendee has no notice, between the vendor and a third person, existing when the contract was made, and which, by mistake, included the same land, is a defect which will render the title invalid, and entitle the vendee to recover the deposit if the vendor fails within a reasonable time to remove the defect.—Bartlett v. McGee, 5, 417.

When a written receipt for money paid contains a "guaranty" that the payee will make a title in the payor to the enumerated premises paid for, which title is not yet in himself, it is the payee's duty to make in the payor the title contemplated by him within a reasonable time after obtaining it.—Stone v. Garnett, 1, 804.

A purchaser is not bound to accept a title resting on the statute of limitations, or to take the risk of determining from-facts which he might learn dehors the record whether or not the statute of limitations can successfully be pleaded against an adverse claim.—McCroskey v. Ladd, 3, 433.

A vendor may be able through litigation to establish a perfect title, and yet be unable to enforce a contract for the sale of his land.—McCroskey v. Ladd, 3, 433.

§ 10. —— Deed from Corporation.

A vendor agreed to convey a good and sufficient title or refund any payments made. Defendants refused to accept the deed offered. It appeared that one of the deeds relied upon by the vendor in the chain of title was executed by the president and secretary of an incorporated association under their private seals, and recited that they were authorized at an annual meeting of the association to make deeds. It was held that since both the recital in the deed from the association and the absence of the corporate seal failed to show any authority from the board of directors to convey, the plaintiff did not offer a good paper title within the meaning of the contract.—McCroskey v. Ladd, 3, 433.

Defendants are not called upon specifically to point out defects in a title where the contract does not require it, and especially where the flaw is in a deed from a dissolved corporation.—McCroskey v. Ladd, 3, 433.

The flaw in the deed from the corporation relates directly to the authority of the officers to act, and is not a defect which can be cured by section 1207 of the Civil Code, which provides that any instrument affecting real property recorded prior to January 30, 1873, shall be deemed to impart notice of its contents to subsequent purchasers and encumbrancers, notwithstanding any defect, omission or informality in the execution of the instrument or in the certificate of acknowledgment or in the absence of any such certificate.—McCroskey v. Ladd, 3, 433.

§ 11. Quantity of Land Conveyed.

Where a contract is made to sell a certain ranch, and the deed executed in pursuance thereof conveys all the land that the vendor has pointed out to the vendee as constituting the ranch, or has proposed to sell to him, and all that the vendee understood to be included in the agreement at the time it was executed, the vendee cannot afterward claim that an adjoining tract belonging to the vendor, and of which another person had possession under a contract of sale, should have been conveyed to him under the agreement as part of the ranch. Gwin v. Sweetser, 3, 531.

§ 12. Vendee's Offer to Pay.

Civil Code, section 1496, provides that, unless an offer of performance be accepted, the thing to be delivered need not be actually produced. Section 1501 declares that all objections to the mode of an offer which could be stated at the time to the person making the offer, and could be then obviated by him, are waived unless then stated. Held, that, in case of an offer to pay money, actual production of it is waived unless demanded at the time.—Green v. Barney, 4, 665.

§ 13. Vendor's Offer to Perform.

Defendant contracted to sell land to plaintiff, and stipulated that the money paid therefor was to be returned in case he failed to execute and deliver a deed "after one year from date" of the contract. It was agreed that time was of the essence of the contract. Held, that the deed was to be delivered one year from the date of the contract, and a tender of it nine days after the expiration of the year was not a compliance with the contract.—Vorwerk v. Nolte, 3, 285.

An action to recover such purchase money is not an action for the rescission of the contract, but one for money due thereunder.—Vorwerk v. Nolte, 3, 285.

§ 14. Representations of Vendor of Fruit Farm.

Where defendant testified that he did not represent that all of the land purchased by plaintiff was suitable for fruit-raising, except that part already planted to fruit trees, and that ten acres in addition to that under cultivation might be rendered suitable for cultivation by a small expenditure, a finding that defendant did not make such representation was supported by the evidence.—Fowler v. Carne, 6, 668.

Where defendant testified that there were fourteen hundred and seventy-six trees on the land purchased by plaintiff, and the written contract specified that there were from fourteen hundred to fifteen hundred, a finding that defendant did not represent that there were sixteen hundred was supported by the evidence.—Fowler v. Carne, 6, 668.

Plaintiff alleged that defendant fraudulently represented that the shares of water stock sold plaintiff were sufficient to irrigate the entire tract purchased by plaintiff, and defendant denied that he represented that plaintiff's shares of water stock would entitle her to a sufficient amount of water to irrigate said lands, or any portion thereof except that part planted to fruit trees. Held, that allowing defendant to amend his answer after the trial by striking out the words, "or any portion thereof except that part planted to fruit trees," was not prejudicial to plaintiff, where the findings of the court supported the answer as it stood prior to the amendment.—Fowler v. Carne, 6, 668.

§ 15. —— Limitation of Action for Relief.

Defendant in an action for balance of purchase price of a fruit farm is not barred by limitations from defendant, and recovering by cross-complaint money paid, on the ground of fraudulent representations, not having till then discovered the misrepresentation as to amount of land, and become convinced of the falsity of plaintiff's representation as to the amount of profits he had realized from the land, and his representation, repeated year after year, that the reason defendant did not obtain such profits was due to his want of experience.—Evans v. Duke, 6, 973.

§ 16. Rescission by Vendee.

Where a contract for the sale of land provides that the vendee may disaffirm the sale at the end of a year, in which event he is to be repaid his purchase money, with ten per cent interest, on giving thirty days' notice of his intention to disaffirm, the vendor cannot complain that the vendee gave more than thirty days' notice of his intention, as this is to the vendor's advantage.—Herberger v. Husmann, 3, 304.

A further provision in the contract of sale that on its disaffirmance the vendee should surrender the title acquired by him thereunder is sufficiently complied with by an offer, in the notice of disaffirmance, to surrender his claim to the land on the repayment to him of the purchase money; and, on the vendor's refusal to make such repayment, the vendee may maintain an action therefor without tendering a release of his rights under the contract, Code of Civil Procedure, section 2074, providing that an offer in writing to deliver a written instrument is, if not accepted, equivalent to a tender of the instrument.—Herberger v. Husmann, 3, 304.

In an action to cancel a sale of land to one, and to enjoin another from removing wood therefrom, on which wood the second defendant claimed a lien by virtue of a promise by plaintiff and the other defendant to pay for cutting it, such second defendant cannot object to the validity of the contract of sale between plaintiff and the first defendant, when offered to prove the issues between them.—Diamond Coal Co. v. Cook, 6, 446.

Under Civil Code, section 1501, providing that all objections to the mode of an offer of performance are waived by the creditor if not stated when the offer is made; and under Code of Civil Procedure, section 2076, providing that a person to whom a tender is made must specify at the time any objection he may have, or be deemed to have waived it, where a grantee in a contract of sale tendered to his grantor possession of land the title to which had failed, but coupled with the tender a condition that the grantor should first pay him the value of improvements thereon, to which condition the grantor did not object at the time, the defect in the tender was waived, and the rescission was good.—Owen v. Pomona Land & Water Co., 6, 438.

Where a grantor's title was derived from one of two conflicting congressional grants, the other of which had been held to be paramount by decisions of the federal supreme court, the fact that this grantee waited from January, 1894, to August, 1896, before he rescinded the contract of sale for failure of title in reliance on the grantor's repeated promises to obtain an act of Congress to cure the defect, and to fix up the title, was not such an unreasonable delay as to amount to laches.—Owen v. Pomona Land & Water Co., 6, 438.

§ 17. —— Grounds for Rescission.

Even if a vendor of land by his own act has put it out of his power to comply with the contract, or has been guilty of such a breach of it that he could not enforce it, the purchaser cannot rescind if he was first in default.—Aikman v. Sanborn, 5, 961.

The fact that a vendor of land fails to perform his contract, or puts it out of his power to perform it, does not amount to a rescission, but is only ground for rescission by the purchaser.—Aikman v. Sanborn, 5, 961.

False representations of vendor that a certain number of acres of the land were under cultivation, and that he had for a number of years obtained certain profits from it, which were fifteen per cent of the purchase price, are ground for rescission.—Evans v. Duke, 6, 973.

§ 18. —— Recovery or Return of Payments.

Plaintiff agreed with one N. and wife to exchange lands, and advanced $500 of the purchase price. N. gave a receipt for the money, and indorsed thereon: "Trade to be finished within two weeks from this date, or this deposit to be forfeited without recourse. Title to prove good, or no sale, and this deposit to be returned." An attachment against plaintiff's husband had been levied on her property, which she refused to procure discharged. N. abandoned the trade, and returned the money to defendants, who had negotiated the exchange of lands for N. Held, that the deposit remained in the hands of defendants as money had and received to plaintiff's use.—Phelps v. Brown, 3, 427.

Where the vendee of land notifies the vendor that he cannot and will not complete the purchase, the vendor need not offer to perform, and by failing to do so does not authorize the vendee to consider the contract as rescinded, so that he can recover the payments made by him.—Cleary v. Folger, 4, 76.

A vendor who, after receiving money on the contract, rescinds it for the vendee's breach, has the burden to show, as against the vendee's claim for return of the money, what damages he has sustained by the breach.—Green v. Barney, 4, 665.

In an action for money paid by plaintiff on a contract for the purchase of land, a recovery can be had only against the person to whom it was paid, and not against a third person, who took a conveyance of the land, and assumed his grantor's contract with plaintiff, as such action is based, not on the contract of purchase, but on the proposition that the contract has been rescinded, and that the vendor has money paid to him without consideration.—Aikman v. Sanborn, 5, 961.

§ 19. —— Evidence.

Where the parties to a suit to rescind a contract for the sale of land and corporate stock stipulated that defendant corporation had published a prospectus of its lands, one of which plaintiff received, it was harmless error to admit the stipulation in evidence, over defendant's objection that the prospectus was incompetent, where the prospectus itself was not offered.—Owen v. Pomona Land & Water Co., 6, 438.

In a suit to rescind a contract for the sale of real estate for failure of title and of corporate stock for misrepresentation, the court properly admitted in evidence an application for the purchase, signed by plaintiff and defendant corporation, which contained representations as to the stock, and recited that a portion of the purchase price of the land and stock was paid, and that the balance was to be paid within ten days after certificate of title, as the recitals tended to prove an agreement to give a good title, and the application was properly construed with the contract.—Owen v. Pomona Land & Water Co., 6, 438.

Where a complaint to rescind a sale of real estate for failure of title alleged a tender of the balance due on the purchase money, which the answer did not deny, and the parties had stipulated that such tender was in fact made, it was not error to exclude evidence offered by defendant to show that the tender was but a mere pretense.—Owen v. Pomona Land & Water Co., 6, 438.

Where plaintiff in an action to rescind a contract for the purchase of land alleged that it was worth only $6,000, but introduced no evidence of its value, error in the admission of evidence of value on the part of defendant was harmless, since the burden to show value was on plaintiff.—Fowler v. Carne, 6, 668.

§ 20. —— Findings and Judgment.

Where an action was brought to cancel a contract for the sale of land to one defendant, and to enjoin another from removing wood from 'the land, and the defendant to the injunction claimed a lien on the wood for cutting it, and asked for foreclosure thereof, the plaintiff's action being equitable, as were also the predominant features of the defense, it was not error for the court to set aside the jury's answers to interrogatories, and substitute findings of his own, though they were contrary to the findings of the jury.—Diamond Coal Co. v. Cook, 6,' 446.

Where plaintiff in an action to rescind a contract for the purchase of land alleged that it was not worth more than $6,000, but introduced no evidence of its value, and defendant and several witnesses testified it was worth from $14,000 to $16,000, and that the shares of stock in a water company sold plaintiff were sufficient to water twenty acres in a year of ordinary rainfall, it cannot be contended that findings that it was worth $15,000, and that the shares of water stock were sufficient to irrigate twenty acres, were not supported by the evidence. Fowler v. Carne, 6, 668.

Where, in a suit to rescind a sale of real estate for failure of title, and of stock in a corporation. for misrepresentation, the complaint alleged that plaintiff had no knowledge of such defect, and relied on defendant's representations and guaranties, which allegations were not denied in the answer, the trial court was justified in finding that such allegations were true.—Owen v. Pomona Land & Water Co., 6, 438.

Judgment for defendant in action for balance of purchase money of land, which rescinds the contract, fixes the amount to be paid defendant, he being charged with rent to date, with interest thereon, and plaintiffs with the amount paid, with interest, and provides that on payment by them he shall deliver possession, subject to his right to enter to remove growing crops, empowers them, by paying the judgment, to prevent his retaining possession while they are paying interest.—Evans v. Duke, 6, 973.

§ 21. Improvements—Recovery of Value of.

Where, in a suit to recover the value of improvements placed on real estate, the parties stipulated to submit the valuation to appraisers, and such appraisement and stipulation were offered in evidence, on which the court based its finding of value, complaint could not be made on appeal that there was no evidence to support the finding.— Owen v. Pomona Land & Water Co., 6, 438.

Civil Code, section 3306, providing that, in case of bad faith, the detriment caused by the breach of an agreement to convey real estate shall be the difference between the price agreed and the value of the estate at the time of the breach, did not apply to an action to rescind a contract of sale of land for failure of title, and plaintiff was entitled to recover the value of improvements placed on the real estate, regardless of whether or not they enhanced the value of the real estate in a corresponding amount.—Owen v. Pomona Land & Water Co., 6, 438.

§ 22. Assignment by Vendee.

Where it appears, in a transaction relating to land, that the title was intended to remain in the obligor and that the instrument is merely a bond to convey when payments are made according to the conditions, the obligee can meantime transfer to a third person nothing but a right to be given a deed upon payment in full.—Willson v. Truebody, 1, 238.

§ 23. Remedies of Vendor.

Where a vendor of real estate has kept all his covenants in a contract of sale, and the vendee refuses to perform his part, the vendor may rescind the contract or sue for specific performance.—Gates v. McLean, 2, 636.

Allowing defendant to prove damages because of plaintiff's failure to complete his purchase is harmless error where he was not allowed to recoup for the reason that plaintiff did not make out his case, and there was therefore nothing against which defendant could recoup.—Cleary v. Folger, 4, 76.

§ 24. —— Right to Claim Forfeiture.

A covenant in an agreement to convey land, which provides that on noncompliance by the purchasers with the terms as to payment the seller shall be free from any obligation to convey, and the purchasers shall forfeit all right thereto, time being made of the essence of the contract, authorizes the seller to avoid the contract or not, at his option, and he is not bound to tender a deed except on payment of the price.—Freeman v. Griswold, 4, 256.

Where a land contract provides that, on noncompliance by the purchaser with the terms as to deferred payments, the seller shall be free from any obligation to convey, and the purchaser shall forfeit all rights thereunder, except a right to occupy the premises as a tenant of the seller so long as the sums paid are equivalent to an annual rent equal to twelve per cent per annum of the price agreed on, with the right to purchase during such time, the seller, by bringing an action to recover the unpaid price, waives his right to treat the agreement to convey as void, and hence this clause, giving a right of occupancy for a certain time to the purchaser, which was to apply only in case of forfeiture, has no application.—Freeman v. Griswold, 4, 256.

§ 25. Rescission by Vendor.

B., having defendant's contract to sell him certain land, died, leaving a balance overdue and unpaid. The contract had not then been rescinded, but defendant made no claim against B.'s estate. Plaintiff, B.'s successor in interest, told defendant that she could not complete the purchase and suggested a division of the land. Defendant refused, but offered to sell her the land, without counting B.'s payments, for a price considerably more than the balance due on the contract. Plaintiff said she would rather keep to the old contract, but was told there was no old contract to keep to. Later, plaintiff wrote defendant that she was now able and willing to pay the amount due, and requested an account, which was furnished, with a letter from defendant's attorney to the effect that defendant did not recognize plaintiff's right to the information. Held, that defendant had rescinded.—Green v. Barney, 4, 665.

The vendor does not rescind the contract by insisting that the purchaser, by failing to make payment as he agreed to in his covenant, forfeited all payments made and his rights under the contract.—Aikman v. Sanborn, 5, 961.

§ 26. Lien of Vendor.

A finding that, after plaintiff sold her land she signed and delivered to a certain person "two unacknowledged deeds to said premises," should not be held to constitute an abandonment of a lien for the purchase price, where it was also found that plaintiff did not waive her lien, and that said person, "being a mortgagee, must account to plaintiff for the profits."—Austin v. Pulschen, 5, 176.

Where plaintiff, in possession of land, which she held under a recorded contract of sale, and upon which there was a lien for the purchase price, agreed to sell the same in consideration that the vendee discharge said lien, and give his notes to her for the payment of a further sum, and that she retain possession until they were paid, and the vendee borrowed money from another, giving him a mortgage on the land therefor, and the sum borrowed was paid to the holder of the first lien, who conveyed directly to the vendee, the mortgage must be postponed to plaintiff's lien, the mortgagee not being entitled to be subrogated to the original lien.—Austin v. Pulschen, 5, 176.

§ 27. —— Priority Over Mechanic's Lien.

The priority of a vendor's lien over a subsequent mechanic's lien for work done on the land with knowledge of the vendor's claim is not affected by the latter's noncompliance with Code of Civil Procedure, section 1192, requiring a person having or claiming an interest in land on which an improvement is to be erected to give notice that he will not be responsible for the cost of the same.—Kuschel v. Hunter, 5, 793.

§ 28. —— Enforcement.

A vendee has rights which must be considered in a resale of property to satisfy the vendor's lien.—Richardson v. Bigler, 1, 43.

In an action to foreclose a vendor's lien, a third party intervened, and asked a foreclosure of an interest claimed by him. Plaintiff denied the allegations of intervener's complaint, and thereupon dismissed his action. Defendant made default. Held, that a decree finding intervener had the interest claimed, but denying him a foreclosure as to such interest, was erroneous.—Greenberg v. California Bituminous Rock, 3, 883.

§ 29. Bona Fide Purchasers—Notice to Grantee.

If one conveys land to another by a deed of bargain and sale and then conveys it, or assumes to do so, to another who has knowledge of the first conveyance, this other takes nothing; a fortiori, the assign of this other takes nothing.—Ellis v. Judson, 2, 169.

Where a vendee signs a purchase money mortgage, payable to the vendor's agent, under the belief that it is payable to the vendor, after having ample opportunity to examine it, he cannot contest its validity as against an innocent purchaser.—Raymond v. Glover, 4, 780.

Defendant knew that M. was not in possession when he conveyed to him, and there was no evidence, except the presumption arising from the deed, that defendant gave any consideration for the land. He knew that M.'s brother had conveyed the land as if it was his own. He did not make inquiries of the occupants of the land, and, although he heard that there was a deed from M. to his brother, there was no evidence that he made any inquiries of M. about it, but he made inquiries of the widow of M.'s brother, and searched the records. Held, that defendant was not a bona fide purchaser.—Bryan v. Tormey, 3, 85.

§ 30. Offense of Selling Land Twice.

A contract to sell land free of encumbrance, which the vendor has previously contracted to sell to another, is not in violation of Penal Code, section 533, providing a penalty for selling land which has been bargained to another with intent to defraud previous or subsequent purchasers, where the previous contract is recognized as an encumbrance which the vendor agrees to settle.—Luchetti v. Frost, 6, 763.

VENUE.

Of larceny. See Larceny, § 4.
Of suit to quiet title. See Quieting Title, § 2.

§ 1. How Determined.

The nature of a cause of action, so far as it determines the venue, must be ascertained from the complaint alone, without considering any amendment which plaintiff may intend to make.—Smith v. Smith, 4, 860.

§ 2. Actions Concerning Realty—Corporations.

A complaint asking that it be adjudged that certain deeds of land are mortgages, and that they have been paid, and that, if it be found that any part of the debt remains unpaid, plaintiffs be admitted to redeem, and that they be let into possession, states a local cause of action, which should be brought in the county in which the land lies. Smith v. Smith, 4, 860.

Code of Civil Procedure, section 392, provides that actions for injuries to real property must be tried in the county in which the subject of the action is situated. Constitution, article 12, section 16, provides that a corporation may be sued in the county where the liability arises or the breach occurs, or in the county where it has its principal place of business. Action was brought against a corporation for injuries to real estate in the county where it had its principal place of business, which was other than that in which the land was situated. Held, that the provision of the constitution did not affect the code provision, and hence refusal to grant defendant's motion for a change of venue to the latter county was error.—Miller & Lux v. Kern County Land Co., 6, 684.

§ 3. Joinder of Local and Transitory Actions.

An action upon a contract whereby defendant was to pay a certain sum for land in case the title thereto was satisfactorily cleared, or to reconvey the land if the title was not so cleared, the complaint, praying for relief in the alternative, is not within Code of Civil Procedure, section 392, providing that actions for the recovery of real property must be tried in the county where the land is situated, but is within section 395, providing that in all other cases the action must be tried in the county in which the defendants reside.—White v. Adler, 5, 215.

§ 4. Change of Venue.
See Divorce, § 8.

Where the court is satisfied from the affidavits that the convenience of witnesses requires the action to be tried in the county in which it was brought a change of venue should be denied.—Prader v. Merchant, 1, 138.

In making an order changing the venue of a case, on application of the defendant and accompanying affidavits, the court acts judicially upon a matter within its cognizance, even though the cause shown for the change be insufficient in fact.—Meininger v. Gluckauf, 1, 113.

A person sued in a state court in a county other than that of his residence is, on proper application being made, entitled to a change of venue.—Foye v. Simon, 2, 216.

A recital in an affidavit by a mutual benefit association to change the place of trial of an action against it from L. to S. county, "that all payments of benefits that have become due and payable to the nominees of any deceased member are made and always have been made by a warrant payable in the city of P.," in S. county, does not controvert an allegation in the complaint that defendant promised to pay at A. in L. county, and justifies the refusal of the motion.—Haas v. Mutual Relief Assn., 5, 180.

A defendant has a statutory right to have the place of trial changed to the county of his residence, and, there being no counter-motion to retain the cause for the convenience of witnesses in the county where it was commenced, the motion should have been granted.—Bailey v. Sloan, 5, 743.

Where, in an action against three defendants, two of whom are residents of the county and the third a resident of another county, it appears the residents, if interested, are proper parties plaintiff, and there is no allegation that they refused to join, the nonresident defendant is entitled to a change of venue to the county of its residence. Read v. San Diego Union Co., 6, 703.

§ 5. —— Case Transferred from Justice's Court.

Where the defendant in an action commenced in a justice's court asks to have the cause transferred to the superior court of the county where he is sued, for the reason that the cause involves the legality of a tax, there is no authority, upon the transfer being made, to transfer the cause to another county for trial.—Powell v. Sutro, 3, 75.

§ 6. Appeal and Review.

An appeal from a refusal of a change of venue will not be considered, when the affidavits on which the application was based are not embraced in the statement or bill of exceptions.—Gliddon & Stratton v. Kerry, 1, 15.

It is proper for a court, after an order refusing a change of venue, to proceed with the trial, notwithstanding notice of appeal from the order.—Hibbard v. Chipman, 1, 16.

The affidavits upon which the motion below was made must, on appeal for alleged error of the trial court in refusing a change of venue, be embodied in the statement of the case or in a bill of exceptions.—Hibbard v. Chipman, 1, 16.

The proper resort for a party aggrieved by an order of the trial court granting an application, upon affidavits, for a change of venue is appeal; mandamus does not apply.—Meininger v. Gluckauf, 1, 113.

Where the evidence on the hearing of a motion for change of venue on the ground of change of residence is conflicting as to whether the residence had actually been changed when the action was commenced, the discretion of the trial court in denying the motion will not be reviewed on appeal.—Conlon v. Gardner, 3, 838.

VERDICT.

In civil cases generally. See Trial, §§ 15–19.

VERIFICATION.

Of pleadings. See Pleading, § 1.

58

VESSELS.
See Shipping.

VIEW BY JURY.
In larceny. See Larceny, § 11.

VOLUNTEER.
Joining in deed. See Deeds, § 6.

VOTING.
See Elections.

VOUCHERS.
Executor's account. See Executors and Administrators, § 34.

WAGES.
See Master and Servant; Work and Labor.

WAIVER.
Of rights by accused. See Criminal Law, § 9.
Of jury. See Jury, §§ 1, 2.
Of statute of limitations. See Limitation of Actions, § 11.
Of redemption. See Mortgages, § 33.
Of objections to tender. See Tender, § 2.

WAREHOUSE.
§ 1. Loss of Liquors by Leakage.
Barrels of spirits were in apparently good condition when received at defendant's warehouse for storage. Six weeks later defendant discovered they were leaking, and immediately notified plaintiff, who found excessive loss by leakage. The evidence showed that the leakage was caused by defective cooperage, but there was no evidence that the barrels were improperly piled, or that the warehouse was improperly constructed, or subject to improper drafts by winds or otherwise, or that it was defendant's duty to continuously inspect them, or that there was any such usage among warehousemen. Held, insufficient to support a verdict that the loss was due to defendant's negligence.—Taussig v. Bode & Haslett, 6, 649.

§ 2. Bona Fide Purchaser of Receipts.
Where brandy manufactured for the owner by a licensed distiller is stored in a United States bonded warehouse, regulated by the act of Congress of March 3, 1877, and the treasury regulations of May 15, 1877, in order to delay the payment of the revenue tax, such laws requiring brandy to be stored in a distiller's name, but not requiring the distiller to be the owner, if the warehouse receipt was issued to the distiller, and he subsequently sold the liquor to another, without anthority, and transferred the receipt to him, the purchaser was a bona fide purchaser for value and without notice, and the owner of the liquor was entitled to a return of his property on paying to such purchaser his payments for warehouse charges and the government tax.—Bliss v. Carroll, 2, 595.

WARRANTS.
Payment by treasurer. See Counties, § 3.
By state to pay claims. See State, § 2.

§ 1. Bona Fide Purchaser.

When a writ of mandate commands a county officer to issue a warrant to a person named in it "or his attorney," and thereupon the warrant is issued to the attorney of that person, if the attorney afterward sells the warrant to one who takes for value and in good faith, the purchaser has a good title.—Sweeney & Co. v. Sutro & Co., 2, 155.

WARRANTY.

On sale of chattels. See Sales.

WASTE.

Injunction against. See Injunctions, § 5.

WATER BILLS.

Liability of tenant. See Landlord and Tenant, § 6.

WATER COMPANIES.

See Waters and Watercourses, §§ 17, 18.

WATERS AND WATERCOURSES.

§ 1. Water Rights in General.

Where, in an action to establish right to water in a stream, a court of equity finds, on sufficient evidence, that the parties have each certain rights in the stream, it may secure enjoyment of those rights by proper regulation of the use of the water.—Barrows v. Fox, 3, 526.

Where the rights of a community to the water of a certain creek were appurtenant to the lands of the individuals composing the community, each individual land owner had an appropriative right to his share of the water.—Hildreth v. Montecito Creek Water Co., 7, 44.

nant thereto, from the date of posting the notice.—Osgood v. El Dorado Water etc. Co., 2, 47.

Where one, from the time of posting notice claiming certain waters, pursues the work of appropriation with due diligence until it is accomplished, the act of Congress of 1866 operates to confirm his claim as of the date of posting the notice, although in the period intervening between the notice and the completion of the work, another person acquires, as against the United States, the title to land through which the stream ran in its natural course.—Osgood v. El Dorado Water etc. Co., 2, 47.

§ 5. Waste of Water.

Under Civil Code, section 1411, providing that an appropriation of running water, to give a right to its use, must be for some useful or beneficial purpose, and that when the appropriator ceases to use it for such a purpose the right ceases, where it is adjudged that plaintiffs are entitled to a certain amount of water from a stream, and that defendants are entitled to the remainder, and it appears that plaintiffs have always used the water by means of a defective flume, the court may direct them to carry the water to which they are entitled by flume and pipe, so that the rest may not be wasted.—Barrows et al. v. Fox, 3, 526.

§ 6. Rights Based on License or Oral Permission.

An oral permission given to divert and use water from a stream is a mere license, which is revocable, and does not vest any estate in the land.—Jensen v. Hunter, 5, 83.

Where a license to construct a ditch is given on consideration that the ditch shall be for the joint use of the licensor and licensee, the right of the licensee to use the ditch can only be lost by abandonment.—Patterson v. Mills, 6, 929.

§ 7. Prescriptive Rights—Adverse User or Possession.

Five years' adverse possession is sufficient to bar an action to enforce a water right.—Evans v. Ross, 2, 543.

Title to a ditch diverting water from a stream on the land of plaintiff's decedent cannot be claimed by adverse possession by one who, after using the water for three years, acknowledged decedent's title by offering to pay for a grant thereof.—Jensen v. Hunter, 5, 83.

The evidence in an action to determine the priority of right to divert the waters of a river claimed by plaintiff, who was a lower riparian owner, by adverse user, showed that plaintiff for a number of years had removed dams erected by defendant, but that the latter had rebuilt them. Plaintiff's ditches were originally constructed under a license from a former owner of defendant's lands, and had originally connected with the ditch of such former owner, and one of the ditches was constructed for the joint use of the parties. Held, insufficient evidence of adverse user to establish plaintiff's prior right. Patterson v. Mills, 6, 929.

It is immaterial that the quantity of water owned by defendant and conducted through the ditch to her land is left indefinite by the evidence, in an action for trespass, where defendant justified under a prescriptive right to the use of a ditch across plaintiff's land as a conduit of water to her lands, and a right of entry for repairing it.—Hart v. Hoyt, 7, 4.

Where one had an appropriative right as a land owner to his share of the water of a certain creek and the water was afterward taken by a company for the purpose of distributing it to those entitled

thereto, and the land owner for eight years was not supplied by
the company, after which he regularly received his share from it,
he did not lose his right by an adverse user of the company during
the intervening period.—Hildreth v. Montecito Creek Water Co., 7,
44.

In an action to quiet title to certain land, evidence held sufficient
to sustain a finding that defendants had acquired a prescriptive right
to the use of waters of a spring located on plaintiff's land and flowing through a pipe line to the land belonging to defendants.—
Higuera v. Del Ponte, 7, 320.

§ 8. Diversion of Water—Action to Enjoin.

Where one of two or more co-owners, in the use of water of a
stream appropriated by them for beneficial purposes, diverts for use
a greater quantity of water than of right belongs to him, so as to
materially diminish the quantity to which the others are entitled, such
parties are entitled to enjoin the wrongdoer from diverting the water
to their injury.—Lorenz v. Jacobs, 2, 296.

Unless the flow in a stream to the land of a riparian proprietor has
been appreciably or perceptibly diminished, he is not entitled to an
injunction against another for wrongfully diverting water from his
stream.—Moore v. Clear Lake Waterworks, 2, 432.

Actions to restrain the diversion, obstruction and use of waters of
a stream, and for damages for the same, are suits in equity to abate
nuisances.—Evans v. Ross, 2, 543.

Where, in an action to establish a water right in a stream, defendants, claiming as appropriators, ask for an injunction to restrain
plaintiffs from taking any water from the stream, it is permissible
for defendants to show the effect on their lands, as to value, of a
deprivation of water as asked by defendants, and that there is no
other available water supply, since this might be necessary to entitle
them to the relief asked.—Barrows v. Fox, 3, 526.

Where one, in draining a marsh from which a stream runs onto another's agricultural land, in connection wherewith it has been used
for irrigating and domestic purposes from time immemorial, diverts
the water intentionally and without benefit to himself, he will be
enjoined.—Bartlett v. O'Connor, 4, 610.

Where suit was brought by an upper riparian owner to compel defendant to desist from taking water from a stream, such compulsory
abandonment cannot constitute a consideration for an agreement by
another owner to allow defendant to divert the water from a point
lower on the stream.—Jensen v. Hunter, 5, 83.

§ 9. Diversion of Water—Action for Damages.

Where each of two defendants made diversion of water for his own
benefit, separately from, and without any collusion, arrangement or
understanding with, his codefendant, and without any consent or
joint action between them, a joint action to recover damages for such
diversion is not maintainable against them.—Evans v. Ross, 2, 543.

In an action for damages for the diversion of water, where a witness has testified only as to the condition of ditches and flumes, and
the work required to clear them, and not as to the amount of the
damage, the action of the trial court in striking out an answer of
the witness, "Yes, sir, I have," given in response to a question by
defendant's counsel as to whether the witness has stated all the
damages, is within its discretion.—Bennett v. Morris, 4, 834.

In an action for the diversion of water from a mine, a witness who
testifies that he knows the claims and ditches involved; that he has
been over the ditches and at the mines of both plaintiff and defend-

ant; that he has resided in the vicinity twelve or thirteen years, and is a miner by occupation, having been engaged mostly in hydraulic mining—is qualified to give his opinion as to whether it is practicable for plaintiff to run his mine if defendant continues to run his in the same way as before.—Bennett v. Morris, 4, 834.

§ 10. Estoppel to Interfere With Irrigation Pipe.

Plaintiffs derive title to the water of a canyon from W., who, while owner, represented to one of the defendants, who he knew was thinking of purchasing certain land, that the right to use water from said canyon therefor was appurtenant thereto. Defendant therefore purchased the land. Subsequently plaintiff's grantors, in order to save waste, proposed to run a pipe across defendant's land. Defendant assented on condition that the pipe should be so laid that he should be enabled to use therefrom the quantity of water to which he had theretofore been entitled. This was done, and defendants used the same until the bringing of this action. Held, that the plaintiff was estopped from interfering with the rights acquired by the defendants to the use of the pipe, and its appurtenances, as long as the same remain as conduit of the water over their land.—Alhambra Addition Water Co. v. Richardson, 2, 722.

§ 10½. Injury to Dam.

Where plaintiff had the right to the water of a ditch and to a dam on defendant's land, which the latter used for the purpose of pasturing stock, defendant was not liable for injuries to the dam by the cattle tramping and treading the same, where plaintiff had the right to enter and protect the dam against such injuries.—Keller v. Fink, 4, 730.

§ 11. Negligence in Repairing Dam.

The evidence in this case failed to show that defendant, a water company, had not used proper care in repairing its dam, the breaking of which injured plaintiff's mining claim, and washed away his tools; and the judgment in plaintiff's favor for damages was reversed, and a new trial ordered.—Weidekind v. Tuolumne Co. Water Co., 2, 695.

§ 12. Injury to Ditch.

A vested right is acquired by the location and construction of a ditch, and to mine it away is recognized by law as an injury; the trespass cannot be justified by custom.—Hill v. Weisler, 1, 724.

When the only damage claimed through the defendant's alleged injury of the plaintiff's ditch is the loss of water sales, the cost or value of the ditch as a structure, separate and apart from the water rights, has nothing to do with determining the damages.—Hill v. Weisler, 1, 724.

In an action against a person for washing away the plaintiff's ditch, causing him a loss of water sales, a variance in describing the ditch is immaterial, if the defendant could not be misled by it, particularly if the ditch was the only one in the vicinity running water at the time and was so identified.—Hill v. Weisler, 1, 724.

§ 13. Canal Diverting American into Sacramento River.

The California act of March 12, 1885 (Cal. Stats. 1885, p. 107), authorizing suits to be brought against the state for damages caused by the destruction of property from the cutting of a canal by order of the levee commissioners, for the purpose of diverting the waters of the American river into the Sacramento river, by virtue of the California act of April 9, 1862, had merely the effect of submitting the state to the jurisdiction of the courts, and did not create any new ground of liability against the state.—Green v. State, 2, 737.

§ 14. Changing Stream as Taking Land for Public Use.

Under the language of the constitution, as it existed prior to the adoption of the new constitution of 1879, if, in pursuance of an act of the legislature, the channel of a river be turned or straightened where it empties into another river, so that the land on the opposite side of the river is destroyed or injured, the damage thus sustained is not a taking of the land for public use; following Green v. Swift, 47 Cal. 536.—Green v. State, 2, 737.

§ 15. Transfer or Conveyance of Water Rights.

Performance of a contract to convey "a good and sufficient water right" for the irrigation of a certain parcel of land was sufficiently tendered by an offer of water certificates issued by an irrigation corporation, guaranteeing the holder a flow of water of the quantity specified in the contract, together with a right of way through a pipe-line reaching the lands to be irrigated for the conveyance of water "represented by said water certificates."—Fairbanks v. Rollins, 6, 99.

A deed by a prior appropriator of water conveyed "all of his right to the use of all the waters of D. creek. Said waters to be taken out at a point . . . . about one mile above the head of S.'s old ditch, and tapping said creek where the B. Co. taps said D. creek. . . . . To have and to hold . . . . the first right to the use of all the waters" thereof. The grantor at that time owned five ditches tapping the stream below the named point of inflow, through which ditches he thereafter continued to divert water, with the grantee's acquiescence. Considerable water still flowed in the stream below the point named, it being from seepage, springs, and other sources. Held, that the intention was to convey a first right only to the point mentioned, and, hence, that the waters below did not become subject to appropriation.—Smith v. Williams, 6, 193.

§ 16. Surface Waters—Obstruction or Interference With.

One over whose lands water spreads during freshets has no right to construct barriers so that he relieves these lands but inflicts the overflow upon the lands of a neighbor.—Castro v. Bailey, 1, 537.

When coterminous tracts of land are in such a position that the lower tract owes a servitude to the other to receive surface water, it cannot be forced back upon the dominant tract by any act of the servient owner.—West v. Girard, 2, 360.

Where the effect of a levee constructed by the defendant was to retain upon the land of the plaintiff, longer than it would otherwise have remained, the accumulated water of floods, and his property was injured thereby, the defendant was held liable for damages.—Montgomery v. Locke, 2, 693.

Under Civil Code, section 801, providing that the right of receiving water from or discharging it upon land, and "the right of having water flow without diminution or disturbance of any kind," may be attached as easements to other lands, the owner of upper land is entitled to the natural and unobstructed flow of the surface water on and across adjoining land, and if the common-law rule is otherwise, it is abrogated by Political Code, section 4468, providing that the common law is the rule of decision "so far as it is not repugnant to or inconsistent with the constitution of the United States, or the constitution or laws of this state."—McDaniel v. Cummings, 3, 137.

Where, from time immemorial surface water had flowed through well-defined channels, from the adjacent country, upon plaintiff's land,

and would still but for the erection by plaintiff of an embankment which diverted the water upon defendants' land, the fact that a change in the conformation of the adjoining country, resulting from its cultivation by strangers, had obliterated the natural channels, and formed new ones, which would cause the water to overflow defendants' lands but for an obstruction erected by strangers many years before such change, will not justify plaintiff in maintaining his embankment, to the injury of defendants.—Drew v. Cole, 3, 765.

The rule that land is subject to the flow of surface water from higher land does not apply to surface water turned on the lower owners by artificial changes made by those owning land above them. Drew v. Hicks, 4, 440.

§ 17. Waterworks and Public Water Supply.

In an act granting a franchise to waterworks proprietors and fixing their relations with a city they propose to supply, a provision whereby, in case of fire, their pipes may be tapped by the fire department free of charge until the introduction of water into the city by some other person, after which they are to "furnish for fire and other municipal purposes their quota or proportion," etc., is to be construed as requiring these proprietors to furnish their quota or proportion free of charge for all municipal purposes.—San Francisco v. Spring Valley Waterworks, 1, 783.

In an act granting a franchise to waterworks proprietors and fixing their relations with a city they propose to supply, the words "shall be introduced into," as employed in the phrase "until such time as water shall be introduced into such city . . . . by some other person"—so employed to mark an event which shall work a change in one feature of these relations—are construed as meaning "shall be provided for."—San Francisco v. Spring Valley Waterworks, 1, 783.

If an act granting a franchise to waterworks proprietors and fixing their relations with a city they propose to supply requires a certain amount of pipe to be laid in the city within a named time, and if subsequently the legislature enlarges this time by an amendment, in no manner changing the words of the act otherwise, the duties of the waterworks proprietors toward the city remain as before except that they have additional time for laying pipe.—San Francisco v. Spring Valley Waterworks, 1, 783.

Where several of those entitled to the waters of a certain creek, as a public use, formed a corporation for the purpose of distributing the water, and all but one of those entitled thereto subsequently became stockholders, the use was not thereby rendered any the less a public one.—Hildreth v. Montecito Creek Water Co., 7, 44.

§ 18. Water Rates—Ordinance Regulating.

A city ordinance providing a "family rate" of $3.75 per month for water furnished for a private dwelling; declaring that where water is used for certain purposes, "or for any other purpose whatever, and no compensation is herein fixed therefor, and satisfactory rates cannot be agreed upon, the meter rates shall govern"; giving any water payer the right to demand a meter and to pay a meter rate on tender of a certain amount for putting in the meter; and declaring the minimum meter rate to be $1.75 per month, does not authorize a water company, putting in a meter without the request of a consumer, to charge him a meter rate instead of a family rate, though it declares the rate per month for water "furnished to consumers through meters" to be a certain amount per 1,000 gallons, and provides that consumers paying the following monthly rates shall be entitled to use the following quantities of water: "$1 monthly, 4,000 gallons," and so on up to $2 per month.—Shaw v. San Diego Water Co., 5, 808.

An ordinance providing a lump sum per month as rate for water furnished a private dweller, and allowing charges according to the amount used only in case the consumer asks for it, does not confiscate property, though the water company has theretofore put in meters of its own accord at its own expense.—Shaw v. San Diego Water Co., 5, 808.

§ 19. Compelling Company to Supply Consumers.

A complaint seeking to compel a water company to supply plaintiff's premises with water, which alleged, in terms, that the water controlled by the defendant had been appropriated to public use, was not so deficient in that regard as to be subject to a general demurrer, though the facts might have been more specifically stated.—Hildreth v. Montecito Creek Water Co., 7, 44.

The waters of a certain creek had been diverted by a ditch and distributed among the neighboring inhabitants, including plaintiff's grantor, for more than five years prior to the formation of a company for the principal purpose of supplying water to the stockholders and others éntitled thereto, whether as riparian owners or as appropriators. This company, with the acquiescence of all parties, diverted the water into pipes, and for twenty-five years delivered it to those entitled thereto. Held, that by a prescription of thirty years, confirmed by an implied contract, plaintiff was entitled to demand that the company continue to supply him his share of the water on payment of reasonable rates. Hildreth v. Montecito Creek Water Co., 7, 44.

Constitution, article 14, section 1, declares the use of water "appropriated for sale, rental, or distribution" to be a public use. A complaint alleged that the waters of a certain creek had been appropriated by a company to public use. It was proved that the company controlling the water of the creek was formed for the principal purpose of distributing it to those entitled thereto by a prior appropriation to public use or as riparian owners. Held, that there was no variance.—Hildreth v. Montecito Creek Water Co., 7, 44.

§ 20. Contract for Water Power.

A contract for the use of water as a motive power for a mill gives the mill no right to use such water for any other purpose.—Fresno Milling Co. v. Fresno Canal & Irr. Co., 4, 592.

Under a contract for the use of water as a motive power the mill owner is not damaged by a failure to deliver the amount of water called for, when an amount equal to the full capacity of plaintiff's mill wheel is delivered.—Fresno Milling Co. v. Fresno Canal & Irr. Co., 4, 592.

§ 21. Contract to Furnish Water for Irrigation.

In an action for breach of a contract to furnish water for irrigation, whereby a large number of grape cuttings planted by plaintiff died, testimony of a witness for defendants that he (witness) procured fifteen thousand cuttings from the lot from which plaintiff procured his, planted them on similar land, and watered and cared for them well, and yet nearly all of them died, though it relates to a collateral matter, is relevant, as tending to prove a fact from which it could be inferred that the loss of plaintiff's vines was not caused by defendants' failure to furnish water.—Remy v. Olds, 4, 240.

WAYS.

See Easements; Highways.

WELL.

Contract to put down. See Contracts, §§ 11–13.

WHARFAGE CHARGES.

See Shipping.

WHARVES.

§ 1. Power of Courts to Prevent Construction.

The district courts have no power to decree the destruction or to enjoin the erection of a wharf, unless it is or will be a nuisance, or is or will be followed by some form of irreparable damage, or unless it is or will be an appreciable hindrance to the execution of some legislative act relating to fishery or to commerce or navigation.—People v. Dennis, 1, 262.

WILLS.

Revocation of trust by will. See Trusts, § 4.

§ 1. Presumption of Compliance With Law.

Where a will on its face does not show that the testatrix subscribed it in the presence of one of the witnesses, or acknowledged to him that she signed it, or declared it to be her will, or that said witness signed it at her request, or in her presence, the law will not presume that all of such acts, being statutory requirements, have been done.—In re Tyler's Estate, 5, 851.

§ 2. Construction.

Testator gave his property to his sister and his nephew, S., and "his sister, my niece," and on the death of his sister added a codicil giving the share of his sister to "the other two residuary legatees therein named, S., and to his sister, my niece, whose name is Marie K., and whose residence is Salzwedel, Germany, share and share alike," and confirming his will save as it was inconsistent with his codicil. The evidence showed that S. had a sister living, but that her name was not Marie K., and that Marie K. was not his niece. Held, that the words referring to Marie K. were used to express the name and residence of testator's niece, and not having accomplished that were to be disregarded as surplusage.—In re Dominici's Estate, 7, 289.

§ 3. —— Education of Children.

Testatrix, after leaving a sum of money to each of her two children, a son and a daughter, divided the estate equally between the children and the husband. In case of the death of the husband before the children's majority, his share was to go to the children. The son was to receive his share at the age of twenty-five, and the daughter at twenty, if she married, the children's education "to be paid for out of the interests of my estate." Held, that the charge for education was upon the whole estate, and that, even conceding the legacies to be vested legacies, distribution could not be had until the charge was satisfied.—In re Berton's Estate, 3, 681.

§ 4. —— Suit by Trustees for Construction.

A complaint by testamentary trustees for a construction of certain trusts in the will, alleging that plaintiffs, who were executors also, had administered on the estate, until by an order or decree of the probate court the funds in their hands as executors were distributed to them as trustees, without stating what disposition, if any, was directed to be made of the trust fund, does not state sufficient facts to enable the court to grant the relief sought, as the will would be superseded by the decree, which is final, a construction of which is all the trustees are entitled to, and an amendment setting out the decree in full should be made.—Goldtree v. Thompson, 3, 61.

§ 5. —— Counsel Fees in Suit Involving Will.

Where a testator leaves a portion of his estate to a charity, and the charity engage in litigation involving the construction of the will, its attorneys' fees will not be chargeable against the whole estate, but only against the portion devised to it.—Hinckley v. Stebbins, 3, 478.

§ 6. Community Property—Disposal of by Husband.

A will of a married man, in terms disposing of all the community property, which states that it "is made with full knowledge of property rights of husband and wife, and with the knowledge and consent of my said wife," indicates the intention of testator to dispose of all his property, including the interest of his wife.—In re Smith's Estate, 4, 919.

Where a will shows that testator meant to dispose of community property, the conveyance by testator's widow of a life estate devised by the will operates as an acceptance by her of the provisions thereof. In re Smith's Estate, 4, 919.

A husband owning community property died, and by his will left all his property to his wife for life, remainder to his children. She borrowed money, and mortgaged the premises as if owner in fee. Held, that on foreclosure the purchaser acquired the widow's undivided one-half and her life estate in the other half.—Webb v. Winter, 6, 768.

§ 7. —— Power of Sale in Will.

A husband has no power to provide in his will for a sale of community property except to pay debts.—In re Wickersham's Estate, 7, 70.

An executor's return of sale of community property under a power in the husband's will is defective where it fails to show that the property was sold for the payment of debts, though it appears that it was sold under the power in the will.—In re Wickersham's Estate, 7, 70.

A wife's interest in community property is adversely affected by a sale thereof under a power in her husband's will.—In re Wickersham's Estate, 7, 70.

Under Code of Civil Procedure, sections 153, 940, 956, providing that the notice of appeal shall state the judgment, order or specific part thereof, appealed from, and that the court on appeal from a judgment may review the verdict or decision and any intermediate order or decision which involves the merits or affects the judgment, the court, on appeal from an order of sale of community property under a power in the husband's will, can review error in including the wife's interest in the order, though it was correct as to the interest of the husband.—In re Wickersham's Estate, 7, 70.

On appeal from an order of sale of community property under a power in the husband's will on the ground that the wife's interest in the property was erroneously included, the executors of the husband could not represent the wife's estate, their interest being adverse.—In re Wickersham's Estate, 7, 70.

Under Code of Civil Procedure, section 1452, providing that heirs or devisees may themselves, or jointly with the executor, maintain an action for the possession of real estate or to quiet title to the same, the heirs of a deceased person are entitled to all actions and defenses necessary to the protection of their property, except those depending on the right of possession; and hence the heirs of a deceased wife are entitled to prosecute an appeal from an order obtained by the executors of the husband for the sale of community property under a power in the husband's will.—In re Wickersham's Estate, 7, 70.

Where a will authorizes the executor to sell the property, if necessary for support of the widow and children, such authority does not include power to mortgage.—Webb v. Winter, 6, 768.

§ 8. Power of Sale—Omitted Children.

Under Code of Civil Procedure, section 1561, providing that "when property is directed by the will to be sold, or authority is given in the will to sell property, the executor may sell any property of the estate without order of the court," and section 1307, providing that children of a testator omitted from a will must inherit from the testator "as if he had died intestate," a power of sale in a will does not authorize the sale of the interests of children not mentioned in the will, without the previous sanction of the probate court required in ordinary cases, and a subsequent confirmation of the sale by the court does not validate it.—Smith v. Olmstead, 3, 223.

§ 9. Contest of Will.

The sufficiency of a bill of contest in a probate proceeding will not be considered by the supreme court when it is raised for the first time on appeal.—In re Bullard's Estate, 6, 688.

Since Civil Code, section 1292, provides that a written will can only be revoked by a writing or by its destruction, a contest interposed to a petition for the probate of a will, which alleged that the property therein disposed of was, after the execution of the will, conveyed to contestant, presents no ground for contest, where it does not also allege that such conveyance declared the will revoked.—In re Tillman's Estate, 3, 677.

§ 10. —— After Probate.

Under Code of Civil Procedure, sections 1330, 1331, providing that, where a will is admitted to probate without contest, any person interested may within one year initiate a contest, and if it shall appear that the will is invalid, etc., the probate must be annulled and revoked, and the powers of the executor must cease, where a contest is initiated in time, and the will found invalid, it must be set aside in toto, and not left standing as to persons not joining in the contest.—Clements v. McGinn, 4, 163.

On the contest of a will on the ground of mental incapacity, the will having been previously admitted to probate, contestants only have the burden of proving the issues raised, and an instruction that the probate of the will raises a presumption of mental capacity, which contestants must also overcome, is properly refused, as imposing an additional burden.—Clements v. McGinn, 4, 163.

§ 11. —— Mental Incapacity.

An averment, in a petition for revocation of the probate of a will, "that at the time of signing said supposed will by him the said James Crozier was not of sound and disposing mind," but, on the contrary, said deceased was at said time of unsound mind, is a sufficient averment of the fact that testator was of unsound mind.—Estate of Crozier, 2, 345.

On the contest of a will on the ground of mental incapacity, declarations of testator are admissible to explain his peculiar actions only when made at about the time of such actions, and therefore a letter by him is not admissible to explain certain conduct, where it is without date, and there is nothing to show when it was written.—Clements v. McGinn, 4, 163.

On the contest of a will, a special finding that testator was not of "sound mind" is a finding of an ultimate fact, and not a mere conclusion of law.—Clements v. McGinn, 4, 163.

§ 12. —— Findings.

Code of Civil Procedure, section 1704, provides that all orders and decrees of the court, or the judge thereof, in probate proceedings, "must be entered at length in the minute-book of the court." Held, that after an order was entered from which an appeal was taken, and while it was pending, the trial court had no power to make any new or further findings or decree in regard to the matters involved.— In re Bullard's Estate, 3, 688.

Findings of facts will not be set aside because they are intermixed with statements of evidence, argument, and conclusions of law. In re Bullard's Estate, 3, 688.

§ 13. —— Compromise and Appeal.

Will contestants who are not heirs at law of a testator, nor related to him, are not parties aggrieved by the denial of their motion for a new trial, within Code of Civil Procedure, section 938, providing that parties aggrieved may appeal.—In re Antoldi's Estate, 7, 211.

A person not a party to a will contest, nor to a compromise resulting therefrom is not bound by it.—In re Dominici's Estate, 7, 289.

WITNESSES.

See Evidence.

Examination of witness in criminal trial. See Criminal Law, §§ 10–14.
Accused as witness. See Criminal Law, § 14.

Testimony of deceased witness. See Evidence, § 4.
Credibility of testimony. See Evidence, § 6.
In action by or against executor. See Executors and Administrators, § 30.
Refreshing memory. See Forgery, § 5.
Competency. See Insane Persons, § 1.
Impeachment in libel case. See Libel and Slander, § 5.

§ 1. Competency.

The question of the incompetency of a witness to testify because of interest must be raised at the trial.—O'Connor v. Hammond, 1, 11.

An official whose duties have compelled a close attention by him to old records and in that connection to a particular signature is a competent witness to prove that signature, although the signatory has been long dead and was never known or seen by the witness.—Garrioch v. Stanner, 1, 490.

§ 2. —— Interest in Case.

Where a witness, who had participated, as a police officer, in the preparation of the case for the prosecution, testified that he was no more than ordinarily interested in the case, and as to experiments made by him, there was no error in excluding the question whether, in view of the experiments, he still testified that he had no more than ordinary interest in the case.—People v. Eaton, 6, 906.

The interest of a deputy sheriff in the outcome of an action against the sheriff and his sureties is not such that he may not be a witness for the defendants on producing a release signed by the sheriff.—Kellogg v. Crippen, 1, 161.

§ 3. Husband and Wife.

The act of the legislature authorizing a woman to be a witness for or against her husband relates to civil, and not criminal, cases.—People v. McFlynn, 1, 234.

In an action for the recovery of personal property, the admission of the testimony of plaintiff's wife against him, without his consent, is ground for reversal, under the Code of Civil Procedure, section 1881.—Fitzgerald v. Livermore, 2, 744.

§ 4. Claimant Against Estate of Decedent.

Code of Civil Procedure, section 1880, disqualifies parties or assignors of parties to an action against an executor or administrator, or persons in whose behalf such action is prosecuted on a claim against the estate of the deceased, from testifying as to facts occurring before the death of the deceased. Held, that the disqualification applies only to those parties who assert claims against the estate.—Todd v. Martin, 4, 805.

Parties to an action or proceeding, or in whose behalf such is prosecuted, against an executor or administrator on a claim or demand against the estate in course of administration, are not competent as witnesses at the trial.—McCausland v. McCausland, 2, 39.

A claim by one asserting herself as the widow for an allowance out of the estate of a deceased person is "a claim or demand" against the estate, in the sense of section 1880 of the Code of Civil Procedure.—McCausland v. McCausland, 2, 39.

§ 5. Credibility—Witness False in Part.

An instruction to the jury that, "if you believe any witness has sworn falsely as to any material fact, you must disbelieve such false statement, and may disbelieve the whole of his or her testimony," is good as far as it goes, and a refusal of it is erroneous; but an instruction that, "if you believe that any witness has willfully testified falsely in regard to any fact material to the issue, you are at liberty to disregard or entirely discard any part of the testimony of such witness," is erroneous, as it is not in accord with section 2061 of the California Code of Civil Procedure, which provides that "a witness false in one part of his testimony is to be distrusted in others."—Brown v. Griffith, 2, 625.

§ 6. Examination of Witness.

Counsel enjoy no right to take a witness out of the hands of opposing counsel during examination; it is only at the discretion of the court that this is allowed, and a refusal to allow it is not error.— Baird v. Duane, 1, 492.

Where a witness states that he "does not consider" or "does not think," etc., such expressions are not expressions of opinion, merely, as witnesses are not required to give their testimony with absolute positiveness.—Prior v. Diggs, 3, 565.

It was not prejudicial error to allow plaintiff to answer the preliminary question: "You may state whether or not you have ever received any injury caused by . . . . defendant," when there follows, without objection, a narration of how the injury was received, and what was said and done by defendant.—Townsend v. Briggs, 3, 803.

Where a part of an answer is not responsive to the question, and a part is directly so, but the whole is relevant, material and competent, it is proper to refuse to strike it out as being irrelevant, immaterial and incompetent, and as being irresponsive to the question. People v. Munroe, 4, 66.

Where a witness responsively answers a question in the affirmative, and then proceeds to state other irresponsive matters, a motion to strike out the whole answer is rightly denied.—Hunt v. Swyney, 4, 108.

A question whether defendant wanted plaintiff "to do anything" at a certain time was rightly excluded as calling for a conclusion.— Whitmore v. Ainsworth, 4, 870.

The issue being whether an instrument, in terms an absolute conveyance, was accepted as such, as contended by plaintiff, or as security, as contended by defendant, a question asked plaintiff, "State what you believed that document to be at the time it was delivered to you," will not be held to ask an opinion as to its legal effect.— Pottkamp v. Buss, 5, 462.

Where one has testified on cross-examination as to the time when, and the circumstances under which, he signed an instrument, a further question on cross-examination, "Do you swear that you signed that instrument as a witness?" calls for a conclusion of law based on the facts stated by him.—Pottkamp v. Buss, 5, 462.

A witness may be asked to examine his account-book to see whether it contains a statement of certain items, the entries having been made by another under his direction, as such testimony is not from memory refreshed by the book.—Grant v. Dreyfus, 5, 970.

It is not error to exclude a question calling for a mere repetition of testimony.—Smith v. Williams, 6, 193.

§ 7. —— Control of Examination by Court.

The trial court's discretion in preventing frequent repetitions of the same question to a witness and in restricting cross-examination is to be upheld, if not abused.—Hewlett v. Steele, 2, 157.

It being in the discretion of the court to permit leading questions, it may, of its own motion, ask questions of witnesses in that form.—People v. Bowers, 2, 878.

Under Code of Civil Procedure, section 2044, providing that the court must exercise reasonable control over the mode of examination, where counsel made a statement to a witness that he was taking a great deal of interest in the case, and wanted to see defendant convicted, expecting witness to answer, there was no error in requiring the examination to be conducted by questions as to interest, instead of by such statements.—People v. Eaton, 6, 906.

§ 8. Cross-examination.
See, also, post, § 10.

A defendant called to the stand by the plaintiff's counsel to testify as to an instrument may be cross-examined by his own counsel and therein made to produce another instrument that modifies the first.—Hawkins v. Kingston, 1, 413.

A witness cannot be asked, on cross-examination, whether she is not in the habit of playing cards for money, and asking for money from her daughter for that purpose, under Code of Civil Procedure, section 2051, providing that evidence of a particular wrongful act is not admissible to impeach a witness.—People v. Bowers, 2, 878.

Where a life insurance agent was called to testify that the mortuary tables in an encyclopedia are in general use, and was not asked on his examination in chief to whom the tables applied, but stated on cross-examination that they applied only to insurable persons, it was not proper cross-examination to ask him "what insurable persons are." Townsend v. Briggs, 3, 803.

Defendant's questions: "Do you know his [plaintiff's] habits as to sobriety?" and "Do you know what his reputation is for sobriety?" were incompetent, as they called for the witnesses' knowledge at the time of the trial, which was two years after the injury was received. Townsend v. Briggs, 3, 803.

Where the testimony of a witness for the prosecution is materially different on the trial from what it was on preliminary examination, the extent to which defendant is to be allowed on cross-examination to go into the present surroundings of the witness, in order to show the motives inducing him to change his testimony, is within the discretion of the court.—People v. Dillwood, 4, 973.

Permitting a witness to be asked on cross-examination whether he had not, at the adjournment after his examination in chief, made a certain statement to a certain person, if error, is harmless, there having been no attempt to prove that his answer, "No," was not the truth.—Willeford v. Bell, 5, 679.

Where, on cross-examination, a witness was asked numerous questions as to whether he had not made certain statements to another, but no time, place or circumstances were specified, it was not error to refuse to permit such others to testify as to such statements for the purpose of impeaching such witness.—Norris v. Crandall, 6, 706.

Under Code of Civil Procedure, section 2044, providing that the court must exercise reasonable control over the examination of a witness, so as to make it as little annoying to the witness as possible, and section 2066, providing that it is the right of a witness to be protected from insulting questions, etc., where a witness testified to certain facts as seen by him, and it appeared from the testimony that the facts were not physically impossible, there was no error in refusing to allow the witness to be asked if he did not know that he

59

was testifying to what was physically impossible.—People v. Eaton, 6, 906.

Where a witness is cross-examined as to collateral matters not testified to in chief, the party conducting the cross-examination is bound by the witness' answers as to such matters, and cannot contradict the same by other evidence for the purpose of impeaching the witness.—Moody v. Peirano, 7, 247.

§ 9. —— As to Genuineness of Note.

On an issue as to the genuineness of the note in suit, plaintiff testified that it was made by defendant for part of the price on sale to him of an interest in a mine by plaintiff and his partner. Plaintiff's testimony in chief was confined to the execution, delivery and nonpayment of the note. On cross-examination he testified that he did not tell his partner on the day of the sale of having taken the note, though they executed the deed together, but told him some time later; whether a week later or two or three months he could not say. Held, that further cross-examination as to how soon after the sale he saw his partner was erroneously excluded.—Taggart v. Bosch, 5, 690.

In such case, there was no direct testimony as to the genuineness of the note, except plaintiff's affirmance and defendant's denial thereof. Plaintiff's partner was ordinarily engaged at the mine, and plaintiff might not have seen him for some months after the sale. The partner testified that he heard of the note the next time after he saw plaintiff, but could not say when that was. Three and a half months after the sale of the mine, plaintiff bought defendant's interest in a liquor business in which they were partners, and, to make the cash payment, borrowed a large sum at the bank, exhibiting the note in suit, which was for $3,000, as one of the securities offered. In addition to the cash payment, plaintiff gave his own notes to defendant for $1,500, nothing being said about the note in suit. Plaintiff's explanation was that he did not want to do anything to interfere with the trade, and that one-half of the note in suit belonged to his partner in the mining business. His explanation of not having told his partner of the note was that their relations were confidential, each doing about as he pleased. The consideration named in the deed of the mine to defendant was $500, and plaintiff testified that the actual consideration was $250 and the note. Plaintiff's partner testified that he understood the consideration to be $250 or $350. Two witnesses testified that defendant told them that it was $250. The expert testimony was equally divided as to the genuineness of the note in suit. Held, that the erroneous exclusion of the cross-examination of plaintiff as to when he next saw his partner after the sale of the mine was prejudicial.—Taggart v. Bosch, 5, 690.

It was error to exclude cross-examination of plaintiff as to whether he had private accounts between himself and defendant, and whether he told the bookkeeper in a liquor business in which they were partners about the note.—Taggart v. Bosch, 5, 690.

§ 10. Impeachment of Witness.
See, also, ante, § 8.

A witness should not be subjected to public insult simply to gratify the spleen of the opposing party in the case, or his attorney, who may be injured by his evidence, or merely to depreciate him before the jury; and compulsion upon a witness to respond to questions material only as affecting his character should be exercised with due regard to this principle.—People v. Snellie, 1, 685.

While evidence other than that of the witness himself, offered to impeach him, must be confined to evidence of general reputation, he may be asked as to collateral facts affecting his standing and having some bearing on his credibility.—People v. Snellie, 1, 685.

While it is proper to prove independent collateral facts in order to place the character of a witness properly before the jury, such facts must be established by the best evidence; parol evidence will not be admissible when it appears that better evidence can be had.—People v. Snellie, 1, 685.

Testimony to show improper relations between the state's witnesses, a man and woman, in order to impeach the woman's testimony, is inadmissible.—People v. Sherman, 3, 851.

A witness cannot on cross-examination, for the purpose of impeaching him, be asked as to his having been in jail, etc., as, under Code of Civil Procedure, section 2051, he cannot be questioned as to particular wrongful acts.—Clements v. McGinn, 4, 163.

Under Code of Civil Procedure, section 2052, it is proper, when the testimony of a witness on preliminary examination is sought to be used to contradict the witness, to require it to be read and shown to the witness on demand.—People v. Dillwood, 4, 973.

To discredit a witness for the prosecution, it may be shown that criminal charges are pending against him, as tending to show a desire to seek favor at the hands of the prosecution, by aiding in the conviction of the defendant. Such charges must be proven by record if oral evidence thereof is objected to.—People v. Dillworth, 4, 973.

Where the court below has made a finding in conformity with a witness' testimony, it is only in exceptional instances that such witness' testimony will on appeal be held to have been impeached by the testimony of others.—Hite v. Hite, 6, 216.

WOOD.
Injunction against cutting. See Injunction, § 5.

WORK AND LABOR.
§ 1. Contract for employment.
§ 2. —— For permanent employment.
§ 3. —— As stage manager of theater.
§ 4. Action for services—Pleadings.
§ 5. —— Evidence and findings.
See Architects; Building Contracts, §§ 4, 5; Master and Servant.
Contract for services. See Contracts, §§ 5, 6.
Convict labor. See Convicts, § 2.

§ 1. Contract for Employment.
In setting forth the agreement, defendant alleged that it was made by G. "as" manager of defendant corporation. The agreement purported to have been made on defendant's behalf, and G. testified that he made it on behalf of defendant. Held, that an objection by defendant that it was on its face not its agreement, but the agreement of G., its manager, was not tenable.—Caffrey v. Omilak Gold & Silver Min. Co., 4, 601.

One who agreed to pay in stock and refuses to deliver it is liable for the amount in money.—Delafield v. San Francisco etc. Ry. Co., 5, 71.

One about to enter the employ of another demanded $100 per week for the term of two years. The employer offered him $75 a week for the first year, and $100 for the second. He declined, but agreed to contract for $90 a week for the first year, and, if business should not then warrant the $10 raise, he would wait until it did. This was

the ground that it varied from that alleged in the complaint.—Delafield v. San Francisco etc. Ry. Co., 5, 71.

§ 5. —— Evidence and Findings.

A finding of the court below on evidence substantially conflicting in an action to recover the value of services rendered will not be interfered with on appeal.—Flanigan v, Davis, 1, 876.

In assumpsit for the value of services in permanent improvements of a vineyard.—Buhman v. Becker, 5, 172.

In action for hauling pipe for third person.—Chapman v. Bent, 6, 740.

Where the court found that plaintiffs had rendered services worth a stated amount, and that they had been paid a named sum, the finding sufficiently made it appear that only the amount named had been paid, and defendant could not object that it did not support a judgment for the difference.—Tyler v. Davis, 3, 670.

In an action for services rendered by plaintiff's assignor, the complaint alleged that they were rendered at the special request of defendant. Defendant, in its answer, admitted that the services were rendered, and set out a copy of the agreement between such assignor and its manager. Held, that it was not error to admit such agreement in evidence against an objection by the defendant.—Caffrey v. Omilak Gold & Silver Min. Co., 4, 601.

In an action for labor in defendant's fish cannery, defendant's testimony was that the balance claimed by plaintiff was covered by a charge against him for defective canning, in accordance with the contract, and that plaintiff had signed a receipt in full, which was read to him before he signed it. Plaintiff's testimony was that the defective canning was due to defective machinery; that plaintiff could not read writing in the English language; that the receipt was not read to him at the time he signed it; that he supposed he was signing only for a payment which he then received. Held, that a verdict for plaintiff will not be disturbed.—Wong Lang v. Alaska Imp. Co., 4, 867.

Where a complaint in an action to recover for work and materials alleges that they were furnished under a contract, which fact is not denied by defendant, the only issue made being as to the contract price, it is error to admit evidence of reasonable value.—Fladung v. Dawson, 5, 286.

Where the only point in dispute on an appeal relates to the value of the services sued for, on which the evidence is conflicting, the verdict of the jury will not be disturbed.—Curry v. Holland, 5, 452.

A complaint alleged that plaintiff was to be paid a reasonable sum for extra work as to a certain contract, and also the performance of the work. The finding showed the performance of the work, its acceptance by defendants on a certain day, and that "defendants agreed to pay therefor the sum of ten dollars." Held, that the finding was not that the work was done for an agreed price; hence there was no variance.—Webb v. Kuns, 6, 97.

WRITS.

See name of writ.

TABLE OF CASES.

60

63

TABLE OF CITATIONS.

[References to volumes are in bold-face figures.]

(1001)

STATUTES—Continued.

STATUTES—Continued.

STATUTES—Continued.

CODE OF CIVIL PROCEDURE.

CODE OF CIVIL PROCEDURE—Continued.

CODE OF CIVIL PROCEDURE—Continued.

SECTION	PAGE	SECTION	PAGE
552	6, 24	662	2, 462; 4, 977
554	2, 149	663	7, 25
555	2, 149; 6, 22, 23, 24	663½	7, 25
556	2, 149	664	1, 889
564	4, 132	667	1, 889; 2, 241, 650; 4, 618
568	5, 75	668	7, 361
578	5, 149, 397, 398; 6, 877	670	2, 270; 3, 65; 7, 162
580	2, 74, 565; 5, 485	671	7, 202
581	2, 347, 434; 3, 588; 4, 501; 5, 393, 395	675	3, 279
		681	3, 611; 6, 668
585	6, 193	682	6, 424
590	5, 878	668	3, 201
592	3, 611; 7, 298	689	4, 772, 775; 5, 165, 310, 339
595	3, 747	694	5, 861; 7, 388
607	4, 695	701	6, 644
622	5, 741	703	6, 645
624	3, 370	705	6, 645
625	2, 736; 3, 369, 370; 7, 280, 282, 284, 286, 287, 288	707	3, 263
		714	2, 568
626	3, 619; 5, 757	715	2, 477
627	5, 360	717	2, 477
631	3, 365	720	2, 477, 479, 568; 3, 252
632	4, 389; 5, 764	723	73
633	4, 389; 5, 311, 312, 764	726	2, 73, 74, 557; 4, 212; 6, 728, 925, 926; 7, 201, 202
634	4, 162		
638	5, 969	731	4, 568
639	4, 550; 5, 969	738	3, 534
643	5, 969	739	4, 299
644	2, 242	752	3, 735
647	2, 680	764	4, 412
648	7, 29	803	2, 542
649	7, 144	838	4, 94
650	7, 144	872	6, 125
652	2, 656; 3, 259	894	2, 654
657	2, 461, 462; 3, 736; 4, 14; 5, 877; 7, 26	938	2, 462; 7, 212
659	2, 150, 402, 460, 462, 536, 616; 3, 97, 549; 4, 192, 299, 681; 5, 317, 778; 6, 163, 165; 7, 26, 27, 62	939	2, 109, 464; 3, 50, 51, 195, 280; 4, 268, 402; 5, 665; 6, 81, 146, 552, 822; 7, 20, 65, 331, 361
660	3, 894	940	2, 303; 3, 280, 545; 4, 677; 6, 278; 7, 73
661	2, 214, 616; 6, 163; 7, 144	941	2, 303, 716; 3, 759

64

CODE OF CIVIL PROCEDURE—Continued.

CODE OF CIVIL PROCEDURE—Continued.

CODE OF CIVIL PROCEDURE—Continued.

CIVIL CODE.

CIVIL CODE—Continued.

CIVIL CODE—Continued.

CIVIL CODE—Continued.

POLITICAL CODE.

POLITICAL CODE—Continued.

PENAL CODE.

PENAL CODE—Continued.

PRACTICE ACT.

PRACTICE ACT—Continued.

CRIMINAL PRACTICE ACT.

PROBATE ACT.

UNITED STATES.

MEXICO.

MISSOURI.

NEW YORK.

PENNSYLVANIA.

TEXAS.